ENCYCLOPEDIA OF CRIME AND JUSTICE

ENCYCLOPEDIA

OF

Crime and Justice

Sanford H. Kadish

EDITOR IN CHIEF

A. F. and May T. Morrison Professor of Law
University of California, Berkeley

VOLUME 1

THE FREE PRESS

A Division of Macmillan, Inc., New York

Collier Macmillan Publishers, London

THE FREE PRESS
A Division of Macmillan, Inc.
866 Third Avenue, New York, N.Y. 10022

Collier Macmillan Canada, Inc.

Printed in the United States of America

printing number

1 2 3 4 5 6 7 8 9 10

Library of Congress Cataloging in Publication Data
Main entry under title:

Encyclopedia of crime and justice.

Includes bibliographies and index.
    1. Crime and criminals—Dictionaries. 2. Criminal
justice, Administration of—Dictionaries. I. Kadish,
Sanford H.
HV6017.E52 1983   364′.03′21   83–7156
ISBN 0–02–918110–0 (set)

CONTENTS

vi   CONTENTS

viii CONTENTS

CONTENTS   ix

x   CONTENTS

EDITORIAL AND PRODUCTION STAFF

FOREWORD

The *Encyclopedia of Crime and Justice* is an attempt, the first of its kind, to draw together in one set of volumes all that is known about criminal behavior and the responses of societies to it. Since its subject is defined by a social phenomenon rather than by an academic discipline, its approach is necessarily interdisciplinary. The Encyclopedia covers all fields of knowledge that have a bearing on understanding the nature and causes of criminal behavior of various kinds, the prevention of crime, the punishment and treatment of offenders, the functioning of the institutions of criminal justice, and the bodies of law that define criminal behavior and govern the processes through which the criminal law is applied.

Crime has been a besetting concern for all societies. In some, including our own, it has appeared endemic, presenting a severe challenge which sometimes seems to threaten the stability of social life. We conceived this Encyclopedia as a contribution to understanding and responding to this challenge in two principal ways: by advancing knowledge and by making it available both to those with a professional interest and to the wider public.

An encyclopedia by definition constitutes an effort to restate what is known rather than to develop new knowledge. But it can also serve as a means of advancing knowledge. In bringing together all that is relevant to the phenomenon of crime into a single work, one can gain new perspectives on what is known and what is not known. Moreover, the discipline of preparing an encyclopedia compels one to develop methods of organizing and structuring enormous bodies of knowledge. This endeavor itself can contribute to understanding by revealing relationships among diverse fields of learning. In addition, encyclopedia articles are a special form of writing. The task of standing back from the subject and describing for the nonspecialist its essential features and significance enables the specialist to develop insights which can illuminate it in a way that more technical writing often fails to do. It is our hope that many of the articles in this Encyclopedia are of this character.

The more traditional contribution of an encyclopedia—making knowledge more readily available to wider audiences—is particularly needed in the area of crime and justice. Those who work in the field cover a wide range of professional roles: lawyers and judges, law enforcement officers, social workers, probation and parole personnel, correctional administrators, and others. Seldom does their training embrace the entire scope of crime and justice. We hope that the Encyclopedia will give access to this wider range of knowledge, as well as to matters which lie directly within their professional concerns. In addition, the Encyclopedia should be useful for students and teachers, not only in professional education in law schools, schools of criminal justice, and departments of criminology, but also in the general education of university, college, and high-school students. It should be of equal importance as a reference tool for academics needing information in fields adjacent to their own, for makers of public policy, such as legislators and government officials, for journalists, and for the interested general public.

It is true, of course, that there is an abundant literature on all of the subjects covered. But access to it is not always easy, and even when it can be reached, often in specialized libraries, labor, time, and expertise are needed to sift out what is essential and relevant to the reader from the mass of published literature—monographs, texts, treatises, studies, commission reports, dissertations, and journal articles. The articles in this Encyclopedia are designed to do this and to present the reader with an integrated account of what is known, based on an expert's assimilation of the literature. Of course, some readers may wish to go further. The list of selected references to important writings on the subjects covered, which is to be found at the end of each article, will facilitate their doing so.

The articles on legal subjects should be especially useful to readers untrained in the law who encounter difficulties in gaining access to the basic materials. These consist of statutes, regulations, decisions of courts, law review articles, legal texts, and treatises, all of which are difficult to comprehend without prior legal study. Indeed, it is regrettable that when lawyers talk law, they talk mainly to themselves. One usually looks in vain for discussions of legal subjects that are neither wrapped in inscrutable legalisms nor so diluted that they fail to convey a sense of the real issues and problems the law confronts. Our aim has been to provide treatments of legal studies that are burdened by neither of these excesses.

It may be useful to comment on some of the decisions we made in the course of preparing this Encyclopedia. While it was inevitable that the work should be primarily American in emphasis, an effort was made to incorporate relevant material from other countries. In the articles within the sphere of the social sciences our authors were asked to respect no national boundaries in presenting their subject, but rather to make an effort to report the best thought in the entire literature. However, in dealing with legal subjects, compromises had to be made. We could not possibly deal with American law adequately and at the same time cover the law in other legal systems as well. This problem was dealt with in two ways. First, we asked our authors to make reference to the law elsewhere when doing so served to illuminate the shape of American law. As it turned out, this meant that English law is treated extensively in the articles, and that European law is discussed occasionally where a comparative analysis is particularly revealing. Second, we commissioned a number of articles to deal explicitly with certain foreign legal systems, such as those on Criminal Procedure: Comparative Aspects, Criminal Law Reform: Continental Europe, Criminal Law Reform: England, and the Adversary System.

As all encyclopedists must, we had to deal with the problem of change. We have done this by trying to present articles which emphasize the stable continuities in the field rather than matters of transitory import, and which view knowledge and understanding as continually evolving. Even a subject like the constitutional limits of police conduct, which changes with almost every term of the Supreme Court, may be presented as an enduring grappling with fundamental issues.

Authorial bias was another inescapable problem. Questions of crime and justice are inextricably bound up with moral and political judgments. People take sides, even—indeed, notably—those who know most about the subject. Therefore, it seemed to us to be mistaken and ultimately misleading to expect a value-free detachment from our authors. But while personal points of view were not out of bounds, we tried to assure that their presentations were evenhanded or at least that all sides of controversial issues were fairly presented to the reader.

The level at which the contributions were to be written was another matter of concern. We wanted the work to be accessible to as large an audience of interested readers as possible without sacrificing that sophistication of treatment required to achieve the special purposes of the Encyclopedia. Accordingly, we asked our authors to direct their writing to the educated lay person who was not a specialist in the field, taking particular care to provide adequate background as well as clear conceptual frameworks for their discussions. Technical terms were to be defined and concepts explicated in language as plain as the material permitted.

While the length of the articles naturally varies— some are as short as 1,000 words, some as long as 10,000—we tended on the whole to favor treatments of larger rather than smaller scope. This preference followed from our conception of the Encyclopedia as a means of advancing learning and from our desire to provide our readers with a vehicle for in-depth study and reference. Thus, for example, there is a single large article on Theft, rather than many short articles on various kinds of theft offenses. Similarly, the subject of Juvenile Justice is dealt with primarily in three substantial articles under a single entry, rather than being split up under a variety of separate entries.

Another issue of importance was the tension between alphabetical and topical arrangements, a tension inherent in an encyclopedia. On the one hand, ease of use and reader convenience favor the alphabet as the principal means of arrangement. On the other hand, an excessive preoccupation with the alphabet can hinder rounded and coherent presentations of the subject. Our solution was to combine alphabetical and topical organization. Articles sharing a general subject matter were grouped together under one main composite entry, which was then placed in alphabetical order. For example, the entry Drugs and Crime comprises three articles: Behavioral Aspects, Legal Aspects, and Treatment and Rehabilitation; the entry Criminal Justice System includes separate articles on Social Determinants, Planning, and Measurement of Performance, preceded by an introductory article providing an overview; and the entry on Prisons offers six articles on various aspects of this broad subject. A glance at the list of entries will reveal many other examples. At the same time, however, we have tried to facilitate the user's search for material by extensive use of blind entries for titles that a reader might plausibly expect to appear, by an exhaustive index, and by cross-references following each article to lead the reader to related material appearing elsewhere in the Encyclopedia.

The principal responsibility for the planning, organization, and editing of the Encyclopedia was that of the members of the Editorial Board, consisting of Professors Francis A. Allen of the University of Michigan, Daniel Glaser of the University of Southern California, Wayne R. LaFave of the University of Illinois, Lloyd E. Ohlin of Harvard University, Franklin E. Zimring of the University of Chicago, and myself. (Dr. Roger Hood of Oxford University and Professor Norval Morris of the University of Chicago made important contributions early in the planning of the Encyclopedia, but regrettably were unable to continue on the Board.) The first and most basic task of the Editorial Board was to reach agreement on

precisely what subjects came within the scope of the Encyclopedia. Once that was determined, these subjects had to be classified into categories that made both conceptual and practical sense. Seven categories were selected: Substantive Criminal Law, General Part; Substantive Criminal Law, Special Part; Criminal Procedure; Criminal Justice Systems; Causes of Crime; Criminal Behavior; and Social Responses, a large category that included prevention, punishment, and treatment of crime. Each category was then assigned to a single editor or to several working together, with some editors involved in more than one category.

The next task was to conceive of each category in terms of composite entries or single articles that together would represent the best coverage of the field. These were first proposed by the editor in charge of the particular category and then decided upon by the entire Editorial Board. The subsequent tasks of preparing descriptions of each article to be written, designating word allocations for each article, and proposing authors were accomplished in the same way. The final task of members of the Editorial Board was to review, appraise, and revise or propose revisions in the submitted manuscripts, and to make the recommendation for publication.

The administrative burdens of carrying out the agreed-upon plan, as well as of initial review of submitted manuscripts, fell to the publisher's staff in New York, under the able direction of Linda Halvorson. Their work in seeing the Encyclopedia through to completion was indispensable, and both personally and on behalf of the Editorial Board I wish to express my gratitude to them for the quality of judgment they displayed and for the excellence of their editorial and administrative work.

SANFORD H. KADISH

INTRODUCTION

The *Encyclopedia of Crime and Justice* offers the professional and lay user a breadth of coverage unavailable in any single existing resource. Its aim is to present information from a variety of disciplines in a way that provides structure and context to the fields covered.

For nonspecialists, the Encyclopedia affords a great deal of flexibility; topics can be pursued individually or as part of a more comprehensive research program. A specific interest in the insanity defense, for example, could lead to further reading about theories of justification and excuse in the criminal law, and about the right to and role of defense counsel. Specialists, who must increasingly be familiar with fields related to their own, will find direction to much useful information: for the criminal attorney, insights into the nature and causes of criminality and data on the efficacy of certain modes of treatment or punishment; for the criminologist, authoritative discussion of substantive and procedural issues in the criminal law.

A glance at the table of contents reveals the many perspectives from which a given topic can be viewed. For example, the entry Prisons offers historical and current coverage, as well as special assessments of issues concerning institutions for youths and for women. Other entries provide cross-disciplinary or comparative perspectives; some deal with concepts, theories, or principles, others with empirical research, and still others with practical applications.

We have tried in a number of ways to ensure the accessibility of the information conveyed. Turning again to the table of contents, one notes that major topics, from Abortion to Youth Gangs and Groups,

are presented as entries. Where a particular topic merits full and separate discussion from a variety of perspectives, these are grouped together under the entry title—for example, the articles Constitutional Aspects and Comparative Aspects under the entry Criminal Procedure. A reader interested in a specific topic can turn to the table of contents; if he does not find it there, he can look for it under its alphabetical location in the body of the Encyclopedia. There, the topic may be found as one of many blind entries dispersed throughout the Encyclopedia to facilitate the reader's search for desired information. For example, a reader seeking information on vandalism will not encounter it in the table of contents, but he will find a blind entry under that designation which will direct him to the entry on Malicious Mischief. A reader pursuing a topic of immediate interest will also find direction to related areas by means of the cross-references that follow each article. Thus, for example, the reader of the article Crime Causation: Psychological Theories is referred to Diminished Capacity, Intelligence and Crime, and Psychopathy, among other entries. Ultimately, full treatment of a topic across entries—that is, in a number of different contexts—may be found by consulting the exhaustive index at the end of the Encyclopedia.

The extensive bibliographies following the articles serve not only to provide documentation but also to indicate resources for further research. These resources include journal articles, scholarly monographs, reference works, textbooks, dissertations, and government documents. All the bibliographies were prepared by the authors of the individual articles, and the items were then verified for completeness and accuracy. Each item refers, where possible, to the most recent, readily available English-language edition; information about reprintings and original dates of publication is provided where appropriate. (For bibliographic sources referred to in the text, the date of publication is provided only where needed to distinguish between two or more works by the same author.)

Full legal citations within the text are the second bridge to outside sources. These citations, again, both document the text and guide the reader to court decisions, statutes, and other legal materials that reflect historical and current thinking and practice in the criminal law. (Readers unfamiliar with forms of legal citation should refer to the Guide to Legal Citations in the front of the Encyclopedia.) Legal citations are provided in the interest of the reader who wishes to pursue a topic in depth, including its significant legal dimensions.

Within the articles themselves, the same concern for accessibility has been paramount. Authors were encouraged not only to provide breadth and depth of coverage, but also to make their presentations meaningful to the nonspecialist. To authors as well as editors, this meant striving for the basics of good writing: a clear agenda of issues to be treated, a full complement of background information, both historical and conceptual, and straightforward prose. Each

article was reviewed by staff members and by the Editorial Board; authors, in turn, reworked and revised where necessary.

To all those who have brought spirited interest and specialized knowledge to bear on the Encyclopedia, thanks and congratulations are due. The editors and authors who contributed their time and expertise merit first note, particularly for their commitment to the unique aims of the project. Edward Sagarin deserves special thanks for serving both as contributor and as informal adviser, and for taking a strong personal interest in the Encyclopedia's development.

Others who worked toward the realization of this project include Charles E. Smith, Publisher; Sylvia Juran, in-house editor; Annette Nathanson, assistant charged with administrative duties; Morton Rosenberg, Production Manager; Joan Greenfield, Designer; Richard Greenbaum, freelance bibliographic and legal researcher; and James Miller, freelance editor. Each devoted special talents to what was, all along, very much a collective effort. It is hoped that this Encyclopedia will bring issues of vital social importance into clearer perspective for professionals and lay readers alike; all of us involved now turn it over to its readership, trusting that this goal has been achieved.

LINDA J. HALVORSON

GUIDE TO LEGAL CITATIONS

The following brief guide to legal citations and the abbreviations used in them is designed primarily for readers unfamiliar with the literature of the law. It is confined to the abbreviations and citation forms used in this Encyclopedia; readers wanting a comprehensive guide to legal citations and abbreviations should consult *A Uniform System of Citation* (the so-called Blue Book), now in its thirteenth edition, published by the Harvard Law Review Association and available at law school bookstores. Extensive lists of legal abbreviations and their meanings can also be found in the *Dictionary of Legal Abbreviations Used in American Law Books* by Doris M. Bieber (Buffalo, N.Y.: Hein, 1979) and in the first appendix to the fifth edition of *Black's Law Dictionary* (St. Paul: West, 1979). Readers wishing more comprehensive information about legal materials should consult *How to Find the Law* by Morris Cohen and Robert C. Berring (St. Paul: West, 1983) or *Fundamentals of Legal Research* by J. Myron Jacobstein and Roy M. Mersky (Mineola, N.Y.: Foundation Press, 1981).

The citation after the name of a case, statute, or treaty tells the reader where to find the full text of the court decision (in the case) or the full text of the material referred to. Below are typical American and British case and statute citations with brief explanations of their structure and the meaning of their various elements.

American state case: *People v. Anderson*, 6 Cal. 3d 628, 493 P.2d 880 (1972)
American federal case: *United States v. Brawner*, 471 F.2d 969 (D.C. Cir. 1972)

1. The first element of a case citation consists of the names of the parties, with the plaintiff—or, in criminal cases, the prosecuting entity—listed first and the defendant last. In the example, therefore, this is the case of (the) People (of the State of California) versus Anderson. In criminal cases, such as the examples above, a governmental unit, rather than an individual, organization, or group is the plaintiff, designated "United States" in federal cases and "State," "People," or "Commonwealth" in state cases. In cases on appeal, such as these, it is usual to list the original plaintiff first in order to retain the same case name throughout the case's entire judicial history, but in some jurisdictions the case on appeal will begin with the name of the appellant (the party initiating the appeal), who is almost always the defendant in the original case.

2. The second element indicates where the case may be found in the appropriate volume of court reports, first in the official reporter (such reporters are published by the United States government and by most of the states) and second, in the unofficial (usually a regional) reporter. Within this element are listed, sequentially, the number of the volume, the abbreviated name of the court reporter, its series (if more than one series has been issued), and the page on which the text of the report (that is, the decision) begins. Further, within this element, the abbreviated name of the jurisdiction also indicates the level of court that decided the case. Thus, in the first example the abbreviation "Cal." indicates that the decision re-

ported is that of the California Supreme Court (as contrasted to an abbreviation such as "Cal. App.," which would indicate a decision of one of the California courts of appeals). The case is reported in volume 6 of the official California Reports, third series, beginning on page 628, and also in volume 493 of the unofficial Pacific Reporter, second series, beginning on page 880. In the second example, the abbreviation "F.2d" indicates that the decision reported is of one of the twelve United States circuit courts of appeals (as contrasted to "U.S.," which would indicate the United States Supreme Court, or "F. Supp.," which would indicate a decision of one the various federal district courts).

3. Within the parentheses is given the year in which the court decision was rendered. As the federal example shows, the parenthetical material may also indicate the specific court that handed down the decision, if the name of the reporter series itself does not convey that information; this is true of all citations to "F.2d." In the example, the parenthetical reference indicates which of the twelve federal circuit courts of appeals rendered the decision—here, the District of Columbia circuit. For those states that do not issue official state reporters, the abbreviated name of the state and the level of the court will be indicated within the parentheses before the date of decision, as in *Spencer v. State,* 263 So. 2d 282 (Fla. App. 1972). Case decisions from states lacking an official reporter for one or more levels of their courts are published in the appropriate unofficial regional reporter.

If the case has any further procedural history (for example, if the decision was later affirmed, modified, or reversed by a higher court), that information will be printed after the basic citation.

British case: *Regina v. McInnes,* [1971] 1 W.L.R. 1600 (C.A.)

The typical British case citation differs slightly in form from the American.

1. After the name of the parties (plaintiff or prosecuting entity first) appears the year in which the decision was published; this is not necessarily the same as the year in which it was rendered.
2. The number after the year is the volume number of that year's published reports. Each year's volumes begin with the number 1; they are not numbered in sequence from the beginning of publication, as are American reports. This is fol-

lowed by the name of the reporter (the official one first if more than one is listed) and the page on which the case report begins.

3. The final element, in parentheses, indicates which court rendered the decision. This element is omitted if the name of the official reporter, for example "A.C.," conveys that information.

American statutes: (1) Bank Protection Act of 1968, as amended, 12 U.S.C. §§ 1729, 1881–1884 (1976 & Supp. IV 1980); (2) Bail Reform Act of 1966, Pub. L. 89-465, 80 Stat. 214 (codified in scattered sections of 18 U.S.C.)

American statutes are cited in two different ways, depending on whether the text of the law in question is codified in one section (or a number of contiguous sections) of the United States Code (U.S.C.). Where this is so the statute is cited as in the first example.

1. The first element is the name of the act (either its actual name or the name by which it is popularly known), followed by the year of its enactment and an indication, if appropriate, of whether the act has been amended since its original passage.
2. The second element consists of the number of the Title (in the example, 12; each Title of the United States Code includes all the laws then in force relating to a particular subject matter, such as criminal law or copyright law) and the section number(s) where the statute has been placed in the code.
3. Finally, there appear in parentheses the edition of the United States Code (a new edition is published approximately every six years) and an indication of where to find any changes or amendments to the statute which have been enacted since the publication of that edition (a multivolume supplement to the code is published annually).

Where the provisions of the statute have been scattered among one or more Titles of the United States Code, the law is cited as in the second example.

1. The first element consists of the name and date of the act.
2. The second element is the public law number. The first group of digits denotes which Congress enacted the legislation; the second, the statute's number in the chronological sequence of all public laws passed by that Congress.
3. There follows the location of the statute's text in the United States Statutes at Large. Until 1946, a volume of this series was published for each Con-

gress; since 1946 a volume has been published for each session of each Congress. The volume number precedes the abbreviation, and the page number on which the text of the statute begins follows it.

4. Finally, in parentheses, is listed the Title(s) (in the example, 18) of the code in or among which the text of the statute has been codified. If the act has been repealed or superseded, that fact will be indicated in parentheses.

British statute: Criminal Appeal Act, 1907, 7 Edw. 7, c. 23 (repealed)

British (or, before 1707, English) statutes are cited by the name of the act, the year of enactment, the year of the monarch's reign (in the example, the seventh year of Edward VII's reign; this practice was discontinued in 1963), and the position of the law in the numerical sequence of all the laws passed that year, the first law of each reign year being numbered chapter (c.) 1. If a particular section of the act is being cited, that will be indicated by "s." followed by the number of the section. If the act or some of its sections have been repealed, that fact will be indicated parenthetically, as in the example.

RICHARD GREENBAUM

ABBREVIATION	FULL NAME	EXPLANATION
A.; A.2d	Atlantic Reporter (First Series; Second Series)	Unofficial reporter containing decisions of the highest courts and of some intermediate appellate courts of Connecticut, Delaware, Maine, Maryland, New Jersey, New Hampshire, Pennsylvania, Rhode Island, and Vermont. *Example:* 189 A.2d 646 (Me. 1933) = Volume 189, Atlantic Reporter, Second Series, page 646 (jurisdiction; year decision rendered).
A.B.M.R.	Army Board of Military Review	An appellate court that reviews decisions of army courts-martial.
A.C.	Appeal Cases (Great Britain)	Part of the official English Law Reports; reports appellate cases decided by the highest courts of England—the House of Lords and the Privy Council. This series of reports begins in 1891.
A.F.B.M.R.	Air Force Board of Military Review	An appellate court that reviews decisions of air force courts-martial.
aff'd,	affirmed	Indicates that the lower-court decision (which appears before *aff'd*) was affirmed by a decision of a higher court (which appears after *aff'd*). Compare *rev'd.*
All E.R.	All England Law Reports	Unofficial but widely cited series containing decisions of English courts, beginning with 1936.
App. Div.; App. Div. 2d (N.Y.)	New York Appellate Division Reports (First Series; Second Series)	Official reports of decisions of the intermediate appellate courts of New York State, the Appellate Division of the Supreme Court of the State of New York.
B.C. Ct. App.	British Columbia (Canada) Court of Appeals	An intermediate appellate court.
BGBl	Bundesgesetzblatt, Teil l (West Germany)	Weekly publication that prints the full official text of all West German federal laws, treaties, and decrees; published since 1949.
c.; ch.	chapter	

ABBREVIATION	FULL NAME	EXPLANATION
C.A.	Court of Appeal (England)	The appellate court in England, from which an appeal is possible only to the Appellate Committee of the House of Lords. It has two divisions: the Civil Division and the Criminal Division.
Cal.; Cal. 2d; Cal. 3d	California Reports (First Series; Second Series; Third Series)	Official reports of decisions of the Supreme Court of California.
Cal. App.; Cal. App. 2d; Cal. App. 3d	California Appellate Reports (First Series; Second Series; Third Series)	Official reports of decisions of the various California courts of appeals, which are intermediate appellate courts.
Cal. Rptr.	California Reporter	Unofficial reporter that prints decisions of all the California courts.
Can. Crim. Code	Canadian Criminal Code	Codification of Canadian criminal law.
Can. S. Ct.	Supreme Court of Canada	Highest Canadian court.
C.C.A.	Court of Criminal Appeal (Great Britain)	Appellate court established by the Criminal Appeal Act of 1907; has been replaced by the Court of Appeal (Criminal Division).
C.C.C.	Canadian Criminal Cases Annotated	Reports of important decisions in criminal and quasi-criminal cases from dominion and provincial courts. Published since 1898; the second series begins with 1971.
C.F.R.	Code of Federal Regulations	A multivolume set, keyed to the Titles of the United States Code and revised annually. It gives the text of all administrative rules and regulations currently in force.
Cir. (as in 1st Cir.)	Circuit	A United States circuit court of appeals (an intermediate-level federal court). There are twelve circuits; the number (or the letters D.C.) preceding the abbreviation indicates from which one the decision emanated.
Cmnd. (No.)	Command (Great Britain) (Number)	A designation affixed to certain reports issued by agencies of the British government and presented to Parliament at the command of the Crown.
C.M.R.	Court Martial Reports	Reports of the decisions of the various courts of military review and of the United States Court of Military Appeals. Published between 1951 and 1978.
Conn. Gen. Stat. (Ann.)	Connecticut General Statutes (Annotated)	A multivolume compilation, supplemented every year, containing all the laws and court rules currently in force in the jurisdiction (state).
C.P.	Court of Common Pleas (England)	One of the four superior courts at Westminster that existed until passage of the Judicature Acts in the second half of the nineteenth century. (The Judicature Acts fundamentally restructured the English court system.)

ABBREVIATION	FULL NAME	EXPLANATION
Cr. Cas. Res.	Court for Crown Cases Reserved (Great Britain)	A court of criminal appeal, established in 1848 to consider questions of law referred by a judge in certain of the lower courts before which a prisoner had been found guilty by verdict. If this court held that the point had been wrongly decided at the trial, the conviction was overturned. The court was abolished in 1907 by the Criminal Appeal Act, which created the Court of Criminal Appeal (C.C.A.)
Crim. App.	Criminal Appeal Reports (Great Britain)	Reports of cases brought under the Criminal Appeal Act of 1907; published since 1909.
C.R.N.S.	Criminal Reports, New Series (Canada)	Annotated reports (decisions) of criminal cases decided in the courts of the various Canadian provinces: 1st Series, 1946–1967; New Series, 1967–1978; 3d Series, 1978—.
Eng. Rep.	English Reports—Full Reprint	A compilation of all reported English cases between 1307 and 1865. Includes most of the material from the contemporary yearbooks.
Entscheidungen BGHSt	Entscheidungen des Bundesgerichtshofes in Strafsachen	Reports of decisions of the German Federal Republic's High Court of Criminal Appeals; published since 1951.
Entscheidungen RGSt	Entscheidungen des Reichsgerichts in Strafsachen	Reports of decisions of the highest court of criminal appeal under the German Empire, the Weimar Republic, and the Third Reich; published from 1880 through 1944.
Eur. Human Rights R.	European Human Rights Reports	Official reports of decisions of the European Court of Human Rights in Strasbourg, France.
Ex.	Court of Exchequer (England)	Originally established by William the Conqueror and later one of the four superior courts at Westminster, although inferior to the King's (Queen's) Bench and Common Pleas.
Exec. Order	Executive Order (United States)	Orders, with the force of law, promulgated by the President. These orders are collected in Title 3 of the Code of Federal Regulations.
F.; F.2d	Federal Reporter (First Series; Second Series)	Official reports of decisions of the federal courts other than the Supreme Court. "F." (begun in 1880) includes decisions of both the federal district courts and the circuit courts of appeals; "F.2d" (begun in 1913) covers decisions of the courts of appeals and the Court of Claims.
F. Cas.	Federal Cases	Reports of decisions of the federal district courts and the federal circuit courts from the establishment of those courts through December 31, 1879.
Fed. Reg.	Federal Register	Official publication, issued daily, containing the text of new and proposed departmental and agency rules and regulations before they are entered in the Code of Federal Regulations. Also contains administrative notices, which are not transferred to the C.F.R.
Fed. R. Evid.	Federal Rules of Evidence	A set of rules governing the introduction and use of various kinds of evidence and the examination of witnesses in all federal trials, civil and criminal.

ABBREVIATION	FULL NAME	EXPLANATION
F.R.D.	Federal Rules Decisions	Reports of opinions, decisions, and rulings (by federal courts and other bodies) involving the Federal Rules of Criminal Procedure and the Federal Rules of Civil Procedure. Published since 1941; covers cases from 1940 on.
Fed. R. Crim. P.	Federal Rules of Criminal Procedure	Rules defining and prescribing proper procedure in all federal criminal cases. Most states have promulgated an analogous set of rules, often called the Code of Criminal Procedure (in New York it is called the Criminal Procedure Law, or CPL).
F. Supp.	Federal Supplement	Official reports of decisions rendered by the various federal district courts, the lowest federal courts.
G.A.O.R.	General Assembly Official Records (United Nations)	Official records of debates and resolutions of the United Nations General Assembly, beginning with its first session in 1946.
H.J. Res. (No.)	House Joint Resolution (Number)	A joint resolution proposed or passed by the House of Representatives of the United States Congress, by number.
H.L.	House of Lords (Great Britain)	As a legislative body, the House of Lords is the upper house of the United Kingdom Parliament; as a judicial body, it is the highest appellate court. It consists principally of the Lords of Appeal in Ordinary—former judges or barristers who are given life peerages and appointed to the House. They sit as Appellate Committees to hear cases and report their conclusions to the House.
H.R. (No.)	House of Representatives (Number)	A bill introduced in the House of Representatives of the United States Congress, by number.
I.L.M.	International Legal Materials	An American journal, published since 1962. Contains selected documents relating to international law, such as treaties and other international agreements, cases, regulations, legislation, and arbitration awards.
I.L.R.	International Law Reports	Unofficial reports of decisions of various international tribunals, and of national courts in cases in which the parties are of different nationalities.
I.R.C.	Internal Revenue Code	Compilation of the tax laws of the United States government. It is also Title 26 of the United States Code.
J.I.	Jury Instructions	Collection(s) of model or pattern instructions or charges given by judges to juries on various points of law.
K.B.	Court of King's Bench (England)	Historically, the highest common-law court in England. During the reign of a queen it is called the Queen's Bench (Q.B.). Under the Judicature Act of 1873 it was merged into the High Court of Justice.
L.N.T.S.	League of Nations Treaty Series	Official collection of bilateral and multilateral treaties and other international agreements signed between 1920 and 1946.

ABBREVIATION	FULL NAME	EXPLANATION
L.R.	Law Reports (England)	Official reports of English appellate cases. In an actual case citation a second abbreviation indicates which specific court or court division decided the case; an example is *Regina v. Prince*, L.R. 2 Cr. Cas. Res. 154 (1875).
Mich. Gen. Ct. R.	Michigan General Court Rules	Code of rules prescribing procedure for all cases, civil and criminal, brought in the courts of Michigan.
Misc.	Miscellaneous Reports	Official reports of the New York State trial courts.
M.J.	Military Justice Reporter	Reports of decisions of the United States Court of Military Appeals and of selected opinions of the courts of military review. Publication began in 1978; the cases reported date back to 1975.
N.E.; N.E.2d	Northeastern Reporter (First Series; Second Series)	An unofficial reporter containing decisions of the highest courts and of some intermediate appellate courts of Indiana, Illinois, Massachusetts, New York, and Ohio.
N.J.L.	New Jersey Law Reports	Compilation of cases decided by the New Jersey Supreme Court and the Court of Errors and Appeals. It was published from 1789 through 1948; subsequently it was merged into the New Jersey Reports (N.J.), which, however, include only decisions of the New Jersey Supreme Court.
N.W.; N.W.2d	Northwestern Reporter (First Series; Second Series)	Unofficial reporter containing decisions of the highest courts and of some intermediate appellate courts of Iowa, Michigan, Minnesota, Nebraska, North Dakota, South Dakota, and Wisconsin.
N.Y.S.; N.Y.S.2d	New York Supplement (First Series; Second Series)	Unofficial reports of the decisions of all New York State courts.
N.Z.L.R.	New Zealand Law Reports	Collection of decisions of the High (Supreme) Court of New Zealand, the highest appellate court, as well as decisions of other New Zealand appellate and special courts.
Op. Att'y Gen.	Opinions of the Attorney General of the United States	Contains formal advisory opinions of the attorneys general of the United States. Most states also publish advisory opinions of their attorneys general.
P.; P.2d	Pacific Reporter (First Series; Second Series)	An unofficial regional reporter containing decisions of the highest courts and of some intermediate appellate courts of Alaska, Arizona, California, Colorado, Hawaii, Idaho, Kansas, Montana, Nevada, New Mexico, Oklahoma, Oregon, Utah, Washington, and Wyoming.
Parry's T.S.	Parry's Consolidated Treaty Series	Unofficial collection of treaties and other international agreements signed between 1648 and 1919.
Pasch.	Pascha (Easter)	The Easter term in the old English court calendar.
P.C.	Privy Council (England)	The principal council of the sovereign, composed of the cabinet ministers and other persons chosen by the monarch. Its Judicial Committee acts as a court of ultimate appeal in certain types of cases from Commonwealth countries.

ABBREVIATION	FULL NAME	EXPLANATION
Phil.	Philippine Reports	Compilation of decisions of the Supreme Court of the Philippines from c. 1900 to the present.
Pub. L.	Public Law	Public laws or acts passed by the United States Congress, as contrasted with private laws (laws passed for the benefit of an individual, a small group of individuals, or a particular locality).
Q.B.	Court of Queen's Bench (England)	See K.B.
Q.B.D.	Queen's Bench Division (England)	Same as Q.B.; see K.B.
rev'd,	reversed	Indicates that the lower-court decision (which appears before *rev'd*) was reversed by a decision of a higher court (which appears after *rev'd*). Compare *aff'd*.
§; §§	section; sections	
S. (No.)	Senate (Number)	A bill introduced in the United States Senate, by number.
S. Ct.	Supreme Court Reporter	Unofficial reporter containing decisions of the Supreme Court of the United States.
S.E.; S.E.2d	Southeastern Reporter (First Series; Second Series)	An unofficial regional reporter containing decisions of the highest courts and of some intermediate appellate courts of Georgia, North Carolina, South Carolina, Virginia, and West Virginia.
S.I.	Statutory Instruments (Great Britain)	A collection of rules, regulations, and orders issued by ministers, departments, and other authorized bodies. Published since 1948.
S.J. Res. (No.)	Senate Joint Resolution (Number)	A joint resolution proposed or passed by the United States Senate, by number.
So.; So. 2d	Southern Reporter (First Series; Second Series)	An unofficial regional reporter containing decisions of the highest courts and of some intermediate appellate courts of Alabama, Florida, Louisiana, and Mississippi.
Star Chamber	Court of Star Chamber (England)	An early English court which evolved to remedy the inability of the common-law courts to bring criminal offenders to justice. Its penalties were severe, its methods cruel, its procedures arbitrary, and its powers were sometimes illegally extended and exercised. Abolished in 1641, it has since become a synonym for the arbitrary and tyrannical exercise of authority.
Stat.	1. United States Statutes at Large	1. Official compilations of the text of newly enacted federal laws. Published for each Congress since the first (1789) and, since the Seventy-ninth Congress (1946), for each session of each Congress.
	2. Statutes	2. A compilation of all the currently effective laws of a given jurisdiction, usually a state.
Supp.	Supplement	

ABBREVIATION	FULL NAME	EXPLANATION
S.W.; S.W.2d	Southwestern Reporter (First Series; Second Series)	An unofficial regional reporter containing decisions of the highest courts and of some intermediate appellate courts of Arkansas, Kentucky, Missouri, Tennessee, and Texas.
T.I.A.S.	Treaties and Other International Acts Series	A collection of treaties and other international agreements and conventions to which the United States is a party. Published since 1945, by the Department of State.
Trade Cas. (CCH)	Trade Cases (Commerce Clearing House)	A privately published case reporter issued as part of a loose-leaf service. It contains cases and administrative decisions dealing with regulation of trade, including antitrust matters. Reference to the cases is typically by paragraph number.
T.S.	Treaty Series (United States Department of State)	Compilation of treaties and executive agreements to which the United States is a party that were signed between January 1908 and November 1944 (ends with No. 994).
U.N.T.S.	United Nations Treaty Series	Official collection of international treaties and other agreements signed since 1946. Continues the League of Nations Treaty Series.
U.S.	United States Reports	Official reports of all decisions of the Supreme Court of the United States.
U.S.C.	United States Code	Official compilation, by Title (subject matter), of all federal laws currently in force. Supplementary volumes are issued annually, and a new edition of the code appears approximately every six years. Two publishers produce annotated versions of the United States Code.
U.S.C.A.	United States Code Annotated	Same as the United States Code, but privately published and containing extensive annotations (summaries of judicial decisions), with references also to law review articles.
U.S.C.M.A.	United States Court of Military Appeals	Reports of cases decided by the named court and of appeals from the boards (since August 1, 1969, courts) of military review, which review the sentences of courts-martial in the various branches of the armed forces of the United States.
U.S. Code Cong. & Ad. News	United States Code Congressional and Administrative News	Unofficial compilation of public laws, legislative histories, executive orders, proclamations, reorganization plans, commentaries, and related materials, beginning with the Seventy-eighth Congress, second session (1944).
U.S.L.W.	United States Law Week	An unofficial weekly publication that prints the full text of the latest United States Supreme Court decisions (substantially before they appear in any of the reporters) and reports all the other actions taken by the Supreme Court. It also contains selected decisions of lower federal courts and of state courts.
U.S.T.	United States Treaties and Other International Agreements	Official collection of treaties and other international agreements to which the United States is a party; published since January 1, 1950.
W.L.R.	Weekly Law Reports (England)	An unofficial reporter, published since 1953, that contains decisions of all the high English courts.

ABBREVIATION	FULL NAME	EXPLANATION
Y.B.	Year Book (England)	Books of case reports in a series extending from the reign of Edward I (1272–1307) to the time of Henry VIII (1509–1547). The reports were written by the prothonotaries (chief scribes) of the courts, at Crown expense, and published annually. Most, but not all, of the Year Book cases are included in the English Reports—Full Reprint (Eng. Rep.).

ABANDONMENT

See ATTEMPT; CONSPIRACY; SOLICITATION.

ABORTION

Introduction

The criminal law has ordinarily used the term *abortion* to describe an intentional termination of pregnancy. Miscarriages or spontaneous abortions, however labeled by the medical profession, are not regarded by the law as abortions at all. Except to the extent that certain nineteenth-century enactments departed from the traditional learning embodied in the common law and in most early abortion statutes, guilt for a criminal abortion lay with the abortionist—that is, the individual who performed the procedure or who supplied to the pregnant woman the materials for it. The woman who sought the abortion or employed the materials furnished to her by the abortionist was not covered by the law (Perkins, p. 139).

The definition of what constitutes the crime of abortion has changed frequently and dramatically between the common-law era and the present day. Religion and shifting mores have, of course, contributed to these alterations in the law. Demographic concerns have exerted an influence as well. But the evolution of modern abortion law also reflects the evolution of obstetric medicine and scientific understanding of the gestational process. Even the United States Su-

preme Court's 1973 invalidation of the abortion restrictions of almost every state and the congressional debates that followed turned, in large part, on differing medical assessments of human reproduction (*Roe v. Wade*, 410 U.S. 113 (1973); *Doe v. Bolton*, 410 U.S. 179 (1973); Cohodas, 1981b).

Historical development

The common law. Modern legal historians dispute whether, and to what extent, abortion constituted a crime at English common law. One view finds that, at most, abortion was an ecclesiastical crime, and concludes that the common law allowed a woman and her abortionist to terminate a pregnancy at all stages of gestation without secular penalties (Means, 1971, pp. 335–362). Another claims that all abortions were at least secular wrongs to the fetus and that only the problems of proving a causal relationship between some abortions and fetal death prevented the punishment of all abortions (Byrn, pp. 814–827). Substantial authority exists, however, for a middle ground: although no penalties attached to abortions before the fetus had quickened, performing a postquickening abortion was a common-law crime, most likely a misdemeanor (Mohr, pp. 3–6; Means, 1968, pp. 411–422).

Consistent with this intermediate position, in the early thirteenth century Henry de Bracton (d. 1268), chancellor of Exeter Cathedral and ultimately a justice of the King's Bench, denounced abortion of a "formed and animated" or a "formed or quickened" fetus as homicide (p. 341). But approximately four hundred years later, Edward Coke wrote that an abortion upon a woman "quick with childe . . . is a great misprision, and no murder" if the fetus dies before being delivered (p. 50). Most American courts have read "great misprision" as "misdemeanor" in applying Coke's statement of the English common law (Means, 1968, p. 420). Similarly, Matthew Hale and William Blackstone, in works published in the eighteenth century, labeled abortion a "great crime," or "misprision," only after quickening, while disclaiming its status as a homicidal offense so long as the fetus died *in utero* (Hale, p. 433; Blackstone, *198).

Several reasons have been offered to explain the critical role of "quickening" (the time when the woman first feels the fetus move within her), a subjective and variable experience usually occurring between the sixteenth and eighteenth weeks of pregnancy. The ancient philosophical theory of "mediate animation," which posited that the fetus attained humanness, or personhood, at some point between conception and birth, provides some insight: when the fetus first makes perceptible, independent movements, it demonstrates that it has reached that status. Destruction of an "animated," or "quick," fetus therefore differed qualitatively from early abortion (*Roe*, 132–134; Means, 1968, pp. 411–418). Alternatively, the nonexistence of an accurate pregnancy test meant that terminating an early pregnancy was indistinguishable from treatment of a "menstrual obstruction," for only after fetal movements had been felt could pregnancy be confirmed (Mohr, p. 4). Finally, the quickening criterion served an important evidentiary function, providing the only indication that an act of abortion had in fact caused destruction of a live fetus rather than merely the expulsion of one that had previously died *in utero* (Byrn, p. 815).

These early observations reveal another point as well. Despite Bracton's treatment of postquickening abortion as homicide, Coke, Hale, and Blackstone agreed that abortion, to the extent that it was a crime, was a distinct offense. Only in cases of live birth and subsequent death from an act of abortion was the fetus (or child) considered the victim of a homicidal crime. Although quickening may have been a sufficient condition for personhood, live birth alone made the child "a reasonable creature, *in rerum natura*" ("in the nature of things"), a necessary criterion for applying the law of homicide (Coke, pp. 50–51; cf. Hale, p. 433; Blackstone, *197–198).

The early statutes. England's first criminal abortion statute, Lord Ellenborough's Act, perpetuated the quickening distinction. Enacted in 1803, it punished as capital offenses postquickening abortions performed by poisoning, while attaching a less strin-

gent sanction, deportation to a penal colony, to all those performed earlier (Malicious Shooting, Stabbing, Poisoning, or Abortion Act, 1803, 43 Geo. 3, c. 58, § 1 (Great Britain) (repealed), cited in Mohr, p. 23).

The first American abortion legislation to supersede the common law received from England was an 1821 Connecticut statute. It imposed life imprisonment for abortion of a woman "quick with child" but, like one part of Lord Ellenborough's Act, only if the method used were poisoning (Conn. Pub. Stats. tit. 22, § 14 (1821) (repealed); Mohr, p. 21). The statute's narrow coverage and its inculpation of only the abortionist, and not the pregnant woman, suggest that the legislature sought to respond to the hazards of certain abortifacients rather than to criminalize abortion per se (Mohr, pp. 22, 24). This conclusion is particularly persuasive in light of other sections of the same statute outlawing a woman's secret delivery of an illegitimate child and her concealment of an illegitimate child (Conn. Pub. Stats. tit. 22, §§ 15, 16 (1821) (repealed)). An 1830 revision of the Connecticut statute, however, did extend the prohibition of abortions to those performed by instruments, but it reduced the penalty to seven to ten years' imprisonment (Conn. Pub. Stats. ch. 1, § 16 (1830) (repealed)).

By this date, Missouri, Illinois, and New York had also acted to ban some abortions (Mohr, pp. 25–26). Yet the underlying purpose of these early legislative efforts—whether protection of maternal health from a procedure perceived to be dangerous, given the limits of existing medical knowledge, or outright opposition to abortion itself—remains unclear (cf. Means, 1968, and Mohr, p. 29). Significantly, New York's law contained two major innovations. First, it punished postquickening abortions resulting in the death of the mother or fetus as manslaughter, thus according the fetus killed *in utero* some of the protection of the homicide law. Second, it allowed the first therapeutic exception for life-saving abortions, thus providing evidence of the state's superior interest in protecting the pregnant woman over the fetus (N.Y. Rev. Stats. pt. IV, ch. 1, tit. 2, § 9 (1829), *as amended by* 1830 N.Y. Laws ch. 320, § 58 (repealed); cf. Means, 1968, pp. 447–449).

By 1841, ten of the twenty-six American states had enacted criminal abortion laws. Half of these followed the common law in punishing only those who performed postquickening abortions. The others, to the extent that they purported to cover earlier abortions, remained unenforceable, for pregnancy itself could not yet be established conclusively prior to quickening. Although during this era some states (for example, Maine) sought to circumvent the difficulties of proving actual pregnancy by including "attempted abortion" in their statutory offenses, this approach proved equally ineffective because the intent to terminate a pregnancy, a necessary element of that crime, was undemonstrable in the absence of quickening; the abortionist could always explain his acts as efforts to treat a suspected menstrual disorder. Finally, because they were enacted as part of a larger campaign initiated by physicians to regulate the practice of medicine, none of the provisions adopted in the United States through 1841 implicated the pregnant woman in the crime of abortion (Mohr, p. 43).

Later legislation and its impact. As abortion became an increasingly popular and publicized practice, not only in the prevention of illegitimacy but also as a method of family planning among white, married Protestants, America's birthrate dropped. In the nineteenth century, as many as one out of every five pregnancies may have ended in abortion (Mohr, p. 76). American legislatures responded to these sociological phenomena by tightening their abortion restrictions. A comprehensive abortion statute enacted in New York in 1845 exemplifies the mid-nineteenth century approach (1845 N.Y. Laws ch. 260, *as amended by* 1846 N.Y. Laws ch. 22 (repealed)). Postquickening abortions resulting in the death of mother or fetus remained manslaughter offenses, in the absence of application of the therapeutic exception. In addition, abortions at all stages of gestation were covered by a provision that punished by a three- to twelve-month jail term anyone who administered, prescribed, or procured any substance for a pregnant woman, or who used any instruments on her, with the intent to induce a miscarriage—although the "pregnant woman" and intent requirements presented substantial proof problems before quickening.

Most significant, however, was the third section of the statute, which made the pregnant woman herself guilty of a misdemeanor punishable by a three- to twelve-month jail term, a $1,000 fine, or both, for seeking to obtain or taking any abortifacient, or for submitting to an operation with the intent to induce a miscarriage. No longer viewing the woman simply as a victim of the crime but rather as an essential target for any effective deterrent efforts, New York was the first to criminalize her complicity (Mohr, pp. 123–125).

Between 1860 and 1880, at least forty restrictive abortion laws were enacted, prompted largely by the intensive lobbying of physicians, who wished not only to refine the standards of their profession by barring midwives and other "irregular" practitioners, but also to disseminate their new understanding of gestation as a continuous process in which quickening played no special role (Mohr, pp. 147–170, 200). Once the fetus was seen as a developing life throughout pregnancy, its destruction could be justified only when necessary to save another life, that of the pregnant woman.

Many of the statutes spawned by the physicians' campaign mirrored the earlier innovations of New York and the other pioneering states. They abandoned the common-law limitations by punishing abortion at any stage of gestation as a felony; holding the pregnant woman as a co-felon; criminalizing attempted abortion, in an effort to obviate the need to prove pregnancy as an essential factual element; labeling any destruction of the fetus, even *in utero*, as manslaughter; outlawing the advertisement of abortion services; and, finally, creating a therapeutic exception for life-saving abortions. Parallel developments in England, after the abolition in 1837 of the quickening distinction and the capital punishment specified in Lord Ellenborough's Act, inculpated the pregnant woman in the abortion crime in 1861 (Mohr, pp. 200–225; 270 n. 10).

Even the federal government of the United States joined the anti-abortion movement in 1873, when, as part of an effort to curb pornography, it enacted a statute prohibiting the advertising or distribution by nonphysicians of any abortifacient (An Act for the Suppression of Trade in, and Circulation of, Obscene Literature and Articles of Immoral Use, ch. 258, § 1, 17 Stat. 598 (1873) (repealed)). Inspired by Anthony Comstock, head of the New York Society for the Suppression of Vice, this law established an enduring link between abortion and obscenity (Mohr, pp. 196–197).

By 1900, all those American states that had not already taken action outlawed or restricted abortion. In the mid-twentieth century the penalties for attempted abortions in the various states ranged from a fine with no imprisonment to ten years' imprisonment; seventeen states authorized longer terms, some as long as twenty-one years, for completed abortions. Ten of these states attached the highest penalty only to postquickening abortions (Model Penal Code, 1980, commentary on § 230.3).

These laws fell far short, however, of halting abortions or protecting the women tempted to undergo them, and mid-twentieth-century statistics presented telling evidence of the failure. Estimates placed the annual number of abortions at 333,000 to 2 million, of which 30 percent to 70 percent were thought to be illegal; 8,000 women may have died each year as the result of abortions. The abortion death rate in

Russia after the relaxation of abortion restrictions was approximately 0.01 percent, as compared to an estimated rate of 1.2 percent in the United States. As many as 90 percent of all abortions in the United States occurred among married women seeking to limit family size, and 90 percent to 95 percent of all premarital pregnancies ended in abortion. Physicians performed more than half the illegal abortions, and hospitals regularly allowed abortions for health-threatening pregnancies, although these were not permitted by law. Despite numerous statutes incriminating the abortion patient, prosecutions were exceedingly rare and reported cases undiscoverable (Model Penal Code, 1959, commentary on § 207.11).

Law reform

The restrictive regime persisted in both the United States and England until the 1960s, when change began on two fronts: statutory liberalizations in the legislatures, and constitutional challenges in the courts.

Statutory revisions. The American Law Institute's publication in 1962 of the proposed official draft of the Model Penal Code, including recommendations for "cautious expansion" of situations justifying abortion, was instrumental in initiating legislative reform. Under the Code, a licensed physician may justifiably terminate a pregnancy if there is substantial risk that continued pregnancy will gravely impair the mother's physical or mental health, if it is likely that the child will be born gravely defective, or if the pregnancy resulted from forcible rape or incest; two physicians must provide written certification of the justifying circumstances. The draft of the Code specified punishment of unjustified abortion as a third-degree felony or, for a pregnancy beyond twenty-six weeks, a second-degree felony (Model Penal Code, 1959, § 207.11). This provision attempted to substitute viability (the capacity of the fetus for extrauterine survival) for quickening, the traditional requirement for the aggravated offense (Model Penal Code, 1980, commentary on § 230.3).

Between 1962, the year of the Code's publication, and 1973, at least eight states adopted its expanded justifications, and numerous others followed the proposal in part. Important influences on the draft's favorable reception included a steadily growing population; recognition that illegal abortion had become a widespread and often harmful reality; increasing realization of the relative safety of abortions performed by competent physicians under aseptic conditions; and the thalidomide tragedy of the early 1960s, which brought new understanding of congenital defects and

heightened public sympathy for women seeking to terminate pregnancies threatened by such abnormalities (Model Penal Code, 1959, commentary on § 207.11; Comment, p. 178).

In 1967, England substantially revised its abortion ban in an enactment (Abortion Act, 1967, c. 87 (Great Britain)) that enlarged the Model Penal Code's justifications. The act permitted the risk of abortions in order to prevent greater risks to the pregnant woman's life, to her physical or mental health, to any existing children of her family, or in the face of substantial risk of the birth of a seriously handicapped child. In life- and health-threatening emergencies, the act suspended its ordinary requirement that two physicians in good faith share the opinion that justifying circumstances exist.

By the end of 1970, legislation in four American states had eclipsed even these reforms: Alaska and Hawaii lifted all substantive restrictions on pre-viability abortions. Washington allowed only those abortions performed before quickening or before the expiration of four lunar months after conception. New York, in the most expansive of the pre-1973 liberalizations, authorized all abortions during the first twenty-four weeks of pregnancy without even the residency and hospitalization requirements contained in the Alaska, Hawaii, and Washington provisions. Significantly, the legislation of all four states, unlike the Model Penal Code and England's Abortion Act of 1967, specified no reasons or justifying circumstances limiting the individual woman's abortion choice (Comment, pp. 181–182).

Judicial review. Ultimately, the judicial forum produced more sweeping changes. In 1973, after a number of successful constitutional challenges in state and lower federal courts to restrictive abortion laws (Comment; Morgan), the Supreme Court held in *Roe v. Wade*, 410 U.S. 113 (1973) that the right of privacy—a liberty shielded by the substantive protections of the Fourteenth Amendment's due process clause—is broad enough to encompass a woman's decision whether or not to terminate a pregnancy.

The constitutional right recognized by a majority of the *Roe* Court could yield only to a compelling state interest. Although protecting human life was argued to be such an interest, the Court was unwilling to decide when life begins, and repudiated the notion that a legal person exists prior to birth. It also rejected the argument that abortion is necessarily a hazardous procedure, noting that early abortion is as safe as, or safer than, its alternative, childbirth. As a result, the *Roe* Court struck down all abortion restrictions in the first trimester of pregnancy. During that stage of gestation, the abortion decision belongs to the physician in consultation with his patient and may rest on all relevant considerations, including health, psychological, social, and economic factors (148–164; cf. *Doe v. Bolton*, 410 U.S. 179, 192 (1973)).

Beginning in the second trimester, when abortion becomes more dangerous, a state's compelling interest in safeguarding maternal health will allow the state, if it chooses, to adopt reasonable abortion regulations designed to achieve that goal (*Roe*, 163–164). Finally, after viability, when the fetus is "potentially able to live outside the mother's womb, albeit with artificial aid," a state may acquire a compelling interest in protecting this "potential life"; at this point, which the Court observed usually occurs at twenty-eight weeks, a state may restrict or even proscribe abortion except when continued pregnancy threatens maternal life or health (153–165).

The Court in *Roe* invalidated Texas's "traditional" abortion law, which was first enacted in the mid-nineteenth century and, as subsequently modified, barred all abortions except those necessary to save maternal life (116–119). In the companion case, *Doe,* the Court also overturned a Georgia statute adopted in 1968 and based on the Model Penal Code's 1962 proposed official draft. A lower court had found even these considerably broadened justifications for abortion unduly restrictive of the personal right of privacy (*Doe v. Bolton*, 319 F. Supp. 1048 (N.D. Ga. 1970)). The procedural provisions of the Georgia statute, including special hospitalization, accreditation, two-doctor concurrence, and residency requirements, were struck down by the Supreme Court on similar reasoning (*Doe*, 192–201).

Together, *Roe* and *Doe* overturned virtually every abortion restriction in effect in the United States. Although opinion polls indicated that most Americans concurred with the holdings (Perry), the Court's decisions provoked considerable public outrage. The so-called pro-life movement decried the Court for having legalized "genocide" ("The Battle over Abortion," pp. 20–21), and more scholarly voices observed that the Justices had usurped the legislative role by substituting their own views on abortion for those of the democratically elected lawmakers of the several states (Ely).

After *Roe* and *Doe*. Numerous legislatures responded by enacting new abortion restrictions designed to fill whatever lacunae *Roe* and *Doe* had left. Subsequent opinions of the Supreme Court, however, have underscored the deference to be accorded both to the pregnant woman's autonomy in childbearing decisions and to her doctor's medical judgment. Thus,

although the Court upheld a law requiring all abortions to be performed by physicians (*Connecticut v. Menillo,* 423 U.S. 9 (1975)), it invalidated another state statute that barred abortion advertising because, in part, "the activity advertised pertained to constitutional interests" (*Bigelow v. Virginia,* 421 U.S. 809, 822 (1975)). In *Planned Parenthood v. Danforth,* 428 U.S. 52 (1976), the Justices struck down both spousal and parental consent prerequisites on the theory that a state could not delegate to a third party a veto over the pregnant woman's abortion choice that the state itself lacked. In the same opinion, the Court found unconstitutional Missouri's prohibition of saline amniocentesis, at that time a popular method of second-trimester abortion. Given the absence of an equally safe available alternative, the Court found the restriction, although purportedly enacted to protect maternal health, a practical bar to all abortions at that stage, in contravention of *Roe* (*Planned Parenthood,* 75–79). But the Court did uphold, although almost without analysis, Missouri's imposition of criminal penalties for abortions performed without the prior written consent of the patient and for failure to comply with special record-keeping procedures (*Planned Parenthood,* 65–67, 79–81).

In the years after *Roe,* the Court clarified its understanding of the critical concept of viability, the point in pregnancy that alone permits fetus-protective actions by an interested state (*Roe,* 163). Because viability varies from fetus to fetus, the *Roe* formula does not permit legislatures to draft abortion restrictions locating viability at a particular number of weeks of pregnancy. Legislatures may, however, adopt provisions such as Missouri's definition of the term, approved by the Court in *Planned Parenthood:* "that stage of fetal development when the life of the unborn child may be continued indefinitely outside the womb by natural or artificial life-supportive systems"(63). "Indefinitely" does not mean forever, and therefore a fetus capable of survival for a time after termination of a pregnancy is an appropriate object of state protection (cf. *Floyd v. Anders,* 440 F. Supp. 535 (D. S.Car. 1977), *vacated and remanded,* 440 U.S. 445 (1979)).

Further, although *viability* necessarily connotes a physician's projection of the capacity of a fetus to survive if the pregnancy is terminated, a statute compelling him to determine whether "the fetus is viable or if there is sufficient reason to believe that the fetus may be viable" is too vague to withstand constitutional scrutiny (*Colautti v. Franklin,* 439 U.S. 379 (1979)). As a result, Pennsylvania could not implement *Roe*'s strictures by requiring a physician to act, to the extent permitted by maternal health considerations, to try to save aborted fetuses he had identified in advance as meeting the "viable . . . or . . . may be viable" standard (*Colautti*, 390–394). Due process for a physician whose primary duties lie with his patient, the pregnant woman, demands a more precise standard for criminal liability. A doctor's failure to protect a live-born infant, however, could make him subject to prosecution under the state's homicide statutes (*Planned Parenthood*, 83–84).

The Supreme Court has also given considerable attention to how far states may go in enacting special abortion restrictions for minors. After invalidating the blanket veto contained in Missouri's requirement that all unmarried females under eighteen years of age must obtain parental consent prior to terminating a pregnancy at any stage (*Planned Parenthood*, 72–75), a majority of the Court held that minors may be compelled to obtain judicial authorization for an abortion (*Bellotti v. Baird*, 443 U.S. 622 (1979)). A minor unable or unwilling to secure parental consent may, if the state wishes, have to go to court for an assessment of her maturity and possibly for permission to terminate her pregnancy. If she is deemed sufficiently mature to reach her own decision, she must be allowed to do so; if she is found too immature, the court may substitute its judgment for hers and resolve the issue in her best interest (647–648) (plurality opinion). Finally, states may require physicians performing abortions upon minors to notify their parents in advance (*H.L. v. Matheson*, 450 U.S. 398 (1981)).

The abortion-funding cases and their consequences. Most of the abortion laws reviewed by the Court, and all those examined above, have been criminal laws—that is, restrictions on abortion accompanied by criminal penalties for noncompliance. Several years after its decisions in *Roe* and *Doe*, however, the Court began to examine a different sort of restriction, that of limitations on the use of public funds or facilities for abortion. The opinions in these cases have, in turn, become increasingly important in subsequent challenges to criminal abortion laws.

The Court has reviewed state and federal programs making public assistance unavailable for abortion while allowing such assistance for other medical care, including treatment incident to childbirth. In doing so, it has articulated a distinction between the "absolute obstacles" to (or "direct interference" with or "undue burdens" upon) individual abortion decisions embodied in the criminal penalties overturned in *Roe* and its progeny, on the one hand, and the legislative policy choices reflected in the provision of financial incentives designed to encourage childbirth, on the other (*Harris v. McRae*, 448 U.S. 297 (1980); *Maher*

v. Roe, 432 U.S. 464 (1977)). Only absolute obstacles need satisfy the rigid compelling state interest test applied in *Roe;* policy choices may validly rest on any legitimate and reasonable basis. Although legislative interests in protecting potential life are not compelling until viability under *Roe*, they are, according to the funding cases, sufficiently legitimate and rational to support selective assistance programs favoring childbirth during all stages of gestation (*Harris*, 312–318, 324–326; Appleton).

The analysis employed in these cases has been applied to criminal abortion laws as well. For example, courts have upheld mandatory waiting periods for abortions and detailed "informed consent" provisions (requiring physicians to give their abortion patients specific information before performing the procedure) on the theory that these laws do not unduly burden or completely thwart the abortion choice. Although perhaps inhibiting the decision to terminate a pregnancy, these statutes are rationally related to the legitimate state purpose of protecting potential life, consistent with the test announced in the funding cases (*Leigh v. Olson*, 497 F. Supp. 1340, 1343, 1346 (D.N.D. 1980); *Women's Community Health Center, Inc. v. Cohen*, 477 F. Supp. 542, 549–550 (D. Me. 1979); cf. *Planned Parenthood League of Massachusetts v. Bellotti*, 641 F.2d 1006, 1021, 1022 (1st Cir. 1981); *Charles v. Carey*, 627 F.2d 772, 784 (7th Cir. 1980)). The Supreme Court's own validation of Utah's parental notification requirement invoked similar reasoning (*H.L.*). Even the written-consent and record-keeping provisions approved in *Planned Parenthood* may be profitably reexamined in light of this subsequent interpretation of *Roe*.

As a result, the threshold consideration in reviewing abortion restrictions, including those accompanied by criminal penalties for noncompliance, may be to classify the restriction as either an "undue burden" on the abortion choice or something less. That classification may, in turn, dictate whether to apply the strict standards of constitutional review used in *Roe* and its immediate successors, or the more relaxed test applied in the funding cases (cf. *Charles*, 777–778).

Legislating when human life begins

The "human-life bill." In 1981, after debates and the taking of medical testimony, the Separation of Powers Subcommittee of the United States Senate Judiciary Committee approved a bill finding that "the life of each human being begins at conception" (U.S. Congress, p. 1). Upon that "factual" basis, the bill extends the Fourteenth Amendment's protection against deprivations of life and liberty without due process of law to "each human life" and "all human beings." It also deprives inferior federal courts of jurisdiction to grant injunctive or declaratory relief in cases challenging abortion restrictions.

If it became law, the bill would allow—or possibly compel—the states to protect human life by criminalizing abortion ("Court, Congress, and the Human Life Statute"; Cohodas, 1981a, p. 386). Its language seems to give states the opportunity not only to reenact the kinds of statutes in effect before 1973 but also to treat abortion as homicide, with all of the gradations in offenses and penalties that most homicide statutes contain. In other words, if a fetus is a legally recognized human being, the protection of its life may be subsumed under the laws that protect other persons. One section of the bill even suggests that such equal treatment must be accorded to all without regard to considerations of "age, health, defect, or condition of dependency." Those provisions would erase the bright line drawn in *Roe* and other cases between all embryos and fetuses (nonpersons), on the one hand, and all infants once born (persons), on the other (*Roe*, 158; *Planned Parenthood*, 83–84; cf. *Keeler v. Superior Court*, 2 Cal. 3d 619, 470 P.2d 617 (1970)).

The bill might also allow states to outlaw some forms of birth control not commonly included in the definition of abortion. For example, the "morning-after pill" and the intrauterine device operate to prevent implantation of a fertilized ovum in the wall of the uterus; if legal protection may begin at the moment of conception, purposeful use of these methods of birth control could be tantamount to murder.

Finally, the bill appears to allow states seeking to ban abortion to ignore the narrow therapeutic exception for life-threatening pregnancies, although to the extent that the pregnant woman herself is potentially liable as a principal or accomplice, she might be able to invoke the justification of self-defense (cf. Thomson). Physicians acting on the behalf of women so endangered by continued pregnancy might similarly try to claim defense of another or, possibly, the justification of necessity.

The constitutional status of the so-called human-life bill remains uncertain. The bill purports to implement the Fourteenth Amendment, whose Section 5 authorizes Congress to "enforce, by appropriate legislation, the provisions of this article." According to its sponsors, the bill does not overturn the Supreme Court's 1973 holdings but instead attempts to fill the factual gap left by the Court's reluctance or inability to pinpoint when human life begins (*Roe*, 159; cf. Cohodas, 1981a, p. 385, and "Court, Congress, and the

Human Life Statute"). Under this view, Congress is simply utilizing its expertise in gathering scientific and medical evidence without substituting its reading of the Constitution for that of the Court. Still, serious questions exist concerning the legitimacy of any legislation that would result in a contraction of a previously recognized constitutional right—here, the pregnant woman's right to privacy (Tribe, pp. 261–275; cf. Estreicher; Sager).

Proposed constitutional amendments. Congress might avoid these particular difficulties if it adopted a constitutional amendment instead of a statute defining human life. The first proposal seeking to extend the protection of the Constitution to the unborn was introduced in Congress on January 30, 1973, seven days after the Court had handed down *Roe* and *Doe* (H.J. Res. 261, 93d Cong., 1st sess., 119 *Cong. Rec.* 2575 (1973)). Several subsequent proposals "guaranteeing the right to life" to the unborn have been introduced, including one which provides that "the paramount right to life is vested in each human being from the moment of fertilization without regard to age, health, or condition of dependency" (S.J. Res. 19, 97th Cong., 1st sess., 127 *Cong. Rec.* S578 (daily ed. Jan. 22, 1981)). Another, with respect to the "right to life," makes *person*, as that term appears in the Fifth and Fourteenth Amendments to the Constitution, applicable to "all human beings, irrespective of age, health, function, or condition of dependency, including their unborn offspring at every stage of their biological development"; it would not, however, "prohibit a law permitting only those medical procedures required to prevent the death of the mother" (S.J. Res. 17, 97th Cong., 1st sess., 127 *Cong. Rec.* S567–570 (daily ed. Jan. 22, 1981)).

Using an alternative approach, the proposed Human Life Federalism Amendment, S.J. Res. 110, 97th Cong., 1st sess., 127 *Cong. Rec.* S10196 (daily ed. Sept. 21, 1981), grants no express fetal right to life, but instead provides that a woman's abortion right "is not secured by this Constitution." The amendment would also give Congress and the states concurrent power to enact abortion limitations, with state laws controlling wherever they are "more restrictive" than federal legislation.

Amending the Constitution presents special problems of passage and ratification. Legislation such as the human-life bill need only pass by a simple majority of each house and would become enforceable when signed by the President. By contrast, Article V of the Constitution requires amendments to be approved by a two-thirds vote of each house and then ratified by three-fourths of the state legislatures. Alternatively, amendments may be proposed at a constitutional convention called by two-thirds of the states, followed by state ratification.

If passed and ratified, all of the proposed amendments noted above would overturn *Roe*. The Human Life Federalism Amendment explicitly excises the *Roe* right from the Constitution. The other two proposals—the "right to life" amendments—would have a similar effect; as the Court observed in *Roe*, if the fetus were recognized as a person, the argument for abortion freedom "of course, collapses, for the fetus' right to life would then be guaranteed specifically" by the Constitution (156–157). Indeed, both right-to-life versions would establish the foundation for treating abortions as criminal homicides, with the grade and degree of the offense determined by the actor's mental state. The version guaranteeing a "paramount right to life" arguably would disallow even abortions necessary to save maternal life. The other version would permit abortions in such cases, but as a result, it contains an internal contradiction, for full fetal personhood protected by the Constitution would seem not to allow an automatic exception (157 n. 54).

The right-to-life proposals' respective use of "fertilization" and "at every stage of their biological development" suggests that they cover use of all post-conception methods of birth control. The due process right that the second of these versions would guarantee, by way of the Fifth and Fourteenth Amendments, raises the possibility of permissible abortions following requisite notice and hearing. The equal protection clause, which is similarly implied, together with the elimination of classifications based on "age, health . . . or condition of dependency," would not only nullify the trimester timetable announced in *Roe* but also would disallow all eugenic abortions.

These right-to-life proposals would inculpate both the abortionist and his patient. Indeed, they could provide the basis for making a pregnant woman who miscarries guilty of involuntary manslaughter or negligent homicide if that event were caused by the necessary degree of carelessness. Under similar reasoning, pregnant women could be made criminally liable for all failures to take appropriate prenatal care.

The impact of the Human Life Federalism Amendment is even more speculative. Even if ratified, its substantive effect will depend upon the precise abortion restrictions that Congress and the states choose to enact. It thus provides a vehicle for limiting abortion freedom by simple legislative majorities. Its deference to "more restrictive" state laws would seem to demand intractable comparisons between, for example, legislation requiring spousal consent for abor-

tions, and legislation allowing abortions where pregnancy results from rape or incest. Would a simple quantitative test, indicating which of these two possible laws would permit fewer abortions, determine the "more restrictive" alternative?

Difficult questions of implementation would also be raised by the right-to-life proposals, if either becomes part of the Constitution. The "paramount right to life" version is drafted in the form of a statement, not in that of a prohibition. Would it obligate all the states to enact legislation banning all abortions? Could a state tolerate abortions performed by private physicians in private facilities by enacting no criminal laws on the subject? The proposal redefining *person* provides that "no unborn person shall be deprived of life by any person" (S.J. Res. 17). It therefore purports to address private action, unlike the Fifth and Fourteenth Amendments, which prohibit only those deprivations of life and liberty inflicted by the government. However, because another section of this proposal empowers both Congress and the states to enforce the amendment "by appropriate legislation within their respective jurisdictions," restrictive federal legislation could well preempt the area (U.S. Const. art. VI, § 2), leaving little room for the states to act at all.

Answers to these questions may be suggested by an analogy to the legislation enacted and the cases decided under the Eighteenth Amendment, the "Prohibition amendment" (*National Prohibition Cases*, 253 U.S. 350 (1920)). The Prohibition amendment, which attempted to translate moral opposition to the consumption of intoxicating beverages into a constitutional rule of law, provides additional guidance as well: its enforcement difficulties and ultimate fate (U.S. Const. amend. XXI) may foretell the destiny of any constitutional amendment designed to ban abortion.

SUSAN FRELICH APPLETON

See also CRIMINALIZATION AND DECRIMINALIZATION; HOMICIDE: LEGAL ASPECTS.

BIBLIOGRAPHY

American Law Institute. *Model Penal Code and Commentaries: Official Draft and Revised Comments.* Philadelphia: ALI, 1980.
———. *Model Penal Code: Proposed Official Draft.* Philadelphia: ALI, 1962.
———. *Model Penal Code: Tentative Draft No. 9.* Philadelphia: ALI, 1959.
APPLETON, SUSAN FRELICH. "Beyond the Limits of Reproductive Choice: The Contributions of the Abortion-funding Cases to Fundamental-rights Analysis and to the Wel-

fare-rights Thesis." *Columbia Law Review* 81, no. 4 (1981): 721–758.

"The Battle Over Abortion." *Time*, 6 April 1981, pp. 20–28.

BLACKSTONE, WILLIAM. *Commentaries on the Laws of England* (1765–1769), vol. 4. Reprint. University of Chicago Press, 1979.

BRACTON, HENRY DE. *On the Laws and Customs of England*, vol. 2. Translated, with revisions and notes, by Samuel E. Thorne. Cambridge, Mass.: Harvard University Press, Belknap Press, 1968.

BYRN, ROBERT M. "An American Tragedy: The Supreme Court on Abortion." *Fordham Law Review* 41 (1973): 807–862.

COHODAS, NADINE. " 'Pro-Life' Interest Groups Try a New Tactic in Effort to Crack Down on Abortion." *Congressional Quarterly Weekly Report* 39, no. 9 (1981a): 383–387.

———. "Protests Force New Hearings in Senate Judiciary Panel on Abortion Legislation." *Congressional Quarterly Weekly Report* 39, no. 17 (1981b): 729–730.

COKE, EDWARD. *The Third Part of the Institutes of the Laws of England: Concerning High Treason, and Other Pleas of the Crown, and Criminal Causes* (1641). London: E. & R. Brooke, 1797.

Comment. "A Survey of the Present Statutory and Case Law on Abortion: The Contradictions and the Problems." *University of Illinois Law Forum* (1972): 177–198.

"Court, Congress, and the Human Life Statute." *Christian Science Monitor*, 17 June 1981, p. 23.

ELY, JOHN H. "The Wages of Crying Wolf: A Comment on *Roe v. Wade*." *Yale Law Journal* 82 (1973): 920–949.

ESTREICHER, SAMUEL. "Congressional Power and Constitutional Rights: Reflections on Proposed 'Human Life' Legislation." *Virginia Law Review* 68 (1982): 333–458.

HALE, MATTHEW. *The History of the Pleas of the Crown* (1736), vol. 1. Edited by W. A. Stokes and E. Ingersoll. Philadelphia: Small, 1847.

MEANS, CYRIL C., JR. "The Law of New York concerning Abortion and the Foetus, 1664–1968: A Case of Cessation of Constitutionality." *New York Law Forum* 14 (1968): 411–515.

———. "The Phoenix of Abortional Freedom: Is a Penumbral or Ninth-Amendment Right about to Arise from the Nineteenth-century Legislative Ashes of a Fourteenth-century Common-law Liberty?" *New York Law Forum* 17 (1971): 335–410.

MOHR, JAMES C. *Abortion in America: The Origins and Evolution of National Policy, 1800–1900*. New York: Oxford University Press, 1978.

MORGAN, RICHARD G. "*Roe v. Wade* and the Lesson of the Pre-*Roe* Case Law." *Michigan Law Review* 77 (1979): 1724–1748.

PERKINS, ROLLIN M. *Criminal Law*. 2d ed. Mineola, N.Y.: Foundation Press, 1969.

PERRY, MICHAEL J. "Abortion, the Public Morals, and Police Power: The Ethical Function of Due Process." *UCLA Law Review* 23 (1976): 689–736.

SAGER, LAWRENCE G. "The Supreme Court, 1980 Term—Foreword: Constitutional Limitations on Congress' Authority to Regulate the Jurisdiction of the Federal Courts." *Harvard Law Review* 95 (1981): 17–89.

THOMSON, JUDITH J. "A Defense of Abortion." *Philosophy and Public Affairs* 1 (1971): 47–66.

TRIBE, LAURENCE H. *American Constitutional Law*. Mineola, N.Y.: Foundation Press, 1978.

U.S. Congress, Senate. *The Human Life Bill—S. 158—Report Together with Additional and Minority Views to the Committee on the Judiciary, United States Senate, Made by Its Subcommittee on Separation of Powers*. 97th Cong., 1st sess., December 1981, Committee Print.

ABSOLUTE LIABILITY

See MISTAKE; *both articles under* STRICT LIABILITY; VICARIOUS LIABILITY.

ACCESSORIES

See ACCOMPLICES; CONSPIRACY.

ACCOMPLICES

An accomplice is a person who is criminally liable for a crime committed by another because he contributed in defined ways to the commission of the other's crime, as by encouraging or helping him. The term *accessory* is often used interchangeably with *accomplice*, but it has a technical meaning at common law that would not cover precisely the same persons who today would be regarded as accomplices.

Accomplice liability occupies a place of fundamental importance in the American legal system. A person is generally not criminally liable for the acts of another, because a basic requirement of Anglo-American law is that guilt must be personal and individual. Plainly, however, legal systems must take account of certain situations in which one who does not physically commit the criminal act should nevertheless be subjected to some criminal sanction for involvement with it. The most common of these situations are those in which one party directs or encourages another to commit a crime, or in some way helps that person to commit it. Doctrines of accomplice liability are designed to cover such situations.

Statutes are usually drafted in such a way that mention is made only of the primary actor, or perpetrator. For example, theft is sometimes defined as occurring when a person takes the property of another with intent to keep it. Doctrines of accomplice liability, whether derived from common law or formulated by statute, serve to extend criminal liability to others besides the actual perpetrator. The doctrines may make a person guilty of a crime when the face of the statute defining the crime may not appear to include that person. Moreover, the effect of the doctrines may be to extend liability to persons who could not directly have violated the statute. For example, a statute may prohibit a federal official from accepting gratuities, yet a person who is not a federal agent may be punishable under such a statute as an accomplice if she assisted the federal agent in violating the statute.

The critical effect of accomplice liability is to subject all accomplices to the same range of possible punishments as the actual perpetrator. Accordingly, an accomplice who aids in a burglary becomes a burglar subject to the same maximum penalty as the person who enters the premises. The fact that the accomplice is subject to the same penalty does not mean, however, that all parties to the crime will actually receive the same sentence. The blameworthiness of the parties may vary, and under the sentencing discretion normally allowed most American judges the parties may receive differing punishments. Depending on the circumstances, the primary actor may be thought more blameworthy, all parties may be thought equally so, or the secondary parties may be seen as deserving an even more severe punishment than the primary actor.

Historical background

The common law made distinctions among various parties to a felony, classifying some as "principals" and others as "accessories." Each of these classifications was subdivided into two further classifications. The four classifications were (1) principals in the first degree; (2) principals in the second degree; (3) accessories before the fact; and (4) accessories after the fact.

Principals and accessories before the fact. A principal in the first degree was the person who was the actual actor, or perpetrator, at the scene of the crime, for example, the person who inflicted the fatal wound on the victim. A principal in the second degree was a person also actually or "constructively" present at the scene of the felony, who aided or abetted the principal in the first degree in the commission of the felony.

Presence, actual or constructive, was the hallmark of the principal, and constituted the critical difference between principals in the second degree and accessories before the fact. At common law, an accessory before the fact was one who commanded, counseled,

encouraged, or aided another in committing a felony ("aided or abetted," to use a shorthand expression), but was not physically or constructively present at the scene of the crime. Under this set of categories, if A encouraged P to rob V, and if B went to the scene with P and served as a lookout while P robbed V, P would have been classified as a principal in the first degree, B would have been considered a principal in the second degree, and A would have been classified as an accessory before the fact.

Accessories after the fact. The fourth category of common-law parties, accessories after the fact, consisted of those persons who gave aid to a known felon, with the purpose of hindering his apprehension, conviction, or punishment. It was critical that the assisting person know that a felony had been committed by the person assisted. It was also necessary that the accessory render an act of positive assistance to elude justice, such as hiding the felon, assisting his escape, or destroying evidence, as distinguished from mere failure to notify authorities. At common law, accessories after the fact were liable for the underlying felony, along with principals and any accessories before the fact, and were subject to the same punishment. Under modern statutes, however, such postcrime conduct is treated as a separate crime carrying a lesser punishment than the underlying felony. Accordingly, discussions of accomplice liability now exclude those who would have been accessories after the fact at common law.

Common-law procedures. Current American treatment of accomplices largely dispenses with the procedural baggage that the common law affixed to the classification of parties. The most notable of the early procedural rules was the requirement that the principal first be convicted (or at least be simultaneously convicted) before an accessory could be tried. This rule, which applied to accessories but not to principals in the second degree, required actual conviction of the principal, not just proof that the crime had been perpetrated by someone. As a result, accessories could not be tried if the principal was never identified or captured, or if he escaped or died. The rule applied as well if there was an acquittal of the principal or if there otherwise was insufficient proof of the principal's guilt, no matter how strong the proof of the accessory's guilt.

Treatment of accomplices under modern law

In the United States, the treatment of accomplices is generally covered by statutes that abrogate most of the common-law procedural rules and distinctions.

These statutes necessarily leave open many questions and are therefore heavily supplemented by court decisions interpreting them—interpretation performed against the background of distinctions and rules developed at common law.

A federal statute provides that "whoever commits an offense against the United States or aids, abets, counsels, commands, induces or procures its commission, is punishable as a principal" (18 U.S.C. § 2 (1976)). It further makes anyone who "willfully causes an act to be done" punishable "as a principal" if the act caused would have been a crime against the United States had it been done directly by that person. This statute applies only to federal crimes. With regard to state crimes, which constitute the bulk of criminal offenses in the United States, state statutes usually articulate the basis for accomplice liability. Borrowing from the common law of principals in the second degree and accomplices before the fact, modern statutes generally hold that one who aids or abets another in the commission of a crime, whether felony or misdemeanor, can be tried and punished as if the secondary party were a principal. Nevertheless, like the federal statute, the various state enactments are generally brief, and are also subject to interpretation and application by the courts of each state. The law in any state may also differ from the applicable federal law. In spite of the dangers of overgeneralization and abbreviation, there still is a great deal of similarity among the laws regarding accomplices.

General principles of accomplice liability. The terms *to aid* and *to abet* (the latter from Middle French *abeter*, "to bait") tend to overlap in most situations. Together, the terms connote activity that encompasses commanding, procuring, instigating, inciting, inducing, encouraging, and counseling, as well as rendering physical assistance. For such activity to engender accomplice liability, it is further required that the activity be accompanied by a culpable mental state (mens rea), usually an intent to promote or facilitate the crime.

Analysis of questions regarding criminal liability, including accomplice liability, is usually divided into inquiries concerning the requisite acts that one must commit to become criminally liable for the crime (the actus reus) and inquiries centering on what accompanying mental state (the mens rea) the defendant must have for criminal liability.

The necessary act. The action that is made the basis for accomplice liability under the typical statutory language covers a wide range of activity. Beyond actions that have to do with initiating the crime, the supplying of physical aid directly or through still another person is a commonly specified method of incurring accomplice liability (for example, handing the perpetrator a weapon, helping to subdue the victim, acting as a lookout, or driving the getaway car). There are instances in which the accomplice aids the perpetrator without the latter's knowledge, as when P attacks V, A puts a weapon within P's reach, and P uses the weapon without realizing that A is present. When the aid is so rendered, this lack of awareness by the perpetrator is legally irrelevant for purposes of establishing the accomplice's liability. The statutory prohibitions generally also cover less tangible support, such as words or acts of encouragement. If no more is found, however, mere presence at the scene is not enough to establish accomplice liability.

Difficult conceptual questions arise when the accomplice's activity is not effective. One such class of activity is present where the possible accomplice tenders aid (other than encouragement), but where it is not clear whether that aid had any actual effect on the perpetrator's commission of the crime. The most noted American case of this kind involved an accomplice who interfered with another's message to a victim warning that the perpetrator was pursuing the victim (*State ex rel. Attorney General v. Tally*, 102 Ala. 25, 15 So. 722 (1894)). The court found that it need not be shown that the killing would not have taken place "but for" the accomplice's aid. Instead, the court concluded that aid which merely rendered it easier for the perpetrator to attain the result was a sufficient basis for liability. Such results emphasize that accomplice liability derives from contributing to a result—promoting or facilitating it—rather than directly causing the result.

An even more acute question involves situations in which the potential accomplice—unknown to the defendant and therefore not covered by the "encouragement" prohibition—attempts to aid but is unsuccessful in doing so. For example, A sets out to help P, who is assaulting a victim, but A is held back by a third person. Such an unsuccessful attempt is thought to be insufficient for accomplice liability in most jurisdictions, but there are those who argue for accountability in these circumstances. The most notable among them are the drafters of the American Law Institute's Model Penal Code, which has influenced a sizable number of state penal codes. The Model Penal Code takes the view that such attempted aid should be treated as criminal when the perpetrator has completed the crime (1962, § 2.06(3)(a)(ii)).

Generally, the mere failure to prevent another from committing a crime is not a basis for accomplice liability. However, in limited situations where the law imposes a duty on a specific person to prevent a crime (a watchman, for example), such a person who fails to prevent the crime may be held liable as an accomplice.

The required mental component. Accomplice liability generally requires fault, and this in turn is associated with a culpable mental state accompanying the required act. Put broadly, the accessory must intend—that is, have as his purpose—the furtherance or facilitation of the perpetrator's criminal conduct. It is not enough that the activity have the effect of encouraging or aiding. For example, the shouting of ambiguous words by A that actually encourage P would not entail accomplice liability in the absence of a finding that A had, in some sense, intended that the words encourage P.

These general formulations of the requirement of intent for accomplice liability mask a host of difficult questions. The requirement of a criminal "intent," or a culpable mental state, is a fundamental prerequisite to most criminal liability. This requirement has led to controversy about which of the many possible mental states should qualify as such "intent."

From pure conscious purpose to assist or encourage a result, lesser states of mind can be visualized as extending along a spectrum. For example, a person could provide some item to another with knowledge that the item will aid a crime, but without a true interest in the use to which the item will be put. Or a perpetrator could in fact be aided by a person who acts with a state of mind reckless of the consequences of the action or even simply negligent with regard to the consequences.

Legislatures, courts, and commentators have reached somewhat varied conclusions with regard to the mental state that should appropriately be treated as "intentional" on the part of the accomplice. Wayne LaFave has noted that these uncertainties may derive from unresolved questions over what, precisely, ought to be the appropriate focus of the criminal law in this area: a concern with the accomplice's mental state regarding his own activity, an awareness by the accomplice of the perpetrator's own mental state, the fundamental fault requirements of the underlying crime, or, perhaps, a combination of these (LaFave and Scott, p. 505). Fundamental disagreements still exist in the criminal law about how much responsibility an actor should assume for the unintended, but probable, consequences of his conduct.

One situation that has proved difficult is that in which the potential accomplice has mere knowledge of the use to which the assisting activity will be put.

The typical case involves a defendant who supplies some common item that will aid the perpetrator, and who acts with knowledge of the criminal use to which the item will be put, but without interest, financial or otherwise, in the perpetrator's action. In many instances, aid supplied with knowledge may, as a matter of evidence, be found by the trier of fact to imply a more purposeful intent to aid, as when a pawnbroker sells a knife with the knowledge that the purchaser will use it in a robbery, and on the understanding that the pawnbroker will receive a share of the robbery proceeds.

Nevertheless, there are cases in which the aider is genuinely neutral toward the criminal conduct of the perpetrator. Recurring problems of this type frequently involve merchants who supply material to a known criminal without any encouragement. Examples might include the routine sale of gasoline for a car known to be used in an illegal activity, the sale of sugar to one known to be illegally distilling liquor, the legal sale of a drug that the pharmacist knows will be used illegally, or the leasing of a house by an owner who knows that it will be used for gambling or prostitution. Some cases accept such knowledge as sufficient for accomplice liability, and some authorities have argued in favor of this position. Other cases, however, generally insist on a more purposeful attitude toward the result. This more widely accepted view is manifested most clearly in the case of *United States v. Peoni*, 100 F.2d 401 (2d Cir. 1938). That view tends to limit accomplice liability to situations in which the purported accomplice "associate[s]" himself with the venture in some way, participating in it as something the accomplice "wishes to bring about," that is, to make succeed. The requirement of a purposive attitude toward the venture reflects a practical concern to avoid putting in jeopardy the freedom of routine individual activity, including everyday mercantile activity. The contrary view reflects a judgment that the knowing giving of aid in the commission of crime provides a sound basis for criminal liability.

The difficulties of each of these positions have led to various hybrid suggestions that seek to ameliorate the results of both extreme views. One suggestion has been that the law ought to treat as significant the amount or nature of the aid: the more substantial the aid, the more acceptable the lesser mental state of mere knowledge as a basis for liability. Such a criterion was originally proposed by an early draft of the Model Penal Code (1953, § 2.04(3)(b)), but it was not adopted in the final draft (1962, § 2.06(3)(b)). Another suggested possibility focuses on the seriousness of the underlying crime. Under this approach, for example, different results might follow if a service-station attendant supplied gasoline to the car of one known to be transporting a kidnapping victim, rather than to a car known to be routinely used for a small lottery. Still another response is to consider assistance given with knowledge as being outside the accomplice liability theory. Rather than treating knowledge as sufficient to make one an accomplice punishable for the underlying crime, an occasional statutory formulation has treated knowledge as the basis for a new offense labeled "facilitation," a crime subject to a lesser punishment than that prescribed for the underlying offense.

Another mens rea problem arises when a person intentionally undertakes some activity but does not intend the consequence or even actually know that the other person will commit a crime, although he *should* know that the other person might. The potential accomplice, for example, could supply what turns out to be aid (such as a car) to someone who should be known to be dangerous (such as an intoxicated driver); the driver then drives recklessly. Courts are not in agreement as to whether this is sufficient for accomplice liability. To find liability under an accomplice theory when the accomplice is reckless or negligent seems to go beyond, or at least stretch to their limits, basic accomplice doctrines regarding mental state.

Some crimes are defined to require no mens rea at all. These crimes are said to entail strict liability, not even negligence. Most courts reject accomplice liability for such crimes, as well as for others, when the person giving aid does so without knowledge or fault. Certain statutes, however, expressly adopt the doctrine of vicarious liability, under which one person is liable for the actions of another solely on the basis of the two individuals' relationship, without respect to fault. An example is a statute making the proprietor of a tavern vicariously liable for his bartender's illegal sale to an underage drinker. When such a statute also makes the perpetrator strictly liable (that is, without regard to any fault on his part), as is the case in the example just mentioned, the liability of the owner is both strict and vicarious. Such a basis for criminal liability is rarely employed because of its inconsistency with principles of individual justice.

Accomplice liability for other crimes. Sometimes the perpetrator goes beyond the express contemplation of the accomplice and commits different or further crimes. These instances involve more than a deviation in the place, instrumentality, time, or means

of accomplishing the contemplated crime, such as using a knife rather than a gun. Deviations of this last kind do not relieve the accomplice of liability. The actor may, however, commit a different crime, for example, robbery and rape, rather than just robbery.

Under the law, the perpetrator does not become a roving general agent for an accomplice. On the other hand, in spite of what might be thought to follow from some of the mens rea rules stated above, neither is the accomplice's liability limited to the precise activity originally contemplated. Instead, when the actor commits a different crime, an accomplice is commonly said to be liable if that crime was "the natural and probable consequence" of the crime contemplated. In cases in which, for example, A aids P in contemplation of P taking money by beating and robbing V, and P kills V in order to overcome V's resistance, the natural-and-probable-consequences test may result in A being deemed guilty not only of robbery but also of homicide. The same result would probably not follow if what A and P had originally contemplated was a larceny.

Differences in liability of perpetrator and accomplices. Although modern law no longer requires conviction of the perpetrator before the accessory can be tried, it is still generally necessary to prove the commission of a crime by a perpetrator before a person can be convicted as his accessory. There are exceptions, however. For example, suppose the perpetrator has a defense of justification, which the aider does not. This would be the case where P kills another, reasonably believing that his own life is threatened, aided by A who knows that P is mistaken and that in fact P is under no danger. A can be convicted of the homicide.

Another example is where the perpetrator's action may be excused but the aider's action may not be, as in the case where P acts under duress but the person aiding him does not. Here again, the aider may be held liable for the crime. It is also possible that the aider can be convicted of a different crime from that committed by the perpetrator. This can happen when each has a different mens rea, as when the perpetrator kills another in a rage engendered by legally sufficient provocation (manslaughter), but the aider acts coolly and without provocation (murder).

In some special situations, one who intentionally aids a perpetrator in committing a crime cannot be held liable as an accomplice. For example, extortion victims or family members who pay ransom to a kidnapper may not be held liable as accomplices of the extortionist or kidnapper; underage participants in statutory rape cannot be held as accomplices of the perpetrator. The reason is that courts interpret such statutes as being designed to protect victims of certain conduct, not to make them criminally liable for being victimized.

Resolution of issues in the courts

As the above discussion illustrates, the possible factual situations that will need resolution are nearly endless. The same can be said of questions as to whether particular activity was "aid" or "encouragement," or whether a defendant entertained a certain intent. Even after it is determined which rules a particular jurisdiction will follow, a host of issues must be resolved, such as whether a particular defendant did or thought a certain thing, whether such activity amounted to aid, or whether the defendant intended a particular consequence. Such issues are normally resolved at trial. Most will be left for resolution to the trier of fact—the jury (or, in a non-jury trial, the judge). The trial judge will determine whether a reasonable jury could find from the evidence that the defendant's activity could, as a matter of law, qualify as aiding or abetting. The judge will also determine whether there is sufficient evidence from which the required mental state could be found (often inferred from acts or words). If the evidence is insufficient, the judge will order the defendant acquitted. Otherwise, the trier of fact will proceed to reach a conclusion as to what actually took place: whether the defendant aided or abetted with the necessary state of mind. In a jury trial, this will be done after the judge instructs the jury about how the law in that jurisdiction defines aiding and abetting, as well as about the other relevant legal rules. The jury will then be left to apply the law to the facts.

The determination of what legal rules a particular jurisdiction follows is a decision that is made in the first place by statute and by court interpretation of the statute. Often, however, the courts are left without a statutory provision on a particular matter, and thus they may look to the common law, to the persuasive reasoning of courts in other jurisdictions, or to writings considered authoritative.

Other grounds of liability

The doctrines of accomplice liability determine the principal ways in which one person may be held liable for the actions of another. However, the law provides other ways as well. One is through the doctrine of vicarious liability, which has been discussed above. Two other ways, which impose a kind of vicarious liability, are through the doctrines of conspiracy and felony murder.

Conspiracy. When two or more people form an alliance for the purpose of committing crime, they may be guilty of the separate crime of conspiracy, whether or not the crime they combined to commit is actually committed. However, the effect of entering into a conspiracy is, under the law of many jurisdictions, to make each conspirator liable for the actions of a fellow conspirator, including criminal actions, so long as those acts are in furtherance of the conspiracy. In a leading case, *Pinkerton v. United States*, 328 U.S. 640 (1946), a defendant who had earlier conspired with his brother to illegally operate a still was held liable for his brother's later acts in operating the illegal still, despite the fact that by the time those acts were committed, the defendant was in prison on another offense. The court held that because the defendant had entered the conspiracy, it was unnecessary to show that he encouraged or aided his brother to commit these particular crimes. The court relied on the theory that each conspirator was an agent of his fellow conspirators and as such was liable for any act done to further the conspiracy. This approach has been criticized as creating a kind of vicarious liability and has been rejected by the Model Penal Code (1953, § 2.04(3)), as well as by several jurisdictions.

Felony murder. A separate and widely employed rule of liability, the felony-murder rule, may also extend accomplice liability. Formulations of the felony-murder rule differ from jurisdiction to jurisdiction, but the rule's effect is to convert into murder certain deaths that take place during the commission of felonies. Thus, killings that might be accidental or otherwise considered as homicide of a lesser degree than murder are defined as murder. The doctrine may not only make the perpetrator of the killing guilty of murder, but it also may have the effect of making any accomplice to the felony liable for the perpetrator's act, and therefore also guilty of murder. Depending on the particular formulation of the felony-murder rule, the interaction of that rule with accomplice liability can create liability for murder when it would not exist under the natural-and-probable-consequences test noted above.

Conclusion

There are substantial areas of agreement in the United States regarding the doctrines of accomplice liability, but there is also considerable variation among jurisdictions concerning who should be considered accomplices and what the extent of their liability should be. These differences mirror wider debates in a heterogeneous society about the proper reach of the criminal law.

JAMES A. STRAZZELLA

See also CONSPIRACY; VICARIOUS LIABILITY.

BIBLIOGRAPHY

American Law Institute. *Model Penal Code: Proposed Official Draft.* Philadelphia: ALI, 1962.
———. *Model Penal Code: Tentative Draft No. 1.* Philadelphia: ALI, 1953.
BLACKSTONE, WILLIAM. *Commentaries on the Laws of England* (1765–1769), vol. 4. Reprint. University of Chicago Press, 1979.
FLETCHER, GEORGE P. *Rethinking Criminal Law.* Boston: Little, Brown, 1978. Includes a helpful comparison of Anglo-American law with several other legal systems.
KADISH, SANFORD H., and PAULSEN, MONRAD G. *Criminal Law and Its Processes.* 3d ed. Boston: Little, Brown, 1975.
LAFAVE, WAYNE R., and SCOTT, AUSTIN W., JR. *Handbook on Criminal Law.* St. Paul: West, 1972.
MILLER, JUSTIN. *Handbook of Criminal Law.* St. Paul: West, 1934.
PERKINS, ROLLIN M. *Criminal Law.* 2d ed. Mineola, N.Y.: Foundation Press, 1969.
SAYRE, FRANCIS B. "Criminal Responsibility for the Acts of Another." *Harvard Law Review* 43 (1930): 689–723.
STEPHEN, JAMES FITZJAMES. *A General View of the Criminal Law of England.* London: Macmillan, 1863.
TORCIA, CHARLES E., ed. *Wharton's Criminal Law,* vol. 1. 14th ed. Rochester, N.Y.: Lawyers Co-operative, 1978.
U.S. National Commission on Reform of Federal Criminal Laws. *Final Report: A Proposed New Federal Criminal Code (Title 18, United States Code).* Washington, D.C.: The Commission, 1971.
WILLIAMS, GLANVILLE L. *Criminal Law: The General Part.* 2d ed. London: Stevens, 1961.

ACCUSATORIAL PROCESS

See ADVERSARY SYSTEM; CRIMINAL PROCEDURE: COMPARATIVE ASPECTS; PROSECUTION: COMPARATIVE ASPECTS; TRIAL, CRIMINAL.

ACQUITTAL

See DOUBLE JEOPARDY; GUILT; TRIAL, CRIMINAL.

ACT, CRIMINAL

See ACTUS REUS; CRIME: DEFINITION OF CRIME.

ACTUS REUS

Problems of definition

The concept of actus reus. In Latin, the term *actus reus* means literally "bad (or evil) act," but in the theory of criminal law it does not necessarily designate either an act or one that is always evil. Rather, *actus reus* is better understood as a term of art whose meaning resides entirely in its technical legal definition. Unfortunately, no single such definition prevails, nor is the term used uniformly among lawyers. Furthermore, here as elsewhere in the law, the literal and ordinary meaning of a term persistently intrudes upon its technical legal meaning.

It is, however, possible to attempt to describe one prevailing and coherent use of the term. It rests on a residual definition: the actus reus designates all the elements of the criminal offense except the mens rea. This definition supposes an exhaustive division of the criminal offense into two components: the mental state of the offender, or mens rea, and "all the rest"— the actus reus. This "residual" view of the actus reus results from the fact that the term comprises a set of elements with no obvious common denominator other than the negative one, namely, that they do not include the offender's state of mind. As the literal meaning of the term implies, the actus reus most commonly consists of a proscribed *act,* such as the hitting of another person while committing the offense of assault. However, the term also includes the harmful *result* of the proscribed act when such harm is included in the definition of the offense—as in homicide offenses, where the actual death of the victim is part of the actus reus—as well as any special *circumstances,* such as the age of the victim in statutory rape, which are mentioned in that definition. Furthermore, as will be seen below, many criminal offenses do not predicate liability on any proscribed *act* at all. Instead, liability may rest on (and the actus reus may accordingly consist of) an *omission,* a *status,* or a *possession.*

It may still be tempting and seem possible to impose a common denominator on the various components of the actus reus by characterizing it as consisting of the "objective" elements of the offense, in juxtaposition to the "subjective" nature of the mens rea. Although this characterization is usually correct, certain exceptions undermine it. The actus reus sometimes includes the state of mind of somone other than the offender. Rape, for example, is defined by the victim's lack of consent to the sexual intercourse. Lack of consent is not part of the mens rea, which pertains only to the state of mind of the accused, but is a *circumstance,* which belongs accordingly to the actus reus.

Although it is impossible to give a comprehensive affirmative definition of the actus reus that would do justice to all its possible components and variations, it must still be recognized that in the great majority of cases criminal liability does rest on a proscribed *act.* The notion of an act plays, therefore, a central role in the paradigmatic case of criminal liability, and its proper definition is accordingly of special significance for the definition of the actus reus.

What is an act? The proper definition of the term *act* or *criminal act* has been the source of considerable scholarly, and sometimes judicial, disputation. Modern American criminal codes, following the American Law Institute's Model Penal Code (§ 1.13(2)), tend to adopt a minimal definition of an act as a "bodily movement." This definition diverges from ordinary or philosophical usage, which, by including within the notion of an act such additional elements as purposefulness and volition, excludes involuntary muscular contractions from the domain of human action.

The minimal legal definition may nonetheless be chosen if one conceives of the actus reus and its various components as part of a technical language whose test is in its clarity and precision, rather than in its fidelity to ordinary usage. It is useful for analytical purposes to have a notion of *act* that pertains solely to bodily movement. Excluding the element of volition from the definition of *act,* for example, allows one to explicitly state and investigate the substantive requirement of a voluntary act as a necessary basis for criminal liability. The adjective *voluntary* would be redundant in a definition of *act* that encompasses the notion of volition, and, it may be argued, clarity of analysis would suffer from the suppression of this adjective.

The problem of an adequate definition of *act* does not, however, admit of easy resolution. Even if the minimal definition were best suited for purposes of legal analysis, its adoption raises all the problems associated with the construction of a professional legal vocabulary divorced from ordinary language. The law is, among other things, a form of rhetorical discourse, which thrives on the richness of allusions and connotations that its terms enjoy in ordinary usage. In arguing that A should not be held responsible for hitting B because she was pushed against him by C, there is undeniable rhetorical force in saying that hitting B was not really A's act at all. Such a statement comports well with ordinary usage (and, naturally, with those legal definitions of *act* that follow it), but would

be false under the minimal definition advocated on analytical grounds.

More broadly, the double challenge posed by the construction of a technical legal language is that of keeping it apart from ordinary language, as well as realizing the very limited, albeit important, purposes for which legal language is useful. Much confusion and error in criminal law, as well as elsewhere in the law, can be traced to a failure to meet these two challenges.

Substantive principles

Two fundamental principles of the criminal law are related to the actus reus. One is the principle requiring an actus reus; the other is the requirement of *voluntariness.*

The requirement of an actus reus. It is a generally accepted principle of the criminal law that liability must rest on a criminal act committed by the defendant. Nonetheless, the exact scope, as well as the precise grounds, of this principle remains somewhat obscure. The scope of the principle depends on how the term *act* in the above formulation is to be understood. If it were to be understood narrowly as a bodily movement, then the stated principle would be honored mainly in the breach. As indicated above, criminal liability is often predicated on various alternatives to an act, notably on omissions, on possession, and, more problematically, on status. Such offenses are not commonly seen as necessarily conflicting with a basic principle of the criminal law.

Alternatively, the principle may be understood to require some element of actus reus as a prerequisite for liability, although not necessarily the element of an act. In the light of our definition of actus reus, the principle, so understood, is equivalent to the proposition that criminal liability cannot rest solely on mens rea or, in less technical terms, that there should be no punishment for mere intentions or other states of mind.

The punishment of criminal intentions. So stated, the principle sounds both trivial and obvious. One needs, therefore, to recall such practices as the burning of heretics to realize that the air of obviousness surrounding the principle in the twentieth century may be quite deceptive. Far from being absurd or pointless, punishment for a state of mind might make perfectly good sense. It might be motivated by two different kinds of concerns. First, certain attitudes or beliefs (for example, racism or anti-Semitism) might be the target of punishment because they were considered, in and of themselves, too repugnant to be tolerated. One who is concerned with the moral fabric of a society in which certain kinds of attitudes or beliefs become prevalent might maintain that criminal legislation should provide at least a symbolic denunciation of—and at best an effective measure against—the spread of such views. Nevertheless, out of what some would describe as greater tolerance and others as greater moral indifference, it seems that hardly anyone (at least in the United States) would seriously suggest that the law adopt or approximate this posture.

The other possible reason for punishing a state of mind is more instrumental. Punishing an individual who harbors a criminal intention may be a way to avert the intended harm. There is, again, nothing pointless or absurd about this. Indeed, although secularization and moral relativism may have diminished public interest in states of mind for their own sake, other developments, notably the rationalization of criminal liability as predicated on the defendant's dangerousness and culpability, have made modern law more hospitable to the idea of punishing on instrumental grounds for mere intentions. The subjectivist view of culpability increasingly taken by the criminal law leads to the conclusion that external factors, including the accused's actual conduct, may be of great probative value as to what his intentions really were; but these factors no longer constitute the *grounds* for liability, as they would under a more retaliatory conception of punishment.

Indeed, modern attempt law comes fairly close to the punishment of mere intentions. What little conduct on the part of the accused is required (and sometimes that is minimal indeed) is explicitly seen as serving an evidentiary role of corroborating the accused's criminal intent (Model Penal Code § 5.01).

The role of the actus reus. The punishment for mental states, proscribed by the principle under consideration, is, accordingly, neither incoherent nor necessarily pointless. Support for the requirement of some form of actus reus must, therefore, rest elsewhere. It is to be found, in abundance, in the exorbitant costs to individual liberty and autonomy that the punishment of mere intentions would surely exact. The difficulties associated with ascertaining psychic events are obvious, and they give rise both to the danger of unfounded convictions and to the perils of increased reliance on confessions. Furthermore, intentions as grounds for criminal liability do not provide clear criteria by which to single out suspects from the rest of the population. All accused persons are

exposed to the intrusions invariably attending police investigations and criminal prosecutions, even when they ultimately result in an acquittal. The primary role of the actus reus is thus to mitigate these dangers. It does so by predicating criminal liability on an observable event that clearly manifests the accused's state of mind, and by reference to which suspects can be identified as reliably and early as possible. The various forms of the actus reus must be assessed by their ability effectively to provide these safeguards.

The concerns underlying the requirement of an actus reus are best satisfied in the paradigmatic case where criminal liability rests on a proscribed act resulting in actual harm. When A shoots and kills B, he unequivocally calls the authorities' attention to himself by means of an event that is objectively ascertainable and likely to be both an embodiment and a demonstration of his culpability and dangerousness.

Criminal liability is not, however, limited to cases resembling this paradigm. First, there are general doctrines that expand the grounds for liability beyond what is required by any particular offense. One can, for example, be punished for an *attempt* to commit a criminal offense where one has neither caused the harm nor concluded the act proscribed by the definition of that offense. Similarly, within the doctrine of *complicity* the accused may be convicted of an offense, even though he did not actually commit the acts explicitly proscribed, on the basis of a broader and vaguer notion of having *aided* the commission of the offense. Such extensions of liability must be examined in light of the concerns that have been ascribed to the requirement of an actus reus.

Criminal liability deviates from the paradigm described above in yet another way: as already indicated, the acta rea of numerous offenses are defined not only by positive criminal acts but also by *omissions, status,* and *possession.* When we later examine each of these "deviant" grounds of liability, we will assess its adequacy in providing the safeguards to individual liberty expected of the actus reus. Before turning to these issues, however, it is necessary to examine the second of the two substantive requirements related to the actus reus, that of voluntariness.

The requirement of voluntariness. The requirement of voluntariness is the legal response to the basic intuition that it would be grossly unfair to punish a person who totally lacked the capacity to conform to the law. Like the requirement of an actus reus, the requirement of voluntariness can also be seen to issue from an underlying concern with individual liberty and autonomy that the substantive criminal law strives to protect. The main virtue of the various formal attributes of the criminal law, it is argued, is that they extend individuals' autonomy by increasing their ability to plan their lives effectively, without fear of unexpected coercive interference by the authorities (Hart). Accordingly, punishment should not be inflicted in situations where the option to comply with the law and thus avoid the risk of punishment is unavailable. In raising a claim of involuntariness, a defendant points to some specific facts which rendered him, at the crucial moment, incapable of obeying the law that he is charged with violating.

Conveniently, the facts that can support such a claim fall into three categories. First, there are the cases commonly referred to as states of automatism, exemplified by diabetic coma, somnambulism, hypnotic suggestion, and epileptic seizure. Second, the lack of control may result from an irresistible external force, such as that exerted by a stronger person who forcibly pulls the accused's finger on a trigger, causing a shot to be fired. Finally, and more problematically, involuntariness may be the product of an irresistible impulse born of mental disease.

Voluntariness and the actus reus. Involuntariness is commonly seen as a claim related to the actus reus rather than to the mental (mens rea) component of the offense. This is because the various facts that can give rise to this claim do not so much negate the defendant's intent, or other states of mind, as render them irrelevant. To illustrate this point, consider the case of the nurse who fails in her duty to provide a life-saving medication to a patient because robbers have tied her up. It is immaterial, although possible, that in her heart she relishes the patient's misfortune. The intimate relation between a claim of involuntariness and the actus reus is reflected in both ordinary and philosophical usages that incorporate in the concept of human action some reference to a possibility of self-activation, or choice, by the agent. The nurse in this example would be fully justified by the conventions of ordinary speech in saying, if blamed for the patient's death, "But I didn't do it." This is different from the excuse appropriate to the denial of intentionality in the case where the harmful act was committed voluntarily but inadvertently. Here a person is likely to escape blame by arguing, "But I didn't *mean* to do it," which implies the agent's concession that he committed the harmful act. By classifying involuntariness as belonging to the actus reus, the criminal law follows this distinction.

The practical significance of classifying voluntariness as belonging to the actus reus (rather than mens rea) component of the offense is that in this way the requirement of voluntariness holds even in strict-liability offenses where no mens rea need be proved. It should, however, be observed that the question of whether to require voluntariness in offenses of strict liability is a normative question to be decided by value judgments or policy considerations; it is not resolved by the conceptual analysis of the term *act* or by the classification of voluntariness as a matter of actus reus. Although insistence on the requirement of voluntariness mitigates the hardships of strict liability in a small number of cases, this is more in the nature of an ad hoc compromise reflecting the law's ambivalence about strict liability, rather than a principled resolution compelled by a comprehensive and consistent normative view.

Voluntariness and free will. To say that voluntariness is a requisite of criminal liability may create the impression that in each criminal case prosecutors are faced with the Herculean task of rebutting determinism and upholding the freewill hypothesis, by demonstrating to judge and jury that the defendant could have behaved differently than he actually did. Nothing could be farther from the truth.

When lawyers speak of voluntariness, they rarely mean to raise metaphysical questions about free will. The criminal law, echoing common beliefs and pervasive ordinary practices, presupposes or—in effect the same thing—postulates that, by and large, people are capable of choosing their course of conduct. Without the possibility of choice, the entire practice of ascribing criminal responsibility, or at least its moral foundation, would be vitiated. Only against the background of such a general presupposition can the notion of voluntariness be understood. What it amounts to is the requirement that in order for conduct to have criminal consequences it must be engaged in under the usual sorts of conditions in which free will is supposed to exist. Only in the exceptional case where, because of some special circumstances, the defendant completely lacks control over his bodily movements in a way that makes the legally mandated conduct impossible, does the claim of involuntariness become a legal issue.

However, keeping the claim of involuntariness within such narrow bounds is no easier than suppressing or suspending the troublesome issue of free will that underlies it. Recognition of a few situations in which a person is said to have been deprived of the capacity to act differently than he actually did is a constant challenge to the determinist strain in our thought, which seeks to deny the presence of such capacity in many, and possibly all, other situations. According to this view, the narrow limits imposed by the law on the claim of involuntariness are dictated by prudential or practical, but morally arbitrary, considerations. For punishment to serve as an effective deterrent, the law must preserve a sufficiently wide range of cases where punishment can be imposed. The law, therefore, can and does recognize involuntariness only when the defendant's determinist account of the criminal event is both of a rare kind and is generally perceived to be clearly convincing. By insisting on these two conditions, the law affirms its commitment to fairness (or justice) without significantly diminishing its effectiveness.

From this perspective, the compromise struck by the law is extremely precarious. There is no escaping the recognition that the requirement of voluntariness is locked in a deadly, and possibly losing, battle with determinism. Scientific (psychological, biological, or medical) explanations, it is argued, almost invariably increase the deterministic element in our view of human conduct. An epileptic seizure supports a claim of involuntariness because the acts in question are accounted for by a determinist medical theory. The more such accounts we possess, the greater the encroachment on the presupposition of voluntariness that underlies the criminal law. Any recognition of a case of involuntariness is bound to take us down a slippery slope, at the end of which we would have nullified the entire criminal law. On the other hand, a refusal to go down the slope, or any attempt to stop somewhere along the way, is bound to be arbitrary and unfair. Take, for example, drug addiction. If, as some courts recognize, addiction is an involuntary condition, then so is the addict's act of using drugs. Furthermore, it has been argued, whatever illegal acts the addict commits in order to obtain drugs are also done under the same compulsion and must, therefore, be deemed involuntary (*Powell v. Texas*, 392 U.S. 514 (1968); *United States v. Moore*, 486 F.2d 1139 (D.C. Cir. 1973), especially Judge Bazelon, 1260).

The main response to this line of argument, greatly influenced by Kantian moral philosophy, takes a radically different view of the place of involuntariness in criminal responsibility. This alternative view does not feel threatened by the premonitions of determinism implicit in the legal requirement of voluntariness. The criminal law, according to this perspective, is based on the subjective experience of moral autonomy and is coextensive with it. By holding us accountable for our actions, the criminal law treats us in the only way in which we should insist that we be treated: with respect and as moral agents. The limits of the criminal law are accordingly determined by the perceived boundaries of our moral autonomy, and the concept

of involuntariness serves to delineate those boundaries. It tries to capture those, and only those, acts that we would be willing, in good faith, to disavow as our own by claiming that "I did not really do it." Seen in this light, the concept of voluntariness does not threaten, but rather expresses, the moral foundation of the criminal law. This view also reduces the temptation to expand the concept of involuntariness beyond its minimal bounds: an expansion of involuntariness implies a corresponding constriction of the sphere of our moral autonomy. As moral agents, we should be most concerned to preserve this sphere intact.

The conflict between these two perspectives can be illustrated by their response to the role of extreme social deprivation in criminal liability. Proponents of the first approach are troubled by the law's refusal to absolve the victims of extreme social deprivation from criminal liability, finding this refusal difficult to reconcile with the law's professed adherence to the requirement of voluntariness. Social conditions, it is argued, may undermine some people's ability to make meaningful choices, and may largely determine their criminal conduct. Proponents of the second perspective retort by pointing to the alarming implications of such an absolution from liability, which amounts to depriving its "beneficiaries" of their status as moral agents, thereby stripping them of their human dignity.

Different forms of the actus reus

In the paradigmatic case, criminal liability is predicated on the defendant's voluntary act. Many criminal offenses deviate, however, from the paradigmatic case by imposing liability without specifying a proscribed act. Instead, liability may rest on an *omission*, on a *status*, or on *possession*.

In considering each of these and the problems they raise, it is important to bear in mind the two substantive principles discussed above. Each of these three forms of the actus reus must be judged by its ability to satisfy the concerns behind the principle that forbids punishment for mere intentions and requires some form of an actus reus. Similarly, each form of actus reus is bound by the requirement of voluntariness: it must provide an opportunity to obey the law and preclude criminal liability when such an opportunity is altogether missing.

Omissions. There are two kinds of cases in which criminal liability rests on an omission. The first, less problematic, category consists of criminal statutes that explicitly impose certain affirmative duties and attach sanctions to the failure to discharge them. The duty to file income-tax returns or to report for the draft are common examples.

In the second, more problematic, breed of offense based on omission, sometimes dubbed "commission by omission," the actus reus is defined as having caused a certain harmful result (such as death), without specifying whether or when passivity, or failure to act, would amount to commission of the offense.

There is nothing unusual in the law's willingness to assign causal efficacy to passivity. This fully comports with ordinary usage, which sometimes completely ignores the distinction between an action and an omission by nonproblematically describing the latter through the use of transitive action verbs. If a mother deliberately fails to feed her baby, who then dies of starvation, she would certainly be said to have *killed* the baby, and there would be nothing odd in supporting such a statement by saying that the baby's death was *her doing*. Within certain limits (discussed below) the criminal law reflects this common judgment—that responsibility for harmful results may rest on failure to act.

Omissions and the role of the actus reus. In doing so, however, the criminal law faces problems, not usually encountered in ordinary judgments, that have to do with its role of curbing official power to protect individual rights and liberties. Unlike a homicide case where liability rests on an act such as shooting, the "negative act" (as an omission is sometimes described) of "not feeding the baby" does not in and of itself single out the mother as the baby's killer; the same description would apply as well to the rest of humanity. Everyone in the world, including the mother, did not feed the unfortunate baby. Indeed, had there been a single benefactor who had undertaken to feed the baby, it would not have died. In this way an omission is less likely than an action to satisfy the need for a clearly ascertainable event that would early and reliably single out suspects from the rest of the population and serve as a necessary trigger to set in motion police investigations. The need for such an event has been identified above as underlying the ban against the punishment of mere intentions, and as providing a criterion of adequacy for the actus reus. This criterion of adequacy is less likely to be met by an actus reus based on an omission than by a positive action.

The reason that we nevertheless feel confident in holding the mother alone liable for the baby's death rests on the moral and legal *duty* owed by a mother to her child. Only against the background of such a duty can we single out the mother's failure to feed the baby as incurring criminal liability. The duty to

act, as well as the factual situation that gives rise to the duty (the maternal relation in the example), accordingly becomes part of the actus reus whenever liability is based on an omission. To assess the adequacy of such an actus reus, we must therefore focus on the nature of the underlying duty: its definiteness, the clarity of the circumstances that create it, and the distinctness or ascertainability of the failure to carry it out.

The duties that commonly underlie criminal omissions are seldom found within the criminal law itself. Rather, courts have recognized various sources of duty as sufficient for the purpose of criminal responsibility. These duties may be created by statute (not necessarily a criminal statute) or by contract; they may result from some special relationship, such as that between spouses, or some special circumstances—for example, accidentally starting a fire may create a duty to attempt to extinguish it.

Omissions and the duty to act. Two diametrically opposed objections can be made against the recognition of the above duties as grounds for criminal liability. On the one hand, many of these duties have been absorbed into the criminal law by way of judge-made rules. They constitute, it may be argued, dangerous extensions of criminal liability, violating the "principle of legality" which requires that criminal liability firmly rest upon, and be strictly limited to, legislative criminal enactments. Where the actus reus component of an offense may be satisfied by the existence of various relations and situations that impose vaguely defined duties, it can no longer serve as a reliable safeguard against unwarranted governmental intrusions into people's lives and liberties. The sprawling and amorphous character that the actus reus assumes frustrates the need for a relatively clear event that will link a person to a harmful occurrence—a need that was said to underlie the insistence upon an actus reus in the first place.

On the other hand, it may be observed that these various duties, broad as they are, do not fully coincide with what many would view as basic moral duties. Specifically, the Anglo-American criminal law does not recognize a general duty to help someone in danger or distress, even in circumstances where common humanity would so require. Failure to save a child drowning in a pond, or to warn a blind person who is about to fall off a precipice, are among the examples commonly given of omissions to act that would generally be viewed as moral outrages but that do not give rise to criminal liability. Some critics see this failure of the law to reflect basic notions of common morality as the product of an individualist ethic that places a high premium on selfishness and that is generally hostile to communal ideals of social solidarity. In response, it could be argued that the road to the fraternity of men and women need not necessarily pass through the jailhouse, and that the greater encroachment on people's liberty involved in imposing wide affirmative duties on them fully justifies the caution with which the criminal law treads in the area of omissions.

It is, however, worth noting that continental European criminal codes generally do contain so-called Good Samaritan provisions, which impose criminal liability for the failure to come to the rescue of others under specified circumstances.

Status offenses. The adequacy of the actus reus becomes more questionable when it takes the form of what is technically known as a *status offense.* The definition of such offenses makes no explicit reference to the accused's conduct, be it active or passive. Rather, it describes a certain state of affairs or a characteristic by virtue of which a person may be punished. Typically, offenses that belong to this category use the term *being,* as in the offense of "being a drug addict" or "being found in a state of intoxication in a public place." Offenses so formulated are commonly found objectionable by courts and commentators alike, although both have some difficulty in articulating the precise grounds for their objection.

Common objections. Status offenses are sometimes attacked as violating the requirement of voluntariness (people should not be held liable for states of affairs or characteristics that they are powerless to change), as well as the constitutional injunction against vagueness and overbreadth in criminal legislation. The first charge is probably true regarding the offense of "being a drug addict," and the second holds with respect to the offense of "being a common scold" or a "vagabond." But neither infirmity is inherent in—and, therefore, necessarily true of—all status offenses. Whatever the objections to making "being a law professor" a criminal offense, they would not rest on grounds of involuntariness or unavoidable vagueness.

Another familiar objection to status offenses is often phrased in terms of the seemingly obvious proposition that people should be punished for what they *do* rather than for what they *are.* However, inspired by existentialist moral philosophy, one could doubt the validity of the distinction between what a person does and what he is. The characteristics or permanent states of affairs by which people define their being are the sum or precipitate of many discrete acts done by them over time. Furthermore, insofar as the distinction does hold, it could be argued to the contrary that

punishment for a single act is justified only if it reveals something of permanence about the defendant's character. Indeed, when an act is strongly influenced by overwhelming external circumstances, thus reflecting little of the agent's own moral character, the criminal law tends to exculpate by means of various excuses, such as duress.

The fervor with which objections are sometimes made to status offenses suggests that the origin of those objections may lie chiefly in the totalitarian connotations of such offenses, and in the fear that they are generally conducive to punishment inspired by social prejudices and self-serving stereotypes. The form of status offenses does call to mind the wholesale criminalization of entire ethnic, cultural, or political groups undesirable to a given regime. The fault in such legislation, however, lies not so much in its form as in its content. One may be justified in feeling that more than a change in the form of a statute is needed in order to abate prejudice and prevent persecution.

Finally, and most important, it is often pointed out that status offenses are frequently a source of abuse by law enforcement authorities. They are commonly used to short-circuit procedural protections, they provide easy pretexts for unwarranted arrests, and they lend themselves to such unreliable methods of proof as evidence of the accused's reputation. According to this line of attack, status offenses do not satisfy the substantive requirement of an actus reus because they fail to specify clearly the event that is necessary to set the law enforcement machinery in motion and that would serve as a clear reference point for assessing the various actions taken by the authorities against a suspect. This charge is certainly true with respect to some status offenses, primarily vagrancy. But here again the charge must be doubly qualified. First, it pertains to only some, not all, status offenses. Second, where it does apply with full force, as in the case of vagrancy, much more than a change in the *form* of the statute would be needed to adequately safeguard the rights of those who are victimized by this legislation.

None of the arguments made against status offenses seem conclusively to condemn this form of criminal legislation. An offense clearly describing a distinctive and easily ascertainable situation over which the accused has control may be innocuous. Yet the many objections made against status offenses have an important cumulative effect. They point out the many pitfalls that attend such legislation and the numerous principles and values that may, although not inevitably, be violated by it. Taken together, the arguments amount to a counsel of caution, suggesting that legislators should avoid the language of "being" or its equivalents in drafting criminal provisions, and that judges should be alerted by such terms to the various specific perils that may lurk in a provision so drafted.

Status and membership. The topic of status offenses is often associated with such dated and somewhat quaint offenses as being a common thief or a common scold, which hardly play a significant role in contemporary criminal law. It is, therefore, important to point out that there is good reason to believe that status offenses may well occupy an increasingly central place in modern criminal jurisprudence. The more social activity—lawful as well as criminal—is conducted by and within bureaucratic organizations rather than by discrete individuals, the more pressure is exerted on the criminal law to impose liability on the basis of one's *membership* or *position* in an organization. Both in the case of organized crime and in the case of offenses committed by lawful organizations, the criminal law faces formidable obstacles in fixing liability on particular individuals for specific acts or omissions.

Consequently, the law may be seen as progressively moving, overtly or covertly, toward fixing liability on the basis of a person's status within, or relation to, an organization. Although this new breed of status offenses has met initially with judicial disfavor (*Lanzetta v. New Jersey*, 306 U.S. 451 (1939)), there is growing evidence that it is gaining ground. If indeed this is the trend, the numerous concerns about status offenses are likely to assume increasing significance.

Possession.

Possession and the role of the actus reus. The possession of certain objects, such as narcotics or stolen property, is sometimes a criminal offense. Here again, as in the case of status offenses, the actus reus of the offense does not specify any conduct, active or passive, as grounds for liability. Rather, liability may be based on the mere physical location of the object. A stolen watch resting in one's bureau drawer or a package of marijuana hidden in the glove compartment of one's car may well satisfy the actus reus element of the relevant possession offenses. Yet there seems little reason for alarm over such provisions. The fact of possession, having to do with the location of a physical object, provides in general a firm, objective foundation for liability. Possession in most cases is a clear and relatively easily ascertainable fact. Furthermore, since possession, as any other offense, must be voluntary, an offense proscribing possession may be seen either as punishing the act of acquisition that preceded the possession, or as imposing a duty to dispose of the specified object, with punishment for the failure to do so.

Knowledge and the definition of possession. With regard to possession, the main question that has been of concern to courts and commentators is the role of knowledge in its definition. Is the physical location of an object sufficient to establish possession, even if the alleged possessor did not know of the object's existence? The analytic framework employed here seems to call for an affirmative answer. Possession is a form of actus reus, and its definition should, therefore, be purged of any reference to the accused's state of mind, which must be relegated to the mens rea component of the offense. Although this analysis will in most cases be entirely satisfactory, it may seem less so with offenses of strict liability where the requirement of mens rea is altogether absent. Imposing punishment for the possession of an object of which the accused knows nothing seems grossly unfair; it has led many to maintain that awareness of the forbidden object is in fact part of the concept of possession, so that such awareness is required even in offenses of strict liability (Model Penal Code § 2.01(4)).

As a mitigation of the hardships occasioned by strict liability, the above position is certainly laudable. This, however, should not blind one to its ad hoc nature. The same degree of unfairness as that involved in punishing for possession without knowledge is present on numerous other occasions where strict liability leads to the punishment of the innocent. Whether this is warranted is a matter of weighing conflicting policies and values. This issue cannot be settled by a conceptual claim about the "true" meaning of possession, just as a conceptual analysis of *act* cannot determine whether the requirement of voluntariness should hold in strict-liability offenses.

Conclusion

It may be well to conclude by qualifying the preceding discussion. The account offered here of actus reus echoes dominant contemporary views, which focus primarily on its role in protecting individual autonomy against potential abuses of the coercive power of the state. However, the persistence and the pervasiveness of an actus reus component (or some close analogue to it) in virtually all systems of criminal justice may well breed a certain degree of skepticism as to the ultimate adequacy of any single rationalization of it. Rational normative analysis of the kind exhibited in this article, as well as in most other writings on the subject, may only scratch the surface of the reality of social institutions as durable and complex as the criminal law, in which the actus reus is a central feature. The present account of actus reus may accordingly be seen as no more than a contemporary interpretation that not so much illuminates the concept under observation as it mirrors the normative predilections of the observers and their time.

MEIR DAN COHEN

See also CRIME: DEFINITION OF CRIME; MENS REA; VICARIOUS LIABILITY.

BIBLIOGRAPHY

AMERICAN LAW INSTITUTE. *Model Penal Code: Proposed Official Draft.* Philadelphia: ALI, 1962.

FITZGERALD, P. J. "Voluntary and Involuntary Acts." *Oxford Essays in Jurisprudence.* Edited by Anthony Guest. London: Oxford University Press, 1961, pp. 1–28.

FLETCHER, GEORGE P. *Rethinking Criminal Law.* Boston: Little, Brown, 1978.

HALL, JEROME. *General Principles of Criminal Law.* 2d ed. Indianapolis: Bobbs-Merrill, 1960.

HART, H. L. A. "Legal Responsibility and Excuses." *Punishment and Responsibility: Essays in the Philosophy of Law.* Oxford: Oxford University Press, Clarendon Press, 1968, pp. 28–53.

HUGHES, GRAHAM. "Criminal Omissions." *Yale Law Journal* 67 (1958): 590–637.

KIRCHHEIMER, OTTO. "Criminal Omissions." *Harvard Law Review* 55 (1942): 615–642.

LACEY, FORREST W. "Vagrancy and Other Crimes of Personal Condition." *Harvard Law Review* 66 (1953): 1203–1226.

LAFAVE, WAYNE R., and SCOTT, AUSTIN W., JR. *Handbook on Criminal Law.* St. Paul: West, 1972.

MORRIS, HERBERT. "Punishment for Thoughts." *On Guilt and Innocence: Essays in Legal Philosophy and Moral Psychology.* Berkeley: University of California Press, 1976, pp. 1–29.

PACKER, HERBERT L. *The Limits of the Criminal Sanction.* Stanford, Calif.: Stanford University Press, 1968.

PERKINS, ROLLIN M. *Criminal Law.* 2d ed. Mineola, N.Y.: Foundation Press, 1969.

———. "Negative Acts in Criminal Law." *Iowa Law Review* 22 (1937): 659–683.

SALMOND, JOHN WILLIAM. *Salmond on Jurisprudence.* 12th ed. Edited by P. J. Fitzgerald. London: Sweet & Maxwell, 1966.

SILBER, JOHN R. "Being and Doing: A Study of Status Responsibility and Voluntary Responsibility." *University of Chicago Law Review* 35 (1967): 47–91.

WILLIAMS, GLANVILLE. *Criminal Law: The General Part.* 2d ed. London: Stevens, 1961.

ADDICTION

See ALCOHOL AND CRIME: TREATMENT AND REHABILITATION; *articles under* DRUGS AND CRIME.

ADMISSIONS

See CONFESSIONS.

ADOLESCENCE

See DELINQUENCY, JUVENILE.

ADULTERY AND FORNICATION

Until the 1950s, almost every state in the United States prohibited extramarital and nonmarital sexual intercourse under criminal statutes condemning adultery, fornication, or lewd cohabitation. Many of these statutes were repealed in the years after World War II, but even before their repeal, memory would have to be stretched to recall a prosecution. In many societies, however, adultery remains a most serious crime, and it often carries the death penalty.

Approximately ten states in the United States retain criminal statutes outlawing adultery, as well as fornication and lewd cohabitation. Some statutes prohibit only "open and notorious" adultery; others prohibit "habitual" adultery. The penalties listed in the statutes are a fine ranging from a maximum of $10 to $1,000, imprisonment for up to five years, or a combination of both. Apart from the ten states prohibiting adultery, fornication, and lewd cohabitation, eight states have statutes prohibiting adultery but no law against fornication or lewd cohabitation. Four states have statutes on adultery and fornication, three have laws on adultery and lewd cohabitation, and two have laws on fornication. Another state, although it has no statutes on adultery or fornication, prohibits open and lewd cohabitation. Only two states (Louisiana and Tennessee) have had no criminal statute prohibiting either adultery, fornication, or lewd cohabitation. The American Law Institute's Model Penal Code recommended dropping all penalties for adult nonmarital sexual behavior, as had been done by many states.

The term *fornication* is often used to refer to heterosexual copulation, but legally it does not refer to such activity between persons who are married to each other. The term derives from the Latin for brothel (*fornix*). The Bible vigorously condemns fornication, and like much other sexual behavior, it was punishable by the ecclesiastical courts of the Church of England. It was a preoccupation of the legal system in Plymouth Colony, and in the period immediately preceding the Revolutionary War it was the subject of 210 of the

370 criminal prosecutions in one Massachusetts county. More recently, the fornication statutes have been used primarily against the male customer of a prostitute, often as a means to coerce his testimony in a prosecution of the woman.

In civil litigation, adultery is now outdated as a basis for a divorce action in view of no-fault divorce laws, but in child custody disputes, courts often encounter, and sustain, the claim that a parent's request for child custody should be denied because the parent has engaged in adulterous conduct. Prior to the no-fault laws, the allegations of adultery were often the result of collusion between the parties to a divorce action in order to bring the case within the requirements of the divorce law. In such circumstances the record in the divorce case obviously could not serve as a basis for criminal prosecution. But even assuming trustworthy evidence of adultery, there would ordinarily have been no criminal prosecution. Convictions were often impossible to obtain, and the criminal statutes were virtually unenforced. Premarital and extramarital sexual intercourse is now widely accepted in the United States as a prerogative of the individual. Indeed, during the countercultural movements of the 1960s, group sex and mate-swapping attracted a good deal of notoriety. Open cohabitation has become quite common.

Adultery was not a crime under the old English common law, but was regarded as a private wrong for which the aggrieved husband had a right of action for damages. The common law defined adultery as sexual relations between a married woman and a man not her husband. Sexual intercourse between a man and an unmarried woman was considered simply fornication by both, regardless of whether or not the man was married. The common law was concerned with illicit intercourse only when it was calculated to adulterate the blood and expose the husband to the maintenance of another man's children and to the risk of their inheriting his property. The term *adultery* in its ordinary sense means pollution or defilement.

In the Middle Ages the English ecclesiastical courts began to punish those who committed adultery and, except for the period between 1640 and 1661, these courts continued to operate until the eighteenth century. As the power of religious institutions waned, secular authorities adopted many of the religious doctrines and provided the relevant sanctions. According to the canon law, adultery consisted of sexual relations between a married person—either a man or woman—and someone other than his or her spouse. In the American colonies, some jurisdictions adopted the canon law definition of adultery, some accepted the common-law definition, and a few combined the two, making both parties guilty of the offense if either, regardless of sex, was married to a third person.

The criminal law on adultery has not had any noticeable effect on the principle of self-help. The "ethics of the duelist and the buccaneer" place a notion of "honor" above life itself. This encourages a violent response from a husband discovering his wife in an act of adultery. Adultery is generally considered sufficient provocation to mitigate a homicide from murder to voluntary manslaughter when a husband discovers his wife in the act of intercourse and kills either her or her paramour. The defense of temporary insanity in such cases is sometimes successfully used. Paramour killing is even made justifiable in a number of states either by statute or by judicial decision.

Various reasons have been given for the prohibition of adultery, namely, that adultery is a violation of the moral sense of the community, that it is an offense against the family, that it corrupts the family line and the unity of the family, and that it is a violation of a man's right of property. None of these reasons, however, speak to the psychological underpinning of the prohibition and the right of self-help. Adultery strikes at a man's (or a woman's) pride.

RALPH SLOVENKO

See also CRIMINALIZATION AND DECRIMINALIZATION; VICTIMLESS CRIME.

BIBLIOGRAPHY

American Law Institute. *Model Penal Code: Proposed Official Draft*. Philadelphia: ALI, 1962.
HONORÉ, TONY. *Sex Law*. London: Duckworth, 1978.
MACNAMARA, DONAL E. J., and SAGARIN, EDWARD. *Sex, Crime, and the Law*. New York: Free Press, 1977.
Note. "Fornication, Cohabitation, and the Constitution." *Michigan Law Review* 77 (1978): 252–306.
SLOVENKO, RALPH, ed. *Sexual Behavior and the Law*. Springfield, Ill.: Thomas, 1965.

ADVERSARY SYSTEM

The term *adversary system* sometimes characterizes an entire legal process, and sometimes it refers only to criminal procedure. In the latter instance it is often used interchangeably with an old expression of continental European origin, "accusatorial procedure," and is juxtaposed to the "inquisitorial," or "nonadversary," process. There is no precise understanding, however, of the institutions and arrangements denoted by these expressions.

Nevertheless, several characteristics are commonly associated by American lawyers with the adversary criminal process. These include a relatively passive tribunal that ideally comprises both judge and jury; the presentation of evidence by the parties through their lawyers, who proceed by direct questioning and cross-examination of witnesses; the representation of state interests by one of the parties—the prosecutor; a presumption that the defendant is innocent until proved guilty; and the principle that he cannot be forced to testify against himself.

The contours of the adversary system remain uncertain because the phrase has been used to describe three distinctive, albeit related, meanings.

The traditional meaning

In Anglo-American jurisdictions the phrase evokes both the aspirations and the actual features of Anglo-American criminal justice. It is incorporated to some extent into American constitutional law through provisions dealing with assistance of counsel and due process of law.

The attributes of "adversariness" change according to context. When techniques of ascertaining facts and deciding legal issues are discussed, a central feature is seen as a confrontational style: prosecution and defense prepare and present their cases to the court, and a decision is reached on the basis of the two alternative versions of fact and law. In this variant, partisan advocates are an essential aspect of the system, with their partisanship supported by canons of legal ethics (Fuller, p. 32). In the case of the public prosecutor, however, there is some equivocation: he is recognized to have a public responsibility that imposes limits upon his partisanship.

When the position of the criminal defendant is at issue, the focus shifts. The mainstay of the adversary system resides in the privilege against self-incrimination (*Malloy v. Hogan*, 378 U.S. 1, 7 (1964)), which implies high obstacles to conviction and an opposition to unbridled crime control. Any lowering of the evidentiary barriers erected to protect the defendant, such as the requirement of a unanimous jury verdict of guilt, is treated as a step away from the adversary ideal.

Adversary features are found not only in the contested trial but also in appellate proceedings, where arguments by the parties must ordinarily precede the decision of the appellate court. Even the pretrial phase of the criminal process is increasingly seen as displaying adversary characteristics. The privilege against self-incrimination, for example, now radiates into the earliest police inquiries, according protection to the suspect. The right to pretrial release and the hostility to preventive detention are also linked to the adversary system. On the other hand, the widespread practice of negotiations between the prosecution and the defense that is termed plea bargaining is usually treated as subverting adversariness. Where the defendant pleads guilty after such negotiations, the core of the adversary system, the contested trial, does not take place.

The adversary system has its distinctive source in liberal ideology. Consider, for example, the image so often used by lawyers of "balancing advantages" between the prosecution and the defense, which makes sense only in light of liberal theories that treat the state interest as analogous to—not superior to—private interests. The presumption of innocence, the requirement of proving guilt beyond a reasonable doubt, and related notions are also suffused with liberal values. Moreover, the passive attitude of the decision-maker has an affinity with the passive laissez-faire ideology.

It is this linkage to ideological currents that has produced two versions of the adversary system in its traditional meaning. In the "classical" variant, the ideal judge is propelled into action only to resolve disputes between the contending parties. The emergence of welfare-state liberalism has generated changes in this version of the idea. Just as modern liberal governments intervene in the economy to correct failures of competitive markets, so, according to this view, an adversary judge should intervene in the trial to redress the competition of the parties. Whereas the classical variant celebrates the parties' dominance over the process, a later variant would curb this dominance (Fuller, p. 41). But there is disagreement as to how far the judge can go in his intervention without negatively affecting the incentives of the prosecution and the defense for the zealous action required by the adversary system. Some see a solution to failures of party competition not in making the judge more active, but rather in replacing "ineffective" advocates by more capable ones.

It is plain that the adversary system in both its traditional senses is inextricably linked to legal ideology. It is praised in many quarters as a palladium of liberty and contrasted with an antipodal "inquisitorial" criminal process, that term serving to convey the worst features of continental European criminal justice prior to its reform in the wake of the French Revolution. Any departure from adversary features is said to imply a lapse into a system where searches are unbridled, the accused is detained without limits, his confession is coerced, counsel is denied him, and he is not accorded the benefit of doubt. This overdrawn polarization is reflected in such important judicial decisions as *Miranda v. Arizona*, 384 U.S. 436, 460 (1966).

The adversary system is extolled not only because of the protection it accords the accused, but also because its competitive style of presenting evidence and argument is thought to produce a more accurate result than an "inquisitorial" alternative, where the judge monopolizes proof-taking. According to this view, the judge who conducts an apparently nonpartisan inquiry cannot truly keep an open mind and lacks sufficient incentives to do a proper job (Hazard, p. 121). The possibility of a tension between the desire to obtain accurate results and to maintain high barricades to conviction is often denied. It is occasionally conceded, however, that high obstacles to conviction lessen the possibility of convicting an innocent person and increase the possibility that the guilty may escape conviction. Hence, by keeping the barriers to conviction high, as mandated by the adversary system, the accuracy of outcomes in the total number of cases—irrespective of the kind of error—can well be decreased. Where this is recognized, proponents of the adversary system accord decisive weight to liberal values: it is better to let a larger number of the guilty go free than to convict a smaller number of innocent persons.

The traditional Anglo-American concept of the adversary system has often been criticized by lawyers from other legal cultures. It has been vigorously questioned whether the clash of two zealous partisans represents the best instrument of discovering the truth. Moreover, the ample opportunities for the defendant to escape conviction have been said to exist mainly for those able to retain high-powered counsel. Finally, the practical importance of the adversary system in America has been doubted in view of the fact that most criminal cases never reach the stage of a contested trial but are settled through negotiations between prosecution and defense in the course of plea bargaining (Taruffo, pp. 259–301).

The adversary system as traditionally understood has its domestic enemies as well. Early in the twentieth century an eminent American legal scholar attacked it as inspired by a "sporting theory of justice" that treats substantively correct outcomes as relatively unimportant (Pound, p. 404). It is testimony to the continuing vitality of the traditional concept, however, that most critics castigate the alleged excesses of the system but fail to formulate alternatives to it. Inspiration for fundamental change is rarely sought in the

modern criminal justice systems of Western Europe, or elsewhere (Weinreb, pp. 117–146; Schlesinger, pp. 382–385).

The traditional concept of the adversary system evokes both actual features of Anglo-American criminal process and its aspirations. Inevitably, therefore, it combines both descriptive and prescriptive elements and cannot be expected to achieve rigorous internal consistency and coherence. It is not so much analytically precise as it is hortatory and rhetorical, aimed at mobilizing consent and at winning points in legal argumentation.

A model of conflict-solving procedure

A second way to view the adversary system is as a theoretical model. Conflict resolution is posited as the goal of the process, and the adversary model is then understood to comprise those procedures that implement this goal most effectively. In this second sense, then, the adversary system is a blueprint designed to promote the choice of certain procedures. Elements of the blueprint and features traditionally classed as adversary do not coincide.

Two methods have been used to construct the theoretical model of the adversary process. One method begins from the initial state of conflict between two sides and conceives of the ideal conflict-solving process as a simulation of, and substitute for, the private war between them. This leads to the central image of proceedings as a contest of two sides before the conflict-resolver. The task is then to develop procedural arrangements logically following from this central image. For example, if the adversary judge were permitted to inquire into facts not in dispute between the parties, the proceedings to determine these facts would "logically" cease to be a party contest. Consequently, the adversary model denies to the judge any independent powers to inquire into facts.

The other method starts from the desired end, which is said to be the acceptance of the court's decision by the disputants. The task here is to identify those procedures most likely to produce such acceptance, beginning with the premise that the goal of acceptance is promoted where the parties are permitted to exercise control over procedural action. In contrast to the first method, which relies on logical analysis, the second relies on observation and experiment. For example, whether participation of lawyers is an integral feature of the model hinges on whether such participation contributes to the control of the parties over the process.

As a model of a conflict-solving process, the adversary system is known in both continental European and Anglo-American legal cultures. Under the label "accusatorial proceedings" the model has a long history on the Continent.

The continental legal culture. Efforts to construct an ideal conflict-solving process are to be found in twelfth-century Roman Catholic ecclesiastical scholarship. By the fourteenth century, Italian students of procedure included in accusatorial proceedings many features now incorporated in the adversary system (Nörr, pp. 93–94). But the most inclusive models of the conflict-solving process are products of rationalist "natural law" scholarship at the turn of the nineteenth century.

These models appear extremely "adversarial" even from the perspective of Anglo-American legal culture. Termed "the party-dominated process" (*Parteiverfahren*) by German legal theorists, they deserve brief description. Under them, the judge cannot initiate or continue proceedings without an actual dispute. Parties control the factual and, to a great extent, the legal boundaries of the cause. Pleadings and stipulations are necessary devices to define and narrow issues, and the judge is not permitted to overrule such mutual arrangements. He is also denied the power to call witnesses on his own initiative. Even his powers of interrogation, otherwise very important on the Continent, are seriously curbed; only those questions can be asked by the bench that are suggested by the litigants. The appropriate role of the party—its "autonomy"—is thought to be incompatible with the duty to testify, and thus a party can invoke a general "right to silence" if called to take a stand. Usually, minimal obligations are imposed on the litigants to disclose evidence or information. "Nobody is expected to supply weapons to his adversary" is the often-invoked maxim.

But this model, so rigorously designed as a contest of two sides before a passive judge, was recommended as a blueprint only for civil cases that were regarded as self-contained private controversies. Because no larger implications were perceived in such lawsuits, judicial passivity seemed appropriate, if not mandated by the requirement of judicial neutrality. Many continental European countries, therefore, enacted codes of civil procedure incorporating features of the recommended theoretical model. The rational implementation of policies toward crime was thought, however, to make the blueprint inapplicable in criminal cases. Though the logic of the party-dominated model might have permitted the public prosecutor to represent the larger interest in crime control, it was viewed as unacceptable to give the other party—the accused—mastery over defensive issues. If this were done, a substantively erroneous result might be imposed on the passive court. For example, an insane defendant could be convicted if, for some strategic reason of his own, he failed to raise the insanity defense.

European procedural theory developed, as a result, a variety of modified blueprints for the criminal process, some of which were built on the "accusatorial principle" or on the "principle of contradiction" (Damaška, p. 560). In their most radical form, they recommended a partial simulation of the party contest, with evidence collected mainly by a nonpartisan but active decision-maker. The facts alleged in the prosecutor's charge constitute the only limit on his inquiry.

The Anglo-American legal culture. In Anglo-American countries, efforts to formulate organizing principles of procedure are mainly the product of the twentieth century. In civil procedure, for example, continental influences have led to the adoption of the twin principles of party prosecution (that the court will take no step in the case except on motion of the party) and of party presentation (that the scope and content of the controversy are to be defined by the parties) (Millar). As a shorthand expression of the characteristics of the classical civil lawsuit, the two principles enjoy a certain currency in scholarly discourse.

In criminal procedure, theoretical study has been devoted principally to the discrepancy between the realities of law enforcement and the aspirations expressed in the traditional concept of the adversary system. But there was another factor that contributed to the emergence of theoretical models. A fascination with empirical science led to the desire to compare the efficiency of some features of the adversary system with the inquisitorial alternatives. Most of the empirical studies focused on alternative ways of developing factual and legal material for decision. For the narrow purposes of this research, an adversary "mini-model" was defined as an arrangement where proof and argument are presented to the decision-maker by two partisan advocates, whereas the inquisitorial mini-model was described as a unilateral official inquiry into facts and law. The two models were then used in laboratory experimentation to test their relative efficacy in counteracting the decision-maker's bias, producing reliable results, or attaining some other goal. For example, since in the adversary model the judge is required to listen passively to both sides of the case before making a decision, it was hypothesized that he would be less likely to become prematurely biased and draw a conclusion too early (Thibaut and Walker, 1975; Sheppard and Vidmar).

The models reviewed here are all based on the assumption that the goal of the process is the resolution of a conflict. They constitute useful guidelines for reform of procedural systems only insofar as these systems are directed toward the same goal. What then is the relation of theoretically posited goals to reality? Conflict resolution as a goal may be restricted to the contested trial in Anglo-American countries, and even here it may be a secondary or only a superficial aim. If the judge refuses to accept the defendant's guilty plea, as he is empowered to in the majority of common-law jurisdictions, the case goes to trial in the absence of a genuine controversy between the prosecution and the defense.

An archetype of Anglo-American process

In its third sense, the adversary system is a procedural type designed by legal comparativists to capture characteristic features of the common-law process, particularly when contrasted with continental systems. For some comparative-law scholars the adversary type is the lowest common denominator of Anglo-American procedures. Consider, for example, the question whether the exclusion from trial of illegally obtained evidence represents a defining feature of the adversary type under this approach. Because the exclusionary rule has not been adopted by all Anglo-American jurisdictions, and because it has been proclaimed by the legislation of several European countries, the answer is in the negative (Hermann, p. 18). Under this approach the precise meaning of the adversary type remains hostage to changes in the law of a single common-law country.

Other scholars conceive of the adversary type as an ideal of procedure that is not fully duplicated in any actual system. This second approach can best be exemplified by analogy with styles in art. To classify a work of art as pertaining to a particular style, it is thought sufficient that the work encompass some, though not all, elements of the stylistic ideal. Similarly, certain features can be viewed as typically adversarial, although they are found only in a small number of actual procedural systems. Of course, in order to be useful, the ideal type of the adversary process must provide a structure in which actual systems can be recognized, albeit in exaggerated or stylized form. This second approach is more widespread and deserves to be followed in some detail.

Most scholars describe the ideal type of the adversary process by focusing their attention on the trial stage of the criminal process and on the three-sided relation among the prosecution, the defense, and the court. This triadic relation is significantly different in continental and Anglo-American countries. In the former, the court tends to monopolize the courtroom

activity; in the latter, the prosecution and the defense take the largest share of action. As a result, the ideal of the judge as a passive umpire, rather than an active seeker of the truth, is taken as the central ideal of the adversary system (Ploscowe, p. 433). But the focus on triadic relations leaves too much out of account. Both in Europe and in Anglo-American countries, important segments of the criminal process unfold in the absence of the judge, or before an official who need not be a judge, such as a public prosecutor or a police official.

The contrast between Anglo-American and continental criminal procedure is best expressed in two basic notions. The first, underlying the inquisitorial type, regards the criminal process as an official inquiry. The second, underlying the adversary type, regards criminal procedure as a regulated contest between the prosecution and the defense. In discussing other meanings of the adversary system, the image of proceedings as a contest has already been encountered. But the comparative perspective highlights some aspects of this contest that are overlooked by a purely domestic vision.

First, the prosecution and the defense prepare two independent cases in advance of the trial, often with a view to possibly avoiding it. Conspicuous by its absence is a nonpartisan agency preparing a single, or "integrative," case. Problems of maintaining a rough equality of the prosecution and the defense thus arise long before the trial. The preliminary detention, for example, does not fit neatly into the adversary type, because it hampers the defendant in preparing his own independent case. But the exclusionary rule glides in smoothly. If in preparing his case the prosecutor breached the law, he should not be permitted to reap advantages from such a "low blow."

Second, various forms of negotiation between the prosecution and the defense are a salient feature of the adversary type. Consider, for example, how easily the practice of plea bargaining fits the "style" of a process based on the notion of contest. It makes little sense to go on with such proceedings if the defendant refuses to oppose the demands of the prosecution. By contrast, in proceedings conceived of as an official inquiry, the defendant need not be asked how he pleads: the trial can go on irrespective of his attitude toward the prosecutorial charges. Inducements to facilitate the task of crime-control agencies exist, of course, in both adversary and inquisitorial systems. But the two are characterized by the different loci of such inducements. In the adversary process, both sticks and carrots are used to persuade the defendant not to contest charges, so that the need for trial is obviated. In the inquisitorial process these inducements are used during the interrogation of the defendant: he is urged to reveal information facilitating the task of the officials conducting the inquiry.

So far we have dealt with the conventional position that attributes the same meaning to the words *adversary* and *accusatorial*. A suggestion has been advanced, however, that comparativists should draw a distinction between the two (Goldstein, p. 1016). Under this approach the adversary process is said to denote only a method of finding facts and deciding legal problems, and is characterized by two sides shaping issues before a relatively neutral judge. The accusatorial system, on the other hand, is a more encompassing concept, which includes the adversary method as its constituent element.

The meaning of this broader concept depends on the contrast with the inquisitorial system, which encompasses the nonadversary method of proof and trial. The contrast turns on the divergent attitudes of state officials. In the inquisitorial system, officials are self-propelling and affirmatively obligated to carry out state policies, but in the accusatorial system they step into action only when a controversy arises and they are requested by the participants to respond. Each attitude entails a variety of consequences and choices among procedural forms, the choice of the proper method of finding facts being only one of many. Ultimately, the contrast between the inquisitorial and the accusatorial modes of proceeding involves two polar views about the role of government in society, that is, whether government should be "reactive" or "proactive" (Goldstein, p. 1017).

The idea of linking the characteristics of the Anglo-American criminal process to political ideology is promising. Important features of the Anglo-American criminal process cannot be reduced to the abstract notion of contest, which is so central to the adversary type. Moreover, some features of Anglo-American justice are in conflict with procedures mandated by notions of a fair contest. For example, the right of the defendant to personally defend himself—a right unique to common law—follows from the tenets of the reactive liberal ideology, but it seriously strains notions of a fair contest (*Faretta v. California*, 422 U.S. 806 (1975)). If more common-law characteristics are to be captured in procedural types, broader organizing principles are needed, and the ideology of reactive government provides one such principle. Consequently, it seems sensible to distinguish between the adversary type, which focuses on the contest design, and the accusatorial type, which centers on a political theory.

But even the broader concept of the accusatorial system fails to account for many striking characteristics of the Anglo-American criminal process when the latter is contrasted to continental systems. From the earliest known attempts to describe the peculiar nature of common-law justice, the participation of the lay jury was regarded as its hallmark, and lay decision-making as one of its most characteristic elements. The law of evidence, for example, is the product of the interaction of the judge, the jury, and the lawyers (Langbein, p. 306). These features elude the adversary type organized around the notion of a contest; the latter can plainly take place with or without a jury. Nor does the accusatorial system, inspired by the reactive philosophy of government, require jury trials; lay adjudicators can be an arm of a totalitarian as well as of a laissez-faire government. Observe, however, how trial by jury reinforces the characteristic Anglo-American image of the criminal process as a contest of the accused and the state before outside arbiters. Where, as on the Continent, the apparatus of justice is dominated by hierarchically organized civil servants, this conception of the criminal process has little credibility. Prosecutors and decision-makers are all too easily traceable to the center of state power. But the contest imagery has far greater plausibility in a procedural system where verdicts are reached by lay persons recruited to serve on the criminal court.

The difficulties involved in expressing the peculiar character of Anglo-American criminal procedure have given rise to increased skepticism as to whether any version of the adversary type can be useful. Those scholars of comparative law who subscribe to the lowest-common-denominator method are clearly justified in their doubts: no single model can be set up to which all Anglo-American criminal procedures conform (Langbein and Weinreb, p. 1551). But even those scholars who are less demanding seem increasingly skeptical. Factors involved in describing the peculiar character of Anglo-American proceedings are too complex and heterogeneous to be captured in a single, internally consistent type of criminal justice.

MIRJAN DAMAŠKA

See also CRIMINAL JUSTICE SYSTEM: OVERVIEW; CRIMINAL PROCEDURE: COMPARATIVE ASPECTS; PROSECUTION: COMPARATIVE ASPECTS; TRIAL, CRIMINAL.

BIBLIOGRAPHY

DAMAŠKA, MIRJAN. "Evidentiary Barriers to Conviction and Two Models of Criminal Procedure: A Comparative Study." *University of Pennsylvania Law Review* 121 (1973): 507–589.

ESMEIN, ADHÉMAR. *A History of Continental Criminal Procedure, with Special Reference to France.* Translated by John Simpson. Editorial preface by William E. Mikell. Introductions by Norman M. Trenholme and William Renwick Riddell. Boston: Little, Brown, 1913.

FULLER, LON L. *The Adversary System: Talks on American Law.* Edited by Harold J. Berman. New York: Random House, Vintage Books, 1961.

GOLDSTEIN, ABRAHAM. "Reflections on Two Models: Inquisitorial Themes in American Criminal Procedure." *Stanford Law Review* 26 (1974): 1009–1025.

HAZARD, GEOFFREY C. *Ethics in the Practice of Law.* New Haven: Yale University Press, 1978.

HERMANN, JOACHIM. "Various Models of Criminal Proceedings." *South African Journal of Criminal Law and Criminology* 2, no. 1 (1978): 3–19.

LANGBEIN, JOHN H. "The Criminal Trial before the Lawyers." *University of Chicago Law Review* 45 (1978): 263–316.

———, and WEINREB, LLOYD L. "Continental Criminal Procedure: Myth and Reality." *Yale Law Journal* 87 (1978): 1549–1568.

MILLAR, ROBERT. "The Formative Principles of Civil Procedure—I." *Illinois Law Review* 18 (1923): 1–36.

NÖRR, KNUT W. *Zur Stellung des Richters im gelehrten Prozess der Frühzeit: Iudex Secundum Allegata Non Secundum Conscientiam Iudicat.* Munich: Beck, 1967.

PLOSCOWE, MORRIS. "The Development of Present-day Criminal Procedures in Europe and America." *Harvard Law Review* 48 (1935): 433–473.

POUND, ROSCOE. "The Causes of Popular Dissatisfaction with the Administration of Justice." *Report of the Twenty-ninth Annual Meeting of the American Bar Association.* Philadelphia: Dando, 1906, pp. 395–408.

SCHLESINGER, RUDOLF. "Comparative Criminal Procedure: A Plea for Utilizing Foreign Experience." *Buffalo Law Review* 26 (1976–1977): 361–385.

SHEPPARD, BLAIR H., and VIDMAR, NEIL. "Adversary Pretrial Procedures and Testimonial Evidence: Effects of Lawyer's Role and Machiavellianism." *Journal of Personality and Social Psychology* 39 (1980): 320–332.

TARUFFO, MICHELE. *Il Processo Civile "Adversary" nell' Esperienza Americana.* Padua, Italy: CEDAM, 1979.

THIBAUT, JOHN W., and WALKER, LAURENS. *Procedural Justice: A Psychological Analysis.* Hillsdale, N.J.: Laurence Erlbaum Associates, 1975.

———. "A Theory of Procedure." *California Law Review* 66 (1978): 541–566.

WEINREB, LLOYD L. *Denial of Justice.* New York: Macmillan, 1977.

AGE AND CRIME

Criminologists have been concerned with the relationship between age and crime ever since the pioneering investigation of the subject by Adolphe Qué-telet in the early nineteenth century. On the basis of a statistical analysis, Quételet concluded that as people age, their rates of involvement in crime decline. Subsequent research seemed to confirm these findings for many types of crimes. Therefore, modern discussion of the prevention and control of crime focuses particularly on juveniles' high rates of involvement.

Whereas criminality has been linked with youthfulness, criminal victimization is popularly thought to occur most often in old age. Newspaper headlines about elderly women mugged by teenagers exemplify the stereotypes of those who commit crimes and those who are victimized by crime. In actuality, however, the evidence concerning the relationship between age and criminality is somewhat ambiguous, and the evidence regarding victimization clearly refutes the stereotype.

Age and criminality

Empirical evidence. Most of the research on the relationship between age and involvement in crime has been conducted with cross-sectional data, drawing on information collected at a single point in time. Some of the studies have been of self-reported infractions, with information elicited from persons of different ages through surveys; other research has been on aggregate rates. Since these rates are generally compiled by law enforcement agencies, they measure participation indirectly, in terms of cases processed by the particular agency. For example, the Federal Bureau of Investigation publishes the numbers of persons arrested for certain kinds of crime each year by police departments, broken down by age categories.

Both types of investigation report broadly similar patterns. Participation in crime rises with age, peaking in adolescence or early adulthood, and then declines. Because most of the self-report studies are based on student populations and are limited in the range of offenses studied, the official sources, for all their limitations, prove more informative. They include older subjects, and cover a wider range of offenses.

Three broad patterns are evident in the official sources (Cline). For burglary, larceny, arson, motor vehicle theft, curfew and loitering violations, running away, and vandalism, the number of arrests in the United States is largest for ages fifteen and sixteen, and declines rapidly with age. A second pattern, found for homicides, forcible rapes, robberies, weapons charges, assaults, drug law violations, forgery and counterfeiting, prostitution, and liquor law violations, has a peak at ages seventeen through twenty-one and a decline with age that is not as rapid as in the first pattern.

A third pattern includes fraud, embezzlement, sex offenses (excluding forcible rape and prostitution), gambling, offenses against family and children, driving under the influence of alcohol, and drunkenness. Here the peak is in young adulthood (ages twenty-one and twenty-two) as in the second pattern, but the decline with age is considerably slower.

To draw conclusions from arrest patterns about how much crime should be attributed to persons of different ages, some assumption must be made about the relation between an individual's age and his risk of arrest following an offense. In the absence of specific information about this relationship, it has generally been assumed that risk of arrest is unaffected by age, but that may not be correct. Presumably, criminals learn from experience how to avoid apprehension, although some evidence supports the possibility that they become better known to the police as they grow older, and thus are caught more readily. Interviews conducted cross-sectionally with convicted felons of different ages confirm that older criminals break the law less frequently than younger ones. It is unlikely, therefore, that the arrest patterns are due solely to variation with age in risk of arrest (Greenwood, Petersilia, and Zimring).

In the 1970s, according to the FBI's *Crime in the United States* (Uniform Crime Reports), roughly a third of all arrests were of persons nineteen years of age or younger. Such figures have been interpreted to show that juveniles commit an especially high amount of crime, but this logic fails to distinguish between numbers of persons arrested and numbers of crimes committed. The distinction is necessary because a given criminal incident can lead to the arrest of more than one person. If the ratio of arrests to crimes were the same at all ages, the distinction could be ignored. However, this is not the case. Juveniles are more likely

than adults to commit crimes in groups. As a result, the ratio of arrests to crimes is higher for younger persons than for adults. When this is taken into account, the proportion of crime attributable to juveniles is considerably reduced (Zimring).

In social statistics, the term *cohort* refers to a group of individuals who experience the same significant life event at about the same time. A *cohort effect* is an influence on a given cohort that persists as the cohort ages. By contrast, a *period effect* is one that does not persist at a later time. Thus, nonenduring effects of a war or depression are period effects, and enduring effects on those who were at a sensitive age during these events are cohort effects. It can be difficult to distinguish *age effects* (patterns of variation in crime rates with age) from cohort and period effects (Glenn; Pullum).

A cohort effect can lead to a decline in crime rates with age in cross-sectional data even in the absence of an age effect. If a given cohort begins committing crimes at the age of fifteen and continues doing so at the same rate in subsequent years, this implies that the cohort experiences no age effect, because its crime rate remains constant as the cohort grows older. In addition, if from one year to the next each subsequent cohort of fifteen-year-olds has a higher crime rate than the one before it—a rate which also remains constant as the cohort grows older—then in any given year, older cohorts will be committing crimes at lower rates than younger cohorts. This creates the false impression that involvement in crime diminishes with age.

Noting a rise in crime rates during the 1960s and 1970s, one should examine whether all or part of the apparent age effects in the arrest data are really cohort effects. This can be done by means of an age-cohort table which follows successive cohorts over a period of time. Table 1 shows the arrest rates on charges of aggravated assault for a number of cohorts over a fifteen-year period.

TABLE 1. *Aggravated assault arrest rates for various age cohorts, 1964–1979 (per 100,000 population)*

| Year | Age | | | | | | | | | |
	15–19	*20–24*	*25–29*	*30–34*	*35–39*	*40–44*	*45–49*	*50–54*	*55–59*	*60–64*
1964	10.3	11.0	8.7	7.6	6.6	5.1	3.2	2.5	1.2	0.7
1969	16.1	16.8	11.6	8.3	6.7	5.6	3.9	2.5	1.5	0.9
1974	24.9	25.4	18.3	12.5	8.9	6.7	4.9	3.4	1.9	1.2
1979	27.2	30.2	21.1	14.1	9.2	6.3	4.4	3.2	2.1	1.1

Number of reporting agencies is 3,977 in 1964, 4,759 in 1969, 5,298 in 1974, and 11,578 in 1979. Population base is total of the jurisdictions reporting, not the population in the given age cohort. Trends for each cohort are indicated by following the figures diagonally downward from left to right. Table is derived from data in four separate reports cited below.

SOURCE: Federal Bureau of Investigation.

According to the table, in any given year the number of arrests per capita peaks in the age 20–24 category. In fact, when rates for each separate year are examined the peak appears at ages 18–19, but the rates for these ages are so much higher than those for ages 15–17, and are so little higher than those for ages 20–24, that the rate for the five-year span covering the ages 20–24 is higher than the rate for ages 15–19. The table also shows that the arrest rate for 15–19-year-olds rose substantially over the period of the study, from 10.3 per 100,000 in 1964 to 27.2 per 100,000 in 1979. Similar increases are evident for other age categories, although they are much less marked for older ages.

If it is assumed that there are no period effects, the effect of age on arrests can be determined by following a given cohort diagonally from the upper left to the lower right. Thus, the 15–19-year-old cohort in 1964 becomes the 20–24-year-old cohort in 1969 and the 25–29-year-old cohort in 1974. The arrest rate of this cohort rises between ages 15–19 and 20–24, much more rapidly than is apparent from the cross-sectional distribution of arrests in 1964. Rather than declining in ages 25–29, as the cross-sectional rates do, the arrest rate for this cohort *rises* slightly, from 16.8 to 18.3 per 100,000.

Only in 1979, when the cohort reaches ages 30–34, does its arrest rate decline, and then only modestly. Similar patterns are seen for the cohorts that are ages 20–24 and 25–29 in 1964. Arrest rates rise slowly or fluctuate at an approximately constant level between 1964 and 1974, and then drop in 1979, when these cohorts are ages 35–39 and 40–44, respectively. The uniformity of these patterns suggests that a period effect is reducing the 1979 rates for all cohorts.

The age-cohort data in the table thus suggest that the arrest rate for aggravated assault does not decline in late adolescence and early adulthood, but only in middle age, if at all. Comparable age-cohort tables for other offenses show that those offenses for which a cross-sectional analysis suggests a peak in mid-adolescence followed by a very rapid decline (for example, burglary) do indeed have an age effect, but that it is not as pronounced as the cross-sectional analysis implies.

It should be emphasized that the behavior of each person within a cohort need not parallel the average or aggregate behavior of the entire cohort. If the number of crimes committed by members of a cohort declines as the cohort becomes older, this might mean that every member of the cohort reduces the frequency of his violations, but it could also mean that some members stop altogether and that others continue with a frequency that is as high or higher than before.

No analysis of aggregate rates can distinguish these possibilities. Only by tracing individuals over time can the change in their patterns of involvement in crime be determined. Alfred Blumstein and Jacqueline Cohen have done this by examining the adult criminal records of a sample of felons arrested in Washington, D.C. They found that age had no consistent and appreciable effect on the arrest rates of recidivists for robbery, aggravated assault, larceny, auto theft, and weapons charges; but for burglary and drugs there was evidence that rates *rose* with age.

An analysis of delinquency in a Philadelphia male birth cohort conducted by Marvin Wolfgang, Robert Figlio, and Thorsten Sellin found a similar pattern. Aggregate involvement in delinquency declined steadily from age sixteen to age thirty, when the study ended. The decline occurred because many boys in the cohort abandoned delinquency as they became older. The study also found that the mean time between the offenses committed by recidivists declined as these individuals grew older. This implies increasing rates of involvement for those who continue in delinquency. In other words, as the cohort becomes older, criminality is increasingly restricted to a small part of the cohort. Within that part, offenses occur more frequently, as measured by arrests.

Theories of age variation in criminality. Criminologists have sometimes referred to the supposed decline in criminality with age as a "maturation effect," implying that delinquency may be a result of physical or mental immaturity. Yet research by Franco Ferracuti has shown that on the average, delinquents are no less and no more physically mature than nondelinquent youths. Cross-cultural studies have examined societies in which young people are much less involved in crime than in the United States. Clayton Hartjen and S. Priyadarsini note that in India only a minute percentage of all crimes can be attributed to juveniles. In the United States, by contrast, roughly a quarter of all arrests are of persons under the age of eighteen. It seems doubtful that these gross variations are caused by the differences in the ages at which Indian and American youths mature. The findings suggest that age differences in criminality are caused largely by social factors, although physical incapacity might help to explain the very low involvement in crime of small children and the elderly.

With varying emphases, Daniel Glaser, Paul Friday and Jerald Hage, and David Greenberg have developed sociological analyses of the age distribution of crime based on the increasing separation of adolescents from adults in modern society, on the differences in the degree to which persons of various ages are integrated into conventional institutions, and on the character of their integration. Low integration in, and alienation from, these institutions can provide motives for violating the law. In addition, low integration implies weak socialization to standards of conventional society, as well as the weakness of informal methods of social control.

Since interest has centered particularly on crimes involving theft and interpersonal violence, and since arrest rates for these offenses peak in the late teenage years and the early twenties, special attention has been devoted to adolescents and the ways they are distinguished from adults, for example, in labor-force involvement. In highly industrialized societies, adolescents enter the full-time paid labor force at much later ages than in nonindustrial societies. The absence of working parents in the home has meant that youths are not subject to the informal social control that exists when they work alongside their parents in the fields or in the kitchen, or when they serve as apprentices or servants in the homes of others. These are the common forms of juvenile employment in preindustrial societies.

Child labor laws, as well as policies that require high school graduation or an age of eighteen to twenty-one for full-time employment, have left many youths either working at part-time, poorly paid jobs, or totally unemployed. When they cannot obtain the income required to meet their perceived needs as consumers, juveniles are likely to consider theft as a means of meeting those needs.

When neither work nor education takes place in the home, parents are less able to exercise control over their children, thereby preventing them from committing thefts or other illegal acts. This reduced interaction may well have weakened parental inculcation of moral standards in children, with the result that youngsters may be more likely to contemplate and commit crimes.

Mandatory school attendance laws, together with high educational requirements for entry-level jobs, expose large numbers of young people to protracted schooling. Students who derive no intrinsic gratification from education, and whose poor academic performance reduces the future occupational benefits of school attendance, are not so much weakly integrated into a conventional institution as forcibly integrated. Their failure to achieve according to school standards, as well as the ridicule of teachers and fellow students, result in low self-regard. This, as well as their resentment at being subjected to a school discipline that

they perceive as pointless, can lead them to violate school regulations as a way of asserting themselves and of showing contempt and hostility to the school.

These experiences can also lead to delinquency outside the school setting, as a way of alleviating frustration and "proving" potency and competence to the delinquent and his peers. In principle, these attributes can be demonstrated in other ways than through crime, for example, through military service, parenthood, or employment. However, the means for doing so do not always exist, and are not always readily created by adolescents. Some delinquent youths have nevertheless integrated well into these conventional institutions when given the opportunity (Gendreau and Ross).

Although vulnerable to court action for status offenses such as truancy, juveniles are treated more leniently than adults for conventional crimes. For example, probation is granted far more readily by juvenile court judges than by criminal court judges, and reformatory sentences are typically much shorter than prison sentences. This official leniency is not compensated by greater informal social control. As noted above, parents are in a poor position to supervise their children when school, home, and workplace are separated. On the other hand, because low grades and a disciplinary record can threaten a child's prospects for further education and employment, school authorities are able to exercise some degree of informal control. However, students who have few future prospects are unlikely to be influenced by these considerations.

It follows that many youths abandon delinquency when they reach the end of adolescence. Employment, leaving school, military enlistment, and marriage eliminate major sources of criminogenic frustration, and at the same time supply informal social control.

Differences among offenses in the age distributions of crime involvement cannot be explained adequately by the above considerations alone, for social integration and social control should inhibit all types of violations in much the same way. An explanation of these variations must include the opportunities to commit offenses, or the motivation at different ages to commit different types of offenses. Since circumstances for theft or assault abound or are easily created, it is unlikely that variation in opportunities can explain differences in the age distributions of these offenses. On the other hand, crimes that by definition can only be committed by the employee of an organization, for example, employee theft, require that the perpetrator be old enough to be employed. The higher the organizational position required for the violation, the older the age at first violation will presumably be.

Little empirical research has been conducted to seek or test explanations for the contrasting peak ages of arrest for the different offenses summarized here. For this reason, there can be no certainty as to the relative importance of the motivations, control considerations, and opportunities that give rise to the various involvement patterns for different offenses. However, the arrest patterns described earlier suggest that adolescence may be a particularly critical period for theft, and adulthood, for drug offenses and assaultive crimes.

Age and victimization

Empirical evidence. A victimization rate represents the chance of becoming the victim of a crime during the course of a year. Information about the age distribution of murder victims comes from police statistics, and for other offenses, from victimization surveys.

In cross-sectional data, different patterns of victimization are seen for different offenses. In the first pattern the chances of being victimized rise, peaking at ages sixteen through nineteen or twenty through twenty-four, and then decline with age. Murder, assault, rape, pickpocketing, burglary, household larceny, and motor-vehicle theft all conform to this pattern. In the second pattern, victimization rates are approximately constant through ages twenty through twenty-four, and then decline. Robbery and larceny exemplify this pattern. Purse-snatching presents a third pattern, in which victimization rates are approximately constant at all ages. With this single exception, victimization rates decline with age. In no case do they rise with age.

Information regarding victimization from other forms of crime is not available, but age distributions can often be inferred from known patterns of eligibility. Home-repair frauds and illegal stock-market dealings are unlikely to victimize teenagers or young adults because ownership of homes and stocks is comparatively infrequent at these ages.

As with crime rates, information about victimization in a single year cannot tell us whether an observed distribution represents an age, cohort, or period effect, or some combination of these. Because victimization surveys have been carried out for only a few years, it is not possible to examine this question by following a given cohort over a number of years, except for homicide. An age-cohort analysis of the age distribution of homicide victims, as reported by the FBI for the period between 1964 and 1979, suggests that chances of being killed in a homicide rise between birth and early adulthood. After that there seem to be few age effects, but pronounced period and cohort effects.

Explanations of age variation in victimization. Comparatively little attention has been given to the explanation of age differences in rates of victimization. If there are such effects, they might be explained in terms of exposure, moral beliefs regarding the acceptability of victimizing persons of different ages, and the measures people of different ages take to avoid victimization.

Where offenses grow out of routine interaction, patterns of victimization will presumably reflect the age patterns typical of the interaction in question. Since many types of interaction commonly involve persons of like ages, a similarity can be expected between the age distribution of victimization and that of commission. However, although there are gross similarities in the two sets of observed distributions, there are also some differences. For example, homicide victims tend to be older than persons arrested for homicide. This is particularly striking because many homicides occur between spouses or lovers, who are generally about the same age. It may be, therefore, that internalized norms concerning acceptable targets of assaultive behavior play a role. If it is considered unfair to strike at someone who is younger, victims will tend to be somewhat older than perpetrators. However, if people are also taught to respect their elders, victims will not be too much older than perpetrators.

Although research has not yet confirmed that moral considerations affect the choice of homicide victims, the infrequency with which very small children are killed, even though they are more vulnerable than older persons, strongly suggests that this may be the case. On the other hand, there may be fewer reasons to kill small children. They are less likely, for example, to be killed in the course of a robbery, because they carry too little cash to be attractive targets for a robber.

A third consideration revolves around age differences in the precautions that people take to avoid victimization. Older people are more fearful of being victimized and, possibly for this reason, reduce their exposure to crime. Individuals with more material possessions have greater incentives to adopt protective measures and are also more likely to have the financial resources to pay for such measures, including taxis, burglar alarms, safe-deposit boxes, and apartments protected by doormen.

Life-style differences can be a contributing factor,

even when they do not reflect attempts to reduce victimization. People who are retired are more likely to be at home than those who are still employed, and dwellings are less likely to be burglarized when someone is at home. People are also less likely to be assaulted by strangers when at home.

Given that the age-cohort analysis for homicide victimization does not indicate that the chance of death through homicide declines with age, variables such as exposure and protection may be more important as determinants of cohort and period effects than as causes of age effects.

DAVID F. GREENBERG

See also CHILDREN, CRIMINAL ACTIVITIES OF; CRIME PREVENTION: JUVENILES AS POTENTIAL OFFENDERS; FAMILY RELATIONSHIPS AND CRIME; JUVENILE STATUS OFFENDERS; POLICE: HANDLING OF JUVENILES; SCHOOLS, CRIME IN THE; *articles under* VIOLENCE IN THE FAMILY; YOUTH GANGS AND GROUPS.

BIBLIOGRAPHY

BLUMSTEIN, ALFRED, and COHEN, JACQUELINE. "Estimation of Individual Crime Rates from Arrest Records." Urban Systems Institute preprint. Pittsburgh, Pa.: Carnegie-Mellon University, School of Urban and Public Affairs, 1978.

CLINE, HUGH F. "Criminal Behavior over the Life Span." *Constancy and Change in Human Development.* Edited by Orville G. Brim, Jr., and Jerome Kagan. Cambridge, Mass.: Harvard University Press, 1980, pp. 641–674.

Federal Bureau of Investigation. *Crime in the United States.* Uniform Crime Reports for the United States. Washington, D.C.: U.S. Department of Justice, FBI, 1964, 1969, 1974, 1979.

FERRACUTI, FRANCO; DINITZ, SIMON; and ACOSTA DE BRENES, ESPERANZA. *Delinquents and Nondelinquents in the Puerto Rican Slum Culture.* Columbus: Ohio State University Press, 1975.

FRIDAY, PAUL C., and HAGE, JERALD. "Youth Crime in Postindustrial Societies: An Integrated Perspective." *Criminology* 14, no. 1 (1976): 347–366.

GENDREAU, PAUL, and ROSS, BOB. "Effective Correctional Treatment: Bibliotherapy for Cynics." *Crime and Delinquency* 25 (1979): 463–489.

GLASER, DANIEL. *Crime in Our Changing Society.* New York: Holt, Rinehart & Winston, 1978.

———, and RICE, KENT. "Crime, Age, and Employment." *American Sociological Review* 4 (1959): 679–686.

GLENN, NORVAL D. *Cohort Analysis.* University Papers: Quantitative Applications in the Social Sciences 5. Beverly Hills, Calif.: Sage, 1977.

GREENBERG, DAVID F. "Delinquency and the Age Structure of Society." *Contemporary Crises* 1 (1977): 189–223.

GREENWOOD, PETER W.; PETERSILIA, JOAN; and ZIMRING, FRANKLIN E. *Age, Crime, and Sanctions: The Transition from Juvenile to Adult Court.* Santa Monica, Calif.: Rand, 1980.

HARTJEN, CLAYTON, and PRIYADARSINI, S. "Delinquency in India: A Comparative Analysis." Unpublished book manuscript, 1981.

PULLUM, THOMAS W. "Parametrizing Age, Period, and Cohort Effects: An Application to U.S. Delinquency Rates, 1964–1973." *Sociological Methodology 1978.* Edited by Karl F. Schuessler. San Francisco: Jossey-Bass, 1978, pp. 116–140.

QUÉTELET, ADOLPHE. *Recherches sur le pendant au crime aux différens âges.* 2d ed. Brussels: Hayez, 1833.

U.S. Department of Justice, Law Enforcement Assistance Administration, National Criminal Justice Information and Statistics Service. *Criminal Victimization in the United States, 1977.* National Crime Survey Report. Washington, D.C.: NCJISS, 1979.

WOLFGANG, MARVIN; FIGLIO, ROBERT E.; and SELLIN, THORSTEN. *Delinquency in a Birth Cohort.* University of Chicago Press, 1972.

ZIMRING, FRANKLIN E. "Kids, Groups, and Crime: Some Implications of a Well-known Secret." *Journal of Criminal Law and Criminology* 72, no. 3 (1981): 867–885.

AGGRAVATING CIRCUMSTANCES

See CRIME: DEFINITION OF CRIME; PUNISHMENT; *articles under* SENTENCING.

AGGRESSION

See CRIME CAUSATION: PSYCHOLOGICAL THEORIES; HOMICIDE: BEHAVIORAL ASPECTS; VIOLENCE.

AIDING AND ABETTING

See ACCOMPLICES.

ALCOHOL AND CRIME

1. BEHAVIORAL ASPECTS   Robin Room
2. LEGAL ASPECTS   Raymond T. Nimmer
3. THE PROHIBITION EXPERIMENT Joseph R. Gusfield
4. TREATMENT AND REHABILITATION Harrison M. Trice

1.
BEHAVIORAL ASPECTS

Alcohol, criminal behavior, and criminal events. In nineteenth-century American thought, the link between alcohol and crime was strong and certain. The showman P. T. Barnum was echoing countless other writers when he stated, in a temperance pamphlet published at mid-century, that "three-fourths of all the crime and pauperism existing in our land are traceable to the use of intoxicating liquors." In many novels, films, and other forms of popular culture influenced by temperance fiction, alcohol was not only linked to violent crime but was almost a necessary precondition. Behind the statistics, many of which trace back to a pioneering empirical investigation by Samuel Chipman, first published in 1834 (Levine in Room and Collins), lay a "scientific" explication in terms of the physiological action of alcohol: "Alcohol has a specific affinity for the brain centers and paralyzes them in the inverse order of their development. It paralyzes the centers of inhibition first and self-control and self-restraint disappear. . . . The center which suffers first and suffers most in the degenerative process constitutes the highest and noblest faculty of the human mind and is the throne of conscience" (Chapple, p. 21).

Substantial scholarly examination of the alcohol-crime link, stimulated by the claims of the temperance movement, was initiated around the turn of the twentieth century. An early landmark in the American literature was John Koren's sophisticated multifactorial analysis in 1899 of the role of alcohol in the causation of crimes. In the wake of this research, a note of caution emerged in scholarly expositions of the alcohol-crime link: "The assurance with which intemperance is held responsible for the mass of criminality has at any rate the merit of being quite natural. When an offense is committed in a state of intoxication or by a habitual user of strong drink, the causal relations seem unmistakable, even inevitable, no matter how infinitely complicated the problem appears to the criminologist. . . . [But] we are still confronted with the question: Assuming that alcohol had never existed, how many and which of the criminal acts perpetrated during a period would not have been committed?" (Koren, 1916). In the polarized atmosphere of the era of national Prohibition (1919–1933) and after Repeal, empirical research on the linkage of alcohol and crime declined, although, as a vestige of the earlier interest, prisoner surveys to this day often retain a few questions relating to alcohol. There was relatively little advance in research design or in theoretically relevant knowledge until the advent of the line of research on alcohol and crime initiated by Marvin Wolfgang (Wolfgang and Strohm; Wolfgang).

For many years, then, the literature on alcohol and criminal behavior and events revolved around a set of "tacit theories" (Roizen and Schneberk in Aarens, Cameron et al.) of the relationship, derived primarily from temperance-era thought, and centering on what Kai Pernanen (1976, pp. 393–399) has named the "disinhibition theory" of the effect of alcohol as an explanation of crimes of violence. The disinhibition theory proposes that alcohol disinhibits behavior pharmacologically—the usual "explanation," now as in Koren's time, is that alcohol suppresses the inhibitory actions of the "higher centers" of the brain.

The present discussion is concerned with alcohol's role in non-alcohol-specific crimes. In the United States, a large part of all reported crimes are accounted for by two alcohol-specific types of crime—drunken driving and public drunkenness; "decriminalization" of the latter offense remains a pious intention rather than a practical reality in much of the country. A third type of alcohol-specific crime—the illicit production, sale, or purchase of alcohol—has been less prominent since the repeal of Prohibition, although it remains a numerically substantial component of juvenile crime.

Empirical evidence on alcohol and crime. Several major reviews of the available literature on alcohol, criminal behavior, and criminal events have appeared (Pernanen, 1976; Aarens, Cameron et al.; Collins; Roizen; Lahelma; Vogt; Aarens, Blau et al.; Coid; Morgan). Taken together, these reviews and analyses offer a well-defined picture of the findings—and of the strengths and weaknesses—of the voluminous empirical literature. But beyond this, in reexamining the theoretical presumptions that underlie the empirical literature, these studies have provided a solid basis for new directions of theoretically grounded empirical work on a variety of aspects of the relationship between alcohol, criminal behavior, and criminal events. Relevant also to such future work are the reconsiderations of theoretical issues in the quite separate literature on drugs and crime (Inciardi; Johnson, 1981a, 1981b) and in the special area of alcohol and disinhibition (Room and Collins).

Both drunkenness and the commission of a crime are, roughly speaking, *events* rather than *conditions* (Aarens, Cameron et al.). The most voluminous part of the empirical literature on alcohol and crime consists of studies of the interrelation of drinking occasions or drunkenness with criminal *events*. The drinking or drunkenness involved can be that of the perpetrator, of the victim (in the case of interpersonal crimes), or of both. The frame of reference for almost all of the studies is the criminal event, and the findings revolve around the percentage of criminal events studied in which drinking or drunkenness was involved. Few studies offer a picture of the association in the opposite direction—the proportion of drunken events that involve criminal activity. Many studies provide no enlightenment on the potential processes linking alcohol and crime beyond a percentage of events in which drinking and crime are conjoined. Given the assumption of intentionality involved in criminal behavior, the alcohol and crime literature has no equivalent of the epidemiological concept of a "control sample," comparing the involvement of drinking or drunkenness in noncriminal events (Aarens, Cameron et al.). Smaller traditions of empirical work bear on the relations between alcohol and criminal *conditions*—on the prevalence of alcoholism among criminals, on the criminal history of alcoholics, and on the intertwining of the "criminal career" and the "alcoholic career" (Collins in Collins).

Types of offenses. The cumulation of studies on alcohol in criminal events allows for substantial comparisons of the rate of occurrence of alcohol factors by type of crime, by sex and age, and by ethnicity and nationality. A lengthy tradition of generalizations on the involvement of alcohol in particular types of crime asserts that drinking is more involved in crimes against the person than in property crimes, and that drinking is more involved in serious than in trivial crimes (Aschaffenburg). The relatively small number of American studies based on arrest-record data on drinking by the offender offer some support to these generalizations. Studies in the tradition of Wolfgang's homicide study show that drinking by the offender is mentioned in police reports for 7 percent of robberies, 24 percent of rapes, 24 percent of assaults, and 55 percent of homicides (Roizen and Schneberk in Aarens, Cameron et al., p. 372). On the other hand, when prisoners are asked whether they were intoxicated during the commission of the offense for which they were incarcerated, no such clear differentiation appears. Reanalysis of a large 1974 American national sample of inmates in state correctional facilities showed substantial proportions who reported drinking (38 percent to 67 percent) and who reported drinking heavily (19 percent to 39 percent) at the time of committing a variety of crimes against persons or property (Roizen and Schneberk in Aarens, Cameron et al., p. 370).

Judy Roizen and Dan Schneberk (Aarens, Cameron et al.), as well as Stephanie Greenberg (Collins), have discussed at some length the potential artifacts—in terms of different populations sampled, different procedures, and response effects—that could contribute to the different results of the two types of study. For example, it has been noted, particularly for sex (McCaghy) and family crimes (Aarens, Cameron et al., p. 554), that offenders may overreport drunkenness as a form of "deviance disavowal." Moreover, Greenberg has argued that drunken arrestees may be more likely than others to be diverted to dispositions other than prison (cf. Speiglman and Weisner), and that police may be more likely to note that the offender had been drinking for some types of crimes than for others. The fact that homicide shows a similar and substantial drinking involvement by the two methods has been noted as a convergence which may be significant, since police and judicial procedures are followed more meticulously for this type of offense. However, the net result of research on alcohol in criminal events must be stated cautiously: it is clear that the offender had been drinking in a relatively high proportion of serious events where the offender is captured, but there appears to be only a weak tendency, subject to exceptions, for drinking by offenders to be associated more with crimes against persons than with crimes against property. Since the bulk of the available literature is concerned with violent interpersonal crimes, the emphasis here will be on alcohol's relation to such crimes.

Sex and age variables. Heavy drinking and criminal behavior show considerable similarity to each other in their distribution by sex and age within the American population. Heavy drinking is more common among men than among women at all ages, and it peaks among men in the general population in their early twenties (Clark and Midanik, p. 35; Collins in Collins, pp. 160–167). This is in contrast to "alcoholism" in clinical settings, which is more concentrated at ages thirty-five to sixty. Men account for 80 percent to 90 percent of those arrested and convicted for serious crimes in the United States. The peak age for numbers of criminal offenders is sixteen; however, for some serious offenses like robbery, "the young adult years may represent the more serious age period" (Collins in Collins, p. 174). The near-coincidence in the gender-age distributions of heavy drinking and crime in the general population of the United States practically ensures some positive correlation between heavy drinkers and criminals in the population as a whole. But "it is not certain that the similar empirical regularities of drinking problems and criminal behaviors in the young adult years have any systematic causal relationship to each other. These two phenomena may each be independently explained by other factors" (Collins in Collins, pp. 205–206).

Ethnic and cultural differences. Contrary to common assumptions in the literature, Roizen's 1981 review concluded that "data from arrest records, prison records, and interviews do not generally support the view that Blacks are more likely than Whites to have been involved in a crime with alcohol present" (Collins, p. 221). For every type of crime, in the 1974 national sample of inmates mentioned above, black males were less likely than white males to report drinking at the time of the crime. Research in the Wolfgang tradition of studies of violent criminal events showed somewhat different results—that "alcohol involvement [was] comparable for Black and White groups"—but this finding also provides little support for the theory that "a disproportionate amount of Black crime is a consequence of drinking" (Roizen in Collins, pp. 224, 232, 252).

More generally, cross-sectional comparisons have long noted substantial differences between nations, as well as between ethnic groups in the United States, in rates and patterns of heavy drinking and drinking-related problems (Mäkelä, Room et al.; Cahalan and Room). Regional comparisons within the United States, and national comparisons between the Nordic countries, have suggested differences in the explosiveness of drinking patterns and in the associated social disruption. The countries or regions with the most explosive drinking styles—Finland as compared, say, to Denmark; and the American South as compared, say, to the Northeast—also have comparatively elevated homicide rates (Christie; Cahalan and Room; Room; cf. Levinson in Room and Collins).

Quantitative empirical studies have shown cultural differences in the association of drinking, violent behavior, and crime (Pernanen, 1982; Graves et al.). These findings converge with one strand of the emerging social-science critiques of the disinhibition theory of the relation of alcohol and crime. Craig MacAndrew and Robert Edgerton collected a broad range of anthropological and other evidence of very wide variations between different cultures and contexts in drunken comportment, suggesting that the link between drinking and violence is at least as much a matter of cultural expectation as of pharmacology. More recent anthropological work (Marshall), as well as evidence from other fields (Room and Collins), has provided further support for this position. Although the literature on variations in the alcohol-aggression link in American subcultures is not well developed (Levinson in Room and Collins), an ethnographic report that drinking and violence seem to have a weaker cultural link among black than among white Americans (Herd in Room and Collins) provides some support for Roizen's conclusions from the quantitative literature, noted above.

Influence on careers in crime. Reviews of the literature (Roizen and Schneberk in Aarens, Cameron et al.; Collins) agree that there is a positive raw correlation between alcoholism as a condition and careers in crime. Roizen and Schneberk made a rough comparison of reported alcohol problems in prison populations and in general population samples of men and concluded that "it is clear that prisoners have a greater incidence of drinking problems than is found in the general population," although "the differences are not as great as might be expected." Looking at the relationship through the other sampling window, "chronic inebriate offenders, excessive drinkers, and alcoholics in treatment have records of criminal behavior far in excess of those expected in a sample of the general population." Roizen and Schneberk note that most of the studies proceed no further after establishing the association, and "spend little effort investigating characteristics of the criminal event for which offenders are incarcerated or major life problems other than drinking." The agenda is "to identify both crime and drinking problems as moral failings of the individual" without attention to the potential contributions of situational or general sociocultural factors (pp. 378, 381–384, 395). It is clear that the empirical relationship of criminal and alcoholic careers is greatly affected by the definitions used, reflecting differences in the life circumstances and chances of those included in the sample. Thus, a Swedish study found wide divergences in the proportion of individuals with criminal records among three samples of different kinds of "alcoholics": 11 percent of voluntary admissions for "alcoholism" in a mental hospital; 42 percent of those hospitalized for acute psychiatric sequels of, and withdrawal symptoms from, excessive drinking; and 77 percent of homeless men receiving social assistance. The proportions with records of "crimes of violence" were, respectively, none, 10 percent, and 27 percent (recalculated from Lindelius and Salum).

As this study suggests, only a minority of even those alcoholics who are entangled in the criminal justice system have records of serious crime. A classic American study of 186 public inebriate offenders found that although they had experienced a total of 3,078 arrests, 77 percent of these were for public intoxication; only one-third of the sample had a criminal history which included serious crime (Pittman and Gordon). Jeremy Coid suggests that both the epidemiological and clinical literatures support a conclusion that there is a special psychiatrically disturbed subgroup in the population of alcoholics with violent proclivities: in his view, there is a "strong association between violence by alcoholics and a prior abnormality of personality, which has led both to violent behavior and the alcoholism itself." Judging from David Pittman and Wayne Gordon's study, "serious crime, if it is committed at all, is committed early in the criminal careers, followed by a longer career of drunkenness offenses" (Roizen and Schneberk in Aarens, Cameron et al., p. 399). Greenberg suggests that such a pattern "may represent those with failed criminal careers. Problem drinking may have prevented a successful criminal career or may be the result of continued failure for other reasons" (Collins, p. 90). Noting that a longitudinal prison study concurred in finding that "criminality by and large preceded the development of a drinking problem" (Goodwin, Crane, and Guze), and that alcoholism as a clinical phenomenon is more a phenomenon of middle age than of youth, Roizen and Schneberk conclude that "if there is a causal connection" between criminal history and alcoholism, then the time-ordering of the behaviors suggest "it is crime 'causing' chronic inebriacy rather than the other way around" (Aarens, Cameron et al., p. 399).

It should be noted that the empirical relations between criminal records, alcoholism diagnosis, and treatment history are likely to be affected by ongoing changes in the American alcoholism treatment and criminal justice systems. There seems to be a general tendency for more and more of those in treatment for alcoholism to be there as court "referrals"—for non-alcohol-specific as well as alcohol-specific crimes (Speiglman and Weisner). Although this reflects the population pressure in the criminal justice system and the expansion of the alcoholism treatment system, it also reflects the operation in the law courts—more at the phase of disposition than at that of determination of guilt (Mosher in Room and Collins)—of the cultural belief in alcohol's criminogenic powers. This trend is likely to produce samples of treated "alcoholics" who are younger and more criminally involved, while lowering the prevalence of "problem drinkers" in prison populations.

Situational factors. Detailed studies of the context of criminal events and of alcohol's place in them have been seen as crucial to an understanding of the nature and strength of the potential links (Pernanen in Collins). But the quantitative empirical evidence available remains rather sparse. A substantial minority of homicides, rapes, and assaults take place in or around bars (Roizen and Schneberk in Aarens, Cameron et al., pp. 322–364). Drawing on ethnographic studies, Roizen suggests that for some populations, taverns may be a particularly important factor in the alcohol-crime link: "among lower-class Blacks, taverns are

both the legitimate settings for interpersonal confrontation and violence, and also places which offer freedom from the norms of everyday life" (Collins, pp. 244–251). In systematic observational studies in Vancouver, British Columbia, Kathryn Graham and her associates found that bars "varied enormously in frequency of aggression"; although "no aggression was seen" in 62 percent of the 185 bars visited, "in 1 bar 14 incidents were recorded in a total of 5 hr of observation." Aggressive incidents were concentrated in bars that were in or near skid row and frequented by patrons who were outside the work force, by those involved in drug dealing, prostitution, and other hustles, and by members of ethnic or other minorities.

Reflecting the weekly cycle of drinking in the general population, homicides involving alcohol are more likely to take place in the evening and on weekends than at other times. A Finnish study found that in homicides and serious assaults the offender was most likely to be drunk when he was an acquaintance of the victim, and least likely to be drunk when they had a close relationship; offenses involving strangers fell in between. The offender was more likely to be drunk in disputes originating on the spot than in revivals of old disputes (Lahelma, pp. 82–86). In interpreting these findings from police reports of assaults, as well as homicide, Pernanen's conclusions (1981) in a Canadian study should be kept in mind: violent incidents were more likely to be reported to the police when the offender and victims were strangers, and when the offender but not the victim had been drinking. Results in American police-report studies suggest that alcohol is about as likely to be a factor in homicides committed in the home as in homicides committed elsewhere. Both inside the home and outside, stabbing is overrepresented and shooting underrepresented as the means of assault in homicides involving alcohol. Alcohol appears to add excess violence to already homicidally violent situations. Homicides involving alcohol are substantially more likely than others to be "victim precipitated," where the victim is "the first to commence the interplay or resort to physical violence" (Wolfgang).

The finding on victim precipitation is related to a more general pattern of association of drunkenness in the offender and in the victim in interpersonal crimes. For robbery, rape, assault, and homicide, American studies show that the offender is more likely to have been drinking if the victim has been drinking, and vice versa. This association is particularly strong for homicide and for rapes involving acquaintances and friends. For these offenses and for assaults, North

American studies suggest that the offender and the victim are about equally likely to have been drinking. For robberies and for rapes involving strangers, it appears that the victim is more likely to have been drinking than the offender.

The special association of the victim's drinking with exploitative crimes should occasion no surprise. In the special context of skid-row drinking, the vulnerability of drunken persons to robbery by "jackrollers" has long been recognized: Edwin H. Sutherland and Harvey Locke described the jackroller as the "worst enemy" of homeless drinkers (p. 120). A study of robbery victims in Helsinki between 1963 and 1973 showed that the median amount taken was considerably greater for drunken than for sober victims (Lahelma, pp. 106–112). A Polish study of injured robbery victims found that two-thirds were definitely "tipsy" and only 6 percent definitely sober. The most common pattern was for the robbery to take place near a restaurant; injuries were usually minor and resulted from slaps or kicks. The victims commonly reported the crime several hours afterward, often claiming an intervening loss of consciousness (Marek, Widacki, and Hanausek). On the general issue of alcohol's "victimogenic" powers, it is suggestive that one of the few clear findings from animal-model studies of alcohol and aggression is that "when given low doses of ethanol, subordinate rodents are more likely to be attacked or injured by dominant animals" (Woods and Mansfield in Room and Collins). However, "alcohol as a victimogenic factor is an important but relatively unexplored aspect of the alcohol and crime question" (Roizen and Schneberk in Aarens, Blau et al., p. 325). The continuing neglect of the issue probably reflects ideological concerns: much of the literature has been oriented toward increasing sympathy and social assistance for the victim, and to establish that victims are often drunk might diminish their perceived blamelessness (Miers, pp. 170, 177, 181–184).

The connection of the victim's drinking with exploitative crimes seems particularly promising as an arena for preventive action. For once, the mechanism of alcohol's involvement in the situation is relatively clear, and the drinking person's intentions and interests tend to be aligned with the aim of crime prevention.

Alcohol as a cause of crime. We turn at last to the vexed question of causation: does alcohol cause crime? Other than for the alcohol-specific offenses, where the answer is a matter of definition, the answer must be, "it depends what you mean." In the first place, any causative connection must be seen as condi-tional: drinking in combination with other factors can result in a crime. The operational test for such conditional causation becomes, Would the crime fail to take place if the alcohol were removed from the situation? With respect to alcohol's victimogenic powers, it seems likely that the answer will be yes. Drunkenness is affecting at least the choice of a victim for the robbers lying in wait outside Polish restaurants and for the jackrollers prowling American tenderloins, and fewer targets of opportunity might well in the long run mean fewer crimes. In terms of criminogenic powers, there seem anecdotally to be circumstances where the answer would be yes. Coid has remarked on the different assumptions in the recent North American literature concerning the criminogenic powers of heroin and alcohol as addicting substances: "Alcoholics are frequently encountered in clinical and forensic practice who have used violence in attempts to obtain more alcohol, or subsequently to escape arrest, but this motivating factor has not been examined in any of the criminal studies found" (p. 9). But mostly when the question of whether alcohol causes crime is asked, the questioner has in mind some version of disinhibition theory as the link between drinking and crime. In his detailed discussions of the potential theoretical connections between alcohol and violent crime, Pernanen (1976; in Collins) elucidates the diversity of possible theoretical connections relevant to disinhibition theory. One of his conclusions is that "no one theory or model will be able to provide the explanation for the totality of the observed statistical association(s) between alcohol use and crime, no matter how grand its scale. Partly, this is due to the fact that the referents of the concepts of both 'alcohol use' and 'crime,' 'criminal behavior,' or 'deviance' are so manifold" (Collins, p. 63).

Often, the question of cause is defined in terms of a biological link: does alcohol pharmacologically make one mean, vicious, or violent? To this question, the converging evidence from various lines of research suggests that the answer may be no (Room and Collins). Pharmacologically, alcohol certainly makes one clumsy, and it certainly makes one feel different—but it seems to be culture and circumstance that determine what meaning and implications this "feeling different" will have. These findings that the link is socioculturally rather than pharmacologically determined are highly controversial—particularly in the United States, given the medical hegemony over alcohol problems and the current return to assumptions of physiological etiology in American psychiatric thought. It should be kept in mind that a sociocultural link is no less "real" than a pharmacological one; paraphrasing the classic sociological dictum, effects that are believed real are real in their consequences. For well over a century, Americans have clearly believed (and have acted and reacted on the basis of the belief) that alcohol has the power to make the drinker act violently and criminally (Levine in Room and Collins).

From a pragmatic policy perspective, the question of cause might well be rephrased to the question, Are crime rates affected by the level or patterning of alcohol consumption? This question is often approached by means of cross-sectional comparison of national or other aggregate alcohol-consumption and criminal statistics. But such analyses—which often show negative raw correlations—are very weak both as tests of cause and in terms of their policy utility. As Klaus Mäkelä notes, "Cultural variations in drinking patterns are based on lasting historical traditions, and they may well be resistant to a certain degree to changes in the level of consumption. To take a somewhat extreme example, we have no reason to believe that the French would start drunken fights should they lower their consumption to the same level as the Scots or the Finns" (1978, p. 333). Far stronger as a test, and far more useful to policymakers, is a study of how criminal behavior in a given culture reacts to changes in the level or patterning of alcohol consumption.

So far, most of the evidence in this direction for non-alcohol-specific crimes comes from Nordic countries. A 1981 collaborative study of seven countries singled out Finland and Poland as "societies with a historic pattern of extreme drinking events and associated consequences" (Mäkelä, Room et al., p. 50). Results from such societies should not be lightly extrapolated to societies where the belief in alcohol's link to violence may not be so firmly established. An additional caution, as Pernanen has noted, is that positive findings in studies of covariation over time of drinking and crime rates in a given population "should not be taken to mean that a causal relationship on the individual level between alcohol use . . . and criminal acts has been established. There may still be common-cause factors on the individual level which explain the statistical associations. . . . It is, for example, possible that when the supply of alcohol is cut down, the frequency of social interaction (through partying, etc.) is also reduced, with a resulting decrease in the probability of interaction and, consequently, interpersonal crime. Thus, the frequency of interaction could be the main explanation of violence in a society" (Mäkelä, Österberg, and Sulkunen, p. 4).

Despite these caveats, aggregate-level studies of temporal changes are probably the strongest existing evidence of the potential importance of alcohol consumption in explaining crime—and are certainly of interest from a policy perspective. In a series of papers, Leif Lenke has conducted time-series analyses of Swedish and other Nordic official statistics on alcohol consumption and violent crime. He concluded that, within a given society, changes in the total consumption of alcohol are likely to induce similar changes in the recorded rates of crimes of violence (1975, 1982; Lahelma, pp. 97–105). In a careful analysis of postwar Finnish data, Esa Österberg (pp. 65–84) showed a generally close relationship between the per capita alcohol consumption and the rates of cases of assault and battery and of associated crimes known to the police. The steep rise in consumption when beer was made much more available in 1969 was matched by a steep rise in assault and battery cases. In general, there was a long-term gradual trend downward in the rate of crimes of violence per liter of absolute alcohol, but "the trend towards less conflict-prone patterns of drinking was apparently interrupted suddenly after the legislative reform of 1969." After 1975, the trend in the direction of fewer consequences per liter seemed to resume (Mäkelä, Österberg, and Sulkunen, pp. 38, 39).

In the 1970s, a small genre of studies of the effects of strikes and other temporary perturbations in the alcohol supply has emerged. Such studies are particularly direct tests of whether crimes are prevented when alcohol is removed, although of course long-term effects might well differ from the short-term effects measured in these studies. In an exemplary series of studies of the strike in the Finnish alcohol monopoly stores in 1972, it was estimated that overall consumption was reduced by about 30 percent, with less impact on middle-class drinking habits and a particularly strong impact on homeless alcoholics. To an "absolutely striking extent," visible public drunkenness disappeared from the Helsinki streets. "Cases of assault and battery were reduced by some 20 to 25 percent," and there were reductions in "such offenses as impeding a public official in the discharge of his duties, violently resisting an officer of the law and disturbing the peace at a public gathering. . . . The fall-off was particularly evident in the rate of aggravated assault. . . . In Helsinki, 95 percent of the persons convicted of aggravated assault and 85 percent of their victims have been under the influence of alcohol at the time of the deed." The rate of cases of "fight injuries sustained by acutely intoxicated persons" appearing at emergency clinics also fell (Mäkelä, 1980, pp. 136, 137); the greatest changes in the case load of a Helsinki emergency hospital service during the strike were reductions in the number of strongly intoxicated patients and in the number of injuries resulting from murder, manslaughter, or assault and battery (Karaharju and Stjernvall). A study of a 1978 Norwegian alcohol monopoly strike in which overall alcohol consumption was estimated to have fallen by only 5 percent to 10 percent nevertheless found "much evidence . . . that skid-row drinkers were strongly affected," including a decline in the rate of "home quarrels" offenses (Horverak).

A last piece of evidence comes from the Gdańsk shipyard strike of 1980, out of which emerged the Polish Solidarity movement. Since accusations of drunken disorderliness had been frequently used by official sources to discredit workers' demonstrations in previous years, the strikers imposed a prohibition on alcohol in the shipyard, a ban quickly picked up and extended by the local government throughout the province. In the succeeding weeks, temporary alcohol bans became a frequent symbolic gesture by both the Polish government and Solidarity, signaling to each other a serious intent and yet a desire to avoid violence (Moskalewicz). A study of the effects of the initial Gdańsk prohibition showed it to be highly effective and widely accepted. Although drinking was not banned per se, most of the respondents in a local survey did not drink at all during the prohibition. Eighty-four percent of the respondents thought that the prohibition had a "large effect" in "reducing the numbers of rows, riots, etc."—second only to the proportion who saw "maintaining discipline during the strikes" as a positive effect of the ban. According to the authorities, "a drop in the number of crimes was noted, although the militia activity in the town was reduced to a minimum." The local ambulance service reported an unusually quiet time (Bielewicz and Moskalewicz).

Besides the ban on alcohol sales, the drop in crime in Gdańsk may well have reflected an increased sense of common purpose, such as has been noted in grave times elsewhere as producing perturbations in social statistics. Such a mixture of abstinence and common purpose was regarded by Gustav Aschaffenburg as having had the same temporary effect in nineteenth-century Ireland: "Father Matthew succeeded, by the power of his personality and his enthusiastic speeches, in making total abstainers of 1,800,000 persons in the course of a few years. The result was that, whereas, in 1828, 12,000 serious crimes were committed in Ireland, in 1841 the number had sunk to 773, the sixteenth part! The slight permanence of this unexampled success proves, it is true, that the method employed was not the right one" (p. 129).

Whatever their applicability outside their national settings, the interrupted time-series and the strike-type studies do pose a challenge to researchers everywhere. In the modern era, most studies of alcohol and crime in English-speaking countries have focused their attention on the relationship as it may exist within the individual psyche—occasionally extending the view to cover factors in the immediate situation of the criminal event. Much remains to be learned, indeed, about the role of alcohol in criminal events, and about the intertwining of drinking and criminal behaviors. But from the point of view of policy, such studies often focus on elements of the connection that are the hardest to change. The studies of change over time reawaken one to the existence of historical change and to the possibility of doing something to prevent crime by influencing the fact, context, and consequences of drinking. This is a worthy agenda for future research and experiment.

ROBIN ROOM

See also ALCOHOL AND CRIME, *articles on* LEGAL ASPECTS *and* TREATMENT AND REHABILITATION; DRINKING AND DRIVING; DRUGS AND CRIME: BEHAVIORAL ASPECTS.

BIBLIOGRAPHY

AARENS, MARC; BLAU, ANNE et al. *The Epidemiological Literature on Alcohol, Casualties, and Crime: Systematic Quantitative Summaries.* Berkeley: University of California, Social Research Group, 1977.

AARENS, MARC; CAMERON, TRACY et al. *Alcohol, Casualties, and Crime.* Berkeley: University of California, Social Research Group, 1977.

ASCHAFFENBURG, GUSTAV. *Crime and Its Repression.* Translated by Adalbert Albrecht. Introduction by Arthur C. Train. Boston: Little, Brown, 1913.

BIELEWICZ, ANTONI, and MOSKALEWICZ, JACEK. "Temporary Prohibition: The Gdańsk Experience, August 1980." Paper read at annual meeting of Alcohol Epidemiology Section, International Council on Alcohol and Addictions, June/July 1982, Helsinki.

CAHALAN, DON, and ROOM, ROBIN. *Problem Drinking among American Men.* Monograph No. 7. New Brunswick, N.J.: Rutgers University, Center of Alcohol Studies, 1974.

CHAPPLE, W. A. "How to Impress the Evils of Alcohol." *Temperance Educational Quarterly* 3, no. 1 (1912): 20–21.

CHRISTIE, NILS. "Scandinavian Experience in Legislation and Control." *National Conference on Legal Issues in Alcoholism and Alcohol Usage, Swampscott, Mass., 1965.* Boston: Boston University, Law-Medicine Institute, 1965, pp. 102–122.

CLARK, WALTER, and MIDANIK, LORRAINE. "Alcohol Use and Alcohol Problems among U.S. Adults: Results of the 1979 Survey." *Report on the 1979 Survey.* By Walter Clark, Lorraine Midanik, and Genevieve Knupfer. Berkeley: University of California, Alcohol Research Group, 1981.

COID, JEREMY. "Alcoholism and Violence." *Drug and Alcohol Dependence* 9, no. 1 (1982): 1–13.

COLLINS, JAMES J., JR., ed. *Drinking and Crime.* New York: Guilford Press, 1981.

GOODWIN, DONALD W.; CRANE, J. BRUCE; and GUZE, SAMUEL B. "Felons Who Drink: An Eight-year Follow-up." *Quarterly Journal of Studies on Alcohol* 32 (1971): 136–147.

GRAHAM, KATHRYN; LA ROCQUE, LINDA; YETMAN, RHODA; ROSS, T. JAMES; and GUISTRA, ENRICO. "Aggression and Barroom Environments." *Journal of Studies on Alcohol* 41 (1980): 277–292.

GRAVES, THEODORE D.; GRAVES, NANCY B.; SEMU, VINETA N.; and SAM, IULAI AH. "The Social Context of Drinking and Violence in New Zealand's Multi-ethnic Pub Settings." *Social Drinking Contexts.* Edited by Thomas C. Harford and Lawrence S. Gaines. NIAAA Research Monograph No. 7. Rockville, Md.: U.S. Department of Health and Human Services, National Institute on Alcohol Abuse and Alcoholism, 1982, pp. 103–120.

HORVERAK, ØYVIND. "The 1978 Strike at the Norwegian Wine and Spirits Monopoly: Effects on the Supply and Consumption of Alcohol and on Some Alcohol-related Problems." Paper read at Twenty-seventh International Meeting of Epidemiology Section, Institute on the Prevention and Treatment of Alcoholism, June 1981, Vienna.

INCIARDI, JAMES A., ed. *The Drugs-Crime Connection.* Beverly Hills, Calif.: Sage, 1981.

JOHNSON, BRUCE D. "The Drug-Crime Nexus (1979–1981): Research on the Drug-Crime Relationship, with Emphasis upon Heroin Injectors as Criminal Repeaters." Working paper. New York: New York State Division of Substance Abuse Services, Interdisciplinary Research Center, 1981a.

———. "Exploring Drug-Crime Relationships: Guiding Relationships and Key Hypotheses." Working paper. New York: New York State Division of Substance Abuse Services, Interdisciplinary Research Center, 1981b.

KARAHARJU, E. O., and STJERNVALL, L. "The Alcohol Factor in Accidents." *Injury* 6 (1974): 67–69.

KOREN, JOHN. *Alcohol and Society.* New York: Holt, 1916.

———. *Economic Aspects of the Liquor Problem: An Investigation Made for the Committee of Fifty under the Direction of Henry W. Farnam.* Boston: Houghton Mifflin, 1899.

LAHELMA, EERO. *Scandinavian Research on Alcohol's Role in Casualties and Crime: A Review Essay and Informative Abstracts.* Berkeley: University of California, Social Research Group, 1977.

LENKE, LEIF. "A Time-series Analysis of Alcohol's Relation to Violent Crime." Paper read at annual meeting of Alcohol Epidemiology Section, International Council on Alcohol and Addictions, June/July 1982, Helsinki.

———. *Våldsbrott och alkohol.* Stockholm University, Kriminalvetenskpliga Institutet, 1975.

LINDELIUS, ROLF, and SALUM, INNA. "Alcoholism and Crime: A Comparative Study of Three Groups of Alcoholics." *Journal of Studies on Alcohol* 36 (1975): 1452–1457.

MACANDREW, CRAIG, and EDGERTON, ROBERT R. *Drunken Comportment: A Social Explanation.* Chicago: Aldine, 1969.

MÄKELÄ, KLAUS. "Differential Effects of Restricting the Supply of Alcohol: Studies of a Strike in Finnish Liquor Stores." *Journal of Drug Issues* 10 (1980): 131–144.

———. "Level of Consumption and Social Consequences of Drinking." *Research Advances in Alcohol and Drug Problems,* vol. 4. Edited by Yedy Israel et al. New York and London: Plenum Press, 1978, pp. 303–348.

———; ÖSTERBERG, ESA; and SULKUNEN, PEKKA. "Drink in Finland: Increasing Alcohol Availability in a Monopoly State." *The Social History of Control Policy in Seven Countries.* Alcohol, Society, and the State, vol. 2. Edited by Eric Single, Patricia Morgan, and Jan de Lint. Toronto: Addiction Research Foundation, 1981, pp. 31–60.

MÄKELÄ, KLAUS; ROOM, ROBIN et al. *A Comparative Study of Alcohol Control.* Alcohol, Society, and the State, vol. 1. Toronto: Addiction Research Foundation, 1981.

MAREK, Z.; WIDACKI, J.; and HANAUSEK, T. "Alcohol as a Victimogenic Factor of Robberies." *Forensic Science* 4 (1974): 119–123.

MARSHALL, MAC. *Weekend Warriors: Alcohol in a Micronesian Culture.* Palo Alto, Calif.: Mayfield, 1979.

McCAGHY, CHARLES H. "Drinking and Deviance Disavowal: The Case of Child Molesters." *Social Problems* 16 (1968): 43–49.

MIERS, DAVID. *Responses to Victimisation: A Comparative Study of Compensation for Criminal Violence in Great Britain and Ontario.* Abingdon, England: Professional Books, 1978.

MORGAN, PATRICIA. "Alcohol and Family Violence: A Review of the Literature." *Alcohol Consumption and Related Problems.* Alcohol and Health Monograph No. 1. Rockville, Md.: U.S. Department of Health and Human Services, National Institute on Alcohol Abuse and Alcoholism, in press.

MOSKALEWICZ, JACEK. "Alcohol as a Public Issue: Recent Developments in Alcohol Control in Poland." *Contemporary Drug Problems* 10 (1982): 155–177.

ÖSTERBERG, ESA. "Indicators of Damage and the Development of Alcohol Conditions in Finland during the Years 1950–1975." Paper read at Second Plenary Meeting of International Study of Alcohol Control Experiences, 1979, Pacific Grove, Calif.

PERNANEN, KAI. "Alcohol and Crimes of Violence." *Social Aspects of Alcoholism.* The Biology of Alcoholism, vol. 4. Edited by Benjamin Kissen and Henry Begleiter. New York: Plenum Press, 1976, pp. 351–444.

———. "Alcohol Use and 'Hidden' Violence." Paper read at Twenty-seventh International Meeting of Epidemiology Section, Institute on the Prevention and Treatment of Alcoholism, June 1981, Vienna.

———. "Ethnic Differences in the Relationship between Alcohol Use and Aggression." Paper read at Medical-Scientific Conference, National Council on Alcoholism, April 1982, Washington, D.C.

PITTMAN, DAVID J., and GORDON, C. WAYNE. "Criminal Careers of the Chronic Police Case Inebriate." *Quarterly Journal of Studies on Alcohol* 19 (1958): 255–268.

ROIZEN, JUDY. "Estimating Alcohol Involvement in Serious

Events." Paper prepared for National Institute on Alcohol Abuse and Alcoholism. Berkeley: University of California, Social Research Group, 1981.

ROOM, ROBIN. "Region and Urbanization as Factors in Drinking Practices and Problems." *The Pathogenesis of Alcoholism: Psychosocial Factors.* The Biology of Alcoholism, vol. 6. Edited by Benjamin Kissin and Henry Begleiter. New York: Plenum Press, 1982, pp. 555–604.

———, and COLLINS, GARY, eds. *Alcohol and Disinhibition.* NIAAA Research Monograph No. 12. Rockville, Md.: U.S. Department of Health and Human Services, National Institute on Alcohol Abuse and Alcoholism, 1982.

SPEIGLMAN, RICHARD, and WEISNER, CONNIE. "Accommodation to Coercion: Changes in Alcoholism Treatment Paradigms." Paper read at annual meeting of Society for the Study of Social Problems, September 1982, San Francisco.

SUTHERLAND, EDWIN H., and LOCKE, HARVEY J. *Twenty Thousand Homeless Men: A Study of Unemployed Men in the Chicago Shelters* (1936). Reprint. New York: Arno Press, 1971.

VOGT, IRMGARD. *Alcohol, Casualties, and Crime: A Review of West German Studies, 1945–1979.* Berkeley: University of California, Social Research Group, 1980.

WOLFGANG, MARVIN E. *Patterns in Criminal Homicide.* Philadelphia: University of Pennsylvania Press, 1958.

———, and STROHM, ROLF B. "The Relationship between Alcohol and Criminal Homicide." *Quarterly Journal of Studies on Alcohol* 17 (1956): 411–425.

2.
LEGAL ASPECTS

The criminal process

On a national basis, more than one million arrests are made annually under public-drunkenness, vagrancy, and related criminal statutes. Most of the arrested individuals are intoxicated when encountered by the police. For many, the arrest is not an isolated event but part of an ongoing series of encounters with the criminal justice system.

These arrests are not distributed evenly across the social spectrum. Rather, whereas upper- or middle-class persons found intoxicated in public are generally ignored or brought home, derelicts in similar condition are routinely arrested and jailed. For such skid-row men, the ceaseless round of arrest, jail, and release accounts for a major part of the criminal justice activity in their locale. The men caught up in this process typically have not acted violently and have broken no other criminal law.

The purpose of arrests. The arrest-and-release cycle imposed on skid-row men is seldom justified in terms of traditional law enforcement objectives. The arrests are not ordinarily viewed as initiating a process of punishment, deterrence, or rehabilitation. Rather, they are most often made to achieve temporary objectives that are in part aesthetic. In many cities, the primary offense of the skid-row derelict is his presence on the street in public view. This presence is aesthetically offensive and to outside observers may appear threatening because of the men's often poor physical condition; thus, the arrests serve to control visibility and perceived threat. The significant variations in arrest rates among cities depend at least in part on the extent to which local policy tolerates a visible skid row, and are not necessarily related to the size of the skid-row population.

A second justification often stated for skid-row arrests is one of social services rather than local aesthetics. According to this view, the skid-row men need to be protected since they are often unable to defend themselves from attacks by other men. In addition, they may be harmed by exposure to the elements. An arrest followed by brief incarceration provides at least short-term respite and protection. In some instances, repeated incarceration may represent the skid-row derelict's only experiences of a sheltered environment.

The service argument is often advanced as a justification for their work by the police officers who make skid-row arrests. The extent and quality of the services provided, however, are minimal. Although many arrestees are severely intoxicated and may need immediate medical attention, most jails have no medical facilities. Physical violence on the streets is an immediate risk, but many jails offer only marginal security. At best, the arrestee may receive no more than a dry floor and a minimal breakfast.

Arrests and the criminal process. Because of the subcultural setting and the absence of rehabilitative services, skid-row arrests are chronic in nature. The same individual may be arrested and rearrested scores of times in a single year. In fact, a personal relationship may develop between the arrestee and an arresting officer. This, in combination with the sheer volume of arrests that may occur, produces a criminal justice process that bears little resemblance to traditional expectations, especially in cities with relatively concentrated skid-row areas and with policies that produce high rates of arrest. Skid-row men may be removed from the streets in groups by patrol vans that make periodic tours of the area. In court, various procedural concessions expedite disposition. The judicial process is oriented toward mass handling of cases. Group arraignments are common, little attention is paid to issues of guilt or innocence, and sentences are routinized or nonexistent. Most arrestees are released on the morning after their arrest.

Alternatives

Although many aspects of the criminal justice process are altered to ensure the efficient handling of skid-row cases, the overall process nevertheless requires significant resources and imposes a significant cost. The cost may be measured in terms of dollars or of a general weakening of the criminal justice system's basic norms. Especially in light of the apparent futility of a cycle of repeated arrests and rearrests, it is not surprising that objections have frequently been raised to the continued use of criminal systems to deal with nonviolent skid-row men. These objections have been based in part on judgments of cost effectiveness but have also involved theoretical considerations as to the appropriate scope of criminal sanctions.

Decriminalization. Public drunkenness arrests are commonly regarded as peripheral to criminal law concerns, mainly because of the view that the criminal sanction should be reserved for cases involving actual or threatened injury to another person or to property (Allen, p. 5). To the extent that criminal sanctions extend beyond this limit, they are regarded as an improper regulation of public morals. This premise would exclude most skid-row arrestees. Although skid-row violence may be common, it is not the primary rationale for the repeated arrest and brief incarceration of men charged with public drunkenness and related offenses. Individuals arrested on these charges pose virtually no threat to others. Their crimes are victimless in nature.

These observations lead to the conclusion that public drunkenness should be decriminalized and that, to the extent that skid-row men need emergency or other services, these should be provided by public or private agencies outside the justice system. Law enforcement within skid-row and similar areas should revert to more traditional concerns related to violent crime.

Total decriminalization offers attractive prospects, but it has seldom been pursued in practice and has not been fully implemented in any jurisdiction. In part, this results from the perceived strength of the countervailing social function of the drunkenness arrests. Although medical and protective functions within the arrest, release, and rearrest cycle are minimal, the aesthetic function may be significant, at least in some cities. Compared with other areas of law enforcement, the arrest of nonviolent skid-row men may appear to be a low-priority police function, and it is. Despite their low priority, however, such arrests serve to enforce the perception that the government is doing something to control skid-row problems; they also minimize the visibility of the men in the area (Nimmer, pp. 144–146). In addition, drunkenness arrests are often viewed as an important element of control in skid row. At least to many outside observers, skid row seems a potentially dangerous area, and recurrent arrests give the impression that this threat is being constrained.

Replacement: the medical alternative. Although total decriminalization has not been achieved, the first half of the 1970s did witness a form of decriminalization in a number of jurisdictions that has had a major national statistical effect. To understand this development, it is necessary to recognize the relationship that has long existed among skid row, drunkenness arrests, and alcoholism. Many skid-row men are alcoholics or are heavy users of alcohol and drugs, and most men who are arrested in skid row are intoxicated at the time of arrest.

As a result, the problem of dealing with skid-row arrests is generally viewed as one involving alcoholism and public drunkenness. To the extent that local arrests are made under vagrancy, loitering, disorderly conduct, or similar statutes rather than public drunkenness statutes, they are described as "alcohol-related." Most decriminalization proposals have the aim of providing services relevant to alcoholism and, in many cases, are contained within more general legislation dealing with alcoholism.

Associating skid-row arrests with alcoholism establishes a connection between the arrest procedure and public-health concerns. Historically, alcoholism has been viewed in pejorative, moralistic terms, but by the late 1960s medical opinion had concurred that alcoholism was an illness. Disagreement continues as to whether the root cause of alcoholism is physical, mental, social, or a combination of these, but the basic view that alcoholism should be dealt with medically has become entrenched and permeates public policy (Jellinek).

By defining alcoholism as an illness, and drunkenness arrests as alcohol-related, policymakers and commentators have strengthened a general desire to decriminalize public drunkenness. They have also provided a method of achieving this result without disregarding the "social" functions historically served by the arrests. Viewed medically, the major problem of skid-row arrests is not that they are an improper use of criminal justice resources, but rather that they attach a negative stigma to sick individuals and deny effective medical care or therapy to the arrestees. From this medical viewpoint, it is possible to devise a process of decriminalization by shifting focus and by relabeling, as well as by placing greater emphasis on short-term medical attention.

Consequently, although a number of alternative systems for dealing with skid-row arrestees have been designed, most reforms proceed on the assumption that the basic objective is to replace the justice system with a more medically relevant system. Illustrative of this approach is the recommendation of the President's Commission on Law Enforcement and Administration of Justice: "Drunkenness should not in itself be a criminal offense. The implementation of this recommendation requires the development of adequate civil detoxification procedures" (p. 1).

Reform and replacement. The medical approach links a social drive for the development of new therapeutic services with a general dissatisfaction over diverting criminal justice resources by police and court involvement in arrests. The proposals for reform thus draw on medical knowledge, criminal justice theory, and cost effectiveness considerations as impetuses for change. During the 1970s, several appellate court decisions sought to reduce criminal handling of skid-row men, for example, *Easter v. District of Columbia*, 361 F.2d 50 (D.C. Cir. 1966) and *Driver v. Hinnant*, 356 F.2d 761 (4th Cir. 1966). The decisions were generally based on the assumption that the arrested men were alcoholics. Reasoning from a legal view which had stated that drug addicts should not be punished for being ill (*Robinson v. California*, 370 U.S. 660 (1962)), several courts concluded that arrest and incarceration for public drunkenness imposed a criminal sanction for conduct that was symptomatic of an illness and thus not voluntary. The result was to preclude such arrests. This view never commanded a majority of the United States Supreme Court (*Powell v. Texas*, 392 U.S. 514 (1968)). However, lower court decisions couched in this language generated several decriminalization reforms. Similarly, during this period a number of states enacted comprehensive legislation to deal with alcoholism as a public-health problem, providing for treatment programs with procedures for voluntary and involuntary commitment. A number of these statutes redefined public drunkenness and related arrests as public-health rather than law enforcement problems. Indeed, procedures to this effect were contained in the model Uniform

Alcoholism and Intoxication Treatment Act, which served as the prototype of much of the legislation in this area (National Conference of Commissioners, p. 57).

As described in the act, the form of decriminalization that emerged essentially involved a replacement of the previous criminal justice model with an analogous system based on medical premises and providing services for alcohol detoxification. Skid-row men were not simply left on the streets or to their own resources, and police pickups were not simply ended. Rather, short-term detoxification programs were established to receive both a walk-in clientele and persons picked up and taken to a treatment center by the police or, in some cases, by civilian patrols. Especially where police were used, detoxification pickups served functions similar to those previously served by arrests. The treatment facility, staffed by volunteers, was oriented toward short-term, emergency medical care and sustenance and typically provided no more than one to three days of treatment. Referrals to more extensive rehabilitation programs were available.

This replacement model became popular during an era in which substantial experimentation with criminal justice alternatives was stimulated by federal funding and numerous research activities. As a result, almost one-half of all the states adopted limited decriminalization. National arrest statistics reflected a one-third reduction in the overall rate of drunkenness arrests by 1975 (Note, p. 1665).

Effects of replacement. By the early 1980s, however, there appeared to be little continued interest in decriminalization by replacement, owing in large measure to the costs of establishing and maintaining such programs. Depending on the size of the facility, the intensity of care provided, and other factors, these costs substantially exceed the costs of maintaining traditional police practices. In addition, there has been a fading of enthusiasm for the medical model on which the detoxification program alternatives were based. With the acceptance of alcoholism as a medical problem and the application of medical knowledge to its cure, there was initially substantial hope that inroads could be made against alcohol problems, even those associated with skid row. Spurred by this enthusiasm, many of the earliest proposed alternatives suggested that rehabilitation was more likely to result from applying the medical rather than the criminal model. As might have been expected, this hope never materialized. Consequently, many of the new systems began to assume the revolving-door character of the older criminal system. Formal labels changed and medical services improved, but this failed to sustain enthusiasm for the replacement systems.

To the extent that the new detoxification programs rely on police actions as the primary referral source, an unanticipated response was noted in at least several cities. Nationally, the rate of skid-row arrests is linked more to local police policy and practice than to the size of the skid-row population or the number of men found intoxicated in public. Thus, for example, even before the adoption of any major reforms, arrest rates in the large Bowery area of New York had traditionally been much lower than in the smaller skid-row sections of Chicago (Nimmer, pp. 35–77). The importance of police policy as a factor in pickup rates was highlighted when replacement reforms were adopted. These reforms rested on a noncriminal definition of drunkenness, and this definitional change affected police policy. In several cities the result was a lowering of the priority attached to skid-row arrests. Being told, in effect, that skid row was not a criminal problem, some departments responded by diverting resources to other issues defined as being clearly within their sphere of interest. This response led to a reduction of arrests and to a reduced number of persons picked up by police and delivered for detoxification. As a result, detoxification programs aimed initially at a clientele that allegedly required police or other personnel to remove them from the streets have tended to become programs oriented primarily toward a walk-in clientele (Aaronson, Dienes, and Musheno, pp. 419–431).

Clarification of issues

The presumed link between disengaging the criminal justice system and implementing a medical alternative for handling skid-row men may be illusory. In fact, two separable issues must be considered. The first focuses on the extent to which the criminal justice system should continue to take part in processing nonviolent skid-row men. The second concerns the type of social and medical services that should be provided to these men.

The first issue is often confused with the question of whether this area should be "decriminalized." As discussed above, decriminalizing public drunkenness in the sense of repealing the relevant statutes is only part of the issue. Such action is, however, a desirable first step. Viewed as a matter of social theory, as a matter of medical science, or simply as a matter of social policy, it is difficult to justify continued application of criminal sanctions to nonviolent skid-row men.

However, even if the statutes are repealed, it is questionable to what extent criminal justice agencies, especially the police, should continue to be involved in noncriminal replacement systems. The arguments favoring such action rest on the belief that local politics require police presence in controlling the outward appearance of skid row, or on the belief that police officers are the most readily available and skilled source of medical emergency aid.

Even accepting either premise, basic operational priorities must be resolved. Although the police must of necessity deal with some emergency situations, it is doubtful whether their continued involvement in this problem area could be justified in light of limited resources and other pressing priorities of a more criminal nature. Perceived political pressure may be weaker than generally believed. As indicated above, in at least some cities a substantial reorientation of police priorities has significantly reduced police involvement.

The second issue poses the question of what public-health or other services should be provided. Here, the range of possibilities is broad. It is important, however, to recognize that the service needs are not defined by historical arrest rates or arrestee populations: arrest patterns are shaped primarily by police policy and resource factors. Rather, the service needs ought to be defined more broadly, at least at the outset. The issue is one of the extent and nature of the services that should be made available to skid-row men in general, and of the extent to which special accommodations are necessary for men who may be intoxicated in public. The primary concern is the need to deal with the social and medical problems that characterize these populations.

RAYMOND T. NIMMER

See also ALCOHOL AND CRIME: THE PROHIBITION EXPERIMENT; CRIMINALIZATION AND DECRIMINALIZATION; DRINKING AND DRIVING; DRUGS AND CRIME: LEGAL ASPECTS; EXCUSE: INTOXICATION; VAGRANCY AND DISORDERLY CONDUCT; VICTIMLESS CRIME.

BIBLIOGRAPHY

AARONSON, DAVID E.; DIENES, C. THOMAS; and MUSHENO, MICHAEL C. "Changing the Public Drunkenness Laws: The Impact of Decriminalization." *Law and Society Review* 12 (1978): 405–436.
ALLEN, FRANCIS A. *The Borderland of Criminal Justice: Essays in Law and Criminology.* University of Chicago Press, 1964.
GRAD, FRANK; GOLDBERG, AUDREY L.; and SHAPIRO, BARBARA A. *Alcoholism and the Law.* Dobbs Ferry, N.Y.: Oceana, 1971.

JELLINEK, ELVIN. *The Disease Concept of Alcoholism.* New Haven: Hillhouse Press, 1960.

National Conference of Commissioners on Uniform State Laws. "Uniform Alcoholism and Intoxication Treatment Act." *Uniform Laws Annotated,* vol. 9. Master ed. St. Paul: West, 1979, pp. 57–110.

NIMMER, RAYMOND. *Two Million Unnecessary Arrests: Removing a Social Service Concern from the Criminal Justice System.* Chicago: American Bar Foundation, 1971.

Note. "Alcohol Abuse and the Law." *Harvard Law Review* 94 (1981): 1660–1712.

PACKER, HERBERT L. *The Limits of the Criminal Sanction.* Stanford, Calif.: Stanford University Press, 1968.

PITTMAN, DAVID J., and GORDON, C. WAYNE. *Revolving Door: A Study of the Chronic Police Case Inebriate.* Glencoe, Ill.: Free Press, 1958.

President's Commission on Law Enforcement and Administration of Justice, Task Force on Drunkenness. *Task Force Report: Drunkenness.* Washington, D.C.: The Commission, 1967.

SCHUR, EDWIN M., and BEDAU, HUGO ADAM. *Victimless Crimes: Two Sides of a Controversy.* Englewood Cliffs, N.J.: Prentice-Hall, 1974.

3.

THE PROHIBITION EXPERIMENT

The Prohibition "experiment" is periodically cited as a test of the legal control of moral behavior. Implications are then drawn for other areas of morals legislation such as drug use, prostitution, abortion, and gambling. However, this analogy between a historical set of events and the scientific test of a hypothesis is both imperfect and misleading. What can be learned from the history of the legislation prohibiting the manufacture and sale of "intoxicating liquors" in the United States is neither as exact nor as unambiguous as the results of an experiment conducted under controlled conditions in a well-equipped laboratory. To speak of a "social experiment" in this context is to utilize a poetic metaphor that may deflect attention away from many important consequences and meanings embodied in the events. Prohibition was not undertaken or opposed in the spirit of experiment, nor was it administered as a controlled test of a hypothesis.

An adequate understanding of the implications of Prohibition for the effectiveness of criminalization and legal control cannot be confined to the 1920s. It must go back to the roots of Prohibition in the century-long temperance movement and the subsequent history of alcohol as a public issue in the United States.

Context is essential to both action and understanding in human events. The analogy to an experiment is misapplied because it imagines social actions as understandable without a context or a history. It treats Prohibition as if it had a fixed meaning devoid of connotations provided by past or subsequent events.

The temperance movement

In December 1917 the United States Congress passed the Eighteenth Amendment outlawing the manufacture, sale, or transportation of "intoxicating liquors." In January 1919 the amendment was ratified by three-fourths of the states, and in January 1920, Prohibition became law. In February 1933, the Twenty-first Amendment, repealing Prohibition, was passed by Congress. It was quickly ratified before the end of that year. This brief encounter with legislation criminalizing commerce in hard liquor, beer, and wine was not an unexpected or bizarre interlude in American public life. It was only one phase in a long history of politics, legislation, common law, and exhortation about alcohol questions in the United States (Krout; Gusfield, 1963).

Popular belief and anti-Prohibitionist sentiment have often explained the passage of the Eighteenth Amendment as an aberration, put over on a quiescent public during wartime. Such an explanation ignores the fact that issues of drinking and its controls were very much in the foreground of American political, social, and legislative life from the 1820s through the 1920s. "Dry" and "wet" have been almost as essential in American politics as "left" and "right."

The antebellum movements. Although during the colonial period alcohol was widely perceived as a beneficial commodity and its excesses generally controlled, by the late eighteenth century widespread drunkenness had occasioned concern. In the decades preceding the Civil War, the temperance movement emerged in the form of organizations, such as the American Temperance Society and the Sons of Temperance, that were committed at first to minimizing and later to eradicating the use of beverage alcohol. A variety of state and local laws were passed, and by the 1850s thirteen states had been dry for varying lengths of time.

The temperance movement was a part of the general reformist impulse that marked American political and religious life in the first half of the nineteenth century. In its earliest phase, before 1826, the movement was dominated by a Federalist local aristocracy that saw in the manners and morals of a rowdy electorate a threat to its own fading power (Gusfield, 1963). By the 1820s temperance took on a tone of self-improvement as artisans, farmers, and industrial workers, often inspired by the religious revivalism of the period, sought their own perfection. During the next decade, improved transportation made whiskey less competitive with other uses of grain, and drinking became a costlier affair (Rorabaugh).

Temperance had become widely accepted in American life by the 1850s. If not necessarily followed by all or even most, it was the public ideal. In an expanding industrial and commercial society, employers and employees no longer thought of alcohol as a permissible accompaniment to the workday or a necessary aid to health and well-being. In an industrializing society, discipline, routinization, and steadiness of pursuit became virtues that contrasted with the erratic habits and spontaneous festivity of an earlier age (Tyrrell). Temperance, abolition, and penal reform were part of a drive toward a more humane and moral society and family (Clark). What in colonial America had been "the goodly creature of God" had become "demon rum" in the new democracy.

The clash of cultures. From one perspective, the rise of the temperance ideal of total abstinence was part of the transformation of the American population from a self-sufficient, rural society into an industrial and commercial one. However, that interpretation is too simple. Except for the Scandinavians, other industrializing societies have not developed so powerful or widespread a movement, nor one that has appeared and reappeared with such persistence for more than a century. Temperance in America owes much to the confrontation between the diverse cultures and religions that streams of immigration brought to the United States.

Most of the European peoples who immigrated to the United States were Roman Catholic. Their concentration in urban areas among the lower classes accentuated the clash with an American-born, Protestant, and rural population. The Irish and the Germans were the bêtes noires of temperance literature in the 1850s, joined by the Mediterranean and Slavic immigrants of the late nineteenth century. For these groups alcohol, in the form of beer, whiskey, or wine, was a part of daily life, and integral to the culture of the community. By the 1850s this was no longer the case among other Americans. Drinking and drunkenness had become isolated and marginal to the daily life of assimilated middle-class Americans—the acts of willful and weak sinners (Gusfield, 1963).

The vision of a dry America found a more pleasing reception among rural, nativist, and Protestant groups than among the new immigrants. Since its inception in 1869, the Prohibitionist party platforms displayed the rhetoric and aims of agrarian populism. Established in 1874, the Woman's Christian Temperance Union developed a number of programs to bring about the assimilation of immigrants into American culture, seeing in total abstinence a major form of acceptance of American values. Bringing the sinner and the immigrant into the mainstream of American life became a major objective of the temperance movement.

In this fashion, the victories and defeats of the movement came to take on symbolic meanings of victory or defeat for the values of middle-class, American-born Protestants. Public approval of total abstinence emerged as a symbol, standing for the dominance of those whose way of life devalued and demeaned drinking and abhorred drunkenness. For some scholars, the schism is seen in Catholic-Protestant and immigrant-native terms (Gusfield, 1963). For others, it is couched in contrasts between religious theologies—basically between evangelical, fundamentalist, and denominational ("pietist") churches and ecclesiastical, hierarchical, and institutionalized ("liturgical") churches (Jensen). For both groups of scholars, however, the alcohol issue in the late nineteenth and the early twentieth century transcended the simple question of abstinence versus indulgence and acquired symbolic significance for a broader set of cultural, religious, and ethnic differences and conflicts.

The coming of Prohibition. By 1906, when the Anti-Saloon League began its agitation for state and national prohibition, the alcohol question had a long history as a significant factor in American politics. The league, by avoiding all other issues and acting as a pressure group in both major parties, was effective in organizing the power of Protestant churches and its members around a single issue—alcohol. Led by the league and its Methodist officials, the movement for prohibition reached its zenith during the period of the great wave of immigration into American cities. In 1906 only three states had prohibition; by 1912 there were ten. In 1919, before the ratification of the Eighteenth Amendment, nineteen more states had passed restrictive legislation and more than 50 percent of the American population lived in dry areas.

The surge of Prohibitionist sentiment and power was abetted by the Progressive reform movement for clean and efficient government. The saloon had become a seat and a symbol of urban corruption, crime, and political manipulation of the electorate. Here, too, the religious and nativist conflicts gain further significance as part of the context for middle-class reform of the saloon as an established institution integrated into the cultures and leisure styles of the new urban immigrants.

Prohibition

When Prohibition was enacted, it was not as an experiment but as a major reform of American life and institutions. Although the temperance movement was concerned with the habitual drunkard, its main goal was total abstinence and the eradication of the liquor traffic. This totality gave the movement its moral character. The political conflict was not an argument over means for preventing alcoholism; it was a process of developing and defining the public values and life styles that would dominate in America—a conflict over the moral status of drinking and the cultural attitudes it implied.

The Prohibition amendment and its enforcing legislation, the Volstead Act (An Act to prohibit intoxicating beverages, and to regulate the manufacture, production, use, and sale of high-proof spirits for other than beverage purposes . . . , ch. 85, 41 Stat. 305 (1919) (repealed)), were thus attempts to define appropriate moral behavior relating to consumption of a commodity and to make the state an agent of cultural persuasion. The emphasis was sociological and institutional: to outlaw the manufacture and sale of liquor and thus make it unavailable. This strategy can be contrasted with alternate psychological approaches, such as that used in the slogan of the liquor industry in the 1980s: "The fault is in the man, not in the bottle." Here institutional change is ignored.

Enforcement and crime. If victory brought satisfaction to the Protestant, nativist, and rural segments of America, its symbolic character increased the resentment and alienation of populations who felt deeply insulted at a level of immediate, day-to-day existence. The expression "striking a blow for liberty" gave support and justification to those, especially in the large cities, who flouted the Prohibition law and kept the bootleggers in diamonds.

The Eighteenth Amendment and the Volstead Act declared a major American industry to be engaged in a criminal activity. Unlike the drug legislation of later decades, they did not criminalize the consumption or purchase of alcohol, but they did place the sale, manufacture, and transportation of a major commodity out of legal bounds. As has long been true of such proscribed goods and services as prostitution, illegal abortion, gambling, and illegal drugs, a lively black market emerged (Merz; Sinclair).

The special character of the commodity made Prohibition productive of organized crime in a manner distinct from that of other black markets. Since alcoholic beverages were still available in other countries, bootlegging was a major smuggling operation, as drugs were in the 1970s and 1980s (Cashman). Transportation was therefore a major aspect of the trade in alcohol. Bootlegging was an enterprise requiring venture capital and business organization, and money, protection against hijacking, and political protection were essential to such a complex undertaking. In such a market, political corruption is a necessary part of operating, and competition is at least as volatile and unwelcome as in the manufacture and sale of automobiles. Much of the sensational gang warfare during Prohibition emerged from efforts to develop and to self-police agreements in restraint of trade. A number of bootleggers in effect died defending the tenets of free enterprise.

That Prohibition was a significant element in the development of organized crime is understandable, given the businesslike character of this victimless crime. Organized crime built on the existing gangs that had controlled prostitution and other black markets before 1920, and by the time of repeal, the underworld was more organized and efficient than it had been before.

The deterrent effects of Prohibition. Was the Prohibition experiment a success? The question possesses an inherent ambiguity that almost defies scientific analysis. Legislation often has meaning on different levels and for different periods of history. As legislation symbolizing the dominance of those classes and religious groups that supported Prohibition, the Eighteenth Amendment acquired significance simply by winning sufficient backing for its passage, regardless of its degree of enforcement. As legislation that sought to change the life styles of Americans, Prohibition could not be gauged until it had been on the books for at least a generation. In fact, some of its impact was not at all evident until after repeal, when restrictions on hours, conditions, and consumer ages displayed some of the lasting educative effects.

Whether or not Prohibition deterred drinkers presupposes the importance of the question's answer to justifications for or against the Eighteenth Amendment. The history of temperance indicates that the passage and continuation of Prohibition was as much a symbolic statement of the public disapproval of drinking as it was an intent to effectuate a change in behavior. The legal scholar should understand that the goal of deterrence does not exhaust the context of issues over which opponents and proponents fought. Prohibition was not championed only as a means of deterring drinking; it was also put forth as a means of reforming the moral attitudes of American life. Considering Prohibition as a moral reform, rather than an experiment in social control, it is doubtful if the arguments about its deterrent effects would have swayed many of its supporters or detractors.

Repeal did not return America to the same situation vis-à-vis alcohol that existed when the Eighteenth Amendment became law and the saloons became speakeasies. Certainly, the newspapers and magazines presented a lurid picture of an America awash in bathtub gin and in easy communication with the local bootlegger; an America that paid little attention to Prohibition except as a matter of ridicule and inconvenience. But such accounts are suspect of more than the pathetic fallacy of converting the experience of a circle of urban journalists into a universal principle. They reflected the world that many journalists saw about them—the world of the metropolitan upper middle class, precisely the group least Prohibitionist in sentiment and most able to spend the money to purchase liquors and wines. A more representative analysis of the 1920s suggests a more varied picture but also underscores the sheer difficulty of answering the question about the impact of the law.

Different accounts of the Prohibition period agree on certain conclusions, cautiously and with recognition of limits in the evidence:

1. Geographic areas where the law was least obeyed were those in which Prohibition had been least supported in elections—best characterized as metropolitan, Catholic, and Jewish. Conversely, areas where Prohibition was most strongly supported were those in which the law was most obeyed—rural, Protestant, and middle-class.
2. The major exception to this generalization was in urban working-class areas of all religious denominations, where the falloff in drinking appears to have been considerable.
3. Both the total consumption of alcohol and the number of deaths from cirrhosis of the liver were lower in the period after repeal than in the decade prior to Prohibition (Gusfield, 1968; Aaron and Musto).

The evidence supporting these conclusions is a variety of statistical data—total amount of grain produced and sold, arrests for drunkenness, hospital admissions for alcoholic psychosis, mortality rates for cirrhosis of the liver, and tax revenues from post-repeal sales—all of which showed decreases. The use of many of these records for any quantitative estimate of alcohol consumption may be questionable, although the tax revenues offer more reliable data than most other sources. Arrest statistics for drunkenness provide especially poor data, since they depend very much on local policies and on the categories used to describe a misdemeanor. Use of the data on deaths from cirrhosis of the liver depends on assumptions about the length of time between the beginning of heavy drinking and the effects of the disease—a time period no longer thought to be very uniform. Alcohol consumption after 1933 was also affected by lower incomes during the Great Depression.

Despite such skepticism about their reliability, these data, together with supplementary material based on impressions of social workers in urban areas, all point in the same direction—toward a decline of alcohol use in pro-Prohibitionist areas and among the rural and urban working class. The available evidence suggests that, contrary to popular belief, Prohibition did decrease the total consumption of alcohol drinking in the United States. The burden of proof thus appears to rest on those who would assert otherwise.

The apparent consensus on the decline in drinking among the working class is consistent with information about other historical periods when costs of alcoholic beverages rose, and perhaps provides the major lesson of the Prohibition period for those interested in controlling total consumption of alcohol. The impact of restrictions on sale and manufacture resulted in a rise in price and a consequent decrease in demand in a segment of the market, especially notable among the less affluent. Not only did prices increase, but as in past periods in American history, transportation costs favored whiskey over beer. The percentage rise in the price of beer (the workingman's drink) was even greater than for hard liquors. Members of the affluent, whiskey-drinking upper middle class became the major customers for alcohol.

The further consequences of Prohibition and repeal. Although the Eighteenth Amendment came under sharper and more organized attack after the mid-1920s, with the victory of Herbert Hoover over Alfred E. Smith it seemed safe from the weapons of a wet siege. Yet four years later, by which time Hoover had become cool to it and Franklin Roosevelt had repudiated it, the Prohibition amendment was ready for the trash heap of history. Whatever else may have contributed to the waning of public passions for a sober America in the midst of the Great Depression, the blocked consumption of alcohol was both a minor issue and a drain on employment opportunities and potential tax revenues. Men of power and wealth who had embraced Prohibition, such as John D. Rockefeller and S. S. Kresge, now leaped off the wagon. Unions, which were always opposed or indifferent to it, now began to petition for redress of jobs. With the Great Depression, the vision of a dry America creating prosperity through sober and disciplined living suffered a decline in belief. The immigrant generation had come of political age just as the Protestant establishment was tilting on its pedestal. The dramatic news of criminal violence and political corruption produced by Prohibition was too great a burden for a crumbling program to bear.

The repeal of the Eighteenth Amendment discredited attempts to control drinking through legal restrictions on the commercial traffic in alcoholic beverages. In addition, it diminished the political importance of the Prohibitionist constituency as shapers of public policy on alcohol after repeal. During the decade following repeal, the role of American Protestant churchmen as leaders of the anti-alcohol movement was taken over by academics, physicians, paraprofessionals, and recovered alcoholics. The stress shifted from the aim of achieving total abstinence and sobriety to the problem of chronic alcoholism—the behavior of a deviant minority of the population. As a corollary, strategies focused on treating the alcoholic rather than controlling the drinking of the general population.

Although American public discussion and action veered sharply away from legal controls, in several ways Prohibition left a legacy of acceptable legal constraints that went beyond those in existence before its passage. Per capita consumption of alcohol never returned to the high point of the early twentieth century, and the general drift away from whiskey and toward beer continued (Aaron and Musto). The comparatively high level of abstainers in the American population remained stable. In more than twelve thousand local-option elections during the two decades after repeal, there was very little change in local law (Gusfield, 1963). At the level of public opinion and personal choice, Prohibition appears to have done little to change attitudes toward drinking and abstinence.

However, the earlier lack of control over saloons was no longer acceptable. All states established Alcohol Beverage Control (ABC) boards. Although often proving to be less regulatory than anticipated, they have served to prevent the issuance of licenses to those with underworld connections. The ABC legislation is one of a number of legislative measures enacted and accepted in American life that perpetuate and expand the concept of beverage alcohol as an "exceptional commodity" more dangerous than most commodities and consequently requiring special legal controls. Restrictions on hours, locations of sales, and special taxes have continued or increased. Laws against public drunkenness and against drinking and driving continue to be enforced, although public-drunkenness legislation is by no means universal in Western countries.

Perhaps most significant has been the increase in the number of minimum-age drinking laws. Availability of alcohol to minors became more restricted at the same time that availability to the general population was widened (Mosher). Indicative of the persisting view that alcohol is a dangerous and exceptional commodity is the failure of many states to alter laws prohibiting the sale of alcohol to persons under twenty-one. The repeal of laws lowering the age in some states has encountered little political resistance despite the decrease of the minimum age to eighteen for most legal purposes.

Although in the post-repeal period alcohol policy was dominated by an emphasis on treatment of alcoholics, by the 1970s attention was again beginning to turn toward questions of prevention through control measures such as taxation and restrictions on sale (Bruun et al.). The ambivalence of American society toward drinking remains characteristic, and still contrasts with the wider acceptance of alcohol in most industrialized societies.

Prohibition was not without its impact on American life. It brought a century-old conflict to a focus, intensified it, and, with repeal, ended its political salience. Despite repeal, America remains a nation of moderate drinking habits in which legal controls and social constraints are accepted and practiced.

JOSEPH R. GUSFIELD

See also ALCOHOL AND CRIME: LEGAL ASPECTS; CRIMINALIZATION AND DECRIMINALIZATION.

BIBLIOGRAPHY

AARON, PAUL, and MUSTO, DAVID. "Temperance and Prohibition in America: An Historical Overview." *Alcohol and Public Policy: Beyond the Shadow of Prohibition.* Edited by Mark Moore and Dean Gerstein. Washington, D.C.: National Academy Press, 1981, pp. 127–183.

BRUUN, KETTIL et al. *Alcohol Control Policies in Public Health Perspective.* Finnish Foundation for Alcohol Studies, vol. 25. New Brunswick, N.J.: Rutgers Center of Alcohol Studies, 1975.

CASHMAN, SEAN D. *Prohibition: The Lie of the Land.* New York: Macmillan, 1981.

CLARK, NORMAN H. *Deliver Us from Evil: An Interpretation of American Prohibition.* New York: Norton, 1976.

Gusfield, Joseph. "Prohibition: The Impact of Political Utopianism." *Change and Continuity in Twentieth Century America: The 1920s.* Edited by John Braeman, Robert H. Bremner, and David Brody. Columbus: Ohio State University Press, 1968, pp. 257–308.

———. *Symbolic Crusade: Status Politics and the American Temperance Movement.* Urbana: University of Illinois Press, 1963.

Jensen, Richard. *The Winning of the Midwest: Social and Political Conflict, 1888–1896.* University of Chicago Press, 1971.

Krout, John A. *The Origins of Prohibition.* New York: Knopf, 1925.

Merz, Charles. *The Dry Decade* (1931). Reprint, with a new introduction by the author. Seattle: University of Washington Press, 1969.

Mosher, James F. "The History of Youthful-drinking Laws: Implications for Current Policy." *Minimum Drinking-age Laws: An Evaluation.* Edited by Henry Wechsler. Lexington, Mass.: Heath, Lexington Books, 1980, pp. 11–38.

Rorabaugh, W. J. *The Alcoholic Republic: An American Tradition.* New York: Oxford University Press, 1979.

Sinclair, Andrew. *Prohibition: The Era of Excess.* Preface by Richard Hofstadter. Boston: Little, Brown, 1962.

Tyrrell, Ian R. "Temperance and Economic Change in the Antebellum North." *Alcohol, Reform, and Society: The Liquor Issue in Social Context.* Edited by Jack S. Blocker, Jr. Westport, Conn.: Greenwood Press, 1979, pp. 45–68.

4.
TREATMENT AND REHABILITATION

Most efforts to alter the behaviors of problem drinkers take place outside criminal justice agencies even though many problem drinkers commit numerous detected or undetected offenses, often serious ones. Assuming that these interventions are to some degree effective, they reduce the overall amount of alcohol-related crime. This article attempts to summarize what is known about the nature and effectiveness of intervention strategies. Such strategies include programs of legal coercion of problem drinkers into treatment; court-related education for persons arrested for driving while intoxicated; job-based programs with "constructive confrontation" for impaired performance; and hospital-based treatment programs, including detoxification services, behavior modification, a wide variety of drug therapies, and various forms of group and individual psychotherapy. These are all frequently associated in one way or another with halfway houses, and typically refer clients to Alcoholics Anonymous (AA). Finally, interveners attempt these various strategies in a wide variety of combinations and permuta-

tions, all against a backdrop of random forces typically called "spontaneous recovery."

Legal coercion of problem drinkers

Compulsory treatment of persons with drinking problems is one form of combating crimes that are ascribed to alcoholism. It may force convicted alcoholic criminals to participate during parole in a clinical program, with a threat of reimprisonment if they disregard clinic appointments. Another example is the mandatory referral of skid-row, "revolving door" alcoholics to treatment programs. Yet another is court-mandated treatment of recidivists for vagrancy and public drunkenness. Another prominent example is the widespread use of probation for persons convicted of operating a motor vehicle while intoxicated. These strategies go against the grain of many therapists and treatment people, who frequently hold the belief that coercion, manipulation, or other use of pressure to participate in therapy is countertherapeutic. The strategy is often applied in municipal courts, where cases of drunken driving, public intoxication, and skid-row offenses are frequent. It attempts to provide a substitute for individual motivation, in the belief that such motivation will emerge from the mandatory attendance at outpatient clinical sessions or involvement in a full-scale inpatient program. Because the criminal justice system has not dealt successfully with the alcoholic offender, the trend toward legal coercion is gaining momentum.

Although there is a tendency among the dozen or so relevant evaluations to conclude tentatively that the coercion strategy is effective, the methodological flaws in these studies suggest caution in accepting their conclusions (Ward). For example, many of them make no effort to control for intervening variables, other than the compulsory treatment, that might explain the favorable results. Furthermore, when cases were assigned to treatment methods other than legal coercion for purposes of comparison, the assignments were not random, resulting in illegitimate comparisons. In addition, rather powerful interest groups may be served by the widespread implementation of enforced treatment: the criminal justice system, whose resources are often threatened because of its inability to deal with problem drinking offenders, and the alcoholism treatment industry, which often is dependent on mandatory court referrals for its clientele.

Nevertheless, there are theoretical reasons for believing the results of the flawed studies. Where clients are employed, married, and have a commitment to conventional society, it seems logical that they would respond. There is a degree of social competence on which the mandated therapy can build. Among the skid-row, revolving-door type, however, these social competencies are probably lacking, throwing any favorable results into question. Even here, however, there is a tendency to see a degree of effectiveness in legal coercion for carefully selected skid-row persons, especially where the penalties for parole violations are harsh.

Drinking-driver programs

Bearing a close affinity to legal coercion are the many Driving While Intoxicated (DWI) programs. These differ from other forms of legal coercion into treatment in that the apprehended offender can refuse to be "directed" into a DWI educational program or clinic and accept the punishment duly assigned (usually by municipal courts), which involves loss of the driver's license as well as a possible fine or jail sentence. There is considerable evidence that these programs do, in fact, identify problem drinkers and alcoholics. Studies on a variety of different populations of drinking drivers with illegally high blood-alcohol content (BAC) at the time of arrest show that approximately half of them can be classified in the "problem drinker" category. An example of these studies is the report of Eric Fine, Pascal Scoles, and Michael Mulligan. In 1974 they studied the drinking pattern of fifteen hundred persons arrested by the Philadelphia Police Department. The vast majority chose to attend the safe-driving school rather than be prosecuted. Forty-eight percent of these reported that during at least twice-a-week drinking sessions they consumed a minimum of five quarts of beer, a fifth of wine, or two pints of liquor. In addition, they described "blackouts," missing meals because of drinking, and other alcohol-related incidents not involving driving.

But prevailing opinion and extant data also cast doubt on the effectiveness of typical DWI programs (estimated at more than 450 in 1978). One reason may be the relatively low intensity of intervention in DWI classes, which are usually largely didactic in nature. Evaluation studies may be represented by Bert Hayslip and his associates and by James Nichols (p. 20). The first study detailed the many problems encountered in evaluating DWI programs: adequate control groups; the relevant criterion of success; intercity differences in laws; separation of problem drinkers from social drinkers caught up in the policing process; the heavy, selective attrition of cases during follow-up; and unreliability of attitude scales. Nichols's study appeared to maintain a randomization

of DWI cases into control and experimental groups (no treatment and DWI exposure, respectively) in eleven locations; it concluded that there were "no consistent differences between the rearrest rates of the treatment and no-treatment groups." One reason for these findings may be the low probability of being rearrested and the relatively high BAC often required to establish drunken driving. The programs may have some effect upon knowledge and attitude, but are not powerful enough to influence such behavior as continuing to abuse alcohol and to drive at the same time.

Job-based interventions

Related to DWI programs, but devoid of any legal coercion, are programs that use a form of pressure called "constructive confrontation" with workers whose job performance has deteriorated, often because of alcohol abuse. There is good evidence that performance deteriorates as problem drinking increases, regardless of occupation, status, or amount of supervision. The central strategy of job-based programs is to use the deteriorating performance of alcoholic employees as a basis on which supervisors and managers confront affected employees with evidence of their impaired performance and simultaneously offer support for rehabilitation, with no stigma attached.

Supervisors do not necessarily need to be able to connect the poor performance directly to alcohol abuse, although they often have excellent reasons to do so. The strategy calls for a supervisor to confront a poor performer solely on the basis of deficiencies in performance and then, in a constructive manner, to tell him about the policy and its offer of nonpunitive help. It is then up to the employee to decide whether to take advantage of this opportunity. Most policies continue the strategy for at least two or three sessions if performance does not return to acceptable levels. In the second or third session, an additional strategy is added, called "crisis precipitation," in which the supervisor warns the employee that continued poor performance will subject him to discipline—initially a temporary layoff or suspension, but eventually discharge. Most policies urge that crisis precipitation be carried out in a constructive context of positive offers of help.

Guiding these specific actions is a written policy that has been adopted by management and promulgated at all levels of supervisors and employees. Such policies vary but usually articulate certain common principles on which job-based intervention strategies are based: alcoholism is a treatable health problem, not a moral weakness; it causes much suffering and poor performance; a constructive approach should be taken to the problem, avoiding self-abasement and emphasizing positive supports; and employees can choose whatever method they wish to regain normal performance with the positive backing of the company. At the same time, the nature of the disorder may call for the creation of a crisis, and job conditions will be used to do this as constructively as possible. Furthermore, every effort is made to incorporate unions, if present, in devising and carrying out the overall strategy. Some version of this strategy is contained in formal statements of thousands of companies. Although the exact number is difficult to determine, the increase since the late 1970s has been enormous, with many policies becoming a routine part of personnel management.

Contrary to the mixed results reported for the other policies discussed so far, the job-based interventions seem to generate consistently remarkable results. A review of twelve evaluative studies (Beyer and Trice) of job-based programs suggested that, taken collectively, these studies probably were accurate in reporting unusually high success rates. Moreover, one detailed evaluation of the job-based policies used a national sample of managers in a large company, one with a long-standing confrontation strategy (Trice and Beyer, p. 492). Using a best-worst criterion of job performance, it demonstrated that the confrontational aspect of the strategy was significantly related to improvements, whereas the constructive dimension was less important.

Formal discipline, such as written warnings and disciplinary layoffs, had no positive effect on job performance. One basic reason for the good results of the alternative strategies described above is their compatibility with the accepted scientific psychological approach to general discipline in the workplace. This can be summarized by the phrases "positive discipline," used by the American Management Association, and "corrective discipline," deriving from collective bargaining and arbitrator decisions.

Clinic-based psychotherapies

The strategy. The bulk of therapeutic interventions tends to take place in organizations variously called clinics, alcoholism treatment centers, or psychiatric centers. Most of these interventions fall under the generic category of "psychotherapy," commonly divided into group or individual psychotherapy and "therapeutic communities," which focus upon large groups of patients. The basic strategy is for a therapist, or therapists, to cultivate a close emotional relationship with patients in order to help them achieve greater self-understanding, objectivity, and personal growth. The therapist attempts to use this relationship to explore the inner feelings of the patient about his life situations, in an effort to restructure the patient's life. Therapy consists of a series of intense discussions between those who seek help and one trained to give it. Often referred to as "counseling" or "casework," this treatment is frequently rendered by social workers, psychologists, and nurses, as well as by psychiatrists.

The treatment proceeds in three phases. The therapist builds a relationship in the initial phase, sets goals, and deals with issues such as health or nutrition. The second phase consists of exploring, trying out, and working through personal decision-making and management of reality, including drinking episodes. The last phase involves reinforcing gains made in the middle period and preparing for termination. Variations on this basic strategy have emerged. Treating more than one patient at a time (group psychotherapy) or using group dynamics in conjunction with individual psychodynamics is frequent. In many clinics, role-playing and psychodrama intensify the process, and pastoral and vocational counseling deal with spiritual and occupational working-through. Psychotherapy is often intermingled with lectures, group discussions, and drug and nutritional therapy, all following detoxification and physical buildup.

Evaluation of psychotherapeutic strategies. Efforts to determine the extent of favorable outcomes from psychotherapeutic interventions are of long standing, but research inadequacies plague them (Sobell, Sobell, and Ward). Therefore, any conclusions about the effectiveness of psychotherapy must be tentative. However, the type of methodological deficiency tends to vary from study to study, so if the studies share common findings, there is reason to believe that the overall results may be accurate. Thus, most sustained efforts directed at large, heterogeneous populations will attain at least 25 percent success on some specific criteria over a short range. All varieties of psychotherapeutic strategy seem to be helpful to a majority of patients (Emrick). In short, most studies are able to demonstrate improvement, but no one therapeutic tactic seems better than another (Edwards et al.).

To the extent that clients with poor prognoses are excluded (selectivity bias), desirable outcomes increase. Yet even here, as in less selective therapies, there is a probability that most patients will return to some type of drinking within a year of discharge. Within this population of patients, however, there are those who, abstinent or not, show substantial improvements in social and psychological functioning. The studies show considerable agreement on predictors for those persons who do respond favorably, but these are not stable items. Prominent among them, however, are a steady work history before admission, including employment at time of admission, and being married (or cohabitating). Higher social status and few arrests predicted a favorable outcome. This profile suggests that the odds for improvements after therapy are relatively high for those who have signs of social competence (Pattison, Coe, and Doerr) such as employment, some occupational status, an ongoing marriage, and little labeling by law enforcement. A randomized study using a population somewhat similar to the social-competence profile described above demonstrated that "advice" given during one morning in a psychotherapeutic setting secured as high a success rate as did much more elaborate therapy (Edwards et al.). This supports the notion that social competence among patients results in higher favorable response rates to treatment. It is probably a factor in the remarkable success rates often reported for job-based programs.

Inadequacies in treatment-evaluation studies. An example of a research flaw that may be difficult to correct is the frequent absence of random placement of patients into different types of treatment, or into control and experimental groups. Unfortunately, the judgment of therapists about a given patient often prevents a random pattern, thereby making impossible the balancing-out of many forces that could be rival explanations of favorable results. There has also been little replacement of randomization by sound "comparison groups," matched on a series of relevant characteristics but with treatment absent for some.

An additional methodological flaw is the frequent use of only one criterion, such as abstinence; this criterion is insensitive to other areas of behavioral change after therapy, for example, an increase or decrease in drinking, and job or marital stability. Abstinence should be one of many criteria (Belasco and Trice), for it is too limited to be the sole yardstick of treatment outcome. Moreover, most evaluation studies fail to demonstrate the reliability or validity of the instruments used to gather data. Another problem rarely resolved is attrition among follow-up subjects. Locating patients twelve to eighteen months after discharge—outcomes probably achieve stability only after this much time—is a formidable task. Rarely do follow-up studies reach even 75 percent or 80 percent of a sample. Often overlooked is the confounding fact that frequent follow-up contacts with patients for research purposes introduce a continuity of treat-

ment, after formal treatment is over, that can influence patient behavior. A "research effect" bias is rarely recognized, much less managed or accounted for.

One of the most insidious problems is the failure to separate various treatment strategies from one another. Compounding this problem is the general practice of mixing persons with different types of drinking problems in one heterogeneous population. The result is that many treatment situations consist of an indiscriminate mix of patients exposed to an equally haphazard collection of treatment strategies, often executed unevenly from patient to patient. Thus, individual psychotherapy may be accompanied by group therapy and lectures; each of these may involve some persons on drug therapy or nutrition therapy. In turn, some of those in group therapy may differentially experience psychodrama and pastoral counseling combined with vocational help and social-worker follow-up. In addition, most patients are exposed to AA, but in varying degrees of intensity. This potpourri makes systematic evaluation difficult. Further compounding the problem is the diversity of occupational groups providing therapy, including psychotherapists (psychologists and psychiatrists), social workers, physicians, clergymen, teachers, lay members of AA, and "counseling" psychologists.

Behavioral treatments and drug therapies. Although drug therapies may be intermingled with psychotherapies, behavioral treatment tends to stand alone as a strategy unto itself. In broad terms, it consists of two types: aversion therapies, which attempt to give the act of drinking itself aversive properties; and operant-conditioning therapies, which attempt to manipulate the results of drinking so as to reduce its frequency. The conditioning approach has as its goal the development of controlled drinking rather than total abstinence. As such, it has generated intense resistance from AA and the National Council on Alcoholism, both of which firmly believe that abstinence is the goal of treatment.

The aversion therapies are of two types: electrical and chemical. In the former, alcoholics receive electric shocks as they imbibe their favorite drink. Such shock sessions may vary from a dozen to twenty. Chemical aversion is similar, but here a chemical nauseant produces uncontrollable vomiting after the drinking of a favorite liquor. There is considerable research evidence that when either of these strategies is used alone it is relatively ineffectual, although chemical aversion in a setting of high expectancy may be more effective because it is related to the realities of the drinking experience.

Operant conditioning attempts to reduce the frequency of drinking by manipulating the results of drinking through tangible experiences. Tactics include training drinkers to sense their own BAC; contrasting drunken behavior with sober behavior by means of videotaping; training, by means of laboratory tasks, in how to cope with stressful life demands without using alcohol; and aversion training for drinking above acceptable BAC levels and for alcoholic "gulping." This combination is called "multifaceted therapy" and often includes some form of aversion therapy. The studies of these strategies suffer fewer of the inadequacies discussed earlier (randomization is standard), but they have not been adequately replicated. In the few available studies, various techniques in the treatment package are removed for experimental purposes, thus setting up tighter experimental comparisons. These studies suggest that "reinforcements and punishment contingencies enforced in a laboratory setting will eventuate in more moderate drinking by alcoholics" (Nathan and Briddell). Unfortunately, there are no assurances in the evaluative studies that the changes effected in the clinic will be reinforced by the natural life conditions to which patients return.

Drug therapies consist of two chemical strategies: the reduction of anxiety by drugs regarded as less addictive than alcohol, leading to lowered use of alcohol; and a chemical "fence" that gives the client very uncomfortable results if alcohol is imbibed while the drug is present. Studies of drug therapies have generally been poorly designed (Baekeland). Dropout rates have been crippling, and the tendency of patients to take drugs in an unprescribed manner has caused confusion. As a result, many of the negative findings regarding drug therapy must be questioned. The few careful studies available suggest that some drugs may definitely be helpful under specific conditions. Thus, Antabuse (a chemical fence) has proved of some value among older, nondepressed persons who are well motivated and rather compulsive in personality makeup, with no history of heart disease. Better-designed studies indicate that among patients who regularly attend outpatient clinics and seem trustworthy, the anxiety-reducing drugs such as Chlordiazepoxide have been of short-term help. These drugs seem to facilitate therapy, but do not appear to be therapeutic in and of themselves.

Alcoholics Anonymous

Probably the best-known and most popular therapy for alcoholism is not a formal one at all. Rather it is a voluntary fellowship of persons who join with one another in an effort to refrain from drinking alcohol. Since the inception of AA in 1939 the number of local groups, each having typically twenty to forty members, has risen to more than sixteen thousand worldwide. Its strategy is a combination of receiving and carrying to others the organization's message, which emphasizes the many problems of drinking and the advantages of sobriety, and which generally seeks to help in any feasible way the nonmember who is "hitting bottom." Newcomers are urged to attend open meetings, at which members openly confess their drinking histories by telling their stories. At closed meetings members share personal problems and give and seek emotional support and counsel from one another.

Clearly, many members of AA are "successes" because their behavior has been changed drastically and is highly visible. They have made a spectacular shift in their lives through a successful identification with AA. Yet it is difficult to estimate how many problem drinkers actually affiliate with AA despite its favorable publicity. That it selects those problem drinkers with certain personal and social characteristics, however, is well known. One study found that affiliative needs, experiences of intense labeling as an alcoholic, proneness to guilt, and physical stability prior to treatment characterized AA members when contrasted with nonaffiliates (Trice and Roman). Estimates of the proportion of problem drinkers who develop a sustained affiliation with AA range from 10 percent to 27 percent; these estimates are high compared with the proportion of problem drinkers reached by the medical profession. Moreover, affiliation means considerable sobriety—often total sobriety—for AA members, which is probably not true for persons under medical treatment.

Nonetheless, numerous opinions hold that AA does not have a higher success rate than other treatments. Evidence supports the conclusion that AA admirably serves a substantial minority of problem drinkers. Other treatments, however, serve segments of the problem-drinking population that are not motivated to conform to AA's Twelve Steps and to its prescribed admission to self and others of powerlessness in the face of alcohol.

Closely aligned with AA are halfway houses, estimated to number well over four hundred in the United States and Canada. Increasingly, these are attracting public funds and being considered in planning social services for problem drinkers. Their strategy is to provide for problem drinkers with few social resources a residence from which, for two weeks up to four months, they can explore and adapt to normal "civilian" life. Usually small in the number of residents (fifteen or twenty) and with a very small staff, they attempt to provide interim primary-group support for "low bottom" alcoholics who have come from inpatient treatment and are attempting to reenter some form of normal living. The rule of abstinence is enforced by a resident staff, and total sobriety is the sole criterion of success. Using this criterion for evaluation, follow-up studies of former halfway house residents have reported between 12 percent and 25 percent success rates. Earl Rubington, using as criteria sober departures, number of sober days, and rates of readmission, reported that of four halfway houses he studied, those with the greater informality (least "institutional atmosphere") had greater success.

Spontaneous recovery

An overarching consideration, but one often ignored in the evaluation of strategies, is that numerous patients seem to improve without treatment; that is, spontaneous remission may well be the rule. Left untreated, a sizable number of problem drinkers will, for a variety of reasons, taper off sharply, often to sobriety, without formal treatment or AA affiliation. Because spontaneous remission and improvement are rather common, they should be taken into account in treatment-evaluation studies. Those studies which have reported on the phenomenon estimate that spontaneous recoveries without treatment range from 4 percent to 31 percent, with a median of 12 percent. Ideally, the spontaneous rate should be calculated to offset reported improvement or recovery rates. In sum, there is a definite chance that desirable changes in drinking behaviors will occur without any formal interventions. Further, where the more intermittent, reactive forms of problem drinking are involved, the in-and-out pattern may be widespread.

HARRISON M. TRICE

See also ALCOHOL AND CRIME, *articles on* BEHAVIORAL ASPECTS *and* LEGAL ASPECTS; DRUGS AND CRIME: TREATMENT AND REHABILITATION.

BIBLIOGRAPHY

BAEKELAND, FREDERICK. "Evaluation of Treatment Methods in Chronic Alcoholism." *Treatment and Rehabilitation of the Chronic Alcoholic.* Edited by Benjamin Kissin and Henri Begleiter. The Biology of Alcoholism, vol. 5. New York: Plenum Press, 1977, pp. 385–440.

BELASCO, JAMES A., and TRICE, HARRISON M. *The Assessment of Change in Training and Therapy.* New York: McGraw-Hill, 1969.

BEYER, JANICE M., and TRICE, HARRISON M. "The Design and Implementation of Job-based Alcoholism Programs: Constructive Confrontation Strategies and How They Work." *Occupational Alcoholism: A Review of Research Issues.*

National Institute on Alcohol Abuse and Alcoholism. Washington, D.C.: The Institute, 1982, pp. 181–239.

EDWARDS, GRIFFITH; ORFORD, JIM et al. "Alcoholism: A Controlled Trial of 'Treatment' and 'Advice.' " *Journal of Studies on Alcohol* 36 (1975): 1004–1031.

EMRICK, CHAD D. "A Review of Psychologically Oriented Treatment of Alcoholism: II. The Relative Effectiveness of Different Treatment Approaches and the Effectiveness of Treatment versus No Treatment." *Journal of Studies on Alcohol* 36 (1975): 88–108.

FINE, ERIC W.; SCOLES, PASCAL; and MULLIGAN, MICHAEL. "Under the Influence: Characteristics and Drinking Practices of Persons Arrested the First Time for Drunk Driving, with Treatment Implications." *Public Health Reports* 90 (1975): 424–429.

HAYSLIP, BERT, JR.; KAPUSINSKI, DAVID; DARBES, ALEX; and ZEH, ROBERT. "Evaluation of Driving-While-Intoxicated Programs: Some Methodological Considerations." *Journal of Studies on Alcohol* 37 (1976): 1742–1746.

NATHAN, PETER E., and BRIDDELL, DAN W. "Behavioral Assessment and Treatment of Alcoholism." *Treatment and Rehabilitation of the Chronic Alcoholic.* Edited by Benjamin Kissin and Henri Begleiter. The Biology of Alcoholism, vol. 5. New York: Plenum Press, 1977, pp. 301–350.

NICHOLS, JAMES L. "The Specific Deterrence Effect of ASAP Education and Rehabilitation Program." Paper read at Annual Meeting of National Safety Conference, Chicago, October 1978.

PATTISON, E. MANSELL; COE, RONALD; and DOERR, HANS O. "Population Variation among Alcoholism Treatment Facilities." *International Journal of the Addictions* 8 (1973): 199–229.

RUBINGTON, EARL. "Halfway Houses and Treatment Outcomes: A Relationship between Institutional Atmosphere and Therapeutic Effectiveness." *Journal of Studies on Alcohol* 40 (1979): 419–427.

SOBELL, LINDA S.: SOBELL, MARK B.; and WARD, ELIOTT, eds. *Evaluating Alcohol and Drug Abuse Treatment Effectiveness: Recent Advances.* New York: Pergamon Press, 1980.

TRICE, HARRISON M., and BEYER, JANICE M. "A Data-based Examination of Selection-Bias in the Evaluation of a Job-based Alcoholism Program." *Alcoholism: Clinical and Experimental Research* 5 (1981): 489–496.

———, and ROMAN, PAUL M. "Sociopsychological Predictors of Affiliation with Alcoholics Anonymous: A Longitudinal Study of 'Treatment Success.' " *Social Psychiatry* 5 (1970): 51–59.

WARD, DAVID A., ed. *Alcoholism: Introduction to Theory and Treatment.* Dubuque, Iowa: Kendall/Hunt, 1980.

AMNESTY AND PARDON

Examples of amnesty and pardon are as ancient as the records of organized society, and these institutions are recognized in almost every contemporary legal system. This universality may be seen as a reflection of the desire appertaining to all systems to "temper justice with mercy." More specifically, it signifies the need for any formal system to maintain a residual power to introduce occasional modifications in implementing its formal norms in order to meet the exigencies of unforeseen situations.

Terminology and etymology

The term *pardon* is first found in early French law and derives from the Late Latin *perdonare* ("to grant freely"), suggesting a gift bestowed by the sovereign. It has thus come to be associated with a somewhat personal concession by a head of state to the perpetrator of an offense, in mitigation or remission of the full punishment that he has merited. *Amnesty,* on the other hand, derives from the Greek *amnestia* ("forgetting"), and has come to be used to describe measures of a more general nature, directed to offenses whose criminality is considered better forgotten. Yet, it is interesting to note that in ancient Greece, amnesties were in fact called *adeia* ("security" or "immunity"), and not *amnestia.* Moreover, the term *pardon* fell into disuse in French law, to be replaced by the term *grâce.*

Clemency is a broader term, often encompassing both amnesty and pardon (Weihofen). Gerald Ford's United States Presidential Clemency Board, on the other hand, specified that it was concerned with granting "clemency, not amnesty." *Clemency,* however, is not usually employed as a legal term.

Historical overview

Early history. The roots of pardon and amnesty are found in ancient law. References to institutions somewhat resembling the modern pardon appear in ancient Babylonian and Hebrew law. The first amnesty is generally attributed to Thrasybulus in ancient Greece (403 B.C.); but fifteen centuries earlier the Babylonian kings, on accession to the throne, would declare a *misharum,* involving a general discharge from legal bonds of both a civil and a penal character. (An analogy may be found in the biblical "jubilee laws.") The Romans, on the other hand, developed a number of forms of clemency, and these influenced subsequent developments in European law.

In medieval Europe the power to grant pardon was held by various bodies, including the Roman Catholic Church and certain local rulers, but by the sixteenth century it usually was concentrated in the hands of the monarch. In post-Reformation England, the "royal prerogative of mercy" was used for three main

purposes: (1) as a precursor to the as-yet-unrecognized defenses of self-defense, insanity, and minority; (2) to develop new methods of dealing with offenders unrecognized by legislation, such as transportation or military conscription; and (3) for the removal of disqualifications attaching to criminal convictions.

Legislative amnesties were frequent in certain civil law countries, such as France, where they were used as an instrument of pacification after periods of civil strife (Foviaux). In England, however, this institution did not take root. The last "Acts of Grace" took place after the Jacobite risings of 1715 and 1745.

The eighteenth century: pardons and the classical school. During the eighteenth century the sovereign's power to grant pardons in individual cases came under attack, notably by Cesare Beccaria in his famous essay *On Crimes and Punishments.* Permitting the sovereign to interfere with the implementation of the laws was perceived as a threat to the concept of the separation of powers in derogation of the autonomy of both legislature and judiciary—although Montesquieu, with whom the concept of the separation of powers is associated, did not oppose the pardoning power. Such interventions were also seen as detrimental to the deterrent powers of the law, which were predicated on the inexorability of its implementation. Finally, the rampant use of pardons (particularly with respect to accomplices to crimes who informed against the principal perpetrators) was seen as a source not only of uncertainties but also of corruption and abuse.

These criticisms bore fruit after the outbreak of the French Revolution with the adoption of the Penal Code of 1791, which abolished all powers of pardon in relation to offenses triable by jury. However, the critics' victory was short-lived, for the pardoning power was revived when Napoleon Bonaparte became consul for life in 1802. Echoes of the eighteenth-century controversy, however, still reverberate today.

The nineteenth century: amnesty and the American Civil War. Article II, Section 2 of the United States Constitution bestows upon the President the power to "grant Reprieves and Pardons for offences against the United States, except in Cases of Impeachment." The first important questions arose in this regard when, in the wake of the Civil War, President Andrew Johnson purported to grant amnesty or a general pardon in favor of southern loyalists. The President was bitterly attacked, it being argued that the power he asserted was in the exclusive purview of Congress, and very different from that specified in the Constitution (L.C.K.). President Johnson seems, however, to have been vindicated in retrospect (at least as regards his constitutional position) by later measures of this type—notably, President Jimmy Carter's general pardon of the Vietnam draft evaders—which have gone unchallenged.

Clemency powers in the twentieth century

The constitutional nature of the clemency powers. Such conflicts in this area between the President and Congress have been symptomatic of the uncertainty attached to the constitutional nature of the clemency powers. Another example, the corollary of the Civil War issue, occurred when in 1939, California's legislature debated the grant of an *individual* pardon (to former labor leader Tom Mooney), and its legal powers to do so were challenged by some academic jurists (Radin).

Traditionally, these powers have been associated with the sovereign authority, and today they are most frequently entrusted to the head of state. This office is generally associated with the executive branch of government, particularly in presidential systems of government. For this reason, the exercise of pardon is often referred to as executive clemency. This, too, is the reason why impeachment has been excluded from the purview of the pardoning power in many jurisdictions: such a power might enable a chief executive to protect his ministers from parliamentary control. It is not altogether clear, however, whether it was in his executive capacity that the sovereign historically exercised these powers; he generally stood at the pinnacle of all three branches of government—legislature, executive, and judiciary—and the precise role of each branch in the decision-making process is controversial. Thus, the mechanism of decision-making, and the involvement of ministers and executive officials, judges, and sometimes even legislators in this process, have varied widely from one jurisdiction to another (Sebba, 1977; Stafford). Furthermore, although acts of clemency are in general immune from judicial review, the grounds for this immunity are sometimes stated to be the executive nature of the act—and sometimes its judicial nature.

Contemporary functions of pardon and amnesty. The term *pardon* is often used generically to describe the power vested in the head of state to grant clemency in individual cases. In this sense it includes such subcategories as full pardon, conditional pardon, commutation, remission, and reprieve. Sometimes, however, it refers only to certain categories. Thus, the United States Constitution refers only to pardons and reprieves, the first term incorporating the remaining subcategories.

In recent times, pardons have served three main functions: to remedy a miscarriage of justice, to remove the stigma of a conviction (and the disabilities thereby entailed), and to mitigate a penalty. The first two objectives are usually achieved by means of a full pardon; the other forms are employed for the purpose of mitigating the sentence. These very different objectives have resulted in some confusion as to the legal effects of a pardon. Thus, a pardon is sometimes held to "blot out guilt"—a necessary outcome where the pardon was brought about by a miscarriage of justice, but an inappropriate result in other cases. A commutation substitutes one recognized form of penalty for another. A conditional pardon is more flexible, the only usual requirement being that the condition attaching to the pardon be reasonable. A remission simply implies cancellation of the penalty, wholly or partly. Finally, a reprieve denotes the deferment of a sentence's execution. This mode is typically adopted in capital cases; the penalty is then commuted to a prison term.

An amnesty typically (1) is enacted by legislation instead of being a purely executive act; (2) is applied generally to unnamed persons, that is, to persons who fulfill certain conditions or a description laid down by the law; and (3) is designed to remove ex post facto the criminality of the acts committed. Amnesties are deemed appropriate after a political, economic, or military upheaval. A newly installed regime may hold a different perception of conduct penalized by its predecessor, whereas a consolidated one may wish to indicate its self-confidence by forgiving its erstwhile opponents. These characteristics differentiate amnesty from pardon, which issues from the head of state rather than the legislature, impinges upon the penalty rather than the conviction, and is granted on an individual basis.

Pardons and amnesty compared. The above distinctions are difficult to apply in the United States and many other countries in the common-law tradition, for three reasons. First, amnesties are rarely resorted to, and few conventions exist in this matter. Second, as noted above, the distribution of power between the legislature and executive in this area is unclear. Third, granting an individual pardon may, in removing the effects of the conviction, have effects as far-reaching as those of a European amnesty. Thus, the United States Supreme Court once went so far as to say that "the distinction between amnesty and pardon is one rather of philological interest than of legal importance" (*Knote v. United States*, 95 U.S. 149 (1877)). In at least one other case, however (*Burdick v. United States*, 236 U.S. 79, 95 (1915)), the Court has indicated the differences between these two concepts, and a state court once declared that "amnesty is the abolition or oblivion of the offence; pardon is its forgiveness" (*State v. Blalock,* 61 N.C. (Phil. Law) 242, 247 (1867)).

This distinction may be illustrated by the measures taken with regard to the Vietnam War evaders and deserters by Presidents Gerald Ford and Jimmy Carter, respectively. Ford established a clemency board to consider for a presidential pardon individual petitioners who were willing to fulfill certain conditions. Carter, on the other hand, proclaimed that all persons convicted of certain offenses under the Selective Service Act were to be unconditionally pardoned, and all pending cases closed. Although the latter measure originated with the President rather than the legislature, and was described as a pardon, its generality, purpose, and breadth of scope suggested an amnesty.

In continental Europe, on the other hand, the older distinctions are becoming increasingly blurred. So-called amnesty laws have been introduced for varied purposes, often to remit penalties rather than to remove the criminality of the offense, and sometimes merely as a device for the reduction of prison populations. Further, a hybrid institution has been introduced, the *grâce amnistiante,* whereby the president is empowered to grant pardon (amnesty?) to selected individuals who fall within certain categories designated by the law. Finally, in Italy, the government has been delegated the power to pass legislation granting either amnesty or pardon (*indulto*).

The future of clemency

Although somewhat neglected by academic writers, clemency is clearly a perplexing area in the scheme of criminal justice. By their very nature amnesties tend to be controversial, since they denote a radical political reassessment of conduct previously designated as criminal. Constitutionally, however, they have presented less of a problem (outside the United States), because they are subject to the same processes and controls as other legislation.

The pardoning power is considerably more problematic. The grant of relief from the processes of criminal justice to selected persons on an individual basis attracts criticism today no less than during the eighteenth century, especially where the decision-making process is often secretive and immune from judicial and political review. The suspicion of favoritism is thus frequently raised. Such criticism may be more vociferous when the pardon is a "blanket" one, unrelated to a specific indictment, as in the case of President Ford's pardon of his predecessor, Richard Nixon.

The functions of the pardon, too, are in modern times seen to be largely anomalous; most of its traditional functions are fulfilled by alternative institutions. Justice is individualized by other methods, such as the discretion of the sentencing judge, parole, and "good time" laws that reduce prison terms for good behavior. Allegations of miscarriages of justice may now lead to a new trial. Removal of the criminal stigma is now achieved in some jurisdictions by restrictions on the disclosure of criminal records or by their expungement. Many European legal systems achieve the same result by "rehabilitation" proceedings. The residual power of the chief executive to modify the inexorable harshness of the law may seem to have been rendered superfluous.

However, at least two considerations seem to operate in favor of retention of the pardoning function. First, the movement away from the rehabilitationist ideal has resulted in a lessening of the power of other existing institutions to individualize the penalty. Fixed sentencing laws have reduced and sometimes removed the court's discretion, and this is often coupled with the abolition of parole. Moreover, the death penalty is undergoing a resurgence, having been legalized by the Supreme Court precisely where discretion as to its application has been restricted. Paradoxically, the increasingly mandatory character of the penal system may necessitate the retention of the pardoning power for those exceptional cases which the formal norms of the written law prove unable to accommodate.

The second consideration in support of retention of the pardoning power is the evidence of history, which seems to indicate the inability of any legal system to survive without it.

LESLIE SEBBA

See also POLITICAL PROCESS AND CRIME.

BIBLIOGRAPHY

BECCARIA, CESARE. *On Crimes and Punishments* (1764). Reprint. Translated with an introduction by Henry Paolucci. Indianapolis: Bobbs-Merrill, 1963.
DUKER, WILLIAM F. "The President's Power to Pardon: A Constitutional History." *William and Mary Law Review* 18 (1977): 475–538.
FOVIAUX, JACQUES. *La Rémission des peines et des condamnations: Droit monarchique et droit moderne.* Preface by Robert Vouin. Paris: Presses Universitaires de France, 1970.
L. C. K. "The Power of the President to Grant a General Pardon or Amnesty for Offences against the United States" (1869). *American Law Register* 8 (n.s.) or 17 (o.s.): 513–532, 577–589.

MONTEIL, JACQUES. *La Grâce en droit français moderne.* Paris: Librairies Techniques, 1959.

MORSE, WAYNE L., ed. *Pardon.* The Attorney General's Survey of Release Procedures, vol. 3. Washington, D.C.: U.S. Department of Justice, 1939.

Note. "Executive Clemency in Capital Cases." *New York University Law Review* 39 (1964): 136–192.

RADIN, MAX. "Legislative Pardons: Another View." *California Law Review* 27 (1939): 387–397.

SEBBA, LESLIE. "Amnesty: A Quasi-experiment." *British Journal of Criminology, Delinquency, and Deviant Social Behaviour* 19 (1979): 5–30.

———. "The Pardoning Power: A World Survey." *Journal of Criminal Law and Criminology* 68 (1977): 83–121.

STAFFORD, SAMUEL P. *Clemency: Legal Authority, Procedure, and Structure.* Denver: National Center for State Courts, 1977.

U.S. Presidential Clemency Board. *Report to the President.* Washington, D.C.: The Board, 1975.

WEIHOFEN, HENRY, and RUBIN, SOL. "Pardon and Other Forms of Clemency." *The Law of Criminal Correction.* 2d ed. Edited by Sol Rubin. St. Paul: West, 1973, pp. 651–696.

ANOMIE

See CRIME CAUSATION: SOCIOLOGICAL THEORIES; CRIMINOLOGY: MODERN CONTROVERSIES; DEVIANCE; PRISONS: PROBLEMS AND PROSPECTS.

ANTITRUST OFFENSES

See ECONOMIC CRIME, *articles on* ANTITRUST OFFENSES *and* THEORY; WHITE-COLLAR CRIME: HISTORY OF AN IDEA.

APPEAL

The system of criminal appeals as we now know it is a relatively recent phenomenon in Anglo-American law. It was not until the enactment of the Criminal Appeal Act of 1907 (7 Edw. 7, c. 23 (repealed)) that a modern and satisfactory system of appellate review was available in England (Meador). In state criminal justice systems, only late in the nineteenth century did the opportunity to appeal become generally available (Orfield). On the federal level, writs of error were authorized on a discretionary basis for the United States circuit courts in 1879 (ch. 176, 20 Stat. 354). Appeal to the circuit courts became available later in some cases, but not until 1928 was the writ of error abolished and review limited to appeals (ch. 14, 45 Stat. 54 (repealed)).

As the opportunities for appeal in criminal cases

expanded and came to be more frequently utilized in the United States, the resulting cases were generally assimilated into existing procedures established for appellate review of civil cases. Thus, although a few states have established specialized appellate tribunals that hear only criminal appeals, in the overwhelming majority of jurisdictions criminal appeals are heard by the same courts that handle other appeals. The latter scheme is preferable, as a "specialized Court is unlikely to attract the continuing attention, interest, and concern of the entire bar" that are needed (American Bar Association, 1980, commentary on standard 21-1.2). Two types of appellate systems are to be found in the states. About half of the states have a one-tier process, which means that the appeal goes directly to the state court of last resort. The remaining states have a two-tier system, ordinarily with appeal as a matter of right to the intermediate appellate court and then discretionary appeal to the second tier (usually but not inevitably called the supreme court). In the federal system, appeals go from the district court to the court of appeals for that circuit, and certain cases may thereafter be taken from the court of appeals to the United States Supreme Court.

Except for provisions in several jurisdictions making appeal automatic when the sentence is death, appeal in criminal cases is elective rather than mandated. Yet appellate review "has become such an integral part of our criminal procedure that it may properly be viewed as an extension of the trial itself" (*Commonwealth ex rel. Neal v. Myers*, 424 Pa. 576, 579, 227 A.2d 845, 846 (1967)). This is not to suggest, however, that appellate courts are like trial courts. For one thing, an appellate court is a multi-judge tribunal, providing "an opportunity for several minds to check the trial decisions made by one mind" (American Bar Association, 1961, p. 14). For another, the appellate court must decide the matters at issue based upon the written record of the proceedings below, whereas the trial court has the advantage of a firsthand observation of the critical events.

Even though, as noted above, criminal appeals are generally processed like civil appeals, criminal appeals have several distinct features. First, they involve a clash of important interests that transcend the individual case—society's interests in effective law enforcement, on the one hand, and individual liberty, on the other. Second, they very often require the state court to resolve matters of federal constitutional law, a result of the fact that much of American criminal procedure has become "constitutionalized." Third, they usually involve institutionalized representation on both sides (prosecutor's office and appellate defender's office), since most criminal appellants are indigent. Fourth, they include a significant number of cases in which the appeal is lacking in substantial merit, a consequence of the fact that the indigent appellant (unlike the typical civil appellant) "has everything to gain and nothing to lose" by taking an appeal (Carrington, Meador, and Rosenberg, pp. 57–60). As for the purposes of appeal in criminal cases, they are: "(i) to protect defendants against prejudicial legal error in the proceedings leading to conviction and against verdicts unsupported by sufficient evidence; (ii) authoritatively to develop and refine the substantive and procedural doctrines of criminal law; and (iii) to foster and maintain uniform, consistent standards and practices in criminal process" (ABA, 1980, standard 21-1.2(a)).

Appeals by the defense

Nature of the right. In the early case of *McKane v. Durston*, 153 U.S. 684 (1894), the Supreme Court noted in dictum that a state is not required by the federal Constitution to provide appellate courts or a right to appellate review at all. This same view has been reiterated in several subsequent opinions, for example, *Ross v. Moffitt*, 417 U.S. 600 (1974) and *Griffin v. Illinois*, 351 U.S. 12 (1956). None of these cases, however, involved a situation in which a state did not provide for any appellate review of criminal convictions. It is unlikely that the Court will have occasion to decide the matter, for (as noted in *Griffin*) "all of the states now provide some method of appeal from criminal convictions" (18). Those appellate rights, even if not constitutionally required, are attended by the equal protection and due process guarantees discussed below.

Most jurisdictions have provisions requiring the court, at the time of sentencing, to notify the defendant of his right to appeal. Typical is Rule 32(a)(2) of the Federal Rules of Criminal Procedure, which has several notable features: notification of the right, including the right to appeal in forma pauperis if indigent, must be given even if the defendant is presently represented by counsel; notification is required only "in a case which has gone to trial on a plea of not guilty," that is, not when the defendant's conviction rests upon his guilty plea; and "if the defendant so requests, the clerk of the court shall prepare and file forthwith a notice of appeal on behalf of the defendant."

Pursuant to the Bail Reform Act of 1966, a federal defendant seeking release pending appeal ordinarily will be released under the same conditions as if he were awaiting trial (18 U.S.C. §§ 3041, 3141–3143, 3146–3152, 3568 (1976)). Release may be denied entirely, however, if any one of four conditions is present: (1) the appeal is frivolous; (2) the appeal is taken for delay; (3) the various conditions of release specified in the act are not sufficient to ensure reasonably that the person will not flee; or (4) those conditions are not sufficient to ensure reasonably that the defendant will not pose a danger to any other person or the community (§ 3148). Many states take essentially the same approach to the matter of release pending appeal.

Equal protection. The criminal appellate process of every state is subject to the requirements of the Fourteenth Amendment's equal protection clause, which means that this process cannot be structured in such a way as to bar indigent defendants from effective appellate review. The principle was first applied by the Supreme Court in *Griffin*, which held that indigent defendants were entitled to a free trial transcript so that they would have "as adequate appellate review as defendants who have money enough to buy transcripts." From *Griffin* it follows, as later held in *Burns v. Ohio*, 360 U.S. 252 (1959), that a state cannot require an indigent defendant to pay a filing fee before permitting him to appeal. Because, as the Court subsequently put it in *Mayer v. Chicago*, 404 U.S. 189 (1971), *Griffin* constitutes "a flat prohibition against pricing indigent defendants out of as effective an appeal as would be available to others able to pay their own way" (196–197), the prohibition extends even to cases in which the challenged conviction is of an ordinance violation punishable by fine only.

Although the Sixth Amendment right to counsel in "all criminal prosecutions," including the right of indigents to have counsel provided for them in all but the most minor cases, is not applicable to the appellate process, the Supreme Court in *Douglas v. California*, 372 U.S. 353 (1963) applied the *Griffin* equal protection principle in ruling that indigents must be afforded counsel on appeal. With respect to "the first appeal, granted as a matter of right to rich and poor alike," the Court in *Douglas* declared that the indigent defendant was entitled to the same type of appeal as a more affluent defendant—that is, one in which "the appellate court passes on the merits of his case only after having the full benefit of written briefs and oral argument by counsel" (356). But in *Ross*, the Court declined to extend *Douglas* to a second-tier discretionary appeal. The Court reasoned that a "meaningful appeal" was possible without counsel in that setting, for counsel on the first appeal would already have prepared a brief and made appellate argument, ensuring that the "defendant's claims of error are organized and presented in a lawyerlike fashion" (615).

Douglas raised the troublesome question of how court-appointed counsel should proceed if he believes that an appeal should not be filed because it lacks merit. In *Anders v. California*, 386 U.S. 738 (1967), the Court held that if after a "conscientious examination" of his case counsel finds an appeal to be "wholly frivolous," he should so advise the court and request permission to withdraw, accompanying that request with "a brief referring to anything in the record that might arguably support the appeal" (744) and with any added points which the defendant may wish to raise personally. The court, not counsel, then decides whether the case is frivolous. Some have criticized *Anders* on the ground that it tends to divert limited public-defender resources from meritorious appeals (Doherty, pp. 1–2). Others have noted that appellate reversals sometimes take place "after appointed counsel has filed an 'Anders' brief explaining that his client's cause was utterly hopeless" (Carrington, Meador, and Rosenberg, p. 77).

Due process. As a matter of Fourteenth Amendment due process, the Supreme Court declared in *North Carolina v. Pearce*, 395 U.S. 711 (1969), a defendant's "exercise of a right of appeal," whether or not the appeal is itself grounded in constitutional claims, "must be free and unfettered." This means, the Court concluded, that "vindictiveness against a defendant for having successfully attacked his first conviction must play no part in the sentence he receives after a new trial," and, indeed, that even an appearance of vindictiveness must be avoided. Consequently, "whenever a judge imposes a more severe sentence upon a defendant after a new trial, the reasons for his doing so must affirmatively appear." Those reasons, which must be made a part of the record, may only "be based upon objective information concerning identifiable conduct on the part of the defendant occurring after the time of the original sentencing proceeding" (725–726).

Pearce has not been applied in slightly different settings where no comparable risk of vindictiveness was present. In *Colten v. Kentucky*, 407 U.S. 104 (1972), it was held inapplicable to sentences imposed following a trial de novo, so that there is no similar due process restriction upon imposition of a higher sentence following the defendant's reconviction after he has exercised his right to be tried anew by a higher-level court. The Court found it especially significant "that the court which conducted Colten's trial and

imposed the final sentence was not the court with whose work Colten was sufficiently dissatisfied to seek a different result on appeal; and it is not the court that is asked to do over what it thought it had already done correctly" (116–117). Similarly, in *Chaffin v. Stynchcombe*, 412 U.S. 17 (1973), the Court upheld a higher sentence imposed by a jury following the defendant's retrial after appellate reversal of his first conviction. The Court stressed that this jury had not been informed of the defendant's prior sentence, and that consequently "there is no basis for holding that jury resentencing poses any real threat of vindictiveness" (28).

Appeals by the prosecution

The Fifth Amendment's guarantee against double jeopardy prohibits prosecution appeal in certain circumstances, most notably when the defendant's trial has resulted in a jury verdict of not guilty (*United States v. Ball*, 163 U.S. 662 (1896)). In the federal system, appeal by the government is permissible in all circumstances when it is not barred by the double jeopardy clause (18 U.S.C. § 3731 (1976)). Several states follow this same approach; a few permit no prosecution appeals; and the others limit the prosecution to (1) pretrial appeals from pretrial orders dismissing an indictment or information, and (2) post-verdict appeals from orders granting a new trial or motion in arrest of judgment following a guilty verdict (Kronenberg).

A considerable number of jurisdictions have also adopted legislation expressly granting the prosecution the right to take an interlocutory appeal from a pretrial ruling granting a motion to suppress evidence alleged to have been illegally acquired. Such provisions have been supported on two grounds. One is that the practical effect of granting a motion to suppress often is to terminate the case since the prosecution, lacking sufficient additional evidence, will be required to request dismissal of the indictment. The other is that the rules relating to searches and seizures and other police practices that lead to suppression motions frequently are uncertain, meaning it is desirable that law enforcement agencies have an opportunity for their policies to be assessed by a higher court (President's Commission, p. 47).

The final-order requirement

Although limited exceptions are sometimes recognized (such as the above-discussed authority of the prosecution to appeal a pretrial suppression of evidence), it may generally be said that appellate review of a case is possible only with respect to those rulings below which are final. Illustrative is the provision (28 U.S.C. § 1291) that grants the federal courts of appeals jurisdiction to review "all final decisions of the district courts." Adherence to this rule of finality has been particularly stringent in criminal prosecutions because "the delays and disruptions attendant upon intermediate appeal," which the rule is designed to avoid, "are especially inimical to the effective and fair administration of the criminal law" (*DiBella v. United States*, 369 U.S. 121 (1962)).

The *DiBella* case provides a useful illustration of this limitation on appeal. There, the Court held that denial of a pretrial motion to suppress evidence which was allegedly obtained illegally was not a final, appealable order, since that ruling was not "fairly severable from the context of a larger litigious process." This is because "the legality of the search too often cannot truly be determined until the evidence at the trial has brought all circumstances to light" (129). But denial of a motion for return of goods allegedly seized illegally is appealable when no criminal prosecution is pending (*United States v. Ryan*, 402 U.S. 530 (1971)). Refusing to permit review under such circumstances, the Court noted, "would mean that the Government might indefinitely retain the property without any opportunity for the movant to assert on appeal his right to possession" (533).

The *DiBella-Ryan* distinction does not mean that a pretrial ruling may never qualify as a final decision. In the civil case of *Cohen v. Beneficial Industrial Loan Corp.*, 337 U.S. 541 (1949), the Court concluded that a pretrial ruling should be deemed "final" for purposes of appeal if (1) the lower court had fully disposed of the question; (2) the decision was not merely a step toward final disposition of the merits of the case, but instead resolved an issue completely collateral; and (3) the decision involved an important right that would be lost, probably irreparably, if review had to await final judgment. Illustrative is the pretrial denial of a motion to dismiss the indictment grounded in the contention that trial is barred by double jeopardy. That ruling is certainly a complete rejection of the claim, is collateral to and separable from the principal issue of the defendant's guilt, and involves a right not to be tried which would be lost if appeal had to await trial (*Abney v. United States*, 431 U.S. 651 (1977)). By contrast, denial of a pretrial motion to dismiss for violation of the defendant's right to a speedy trial is not appealable, since "most speedy trial claims . . . are best considered only after the relevant facts have been developed at trial" (*United States v. MacDonald*, 435 U.S. 850, 858 (1978)).

Mention must also be made of the possibility of review through contempt. In *Cobbledick v. United States*, 309 U.S. 323 (1940), the Court held that an order denying a witness's motion to quash a grand jury subpoena was not a final order and therefore was not appealable. This is because a witness should not be allowed to halt so easily the orderly progress of a grand jury's criminal investigation. But, the Court added, the result would be otherwise if the witness refused to comply with the subpoena and was then held in contempt; at that point "the witness' situation becomes so severed from the main proceeding as to permit an appeal."

Scope of appellate review

Moot cases. An appellate court will not review the trial court's decision in a case, civil or criminal, where the appeal has become "moot." The traditional view has been that a criminal appeal is moot when the sentence imposed by the trial court has been fully satsified—that is, when the defendant has paid his fine and served the full period of imprisonment or probation. Some jurisdictions still adhere to that position, although most now recognize some significant departures from it. The most extreme opposing view is that defense appeal from a conviction is never moot because the "stigma of guilt" remains even after the sentence has been served. One departure of a more limited nature, related to cases in which the defendant paid a fine, is that the appeal is not moot if state law permits remittance of a fine paid on an invalid conviction. A second departure, grounded in the sensible notion that a state should not be able to prevent appellate review simply by having a slow or inefficient appellate process, results in appeal being permitted where the defendant was denied a stay of sentence and then, because of the slowness of the appellate process, completed his sentence before the appeal was reached.

However, the most commonly recognized departure from the fully-satisfied-sentence position is the so-called collateral consequences doctrine. As explained in *Sibron v. New York*, 392 U.S. 40 (1968), it is very often possible that a criminal conviction will result in other adverse collateral legal consequences for the defendant, such as use of that conviction to impeach his character if he chooses to put it in issue in any future criminal trial. Given this possibility, it is better to determine the validity of that conviction now, "when the dispute is fresh and additional facts may, if necessary, be taken without a substantial risk that witnesses will die or memories fade" (57), rather than to wait until some time, perhaps in the distant future, when the conviction is challenged collaterally. This interest is shared by both the convicted defendant and the state, and thus the doctrine is also relevant in the case of a state's opposition to dismissal of an appeal (*Pennsylvania v. Mimms*, 434 U.S. 106 (1977)).

Concurrent sentence doctrine. Prior to *Sibron*, federal appellate courts traditionally followed the rule that where the defendant had been sentenced to equal concurrent sentences on different counts of an indictment, the court would not consider challenges to the remaining counts once conviction on any one count was found to be valid. But the Court concluded in *Benton v. Maryland*, 395 U.S. 784 (1969) that in light of *Sibron* the concurrent sentence doctrine could not be justified on mootness grounds. The Court in *Benton* took note of the contention that the "concurrent sentence rule may have some continuing validity as a rule of judicial convenience" (791), but found it unnecessary to resolve this dispute.

Although most federal courts have continued to apply the concurrent sentence doctrine as a matter of discretion, treating it as a rule of "judicial convenience," some have rejected the doctrine outright (*United States v. Vargas*, 615 F.2d 952 (2d Cir. 1980)). Some states have also rejected the doctrine.

Issues not properly raised. Appellate courts ordinarily will not consider objections that were not properly presented at the trial level and consequently were not ruled upon by the trial court. This means that an appellant is not likely to obtain review of issues which he failed to raise in a timely fashion before the trial judge—as required, for example, by statutes and rules of court specifying the time at which one must object to the admission of illegally seized evidence, to the composition of the grand jury, to an indictment or information, or to denial of a speedy trial; or at which one must make post-verdict motions.

Various exceptions are recognized to the general rule that the failure properly to raise an issue at the trial level ordinarily precludes appellate review. For one thing, if the procedural requirement itself violates due process because it fails to provide the defense with a reasonable opportunity to raise an objection at the trial level, then that requirement will not bar appellate review (*Reece v. Georgia*, 350 U.S. 85 (1955)). For another, some states will allow appeal where it appears that barring the appeal would not prevent the defendant from obtaining federal court review of

the conviction by a writ of habeas corpus (*State v. Carufel*, 106 R.I. 739, 263 A.2d 686 (1970)). Finally, lack of a timely objection might not bar an appeal raising a most fundamental issue going to the jurisdiction of the trial court, such as a double jeopardy question (*People v. Michael*, 48 N.Y.2d 1, 394 N.E.2d 1134 (1979)).

Plain error. The rule in the federal courts, just as in most state courts, is that an appellate court will consider a trial error not properly presented below—or, indeed, not even raised on appeal—if it is a plain error "affecting substantial rights" of the defendant (Fed. R. Crim. P. 52(b)). As the Supreme Court once explained: "In exceptional circumstances, especially in criminal cases, appellate courts, may, of their own motion, notice errors to which no exception has been taken, if the errors are obvious, or if they otherwise seriously affect the fairness, integrity, or public reputation of judicial proceedings" (*United States v. Atkinson*, 297 U.S. 157, 160 (1936)).

Although an appellate court is more likely to recognize plain error if the evidence against the defendant is barely sufficient, it must be emphasized that the plain-error rule serves to ensure both that the innocent are not convicted and that the guilty are fairly convicted. The plain-error rule is a departure from the notion that in an adversary system a party must look to his counsel to protect him, and thus appellate courts are more likely to find plain error if it appears that the trial representation of defense counsel was questionable. Yet another situation in which plain error is more readily found is that in which the appellant is under sentence of death.

Harmless error

Not involving constitutional rights. Even if appellate review does extend to a certain issue and even if the appellate court finds that a statute or rule of court was not fully complied with or that some other comparable violation of law occurred at the trial level, it is not inevitable that the conviction will be reversed. The rule in the federal courts, for example, is that "any error, defect, irregularity or variance which does not affect substantial rights shall be disregarded" (Fed. R. Crim. P. 52(a)). The states generally take the same approach.

This harmless-error rule reflects the notion that "a defendant is entitled to a fair trial but not a perfect one" (*Lutwak v. United States*, 344 U.S. 604, 619 (1953)). There is no agreement, however, as to just how demanding the harmless-error standard should be. At one extreme, it is contended that "unless the appellate court believes it highly probable that the error did not affect the judgment, it should reverse" (Traynor, p. 35). At the other is the view that appellate affirmance is proper if it is more probable than not that the error did not materially affect the verdict (*United States v. Castillo*, 615 F.2d 878 (9th Cir. 1980)). In any event, appellate courts are more likely to find the error to be harmless if the evidence of the defendant's guilt is overwhelming, if the trial was by a judge rather than a jury, or if the jury was given effective instructions to disregard the error.

Involving constitutional rights. It is another matter if the error that has occurred amounts to a violation of the defendant's constitutional rights. For one thing, as the Supreme Court recognized in *Chapman v. California*, 386 U.S. 18 (1967), "there are some constitutional rights so basic to a fair trial that their infraction can never be treated as harmless error" (23). The Court in *Chapman* mentioned the rule against coerced confessions, the right to counsel, and the right to an impartial judge; doubtless there are several others. But in the same decision the Court also recognized that there are "some constitutional errors which in the setting of a particular case are so unimportant and insignificant that they may, consistent with the Federal Constitution, be deemed harmless, not requiring the automatic reversal of the conviction" (22). Examples include the admission of illegally obtained evidence and prosecutorial comment on the defendant's failure to take the stand.

The Supreme Court in *Chapman* went on to hold that even when the nature of the constitutional violation is such that it might be harmless error, it is required as a matter of constitutional law that the appellate court apply a very exacting test. Reversal is required unless the court is "able to declare a belief that it was harmless beyond a reasonable doubt" (24), and the burden of proof in this respect must be placed upon the prosecution. One view of this test is that it is too strict, amounting almost to a rule of automatic reversal, in that an appellate court can rarely say that it was virtually certain the error had no effect (Traynor, pp. 43–44). Another view is that it is too generous, in the sense that an inherent difficulty with the harmless-error rule is that a certain constitutional error, such as the admission of impermissible evidence, may have significantly affected the strategies of both sides in ways that will not be apparent to the appellate court (Saltzburg, pp. 988, 990). But the Supreme Court has, if anything, made the test less demanding. Although in *Chapman* the Court criticized the notion that error is harmless if there is overwhelming evidence of guilt, in later cases the Court has given em-

phasis to the weight of the evidence showing guilt (*Harrington v. California*, 395 U.S. 250 (1969)).

WAYNE R. LaFAVE

See also COUNSEL: RIGHT TO COUNSEL; COURTS, ORGANIZATION OF; CRIMINAL PROCEDURE: CONSTITUTIONAL ASPECTS; DOUBLE JEOPARDY; HABEAS CORPUS.

BIBLIOGRAPHY

American Bar Association. "Criminal Appeals." *Standards for Criminal Justice*, vol. 4, 2d ed. Prepared with the assistance of the American Bar Foundation. Boston: Little, Brown, 1980, chap. 21.
——, Section of Judicial Administration. *Internal Operating Procedures of Appellate Courts.* Prepared in cooperation with the Institute of Judicial Administration in the Study of Appellate Courts. Chicago: ABA, 1961.
CARRINGTON, PAUL D.; MEADOR, DANIEL J.; and ROSENBERG, MAURICE. *Justice on Appeal.* St. Paul: West, 1976.
DOHERTY, JAMES J. "Wolf! Wolf!: The Ramifications of Frivolous Appeals." *Journal of Criminal Law, Criminology, and Police Science* 59 (1968): 1–3.
KRONENBERG, JERRY. "Right of a State to Appeal in Criminal Cases." *Journal of Criminal Law, Criminology, and Police Science* 49 (1959): 473–482.
MEADOR, DANIEL. *Criminal Appeals: English Practices and American Reforms.* Charlottesville: University Press of Virginia, 1973.
ORFIELD, LESTER B. *Criminal Appeals in America.* Introduction by Roscoe Pound. Boston: Little, Brown, 1939.
President's Commission on Law Enforcement and Administration of Justice, Task Force on the Administration of Justice. *Task Force Report: The Courts.* Washington, D.C.: The Commission, 1967.
SALTZBURG, STEPHEN A. "The Harm of Harmless Error." *Virginia Law Review* 59 (1973): 988–1032.
TRAYNOR, ROGER. *The Riddle of Harmless Error.* Columbus: Ohio State University Press, 1970.

ARRAIGNMENT

Arraignment is the stage of the criminal process at which the defendant is advised of the formal charges against him and called upon to enter a plea. In most jurisdictions, he may enter a plea of not guilty, guilty, or nolo contendere. If the defendant stands mute (refusing to enter a plea), a plea of not guilty is entered on his behalf.

A plea of nolo contendere—sometimes referred to as a plea of *non vult contendere*, or *non vult*—is a means by which the defendant may assert that he does not wish to contest the charges against him. Such a plea may not be entered as a matter of right but only with the consent of the judge receiving the plea, and judges will not as a rule accept such pleas without the prosecutor's concurrence. In most respects, the plea of nolo contendere is the practical equivalent of a guilty plea. A defendant entering such a plea will be subject to the same sentence as if he pleaded guilty, and the plea may be admitted against him in subsequent criminal proceedings for perjury or false statement. From the perspective of the defendant, the plea's sole practical benefit is that in contrast to a guilty plea, or a conviction following a not-guilty plea, a plea of nolo contendere may not be admitted into evidence in a subsequent civil action as proof of the fact that the defendant committed the offense to which he entered the plea. Thus, a defendant entering this plea to criminal tax fraud or antitrust violations will not be precluded from contesting the civil actions usually associated with such offenses.

The effect of a defendant's plea of not guilty is to precipitate a trial at which the prosecutor will be required to establish the defendant's guilt beyond a reasonable doubt. On the other hand, a valid plea of guilty will constitute a legally binding admission of guilt and a waiver of all defenses except such as would absolutely negate the power of the prosecution to bring charges against the defendant or of the court to consider such charges (*Blackledge v. Perry*, 417 U.S. 21 (1974); cf. *Tollett v. Henderson*, 411 U.S. 258 (1973)). Although precise figures are not available, it appears that in most jurisdictions between 80 percent and 90 percent of all criminal defendants eventually plead guilty. Therefore, the important issues relating to arraignment concern the procedures employed in the preplea colloquy to ensure that guilty pleas entered by defendants will be valid. Accordingly, it is necessary to examine the requirements of a valid preplea colloquy—that is, to determine what information should appear in the record before a judge may properly accept a guilty plea. In addition, it is appropriate to explore the effect of a valid preplea colloquy upon a defendant's right to withdraw his guilty plea—that is, to examine the law relating to the defendant's right to withdraw the plea when the preplea colloquy requirements have been complied with and when they have not been complied with.

Requirements of the guilty-plea colloquy

In the federal courts, Rule 11 of the Federal Rules of Criminal Procedure provides detailed guidelines for the judge to follow before accepting a guilty plea. Although the states are not constitutionally required to comply with Rule 11, the rule has provided a model of accepted procedure that many states have chosen to emulate (Pa. R. Crim. P. 311; Mich. Gen. Ct. R. 785.7(3)). States that have elected not to pattern their procedures after Rule 11 are bound by some constitutional constraints. At a minimum, the state preplea colloquy must "affirmatively disclose that a defendant who pleaded guilty entered his plea understandingly and voluntarily" (*Brady v. United States*, 397 U.S. 742, 747 (1970); *Boykin v. Alabama*, 395 U.S. 238 (1969)).

Under the guidelines provided by Rule 11, a judge may not properly accept a guilty plea until three central requirements are satisfied. First, by personally addressing the defendant in open court, the judge must determine that the defendant is entering the plea voluntarily and intelligently. Second, if there has been a plea agreement (that is, an agreement under which the defendant agrees to plead guilty in exchange for a prosecutorial concession, such as a reduction of charge or a favorable sentencing recommendation) between the defendant and the prosecutor, the agreement must be disclosed and made a part of the record, and the defendant must be informed whether the judge will honor the terms of the agreement. Finally, before entering judgment on a plea of guilty, the judge must satisfy himself that there is a factual basis for the plea.

Of course, determining whether these requirements have been satisfied is not always easy. In order to ensure that the defendant's plea be intelligent, Rule 11(c) specifies certain areas of inquiry. Thus, the judge must determine that the defendant understands he has a right to plead not guilty and to be tried by a jury with the assistance of counsel, and that he understands the nature of the charge to which he is pleading guilty and is aware of the possible penalties, including the mandatory minimum sentence, if any, and the maximum sentence provided by law. Predictably, the extent of inquiry required in each of these defined areas has been the subject of litigation. The problems related to explaining the nature of the charge are exemplified by the Supreme Court's decision in *Henderson v. Morgan*, 426 U.S. 637 (1976). In that state case, the defendant entered a plea to second-degree murder but, in explaining his version of the offense, noted that he "meant no harm" to the victim when he entered her room with a knife. The Court held that under the circumstances of the case, the judge's failure to explain to the defendant that the crime of second-degree murder included intent to kill as a required element vitiated the constitutional validity of the guilty plea. In a footnote, the Court delineated the scope of *Henderson*'s holding. While not requiring a full explanation of every element of the offense to which a plea is to be entered, the case does impose a duty upon the judge to explain any "critical element" of the offense before accepting a plea (*Henderson*, 647, n. 18). A "critical element" of an offense would be one that the defendant would need knowledge of in order to understand the true nature of the charge against him (*United States v. Coronado*, 554 F.2d 166 (5th Cir. 1977)).

Explaining the possible penalties involved is generally fairly straightforward. The judge can merely describe to the defendant whatever statutory penalties are provided. A problem may arise, however, as to whether the defendant should also be informed of collateral consequences that might result from the plea. In general, the judge is not required to inform the defendant that conviction can result in such collateral consequences as deportation, loss of the right to vote, or loss of the right to operate a business licensed in the state (Note, pp. 875–876). However, when a defendant's guilty plea will render him ineligible for parole, there is a split of authority as to whether the defendant should be so advised prior to acceptance of the plea, as can be seen in a comparison of cases such as *Durant v. United States*, 410 F.2d 689 (1st Cir. 1969) and *Sanchez v. United States*, 417 F.2d 494 (5th Cir. 1969). The Supreme Court has stated that when the guilty plea will subject the defendant to a special term of parole in addition to the statutory prison sentence provided, this information should be disclosed to the defendant (*United States v. Timmreck*, 441 U.S. 780, 784 (1979)).

Perhaps Rule 11's most troubling aspect stems from the obligation it imposes upon the judge to ensure that there is a "factual basis" for the plea of guilty. In the typical case, this requirement can easily be satisfied. The prosecutor will present (or read into the record) evidence that would establish at least a prima facie case against the defendant, and the defendant will admit that the facts alleged by the prosecutor are true. A problem arises, however, when the defendant either refuses to admit, or affirmatively denies, the facts alleged by the prosecutor. Under those circumstances, what evidence, if any, will be sufficient to satisfy the factual-basis requirement?

The Supreme Court dealt with the constitutional aspects of this problem in *North Carolina v. Alford*, 400 U.S. 25 (1970). In that case, the North Carolina defendant was originally charged with first-degree murder, a capital offense. He entered a plea to second-degree murder, after which the trial court received a summary of the state's case, including testimony from witnesses

that the defendant declared his intent to kill the victim and later stated that he had carried out the killing. The defendant then took the stand and testified that he had not killed the victim but was nevertheless pleading guilty because he wanted to avoid the death penalty. The Supreme Court held that the trial judge did not commit constitutional error in accepting the plea.

While *Alford* affirms that a factual basis for a guilty plea may be established even though the defendant denies responsibility for the offense charged, the case does not adumbrate the level of evidence required to meet the factual-basis requirement in the face of a defendant's refusal to admit guilt. In *Alford*, strong evidence of the defendant's guilt was presented by witness testimony. But whether a lesser quality and magnitude of evidence would be sufficient to satisfy the factual-basis requirement is a question that is not resolved by either *Alford* or subsequent cases.

Another perplexing issue raised by the *Alford* decision concerns the trial judge's discretion to refuse to accept a guilty plea in cases in which defendants refuse to acknowledge their guilt. In a footnote, the Supreme Court specified that it would not delineate the scope of a federal or state judge's discretion to refuse to accept a plea in this situation (*Alford*, 38, n. 11). As a result, there is no uniformity of view on this point among the federal courts. For example, in *United States v. Gaskins*, 485 F.2d 1046 (D.C. Cir. 1973), where strong evidence of the defendant's guilt was presented, the trial judge abused discretion in refusing to accept a plea. On the other hand, *United States v. Biscoe*, 518 F.2d 95 (1st Cir. 1975) rejected *Gaskins*'s approach and found that the trial judge did not abuse discretion in refusing to accept a plea. Neither is there uniformity among the states (Alschuler).

The defendant's remedies

To what extent will a trial judge's failure to comply with Rule 11 prior to accepting a guilty plea give rise to a defendant's right to withdraw or vacate that plea? The Supreme Court has addressed this issue, and the Court's decisions have, of course, provided important guidance for state courts with preplea guidelines patterned after Rule 11. In *McCarthy v. United States*, 394 U.S. 459 (1969), a trial judge had failed to address the defendant personally and to determine that his plea was made voluntarily and with an understanding of the nature of the charge. Rejecting the government's claim that it should be allowed to prove that the defendant's plea was in fact a voluntary and intelligent one, the Court held that this violation of Rule

11 should automatically afford the defendant an opportunity to plead anew. The controlling rationale articulated by the Court was that "prejudice inheres in a failure to comply with Rule 11, for noncompliance deprives the defendant of the rule's procedural safeguards, which are designed to facilitate a more accurate determination of the voluntariness of the plea" (*McCarthy*, 471–472).

Despite *McCarthy*'s unequivocal statement, *Timmreck* held that the failure to explain to the defendant that he would be subject to a mandatory special parole term of at least three years, a failure that the Court characterized as a "technical violation" of Rule 11, would not, in the absence of a showing that the defendant would not have pleaded guilty if he had been properly advised by the judge, entitle the defendant to vacate his plea. Much of *Timmreck*'s analysis seemed to turn upon the fact that the defendant had exhausted his right to attack his guilty plea on appeal and was instead attacking his conviction by seeking federal habeas corpus relief. Indeed, the Court at one point strongly intimated that if a "technical violation" of Rule 11 were established on a defendant's direct appeal, this would mandate a vacation of the defendant's guilty plea (*Timmreck*, 784). Nevertheless, at least one lower federal court has read *Timmreck* as imposing a dual standard for review of Rule 11 violations on appeal. In *United States v. Dayton*, 604 F.2d 931 (5th Cir. 1979), the Fifth Circuit distinguished between the "core" and "peripheral" requirements of Rule 11. Core requirements include advice to the defendant to ensure that he understands the nature of the charges against him, the consequences of the plea (that is, the possible prison sentences and waiver of jury trial), and his right to an attorney, as well as the requirements that the record show the plea was voluntary and that there is a factual basis for its accuracy. Violation of any of these requirements automatically mandates automatic reversal of the defendant's conviction and an opportunity for him to plead anew. On the other hand, a violation of a provision of Rule 11 not within one of these core categories will not result in the vacation of the defendant's guilty plea unless it appears that the trial judge's determination that the preplea colloquy meets the specific requirements of Rule 11 is "clearly erroneous." While it appears inconsistent with the rationale articulated in *McCarthy*, *Dayton*'s approach or something resembling it may commend itself to the Supreme Court, which has manifested an increasing lack of patience with prophylactic rules that jeopardize the finality of criminal convictions.

The question of the extent of a defendant's remedy may also arise in cases in which the guidelines provided by rules such as Rule 11 have been complied with. Obviously, threats or promises occurring prior to the preplea colloquy could taint the validity of the plea itself without being subject to detection at the preplea colloquy. In *Blackledge v. Allison*, 431 U.S. 63 (1977), the Court manifested at least limited agreement with this analysis. Prior to accepting the defendant's guilty plea, the trial judge conducted the preplea colloquy in accordance with North Carolina law. After acceptance of the plea, the defendant was sentenced to seventeen to twenty-one years in prison. Based on the record of the colloquy, the judge's acceptance of the plea was constitutionally valid. However, the defendant claimed that the plea was in fact induced by an unfulfilled promise. His attorney had told him that an agreement had been reached with the prosecutor and judge whereby if he pleaded guilty he would receive a sentence of only ten years, but had cautioned him nonetheless to answer the questions of the judge (including a question as to whether the plea was induced by a promise) as he in fact did. The Court stated that "the barrier of the plea or sentencing proceeding record, although imposing, is not invariably insurmountable" (*Allison*, 74). Noting that when the procedures of Rule 11 are followed a defendant making such a contention would be entitled to an evidentiary hearing only in extraordinary circumstances, the Court held that in the situation presented in *Allison*, the defendant should be permitted an opportunity to establish the accuracy of his detailed allegations. Thus, the Court refused to adopt a rule that would allow a valid preplea colloquy to constitute an impenetrable barrier to specific allegations that the plea was in fact "so much the product of such factors as misunderstanding, duress, or misrepresentation by others as to make [it] a constitutionally inadequate basis for imprisonment" (*Allison*, 75).

The claim alleged in *Allison* suggests that another important issue relating to remedy concerns the relief that should be afforded a defendant who can prove that his guilty plea was entered in exchange for an unfulfilled promise by the government. If the defendant in *Allison* could demonstrate that the prosecutor offered him a ten-year sentence in exchange for his plea of guilty, should the defendant be entitled to specific performance, that is, to have his sentence reduced to ten years? Should the relief granted be merely to vacate the guilty plea and to permit him to plead anew? Or, finally, should the defendant be permitted to elect either of these remedies?

The Court intimated that a defendant who is sentenced in violation of the terms of a plea agreement may be entitled to specific performance (*Allison*, 72). This would be consistent with the decisions of some state and federal lower courts, for example, *Palermo v. Warden*, 545 F.2d 286 (2d Cir. 1976) and *State v. Tourtellotte*, 88 Wash. 2d 579, 564 P.2d 799 (1977), and it accords with the view of commentators who have suggested that "it is fundamentally unfair for the state to create and then destroy a defendant's expectation" (Westen and Westin). Nevertheless, the Supreme Court has provided no definitive guidance on this issue.

An even more problematic issue arises when, upon showing that the government has breached a plea agreement, the defendant asserts that the appropriate relief is to allow him to plead anew. This issue was presented, but not decided, in *Santobello v. New York*, 404 U.S. 257 (1971), in which the Court found that the terms of a guilty-plea agreement were breached by the prosecution. One prosecutor had agreed to make no recommendation as to sentence, but after the guilty plea was entered, a new prosecutor recommended that a maximum one-year sentence be imposed. Although the relief sought by the defendant was vacation of the guilty plea, a majority of the Court refused to decide what ultimate relief should be afforded the defendant and merely remanded the case to the state court, directing it to determine in the first instance whether the defendant should be entitled to vacate his plea or whether the remedy of specific performance would be constitutionally sufficient. Despite this limited holding, however, four of the seven Justices sitting in *Santobello* seemed to indicate that in a case of this sort, the defendant should ordinarily be entitled to the remedy of vacating his plea. Thus, while the defendant's remedy for a breached plea bargain is still an open question, it is at least arguable that in such a case the defendant may elect between the remedies of specifically enforcing the bargain and vacating the guilty plea.

WELSH S. WHITE

See also both articles under BAIL; COUNSEL: RIGHT TO COUNSEL; *both articles under* GUILTY PLEA.

BIBLIOGRAPHY

ALSCHULER, ALBERT W. "The Defense Attorney's Role in Plea Bargaining." *Yale Law Journal* 84 (1975): 1179–1314.

BARKAI, JOHN L. "Accuracy Inquiries for All Felony and Misdemeanor Pleas: Voluntary Pleas but Innocent Defendants?" *University of Pennsylvania Law Review* 126 (1977): 88–146.

DIX, GEORGE E. "Waiver in Criminal Procedure: A Brief for More Careful Analysis." *Texas Law Review* 55 (1977): 193–268.

ISRAEL, JEROLD H. "Criminal Procedure, the Burger Court, and the Legacy of the Warren Court." *Michigan Law Review* 75 (1977): 1319–1425.

KAMISAR, YALE; LAFAVE, WAYNE R.; and ISRAEL, JEROLD H. *Modern Criminal Procedure*. 5th ed. St. Paul: West, 1980.

LOMBROS, J. "Plea Bargaining and the Sentencing Process." *Federal Rules Decisions* 53 (1972): 509–523.

NEWMAN, DONALD J. *Conviction: The Determination of Guilt or Innocence without Trial*. Boston: Little, Brown, 1966.

Note. "Guilty Plea Bargaining: Compromises by Prosecutors to Secure Pleas." *University of Pennsylvania Law Review* 112 (1964): 865–876.

SALTZBURG, STEPHEN A. "Pleas of Guilty and Loss of Constitutional Rights: The Current Price of Pleading Guilty." *Michigan Law Review* 76 (1978): 1265–1341.

TIGAR, MICHAEL E. "Waiver of Constitutional Rights: Disquiet in the Citadel." *Harvard Law Review* 84 (1970): 1–28.

WESTEN, PETER. "Away from Waiver: A Rationale for the Forfeiture of Constitutional Rights in Criminal Procedure." *Michigan Law Review* 75 (1977): 1214–1261.

———, and WESTIN, DAVID. "Constitutional Law of Remedies for Broken Plea Bargains." *California Law Review* 66 (1978): 471–539.

ARREST AND STOP

The Fourth Amendment states in part, "The right of the people to be secure in their persons . . . against unreasonable searches and seizures, shall not be violated. . . ." Since arrest and detention involve seizure of the person, they are subject to the Fourth Amendment's requirement that there be probable cause to justify the government's intrusion on the citizen's privacy.

The definition of *arrest and stop*

The traditional definition of *arrest* is the deprivation of a person's liberty by legal authority. The logical conclusion arising from full acceptance of this definition would be that an arrest, and therefore a Fourth Amendment seizure, occurs whenever a person's liberty has been restricted by law enforcement officers to the extent that he is not free to leave of his own volition. While the Supreme Court appeared for many years to accept this rather restrictive definition, the decision in *Terry v. Ohio*, 392 U.S. 1 (1968) made it clear that every detention of citizens by police officers need not be justified by probable cause. Indeed, the definition of *arrest* can perhaps be understood by examining what encounters do not constitute arrest.

In *Terry*, an experienced police officer observed three unknown men conducting themselves in a manner that suggested the planning of an imminent robbery. With his suspicion aroused, but clearly without probable cause to make an arrest, the officer stopped and patted down, or frisked, the men, finding weapons on two of them. The holders of the two guns were arrested and convicted of possession of a concealed weapon.

The Supreme Court ruled that the officer's actions in stopping the suspects were constitutional. Clearly, the suspects were not free to leave. Equally clear was the absence of probable cause for arrest. Nevertheless, the Court held that the Fourth Amendment permits some stopping that is not an arrest: "It is quite plain that the Fourth Amendment governs 'seizures' of the person which do not eventuate in a trip to the station house and prosecution for crime—'arrests' in traditional terminology. It must be recognized that whenever a police officer accosts an individual and restrains his freedom to walk away, he has 'seized' that person" (*Terry*, 16).

The *Terry* decision was the first time that the Court explicitly recognized an exception to the general rule that seizures of the person under the Fourth Amendment must be based on probable cause. After *Terry* the Court suggested that a brief detention of a suspect to obtain his fingerprints would be permitted without full probable cause to arrest. In *Davis v. Mississippi*, 394 U.S. 721 (1969), the Court stated, "It is arguable . . . that, because of the unique nature of the fingerprinting process, [detentions for the sole purpose of obtaining fingerprints] might, under narrowly defined circumstances, be found to comply with the Fourth Amendment even though there is no probable cause in the traditional sense" (*Davis*, 727).

Since *Davis*, however, the Court has held that the police need full probable cause to arrest an individual before they may compel him to go to the station house for interrogation. In *Dunaway v. New York*, 442 U.S. 200 (1979), the majority distinguished the on-street stop on the ground that a station-house detention is more intrusive and involves few of the special problems of investigation on the street. The Court concluded, "Detention for custodial interrogation—regardless of its label—intrudes so severely on interests protected by the Fourth Amendment as necessarily to trigger the traditional safeguards against illegal arrest" (*Dunaway*, 216).

Terry therefore authorizes officers, on the ground of reasonable suspicion, briefly to stop a suspicious individual in order to determine his identity or to maintain the status quo while obtaining more information. The officer is allowed to conduct a pat-down—"a carefully limited search of the outer clothing in an attempt to discover weapons which might be used to assault him" (*Terry*, 30–31).

In 1981 the Court in *United States v. Cortez*, 449 U.S. 411 (1981) had occasion to interpret its standard of reasonable suspicion. In *Cortez*, customs and immigration authorities had observed footprints in the desert leading to an Arizona back road about twenty miles north of the Mexican border. The officers suspected this to be a pickup point for illegal aliens. Further, the officers reasoned that the pickups were probably made on weekends between midnight and 6:00 A.M. by someone driving a car large enough to carry several persons that would come from, and return to, Phoenix, some miles east. On the first night of their stakeout, they observed several passing cars, one of which was a camper van. The van returned past the monitored point two hours later. When the officers stopped the van, the driver opened the back, revealing the illegally smuggled aliens. The only question addressed by the Supreme Court was the reasonableness of the stopping. Writing for the majority, Chief Justice Warren Burger said the test of reasonable suspicion to ground a permissible stop is to view the "whole picture" as it would be interpreted by trained law enforcement personnel. Applying this test, Burger concluded that the standard of reasonable suspicion had been met to justify the stopping of Cortez's van. As *Cortez* indicates, most reasonable suspicion cases are likely to be very fact-specific and decided on a case-by-case basis with some preference running in favor of accommodating the needs of effective police investigation.

The same concern for effective police investigation underlies the Supreme Court's decision in *Michigan v. Summers*, 452 U.S. 692 (1981), that a warrant to search for contraband founded on probable cause implicitly carries with it the limited authority to detain occupants of the premises while the search is conducted. Here, Detroit police had a warrant to search Summers's house for narcotics. When the police went to the house to execute the warrant, Summers was walking down the steps outside. The police asked Summers to help them enter the house, and detained him while they searched the premises. During the search, the police discovered illegal drugs and arrested Summers. They then searched Summers's person and found heroin in his coat pocket. Summers was charged with possession of the heroin found in his pocket. The Michigan courts had ruled Summers's detention unlawful, but the Supreme Court reversed that decision.

Writing for the majority, Justice John Paul Stevens first concluded that the detention of Summers was a seizure within the meaning of the Fourth Amendment. The Court reaffirmed the general rule that seizures of the person (arrests) must be based on probable cause. Relying on *Terry,* however, Stevens noted, "Some seizures admittedly covered by the Fourth Amendment constitute such limited intrusions on the personal security of those detained and are justified by such substantial law enforcement interests that they may be made on less than probable cause, so long as police have an articulable basis for suspecting criminal activity" (*Summers,* 699). In making the determination that the detention of Summers was permissible under the Fourth Amendment, the Court analyzed both the character of the official intrusion and its justification. Of prime importance in assessing the intrusion was the fact that the police had a valid search warrant for Summers's house. According to the Court, the brief detention was surely less intrusive than the substantial invasion of privacy involved in the search of the house. Further, the Court felt the detention unlikely to be exploited or prolonged by police and of little inconvenience or stigma to the detainee, since he was only being asked to remain in his own home.

In assessing the justification for the detention, the Court found several factors important. First, there is a legitimate law enforcement interest in preventing flight when incriminating evidence is found during the search. Second, there is an interest in minimizing potential harm to police. Third, the orderly completion of the search may be facilitated if the occupants are present. The key to *Summers* seems to be the existence of the warrant and the Court's notion that "a judicial officer has determined that police have probable cause to believe that someone in the home is committing a crime" (*Summers,* 703).

Taken together, *Terry, Davis, Dunaway,* and *Summers* seem to make it clear that police may detain on reasonable suspicion for on-street investigation, perhaps to secure a sample of a suspect's fingerprints but not to compel station-house interrogation. The police may detain occupants in the execution of a valid search warrant, which in and of itself supplies sufficient suspicion to justify the detention. Other detentions must be based on probable cause.

Probable cause

While the language of the Fourth Amendment itself only requires probable cause for the issuance of war-

rants, probable cause has long been interpreted as the standard of reasonableness justifying detention outside the *Terry* context.

The probable cause standard in the arrest context has been defined by the Supreme Court as turning on "whether at that moment [of arrest] the facts and circumstances within [the officers'] knowledge and of which they [have] reasonably trustworthy information [are] sufficient to warrant a prudent man in believing that the [suspect] had committed or was committing an offense" (*Beck v. Ohio,* 379 U.S. 89, 91 (1964)). The *Beck* formulation notes two potential sources of information: "trustworthy" secondary data and personal knowledge.

Probable cause deriving from outside sources. As indicated above, the Supreme Court has clearly established that secondary data—that is, information not within the officer's personal knowledge—can be sufficient grounds for an arrest. Thus, such police practices as relying on reports from other jurisdictions can support valid arrests (*Whiteley v. Warden,* 401 U.S. 560 (1971)). A more complicated credibility issue arises when the information relied on is supplied by an informant.

Most of the Supreme Court's adjudication on the required credibility of informants has arisen in cases involving search warrants rather than arrest warrants. In this particular area, the considerations in both contexts are virtually identical: thus, the so-called *Aguilar-Spinelli* test sets out the standards for use of informants here as well as in the search context.

In *Aguilar v. Texas,* 378 U.S. 108 (1964), the Court first enunciated the two requirements for a valid informant-based warrant: the affidavit must set forth sufficient underlying circumstances to demonstrate to a neutral and detached magistrate how the informant reached his conclusion, and it must establish the reliability or credibility of the informant (*Aguilar,* 121). As the Court explained in *Spinelli v. United States,* 393 U.S. 410 (1969), the absence of a statement detailing the manner in which the informant's data were gathered renders it especially important that "the tip describe the accused's criminal activity in sufficient detail that the magistrate may know that he is relying on something more substantial than a casual rumor . . . or an accusation based merely on an individual's general reputation" (*Spinelli,* 416).

There must also be some basis for crediting the reliability of an informant. Particularly when information comes from a police informant—that is, one who is, or has been, involved with crime and seeks some sort of quid pro quo for his assistance, such as a promise that he will not be prosecuted—the police may not rely on such hearsay information unless the informant has a solid reputation for credibility (*Draper v. United States*, 358 U.S. 307 (1959)). The affidavit may support the reliability and credibility of the informant by setting out the informant's prior usefulness or by asserting that the informant has made a declaration against his "penal interest," such as "The informant said he bought illegal liquor from Harris" (*United States v. Harris*, 403 U.S. 573 (1971)). Where the source of the information is not a police informant but merely an average law-abiding citizen, no special showing of credibility is required.

Probable cause deriving from personal knowledge. Often an arresting officer will be acting on personal knowledge. It is clear that such knowledge must be specific; mere knowledge that a suspect has a prior record, coupled with an unidentified informant's tip alleging current criminal activity, has been held insufficient ground for a lawful arrest (*Beck*).

As in defining arrest, it is sometimes helpful in analyzing what constitutes probable cause to look at what does not. It appears, for example, that the mere failure of a suspect to identify himself is not adequate to supply probable cause (*Brown v. Texas*, 443 U.S. 47 (1979)). Nor may a valid arrest rely on an individual's failure to protest his innocence when he is found with suspects for whom probable cause exists (*United States v. Di Re*, 332 U.S. 581 (1948)).

Similarly, *Di Re* also stands for the proposition that the mere presence of an individual in the company of others who are properly suspected of criminal activity does not constitute probable cause. Subsequent cases, however, have made clear that there are limits to this principle. The difficulties here have largely come with possessory offenses. The Court, in *Johnson v. United States*, 333 U.S. 10 (1948), held that a tip that opium was being smoked, coupled with the smell of opium outside a hotel room, did not give rise to probable cause to arrest the person in the room. While there was probable cause to believe a crime was being committed, there was insufficient information to determine who was committing it. Yet, in *Ker v. California*, 374 U.S. 23 (1963), the Court upheld the arrest of a married couple found in their kitchen with a brick of marijuana, even though the tip leading them there linked only the husband to the contraband. The Court reasoned that the combination of her presence in a small kitchen with obvious contraband, coupled with information that her husband had been using the apartment as a base for his drug activities, gave sufficient ground for a reasonable belief that they were both in possession of marijuana.

The requirement that probable cause be linked specifically to the arrestee is again mentioned by the Court in *Ybarra v. Illinois*, 444 U.S. 85 (1979). There the police procured a valid warrant to search a tavern believed to be the center of drug activity. In executing the warrant, the police searched about a dozen of the tavern's patrons, including Ybarra. While the case thus actually dealt with the legitimacy of the search rather than an arrest, the Court stated that "where the standard is probable cause, a search or *seizure of a person* must be supported by probable cause particularized with respect to that person. This requirement cannot be undercut or avoided by simply pointing to the fact that coincidentally there exists probable cause to search or seize another or to search the premises where the person may happen to be" (*Ybarra*, 91; italics added). *Ybarra* thus reinforces the requirement that probable cause be particularized to the person arrested; mere presence at a place connected with criminal activity or in the company of suspected criminals is inadequate.

The warrant requirement

While exceptions to the warrant requirement in the search context are rather narrowly drawn, warrantless arrests are the rule rather than the exception. The traditional common-law rule was that an arrest warrant was not required when the arresting officer had probable cause to believe that a felony had been, or was being, committed by the arrestee or that a misdemeanor was being committed by the arrestee in the officer's presence.

In *United States v. Watson*, 423 U.S. 411 (1976), the Court held that the police may rely on these broad common-law powers to arrest without a warrant in a public place. Watson argued that his warrantless arrest was unlawful because the police had time to secure a warrant and failed to do so before arresting him in a public restaurant. The Supreme Court held that the police may constitutionally make nonemergency arrests in public places without securing an arrest warrant. While the Court in *Watson* acknowledged its often-stated judicial preference for arrest warrants, it refused "to transform this judicial preference into a constitutional rule when the judgment of the Nation and Congress has for so long been to authorize warrantless public arrests on probable cause" (*Watson*, 423).

The Court has also held that where the police attempt a nonemergency arrest in a public place and the suspect retreats into a private area, the police may pursue the suspect into the private area without a warrant. In *United States v. Santana*, 427 U.S. 38

(1976), the police with cause to arrest Mrs. Santana arrived at her house to find her standing in the front doorway. When she saw the officers approaching, she retreated into the vestibule and closed the door behind her. The officers followed her inside and there arrested her without a warrant. The Supreme Court affirmed the validity of her arrest. When Mrs. Santana stood in the doorway, the Court explained, "she was not in an area where she had any expectation of privacy" (*Santana*, 42) and her arrest at that point without a warrant would have been reasonable under the *Watson* public-arrest analysis. When she retreated into her house, she created exigent circumstances that justified a warrantless entry under a "hot pursuit" rationale. Little more, however, can be derived from *Santana* than a rule affirming that under certain circumstances, police are permitted to make warrantless entries into a private dwelling if the arrest action began in a public place.

The *Watson* court was careful to restrict its holding to arrests in public places. By contrast, in *Payton v. New York*, 445 U.S. 573 (1980), the Court concluded that an arrest warrant is required to make a nonemergency arrest of a suspect in his home. Justice Stevens, writing for a six-justice majority, emphasized that the sanctity of the home was a primary concern of the Fourth Amendment and noted that while the common law had clearly allowed warrantless arrest in public places, there was no clear authority supporting warrantless entries into a home for a routine arrest. Nor was there unanimity among the circuits or the state courts about the constitutionality of such a procedure. Indeed, to refute the state's claim of impracticality, Justice Stevens pointed to those jurisdictions that had already adopted a warrant requirement for nonemergency arrests in a suspect's home.

While *Payton* thus establishes that a warrant is required to enter a suspect's home to arrest him in the absence of exigent circumstances, the opinion makes no effort to define *exigency*. It is quite possible that courts will continue to employ the definition of exigency used to justify the warrantless entry in the prominent case of *Dorman v. United States*, 435 F.2d 385 (D.C. Cir. 1970): (1) the offense is grave; (2) the suspect is reasonably believed to be armed; (3) the police have a high degree of probable cause; (4) there is an especially strong reason to believe that the suspect is on the premises; (5) it is likely that the suspect will escape if not quickly apprehended; and (6) the entry may be made peaceably (*Dorman*, 392–393).

In *Steagald v. United States*, 451 U.S. 204 (1981), the Supreme Court ruled that police who have a warrant for the arrest of a suspect have no authority to search third parties' homes without first obtaining a separate search warrant.

After some warrantless arrests, the suspect may be entitled to a prompt judicial determination of probable cause to detain (*Gerstein v. Pugh*, 420 U.S. 103 (1975)). The warrantless arrest of suspects is justified by exigencies that disappear once the subject is in custody. At that point, the suspect's right to be free from unlawful detention becomes paramount. Because of the high stakes involved in the deprivation of liberty, the detached judgment of a neutral magistrate is essential. This does not, however, mean that a *Gerstein* hearing need be formal. The Court has approved a hearing that is typically informal and brief and that may not require the suspect's presence.

Gerstein does not give the accused a right to this hearing after every arrest. The return of a grand jury indictment satisfies the probable cause determination required to detain a suspect, pending trial. Similarly, a person arrested pursuant to a warrant has received an adequate prior judicial determination of probable cause to detain.

Further, this probable cause determination is required only when a "significant restraint on liberty" is involved. *Gerstein* explains that the restraint must be something more than the condition that the suspect return for trial. On the other hand, the mere fact of pretrial release does not mean that there is no significant restraint on liberty, since many conditions can be attached to liberty. The opinion offers little guidance on the issue other than to say, "We cannot define those [conditions] that would require a prior probable cause determination, but the key factor is a significant restraint on liberty" (*Gerstein*, 125, n. 26).

Arrest procedure

Method of entry: no knock and nondeadly force. At common law, officers were entitled to break into a house to effect an arrest only after announcing their authority and purpose; this notice requirement was later relaxed in exigent circumstances. In the modern era, the standards for arrest entries have generally been set by statute. The federal statute 18 U.S.C. § 3109 (1976) is typical in applying to arrests with or without a warrant and allowing an officer to break open any window or door if, after giving notice of his authority and purposes, he is refused admittance.

The Court has not made clear whether the standard set by Section 3109 represents the minimum standard of conduct or, indeed, whether any of the issues involved in arrest entry procedure rise to constitutional significance at all. The Court has broached the subject in such cases as *Ker.* By upholding the California Supreme Court's affirmance of a silent entry based on the need to prevent the destruction of evidence, the Court necessarily held that no-knock entries in exigent circumstances do not constitute a Fourth Amendment violation.

The Court has made it clear that Section 3109's requirement of announcement of purpose in normal circumstances is to be construed strictly (*Miller v. United States,* 357 U.S. 301 (1958)). Further, the fact that a door is unlocked does not release officers from the announcement and identification requirements (*Sabbath v. United States,* 391 U.S. 585 (1968)).

Deadly force. While the Supreme Court has never had occasion to address the legitimacy in either a statutory or constitutional context of the use of deadly force to arrest, virtually every state has a statute or police regulation limiting the use or threat of violence in the apprehension process. A typical example is set forth in the American Law Institute's Model Penal Code, Section 120.7, which would authorize such force as is reasonably necessary to effect the arrest or prevent the suspect's escape. Under the Code's formulation, deadly force is authorized when the arrest is for a felony, when the use of such force creates no substantial risk to bystanders, and when the officer reasonably believes that the felony involved the use of deadly force or threat thereof or there is a substantial risk that the arrestee would cause other deaths or serious bodily harm if deadly force is not employed.

CHARLES H. WHITEBREAD

See also CRIMINAL PROCEDURE: CONSTITUTIONAL ASPECTS; EXCLUSIONARY RULES; SEARCH AND SEIZURE.

BIBLIOGRAPHY

AMERICAN LAW INSTITUTE. *A Model Code of Pre-arraignment Procedure.* Philadelphia: ALI, 1975.

————. *Model Penal Code and Commentaries: Official Draft and Revised Comments.* Philadelphia: ALI, 1980.

BLACK, DONALD J. "Social Organization of Arrest." *Stanford Law Review* 23 (1971): 1087–1111.

BOGOMOLNY, ROBERT L. "Street Patrol: The Decision to Stop a Citizen." *Criminal Law* 12 (1976): 544–582.

CANTRELL, CHARLES L. "Reasonable Cause in Warrantless Arrests: An Analysis of Some Selected Factors." *American Journal of Criminal Law* 6 (1978): 267–285.

COOK, JOSEPH G. "The Art of Frisking." *Fordham Law Review* 40 (1972): 789–804.

————. "Probable Cause to Arrest." *Vanderbilt Law Review* 24 (1971): 317–339.

COUNTRYMAN, VERN. "Search and Seizure in a Shambles?

Recasting Fourth Amendment Law in the Mold of Justice Douglas." *Iowa Law Review* 64 (1979): 435–460.

LAFAVE, WAYNE R. *Arrest: The Decision to Take a Suspect into Custody.* Report of the American Bar Foundation's Survey of the Administration of Criminal Justice in the United States. American Bar Foundation Administration of Criminal Justice Series. Boston: Little, Brown, 1965.

————. " 'Case-by-case Adjudication' versus 'Standardized Procedures': The Robinson (*U.S. v. Robinson,* 94 Sup. Ct. 467) Dilemma." *Supreme Court Review* (1974): 127–163.

————. "Probable Cause from Informants: The Effects of Murphy's Law on Fourth Amendment Adjudication." *University of Illinois Law Forum* (1977): 1–68.

————. " 'Street Encounters' and the Constitution: *Terry, Sibron, Peters* and Beyond." *Michigan Law Review* 67 (1968): 40–126.

PROJECT ON LAW ENFORCEMENT. *Policy and Rulemaking: Stop and Frisk.* Washington, D.C.: Police Foundation, 1974.

WHITEBREAD, CHARLES H. *Criminal Procedure: An Analysis of Constitutional Cases and Concepts.* Mineola, N.Y.: Foundation Press, 1980.

ARREST RATES

See articles under CRIME STATISTICS.

ARSON

1. BEHAVIORAL AND ECONOMIC ASPECTS   James A. Inciardi
2. LEGAL ASPECTS   Denis Binder

1.
BEHAVIORAL AND ECONOMIC ASPECTS

The earliest scientific writings on arson were produced during the late eighteenth century by a group of German psychiatric theorists, who concluded that the crime was characteristic of physically and mentally retarded females from rural areas who were undergoing the stresses of puberty. These theorists classified arson under the rubric of "instinctive monomania," which according to prevailing legal codes defined arsonists as insane and not accountable for their actions. During the decades that followed, the terms *monomanie incendiaire* and *pyromania* appeared in the literature, which described arson as an impulsive act and a distinct mental disorder. From the 1820s through the 1930s, arson was studied in relation to psychiatry, psychology, and the law. The prevailing issue concerned the medicolegal understanding of the term *irresistible impulse:* was incendiarism generally impulsive behavior resulting from some form of mental aberration, and was a person legally responsible if motivated to commit a crime only by some irresistible impulse?

Later in the twentieth century, those studying arson began to examine other areas and motivations, and it was quickly learned that the phenomenon was not restricted to mentally ill or defective persons but could be found among otherwise "normal" individuals as well, whose actions emerged from a wide range of personal motives.

Offender types. Since the 1950s, studies of arsonists have generally focused on arrested, institutionalized, and paroled individuals. Six separate behavioral categories seem consistently to emerge. The works of the Columbia University psychiatrists Nolan Lewis and Helen Yarnell and of the sociologist James Inciardi have found that the offenders commit arson for purposes of revenge, vandalism, or crime concealment. Some seek to collect insurance; others set fires in search of excitement or are impelled by an irresistible impulse (pyromaniacs).

1. Revenge arsonists, the most prevalent type, are persons who, as the result of arguments or feelings of jealousy or hatred, seek revenge by fire. The victims are typically family members and relatives, employers, or lovers. In retaliation for real or imaginary wrongs, revenge arsonists set ablaze their victims' property or the premises in which they reside. These arsonists appear to be the most potentially dangerous of all the types. They set occupied dwellings afire with little thought as to the safety of those within, thinking only of the revenge they must have on their specific victims. Furthermore, they are often intoxicated at the time of the offense. No elaborate incendiary devices are employed, typically only matches and gasoline. Although their crimes are premeditated, they take few steps to conceal their identities and are thus easily detected by alert investigators.

2. Vandalism arsonists include teenagers who willfully destroy property solely for purposes of fun and sport, although at times revenge motives may be partially present. As opposed to other arsonists, who work alone, vandalism arsonists usually have at least one accomplice. They tend to set their fires at night in churches, school buildings, and vacant structures.

3. Crime-concealment arsonists set fire to premises where they have committed other offenses. The crime is usually burglary but sometimes murder, and the arson is an attempt to cover the traces of the criminal or obliterate the proof that another crime has taken place. Such fires are usually set at night in unoccupied dwellings or places of business.

4. Insurance-claim arsonists include insolvent property owners, small-business operators, and other individuals who, because of extreme financial pressure, incinerate their own property to collect the insurance on what has been destroyed. As a rule they do not set fire to occupied dwellings, and their offenses generally take place in the daytime.

5. Excitement arsonists set buildings ablaze for the thrill connected with fires. Some like setting or watching fires, while others enjoy viewing the operations of the fire fighters and fire equipment. (Occasionally a volunteer fireman is found among them.) Their offenses take place at night, they rarely set ablaze anything but inhabited buildings, and they are usually intoxicated at the time of the offense.

6. Pyromaniacs are pathological firesetters. They seem to have no practical reasons for setting the fires and receive no material profit from them. Their only motive seems to be some sort of sensual satisfaction, and the classic "irresistible impulse" is often a factor. The behavior of pyromaniacs was best described during the early 1950s by Lewis and Yarnell in their well-known study *Pathological Firesetting:*

The reasons for the fires are unknown; the act is so little their own that they feel no responsibility for the crime. . . . These offenders are able to give a classical description of the irresistible impulse. They describe the mounting tension; the restlessness; the urge for motion; the conversion symptoms such as headaches, palpitations, ringing in the ears, and the gradual merging of their identity into a state of unreality; then the fires are set. . . . Once they have started the fires, thrown the neighborhood into confusion, and are assured the fire engines are working, the tension subsides, and they can go home and drop into a peaceful sleep. The majority of pyromaniacs, incidentally, start fires in their own neighborhood. With some the impulse asserts itself episodically with extended periods of "normality" intervening; with others, it controls them night after night; in either instance they almost always have to set a fire when the impulse appears. Such offenders will continue, each fire being a facsimile of the first, until a more powerful force, usually embodied in the "arm of the law," steps in and commands them to stop [p. 87].

These are the mysterious "firebugs" who terrorize neighborhoods by going on solitary firesetting sprees, often nocturnal, during which they touch off trash fires in one building after another without regard to property or life. Many are low-grade mental defectives, persons who derive sexual satisfaction from watching fires, or chronic alcoholics, and they encompass the full range of ages.

Many pyromaniacs bring arrest upon themselves by making certain that the identity of the firebug will be easily found, by being conspicuously present watching all of the fires, by repeatedly contacting police or fire officials as to the whereabouts of fires or with information about the "identity" of local arsonists, or by going directly to the police and asking to be protected from their own "criminal desires." Once they are arrested the irresistible impulse ceases, and for some it never returns. The sprees of pyromaniacs last from a few days to a few months or even years, but discovery and arrest tend to put an end to each particular episode.

These six types are those that are most familiar to criminal justice authorities, but there are other, less common, varieties. Inciardi described a pattern of arson that was characteristic of some mental defectives who had been in institutions almost since birth. They had grievances against the institution and learned that setting fires would result in transfer to another facility. Rather than burning institutional property, they would escape confinement to burn farm buildings in the immediate vicinity; this would ensure a criminal complaint and conviction. The median intelligence quotient of persons in this category is under 70. However, in their new prison setting, they would be found to be in the low normal-intelligence range, ensuring them parole and ultimate "escape" to a more normal noninstitutionalized environment.

New York Fire Marshal Angelo Pisani identified what he called the "welfare fraud firesetter," typically a woman who incinerates her own residence when no one else is present. For such a recipient of public assistance, fire is viewed as a mechanism for obtaining new housing as well as funds to replace clothing, furniture, and other household goods that were allegedly destroyed in the fire.

Lewis and Yarnell have identified a number of distinct arsonist types, including the "would-be hero" arsonists, who are motivated primarily by vanity. These individuals are described as "little" men with grandiose social ambitions whose natural capacities doom them to insignificance. They are basically exhibitionists who set significantly large fires, but instead of playing the role of hero by saving lives or helping to extinguish the flames, they turn in the alarms and identify themselves as those who discovered the fires. Lewis and Yarnell have also identified various categories of vagrant arsonists of all ages. These are basically wanderers who start brushfires or incinerate vacant buildings, railroad property, bridges, and farm property for the vicarious pleasure they derive from such destruction.

Arson for profit. Although the insurance-claim arsonists and the welfare-fraud arsonists represent longstanding types with economic motives for arson, since the early 1970s newer and more pervasive forms of arson for profit have become evident. A common pattern involves the purchase of property in decaying inner-city neighborhoods at a low price, followed by several changes of ownership in order to double or triple its paper value. Insurance is obtained, promises of rehabilitation are made, and fire then breaks out. An alternative pattern is manifested by owner-set fires in large inner-city apartment buildings, the rental profits from which have diminished over the years owing to decaying neighborhoods and economic recession. The annual taxes on such properties often exceed the rental income, reducing the market value to near zero. Incineration then becomes the only economically viable method of disposing of the building. Another type of arsonist, often referred to as a "fire stripper," burns buildings and then scavenges them for plumbing, wiring, and fixtures exposed in the gutted structure.

Little is known about those involved in arson for profit, for few are arrested and convicted. Federal Bureau of Investigation data since 1970 reflect considerable consistency regarding those arrested for arson: the vast majority are males under the age of twenty-five. But studies of imprisoned and paroled arsonists fail to detect many arson entrepreneurs, or "professional torches."

Fire insurance companies, however, have provided at least some insight into the dynamics of arson for profit and "arsonists for hire." So-called fire brokers, to give an example, specialize in locating failing businesses or decaying properties for persons who intend ultimately to "sell" them to an insurance company. Such brokers make arrangements for the legitimate sale of the targeted property, the inflated insurance, the fire, and the insurance settlement. Their fees range from 10 percent to 20 percent of the insurance value. These brokers generally work in conjunction with "arson co-ops," or rings that specialize in sophisticated methods of property incineration.

There is also evidence that organized crime is involved in the arson business, offering property owners package deals that begin with the fire and end with complete arrangements for settlement. Insurance investigators also believe that many fires result from extortion by underworld loan sharks, who arrange for incendiary fires and insurance settlements in order to force their principals to pay outstanding debts.

Arson and collective violence. The great Albany fire of 1793 has been documented as an illustration of how arson, combined with rioting, has been a mechanism for venting the grievances and frustrations of servitude and oppression (Gerlach). Similar phenomena were the ghetto riots of the 1960s, the racial outbreaks in Miami in 1980, and prison uprisings during the 1970s and 1980s. Studies of this behavior have shown that the fires associated with mob violence are not necessarily the work of arsonists but that they simply go hand in hand with the accompanying property destruction and looting. The persons participating in such incidents have rarely been arrested for arson and therefore have remained unstudied, but analyses of the spatial distribution of fires during riots suggest that these fires occur more often in neighborhoods where the median income is at or below the poverty line and where the participants have the least to lose in terms of personal property that could be destroyed by fire.

Statistical and economic issues. Since 1970 arson has been referred to as the fastest-growing major crime, and in 1979 the FBI began including it as an "index crime" in its Uniform Crime Reports. It is estimated that one in four fires is intentionally set and that no less than one thousand deaths and three thousand injuries each year result from arson. The number of arson fires annually is believed to exceed one-half million, with some 30 percent involving buildings and other structures, 10 percent involving vehicles, and the balance directed at outdoor targets ranging from forests to city trash cans. The direct costs of arson in the United States approach $2 billion annually, but estimates suggest that the indirect costs—lost tax revenue and wages, unemployment insurance payments, relocation costs, and other economic ripple effects—are five to ten times higher.

Opinions differ as to the proportional distribution of each type of arsonist and the various patterns of arson. Insurance and arson investigators maintain that arson for profit accounts for the majority of suspicious fires, but this has not been confirmed in any data source. By contrast, studies by the Law Enforcement Assistance Administration (U.S. Department of Justice) indicate that vandalism accounts for some 42 percent of all incendiary fires, followed by arson for revenge at 23 percent, pyromania at 14 percent, arson for profit at 14 percent, and other motives at 7 percent.

The amount of information dealing with arson and arsonists is severely limited, owing to numerous difficulties in collecting comprehensive and reliable data. First, arson does not always appear to be a crime at the time of occurrence. Many fires are classified as suspicious, but subsequent investigations cannot always document whether a crime did indeed occur. Second, most police agencies are not adequately trained and equipped in the areas of fire science and investigation. Third, the legislative authority to investigate suspicious fires is typically in the hands of state and local fire marshals or municipal fire service companies, with the communication of arson data to law enforcement agencies only on a voluntary basis. Fourth, the majority of fire fighters in the United States serve as unpaid volunteers and this results in substandard investigation into the causes of fires. Fifth, rates and trends in arson are generally drawn from arrest statistics, and the unreliability of such data as measures of the incidence and prevalence of crime has been well documented. Sixth, and most important, arson is a low-risk crime, thus yielding few samples of offenders for scientific study. The offense is difficult to prove unless there is a confession or an unimpeachable witness—both unlikely, given the nature of the crime and the criminal. Furthermore, many prosecutors avoid filing formal charges unless the evidence is strong, because the conviction rates for arson are low; and most insurance companies are reluctant to question claims, because they fear civil suits for punitive damages if they turn down a legitimate claim.

JAMES A. INCIARDI

See also ARSON: LEGAL ASPECTS; RIOTS: BEHAVIORAL ASPECTS.

BIBLIOGRAPHY

Federal Bureau of Investigation. *Crime in the United States, 1980.* Uniform Crime Reports for the United States. Washington, D.C.: U.S. Department of Justice, FBI, 1981.

GERLACH, DON R. "Black Arson in Albany, New York, November 1973." *Journal of Black Studies* 7 (1977): 301–311.

HURLEY, W., and MONAHAN, T. M. "Arson: The Criminal and the Crime." *British Journal of Criminology* 9 (1969): 4–21.

INCIARDI, JAMES A. "The Adult Firesetter: A Typology." *Criminology* 8 (1970): 145–155.

LEWIS, NOLAN D. C., and YARNELL, HELEN. *Pathological Firesetting (Pyromania).* New York: Nervous and Mental Disease Monographs, 1951.

PISANI, ANGELO L. "Adult Firesetting Behavior: A Typology." Master's thesis, City University of New York, John Jay College of Criminal Justice, 1981.

U.S. Congress, Senate, Committee on Governmental Affairs. *Arson-for-Hire: Hearings before the Permanent Subcommittee on Investigations of the Committee on Governmental Affairs.* Washington, D.C.: Government Printing Office, 1978.

U.S. Department of Justice, Law Enforcement Assistance Administration, National Institute of Justice. *Arson and Arson Investigation: Survey and Assessment.* Prepared by John F. Boudreau et al. Washington, D.C.: The Institute, 1977.

2.
LEGAL ASPECTS

Common-law arson. By the mid-eighteenth century, common-law arson was well established as the malicious and willful burning of the house of another by day or by night (Coke, p. 66). The common law viewed arson, like burglary, as a crime against the security of habitation rather than a crime against property. A *house* was defined for both crimes as the dwelling house of the occupant, in addition to the buildings located within the curtilage. *Curtilage* meant the yard or space of ground near the dwelling house, contained in the same enclosure and used in connection with it by the household, and the parcel of buildings or structures contained therein. Barns were generally included in the curtilage. It was quite foreseeable that a fire in any building within the curtilage could spread to the dwelling and endanger the occupants. Thus, a sufficient threat to quiet possession occurred even if the actual dwelling place escaped harm.

Since arson protected habitation, the burning of an unoccupied house did not constitute arson: there could be no arson if the fire occurred before the first resident moved in, after the dwelling was vacated, or in a period between residents. On the other hand, a dwelling retained its occupied status during the temporary absence of the occupant; it was unnecessary that he be present in the dwelling at the time of the burning.

The use of the building determined its status. A permanency of dwelling was necessary. Burning a place where transients stayed, such as a hotel, did not constitute arson under the common law. Neither did the burning of institutions, such as jails or hospitals, unless someone also lived in the building as a permanent resident.

Since arson was viewed as a crime against the security of habitation, the building burned had to be that of another. It was not arson to burn the house one occupied, whether or not the occupant owned it, even if the burning threatened the lives of others in the house. The burning of one's own dwelling to collect insurance did not constitute common-law arson. It was generally assumed in early England that one had the legal right to destroy his own property in any manner he chose.

Arson was legally regarded as a heinous and aggravated offense both because it threatened human life and the security of habitation and because it evidenced a moral recklessness and depravity in the perpetrator. Arson was thus a capital offense until more lenient statutes were enacted in the nineteenth century.

Although it was not common-law arson to burn one's own house, it was a common-law misdemeanor ("houseburning") if the burning was intentional and the house was situated in a city or town, or, if beyond those limits, was still so near other dwellings as to create danger to them. Any malicious destruction of, or damage to, the property of another not amounting to common-law arson constituted a common-law misdemeanor known as malicious mischief.

The common law required an actual burning or ignition of some part of the building, at least to the extent of charring the wood. A mere smoking, scorching, or discoloration of the wood was insufficient. The general rule was that a slight charring, no matter how small, was sufficient.

Since the common law required that the fire damage the structure, setting fire to personal property within the building would not constitute arson unless the fire spread to the building itself. An attempted burning did not constitute arson. Similarly, it was no crime under the common law to prepare a building for a fire.

Corpus delicti. To have established the corpus delicti of arson at common law, the proof must have shown that there had been a burning of a structure or property protected by law, and that the fire had resulted from the criminal act of some person. It also had to be shown that the defendant was the criminal agency. The common law presumed that all fires resulted from accident, negligence, or natural causes. Therefore, direct or circumstantial evidence that the fire was of incendiary origin and that the defendant was the guilty party was required.

The requisite mens rea consisted of a willful and malicious intent to burn. The word *willful* meant the arsonist must have started the fire intentionally. The requisite intent could be viewed as the general, unlawful purpose to damage or destroy certain property. While the intent could be inferred from the act, more than negligence had to be shown. In some cases negligent burnings could be punished as a lesser offense, such as negligently burning prairie land or timberland.

Malice was an essential element of common-law arson, and had to be established independently of any showing of willfulness. Malice was generally construed as a desire to injure the victim of the unlawful act, and was readily inferred from the nature of the act or the circumstances surrounding it, so that liability generally resulted if the burning were intentional. Motive was not an element of arson, although motive was often used to infer intent, such as the overinsuring of property. The existence of a motive may have helped establish the corpus delicti of arson by showing both that the fire was intentional in origin and that the defendant was culpable. Conversely, the absence of a motive may have made proof of the essential elements less persuasive.

Direct evidence of arson is frequently unavailable since the crime is ordinarily committed under the cover of darkness, clandestinely, and in a manner intended to divert suspicion. Thus, circumstantial evidence, and reasonable inferences based thereon, were generally used to establish the crime and the culprit.

Statutory arson. Owing to the narrow confines of arson under the common law, statutes were enacted in every state beginning in the early 1800s (as, for example, in the *Acts Passed at the First Session of the Legislative Council of the Territory of Orleans . . . ,* p. 416), greatly expanding the crime to include the criminal burning of almost every type of property. The statutory scheme remained far from uniform through the early 1900s, but statutes generally protected property as well as habitation. The burning of one's dwelling constituted arson, whether or not the intent was to collect insurance. A few of the earliest statutes imposed a harsher penalty if the burning occurred at night. Modern statutes take note of the time of the arson only in determining the grade or degree of the crime. Statutory arson also included situations in which chattels (personal effects) were burned in a building without spreading to the structure. A few statutes followed the common-law distinctions between dwelling houses and other buildings. Some distinguished between occupancy and vacancy.

Statutes commonly divide arson into various degrees. First-degree arson is directed at the endangering of life rather than of property, whereas the lesser degrees relate to the value of the damaged property, the motive, or the type of property burned. The penalties differ according to the degree of arson.

A typical Alabama statute provided that arson of the first degree consisted of the willful burning of a dwelling or structure in which a person was present at the time, or of any inhabited dwelling. Arson of the second degree included the willful burning of a public building, manufacturing establishment, storage place, vessel, or uninhabited dwelling. Third-degree arson consisted of the willful burning of a house or vessel, bridge gate, or causeway (Code of Ala., §§ 3289, 3290, 3293 (1923)). Many other statutes provide for aggravated arson, which covers that form of arson which does or could result in injury to persons, and simple arson, which is all other arson.

Statutes generally require the act to be "willful" or "malicious," or some combination of these terms. Regardless of the word or phrase used, the interpretations have generally been in accordance with the common law.

Under the common law, damage caused by an explosive could not be considered arson since there was no burning. Many states have solved this problem by statutorily defining arson to include injury to property resulting from the use of an explosive, whether or not a burning actually occurs. Most modern statutes include "explosive" in the means of destruction or damage performed by arsonists (N.Y. Penal Law (McKinney) § 150.10 (1975 & 1981–1982 Supp.)).

Model arson statutes. The Model Arson Law, proposed in the early 1920s by the National Board of Fire Underwriters, enlarges criminal liability for preliminary behavior by punishing not only what would be attempted arson at common law, but also the preparation of a building for burning. In addition, a separate category is established for the intentional burning of any property insured against loss or damage by fire with the purpose of injuring or defrauding the insurer. This provision applies to the accused's own property. It should be noted that while arson requires only a general intent, arson to defraud requires a showing that the burning was specifically for the purpose of collecting insurance. Accessories to arson are liable as principals under the Model Arson Law.

The American Law Institute's Model Penal Code provisions on arson have not been widely followed (§ 220.1). Under these proposals arson is defined as the destruction of a "building or occupied structure" or the damaging of any property with intent to collect insurance. The Code's provisions differ from those of the above-mentioned Model Arson Law in several ways. First, they include explosions as a category of arson. Second, they insert in the definition of intent a requirement that the act be done "with the purpose of destroying property." Third, they exclude the actor's own building or structure, unless it was insured. Finally, they unequivocally designate as arson the burning of any property, chattels as well as buildings, with the purpose of collecting insurance.

In addition to the crime so defined, the Code provides lesser felony penalties for reckless burnings or explosions that threaten bodily injury or damage to buildings or occupied structures of another. Other types of property damage by fire are treated as misdemeanors.

In 1978 several insurance associations prepared a model arson penal law, which is similar in several respects to the Model Penal Code. In the proposal a first-degree felony offense of "aggravated arson" encompasses cases of death or bodily injury resulting from arson. The second- and third-degree offenses resemble the Model Penal Code provisions, and include unoccupied structures. Specific penalties are provided for the damage of any property when the purpose is to defraud the insurer.

The history of arson law in the Anglo-American legal systems has been one of general expansion in the reach of the criminal law. Modern urban conditions and political unrest ensure that the evolution of the law will continue during the years ahead. In the meantime, considerable variations in particular provisions of the law of arson may be expected to persist among the various American jurisdictions.

DENIS BINDER

See also ARSON: BEHAVIORAL AND ECONOMIC ASPECTS; MALICIOUS MISCHIEF.

BIBLIOGRAPHY

Acts Passed at the First Session of the Legislative Council of the Territory of Orleans Begun and Held at the Principal in the City of New-Orleans on Monday the Third Day of December in the Year of Our Lord One Thousand, Eight Hundred and Four and of the Independence of the United States the Twenty-ninth. Published by Authority New-Orleans. Printed by James M. Bradford, Printer to the Territory, 1805.

AMERICAN LAW INSTITUTE. *Model Penal Code: Tentative Draft No. 11.* Philadelphia: ALI, 1960.

ARSON PROJECT. "Arson Fraud: Criminal Prosecution and Insurance Law." *Fordham Urban Law Journal* 7 (1978–1979): 541–615.

BRAUN, WILLIAM C. "Legal Aspects of Arson." *Journal of Criminal Law, Criminology, and Police Science* 43 (1952): 53–62.

COHN, HERMAN H. "Convicting the Arsonist." *Journal of Criminal Law, Criminology, and Police Science* 38 (1947): 286–303.

COKE, EDWARD. *The Third Part of the Institutes of the Laws of England: Concerning High Treason, and Other Pleas of the Crown, and Criminal Causes.* 2d ed. London: W. Lee & D. Pakeman, 1648.

CURTIS, ARTHUR F. *A Treatise on the Law of Arson, Covering the Decisions of All American States and Territories, and Including Those of England and the British Colonies.* Buffalo, N.Y.: Dennis, 1936.

HOPPER, WILLIAM H. "Arson's Corpus Delicti." *Journal of Criminal Law, Criminology, and Police Science* 47 (1956): 118–130.

———. "Circumstantial Aspects of Arson." *Journal of Criminal Law, Criminology, and Police Science* 46 (1955): 129–134.

NOTE. "Arson—Statutory Change of Common Law Requisites." *Michigan Law Review* 25 (1927): 450–453.

NOTE. "Proof of the Corpus Delicti in Arson Cases." *Journal of Criminal Law, Criminology, and Police Science* 45 (1954): 185–191.

PERKINS, ROLLIN M. *Criminal Law.* 2d ed. Mineola, N.Y.: Foundation Press, 1969.

SADLER, PAUL, JR. "The Crime of Arson." *Journal of Criminal Law, Criminology, and Police Science* 41 (1950): 290–305.

ASSASSINATION

In the eleventh century the Shiite Ismaili convert Hasan ibn-al-Sabbah (c. 1050–1124), "the Old Man of the Mountain," appeared in Islamic Persia and for nearly fifty years led the struggle against both Sunni orthodoxy and Turkish rule. Hasan shrewdly combined emotional appeals to the downtrodden, intellectual appeals to the more enlightened, and insistence upon total obedience to himself as the Asas, or Imam, the "true teacher." Persecuted and hunted, he established the mountain fortress of Alamut, which "became the greatest training center of fanatical politico-religious assassins that the world has known" (Franzius, p. 45). Facing the vastly superior forces of his enemies, Hasan avoided open war as much as possible, relying instead upon his *fidais* ("devoted ones"). These young men he sent singly or in small bands to kill military, political, and religious leaders aligned against him. Such was the suicidal fanaticism of Hasan's skilled killers that it was widely believed they must be stimulated by hashish. They were called "hashish-eaters," apparently shortened in Arabic usage to *Assassins*, which may also connote *Asasi* ("followers of the Asas") and perhaps in addition, "followers of Hasan" (Franzius, pp. 47–48).

Defining assassination

In time, *assassin* came generally to mean one who killed an unsuspecting victim without warning, but the original sense of political purpose was never quite lost, and in the twentieth century has become increasingly strong. It is now redundant to speak of "political" assassination. To assassinate is to kill for a political reason—to secure or resist authority, to eliminate a rival for power, to prevent or avenge a political defeat, or to express a political grievance.

Political motivation distinguishes assassination

from other deadly interpersonal violence. Unfortunately for analytic rigor, motivation is extremely difficult to establish. Indeed, after a useful discussion of the problems (pp. 16–23), Murray Havens, Carl Leiden, and Karl Schmitt remarked at the end of their research that "perhaps attempts to determine motives are irrelevant, for once the act has been committed the public manufactures its own motive in harmony with its own political predilections" (p. 150). Political motives, like others, are often hidden or unclear, and cannot merely be inferred from the political significance or prominence of a target (Kirkham, Levy, and Crotty, pp. 267–268). Heads of state may be the victims of nonpolitical violence; ordinary citizens may die as political surrogates or pawns. Nonetheless, it has been generally assumed that only attacks upon important officials and other politically influential persons are politically inspired, and that common folk are too insignificant to draw the assassin's fire. Both assumptions are questionable.

The meaning of *political* blurs as power concerns and struggles permeate society and as the interdependence and interpenetration of different loci and forms of authority increase. Any area of social life, from religion and education to industry and entertainment, can be politicized, serving as a base, vehicle, or object of power struggles. Whoever emerges as a leading figure may have, or be seen as having, political significance as actor or symbol, in the sense once associated almost exclusively with the leaders of governments and parties. Charismatic figures are especially likely to attract the attention of an established or aspiring power-wielder who sees the potential value and danger of anyone who sways others.

The modern theory of assassination and terrorism, as developed particularly by the Russian nihilists of the 1860s and 1870s, initially designated the secret police and certain other state officials as appropriate targets. Political rivals soon were included, as well as influential "obstacles" in various social institutions. Since the nineteenth century, the principle of specifying individuals as targets has been extended to groups and categories of people viewed as class, national, ethnic, or racial threats. The ultimate extension of the principle is to specify (as have such international terrorists as the Japanese Red Army and the Black September faction of the Palestine Liberation Organization) that death is appropriate for all who live as "part of the problem"—that is, who try to carry on a normal life instead of joining in the war to destroy the existing unjust world system. In such terms, every killing is an assassination, serving the political aim of demonstrating that all are guilty until all injustice

is eliminated from the world. One major consequence is that the meaning of *assassination* shifts not only to include common as well as prominent people, but also to include the killing of many as well as of one or a few. Assassination finally becomes synonymous with terror—random violence whose victims are selected by chance instead of design, irrespective of the varying innocence and political power of individuals.

The logic of terrorist theory thus leads to a concept of assassination in which the element of specification is ultimately dissolved. Yet even terrorists find it necessary to make distinctions and set priorities. Dangerous adversaries must be distinguished from innocent bystanders. Opportunities must be weighed with regard to potential risks and benefits. Resources have to be matched to opportunities. Targets have to be selected with due regard for their tactical importance. This suggests that assassination is characterized by selection rather than by specification. The point is that victims are selected because of the anticipated impact of the timing, place, or manner of their death. Their attributes as individuals may or may not be relevant concerns and, in any case, will be secondary ones. Symbols, positions, and relationships—not people—are the targets of assassination.

Thus, the definition of *assassination* is as follows: a politically motivated killing in which victims are selected because of the expected political impact of their dying. Their individuality is irrelevant as such, although particular attributes may be assessed as enhancing or reducing their significance as potential victims. Significance is not only or necessarily a function of power or prominence. People may be more shocked by the bombing of school buses and churches than of police cruisers and government buildings. Political opponents may be affected more by the loss of their children than of their leaders. Of course, the political repercussions of assassination will not necessarily be what the assassin expects—the weakening or elimination of opposition. In any case, it is the political purpose of a killing, not its victim or its aftermath, that makes it an assassination.

Assassination and the law

The legal status of assassination is ambiguous in both domestic and international law. Killing or endangering the sovereign, members of his family, or his chief representatives has always been abhorrent in English common law, and was formally defined as treason in the fourteenth century ("Treason Act," 25 Edw. 3, stat. 5, c. 2 (1351) (England)). The concept of treason has since been extended beyond personal fealty to include violence against the constitutional system by anyone having a duty of allegiance. The law of treason has, however, rarely been invoked (Law Commission). Indeed, the English legal system has been characterized by its nonrecognition of political offenses as such. Political motivation has been accorded scant consideration as even a mitigating factor, in contrast to the tradition established in continental legal systems. There is no recognized political defense in English law. Thus, assassination as a form of treason is extremely circumscribed, and most assassinations are treated as common-law crimes without political import.

Canada, the United States, and some other nations formerly British-ruled follow the English model on this question. Under Canadian law it is high treason to injure or restrain the reigning monarch, to war against Canada, or to aid enemy forces. It is treason to use force or violence to overthrow the federal government or a provincial government, and it is an indictable offense to use violence to intimidate members of the federal or provincial parliaments. The minimum penalty for high treason and for using violence to overthrow government is life imprisonment without parole eligibility for twenty-five years. Alternatively, assassination may be dealt with as first-degree murder, which would include the murder of a police or prison employee acting in the course of his duties, whether or not the murder was planned and deliberate (Can. Crim. Code pt. II, ss. 46–47, 49, 51; pt. VI, ss. 213, 214; pt. XX, s. 669 (1982)).

In the United States, Congress reacted in 1965 to President John F. Kennedy's assassination by making it a federal offense punishable by death or life imprisonment to assassinate the President, President-elect, Vice-President, Vice-President-elect, or anyone legally acting as President (18 U.S.C. § 1751 (1976)). Subsequently, it was also made a federal offense to assassinate an incumbent or elected member of Congress. To war against the United States or to assist its enemies constitutes treason; and it is an offense to advocate the forcible or violent overthrow of the federal or any state government, or the assassination of any officer of such governments (18 U.S.C. §§ 2381, 2385 (1976)). Otherwise, assassination is a common crime to be dealt with by the state or other government in whose jurisdiction it occurs.

Until the nineteenth century the European monarchs generally agreed that regicide is intolerable, and considered the offender against government the most despicable of criminals. In 1833, Belgium initiated the doctrine that political offenders were not to be extradited. Most other nations followed suit, but the ensuing treaties typically required extradition of assassins and other violent offenders as common criminals unless their acts occurred in the course of a political disturbance or were "proportionate"—that is, not excessive in view of the aims and circumstances of the act (Kittrie, pp. 358–360). Beginning with the reaction against late-nineteenth-century anarchist violence, the political defense of assassination and other political violence has been increasingly unlikely to prevent extradition. In particular, war crimes and crimes against humanity are widely considered to be extraditable offenses. However, there have been many exceptional cases, and the international community remains sharply divided on how to define and deal with terrorist killings and other politically motivated violence (Green).

The legal situation is, then, that assassination may be defined domestically as treason, an "allied offense," or a common crime. Under international law, it may be defined as a nonextraditable political offense (albeit "complex" rather than "pure"), as an extraditable common crime, or as a crime against humanity or against the laws of war. In both domestic and international law, the legal status of any particular assassination depends upon the political concerns and relative power of the various authorities and of any private parties involved or interested in its occurrence.

Causes and patterns

How one approaches the problem of explaining assassination depends upon one's assumptions about political violence. If violence for political reasons is considered to be unusual and unjustifiable, the causes of assassination are expected to lie in the psychopathology of individual killers. If political violence is thought to be aberrant but sometimes justifiable, or at least understandable, causes are sought in threatening or oppressive social conditions, which in principle can be changed so as to eliminate the violence. If violence is seen as an intrinsic dimension and a common instrument of politics, causes are to be found in the varying fortunes and tactics of social groups attempting to defend or increase their life chances. A developed scientific theory of assassination presumably would avoid moral assumptions about political violence and would encompass all three causal sources, treating them as sets of variables whose interrelationships result in an increasing or decreasing probability of assassination attempts. No such theory yet exists. As a first step, the following hypotheses are to be considered: (1) The more threatening or oppressive social conditions are for a particular group, the more likely the group is to resort to assassination and other forms of violence. (2) Individuals with certain psychopathologic characteristics are more likely to be selected for the actual work of killing; alternatively, those selected develop psychopathologic characteristics because of the guilt, isolation, fear, suffering, or other experiences associated with their "dirty work."

Oppression, threat, and assassination. Research on the social causes of assassination indicates that oppression is probably less important than threat in affecting the probability of assassination. Feliks Gross has defined *oppression* as "acts of physical brutality, including killing and limitation of freedom, humiliation of persons, economic exploitation, deprivation of elementary economic opportunities, confiscation of property" (p. 86). His examination of eastern European and Russian history led to him hypothesize that even foreign domination causes assassination only if it is perceived as oppression, if a political party exists with "an ideology and tactics of direct action," and if there are "activitist personality types" ready to use violence (p. 89). Gross concludes that socioeconomic conditions have had little or no causal significance with regard to the use or increase of assassination. Ethnic and nationalist conflicts appear to be far more important factors in encouraging assassination and other political violence. With respect to the class factor, political violence tends to be the work of higher-class visionaries and activists, in contrast to the lower-class predatory types who engaged in "common criminal violence" (p. 93).

The most systematic available evidence concerning the linkage between socioeconomic conditions and assassination is found in a report compiled for the United States National Commission on the Causes and Prevention of Violence (Kirkham et al.); the report includes an abbreviated earlier draft of the Gross study. This cross-national comparative study indicates that assassination is associated with political instability, which in turn reflects such factors as a low level of socioeconomic development, a high level of relative deprivation, and a high rate of socioeconomic change. Other contributing factors are a government neither very coercive nor very permissive, and high levels of externalized aggression and hostility toward foreigners, among minority and majority groups, and among individuals, as indicated by high homicide and low suicide rates (pp. 113–169). The United States is exceptional in combining an advanced level of socioeconomic development with the other features. However, as the report noted, blacks and other major sectors of the American population do generally live under

conditions internally approximating those found to be associated with relatively high levels of political violence in the cross-national analysis (p. 167). Both the cross-national and the case analyses in the Kirkham report suggest that socioeconomic conditions must interact with political and cultural factors to become significant in causing assassination and other political violence.

It appears that oppression becomes causally relevant only when it is interpreted as threat, whereas perceived threat in itself is sufficient to encourage political violence. One major implication of this general proposition is that economic conditions must become political factors to affect the level of political violence. A further implication is that political conditions must be interpreted as threatening in order to be causally significant. The process of interpretation is, then, the key to creating situations in which the probability of assassination and other political violence is significantly increased.

Threats may be real whether or not perceived. For a group to have fewer resources while another has more implies a present or potential threat to the life chances of the disadvantaged. The greater the difference, the greater the likelihood that the more advantaged group is living in part at the expense of the less advantaged (assuming they are bound together economically and politically in a real, if not necessarily formal, sense). Certainly, the less advantaged live more precariously and are more vulnerable to life's miseries. For them, it is not difficult to see or believe that inequality is threatening. At the same time, the more advantaged will readily see or believe that underclass discontent or gains are threatening. At any given moment, the available resources are finite; the pie cannot be shared without someone having less if another is to have more. Both sides are likely to feel threatened by change—particularly by high rates of socioeconomic change—because it is difficult to predict just who will win and who will lose in the course of events.

The perceived threat posed by existing or changing economic or political conditions does not of itself necessarily produce violence. What is required is that an enemy be identified and that potential assailants be mobilized. Historically, this last step has been accomplished by a campaign of vilification of visible members of a targeted group (government, party, class, religion, nationality, race, or ethnic category), as well as of the group as a whole (Gross, pp. 90–91; Kirkham et al., pp. 225–228). Responsibility for the threatening economic or political conditions is placed squarely upon the targeted individuals and groups, who are depicted as entirely reprehensible, irredeemably monstrous, and perhaps even subhuman.

Unchecked, vilification produces a climate of extremism because the targets of the campaign tend to respond in kind. In such a climate, some individuals experienced in using violence may be deliberately recruited as assassins (hired killers). Others (political actors) may progress in stages of activism from minimal political involvement to the conclusion that assassination is tactically essential. Still others (expressive reactors) may simply be caught up in the excitement of political conflict, finding in the rhetoric of vilification a means and focus for expressing their discontent, perhaps in assassination. Although individual cases exhibit some overlap and movement among them, these types—hired killers, political actors, and expressive reactors—must be analytically distinguished if the psychology of assassins is to be explored fruitfully.

The psychology of assassins. Psychological profiles of assassins are derived from limited and unrepresentative samples biased in several ways. First, assassins who *attack* governmental and other institutional figures have been studied, rather than assassins acting on behalf of such figures. Second, assassins of chief executives and other prominent individuals have been studied, to the virtual exclusion of those who kill minor officials and ordinary people. Third, only assassins who have been caught have been studied, so that almost nothing is known about those who are deterred or who escape detection and capture. Fourth, analysis has focused upon expressive reactors, with little or no attention having been given to hired killers and political actors. Fifth, the presumption of psychopathology has been strong in both the selection of subjects for study, usually by psychiatrists, and in the analysts' common tendency to see political (and other) violence as intrinsically abnormal and irrational. Finally, the possibility of organized, tactical assassination has tended to be discounted in favor of an image of the assassin as typically a loner without coherent political motivation and unable to act in concert with others to further political aims.

Research on assassins and assailants of American presidents has found nearly all (excepting the Puerto Rican nationalists who attacked Blair House during President Harry Truman's temporary residency there) to be "mentally disturbed persons who did not kill to advance any rational political plan" (Kirkham et al., p. 62). They lacked a normal childhood relationship with a parent, had difficulty in making friends (especially with women), tended to identify with a cause or ideology, and had difficulty in working cooperatively with others.

Albert Ellis and John Gullo found assassins other than "paid gunmen" and political agents to be characterized by sexual impotence, self-hatred, lack of frustration tolerance, magical thinking, extreme moralism and hostility, and grandiosity in self-claims, ambitions, and views about the significance of their deeds. Assassins were found to have long histories of psychological disturbance, to have experienced a life crisis shortly before the assassination, and to kill without aim or sense "as far as their political beliefs and aspirations are concerned" (pp. 190–250).

Irving Harris has suggested that to understand assassins one must look beyond psychopathology to the more normal psychology of the "rebellious-rivalrous personality," a type who "finds authority and restrictions irksome and strives for a redistribution of hierarchical status by competing with the successful limelighted rival" (pp. 199–200). Such persons feel that they should have greater social visibility and recognition and that there is an intolerable discrepancy between their actual status and the status they deserve. "Constructive and integrative" variants attempt to resolve their problems by becoming social critics of "unwarranted and unfair bigness" or writers of fiction expressing "residual rancor." The "destructive, poorly integrated" variants are marked by "Factor X"—"the unrealistic self-inflation which, when added to the rebellious-rivalrous personality, predisposes the person to assassination" (p. 214). Harris notes that the profile may also fit looters and vandals, and points to the lack of research conducted on female assassins.

From the sparse evidence available, it may be concluded that the expressive-reactor assassin is a markedly unstable person, unloved and unloving, who is predisposed to seek in assassination a way to satisfy his craving for recognition and significance. Such assassins typically act alone, but would seem to be likely candidates for use as pawns and scapegoats. In historical and comparative perspective, only a minority of assassins can be described as expressive reactors. Their salience in the literature is disproportionate and misleading, having more to do with the manner of their selection for study than with political realities.

The hypothesis of prior psychopathology is supported for expressive reactors, but seems unlikely to be verified for hired killers or political actors. Subsequent psychopathology might occur in expressive reactors denied publicity, and perhaps in hired killers who lack or lose supportive relationships. Political actors, however, are unlikely to exhibit either prior or subsequent psychopathology, on the evidence of many who have been or who become productive citizens, reliable bureaucrats, and even prime ministers.

The impact of assassination

Established political orders and movements are rarely affected in any clearly significant way by assassination. Leaders are replaced and rivals displaced, but their successors usually lack the inclination or resources to accomplish more than incremental changes in the structures and programs that they inherit. Although a sometimes efficient and even institutionalized way of transferring power, assassination is more likely to be politically significant as a symptom than as an instrument. Nonetheless, the lack of immediate and dramatic effects does not negate the possibility of long-term or less-obvious consequences. Nor can evidence indicating the generally low impact of isolated assassinations, particularly by expressive reactors, be used to discount the possibility that tactical assassinations may have considerable impact.

Havens, Leiden, and Schmitt have provided a rough scale of possible effects from the least to the most consequential: no discernible changes, personnel changes, policy changes, systemic changes, social revolution, disappearance of the political system (pp. 37–39). Their comparative analysis of ten cases indicates that the assassination of major political leaders is seldom followed by more than personnel or trivial policy changes, and demonstrates that it is extremely difficult to establish the causal significance of assassination in relation to whatever changes do subsequently occur.

The impact of assassination varies according to the political milieu. Assassination undermines democratic institutions insofar as it deters able persons from seeking positions of leadership, reduces the public's sense of security, or leads to political repression and vigilantism. In more totalitarian systems it encourages opportunism and autocracy, inhibits creative effort and cooperation, and therefore probably reduces the capacity for collective adaptation to environmental and internal changes. Where economic and political instability are endemic, as in much of the Third World, assassination makes it even less likely that able leaders will emerge or have time enough to do whatever they might to improve the situation. In short, where political order is lacking, assassination helps to prevent its achievement; where it is established, assassination contributes to its erosion or ossification.

Assassination is most likely to be an effective tactic when the goal is a limited one (such as retaliation, discipline, or elimination of a rival or an obstacle) and when it has organizational support. It is least likely to occur or affect political life when most people are content and when peaceful mechanisms for transferring power have been established. This generalization is qualified by the internationalization of political conflict and by the perpetuation of internecine struggles among emigrants and travelers abroad. The consequence is likely to be a higher incidence of assassinations—many of them "imported"—than would otherwise be expected in the Western democracies. Like other forms of violence, assassination is part of the cost of having a relatively open and permissive society.

AUSTIN T. TURK

See also both articles under HOMICIDE; TERRORISM.

BIBLIOGRAPHY

BELL, J. BOWYER. *Assassin!* New York: St. Martin's Press, 1979.

BORNSTEIN, JOSEPH. *The Politics of Murder.* New York: William Sloane Associates, 1950.

CAMELLION, RICHARD. *Assassination: Theory and Practice.* Boulder, Colo.: Paladin Press, 1977.

ELLIS, ALBERT, and GULLO, JOHN M. *Murder and Assassination.* New York: Lyle Stuart, 1971.

FRANZIUS, ENNO. *History of the Order of Assassins.* New York: Funk & Wagnalls, 1969.

GREEN, L. C. "Terrorism and the Courts." *Manitoba Law Journal* 11, no. 4 (1981): 333–358.

GROSS, FELIKS. *Violence in Politics: Terror and Political Assassination in Eastern Europe and Russia.* The Hague: Mouton, 1972.

HARRIS, IRVING D. "Assassins." *Violence: Perspectives on Murder and Aggression.* Edited by Irwin L. Kutash, Samuel B. Kutash, Louis B. Schlesinger, and associates. Foreword by Alexander Wolf. San Francisco: Jossey-Bass, 1978, pp. 198–218.

HAVENS, MURRAY CLARK; LEIDEN, CARL; and SCHMITT, KARL M. *The Politics of Assassination.* Englewood Cliffs, N.J.: Prentice-Hall, 1970.

HYAMS, EDWARD. *Killing No Murder: A Study of Assassination as a Political Means.* London: Thomas Nelson, 1969.

INGRAHAM, BARTON L. *Political Crime in Europe: A Comparative Study of France, Germany, and England.* Berkeley: University of California Press, 1979.

KIRKHAM, JAMES F.; LEVY, SHELDON G.; and CROTTY, WILLIAM J. *Assassination and Political Violence: A Report to the National Commission on the Causes and Prevention of Violence.* Reprint, with an introduction by Harrison E. Salisbury. New York: Bantam Books, 1970.

KITTRIE, NICHOLAS N. "A New Look at Political Offenses and Terrorism." *International Terrorism in the Contemporary World.* Edited by Marius H. Livingston, with Lee Bruce

Kress and Marie G. Wanek. Westport, Conn.: Greenwood Press, 1978, pp. 354–375.

Law Commission. *Codification of the Criminal Law: Treason, Sedition, and Allied Offences.* Working Paper No. 72. London: Her Majesty's Stationery Office, 1977.

LEWIS, BERNARD. *The Assassins: A Radical Sect in Islam.* New York: Basic Books, 1968.

MCCONNELL, BRIAN. *Assassination.* London: Leslie Frewin, 1969.

RAPOPORT, DAVID C. *Assassination and Terrorism.* Toronto: Canadian Broadcasting Corporation, 1971.

WILKINSON, DORIS Y., ed. *Social Structure and Assassination Behavior: The Sociology of Political Murder.* Cambridge, Mass.: Schenkman, 1976.

ASSAULT AND BATTERY

Assault and battery are two distinct common-law crimes that exist in all American jurisdictions, usually as statutory misdemeanors. Battery involves actual physical contact with the victim and is defined as conduct producing a bodily injury or an offensive contact. Assault, on the other hand, does not include physical contact with the victim and is classified as either an attempt at battery or an intentional frightening of another person. Although the term *assault and battery* is frequently used when a battery has been committed, one who commits a battery cannot also be punished for committing an assault, since the lesser offense of assault blends into the actual battery.

Battery

Battery, which requires physical contact with the victim, is broken down into three separate elements: the defendant's conduct, his mental state, and the harm done to the victim. Although many statutes do not define battery with specificity, or even list these elements, it is a widely recognized principle of law that each of them must be met.

Conduct. A defendant's conduct in a case of battery encompasses the physical acts he performs in committing the crime. Battery may be committed either by directly touching a person or indirectly applying force to him. It is clear that intentionally striking someone should be classified as a battery, but it is less clear that a battery charge should result from an injury not directly caused by the defendant. The latter result is often reached by modern courts, however. Consequently, one may commit a battery by causing injury through poisoning. One may also be liable for directing another person to make physical contact. Battery, therefore, may result when a person is forced to touch something that is repulsive to him or when one is injured in a dangerous situation intentionally created by the defendant. Additionally, if the other elements of battery are present, some cases have held persons criminally responsible when neglect of a duty to act causes injury in another—for example, when a lifeguard fails to warn swimmers of dangerous undercurrents.

Mental state. A defendant is held to be culpable in a battery charge if he acts with either an intent to injure or with criminal negligence. In some jurisdictions it is sufficient if he commits an unlawful act, regardless of his intent. Culpability is apparent when one acts with intent to injure, but one is usually not liable for committing a battery when he possesses no intent to injure. Hence, it is not a battery to grab someone in order to rescue him or to prevent him from doing something dangerous.

The use of criminal negligence to supply the requisite intent for battery is not always accepted, for negligence is not normally sufficient to prove the mental state needed for the criminal act. Some courts state that criminal negligence supplies the intent, thus equating this negligence with a simple intent to injure. Other states have statutes that make battery a minor misdemeanor when one acts in reckless disregard of the risk of causing injury to another.

If criminal negligence is held sufficient to warrant a charge of battery, the term *negligence* requires definition. For criminal liability, more than ordinary lack of due care should be required. Most jurisdictions defining batteries based on negligence require actions that create an unreasonable and high risk of harm to others. Although there is no single definition, it is generally accepted that the risk should be one a reasonable person would be clearly aware of, even if the defendant does not perceive it. It may seem wrong to criminally punish someone for harmful acts he does not intend. Nevertheless, one should be responsible for actions that would be recognized as harmful by most persons and that outrage and injure the general public.

In only a few jurisdictions is the unlawful-act standard applied in battery cases. The question of intent is again applicable, in connection with both the injury and the act itself. One who is consciously acting unlawfully should be responsible for the results of his actions, regardless of his intent. However, if he is unaware that he is acting unlawfully, it is more difficult to argue that criminal liability should automatically follow. Some states have dealt with this problem by ruling that liability results if the act is bad in itself (*malum in se*) but not if it is simply prohibited conduct (*malum prohibitum*); *malum prohibitum* acts, however, may be sufficient if the defendant is either criminally negligent or intends to cause injury.

Harm to the victim. The final element necessary for battery is the harmful result to the victim. This element is satisfied by virtually any type of bodily injury; indeed, many states have statutes that permit any offensive touching to qualify as a battery. Some cases have held that forcing a child to touch parts of the defendant's body created criminal responsibility, even when the defendant himself did not do any actual touching. In such situations, the defendant is viewed as having caused the act just as if he had touched the victim, since he initiated and controlled the situation, and the victim felt personally violated by the defendant.

Aggravated battery. The crime of aggravated battery, punishable as a felony and specifically defined by statute, exists in many states. Examples of such crimes are actions taken with intent to kill or to rape. Usually, the defendant must have intended to cause the specific result; otherwise, the crime is considered as a regular battery charge. Batteries based on criminal negligence are generally not considered sufficiently egregious to warrant a felony charge. Where a defendant did not intend to commit a felony, it seems unjust to convict him of the more serious charge.

Assault

An assault is classified as either an attempted battery or an intentional frightening of another person; physical contact is not an element of the crime in either of these situations. Many states do not define assault, and some states list it under attempt rather than under assault.

Attempted battery. In assaults resulting from attempted battery, there must be a specific intent on the part of the defendant to cause injury. The theory behind this requirement is that one cannot be guilty of attempting a battery if he lacks the intent to commit a battery. In some states there is an additional requirement of a present ability to commit the crime, on the assumption that a defendant cannot have attempted a battery if he was unable to act at the time.

Intentional frightening. Most states classify as assaults those acts that are designed to frighten another. Thus, one is liable for committing an assault when, intending to cause another person reasonable apprehension of immediate bodily harm, one acts to create such apprehension. In such assaults the defendant does not plan actually to harm the victim, but merely to frighten him. Some states do not classify an intentional frightening as a crime of assault, believing that such acts are not serious enough to warrant criminal punishment. There is a strong argument in favor of the viewpoint that intentional frightening should be left to tort law, where the defendant is held responsible more for causing harm to the plaintiff than for acting dangerously.

In the majority of states, the first requirement of intentional frightening as an assault is an actual purpose to frighten. It is not necessary that one have the ability to harm someone, because this assault focuses on intent rather than on present ability. Thus, when one points an unloaded gun at another with the intent to frighten, one is guilty of committing an assault even though it is impossible for him to fire.

A second requirement for a successful assault charge is that the victim actually be frightened by the defendant's actions. In addition, the defendant's conduct must be of the sort to arouse a reasonable apprehension of bodily harm in the average person. Thus, it is not sufficient to say something that frightens another, if a reasonable person would not be placed in fear of bodily harm by such conduct.

Proving fright on the part of the victim can be difficult. Some courts have created a distinction between immediate fear and reasonable apprehension, stating that reasonable apprehension may be a response of which the victim is not immediately aware. One may be so startled by the defendant's acts that one's reaction is delayed, but this should not automatically mean that one is not frightened. When a person is threatened with a gun, it is irrelevant whether the gun is loaded. Just as an unloaded gun may be used to fulfill the intent requirement, it may also serve to cause apprehension. If a gun is used, the victim's apprehension is normally proven unless it is shown he knew the gun was unloaded.

Conditional assault. In addition to the above two types of assault, there is a third category, that of conditional assault. This is an assault that arises only under certain conditions, usually failure of the victim to act as the defendant directs. If a defendant threatens to shoot another unless that person leaves the property, he is guilty of committing an assault even though the victim departs. The defendant is not protected from an assault charge simply because the victim complied with the condition. The fact that the defendant would have harmed the victim if the condition had not been satisfied is enough to supply the requisite intent.

Aggravated assault. As with batteries, assaults may be charged in an aggravated form. Acts such as assault with intent to kill or to rape are punishable as felonies rather than misdemeanors. Many statutes provide that the use of a deadly weapon automatically creates an aggravated assault. What constitutes a deadly weapon, however, is not always certain. Most courts hold that a dangerous weapon per se is an instrumentality designed and constructed to produce death or great bodily harm. Thus, a riding crop is not a dangerous weapon per se even though it may be used to inflict excessive bodily harm. The riding crop may still be a dangerous weapon, however, if the trier of fact decides that it has been used in a way that makes it dangerous. Guns are almost always considered dangerous weapons per se.

Defenses to assault and battery

Although one is usually liable for committing either an assault or a battery when he commits the elements discussed above, there are defenses to both crimes. Perhaps the most popular defense is the claim of self-defense. The defendant will argue that he committed the assault or the battery only because it was necessary to protect himself from attack. In other situations the defendant may seek to prove that he acted properly to protect another from harm. Although that person may have been touched in a forcible or offensive way, the defendant's actions are justified because they were prompted by a desire to help or rescue the person who was in a dangerous situation.

The consent defense is claimed where the victim permits the defendant to commit certain acts. The issue of consent often arises in cases involving sexual assaults, where the victim alleges that an attack occurred, and the defendant claims consent was given. In other areas, consent may also act as a defense to a charge of assault or battery, such as a situation in which the defendant grabs someone while playacting. Many courts, however, hold that consent is no defense when the act violates public policy, especially when the battery is severe. Hence, a battery is normally committed when two people agree to fight each other.

The issue of consent has become very important in the areas of sports and domestic relationships. In sports, the issue is whether excessive violence in a game exposes players to criminal liability. Although the elements of battery are present, it is argued that the players consent to these actions before the game starts. Consent is presumed by the players' participation in the sport. The question remaining is to what specific acts the players have given their consent. When some participants become rougher than may be reasonably necessary, can it be assumed that an injured player consented to this violence? There is as yet no definite answer to this, but as more sports-related prosecutions are brought, the answers will undoubtedly be forthcoming.

Interest in prosecuting domestic batteries has increased greatly as awareness of the problem developed. It is clear that in most domestic battery cases there is no actual consent given, so that consent should not operate as a defense to a criminal offense. The mere fact that the defendant was married to the victim should not operate as a defense. Still, government officials are properly reluctant to prosecute routinely in this area because of the presence in many cases of more appropriate forums for the resolution of disputes.

The common-law crimes of assault and battery raise many interesting and difficult questions involving the elements of the offenses, the defenses to them, and the situations in which they should be charged. Perhaps most important is the need to clarify the societal interest in imposing criminal sanctions on such activities. Particularly when the defendant has not seriously injured the victim or did not intend adverse consequences, the civil tort remedy may be a preferable way of dealing with the problem.

PAUL MARCUS

See also ATTEMPT; MAYHEM.

BIBLIOGRAPHY

American Law Institute. *Model Penal Code: Tentative Draft No. 10.* Philadelphia: ALI, 1960.
Comment. "The Consent Defense: Sports, Violence, and the Criminal Law." *American Criminal Law Review* 13 (1975): 235–248.
LaFave, Wayne R., and Scott, Austin W., Jr. *Handbook on Criminal Law.* St. Paul: West, 1972.
Note. "Consent in Criminal Law: Violence in Sports." *Michigan Law Review* 75 (1976): 148–179.
Perkins, Rollin M. "An Analysis of Assault and Attempts to Assault." *Minnesota Law Review* 47 (1962): 71–91.
———. "Non-homicide Offenses against the Person." *Boston University Law Review* 26 (1946): 119–206.
Prosser, William L. *Handbook of the Law of Torts.* 4th ed. St. Paul: West, 1971.

ASSISTANCE OF COUNSEL

See ADVERSARY SYSTEM; *both articles under* COUNSEL; TRIAL, CRIMINAL.

ATTEMPT

To be punishable as a criminal attempt, conduct must consist of an intent to perform an act or to bring about a result that would constitute a crime, together with some substantial steps taken in furtherance of that intent. This article describes the historical development of criminal liability for attempts, the policies served (and disserved) by punishment in attempt cases, and the current scope of liability for attempts in American law.

History

There was no general crime of attempt in the early English common law. Historians have uncovered scattered decisions, dating back as far as the fourteenth century, in which courts did convict of felony the perpetrator of an unsuccessful attempt. But punishment of attempts was at most sporadic, and was limited to cases in which rather serious harm had occurred in any event. During the sixteenth century, the Court of Star Chamber began to correct perceived shortcomings in the common law, by affording needed remedies that were unavailable in the common-law courts. Cases involving attempts to coin money, threats, and attempted dueling were held punishable in the Star Chamber. The court apparently did not develop a general doctrine of criminal attempts, however (Hall, pp. 561, 567–568).

The Court of Star Chamber was abolished in 1641, and historians disagree about whether its jurisprudence had any influence on subsequent developments (cf. Sayre, p. 829; Meehan, pp. 153–154; Hall, p. 569). In any event, more than a century elapsed before anything like the modern theory of attempt was suggested in the common-law courts. The first decision of consequence, *Rex v. Scofield*, Cald. 397 (1784), held that the defendant was properly charged with a misdemeanor for an unsuccessful attempt to burn down a house. Subsequently, in *Rex v. Higgins*, 102 Eng. Rep. 269, 275 (K.B. 1801), the court upheld an indictment charging an unsuccessful attempt to steal and stated in broad terms that "all such acts or attempts as tend to the prejudice of the community, are indictable."

The principle enunciated in *Higgins* was quickly accepted by courts and commentators, and it was soon considered settled that an attempt to commit either a felony or a misdemeanor was itself indictable as a crime. This remains the rule in the United States. In most jurisdictions, the rule is reflected in statutes specifying the punishment applicable to cases of attempt. The term *attempt* itself, however, is often left undefined, so that its meaning must be drawn from the common-law sources. In a few jurisdictions, the penal statutes may not provide explicitly for punishing criminal attempts, but such attempts nevertheless remain punishable as "common-law crimes," unless the law of the jurisdiction requires that all criminal offenses be defined by statute.

Why did the law punishing attempts develop so slowly, and why did the general theory of attempts win acceptance only in relatively recent times? Part of the explanation lies in the availability, probably throughout history, of other means for dealing with threatening or dangerous behavior. In earlier times dangerous persons could be required to give a pledge as a guarantee of good behavior, under the systems of frankpledge and of surety for the peace. Moreover, some substantive crimes, such as vagrancy or unlawful assembly, could be used to punish attempt-like behavior, and such offenses as assault and burglary were undoubtedly developed as a means of reaching conduct that was merely preparatory to the infliction of actual harm. Even today, many statutes treat as completed substantive crimes conduct that involves only steps toward the commission of some specific offense, for example, possession of burglary tools with intent to commit burglary. A general crime of attempt was, and is, necessary only to the extent that there remain gaps in the network of substantive offenses relating to specific kinds of attempts.

Another factor in the belated acceptance of attempt principles may have been a tendency to view the criminal law as concerned primarily with vengeance or retaliation. At the earlier stages of common-law development, crime and tort were not yet neatly differentiated. Even though public prosecution and punishment now have become distinct from the private lawsuit to recover damages, the retaliatory principle—an eye for an eye—may still figure prominently in attitudes about punishment.

Policies

Why should the criminal justice system trouble itself to prosecute and punish persons whose conduct has not actually harmed other individuals or society generally? The question is important not only for appreciating the theoretical underpinnings of attempt crimes but also for understanding the various rules that govern the scope of attempt liability under prevailing legal doctrine.

For those modern theorists who view the criminal

process as centered on a principle of retaliation for damage inflicted on society, punishment for attempt must remain a mystery or, perhaps, an unjustified aberration. Some writers, such as Lawrence Becker, have suggested that the attempt does actually injure society because the very threat of harm upsets the social equilibrium and gives rise to a sense of tension or disorder (pp. 273–276). This insight applies particularly to situations involving highly dangerous and widely observed threats. The notion does not, however, afford a fully satisfying explanation for attempt liability. The importance of punishment in attempt cases usually seems much more closely tied to the gravity of the threatened harm than it is to an elusive "actual" harm associated with a disturbance of the social equilibrium.

Attempt liability therefore seems more plausibly explained, and justified, by reference to the forward-looking purposes of punishment—deterrence of future crime, restraint of the dangerous offender, and rehabilitation. The deterrence justification has been somewhat controversial and remains perhaps only a subsidiary justification for attempt liability. Some scholars suggest that punishing attempts cannot add significantly to the deterrent efficacy of the criminal law, because the person punished was in any event willing to risk the sanction authorized for the completed crime, which by hypothesis he intended to commit (Model Penal Code, 1960, commentary on § 5.05; Michael and Wechsler, pp. 1295–1298). The point cannot, of course, hold true for those crimes that, when successfully committed, are likely to go undetected (a "perfect" murder) or unpunished (treason is the classic example). Putting aside these relatively unusual examples, there remain many recurrent situations (such as "victimless" crimes investigated by police decoys), in which the penalties applicable to an attempt could significantly affect the calculus of risks involved in a given criminal plan (Schulhofer, pp. 1538–1539).

Restraint and rehabilitation appear to be the principal functions of punishment for attempt. A criminal attempt manifests a disposition toward dangerous behavior that often warrants confinement of the offender to protect the public and to permit rehabilitative efforts if possible. The man who shoots to kill but misses might in a sense be less dangerous than one who kills on the first shot (because the latter may appear a more skilled marksman), but both pose substantial threats to society. Indeed, the man whose attempt has failed may actually be more dangerous, since if not restrained he might try again to harm the intended victim.

Practical considerations of law enforcement reinforce these broad concerns of penal policy. Police on patrol should have power to investigate suspicious activity and, if possible, to prevent injury from being inflicted. If an officer observes someone about to commit a crime, he can warn the individual and, under some circumstances, detain him temporarily, but the officer would have no power to arrest the person unless there was probable cause to believe that a crime had already been committed. The law of attempts and related attempt-like crimes permits police officers to intervene effectively in potentially dangerous situations before serious, often irreparable, injury has occurred.

This "early intervention" function in attempt law draws attention to the dangers that accompany a vigorous extension of criminal liability for attempts. The law of crimes must not only provide for punishment when useful and otherwise justified, but must serve to safeguard *from* punishment those individuals whose behavior does not warrant criminal sanctions. This latter, safeguarding function has been associated with a tradition of limitations on the proper scope of criminal responsibility, including two notions particularly relevant here—reluctance to impose criminal liability in the absence of personal culpability, and an insistence that the behavior subject to criminal sanctions be clearly specified by standards that are reasonably ascertainable in advance. Both of these limiting notions can be infringed by expansive liability for attempts.

The culpability notion limits punishment to those whose conduct is morally blameworthy, in the sense that they have consciously chosen to do an act that society regards as wrong. Although the criminal law sometimes departs from the culpability requirement (strict liability offenses are an example), there is usually a sense that such departures are at best unfortunate and narrowly circumscribed exceptions. A penal law that authorized restraint and rehabilitation of any person identified as dangerous to society would in effect create a general power of preventive detention, in direct violation of the culpability requirement. Yet is this not precisely what occurs in the law of attempts? Attempt doctrine can escape the moral objections to general preventive detention, but only when the evil intentions are accompanied by definite acts (for without acts there has been no exercise of choice), and only when the acts proceed far enough to involve clearly culpable threats rather than blameless fantasy. The preceding concern prompts an unwillingness to punish all preparatory behavior as a criminal attempt, but courts and legislatures have been unable to delineate with precision the point at which preparations have gone far enough to warrant criminal liability. As a result, the behavior punishable as an attempt often cannot be distinguished readily from noncriminal preparation. Liability turns on a standard whose application cannot always be predicted reliably in advance.

Although attempt liability thus appears solidly grounded in the restraining and rehabilitating functions of the criminal law and, to a lesser extent, in the deterrent function, the concerns just mentioned have prompted some uneasiness about imposing criminal responsibility for attempts. As a result, legal doctrine continues to erect complex limitations on the scope of liability for unsuccessful efforts to commit crime.

Modern law

To indicate the scope of liability for attempts in modern American law, the following will be considered: (1) the required state of mind, or mens rea; (2) the required acts, or actus reus; (3) liability when the offender desists before completing the intended crime (the problem of "abandonment"); (4) liability when the accused could not possibly carry out the intended crime (the problem of "impossibility"); and (5) the severity of punishment for attempt (the problem of "grading").

The mens rea. A criminal attempt is traditionally defined as an intent to perform an act or to bring about a result that would constitute a crime, together with some substantial steps taken in furtherance of that intent. In accordance with this definition, it is apparent that the state of mind, or mens rea, required is the actual intent or purpose to achieve the proscribed result; mere recklessness or negligence will not suffice.

The usual requirement of intention or purpose can appear anomalous when the many situations are considered in which the *completed* crime may be committed by recklessness, negligence, or even on a strict-liability basis. Suppose, for example, that a construction worker dynamites a hillside, with no intent to kill anyone, but with a reckless disregard for the lives of people residing nearby. If one of those people is killed by the explosion, the worker will be guilty of murder; recklessness is sufficient for liability. However, if the person injured by the explosion eventually recovers, the worker would not be guilty of murder and could not even be convicted of attempted murder because he was merely reckless and did not *intend* to kill.

How can this gap in attempts liability be explained?

If, in the event of death, the conduct should be punished as murder, then why does the identical behavior not remain a proper subject of penal sanctions when the victim luckily survives? One answer is definitional. An attempt, by the very meaning of the word, implies that the actor was *trying* to achieve the forbidden result, and this simply cannot be said of the construction worker. This view does not leave us with a very satisfying reason for not punishing the conduct, but rather focuses solely on the inelegance of referring to the conduct as an "attempt."

Some legislatures have relaxed to a limited degree the requirement of purpose or intention: one approach has been to create a specific offense of reckless endangerment, so that such conduct need not be prosecuted as an attempt (Pa. Cons. Stat. Ann. tit. 18, § 2705 (1973); Model Penal Code, 1962, § 211.2).

The actus reus. The courts hold that certain preliminary activities, designated "mere preparation," are not punishable even when accompanied by the requisite intent. Attempt liability attaches only when the defendant goes beyond mere preparation and begins to carry out the planned crime.

How can one determine the location of this line dividing mere preparation from the punishable attempt? Suppose, for example, that a defendant announces his desire to blow up the office of a former employer, collects a supply of matches, old newspaper, and kerosene, buys dynamite and a long fuse, places the dynamite and other material in the building, and finally lights the fuse. At what point in this sequence of events has the defendant committed a punishable attempt? Cases confronting such questions have invoked a considerable variety of analytic devices and have come to widely divergent results. The most important approaches are those requiring either commission of the last necessary act, commission of an act proximate to the result, or commission of an act that unequivocally confirms the actor's intent. The Model Penal Code's approach combines elements of these three. After discussing these approaches, this section considers one other actus reus problem, the possibility of punishing "attempts to attempt."

The last-act test. Under the last-act test, suggested in *Regina v. Eagleton*, 6 E. Cox, Crim. Cas. 559 (C.C.A.) (London, 1855), the disgruntled employee in the example above would be guilty of attempt only after lighting the fuse. At that point, although the attempt may still miscarry, the actor has done everything that appears necessary to carry it through to completion. The last-act test is designed not only to ensure that the defendant's intent is serious, but also to provide an incentive for him to desist by enabling him to avoid liability right up to the last possible moment. The last-act test seems much too strict, however, in terms of the "early intervention" function of attempt law. A defendant who follows a victim, draws a gun, and takes careful aim could not be charged with attempt, because he had yet to pull the trigger. For these reasons, no contemporary court would insist strictly upon commission of the last necessary act (Model Penal Code, 1960, commentary on § 5.01). Attempt liability attaches at an earlier point, and the needed incentive to desist is provided by a separate defense of "abandonment," discussed below.

The proximity test. To avoid the practical difficulties of the last-act test, many courts apply a "proximity" test requiring only that the defendant's preparatory actions come rather close to completion of the intended crime. But how close is close enough? Two examples will indicate the difficulties of the proximity test. In *Commonwealth v. Peaslee,* 177 Mass. 267, 59 N.E. 55 (1901), the defendant arranged combustible material in a building and left. Later, intending to set off the blaze, he drove within a quarter mile of the building and then decided to turn back. Writing for the court, Justice Oliver Wendell Holmes suggested that this might be a punishable attempt. In *People v. Rizzo,* 246 N.Y. 334, 158 N.E. 888 (1927), the defendants spent considerable time driving around the streets of New York searching for a payroll clerk whom they intended to rob. The police arrested them before they could find the clerk, but the New York Court of Appeals held that this was not a punishable attempt. In such cases, courts may be thinking of proximity primarily in a physical or spatial sense; in *Peaslee* the defendant had driven most of the way to the building, whereas in *Rizzo* the payroll clerk was never located at all and the defendants seemingly never came "close" to actually putting their plan into action. However, this sort of spatial proximity is not only hard to specify, but totally unrelated to the purposes of attempt law. Preliminary acts should become punishable when they establish that the intent is likely to be put into action, that the individual is sufficiently dangerous to require restraint, and that there is a dangerous probability of success requiring deterrence and early police intervention. From all of these perspectives the case for punishment is at least as strong in *Rizzo;* indeed, the defendant in *Peaslee* was, if anything, *less* deserving of punishment because he apparently chose voluntarily to abandon his plan. Some courts have attempted to adapt the proximity test more satisfactorily to the purposes of attempt law by focusing on whether the acts involve a dangerous

proximity to success or demonstrate that the actor was unlikely to desist, but these approaches also prove difficult to apply with objectivity and consistency.

The equivocality approach. Reluctance to punish "mere preparation" is based in part on concern that very preliminary acts may not confirm that the defendant seriously plans to put his intent into action. Accordingly, some authorities have suggested that to be punishable, a preliminary act must be "of such a nature as to be in itself sufficient evidence of the criminal intent with which it is done. A criminal attempt is an act which shows criminal intent on the face of it" (*Rex v. Barker,* [1924] N.Z.L.R. 865, 874 (C.A.)). American cases sometimes appear to speak approvingly of this requirement that the acts unequivocally confirm the criminal intent, and this approach does in theory appear consistent with the purposes of attempt law. Nevertheless, the equivocality approach, if applied literally, would often prove even stricter than the last-act approach. A defendant might approach a haystack, fill his pipe, light a match, light the pipe, and perhaps even toss the match on the haystack. The acts alone are not wholly unequivocal, but it is hard to imagine a court holding that regardless of any other evidence of intent, the acts themselves do not go far enough (Williams, p. 630).

The Model Penal Code approach. The Model Penal Code borrows from the concepts of proximity and equivocality but treats both in rather flexible fashion. Less suspicious of confessions and other direct evidence of intent, the Code relaxes the traditional insistence on very substantial preparation. Under the Code, an attempt must include "an act or omission constituting a substantial step in a course of conduct planned to culminate in . . . commission of the crime" (1962, § 5.01(1)(c)). The substantial-step requirement reflects proximity notions, but shifts the emphasis from the significance of the acts still required to the significance of what the defendant has already done. The Code also specifies that an act cannot be deemed a "substantial step" "unless it is strongly corroborative of the actor's criminal purpose" (§ 5.01(2)). The Code thus incorporates the concerns underlying the equivocality test, without being burdened by the impractical rigidity of that approach.

Attempts to attempt. Many substantive crimes are in effect attempts to commit some other offense. Assault, for example, is essentially an attempt to commit a battery; burglary (breaking and entering a structure with intent to commit a felony therein) is essentially an attempt to commit some other felony. Sometimes a defendant charged with attempted assault or attempted burglary will argue that the alleged conduct should not be punishable because it amounts to no more than an attempt to attempt. Such arguments may suppose the conceptual impossibility of such an offense, or they may reflect the view that conduct not amounting to an attempt is necessarily "mere preparation." Neither position is plausible. Concerns about imposing attempt liability at an excessively early point need to be faced, but in principle there is no reason why preparations to commit burglary, for example, might not pass the realm of mere preparation, even though the burglary itself was not successfully perpetrated. Consider the case of a masked man caught in the act of picking the lock of an apartment door. In such a case, a charge of attempted burglary is clearly justified, and the courts so hold (Model Penal Code, 1960, commentary on § 5.01).

Abandonment. Once the defendant's conduct has moved from "mere preparation" into the realm of a punishable attempt, can he nevertheless avoid liability if he has a genuine change of heart and decides to abandon his plan? Many cases appear to give a negative answer to this question. Just as a defendant who has stolen property cannot avoid liability by making restitution, the courts often say that once the defendant's attempt goes far enough to be punishable, a crime has been committed and subsequent actions cannot change that fact, although they may have a bearing on the appropriate sentence (Perkins, pp. 319, 354).

Whatever the logic of this view, one of its consequences is to reinforce traditional objections to imposing liability at relatively early stages of preparatory conduct. In the absence of an abandonment defense, early liability eliminates a significant incentive to desist and appears unfair to the defendant who has had a genuine change of heart, as in *Peaslee*. Such concerns generate pressure to reject early liability even when there is no hint of possible abandonment by the defendants in the case actually at hand, as in *Rizzo*. In short, in the absence of an abandonment defense, the line between preparation and attempt may fall so early as to seem unfair to the defendant who voluntarily abandons his plan, yet fall too late to meet proper law enforcement objectives with respect to the defendant who apparently would have carried his plan through to completion.

One way to avoid this dilemma is to recognize that voluntary abandonment is a complete defense to a charge of criminal attempt. Although the common-law decisions appear unsettled or in conflict with respect to the status of such a defense (Rotenberg, pp. 596–597), many statutory codifications have adopted

it. For example, a New York statute (N.Y. Penal Law (McKinney) § 40.10(3) (1975)) provides a defense to an attempt charge when "under circumstances manifesting a voluntary and complete renunciation of his criminal purpose, the defendant avoided commission of the crime attempted" (cf. Model Penal Code, 1962, § 5.01(4)).

In jurisdictions that recognize an abandonment defense, it is necessary to determine when the abandonment is genuinely "voluntary." Given the rationale of the defense, it seems clear that abandonment should not be considered voluntary when prompted by realization that the police or the victim have detected the plan, or when the defendant is simply postponing the attempt until a more favorable opportunity presents itself. The Model Penal Code provides that "renunciation of criminal purpose is not voluntary if it is motivated in whole or in part, by circumstances, not present or apparent at the inception of the actor's course of conduct, which increase the probability of detection or apprehension or which make more difficult the accomplishment of the criminal purpose" (1962, § 5.01(4)).

Impossibility. Courts and commentators have struggled for generations over the question whether an accused should be punishable for attempt when, for reasons unknown to the defendant, the intended offense could not possibly be committed successfully under the circumstances. The problem arises in a great variety of settings. The accused, for example, may attempt to kill with a pistol that is unloaded or defective, or he may shoot at an inanimate decoy rather than at the intended victim. A would-be pickpocket may reach into an empty pocket, or a drug dealer may purchase talcum powder, believing it to be narcotics.

Some courts have sought to resolve such cases by distinguishing between "legal" and "factual" impossibility. Factual impossibility is said to arise when some extraneous circumstance unknown to the defendant prevents consummation of the crime, and in this situation the attempt is punishable. Legal impossibility, on the other hand, arises when the intended acts, even if completed, would not amount to a crime, and it is said that in this situation the attempt should not be punishable.

In application, these concepts of legal and factual impossibility have proved elusive and unmanageable. In one case involving a charge of attempt to smuggle letters out of prison without the knowledge of the warden, the plot was discovered by the warden, although the accused remained ignorant of this fact. The court treated the case as one of legal impossibility and reversed the conviction for attempt (*United States v. Berrigan*, 482 F.2d 171 (3d Cir. 1973)). It is apparent, however, that the situation could as readily be characterized as one of factual impossibility, and the same is true of attempts to pick an empty pocket, to shoot at a dead body believed to be alive, and so on. Some commentators have sought to clarify the categories by introducing further distinctions between "intrinsic" and "extrinsic" factual impossibility (Comment, pp. 160–162). One court has suggested a still more sophisticated taxonomy involving six ostensibly distinct categories (*Regina v. Donnelly*, [1970] N.Z.L.R. 980, 990 (C.A.)).

All of these efforts at classification ultimately founder, however, because generally speaking the reasons for punishing unsuccessful attempts apply as much to one category as to any of the others. When the defendant has fired at a decoy or used an unloaded weapon, the circumstances may, of course, raise a question about whether he actually intended to kill, but the question of intent must be faced and resolved with care in every type of "possible" or "impossible" attempt. In fact, the use of undercover agents or cleverly disguised decoys may provide particularly reliable *confirmation* of intent, even though such tactics would arguably raise a problem of "legal impossibility" under some of the traditional taxonomies. So long as it can be proved that the accused acted with intent to commit the offense and that his conduct would constitute the crime if the circumstances had been as he believed them to be, the defendant is just as culpable and in general just as dangerous as the defendant who successfully consummates the offense. Nearly all of the modern statutory codifications have taken this view, specifying that neither factual nor legal impossibility is a defense "if such crime could have been committed had the attendant circumstances been as such person believed them to be" (N.Y. Penal Law (McKinney) § 110.10 (1965); cf. Model Penal Code, 1962, § 5.01(1)(a)).

There remains one type of "legal impossibility" that fails to satisfy the proviso just quoted. Suppose that the accused has attempted to smuggle expensive lace past a customs officer but that (unknown to the accused) this item has recently been removed from the list of goods subject to duty. Here, even if the accused had accomplished everything he set out to do, his acts will not violate any provision of law. It is true that the accused thought he would be committing a crime, but since the goal he seeks to achieve is not in fact prohibited, the purposes of attempt law do not call for punishment (Kadish and Paulsen, pp. 362–366). In this type of situation, sometimes called a case

of "genuine" legal impossibility, the attempt would not be punishable even under revised statutory provisions that otherwise reject both factual and legal impossibility as defenses.

Grading. Statutory provisions specifying the penalty applicable to a criminal attempt vary widely among American jurisdictions. A specific punishment may be provided for all attempts, or different penalty ranges may be specified according to the seriousness of the crime attempted. Under some statutes, for example, the maximum penalty is one-half that provided for the completed crime. Although a few states provide the same maximum penalty for attempt and for the corresponding completed crime, this approach still appears to be the minority view; despite other variations in detail, in most jurisdictions an attempt will be punished much less severely than the completed crime (Model Penal Code, 1960, appendixes A and B to § 5.05).

What is the justification for this prevalent grading pattern? Relative leniency seems appropriate in the case of defendants who have crossed beyond the domain of "mere preparation" but who nevertheless have yet to carry out every step that appears necessary to consummate the crime. When the attempt is incomplete in this sense, the intent and the dangerousness demonstrated are inevitably more ambiguous than when the actor has taken the decisive final step. Moreover, the lower penalty preserves some incentive for the actor to avert the threatened harm, even when he may be unable to meet the requirements for a complete defense of voluntary abandonment.

In contrast, the prevalent pattern of leniency for attempts appears difficult to justify when the defendant has carried out every step that appears necessary for successful completion of the offense, as, for example, when a defendant shoots at someone intending to kill, but the victim survives the wounds inflicted. In such a case the difference between a successful consummation of the crime and an unsuccessful attempt may result from fortuitous factors wholly beyond the control of the actor, and the sharp difference in applicable penalties appears anomalous.

It is sometimes suggested that the successful actor may be more dangerous or more culpable than the one whose attempt fails. Neither of these arguments can be considered valid over the general range of attempt situations (Schulhofer, pp. 1514–1517, 1588–1599). The Model Penal Code accepts that premise, and concludes that generally the maximum penalty for attempt should equal that for the completed crime. The Code provides, however, that in the case of the most serious felonies the penalty for attempt should be less severe than for the completed offense (1962, § 5.05(1)). The rationale for this limited exception to the general approach of equal treatment is that in this situation the use of severe sanctions can be minimized without impairing the deterrent efficacy of the law (Model Penal Code, 1960, commentary on § 5.05). The Model Penal Code rationale turns out to depend on a number of complex and problematic assumptions. Although the Code's goal of limiting the use of the most severe sanctions appears attractive, it proves difficult to show with any degree of generality that the Code's approach in fact has this effect; leniency for unsuccessful attempts may instead work to perpetuate unnecessarily severe and vindictively harsh sentences in the case of completed crimes (Schulhofer, pp. 1562–1585).

Intuitively, the most plausible explanation for more lenient treatment of attempts is that the community's resentment and demand for punishment are not aroused to the same degree when serious harm has been averted. This explanation, however, raises further questions. Can severe punishment (in the case of completed crime, for example) be justified simply by reference to the fact that society "demands" or at least desires this? To what extent should the structure of penalties serve to express intuitive societal judgments that cannot be rationalized in terms of such instrumental goals as deterrence, isolation, rehabilitation, and even retribution—that is, condemnation reflecting the moral culpability of the act? Conversely, to what extent should the criminal justice system see its mission as one not of expressing the intuitive social demand for punishment, but rather as one of restraining that demand and of protecting *from* punishment the offender who, rationally speaking, deserves a less severe penalty? Answers to such questions must be sought beyond the confines of attempt doctrine, for they reflect wider problems of democratic theory and normative political philosophy.

STEPHEN J. SCHULHOFER

See also ASSAULT AND BATTERY; CONSPIRACY; SOLICITATION.

BIBLIOGRAPHY

AMERICAN LAW INSTITUTE. *Model Penal Code: Proposed Official Draft.* Philadelphia: ALI, 1962.

———. *Model Penal Code: Tentative Draft No. 10.* Philadelphia: ALI, 1960.

BECKER, LAWRENCE C. "Criminal Attempt and the Theory of the Law of Crimes." *Philosophy and Public Affairs* 3 (1974): 262–294.

Comment. "Why Do Criminal Attempts Fail?: A New Defense." *Yale Law Journal* 70 (1960): 160–169.

HALL, JEROME. *General Principles of Criminal Law.* 2d ed. Indianapolis: Bobbs-Merrill, 1960.

KADISH, SANFORD H., and PAULSEN, MONRAD G. *Criminal Law and Its Processes: Cases and Materials.* 3d ed. Boston: Little, Brown, 1975.

MEEHAN, EUGENE R. "The Trying Problem of Criminal Attempt: Historical Perspectives." *University of British Columbia Law Review* 14 (1979): 137–161.

MICHAEL, JEROME, and WECHSLER, HERBERT. "A Rationale of the Law of Homicide." *Columbia Law Review* 37 (1937): 701–761, 1261–1325.

PERKINS, ROLLIN M. "Criminal Attempt and Related Problems." *UCLA Law Review* 2 (1955): 319–355.

ROTENBERG, DANIEL L. "Withdrawal as a Defense to Relational Crimes." *Wisconsin Law Review* (1962): 596–607.

SAYRE, FRANCIS B. "Criminal Attempts." *Harvard Law Review* 41 (1928): 821–859.

SCHULHOFER, STEPHEN J. "Harm and Punishment: A Critique of Emphasis on the Results of Conduct in the Criminal Law." *University of Pennsylvania Law Review* 122 (1974): 1497–1607.

WILLIAMS, GLANVILLE. *Criminal Law: The General Part.* 2d ed. London: Stevens, 1961.

AUTOMOBILES AND CRIME

See DRINKING AND DRIVING; ECOLOGY OF CRIME; TRAFFIC OFFENSES.

AVERSIVE CONDITIONING

See CRIME CAUSATION: PSYCHOLOGICAL THEORIES.

B

BAIL

The article on THE RIGHT TO BAIL *discusses the extent to which the United States Constitution and applicable statutes grant a right to release on bail before, during, or after a criminal trial and the extent to which they permit denial of such release. The second article within this entry,* BAIL REFORM, *describes and assesses recent efforts to make pretrial release more readily available.*

1. THE RIGHT TO BAIL   Wayne R. LaFave
2. BAIL REFORM   Caleb Foote

1.
THE RIGHT TO BAIL

The concept of bail has been traced back to the system of frankpledges adopted in England following the Norman Conquest. Under that system, the community as a whole was required to pledge its property as security for the accused's appearance at trial. The concept of community responsibility eventually dissolved, but there remained the capacity of the accused to retain his freedom pending trial by posting security. Release upon posting bail became available in Anglo-American law for all but capital cases.

Pretrial release procedures

The federal Bail Reform Act. The federal Bail Reform Act of 1966, 18 U.S.C. §§ 3146–3151 (1976), which governs bail and release practices in the federal courts, declares that anyone charged with a noncapital offense shall "be ordered released pending trial on his personal recognizance or upon the execution of an unsecured appearance bond in an amount specified by the judicial officer, unless the officer determines . . . that such a release will not reasonably assure the appearance of the person as required" (§ 3146(a)). In the event of such a determination, the judicial officer is required, "in lieu of or in addition to the above methods of release," to "impose the first of the following conditions" which "will reasonably assure the appearance of the person for trial or, if no single condition gives that assurance, any combination of the following conditions: (1) place the person in the custody of a designated person or organization agreeing to supervise him; (2) place restrictions on the travel, association, or place of abode of the person during the period of release; (3) require the execution of an appearance bond in a specified amount and the deposit in the registry of the court, in cash or other security as directed, of a sum not to exceed 10 per centum of the amount of the bond, such deposit to be returned upon the performance of the conditions of release; (4) require the execution of a bail bond with sufficient solvent sureties, or the deposit of cash in lieu thereof; or (5) impose any other condition deemed reasonably necessary to assure appearance as required, including a condition requiring that the person return to custody after specified hours" (§ 3146(a)).

The federal act also specifies the factors that are to be taken into account in determining which conditions will reasonably assure appearance: "the nature and circumstances of the offense charged, the weight of the evidence against the accused, the accused's family ties, employment, financial resources, character and mental condition, the length of his residence in the community, his record of convictions, and his record of appearance at court proceedings or of flight to avoid prosecution or failure to appear at court proceedings" (§ 3146(b)).

A person who is unable to meet the conditions of release imposed or who is released on condition that he return to custody after specified hours is entitled to a prompt reconsideration of such conditions and, if they are not removed, to have the judge set forth in writing the reasons for them. Subject to the same limitations, the judicial officer may at any time amend his order to impose additional or different conditions of release. One who has been unable to obtain his release at all, or except upon the condition that he return to custody after specified hours, is entitled to a prompt appeal.

State practice. The typical state statute declares that the objective of bail is to secure the defendant's attendance at the proceedings against him and to prevent his punishment before conviction. Some of these statutes furnish no guidance on the question of the factors to be taken into account, while others provide a detailed list of factors in the manner of the federal act.

Typically, an arrested defendant is taken to the nearest station house and then transported to the city jail within twenty-four hours. For defendants charged with a minor offense listed in a fixed bail schedule, the first opportunity for release comes at that time. Those defendants unable to obtain their release at the station must await their appearance before a judicial officer, often the following morning, at which time the judge will set the terms of release. Defendants who obtained their release earlier, if their cases are not immediately disposed of at their subsequent court appearance, may have the amount of their bail revised upward or downward.

Judges are inclined to give primary consideration to the seriousness of the offense charged, most likely because it is a factor that is clear-cut and easy to apply. The strength of the case against the defendant, as communicated by the prosecutor or police, is also an important yardstick in practice. A third factor considered very relevant is the defendant's prior criminal record. In many localities it is unusual for the judge to determine or consider other facts about the defendant's background and character, for example, whether he is employed and how long he has resided in the community. The common explanations for this are that the judges believe they are overworked and do not have time to inquire into such matters, and

that they doubt defendants can be trusted to supply truthful answers to such inquiries.

In response to that problem, bail projects are now in operation in many major cities. In the typical project, project personnel (1) interview defendants in custody to obtain information about their backgrounds and ties to the community; (2) verify the information provided by the defendants; (3) determine (often by a point system, such as + 3 for a steady job, + 1 for continued local residence, and − 1 for prior violent-felony conviction) which defendants qualify for nonfinancial release; (4) submit release recommendations to the court; and (5) attempt to ensure that persons released return to court as scheduled.

As for the methods by which a defendant may obtain pretrial release in the state courts, one frequently used procedure is cash bail. Once he has learned the bail figure, the defendant may raise the full amount of the bond through personal savings or money supplied by friends and family. If he shows up for all required court appearances, the entire amount is usually returned to him. But if, as is often the case, the defendant must rely upon the services of a bail bondsman, then he will have to pay a fee usually not less than 10 percent of the bond amount, a payment which is not recoverable by the defendant.

Another method by which pretrial release may be obtained in many locales is via the 10 percent plan. The defendant pays 10 percent of the bond directly to the court and then recovers most or all of that amount if he appears in court as scheduled. Yet another possibility is that a defendant may obtain his release on a property bond, which means he offers property as bail in lieu of cash. Still another possibility is personal bond, sometimes referred to as personal surety or release on own recognizance (ROR), which is used when the judge concludes that the defendant is sufficiently motivated to appear that he can be released on his own signature without bail. In addition to or in lieu of these methods, some localities utilize daytime release, release to the custody of an approved individual or organization, or release on conditions.

Constitutionality of limits on pretrial freedom

Amount of money bail. The Eighth Amendment, also applicable to the states through the Fourteenth Amendment due process clause, provides in part: "Excessive bail shall not be required." The traditional question which has been raised under this provision is that of what amount of money bail may constitutionally be required of a defendant. The leading case is *Stack v. Boyle*, 342 U.S. 1 (1951), involving twelve petitioners who had been charged with conspiring to advocate the overthrow of the government by force or violence. Bail was fixed in the district court in the uniform amount of $50,000 for each petitioner. The petitioners then moved to reduce bail on the ground that it was excessive, and in support submitted statements as to their financial resources, family relationships, health, prior criminal records, and other information. Although the only response of the government was a certified record showing that four other persons previously convicted of this offense had forfeited bail, the district court denied the motion. The court of appeals affirmed, but the Supreme Court ruled that bail had "not been fixed by proper methods."

One respect in which the *Stack* decision is important is in its specification of the purpose of bail which may be legitimately taken into account in setting the amount. The Court declared that "the modern practice of requiring a bail bond or the deposit of a sum of money subject to forfeiture serves as additional assurance of the presence of an accused. Bail set at a figure higher than an amount reasonably calculated to fulfill this purpose is 'excessive' under the Eighth Amendment" (5).

In addition, *Stack* stresses that setting an amount of bail which properly serves this single purpose requires an assessment of the facts of the particular case. The Court declared that "standards relevant to the purpose of assuring the presence of that defendant" must "be applied in each case to each defendant" (5). The "traditional standards" recognized by the Court in *Stack* were " 'the nature and circumstances of the offense charged, the weight of the evidence against him, the financial ability of the defendant to give bail and the character of the defendant' " (5 n. 3). It was relatively easy to find noncompliance with the Eighth Amendment in *Stack,* for (as the Court noted) "bail for each petitioner has been fixed in a sum much higher than that usually imposed for offenses with like penalties and yet there has been no factual showing to justify such action in this case" (5).

One question that might be raised under the *Stack* formulation is whether there may be circumstances under which no amount of bail will suffice to ensure the defendant's appearance at the proceedings against him. This issue has not often been litigated, most likely because a court confronted with a high-risk defendant will in all probability proceed to set the bail in an unreachable amount rather than deny bail altogether. But with some defendants, especially those alleged to be major drug dealers, who are in a position

to post bail in amounts exceeding $1 million, the question is taking on increasing importance. In *United States v. Abrahams,* 575 F.2d 3 (1st Cir. 1978), the court concluded that the instant case was "the rare case of extreme and unusual circumstances that justifies pretrial detention without bail" (8). The defendant, charged with fraud (punishable by up to five years' imprisonment and a $10,000 fine), had three previous convictions, was an escaped prisoner from New Jersey, had given false information at the previous bail hearing, had failed to appear on the previous bail of $100,000, had failed to appear in a California case and was a fugitive from that state, had used several aliases in the past, and in the last two years had transferred $1.5 million to Bermuda. These facts, the court concluded, supported the district court's findings that "none of the five conditions spelled out in" the federal act, "or any combination thereof, will reasonably assure the appearance of defendant for trial if admitted to bail" (5).

Poverty and pretrial release. As for the relevance of the defendant's indigence upon the Eighth Amendment bail question, *Stack* is itself instructive, for it expressly states that "the financial ability of the defendant to give bail" is one of the factors which must be taken into consideration. This is certainly sensible, but it is a substantial jump from that truism to the proposition that an amount of bail which a defendant cannot meet because of his poverty is thereby "excessive" under the Eighth Amendment. Courts have refused to take that leap; they instead continue to adhere to the proposition that bail "is not excessive merely because the defendant is unable to pay it" (*Hodgdon v. United States,* 365 F.2d 679, 687 (8th Cir. 1966)).

As for an equal protection claim, note must be taken of the oft-quoted comments of Justice William O. Douglas in *Bandy v. United States,* 81 S. Ct. 197 (1960). Observing that the Court had held in *Griffin v. Illinois,* 351 U.S. 12 (1956) "that an indigent defendant is denied equal protection of the law if he is denied an appeal on equal terms with other defendants, solely because of his indigence" (*Bandy,* 197), Justice Douglas opined that it must be similarly unconstitutional for "an indigent [to] be denied freedom, where a wealthy man would not, because he does not happen to have enough property to pledge for his freedom" (198). Some have argued that this position has been bolstered by such cases as *Williams v. Illinois,* 399 U.S. 235 (1970) and *Tate v. Short,* 401 U.S. 395 (1971), deemed to provide a close analogy because they held that the equal protection clause bars subjecting indigent defendants to sentences of imprisonment beyond that which other defendants could receive. However,

Williams and *Tate* did not bar imprisonment for indigents merely because a wealthier defendant would probably escape such a consequence by being fined instead, and *Griffin* has since been given a rather narrow interpretation by the Supreme Court. Thus it is not surprising that courts have not been inclined to accept the equal protection argument that bail is unconstitutional when set in an amount a particular indigent defendant cannot meet (*Bellamy v. Judges*, 41 A.D.2d 196, 342 N.Y.S.2d 137 (1st Dept. 1973)).

Because of bail reform efforts in recent years, the dimensions of the debate concerning the indigent defendant have changed somewhat. Where, as is true under the federal act, nonfinancial alternatives must be considered by the judge, the argument has been made that in the case of an indigent defendant the judge is obligated to select one of those alternatives. But that argument has not prevailed because "carried to its logical conclusions, every indigent person would always be released on non-financial conditions and the requirement for reasonable bail would be meaningless" (*United States v. Cook*, 442 F.2d 723, 724 (D.C. Cir. 1970)).

A more compelling argument, and one of particular importance in those jurisdictions which have not adopted bail reforms in the manner of the federal act, is that money bail may no longer be constitutionally viewed as the sole means of pretrial release or even as the preferred means of gaining pretrial freedom. Important here is *Pugh v. Rainwater*, 557 F.2d 1189 (5th Cir. 1977), which held that "equal protection standards are not satisfied unless the judge is required to consider less financially onerous forms of release before he imposes money bail" (1201). This would mean, as the court later put it on rehearing en banc, 572 F.2d 1053, 1058 (5th Cir. 1978), "that in the case of an indigent, whose appearance at trial could reasonably be assured by one of the alternative forms of release, pretrial confinement for inability to post money bail would constitute imposition of an excessive restraint."

As bail reform efforts result in alternative methods of release being provided, other equal protection issues can arise, as is illustrated by *Schilb v. Kuebel*, 404 U.S. 357 (1971). At issue there was a state statute which provided, regarding a defendant not released on his own recognizance, that he could either deposit cash equal to 10 percent of the bond, in which case 10 percent of the amount deposited (that is, 1 percent of the amount of the bond) would be retained by the state as "bail bond costs" even if the defendant appeared as required, or else he could deposit the full amount of the bail, in which event there would

be no charge or retention if the defendant appeared as required. Although the defendant claimed that this meant a charge was imposed only on the nonaffluent and thus constituted a denial of equal protection, the Court concluded otherwise, finding that the distinction drawn by the statute was not "invidious and without rational basis." The defendant's assumption that the affluent would always opt for the full-deposit alternative and thus escape the charge was itself doubted by the Court, which noted that "in these days of high interest rates" it would make more sense for an affluent person to post only 10 percent and earn interest on the balance.

Opportunity to prepare a defense. Although there is little reason to doubt the proposition that pretrial detention has a significant adverse impact upon the ability of a defendant to vindicate himself at trial or to secure leniency in sentencing, courts have not been receptive to post-conviction claims by defendants that they were entitled to relief because their pretrial incarceration in some way interfered with preparation of their defense. However, a particularized claim made during the time of pretrial detention will sometimes produce limited relief, as is illustrated by *Kinney v. Lenon*, 425 F.2d 209, 210 (9th Cir. 1970). There, the juvenile defendant, in custody awaiting trial on charges arising out of a schoolyard fight, alleged that "there were many potential witnesses to the fight, that he cannot identify them by name but would recognize them by sight, that appellant's attorneys are white though he and the potential witnesses are black, that his attorneys would consequently have great practical difficulty in interviewing and lining up the witnesses, and that appellant is the sole person who can do so." The court concluded that the defendant's detention was infringing upon his constitutional right to compulsory process to obtain witnesses in his behalf, which "as a practical matter would be of little value without an opportunity to contact and screen potential witnesses before trial." Thus, the court held that release of the defendant into the custody of his parents was necessary to protect "his due-process right to a fair trial."

Constitutionality of mandating pretrial detention

Preventive detention. The Eighth Amendment prohibition on "excessive" bail means that in setting pretrial release conditions there is but one legitimate consideration: What is necessary to provide a reasonable assurance that the particular defendant will subsequently appear at the proceedings against him? There is no question, however, but that bail determinations are sometimes influenced by such considerations as the accused's assumed danger to the community. Especially in earlier days, when there was almost exclusive reliance upon money bail and little opportunity for a defendant to obtain review of his bail setting, this could quite easily occur. Because of the sub rosa character of such action, the concept of "preventive detention" (pretrial custody of a defendant for the purpose of protecting some other person or the community at large) did not receive close scrutiny.

Since the mid-1960s, by comparison, the subject of preventive detention has been much debated. This is largely attributable to bail reform activities, for as alternatives to money bail were implemented and as judicial review of the conditions set for defendants as yet unable to obtain their relief was mandated, it became increasingly likely that those defendants perceived by some as "dangerous" would obtain their freedom pending trial. This concern has produced some legislative activity, most notably the District of Columbia preventive detention law, D.C. Code §§ 23-1322–23-1331 (1973), which authorizes pretrial detention of a defendant for up to sixty days, after which he is eligible for release if his expedited trial has not yet commenced. Such detention is permitted only upon a showing that "there is no condition or combination of conditions of release which will reasonably assure the safety of any other person or the community" (§ 23-1322(b)). In addition, the defendant must fall into one of the following categories: (1) a person charged with a "dangerous crime" (such as robbery, burglary, rape, arson, or sale of narcotics), upon a finding that there is a "substantial probability" that he committed the charged crime; (2) a person charged with a "crime of violence" (such as murder, rape, robbery, burglary, arson, or serious assault), upon a like finding, if in addition that person is an addict, has been convicted of such a crime within the past ten years, or allegedly committed the charged crime while on bail, probation, or parole regarding such a crime; or (3) a person charged with any offense who, "for the purpose of obstructing or attempting to obstruct justice, threatens, injures, intimidates, or attempts to threaten, injure or intimidate any prospective witness or juror" (§ 23-1322(a)).

No state has yet seen fit to adopt such a full-scale preventive detention scheme, but there nonetheless has been some activity at the state level. Nearly half of the states presently permit some consideration of defendant dangerousness in the pretrial release determination. In addition, many states by statute, court rule, or court decision permit revocation of release because of commission of a crime or other misconduct. Moreover, preventive detention objectives are also served by state laws that permit the denial of bail to defendants charged with certain serious noncapital offenses. This includes provisions that actually specify certain noncapital crimes as not bailable and those that have been construed to allow denial of bail for certain crimes which would be capital but for constitutionally defective sentencing procedures.

The Eighth Amendment ambiguity. Whether the Eighth Amendment confers a right to bail that would render at least some of these preventive detention schemes unconstitutional is unclear. A literal reading of the relevant language of the amendment, "Excessive bail shall not be required," indicates no such right. The Supreme Court has never decided the issue, but has from time to time used language helpful to those on both sides of this debate. The lower courts have confronted the question infrequently, and are divided on the issue.

Those holding to the view that the Eighth Amendment does *not* encompass a right to bail find it useful to trace the excessive bail provision back to a comparable provision in the English Bill of Rights, 2 Wm. & Mary, Sess. 1, c. 1 (1689). The latter provision, it is noted, was not prompted by the well-established statutory provisions that carefully enumerated which offenses were bailable and which were not, but rather by judicial circumvention of the protections of the Habeas Corpus Act through setting prohibitively high bail for bailable offenses. The English excessive bail clause, therefore, was developed as a specific remedy for judicial abuse of the bail procedure otherwise established by law and did not, in and of itself, imply any right to bail. This distinction, it is argued, was recognized in the colonies and early states, as reflected by three significant developments: (1) several states dealt with the right to bail by statute, thus indicating an understanding that the subject was open to legislative limitation; (2) several states adopted constitutional provisions that were explicitly directed to limiting the power of the judiciary; and (3) several states adopted constitutional provisions that granted a right to bail and also an excessive bail clause, manifesting a recognition that the latter did not encompass the former.

The view that the Eighth Amendment does not confer a right to bail is also claimed to be consistent with the contemporary understanding when the amendment was considered and adopted. It is pointed out that some of the states proposing an excessive bail clause for the federal Constitution had such a clause and also a right to bail provision in their state constitutions, and thus would have proposed both had they desired a constitutional right to bail against the federal government. Also noteworthy is the fact that in the same session in which Congress considered and approved the Bill of Rights, it drafted and enacted the Judiciary Act of 1789, ch. 20, 1 Stat. 73, which established a statutory right to bail in noncapital cases. This view of history, it is argued, was accepted by the Supreme Court in *Carlson v. Landon*, 342 U.S. 524, 545 (1952), when it stated that the excessive bail clause "has never been thought to accord a right to bail in all cases, but merely to provide that bail shall not be excessive in those cases where it is proper to grant bail."

This argument for a narrow reading of the Eighth Amendment concludes with the contention that such an interpretation is consistent with the general constitutional scheme. In response to the objection that it would make little sense to prohibit judicial imposition of excessive bail but not forbid the legislative denial of bail altogether, it is said that such a construction squares with the fact that the chief concern of the Bill of Rights generally is the conduct of the judicial branch of government.

As for those holding to the view that the Eighth Amendment does include a constitutional right to bail, they take a somewhat different view as to the significance of the amendment's English antecedents. They agree that English law denied bail for some offenses, but find no evidence that such a denial was ever permitted for the purpose of protecting the community. In any event, so the argument proceeds, the English history is not controlling here because from the very beginning the American concept of bail differed significantly from that of the English. This is reflected by the fact that most states include in their state constitutions a provision that "all persons shall be bailable." And while these state constitutional provisions contain an exception for capital cases, this hardly reflects acceptance of the concept of preventive detention. Rather, these provisions were enacted in this form because it had been thought that most defendants facing a possible death penalty would probably flee regardless of what bail was set.

Those favoring a broader reading of the Eighth Amendment to include a right to bail contend that this is the only logical construction of the bail provision. Thus, the argument proceeds, to read the amendment as barring judicial setting of excessive bail but not legislative denial of bail would make it virtually meaningless. This is because the interests at stake, both the government's and the individual's

are identical whether a legislature or a court has made the basic decision resulting in the defendant's pretrial imprisonment. Moreover, interpretation of the bail clause as limited to judicial abuse is inconsistent with the general approach taken in the Bill of Rights, which is concerned primarily with curtailing the powers of Congress. This is evident within the Eighth Amendment itself, for the prohibitions on cruel and unusual punishments and excessive fines have traditionally been viewed as limitations on legislative abuse.

As for the *Carlson* case, it is noted that the language quoted above was dictum set out in the context of a civil rather than a criminal case, in which the actual holding was that bail could be denied to prevent sabotage by alien Communists pending their deportation. More relevant, so the argument proceeds, is the Court's declaration in *Stack* that unless "this right to bail before trial is preserved, the presumption of innocence, secured only after centuries of struggle, would lose its meaning" (4).

Other constitutional objections. The language just quoted has understandably prompted the argument that preventive detention schemes are unconstitutional simply because they run afoul of the presumption of innocence. But while it is now generally accepted that the presumption of innocence has constitutional stature, as currently viewed by the Supreme Court it appears to have no bearing upon the preventive detention issue. The Court in *Bell v. Wolfish*, 441 U.S. 520, 533 (1979) concluded that the presumption "is a doctrine that allocates the burden of proof in criminal trials" and requires the fact finder "to judge an accused's guilt or innocence solely on the evidence adduced at trial and not on the basis of suspicions that may arise from the fact of his arrest, indictment, or custody or from other matters not introduced as proof at trial," and that it has "no application . . . before his trial has even begun."

A particular preventive detention scheme might nonetheless be vulnerable to an attack on due process grounds on the theory that it amounts to an impermissible imposition of punishment. As the Supreme Court recognized in *Bell*, the Constitution "includes freedom from punishment within the liberty of which no person may be deprived without due process of law," so that generally "punishment can only follow a determination of guilt after trial or plea" (536 n. 17). But the Court in *Bell* deemed it beyond dispute that pretrial incarceration is not inevitably "punishment" within the meaning of this doctrine. As for how to draw the "distinction between punitive measures that may not constitutionally be imposed prior to a determination of guilt and regulatory restraints that may" (537), the Court identified a series of three factors: (1) whether "the disability is imposed for the purpose of punishment or whether it is but an incident of some other legitimate governmental purpose"; (2) in the absence of an intent to punish, whether "an alternative purpose to which [the restriction] may rationally be connected is assignable for it"; and (3) if there is such a purpose, a "legitimate governmental objective," whether the disability "appears excessive in relation to the alternative purpose assigned [to it]" (538, 539). Whether a preventive detention statute of a particular magnitude is or is not excessive in this sense is certainly a matter on which there might be a difference of opinion.

There is also the possibility that a preventive detention scheme could be questioned on equal protection grounds; it might be argued that a process which selects only from those charged with crimes is arbitrary. Lending some support to this view is *Jackson v. Indiana*, 406 U.S. 715 (1972), holding that "pending criminal charges" provide no justification for incarcerating incompetents under less demanding standards than those applying to mentally ill persons not so charged. Yet authority is to be found that a legislative body may rationally conclude that those charged with a particular type of offense are likely to repeat their crimes, so that preventive detention for persons so charged may be legislatively authorized (*Parker v. Roth*, 202 Neb. 850, 278 N.W.2d 106 (1979)).

Finally, even if a particular preventive detention scheme suffers from none of the previously discussed constitutional defects, the procedures for determining which individuals will actually be confined must be fair in a procedural due process sense. Even in a situation in which it is conceded that the defendant has no absolute right to bail, a fair adjudicatory procedure must be followed. Just what constitutes fair procedure for due process purposes depends to some extent upon the circumstances and matter at issue. Thus, in *Gerstein v. Pugh*, 420 U.S. 103, 119 (1975), concerning the judicial determination of probable cause after a warrantless arrest, the Court held that "the full panoply of adversary safeguards—counsel, confrontation, cross-examination, and compulsory process for witnesses" is not constitutionally required. On the other hand, in *Morrissey v. Brewer*, 408 U.S. 471 (1972), concerning parole revocation, the Court ruled that the parolee was entitled to notice, an opportunity to present evidence, and a right to confront and cross-examine adverse witnesses. In *United States v. Edwards*, 430 A.2d 1321 (D.C. App. 1981), upholding the District of Columbia preventive detention law, the majority ruled that *Gerstein* rather than *Morrissey* governed be-

cause it concerned a hearing with a similar issue: "whether the accused may be detained pending trial." That reasoning is unconvincing. As a partly dissenting opinion noted, *Gerstein* is hardly analogous because it involves only a probable cause determination, which (1) is not a basis for further detention per se but only for requiring bail; and (2) is much less complicated than the "far more complex, inherently speculative prediction that the accused is likely to be dangerous in the future" (*Edwards*, 1353).

Special situations

Capital cases. Forty states have adopted constitutional provisions declaring that all offenses are bailable, "except for capital offenses, where the proof is evident, or the presumption great." Although, as we have seen, there is considerable uncertainty regarding whether the Eighth Amendment creates a right to bail, and if so to what extent, it is generally assumed that the exception in these state constitutional provisions does not offend the federal Constitution. As the Supreme Court declared in *Carlson:* "The Eighth Amendment has not prohibited Congress from defining the classes of cases in which bail shall be allowed in this country. Thus, in criminal cases it is not compulsory where the punishment may be death" (545).

In states with these provisions, legislative abolition of the death penalty has been consistently held to mean that persons charged with offenses formerly subject to capital punishment are in all cases bailable. But there has not been agreement as to how these constitutional provisions should be applied when the legislature has provided for the death penalty but has done so in such a way that imposition of the penalty is constitutionally barred. Under the penalty theory, illustrated by *Commonwealth v. Truesdale*, 449 Pa. 325, 296 A.2d 829 (1972), the notion is that these constitutional provisions are based upon the "strong flight urge because of the possibility of an accused forfeiting his life," and thus are inapplicable once that possibility is removed by either the legislature or the courts. Under the classification theory, as represented by *People v. Anderson*, 6 Cal. 3d 628, 657 n. 45, 493 P.2d 880, 900 n. 45 (1972), it is stressed that the "underlying gravity of those offenses endures and the determination of their gravity for the purpose of bail continues unaffected by [the] decision" that the death penalty is unconstitutional.

Because these constitutional provisions prohibit bail only in those capital cases where "the proof is evident, or the presumption great," a defendant is not barred from obtaining his release on bail merely because he has been charged in such a way that he could receive the death penalty. Rather, these provisions contemplate "that bail should be denied when the circumstances disclosed indicate a fair likelihood that the defendant is in danger of a jury verdict" for an offense punishable by death, since "only in instances where such likelihood exists is his life in jeopardy and the well recognized urge to abscond present" (*State v. Konigsberg*, 33 N.J. 367, 377, 164 A.2d 740, 745 (1960)). As for where the burden of proof lies, one line of cases takes the view that since the defendant is entitled to bail only on application and when he so applies is trying to change the status quo, the burden is rightly on him to show that the proof is not evident or that the presumption is not great. The other and better view is that these constitutional provisions confer a right to bail except under the limited circumstances specified and that the burden should rest on the party relying on the exception, that is, the prosecution.

During trial. Once the defendant's trial has commenced, he is in a somewhat different position regarding his right to be at large on bail or other form of release. As the Supreme Court recognized in *Bitter v. United States*, 389 U.S. 15, 16 (1967): "A trial judge indisputably has broad powers to ensure the orderly and expeditious progress of a trial. For this purpose, he has the power to revoke bail and to remit the defendant to custody. But this power must be exercised with circumspection. It may be invoked only when and to the extent justified by danger which the defendant's conduct presents or by danger of significant interference with the progress or order of the trial." Thus bail may be revoked during trial where a defendant has made threats to government witnesses, or where he has engaged in obstructive misconduct during the course of the trial.

Pending appeal. Once the defendant's trial is completed and he has been convicted, his situation with respect to his release, even if he plans to take an appeal, changes significantly. The typical state constitutional provision guaranteeing a right to bail is limited to the time "before conviction," and this distinction is ordinarily observed in state statutes just as it is in the federal Bail Reform Act. The act declares that a person "who has been convicted of an offense and is either awaiting sentence or sentence review . . . or has filed an appeal or a petition for a writ of certiorari" is to be dealt with under the pretrial release provisions "unless the court or judge has reason to believe that no one or more conditions of release will reasonably assure that the person will not flee or pose a danger to any other person or to the community. If such a risk of flight or danger is believed to exist, or if it appears that an appeal is frivolous or taken for delay, the person may be ordered detained" (§ 3148).

The United States Supreme Court held as early as 1894 that there is no constitutional right to bail pending appeal from a conviction (*McKane v. Durston*, 153 U.S. 684 (1894)). A defendant who has been convicted and has little hope for reversal might be strongly tempted to flee, and one with greater hope for reversal might be tempted to tamper with witnesses who had been especially useful to the prosecutor so as to minimize the chances of conviction after remand. Another reason given is that "the presumption of innocence and the right to participate in the preparation of a defense to ensure a fair trial—are obviously not present where the defendant has already been tried and convicted" (*Gallie v. Wainwright*, 362 So. 2d 936, 941 (Fla. 1978)).

Probation or parole revocation. Even assuming a constitutional right to have bail set in other circumstances, it does not follow that a defendant held pending a revocation hearing for an alleged violation of probation or parole has a right to bail. As explained in *In re Whitney*, 421 F.2d 337, 338 (1st Cir. 1970), such a person "has been convicted of a crime, subjected to the sanctions prescribed by law, and has been granted conditional release in order to serve the interests of society." Thus the "interests which the government may protect at this stage of the process are properly much broader than before trial."

Material witnesses. Section 3149 of the federal act provides that if the testimony of a person is material in a criminal proceeding and it is shown "that it may become impracticable to secure his presence by subpoena," then the release conditions otherwise provided for in that act shall be utilized. Detention of a material witness for inability to comply with the conditions set is not allowed "if the testimony of such a witness can adequately be secured by deposition, and further detention is not necessary to prevent a failure of justice." In such case release may be delayed "for a reasonable period of time until the deposition of the witness can be taken."

Nearly all of the states have enacted provisions dealing with the pretrial confinement of material witnesses. Typically these statutes provide that a prospective witness in a case involving a felony or major crime can be brought before a judge on application of counsel, generally the prosecutor. The magistrate determines the importance of the witness to the case and gives the witness the option of posting some form of bail or recognizance, either personal or with sureties. If the witness must post bail but refuses or fails to do so, he can be confined until he has given his testimony or the case is dismissed. Several states authorize the taking of depositions for preserving testimony so that the witness may be released when the deposition is obtained, and some have adopted alternatives to incarceration such as placing the witness in the custody of another person.

WAYNE R. LaFAVE

See also APPEAL; ARRAIGNMENT; CAPITAL PUNISHMENT; JAILS; TRIAL, CRIMINAL.

BIBLIOGRAPHY

American Bar Association. "Pretrial Release." *Standards for Criminal Justice*, vol. 2. 2d ed. Prepared with the assistance of the American Bar Foundation. Boston: Little, Brown, 1980, chap. 10.
BASES, NAN C., and McDONALD, WILLIAM F. *Preventive Detention in the District of Columbia: The First Ten Months.* New York: Vera Institute of Justice, 1972.
CARLSON, RONALD L., and VOELPEL, MARK S. "Material Witnesses and Material Injustice." *Washington University Law Quarterly* 58 (1980): 1–53.
COHEN, RICHARD A. "Wealth, Bail, and the Equal Protection of the Laws." *Villanova Law Review* 23 (1978): 977–1040.
FOOTE, CALEB. "The Coming Constitutional Crisis in Bail." *University of Pennsylvania Law Review* 113 (1965): 959–999, 1125–1185.
HUNTER, ELMO B. "The Bail Reform Act of 1966." *University of Missouri at Kansas City Law Review* 40 (1972): 295–308.
MEYER, HERMINE H. "Constitutionality of Pretrial Detention." *Georgetown Law Journal* 60 (1972): 1139–1194, 1381–1474.
MITCHELL, JOHN N. "Bail Reform and the Constitutionality of Pretrial Detention." *Virginia Law Review* 55 (1969): 1223–1242.
THOMAS, WAYNE H. *Bail Reform in America.* Berkeley: University of California Press, 1976.
TRIBE, LAURENCE H. "An Ounce of Detention: Preventive Justice in the World of John Mitchell." *Virginia Law Review* 56 (1970): 371–407.
WICE, PAUL B. *Freedom for Sale: A National Study of Pretrial Release.* Lexington, Mass.: Heath, Lexington Books, 1974.

2.
BAIL REFORM

The question of what to do with an accused person between arrest and judgment poses a severe conflict for any system of criminal law. For the accused, pretrial imprisonment means the imposition of what amounts to punishment before determination of guilt,

disruption of family and employment relationships, obstruction of self-help in the preparation of a defense, and reduction of bargaining leverage in plea or sentencing negotiations. Conditional release pending trial, however, affords the defendant the opportunity to flee, to engage in criminal activity, or to corrupt the trial process by intimidating witnesses or destroying evidence. This inherent tension between fairness for the accused and the reduction of risks for the state is aggravated in modern society because of the typically deplorable conditions of the local jails in which pretrial detainees are confined and because the pretrial period may be prolonged for months or even years owing to court congestion, bureaucratic lethargy, pretrial tactics, or the complexity of preparing certain kinds of cases for trial.

Bail as a mechanism by which a balance is struck between these competing demands goes back at least to the time of Plato, who described how, in murder cases, the prosecutor must "demand bail from the defendant; and the latter shall provide three substantial securities . . . who guarantee to produce him at the trial, and if a man be unable or unwilling to provide these sureties, the court must take, bind and keep him, and produce him at the trial of the case" (p. 261). While bail has virtually disappeared in modern continental European practice, it has remained a mainstay of English and American pretrial procedure, although by the nineteenth century the deposit of financial security had replaced personal sureties as the deterrent against the accused's flight.

The right to bail is not a right to conditional liberty pending trial, but merely assures the accused of a prompt determination of the conditions under which a release from pretrial detention can be obtained. Thus, at the defendant's first court appearance after arrest and after a hearing that is typically brief and perfunctory, the judge will decide the amount of bail which is required or set other conditions by which conditional liberty will be allowed. When the accused, his family, or his friends can afford it, they can post cash or property as security, but economic realities and the amounts required are such that most defendants choose, or are forced to rely on, the purchase of an appearance bond from a bail bondsman. The bond premium is usually about 10 percent of the required amount of bail, and as with other forms of risk insurance, it is not refundable. In addition, the bondsman can require the accused to provide collateral against all or part of the bond. If a bond cannot be obtained or afforded, as happens in a substantial proportion of cases, in the traditional bail system the accused remains in jail. If he has been conditionally released but fails to appear when required, the security is subject to forfeiture.

Since the early 1960s, the active bail reform movement (discussed below) has resulted in two modifications of traditional bail practice. One has been the greatly increased use of forms of conditional release that do not require the posting of financial security. The most common method, especially frequent in the cases of minor offenders, is release on the accused's unsecured promise to appear ("release on own recognizance," or ROR), backed up in many jurisdictions by pretrial release agencies created to screen eligibles for ROR and to keep track of those who are released. Other methods include increased use of a summons to appear instead of an arrest, and a plan by which the accused deposits 10 percent of the required bail with the court as if he were purchasing a bond, the difference being that most of the deposit is refunded upon compliance with the conditions of release. Second, this reform effort to reduce dependence on money bail has resulted in growing sentiment in favor of some form of "preventive detention" that would permit denial of pretrial release to all defendants, rich as well as poor. As enacted in a few jurisdictions, this applies to some limited classes of defendants despite the fact that they are not accused of capital crimes, the only previously widespread traditional ground for possible denial of bail.

Need for reform

Role of the bondsman. The nature of the money bail system handicaps any judicial ability to control whether or not the accused remains in jail. As a private businessman, the bondsman can reject clients on his own terms. Although premium rates are regulated by the states, the bondsman can manipulate the economic realities for persons of limited means by demanding as much collateral as in his unreviewable business judgment he deems advisable; a client who can afford the premium but not the required collateral, or one who is refused a bond under any conditions, has no recourse. Thus the judge's bail decision is two steps removed from the actual outcome. The judge will often not know how much cash the defendant has or how much additional security he will have to put up, and he has no control over the practices of bondsmen, who "hold the keys to the jail in their pockets" (*Pannell v. United States*, 320 F.2d 698, 699 (D.C. Cir. 1963)).

Earlier in the twentieth century many bondsmen operated independently, putting up property they owned as security. This practice was a fertile source of the abuse of "straw bail," where the same property was used as security over and over again at the same time. To minimize their risk, bondsmen relied on the low rate of absconding and on the frequency with which forfeitures after default would not be imposed or would be at least partially remitted. The trend, however, has been away from independent entrepreneurs, and since mid-century most bondsmen have been agents of surety companies. While this provides the government with a financially responsible surety, the risk is still largely borne by the individual bondsman, since surety companies usually retain part of each agent's premiums in a fund to protect against the losses which that agent incurs.

In return for such delegation to private business of this substantial part of pretrial practice and decision-making, the government is entitled to the bondsman's services as quasi-probation officer in supervising the releasee and seeing that he comes to court on time, and as quasi-policeman in tracking him down and bringing him back if he absconds. It is also entitled to the bondsman's aid as guarantor for the payment of "damages" to the state in the amount of the bond when default occurs. The value of these services is questionable: bondsmen usually cannot afford much (if any) time for supervision, their resources for locating fugitives cannot begin to approach those available to the police or the Federal Bureau of Investigation, and the most immediate effect of strict forfeiture enforcement would be to make the bondsman more restrictive in his bonding practice and thereby to accentuate jail overcrowding and bias against lower-income defendants. In some cities, indeed, bondsmen have gone "on strike" to protest high forfeiture rates, a tactic calculated to flood the jails and cripple the courts.

Excessive bail. Referring to the bail system's exclusive reliance on financial deterrents against flight, a puzzled Alexis de Tocqueville observed in his *Democracy in America* (1835): "It is evident that such a legislation is hostile to the poor and favorable only to the rich." Yet prior to the emergence of the bail reform movement a century and a quarter later, almost no consideration was given to methods by which the pervasive discrimination against the poor that was inherent in bail might at least be mitigated.

The only United States Supreme Court case squarely on the issue of excessive bail did not involve indigents, but the Court's holding and dicta in the opinions afford no resolution of the problem of poor defendants (*Stack v. Boyle*, 342 U.S. 1 (1951)). Justice Robert H. Jackson, concurring, said that setting high bail to keep defendants in jail "is contrary to the whole policy and philosophy of bail," but he then added: "This is not to say that every defendant is entitled to such bail as he can provide, but he is entitled to an opportunity to make it in a reasonable amount" (5, 10). Reflecting prevailing law in both state and lower federal courts, the Court made it clear that the basic standard for what is "reasonable" is the amount "usually fixed" for the offense charged.

Such an interpretation places limits on the extent to which bail can be increased above the norm and restricts the imposition of higher amounts to cases where a defendant who could make normal bail is shown to pose a special high risk of flight. But the converse does not follow; if the amount required falls within the usual range for the crimes charged, refusal to lower it because of circumstances demonstrating low risk and restricted financial assets does not violate the Eighth Amendment. The extent in actual practice of bias against the poor that results from application of this dual standard will depend upon what levels of bail have been established as normal by custom and precedent. The pervasiveness of bias, however, is obvious from the size of detention populations, and was demonstrated empirically long ago by Arthur Beeley in Chicago (1927) and by Wayne Morse and Ronald Beattie in Oregon (1932). Their research was ignored and forgotten until resurrected as part of comprehensive empirical examinations of the bail system carried out by the University of Pennsylvania Law School in Philadelphia in 1954 and 1958 (Foote, Markle, and Woolley; Note) and by the Manhattan Bail Project in New York City in 1958 (Ares, Rankin, and Sturz).

With varying emphasis and documentation, all these studies showed (1) that bail was routinely set in the normal range for the offense charged without regard for ties to the community; (2) that from one-half to two-thirds of felony defendants could not make bail in these amounts; (3) that up to one-fourth of those charged with bail as low as $500 could not make that amount; (4) that nonfinancial ROR was extremely rare; (5) that from one-fifth to one-third of those detained in jail for want of bail were ultimately never convicted; (6) that detention conditions were deplorable and more restrictive than those imposed on convicted felons; and (7) that jailed defendants, as compared with those who were bailed, were subject to prejudice in the disposition of their cases.

Reform efforts

The Vera experiment. It was against this background that the bail reform movement erupted with astonishing rapidity in the 1960s. Some of the more obvious explanations for such a sudden outburst of activity after decades of neglect are easy to identify: (1) the climate engendered by the approach to criminal justice of the Warren Court, especially its decision on the appeal rights of indigents in *Griffin v. Illinois*, 351 U.S. 12 (1956); (2) the incoming Kennedy administration's generally liberal approach to domestic problems and its particular emphasis on a "war on poverty"; (3) the available documentation of the extent of prejudice against indigents provided by the 1954 and 1958 University of Pennsylvania studies; and (4) the creation in 1961 of the Vera Foundation and Institute by New York philanthropist Louis Schweitzer for the purpose of promoting and initially funding reform of pretrial detention. The movement's rapid growth was facilitated by increasing strain on detention facilities caused by sharply accelerating arrest rates. There was also concern to develop alternative criteria for pretrial detention, because it was recognized that a bail system based exclusively on money might not survive a constitutional challenge before a Supreme Court that, in its *Griffin* decision, had stressed the rights of indigents under the equal protection clause.

Whatever the reasons, the Vera program was the right idea at the right moment. Under the energetic direction of Herbert Sturz, Schweitzer's associate, the Vera Institute obtained the cooperation of a group of New York judges for the experimental Manhattan Bail Project. The project promoted increased use of ROR, developed nonfinancial criteria for rapid screening of arrested persons to identify those deemed to pose little risk of flight, and created and staffed an agency to do the screening and to follow up ROR releasees in order to reduce the number who would fail to appear. Vera assumed that a defendant's residential, family, and employment ties to the community were valid predictors of his likelihood to comply with the conditions of pretrial release. The project developed a scale by which to score these variables on the basis of information supplied by the defendant and verified it rapidly, usually by telephone. If the defendant scored above a cutoff point, the project's favorable prognosis was reported to the judge for his consideration in reaching his pretrial release decision (Ares, Rankin, and Sturz; Friedman).

An early and very influential evaluation of the Vera project compared the pretrial release outcomes of a control group in which bail was set in the traditional manner with an experimental group processed under the Vera plan (Ares, Rankin, and Sturz). Many more defendants were released on ROR in the experimental group without any increase in the fail-to-appear rate, which did not exceed 1 percent in either group. This was widely cited as a demonstration that the number of releases could be greatly increased without an appreciable increase in risk, and the study doubtless contributed substantially to the increased willingness to use ROR which followed. The finding was also interpreted as an indication that the Vera selection procedure was an effective discriminator of good and bad risks, and the method was later widely copied in other projects. This confidence was unwarranted, however, for the study was unable to show the relative importance in causing a low failure-to-appear rate of the original selection and of subsequent follow-ups to encourage compliance. Nor could it demonstrate that those who failed to win a Vera-approved release might not have complied just as successfully as those actually released.

Perhaps just as important in promoting the creation of similar programs, Vera soon enlisted the enthusiastic cooperation of Robert Kennedy's Justice Department. The 1964 report of the United States Attorney General's Committee on Poverty and the Administration of Federal Criminal Justice, chaired by Francis Allen, placed major emphasis on the bail system's discriminatory impact on the poor, and Kennedy followed this up by an order to all United States attorneys to accept ROR for low-risk defendants. In 1964, only a decade after the Philadelphia bail study had suffered the same apathetic neglect as its predecessors, a national bail conference co-sponsored by Vera and the Department of Justice brought together in Washington judges and criminal justice administrators from across the nation and propelled an attack on traditional bail to the forefront of the reform agenda. A 1964 report to the conference by Daniel Freed and Patricia Wald provided a concise analysis of the problems and proved to be an influential stimulus to change. Two years later, the department obtained congressional passage of the federal Bail Reform Act of 1966, 18 U.S.C. §§ 3146–3150, which in effect created a presumption in favor of ROR and permitted money bail to be imposed only if three prescribed alternative forms of nonfinancial release would not "reasonably assure the appearance of the person for trial."

Diffusion. Vera-type pretrial programs spread rapidly to many cities; Wayne Thomas has provided a detailed account of the movement's growth during the first decade of its existence, and critical assessments of its accomplishments have been published by John Goldkamp and Malcolm Feeley (1983). The evolution of the original Manhattan project provided

a preview of what was to happen in many other parts of the country. In its first year it was entirely financed by Schweitzer, but it was soon recognized that if the program was to survive it would have to be incorporated into the governmental structure of the criminal justice system, and in 1964 it was absorbed into New York City's Probation Department. The adverse effects of bureaucratization were perhaps inevitable, for as was true of all city agencies, the project's budget was precarious and its survival depended upon reaching accommodation with judges, prosecutors, and the city's political system. In any event, requirements for release were tightened up, there was a sharp decline in the proportion of interviewed defendants who were recommended for release, and as time went on the operation's effectiveness in obtaining ROR releases declined. After nine years the Vera Institute obtained a transfer of the program to the federally funded Pretrial Services Agency.

Impact of reform

The significance of these developments in actual practice is difficult to appraise. Unquestionably, the use of ROR has resulted in the conditional release of large numbers of predominantly less serious alleged offenders who would previously have been required to post bail that some or many could not have afforded. But at the same time, detention facilities have continued to be crowded with pretrial detainees jailed for want of bail. The apparent contradiction is explained by the rapid increase in the number of arrests during the 1960s and 1970s and by the fact that many of those released on ROR could have purchased a bond if it had been necessary. Thus "bail reform" remains substantially unfinished; in practice in most jurisdictions the majority of those charged with more serious crimes, and many lesser offenders as well, continue to be jailed. This widespread persistence of de facto preventive detention through the operation of the traditional bail system suggests that the seemingly radical incursion on the right to bail of formal preventive detention provisions may have only limited significance in actual practice.

CALEB FOOTE

See also BAIL: THE RIGHT TO BAIL.

BIBLIOGRAPHY

ARES, CHARLES E.; RANKIN, ANNE; and STURZ, HERBERT. "The Manhattan Bail Project: An Interim Report on the Use of Pre-trial Parole." *New York University Law Review* 38 (1963): 67–95.

BEELEY, ARTHUR. *The Bail System in Chicago* (1927). Reprint. University of Chicago Press, 1966.

FEELEY, MALCOLM M. *Court Reform on Trial.* New York: Basic Books, 1983.

————. *The Process Is the Punishment: Handling Cases in a Lower Court.* New York: Russell Sage Foundation, 1979.

FOOTE, CALEB. "The Coming Constitutional Crisis in Bail." *University of Pennsylvania Law Review* 113 (1965): 959–999; 1125–1185.

————; MARKLE, JAMES P.; and WOOLLEY, EDWARD A. "Compelling Evidence in Court: Administration of Bail in Philadelphia." *University of Pennsylvania Law Review* 102 (1954): 1031–1079.

FOOTE, CALEB, ed. *Studies on Bail.* Philadelphia: University of Pennsylvania Law School, Institute of Legal Research, 1966.

FREED, DANIEL J., and WALD, PATRICIA M. *Bail in the United States, 1964.* Working paper for the National Conference on Bail and Criminal Justice, May 27–29, 1964. Washington, D.C.: U.S. Department of Justice, 1964.

FRIEDMAN, LEE S. "The Evolution of Bail Reform." *Policy Sciences* 7 (1976): 281–313.

GOLDKAMP, JOHN S. *Two Classes of Accused: A Study of Bail and Detention in American Justice.* Cambridge, Mass.: Ballinger, 1979.

MORSE, WAYNE L., and BEATTIE, RONALD H. "Survey of the Administration of Criminal Justice in Oregon." *Oregon Law Review* 11 (1932): Supp., pp. 1–221.

National Center for State Courts. *An Evaluation of Policy Related Research on the Effectiveness of Pretrial Release Programs.* Denver: The Center, 1975.

Note. "A Study of the Administration of Bail in New York City." *University of Pennsylvania Law Review* 106 (1958): 693–730.

PLATO. *Laws,* vol. 2. Translated by R. G. Bury. Loeb Classical Library. Cambridge, Mass.: Harvard University Press, 1926.

ROESCH, RONALD. "Predicting the Effects of Pretrial Intervention Programs on Jail Populations: A Method for Planning and Decisionmaking." *Federal Probation* 40 (1976): 32–36.

THOMAS, WAYNE H. *Bail Reform in America.* Berkeley: University of California Press, 1976.

TOCQUEVILLE, ALEXIS DE. *Democracy in America* (1835). 2 vols. Foreword by Harold J. Laski. New York: Knopf, 1945.

U.S. Attorney General's Committee on Poverty and the Administration of Federal Criminal Justice. *Report: Poverty and the Administration of Federal Criminal Justice.* Washington, D.C.: U.S. Department of Justice, 1964.

WALD, PATRICIA. "Pretrial Detention and Ultimate Freedom: A Statistical Study." *New York University Law Review* 39 (1964): 631–640.

————. "The Right to Bail Revisited: A Decade of Promise without Fulfillment." *The Rights of the Accused.* Edited by Stuart S. Nagel. Beverly Hills, Calif.: Sage, 1972, pp. 189–195.

WICE, PAUL B. *Freedom for Sale: A National Study of Pretrial Release.* Lexington, Mass.: Heath, Lexington Books, 1974.

ZEISEL, HANS. "Bail Revisited." *American Bar Foundation Research Journal* (1979): 769–789.

BANISHMENT AND EXILE

In the context of criminal justice, both banishment and exile refer to the expulsion or removal of persons from a community or country as punishment. The penalties have been termed society's most primitive form of self-defense (Hentig).

Origins. Under prehistoric tribal laws, offenders were declared outcast and driven from the group. Banishment in diverse forms was the penalty in ancient Greece and Rome for homicide and other serious offenses. Under Anglo-Saxon law, offenders could be condemned as outlaws and deprived of the benefits and protection of the law. England later allowed arrested persons to "abjure the realm," that is, to swear to depart and never return. In colonial America banishment from the jurisdiction was employed as a penalty for nonresident offenders, although not extensively.

The Roman Empire developed two forms of banishment, relegation and deportation. Relegation consisted in exclusion from a particular city or region, whereas deportation involved transportation from Italy for life, together with loss of civil rights and confiscation of property. Its use was restricted to upper-class transgressors of the law. Originally confined to political offenders, it was extended to include a variety of criminal offenders.

Transportation. The use of extraterritorial transportation for criminals on a large scale originated in Europe, when Portugal and Spain used criminals and vagrants as colonizers in the fifteenth and sixteenth centuries. In 1598 the British Parliament authorized transportation, and offenders were sent to Virginia after its foundation in 1607. Seventeenth-century Russia and eighteenth-century France adopted transportation, sending offenders to Siberia and French Guiana, respectively. Throughout the eighteenth and nineteenth centuries, transportation to penal colonies or distant settlements became widespread; it was taken up by other European countries, including the Netherlands, Denmark, and Italy.

The English system. It is estimated that in the first half of the seventeenth century no more than 50 British convicts a year were transported to America. In

1655 the practice of pardoning criminals on condition that they accept transportation to the colonies began, and by the end of the century about 4,500 had been transported in this way.

In the eighteenth century transportation became one of the principal sanctions of the English criminal law. The numbers transported rose from an average of 500 a year in the first half of the century to an average of 1,000 a year between 1750 and 1776. In addition, prior to the American Revolution about 7,500 convicts were sent to America from Ireland. Most went to Virginia and Maryland, but all thirteen British colonies in America received some.

The Revolution ended transportation to America, but in 1788 it was resumed to the newly discovered continent of Australia. In the first decade of the nineteenth century an annual average of about 400 offenders were transported, but the numbers increased until, in the 1830s, the average exceeded 5,000 annually. Thereafter the numbers declined, and by 1868, when the system was abolished, about 500 were being sent each year. An estimated total of nearly 162,000 men and women were transported to Australia. In both America and Australia, transportation served an economic as well as a penal function, providing cheap labor for the development of colonial territories.

The Russian system. In Russia, transportation to Siberia served the dual purpose of eliminating criminals and contributing to the population and development of new territory. In the seventeenth century it was used only for disabled criminals already punished by such methods as branding or tongue removal. In the eighteenth century personal mutilation and death were abolished as penalties and replaced by exile to Siberia as punishment for both political and criminal offenses. In addition, the use of exile was extended to a great variety of minor offenses.

It is not known how many offenders were exiled prior to the establishment in 1823 of the Bureau of Exile Administration, the first organization to keep records on exiled persons. By the 1860s an average of 14,600 offenders a year were exiled with or without confinement, and this rose to 18,000 by the 1880s. It is estimated that between 1800 and 1914 about 1 million persons were banished to Siberia. No official figures have been published since 1917, but journalistic and émigré accounts suggest that in the Soviet Union the system has continued on a vastly greater scale than under the czars.

Conclusion. Banishment and exile reflect what Max Grünhut calls "the tendency to get criminals out of sight" (p. 73). With the major exception of the Soviet Union, the penalties are seldom used. The function of eliminating or removing the offender from society, apart from the vestigial form of the deportation of criminal aliens, has been largely taken over by imprisonment.

GORDON HAWKINS

See also PENAL COLONIES; PUNISHMENT.

BIBLIOGRAPHY

GRÜNHUT, MAX. *Penal Reform: A Comparative Study.* Reprint. Montclair, N.J.: Patterson Smith, 1972.
HENTIG, HANS VON. *Punishment: Its Origin, Purpose, and Psychology.* London: Hodge, 1937.
IVES, GEORGE. *A History of Penal Methods: Criminals, Witches, Lunatics.* Reprint. Montclair, N.J.: Patterson Smith, 1970.
KENNAN, GEORGE. *Siberia and the Exile System.* Reprint. Abridged ed. University of Chicago Press, 1958.
SELLIN, THORSTEN. *Slavery and the Penal System.* New York: Elsevier Scientific, 1976.
SHAW, A. G. *Convicts and the Colonies: A Study of Penal Transportation from Great Britain and Ireland to Australia and Other Parts of the British Empire.* London: Faber & Faber, 1966.
SMITH, ABBOT EMERSON. *Colonists in Bondage: White Servitude and Convict Labor in America, 1607–1776.* Reprint. New York: Norton, 1971.

BANK ROBBERY

Under the federal Bank Robbery Act of 1934, as amended, 18 U.S.C. §§ 2113, 3231 (1976), banks, credit unions, and savings and loan associations that are (1) organized under federal law, (2) part of the federal system, or (3) federally insured are protected. This section of the United States Code defines *bank* as any banking or trust institution that is organized and operating under United States law and that is either a member of the Federal Reserve System or has its deposits insured by the Federal Deposit Insurance Corporation (FDIC). Concurrently, this statute also applies to those savings and loan associations that have their accounts insured by the FDIC (§ 2113(f), (g)).

The act makes it a federal offense for anyone to take or attempt to take by force and violence or intimidation anything of value belonging to one of the protected institutions, or anything that is in one of the protected institution's care, custody, control, management, or possession (§ 2113(a)). The statute divides the offense of bank robbery into various stages, making criminal the acts that constitute the steps of the crime.

First, the entering of a protected bank or savings and loan association with the *intent* to commit a felony therein is a crime. Second, Section 2113(b) addresses the stage of taking and carrying away the property of the protected institution. The escape phase of the robbery is regarded as part of the robbery itself, not as a separate event that takes place afterward. Hence, any party assisting or participating in that phase of the robbery becomes a principal to the crime itself (*United States v. von Roeder*, 435 F.2d 1004 (10th Cir. 1970), *vacated and remanded sub nom. Schreiner v. United States*, 404 U.S. 67 (1971)). Third, Section 2113(c) deals with what one does with the stolen property. Any other party who becomes involved in this stage of the act is subject to the same punishment he would have incurred if he had robbed the bank. Fourth, Section 2113(d) makes the acts described in sections 2113(a) and 2113(b) subject to a heavier penalty if anyone's life is put in jeopardy with the use of a dangerous weapon or device or if the person committing or attempting to commit the offense assaults any person. Finally, Section 2113(e) allows a jury to authorize the death penalty if any offense described within the act is accompanied by a killing or a kidnapping.

The question is commonly posed whether an unlawful entry and a robbery that follows are two separate offenses, consecutively punishable. The United States Supreme Court in *Prince v. United States*, 352 U.S. 322 (1957) answered in the negative. The Court concluded that the unlawful-entry provision was included in the act to cover an instance in which a person entered a bank intending to rob it but became frustrated before doing so. Conversely, the Court stated, where one entered a bank intending to rob it and did rob it, the two crimes merged. The provision of the act that addresses the receiving of stolen property is intended not to increase the robber's punishment, but rather to punish the ones who eventually and knowingly receive the stolen money (*Heflin v. United States*, 358 U.S. 415 (1959)).

Section 2113(e), which deals with kidnapping and murder, especially where these acts are committed after the robbery and in an attempt to avoid apprehension, may provide separate and distinct crimes from the robbery provision (*United States v. Parker*, 283 F.2d 862 (7th Cir. 1960); *Duboice v. United States*, 195 F.2d 371 (8th Cir. 1952); *Clark v. United States*, 184 F.2d 952 (10th Cir. 1950)). However, it has been suggested that the entire statute creates a single offense, with various degrees of sentences allowed for the increasing severity of the crime (*United States v. Drake*, 250 F.2d 216 (7th Cir. 1957); *Simunov v. United States*, 162 F.2d 314 (6th Cir. 1947); *Wells v. Swope*, 121 F. Supp.

718 (N.D. Cal. 1954)). From the Supreme Court's decision in *Prince*, this latter view appears to be supported, even though the Court did not expressly overrule the other cases.

Depending on the facts of the alleged violation of the Bank Robbery Act, various sentences may be imposed on the offender on the different counts of the indictment without constituting double jeopardy (*United States v. Koury*, 319 F.2d 75 (6th Cir. 1963)). However, if the defendant is charged with separate counts of jeopardizing the lives of different persons, this is generally regarded as but one offense, and only one sentence may be imposed (*McDonald v. Johnston*, 149 F.2d 768 (9th Cir. 1945); *McDonald v. Hudspeth*, 129 F.2d 196 (10th Cir. 1942)). Analogous to this reasoning, as shown in *United States v. McKenzie*, 414 F.2d 808 (3d Cir. 1969) and *Holbrook v. Hunter*, 149 F.2d 230 (10th Cir. 1945), where one is charged with committing a robbery and also with assault, only one sentence may be imposed.

ROBERT L. BOGOMOLNY

See also FEDERAL CRIMINAL JURISDICTION; FEDERAL CRIMINAL LAW ENFORCEMENT; ROBBERY.

BIBLIOGRAPHY

Comment. "A General Sentence Is to Be Imposed for a Conviction Consisting of Several Counts Charging Violation of the Federal Bank Robbery Act but the Term Shall Not Exceed the Maximum Permissible Sentence on the Count that Carries the Greatest Maximum Sentence." *Houston Law Review* 9 (1972): 579–586.

CONKLIN, JOHN E. *Robbery and the Criminal Justice System*. Philadelphia: Lippincott, 1972.

DRECHSLER, C. T. "Annotation: Validity and Construction of Federal Bank Robbery Act." *American Law Reports Annotated*, 2d series, vol. 59. Rochester, N.Y.: Lawyers Co-operative, 1958, pp. 946–1011.

O'KEEFE, JOSEPH JAMES. *The Men Who Robbed Brink's: The Inside Story of One of the Most Famous Holdups in the History of Crime, as Told by Specs O'Keefe to Bob Considine, in Cooperation with the FBI*. New York: Random House, 1961.

WHARTON, FRANCIS. *Wharton's Criminal Law*, vol. 4. 14th ed. Edited by Charles E. Torcia. Rochester, N.Y.: Lawyers Co-operative, 1978.

BATTERY

See ASSAULT AND BATTERY.

BEHAVIORAL THEORY

See ALCOHOL AND CRIME: TREATMENT AND REHABILITATION; *articles under* CRIME CAUSATION; DELINQUENT AND CRIMINAL SUBCULTURES; DEVIANCE; EDUCATION AND CRIME.

BEHAVIOR, TYPOLOGIES OF CRIMINAL

See TYPOLOGIES OF CRIMINAL BEHAVIOR.

BIGAMY

Scholars, codifiers, and legislators have commonly classified bigamy as an "offense against the family." It may be that the universal legislative practice of prescribing penal sanctions for multiple marriage reflects a consensus that such behavior is either so common or so threatening to family stability that it requires criminal stigmatization. It is much more likely, however, that this legislative unanimity is the product of the powerful influence exerted on the criminal law by historical precedent and moral fervor.

Prior to 1603 in England, the social problems caused by bigamy—problems produced when a person marries another prior to the termination of an existing marriage by divorce, annulment, or death—were the exclusive province of ecclesiastical courts and Church authorities. In the early seventeenth century, when "reform" of the law with respect to bigamy took place, the scope of criminal sanction and religious notions of immoral conduct were widely considered coterminous. It is not surprising, then, that in 1603, during the reign of King James I, the House of Commons made bigamists felons. Nor should it be surprising that twentieth-century criminal law reformers, influenced as they have been by the virtues of "decriminalization," have stirred (largely unresolved) controversy as to the propriety of maintaining criminal sanctions against bigamy.

The origins and aims of the original statute were clear enough: prohibitions against bigamy were designed to reinforce, through threat of the death penalty, the Church's command that marriage be indissoluble. Despite the importance of this purpose, there is no evidence that the crime was ever enforced with the vigor employed against "real" criminals—*vigor* having the meaning of investigative thoroughness and prosecutorial zeal.

An argument can be made, of course, that defining bigamy as a crime protects against real injury. The American Law Institute's Model Penal Code notes that

bigamy . . . seeks legal sanction for what amounts to a . . . special provocation to the first spouse. . . . Bigamy may also undermine the property interests of the first spouse by setting up a new spouse-claimant under community property or inheritance laws. Bigamy contemplates a permanent abandonment of the prior spouse or a continuing division of the bigamist's time and money between two or more families. There is thus a high likelihood that a second alliance concluded under color of law will prejudice a prior marriage by resulting in desertion and non-support and some justification for punishing bigamous relations independently of separate criminal offenses that may apply [commentary on § 230.1].

Yet the Code's assessment of the danger of bigamous behavior is tokened by the fact that it relegates bigamy to misdemeanor status, and bigamy is included in most commentators' lists of "victimless crimes." In a divorce-prone and divorce-permissive society, the bigamist's first spouse has little interest in marital exclusivity worthy of protection by criminal sanction. The second "spouse's" interest, if any, assumes that he or she is ignorant of the bigamy and that the injury is likely to be financial; this injury can thus be protected by sanctions against theft. An ahistorical defense of defining bigamy as a crime might point to the risk that plural wives are especially likely to be denied "personhood"; yet it is probably also true that social mores and religious norms will prevent "old-fashioned" bigamy as well as will criminal sanctions. Commentators have often concluded that the social interest consists more in asserting that bigamy is a crime than in enforcing criminal sanctions against it. Therefore, as is usually the case when the penal interest is exemplary, the offense is occasionally and capriciously enforced against defendants who are no more culpable than are a host of violators whose behavior is officially ignored. Interestingly enough, the civil law's sanctions—invalidation of the second marriage and denial of the benefits of marital status to either "spouse"—present just as dismal a picture: infrequent and capricious application, almost exclusively at the behest of a person likely to benefit financially if the sanctions are applied.

The ancient lineage of the offense, its exemplary function, and the scarcity of prosecutions all help to explain some of the unusual features of the crime. Its parameters remained almost unchanged from the time of James I until in the 1950s the preliminary draft of the Model Penal Code gave impetus to criminal law reform in the United States. Thus, most states maintained some version of the Jacobean exception for marriages of a person "whose Husband or Wife shall be continually remaining beyond the Seas by the Space of Seven Years together." Despite the strength of mens rea notions in criminal law jurisprudence, many state courts stubbornly refused to exculpate a defendant who reasonably but erroneously believed that his marriage was nonbigamous. The Model

Penal Code's recommendation that the "mistake of fact" problem be treated similarly to other mens rea issues has influenced subsequent state reforms (commentary on § 230.1). Nor has the crime of bigamy frequently fallen victim to the traditional understanding that "criminal statutes must be strictly construed in favor of the defendant" (LaFave and Scott, p. 72). In *Reynolds v. United States*, 98 U.S. 145 (1878), for example, the United States Supreme Court saw no need to narrow the scope of the federal bigamy statute in order to exclude Mormons engaging in plural marriage under a claim of religious right. The Court was unanimous in holding that the statute, as construed, did not violate the freedom-of-religion strictures of the First Amendment. In the present, more permissive, era the Court has affirmed the First Amendment holding, while giving prosecutors considerable authority to deter bigamous behavior. In *Cleveland v. United States*, 329 U.S. 14 (1946), the Court upheld the constitutionality of the Mann Act—which prohibited the interstate transportation of "any woman . . . for prostitution or debauchery, or for any other immoral purpose"—after interpreting it to allow the conviction of a Mormon for traveling from one state to another in order to cohabit with his bigamous wife.

The twentieth century's most celebrated bigamy prosecution deserves special attention. A Caldwell County, North Carolina, couple traveled to Nevada (the American capital of "migratory divorce" at the time), divorced, remarried, and returned to Caldwell County to enjoy (reconstituted) connubial bliss. The local prosecutor twice convicted Mr. and "Mrs." Williams of bigamous cohabitation. The Supreme Court reversed the couple's first conviction and by a narrow majority affirmed the second. But the Court's interest in the Williamses' plight proceeded not from any concern about the crime of bigamy, but because their migratory divorce and North Carolina's refusal to be bound by it implicated serious questions concerning the Constitution's full faith and credit clause (*Williams v. North Carolina*, 325 U.S. 226 (1945); *Williams v. North Carolina*, 317 U.S. 287 (1942)).

A significant proportion of marriages are now terminated by judicial decree rather than by death, and such a decree can be obtained fairly quickly and inexpensively, either in the spouses' domicile or in a "divorce mill" state. Under these circumstances, most plural marriages are likely to be "serial" rather than simultaneous, and traditional bigamy is more likely to be the product of bad legal advice (or no legal advice) than of criminal intent. Thus, the continuance of the crime of bigamy allows prosecutors in communities that adhere to traditional monogamous mar-

riage values to harass dissenters who travel to other states to change spouses. Whether perpetuating draconian penalties for bigamy currently serves any purpose related to marital stability or the protection of innocent marriage partners is seldom addressed. This question will not be faced so long as legislators continue to be fearful of destabilizing the criminal law status quo.

ROBERT J. LEVY

See also ADULTERY AND FORNICATION; CRIMINALIZATION AND DECRIMINALIZATION; *both articles under* STRICT LIABILITY.

BIBLIOGRAPHY

American Law Institute. *Model Penal Code: Official Draft and Revised Commentaries.* Philadelphia: ALI, 1980.

LaFave, Wayne R., and Scott, Austin W., Jr. *Handbook on Criminal Law.* St. Paul: West, 1972.

BILL OF RIGHTS, AMERICAN

See CRIMINAL PROCEDURE: CONSTITUTIONAL ASPECTS.

BIOLOGY AND CRIME

See CRIME CAUSATION: BIOLOGICAL THEORIES.

BLACKMAIL AND EXTORTION

Theft may be accomplished by many methods: threat, force, false pretense, stealth, and breach of trust (Allen). Theft by certain kinds of threats is called blackmail or extortion; by others, it is called robbery. The distinction traditionally drawn between robbery by intimidation and blackmail or extortion is that a person commits robbery when he threatens to do *immediate* bodily harm, whereas he commits blackmail or extortion when he threatens to do bodily harm *in the future*.

Extortion by a public official is sometimes distinguished from bribery by the intent of the person making the payment. If the payment is voluntary and the person paying the official is seeking an advantage to which he is not otherwise entitled, he and the public official are both guilty of bribery. If, on the other hand, the person makes the payment because of coercion, he is deemed the victim of the public official's crime of extortion. Although some authorities argue that extortion cannot be committed where bribery occurs, the reality is that a public official sometimes extorts money at the same time that a citizen is offering a bribe.

In the eighteenth century, blackmail and extortion were different crimes. Both involved gaining property by threats, but extortion was committed by public officials, whereas blackmail was committed by private citizens. Now that all crimes are defined by statute, the terms *blackmail* and *extortion* are often used interchangeably. Yet in common parlance, they connote somewhat different behaviors. Blackmail generally refers to a threat seeking hush money, and extortion, to a threat of physical harm to person or property or to a threat made by a public official. Many modern statutes, however, do not use either term, referring to behavior usually considered blackmail or extortion by such names as criminal coercion or theft.

Extortion by a public official. *Extortion* is an older term than *blackmail*. In England the earliest extant statute setting out the crime of extortion was the Statute of Westminster, the First, 3 Edw. 1, cc. 24–31 (1275) (England) (repealed), which prohibited extortion by a "sheriff or other royal official." This statute may have been derived from Roman law of the second century A.D., which forbade public officers to profit from their offices. Although extortion continued intermittently as a statutory crime, it was for many centuries primarily a common-law (case-law) crime. According to William Blackstone, extortion at common law was "an abuse of public justice, which consists in an officer's unlawfully taking, by colour of his office, from any man, any money or thing of value, that is not due him, or more than is due, or before it is due" (*141).

Extortion at common law had five elements, which have remained under most modern extortion statutes. First, the fee must be *unlawful*, that is, not due at all, not due at the time collected, or larger than due. Second, the fee must be collected by a *public officer*. It is usually thought to be irrelevant whether the extortionist is an official of local, state, or national government so long as the crime has been committed within the jurisdiction. Third, the fee must be collected *under color of office*. If a public official receives money for additional services actually performed in a private capacity, this is usually not extortion (Perkins, pp. 369–370).

Fourth, at common law the fee had to be actually *received*. This requirement has been relaxed under many modern statutes to punish the extorting of a promise to pay an unlawful fee. Fifth, the fee must be taken *corruptly*. At common law and in most jurisdictions, an official who takes an unlawful fee because of an honest mistake has not committed blackmail. Even where the word *corruptly* has been omitted from the statutory definition of extortion, an official usually cannot be convicted if he acted honestly and in good faith (Perkins, p. 371).

Blackmail and extortion by a private person. The first references to blackmail date from the sixteenth century, when the Scottish Parliament made it a crime to obtain property by certain written threats of physical harm to person or property (Scot. Parl. Acts Jas. VI, c. 27 (1567) (Scotland) (repealed); Scot. Parl. Acts Jas. VI, c. 59 (1587) (Scotland) (repealed)). Later, some types of blackmail were outlawed in parts of England (43 Eliz. 1, c. 13 (1601) (England) (repealed)). In 1722 the repressive Waltham Black Act (officially known as the Criminal Law Act, 9 Geo. 1, c. 22 (1722) (Great Britain) (repealed)) authorized the death penalty throughout the country for making certain written threats that demanded property as the price for refraining from physically injuring person or property. Because blackmailers began obtaining property by sending extortionate letters without making any demands in them, a 1754 statute removed the requirement of a demand (27 Geo. 2, c. 15 (1754) (Great Britain) (repealed)). A few years later, blackmail was expanded to include certain written threats to accuse a person of an infamous crime with an intent to gain (30 Geo. 2, c. 24 (1757) (Great Britain) (repealed)).

Not until 1843 was gaining by threatening to expose embarrassing but noncriminal behavior made a crime (Hepworth, p. 14). Various English blackmail statutes were collected, restated, and revised in 1916 and 1968, as well as several times in the nineteenth century (Tooher). Blackmail was also a misdemeanor at common law (*Regina v. Woodward*, 88 Eng. Rep. 949 (Q.B. 1707)). However, this misdemeanor was rarely prosecuted, and it fell into disuse as the blackmail statutes mentioned above were passed.

Some commentators have argued that the offense of blackmail was created by statute to plug a loophole in the law of robbery. At common law, robbery was the taking of property by actual force or the threat of imminent force to the victim. In the eighteenth century, robbery was expanded case by case to include taking property by two other types of threats: (1) the threat to destroy the victim's house by mob violence, and (2) the threat to publicly accuse the victim of sodomy, whether or not the accusation was true. Sodomy was so despised that Blackstone refused even to mention it by name, referring to it as "the infamous crime against nature . . . the very mention of which is a disgrace to human nature" (*215). Some commentators have suggested that physical force is implicit in the accusation of sodomy because of the possibility of mob violence, and in the threat to destroy a house because of danger to the occupants.

Modern American statutes vary considerably in the ways they define blackmail or extortion by a private person. Some statutes require that the threat accomplish its purpose. Under such a statute an unsuccessful threat may usually be prosecuted as a criminal attempt. But most modern statutes do not require that the extortionate threat succeed; the making of the threat is enough.

The statutes also vary with regard to what must be demanded for the behavior to be illegal. Some statutes, for example, prohibit the obtaining of "property," "any pecuniary advantage," or, more broadly, "any valuable thing." A few statutes prohibit inducing someone "to do or refrain from doing any act against his will."

American blackmail and extortion statutes, unlike those in England, usually enumerate the types of prohibited threats. In the state statutes, the most common types of prohibited threats (however defined) are: (1) the threat of personal injury; (2) the threat to injure property (whether or not such an injury is physical); (3) the threat to accuse of a crime; and (4) the threat to expose any matter that would damage personal or business reputation, or that would expose the victim to hatred, contempt, or ridicule.

Many other threats, often overlapping with the above four, are prohibited under some state statutes: (1) the threat to commit any offense; (2) the threat to commit any felony; (3) the threat to physically confine or restrain; (4) the threat of physical harm to property; (5) the threat to impair credit; (6) the threat to expose a secret; (7) the threat to cause or continue a strike or boycott, if a labor representative is seeking a personal payoff for not striking or boycotting; (8) the threat to give or withhold testimony or information about another's legal claim or defense; (9) the threat of a public official to take or withhold action against anyone or anything; and (10) the threat to inflict any other harm that would not benefit the threatener.

Because some of these prohibited threats often have legitimate uses, some jurisdictions give the threatener an affirmative defense that he genuinely believed that the property sought was due him. Other jurisdictions allow this "claim of right" defense only when the amount sought was previously ascertained, as with a preexisting debt or liquidated damages. But many jurisdictions have not yet recognized the claim-of-right defense in any form.

Modern federal statutes. Federal statutes make many particular kinds of extortion or blackmail illegal. For example, extortion by officials of the federal government is a crime (18 U.S.C. § 872 (1976)). It is blackmail to demand or receive a valuable thing by offering not to inform against anyone who has violated federal law (18 U.S.C. § 873 (1976)). Moreover, extorting kickbacks from public-works employees is illegal (18 U.S.C. § 874 (1976)). It is also prohibited to mail or transmit in interstate commerce certain threats with the intent to extort, including threats to injure person, property, or reputation; to kidnap; or to accuse of a crime (18 U.S.C. §§ 875–877 (1976)). Another statute, the Travel Act of 1961, as amended, 18 U.S.C. § 1952 (1976), makes it illegal to travel between states or use interstate commerce to distribute the proceeds of extortion. The federal criminal code also makes it a crime to make, finance, or collect extortionate extensions of credit (18 U.S.C. §§ 891–894, 896 (1976)). An extortionate extension of credit is defined as one that, it is understood, will be enforced by violence or other criminal means.

The federal extortion statute that has generated the most litigation is the 1946 "Hobbs Act" amendment to the Anti-Racketeering Act of 1934 (ch. 537, 60 Stat. 420 (1946)), which prohibits racketeering in interstate commerce. The act prohibits robbery, extortion, and threats of violence to person or property in furtherance of robbery or extortion, when these would affect interstate commerce. It also prohibits attempts and conspiracies to commit these unlawful acts.

The most controversial interpretations of the Hobbs Act have been in the area of labor extortion. In *United States v. Teamsters Local 807,* 315 U.S. 521 (1942), the United States Supreme Court restricted the operation of the Hobbs Act's predecessor, the Anti-Racketeering Act of 1934 (subsequently amended by 18 U.S.C. § 1951 (1976)), so that it did not cover labor violence used to seek work or wages. To correct what it perceived as an outrageous decision, Congress passed the Hobbs Act.

Unfortunately, the language of the Hobbs Act was not specific enough to prevent the Supreme Court from once again providing an exemption for labor unions that extort wages or work by violent means. In *Enmons v. United States,* 410 U.S. 396 (1973), the Court held that no extortion had occurred, although a union had allegedly blown up a power station to enforce its demands for higher wages. Apparently, only two basic types of union extortion are illegal under the Hobbs Act: where the work sought is totally unwanted or unneeded, and where a union official is seeking a personal payoff or kickback. In essence, the Supreme Court has refused to apply the Hobbs Act to unions that seek almost any legitimate objective, no matter what means are used to obtain that objective.

The paradox of blackmail. The Supreme Court's problems in interpreting the Hobbs Act stem in part from a failure to understand one of the most intractable intellectual problems in the criminal law—what has been called the paradox of blackmail. In short, what is wrong with blackmail, and why is it illegal? The answers to these questions have eluded the best efforts of some of the leading legal scholars of the twentieth century. The problem, as stated by Glanville Williams, is that "two things that taken separately are moral and legal whites together make a moral and legal black" (p. 163). For example, if I threaten to expose a businessman's income-tax evasion unless he gives me a lucrative contract, I have committed blackmail. I have a legal right to expose and to threaten to expose the tax evasion, and I have a legal right to seek a lucrative contract, but if I combine these rights I have committed blackmail. If both ends and means are otherwise legal, why is it blackmail to combine these legal ends and means? Therein lies the paradox.

Many theories have been offered to explain this paradox. Arthur Goodhart suggested that the distinction between blackmail and situations that are not blackmail lies in what the threatener is offering to refrain from doing (pp. 175–189). According to Goodhart, seeking money to refrain from taking an *immoral liberty* (right), such as exposing someone's extramarital affair, is blackmail; whereas seeking money to refrain from taking a *moral liberty,* such as cutting down trees on one's own land, is not blackmail. The problem with Goodhart's theory is that blackmail is not limited to threats to take immoral liberties. It can be committed when the blackmailer obtains money by threatening to take a moral liberty, such as reporting a crime or a civil regulatory infraction.

Lord Atkin, in the British case of *Thorne v. Motor Trade Assn.,* [1937] 3 All E.R. 157 (H.L.), offered a second theory. He argued that blackmail is not committed when lawful business interests are furthered. But Atkin's theory is not able to explain why blackmail can be committed when a person seeks a lawful business interest. For example, a newspaper publisher commits blackmail if he obtains advertising by threatening to publish a true story damaging the advertiser's reputation. Yet both what he seeks and what he threatens to do further lawful business interests.

Harry Ball and Lawrence Friedman have argued

that "the criminality of blackmail represents a social judgment that one may not manipulate as an income-producing asset knowledge about another person's past" (pp. 205–206). Ball and Friedman, however, do not adequately distinguish blackmail from legitimate sales of information about a person's past, such as genealogy, biography, and reporting.

In Robert Nozick's view, on the other hand, blackmail is an unproductive economic exchange—the blackmail victim would prefer that the blackmailer had not dealt with him or had never existed at all (pp. 84–86). But in many legitimate economic exchanges, one party wishes that the other had never existed. For example, an inventor or other talented individual may threaten to sell his invention or services to a competing manufacturer. The manufacturer may wish that the individual or his invention had never existed at all, and yet he may legitimately buy the invention or services to keep them out of the hands of competitors. Nozick's theory cannot explain why this behavior does not involve blackmail.

Offering another economic theory, William Landes and Richard Posner view blackmail as an unconventional form of "private enforcement of law—the blackmailer induces his victim, the violator of the legal or moral rule, to pay him a sum up to the amount the violator would be willing to pay to avoid punishment" (p. 2). Landes and Posner argue that blackmail is prohibited where private enforcement is prohibited. Where the blackmailer threatens to expose behavior that violates a moral but not a legal rule, these authors contend that blackmail is not allowed because of a social judgment that resources expended in enforcing that moral rule would be wasted. Thus their theory is unable to distinguish between blackmail and legitimate ways to enforce moral rules, such as withholding business or terminating an employee, both of which they view as enforcement.

A sixth theory, advanced by Douglas Ginsburg, argues that blackmail is wasted economic activity: the blackmailer expends resources searching out information, only to suppress it. Yet Ginsburg cannot explain why selling inadvertently acquired information is illegal; no resources are expended in obtaining such information. For example, a female rape victim who blackmails a male rapist acquires the damaging information without expending resources searching out the rape.

According to Jeffrie Murphy's theory, without a law of blackmail there would be incentives for invasions of privacy. Murphy's theory, like Ginsburg's, cannot explain why it should be blackmail to sell inadvertently acquired information; that information was not acquired because of any incentives to invade privacy.

Thus, none of these theories are adequate to resolve the paradox of blackmail. The inadequacies are of two types. First, a given theory may not explain why some behavior that fits its rationale for blackmail is not blackmail. Second, a theory may not explain why some behavior that does not fit its rationale for blackmail is blackmail.

Although blackmail and extortion are illegal in every jurisdiction, legislators have defined the crimes in a number of different ways. Thus behavior that is criminal in some jurisdictions is legal in others. Even where the illegality of particular behavior is admitted, scholars and judges cannot agree on why that behavior ought to be illegal.

JAMES LINDGREN

See also both articles under ORGANIZED CRIME; THEFT.

BIBLIOGRAPHY

ALLEN, FRANCIS A. "Offenses against Property." *Annals of the American Academy of Political and Social Science* 339 (1962): 57–76.

BALL, HARRY V., and FRIEDMAN, LAWRENCE M. "The Use of Criminal Sanctions in the Enforcement of Economic Legislation: A Sociological View." *Stanford Law Review* 17 (1965): 197–223.

BLACKSTONE, WILLIAM. *Commentaries on the Laws of England* (1765–1769), vol. 4. Reprint. University of Chicago Press, 1979.

CAMPBELL, A. H. "The Anomalies of Blackmail." *Law Quarterly Review* 55 (1939): 382–399.

GINSBURG, DOUGLAS H. "Blackmail: An Economic Analysis of the Law." Unpublished manuscript, 1979.

GOODHART, ARTHUR L. *Essays in Jurisprudence and the Common Law.* Cambridge, England: Cambridge University Press, 1931.

HEPWORTH, MIKE. *Blackmail: Publicity and Secrecy in Everyday Life.* London: Routledge & Kegan Paul, 1975.

LANDES, WILLIAM M., and POSNER, RICHARD A. "The Private Enforcement of Law." *Journal of Legal Studies* 4 (1975): 1–46.

LINDGREN, JAMES. "Unraveling the Paradox of Blackmail." Unpublished manuscript, 1982.

MURPHY, JEFFRIE G. "Blackmail: A Preliminary Inquiry." *Monist* 63 (1980): 156–171.

NOZICK, ROBERT. *Anarchy, State, and Utopia.* New York: Basic Books, 1974.

PERKINS, ROLLIN M. *Criminal Law.* 2d ed. Mineola, N.Y.: Foundation Press, 1969.

TOOHER, L. G. "Developments in the Law of Blackmail in England and Australia." *International and Comparative Law Quarterly* 27 (1978): 337–377.

WILLIAMS, GLANVILLE. "Blackmail." *Criminal Law Review* (1954): 79–92, 162–172, 240–246.

WINDER, W. H. D. "The Development of Blackmail." *Modern Law Review* 5 (1941): 21–50.

BLAMEWORTHINESS

See CRIME: CONCEPT OF CRIME; GUILT; PUNISHMENT.

BODILY HARM

See ASSAULT AND BATTERY; HOMICIDE: LEGAL ASPECTS; MAYHEM.

BREACH OF PEACE

See TRESPASS, CRIMINAL; VAGRANCY AND DISORDERLY CONDUCT.

BREAKING AND ENTERING

See BURGLARY.

BRIBERY

The act or practice of benefiting a person in order to betray a trust or to perform a duty meant to be performed freely, bribery occurs in relation to a public official and, derivatively, in private transactions. This article will deal with both species in terms of (1) the tradition, (2) modern law, and (3) problems.

The tradition

Roots. Like many American legal concepts, the notion of bribery has its roots in the ancient Near East. As in most archaic societies, peaceful relations with strangers were here established in two ways, by gift and by contract. The gods or God were similarly made approachable by offerings or covenants. Against the norm of reciprocal relations ran two concepts. First, the ruler was the protector of the powerless, of "the widow and the orphan," as texts from Lagash (2400 B.C.), Babylon (1700 B.C.), and Israel (600 B.C.) expressed it. Second, man was judged by the gods impartially, as shown by the scales in the judgment scene of the Egyptian Book of the Dead (2500 B.C.). A ruler who aids the powerless is not responsive to gifts, nor is one who judges in the place of the gods. These religious insights crystallized in an image of a judge who does not take gifts for his judgment, an ideal apparent in Egyptian texts by 1500 B.C. The ideal received an expression of great influence on Western culture in Deuteronomy (seventh century B.C.), where it was stated that God in judging "does not take reward" (Deut. 10:17) and man in judging should not "take reward" (Deut. 16:19). The total biblical message on reciprocity was mixed but provides the main religious outlook from which the bribery prohibition of the West developed.

Biblical hostility to bribery was reinforced by a political tradition that appeared in the Greek city-states and had a strong impact on the ideals of the Roman Republic. The classic expression was provided by Cicero in his prosecution of Verres (whose name in Latin means "hog"), among the worst of whose offenses was "taking money for judgment," a crime described as "the foulest" (*Against Verres*, pp. 2, 3, 78). The essential sanction was supernatural, and climactically Cicero called on various gods to punish Hog.

The antibribery ethic, reflecting the biblical and classical sources, was conveyed by Christian moralists like Augustine and reinforced by the special aversion developed against a subspecies of bribery, the sin of simony, or sale of spiritual offices or goods. Denounced as a heresy, simony was the periodic object of reformers from Gregory I (A.D. 600) to Gregory VII (A.D. 1073). The notion of a spiritual domain that should not be sold complemented that of nonvendible justice. Papal pronouncements such as Innocent III's *Qualiter et quando* of 1205 (Gregory IX, "Decretales") insisted that judges must put aside "favor and fear" and "have God alone before their eyes."

Secular law followed suit. The antibribery ethic was firmly set out in Henry de Bracton's great mid-thirteenth-century treatise on English law (pp. 302–303), where the taking of bribery was condemned by biblical and Roman law and the judge who takes was said to be "corrupted by filth." Two notions, central to the idea of a judge in English law, were embodied in the antibribery ethic: trust should not be betrayed, acts of judgment cannot be sold. All subsequent development flows from these two ideas.

Literature and linguistics. The strongest teacher of the prohibition of bribery was literary. At the center of the European tradition stood Dante's *Divine Comedy*, in which bribery and simony constituted sins of fraud, more reprehensible than sins of violence because they involved misuse of man's intellect; those who sold secular justice were punished even more severely than the ecclesiastics, by immersion in a boiling, sticky pitch. Lucca, where "No becomes Yes for money," is eternally stigmatized as a symbol of civic corruption (*Inferno*, canto 21). Shakespeare fixed the English literary-moral tradition, especially with passages on bribes and corruption in *Julius Caesar* (act 4, scene 3) and with an entire play, *Measure for Measure*, which contrasts Christian spiritual reciprocities with foul redemption by a bribe. From Shakespeare to Henry Adams (*Democracy*) and Robert Penn Warren (*All the King's Men*), the moral offensiveness of criminal bribery has been a significant theme in English and American literature.

The classical languages had a single word—*shohadh* in Hebrew, *doron* in Greek, and *munus* in Latin—meaning gift, reward, bribe. The ambiguity reflected moral and legal ambivalences. By the sixteenth century, English used *bribe* unambiguously in its present moral and legal sense. By the same period *to bribe*, *bribery*, and *briber* were in use, as well as the colloquial expression *to grease*, meaning *to bribe*. *Bribee*, *graft*, and *grafter* are nineteenth-century terms, the latter two American. *Slush fund*, a source from which bribes are paid, and *payoff* are twentieth-century Americanisms. The association of bribes with dirt, dirty hands, and grease goes back to classical times. Euphemisms for bribe are *gift*, *gratuity*, *reward*, *contribution*, and *kickback*. *Conflict of interest* is sometimes used for a good-faith dilemma, sometimes as a euphemism for a situation produced by bribery.

Paradigms. In the Anglo-American tradition there have been several cases in which the defendant was so prominent that his prosecution was exemplary. (1) The paradigmatic trial of a bribe-taking judge was that of Francis Bacon, chancellor of England, convicted by the House of Lords in 1621. (2) The classic trial of a corrupt administrator was that of Governor-General Warren Hastings of Bengal, impeached by the House of Commons in 1787. Although ultimately acquitted, Hastings was irretrievably damaged in reputation, and his prosecution by Edmund Burke, modeled on Cicero's of Hog, set the standards for the nineteenth-century British civil service. (3) The trial of Oakes Ames, a Massachusetts congressman and a central figure in the Union Pacific–Credit Mobilier scandal, served as a double paradigm for bribers and legislators. Ames was censured by the House of Representatives in 1873 for bribing members of Congress. Legislative investigation created each paradigm. In each, multiple acts of bribery were established. The essential sanction in each was public shame.

Modern law

Nonstatutory sanctions. Bribery, along with treason, is one of two crimes for which the United States Constitution (art. II, sec. 4) specifically prescribes impeachment for the President, Vice-President, and "all civil officers of the United States." Two federal judges have been impeached and convicted of corruption; more than a dozen others have resigned in the face of threatened impeachment. Indication of investigation has produced other resignations, most notably of a Justice of the Supreme Court.

Since 1873, Congress has censured members for bribe-taking or bribe-giving, and in 1980 it actually expelled a member after his criminal conviction. A more common sanction has been electoral, although belief that a candidate is a bribe-taker is more apt to act as a comparative disadvantage than an absolute disqualification. Lawyers convicted of bribery are subject to disbarment. In descending order of frequency, electoral disadvantage, forced or prudential resignation, disbarment, censure, impeachment, and expulsion have been sanctions for bribery in high American office. In enforcing them, the role of the press has been crucial.

Statutes. Modern statutes, state and federal, have four common characteristics. (1) They apply equally to receivers and givers. (2) They are comprehensive, including as officials all employees of government and those acting in a government capacity, such as jurors and legislators. More recent statutes include party officials and even party employees. (3) They treat bribery as a crime that can be committed by the briber even though the bribee is not influenced. (4) They treat bribery as a felony.

American statutes differ in that some treat a bribe as any "benefit," thereby including nonpecuniary favors, whereas others restrict the term to pecuniary benefits. Some, such as the New York Penal Code, permit extortion to be a defense for the bribe-giver (N.Y. Penal Law (McKinney) § 200.05 (1975)), but this defense is disapproved by the Model Penal Code (§ 240.1). Older statutes use *corruptly* to qualify the condemned giving and receiving, whereas more recent ones eliminate *corruptly* and speak more specifically. An essential component of modern statutes is an antigratuity provision making it criminal to confer any benefit on an official "for or because of any official act" (18 U.S.C. § 201). Excepted, of course, are benefits provided by law. The provision eliminates a need to show that the benefit was "to influence" performance. The giver is guilty if he gave for the act; the recipient is guilty if he took on account of the act. Some statutes also criminalize compensation for a past official act, obviating difficulty in proving bribery (Model Penal Code § 240.3). Some statutes also criminally forbid private employment in a matter on which, as an official, one had acted, assimilating such conflicting interest to a bribe. An example of such a statute is the Bribery, Graft, and Conflicts of Interest Act of 1962, as amended, 18 U.S.C. §§ 201–208 (1976 & Supp. IV 1980).

Prosecutions. Neither the state nor the federal statutes have been systematically and uniformly enforced against all offenders. Usually either political investigation or particularly outrageous corruption has triggered prosecution. Routine federal cases show topicality: bribees were prohibition agents in the 1920s, draft-board members in the 1940s, revenue agents in the 1950s. Celebrated convictions include those of Secretary of the Interior Albert Fall for accepting bribes in connection with the Teapot Dome oil leases (*Fall v. United States*, 49 F.2d 506 (D.C. Cir. 1931)) and of Circuit Court Judge Martin Manton (*United States v. Manton*, 107 F.2d 834 (2d Cir. 1938)).

The 1970s were marked by a more sustained federal effort, in particular by the temporary Watergate Special Prosecution Force, by the permanent Office of Public Integrity in the Justice Department, and by the project known as Abscam, where the use of decoys and the filming of transactions led to the conviction of half a dozen members of Congress and a senator.

Auxiliary legislation. Evidentiary difficulty in proving bribery, conceptual difficulty in distinguishing bribes from campaign contributions, and experience with the effect of money on elections have led to the adoption of state and federal laws generically known as anticorrupt practice acts. Typically, these limit the amount of campaign contributions, require that they be made only to identified committees, specify that they be reported, and prohibit certain classes of contributors from contributing anything. For example, a federal corrupt practices act, a product of the Progressive era, first prohibited contributions to a federal election by any corporation of any kind, then was amended to bar political solicitations from federal employees or contributions by contractors, and afterward was further amended to include contributions by labor unions (18 U.S.C. §§ 597, 599, 602 (1976 & Supp. IV 1980)). Offenses under such statutes have, in general, been misdemeanors rather than felonies. The laws have been limited and sometimes invalidated by federal or state constitutional requirements.

For the most part the effectiveness of these statutes has rested chiefly on their being observed by law-abiding corporate managers, lawyers, auditors, and campaign officials. Before the 1970s there was almost no criminal enforcement of the federal law against corporations, contractors, or candidates. The Securities and Exchange Commission (SEC), by requiring the confession of illegal contributions by corporations with stock registered under the Securities Exchange Act, and the Watergate Special Prosecution Force, showed that the laws were often violated. John McCloy's report on Gulf Oil was particularly revealing, disclosing that a slush fund had been maintained for fifteen years, from which leading American politicians, including Senate Majority Leader Lyndon Johnson, were supplied with envelopes containing cash. The difference between such access payments and bribes was difficult to detect.

While federal agencies began to give vigor in the 1970s to the Corrupt Practices Act, federal involvement in prosecuting state and local bribery underwent an enormous expansion. Mail fraud law was used to catch the bribery of Governor Otto Kerner of Illinois. Failure to report the income led to the prosecution of Vice-President Spiro Agnew for bribes taken as governor of Maryland. In addition, on the books were (1) the Travel Act of 1961, as amended, 18 U.S.C. § 1952 (1976), making it a federal felony to use interstate facilities to commit what was bribery under state law; and (2) the much older Hobbs Act, 18 U.S.C. § 1951 (1976), covering any act affecting interstate commerce and defining extortion as obtaining property from another person with that person's consent "under color of official right." This definition was interpreted to include payoffs expressly or tacitly sought by a governor, a state legislator, a city alderman, or a policeman (for example, *United States v. Braasch*, 505 F.2d 139 (7th Cir. 1974)).

These laws were eventually overshadowed by the Racketeer Influenced and Corrupt Organizations (RICO) Act of 1970, 18 U.S.C. § 1961, punishing as "racketeering" any "pattern" (two or more acts) of bribery. Under this act, bribe-taking bail bondsmen, sheriffs, and traffic court employees—typical small-time grafters—as well as state revenue officials, state senators, and a state governor, were federally indicted as racketeers. Acquittal under state law was no defense to the federal crime, and state statutes of limitations did not apply. Armed by RICO with powerful weapons, the Justice Department became a formidable adversary of local corruption. By the 1970s, state officials were being federally prosecuted at the rate of several hundred per year.

Foreign corrupt practices. In the 1970s the SEC took the position that payments of bribes overseas constituted material information, to be disclosed on reports to the SEC. More than four hundred American companies confessed to making such payments. A small percentage of registered corporations, they included such giants as Lockheed Corporation, which spent $6 million a year in overseas bribes. In response

to public furor, Congress enacted the Foreign Corrupt Practices Act of 1977, 15 U.S.C. §§ 78m, 78dd-1–dd-2 (Supp. IV 1980). This legislation was notable in four respects: (1) The statute made it a crime to bribe an official of *another* country, an extension of jurisdiction never attempted before in regard to bribery. (2) It applied only to bribers, whereas other bribery laws apply to bribees as well. (3) Under criminal penalty, it required one class of bribers, those registered under the securities laws, to make a public report of its crime. (4) As to all bribers, it was *more* stringent than federal law on bribery in the United States in that (*a*) it applied to bribing political parties; (*b*) it applied to all domestic businesses and all American citizens; and (*c*) it specified a heavier financial punishment, up to $1 million. The act's effect has depended on cooperation by lawyers, auditors, corporate managers, and outside directors.

Commerce and contests. Criminal statutes against the bribery of private persons began with New York in 1881. They were enacted in England and several states in the early twentieth century, numbered seventeen by 1934, and doubled by 1980. The earlier statutes tended to specify employments—gardeners in Maryland, chauffeurs in Illinois! The more recent tendency, reflected in the Model Penal Code, has been to include all employees, agents, and fiduciaries. Seeking to reach payola in the recording business, the Code, followed by several states, also includes anyone who professionally is a disinterested expert. The statutes in substance make it a crime to confer a benefit on a fiduciary with intent to influence the recipient's conduct in his principal's affairs. Consent of the principal is a defense, and penalties vary. The statutes have sometimes been invoked civilly to invalidate a contract, but they have rarely led to criminal convictions. Persons injured have more incentive to hold the bribee liable for the bribe or to make the briber turn over his gain.

Between 1947 and 1980, thirty-four states made it a crime to influence sporting contests by bribes to officials or participants. The state statutes are rarely used, but occasionally they have been harshly applied—for example, ten years' sentence of imprisonment was imposed for fixing a basketball game in Iowa. Concern with the effect on sports of professional gamblers connected with organized crime led in 1964 to a federal law which has been extended to apply to jockeys rigging their own race (18 U.S.C. § 224 (1976)). Responding to rigged television contests, the Model Penal Code (§ 224.9) and eight states have included not only sports but every "publicly exhibited contest." The Code and three states specified a criminal penalty for any participant who knows that the contest has been fixed.

Dynamism. Modern bribery law has tended to expand enormously those subject to the criminal law, to increase the acts covered, to multiply indirect attacks on bribery, to develop more effective techniques of detecting the crime, to expand federal jurisdiction at home and abroad, to increase the number of prosecutions, and to increase the severity of sanctions. The movement of the law has been the reverse of Henry Maine's famous dictum, "from status to contract." The law here has gone from reciprocity to nonreciprocity, determined by status. Its continued expansion could be confidently predicted, were it not for three problems now to be addressed.

Problems

Quantification. Bribery is not normally reported by briber or bribee, nor boasted of. No statistics exist as to the number or amount of bribes or the percentage of transactions affected by them. Consequently, although many historians speak of a government, a country, or an era as "corrupt," there is no quantifiable evidence on which they rest their judgments. By extrapolation from the disparate data available, guesses conceivably might be made that would compare one regime with another as more or less corrupt. But such comparative guesses have not been developed. Historians often take an era in which there is greater legislation against bribery or greater prosecution of it and conclude that this period was more corrupt than an era without legislative or prosecutorial activity. Nothing could be more fallacious. Greater activity indicates greater opposition to bribery and has no necessary connection with an increase in bribery. To take a contemporary American comparison, were the 1970s more corrupt than the 1950s? No one has done the work that can provide a rational answer to this question.

Since bribery is an unquantified phenomenon, it is impossible to say whether the multiplication of laws and prosecutions is reducing it, keeping even with it, or falling behind. In the absence of a quantitative basis for evaluating the efficacy of criminal law in this area, the success of the law is measured in terms of its symbolic impact. The law is more specially vindicated when a powerful person is subjected to it. Hence bribery prosecutions often have a political aspect.

Prosecutorial discretion. Prosecutorial discretion determines to a very large degree the application of the law. Discretion exists at the federal level as to state crimes. Virtually any local bribery has an aspect

touching interstate commerce and thus could be federally prosecuted. Prosecution depends on decisions by regional district attorneys and by Washington. Discretion also exists at the charging level. For example, a campaign contribution by a corporation, criminal under federal law, can be prosecuted for having been made or accepted (a misdemeanor); for not being reported (a misdemeanor usually treated lightly); for being made by a federal contractor (a felony; most corporations are federal contractors to some extent); for being a gratuity (a more serious felony); or for being a bribe (a very serious felony).

Prosecutors again have discretion to interpret custom to modify the statutes. A Christmas present to a mailman, for example, is a federal felony if the antigratuity law is read literally. Prosecutorial discretion saves the law from being absurd. In a more debatable exercise of discretion, no prosecutor charged Governor Nelson Rockefeller of New York with a crime for giving large loans, as much as $500,000, to public employees in literal violation of an antigratuity statute. In a more central area of concern, many legislative deals or compromises fall literally within the terms of a bribery statute. The older type of statute, providing that giving must be done "corruptly," has left the prosecutor to interpret this vague term with the help of custom to exclude the legislative arena.

Historically, prosecutors have depended on chance to bring cases to their attention. To take the example of a particularly elaborate investigation, the congressmen prosecuted in Abscam became targets when criminal middlemen boasted that they could deliver them. No overall plan to test the members of Congress existed. Since the mid-1970s it has been the conscious policy of the Justice Department to give priority to cases involving high federal or state officials—members of Congress, judges, and governors. This exercise of discretion, rationally defensible, could be followed by a second exercise of discretion, to monitor closely the activities of, say, all members of Congress. Experienced observers suggest that almost any area of government, if probed, will yield evidence of corruption. To what extent shall the prosecutor with limited resources wait for an informant? To what extent shall he probe? The bite of the law depends on his decision. The political power resident in his exercise of discretion is substantial. Coupled with the political aspect of many bribery cases, prosecutorial discretion means that bribery, to an extent unusual in the criminal law, is a crime whose prosecution depends on political, but not necessarily partisan, choices.

Rigorism, cynicism, and relativism. Reciprocities run through human relations, including the political.

They can as easily be removed from society as moisture from the atmosphere. Confronted with their ubiquity, one can take three positions. (1) *The rigorist*—every bargain, every looked-for reciprocation in the area of political judgments, is wrong. Each judgment is to be made on its merits. The standards applied to judges should apply equally to presidents, legislators, and voters. (2) *The cynical*—most political reciprocities go uncondemned and unpunished. Legislators logroll, presidents use patronage, voters are rewarded by bills that favor their interest. The isolation of a few specific trades as corrupt is hypocritical pretense. In the main, reciprocities rule. A Marxist view of Western society approaches the cynical, even though actual communist societies afford a basis for even greater cynicism. (3) *The relativist*—custom determines which reciprocities are bad and which are acceptable. No trade is intrinsically evil. The antibribery ethic is sufficiently enforced by a few spectacular cases showing the kinds of trades our society rejects.

Each of these positions has an effect on the criminal law. The internal dynamism of the antibribery ethic pushes toward rigorism. The result is perceptible in the Model Penal Code and modern statutes struggling with definitions that will not make a criminal prosecutor the judge of legislative compromises and election promises. The cynical view is the inevitable reaction to rigorism when it becomes apparent that all reciprocity cannot be eliminated. The view undermines enforcement and even observance of the law. The relativist position is that of the liberal, comfortable with society as it is, who believes that ideal disinterestedness in political judgments can be encouraged if not guaranteed and that its violation can be vindicated in flagrant instances. The relativist, however, has little reason to condemn corruption abroad and, viewing what constitutes corruption as arranged by social convention, has a small moral investment in the criminal law. The removal of moral fire from the law weakens its efficacy.

Conclusion

There exists, however, a fourth position, the social-personalist one. It holds bribery to be a moral issue, that is, it affects both the good of society and the good of persons—the good of society by its impact on the ideals of the society, the good of persons by involving them in acts unworthy of their nature. A breach of trust and a sale of what should not be sold, bribery violates a divine paradigm set out in Jewish tradition and Christian tradition. Because of its deep moral content, the antibribery ethic requires embodiment in the law.

The social-personalist position denies the cynic's charges of hypocrisy, insisting that selective, symbolic, and dramatic enforcement is educative. It challenges the relativist's belief that all is conventional, pointing to fundamental needs for trust, gratuitous action, and disinterested judgment that are protected, although imperfectly and variously. It has affinities with the rigorist position, rejoicing in the expansion of the ethic, especially its belated inclusion of legislators; yet it differs from the rigorist position by rejecting its reliance on criminal sanctions, in particular imprisonment. Rooted in history, the fourth position favors attacking bribery in multiple ways.

In particular, these measures should be considered. (1) *Increasing the legal profession's efforts against bribery.* Lawyers have been very frequently involved in modern bribery as advisers, bagmen, couriers, directors, lobbyists, or recipients. Meanwhile law schools, like legal scholars of every era, ignore the profession's involvement. A key class of participants could be educated, disciplined, and motivated to take a more active stand against bribery. (2) *Extending the requirements of the Foreign Corrupt Practices Act to all corporations as to domestic bribes and political contributions.* There is no reason to be more concerned with corruption overseas than at home. The record-keeping provisions and heavy financial penalty of the act are appropriate deterrents to use against all corporations. (3) *Relying more on disgrace, censure, and electoral reprisals than on imprisonment.* At a time when there are general doubts about incarceration, it is odd to rely on it as a remedy here. Historically, bribery has been punished by shame attached to acts unworthy of human persons.

JOHN T. NOONAN, JR.

See also FEDERAL CRIMINAL LAW ENFORCEMENT; OBSTRUCTION OF JUSTICE; WHITE-COLLAR CRIME: HISTORY OF AN IDEA.

BIBLIOGRAPHY

AMERICAN LAW INSTITUTE. *Model Penal Code and Commentaries: Official Draft and Revised Comments.* 3 vols. Philadelphia: ALI, 1980.

BOND, EDWARD A., ed. *Speeches of the Managers and Counsel in the Trial of Warren Hastings.* 4 vols. London: Longman, 1859–1861.

BORKIN, JOSEPH. *The Corrupt Judge: An Inquiry into Bribery and Other High Crimes and Misdemeanors in the Federal Courts.* New York: Clarkson Potter, 1962.

BRACTON, HENRY DE. *On the Laws and Customs of England,* vol. 2. Translated with revisions and notes by Samuel

E. Thorne. Cambridge, Mass.: Harvard University Press, Belknap Press, 1968.

CICERO, MARCUS TULLIUS. *Against Verres.* Translated by L. H. G. Greenwood. Cambridge, Mass.: Harvard University Press, 1928–1935.

GREGORY IX (POPE). "Decretales" (1234). *Corpus Juris Canonici*, vol. 2. 2d Leipzig ed. Edited by Emil Albert Friedberg and Aemilius Ludwig Richter. Graz, Austria: Akademische Druck und Verlagsanstalt, 1955, cols. 1–927.

MCCLOY, JOHN J.; PEARSON, NATHAN W.; and MATTHEWS, BEVERLY. *The Great Oil Spill: The Inside Report—Gulf Oil's Bribery and Political Chicanery.* New York: Chelsea House, 1976.

NOONAN, JOHN T., JR. "Bribes." Forthcoming publication, 1983.

Note. "Campaign Contributions and Federal Bribery Law." *Harvard Law Review* 92 (1978): 451–469.

Note. "Control of Nongovernmental Corruption by Criminal Legislation." *University of Pennsylvania Law Review* 108 (1960): 848–867.

RUFF, CHARLES F. C. "Federal Prosecution of Local Corruption: A Case Study in the Making of Law Enforcement Policy." *Georgetown Law Journal* 65 (1977): 1171–1228.

BURDEN OF PROOF

The principal purpose of most trials is to resolve a dispute about facts. Both parties present evidence to a fact finder, either judge or jury, who evaluates the evidence and resolves the controversy. A number of rules of law guide the fact finder in evaluating the evidence; most important of these are the rules that tell the fact finder who should have the benefit of the doubt.

These rules are typically expressed as statements about which party must carry the burden of proof, and how heavy the burden is. For example, in most civil cases, the plaintiff has the burden of proof, and the burden is to prove the case "by a preponderance of evidence." In some cases, the plaintiff has the burden of proof "by clear and convincing evidence," which is a heavier burden than proof by a preponderance of evidence. Finally, in criminal cases it has long been the general rule that the prosecution has the burden of proof, and the burden is to prove guilt "beyond a reasonable doubt."

The reasonable doubt rule

In 1970, the United States Supreme Court declared that the reasonable doubt rule in criminal cases was required by the United States Constitution. In the case of *In re Winship*, 397 U.S. 358 (1970), the Court held that the "Due Process Clause protects the accused against conviction except upon proof beyond a reasonable doubt of every fact necessary to constitute the crime with which he is charged" (364).

The holding in *Winship* restated the general understanding of the rule governing proof in a criminal case, and therefore it was not especially controversial. At the same time, however, by articulating a constitutional basis for the rule, *Winship* laid the foundation for litigation over the proper scope of this newly articulated constitutional rule.

One question that has generated some controversy is whether the rule applies in contexts that are not clearly criminal prosecutions, but are similar in some respects to criminal cases. *Winship* itself extended the rule from ordinary criminal cases to certain types of juvenile delinquency proceedings. In general, the Court has declined to hold that proof beyond a reasonable doubt is required in noncriminal proceedings, although it has held that sometimes the Constitution requires the government to prove its case by the intermediate standard of "clear and convincing evidence." For example, the state must prevail by clear and convincing evidence in proceedings for compulsory psychiatric hospitalization (*Addington v. Texas*, 441 U.S. 418 (1979)) and in proceedings to terminate parental rights (*Santosky v. Kramer*, 455 U.S. 745 (1982)).

A second controversial question is whether the rule applies to every issue in a criminal case, or whether particular issues may be excluded from the rule. Although most states have long adhered to the general rule that the prosecution must prove guilt beyond a reasonable doubt, each state has also developed its own idiosyncratic list of exceptions. Defendants have been required to prove self-defense, duress, insanity, entrapment, renunciation, and mistake. They have been required to prove that their conduct falls within a specific exception written into the statutory definition of a particular crime, and also to prove threshold matters such as the running of the statute of limitations and mental incompetence for trial.

Some state criminal codes use the term *defense* to describe an issue for which the state intends to assign the burden of proof to the defendant. Other state criminal codes use the term *affirmative defense* for this purpose. Still other codes use neither term, and simply state that the burden of proof for all issues is on the state except where the statute expressly states otherwise.

Both the reasonable doubt rule and some of its exceptions have relatively ancient roots. The reasonable doubt rule has been recognized in Anglo-American law at least since 1798, and probably for several centuries before that (May, pp. 656–658; Morano, pp. 515–519; Green, p. 424 n. 45). Exceptions to the rule were also apparently recognized in the eighteenth and nineteenth centuries (Fletcher). But not until the rule acquired constitutional standing in 1970 did courts begin to seek criteria to govern its application.

The Supreme Court has provided little guidance in determining which issues are governed by the rule. In a pair of very similar cases, the Court reached virtually opposite conclusions. Both cases involved statutes that shifted to the defendant the burden of proving that the crime was not murder but only the less serious crime of manslaughter. In *Mullaney v. Wilbur*, 421 U.S. 684 (1975), the Court invalidated a state statute requiring the defendant to prove provocation, but two years later, in *Patterson v. New York*, 432 U.S. 197 (1977), the Court, without overruling *Mullaney*, upheld a statute requiring the defendant to prove "extreme emotional disturbance." The opinions in the two cases survey the factors that have been thought relevant by lower courts and commentators in deciding when the Constitution permits such burden-shifting, but in neither case did the Court offer a framework for analyzing the problem in the future.

Commentators have proposed various criteria for determining which issues in a criminal case are governed by the reasonable doubt rule. In order to evaluate these criteria, it is useful to consider the purposes of the constitutional rule.

Reasons for the rule. Two distinct functions are generally attributed to the requirement that the government prove guilt beyond a reasonable doubt. First, the rule is meant to affect the outcome of individual cases, reducing the likelihood of an erroneous conviction. Second, the rule is meant to symbolize for society the great significance of a criminal conviction. The *Winship* Court invoked both purposes, reasoning that the rule was required both to protect the important interest of the accused individual in avoiding incarceration and stigma, and to command the respect and confidence of the community in the moral force of the criminal law.

The reasonable doubt rule reduces the chance of erroneous conviction simply by reducing the chance of any conviction. It puts a thumb on the defendant's side of the scales of justice, in order to implement "a fundamental value determination of our society that it is far worse to convict an innocent man than to let a guilty man go free" (*Winship*, 372 (Justice Harlan concurring)).

The reasonable doubt rule fulfills its symbolic function by singling out criminal convictions as peculiarly serious among the adjudications made by courts. The rule reaffirms the special opprobrium that attaches to criminal convictions, and the special importance of protecting individuals against the state's power to convict. It follows, then, that exceptions to the rule are appropriate only for those issues which for some reason do not require the special safeguards against error that attach to other issues in a criminal case.

There are, of course, empirical questions about whether the rule in practice has its intended effect. The available studies are inconclusive, but they suggest that the instruction on the burden of proof can affect the outcome of a case (L.S.E. Jury Project; Simon, 1969, 1970; Simon and Mahan).

Issues that should be governed by the rule. Commentators have suggested a number of different approaches to the problem of deciding which issues in a criminal case should be governed by the reasonable doubt rule. At one extreme, the rule might apply to every issue in a criminal case, without exception, governing the proof of every fact that the criminal law makes relevant to a criminal conviction. At the other extreme, the rule might apply only to those issues for which the legislature has made no explicit exception. The Supreme Court has plainly rejected both extreme positions in *Mullaney* and *Patterson*. Under these cases some exceptions are permitted, but there are constitutional limits on the power of the legislature to make exceptions. Although the Court has not specified the criteria for permissible exceptions, commentators have suggested several criteria.

First, and least controversial, is the view that the Constitution permits an exception for issues in a criminal case that do not directly relate to guilt or innocence. In the course of a criminal prosecution, it may be necessary to decide whether the case is properly before the court, or whether particular items may be admitted into evidence. These decisions may well determine whether it is possible as a practical matter to convict the defendant, but they do not determine whether the defendant is in fact guilty. For that reason, the Constitution does not impose the reasonable doubt rule on such determinations, although the rule may nonetheless be required as a matter of state law (*Lego v. Twomey*, 404 U.S. 477, 486–487 (1972) (voluntariness of a confesssion); Saltzburg). Thus, the Constitution does not require proof beyond a reasonable doubt of jurisdiction and venue, of timely prosecution, or of the defendant's mental competence for trial. Nor does it require proof beyond a reasonable doubt that a hearsay statement fits within an exception to the hearsay rule.

A second, somewhat more controversial, proposal is an exception for issues that present special problems of proof. It is suggested that the defendant should bear the burden of proof on an issue if the defendant has better access than the prosecution to the significant evidence on that issue. The rationale is that a defendant with control over the relevant evidence has a great incentive to withhold the evidence, mislead the jury, and prevail because of the prosecution's inability to meet its burden of proof. This strategy could be prevented by a rule shifting the burden of proof to the defendant. On this theory, the burden of proof might be assigned to the defendant on the issue of insanity, of intent, or of special permission or a license to do the otherwise prohibited act. The problem with shifting the burden of proof to the defendant for this reason is that it accomplishes too much. It not only elicits evidence from the defendant, but it also continues to tilt the scales against the defendant even after all the evidence has been produced. A better solution to the problem of access to evidence would shift to the defendant the burden of coming forward with enough evidence to raise the issue, and then leave with the government the ultimate burden of proof after all the evidence is in.

A third proposed criterion for identifying exceptions to the reasonable doubt rule has become the center of a major debate, with significance beyond the details of the rule. This controversy raises basic questions about the relationship between substantive law and procedure, as well as about the relationship between state legislatures and the federal Constitution on matters of criminal law. Some commentators have argued that the reasonable doubt rule should not apply to the proof of any fact that the legislature could constitutionally have omitted from its substantive criminal law. They argue that if the legislature has the constitutional power to make a fact irrelevant to guilt, then it must also have the power to choose its own rules for proving that fact. Put differently, if the legislature has created a gratuitous defense, then that issue is exempt from the requirement that the government prove its case beyond a reasonable doubt. Other commentators argue that legislative power to eliminate a defense does not entail the power to shift to the defendant the burden of proof. They maintain that both the practical and the symbolic functions of the reasonable doubt rule apply with full force where a gratuitous defense is concerned.

The controversy over this proposed formulation is set forth in a pair of articles by Barbara Underwood and by John Jeffries and Paul Stephan. Jeffries and Stephan argue that it is both illogical and unwise to impose strict procedural requirements on the proof of a gratuitous defense. It is illogical, they say, because only if the Constitution requires the state to prove a particular fact as a prerequisite to conviction does the Constitution also require the state to prove that fact beyond a reasonable doubt. It is unwise, they argue, because state legislatures have often been willing to enact generous new defenses to crime only in conjunction with rules that shift the burden of proof to the defendant. To prohibit such compromises, they contend, would stifle reform of the criminal law.

Underwood argues, by contrast, that the power to eliminate an issue from the criminal law does not entail the power to alter the rules of proof for that issue. In her view, the Constitution allocates to the states very broad power to define the substantive criminal law, but it imposes rigorous procedural requirements on the process of proving whatever facts the state has made criminal. Thus, the Constitution does not permit a state to adopt a controversial defense, and then limit it by shifting the burden of proof to the defendant. Instead, the state must resolve controversies over criminal law policy by making adjustments and compromises in the content of the substantive criminal law.

For example, a state legislature might be divided over a proposal to exempt from the narcotics law those who possess narcotics solely for personal use. A procedural compromise would be to adopt the defense in full, and to limit it by shifting the burden of proof to the defendant. A substantive compromise would be to adopt the defense in part, exempting only those who possess narcotics for personal use in specified small quantities, or in the privacy of the home. If the Constitution prohibits the procedural compromise, then the legislature must adopt or reject the defense or find a substantive compromise.

Two propositions provide much of the support for the view that gratuitous defenses should be exempt from the reasonable doubt rule. First, its proponents claim that the exemption is necessary to promote reform of the criminal law. Second, they claim that the Constitution imposes meaningful limits on the substantive criminal law, and that these limits provide a suitable guide for determining the scope of the reasonable doubt rule. Both claims are highly controversial.

It is, of course, difficult to determine whether in fact reform would be stifled if the burden-shifting device were prohibited. Legislatures might instead adopt reforms without burden-shifting, or they might find satisfactory substantive compromises. Moreover, the argument that burden-shifting is necessary for legislative reform does not require an exception from the reasonable doubt rule for all gratuitous defenses. It requires an exception only for those new gratuitous defenses that result from legislative compromise. Justice Lewis Powell has suggested that he would favor such an approach. He would make no exception for traditional defenses, whether or not gratuitous, but only for "new ameliorative defenses" that might be the product of legislative compromise (*Patterson*, 227–230 (Justice Powell dissenting)).

The second proposition is equally questionable. Commentators have long urged the Court to develop a body of constitutional criminal law, but the Court has consistently refused to do so. Moreover, in the future it is likely to continue to avoid the morass of reviewing in detail state substantive criminal law. Under those circumstances, if the reasonable doubt rule applies only to constitutionally necessary facts, then it may have almost no application at all.

The gratuitous character of a defense is not by itself sufficient to exempt that defense from other constitutional requirements of fair procedure. Even a defendant raising a gratuitous defense has the right to trial by jury, to counsel, to confrontation, and to compulsory process. If an issue is exempt from the requirement of proof beyond a reasonable doubt, the reason must not be solely that the defense is gratuitous, but that for some reason it is less important to protect the defendant against error.

Presumptions as burden-shifting devices

Closely related to rules that regulate the burden of proof are rules of law that establish presumptions. These rules come in many variations, but they all instruct the fact finder to infer one fact from evidence that directly proves some other fact. Thus, in a criminal case such rules may seem to relieve the prosecution of its burden of proof, or to shift the burden of proof to the defendant, in violation of the constitutional requirement.

The Supreme Court has recognized that some forms of presumptions shift the burden of proof to the defendant in an unconstitutional manner. In *Sandstrom v. Montana*, 442 U.S. 510 (1979), the Court found constitutional error in an instruction that "the law presumes that a person intends the ordinary consequences of his voluntary acts" (513). That instruction, in a prosecution for "deliberate homicide," shifted to the defendant the burden of proving he did not intend to cause death.

By contrast, in *County Court v. Allen*, 442 U.S. 140 (1979), the Court upheld an instruction that "upon proof of the presence of the machine gun and the hand weapons, you may infer and draw a conclusion that such prohibited weapon was possessed by each of the defendants who occupied the automobile at the time when such instruments were found" (161 n.

20). That instruction, in a prosecution for criminal possession of a weapon, was held to be merely permissive and not burden-shifting, because it left the jury free to credit or reject the inference.

From these and earlier cases, several principles emerge. If the reasonable doubt rule applies to an issue, then the rule cannot constitutionally be circumvented by a presumption. Both the issue of intent in *Sandstrom* and the issue of possession in *County Court* were clearly subject to the reasonable doubt rule. For such issues, there can be no mandatory presumptions, even if they are rebuttable, because such presumptions are burden-shifting. The state may, however, use presumptions that merely authorize a permissible inference or invite the fact finder to consider it.

Neither *Sandstrom* nor *County Court* dealt with issues outside the scope of the reasonable doubt rule. For such issues there can be no constitutional objection to the burden-shifting character of a presumption, although the Constitution requires that any presumption, whether burden-shifting or not, have some rational basis.

BARBARA D. UNDERWOOD

See also CRIMINAL PROCEDURE: CONSTITUTIONAL ASPECTS; TRIAL, CRIMINAL.

BIBLIOGRAPHY

ALLEN, RONALD J. "Structuring Jury Decisionmaking in Criminal Cases: A Unified Constitutional Approach to Evidentiary Devices." *Harvard Law Review* 94 (1980): 321–368.

ASHFORD, HAROLD A., and RISINGER, D. MICHAEL. "Presumptions, Assumptions, and Due Process in Criminal Cases: A Theoretical Overview." *Yale Law Journal* 79 (1969): 165–208.

FLETCHER, GEORGE P. "Two Kinds of Legal Rules: A Comparative Study of Burden-of-Persuasion Practices in Criminal Cases." *Yale Law Journal* 77 (1968): 880–935.

GREEN, THOMAS A. "The Jury and the English Law of Homicide, 1200–1600." *Michigan Law Review* 74 (1976): 413–499.

JEFFRIES, JOHN C., JR., and STEPHAN, PAUL B., III. "Defenses, Presumptions, and Burden of Proof in the Criminal Law." *Yale Law Journal* 88 (1979): 1325–1407.

L.S.E. Jury Project. "Juries and the Rules of Evidence." *Criminal Law Review* (1973): 208–223.

[MAY.] "Some Rules of Evidence: Reasonable Doubt in Civil and Criminal Cases." *American Law Review* 10 (1876): 642–664.

MORANO, ANTHONY A. "A Reexamination of the Development of the Reasonable Doubt Rule." *Boston University Law Review* 55 (1975): 507–528.

NESSON, CHARLES R. "Reasonable Doubt and Permissive

Inferences: The Value of Complexity." *Harvard Law Review* 92 (1979): 1187–1225.

SALTZBURG, STEPHEN A. "Standards of Proof and Preliminary Questions of Fact." *Stanford Law Review* 27 (1975): 271–305.

SIMON, RITA JAMES. " 'Beyond a Reasonable Doubt': An Experimental Attempt at Quantification." *Journal of Applied Behavioral Science* 6 (1970): 203–209.

————. "Judges' Translations of Burdens of Proof into Statements of Probability." *Trial Lawyer's Guide* (1969): 103–114.

————, and MAHAN, LINDA. "Quantifying Burdens of Proof: A View from the Bench, the Jury, and the Classroom." *Law and Society Review* 5 (1971): 319–330.

UNDERWOOD, BARBARA D. "The Thumb on the Scales of Justice: Burdens of Persuasion in Criminal Cases." *Yale Law Journal* 86 (1977): 1299–1348.

BURGLARY

Burglary is a crime that involves entering or remaining in a building for the purpose of committing a theft or some other crime. The essence of burglary is the entry and the intent, and generally it does not matter whether the theft or other crime is ever completed or not.

Legal definition. Modern burglary is best understood by comparison with the older English law. This law sought to protect the home against nighttime invaders and required proof of six elements: (1) breaking and (2) entering (3) the house (4) of another (5) in the nighttime (6) for the purpose of committing a felony inside.

Since the purpose was to protect the home, the common-law definition of burglary did not cover entries invited or allowed by the dwellers. It required a "breaking," or the making of an opening into the house. Originally there may have been a need for physical violence, such as forcing a lock or breaking a window. Ultimately, however, the rule developed that a breaking had taken place if the intruder moved some part of the house. Opening an unlocked door or even an already partially open window was thus a breaking, but entering a fully open door or window without widening the opening was not. Opening or forcing a closed inside door was also a breaking, as was entry by intimidation, impersonation, or use of an inside confederate.

The second requirement was an entry, and any intrusion of the would-be burglar's body, no matter how brief, was enough to establish this. Thus, if the invader put part of his hand into the house to open the window, or part of his foot while kicking out the window, that was an entry. Intruding instruments into the house was different, however, and did not constitute an entry unless used to achieve the intruder's felonious purpose. Extending a crowbar or some other instrument into the house to open the window, for example, was not an entry unless the tool was then used to reach some property inside the house. It was not necessary for the entry to take place at the same time or even on the same day as the breaking, but it had to be connected with the breaking and be made through the opening so created.

Because burglary was a crime designed to protect the habitation, the third common-law requirement was that the breaking and entering concern a dwelling house. This meant all structures that were places of human habitation, whether the occupants were present or not. It did not include unfinished houses and such buildings as stores and factories. Barns, stables, and other outbuildings were included, however, even though no person lived in them, if they were associated closely enough with the house.

The fourth requirement was that the dwelling be that of another. One who broke and entered his own house for the purpose of committing a felony was not guilty of burglary. Occupancy, rather than ownership, determined whether the dwelling was that of another, however, so that a landlord could burglarize the premises of his tenant.

The fifth requirement was that the crime be committed at night. This began not at sunset but when the countenance of a man could no longer be made out from the natural light. The fact that the intruder was visible because of moonlight or artificial light was not a defense, however.

The sixth requirement was that the intruder intended to commit a felony, such as murder, rape, or larceny, within the dwelling house. Any intent to steal was sufficient, since all theft was considered a felony (even though only larceny of twelvepence or more was punishable by death). If the purpose of the entry was merely to look around or even to strike someone, however, there was no burglary. This was true even if the invader later decided to steal property, or if the person assaulted died.

Modern changes. Modern statutes and judicial decisions have greatly expanded the crime, everywhere extending it to both daytime events and to most buildings. An even more radical change has been introduced by more than two-thirds of the American states. By eliminating the breaking requirement that was at the heart of the original crime, these states have placed the principal emphasis upon intent and have expanded burglary to include all entries with an improper mental state into buildings. Walking into an open store with the intention of shoplifting thus becomes a burglary.

Many jurisdictions have also broadened the crime by eliminating the necessity of intending a felony and requiring only that some crime be intended. Coupled with the change in the breaking requirement, this means that going to a friend's house to smoke marijuana or to cheat on income taxes is a burglary. Another common expansion has been to modify the definition of entry so that it covers persons who unlawfully remain in structures as well as those who enter unlawfully.

Even these extraordinarily wide boundaries have not been enough for some states. California, for example, punishes entries into tents, mines, telephone booths, and locked autos (Cal. Penal Code § 459 (1970 & 1982 Supp.)), and New York once made any crime committed in a building a burglary, regardless of how the actor entered or with what intent (N.Y. Penal Law § 404 (McKinney) (1967, Appendix)).

One of the consequences of the broadened definition has been the inclusion of many offenses of less severity than common-law burglary. This has led most states to create a number of different gradations of the offense for sentencing purposes. New York, for example, has three such grades of burglary, with maximum punishments of seven, fifteen, and twenty-five years. The lowest punishments are for entry into a building with the intent to commit a crime, and the most serious is for entry into a dwelling aggravated by the infliction of a personal injury or by the presence or use of a weapon (N.Y. Penal Law §§ 140.20–140.30 (McKinney) (1975 & 1981–1982 Supp.)).

Criticism of the modern definition. Legal commentators have severely criticized the burglary concept, particularly the extended modern definitions. Because every burglary by definition involves an intent to commit some other crime, they suggest that the law would be more rational if burglary were simply absorbed into the general law of criminal attempts. They make five major criticisms of the modern formulations.

First, it is argued that the modern extensions of burglary have destroyed whatever central concept there may once have been and that the crime now has no coherent purpose. Second, critics hold that one major effect of the separate burglary category is to upgrade the punishment for crimes attempted in buildings in ways that are erratic and anomalous. Definitions which make stealing from an outside market larceny but entering an open store intending to steal the same items subject to more severe penalty are seen as particularly capricious.

Third, it is pointed out that burglary creates double punishment. If a burglar completes the theft or other crime that he intended, he may in most jurisdictions be convicted and punished for both the burglary and the theft or other crime. Under the more general law of criminal attempt, the attempted crime would be merged with the completed one so that the perpetrator could be convicted and punished only once.

Fourth, critics contend that earlier problems in the law of criminal attempts have now been cured. It is true that the early English common law did not make attempts criminal and that the later common law made attempts difficult to prove and punishable with very light penalties. The purpose that burglary served during these periods is no longer important, however, because modern law makes criminal attempts easier to prove and the penalties more appropriate.

Fifth, it is argued that because of their breadth, the modern extensions are not consistently enforced and that it is consequently unfair for police, prosecutors, and judges to apply them selectively.

Despite these criticisms, the American Law Institute retained the crime in its Model Penal Code (§ 221.1). Arguing that the concept of burglary was too deeply embedded in Anglo-American legal thought to be abolished, the Institute recommended narrowing the crime to unprivileged entries of buildings or occupied structures with the intent to commit a crime. This definition retains the core of the breaking idea but eliminates the technicalities. It prevents the application of burglary to shoplifting and to stealing from such places as unoccupied phone booths, cars, and caves, and eliminates double punishment except in those situations in which the crime intended is a serious one, such as murder, manslaughter, kidnapping, rape, arson, or robbery. Using a somewhat similar approach, the Theft Act, 1968, c. 60 (Great Britain) also retained burglary as a separate crime.

Related crimes. Theft is by far the most common reason for breaking into houses and stores. If property is taken, the thief is guilty not only of burglary but also of larceny. In some modern extensions, a person who enters a store with the intention of shoplifting is guilty of burglary at the moment of entry and before any theft has been consummated. Persons who decide to steal after they have already entered the building, however, are generally not guilty of burglary and may be charged only if they attempt or complete a larceny.

Because burglars are usually not seen while they are invading buildings, apprehensions and prosecutions are often difficult. Legislatures have consequently created offenses that make it easier to intercept burglars in preparatory acts or after the burglary has taken place. One such crime is that of possessing burglary tools. This crime is generally not limited to the possession of tools, such as picks or dummy keys, that are specifically useful in burglaries, but includes the possession of any tool or object with the intent to commit a burglary or with the knowledge that it will be used in a burglary.

A second crime that aids in the capture of burglars punishes the receiving or possessing of property with the knowledge that it has been stolen. This crime makes it risky for burglars openly to sell or transport property they have taken, particularly property that can be traced to the victim. Legal rules in some states go even farther and provide that the unexplained possession of stolen property gives rise to a presumption that the possessor is the burglar or the thief.

A third related crime is that of criminal trespass or prowling. Although neither the name nor the provisions of this crime are uniform, many jurisdictions punish prowling or wandering near private residences at night. This makes it possible to apprehend suspicious persons before any breaking has taken place.

If a burglar intentionally shoots or seriously injures a victim and the victim dies, the burglar is guilty of murder. Under the older English law, even an accidental shooting by a burglar that ended in the death of the victim was murder because of the felony-murder doctrine, which provided that killings committed in the course of a felony constituted murder. Regarding burglary as not inherently dangerous enough to warrant use of this drastic rule, some states no longer apply the rule to burglary.

History. The modern tendency to revise and reshape burglary has ancient roots. Although English law has protected the home from outside invasion for as far back as legal records exist, burglary in the form described by the classic common-law writers did not emerge until the late fifteenth or mid-sixteenth century—well after such other common-law felonies as murder, robbery, and arson.

Burglary seems to have evolved out of the old Anglo-Saxon crime of *hamsocn,* or housebreaking, a very serious crime. This crime was aimed more at violence than at theft and punished breaches of the peace of the house, such as assaults or entries to commit an assault. What is known of the earliest forms of burglary suggests that the crime could be committed during the day as well as at night and that it did not always require a breaking. At times it required an actual theft inside the house with the dwellers present, at other times a robbery inside the house, and at still other times a breaking but with the dwellers present and placed in fear.

Although the refinement of burglary in the late fifteenth or mid-sixteenth century into its classic common-law form settled some issues, others remained unresolved, and over the next century and a half, Parliament passed at least a dozen statutes filling gaps and raising penalties for such offenses as daytime theft from the home.

Common-law burglary was a capital felony in England until the 1830s. In the United States it remained a capital crime in three states until the early 1960s: there were eleven executions for burglary between 1930 and 1957.

Since antiquity, virtually all legal systems have given special protection to the home. Some have used formulations such as common-law burglary; others, however, have done so without a separate crime focused on breaking and entering with criminal intent. Modern French law, for example, treats theft from the home after entry by stealth as an aggravated form of theft but has no separate criminal category for burglary. West German law, on the other hand, makes the unlawful entry of homes or businesses a separate crime, without regard to the intent.

Types of behavior. Burglary is a difficult crime to describe empirically because the definition varies so much from place to place. Modern surveys of crime victims solve this problem by limiting burglary for statistical purposes to the breaking and entering of buildings. Using this relatively narrow definition, the authors of these surveys have suggested that two-thirds or more of the burglaries committed in the United States are never reported to the police.

Adopting a different approach, the Federal Bureau of Investigation's Uniform Crime Reports instructs police departments to regard any unlawful entry of a structure in order to commit a felony or a theft as a burglary. More than 85 percent of the burglaries so reported involve forcible or attempted forcible entries, which are illegal in all states. Less than 15 percent involve such entries as those to shoplift, which are unlawful in only some states. Since shoplifting is a very widespread crime, these figures suggest that it is not routinely treated as burglary.

Two-thirds of the burglaries reported to the police involve residences; one-third involve stores, offices, and other structures. Of those burglaries for which a time can be fixed, less than half the residential, but more than three-quarters of the commercial, burglaries take place at night. A fifth or more of the entries of residences are through unlocked doors or windows.

Ninety percent or more of all burglaries are for the purpose of theft, and most do not involve any confrontation with building occupants. Some burglaries are committed for the purpose of assault or rape, however, and do involve violence. A few burglaries for the purpose of theft also end in violence when the thief is surprised in the act.

Burglary is primarily a stranger-to-stranger crime—that is, a crime in which the offender does not know the victim. A small percentage, however, involve such acquaintances as former spouses, boyfriends, or roommates.

Characteristics of offenders. Burglars who break into stores and houses are generally not seen. What is known about burglars therefore comes primarily from information about persons arrested for burglary. This information is incomplete, since in the United States offenders are arrested in less than 20 percent of all burglaries.

Most arrested burglars are male and young: more than 90 percent are male, and more than 80 percent are under twenty-five years of age. Nearly half are under eighteen, and almost a fifth under fifteen. However, older offenders probably commit a higher proportion of the burglaries than these figures suggest. They operate alone more often, and they tend to commit more burglaries before being caught.

Some common kinds of burglars are first offenders, teenage burglars, persistent thieves and hustlers, drug addicts, habitual burglars, and safecrackers and other skillful planners.

Self-report studies indicate that large numbers of youths, particularly males, admit to having committed at least one burglary. For most, this is part of the growing-up process, and they do not continue further with a burglary career.

A sizable number of teenagers, however, do commit more burglaries. These youths tend to operate in groups or gangs, to commit daytime burglaries, and to limit their burglaries to within a mile or two of their homes.

Persistent thieves and hustlers tend to be drifters, seeking to pick up money in whatever way they can. They often commit shoplifting and other forms of theft, as well as burglary.

Burglary is one of the crimes commonly committed by heroin addicts to support their habit. Although estimates that attribute nearly all burglaries to addicts are almost certainly faulty, reliable studies suggest that addicts may account for a quarter or more of all burglaries in some American cities.

Habitual burglars develop the crime into a business. They learn how to get in and out of homes or stores quickly, to deal with alarm systems, to identify the items of greatest value, and to dispose of property efficiently. When arrested, this kind of burglar can often identify scores or even hundreds of burglaries for which he is responsible.

Most burglars seek money or valuables that can be taken quickly and easily. Safecrackers are a small group of burglars who are willing to run greater risks for greater rewards. Their crimes often require a knowledge of explosives or incendiary devices and considerable skill and planning.

FLOYD FEENEY

See also ATTEMPT; THEFT; TRESPASS, CRIMINAL.

BIBLIOGRAPHY

American Law Institute. *Model Penal Code: Proposed Official Draft.* Philadelphia: ALI, 1962.
———. *Model Penal Code: Tentative Draft No. 11.* Philadelphia: ALI, 1960.
BENTIL, J. KODWO. "Elements of Burglary." *Solicitor's Journal* 124 (1980): 551–553.
CONKLIN, JOHN E., and BITTNER, EGON. "Burglary in a Suburb." *Criminology* 11 (1973): 206–232.
Federal Bureau of Investigation. *Crime in the United States, 1980.* Uniform Crime Reports for the United States. Washington, D.C.: U.S. Department of Justice, FBI, 1981.
IRWIN, JOHN. *The Felon.* Englewood Cliffs, N.J.: Prentice-Hall, 1970.
LAFAVE, WAYNE R., and SCOTT, AUSTIN W., JR. *Handbook on Criminal Law.* St. Paul: West, 1972.
LOW, PETER, and JEFFRIES, JOHN C., JR. "The Crime of Burglary under the Model Penal Code." *Practical Lawyer* 26, no. 8 (1980): 33–50.
MOYLAN, CHARLES E., JR. "The Historical Intertwining of Maryland's Burglary and Larceny Laws, or the Singular Adventure of the Misunderstood Indictment Clerk." *University of Baltimore Law Review* 4 (1974): 28–58.
Note. "Statutory Burglary: The Magic of Four Walls and a Roof." *University of Pennsylvania Law Review* 100 (1951): 411–445.
PERKINS, ROLLIN M. *Criminal Law.* 2d ed. Mineola, N.Y.: Foundation Press, 1969.
SCARR, HARRY A.; PINSKY, JOHN L.; and WYATT, DEBORAH S. *Patterns of Burglary.* 2d ed., rev. and enlarged. With an annotated bibliographic guide to literature on burglary, burglars, and burglarizing. Washington, D.C.: U.S. Department of Justice, Law Enforcement Assistance Administration, National Institute of Law Enforcement and Criminal Justice, 1973.
SMITH, JOHN C. *The Law of Theft.* 3d ed. London: Butterworths, 1977.

BUSINESS CRIMES

See CORPORATE CRIMINAL RESPONSIBILITY; *articles under* ECONOMIC CRIME; WHITE-COLLAR CRIME: HISTORY OF AN IDEA.

C

CAPITAL PUNISHMENT

The death penalty is most conveniently examined in two stages, beginning with a study of the major developments and trends in law and policy that have characterized it during the twentieth century and that probably will shape its future as well. A review and evaluation of the major types of arguments that have been used to attack or defend it will follow. As a supplement to the discussion of these two major topics, which focus mainly on the death penalty in the United States, a brief look at the status of the death penalty elsewhere in the world will help put modern issues into better perspective.

Developments in law and policy

The status of the death penalty at any given time can be assessed by a careful study of the factors that affect its administration. These may usefully be grouped under the following major headings: (1) the variety and scope of capital laws; (2) the volume and rate of death sentences and executions; (3) the role of appellate courts in shaping the law of capital punishment; (4) the search for effective and humane methods of execution; (5) the setting in which executions are carried out; and (6) the struggle over the complete abolition of the death penalty.

Variety and scope of capital laws. During the American colonial period (1600–1775), as well as in England at the same time, the penalty of death by hanging was imposed not only for murder but also for many other felonies against the person, the state, and property. Capital statutes varied considerably among the colonies, and when the nation was constituted in 1789 there was no uniformity in the death-penalty laws in force in the thirteen states. This diversity in the substantive law of capital crimes has remained one of the most characteristic features of the death penalty in the United States. In 1960, for example, the statutes of the nation's fifty-three jurisdictions (fifty states, District of Columbia, federal civil and military) authorized the death penalty as follows. One or more forms of murder was punishable by death in forty-four jurisdictions, thirty-four authorized death for one or more forms of kidnapping, nineteen punished rape or other forms of sexual assault with death, ten punished robbery with death, and two or more jurisdictions had a death penalty for such other crimes as assault by a life-term prisoner, burglary, arson, and train wrecking.

In contrast to this variety of capital offenses, relatively few convicted felons have been sentenced to death and executed. For example, out of the thousands convicted in 1960 of murder, rape, and other nominally capital offenses, only 113 persons were sentenced to death and only 56—half that number—were actually executed. For decades this kind of disparity has been typical of the actual practice involving capital punishment. Despite the wealth of capital statutes and the volume of capital offenders, few persons have been sentenced to death and even fewer actually executed.

From the earliest history of the nation, various factors have been at work to limit the impact of the death penalty. The colonies inherited from English criminal law two such moderating factors. One of them, benefit of clergy, ceased to have effect after the eighteenth century. The other, still practiced today, was the prerogative of executive clemency. Of far greater importance were two novel departures from English common and statutory law: the introduction of discretionary capital sentencing, and the introduction of degrees of murder.

Under the common law, all murder was punishable by death and all death penalties were mandatory. Provocation reduced murder to manslaughter at common law (voluntary manslaughter). Very early in the nation's history, legislatures modified the stringency of both these rules. A 1642 Massachusetts statute made the death penalty for rape optional with the sentencing court, and flogging or other public humiliation quickly became the alternative sentence in most cases. A Pennsylvania statute of 1794 confined capital punishment for murder to "first degree" murder (premeditated and deliberate killings and felony murder, that is, any homicide committed during the course of arson, burglary, rape, robbery, or other specified felony). By the mid-twentieth century, mandatory death penalties were rare and typically confined to crimes hardly ever committed, for example, treason. The trends, therefore, have been to confine the death penalty to the gravest crimes, to repeal it for lesser crimes, to limit its scope still further by reducing the number of homicides that qualify as capital murder, and to empower the sentencing court to grant mercy in the form of an alternative punishment of long-term imprisonment.

The rationale for reductions in the number of capital offenses was twofold. On the one hand, they prevented jury nullification, a problem notorious in England, where under the "bloody code" that prevailed prior to 1800, juries refused to convict obviously guilty defendants because a death sentence was deemed too severe. Conversely, degrees of murder and discretionary sentencing tended to limit the severest penalty—death—to those offenders whom the community regarded as the worst among the bad, thereby making it the appropriate punishment on deterrent and retributive grounds. Close scrutiny of actual practice, both historical and modern, tends to cast doubt on the legitimacy of the latter rationale. Nevertheless, the trends cited have continued to prevail.

Rulings by the United States Supreme Court in the 1970s have effectively reinforced these trends. Under *Woodson v. North Carolina*, 428 U.S. 280 (1976) and *Roberts v. Louisiana*, 431 U.S. 633 (1977), the mandatory death penalty for murder, including the murder of an on-duty law officer, has been declared an unconstitutionally "cruel and unusual punishment." Since *Coker v. Georgia*, 433 U.S. 584 (1977), the death penalty for rape (where the victim is otherwise unharmed) has been prohibited on the same ground; the same rationale was used to strike down the death penalty for kidnapping (*Eberheart v. Georgia*, 232 Ga. 247, 206 S.E.2d 12 (1974), *vacated and remanded* 433 U.S. 917 (1977)). The constitutionality of the death penalty for such typically federal crimes as treason, espionage, air piracy, and other nonhomicidal offenses had not (as of 1980) reached the courts. Thus, constitutional interpretation has effectively confined the death penalty to the punishment of certain forms of murder (and, as of 1980, statutes in thirty-four states so provided), even though legislative enactments during the 1970s showed strong inclinations in many jurisdictions to retain certain nonhomicidal crimes as capital offenses, and even in some cases to preserve the death penalty as a mandatory punishment.

Volume and rate of death sentences and executions. Between 1930 and 1980, 3,860 persons were executed for eight different crimes. The vast majority—3,335, or 86 percent—were executed for murder; 455, or 12 percent, for rape; and the rest—70, or 2 percent—for armed robbery, kidnapping, burglary, sabotage, aggravated assault, or espionage (U.S. Department of Justice). The number of death sentences during this period and the proportions sentenced for each crime are not known.

Almost all persons sentenced to death and executed have been male. Since 1930 only thirty-two women (twelve of them nonwhite) have been executed, all but two for the crime of murder. The racial breakdown shows that since 1930, 54 percent of all persons executed were nonwhite and 89 percent of the persons executed for rape were nonwhite.

National records show that during the twentieth century executions reached a peak in the mid-1930s, after which they steadily declined. The annual average during the 1930s was 167; during the 1940s, 128; in the 1950s, 72; and 19 in the 1960s. Concurrently, executions became increasingly confined to the South and West. In the 1970s only three persons, all male and all white, were put to death. Two of them refused to permit any challenge to the legality or constitutionality of their death sentences.

The decline in executions since the mid-1930s may be somewhat deceptive, in that the supply of death sentences has not diminished at the same rate. During the 1970s, an average of 160 persons were sentenced to death annually, whereas during the previous decade the average was 113. Only a few of these sentences were carried out, owing primarily to appellate litigation over the constitutionality of the death sentence, discussed below. Indeed, it became characteristic during the 1970s for death rows around the nation to fill steadily with persons awaiting execution, and then suddenly to empty as death sentences were overturned by the hundreds. Even so, during 1981 more than 800 persons in twenty-nine jurisdictions were awaiting execution.

Whether executions will become as frequent as they were in the 1930s is unlikely, and depends on a number of factors. True, trial juries throughout the nation during the 1960s and 1970s showed little reluctance to convict and sentence murderers to death; chief executives also showed no inclination to use the power of clemency to nullify all or even many of the death sentences meted out by trial courts. Legislatures have repealed some nonhomicidal capital statutes, but very few death sentences and executions had resulted from these laws. The chief obstacle to a large volume of executions has been the critical role of the Supreme Court in nullifying death sentences.

Role of appellate courts. By far the single most dramatic development affecting the death penalty in the United States since the 1920s has been the increasingly prominent role played by the federal appellate courts in supervising several aspects of the death penalty.

Prior to the 1960s, interventions by the appellate courts in capital cases were confined largely to two areas. One concerned the review of the *methods* of carrying out the death penalty. Litigation on this issue was conducted for decades on the unargued assumption that the death penalty itself was not an unconstitutionally "cruel and unusual punishment." The other area concerned various requirements of *procedure* affecting the conviction and sentencing phases of a capital trial under constitutional standards, such as those provided by the due process and equal protection clauses of the Fourteenth Amendment. The pioneering case in this area, famous during the 1930s as the "Scottsboro boys" rape trial, held that it was a violation of due process for capital defendants to face trial without prior counsel (*Powell v. Alabama*, 287 U.S. 45 (1932)).

Not until the late 1960s was the constitutionality of the death penalty challenged directly (Meltsner; Bedau, 1977). The initial challenges were addressed to procedural issues, in particular the practice of holding a "unitary trial" to settle issues of both guilt and sentencing, and the practice of exercising discretion without using any standards in sentencing to determine whether to punish a convicted offender with death or with imprisonment. Subsequent challenges were addressed to the substantive question of whether the death penalty, however administered, was in violation of the Eighth Amendment as a "cruel and unusual punishment." These challenges were in part prompted by the dissent of three Supreme Court Justices to the denial of certiorari in *Rudolph v. Alabama*, 375 U.S. 889 (1963), in which they argued that the Court should hear argument on whether the death penalty for rape was a "cruel and unusual punishment"—an unprecedented display of concern on the highest federal bench over the constitutionality of capital punishment.

Four years later, in 1967, in response to a class-action habeas corpus petition initiated by the NAACP Legal Defense and Educational Fund on behalf of its death-row clients, federal district courts in Florida (*Adderly v. Wainwright*, 272 F. Supp. 530 (M.D. Fla. 1967)) and in California (*Hill v. Nelson*, 272 F. Supp. 790 (N.D. Cal. 1967)) granted a stay of execution to all death-row inmates in these two states, pending review of various constitutional objections to the death sentence. These class-action stays were the source of the de facto national moratorium on executions between 1967 and 1977.

From 1968 to 1971, the Supreme Court disposed of the procedural objections without granting any of the claims raised in opposition to capital punishment (*Maxwell v. Bishop*, 398 U.S. 262 (1970); *McGautha v. California*, 402 U.S. 183 (1971)). In particular, the Court turned back the challenge that the chief effect of the exclusionary rule which summarily excluded from jury duty veniremen who declared conscientious objection to the death penalty was to create a "conviction-prone" jury (*Witherspoon v. Illinois*, 391 U.S. 510 (1968)). Nevertheless, the Court did forbid the prosecution from abusing the rule to obtain a "hanging jury." (As Welsh White has shown, it has proved difficult to give this vague ruling full effect.) This set the stage for the Supreme Court to confront the ultimate constitutional question of whether the death penalty per se was "cruel and unusual punishment."

In 1970, a federal circuit court ruled that the death penalty for rape was "disproportionate" to the crime and was therefore an unconstitutional "cruel and unusual punishment" (*Ralph v. Warden*, 438 F.2d 786 (4th Cir. 1970)). Two years later, with more than six hundred persons under sentence of death in thirty-three states, the Supreme Court handed down its ruling in *Furman v. Georgia*, 408 U.S. 238 (1972). The Court majority did not face squarely the question of whether the death penalty was per se unconstitutional. Instead, it held that the death penalty, as then administered by trial courts with no standards to govern their exercise of sentencing discretion, was unconstitutional under the Eighth and Fourteenth amendments. At one stroke, this ruling in effect abolished all death penalties throughout the nation. (A small handful of the persons then on death row who had been sentenced under the few remaining mandatory capital statutes were not affected by the ruling.)

Most legislatures promptly reacted to *Furman* in one of two ways: by enacting new mandatory death statutes, or by enacting new death statutes with provisions for a bifurcated (two-stage) trial. These latter statutes typically directed the trial court in a capital case to conduct a post-conviction hearing to consider evidence specifically introduced for its relevance to the choice of sentence—death or life imprisonment. A death sentence would then be based on evidence that "aggravated" the defendant's guilt (for example, his prior criminal record); a life sentence would be based on evidence that "mitigated" his guilt (for example, his youth). Both the aggravating and mitigating factors were specified by statute. Automatic review by the state supreme court of each death sentence in order to guarantee equitable sentencing was also a typical requirement of these post-*Furman* capital statutes.

In 1976 the Supreme Court invalidated the mandatory death penalty for murder (*Woodson*) on the ground that it was inconsistent with the "particularized" sentencing required by *Furman*. At the same time, the Court resolved the issue left open in *Furman* by holding that the death penalty is not necessarily cruel and unusual punishment, and upheld three different statutory models incorporating the principle of guided discretion and the bifurcated trial (*Gregg v. Georgia*, 428 U.S. 153 (1976); *Jurek v. Texas*, 428 U.S. 262 (1976); *Proffitt v. Florida*, 428 U.S. 242 (1976)). The Court decided in each case that the legislature had adopted statutory provisions reasonably designed to remedy the defects that were condemned in *Furman*, and that there were no adequate grounds for ruling the death penalty per se unconstitutional.

Whether the specific ills that provoked the *Furman* ruling—arbitrary and racially biased death sentences in particular—were in fact fully or even partially alleviated by the post-*Furman* guided discretion statutes has remained a matter of dispute. The appellate courts have been reluctant to confront the issue directly. Studies of conviction and sentencing patterns in several states since 1976 suggest that however color-blind the statutes may be, the actual practice of the trial and state appellate courts has been to sentence to death with greater frequency those offenders (white or black) who kill whites than those who kill blacks.

Thus, despite the infrequency of federal death sentences (fewer than 1 percent of all capital sentences in this century have issued from federal courts), the federal courts have exercised an increasingly important supervisory role in the nation's capital jurisprudence. Whether in future decades the Supreme Court will rule directly against the death penalty, thereby extending *Furman* and overruling *Gregg, Jurek,* and *Proffitt,* remains uncertain. What is more likely is that the federal courts will continue to scrutinize capital statutes and capital sentencing procedures with great care and not hesitate to break new ground to nullify death sentences, even though these sentences were issued under nominally constitutional statutes (Radin, 1978, 1980). In such ways, the Supreme Court has acknowledged that "death is different" (*Gardner v. Florida*, 430 U.S. 349, 357 (1977)). This realization probably will continue to distinguish its treatment of capital cases from the rest of its criminal jurisprudence.

State appellate courts, with rare exceptions, have not used their constitutional authority to overturn death sentences in a manner parallel to that of the federal courts. This has been so despite the presence in most states of constitutional provisions for due process and against cruel and unusual punishments similar to those in the federal Constitution. In a precedent-breaking ruling a few months before *Furman* was announced, the California state supreme court held that capital punishment was per se a violation of the state's constitutional prohibition against "cruel or unusual punishment" (*People v. Anderson*, 6 Cal. 3d 628, 493 P.2d 880 (1972)). This ruling was promptly nullified by passage of an initiative amending the state constitution. In 1976, the Massachusetts state supreme court ruled that the mandatory death penalty for felony-murder based on rape was in violation of the state constitution (*Commonwealth v. O'Neal*, 369 Mass. 242 (1975)), and in 1981 it ruled that the death penalty for any crime would be similarly unconstitutional (*District Attorney for the Suffolk District v. Watson*, 411 N.E.2d 1274 (Mass. 1980)). These rulings, however, are quite unusual; most state appellate courts have given relatively perfunctory review of their own lower-court death sentences and have rarely ruled against the penalty, as distinct from overturning the conviction itself.

The search for effective and humane methods of execution. During the twentieth century, persons have been lawfully executed in the United States by one of five methods: hanging, shooting, electrocution, lethal gas, or lethal injection. The constitutionality of each has been tested and upheld: hanging (by inference) in *Medley, Petitioner*, 134 U.S. 160 (1890); shooting in *Wilkerson v. Utah,* 99 U.S. 130 (1879); electrocution in *In re Kemmler,* 136 U.S. 436 (1890); lethal gas in several state court decisions, for example, *State v. Gee Jon,* 46 Nev. 418, 211 P. 676 (1923) and *People v. Daugherty,* 40 Cal. 2d 876, 256 P.2d 911 (1953), *cert. denied,* 346 U.S. 827 (1953); and lethal injection in *Ex parte Granviel,* 561 S.W.2d 503 (Tex. Ct. Crim. App. 1978). In 1980, four states still favored hanging, the traditional method for executing ordinary felons. One state, Utah, required the use of the firing squad, a method of execution elsewhere associated with punishment for military offenses or with capital crimes under martial law.

In an effort to improve on the uncertainty and inhumanity of hanging, New York introduced the electric chair and first used it in 1890 to carry out a death sentence. In 1980, most American death-penalty jurisdictions (seventeen) still authorized this method in preference to others. Nevada was the first jurisdiction to adopt execution by lethal (cyanide) gas chamber, and in 1924 used it to put to death a convicted murderer. Several other states adopted this technique during the next two decades; as of 1980, it was the lawful method of execution in ten states. In 1977 a fifth method of execution, lethal injection, was adopted by the Oklahoma legislature. This method, which involves a massive intravenous dose of barbiturates, had been adopted by three other jurisdictions as of 1980; during 1982 two states authorized lethal injection as an optional mode of execution. In December 1982 Texas became the first jurisdiction to carry out a death sentence by this means. The federal government in its criminal jurisdiction has traditionally carried out executions by whatever method is authorized in the state in which the federal prisoner's death sentence is carried out. Under military law, hanging or a firing squad is authorized.

From a scientific and humane perspective, the relative merits of these various methods have never been adequately settled. In 1953, the Royal Commission on Capital Punishment investigated the matter and cautiously endorsed the traditional British method of hanging. The American Medical Association adopted in 1980 a resolution urging physicians not to participate in any execution by lethal injection, on the ground that this was "a corruption and exploitation of the healing profession's role in society" (Curran and Casscells, p. 230). The effects of hanging, electrocution, and the firing squad on the body of the prisoner, as well as on the official witnesses to the execution, have little to recommend them; each of these methods can result in cruelty and brutality if improperly administered. Both lethal gas and lethal injection

have unfortunate associations owing to the notorious employment of these methods by the Nazis in their genocidal crimes and "medical experiments" during World War II. It is generally conceded that the ideal method of execution for a civilized nation has yet to be invented and adopted.

The setting: public vs. private executions. Executions in the United States are invariably carried out behind prison walls, shielded from the public gaze but witnessed by authorized invited observers. The number and status of such witnesses vary considerably according to the statutes and prison regulations of each jurisdiction. In earlier centuries, a hanging was typically a public affair and the occasion for revelry, often attended by thousands. Beginning in the 1830s, the venue and environment of legal executions were progressively controlled by law. Not until a century later, however, was the time-honored practice of public execution finally outlawed. The last persons to be executed in public in the United States were a black rapist (hanged in Kentucky in 1936) and a white murderer (hanged in Missouri in 1937).

Since the development of television in the 1950s, some have advocated that executions be broadcast "live." Defenders of the death penalty have argued that this would enhance the deterrent effect; some abolitionists have thought it might so repel and disgust the general public, which for decades has had little direct knowledge about actual executions, that it would increase opposition to executions. An attempt in 1977 to force prison authorities in Texas to permit public television to cover an execution was rebuffed in federal courts (*Garrett v. Estelle,* 556 F.2d 1274 (5th Cir. 1977)), partly on the ground that the issue was moot, the execution having been indefinitely postponed.

Abolition vs. retention of the death penalty. Efforts to abolish the death penalty for all crimes in the United States have a long history (Mackey) but have met with uneven success. When Michigan accepted statehood in 1847, it had already abolished the death penalty for murder (although not for treason), thereby becoming the first "abolitionist" jurisdiction in the English-speaking world. During the mid-nineteenth century Rhode Island (1852), Wisconsin (1853), Iowa (1872), and Maine (1876) followed Michigan's lead; but the Civil War (1861–1865) effectively ended any trend toward further abolition elsewhere in the nation.

Not until the Progressive era, terminated by America's entry into World War I, did a number of states again abolish the death penalty: Kansas (1907), Minnesota (1911), Washington (1913), Oregon (1914),

South and North Dakota and Tennessee (1915), Arizona (1916), and Missouri (1917). During the next two decades, however, most of these states restored capital punishment, and no legislature voted to abolish the death penalty for murder anywhere in the United States for another forty years, until hanging for murder was repealed in Delaware in 1958. Within the next decade, Oregon (1964), New York (1965), West Virginia (1965), Vermont (1965), and New Mexico (1969) either abolished their capital statutes for murder or severely limited them to certain types of homicide, for example, killing a law officer on duty. During the 1970s, several of these states restored the death penalty. The reasons why some states abolished it and why some then reintroduced it are not fully understood.

By 1980, thirty-four states had retained or restored the death penalty for murder, and several had tried to keep it for certain nonhomicidal crimes, although Supreme Court decisions nullified most of these efforts. The record thus shows that few legislatures in this century have had more than sporadic inclinations to repeal the death penalty for murder. Whether the climate of abolitionist sentiment that affected much of the nation outside the South in the second decade of the twentieth century and again in the 1960s will return, and whether it will penetrate for the first time into the Sun Belt region—where most capital statutes and most death sentences are to be found—remain to be seen.

One factor in legislative decisions to retain, abolish, or restore the death penalty is the legislature's perception of the public's attitude. Survey research during the 1960s showed abolitionist sentiment nationwide to be nearly even with retentionist sentiment; this gave ardent abolitionist groups more leverage with legislatures than in earlier decades, when polls showed that the public favored the death penalty by a wide margin. By the early 1970s, however, there had been a significant shift in public opinion, and all polls showed that the public favored the death penalty by a margin of two (or even three) to one, a reversion to the pattern of public attitudes that had prevailed during the 1930s.

Defense of the death penalty during the 1970s became a plank in the legislative programs of such organizations as the International Association of Chiefs of Police and the National District Attorneys Association. Public attitudes favoring the death penalty during the 1970s, however, were not primarily the result of effective lobbying by pro-death-penalty groups. They seem rather to have been caused by (1) increased fear of victimization; (2) belief in the deterrent effec-

tiveness and retributive appropriateness of execution for murderers; and (3) a view of the death penalty as a symbol of a "get tough" attitude toward criminals that accompanied the rise of a general conservative sociopolitical ideology. Attitudes in favor of the death penalty rarely have reached the level of clamor for actual executions, however. The failure to execute nearly two thousand persons during the 1960s and 1970s, owing to appellate court decisions remanding them to lower courts for resentencing to imprisonment, caused little public outcry.

Organized efforts to abolish the death penalty emerged in the 1920s with the formation of the American League to Abolish Capital Punishment (disbanded in 1972). During the 1960s, multi-issue civil liberties and civil rights groups, such as the American Civil Liberties Union and the NAACP Legal Defense and Educational Fund, undertook to attack the death penalty in the legislatures and the courts. In 1976 the National Coalition against the Death Penalty was formed, consisting of more than fifty major national and regional organizations in the fields of religion, law, civil liberties, and civil rights (U.S. Congress, House, pp. 30–31).

Some have argued that the very success of abolitionist efforts for more than a century best explains the failure to secure complete national abolition. Degrees of murder, jury discretion in sentencing, automatic appellate court review, executive clemency, replacement of hanging by purportedly more acceptable modes of execution, repeal of most nonhomicidal capital statutes, virtually total refusal to sentence or execute women—all these limit the death penalty and thus restrict to a narrow scope its morally troubling aspects. It consequently plays a minor role in the actual protection of the public against crime. Conversely, its symbolic value looms quite large in the minds of those who are anxious over what they regard as the decay of traditional values and the erosion of law and order and of firm measures against convicted or would-be criminals.

Arguments for and against capital punishment

The reasons advanced for and against the death penalty can be conveniently divided into *religious* and *secular*, and the latter can be further subdivided into considerations that rest primarily on appeals to *justice*, in contrast to those that rest primarily on appeals to *social utility*.

Jewish and Christian views.
Biblical attitudes. The Bible frequently and unequivocally endorses the death penalty as the proper

mode of punishment for many crimes. The Mosaic code mentions murder, kidnapping, witchcraft, idolatry, sodomy, adultery, incest, blasphemy, and several other offenses as punishable by death. The method of execution was to be either by stoning or by burning; hanging was originally a posthumous insult to the offender. Crucifixion was later introduced by the Romans. Opponents of the death penalty sometimes point to the biblical story of the first murderer, Cain, whom God did not punish with death but with banishment and a curse (Gen. 4:8–15). Proponents of the death penalty reply by citing the Noachian commandment, "Whosoever sheddeth man's blood, by man shall his blood be shed" (Gen. 9:6). The biblical *lex talionis* ("eye for eye, tooth for tooth, life for life"), probably a borrowing from the Code of Hammurabi, is also often cited as proof of divine authority for the death penalty. But most biblical scholars today construe this as a limitation on merited punishment (*no more than* a life for a life), and they point out as well that post-biblical Talmudists favored a penology built around monetary compensation rather than bodily injury, thereby reflecting a shift from punishment as retaliation in kind to proportional punishment (Cohn).

Modern attitudes. Since the 1950s, most Jewish and Christian religious groups in the United States have publicly opposed the death penalty as inconsistent with the fundamental religious theme common to both the Old and the New Testament—the redemptive and forgiving power of a just God (U.S. Congress, House, pp. 32–69). Some orthodox Jewish sects and fundamentalist Christian churches, however, cling to an older view (common enough among all Protestant clergy during the nineteenth century) that supports current death penalties—especially for murder—by appeal to the punitive doctrines proposed in the oldest books of the Bible. Both proponents and opponents of the death penalty have also appealed to the biblical idea of the *sanctity* of human life as decisive for their outlook. Proponents have insisted that murder violates that sanctity, and that the Bible authorizes punishment by death as the appropriate way to vindicate this principle. In the view of opponents, since the Bible teaches that no human society has the purity and justice to inflict death as a punishment, for a secular government to act as though it does is to claim the prerogatives of God.

Issues of justice and human rights. With the rise of rationalist thought in European culture during the Renaissance and Enlightenment (1550–1750), and the concurrent decline in an exclusively religious foundation for moral principles, philosophers and jurists in-

creasingly lent their support to the doctrine of "the rights of man" as the foundation for constitutional law and public morality. The most influential continental, British, and American Enlightenment thinkers—John Locke, Jean-Jacques Rousseau, Cesare Beccaria, William Blackstone, Immanuel Kant, and Thomas Jefferson—all agreed that the first and foremost of these rights is "the right to life." Few of these thinkers, however, opposed the death penalty (Beccaria was the notable exception); most endorsed it explicitly. They argued, typically, that since each person is born with a "natural" right to life, murder must be viewed as a violation of that right; accordingly, executing the murderer is not wrong since the murderer has forfeited his own right to life by virtue of his crime.

Modern thinkers, under the influence of the human rights provisions advocated by the United Nations in various resolutions, declarations, and covenants, have sought to appeal to a more complex line of considerations embedded in other human rights, as well as in the idea of the right to life. This view was advocated most prominently in the 1970s by Amnesty International, the human rights organization awarded the Nobel Peace Prize in 1978 for its worldwide campaign against torture. On this view, the death penalty violates human rights because (1) its administration is inevitably surrounded by arbitrary practices and unreliable procedures that violate offenders' rights (Black); (2) erroneous executions are an irrevocable and irremediable violation of the right to life; and (3) there are less severe and equally effective alternatives—notably, long-term imprisonment.

In the United States since the 1960s, these themes have been argued most vigorously by the American Civil Liberties Union and by attorneys for the NAACP Legal Defense and Educational Fund and the Southern Poverty Law Center on behalf of nonwhite and indigent clients accused of murder. Their basic argument has been that the death penalty as it is actually used in contemporary American criminal justice systems is inherently and irredeemably class- and race-biased, so that a self-respecting civilized society cannot afford to employ it.

Racism. The central evidence for the main criticism—racist administration of the death penalty—comes from research conducted in several states, particularly in the South, in which it has been shown that a person is more likely to be sentenced to death if the victim is white than if nonwhite (Bowers and Pierce, 1980a). These results are consistent with the generally acknowledged results of earlier research on the death penalty for rape, in which it was shown that the overwhelming preponderance of death penalties for black offenders could be explained only by the race of the offender taken in conjunction with that of the victim: the death penalty was highly probable only if the victim was white (Wolfgang and Riedel).

Defenders of the death penalty have, or could have, replied as follows: (1) all current capital laws are color-blind and impose equal liability on all persons regardless of race, color, class, or sex of offender or of victim; (2) racism in the current administration of the death penalty cannot be inferred from evidence relating to the admittedly racist practices of the distant past; (3) the evidence tending to show that the race of the victim is the chief explanation for whether an offender is sentenced to death (white victim) or to prison (non-white victim) is incomplete and inconclusive; (4) since justice requires that all murderers be sentenced to death and executed, some racial bias (if there is any) in the day-to-day administration of capital punishment is merely another case of the regrettable but tolerable imperfect enforcement of a just law; and (5) the deterrent and incapacitating effects of executions provided by even a somewhat racially biased death penalty are better for society than are the results of a less potent (even if less biased racially) alternative mode of punishment.

Retribution. Many defenders of the death penalty rest their position on principles of retributive justice and the appropriateness of moral indignation at murder, which they believe can be expressed adequately only by punishing that crime (and others, if any, no less heinous) by death. Whether such retributive reasoning has its origins in a passion for vengeance is less important than whether the principles to which it appeals are sound. Most opponents of the death penalty do not dispute (1) the principle that convicted offenders deserve to be punished; (2) the principle that a suitable punishment is, like a crime itself, some form of harsh treatment; and (3) the principle that the severity of the punishment should be proportional to the gravity of the offense. What is disputed is whether the third principle *requires* the death penalty for murder (and other crimes) or whether this principle is merely *consistent* with such a punishment, so that the further step in favor of death as the ideally fitting penalty must be taken by reference to other (perhaps nonretributive) considerations. Making the punishment fit the crime in any literal sense is either impossible or morally unacceptable, given the horrible nature of many murders. Interpreting the third principle so that it entails "a life for a life" thus verges on begging the question. As a result, the focus of controversy between proponents and opponents of

the death penalty who agree in arguing the issue primarily on grounds of retributive justice is on how closely it is necessary and desirable to model a punishment on the crime for which it is meted out. It is perhaps noteworthy that the most influential proponents of the "new retributivism" do not advocate capital punishment for any crimes (von Hirsch).

Utility and the prevention of crime. Quite apart from considerations rooted in principles of retributive justice or of constitutional law, arguments for and against the death penalty often proceed by reference to essentially utilitarian considerations, in which the consequences for overall social welfare—especially as this involves the reduction of crime—are the criteria to which both sides appeal. For example, defenders of the death penalty have argued that executions are a far less costly mode of punishment than any alternative. Abolitionists have replied that this is untrue if one takes into account the enormous cost to society of the extremely complex and lengthy litigation that surrounds a capital case, beginning with the search for an acceptable jury and culminating in postsentencing appeals and hearings in both state and federal courts. The chief issue of utilitarian concern, however, has always been whether the death penalty is an effective means of preventing crime and whether it is more effective than the alternative of imprisonment.

Incapacitation. Both sides concede that execution is a perfectly incapacitative punishment and that in this respect it is preferable to imprisonment. How much difference this makes to the crime rate is a matter of sharp dispute: the issue turns on (1) whether persons who have been executed would have committed further capital (or other) offenses if they had not been executed, and (2) whether persons convicted and imprisoned for capital crimes but not executed will commit further capital offenses when and if released. There is no direct evidence available regarding the first question. Evidence relevant to the second question from parole and recidivism records indicates that a very small number of capital offenders commit subsequent crimes. Roughly 1 convicted homicide offender out of every 340 such persons released from prison commits another homicide within the first year after release (U.S. Congress, Senate, pp. 207–211). Defenders of the death penalty often argue that it is inexcusable for society not to take measures guaranteeing that a convicted murderer is incapable of repeating his crime. Abolitionists argue that the alternatives open to society, if it abandons the present system of parole and release practices, are even worse: either society must execute *all* convicted murderers, at intolerable moral cost (these thousands of executions are unnecessary, since so few murderers recidivate), or society must imprison *all* convicted murderers until their natural death, also intolerable because of the prison management problems that such a policy would create.

General deterrence. Still more important and controversial is the adequacy of the death penalty as a general deterrent. During the 1950s, evidence based on several different comparisons convinced most criminologists that there was no superior deterrent effect associated with the death penalty. The comparisons were between homicide rates in given states before, during, and after abolition; homicide rates in given jurisdictions before and after executions; homicide rates in adjacent states, some with and others without the use of capital punishment; and rates of police killings in abolitionist and death-penalty jurisdictions (Sellin, 1959, 1980). In the 1970s, this conclusion was challenged by research which used new methods borrowed from econometrics and which asserted that each execution in the United States between 1930 and 1969 prevented between eight and twenty murders (Ehrlich). Subsequent investigators, however, soon showed that the alleged deterrent effect was an artifact of arbitrary if not dubious statistical methods. A panel of the National Academy of Science (NAS) went even further and expressed extreme skepticism about the results of all available research studies; none, the panel said, provided any useful evidence on the deterrent effect of capital punishment (Blumstein, Cohen, and Nagin). No reliable scientific investigations support the commonsense inference that since the death penalty is more severe than long-term imprisonment, the death penalty must be a better deterrent.

It is difficult to say whether skepticism (as recommended by the NAS panel) or a more positive conclusion against the deterrent efficacy of the death penalty is justified by the totality of all research. Some research, based on the study of executions and homicides in New York, has even suggested the initially implausible hypothesis that executions may actually exert a "brutalizing" effect upon society and that instead of deterring murders it incites them (Bowers and Pierce, 1980b). What does seem true is that any argument for the death penalty based primarily on the claim of its superior deterrent efficacy is untenable. It is worth noting that the Supreme Court, in its series of death-penalty decisions during the 1970s, skirted this controversy and never spoke with a clear and unanimous voice one way or the other. (The sole exception is its decision in *Gregg*, where the majority of the Court conjectured that in such cases as "calcu-

lated murders," for example, terrorist attacks, sanctions less severe than death may not be adequate.) How much evidence proponents of the death penalty should be expected to produce in favor of the superior deterrent power of executions is also unclear, and perhaps imponderable.

Burden of proof. It seems reasonable to many observers for the proponents to have the burden of proof, since they advocate the more severe and irreversible penalty. Some defenders of the death penalty counter by claiming that it is better to put to death someone convicted of murder, on the chance that doing so will prevent (either by incapacitation or by general deterrence) a future murder, than it is to risk the lives of the innocent by using some less severe punishment (Van den Haag). Others argue that the proper foundation for the death penalty is not its deterrent efficacy—or, indeed, any other essentially utilitarian consideration—but reasons rooted in retributive justice (Berns). Both of these responses by advocates of the death penalty imply that burden-of-proof considerations really fall on the other side, or else should play no role in a moral and rational evaluation of the entire question.

International status

Capital punishment abroad is difficult to describe with accuracy, both because in many countries reliable official information is not available, and because practices are often radically at variance with constitutional and statutory provisions (Amnesty International; López-Rey). Even a brief and selective survey will, however, put into better perspective the history, status, and trends to be found in the United States.

Western hemisphere. Canada abolished the death penalty, except for certain offenses under its military code, in 1976. Mexico has abolished the death penalty for all crimes in twenty-six of its thirty-two jurisdictions. In many other Latin American nations there has been historic opposition to the death penalty: Venezuela abolished all death penalties in 1863, Ecuador in 1897, and Colombia in 1910. But executions have often been widespread in the aftermath of revolutionary or counterrevolutionary upheavals, as in Cuba after the revolution of 1959, and in Chile in 1973. Executions are usually carried out in private, by hanging or firing squad.

Europe. Most of the countries of Western Europe have abolished the death penalty. Portugal was the first (1867), but its neighbors, Spain (1975) and France (1981), were among the last. Some nations, for example, Switzerland, retain the death penalty for certain crimes committed during wartime; others, such as Belgium, have not officially abolished it, but any death penalty is automatically commuted to life imprisonment. In the Soviet Union and the other Communist-bloc countries of Eastern Europe, as well as in Greece, Turkey, and Yugoslavia, executions (either by firing squad or by hanging) have been more than occasional, and many offenses are punishable by death.

Asia, Africa, and the Middle East. Every country in these regions retains the death penalty for one or more crimes, and some use it extensively. In Israel, only one person has been executed (Adolf Eichmann in 1962), and the only capital offenses are genocide, crimes against humanity, and crimes against the Jewish people. In Saudi Arabia, Oman, and the Yemen Arab Republic, Islamic law derived from the Koran is the basis of capital punishment for several crimes against persons, property, and the state. In 1977, considerable publicity surrounded Saudi Arabia's execution by stoning of three men for rape, and by beheading of three others, two of whom had been convicted of kidnapping and indecent assault (sodomy) and one of kidnapping and raping a young girl. In Iran under the Shah, drug smugglers and peddlers were executed by the hundreds; after the Shah was deposed in 1978, revolutionary councils ordered the executions of thousands for political and other crimes.

Pakistan officially reported that during the late 1970s as many as 800 persons a year were executed for various offenses. In India, however, executions have been rare even though the penal code authorizes the death penalty for many crimes. In Japan, according to unofficial estimates, 16 persons a year on the average were executed between 1954 and 1974. In China, where no official or unofficial estimates are available, it is known that there were dozens of executions during the 1970s for murder as well as for political crimes. South Africa has one of the highest rates of judicial execution in the world; in 1978, for example, 132 persons (all but one nonwhite) were executed by hanging for criminal offenses. In 1979 there was one execution for a politically related offense under Terrorism Act 83 of 1967, as amended, § 2(1)(c) (South Africa), the first such execution since the mid-1960s. In many other African countries, executions are public, and no more than the barest judicial formalities are observed during trial and sentencing of capital offenders.

The United Nations. Of some influence throughout the world has been the interest in the death penalty shown by various bodies within the United Nations, notably the General Assembly and the Economic and Social Council (ECOSOC). The General Assembly first addressed the issue in 1959; the following year a report was tendered to ECOSOC, fully describing the general trends worldwide in the use of the death penalty. ECOSOC urged further research and recommended that de facto abolitionist countries adopt abolition de jure; this recommendation was endorsed by the General Assembly in 1963. The International Covenant on Civil and Political Rights, adopted by the General Assembly in 1966, came into force in 1976 and called for strict procedures in the use of the death penalty (art. 6). After several years of intermittent debate and controversy, the General Assembly resolved in 1971 that "in order fully to guarantee the right to life, provided for in Article 3 of the Universal Declaration of Human Rights, the main objective to be pursued is that of progressively restricting the number of offenses for which capital punishment may be imposed, with a view to the desirability of abolishing this punishment in all countries" (General Assembly Resolution 2857 (XXVI), 20 Dec. 1971; cited in Amnesty International, p. 28).

HUGO ADAM BEDAU

See also CRUEL AND UNUSUAL PUNISHMENT; PUNISHMENT.

BIBLIOGRAPHY

Amnesty International. *The Death Penalty.* London: Amnesty International Publications, 1979.

BEDAU, HUGO ADAM. *The Courts, the Constitution, and Capital Punishment.* Lexington, Mass.: Heath, Lexington Books, 1977.

———, ed. *The Death Penalty in America.* 3d ed. New York: Oxford University Press, 1982.

———, and PIERCE, CHESTER M., eds. *Capital Punishment in the United States.* New York: AMS Press, 1976.

BERNS, WALTER F. *For Capital Punishment: Crime and the Morality of the Death Penalty.* New York: Basic Books, 1979.

BLACK, CHARLES L., JR. *Capital Punishment: The Inevitability of Caprice and Mistake.* 2d ed. New York: Norton, 1981.

BLUMSTEIN, ALFRED; COHEN, JACQUELINE; and NAGIN, DANIEL, eds. *Deterrence and Incapacitation: Estimating the Effects of Criminal Sanctions on Crime Rates.* National Research Council, Panel on Research on Deterrent and Incapacitative Effects. Washington, D.C.: National Academy of Sciences, 1978.

BOWERS, WILLIAM J. *Death as Punishment.* Boston: Northeastern University Press, 1982.

———, and PIERCE, GLENN L. "Arbitrariness and Discrimination under Post-*Furman* Capital Statutes." *Crime and Delinquency* 26 (1980a): 563–635.

———. "Deterrence or Brutalization: What Is the Effect of Executions?" *Crime and Delinquency* 26 (1980b): 453–484.

COHN, HAIM H. "The Penology of the Talmud." *Israel Law Review* 5 (1970): 53–74.

CURRAN, WILLIAM J., and CASSCELLS, WARD. "The Ethics of Medical Participation in Capital Punishment by Intravenous Drug Injection." *New England Journal of Medicine* 302 (1980): 226–230.

EHRLICH, ISAAC. "The Deterrent Effect of Capital Punishment: A Question of Life and Death." *American Economic Review* 65 (1975): 397–417.

———, and MARK, RANDALL. "Fear of Deterrence: A Critical Evaluation of the 'Report of the Panel on Research on Deterrent and Incapacitative Effects.'" *Journal of Legal Studies* 6 (1977): 293–316.

LÓPEZ-REY, MANUEL. "General Overview of Capital Punishment as a Legal Sanction." *Federal Probation* 44 (1980): 18–23.

MACKEY, PHILIP E., ed. *Voices against Death: American Opposition to Capital Punishment, 1787–1975.* New York: Franklin, 1976.

MELTSNER, MICHAEL. *Cruel and Unusual: The Supreme Court and Capital Punishment.* New York: Random House, 1973.

RADIN, MARGARET JANE. "Cruel Punishment and Respect for Persons: Super Due Process for Death." *Southern California Law Review* 53 (1980): 1143–1185.

———. "The Jurisprudence of Death: Evolving Standards for the Cruel and Unusual Punishment Clause." *University of Pennsylvania Law Review* 126 (1978): 989–1064.

Royal Commission on Capital Punishment, 1949–1953. *Report.* Cmd. 8932. London: Her Majesty's Stationery Office, 1953.

SELLIN, THORSTEN. *The Death Penalty: A Report for the Model Penal Code Project of the American Law Institute.* Philadelphia: ALI, 1959.

———. *The Penalty of Death.* Beverly Hills, Calif.: Sage, 1980.

U.S. Congress, House, Committee on the Judiciary, Subcommittee on Criminal Justice. *Sentencing in Capital Cases: Hearings on H.R. 13360,* 95th Cong., 2d sess. Washington, D.C.: Government Printing Office, 1978.

U.S. Congress, Senate, Committee on the Judiciary. *Capital Punishment: Hearings on S. 114,* 97th Cong., 1st sess. Washington, D.C.: Government Printing Office, 1981.

U.S. Department of Justice. *National Prisoner Statistics: Capital Punishment.* Washington, D.C.: The Department, annually under various titles since 1950.

VAN DEN HAAG, ERNEST. *Punishing Criminals: Concerning a Very Old and Painful Question.* New York: Basic Books, 1975.

VON HIRSCH, ANDREW. *Doing Justice: The Choice of Punishments.* Report of the Committee for the Study of Incarceration. Preface by Charles E. Goodell. Introduction by Willard Gaylin and David J. Rothman. New York: Hill & Wang, 1976.

WHITE, WELSH S. "Death-qualified Juries: The 'Prosecution-Proneness' Argument Reexamined." *University of Pittsburgh Law Review* 41 (1980): 353–406.

WOLFGANG, MARVIN E., and RIEDEL, MARC. "Race, Judicial Discretion, and the Death Penalty." *Annals of the American Academy of Political and Social Science* 407 (1973): 119–133.

CAREER CRIMINALS

See both articles under CRIMINAL CAREERS; *both articles under* PROFESSIONAL CRIMINAL.

CAREERS IN CRIMINAL JUSTICE

1. CORRECTIONS	David E. Duffee
2. LAW	Sue Titus Reid
	Lorna Keltner
3. POLICE	Peter K. Manning
4. PROBATION AND PAROLE SUPERVISION	Harvey Treger

1.
CORRECTIONS

Many older prisons in the United States are staffed by persons who chose a career in corrections mainly because members of their family did so before them. Correctional work as a career option has usually been given low status both by the general public (Joint Commission on Correctional Manpower and Training) and by prison employees (May). Moreover, systematic study of correctional employment, particularly in custody, has rarely been undertaken (Ross, p. 1). This article surveys the historical development and present status of correctional careers, as well as the issues that are likely to influence them and correctional policy in the future.

Historical development. In 1777, John Howard's classic *The State of the Prisons in England and Wales* indicated the conditions of early prison employment in Europe, not so much from what he described as from what he recommended. Howard stated emphatically that nothing is more important to the efficient management of a prison than an honest, nondrinking, and nongambling warden. He also recommended that both the warden and the turnkeys should be salaried so that neither would have to depend on fees extracted from inmates. The simplicity of the division of labor in 1777 is reflected in Howard's suggested staffing: a warden, a matron, some turnkeys, a manufacturer (to supply inmates with employment), and some taskmasters.

According to Gustave de Beaumont and Alexis de Tocqueville, before the penitentiary movement and its emphasis on the moral uplifting of prisoners that began in the 1790s, only crude, ill-bred persons could be attracted to prison jobs. The movement made prison administration itself a moral calling. The two

French visitors stated that the "inferior agents, the underwardens," did not match the caliber of the wardens but were for the most part "intelligent and honest men." Yet early American accounts of prison employment indicated that it could be debilitating, and that only constant monitoring by outside prison inspectors could keep the staff honest and humane.

Three important lessons may be gleaned from the historical material. First, the weight of public opinion is crucial to the quality of prison work. Second, there were (and still are) tremendous variations in the level of prison life and the nature of prison work from one prison to another. Finally, it is obvious that the prison guard played various roles; indeed, Beaumont and Tocqueville's observation that most guards had special technical knowledge in the areas in which offenders worked, and were responsible for instruction as well as security, is still valid.

The next important change in the history of correctional careers did not occur until the first three decades of the twentieth century, with the growth of social work, psychological treatment, the child-saving movement, and institutions for juveniles (Platt). In the new juvenile institutions, work roles were usually structured differently from those in adult institutions. The custodial role of the cottage parent in a training school is less austere than that of the guard in a prison, involving closer working relationships with the counseling and educational staffs. Thus, juvenile institutions provided a different model for custodial work, one often also evident in women's institutions and in small community facilities such as halfway houses.

Institutions for juveniles brought to corrections an influx of social workers, psychologists, and other treatment specialists, and after 1930 a movement to add such personnel to adult correctional staffs became important (Dession). Whether or not the new specialists were effective, their presence in prisons had a radical influence both on the public image of corrections and on work structure. Since these staff members were now expected to improve offenders, any lack of improvement could be called an administrative failure. Additionally, the new workers disrupted power inside the institutions by establishing a new line of authority that reached from inmates to warden or superintendent without going through custodial channels (Zald).

The labor force. More people are employed in corrections in the 1980s than ever before, and the demand for correctional staff seems likely to increase through the end of the twentieth century. The most accurate statistics on correctional employment do not list community corrections and institutional employ-

ment separately (Hindelang, Gottfredson, and Flanagan, p. 132). They indicate that in 1971 there were 106,045 full-time employees in state corrections and another 66,776 in local corrections. By 1978 state corrections had increased by 43 percent and local corrections by 53 percent. Public juvenile corrections witnessed a staff growth of 41 percent from 1970 to 1977. The 1978 National Manpower Survey of the Criminal Justice System (U.S. Department of Justice), known as the NMS, projected for the period between 1974 and 1985 a 58 percent increase in employment in both adult prisons and local jails and a 71 percent increase in local juvenile corrections, but a 17 percent drop in state juvenile institutions. The juvenile figures projected a smaller teenage population and the continued growth of community programs for youths.

The NMS reported (pp. 15–24) that as of 1974, 62.9 percent of state prison staff members worked in custody, 10.4 percent in treatment and education (including teachers, social workers, psychologists, psychiatrists, and medical personnel), and 26.6 percent in administrative, maintenance, and clerical positions. In jails, on the other hand, 73.2 percent of the force was custodial; 7.2 percent in treatment, educational, and medical positions; and 19.6 percent in other areas. The juvenile institution work force was more evenly split: 12 percent in administrative positions, 41 percent in child care, 31 percent in education and training, and 15 percent in other positions.

Salaries for correctional workers vary considerably from state to state but are relatively low everywhere. As of August 1979, the annual salaries for entering custodial officers ranged from $18,228 in Alaska to $7,812 in West Virginia. The mean minimum was $10,739, and the mean maximum, $14,074. Guards in county jails earned appreciably less (Hindelang, Gottfredson, and Flanagan, p. 144). Corrections offers some of the poorest working conditions and lowest salaries in the criminal justice field.

Structure. The composition of the labor force in correctional and juvenile institutions is actually much more complex than the above survey indicates. Specialization abounds and is increasing. In 1969 the Joint Commission on Correctional Manpower and Training listed (p. 73) forty-four common personnel categories in adult and juvenile institutions. Many of these categories represented very few people, since one-fourth included administrative posts such as warden, business manager, and director of classification, and another one-fourth, such professionals as teachers, counselors, and psychologists. An increasing number of persons work in, but not for, correctional institutions; prison parole officers are traditional examples. Conversely, some prison employees work outside the institution much of the time—for example, in work-release and community-liaison programs. There are also a significant but unknown number of volunteers who devote from a few hours a month to many hours a week to prisons and training schools in a variety of capacities, including, in at least one state, front-line custodial roles (League of Women Voters of Wisconsin).

A number of correctional careers may not involve daily entrance to the prison but significantly influence what happens inside it. Most important are the central office staffs in state departments or bureaus of corrections. Union organizers and managers are also influential, as are researchers from universities, research centers, and consulting firms. Psychological, medical, and management experts in part-time capacities constitute another important group.

Finally, special attention might be paid to the employment of ex-offenders. In some states, they work as aides to the regular professional staffs or in specially created posts. The presumed justification for considering them a separate category of employee is that ex-offenders may have special skills which make them complementary to, but different from, other employees. The obvious disadvantage of this view is that the special positions created for them become dead-end careers, unless provision is made for lateral transfer. Other states have shied away from the separation of such employees and claim to consider ex-offenders on a competitive basis with nonoffenders for the same positions (Hindelang, Gottfredson, and Flanagan, p. 157).

Organization. A prison or juvenile-institution staff typically comprises several relatively autonomous, poorly coordinated subbureaucracies, such as those for treatment, custody, and maintenance in the one and for child care, treatment, and education in the other. Each division has its own front-line mid-level supervisors and chief executives, linked only by their common subordination to a warden. Such standard bureaucratic divisions and positions are now highly entrenched in larger and more custodially oriented institutions.

In contrast, staffs in smaller institutions, such as work-release centers, camps, and ranches, are often relatively well integrated, even if some staff members wear uniforms and others do not. In the larger institutions, the separate specialties are frequently in conflict with one another because their responsibilities with the inmate population differ and cannot always interconnect. Because of lack of communication, various prison staff groups often adopt remarkably different ideologies about offenders and prison work. Although some of the expressed value differences reflect differences between jobs (for example, guards are more concerned with safety than are counselors), the various staff groups frequently view themselves as more autonomous than their work objectives warrant. Training and organization that bring the different staffs together in an atmosphere of mutual exchange can reduce conflict and misunderstanding, but the maintenance of an enduring collaboration—for example, between guards and counselors or teachers—is usually difficult.

Some prisons have attempted new remedies for staff divisiveness. Thus, in the unit plan, larger prisons are subdivided into relatively autonomous smaller components in which officers and administration work jointly on their common problems.

Prison careers: a longitudinal picture.

Education and training. Because crime and corrections are not likely to disappear, prison work is presumed to provide job security, especially to custodial staffs. In many states these employees need only a high-school education or less. Perhaps for some who have little schooling or technical skill, prison work can assure more stable employment than other available options, but overall it has been found that few youths aspire to work in correctional jobs at any level (Joint Commission).

Correctional counselors and probation and parole agents, on the other hand, are generally expected to complete a more demanding course of instruction. Beginning in the late 1960s, several hundred colleges initiated criminal justice programs that provided training for young people planning these careers. The general requirement for most counselors is a bachelor's degree, although many systems prefer master's degrees. Graduate degrees are important when treatment personnel are considered for promotion. Many jurisdictions also require civil service examinations of job applicants and merit examinations for promotions.

As might be expected, the amount and quality of in-service training for correctional employees vary greatly. Nevertheless, the NMS estimated that in 1974, 94 percent of all correctional officers worked in facilities where at least some form of entry-level training was available (p. 92). Total lack of training is most common at small facilities, particularly rural jails. A particular deficiency is that of training in treatment skills for correctional officers.

Problems in correctional work. Most studies of persons entering a correctional career report that a major reason for seeking such employment is a desire to work with people. Once employed, both guards and counselors often state that "helping people" is the main source of satisfaction in their work. However, cynicism and disappointment tend to develop early in correctional careers. Counselors discover that little counseling is done and that most of their time is taken up in minor administrative work. Correctional officers and child-care workers often learn that there is little opportunity to help those in their charge and that they are sanctioned by management or by other custodial workers for conversing freely with the offenders they are seeking to aid. Neal Shover suggests that competent counselors move on rapidly to other types of work or, alternatively, seek promotion to managerial positions, which generally entail fewer frustrations but also much less contact with inmates (p. 349).

"Flight from the client" is not characteristic of counseling alone. In many prisons, correctional officers seek custodial jobs that will take them away from the cellblock or dormitory. Bidding for safer jobs with less inmate contact has become a major issue in states where these employees are unionized. The evidence suggests that some officers seek prison niches where they will have the least trouble and frustration.

Many prisons also experience problems with staff turnover. The NMS (p. 45) found a 19.1 percent mean annual turnover rate for correctional officers and 27.2 percent for child-care workers. Turnover among professional staffs dropped drastically from 1967 to 1974 but remained high among custodial personnel. At smaller facilities these rates are often much higher. Absenteeism is an equally difficult problem, amounting in some prisons to 15 percent on any given day.

Are there then successful correctional careers? The answer is yes—but not as many as there could be. Despite higher turnover rates at smaller facilities, available evidence suggests that it is in such facilities that employees find most satisfaction in their work, cooperate most with other staff categories, and have maximum opportunities to interact meaningfully with the persons in their charge. In larger institutions the personnel most satisfied with their work, the security forces in particular, are in the few positions that offer relative isolation from the more bureaucratic aspects of the facility and provide for closer, more informal relationships with inmates and staff members.

Issues in correctional careers.

Employment of women and minorities. Institutional staffs have consisted mainly of white males, particularly in supervisory positions, although challenges to that situation have increased. Until the 1970s, women's roles in corrections were generally limited to clerical work and some counseling, except in the small

number of women's prisons. Equal-opportunity programs have forced correctional and other agencies to demonstrate good reasons for restricting recruitment to males, but women have far to go to reach equality in correctional career opportunities. For example, in 1974 only 1.4 percent of the women employed in correctional institutions were in administrative positions; 19 percent were in professional roles, such as counseling; 41.6 percent were in clerical jobs; and only 12.5 percent were employed in custodial work, usually in women's facilities. In contrast, 5.1 percent of male employees had administrative posts, 23 percent were classified as professionals, 2.2 percent were in clerical positions, and 47.7 percent worked in custody (NMS, p. 53).

Perhaps more important is the issue of minority recruitment. As of 1981, the majority of prisoners in most states belonged to ethnic minorities, but most staff members were white. Minority representation in the administration of prisons is generally less than in the guard force. In 1975, 9 percent of prison administrators were drawn from minority populations, as compared to 13 percent in the juvenile system (NMS, pp. 51–53). Steps have been taken in many states to reduce this racial imbalance, and since 1974, minorities have been increasingly represented in the yearly recruitment figures. But it is doubtful that greater minority recruitment alone will solve the problem.

Unionization. Unionization of prison staffs is a fairly new phenomenon. The first guard unions with collective bargaining rights were established in Washington, D.C. in 1956 and in New York City at about the same time. By 1981 twenty-nine out of fifty-two (including federal and District of Columbia) jurisdictions reported unionization of prison staffs, with twenty-one of these organizations established since 1970 (Hindelang, Gottfredson, and Flanagan, pp. 147–149).

Available data suggest that unions are becoming more vociferous in their demands and more militant in their tactics. Between 1976 and 1979 fourteen states reported at least one union action, such as a strike or an instance of collective bargaining, and certain prisons have experienced repeated strikes. In the long run, perhaps more significant than such infrequent but massive disruptions is the impact of union organization on the daily decision-making within the prison. Unionization has significantly reshuffled the balance of power in the prison. Many states now have a tripartite division—inmates, administration, and union. This does not mean that there are always three sides to every prison conflict, or that all staff members side with the union. But it does mean that the old-style accommodations between the keepers and the kept are now more complex and probably less stable, because a separate recognized interest group (or groups) has entered the picture.

Some forecasters suggest that unionization will lead to a greater polarization of staff and inmates. Others are less certain, pointing out that on some issues pro-union guards and inmate groups have relatively compatible concerns. Some unions may not oppose inmate groups or treatment programs so much as they may demand that custodial personnel should have a hand in determining when and how treatment is implemented. Different unions in different states often have different or opposite viewpoints. Consequently, some types of correctional careers are shaped by the policies and practices of the prevailing union.

Career supports. There is a growing concern for the development of supports of various kinds to provide correctional workers with a fuller and more satisfying career experience. In addition to professionalization and unionization, important career-support movements include (1) attempts by such organizations as the American Correctional Association (ACA) to promote the image of corrections as an important societal institution; (2) attempts by the ACA to accredit correctional institutions and to establish standards for various aspects of correctional work; and (3) attempts to deal with the psychological pressures of correctional work, either by providing training in coping with stress, frustration, cynicism, and alcoholism or by seeking to restructure the correctional enterprise so that work pressures will be reduced and a sense of accomplishment and effectiveness increased.

DAVID E. DUFFEE

See also CORRECTIONAL TREATMENT; EDUCATIONAL PROGRAMS IN CRIMINAL JUSTICE; JAILS; *articles under* PRISONS.

BIBLIOGRAPHY

BEAUMONT, GUSTAVE DE, and TOCQUEVILLE, ALEXIS DE. *On the Penitentiary System in the United States and Its Application in France* (1833). Translated by Francis Lieber. Introduction by Thorsten Sellin. Foreword by Herman R. Lantz. Carbondale: University of Southern Illinois Press, 1964.
DESSION, GEORGE. "Psychiatry and the Conditioning of Criminal Justice." *Yale Law Journal* 47 (1938): 319–340.
GALVIN, JOHN J., and KARACKI, LOREN. *Manpower and Training in Correctional Institutions.* Staff Report of Joint Commission on Correctional Manpower and Training. Washington, D.C.: The Commission, 1969.
HINDELANG, MICHAEL; GOTTFREDSON, MICHAEL; and FLANAGAN, TIMOTHY, eds. *Sourcebook of Criminal Justice Statistics, 1980.* Washington, D.C.: U.S. Department of Justice, Law

Enforcement Assistance Administration, National Criminal Justice Information and Statistics Service, 1981.
HOWARD, JOHN. "The State of the Prisons in England and Wales" (1777). *Penology.* Edited by George Killinger and Paul Cromwell. St. Paul: West, 1973, pp. 5–11.
JACOBS, JAMES B., and GREAR, MARY P. "Drop-outs and Rejects: An Analysis of the Prison Guard's Revolving Door." *Criminal Justice Review* 2, no. 2 (1977): 57–70.
Joint Commission on Correctional Manpower and Training. *The Public Looks at Crime and Corrections.* Report of a survey conducted by Louis Harris and Associates. Washington, D.C.: The Commission, 1968.
League of Women Voters of Wisconsin. "Changing of the Guard: Citizen Soldiers in Wisconsin Correctional Institutions." *Prison Guard/Correctional Officer.* Edited by Robert R. Ross. Toronto: Butterworths, 1981, pp. 169–189.
MAY, EDGAR. "Prison Guards in America: The Inside Story." *Corrections Magazine* (1976): 4–5, 12, 35–40, 44–48.
PLATT, ANTHONY. "The Rise of the Child-saving Movement: A Study in Social Policy and Correctional Reform." *Annals of the American Academy of Political and Social Science* 381 (1969): 21–38.
ROSS, ROBERT R., ed. *Prison Guard/Correctional Officer.* Toronto: Butterworths, 1981.
SHOVER, NEAL. " 'Experts' and Diagnosis in Correctional Agencies." *Crime and Delinquency* 20 (1974): 347–358.
U.S. Department of Justice, Law Enforcement Assistance Administration, National Institute of Law Enforcement and Criminal Justice. *Corrections.* National Manpower Survey of the Criminal Justice System, vol. 3. Washington, D.C.: The Institute, 1978.
ZALD, MAYER. "Power Balance and Staff Conflict in Correctional Institutions." *Administrative Science Quarterly* 6 (1962): 22–49.

2.
LAW

The role of legal education

The early American tradition of training lawyers followed the English practice of apprenticeship. Aspiring young men became competent as they worked in law offices, read the law, and observed and assisted attorneys at work.

In the 1700s, proprietary law schools, generally private and not affiliated with universities, were founded. They maintained an emphasis on the practical aspects of law but also made strides toward systematizing legal education, thus removing the main objection to the apprentice system—the lack of standards or procedures for controlling quality legal education. Bar associations were also developing at this time and gained control over the education of lawyers as well as over admission to the bar. In the 1800s, however, their influence diminished, with the result that almost anyone who was allegedly of "good moral character" could enter the practice of law.

After this period, the university-affiliated law school developed, apparently to give legal education respectability as well as to confer degrees. In 1870, Christopher Columbus Langdell became the dean of the Harvard Law School and initiated the case method of instruction characteristic of modern legal education. No emphasis was placed on clinical education or practical experience; thus, formal legal training differed significantly from the apprenticeship and proprietary approaches.

In 1900 the Association of American Law Schools (AALS) was formed at the request of the American Bar Association's (ABA) Section of Legal Education. The AALS was to establish minimum standards for member law schools. Later, the ABA began accrediting law schools (American Bar Association, 1980, pp. 3–4).

The basic function of formal legal education has traditionally been to teach students how to "think like a lawyer." Although legal writing, oral advocacy, and trial practice are included in the curriculum, they do not receive the same emphasis as legal reasoning skills. It is not intended that students will be fully competent lawyers upon receiving a law degree. "This view of legal education stresses the role of experience and training after law school (a period of informal apprenticeship or professional development) in the development of a full-fledged, competent lawyer" (American Bar Association, 1979, p. 11).

In the 1960s a movement toward greater emphasis on clinical legal education emerged. Increasing attention was paid to the issue of trial lawyer competency, especially after Chief Justice Warren Burger's 1973 declaration that "the modern law school is failing in its basic duty to provide society with people-oriented and problem-oriented counselors and advocates to meet these broad social needs." Others argued that law faculties had no right to demand three years of rigorous study from students without preparing them to practice law (Littlejohn, p. 10). In response to the concern with inadequate preparation of trial attorneys, several ABA and judicial groups have recommended that courses in trial skills should be available to all students (Devitt; American Bar Association, 1980; Kahn and Kahn; Burger).

A new emphasis on courtroom preparation is critical to future criminal lawyers, but "innovation in legal education comes hard, is limited in scope and permission, and generally dies young" (American Bar Association, 1980, p. 8). Edward Devitt has noted that trial-skills classes have a poor reputation among law faculties; law professors tend to classify them as vocational or trade training, and full funding is often denied them. Devitt suggests that experienced attorneys should donate their services and that federal courts should institute student practice rules to provide practical, supervised trial experience. Finally, he recommends a new emphasis on continuing legal-education programs in trial skills (p. 1802).

The prosecuting attorney

Attorneys who practice in the area of criminal law may be categorized as prosecution (district or prosecuting attorneys) or defense (private defense attorneys or public defenders). Bill Davidson writes:

The Prosecutor, reviled, unloved, unknown—except for the occasional Tom Dewey or Frank Hogan. On television and in fiction generally he's the ruthless Cromwell to the defense attorney's dashing King Charles. In the movies most often he's the plodding Watson to the super-detective Holmes. In the press, the F. Lee Baileys and the Edward Bennett Williamses outscore him ten to one in paragraph space. . . . yet though he and legions of experts he commands are the cornerstone of the democratic American system of justice and law enforcement—what the prosecutor does and how he does it are almost totally unknown to the vast majority of the American public [p. vii].

Joan Jacoby states that the lack of historical research on prosecuting attorneys can be explained by noting that the office of prosecuting attorney originally had little stature and power and only gradually evolved to a key position in law enforcement with great authority and discretion (p. 6).

One study of prosecutors in Alabama and California found their median age to be 33.9 years. The prosecutors did not have remarkable academic records, and more than 60 percent had less than two years of experience; only one-fifth had more than five years' experience as prosecutors (Felkenes). Abraham Blumberg emphasizes that the position of prosecutor is used by many attorneys to acquire trial experience rapidly or as a springboard for political office: "As a practical matter, many important public and political careers have had their genesis in a prosecutor's office. The job can be a prosaic internship to an otherwise routine career as a criminal defense lawyer, or a launching platform for a gubernatorial office, or even the presidency. It is an office rich in career possibilities, if not in monetary compensation" (p. 122). It is also a position used by some attorneys as a training ground for corporate practice (Jacoby, p. 36).

One of the several reasons for the short-term careers of most prosecuting attorneys may be the pressures and strains of the position. Prosecutors are leaders in community law enforcement and are expected to be relentless in reducing crime. On the other hand, they are expected to use the power of their office fairly and without oppression, and to protect the rights of all parties, including defendants who may be guilty. "The conflicts of these demands exert pressures on a prosecutor which his sense of fairness as a lawyer may reject, and with which his capacities as a human being cannot cope. Little wonder you cannot think of a single human being who is eminently qualified to be a district attorney" (Jacoby, p. 15). Prosecutors also encounter many of the stresses and strains common to the position of defense attorneys.

The defense attorney

Defense attorneys may be in private practice or working in public-defender systems. The distinctions will be noted, followed by a discussion of some of the common characteristics of both types.

Private defense attorneys. In his introduction to Paul Wice's detailed study of private defense attorneys, Fred Cohen comments: "Beset by health problems, economic hardships, professional and social ostracism; unaided by a continuing infusion of new blood, and criticized as to their competence from sources as lofty as Chief Justice Burger and as close as their fellow practitioners, this once romantic breed of lawyers seems to face extinction" (p. 9). The Wice study gives a demographic identification and description of 180 private defense attorneys across the country and describes their professional folkways. The work is important to the study of criminal lawyers because there is little scholarly research in the field and because the number of private criminal lawyers is shrinking, primarily owing to the growth in public-defender systems. "To study criminal lawyers today offers one an unusual opportunity to witness the decline of a fascinating and critical element of our legal system as it fights for its survival" (Wice, p. 15).

Classification systems. Wice discusses the various methods of classifying private attorneys as defense attorneys (pp. 32–38). One classification system is based on the proportion of the lawyer's total practice that is devoted to criminal law. Another distinguishes between those trial lawyers who have only a few clients willing to pay the high fees for their skilled services in the courtroom, and "wholesalers," those skilled in negotiating plea bargains who rely on a volume business for their income. A third scheme classifies lawyers according to whether they practice at the federal or the state level. A fourth method looks at the seriousness of the crimes handled as it relates to the severity of the possible punishment. Another scheme classifies lawyers according to their incomes.

None of these schemes is entirely adequate, and Wice proposes a scheme combining many of the above features. The lowest category of criminal lawyers would appear to consist of wholesalers who rarely go to trial, who practice in the state courts, and who handle less serious cases with less chance of achieving financial success. At the opposite end of the spectrum are lawyers who frequently try cases, who have good reputations based on their courtroom abilities, who often seem to take on either state cases or federal suits, and who often achieve great financial success. Wice notes that this model works well with the exception of the plea bargainers, who can earn large salaries from the turnover and volume of cases they handle.

Career patterns. The majority of lawyers interviewed in Wice's study downplayed the mythical romance of criminal law work; most stated that they entered the field because of economic necessity. Wice says this may be because the only jobs available to young lawyers were with small firms that handled criminal cases. "Many simply had to take the plunge and hang out a shingle for themselves until, after several months of near starvation, they discovered the one or two cases that would come along and provide their first victory" (pp. 85–86).

Most lawyers in private practice enter the criminal law field later than is usually the case among private attorneys in other fields. In the Wice study, 75 percent of the attorneys were between the ages of twenty-five and thirty-five when they began practicing criminal law. Most had previously held full-time jobs in unrelated areas and could not answer when asked why they had chosen criminal law, since they had not specifically plotted a career in this field. About one-third had held two jobs before going into private criminal law practice. They had either moved from a government job to the prosecutor's office or from the prosecutor's office to a small firm or a government job. The highest number, 38 percent, had been in a prosecutor's office before beginning a criminal law specialization; 14 percent had been with a different criminal law firm; 13 percent had held nonlegal business jobs; and 12 percent had been with a public defender's office (Wice, pp. 82–83). The lawyers stated that the prosecutor's office had more prestige than the public defender's and that it offered the best opportunity to develop good relations with the courts and the police. Further, working in the prosecutor's office gave them excellent training in knowing how the opposition prepares a case and thus enhanced their ability to do defense work.

Organizational structure of the private criminal bar. Most of the attorneys in the private criminal bar practice as "solos" or in small firms. In his 1962 study of Chicago lawyers, Jerome Carlin found that "although once held in the highest esteem as the model of a free, independent professional, today the individual practitioner of law, like the general practitioner in medicine, is most likely to be found at the margin of his profession, enjoying little freedom of choice of clients, type of work, or conditions of practice" (p. 206). Later studies have shown that the percentage of solo attorneys in private practice continues to decline. One source indicates that between 1945 and 1970 the proportion of lawyers in private practice decreased from two-thirds to one-half, with the number continuing to decline in the 1970s (Laumann and Heinz, p. 158).

Public-defender systems. Authorities have attributed the decline in the numbers of private criminal attorneys to the development of public-defender systems. Wice points out that jurisdictions with very good defender organizations leave only 20 percent to 30 percent of the criminal cases for the private bar (p. 50). Furthermore, nearly two-thirds of all defendants are indigent, and the decisions in *Gideon v. Wainwright,* 372 U.S. 335 (1963) and *Argersinger v. Hamlin,* 407 U.S. 25 (1972) require that in such instances the state must provide counsel. "It is this development, more than any other, which has sounded the death knell for the private practice of criminal law" (Wice, p. 214). In the ten years between *Gideon* and *Argersinger,* the percentage of counties with public-defender systems increased from 3 to 28, with the latter figure including approximately two-thirds of the population of the United States (Ligda, p. 321).

Public-defender systems developed as an expedient method of processing large numbers of cases, and they typically involve salaried attorneys who spend most of their time defending indigents accused of crimes. A number of studies support the stereotype of public defenders as "faceless bureaucrats," "public servants," "insidious technocrats," or "dangerous do-gooders." Anthony Platt and Randi Pollock, however, found that most of the recruits were white males with working- or lower-middle-class origins and liberal political backgrounds who did not plan to make a career in the department and remained only about two and a half years. They began their careers with idealism, humanitarianism, and enthusiasm, but they left the

system embittered, cynical, and alienated from political action. They saw their work mainly as "ameliorism and Band-Aid reform" and came to regard themselves as "mediators between the poor and the courts, resigned to seeking occasional loopholes in the system, softening its more explicitly repressive features and attempting to rescue the victims of blatant injustices." Most of their clients responded with resentment, ingratitude, or indifference (p. 260).

Wice found that few public defenders entered private defense practice; the financial security of the defender's office generally outweighed the difficulty and uncertainty of private practice. After two or three years many public defenders, disillusioned by their inability to win more than a few cases and by the scornful attitudes of defendants, were ready to discard defense work. More former public defenders moved into prosecutorial work than into private practice as defense counsel. Wice attributes this to the higher pay and prestige of prosecutorial work as well as to the opportunities it offered for entering politics (p. 85).

Demographic and personality characteristics of defense attorneys. Some studies of defense attorneys distinguish characteristics of private, as compared to public, defenders, but many studies do not make this distinction. Of the approximately four hundred thousand lawyers in the United States in 1978, only an estimated ten thousand to twenty thousand attorneys in private practice accepted criminal cases more than occasionally, and only about four thousand were employed by public-defender systems. Of those interviewed by Wice only 11 percent were black, a proportion that is close to the percentage of blacks in the national population. Wice attributes this low percentage to the past years of discrimination and to a new trend among young black lawyers of going into politics or financially rewarding civil practices instead of less prestigious criminal work. The young black lawyers in criminal practice are typically found in public-defender offices because there they have "regular paychecks, no discrimination and social respectability" (p. 65). Chicanos are even more poorly represented among criminal lawyers, as are Cuban-Americans.

A look at the ethnic and religious backgrounds of criminal lawyers in the Wice study revealed that 50 percent were Jewish, 30 percent were Catholic, and 20 percent were Protestant. Since only 5 percent of the national population is Jewish, these figures reflect a significant overrepresentation of Jewish criminal lawyers. Many Jewish lawyers explained that past discrimination had kept them out of the larger firms practicing civil law and that they had been forced into solo practice or small firms, many of which handled criminal cases.

Only 3 percent to 4 percent of the criminal lawyers in the United States are women. Male defense attorneys in Wice's study tended to explain this as a reflection of the "sleazy clientele, possible physical risks," and, most commonly, "women's lack of the necessary combative nature in the courtroom." Wice noted that with the increasing enrollment of women in law schools and with more women in district attorneys' and public defenders' offices, the number of women practicing in private defense work might increase (p. 68).

Although defense attorneys in public-defender systems are often very young, Wice found that of the private defense bar, 70 percent were between the ages of thirty and fifty; the median age was forty-two. Very few were young criminal attorneys, a situation attributed to the years generally spent as apprentices in prosecutors' or public defenders' offices. Several attorneys indicated that the small percentage of older criminal lawyers was probably the result of professional "burnout." Many criminal lawyers nearing the age of fifty said that they were in the process of terminating their careers or at least cutting down on the number of criminal cases they handled. Those who did remain past the age of sixty (10 percent of Wice's sample) were financially successful and could be selective in deciding which criminal cases to accept (pp. 63, 65).

Earlier studies of criminal defense lawyers had revealed that the majority were from lower socioeconomic backgrounds (Wood, pp. 35–36). Wice, however, found that 23 percent had parents who were engaged in professional occupations, 63 percent were from middle-class families, and only 13 percent were from working-class families (p. 71).

Wice states that although it is difficult to generalize about personality characteristics, some basic traits are shared by the majority of criminal lawyers. He found the typical lawyer to be highly cynical but also idealistic, aggressive or combative, and possessed of a very strong ego. The nature of defense trial work demands an ability to face an antagonistic judge, a hostile prosecutor, critical jurors, and a room full of other attorneys, reporters, and courtroom regulars, as well as skill in dealing with the accused and his family. It is also important that a good trial attorney be an actor, able to disguise his real feelings when presenting the case, since the defendant is often judged by the performance of counsel (pp. 75–76).

Problems of criminal defense practice. Wice found a variety of physical and mental problems among defense attorneys: lawyers characterized their heart conditions, stomach troubles, and hypertension as "occupational hazards." He found that many defense attorneys were overweight, and he repeatedly spoke to lawyers who admitted to alcoholism or who knew criminal lawyers with serious drinking problems. Marital discord is also common: more than 40 percent of Wice's sample had been divorced, and many others mentioned a nonexistent family life which they blamed on the long working hours and the strong egos that led to much selfish behavior (pp. 76–80). A study of the Homicide Task Force of the Cook County (Chicago) public defender's office found similar problems. The attorneys in this group defend only those charged with murder. Many have left because of burnout. "Others have seen their marriages end in divorce or developed psychosomatic problems from the pressure" (McClory, p. 45).

Burnout is described as "a syndrome of emotional exhaustion, in which the attorney has very little concern, sympathy or respect for clients." Cynicism grows, and attorneys think of clients in derogatory terms, believing they deserve their problems. The attorneys begin to "process people like machines [and] lose their enthusiasm, their creativity and their commitment." Family relationships as well are endangered, reflecting the difficulties encountered at work. Burnout may begin with excessive case loads, long hours, and the impossibility of any meaningful contact between the attorney and the client. This, combined with low pay and the lack of intellectual stimulation and of prestige, may lead to resentment, frustration, and finally disillusionment and burnout (Maslach and Jackson, pp. 52–53).

Wice reported that the majority of his sample were upset with the low status and low pay of their profession. They believed that they were identified with their clients and accused of unscrupulous behavior in defense work and of ignoring the welfare of society. Noting that the practice of criminal law is no longer lucrative, they pointed out that the emotional, physical, and moral hazards they encounter are not offset by financial rewards (p. 218).

Conclusion

Because of these problems, many young attorneys are reluctant to enter the practice of criminal law even when they have an intense interest in that area. In discussing this issue, Paul Hoffman concluded: "Far better to be ensconced in a skyscraper office pushing papers across a desk than to confer with clients through the bars of a jail cell. Far better to practice in a civil court among men of substance than in a criminal courtroom crowded with the dregs of society. Far better to have a corporation on a regular retainer than to have to badger clients for fees. And United States Steel never issues a midnight summons calling its counsel to some police precinct house. . . . So the criminal bar has become a netherworld of the legal profession" (p. 23).

An earlier study, however, found that criminal lawyers were as satisfied with the practice of law as were civil lawyers, although criminal lawyers did more often indicate a desire to change their specialty (Wood, p. 51). Changing conditions in the practice of criminal law, as described above, might explain the lack of such general satisfaction. Still, it is important to emphasize that some attorneys do enjoy the practice of criminal law. Perhaps they are able to "redefine the situation," as sociologists would say. Instead of dwelling on the fact that they seldom win cases, they redefine the meaning of *win*. Rather than discuss victories or acquittals, they emphasize the optimum plea bargain and seek to shorten the amount of incarceration time or to obtain alternative sentencing dispositions. Others survive by concentrating on the rare acquittals. Many like the independence, excitement, and unpredictability of criminal law work, and enjoy the opportunities it affords for working with people.

SUE TITUS REID
LORNA KELTNER

See also CAREERS IN CRIMINAL JUSTICE, *articles on* CORRECTIONS, POLICE, *and* PROBATION AND PAROLE SUPERVISION; EDUCATIONAL PROGRAMS IN CRIMINAL JUSTICE.

BIBLIOGRAPHY

American Bar Association. *Law Schools and Professional Education: Report and Recommendations of the Special Committee for a Study of Legal Education.* Chicago: ABA, 1979.
———. "Report and Recommendations of the Task Force of the American Bar Association Section of Legal Education and Admission to the Bar." *Lawyer Competency: The Role of the Law School.* Chicago: ABA, 1980.
BLUMBERG, ABRAHAM S. *Criminal Justice: Issues and Ironies.* 2d ed. New York: New Viewpoints, 1979.
BURGER, WARREN E. "Annual Report on the State of the Judiciary, 1980." *American Bar Association Journal* 66 (1980): 295–299.
CARLIN, JEROME EDWARD. *Lawyers on Their Own: A Study of Individual Practitioners in Chicago.* New Brunswick, N.J.: Rutgers University Press, 1962.
DAVIDSON, BILL. *Indict and Convict: The Inside Story of a Prosecutor and His Staff in Action.* New York: Harper & Row, 1971.
DEVITT, EDWARD J. "Law School Training: Key to Quality

Trial Advocacy." *American Bar Association Journal* 65 (1979): 1800–1802.
FELKENES, GEORGE T. "The Prosecutor: A Look at Reality." *Southwestern University Law Review* 7 (1975): 98–123.
HOFFMAN, PAUL. *What the Hell Is Justice: The Life and Trials of a Criminal Lawyer.* Chicago: Playboy Press, 1974.
JACOBY, JOAN E. *The American Prosecutor: A Search for Identity.* Lexington, Mass.: Heath, Lexington Books, 1980.
KAHN, MICHAEL H., and KAHN, LISA DAVIDSON. "Specialization in Criminal Law." *Law and Contemporary Problems* 41 (1977): 252–292.
LAUMANN, EDWARD O., and HEINZ, JOHN P. "Specialization and Prestige in the Legal Profession: The Structure of Deference." *American Bar Foundation Research Journal* (1977): 155–216.
LIGDA, PAUL. "Some Thoughts on Defender Office Management." *National Journal of Criminal Defense* 1 (1975): 321–330.
LITTLEJOHN, BRUCE. "Forum: The Law School's Role in Lawyer Competency." *Trial* 16, no. 4 (1980): 10–12.
MASLACH, CHRISTINA, and JACKSON, SUSAN E. "Lawyer Burn Out." *Barrister* 5 (1978): 8, 52–54.
McCLORY, ROBERT. "Murder Is Their Business." *Student Lawyer* 8, no. 1 (1979): 13–16, 45.
PLATT, ANTHONY, and POLLOCK, RANDI. "Channeling Lawyers: The Careers of Public Defenders." *The Potential for Reform of Criminal Justice.* Edited by Herbert Jacob. Beverly Hills, Calif.: Sage, 1974, pp. 235–262.
WICE, PAUL B. *Criminal Lawyers: An Endangered Species.* Foreword by Fred Cohen. Beverly Hills, Calif.: Sage, 1978.
WOOD, ARTHUR LEWIS. *Criminal Lawyer.* New Haven: College and University Press, 1967.

3.
POLICE

Introduction

The word *career* is used here to denote a set of positions occupied sequentially, with which are associated prestige and other rewards. This definition is well suited to the study of bureaucratic careers within relatively stable and orderly systems, and of fairly well demarcated types of occupations. Although policing manifests these criteria, other frames of reference, especially those with a subjective conception of the meaning of *career*, are also useful in police studies (Blankenship).

Such definitions are useful insofar as a person lives his work-life within two systems of evaluation: the everyday world of personal interaction and exchange in local circles, and the more distant sphere of evaluation within the occupational hierarchy (Tausky, p. 141). Clearly, the informal, or face-to-face, world is highly patterned by the structural effects of encompassing systems of work evaluation and ranking.

A primary concern in the study of police careers should be their variation with respect to types of police systems, but particular attention will be given here to the Anglo-American type found in the United States, Canada, the United Kingdom, Australia, and New Zealand. Analyses such as this, which locate the study of careers in law enforcement in historical, comparative, and longitudinal perspectives, are much needed (Bayley, 1975, 1979).

Policing: problems and types of solutions

The fundamental defining characteristic of police in all societies is their monopoly on the legitimate use of violence. In democratic societies, the police are expected to act in asymmetrical relation to the army; the army acts in dire situations that threaten the stability of the state, in tandem with the police, and only after the police have been deployed. First-line formal social control lies with the police, and their responsibility for employing violence can only be shared, never eschewed nor conceded to the army in the first instance. Police hold this capacity to exercise non-negotiable coercion, up to and including death, in order to regulate social relations within a politically defined unit. They do so in the name of that collectivity (Bayley, 1975, p. 328). The growth of the state, especially in European societies, has been accompanied by the establishment of armed, uniformed, and disciplined police forces that represent the law and the state and that arrogate to themselves the responsibility for maintaining social order. Police organizations are embedded in social, cultural, and political contexts, which include formal and informal normative structures, institutional practices and technologies, and such cultural traditions as the relative importance of self-help or revenge, respect for the state and law, and the standing of the police as representatives of a social or legal order (Bordua).

Several further characteristics of police, identified by David Bordua and David Bayley (1980), have arisen either from fundamental dilemmas historically facing police, or from recurrent problems that police have encountered and recognized as salient in their social environment (Manning, pp. 104–111). Internally, police must maintain discipline and loyalty. In the external environment, they attempt to maintain political neutrality, to exercise impartial law enforcement, and to be seen as committed to legality, both procedurally and substantively. From the perspective of strategic control or mobilization, they attempt to regulate the

social environment by deploying positions across time and space and by allocating levels of staff to those positions. These functional dimensions of policing are diversely rooted in the social structures of contemporary societies.

In order to understand the patterning of police careers in the United States, alternative police systems should be at least appreciated. An unpublished paper by Bayley suggests differentiation of the Anglo-American from (1) an *Asian* type that is highly integrated with its community and relies on community controls before taking legal action, and (2) an *authoritarian* type that is highly integrated with a centralized state and has little formal legal restriction on police action for political purposes. These types of police systems are the product of past solutions to routine social-control dilemmas. The Anglo-American type has features that organize objective career options and constrain career choice differently from the other types.

The Anglo-American type. Anglo-American policing attempts to produce political neutrality by means of civil service protections for officers and procedural or legalistic protections for citizens, and it attempts similar modes of control over police and public commitment to legality. Some of the actions of the police are reviewed by other elements of the criminal justice system. Discipline and loyalty, which were primary concerns of Charles Rowan and Richard Mayne, the architects of the London Metropolitan Police, and which in large measure have been the paradigm for Anglo-American policing, are expected to be controlled by recruitment practices and by harsh punishment for violations of rules and regulations. In many ways, the occupational culture, as well as wages and retirement benefits, is a substantial source of control. The degree of control provided by general occupational commitment varies, as discussed below. Efficient functioning is based to a considerable degree upon local community standards, although the scope of external funding, control, and accountability varies within Anglo-American societies. Crime control of this type focuses on the apprehension of perpetrators and the management of already completed crimes, rather than on prevention or deterrence. Finally, in such systems mobilization patterns are semicentralized or decentralized when compared with the Asian and authoritarian systems.

In Anglo-American societies, the police apply coercion to citizens in order to protect the latter from one another and to mediate between the citizens and the state. In addition, the police operate within the bounds of legally defined procedures, rules, and regulations; they define their mission in terms of crime control after the commission of crimes; and they are semicentralized or decentralized with respect to recruitment, socialization, command and control functions, and mobilization. These patterns have determined the types of police careers that are possible.

Recruitment and centralization

There are two principal sources of career patterning in the Anglo-American system: the degree of *centralization of authority* and the permitted extent of *lateral entry* into police organizations from without. Centralization can be viewed in this case as the degree of aggregation of command authority, and should be distinguished from the locus of accountability and supervision. Lateral entry varies both in degree and kind.

When compared to other police systems, the Anglo-American variants, especially those of Canada and the United States, are "the extreme cases of decentralized command. Canada has almost seven hundred autonomous police forces, several provincial forces and the Royal Canadian Mounted Police. In the United States, the situation is so chaotic that no one knows for sure how many police forces there are" (Bayley, 1979, pp. 125–126). It is safe to say that in the United States there are some 17,500 forces, with about 2.2 officers per thousand persons; in England and Wales, there are some 106,000 officers, also amounting to about 2.2 per thousand.

The distinctions concerning entry that are most relevant to the patterning of police careers include recruitment and training, as well as the absolute and relative number of officers employed. Whereas England is semicentralized with respect to societal control of recruitment and authority, Canada and the United States are decentralized. All three systems, however, recruit new officers almost exclusively at the lowest rank. England recruits according to a single standard and hires locally except at the highest levels (assistant chief constable, deputy chief constable, and chief constable). Training and allocation are controlled regionally. In the United States and Canada, allocation, hiring, and training are done locally, except for the training facilities of the Royal Canadian Mounted Police and a few specialized schools in both countries operated at the federal level. In these systems, the position of chief is the single post for which a broad search is undertaken and for which lateral entry is permitted; the primary constraint on lateral entry is that retirement benefits are often state- or city-vested and may be lost by a move from one post to another. In Canada and the United States, it is legally acceptable to hire a "civilian" without police

experience for a position at the top of a police hierarchy, such as a director of public safety. In England, on the other hand, the preference is to recruit and hire from other forces senior command officers with fifteen to twenty years' experience.

Although in theory lateral entry is permitted, in practice these systems assume that all officers enter at the lowest level and "work their way up" through the ranks. More importantly, perhaps, they are assumed to work their way up within the same police organization in which they began their career. All police careers of the Anglo-American type must be seen against this assumptive background. In turn, these interactions of degree of centralization and the mode of recruitment and training produce career paths that are subject to a number of other social influences.

Influences shaping police careers

Four significant sources shaping police careers that vary by degree of centralization are: (1) class, race, and ethnicity; (2) the degree of political influence on promotions and appointments; (3) links to the military system; and (4) elitist training and leadership.

In semicentralized systems such as the British, class and ethnicity affect recruitment generally, but not in a manner that applies specifically to certain positions. The degree of involvement in politics is modest, and the "law" and the "state" are separated in thought, if not in action. The military is a prime source for the recruitment of personnel and for a style of police behavior that is much emulated among officers, but military influence is systematically excluded from police matters except in times of declared national crisis. Veterans are given preference for places in the police service after the cessation of hostilities, and standards for age, formal examinations, and interviews are relaxed for them. Elitism is a cyclic affair, more related to external political attempts to control the police than to internal dynamics.

In decentralized systems such as those of Canada and the United States, class, race, and ethnicity have a general effect on recruitment and a ceiling effect on achievement. Few blacks and members of other minorities rise to command positions, although this situation may be changing. Local political pressures and trends have very strong effects on policing, but national issues have relatively little impact. Links to the military are weak and follow a pattern in domestic affairs of the military acting only in concert with the police rather than unilaterally, and of the police normally acting unilaterally. Other informal military influence ebbs and flows according to the number of veterans recruited after a major war. Elitist training is eschewed. Education, especially in the United States, has been viewed by police as a means for enhancing job security or increasing pay.

During the 1970s there was a tremendous federal investment in the direct funding of officers' enrollment in colleges, especially in criminal justice programs: the amount spent rose from $6.5 million in 1969 to $40 million in 1977. As a result, the number of police-related college programs increased from 125 in 1965 to 1,245 in 1976, and the percentage of officers with some college education rose from 20 percent in 1960 to 32 percent in 1970 and 46 percent in 1975. This impact has been differential by rank, with almost 60 percent of line investigation officers (detectives) and superiors receiving some college education, whereas 47 percent of patrol officers and 42 percent of management personnel have attained similar educational levels. There is some evidence that educated officers are given lower performance ratings *because* they are educated (Sherman, pp. ix, 36, 186–187; Van Maanen). The overall evidence pertaining to the impact of education upon performance, in the words of one comprehensive summary of empirical research on the subject, is "scant, conflicting and ambiguous" (Bennett and Haen, p. 149).

Careers and success

There are two major divisions in career orientation in semicentralized and decentralized police systems. The first is between those with the rank of sergeant or higher, and lower participants. The second is between officers oriented toward career advancement based on efforts to secure higher rank, and those inclined toward permanent accommodation or anchored in what they have thus far achieved (Tausky).

Among those who accept their current rank, there are at least two subtypes. The first is the *accommodative*—officers oriented toward achieving the maximum autonomy and reward (excluding corrupt actions) within the limits of a position. Informal rewards often exist in unique form within particular segments of a force (Dalton). These segment-based rewards might include such formal rewards as opportunities for overtime, time off, and other perquisites of office (Manning, pp. 151–159). Investigative work generally is thought of in this way in Anglo-American societies. The second subtype is the *indifferent*—those who seek neither upward mobility nor lateral movement to obtain greater informal rewards or status recognition. Within a given rank, officers who are accommodating and indifferent to mobility devalue the apparent ad-

vantages ascribed to higher positions by their occupants, relatively overvalue their present positions, and emphasize their achievements up to that point. They may be termed *laterally bonded.* This type of bond appears to be stronger, or at least more durable, for lower-ranking personnel (sergeants and those below) than for higher-ranking personnel. Such bonding is sometimes glossed with the term *occupational subculture,* although the differential attachment of individuals by organizational segments or ranks is seldom considered (Van Maanen). The relative degree of bonding produces the cynical use of the subculture as a protection, as evidenced by lying, fabrication of evidence, the making of false statements to the media, and legitimated irresponsibility at the administrative level.

Those who seek higher rank are oriented toward the position they hope to reach and may seek lateral moves within their rank, such as to detective work or vice investigation, because these promise greater visibility or opportunities for vertical promotion. Such officers are seeking another route to prestige and responsibility—an escalator in rank, as it were (Becker and Strauss, p. 254). They are willing to shed or devalue their current positions, especially in terms of informal rewards or perquisites, and to "pay the price" of upward mobility. Furthermore, among those who are upwardly anchored, avenues or escalators to promotion vary from department to department, depending on the status characteristics that are thought to be relevant to advancement, such as age, sex, race, ethnicity, education, sponsorship, and religion.

It would appear that the higher one rises in the organization, given the *serial,* or apprenticeship, type of training that characterizes police worldwide, the more pertinent are one's personal characteristics, sponsors, and anchorage. This may vary by the degree of codification of the evaluation procedures. As one moves above the rank of sergeant, matters of personal style, dress, and contacts outside the organization are more influential. Hence, the higher participants tend to share less lateral bonding and are more sensitive to external political forces with respect to career contingencies.

The capacity to manage persistent force-wide political problems in a somewhat more abstract or managerial style is also sought. This should be seen in the context of the tendency of police organizations to move from crisis to crisis and to be characterized by "crisis management" (Wilson, p. 69). The value placed on this skill is thus relative to the degree of systematic management and planning that is sought and rewarded.

Patterns of commitment to police careers

In those societies that do not instill powerful bureaucratic controls to insulate the police from the community, recruitment and training become more salient. "Bureaucratization is a device whereby commitment to the occupational organization or occupational community and its norms of superordination and service takes precedence over extraoccupational social commitments" (Bordua, p. 176). This is a variable across nations, historically, and at different levels within the bureaucratically organized police. Even within relatively bureaucratic organizations, the degree of commitment varies both within and across ranks, it being generally understood that greater commitment is found among participants of higher ranks (Manning, pp. 145–151). These variations are important in patterning the types of careers possible within decentralized and semicentralized bureaucratic systems.

The kinds of commitment made most likely in decentralized systems have emerged from mechanisms initiated by the early leaders of the British police, Rowan and Mayne: police were insulated from the community and isolated in police barracks, given low pay, chosen on merit, promoted from within, and fully housed, clothed, and equipped (Radzinowicz; Miller). The working-class culture of the police, which emphasizes masculine toughness, action, and here-and-now solutions and which deprecates abstraction and "paperwork," provides the stylistic content of Anglo-American occupational culture. A "working class" culture content appears to exist in some sort of tacit exchange for the limited forms of reward and participation granted to lower-ranking personnel in the organization (Katz, p. 212). The autonomy allowed produces commitment and loyalty, and the extension of work into everyday life (policing is everywhere viewed as a twenty-four-hour-a-day job) is shared with other traditional (and more prestigious) professions, such as the clergy, college teaching, and the law. Conversely, those who are primarily oriented toward money as a means of achieving their goals are disadvantaged for promotion in systems where overtime benefits, freedom from duty demands when off duty, and time for home and family are foregone by those who rise above the rank of sergeant. Above that rank there are periods in which effective pay (taking into account travel time, loss of overtime pay, and increased hours worked) is reduced by promotion. On a monthly basis, absolute pay for command officers is frequently less than for those in the constable rank.

The bases of commitment within the system change from extrinsic to intrinsic as one moves up the positional ladder. This movement is differentially affected by the degree of formal assessment of officers: the more formalized the evaluation of officers, the more intrinsic their commitment tends to be. The benefits associated with promotion in rank are formalized as well, so that they are more predictable and less likely to be based on seniority. Achieving seniority rewards such extrinsic commitments as ensuring retirement or steady raises. Careers are also cast within a changing organizational context. As organizations change, career opportunities and the shape of the positional distribution also change.

The organizational context of careers

These variations in commitment by rank and by segment of the organization suggest that the concept of *organizational context* of careers is useful in discussing careers in the Anglo-American system. The organizational context of careers refers to the degree and kind of structure that the organization has provided for the norms of achievement or assessment. The standards utilized for judging accomplishment, promotion, and rewards can range from highly codified to noncodified, and may be subject to external redefinition.

In decentralized and semicentralized systems, norms are codified with respect to each position, with entry-level acceptance through promotion to sergeant being based on an examination, and with varying weights given to personal interviews and performance evaluations by supervisors. In general, police undervalue written records and performance evaluations, and trust the judgment of colleagues. At ranks above sergeant, promotional boards are assembled and interviews are combined with performance evaluation and examinations. Above the lieutenant or inspector level, interview boards become the deciding factor, and other criteria act as screening mechanisms.

More formalized standards generally are correlated with increased use of technology, greater numbers of college-educated officers, lessened corruption, and a greater degree of control and supervision of officers through computerized, or at least radio-based, systems of command and control. Increased capacity to keep accurate records, to develop planning and research potential, and to apply rational administrative practices are all associated with more codified standards in police departments (Wilson; Bordua and Reiss).

Tactics of police socialization

All occupations socialize persons with respect to the proper attitude toward the work and provide newcomers with skills relevant to the tasks they are expected to accomplish. John Van Maanen and Edgar Schein assert that tactics of organizational socialization refer to "the ways in which the experiences of an individual in transition are structured for him by others in the organization" (p. 230). These authors contend that there are at least eight types of tactics, not mutually exclusive, each having an implicit continuum from high to low. In this view, programs for socialization of the police in Anglo-American societies are *formal, collective, sequential, fixed, serial,* and *closed* and involve *investiture.* That is, socialization to the police career in Anglo-Saxon systems is formal, segregated from the workplace, carried out according to very specific directives, and intended to prepare a person to assume higher status in the organization. It is done in cohorts of recruits entering at the same time, and is characterized by a discrete and identifiable sequence of fixed stages through which one must pass—for example, recruit school, probation period, and first formal assignment. In such serial socialization, "experienced members groom newcomers who are about to assume similar roles in the organization" (p. 247). The closed socialization activities of the police bind together the cohort of individuals who are inducted as a group into the common life and purpose of the organization. Police socialization is oriented to investiture in the new status and involves the "stripping" of old statuses. Recruits are told that they are to *add* to their present attitudes and skills, as well as to divest themselves of old attitudes, that is, to undergo desocialization prior to this augmenting process of socialization.

Police forces attempt to induce an attitude toward the vicissitudes of the work that is relatively continuous from academy studies to on-the-street training and thence to first assignment. On the other hand, the recruit is given new knowledge and strategy rules for making decisions and is divested of previous civilian views. Recruits on the street are typically told to forget all that they learned—knowledge content and strategies—in the academy, albeit the attitude learned in academy training is one of cynicism toward civilians and lawyers. Their colleagues thus legitimate a formalist adherence to rules and regulations so as to avoid mistakes or "rocking the boat" (Van Maanen; Harris).

Police careers and society

The results of training police in societies using formal, collective, sequential, fixed, and serial investiture tactics are frequently noted. Such a socialization pattern produces collectively oriented persons with strong cohort ties who are internally separated by slightly differing cohort experiences. They are integrated vertically by shared bases of such experience (there is a cohort-age effect and a rank effect in time, as well as a general effect of policing) and strongly identify with their on-the-job trainers.

It should be noted that work such as policing depends heavily on the personal knowledge of more experienced colleagues rather than on the academy for the teaching of actual practices, rules of thumb, and taken-for-granted meanings. This assemblage of tactics found in other traditional and honorable occupations, such as fire departments and the military, powerfully links the sentiments, role, and career of the officer with a societal structure. It reinforces a traditional, unchanging, collective-oriented, and interlinked occupational world.

Identification with the traditional occupational and societal values that the police represent, as well as their links with the ongoing institutional structure and civic culture, ensures a remarkable stability of the police ethos and organization in many societies. Bayley comments, after summarizing materials drawn from his analysis of police forces in Western Europe and North America, that "police systems exhibit an enormous inertial strength over time; their forms endure even across the divides of war, violent revolution, and shattering economic and social change" (1975, p. 370). Police systems of supervision and training change little with the passage of time, and the stabilizing effects of authority are reflected almost directly in the ways in which core institutions socialize members. Conversely, one could argue that changes in the socialization methods of the police will be sensitive harbingers of change within the police, as well as in the society at large.

PETER K. MANNING

See also CRIME PREVENTION: POLICE ROLE; EDUCATIONAL PROGRAMS IN CRIMINAL JUSTICE; *articles under* POLICE.

BIBLIOGRAPHY

BAYLEY, DAVID H. "The Police and Political Development in Europe." *The Formation of National States in Western Europe.* Edited by Charles Tilly. Princeton, N.J.: Princeton University Press, 1975, pp. 328–379.

————. "Police Function, Structure, and Control in Western Europe and North America: Comparative and Historical Studies." *Crime and Justice: An Annual Review of Research*, vol. 1. Edited by Norval Morris and Michael Tonry. University of Chicago Press, 1979, pp. 109–143.

————. "A World Perspective on the Role of Police in Social Control." Paper presented to Royal Canadian Police College, Ottawa, August 1980.

BECKER, HOWARD S., and STRAUSS, ANSELM L. "Careers, Personality, and Adult Socialization." *American Journal of Sociology* 62 (1956): 253–263.

BENNETT, RICHARD R., and HAEN, MARSHALL I. "Criminal Justice Education in the United States: A Profile." *Journal of Criminal Justice* 7 (1979): 147–172.

BLANKENSHIP, RALPH L. "Organizational Careers: An Interactionist Perspective." *Sociological Quarterly* 14 (1973): 88–98.

BORDUA, DAVID J. "The Police." *International Encyclopedia of the Social Sciences*, vol. 12. New York: Macmillan and Free Press, 1968, pp. 174–181.

————, and REISS, ALBERT J., JR. "Law Enforcement." *The Uses of Sociology*. New York: Basic Books, 1967, pp. 275–303.

DALTON, MELVILLE. *Men Who Manage: Fusions of Feeling and Theory in Administration*. New York: Wiley, 1959.

HARRIS, RICHARD N. *The Police Academy: An Inside View*. New York: Wiley, 1973.

KATZ, FRED. "Explaining Informal Work Groups in Complex Organizations: The Case for Autonomy in Structure." *Administrative Science Quarterly* 10 (1965): 204–223.

MANNING, PETER K. *Police Work: Essays on the Social Organization of Policing*. Cambridge, Mass.: MIT Press, 1977.

MILLER, WILBUR R. *Cops and Bobbies: Police Authority in New York and London, 1830–1870*. University of Chicago Press, 1977.

RADZINOWICZ, LEON. *Grappling for Control*. History of English Law and Its Administration from 1750, vol. 4. London: Stevens, 1968.

SHERMAN, LAWRENCE W., and National Advisory Commission for Higher Education for Police Officers. *The Quality of Police Education*. San Francisco: Jossey-Bass, 1978.

TAUSKY, CURT. *Work Organizations: Major Theoretical Perspectives*. Itasca, Ill.: Peacock, 1970.

VAN MAANEN, JOHN. "Police Socialization: A Longitudinal Examination of Job Attitudes in an Urban Police Department." *Administrative Science Quarterly* 20 (1975): 207–228.

————, and SCHEIN, EDGAR. "Toward a Theory of Organizational Socialization." *Researching Organizational Behavior*. Edited by Barry M. Staw. New York: JAI Press, 1979, pp. 209–269.

WEBER, MAX. *The Theory of Social and Economic Organization*. Translated by A. M. Henderson and Talcott Parsons. Edited with an introduction by Talcott Parsons. New York: Oxford University Press, 1947.

WILSON, JAMES Q. *Varieties of Police Behavior: The Management of Law and Order in Eight Communities*. Cambridge, Mass.: Harvard University Press, 1968.

4.
PROBATION AND PAROLE SUPERVISION

Profile of probation and parole officers. There are 3,285 state and local probation and parole agencies in the United States, 1,563 of these on the state level. Most of the probation agencies are small and employ fewer than ten officers. They are organized in a variety of ways, primarily under the judiciary. There are also federal probation officers attached to each federal district court who supervise not only persons placed on probation by these courts but also persons paroled from federal prisons to these districts, as well as a few parolees from military court-martial sentences.

A 1979 national survey of probation officers in small agencies indicates that 93 percent are white. Seventy-nine percent are male and 70 percent are under 40 years of age; most (54 percent) have 5 years or less of experience, with the mean 6.8 years. Ninety-seven percent are employed full time; 74 percent are in line positions, 12 percent are chief probation officers, 8 percent are supervisors, and 2 percent are directors of court services (Thomson and Fogel). This suggests a need for increased recruitment and selection of minorities and women.

There are some 36,600 probation officers in the United States. The highest educational requirement throughout the country for entry-level probation and parole officers is the bachelor's degree. Connecticut, New York, North Carolina, North Dakota, and Wisconsin require the master's degree for higher-level classifications, with only Wisconsin requiring a master's degree in social work (*Sourcebook of Criminal Justice Statistics*). The highest salary for probation and parole officers ($32,110 in 1980) is in the federal service.

Selection of personnel. If the goals of probation and parole are primarily rehabilitative through direct service, applicants should have a demonstrated ability to establish positive relationships with a wide range of people and to cope with manipulative or aggressive behavior by setting limits and giving emotional support; a knowledge of human growth, psychopathology, and community resources; and an understanding of legal and organizational systems. If the goals are primarily social control through client compliance with rules, an individual who can follow up on details, ensure that people conform to agreed conditions, and be satisfied with minimal personal involvement is a good candidate. In either of these roles, the ability to communicate clearly and concisely, both orally and in writing, is needed, in addition to flexibility in working with other professions and viewpoints. Also required are positive attitudes toward authority and the criminal justice system, personal stability, and high moral and social values. Other factors likely to influence appointments are the applicant's personality and demeanor, his ability to cooperate with colleagues, his motivation and interest in the work, his understanding of and orientation toward the job, and his acceptance of the court and probation philosophy.

One issue in the selection of probation and parole officers is whether candidates with backgrounds similar to those of the clients can develop closer and more influential relationships with them than can persons with dissimilar backgrounds. Donald Cressey (1965) and others have suggested using ex-offenders—who can readily understand criminal verbalizations—for the rehabilitation of offenders, which is essentially a process of changing offenders' self-concepts through role reversal. One test of this approach was made in the Ohio Parole Officer–Ex-offender Aide Project, in which former parolees were compared with parole officers in terms of their relative effectiveness as parole supervisors. Over a two-year period the performance of both groups proved equally effective, as measured by client attitudes and supervisor ratings (Scott).

Socialization. Socialization as a probation officer begins prior to employment, and continues on both formal and informal levels through training, interaction with other personnel, membership in professional associations, and the reading of professional literature.

A perennial issue concerns the kind of education that best fits the needs of probation and parole officers. Should it center on social work, criminology, corrections, sociology, psychology, public administration, education, law, or law enforcement? There is no evidence to indicate the superiority of any single academic program as preparation for this line of work (Senna); an interdisciplinary education appears to be the best means of preparing one to work cooperatively with a variety of persons and agencies.

Since approximately 1900, social work (and later, more specifically, social casework) was the preferred training for probation and parole officers. By 1967 the President's Commission on Law Enforcement and Administration of Justice recommended the master's degree in social work because it provided theoretical understanding as well as an array of skills for planning programs and for delivering and evaluating services. The Joint Commission on Correctional Manpower and Training complained that graduate schools of social work could not meet the demand for correctional personnel and that social workers in corrections

lacked opportunities for utilizing their knowledge and skills. Since persons with a bachelor's degree were performing the probation officer's tasks effectively, it was recommended that this degree in any behavioral science become an entry-level standard for probation officers. By the 1970s, the primary function of the probation officer was viewed as that of a community resource expert engaged in case management and referral rather than counseling and surveillance.

Preservice training of newly appointed probation and parole officers sensitizes them to the values, behavior norms, and formal and informal power structures of the job setting and affords opportunities to develop successful relationships with colleagues. It also gives administrators information for planning future employee-development programs.

Individual and group supervision provides ongoing communication between field staff and administration. It constitutes a learning process that helps officers cope with difficult problems and situations, and it facilitates the transmission of information about laws, court decisions, and administrative policies (Cohn). Supervision also fosters consistency in decision-making. For the administrator, supervision provides information useful in determining agency policy and program development, as well as a means of identifying gaps in community resources. Consultation with outside legal, medical, social-work, psychological, and psychiatric experts can reduce bias in the interpretation of information and provide resources for staff development.

In-service training continues officer socialization. Especially needed when innovations are planned or implemented, it serves officials as a source of feedback on staff reactions to change. It also encourages further growth and development of the officer, contributes to staff morale, and can improve the quality of supervision of offenders.

Informal socialization, which often occurs unconsciously through interaction with associates in the criminal justice system, becomes manifest when judges and probation officers label one another. Thus, some judges classify probation officers as too permissive, too stringent, or inconsistent. This is similar to the types of probation and parole officers classified by Lloyd Ohlin, Herman Piven, and Donnell Pappenfort: the "punitive officer," the "protective agent," and the "welfare worker." Daniel Glaser later developed a fourfold classification based on high or low emphasis on control and assistance: the paternal officer, the punitive officer, the welfare worker, and the passive officer.

The judge may use such assessments as clues to

officer bias when reviewing presentence investigations and progress and violation reports. Similarly, probation officers, through their own experience and their conversations with others, learn about judges' biases—for example, that one judge never grants probation to an income-tax violator or a narcotic seller. As a result, the officers may never recommend probation in such cases and are thus co-opted, especially if they need a judge's approval to be promoted. Insufficient recognition of such practices limits the criminal justice system's potential for improved decision-making.

Progression in role. In 1970 the Joint Commission documented a lack of upward mobility in the probation and parole field in the United States. Lateral entry—which permits qualified personnel to move from one agency to another—was available in 70 percent of the states, but mostly at beginning levels. Proponents argue that lateral entry may expand opportunities for individuals, and increase overall flexibility in dealing with changing regional demands for probation and parole services. It would be fostered by standard civil service requirements and a national portable retirement system. The traditional model of starting at the bottom and working up to the top solely on the basis of seniority is less common than it once was. Fair-employment practice guidelines require that many positions be advertised and that opportunities be made available to qualified individuals within and outside of public agencies. The increasing need for persons with specialized technical skills for innovative programs, computerized information systems, and cost-effectiveness evaluations encourages recruitment from universities and the business community.

The differences between probation and parole. Parole officers work with clients who move from closed and structured institutions to the more free and open society at large. As a rule, parolees find returning to life on the outside especially difficult and usually require more assistance then probationers, who have never left the community. Assistance may be needed in obtaining food and shelter and in coping with everyday realities and relationships. Parole officers need to be aware of the effects of closed institutions on those whom they supervise. Evidence indicates that for the vast majority of inmates, the maximum-security prison environment results in mental, emotional, and behavioral debilitation and in further incapacity to adapt to stress in the outside world. Inmates who adjust to life on the inside become less able to function outside in the free world (De Wolfe and De Wolfe).

In juvenile probation, officers must work closely with the family and with others who affect the child, for example, school and community agencies. When a probationer is in late adolescence, a period during which individuals normally seek greater independence, the probation officer may concentrate his efforts more on the youth than on the family.

Alienation of probation and parole officers. People entering the fields of probation and parole are often viewed as on the fringes of the social-work profession. There is much discomfort among social-work educators and practitioners with regard to the coercive nature of the criminal justice system, because of its perceived incompatibility with the more permissive treatment values of social work. Probation and parole officers may undergo an alienation from other professional groups that is similar in some ways to the experiences of their clients with people, agencies, or institutions reluctant to provide services and opportunities. This tendency to view probation and parole officers as marginal professionals impedes the growth of the justice system. To remedy this condition, probation and parole officers must maintain a positive attitude about their own services as well as about the prospects of the offenders they deal with.

Principal issues. Issues that invite the concern of probation and parole officers include the following:

Goals. Administration and staff often do not possess a clear understanding of their working philosophy and objectives, so that individual rather than organizational aims are pursued. Therefore, goals should be stated in clear and measurable terms.

Dispositions. Should case dispositions be recommended to the court or parole authority by probation or parole officers in their presentence or violation reports? Such recommendations are often the most difficult and agonizing aspect of an officer's job, necessitating supervision and consultation. Alternatively, when such advice is not solicited from officers, they need only present relevant data, with their sources and interpretation.

Co-optation. The demands of the larger justice system may be seen by probation and parole officers as impinging on their personal orientations and ideologies. However, cooperative relationships with others in this system can be fostered by an appreciation of the interdependence of roles, a respect for co-workers' contributions, and an ability to work with differences in orientation and values. In addition, affiliation with professional associations and educational institutions constitutes an important source of continuing guidance and support. The work of probation and parole officers is properly seen both as a unique contribution to, and an interdependent part of, the larger criminal justice system.

Assistance versus control. Should the probation and parole officer's role consist primarily of assistance or of control? In practice, both functions may exist simultaneously if mandated or if an officer believes both to be appropriate. If an offender needs limits placed on his behavior, assistance becomes control. The principal issue here is public doubt as to the effectiveness or justice of an officer counseling or providing other aid to the same offender on whom he must also impose controls. Underlying this may be the concern of whether or not a person who has violated society's laws is deserving of assistance.

Treatment. Does the state have a right to intervene in a person's life if it cannot prove that what it offers will be beneficial? The issue is often one of self-determination: can clients be helped against their will? When treatment goals are set by the court, should clients be consulted? Some believe that offenders, by virtue of their conviction, do not deserve such self-determination. Norval Morris has advocated avoiding abuse of human rights in imposing rehabilitation by limiting power over an offender's life to what would be done if reform were not a goal, and by basing correctional practice on the extent to which reform is achieved by various sanctions.

Organization of services. Should probation and parole services be organized so that officers are primarily counselors who provide an array of services centralized in the probation office, or should they be primarily case managers who refer, coordinate, and monitor services provided by contracting and participating private and public agencies? The officers' educational emphasis and preparation will be different for each of these roles. Which arrangement is most cost-effective and best serves and protects the community?

Unionization. A modern trend in probation and parole is the unionization of public employees. Probation and parole officers are joining labor unions for collective negotiation of wages and working conditons. The officers are divided on unionism, since it conflicts with some conceptions of an autonomous profession. Nevertheless, unions will probably have a continuing impact on recruitment, job classification, salary levels, and other aspects of employment, as well as on the quality of services delivered.

The future. The last two decades of the twentieth century are likely to witness the greatest changes yet in the roles of probation and parole officers. Their careers will depend on public policy toward offenders, availability of resources, priorities for human services, and arrangements for delivering these services. The greatest demand will be in state and local criminal justice systems in the areas of greatest population growth. At the federal level, the volume of referral to probation and parole will diminish because of decreased appropriations, the diversion of more offenders to local agencies, and the concentration of federal law enforcement and prosecution on white-collar crime. With a tight labor market and increased competition for jobs, personnel will be sought who have multiple skills and graduate education.

With limited financial resources at state and local levels, however, probation and parole services will be Spartan. Agencies will focus on survival and on the most effective use of resources. Parole will gradually be diminished, with discharges effected earlier as the limits of institutional space and budget are reached. Aftercare assistance will be increasingly available on a voluntary basis from private agencies. In probation, a parallel development in the private sector will occur. Officers will have less direct work with clients and will be involved to a greater extent in referral, advocacy, supervision, and training. There will be more emphasis on consultation with probation aides drawn from the same neighborhoods as the offenders and with private agencies receiving public funds. Experimentation with a variety of such public-private agency arrangements for probation and parole services will continue for the foreseeable future, although such ventures are opposed by the unions recruiting correctional personnel.

With continuing inflation, the costs of incarceration will escalate. As a result, there will be increased demands for more selectivity in sentencing persons to prison and in screening out those who can safely be diverted from the system. More community alternatives will be demanded, such as police–social-work programs, pretrial services, deferred prosecution, fines, public-service sentences, restitution, and probation, which can provide control and protection at costs supportable by public opinion and through appropriation. Services will be concentrated at early and critical points, especially prior to adjudication. There will be increased accountability for services provided, and results will be analyzed in terms of cost benefits and public safety. Controversial areas will include determining criteria for estimating the relative value of benefits derived from different kinds of services, and dealing with the reactions of criminal justice personnel to change. Careful collation and cross-checking of computerized data for many agencies could reduce the nonproductive duplication of services. If this does not foster the overorganization and overmechanization of probation and parole supervision, the beneficiaries of such changes may comprise not only the public and the system's operators but also its clients.

HARVEY TREGER

See also EDUCATIONAL PROGRAMS IN CRIMINAL JUSTICE; PRETRIAL DIVERSION; *articles under* PROBATION AND PAROLE; SENTENCING: PRESENTENCE REPORT.

BIBLIOGRAPHY

COHN, YONA. "Toward Job-related In-service Training in Corrections: Reflections on Designing Training Programs." *Federal Probation* 44 (1980): 48–57.
CRESSEY, DONALD R. "Changing Criminals: The Application of the Theory of Differential Association." *American Journal of Sociology* 61 (1955): 116–120.
———. "Theoretical Foundations for Using Criminals in Rehabilitation of Criminals." *The Future of Imprisonment in a Free Society.* Key Issues, vol. 2. Edited by Hans W. Mattick. Chicago: St. Leonard's House, 1965, pp. 87–99.
DE WOLFE, RUTHANNE, and DE WOLFE, ALAN S. "Impact of Prison Conditions on the Mental Health of Inmates." *Southern Illinois University Law Journal* (1979): 497–533.
GLASER, DANIEL. *The Effectiveness of a Prison and Parole System.* Indianapolis: Bobbs-Merrill, 1964.
Joint Commission on Correctional Manpower and Training. *Staff Report: Perspectives on Correctional Manpower and Training.* Baltimore: American Correctional Association, 1970.
MORRIS, NORVAL. "Impediments to Penal Reform." *University of Chicago Law Review* 33 (1966): 627–656.
OHLIN, LLOYD; PIVEN, HERMAN; and PAPPENFORT, DONNELL M. "Major Dilemmas of the Social Worker in Probation and Parole." *National Probation and Parole Association Journal* 2 (1956): 211–225.
President's Commission on Law Enforcement and Administration of Justice. *The Challenge of Crime in a Free Society.* Washington, D.C.: The Commission, 1967.
SCOTT, JOSEPH E. *Ex-offenders as Parole Officers.* Lexington, Mass.: Heath, Lexington Books, 1974.
SENNA, JOSEPH J. "The Need for Professional Education in Probation and Parole." *Crime and Delinquency* 22 (1976): 67–74.
Sourcebook of Criminal Justice Statistics, 1976. Washington, D.C.: U.S. Department of Justice, Law Enforcement Assistance Administration, National Criminal Justice Information and Statistics Service, 1977.
THOMSON, DOUG, and FOGEL, DAVID. *Probation Work in Small Agencies: A National Study of Training Provisions and Needs.* Final Report on Grant AN-9 from the National Institute of Corrections. Chicago: University of Illinois at Chicago Circle, Center for Research in Criminal Justice, 1980.

CAUSATION

Introduction

The role of causation in the criminal law. To be held liable for certain offenses, one must have caused a harmful, proscribed result. Homicide is the most common example. To be convicted of a homicide offense, such as murder or manslaughter, the defendant must be proved to have caused the death of another human being. In legal analysis, the factual grounds for liability in such a case are commonly divided into three components: the harmful result (that is, the victim's death), the defendant's conduct (for example, pulling the trigger), and a causal connection between these two.

Although the concept of causation is thus implicitly invoked in all cases in which liability depends on the occurrence of a certain result, it is explicitly considered in relatively few. In the straightforward, paradigmatic case (where, for example, the bullet shot at the victim lodged in his heart), there is hardly any reason to raise the question of causation as an independent issue. To resort to any tests or guidelines as to whether a causal connection exists in this case is quite unnecessary, possibly confusing, and consequently never done. The three components mentioned above—the defendant's conduct, the victim's death, and the causal relation—are all comprehended in and adequately rendered by the verb *to kill*. Familiarity with such transitive verbs, and facility in applying them in numerous situations, are all that is needed for the legal resolution of the factual component in the model homicide case. But if in the paradigmatic case of homicide there is hardly any occasion to deal with questions of causation, there are numerous other cases where the issue does occupy a central and often perplexing role. Consider, for example, the following situations:

1. On a cold winter night the defendant and his wife had a fierce quarrel, after which the wife left for her parents' home. She remained outdoors for the rest of the night, however, and froze to death (*State v. Preslar*, 48 N.C. (3 Jones) 421 (1856)).
2. The defendant wounded the victim, who was hospitalized. At the hospital the latter contracted scarlet fever and died from the disease (*Bush v. Commonwealth*, 78 Ky. (1 Rodman) 268 (1880)).
3. The defendants robbed a store. The proprietor, who had a heart disease, was shaken by the robbery and died of a heart attack (*People v. Stamp*, 2 Cal. App. 3d 203, 82 Cal. Rptr. 598 (1969)).

These are situations in which the application of the transitive verb *to kill* to the defendant's acts seems forced and problematic, if not outright wrong. They force one, therefore, to confront the aforementioned tripartite division of the relevant criminal transaction, and in particular to consider explicitly whether a causal relationship exists in each of these cases between the defendant's acts and the victim's death.

In dealing with this issue, the law resorts to a variety of rules and guidelines, often referred to as "tests," which in conjunction are supposed to define and elucidate the concept of causation and guide its application to particular cases.

The conventional analysis of legal causation. Conventional analysis divides the causal relation, and consequently the tests offered to guide inquiry, into two main components, commonly referred to as *cause in fact* and *cause in law*. According to this analysis, not just *any* factual causal relationship can support criminal liability. To be of legal relevance, the causal relationship must satisfy some further criteria, or tests, which are subsumed under the category of *cause in law*. Of these two categories, cause in fact, which is mainly identified with the "but for" test (discussed below), is less problematic, but also less informative. Most of the difficulties in defining the legal concept of causation are encountered in trying to spell out the additional criteria that must be satisfied for there to exist not merely a factual but a legally sufficient causal relation, one that may support conviction and punishment for a harmful occurrence.

Numerous tests are invoked by courts and commentators to determine the existence of a legally sufficient causal relation. Most salient among these is the *foreseeability* test: that the actual harm must have been reasonably foreseeable by the accused when he committed the relevant act. Another is the *novus actus interveniens* ("new intervening act") test. This test suggests that a causal relationship that would otherwise have existed between the accused's act and the ensuing harm is negated if the immediate cause of the harm was the intervention of another agent's voluntary act. Finally, there is the *proximity* test, which requires that the causal chain, measured by the number and duration of events between the accused's conduct and the harm, not be excessively long.

The Model Penal Code's formula. The attempt to construct this set of guidelines has not, however, proved successful. One has the feeling that although the various tests provide different approximations to the notion of causation, the concept itself remains elusive. The various tests may be likened, to use a well-worn image, to the reports about the elephant that were obtained from the five blind men. In the case of causation, however, the enterprise has been marked by such Herculean efforts and such meager results that one begins to suspect there may be more than a single animal to be described. One may conclude that the concept of causation is (in the law as elsewhere) too basic to be amenable to complete analysis in terms of other, simpler concepts. At the same time, one realizes that it is so intricately woven into the fabric of the law that its perplexities and puzzles are but the reflection of much that is perplexing and unsettled in the theories and practices of which it is a component.

Support for this bleak view can be gathered from the fact that the drafters of the most influential modern criminal code, the American Law Institute's Model Penal Code, have to a large degree despaired of providing an illuminating definition of causation or a set of meaningful guidelines for its application. In addition to the but-for test of causation, the Code also requires that the result, to be causally linked to the defendant's conduct, must not be "too remote or accidental in its occurrence to have a [just] bearing on the actor's liability or on the gravity of his offense" (§ 2.03).

The drafters' admission of failure to provide a workable definition of legal causation consists in the insertion into the definition of the bracketed word *just*, which renders the provision transparently circular. Whether and with what severity the defendant can justly be held criminally liable supposedly depends, in part, on whether he can be said to have caused the harm attributed to him. To know whether the defendant can be justly punished, one must therefore first be able to ascertain whether the causal relation, as legally defined, exists. The point of this definition is, however, defeated if it specifies, as the Model Penal Code in fact does, that in order to establish the causal relation one must first be satisfied about whether the defendant can justly be held liable for the harm in question. In this way causation and liability circle about each other, neither providing independent support for ascertaining the other.

Based on this experience, the United States National Commission on Reform of Federal Criminal Laws omits altogether from its draft of a proposed federal criminal code a provision defining causation, stating in its report that "an explanation of causation which is likely not to be helpful to a jury and is as likely as not to be confusing should not be included" (p. 144).

Given this impressive admission that despite the perceived flaws in the Model Penal Code's provision on causation it may not be possible to improve upon it, it would seem sensible to give up at this point further attempts to resolve the difficulties concerning the legal definition of causation. It might be more fruitful instead to try to diagnose in some detail their source.

The insufficiency of cause in fact

The most basic and widely accepted of the tests used to ascertain the existence of a causal relation is the so-called but-for test, or, in its Latin form, the sine qua non test. The aim of this test is to capture the intuitive idea that for A to cause B means (at least) that if A had not happened, neither would B. To find out whether A is the cause of B one must, according to this test, conduct a mental experiment in which one eliminates A and then asks whether B would have happened nonetheless. If the answer is negative, then A is a but-for cause of B.

The test is generally useful in that in most cases it leads to judgments that comport with common intuitions about causation. Yet it suffers from some difficulties. First, but-for is not always a necessary condition for a causal relation. This is evident in situations of *joint causation*, in which the outcome is causally overdetermined. The examples commonly given are those of two defendants who simultaneously but independently shoot the victim, each inflicting a mortal wound, or of two defendants who each started a fire at a different part of the burned house. Applying the but-for test to these cases leads to the paradoxical conclusion that neither of the defendants caused the victim's death in the first case or the fire in the second.

The fact that one can so easily grasp the paradox and that one is willing to depart from the but-for test for the sake of a sounder result is instructive as to the relation between the but-for test and the causal connection it helps establish. The but-for test should not be mistaken for a definition or even an explanation of causal relations. The ability to make causal judgments is prior to, and in a sense more basic than, the notion of but-for. Indeed, the very ability to use the test presupposes a familiarity with causal relations. In order successfully to conduct the mental experiment called for by the but-for test, one must already possess a firm notion as to what kinds of things bring about (cause) other things. The but-for test is only of heuristic value, helping on some, but not all, occasions to satisfy ourselves that a causal relationship between two events exists.

The second difficulty with the but-for test is its frequent indeterminacy. In many cases people resort to a test of a causal relation rather than relying on their immediate perception of its existence or absence, precisely because the answer to the counterfactual question suggested by the but-for test is not clear. The test may, therefore, be of little use when it is most needed. A speeding car kills a pedestrian. Could one say, with any degree of assurance, that but for the speeding the pedestrian would not have died? The impact would have been weaker. But could it not have been fatal nonetheless? Or consider the parents who failed to take their ailing child to the doctor, with fatal consequences (*State v. Williams*, 4 Wash. App. 908, 484 P.2d 1167 (1971)). Given all that is known about the vagaries of medical treatment, would it not be possible for the child to have died of the disease despite timely care? Yet, one may feel quite strongly that, given the extreme dangerousness of their conduct, both the driver in the one case and the parents in the other case should be held respectively responsible for the deaths that occurred.

Finally, the essentially auxiliary function of the but-for test must be emphasized. The test comes into play only *after* an initial selection process that has generated relatively few candidates for bearing the causal brunt. The but-for test would do a very poor job if it were to be systematically employed from the outset as a means of narrowing the list of events that could serve as legally relevant causes: but for Adam and Eve, the present article would not have been written. This problem is further compounded by the fact that the but-for test does not distinguish between actions and omissions. A failure to act can easily satisfy the but-for test and thus become as causally effective as an action: *but for* the bystander's failure to come to the baby's rescue, the baby would not have drowned in the pond. Although in this case the but-for test seems to comport with our intuitive judgment, the consequence of recognizing omissions as but-for causes is to expand infinitely the range of events captured by this test as causally relevant to any given harm. Not only is this article the product of a chain of but-for causes leading straight back to Adam and Eve, but every possible event along the way which might have interrupted that chain (but did not) is also causally implicated in its writing. Consequently, when "causing death" is made the basis of a criminal offense, the criminally relevant conduct cannot be located merely by relying on the but-for test, leading as it does to a virtually infinite universe of potential causal factors. Indeed, as was already pointed out, legal causal analysis proceeds beyond the questions of *cause in fact* by invoking the concept of *cause in law*. Only causal relations that satisfy this additional set of criteria (sometimes designated by the technical but somewhat confusing term *proximate cause*) are legally relevant.

The failure to articulate a definition of legal causation that would do justice to the richness and complexity of the actual use of this concept in the law has already been noted. The obstacles that can account for this failure, and for the improbability of achieving any fully adequate definition of legal causation or of a consistent and workable set of guidelines for its application, should now be examined.

The analysis of cause in law

Two strategies are commonly employed to investigate the legal concept of causation: a functional analysis and an ordinary-language analysis. Functional analysis proceeds from the vision of the law as an instrument that serves some relatively specific social goals. The meaning of causation, like that of other legal concepts, must be derived from, or determined by, its role in serving those goals. The second strategy views the legal use of causation as derived from, and reflecting, the use made of this term in ordinary language. Accordingly, to elucidate the legal concept of causation one must investigate the ordinary usage of causal terminology in contexts analogous to those that interest the law. More specifically, understanding the meaning of causation in the criminal law requires an investigation into the role played by this concept in everyday discourse when ordinary people assign blame and ascribe responsibility. Both of these strategies, however, have certain limits that frustrate a complete resolution of the problems of legal causation.

The limits of functional analysis.

The irrelevance of actual harm. The concept of causation establishes a link between the accused's conduct and a harmful event, for example, the victim's death. A functional analysis of causation would derive the legal meaning and contours of this concept from the answer to the question, What purpose is served by linking the harmful event to the accused's conduct? Only by answering this question would one be able to specify the sort of link that is sought.

The functional analysis of causation is, therefore, greatly impeded by discovering that there is considerable difficulty in establishing the relevance of the occurrence of actual harm to criminal liability or severity of punishment. If the purposes commonly ascribed to the criminal law do not rationally require that criminal liability depend on actual harm, one can hardly expect to derive from those purposes the necessary link between the harm and the defendant's conduct.

The rational and moral grounds for punishment, it has been argued, should lead one to focus on the defendant's conduct and state of mind or degree of culpability, not on whether some harmful result actually followed from that conduct (Schulhofer). The following illustration will convey the essence of the argument for the irrelevance of actual harm to criminal liability.

Imagine two cases, in both of which the respective defendants shoot their victim with intent to kill. In both cases the bullets lodge in the respective victim's chest. Both victims undergo surgery. The cases are identical in all respects but one: in the first case the victim dies of the wound, and in the second, he is saved by the operation. Rationally, what does this difference in outcome have to do with the proper criminal disposition of the two defendants? Both have demonstrated precisely the same degree of dangerousness and culpability; indeed, the hypothetical facts could be easily manipulated so as to make the second defendant more culpable, morally speaking, than the first. It can be argued that their treatment by the criminal law should not reflect the fortuity that one victim had a better surgeon or better luck than the other. Neither considerations of deterrence nor calculations of the two defendants' just deserts can support differential legal treatment. Consequently, any attempt to base the analysis of causation on grounds of policy must fail: if the fact of the first victim's death is irrelevant to the policies served by the criminal law, the same must be true of the causal relation between that death and the defendant's shooting. We can, therefore, entertain little hope for deriving guidelines for the legal use of causation from its function in serving the criminal law's goals.

That the actual death of the victim is somehow relevant to determining the accused's criminal liability is nonetheless a widely shared and deeply entrenched intuition, one that is as persistent as it is resistant to any convincing rationalization. The legal concept of causation may accordingly be seen as a corollary of this intuition. Although the intuition itself resists rationalization by reference to the goals of the criminal law, it can still be demonstrated that the *fact* of its existence and pervasiveness is relevant to the criminal law's ability to discharge its main functions. As will now be shown, the law's recognition and adoption of the way in which people ordinarily relate the occurrence of harm to blame and punishment may serve both retribution and deterrence—the two goals most commonly ascribed to the criminal law.

Causation and retribution. As used here, *retribution* stands for a cluster of divergent ideas. They have in common, however, the view that the infliction of punishment is the proper social response to the harm suffered as a result of the commission of a crime. This view is doubtless the expression of a widely held and deep-seated sentiment about the relationship between crime and punishment. One may condemn that sentiment by characterizing it as a crude urge for vengeance, or dignify it with a loftier image according to which punishment is needed to expunge the "tainting" effect of crime or to restore a social equilibrium disturbed by the crime's commission. But it is hard to deny both the pervasiveness of that underlying sentiment and the influence it actually exerts on the criminal law, even in the absence of compelling rational arguments to support it. Seen in this light, the issue of causation must be referred to this sentiment—call it the retributive urge—that animates the practice of blame and punishment. Posed in connection with the retributive goal of punishment, the question of causation (namely, "Is there a causal relation between A's conduct and B's death?") amounts to asking whether punishing A is necessary to satisfy the retributive urge aroused by the fact of B's death.

Two conclusions about the investigation of the legal concept of causation are implied by these comments. First, to the extent that causation plays a role in serving the retributive goal of punishment, its elucidation compels us to investigate the ordinary use of causal notions in the context of blaming others for harm done. Second, in conducting this investigation it is likely to become apparent that, as an element of the retributive urge, the concept of causation is inextricably bound up, in ordinary usage, with the entire complex of blaming. As will be discussed below, the statement that A caused B's death may, in ordinary speech, be as much a conclusory statement, based on the prior tacit judgment that A deserves to be punished for B's death, as it is an independent statement of fact which leads to that conclusion. Put differently, in ordinary usage the concepts of causation and blame or deserts often reverse the idealized roles usually assigned to them in moral and legal theory. According to that theory, one would expect the conclusion that A should be punished for B's death to be based, in part, on the judgment that A caused B's death. In fact, the conclusion that A deserves to be punished may be directly and intuitively generated by the retributive urge, preceding and merely rationalized by the finding of a sufficient causal relationship between A's acts and B's death.

The view of causation as playing a role in the law's wish to satisfy the retributive urge helps explain a central feature of causal judgments in the criminal law: their dependence on the availability of alternative potential bearers of responsibility. This feature of legal causation has three different manifestations, of which only the first enjoys the status of an explicitly recognized "rule," whereas the other two exert a tacit influence on causal judgments.

Consider first the rule known as *novus actus interveniens* ("new intervening act"). As noted above, according to this rule the causal relation that otherwise would be said to exist between A's act and a certain harmful event is interrupted if a voluntary act by B intervenes between A's act and the result and is its immediate (but-for) cause. If A, for example, sets fire to a pile of wood in order to burn down a house, and as the flames in the wood are about to flicker out B deliberately pours some gasoline on them, rekindling the fire, it is B, not A, who will be said to have burned down the house—even though a but-for connection exists between A's acts and the harm. In such cases, it has been argued, "the intervention of the responsible actor diverts our retributive wrath from the defendant" (Williams, 1978, p. 338).

Causal judgments also seem to depend on the availability of alternative bearers of responsibility in cases of what one may call *scapegoating*. In such cases, the retributive urge precedes the perception of anyone's culpability and seeks some as-yet-unidentified, and possibly nonexistent, target. The retributive urge is likely to exhibit overtones of scapegoating when the harmful event is particularly dramatic or otherwise unnerving, as when a fire breaks out in a public place, claiming hundreds of lives (*Commonwealth v. Welansky*, 316 Mass. 383, 55 N.E.2d 902 (1944)). In such a case the concept of causation may sometimes prove to be quite flexible, and responsive to the intensity of the retributive urge. In the absence of some direct and obvious causes of the calamity, the needed target for the public outrage is sometimes located at a distance, and a causal relation that would otherwise be deemed too tenuous is nonetheless sustained.

Finally, the dependence of causal judgments on the availability of alternative bearers of responsibility is reflected in what may be called *symbolic absolution*. Consider the case of a police officer who in a fusillade with a gang of bank robbers shoots and kills an innocent bystander. Here the impulse at work may be to shield the police officer from becoming, because of his causal proximity to the bystander's death, the target of the public retributive urge, and symbolically vindicate his conduct by allocating responsibility for the killing to some other agent. By finding, as the law sometimes does, a sufficient causal connection between the robbers' shooting and the bystander's death, an account of the killing is given that bypasses the role played by the policeman. This ensures that the entire blame for the killing falls on the robbers and that none of it attaches to the officer (*Commonwealth v. Almeida*, 362 Pa. 596, 68 A.2d 595 (1949); later overruled in *Commonwealth ex rel. Smith v. Myers*, 438 Pa. 218, 261 A.2d 550 (1970)).

Causation and deterrence. The goal of deterrence is most directly served not by the actual imposition of punishment, but rather by the threat of punishment. It is people's *belief* that prohibited conduct will result in a criminal sanction that is expected to reduce the incidence of crime. Actual punishment, accordingly, is only indirectly justified by the goal of deterrence: it is called for merely in order to lend credibility to the initial threat. The imposition of punishment is a mode of emphatic communication, and is to be assessed according to its ability to convey the desired message. Consequently, the question of causal relationship asked from the perspective of deterrence becomes, Is punishing A for B's death likely to increase people's awareness that the threat of punishment for homicide is serious? Conversely, is failure to punish A for B's death likely to weaken people's belief in the seriousness of the threat of punishment for homicide?

What needs to be emphasized about this way of posing the causal question is that in resolving the causal issue in the context of the deterrence goal one is again, as in the case of retribution, referred to the perceptions of ordinary people. To promote deterrence, the legal concept of causation must coincide with the corresponding ordinary notion that leads people to associate a harmful event (B's death) with a certain action (A's shooting), and consequently to expect that the threat of punishment for killing will be carried out against A on these grounds.

The goal of deterrence is sometimes thought to lead to a "foreseeability" test of causation. According to this test, a defendant can be held criminally liable only for the but-for results of his conduct that he could have foreseen. The reasoning supporting this proposition is as follows. Supposedly, in order to act as an effective deterrent, the threat of punishment must be taken into consideration by the agent when he contemplates his criminal behavior. According to this simplified model of rational decision-making, the agent will assign to the criminal option the negative value represented by the probability and severity of punishment. In doing so, he can do no better than take into consideration all the *foreseeable* outcomes of the contemplated conduct and the punishment attached to them. To punish for unforeseeable consequences is, therefore, pointless as far as deterrence is concerned.

This argument is flawed in two ways. First, knowledge that punishment may be visited on unexpected, as well as on expected, results of a prohibited course of conduct must augment the overall negative value placed by the rational individual on that conduct, and will thereby increase the deterrent effect of the law. Second, the argument confuses considerations relevant to the threat of punishment with considerations about its actual imposition. The question of what punishment should be imposed in a particular case is always a post-factum question, and its resolution does not depend on the defendant's own calculations; it is already known that his calculations led him in fact to the commission of the crime. Rather, the issue of actual punishment must be decided, as noted above, in light of the message that the imposition or withholding of a certain punishment in a given case is likely to convey to people in general about the seriousness of the relevant legal threat. This decision does not depend logically and directly on the foreseeability of the harm caused. The issue of foreseeability may still be relevant, but only indirectly, mediated by ordinary people's common notions of causal relations. Foreseeability is relevant to causation as seen from the deterrence perspective only insofar as people's association of a harmful event with particular conduct coincides with the antecedent foreseeability of that event.

From these remarks it may be concluded that the functional approach to the legal concept of causation—the attempt to derive its content from the goals of retribution and deterrence—refers us to the use of causal notions in ordinary language. In order to serve the function of satisfying a widespread retributive urge, and in order to promote deterrence by conveying the seriousness of the legal threat, the legal notion of causation must comport with people's common perceptions of the connection between an act and its effects. The investigation of causation in the criminal law is in this way reduced to the investigation of the role played by that notion in shaping everyday judgments about responsibility and blame. The concept of legal causation is, therefore, unlikely to enjoy a greater degree of rigor and precision than does its counterpart in ordinary language.

It is now necessary to examine briefly the use of causal language in ordinary life in the context of blaming and the ascribing of responsibility. As it turns out, in light of their ambiguities and obscurities, ordinary causal notions compound rather than dispel the difficulties of reaching a clear and workable definition of legal causation.

Ordinary and legal usage of causation.

The ordinary use of causal language. To reproduce ordinary causal language in legal rules or guidelines is a particularly onerous task because of the multiplicity of meanings and forms that such language assumes, and because of the uncertainty as to which of these is to be followed. To illustrate this point, consider the following statements: (1) "A killed B"; (2) "A caused B's death"; (3) "B was killed by A"; (4) "B's death was caused by A"; and (5) "B died as a result of A."

These five statements may seem equivalent and interchangeable descriptions of the same event, all implying a casual connection between A and B's death. According to this interpretation it is this single causal connection, rendered in five different ways, that is the subject of the law's interest and that should be captured by the legal definition of causation. This, however, is not the case. As the following examples illustrate, each of the above descriptions may be appropriate in situations where the others are not.

(*a*) A shoots at B, hitting him in the chest, and B dies instantaneously.

(*b*) A threatens to kill B. B, trying to escape, jumps out the window and suffers fatal injuries.

(*c*) B lies on the railroad tracks and is hit, fatally, by a train.

(*d*) B commits suicide after learning that A, the woman he loves, has married another man.

(*e*) B undergoes an unsuccessful surgical operation and dies of hemorrhage.

Relating these events to the aforementioned causal descriptions, it would seem that description (1) fits (*a*) very well: no one would hesitate to describe the situation by saying that A killed B. This, however, would not be the natural way to describe (*b*). Here one would be inclined to deny that A in fact killed B (as she threatened she would) but still hold that A caused, by her threats, B's death. In (*c*), one would probably not even be willing to go so far as to contend that the train, much less its engineer, caused B's death. The most natural way to account for the situation seems to be by resorting to the passive voice and saying that B was killed by a train. In (*d*), one is unlikely to say that B was killed by A (or by A's marriage), but one may nonetheless say that B's death (or suicide) was caused by A's marriage to another man.

Finally, in (*e*), the most appropriate account seems to be that B died as a result of the operation; to say that B's death was caused by the operation (or by the surgeon) sounds somewhat too strong.

If these illustrations correctly capture different shades of ordinary causal statements, then to say that A caused B cannot be understood as a factual, morally neutral common denominator of all these cases, as the legal preoccupation with "the concept of causation" may lead one to believe. Rather, the term *cause* is one among a number of contenders for the adequate description of a given situation. As such, it carries a set of unique linguistic connotations, different from those of other competitors, such as the transitive verb *to kill* or the passive voice *was the result of.* Each description conveys a different degree of willingness to ascribe responsibility to A for B's death or to blame him for it, which in turn seems to be a product of a complex set of considerations. All of these considerations bear on the choice of language, but none of them determines it uniquely or exclusively. Merely from looking at the five examples, one can readily discern a number of such considerations: among others, whether there was any direct physical impact of A on B, whether A's conduct was wrongful, whether B's conduct was wrongful, and the nature of A's intent relative to B's death.

Two conclusions follow from these illustrations. First, causal language, as it is used in ordinary speech, is not a mere report of objective factual relations, but rather is replete with normative judgments and is influenced by beliefs about the actor's state of mind. Second, the term *cause* in ordinary speech does not designate, as it is expected to do in the law, an abstract concept that serves as a common denominator of all causal relations. Rather, it is used, as just demonstrated, to capture a specific subset of causal relations—the product of a special combination of the various factors that are relevant to the formation of a causal judgment. Other combinations of these factors would lead, in ordinary speech, not to denial of a causal relation, but to the adoption of a different description by resorting to the appropriate transitive verb, to the passive voice, or some analogous device.

Legal implications. These two observations help account for the difficulties and uncertainties that plague the concept of causation in the criminal law. The first point—that ordinary causal judgments incorporate normative and subjective considerations as well as factual ones—makes causation a difficult concept to handle for a legal system that professes commitment to the analytical and institutional separation of such considerations. The criminal law's professed ideology insists on a sharp separation between the normative and the factual. Normative issues are seen as a matter of law. They are the province of the legislature, which provides general guidelines in the form of rules. The application of these rules to the particular case is the task of the judge. Matters of fact, on the other hand, are within the domain of the jury, which is charged with making a determination of what has actually happened in a particular case.

Within the realm of facts, furthermore, criminal law doctrine draws a sharp line between "objective"—directly observable, or "public"—facts that roughly fall under the category of actus reus, and "subjective," or psychological, facts about the accused's state of mind, which serve as a measure of his culpability and are subsumed under the term *mens rea*. To fit into this schema, issues of causation are commonly categorized as matters of fact rather than of law and, within the second dichotomy, as part of the actus reus. They are part of the report of the external, observable facts, to the exclusion of questions of culpability, which are relegated to the mens rea category. "Did A cause B's death?" is, according to this professed scheme of the structure of criminal responsibility, a factual matter that, together with A's having the necessary guilty mind, and the existence of a prohibitory criminal norm, will lead to the imposition of criminal liability on A.

Having observed the way causal language is ordinarily used, one can now appreciate the amount of resistance that the concept of causation is likely to exert to being "boxed" in this way. Rather than play a modest role within the actus reus as part of the factual finding, the concept of causation constantly strives to invoke both subjective and normative considerations. Consequently, causation plays a kind of subversive role, threatening to collapse, or expose the untenability of, both dichotomies—that between facts and norms and that between actus reus and mens rea—which play such a fundamental role in the ideology, the doctrine, and the institutional structure of criminal law.

The second feature of ordinary causal language that has been observed is an equal source of trouble for the legal use of causal terminology. There is a fatal ambiguity in presenting the jury with a question such as "Did A cause B's death?" as one of the determinative factors in reaching a verdict. On the one hand, this question may be meant to be neutral as between the various descriptive forms previously identified as current in ordinary speech. It may aim at some minimal common denominator, allegedly present in all the events considered, to the exclusion of those factors that in ordinary speech lead to the tendency to distinguish between those descriptions and to choose one over the others. On the other hand, the question, so posed, is likely to be interpreted by the jury, consciously or unconsciously, as taking sides in the competition among the various descriptive candidates, choosing one particular descriptive form over the others as adequate for the purpose of imposing criminal liability.

If this is the interpretation that the members of the jury give to the instruction phrased in causal terms, then their judgment will indeed be colored by the entire array of considerations that usually would lead one to adopt the particular descriptive language used in the instruction. In other words, by being asked to decide whether A caused B's death, the jury may see itself invited to decide whether the case under consideration would be most adequately captured by description (2) as opposed to description (1) or descriptions (3)–(5) on the list above. Whether the instruction to the jury is given in one or the other of the various descriptive formulas ("Did A kill B?" or "Did A cause B's death?" or "Did B die as a result of A's actions?" and so forth) is, accordingly, likely to influence their substantive judgment in the case at hand. Although it is possible that the imposition of a criminal sanction is always appropriate only when all the relevant factors lead to the adoption of description (2) ("Did A cause B's death?"), there is no reason to believe that this indeed is the case, nor that such a determination underlies the use of the term *cause* in the law.

The same problem, viewed from the perspective of the lawyer or legal scholar, helps account for the elusiveness of the concept of causation, an elusiveness that frustrates his attempt to define it. As this discussion suggests, the lawyer's "concept of causation" resists definition and uniform application because it is a mere phantom that conceals a wide range of linguistic forms, each with its different meaning and set of implied considerations and connotations. Although the various legal "tests" can capture with some degree of accuracy one or another of these linguistic forms, one should not expect any single definition or test adequately to render their entire range.

MEIR DAN COHEN

See also ATTEMPT; HOMICIDE: LEGAL ASPECTS; PUNISHMENT.

BIBLIOGRAPHY

American Law Institute. *Model Penal Code: Proposed Official Draft.* Philadelphia: ALI, 1962.

EDGERTON, HENRY W. "Legal Cause." *University of Pennsylvania Law Review* 72 (1924): 211–244, 343–375.

FLETCHER, GEORGE P. *Rethinking Criminal Law.* Boston: Little, Brown, 1978.

HALL, JEROME. *General Principles of Criminal Law.* 2d ed. Indianapolis: Bobbs-Merrill, 1960.

HART, H. L. A., and HONORÉ, A. M. *Causation in the Law.* Oxford: Oxford University Press, Clarendon Press, 1959.

LAFAVE, WAYNE R., and SCOTT, AUSTIN W., JR. *Handbook on Criminal Law.* St. Paul: West, 1972.

MORRIS, NORVAL, and HOWARD, COLIN. *Studies in Criminal Law.* Oxford: Oxford University Press, Clarendon Press, 1964.

MUELLER, GERHARD O. W. "Causing Criminal Harm." *Essays in Criminal Science.* Edited by Gerhard O. W. Mueller. South Hackensack, N.J.: Rothman, 1961, pp. 169–214.

PERKINS, ROLLIN M. *Criminal Law.* 2d ed. Mineola, N.Y.: Foundation Press, 1969.

RYU, PAUL K. "Causation in Criminal Law." *University of Pennsylvania Law Review* 106 (1958): 773–805.

SCHULHOFER, STEPHEN J. "Harm and Punishment: A Critique of Emphasis on the Results of Conduct in the Criminal Law." *University of Pennsylvania Law Review* 122 (1974): 1497–1607.

U.S. National Commission on Reform of Federal Criminal Laws. *Working Papers,* vol. 1. Washington, D.C.: The Commission, 1970.

WILLIAMS, GLANVILLE. "Causation in Homicide." *Criminal Law Review* (1957): 429–440, 510–521.

———. "Causation in the Law." *Cambridge Law Journal* (1961): 62–85.

———. *Textbook of Criminal Law.* London: Stevens, 1978.

CENSORSHIP

See LIBEL, CRIMINAL; *both articles under* OBSCENITY AND PORNOGRAPHY; SEDITION.

CENSORSHIP, PRISON

See PRISONERS, LEGAL RIGHTS OF.

CERTAINTY OF PUNISHMENT

See DETERRENCE.

CHARGING

The charging decision is a determination of whether a person should be formally accused of a crime and thus subjected to trial if he does not first plead guilty. In minor cases, most notably those involving lesser traffic offenses, this decision is commonly made exclusively by police. The ticket given the violator serves as the charge, and the case goes directly to court for trial or plea without prosecutorial review. In other cases the prosecutor plays the central role, with the police nonetheless exercising considerable influence in both a negative and positive sense. The overwhelming majority of cases that reach the prosecutor are brought to his attention by police after they have made an arrest, a decision as to which they exercise vast and largely uncontrolled discretion. Thus, if in a particular instance an officer decides not to arrest, doubting whether the evidence is sufficient or whether any good purpose would be served by invoking the criminal process, he has in effect virtually assured that there will be no prosecution. As for positive influence, police sometimes accomplish this by an especially solid presentation of their evidence or by articulation of some law enforcement interest that presumably would be served by prosecution.

In many locales certain crimes such as nonsupport and the passing of bad checks are unlikely to come to official attention unless reported directly to the prosecutor by a concerned citizen. Here again, a decision not to bring the matter before the prosecutor virtually assures no charge. As for positive influence, in these kinds of cases (and to a lesser extent in cases first handled by the police) the complainant may prompt a charge by expressing strong interest in, or promising full cooperation in, the prosecution.

In most jurisdictions there are institutional checks upon the prosecutor's charging power in serious cases, so that he exercises this power affirmatively only with the concurrence of another agency. In the federal system as a Fifth Amendment requirement, and in half the states as a matter of state law, a felony charge must be approved by a grand jury unless the defendant has waived that right. And unless the grand jury has first acted, most jurisdictions require that a felony charge be approved by a judicial officer at a preliminary hearing, again unless the defendant has waived that protection.

Various charging documents are used, depending upon the circumstances. An indictment is prepared by the prosecutor and then endorsed by the grand jury when it approves the prosecutor's decision to charge. An "information" is signed under oath by the prosecutor; it is used when the defendant has waived, or when the law otherwise does not require, indictment. A complaint, sworn to by some other person with knowledge of the offense, often a policeman but sometimes a victim or witness, is a sufficient charging document for minor offenses in most jurisdictions and is also used as a temporary charge in those cases awaiting grand jury action.

The charging decision will frequently entail consideration of the following: (1) whether there is sufficient evidence to support a prosecution; (2) if so, whether there are nonetheless reasons for not further subjecting the defendant to the criminal process; (3) if so, whether nonprosecution should be conditioned upon the defendant's participation in a diversion program; and (4) if prosecution is to be undertaken, what offense or offenses should be charged.

As for the first of these, it is commonly said that a prosecutor should institute a charge only if it is "supported by probable cause" (American Bar Association). Presumably this means something more than the probable cause required for police to arrest, which is based upon "the factual and practical considerations of everyday life on which reasonable and prudent men, not legal technicians, act" (*Brinegar v. United States*, 338 U.S. 160 (1949)). The prosecutor, as a legal technician, often will have to consider whether his charge will withstand review by the grand jury or preliminary hearing judge, and therefore the standard imposed by law on these agencies might be viewed as the evidentiary test for charging. In some jurisdictions that standard is "probable cause," a substantial likelihood that the defendant committed the crime, while in others it is a "prima facie case," evidence that if unexplained would allow a finding at trial of guilt beyond a reasonable doubt. But as a practical matter a prosecutor is likely to require evidence indicating a high probability of conviction, since he is interested in having an impressive conviction record and in not wasting his limited trial resources.

As for the second question, it is important to recognize that American prosecutors have traditionally exercised considerable discretion in deciding whether as a matter of enforcement policy prosecution is called for in a given case. There are various reasons why this is so: (1) because of legislative "overcriminalization," the tendency of legislatures to make conduct criminal without regard to enforceability or changing social mores; (2) because of limitations in available enforcement resources and the prosecutor's need to use the scarce resources of his office and other agencies not randomly but in a way that will be most effective; and (3) because of a need to individualize justice, as where the mere fact of prosecution would be unduly harmful in light of the mitigating circumstances. If the prosecutor fails to charge for one of these reasons, the grand jury and preliminary hearing judge will not be involved, but this does not mean they will never confront such issues. A grand jury, sometimes acting in concurrence with the prosecutor's wishes and sometimes in opposition to them, may refuse to indict a defendant against whom there is ample evidence because of a belief that prosecution would result in a miscarriage of justice. A preliminary hearing judge is supposed to be concerned only with evidence sufficiency, but on occasion a finding of insufficiency may mask a decision that prosecution is unwarranted for some other reason.

The third question has to do with whether some middle ground between prosecution and no action would be appropriate. Diversion is "the disposition of a criminal complaint without a conviction, the noncriminal disposition being conditioned on either the performance of specified obligations by the defendant, or his participation in counseling or treatment" (National District Attorneys Association). The diversion alternative is sensible only if sufficient community resources are available and are utilized in instances that otherwise should have resulted in prosecution.

As for charge selection, sometimes it is simply a matter of whether the charge should be of a greater or lesser crime—for example, felony burglary versus misdemeanor breaking and entering. This involves judgments about both evidence sufficiency (whether the greater crime can be proved at trial) and enforcement policy (whether prosecution for the greater crime would be unduly harmful to this defendant). However, sometimes the prosecutor will initially charge a defendant with a higher offense than can be proved or than would be "just," hoping to use that charge as leverage to obtain a guilty plea to a lesser crime. When the defendant has committed a series of crimes over time or has violated several criminal statutes on one occasion, the prosecutor must decide how many charges to bring. Resort to multiple charges is most common when undertaken to encourage a plea of guilty to one of the crimes or when deemed necessary to provide the judge with a sufficient range of sentencing options.

WAYNE R. LaFAVE

See also GRAND JURY; *both articles under* GUILTY PLEA; INFORMAL DISPOSITION; PROSECUTION: PROSECUTORIAL DISCRETION.

BIBLIOGRAPHY

American Bar Association. *Code of Professional Responsibility*, DR 7-103(A). Chicago: ABA, 1969.
ARENELLA, PETER. "Reforming the Federal Grand Jury and the State Preliminary Hearing to Prevent Conviction without Adjudication." *Michigan Law Review* 78 (1980): 463–585.
LaFAVE, WAYNE R. "The Prosecutor's Discretion in the

United States." *American Journal of Comparative Law* 18 (1970): 532–548.

MILLER, FRANK W. *Prosecution: The Decision to Charge a Suspect with a Crime.* American Bar Foundation Administration of Criminal Justice Series. Edited by Frank J. Remington. Boston: Little, Brown, 1970.

————, and REMINGTON, FRANK J. "Procedures before Trial." *Annals of the American Academy of Political and Social Science* 339 (1962): 111–124.

MILLS, RICHARD. "The Prosecutor: Charging and Bargaining." *University of Illinois Law Forum* (1966): 511–522.

National District Attorneys Association. *National Prosecution Standards.* Chicago: The Association, 1977, p. 152.

NIMMER, RAYMOND T. *Diversion: The Search for Alternative Forms of Prosecution.* Chicago: American Bar Foundation, 1974.

CHILD ABUSE

See VIOLENCE IN THE FAMILY: CHILD ABUSE.

CHILDREN, CRIMINAL ACTIVITIES OF

Whereas a great deal of public and professional attention is focused on the serious, violent, and other criminal activities of people variously described as youthful offenders, teenagers, adolescents, or juveniles, little study has been made of crime committed by pubescent or prepubescent children. The public learns of such events, including particularly murder, as individual instances that reach the newspapers from time to time, with anonymity often shielding the child from the glare of publicity. When the offense is less chilling than homicide or forcible rape, those learning of burglaries or bank robberies committed by a child, not yet five feet tall and perhaps still counting the years with single digits, react as if it were a caper unworthy of serious consideration.

Adolescence and the teenage years are widely regarded as difficult, and youths of those ages are seen as sometimes ungovernable, irascible, rebellious, and likely to experiment with alcohol and drugs. Yet the preteen remains as though robed in a cloak of pristine innocence. Malevolent activities are not expected, and if they surface, they must be treated as deriving from a mind incapable of knowing the nature and gravity of the act. If this attitude is successful in protecting the child of three or four years of age who might cause serious injury or even death to a sibling or playmate, it cannot easily be extended to exculpate the child between the ages of, say, eight and twelve.

The age of seven was traditionally the minimum at which criminal responsibility was assigned to a child, and by age twelve or thirteen (depending upon the time, jurisdiction, and nature of the offense) the child had reached the point where delicts qualified him for the status of juvenile delinquent. The age grouping in between remained a legal arena in limbo, recognized since the seventeenth century as a period of at least diminished culpability. Prior to the age of seven, it was considered unlikely that a child had mentally progressed enough to comprehend the nature of a criminal action; after the onset of the teenage years, it was assumed that both physical and mental maturity had progressed, if not to the reasoning power of adulthood, then at least to the point where adult responsibility could be imputed, perhaps only as a legal fiction necessary for social defense.

During the years between early childhood and the first signs of maturation, the law, although not totally absolving the perpetrator of legal guilt, permitted a youth to claim that the innocence of years mitigated any criminal intent. Judges were not required to accept the claim and could even impose the most severe penalties, such as death, if deemed appropriate, although in fact they seldom did.

Extent and nature of child criminality. Persons twelve years old and under constitute approximately 19 percent of the total population of the United States. From this figure, one ought properly to eliminate all those who have not reached their seventh birthday, leaving about 9 percent of the population in the category under study. Those ten and under accounted for some 0.8 percent of arrests in an average year in the late 1970s and early 1980s (the years on which the findings here are based), according to the Federal Bureau of Investigation's Uniform Crime Reports. Children aged eleven and twelve were responsible for 1.4 percent of arrests, with the figure rising each succeeding year until the age of eighteen and then leveling off. Clearly, the group under the age of thirteen had not yet developed its potential for criminality.

Most of the arrests are for status offenses (acts that are not crimes if committed by an adult), for disorderly conduct, or for "all other offenses (except traffic)," and one might assume that serious criminality is not concealed behind such labels. Of somewhat more than two hundred thousand arrests of children twelve years old and under in one typical year, more than one-fourth may be eliminated because the children were apprehended as runaways, for curfew or loitering violations, or on some charge where one had little reason to suspect serious criminality. There were more than twenty-nine thousand arrests in this age group for vandalism, but dismaying as such acts are, they probably do not represent a major danger for society.

Other data do not lead to sanguine conclusions about the innocence of these children. Some twelve hundred of them were arrested in a typical year on weapons charges, and even though this makes up slightly less than 1 percent of persons of all ages booked for this crime, it is nonetheless particularly chilling to contemplate children of such tender years with deadly weapons in their possession. Similarly frightening is a figure of about two hundred arrests of children not yet thirteen years of age on the charge of drunken driving.

In a more serious category, children who have not yet reached their thirteenth birthday are strongly represented in arrests for property crime, particularly larceny-theft, and they account for a considerable number of burglaries. Children of twelve and under commit a surprising proportion of automobile thefts, although in some instances they may have been accomplices of an older youth. They account for one out of six arson arrests, but as one might not expect, in a single and not atypical year, children ten and under accounted for fourteen arrests for murder and non-negligent homicide, and sixty-six for forcible rape—a small number, and certainly a minute percentage compared to older youths, yet not small when the age of the perpetrator is considered.

It is difficult to know whether the data in the Uniform Crime Reports exaggerate or understate the extent of the involvement of children in serious criminality. On the one hand, the likelihood of a child criminal avoiding apprehension is far less than that of an older youthful offender or an adult. The child does not have the mental acumen, physical agility, or strength required to carry out crimes with the success of older persons. Many childhood crimes are crudely executed, and arrest is speedily accomplished. By contrast, for most crimes other than murder, a child is more likely than an adult to be chastised, perhaps reported to parents, and diverted to a counseling center. In one fashion or another, arrests and serious charges tend to be avoided.

What types of incidents constitute serious childhood crimes? The murders have frequently been of family members or playmates. Murdered parents were usually reported to have been strict, and the child's resentment was strong. Homicidal children fall into two categories, almost polar opposites: some had been chronically angry, destructive, violent, and threatening; others had been quiet, subdued, withdrawn, and ready to explode, but without any outward signs of their inner turmoil. Other than the murders that crop up in newspaper reports from time to time, little is known of the young people who find their way into crime statistics in the youngest of recorded age groups.

Etiology. The phenomenon of serious child criminality has not yet been sufficiently studied for conclusions to be drawn as to causation. Clinicians, whose reports are based on a few in-depth case histories, have made several suggestions, including inborn predilection for violence, the effects of television violence on the young, or early manifestations of psychopathy or sociopathy. The lower age of onset of puberty, which appears to have dropped by a full year since the turn of the century, might account for increased violent crime, particularly rape, in preteen children. The notion of a "bad seed," once popularized on American stage and screen, is hardly proved, for it was based on a biological determinism that is today disdained by almost all criminologists who are biologically oriented. Evidence of the appearance of psychopathological symptoms at an early age is similarly not forthcoming, based at least on follow-up studies that sometimes reveal good adult adjustment (Robins), unless one postulates psychopathology as a childhood phenomenon that might be outgrown.

In some, but not all instances, the child appears not to have understood the enormity of his act or, in the case of murder, its irreversibility. In fact, Jean Piaget has asserted that the finality of death is beyond the conception of small children. For predatory and property crimes, as well as holdups and burglaries, it may be suggested that there is an epidemiology to crime, and that as it increases it takes on a dynamism of its own. Growing from its own momentum, it extends to new groups hitherto much less represented in the ranks of offenders, including women, rural dwellers, and children. Thus, crimes such as chronic mugging, robbery, and burglary may be understood as part of the ambience surrounding the children, although generally perpetrated by older youths, who may be subcultural role models for the children. For other types of crimes, clinicians may have a great deal to offer, despite heavy reliance upon case-study analyses. Such analysis, however, does not permit confident generalizations, since there is no way to determine if the particular offenders are representative of their kind.

Not unexpectedly, clinical researchers have focused on the relatively infrequent but particularly aggressive violent child-offender. Some clinicians find that homicidal aggression is usually characterized by intense impulsiveness, a conclusion evident in studies of children who kill (Sorrells). A psychiatrist, Henry DeYoung, noting that the majority of adult homicides are committed among family members or close acquaintances, said that the same was true of childhood homicides. They are almost invariably sudden explosions that could not have been predicted.

Nevertheless, it is unlikely that impulsiveness is sufficient to explain the gamut of violent outbursts. At times, researchers have suggested that violence-prone children either suffer from a severe neurological or psychological disturbance, usually labeled as psychopathy or schizophrenia, or that they manifest extreme antisocial behavior characterized by aggressiveness, assaultiveness, temper outbursts, and arson (Adams; Bender and Curran; Conklin; McQuaid). In addition, a propensity to torture small animals, and significantly lower intelligence quotients, have been consistently found in the behavior of youngsters who act out their aggressive desires (Felthous; Hays, Solway, and Schreiner).

By contrast, some researchers report that homicidally aggressive youths are indistinguishable in their psychological makeup from other youths (Adams; Washbrook). They attribute aggression to deprivation of parental love, sibling rivalry, or family situations in which destructive reactions are unconsciously programmed into the child. These researchers conclude that although the act itself may have been situationally impulsive, the motivation behind it probably was not.

Research on the etiology of crime may be of importance for those studying serious child offenders, since it is these children who respond with particular intensity to the turbulent processes associated with maturation. Many findings concerning the intricacy of these phenomena have been reported. For example, in *Vulnerabilities to Delinquency*, Dorothy Lewis and other authors examine much of the available medical research on genetic, endocrine, and neurochemical disorders in relation to early delinquency patterns. Some of these disorders have been linked to particularly serious criminality because of their apparent connection with biologically controlled aggressive tendencies. The psychological disorder perhaps most directly associated with antisocial behavior problems, although these may not necessarily be serious, is hyperactivity. This disorder, called ADDH (attentional deficit disorder with hyperactivity) by medical professionals, is often characterized by excessive motor activity and an inability to concentrate for even brief periods of time.

Both these factors may be influential in the development of delinquent tendencies, possibly as a result of an interruption of normal learning processes and an early identification as a "troublemaker." Of particular interest, too, is the timing of the onset of ADDH and the effects of the biological transformation on actual behavior. The disorder appears most visibly in the prepubescent years, and certain physiological functions occurring at this time, such as the increase in hormonal production, have been linked to aggressiveness. Thus, as the child responds to physiological functions, he may also begin to suffer from the early stigmatization associated with hyperactivity.

Reaction: punishment, therapy, and outlook. Diminished responsibility is generally assumed for children under a given age, and this is expressed by the view that they cannot be tried or punished as adults. In New York State, children aged thirteen and over can be tried as adults for homicide and a few other major crimes, but such trial, and subsequent punishment, are seldom invoked. The United States Supreme Court, in its landmark decision *In re Gault*, 387 U.S. 1 (1967), ruled that children accused of delinquent or criminal acts are entitled to representation by counsel and other constitutional rights. This decision notwithstanding, children nevertheless generally continue to be processed rather than tried, constitutional safeguards are few (but anonymity is protected), and children can be sent to juvenile detention centers, homes, industrial schools, or other facilities for periods extending to their twenty-first birthday.

In such centers, the individual therapy that many criminal youths require is seldom forthcoming. Where therapy is offered, results have often been promising. However, it is sometimes suspected that the youths who respond to this therapy are those who have made a single serious error and whose greatest problem will be in adjustment to life with memories of their crime and the burden of their guilt. This is particularly true of family and other homicides.

Although preteen children are not likely to lose their historical protection from the harshest of punishments, increased institutional time may well begin to replace alternative dispositions, such as probation. Some will argue that this is desirable since it eliminates the putative mollycoddling of past practices. But the findings of cohort studies, in conjunction with fiscal frugality and a widespread pessimism about rehabilitative efforts, suggest that these criminal children may well carry the stigma of the public's vengeance into their later careers of crime.

EDWARD SAGARIN
ALLAN SHORE

See also AGE AND CRIME; EXCUSE: INFANCY; FAMILY RELATIONSHIPS AND CRIME; *articles under* JUVENILE JUSTICE; JUVENILE STATUS OFFENDERS; SCHOOLS, CRIME IN THE; YOUTH GANGS AND GROUPS.

BIBLIOGRAPHY

ADAMS, KATHRYN A. "The Child Who Murders: A Review of Theory and Research." *Criminal Justice and Behavior* 1 (1974): 51–61.

BENDER, LAURETTA. "Children and Adolescents Who Have Killed." *American Journal of Psychiatry* 116 (1959): 510–513.

——, and CURRAN, FRANK J. "Children and Adolescents Who Kill." *Journal of Criminal Psychopathology* 1 (1940): 297–322.

CONKLIN, EDMUND S. *Principles of Adolescent Psychology.* New York: Holt, 1935.

DEYOUNG, HENRY. "Homicide (Children's Division)." *Human Behavior* 5, no. 2 (1976): 16–21.

Federal Bureau of Investigation. *Crime in the United States. Uniform Crime Reports for the United States.* Washington, D.C.: U.S. Department of Justice, FBI, annually.

FELTHOUS, ALAN R. "Aggression against Cats, Dogs, and People." *Child Psychiatry and Human Development* 10 (1980): 169–177.

HAYS, J. RAY; SOLWAY, KENNETH S.; and SCHREINER, DONNA. "Intellectual Characteristics of Juvenile Murderers versus Status Offenders." *Psychological Reports* 43 (1978): 80–82.

LEWIS, DOROTHY O., ed. *Vulnerabilities to Delinquency.* New York: SP Medical and Scientific Books, 1981.

MCQUAID, P. E. "Child Criminals?" *Irish Medical Journal* 71 (1978): 515–518.

PIAGET, JEAN. *The Language and Thought of the Child* (1926). 3d ed., rev. and enlarged. Preface by E. Claparède. Translated by Marjorie Gabain. New York: Humanities Press, 1959.

ROBINS, LEE N. *Deviant Children Grown Up: A Sociological and Psychiatric Study of Sociopathic Personality.* Baltimore: Williams & Wilkins, 1966.

SORRELLS, JAMES M. "Kids Who Kill." *Crime and Delinquency* 23 (1977): 312–320.

WASHBROOK, R. A. H. "Bereavement Leading to Murder." *International Journal of Offender Therapy and Comparative Criminology* 23 (1979): 57–64.

WOLFGANG, MARVIN E.; FIGLIO, ROBERT M.; and SELLIN, THORSTEN. *Delinquency in a Birth Cohort.* University of Chicago Press, 1972.

ZENOFF, ELYCE H., and ZIENTS, ALAN B. "Juvenile Murderers: Should the Punishment Fit the Crime?" *International Journal of Law and Psychiatry* 2 (1979): 533–553.

CHILDREN, RIGHTS OF

See articles under JUVENILE JUSTICE; POLICE: HANDLING OF JUVENILES.

CHINESE LAW

See COMPARATIVE CRIMINAL LAW AND ENFORCEMENT: CHINA.

CHOICE OF EVILS

See JUSTIFICATION, *articles on* NECESSITY *and* THEORY.

CITIES AND CRIME

See ECOLOGY OF CRIME; URBAN CRIME; YOUTH GANGS AND GROUPS.

CIVIL COMMITMENT

See articles under DRUGS AND CRIME; EXCUSE: INSANITY.

CIVIL DEATH

See CONVICTION: CIVIL DISABILITIES.

CIVIL DISABILITIES

See CONVICTION: CIVIL DISABILITIES.

CIVIL DISOBEDIENCE

See JUSTIFICATION, *articles on* NECESSITY *and* THEORY.

CLASS AND CRIME

Introduction. For centuries, ideas on the etiology of crime have had a "wealth" component. Wealth includes any number of socioeconomic class or status indicators, among them family income, education, occupation, neighborhood status, and receipt of welfare payments. Crime refers to events prohibited by the criminal law. As noted below, how and what one chooses to define as criminal have a great impact on the magnitude and even the direction of the crime-status relation.

In 1916, Willem Bonger (1876–1940) asserted that Thomas More (1478–1535), the author of *Utopia*, was the first to relate crime and economic conditions in a "scientific way." Whether or not Bonger was correct, it is clear that belief in the causal relationship of poverty and crime has been popular for centuries. The most influential modern source of this view, of course, was Karl Marx (1818–1883), and Bonger was a leading

Marxist criminologist. An important question is how well this view squares with available data.

The systematic collection of data on offenses, arrests, and convictions began in Europe in the early nineteenth century, pioneered by Adolphe Quételet (1796–1874). Almost at the outset of his inquiry, Quételet applied literary and occupational measures of social status to offenders (pp. 84–85). The lack of such data for the general population prevented accurate assessments of class-crime relationships, but that did not dissuade Quételet from concluding that the greatest number of crimes take place among the lower classes (p. 85).

Ecological correlates from official data. In the United States, crime and delinquency were studied primarily as an outgrowth of work conducted on the more general topic of urban ecology by William I. Thomas, Robert Park, Ernest Burgess, Louis Wirth, and others at the University of Chicago early in the twentieth century. Frederic Thrasher's seven-year observational study of 1,313 gangs in Chicago located them on Burgess's concentric rings model of urban growth in order to illustrate the gangs' concentration in the poverty belt: "a region characterized by deteriorating neighborhoods, shifting populations, and the mobility and disorganization of the slum. . . . This zone is a distinctly interstitial phase of the city's growth. . . . As better residential areas recede before the encroachments of business and industry, the gang develops as one manifestation of the economic, moral, and cultural frontier which marks the interstice" (pp. 20–31). Actually, Thrasher seemed to use the term *gang* as a synonym for lower-class delinquents who resided in deteriorating neighborhoods, or slums.

Almost simultaneously with Thrasher's work, studies were made by Clifford Shaw and Henry McKay (1931) for the United States National Commission on Law Observance and Enforcement. Although Shaw and McKay came from the same urban-studies tradition at the University of Chicago as Thrasher, his work was almost entirely qualitative, whereas theirs was quantitatively and graphically oriented. Shaw and McKay presented data from several cities, but primarily from Chicago, where they used three main sources: (1) more than nine thousand alleged delinquent boys dealt with by police probation officers in 1926; (2) more than eight thousand alleged delinquent boys brought before the juvenile court of Cook County from 1917 to 1923; and (3) more than twenty-five hundred delinquent boys committed to correctional institutions in Cook County between 1917 and 1923. Rates were calculated as the percentage of all boys ten through sixteen years of age alleged to be delinquents.

Shaw and McKay were able to obtain "rates of family dependency"—measures based on the proportion of families in each city area receiving financial aid—in 113 one-mile-square areas of Chicago, grouped into five categories. They found, for example, that among the more than eight thousand boys in their 1917–1923 juvenile court series, the ecological coefficient of correlation between family dependency and court appearance was in excess of .7 (1931, p. 77). (This coefficient indicates the extent to which one statistic can be predicted by another. It varies from zero for no relationship to 1.0 for perfect prediction, but is preceded by a minus sign if the prediction is inverse, that is, if the higher the rate is for one statistic, the lower the rate is for the other. The coefficient of .7 indicates that rates of court appearance for the city areas can be predicted quite well by the rates of family dependency for these areas.) Another measure of dependency available to them was children in families who had received financial aid under the Mothers Pension Act during the period from 1917 to 1923; its ecological correlation with rates of delinquency across the 113 areas was .6.

In their subsequent work, *Juvenile Delinquency and Urban Areas,* Shaw and McKay examined and updated other indexes of economic status in Chicago, as well as Philadelphia, Boston, Cincinnati, Cleveland, and Richmond, Virginia. These correlations were often computed across 140 one-mile-square areas of Chicago without categorizing them into a small number of groups, as had been done in their earlier work. They found, for example, that the correlation between the percentage of families on relief in 1934 in these areas and the rates of delinquency from the 1927–1933 juvenile court series was .89, whereas median monthly rentals were correlated −.61 and homeownership −.49 with the same rates of delinquency (1969, pp. 148–152).

Up to this point, discussion has been limited to the association between various indicators of socioeconomic status and rates of delinquency across *areas.* Such correlations more often than not overestimate the magnitude of the relation found when the unit of analysis shifts to the individual; for rare types of events, such as serious crime, they can even be spurious, a phenomenon known in statistics as the "ecological fallacy."

Individual correlates from official data. As used here, official data include police contacts or arrests, court appearances, and sentences meted out by the courts, ranging from probation to imprisonment.

Bonger presented a systematic theory of the causes of crime, arguing that capitalist societies were held together not by consensus but rather by force and that the ruling and the ruled were sorted out by the system of production, which is often characterized by unrestrained competition:

I have already spoken of the influence exercised by bad material surroundings on a man's character; I have pointed out the moral consequences of bad housing conditions, and also that he becomes embittered and malicious through the lack of the necessaries of life. All this applies to the proletariat in general, but much more strongly still to those who do not succeed, for any reason, in selling their labor, that is the lower proletariat. . . . All the statistics cited show then that the poor supply a very great proportion of convicts, in every case a greater proportion than they bear to the general population, and the well-to-do form only a small part [p. 435].

Empirical support for concluding that a link existed between class and crime was mustered by Bonger from citations to educational and occupational characteristics of prison inmates compared to those of the general population (p. 425). He showed, for example, that of more than eighty thousand prisoners held in the United States and counted by the Bureau of the Census for the 1890 census, nearly one-fourth were classified as illiterate, as contrasted with 13 percent of the general population over the age of ten. These findings were replicated for many European countries as well (pp. 407–447). Thus, Bonger demonstrated that an inverse relation between class and crime at the individual level existed when imprisonment was used as the crime criterion.

Using a quite different official measure of crime, rearrest of felons released from prisons, Richard Berk, Kenneth Lenihan, and Peter Rossi (1980) analyzed samples of more than two thousand ex-offenders from Georgia and Texas in an experimental group that received $60 per week if unemployed after release from prison. Berk and his associates found that arrests under conditions of unemployment increased for both property and nonproperty offenses, but that "payments appear to reduce arrests." These findings led them to conclude that "poverty is apparently causally related to crime at the individual level" (p. 784).

Thus, statistical studies using very diverse official criteria have been employed for the last century and a half to study the class-crime relation. But for a variety of reasons—not the least of which is the potential for class-related biases to enter at every stage in the criminal justice system—many sociologists have been dissatisfied with all official criteria.

In the mid-1950s, F. Ivan Nye and James Short published the first class-focused systematic analyses of juvenile delinquency using as a criterion a variable other than an official record. They surveyed high-school students, asking them to check on a list of delinquent acts those in which they had been involved, whether or not these violations ever came to the attention of law enforcement officials. The use of this "self-report" method increased substantially thereafter, so much so that researchers interested in questions relating to the causes of crime have virtually abandoned their earlier sole reliance on arrest and other official indicators of juvenile or criminal conduct.

Early research on the class-crime relationship using official individual-level data was limited. In fact, John Braithwaite's comprehensive review of the American literature on this topic prior to the 1957 Nye and Short article found only four studies of juvenile delinquency and five of adult crime that used official statistics on individuals. All these studies showed ". . . lower class juveniles to have substantially higher offense rates than middle class juveniles. Among adults, all . . . studies found lower class people to have higher crime rates" (p. 38). Since the publication of Nye and Short's work, much more research using official criteria for both juveniles and adults has been completed. In the American studies of juveniles using an official criterion reported by Braithwaite, slightly less than one-third did not show substantial differences between lower-class and middle-class youth; among adults, the studies he reported were unanimous in showing lower-class adults to be more criminal than the other social-class groups.

What might account for this disagreement between the studies using official criteria for juveniles and adults since the mid-1950s? Perhaps the most plausible hypothesis is that juveniles do not have to do much in order to appear on "official" records. From the late 1950s through the 1970s, juveniles appeared on police blotters, and were even incarcerated in institutions, for offenses as innocuous as truancy, running away from home, or violating liquor laws. On the other hand, the behavior required for an adult to be noticed and reacted to is generally much more serious. As prisons become more crowded, the threshold point required for officials to notice and take action on adult lawbreaking can be expected to rise even higher. Thus, offense seriousness is central to this issue.

Individual correlates from survey data for juveniles. It is useful to examine the reliability and validity of the self-report as a source of offense data. Reliability—the extent to which an instrument consistently gives the same results—has been shown to be in the generally acceptable range for psychological tests.

The most common methods of assessing reliability, such as test-retest, have produced correlation coefficients in the .8 to .9 range, strongly suggesting that respondents report *consistently* on their norm-violating behavior.

More difficult to determine is the validity of the responses given, that is, their overall accuracy. A comparison of information reported by the respondent with that available from some other source, such as police or court records and reports from teachers or friends, suggests that the correlation between rates from the two sources is often as high as .5 to .7 among whites. At the same time there is evidence to support the view that among blacks, especially black males, the accuracy of self-reports may be substantially lower (Hindelang, Hirschi, and Weis). The implications of this possible differential validity by race require further investigation, particularly in light of the relationship between race and social class.

The most advantageous aspect of the survey procedure for studying correlates of law violation among juveniles is that the survey can be collected independently of official data and of any biases that might be introduced by the use of official indicators—police contact, arrest, probation, institutionalization, or any other record of government actions. From an etiological perspective, the least advantageous aspect of the survey procedure for this purpose is the fact that serious lawbreaking is only rarely reported with sufficient frequency for the required analyses in the relatively small samples typically used in these surveys. This is particularly true in mixed class, race, or sex samples, especially if there is no attempt made to select the most crime-prone cases within strata.

Nye and Short reported that eleven of their twenty-three offenses, included in the research of most subsequent investigators, formed a scale of increasing degree of delinquency, but four of the most serious were reported too infrequently among the high-school students to remain in the scale: running away, stealing items of medium value (between $2 and $50), stealing items of large value (more than $50), and selling narcotics. Items retained included stealing small items (worth less than $2), buying or drinking beer, and having heterosexual intercourse. None of these offenses placed higher than 125 out of 140 offenses ranked for perceived seriousness by the public in a national survey made in the early 1980s (Hindelang, Hirschi, and Weis).

Perhaps the best-known national self-report surveys are those conducted by Martin Gold in 1967 and 1972 (Williams and Gold; Gold and Reimer). The first was a national probability sample of about eight hundred

fifty youths thirteen to sixteen years of age and diverse in social class. Fewer than thirty-four cases (4 percent) had police records—too few to expect many serious offenses. Yet throughout the text, Jay Williams and Gold used social class to contrast the correlates of *official* delinquency on the one hand and the correlates of self-reports of delinquency *behavior* on the other (pp. 210, 211, 217). They compared police contact and court appearance statistics of official delinquency to their self-reported delinquent behavior and reported—virtually without comment—that none had any statistically significant relationship to social status, as measured by occupation of parents.

In Gold's latter study the average number of cases was fewer than 100 in each of his three categories of social class tabulated separately for boys and girls, which is too small in a general population survey to generate the number of cases of serious delinquent behavior (such as drug use, larcenies, burglaries, and robberies) required for meaningful analysis. As in the earlier study, Gold and David Reimer found that parent's occupation, as a measure of social class, had little significant relationship to rates of self-reported delinquent behavior.

Delbert Elliott and Suzanne Ageton have reported national survey results on a panel study of 1,726 youths (less than three-fourths of those originally selected to be sampled), eleven to seventeen years old and heterogeneous in sex, race, and class. They were contacted between January and March 1977 regarding offenses committed during 1976. The total self-reported delinquency scale has several subscales: predatory crimes against persons, predatory crimes against property, illegal service offenses (such as prostitution), public disorder offenses, hard-drug use, and juvenile status offenses (such as truancy).

The results presented for "lower," "working," and "middle" class groups differed significantly on the total delinquency scale and the subscale for predatory crimes against persons, but were related to none of the other five subscales. Without information on sex and age effects, however, it is difficult to reach confident conclusions about the effects of social class from these data on self-reported delinquency.

John Johnstone has published the results of a questionnaire survey for data collected from about twelve hundred adolescents in more than 220 census tracts of the Chicago metropolitan area. Responses were cross-tabulated by status of *area* and family status of the *individual* respondent, using educational, occupational, and income indicators. Hence, this procedure uses both ecological- and individual-level measures. Johnstone reported that for no type of crime was the rate of self-reported illegal behavior highest for lower-class persons living in lower-class areas. Although the highest scores on all seven of his indexes were reported by the lowest-status persons, rates for aggressive behavior, theft offenses without violence, robbery, and drug use were highest among lower-class persons residing in middle-class areas. The rates of status violations, automobile thefts, and Uniform Crime Reports offenses and arrests were highest among lower-class respondents living in high-status areas. The author has suggested that these findings indicate that some mechanism such as the relative deprivation of a person in comparison to others living in the same area (rather than the absolute level of deprivation) may account for the distribution of results. In any event, the data suggested that the class-delinquency relationship may be much more complex than typically portrayed in sociological theory.

Some further methodological criticisms of these studies include the following:

1. Doubts as to the validity of the father's occupation as an index of occupations across communities: a "salesperson" in a poor neighborhood may be a minimum-wage store clerk, and a "salesperson" in an upper-class neighborhood may be an affluent seller of luxury properties; similarly, a "professional" may be a low-paid barber or a high-income physician

2. Evidence that self-report delinquency rates do not vary with occupation of father within any school (which is frequently the sampling unit for such studies) but vary markedly with the average parental status of the students in different schools (Clark and Wenninger)

3. Evidence that the most serious "career delinquents" come disproportionately from the poorest families (Reiss and Rhodes)

4. Evidence that the students who are both poorest and most delinquent are also most frequently absent from school when questionnaires on self-reported delinquency are distributed (McDonald)

Braithwaite's comprehensive survey summarized the results of thirty-four self-report studies conducted in the United States. Half showed no support for the notion that class affects self-reported delinquency, and the other half showed at least some support for a social status–delinquency association. Thus, taken in toto, American self-report surveys of adolescents have provided no clear answer to the class-crime question.

Individual correlates from survey data for adults. Charles Tittle and Wayne Villemez conducted one of the few self-report studies on American adults. The sample consisted of persons aged fifteen or over residing in New Jersey, Iowa, and Oregon. Nearly thirty-five hundred households were approached, and the final response rate was 57 percent. Data gathered in one-hour interviews included how often in the preceding five years the respondents had stolen an item worth between $5 and $50, or more than $50; gambled illegally; physically harmed someone; cheated on income taxes; or smoked marijuana. Among the 749 white males in this group, the strongest relationship was that between social class (as measured by a combination of family income, occupation, and education) and the respondent's cheating on his income tax, but this relationship was not very strong. Among the 69 black males interviewed, moderately strong relationships were found between social class and assault, and between social class and the use of marijuana. It is important to note that all three of these offenses were related to class in the direction *opposite* to that predicted by most conventional theories—that is, higher-class individuals more often admitted crimes. Among the 1,006 white and 64 black females interviewed, none of the six offenses was significantly related to social class.

Jerald Bachman, Patrick O'Malley, and Jerome Johnston questioned a nationally representative sample of high-school students about delinquent and criminal behaviors in which they may have been involved, beginning in about the seventh grade and continuing until five years after high school. When the survey began in 1966 the sample consisted of just over twenty-two hundred boys; in 1974 the survey was still in contact with more than sixteen hundred young men. In that year, their median age was twenty-three years, 8 percent of them were black, and just under one-half were single.

The young men's educational attainment then was found to be negatively correlated with interpersonal aggression. Those who were unemployed in 1974, as contrasted with those who were employed, had a history of greater delinquency, particularly interpersonal aggression; moreover, those with a history of delinquency had lower-status jobs at the end of the study. The authors concluded:

It appears that unemployment and delinquency are indeed correlated and the relationship is not altogether simple or straightforward. Those in the ranks of the unemployed [in 1974 at age 23] began the study with slightly higher levels of delinquency, but those differences in delinquency increased and were fairly substantial at the end of the study. The relationship was . . . particularly pronounced among high school dropouts [pp. 182–183].

As these authors later noted, unemployed young men in the sample produced misleadingly low correlations because their proportion was so small. Young men unemployed in 1974 reported twice as much interpersonal aggression and illicit use of drugs as did their employed counterparts (p. 199).

The theme that there are a small number of respondents who produce "misleadingly low correlations" repeats itself throughout the survey literature. It is a critical shortcoming of the self-report technique, and until it is remedied it can be expected to produce offense measures that cannot be strongly related to normally distributed social-class variable measures. This problem is related to the problem of the seriousness of reported offenses noted above.

Other offenses. Among the important issues thus far virtually ignored here is that of the class-crime relationship for other than street crimes, including white-collar offenses, organized crime, and occupational lawbreaking. Since white-collar and occupational crime are generally defined as offenses of particular social-class levels, however, they cannot be correlated with differences in class categories. Although researchers could investigate their linkage to more variable indexes of the participant's class origins, such as parental status, this apparently has not been done.

Organized crime, such as racketeering, large-scale prostitution, gambling, and narcotic trafficking, is generally reported to recruit mainly persons from lower social-status groups, but to move some upward in status over generations and to recruit some higher-status individuals. As far as can be determined, no valid systematic, empirical work on the relation between status and organized crime has been done.

Interpreting the social-class–crime relation. The research data for the American studies reviewed above suggest that there is a small but consistent inverse correlation of social class with street crime for both adults and juveniles when the criterion is an official measure—police, court, or institutional record. When the criterion is a self-report measure generated by a survey, the results from studies of adolescents are far from unanimous. About half of the American studies support the hypothesis of an even smaller inverse relationship between various social-class indicators and reported illegal behavior, and half provide no support for the hypothesis. Among adults, survey-generated criteria of crime are available from too few American studies, and they yield findings too diverse to warrant any confident conclusions.

In twentieth-century American criminology the importance of class status as a precursor of crime and delinquency seems to be derived primarily from theories that were inspired by the early ecological studies based on official data. No other sociological variable in the study of crime causation has been able to muster so much allegiance over so long a period with so little empirical data on individuals to sustain it. Compared to other demographic and social variables, class does not fare very well as a correlate of offending. For example, Quételet argued convincingly, with data from the early nineteenth century, that age "is undoubtedly the cause which operates with most energy in developing or subduing the propensity to crime" (Sylvester, p. 41). In our time, victimization survey data (based, of course, on reports of victims) have shown that other basic demographic variables such as sex, age group, and race account for much of the variance in incidence rates of offending (Hindelang). Further, theorists such as Travis Hirschi, who do not use social class as an important explanatory variable, generally are able to account for the distribution of criminal behavior far better than are those who rely solely or primarily on social class to explain the phenomenon. Thus, it is not only a question of *whether* the hypothesis that there is no statistically significant crime-class relationship can be rejected, but whether very *much* of the variance in criminal conduct can be accounted for by social class. Available evidence suggests that it is primarily on these latter grounds that social class falls short as *the* explanation of criminal behavior in twentieth-century America.

Assuming that class and crime are inversely related, what would generate research data more consistent with class-based theories? The most fundamental problem relates to the seriousness of offenses. Surveys of the general population must be designed so that they report crimes serious enough to result in arrest. Without stratifying samples by variables known to be related to high probabilities of reporting serious offending, and without drawing wastefully large samples designed to be representative of the general population, accomplishing this task is not easy. Sample sizes used in victimization surveys involving as many as 130,000 persons interviewed twice per year yielded fewer than 120 reports of rapes and 800 reports of robberies for the entire United States.

When one considers the problem of nonresponse—the failure of respondents to report their own known offenses to survey interviewers—as suggested by the results of reverse record check studies (Hindelang, Hirschi, and Weis), it seems unlikely that serious offenders will be as forthright or cooperative as victims in self-reports, even if stratification or huge sample sizes were feasible. However, official reports of offender attributes have become "disvalued" by (1) an ever-declining clearance of crimes by an arrest, and (2) an ever-increasing diversion of offenders to permit their avoidance of the juvenile or adult justice systems.

MICHAEL HINDELANG

See also CRIME CAUSATION, articles on ECONOMIC THEORIES, POLITICAL THEORIES, and SOCIOLOGICAL THEORIES; EDUCATION AND CRIME; RACE AND CRIME; UNEMPLOYMENT AND CRIME; WHITE-COLLAR CRIME: HISTORY OF AN IDEA.

BIBLIOGRAPHY

BACHMAN, JERALD G.; O'MALLEY, PATRICK M.; and JOHNSTON, JEROME. Adolescence to Adulthood: Change and Stability in the Lives of Young Men. Ann Arbor: University of Michigan, Institute for Social Research, 1978.

BERK, RICHARD A.; LENIHAN, KENNETH J.; and ROSSI, PETER H. "Crime and Poverty: Some Experimental Evidence from Ex-offenders." American Sociological Review 45 (1980): 766–786.

BONGER, WILLEM A. Criminality and Economic Conditions. Translated by Henry P. Horton. Preface by Edward Lindsey. Introduction by Frank H. Norcross. Boston: Little, Brown, 1916.

BRAITHWAITE, JOHN. "The Myth of Social Class and Criminality Reconsidered." American Sociological Review 46 (1981): 36–57.

CLARK, JOHN P., and WENNINGER, EUGENE P. "Socio-economic Class and Area as Correlates of Illegal Behavior among Juveniles." American Sociological Review 27 (1962): 826–834.

ELLIOTT, DELBERT S., and AGETON, SUZANNE S. "Reconciling Race and Class Differences in Self-reported and Official Estimates of Delinquency." American Sociological Review 45 (1980): 95–110.

GOLD, MARTIN, and REIMER, DAVID. "Changing Patterns of Delinquent Behavior among Americans Thirteen through Sixteen Years Old: 1967–1972." Crime and Delinquency Literature 7 (1975): 483–517.

HINDELANG, MICHAEL J. "Variations in Sex-Race-Age Specific Incidence Rates of Offending." American Sociological Review 46 (1981): 461–474.

———; HIRSCHI, TRAVIS; and WEIS, J. Measuring Delinquency. Beverly Hills, Calif.: Sage, 1981.

HIRSCHI, TRAVIS. Causes of Delinquency. Berkeley: University of California Press, 1969.

JOHNSTONE, JOHN W. C. "Social Class, Social Areas, and Delinquency." Sociology and Social Research 63 (1978): 49–72.

McDONALD LYNN. Social Class and Delinquency. Hamden, Conn.: Archon Books, 1969.

NYE, F. IVAN, and SHORT, JAMES F., JR. "Scaling Delinquent Behavior." American Sociological Review 22 (1957): 326–331.

QUÉTELET, ADOLPHE. A Treatise on Man and the Development of His Faculties (1835). Facsimile reproduction; with an introduction by Solomon Diamond. Gainesville, Fla.: Scholars' Facsimiles and Reprints, 1969.

REISS, ALBERT J., and RHODES, ALBERT L. "The Distribution of Juvenile Delinquency in the Social Class Structure." American Sociological Review 26 (1961): 720–732.

SHAW, CLIFFORD R., and McKAY, HENRY D. Juvenile Delinquency and Urban Areas: A Study of Rates of Delinquency in Relation to Differential Characteristics of Local Communities in American Cities (1942). Rev. ed. University of Chicago Press, 1969.

———. Social Factors in Juvenile Delinquency: A Study of the Community, the Family, and the Gang in Relation to Delinquent Behavior. Report on the Causes of Crime, vol. 2. Prepared for the U.S. National Commission on Law Observance and Enforcement [Wickersham Commission]. Washington, D.C.: The Commission, 1931.

SYLVESTER, SAWYER F., JR. ed. The Heritage of Modern Criminology. Cambridge, Mass.: Schenkman, 1972.

THRASHER, FREDERIC M. The Gang: A Study of 1,313 Gangs in Chicago. 2d rev. ed. University of Chicago Press, 1936.

TITTLE, CHARLES R., and VILLEMEZ, WAYNE J. "Social Class and Criminality." Social Forces 56 (1977): 474–502.

WILLIAMS, JAY R., and GOLD, MARTIN. "From Delinquent Behavior to Official Delinquency." Social Problems 20 (1972): 209–229.

CLEMENCY

See AMNESTY AND PARDON; PROBATION AND PAROLE: RELEASE AND REVOCATION.

CODIFICATION

See articles under CRIMINAL LAW REFORM.

COERCED CONFESSIONS

See CONFESSIONS.

COERCION

See EXCUSE, articles on DURESS and SUPERIOR ORDERS.

COHORT STUDIES

See CRIMINOLOGY: RESEARCH METHODS.

COLLATERAL ATTACK

See HABEAS CORPUS.

COMMERCIALIZED VICE

See GAMBLING; both articles under OBSCENITY AND PORNOGRAPHY; both articles under PROSTITUTION AND COMMERCIALIZED VICE.

COMMON-LAW CRIMES

See CRIME: DEFINITION OF CRIME; CRIMINAL LAW REFORM, *articles on* CURRENT ISSUES IN THE UNITED STATES, ENGLAND, *and* HISTORICAL DEVELOPMENT IN THE UNITED STATES.

COMMUNITY CORRECTIONS

See CORRECTIONAL TREATMENT; PRETRIAL DIVERSION; *articles under* PROBATION AND PAROLE.

COMMUNITY CRIME CONTROL

See CRIME PREVENTION: COMMUNITY PROGRAMS.

COMMUTATION OF SENTENCE

See AMNESTY AND PARDON; PROBATION AND PAROLE: RELEASE AND REVOCATION.

COMPARATIVE CRIMINAL LAW AND ENFORCEMENT

Discussions of criminal law and enforcement in various countries are to be found in many of the articles in this Encyclopedia devoted to particular subject matters. This entry contains overall treatments of criminal law and enforcement in four cultures whose law has developed, to a greater or lesser degree, outside the main Western tradition.

1. CHINA   Stanley Lubman
2. ISLAM   David F. Forte
3. PRELITERATE SOCIETIES   Laura Nader
                            Philip Parnell
4. SOVIET UNION   Harold J. Berman

1.
CHINA

Introduction

The contemporary Chinese criminal process is best understood as it reflects issues arising out of China's attempted transition to postrevolutionary stability. Since the establishment of the People's Republic of China (PRC) in 1949, law has been highly politicized, reflecting the commitment of the Chinese Communist Party (CCP) to destroy entire economic classes and to construct a new social order. Basic political and economic policies have changed frequently and some-

times violently, inhibiting the stability of legal institutions. Meanwhile, the Chinese leadership has not clearly and consistently apportioned power among agencies of the state and the CCP, a fact that has further retarded differentiation of the formal criminal process from other instruments of state power. Beneath these difficulties lies the inhospitability of traditional Chinese values to certain aspects of the Western-style formal criminal process that China has adopted.

Since 1978, China has given considerable attention to building a legal system with a formal criminal process at its core. After three decades during which policy, political institutions, and law were intertwined, attempts were made to disengage these elements from one another. However, the functional specialization of the criminal process institutions is likely to become meaningful, if it does so at all, only over a long period of time, during which they will probably remain fragile.

The traditional and revolutionary background of contemporary Chinese law

Traditional Chinese law. Chinese law has a complex background which includes both traditional institutions that preceded it for many centuries—and may continue to influence it—and more recent revolutionary experimentation that has kept institutions fluid since 1949. Four aspects of traditional Chinese law are especially significant because they mutually reinforced each other, and also limited the evolution of concepts of individual rights that could be vindicated or protected by agencies of the state.

The dominance of informal means of settling disputes and punishing minor offenses. The traditional imperial bureaucracy descended territorially only to the level of the *xian* (county) magistrate, who in the Qing dynasty (China's last, 1644–1911) was the sole official appointed by Peking to govern an area with a population of perhaps 200,000 to 250,000 persons. Each magistrate had a large jurisdiction, and the resources available to him for maintaining order were limited. Authority to punish many offenses was, in fact, lodged in the clans (which united all persons descended from common ancestors), the local gentry (men who had passed at least one of the imperial examinations or obtained the status by purchase), landlords (not necessarily gentry), village heads, merchant guilds, and, of course, the family. All of these were self-regulatory to a considerable extent. Without official intervention they served to heal or suppress much social conflict by providing means to settle disputes informally, by exerting pressure on disputants or other violators of social order to preserve social harmony, or by administering punishment directly.

The lack of functional separation between law and bureaucracy. Traditional China long had intricate criminal codes. The oldest surviving one dates to the Tang Dynasty (A.D. 618–906); the most recent was that of the Qing, compiled in definitive form in 1740. Its 436 sections were supplemented by 815 substatutes, which were imperial edicts issued over the years as authoritative and binding precedents. Records of past cases were preserved, particularly in official and unofficial commentaries; although past cases had no binding precedental authority, they provided guidance to judges. Specialized legal officials in provincial capitals and in Peking reviewed all serious cases, and local magistrates were assisted by legal secretaries with specialized knowledge.

However, administration of law at the county level—where most cases began and ended—was for the most part overseen by the local magistrates, who generally lacked legal training. As an activity of government, law attained little functional specialization and no autonomy. As Max Weber commented, "Chinese administration of justice constitutes a type of patriarchal obliteration of the line between justice and administration" (Rheinstein, p. 264). At the same time, penal law served as an important instrument in maintaining social order and the total cosmic order that it was assumed to reflect. Criminal and civil liability were not distinguished from each other, and "the official law always operated in a vertical direction from the state upon the individual, rather than on a horizontal plane directly between two individuals" (Bodde and Morris, p. 4).

Popular fear and avoidance of the legal system. Resort to formal judicial procedure was viewed as signifying a serious breakdown in the social order. Legal procedures were not designed to give litigants comfort, but served rather to discourage them and others from utilizing the formal judicial process. In the inquisitorial system that prevailed, the magistrate was allowed to torture the parties; accused criminals could not be sentenced until they confessed; and no professional class of lawyers was allowed to act as intermediaries. Indeed, the men who assisted litigants in drawing up the documents required in lawsuits were commonly known as "litigation tricksters." The fees and bribes that had to be paid to officials were high and even ruinous. Although property and inheritance matters were sometimes litigated, the formal legal system was generally avoided by most who could escape its reach.

The subordination of law to a dominant state philosophy. Law was so thoroughly identified in traditional China with punishment that there was only a criminal code, and no civil code as such. The criminal code reinforced the state philosophy of Confucianism and the hierarchical social order which that philosophy served to justify. For example, the punishments prescribed by the criminal code for murder varied according to the difference in status between murderer and victim in the social hierarchy or within a family. Thus, if the accused had committed a murder in pursuit of his familial duties—such as revenge for the murder of his father—he could be allowed special consideration or pardon after conviction. In all societies, law reflects and supports the dominant ideological and ethical systems, but the extent to which it explicitly performed these functions in Chinese society to reinforce ideas of hierarchy and subordination made it arguably unique.

The period from 1911 to 1949.

The failure of law reform. Throughout the first half of the twentieth century, before the Communist victory in 1949, law reform was retarded by the warlordism, continuous exploitation from abroad, corruption, invasion by Japan, and civil war that wracked China. Before the fall of the Qing dynasty, the criminal code was revised, and legal scholars and a newly created supreme court worked to adapt Western legal concepts to Chinese needs. After the overthrow of the Qing and the establishment of the Republic, legal education was introduced in the universities and a bar was established. By the mid-1930s, civil and criminal codes had been promulgated, as well as procedural codes in both areas.

However, the new codes were not vigorously enforced. They were largely ignored outside the cities; judges were poorly trained and often corrupt; and the courts were inaccessible to all but a few and heavily subject to political controls by an authoritarian government. The procedural codes, borrowed from abroad, were too formalistic and complicated for the Chinese situation. The disintegration of Chinese society that was accelerated by the war with Japan and that culminated in the collapse of Guomindang (Chinese Nationalist Party) rule could only have lowered the expectations which the Chinese people might have had of the legal system.

The criminal process during the CCP's revolutionary struggle. The ideology, organization, and tactics that the Chinese Communist Party developed while leading the greatest peasant revolution of the twentieth century were inconsistent with the existence of a meaningful formal legal system. In the area that earliest came under Communist rule, the Jiangxi Soviet (which lasted only three years, from 1931 to 1934), the criminal process was politicized by the need to extirpate "counterrevolutionaries" and "class enemies," and was marked by reliance on the police to investigate, arrest, and punish such opponents. During the later 1930s and the 1940s, when the party served an apprenticeship to nationwide power by ruling large, mostly rural areas, it gained further experience in politicizing the criminal process. By the time the Chinese Communist Party gained total victory in 1949, it had developed methods of political leadership, articulated by Mao Zedong, that decisively stamped legal as well as other governmental institutions.

Maoism emphasized popular participation and decentralization. Mobilizational mass "campaigns" led by the revolutionary elite of the party were used not only to accomplish economic and social changes, but also to carry out many ordinary affairs of government. Deeply antibureaucratic, Maoism opposed the development of technically expert specialists in bureacratic organizations, including the courts. The function of law was to serve policy and mobilize support for the party. Although some attention was given to regularizing criminal procedure, much more emphasis was placed on serving the "mass line." This involved extensive participation of the populace in carrying out policy by organizing small groups of citizen "activists" to assist the police, using mediational dispute settlement to engage in propaganda while settling disputes, and blending adjudication with mass meetings and rallies to attack landlords, "class criminals," and other class enemies (Leng, 1967, pp. 1–26).

Chinese law since 1949

Early politicization of law. For most of the PRC's first thirty years of existence, the formal criminal process reflected the highly politicized Maoist mobilizational style of government. During the first four years of Communist rule (1949–1953), the party reorganized Chinese society. The new Communist government abolished the Nationalist codes and did not substitute new ones. Some penal norms punishing counterrevolutionary activity and corruption were adopted in the course of violent mass campaigns, but they were broad and imprecise. Although regulations providing for hierarchies of courts and the procuracy (a prosecutorial organ) were promulgated, in practice the lower-level courts were not established at all, were used only to implement specific campaigns, or were displaced by special ad hoc tribunals. Most of the

law-trained judges and clerks who had previously worked for the overthrown Guomindang regime were quickly purged and replaced by politically reliable cadres. Procedural and substantive rules and principles, such as *nulla poena sine lege* and even the basic principle that cases should be decided "on the merits," were criticized as tools of reaction.

During the early years of Communist rule, too, all families were classified by "class origin," a designation indicating their economic status and political coloration at the time of the Communist victory. As a result, some persons—and later their children—were permanently labeled as "counterrevolutionary," "landlord," "bourgeois," or (former Guomindang) "bureaucrat," while most Chinese were denominated "poor peasants" or "workers." Those classed as opponents of the regime or as otherwise undesirable elements were often grouped together as the "four bad elements," namely, "landlords," "rich peasants," "counterrevolutionaries," and (ambiguously and redundantly) "bad elements." These classifications, entered in each person's dossier as an index of loyalty and reliability, often critically influenced the severity of any sanctions applied to them.

Creation of an apparatus of control. During the early years the party also created an elaborate apparatus for surveillance, control, and sanctioning. A public-security (that is, police) hierarchy was organized from the Ministry of Public Security in Beijing downward to local rural and municipal neighborhood police stations. Public security control was augmented by "security defense committees" of activists who reported suspicious activities of fellow residents to the police. Other activists headed "mediation committees," urban "residents' committees," and "residents' small groups" (to which all urban residents belonged) and carried out propaganda and organization work in such mass organizations as the Young Communist League and the China Women's Association. The public-security apparatus reached into such functional units as government bureaus, economic and commercial enterprises, and schools. Of course, Communist party branches and cells were embedded in police and other governmental units, as well as in the mass organizations. Policy implementation in all territorial and functional units was guided by a vast party hierarchy, which was at all times parallel to but distinct from other organizations.

During the first years of the PRC the police, under close party leadership, dominated the formal process that administered serious "criminal" sanctions, ranging from confinement in police-run "labor reform" camps to the death sentence. Trials were conducted principally in conjunction with mobilizational campaigns, and were public if party officials felt that a public trial possessed particular educational importance. Other police-controlled sanctions included minor fines and short periods of confinement in police-run detention centers for less serious offenses, as well as a regimen of "control," which was first applied to former landlords and minor counterrevolutionaries who had not been linked with serious crimes. Later such a regimen was extended to other persons deemed to deserve stigmatization and surveillance without prison confinement.

In every economic, educational, and governmental unit, police and party cadres handled "personnel" and "security" matters and labor discipline, and applied administrative sanctions such as dismissal, demotion, entry of demerits in dossiers, reductions in salary, and job reassignments. The Communist party and its adjunct, the Young Communist League, created their own internal mechanisms for discipline. Finally, in every urban street and, less effectively, throughout the vast Chinese countryside, the activist-augmented cadre apparatus directly controlled or influenced application of an assortment of informal punishments, such as public criticism of varying intensity in small or large groups. Courts and the procuracy figured little in sanctioning except to formalize the most serious punishments in order to propagandize party policies and educate the masses with regard to desired behavior.

Legality and discipline. By 1953 the Chinese Communist leadership had consolidated its control, and the leadership shifted its aim to industrialization under Soviet-style five-year plans. At the same time, it showed greater interest in establishing a formal judicial system, and professed adherence to the relatively more regularized and centralized Soviet models. To Western eyes, Stalinist legal institutions may hardly seem regular, but they did present a more bureaucratic contrast to previous Chinese practices. The emphasis on building new legal institutions was consistent with the Stalinist inspiration, which stressed not legality but the discipline necessary in the drive for "economic construction."

The period from 1953 to 1957: tentative regularization. In 1954 a constitution was adopted, organizational legislation was promulgated for the courts and procuracy (Law of the PRC for the Organization of People's Courts; Law of the PRC for the Organization of People's Procuracies), and rules on arrest and detention were established (Arrest and Detention Act of the PRC). New policies on the formal criminal process were evidenced by a tripartite division of functions, at least in form: (1) the police were to investigate suspected offenses and make arrests after approval by the procuracy; (2) the procuracy, made formally independent as in the Soviet Union, rather than attached to the courts as in the Guomindang system and in Jiangxi, was to approve arrests, verify evidence, and make formal accusations; and (3) the courts were to determine guilt in public trials at which the accused had a "right to defense" and which were in principle to be conducted by panels consisting of one judge and two citizens acting as "people's jurors."

At various times from 1954 to 1957 sporadic attempts were made to implement these new measures. However, political campaigns continued to link the activity of the courts to the promotion of specific policies, such as suppressing grain thefts or collectivizing agriculture. For barely a year, from mid-1956 to June 1957, criminal procedure was briefly and tentatively regularized, probably only in China's largest cities, and unevenly even there.

The formal criminal process as administered was adjudicatory only in form and remained dominated by the police and by party officials within the "political-legal" system, as the three organs of police, procuracy, and courts were called. In most cases, the procuracy and courts only confirmed police recommendations on disposition. Public trials, if held, were used to confirm decisions already reached by the police and the procuracy and to demonstrate the defendant's guilt. If police, procuracy, and courts differed, their disagreements were resolved by consultations that crossed the often-blurred lines between party and government. Local party secretaries usually exercised considerable power in these consultations.

Although defendants were entitled to be represented at their trials by defense counsel, lawyers' offices, which were opened intermittently from 1955 to 1957, remained very small. Defense lawyers were criticized in 1957 for being too closely linked with the "enemies" who were the objects of the criminal process. After conviction, defendants could theoretically appeal, but very few did; some cases, however, were reviewed as an internal bureaucratic matter by the trial courts, the higher-level courts, the Ministry of Justice, and the police, sometimes acting together.

At all times during the first thirty years of the PRC, promulgated laws were less important than directives transmitted through the Communist party apparatus, statements by Chinese leaders reported in the media, and "campaigns" intended to popularize and implement policies. Promulgated statutes and regulations on substantive criminal law and criminal procedure remained both scattered and tentative, and their practical effects and implementation varied constantly with shifts in official policy. Unpromulgated internal rules guided the police and the party in defining offenses and applying sanctions.

Outside the courts, many minor disputes and petty offenses were handled by groups of activists at the lowest-level units of local government, such as those in the neighborhoods of China's cities. The organizations that are places of work for many millions of Chinese, for example, factories, schools, and government offices, wielded extensive power to define and punish misbehavior.

The defeat of earlier liberalizing trends: law in the service of politics. For one notable brief period, in 1956 and 1957, some Chinese leaders seemed willing to increase the regularity of the legal system. Even Mao stated in early 1957 that large-scale mass movements were basically over. Six months later, Mao reversed himself. Concern for regularizing the institutions of the state, including those of the still-emerging legal system, which had grown during the blossoming of the "hundred flowers," was condemned as "rightist," and by mid-1957 the slow development of the legal system was arrested.

For a decade thereafter, until the disorder of the Cultural Revolution, the police and the party dominated the criminal process. The newly created bar withered away. In the small number of law schools that existed by 1957, where much legal education had consisted of highly abstract discourse on Soviet principles, curricula were heavily politicized by infusions of Mao Zedong thought. Criminal law and procedure remained uncodified. The principal penal legislation, in addition to a 1951 act on counterrevolutionaries (Act of the PRC for Punishment of Counterrevolution), consisted of two laws providing for wholly extrajudicial punishments. The 1957 Public Security Regulations authorized the police to detain persons for limited periods of time for minor offenses. Another law issued in 1957 permitted the police and many other organizations, such as schools and factories, to send "rightists" and other very broadly defined classes of persons to police-run camps for "labor rehabilitation" for an indefinite period (Decision of the State Council of the PRC Relating to Problems of Rehabilitation through Labor).

During the Great Leap Forward of 1958 to 1960, most of whatever separation of functions had appeared was undone by insistence on the "mass line," which involved carrying out investigations and trials on the spot, "simplifying" procedures, and waging class warfare. From 1961 to 1965, a period of slow recovery from the Great Leap, the intensity of these emphases abated somewhat from time to time, but the essence of policy remained a blending of law and politics.

The Cultural Revolution. The Cultural Revolution drastically affected the institutions of the criminal process. Before it took place, the Chinese police possessed immense power as a major instrument of coercion. By 1970 many police cadres had been purged; the army was in some places directly supervising the police, the courts, and the procuracy; and some police functions had been distributed to new activist organizations. Between 1966 and 1969, the police, the procuracy and the courts were first severely criticized and their activities virtually suspended, and then they were partially reorganized. During the same period, too, China's cities and some portions of the countryside experienced a general disruption of public order, which included widespread violence and many deaths. New and flamboyantly named organizations of young people, all claiming to be supporters of Chairman Mao's continuing revolution, attacked persons considered to be bourgeois and fought bitterly among themselves, sometimes to the death. Crime appeared to an extent unknown in China since 1949, and the army had to intervene to maintain order.

With the end of the Cultural Revolution, the army's role in peacekeeping receded. Army leader Lin Biao's attempt to seize power reaffirmed the determination of Mao and other Chinese leaders to maintain control over the army, and by 1972 the police again patrolled the streets. Parapolice groups, which had appeared in the cities during the Cultural Revolution, were disbanded, gradually assimilated into urban militia forces, or placed under their control. The courts resumed activity, although certainly no more vigorously than before the Cultural Revolution. A new constitution adopted in 1975 contained only limited references to judicial activity, and the procuracy disappeared from view. However, with the overthrow of the "Gang of Four" in 1976, a new stage was inaugurated. After several years during which the power of a newly pragmatic leadership was consolidated, formal legal institutions began to receive attention that they had not known for more than twenty years.

Basic institutions of the contemporary criminal process

Codification. Not until late in 1977 was the need for law codes stressed publicly, for the first time since 1957. Codification proceeded surprisingly quickly, and in July 1979 the Second Session of the Fifth National People's Congress adopted codes of criminal law and criminal procedure, as well as new laws in other areas (The Criminal Law of the People's Republic of China; The Criminal Procedure Law of the People's Republic of China).

The Criminal Law of the PRC. The classes of offenses provided by the criminal code are as follows: (1) counterrevolutionary offenses; (2) offenses endangering public security; (3) offenses against the socialist economic order; (4) offenses infringing upon the personal and economic rights of citizens; (5) offenses of encroachment on property; (6) offenses against public order; (7) offenses against marriage and the family; and (8) malfeasance.

The range of punishments is as follows:

1. Public surveillance (three months to two years), under which the offender is allowed to continue to reside in his home, but works (at standard wages) under the "supervision of the masses" and must report to the police and the civil officials at his place of residence (that is, a rural commune or urban neighborhood)
2. Detention (five days to six months), with work at nonstandard wages and home leave once or twice monthly
3. Imprisonment at a prison or labor reform camp for six months to fifteen years
4. Life imprisonment
5. The death sentence, which may be suspended for two years, after which the offender is executed or his sentence commuted to life imprisonment or imprisonment for fifteen to twenty years

Fines, deprivation of rights, and confiscation of property are ancillary punishments.

The new code retained the concept of "counterrevolutionary crimes," which are conspicuous by reason of the detail with which they are defined as compared to other offenses. The code also employs the principle of analogy, although offenders may be punished by analogical application of the code only after approval by the Supreme People's Court. The code makes a notable departure from previous reluctance, since 1949, to define substantive crimes, but it does not necessarily signal a firm commitment to depoliticize the formal criminal process.

The Criminal Procedure Law of the PRC. The Criminal Procedure Law expresses the basic tripartite division of functions among the principal institutions of the formal criminal process, providing that

the public security organs are in charge of investigation, detention and preparatory examination in criminal cases; the people's procuracies are responsible for approving arrest, conducting procuratorial control (including investiga-

tion) and initiating public prosecution. The people's courts are responsible for adjudication. No other organ, organization or individual has the right to exercise these powers [art. 3].

In criminal proceedings, the court, the procuracy, and the police must "take facts as their basis and law as their criterion" (art. 4), and should "have a division of labor and separate responsibilities and coordinate with and restrain one another in order to guarantee the accurate and effective enforcement of the law" (art. 5). The basic differentiation of function is itself noteworthy, because it expresses the exclusive power of the legal-bureaucratic organizations to impose the sanctions contemplated under the criminal law. Noncriminal sanctions, including police-administered detention and "education through labor" for up to three years, remain, however, outside the province of the code. Even this is more limited than before, however; previously, work and residential units had often taken it upon themselves to punish offenders, a power they can no longer exercise. At the same time, though, the role of the party, which is unmentioned, remains more ambiguous.

The Law requires the police to obtain warrants before arrest of a suspected offender, to promptly notify the detainee's family after the arrest, and to begin interrogation within twenty-four hours of any apprehension or arrest. The procuracy must be notified of the arrest within a stated time limit, and must either approve the arrest or order release of the detainee within three days.

During the "investigation" stage, the accused and witnesses are interrogated, all other evidence obtained, and the indictment prepared. In principle, detention pending investigation may not exceed two months, although the procuracy may obtain a one-month extension from the next-higher level procuracy. The use of torture, threat, intimidation, or any other illegal means to obtain a confession is strictly forbidden.

If the procuracy finds "conclusive and sufficient" evidence of guilt, it must file an indictment with the court. Trials are conducted by panels composed of one judge and two "people's jurors," or assessors. The record is first reviewed by the panel, which decides whether to proceed to a public trial. At the trial, an accused has a right to defense by a lawyer, a relative, a guardian, a citizen recommended by the accused's unit or other organization, or a "defender" appointed by the court. The role of the defender is to present "materials and opinions proving that the defendant is not guilty, that his crime is minor, or that he should receive a mitigated punishment or be exempted from criminal responsibility, safeguarding the lawful rights and interests of the accused" (art. 28).

The drafters did not go so far as to create a presumption of innocence. Rather, the Law says that all evidence used as the basis of judgment must be verified; no defendant may be convicted on the basis of his confession alone. Debate on the presumption of innocence, which occurred in 1957 until it was criticized as "rightist," has continued after promulgation of the law on criminal procedure.

Review of a trial court decision may come about by a variety of means: the judgment may be reviewed as an administrative matter by the court that rendered it, by a higher-level court, or after the procuracy has lodged a protest. These procedures may lead to an increase or decrease in a convicted defendant's sentence, or to a reversal of a conviction. The defendant may appeal, too, and, abandoning an earlier practice, the appellate court may not increase his sentence if review has been initiated in this manner.

The courts. China has three types of courts, provided for in the Organic Law for People's Courts, 1979: the Supreme People's Court in Beijing, local people's courts, and special courts (including military, railway transport, water transport, forestry, and other unspecified types). The organizational law of the courts states that all citizens must be treated equally before the law, and declares that they have the right to public trial and to defense by a lawyer or other person designated by the accused. Cases are to be decided by a panel of judges sitting with two "assessors" chosen from the masses. Within the courts, "judicial supervision" is to be exercised by "judicial committees" (sometimes translated as "adjudication committees"), which are to "sum up judicial experience, discuss major difficult cases and other issues regarding judicial work."

The hierarchy of people's courts has three levels: the "basic" level (in rural counties or in districts in major cities), the "intermediate" level (essentially in provincial districts and in districts in major cities), and the "higher" level (provincial or citywide in major cities). At the apex of the judicial pyramid is the Supreme People's Court. According to the Criminal Procedure Law, only one appeal to the next higher level is technically possible, except in cases involving the death penalty, which may be taken to the Supreme People's Court. At a time of great concern that serious crimes be punished expeditiously, the Standing Committee of the National People's Congress, China's legislature, temporarily reduced the jurisdiction of the Supreme People's Court by deciding that from July

10, 1981, to the end of 1983 most cases involving the death sentence could not be appealed beyond the "higher" level people's courts (Decisions on Death Sentences).

The procuracy. The procuracy is charged both with prosecuting offenders and upholding the lawfulness of the prosecution. It must not only obey the law itself, but must also check unlawfulness on the part of the public security departments or the courts. Further complicating its tasks, however, is the fact that the procuracy is also supposed to follow the leadership of the Communist party—but without, at the same time, violating its own independence under the law (Organic Law for People's Procuracies, 1979).

Using a formulation which has apparently become standard, published discussions state that the task of the local party committee is to exercise its leadership over questions of "line, principles, and policy." The implicit but important distinction is one between permissible *general* guidance and improper interference in the disposition of *individual* cases. Whether paradoxical or not, the party must itself supervise the procuracy's strict enforcement of the law.

The role of the lawyer. Although no lawyers were trained during the Cultural Revolution and for years afterward, law departments at universities under the jurisdiction of the Ministry of Education and four law schools under the jurisdiction of the Ministry of Justice, all of which had existed before the Cultural Revolution, were reopened in the late 1970s, and additional law departments have been established. By 1982 there were more than eight thousand law students in China. Lawyers are to be paid by the state, are not allowed to have "personal offices," and must remit their fees to the state (Text of Provisional Regulations on Lawyers). The Chinese lawyer must "serve the cause of socialism" and "protect the interest of the state and the collective" on the one hand, and, on the other, protect the "legitimate rights and interests of the citizens." By early 1982, it was estimated that approximately fifty-five hundred lawyers were at work in these offices.

In a society lacking a tradition of an independent bar and in which opponents of the state have not been lightly tolerated, lawyers have not hastened to become vigorous defenders of their clients. It is essential to recall that the Chinese concept of a public trial has been, since the earliest days of CCP rule over "liberated areas," more limited than comparable proceedings in the West. In no Communist-ruled portion of China has the trial been used to resolve contested issues of fact; the trial has consistently been regarded as a pre-conviction stage at which the sufficiency of the written record to confirm a verdict of guilty is established. This is one reason why the Chinese have rejected some Western criticisms of the trial of the "Gang of Four" as a show trial. It was never assumed that the trial would hear disputed facts; rather, it was to consider only uncontested facts which clearly established the defendants' guilt.

The usefulness of lawyers has been emphasized by official policy and illustrated by media articles and broadcasts intended to educate the populace and officials alike about the appropriateness of institutionalizing the bar. At the same time, Chinese lawyers are reminded that they must behave as responsible upholders of proletarian justice, and must avoid using the "tricks" which bourgeois lawyers allegedly employ to assist guilty clients despite their guilt. Some must recall, too, that certain energetic lawyers who urged courts in the mid-1950s to find their clients innocent were later criticized for protecting criminals.

Conclusions

The institutions described above have only recently been placed—or reestablished—alongside an apparatus of political control that long antedates them. Some of the trends and conflicts that are likely to persist are summarized below, and perspectives from which developments in the Chinese criminal process can appropriately be viewed are suggested.

Law and politics.

Party control. The grasp of the party on the courts is likely to remain an issue for a long time. Soon after the new codes were adopted, some public discussions urged that law should be superior to policy. Proponents of this viewpoint argued that party leadership should be extended over "principles and policies," but that party committees (every court has one) should not interfere in the decision of specific cases. However, since then, Chinese media discussions have continued to refer to party committees engaging in such interference. Party dominance has been too long-lived and too firm to yield very easily to the courts.

Equality before the law. The existence of a revived formal criminal process also raises the issue of whether it will be used to punish state and party officials. Before the Cultural Revolution, cadres were punished (if at all) administratively for offenses against discipline, Communist morality, law, or all three. Standard administrative punishments were "demerits"—warnings of various degrees of severity, demotion, transfer, and dismissal. Party members could also be sanctioned by suspension of their party membership or dismissal from the party. The party

continues to employ its own disciplinary inspection commissions to investigate and punish breaches of discipline, which may often constitute offenses against law as well.

Equality of all before the law, a principle affirmed in the Criminal Procedure Law, would require that party officials be tried in the courts if their conduct violates the criminal code, and that they cease to use their influence to prevent punishment of relatives and friends. Judicial trial and conviction of some party members soon after the criminal code and Criminal Procedure Law were adopted suggest that the Chinese leadership may begin to expand the role of the criminal process in sanctioning officials and party members for conduct which violates the criminal law, ranging from clearly criminal acts such as theft of public funds to serious lapses of judgment. However, the long subservience of the courts to the party will not soon be overcome.

The use of politicized standards for decision. It remains to be seen, too, whether the Chinese criminal process will be depoliticized by abandoning the former practice of identifying all persons according to their socioeconomic class and their general attitude toward Communist rule, with punishments varying accordingly. The use of criteria of "class status" has been criticized in legal texts and journals as inconsistent with the principles of criminal responsibility and punishment laid down in the criminal code.

In the past, mobilizational campaigns frequently disrupted the regular operation of sanctioning processes in almost every year between 1949 and 1966. The Cultural Revolution plunged the entire nation into disorder for years, and it was not until 1979 that campaigns were generally eschewed as a tool of government.

Both in campaigns and otherwise, since 1949 the Chinese courts have been used explicitly as tools to implement party and state policies. Typically, as with all other Chinese governmental agencies, short-term goals consistent with campaigns have frequently been set for the courts, such as punishing economic crimes severely. Courts have been publicly congratulated for explicitly and vigorously applying harsh penalties in such cases.

Insulation of the courts from the pressures and disorder of mass campaigns may remain particularly difficult as long as the party continues to profess devotion to the "mass line." This was recognized in the case of nationwide drives to punish economic crimes severely, which were launched soon after the codes were promulgated and which brought about the enactment of amendments to the criminal code that increased penalties for certain economic crimes. If a style of justice associated with campaigns continues to stamp judicial administration, functional specialization and judicial independence—goals given support in some statements by Chinese leaders—will be inhibited.

Less overt a political influence on the courts than varying punishments according to class or campaign, but noteworthy because of its importance, is the continued use of courts to promote and symbolize the discipline needed for China's economic modernization, much as the courts in the 1950s were called on to assist industrialization.

One form of indiscipline that has provoked the use of the criminal process is open political dissidence. In a crackdown in 1979 a number of dissidents were punished, including one who, after a highly publicized trial, was sentenced to fifteen years in prison for disseminating "counterrevolutionary" propaganda and revealing military secrets. In addition, wide publicity has been given to severe sentences meted out to criminals, open trials, and "rallies" at which sentences have been announced in stadiums. A few highly publicized proceedings have ended with the convicted offender marched off to prompt execution.

Another response to the perceived need for discipline has included a strengthening of the power of the police. The regulations on police punishment of minor violators of public order, already mentioned, which were originally published in October 1957, were republished in February 1980. Under these regulations, the police may warn, fine, or place under "administrative detention" for limited periods of time persons who commit certain minor offenses against "public order." Also republished in early 1980 were the regulations on "education through labor," which were first issued in 1957. Under this law, offenders who fall into certain rather broadly defined categories can be punished by "nonjudicial departments" (that is, the police) with sentences of up to three years of "labor reeducation" (1957 Regulations on Reeducation through Labor Published).

Concepts of law.

Law as process. At issue are nothing less than basic Chinese conceptions of law. At the time the new codes were promulgated and in the years immediately following, official policy statements expressed a commitment to establishing formal legal institutions and to promulgating new legal rules. There seems to be reluctance to regard law as a *process* involving interpretation of laws in the course of applying them to specific situations. Much public discussion, as well as statements by Chinese leaders, has seemed to assume that with the promulgation of the new laws and the setting

into place of courts to apply them, a satisfactorily regularized legal system would appear.

But regularization is not likely to occur so quickly. Regularization cannot be produced merely by a desire to regularize or by a campaign; it is more likely to emerge, as the outcome of sustained incremental effort. Only if it is so fostered is it likely to endure.

The function of rules. Substantive and procedural rules can only develop meaningful functions over a period of years after codification. Earlier in the history of the PRC, policies were expressed in formal norms that were characterized by a high degree of generality, and local officials were permitted considerable latitude in interpreting them. These norms have often been quite vague, not only by Western standards but also by those of the Chinese officials who were required to enforce them. For example, the 1957 statute on "labor rehabilitation" punished, inter alia, "those counterrevolutionaries and anti-socialist reactionaries who, because their errors are minor, are not pursued for criminal responsibility [and are expelled from an educational or work unit]."

Much Chinese practice suggests that statutes were used in the past less as specific guides than as general and often exhortative policy statements. Leaders may have expected only partial compliance, and may have been prepared to abandon or alter the rules if circumstances required. In the past, too, there has been a high degree of inconsistency between normative language and official conduct. For example, much police sanctioning was done without formal authority; statutes defining and scaling sanctions were repeatedly disregarded; and direct sanctions were decided by ad hoc groups during political campaigns. In addition, internal, secret directives were used to guide cadre discretion, although some of them were probably as ambiguous as the public ones. Cadres have complained about the lack of clarity of both internal and promulgated rules.

Assumptions about rational grading of sanctions. Penal legislation commonly aims at scaling criminal punishment in accordance with the seriousness of the crimes. Most legal systems assume that there are legal and moral reasons for making punishments proportionate to crimes. In theory, Chinese sanctions are arranged in ascending order of severity and formality, beginning with the mildest of rebukes by a cadre, continuing through more intense forms of group criticism, and extending to formal trial and the death sentence. Police-administered sanctions such as "control," short-term detention, warnings, and fines for minor offenders and intermediate confinement in labor camps for more serious offenders fall between nonjudicial criticism in residential or work units and sentences imposed through the formal criminal process.

In practice, however, the application of sanctions has been considerably less measured than the analytical scheme might suggest. For example, the consequences of informal sanctions have sometimes been as severe as more formal punishment, involving permanent stigmatization and limitation in future career opportunities.

Law and administration: the criminal process and Chinese conceptions of bureaucracy. Both the history and the likely future evolution of the Chinese criminal process are linked to leadership attitudes toward administration. To what extent will legal institutions be allowed to become differentiated from other bureaucratic institutions and permitted to develop unique doctrine and decision-making processes? China has long been involved in a struggle to adapt institutions developed during the party's rise to power to the different task of modernizing a nation. The transformation of revolutionary innovators into bureaucrats and administrators has been perceived by some Chinese leaders, especially Mao, as a threat to the revolution. Bureacracy erodes mobilization, increases functional specialization, and creates networks of influence and corruption. These were major problems that provoked Mao to begin the Cultural Revolution, and they may again be viewed as major problems.

The history of the criminal process in the PRC has seen a struggle between two different conceptions of the criminal process, which are in turn grounded in different political styles. One conception is mobilizational, and treats judicial trials as exercises in mass education that demonstrate the guilt of the accused and thereby aid policy implementation and maintain revolutionary fervor. In a competing, more routinized model, cases are disposed of in a manner less explicitly oriented toward policy considerations and more hospitable to the use of legal doctrine and legal skills, increasing rationality and reducing cadre arbitrariness. From these competing conceptions arise Chinese analogues, albeit distant ones, to what one scholar has suggested as competing models of the American criminal process, one in which it is an "assembly line" and another in which it is an "obstacle course" (Packer, pp. 149–173). In one Chinese analogue, the criminal process is a routinized handling of putatively guilty suspects; in the other, the process must include checks on official arbitrariness that would prevent unjust convictions, even if they would also slow administration of the process.

However, even though the opposition of such concepts can be discerned in China, models such as those mentioned above, derived from the Anglo-American criminal process, may be used only with great caution in analyzing the Chinese process. Illustratively, the conventional Anglo-American division of the formal criminal process into separate stages of pretrial, trial, and post-conviction review, each with considerable finality, is regarded very differently in China. The formal process has been treated in China more like a continuous inquiry into the facts of a case, the identity of the offender, the responsibility of the accused, and the appropriateness of the punishment; the resulting fluidity is likely to persist.

Some concepts derived from Chinese traditions may be helpful only in understanding contemporary institutions, and may, eventually, perhaps also help to reinforce the autonomy of a formal criminal process. For example, Chinese Communist ideology and organization emphasize a strongly hierarchical view of political authority. The traditional Chinese criminal process was also shaped by a deep commitment to a hierarchical political system. The history of the criminal process in the Romanist systems of Europe demonstrates that a hierarchical political authority can produce a non-adversarial formal criminal process in which arbitrariness and unfairness may be controlled by institutions associated with bureaucratic professionalism (Damaška, 1973, 1975). Although the allocation of functions among institutions differs from that in Anglo-American systems, each is able to aim at upholding similar values. It may be that if the promotion of bureaucratic professionalism is linked to the contemporary Chinese preference for hierarchical order, greater regularity in the Chinese criminal process may also be brought about, although some other values contending for dominance will be unique to China. Regardless of the eventual outcome, the strength or weakness of the formal Chinese criminal process is likely to continue to reflect the style and dynamics of bureaucratic administration generally in China.

Since 1949, mass-line and bureaucratic models have alternated and competed. During the periods of relatively greater politicization, official policy emphasized the function of the criminal process to assist mobilization of the masses to carry out policy. During periods of consolidation, recovery, or retrenchment, stress was placed on achieving bureaucratic efficiency and on reducing arbitrariness and errors. In the late 1970s, when the Chinese leadership committed the nation to a sustained effort at economic modernization, the old mobilizational style of administration was explicitly declared to be inappropriate, and far greater emphasis than before was placed on economic rationality and efficiency. It was as part of a new stage in China's efforts to modernize that codes of criminal law and criminal procedure were adopted, for the first time in the history of the PRC. Codification, however, raises the issue once again, and more acutely than in the past, of the choice among competing models of the criminal process. Although mobilizational politics and the style of judicial administration derived from it have avowedly been cast off, it may be too early to tell whether a commitment has been made to the firm choice of clear alternatives, either in law or in politics, and to limiting Communist party restraints on the growth of law and courts. How the criminal process develops in the future will depend to a considerable extent on the continued impact of the revolutionary and traditional influences that have shaped it in the past—and in some measure too, on whether the drive to modernize China economically will cause these influences to be attenuated or transcended.

STANLEY LUBMAN

See also ADVERSARY SYSTEM; CRIMINAL LAW REFORM, *articles on* CONTINENTAL EUROPE *and* ENGLAND; CRIMINAL PROCEDURE: COMPARATIVE ASPECTS.

BIBLIOGRAPHY

Act of the PRC for Punishment of Counterrevolution, 1951. Translated by Jerome A. Cohen and David Finkelstein. *The Criminal Process in the People's Republic of China, 1949–1963: An Introduction.* By Jerome A. Cohen. Cambridge, Mass.: Harvard University Press, 1968, pp. 299–302.

Arrest and Detention Act of the PRC, 1954 (in part). Translated by Jerome A. Cohen and David Finkelstein. *The Criminal Process in the People's Republic of China, 1949–1963: An Introduction.* By Jerome A. Cohen. Cambridge, Mass.: Harvard University Press, 1968, pp. 360–362.

BAO, RUO-WANG, and CHELMINSKI, RUDOLPH. *Prisoner of Mao.* New York: Coward, McCann & Geoghegan, 1973.

BERMAN, HAROLD J.; COHEN, SUSAN; and RUSSELL, MALCOLM. "A Comparison of the Chinese and Soviet Codes of Criminal Law and Procedure." *Journal of Criminal Law and Criminology* 73 (1982): 238–258.

BODDE, DERK, and MORRIS, CLARENCE. *Law in Imperial China: Exemplified by 190 Ch'ing Dynasty Cases, Translated from the Hsing-an hui-lan.* With historical, social, and juridical commentaries. Cambridge, Mass.: Harvard University Press, 1967.

COHEN, JEROME A. "Chinese Mediation on the Eve of Modernization." *California Law Review* 54 (1966): 1201–1226.
_____. *The Criminal Process in the People's Republic of China, 1949–1963: An Introduction.* Cambridge, Mass.: Harvard University Press, 1968.
_____. "Reflections on the Criminal Process in China."

Journal of Criminal Law and Criminology 68 (1977): 323–355.

Constitution of the PRC, 1954. *Documents of the First National People's Congress of the People's Republic of China.* Peking: Foreign Languages Press, 1955, pp. 131–163.

Constitution of the PRC, 1978. *Documents of the First Session of the Fifth National People's Congress of the People's Republic of China.* Peking: Foreign Languages Press, 1978, pp. 125–172.

The Criminal Law of the People's Republic of China. Translated by Jerome A. Cohen, Timothy A. Gelatt, and Florence M. Li. *Journal of Criminal Law and Criminology* 73 (1982): 138–170.

The Criminal Procedure Law of the People's Republic of China. Translated by Jerome A. Cohen, Timothy A. Gelatt, and Florence M. Li. *Journal of Criminal Law and Criminology* 73 (1982): 171–203.

DAMAŠKA, MIRJAN. "Evidentiary Barriers and Two Models of Criminal Procedure: A Comparative Study." *University of Pennsylvania Law Review* 121 (1973): 507–589.
_____. "Structures of Authority and Comparative Criminal Procedure." *Yale Law Journal* 84 (1975): 480–544.

Decision of the State Council of the PRC Relating to the Problems of Rehabilitation through Labor, 1957. Translated by Jerome A. Cohen and David Finkelstein. *The Criminal Process in the People's Republic of China, 1949–1963: An Introduction.* By Jerome A. Cohen. Cambridge, Mass.: Harvard University Press, 1968, pp. 249–250.

Decisions on Death Sentences. *Foreign Broadcast Information Service, Daily Report, People's Republic of China* 81–112, 11 June 1981, p. K4.

FAIRBANK, JOHN K., ed. *Late Ch'ing, 1800–1911.* The Cambridge History of China, vol. 10. Cambridge, England: Cambridge University Press, 1978.

GELATT, TIMOTHY A. "The People's Republic of China and the Presumption of Innocence." *Journal of Criminal Law and Criminology* 73 (1982): 259–316.

GINSBURGS, GEORGE, and STAHNKE, ARTHUR. "The People's Procurorate in Communist China: The Institution Ascendant, 1954–1957." *China Quarterly* 34 (1968): 82–132.
_____. "The People's Procurorate in Communist China: The Period of Maturation, 1951–1954." *China Quarterly* 24 (1965): 53–91.

Harvard Law School. *Preliminary Union List of Materials on Chinese Law, with a List of Chinese Studies and Translations of Foreign Law.* Studies in Chinese Law No. 6. Cambridge, Mass.: Harvard Law School, 1967.

HSIA, TAO-TAI. *Guide to Selected Legal Sources of Mainland China: A Listing of Laws and Regulations and Periodical Legal Literature, with a Brief Survey of the Administration of Justice.* Washington, D.C.: Library of Congress, 1967.

Law of the PRC for the Organization of People's Courts, 1954. Translated by Jerome A. Cohen and David Finkelstein. *The Criminal Process in the People's Republic of China, 1949–1963.* By Jerome A. Cohen. Cambridge, Mass.: Harvard University Press, 1968, pp. 425–566 *passim.*

Law of the PRC for the Organization of People's Procuracies, 1954. Translated by Jerome A. Cohen and David

Finkelstein. *The Criminal Process in the People's Republic of China, 1949–1963.* By Jerome A. Cohen. Cambridge, Mass.: Harvard University Press, 1968, pp. 379–566 *passim.*

Lectures on the General Principles of Criminal Law in the People's Republic of China. Washington, D.C.: U.S. Department of Commerce, Office of Technical Services, Joint Publications Research Service, 1962.

LENG, SHAO-CHUAN. "Criminal Justice in Post-Mao China: Some Preliminary Observations." *China Quarterly* 87 (1981): 440–469.

———. *Justice in Communist China: A Survey of the Judicial System of the People's Republic of China.* Dobbs Ferry, N.Y.: Oceana, 1967.

LI, VICTOR H. *Law without Lawyers: A Comparative View of Law in China and the United States.* Boulder, Colo.: Westview Press, 1978.

———. "The Public Security Bureau and Political-Legal Work in Hui-Yang, 1952–64." *The City in Communist China.* Edited by John Wilson Lewis. Stanford, Calif.: Stanford University Press, 1971, pp. 51–74.

———. "The Role of Law in Communist China." *China Quarterly* 44 (1970): 66–111.

LIN, FU-SHUN. *Chinese Law, Past and Present: A Bibliography of Enactments and Commentaries in English Text.* New York: Columbia University, East Asian Institute, 1966.

LUBMAN, STANLEY. "Form and Function in the Chinese Criminal Process." *Columbia Law Review* 69 (1969): 535–575.

———. "Mao and Mediation: Politics and Dispute Resolution in Communist China." *California Law Review* 55 (1967): 1284–1359.

McALEAVY, HENRY. "The People's Courts in Communist China." *American Journal of Comparative Law* 11 (1962): 52–65.

MICHAEL, FRANZ. "The Role of Law in Traditional, Nationalist, and Communist China." *China Quarterly* 9 (1962): 124–148.

1957 Public Security Regulations Published. *Foreign Broadcast Information Service, Daily Report, People's Republic of China* 80–039, 26 February 1980, pp. L8–L15.

1957 Regulations on Reeducation through Labor Published. *Foreign Broadcast Information Service, Daily Report, People's Republic of China* 80–039, 26 February 1980, pp. L4–L5.

"NPC Promulgates New Regulations on Arrests, Detentions." *Foreign Broadcast Information Service, Daily Report, People's Republic of China* 79–039, 26 February 1979, pp. E2–E5.

Organic Law for People's Courts, 1979. *Foreign Broadcast Information Service, Daily Report, People's Republic of China* 79–146, Supp. 019, 27 July 1979, pp. 20–27.

Organic Law for People's Procuracies, 1979. *Foreign Broadcast Information Service, Daily Report, People's Republic of China* 79–146, Supp. 019, 27 July 1979, pp. 27–33.

PACKER, HERBERT L. *The Limits of the Criminal Sanction.* Stanford, Calif.: Stanford University Press, 1968.

Qing Code (in part). *Ta Tsing Leu Lee: Being the Fundamental Laws of the Penal Code of China.* Translated by George T. Staunton. London: Cadell & Davies, 1810. Reprint, with a selection from the supplementary statutes. Taipei, Taiwan: Ch'eng-wen, 1966.

RHEINSTEIN, MAX, ed. *Max Weber on Law in Economy and Society.* Translated by Edward Shils and Max Rheinstein. Cambridge, Mass.: Harvard University Press, 1954.

State Council Supplementary Regulations. *Foreign Broadcast Information Service, Daily Report, People's Republic of China* 79–232, 30 November 1979, p. L3.

Text of Provisional Regulations on Lawyers. *Foreign Broadcast Information Service, Daily Report, People's Republic of China* 80–169, 28 August 1980, pp. L6–L9.

VOGEL, EZRA F. "Preserving Order in the Cities." *The City in Communist China.* Edited by John Wilson Lewis. Stanford, Calif.: Stanford University Press, 1971, pp. 75–93.

WHYTE, MARTIN K. "Corrective Labor Camps in China." *Asian Survey* 13 (1973): 253–269.

2.

ISLAM

Islamic law does not possess a concept of penal law comparable to that of modern Western systems; instead, it categorizes its offenses by the types of punishments they engender. There are offenses to which are affixed a specified punishment (*ḥadd*); those for which the punishment is at the judge's discretion (*taʿzīr*); those offenses in which a form of retaliatory action or blood money is inflicted against the perpetrator or his kinsmen by the victim's kinsmen (*jināyāt*); offenses against the public policy of the state, involving administrative penalties (*siyāsa*); and those offenses that are corrected by acts of personal penance (*kaffara*).

The classical, sacred law of Islam, the *sharīʿa*, deals primarily with *ḥadd*, *taʿzīr*, and *jināyāt* offenses. Those offenses are to be adjudicated before the judge (*qāḍi*) of the *sharīʿa* courts. Secular tribunals handle administrative offenses under the state's *siyāsa* jurisdiction. Acts of personal penance, or *kaffara*, are usually undertaken voluntarily by the individual outside of any tribunal or court.

The main form and content of the *sharīʿa* arose during the first three and a half centuries after the death of Muhammad in A.D. 632, through the development of "schools of law," which were groupings of legal specialists. There are today four major surviving schools of law in orthodox, or Sunnī, Islam. They are the Maliki, the Ḥanāfi, the Shafiʿī, and the Ḥanbali.

Only during the first century of Islam and later in some parts of West Africa did the *qāḍi* have any authority to develop Islamic penal law through case adjudications. For the most part, the *sharīʿa* has been the province of legal specialists, who are often also religious leaders and who make it the subject of life-long study. Formally, the *shari̇'a* finds its basis in four sources: the Qur'ān (Koran), traditions ascribing certain actions and attitudes to Muhammad, the consensus of jurists on certain legal principles, and additional rules devised by reasoning from analogy. In point of fact, penal law in Islam is significantly influenced not only by the formal sources of the *shari̇'a* but also by pre-Islamic Arabic custom, by the rulings of the judges in the early years of the Islamic empire, by practices from other legal traditions, and by the secular history of the Islamic states.

The portion of the *shari̇'a* dealing with criminal matters is one of its less developed parts, particularly when compared to the law of contract, succession, property, and marriage and divorce. In addition, the extent to which the *shari̇'a* in general has been followed by Islamic societies has varied over time and by locality. The penal provisions have frequently been the least well observed.

There is no clear dividing line between religious and secular offenses in classical Islamic law. The religious element is present in all the categories of offenses, except for some offenses permitted under the administrative discretion (*siyāsa*) of the state. Some variations among the several schools in the interpretation of Islamic penal law are given below. It should be noted, however, that the variety of views is not complete as presented and that alternatives exist.

Specified punishments (*ḥadd*)

Islamic law denotes five "Koranic offenses," which are regarded as offenses directly against Allah and which compel a specific punishment. Theoretically, these offenses find their source in the Koran, although many aspects are post-Koranic developments.

Unlawful intercourse (*zinā'*). The offense of unlawful intercourse consists in having sexual relations with any person not one's lawful spouse or concubine. Thus, if a man marries and has intercourse with a woman not legally capable of becoming his wife, such as a near relative, a fifth wife while four are still living, or a girl below the age of puberty, he violates the prohibition against unlawful intercourse. Strictly speaking, Islamic law has no general conception of adultery as a violation of the marital contract between two persons. It is not a legal basis for divorce, for example. Unlawful intercourse both within and outside of marriage is an offense against God.

The punishment for *zinā'* is either death by stoning or a specified number of lashes. The penalty of death by stoning is not in the Koran but was inflicted as punishment by the first caliphs who succeeded Muhammad. According to some scholars, stoning was adopted from Mosaic law and was incorporated into Islamic law by a later tradition in which Muhammad was said to have approved the practice. Stoning can only be inflicted on one who has been convicted of unlawful intercourse, is not a minor, is mentally competent, is free, and has already had lawful sexual intercourse in marriage. For all others, the punishment is a hundred lashes, or fifty lashes if the convicted person is a slave. In some cases, banishment is added as a penalty.

Even with certain modifications, the *ḥadd* punishments for unlawful intercourse strike many as unnecessarily harsh. Indeed, Islamic jurists have hedged about the crime with so many evidentiary requirements as to make conviction virtually impossible.

As with most *ḥadd* offenses, an action for *zinā'* must normally be brought against an accused within one month of the offense. The proof must affirmatively show not only that unlawful intercourse took place but also that the act was voluntary. For conviction, Islamic law requires either the testimony of four eyewitnesses, instead of the normal two, or the confession of the accused. The witnesses must be competent adult male Muslims. Non-Muslims may testify in cases in which a non-Muslim is charged with *zinā'*. The witnesses must testify that they all saw the same act of unlawful intercourse at the same time. The magistrate who receives their testimony is charged with examining the witnesses assiduously, for they must not only testify to the fact of intercourse but also to its unlawfulness—that is, they must testify that the parties were not married to each other and that the act was voluntary.

Many jurists state that it is meritorious for witnesses to refrain from coming forward so that the accused can settle the offense privately with God. An additional incentive for silence lies in the fact that if the accusation is dismissed, those who testified are subject to the *ḥadd* punishment for false accusation of adultery (discussed below). Even if the case is dismissed for a technical reason, such as the minority of one of the witnesses, all the other witnesses can be charged with false accusation of adultery. If one is convicted by testimony, the four witnesses must be present at the execution and must throw the first stones. Otherwise, the death penalty is not carried out.

Alternatively, one can be convicted of *zinā'* by a personal confession. Again, however, the offender is encouraged to be silent and to turn to God privately for forgiveness. If he does confess, a retraction at any time will void the confession. The magistrate is urged to give the self-accused every opportunity for retraction. Any person who is not liable for the *hadd* punishment for *zinā'* because of any of the limitations listed above may still be prosecuted under the criminal law of discretionary punishment, or *ta'zīr* (discussed below).

False accusation of unlawful intercourse (*kadhf*). Anyone who is competent and adult, whether male or female, Muslim or not, slave or free, is liable if he falsely charges another person with unlawful intercourse if the slandered party is free, adult, competent, Muslim, and not previously convicted of unlawful intercourse. False accusation (*kadhf*) occurs also when one is charged with being illegitimate. Only those who are the objects of the slander (the alleged fornicator or the alleged bastard) or their heirs may bring a charge of *kadhf*.

The *hadd* punishment for *kadhf* is eighty lashes for free persons or forty lashes for a slave. Proof is obtained by normal Islamic penal procedure, either by confession (in this case retraction will not be suggested by the judge) or by the testimony of two adult male free Muslims. The person accused of slander may defend himself by proving that unlawful intercourse actually took place, but he would have to produce the four male witnesses as required by the law on *zinā'*. Those slanders not falling under the strict rules regarding *kadhf* are punished under *ta'zīr*.

Islamic law treats as a special case the accusation by a husband of his wife's adultery, either directly or by denying paternity of her child. The procedure is known as *li'ān*. A husband may charge his wife with infidelity without risk to himself if he swears four times by Allah that he is speaking the truth and, at a fifth oath, calls down a curse upon himself if he is lying. The wife may answer the charge similarly by swearing four times by Allah that she has not sinned and, at a fifth oath, by calling down a curse upon herself if she is not speaking the truth.

If the husband makes an accusation of adultery without using the *li'ān* formula, he is liable to the *hadd* punishment for *kadhf*. The Hanāfi imprison the husband until he pronounces the *li'ān*. If he still refuses, he is declared a liar and given the lashes. If, after an accusation by *li'ān*, the wife does not deny the charge by the *li'ān* formula, this is taken as a tacit confession, and she is subject to the *hadd* punishment for *zinā'*. The *li'ān* is the only legal means by which a man may contest the paternity of his child.

Drinking of wine or intoxicating beverages (*shurb*). The prohibition against drinking wine grew by historic stages in the Koran. Ultimately, drinking was prohibited altogether as Muhammad became scandalized at the drunkenness present in much of Arabic society at the time.

The punishment for drinking intoxicants or for drunkenness is eighty lashes for a freeman and forty for a slave. The punishment is not prescribed in the Koran but was established later and analogized from the punishment for the *kadhf*. The Shafi'ī school limits the punishment to forty and twenty lashes, respectively.

Besides proof by a retractable confession, evidence can be given by two male adult Muslims who saw the accused drinking an intoxicant, smelled the odor of alcohol on his breath, or saw the accused in a state of drunkenness. The accused must be shown to have acted voluntarily and to be competent to stand trial.

Theft (*sariqa*). The *hadd* punishment for theft is the amputation of a hand. However, here too the Islamic jurists have severely limited the kinds of instances to which the punishment may apply. To be guilty of theft, one must be a competent adult and have the mental intention to steal. The act must consist of the removal by stealth of a certain kind of item of a minimum value that is owned by another person.

The stealth requirement means that the item taken must be in a private residence or be under guard and that the thief is not an invited guest. In the Hanāfi school, theft of items in shops, bazaars, or other places open to the public does not incur the *hadd* penalty. The Maliki, however, apply the *hadd* penalty in such cases. The *hadd* penalty does not apply to pickpockets or to one who enters a home stealthily and steals but leaves the residence openly, unless he is trying to escape imminent apprehension. A thief is not subject to the *hadd* if he is caught stealing an item but has not yet left the residence. One who receives a stolen item is not subject to the *hadd* unless he assisted the thief in breaking into the residence. There are additional variations in the above rules.

The minimum value of the stolen item is set at different levels by different jurists. If a person stole different items at different times, even in the same evening, at least one item must be of the minimum value. If there are accomplices in the theft, the value of the thing taken is divided by the number of accomplices. The result must equal or exceed the required minimum value.

The item that is stolen must be a form of property legally capable of ownership. For example, since Muslims are forbidden to own wine, the theft of wine is not regarded as a *hadd* offense. For some jurists, books are not subject to theft, since Islamic law did not develop a law protecting intellectual property and the thief is presumed to be seeking not the physical book but its contents. The Ḥanafi school even exempts the stealing of a free child, for a free person cannot be owned.

The purloined item must be owned by another person. It is not theft if one takes something in which he has a part interest. Also excluded is the taking of property by one's husband, wife, or near relative; by a guest from his host; by a slave from his master; or, in the Maliki school, by one whose accomplice is an ascendant relative of the owner of the stolen property.

Except in cases in which the thief confesses, the charge must be brought by the owner of the thing stolen. If the accused is convicted, the owner must be present at the punishment or it will not be performed. If the thief returns the stolen item before a charge is lodged, he cannot be accused. Finally, if one is poor and steals out of need, he does not have the requisite mental intention to have committed the act of theft. Depending on the circumstances, if a charge of theft under the rules of *hadd* punishments cannot be brought, the offense is reduced either to one of discretionary punishment (*ta'zīr*) or to usurpation of another's property, which is only a civil offense.

In the relatively unlikely circumstance that one is convicted for the *hadd* offense of thievery, his right hand will be amputated and the wound cauterized. If he is subsequently convicted of other thefts, the amputations proceed to the left foot, left hand, and right foot.

Highway robbery or brigandage (*qaṭ'al-ṭarīq*). The crime of highway robbery is an extremely serious offense, since it threatens the calm and stability of society itself. Two kinds of offenses are covered by the prohibition: robbery of travelers who are far from aid, and armed entrance into a private home with the intent to rob it. Both Muslims and non-Muslims are protected from robbers by this law.

If one is convicted of *qaṭ'al-ṭarīq*, the punishment is amputation of the right hand and left foot for the first offense and amputation of the left hand and right foot for the second offense. If murder took place during an attempted robbery, the punishment is death by the sword. If there was murder accompanied by an actual theft, the penalty is crucifixion. The body is to be hung for three days. Unlike the normal case of murder, where the relatives of the victim have a choice of retaliation, blood money, or pardon of the offender, the death penalty here is mandatory. All accomplices must be treated in the same way. If one (a minor, for example) cannot be given the *hadd* punishment, neither can any of the others.

Discretionary punishment (*ta'zīr*)

Ta'zīr did not enter Islamic law from the customary Arabic law, which provides the basis for the tort-based law of retaliation, nor is it based on the *hadd* crimes listed in the Koran with their subsequent glosses. Rather, *ta'zīr* developed in the early Islamic empire of the Umayyads (A.D. 661–750) and grew out of the discretionary punishments the *qādi* imposed when he was part of the imperial bureaucratic apparatus. This practice became incorporated into the official structure of Islamic law during the early development of the various schools of law. Much of the later growth of penal law within the Islamic empires was ignored by the schools after their doctrines had hardened.

Ta'zīr was designed to punish those who violate the law and act against God or man. The objective of the punishment was prevention of the recurrence of the crime, deterrence to others, and reform of the guilty party. The judge would attempt to accomplish those objectives by varying the punishment according to the circumstances of the case, of the convicted party, and of society. Consequently, acts of reparation and repentance by the offender are relevant to a judge's sentence. So also are interventions made before the court on behalf of the offender; such interventions are forbidden in cases dealing with *hadd* offenses.

The punishments cover a range of severity, as follows: (1) a private admonition to the guilty party, sometimes by letter; (2) a public reprimand in court; (3) a public proclamation of the offender's guilt; (4) a suspended sentence; (5) banishment; (6) a fine; (7) flogging; (8) imprisonment; and (9) death. The schools are divided on some of the punishments. The Ḥanafi school and some of the jurists of the Shafi'i school deny that fines are a legitimate punishment in Islamic law; the other schools accept the validity of fines.

Similar differences arise on the issues of flogging and death. The general rule in all of the schools, except the Maliki, is that no punishment in *ta'zīr* can exceed a *hadd* penalty. Although the death penalty is to be used only in extreme cases, all the schools allow it.

For one to be subject to *ta'zīr*, he must be fully competent. The standard of proof is less strict than in cases of *hadd*: either a confession or the testimony of two witnesses is sufficient for conviction. Some jurists permit one of the witnesses to be a woman. In *ta'zīr*, a confession is not retractable. Certain legal specialists teach that a judge may proceed on his own knowledge without the need of confession or witnesses.

Offenses under *ta'zīr* include perjury, usury, and slander. Many thefts, acts of unlawful intercourse, and false accusations of adultery that escape the rigorous rules under the *ḥadd* punishments can be dealt with under *ta'zīr*. For example, only under *ta'zīr* can a non-Muslim be protected from the *kadhf*. *Ta'zīr* is the most important area of classical Islamic criminal law, since it has traditionally included the bulk of criminal offenses. Because the central aspect of *ta'zīr* is discretionary punishment by the judge, and because Islamic law categorizes offenses according to their penalties, there has never developed a rigorous code of penal offenses under *ta'zīr* within the classical schools of law. Some Islamic rulers and states have indeed codified penal offenses, but where punishments have also been specifically required, such a codification would not fit into the traditional category of *ta'zīr*.

Homicide and bodily harm (*jināyāt*)

The attitude of Islamic law toward homicide and bodily harm straddles the areas of tort and of crime. Pre-Islamic Arabia treated attacks against one's tribesman as an attack on the tribe itself. Such an attack could result in a blood feud between the two tribes where any member of the other tribe was an object of vengeance. Through arbitration, justice could sometimes be secured by retaliation against the specific offender or by the payment of blood money to the victim's tribesmen.

Islamic law accepted the basic structure of the traditional Arabic law of homicide and bodily harm, but modified it in three ways: (1) the blood feud was abolished; (2) vengeance could be exacted only after a trial before a judicial authority, which determined the guilt of the accused; and (3) punishment was scaled according to the offender's degree of culpability and the harm inflicted on the victim. There is a wide variety in the interpretation of the rules by the various schools of law.

Three kinds of punishments can be permitted in cases of proven homicide or bodily harm: retaliation, blood money, and penitence. The punishments are applicable only if the victim is harmed or killed within a Muslim state.

Where retaliation (*qiṣāṣ*) is applied, the guilty party is liable to the same degree of harm as he inflicted on his victim. In the case of homicide, the nearest kinsman of the victim performs the retaliation. Where there is bodily harm, the victim is entitled to perform the act of vengeance. In all schools except the Ḥanāfi, the general rule is that retaliation is allowed only in cases in which the victim was equal or superior to the attacker in terms of freedom and religion.

With a few exceptions among the opinions of the jurists, the general rule is that in nearly all cases, a father may not be killed in retaliation for murdering his child, but the child can be subject to the penalty for patricide. The same formula applies to homicidal actions between masters and slaves. The Ḥanāfi school is alone in holding that a freeman may be subject to retaliation if he kills the slave of another.

Retaliation can come about if, after proper conviction, the nearest relative of the victim (or the master, in the case of a slave) demands it. The schools differ on the question of which relatives have standing to demand retaliation and which have the right to inflict a capital retaliation. If the victim has no living relatives, the right of retaliation falls to the state, which can execute the offender.

In the case of wounding, the victim must demand retaliation. Before he dies from his injuries, a wounded man can, on his own, remit retaliation for the offender. If the guilty party dies before retaliation can be inflicted on him, the case lapses entirely in the Maliki and Ḥanāfi schools, but the Shafi'ī and the Ḥanbali allow blood money (*diya*) to be paid. If many persons participated in the murder, all can suffer retaliation if the action of any one of them would have resulted in death.

A murderer is to be killed in the same way as he killed, according to the Maliki and Shafi'ī schools. The Ḥanāfi require execution by the sword and punish any other form of execution by *ta'zīr*. The Ḥanbali jurists are divided on the issue. If a person is entitled to inflict retaliation but inflicts it before proper judicial procedure has been completed, he is subject to *ta'zīr*. If a man avenges a killing without any possible legal entitlement, he himself is subject to the law of retaliation.

In cases of bodily harm, an exact equivalence of harm is inflicted on the perpetrator: a hand for a hand, a tooth for a tooth. Loss of sight can be avenged, but not the loss of an eyeball, for the injury cannot be exactly duplicated. Neither can retaliation be inflicted for the loss of the nose or penis. Only blood money is permitted as punishment in those cases.

If there was an attack by many, all the perpetrators suffer the same loss as the wounded victim, but this is not permitted in the Ḥanāfi school. Nor do the Ḥanāfi permit retaliation for wounding between men and women or between slaves. When retaliation is allowed, all schools except the Maliki allow the victim to return the wound. The Maliki assign an expert to inflict the punishment. Any excess harm is punishable by *ta'zīr*.

The second form of punishment is blood money. The *diya* is sometimes an alternative to retaliation, at the option of the nearest relative of the slain person or of the wounded victim. At other times, depending on the circumstances of the crime, *diya* and forgiveness are the only options available.

The traditional *diya*, as taken over from Arabic custom, is set at two levels. In serious cases the heavier *diya* is imposed, set at a hundred female camels equally divided between one-, two-, three-, and four-year-olds. In less serious cases the lighter *diya* is imposed, amounting to eighty female camels, similarly divided by age, in addition to twenty one-year-old male camels.

The *diya* is paid by the near relatives of the offender to the heirs of the deceased, or to the wounded victim. If the near relatives cannot be found, the state assumes the obligation to pay the *diya*. In all but the Ḥanāfi school, the full amount of the *diya* is due only when the victim is a free male Muslim. If the victim is a *ḍimmi* (a non-Muslim protected by treaty) or a *musta'min* (a non-Muslim under safe-conduct pass), the *diya* ranges from one-third to one-half of that for a Muslim except in the Ḥanāfi school, which requires full payment. The *diya* for a murdered slave is his market value.

The *diya* for bodily injury is a proportion of the payment for loss of life. If there is only one of a bodily part, such as the nose, the *diya* is the same as for loss of life. If there are more than one, the *diya* is proportionately smaller—for example, one-half for an arm, a leg, or an eye; one-tenth for a finger; a third of one-tenth for each joint of a finger; and one-twentieth for a tooth. The jurists have established an elaborate scale of payments. If an injury falls outside of the defined examples, compensation is paid on the basis of the "actual harm suffered" (but does not include any pain and suffering endured). The *diya* for a woman is half that of a man, but in no case, such as for partial injuries, is it to fall below a third of what a man would receive.

The third form of punishment is penitence (*kaffara*), but penitence is never the sole required punishment. When imposed, it is attached in certain kinds of cases to the payment of *diya*. An act of penitence consists in freeing a Muslim slave or, if one has no slaves, in fasting during daylight hours for two consecutive months.

Generally speaking, Islamic law holds that those entitled to retaliation or *diya* may remit the punishment on their own accord or may agree to any level of settlement, although not normally higher than the legal *diya*.

Most schools divide homicide into three categories;

the Ḥanāfi have developed five. The first category is that of *willful homicide*. This is an action resulting in death that was undertaken with no legal excuse, with the intention to wound or kill, and by means of an instrument that normally causes death. The punishment is retaliation or, if remitted, the heavier *diya*, plus loss to the offender of any rights of inheritance from the deceased, although the Maliki and some Shafi'i do allow the guilty party to receive a bequest from the will of the deceased. More than any other school, the Maliki define willful homicide by ideas of intent and actual causality that are similar to those in modern Western law. Many jurists in the Shafi'i school, on the other hand, do not require an independent proof of intent. Any attack with a dangerous weapon is sufficient.

All schools except the Ḥanāfi categorize as willful homicide death resulting from intentional false testimony at trial, as well as death caused by intentionally withholding food and water. The Shafi'i and the Hanbali also term as willful homicide any fatal action resulting from repeated blows, no one of which would normally cause death. Of course, homicide as part of highway robbery is a *hadd* offense and is punished by execution.

In *quasi-willful homicide*, there is an intent to kill or wound with an instrument not normally known to be fatal. If death results, the punishment consists of the heavier *diya*, acts of penitence, and loss of inheritance rights, but here too the Shafi'i allow a bequest granted by will to stand. If only bodily harm results, the offense is then one of willful wounding, the punishment for which is retaliation or, if remitted, the appropriate proportion of the *diya*. The Maliki have no separate category of quasi-willful homicide. If the instrument did in fact cause death by the willful act of the perpetrator, then it is a case of willful homicide.

Accidental homicide is a type of homicide in which the offender either did not intend to kill a person or he did intend to kill a person but believed that he was acting legally. For example, if one shoots at an animal but misses and kills a person instead, if one believes he is shooting at a deer but in reality is shooting at a human being, or if during wartime one kills a Muslim under the impression that he is a non-Muslim, the case will be treated as accidental homicide. The punishment is payment of the lighter *diya*, the obligation to perform acts of penitence (except in the Ḥanāfi school), and the loss of inheritence rights in the Ḥanāfi and the Ḥanbali schools. The Ḥanāfi and the Shafi'i categorize as accidental homicide a case in which one intends to kill a specific person and kills another person by mistake. The Ḥanbali and Maliki schools term that action willful homicide.

In *quasi-accidental homicide*, one of the two other categories added by the Ḥanāfi, death is caused without intent to harm and without a deadly instrument, as when a sleeping person falls out of a house or tree and kills someone below. The penalty is the same as in cases of accidental homicide. The second of these categories is that of *indirect homicide*, wherein some instrumentality not directly controlled by the killer at the time of death causes the death of the victim, as when someone falls into a pit dug by the guilty party and dies. The penalty is the lighter *diya* (or its proper proportion in cases of bodily injury). There are myriad other examples of what does or does not constitute culpable behavior under indirect homicide.

Procedurally, the charge of homicide must be brought by the nearest relative of the deceased, or by the wounded victim. Proof is by retractable confession or by testimony of two male witnesses. In addition, there is the unusual procedure known as *kasama*, whereby the oaths of fifty reliable persons who are not witnesses are accepted as proof where incomplete evidence has created a presumption of guilt. The Maliki school utilizes *kasama* to complete proof. The Ḥanāfi use it to prevent a conviction.

In a number of instances, killing or inflicting bodily injury is excused. Of course, retaliation properly applied after an adjudication of guilt is permitted. There is no culpability if a man kills his wife, daughter, or sister as well as her lover if he discovers them in an act of unlawful intercourse, and none, except in the Maliki school, for harm or death inflicted with the consent of the victim.

Self-defense is permitted if it is an act of resistance to an unlawful assault and if it is proportionate to the danger. Preemptive action is allowed to forestall an imminent attack. However, in the Ḥanāfi school, one must pay the heavier *diya* if he uses a deadly weapon to kill a minor or insane person in self-defense. Killing combatants in lawful war is permitted and, in many cases, may take on an obligatory nature. One is permitted to kill male non-Muslims who refuse to pay the obligatory poll tax and who also refuse to convert to Islam.

There is also the special case of the apostate from Islam. The schools are divided on the issue. For some jurists, an apostate may be killed with impunity, without a trial. Others demand a trial first. A male apostate is given three days to repent before execution; a female is imprisoned and beaten until she repents. Some jurists classify apostasy as a *ḥadd* offense; others, as *siyāsa* (discussed below). It should be emphasized that some modern Muslim jurists assert that the penalty for apostasy was a later accretion and has no authority from the Koran or elsewhere.

Discretionary administrative penalties (*siyāsa*)

Under Islamic law, the secular authorities do not possess a power to legislate independently of the *sharīʿa*, but the state may develop public policies by enacting and enforcing administrative regulations. The regulations are designed to help effectuate the *sharīʿa* and to regulate those areas in which the *sharīʿa* has left gaps. *Siyāsa* regulations are not supposed to conflict with the provisions of the *sharīʿa*. Nonetheless, it has been through the mechanism of *siyāsa* that the Islamic states have supplanted many of the penal requirements of the *sharīʿa*.

From the earliest days, the Islamic states have employed a number of means to control the content and the process of criminal law. Much of the ill-defined area of *taʿzīr* has been taken over by enacting specific regulations and penalties. Most significantly, early rulers withdrew much, if not most, criminal jurisdiction from the *qādi* in the *sharīʿa* courts and lodged it in their own secular courts, staffed by imperial appointees. Even the judges themselves were appointed by secular authority. The jurists of Islamic law have explicitly recognized the right of a ruler to limit the jurisdiction of the *qādi* to whatever extent the ruler wishes. Even where the *qādi* retains jurisdiction, he is dependent on the government to enforce the judgment. The combination of *siyāsa* and the power over jurisdiction effectively shifted the definition and enforcement of criminal regulations to the state, although the *sharīʿa* significantly influenced the content of the secular criminal law.

A number of institutions gave the state effective control over criminal law matters. Originally instituted for the purpose of preserving public order, the *shurṭa*, or police, soon became a competitor for power with the *qādi* courts. Suspicion was cause enough for the *shurṭa* to arrest and punish persons without the evidentiary and substantive limitations of the *sharīʿa*. The state also took over from the former Sassanian kings of Persia (A.D. 226–641) a set of tribunals with equity jurisdiction (*maẓālim*). Many of the *siyāsa* regulations were enforced by the *maẓālim* courts. The *sharīʿa* courts retained dominance in the areas of succession and family law and, to some extent, in cases involving contracts, property, and personal injury.

In the former Byzantine provinces, the Islamic empire continued the use of the "inspector of the market" (*ḥisba*), who enforced the rules regulating trade, commerce, health, and traffic. The duties of the office were expanded to include punishment of offenses against Islamic morals, here too without the procedural protections of the *sharīʿa* courts.

In the nineteenth and twentieth centuries, two overlapping reform movements directed the law even farther away from the traditional rules of the *sharī'a*. One group of Muslim law reformers sought to reinterpret the values and sources of Islamic law outside of the confines established by the schools of law. Another group of reformers, influenced by Western structures of law, has had significant impact on Islamic states. Particularly in the case of criminal law, virtually every Islamic country has adopted a European-style criminal code. In most states, *sharī'a* courts have been abolished or restricted to cases involving personal status. Only in Saudi Arabia, Yemen, and Afghanistan have the *sharī'a* and its courts been maintained with wide jurisdictional powers. Other Islamic nations, such as Pakistan and revolutionary Iran, have made uncertain moves toward reestablishing Islamic law. Colonel Mu'ammar al-Qaḏafi proclaimed the reimposition of the *ḥadd* punishments in Libya, but mainly as a measure seeking Muslim legitimization of his overthrow of the royal house. Despite the rhetoric, Libyan criminal law remains of the European type.

In Saudi Arabia, the *sharī'a* courts are the primary courts of the nation, having jurisdiction over most matters covered by the *sharī'a*. Judges follow the Ḥanbali school, but a 1961 governmental decree permits a *qāḏi* to go beyond the Ḥanbali rules if the decision is faithful to the sources of Islamic law. Under its *siyāsa* jurisdiction, the government has established boards that adjudicate cases arising under administrative decrees in the areas of commerce, labor, taxes, and traffic. It has also legislated penalties, such as fines and imprisonment, that the *qāḏi* imposes in addition to the requirements of the *sharī'a*. The Saudi government has established higher courts—unknown to traditional Islamic law—that can hear appeals from *qāḏi* judgments. It also operates *maẓālim* courts.

Acts of penitence (*kaffara*)

Kaffara consists in the performance of certain acts of penitence to cover or expiate sinful acts. The acts of penitence are the freeing of a Muslim slave, fasting during daylight hours (while also abstaining from sexual intercourse), or, in some cases, giving alms to the poor. In rare cases, *kaffara* is accomplished by the sacrifice of a goat, sheep, camel, or cow.

Although the lawbooks prescribe *kaffara* for certain sins, the imposition of the penance is almost always voluntary. Only in exceptional cases can a *qāḏi* require *kaffara*. Offenses for which *kaffara* is prescribed include breaking an oath, perjury, breaking fast during the holy month of Ramadan, or hunting or breaking other rules while in a consecrated state for the holy pilgrimage to Mecca.

Summary

The description of the types of offenses under Islamic penal law illustrates the basic distinctions that Islam makes in categorizing wrongful behavior. (1) Where there is an offense against God, a sanction is appropriate, whether it be *ḥadd*, *ta'zīr*, or *kaffara*. (2) Offenses solely against man are compensated under the civil law. (3) Some offenses are characterized as against both God and man, as seen in the law of homicide and bodily harm. (4) Only under *siyāsa* has there developed historically the concept of offenses against the state.

DAVID F. FORTE

See also ADVERSARY SYSTEM; CRIMINAL LAW REFORM, *articles on* CONTINENTAL EUROPE *and* ENGLAND; CRIMINAL PROCEDURE: COMPARATIVE ASPECTS.

BIBLIOGRAPHY

ANDERSON, JAMES N. D. "Homicide in Islamic Law." *Bulletin of the School of Oriental and African Studies, University of London* 13 (1951): 811–828.

———. *The Maliki Law of Homicide.* Zaria, Nigeria: Gaskaya Corporation, n.d.

BAROODY, GEORGE M. "Crime and Punishment under Hanbali Law." Master's thesis, American University at Cairo, 1962.

BASSIOUNI, M. CHERIF, ed. *The Islamic Criminal Justice System.* London and New York: Oceana, 1982.

DONALDSON, DWIGHT M. *Studies in Muslim Ethics.* London: SPCK, 1953.

MAYER, ANN ELIZABETH. "Libyan Legislation in Defense of Arabo-Islamic Sexual Mores." *American Journal of Comparative Law* 28 (1980): 287–313.

RAHIM, ABDUR. *The Principles of Muhammadan Jurisprudence According to the Hanafi, Maliki, Shafi'i, and Hanbali Schools* (1911). Reprint. Westport, Conn.: Hyperion Press, 1981.

SCHACHT, JOSEPH. *An Introduction to Islamic Law.* Oxford: Oxford University Press, Clarendon Press, 1964.

SOLAIM, SOLIMAN A. "Saudi Arabia's Judicial System." *Middle East Journal* 25 (1971): 403–407.

VICKER, RAY. "Moslem Justice." *Wall Street Journal*, 11 May 1979, pp. 1, 30.

3.
PRELITERATE SOCIETIES

Emerging problems

Preliterate societies do not constitute a single type of society but a whole assortment of societies. Just as most people speak about English, Soviet, or Chinese law, an anthropologist speaks about Tongan,

Tiv, or Zapotec law. Any study of criminal law in preliterate societies must take this diversity into account. The comparative perspective, however, need not stress only the differences among preliterate societies, or between preliterate societies and our own, but may uncover similarities as well. The inhabitants of Mexican mountain villages are generally peaceful, whereas New Guinea highland communities tend to be warlike. Melanesians settle most of their disputes through negotiation, and so do Americans. Both the Lenje of Zambia and the Japanese stress restitution. Clearly, in trying to understand human behavior, Western concepts present difficulties. The concept of crime, for example, an idea related to the development of the state, becomes problematic when applied cross-culturally in societies with little or no government. The world of preliterate and literate societies presents a rich laboratory in which to examine the problem of universal categories.

Early studies. Nineteenth-century anthropologists interested in preliterate law were armchair speculators who first investigated the differences between Western and non-Western law. Two viewpoints emerged. Some theorists, such as Emile Durkheim, described primitive law as penal and repressive in contrast with that of more advanced and specialized societies, which generally used restitutive sanctions. Others, like Leonard Hobhouse, challenged that distinction, arguing instead that as human societies become more advanced, their legal systems progress from a reliance on self-redress to formal sanctions of punishment or restitution.

Later generations of anthropologists studied societies through actual fieldwork, which revealed that the models developed by armchair anthropologists were either oversimplified or wrong. These "newer" anthropologists were struck by the wide diversity in social organization and attempted to understand and then explain the ways in which different societies manage the serious wrongs that might endanger their peace and security.

The most powerful break with the past was made by Bronislaw Malinowski, a field observer of the first rank who used his detailed observations to destroy widespread myths about law and order among preliterate peoples. In *Crime and Custom in Savage Society* (1926) he argued persuasively that people do not automatically conform to rules of conduct in what were then called the "simpler societies": positive inducements were as important as sanctions in inducing social conformity. Malinowski also called attention to the important connection between social control and social relations, an idea that foreshadowed a generation of anthropological research on how peace could

be achieved in societies that Malinowski described as lacking in central authority, codes, courts, and constables. His definition of *crime* was "the law broken." Precision in definition defied Malinowski, who wrote that crime in Trobriand societies could be only vaguely defined as an "outburst of passion, sometimes the breach of a definite taboo, sometimes an attempt on person or property (murder, theft, assault), sometimes an indulgence in too high ambitions or wealth, not sanctioned by tradition, in conflict with the prerogatives of the chief or some notable" (p. 99).

A. R. Radcliffe-Brown, a contemporary of Malinowski, was more jurisprudential in approach. In 1933 he made use of Roscoe Pound's definition of *law* as "social control through the systematic application of the force of politically organized society" (p. 202). Radcliffe-Brown had studied the Andaman Islanders of the Bay of Bengal, a people he described as without any law at all. By defining *law* in terms of organized legal sanctions, Radcliffe-Brown concluded that in some simpler societies there is no law. He did not find terms such as *civil law* and *criminal law* useful in analyzing data from other societies; instead, he observed a distinction between public law (which made use of penal or repressive sanctions) and private law (which emphasized restitutive sanctions). Like Malinowski, Radcliffe-Brown viewed crimes as acts that cause the entire community to react in anger and that engender a collective feeling of moral indignation.

Modern approaches. Today most anthropologists of law do not define *crime*, nor do they attempt to impose such distinctions as those between crime, tort, delict, sin, and immorality on their data. Hardly any anthropologist would accept as valid the distinction between public and private law. The problem of distinctions is discussed, but anthropologists increasingly report data without attempting to categorize them in terms of Western legal thought; instead they adopt, for purposes of analysis, the categories used by the people studied or of the social scientist, and eschew attempts to define *crime* in a universal manner.

Diverse concepts of crime. Antisocial conduct is a universal aspect of group life, but the forms it takes and the reactions it provokes vary according to each group's culture and social organization. In some societies today infanticide, cannibalism, theft, or the selling of products known to be harmful fall in the area of conduct approved by authorities, but standards of good and bad behavior are not constant over time. Records covering the Tswana peoples of Africa over a hundred-year period indicate not only that "crimes" are in a state of flux but also that crime is not necessarily disapproved of by all members of society. In one example, Isaac Schapera observed that a "civil" wrong was treated as such by one chief, made a "penal" offense by another, and denied legal recognition by a third. Notions of specific wrongs may be internalized by and reflect the behavioral norms of a group, or they may be ordered from above. Schapera's study indicates that native law is not static and that it was founded on deliberate enactment as well as custom.

Since there are no wrongs that are universal to preliterate societies and no behavior that is bad in itself, the nature of an act alone cannot be used to determine its social or legal meaning. For the Ontong Javanese, as for many societies, killing kin is murder and killing non-kin is not. Among the Tiv of Nigeria, killing thieves or witches may be permissible.

The relationship of all the parties concerned may determine whether an act is regarded as a crime. For the Kapauku of New Guinea, intraconfederacy killing is murder, whereas killing outside the confederacy is warfare if approved by the elders; otherwise, starting a war is a crime punishable by death. In New Guinea an offense is defined more by the social context than by the nature of the act; there are no broad distinctions between types of offenses, and opinions about what constitutes the "same" crime vary widely from group to group or among individuals in a group. Among the Kipsigi of Kenya the same offense will meet with different consequences according to the political differences between the opposing parties.

The task of discovering the factors that determine the seriousness of an act has encouraged a relativistic approach, since categories in some societies may bear no resemblance to standard Western ones. There is, for example, no special Lozi term for *crime*, although Max Gluckman (1965, p. 4) reports a distinction between *wrong* and *great wrong*. The Tiv rank acts by their social consequences, the most serious being incest, homicide, and sometimes adultery. The Yakan of the Philippines distinguish between wrongs that can lead to disputes, and wrongs against God (or moral wrongs), which do not bring legal consequences to the offender. Among the Jalé of the New Guinea highlands, intention is less important than consequence in defining an act as an offense. Attempted murder is not a crime since it inflicts no harm, but if a woman dies in childbirth the husband is as responsible for the death (since he impregnated her) as is a man who kills another in a fight. Among the Zinacantecan of southern Mexico, circumstances surrounding an offense are crucial; if an offense is committed when the offender is not under the influence of alcohol, or is a repeated offense, the act is considered serious enough to require punishment as well as the compensation sufficient for lesser offenses.

Radcliffe-Brown's distinction between public and private law has not been found useful by modern anthropologists because of the difficulty in determining whether an offense is against the individual or the society, as Karl Llewellyn and E. Adamson Hoebel have shown with regard to Cheyenne society. Often it is both.

Diverse concepts of punishment. Early notions about sanctions in preliterate societies are not supported by the data. Durkheim's theory that a repressive and penal law characterizes the "inferior societies" is incorrect. As a matter of fact, restitution plays a predominant role in face-to-face societies. Restitution is the process whereby money or services are paid by the offender or the offender's family to the victim or the victim's family: it may be paid in kind (a life for a life) or in equivalence (a wife for a life). There are various forms of liability: absolute and contingent, collective and individual. Klaus-Friedrich Koch has proposed that the distinction between absolute and contingent (relative) liability depends upon the availability of third parties to facilitate review of a case. Without formal governmental control or indigenous third-party mechanisms, liability will be absolute. Similarly, collective responsibility is likely to prevail where descent groups are the primary units in the organization of a society.

Among the Berbers of the Atlas Mountains of Morocco, restitution follows a pattern of collective and contingent liability. After an act of physical aggression, the culprit and his close kinsmen escape to a sanctuary provided by the religious leaders for a cooling-off period, which is then followed by a period of mediated negotiation between the victim's group and that of the offender. Compromises usually recognize degrees of seriousness of the act and the status of the victim; the higher the victim's status, the greater the restitution. The Egyptian bedouin of the western desert regard the consequence of the act and the status of both parties as the primary determinants of the amount of restitution. The Ifugao of northern Luzon recognize a scale of payment that varies according to the social position of the injured party and the offender; higher payments accompany higher positions.

The reparation process may function as a deterrent, since the process implicates kin groups on both sides. Once a reparation has been agreed on, the victim is often urged to avoid further conflict with the offender so as not to forfeit the kin's right to compensation, and the members of the offender's group usually have a vested interest in keeping him in line because they are paying for his actions. The threat of a mutually destructive feud gives added incentive to abide by the agreement. However, a society that uses restitution as a strategy may also use retaliation, raids, property seizures, and fines. Retaliative sanctions are systematized through rules governing how the injured party may strike back and how much the injured parties should demand for righting a wrong or punishing an individual.

Restitution can be found in societies both with and without formalized political systems. Even societies without such systems—the Yurok of California, the Ifugao of Luzon, or the bedouin of Egypt—can have very sophisticated, even if unwritten, indemnity codes. Such substantive law can develop independently of legal procedures, courts, and complex political organization. On the other hand, a society can have a formal court system and not use it. In Japan the question of restitution is settled almost entirely extrajudicially, by agreements between victim and offender.

Finally, restitution is used sparingly in preliterate societies, most often in cases of murder, theft, debt, adultery, and property damage. The restitutive sanction, whether collective or individual, restores social equilibrium by addressing the needs of the victim or the victim's kin, by restating social values, and by providing a means for reintegrating the offender into the mainstream without too much stigma. Among the Valley Zapotec of Mexico, who follow the law of both the village and the state, the process of reintegration into the village begins after the offender's release from jail. This process entails a gradual resumption of relationships between the offender and the community by means of material and interpersonal exchanges. By Zapotec definition, ex-offenders build up social relationships by exchange as a means of removing stigma. The Zapotec do not keep the deviant permanently on the margin of society but reintegrate him through the resumption of social interchange and through a "collective amnesia" which serves to deny that the crime ever occurred in the first place.

Habitual misbehavior is considered more threatening than single offenses in preliterate as in complex societies. The custom of group lynching among the Kamba of East Africa was reserved for habitual thieves or sorcerers. These community killings involved no blood guilt but did require consent of an offender's nearest relatives. The Tiv are critical of Nigerian state law, which punishes single murders harshly while denying the community the right to execute habitual offenders for behavior that the Tiv see as more dangerous. The Tiv judge a person's general behavior, rather than a specific wrong.

Social control and the state. The evolution of the state and the growth of governmental machinery for regulating social relations provided the political con-

text for the development of penal criminal law. In large and complex societies, in which social differentiation is great and conflicting values are juxtaposed, a small number of people representing the powerful interests of the state define what the law will call criminal. The criminal act becomes an act against the state. As the initiator of third-party hearings, the offended merely becomes the victim, and loses the important status of plaintiff.

With the emergence of the state, there is an increasing reliance on penal sanctions to deter antisocial behavior. In preliterate or prestate societies the legal sanction, whether penal or restitutive, represents only one means of enforcing conformity to norms. Control mechanisms such as sorcery and suicide, which had often been labeled as criminal behavior by Western observers, were seen by Malinowski as legal and socially rehabilitative mechanisms—behaviors that supported the preliterate social order. Beatrice Whiting's work on Paiute Indians reported that sorcery was found in societies with decentralized political systems, and she argued that sorcery is an important mechanism of social control in decentralized systems. A study of purely criminal law among preliterate peoples misses just such important phenomena of their legal life.

Radcliffe-Brown argued that in preliterate societies there is a close connection between religious behavior and the sanctions of criminal law. In fact, supernatural sanctions may be more threatening to an offender than physical retaliation against him or material compensation to his victim, because they are so vague and unpredictable. Public shame and ridicule or the sanction of supernaturally imposed sickness both constitute a means for societal regulation. When formalized legal sanctions coexist with less formal controls, the latter have often been more effective in restraining disruptive social conduct and strengthening the cohesion of social relations. It is important to realize that courts, police, and the like are not necessary to achieve order in societies where there is a wide range of checks on human conduct that are functionally equivalent to enforcement agencies in state societies. Among the eighteenth-century Iroquois, for example, theft and vandalism were almost unknown. Public opinion in the form of gossip and ridicule was sufficient to deter most members of the tribe from such property crimes.

Crime and social structure

Order and disorder. Theories have been proposed to explain the relation between modes of production and the organization of social controls. For example, a number of anthropologists have observed that hunters and gatherers do not develop means for adjudicating disputes, but rather for avoidance of disputes. Order and disorder are present in both small and large societies. For this reason, the presence or absence of order (however one measures order) is not easily explained by theories of size, means of livelihood, or ecology. Although understanding diversity in relation to law is crucial to understanding prestate societies as a group, law as it relates to order can never be comprehended by scientific rules of evidence except in the context of the particular society that houses this law.

A productive approach to an examination of order and disorder is to analyze the influence of social organization. Most ethnographic studies of a specific society describe how relationships or institutions function to coordinate social activities or to organize social relations, or they describe how the society is disordered by just such factors. In the social organization of the Mexican Zapotec town of Talea, the binding force of reciprocity and the principles of social organization provide systematic ordering (Nader). The ties that link citizens are those of kinship, locale, common work interests, friendships, and shared obligations and values. Three dimensions of Talean social organization best indicate the manner in which principles of social control operate outside of governmental organization.

First, in Talea, all groups, whether kinship, governmental, or religious, are organized hierarchically according to sex, age, wealth, or experience. Second, a value is placed on symmetry (a term that translates as *equality* only in some contexts), which serves to level relationships. Such leveling mechanisms as those that redistribute wealth from the rich to the poor mediate the harsher aspects of hierarchy but do not sabotage the virtues of superordinate-subordinate relationships. The third dimension of Talean social organization brings people together as groups or as individuals, and at the same time divides them by linking some of them with different groups. These three dimensions stratify, level, and integrate the town: they reinforce hierarchy and symmetry by buttressing traditional and changing values, and they strengthen the linkages by ensuring the presence of third parties in case of dispute. Asymmetry is both unappealing and dangerous; it is often the underlying cause of envy, witchcraft accusations, and court disputes. The integrative links between individuals and groups provide a safety valve and cool most disputes before excessive pressure builds up.

The Taleans are therefore a relatively peaceful people, unlike their neighbors in the mountains, the people of Yalalag, who have a high annual rate of violent killings. Yalalag, divided into two traditionally opposed parts, each with its own leaders, illustrates that without a social organization which links groups together, institutions for the peaceful settlement of disputes do not develop. Although Talea and Yalalag are similar in cultural history, size, ecology, and economy, differences in social organization have produced different means for managing problems and disputes. The Taleans tend to use third-party mechanisms, whereas the people of Yalalag use self-help tactics such as assault, battery, and killing.

The social correlates of relatively violent or peaceful societies have been the subject of extensive research. For example, studies on preliterate societies have correlated place of residence after marriage with the management of conflict. H. U. E. Thoden van Velzen and W. Van Wetering have examined the question of residence and violence cross-culturally and have found a consistent relationship between the predominant use of passive means of managing conflict, and the use of matrilocal residency rules, which locate married couples with maternal relatives. They also recognized the relationships between residence with the paternal relatives of the group, the development of mutually exclusive fraternal interest groups, and the frequent use of physical violence among males within such societies.

Koch found a relationship between patrilocality and the use of physical violence in the Jalé society of western New Guinea. In the New Guinea highlands most disputes are of the intermunicipal sort, like contemporary international conflicts in which a sovereign power does not exist. The Jalé are a farming people who live in villages divided into two or more wards. The wards form the principal war-making units in intravillage and intervillage conflicts. There are no political and judicial offices, and thus self-help—often in the form of violent retaliation—is an institutionalized method of resolving conflicts when negotiation fails.

A number of problems are evident in Jalé conflict management. The first is the snowball effect of inadequate procedures to deal with grievances: if there are no authorities capable of settling conflicts, even minor disagreements may escalate into war between whole villages. A second is the potential of every retaliation to generate new troubles. Brakes are provided by kinship and residence, but these are not strong enough to prevent escalation in any particular conflict. Such results support the proposition that both the style of conflict resolution and the occurrence of conflict derive from a society's principles of human association.

The factor of early environment. A cross-cultural study of the correlates of crime by the psychologists Margaret Bacon, Irvin Child, and Herbert Barry examined the frequency of theft and personal crimes (defined to include assault, rape, suicide, sorcery, murder, and making false accusation) in forty-eight preliterate societies. They found that both types of offense are more frequent in societies having polygynous mother-child households than in those societies with monogamous, nuclear households.

Whiting expanded on this work and examined the idea associating household organization and conflict frequencies in six cultures. Her study combined social, structural, and psychological variables to test this hypothesis: If, during the first two or three years of life, a boy is frequently with the mother and only infrequently with the father, he will identify strongly with his mother; if, later in life, he is living in a world dominated by men, he will face internal conflict, which may lead to attempts to prove his masculinity. The "masculine protest hypothesis" was concerned with the sex identity conflict theory: where the father has less importance in infancy and where men have higher prestige and salience from childhood on, violence becomes an expression of "protest masculinity," as among the Gusii of Kenya or the Khalapur Rajput of India.

Witchcraft in preliterate societies. Like killing, the act of sorcery or witchcraft is not necessarily a wrong; rather, it depends for its cultural meaning on the context and locus of the action and on who is involved. Furthermore, in many societies there is no division between the natural and the supernatural. For the Mexican Zinacantecans, earthly conflicts are only manifestations of conflicts between supernatural beings and people, often expressed by means of witchcraft. The Kapauku of New Guinea consider killing by arrow, by sorcery, or by forced violation of food taboos to be identical crimes, since all are attacks on people. The Gwembe Tonga of Zambia treat poisoning and sorcery in the same manner; the Tonga reason that they are functionally identical, since both are covert attacks which make people fall sick. The Barotse and Gisu of Zambia and Kenya and the Sepik of Melanesia believe that no death or illness is entirely natural. Each death brings the question, "Who has caused this?"

In witchcraft societies people usually fear sorcery, although not everyone condemns it. At times sorcery is condemned, but sorcerers are not punished. The Sepik rarely accuse anyone of sorcery, because they fear reprisals from evil spirits. Among the Gisu, a sorcerer will be killed if the whole community agrees

to the killing. In many societies sorcery was formerly sanctioned by death, but today this penalty is considered illegal under state law, and indeed, such traditional punishment is now defined as murder by some national legal systems.

The identity of the initiator of witchcraft is important, especially since witchcraft itself is frequently inferred from death or sickness rather than directly observed. Among the Azande of the Sudan, people accused of witchcraft are usually those whom people in the community already had cause to hate. Women can be vulnerable to charges of witchcraft in patrilineal societies, where they are seen both as outsiders and as a divisive force. Men may or may not accuse lineage members, depending on whether rivalry or solidarity is paramount.

Some have examined witchcraft as an index to social disorder. Agricultural, rather than pastoral, communities tend to have witchcraft outbreaks as a response to overpopulation. Witchcraft in such settings allows people an excuse to leave the community either because they have been accused or because they are afraid of being witched (Colson). Gluckman connected the witchcraft outbreak of 1957–1958 among the Barotse with societal strain caused by the young going off to work and bringing back money, which resulted in a loss of prestige by the powerful tribal elders. The accusations of witchcraft in this case were by the young against the old. Waves of witchcraft accusations may be connected with changing times, as among the Barotse; with stress and periods of unrest, as among the Tonga; and with the absence of centralized political machinery, as among the Paiutes of the United States. During Great Britain's colonial period, the use of witchcraft by indigenous peoples led to heated debates among British administrators, who were called upon to maintain the native customary law according to their policy of indirect rule, which respected indigenous law.

Generalizing about small-scale societies

Most stereotypes of preliterate societies have not withstood the empirical test. Preliterate societies, like modern ones, support various, and sometimes contradictory, systems of rules. Adjectives that apply to the law of some African societies—communal, restitutive, cloaked with magic-religious beliefs—do not apply to the Australian aborigines, the Plains Indians of North America, or other societies that may be more individualistic and dominated by practical, rather than litigious, thinking in relation to law.

One can no longer argue that small, face-to-face

societies are more peaceful or that large and complex societies, where relations between strangers predominate, are more naturally crime-prone. It is not true that preliterate societies use negotiation to the exclusion of arbitration or mediation, or that industrial societies use adjudication to the exclusion of negotiation. Collective liability is as much a part of the thinking of contemporary insurance companies as it is of traditional Berbers. Preliterate law may be flexible and highly effective or highly unpredictable and destructive because of the absence of formalized controls. There are wide differences in the degree to which societal wrongs are recognized and punished. Research on exogamy rules (patterns of marrying outside the group) has revealed that official sanctions vary from one society to another in response to violation of these rules and include death, fines, beating, banishment, and invoking the disapproval of supernatural forces.

The rare attempts by anthropologists to define the nature of "primitive" crime have frequently placed undue emphasis on categories drawn from Western cultures and have paid little heed to the wide range of variation that exists among preliterate societies. Although few efforts have been made to produce a definition of crime that can be applied cross-culturally, it seems clear that the results of norm violations across cultures are loss of status and change in social position. The development of a cross-cultural understanding of crime may lie in the study of those normative violations that consistently result in downward change in the social rank for the violator. Such patterns will vary in meaning with authority structures that may be consensual or authoritarian. In preliterate societies the numerous combinations of structures provide means for preventing the escalation of conflicts, and yet they also generate interconnecting systems of behavior in the domains of kinship, economics, politics, and law that give the air of suitability to acts which, to the Western mind, may appear deviant.

Essentially, similarities in social structure and culture will produce similarities in criminal offenses and in the management of such offenses. In small-scale settings, where people know one another and share a broad range of personal ties, there is a special kind of indirect social control that is absent from, or almost inoperative in, settings where anonymity functions as an escape from the controls of kin and neighbor. In this second setting, criminal offenses are increasingly a result of the interaction between people who do not know one another. In the West, such offenses are met directly with sanctions that are likely to be repressive and penal rather than restitutive. Gluckman

(1967) has noted that the range of relevance is narrow in cases involving strangers and broad in those involving kinsmen. A dispute between two parties who are strangers need not end in reconciliation, but rather can be adjudicated and end in a clear decision. Changes in relationships between disputants and population movements accompany modernization processes. With the development of state law, which monopolizes the legitimate use of violence and social control in general, other systems of control cease to be important, and there is increased dependence on police enforcement.

Preliterate societies in the modern world

Surviving preliterate societies are increasingly being encapsulated by the modern bureaucratic state, a process that began under colonial governments and has developed further under conditions of independence. Creating central administrations has had a pervasive influence on local communities by acting as a brake on intervillage hostilities. Elizabeth Colson reports that before becoming subjects of the British colonial administration, the Valley and Plateau Tonga of Zambia lived in fear of intervillage raids. Of course, the fear of violence in such societies led to avoiding and preventing violence, but where insecurity was common, colonial governments may have been welcomed as allies.

On the other hand, political encapsulation brings into contact different systems of right and wrong, different ideas about authority, and different processes of treating wrongdoers. In addition, encapsulation may establish "insider-outsider" distinctions that were absent prior to the introduction of modern politics, and may open opportunities for those who see an advantage in using violence to gain their own ends. Among the Maya Indians of Guatemala, an encroaching Guatemalan state system has been associated with the disintegration of village leadership and with increased resort to homicide for the management of problems and disputes in the community. Alternatives to, and controls over, the use of physical violence resulted from the nature of contact between the two types of systems—state and village. The contact between local and state organizations produced a similar result among the Sidamo of southwest Ethiopia. The Sidamo have increasingly neglected procedural rules of community law, developed a preference for revenge, and refused to accept traditional sanctions. The increased use of national courts underlies these changes.

However, not all contacts between indigenous and

state systems of control produce similar results. The mountain Zapotec have developed ways of settling disputes and political strategies that effectively control the amount and impact of state judicial involvement in village affairs. It is considered a serious offense against the Zapotec village to aid the state in gaining control over the processing of a dispute, but most villages are able to maintain control over their customary boundaries of authority by maintaining effective mechanisms for local dispute settlement. Indigenous communities may not define the state system of law as "legal" when the state actively participates in those disputes that villagers wish to settle among themselves.

Although crimes, from the Western perspective, are violations of the law, violations of the law from the cross-cultural perspective are not necessarily crimes. Radcliffe-Brown's definition of *crime* in primitive societies as a violation of public order is cross-culturally inapplicable if the exercise of a penal, rather than a civil, sanction is at issue. Research on preliterate societies has not yet established that the cost to the victim is the criterion commonly applied in classifying behavior as criminal or in establishing the severity of the offense. What has been established is that societies without criminal populations are those which prevent individuals from obtaining criminal status through their behavior, not those which prevent violations of the "law." The record on world societies has well illustrated that crime is a cultural construct.

LAURA NADER
PHILIP PARNELL

See also ADVERSARY SYSTEM; CRIMINAL LAW REFORM, *articles on* CONTINENTAL EUROPE *and* ENGLAND; CRIMINAL PROCEDURE: COMPARATIVE ASPECTS.

BIBLIOGRAPHY

BACON, MARGARET K.; CHILD, IRVIN L.; and BARRY, HERBERT, III. "A Cross-cultural Study of Correlates of Crime." *Journal of Abnormal and Social Psychology* 66 (1963): 291–300.
COLSON, ELIZABETH. *Tradition and Contract: The Problem of Order.* Chicago: Aldine, 1974.
DURKHEIM, EMILE. *The Division of Labor in Society* (1893). Translated by George Simpson. New York: Free Press, 1964.
GLUCKMAN, MAX. *The Judicial Process among the Barotse of Northern Rhodesia.* 2d ed. with corrections and two additional chapters. Manchester, England: Manchester University Press for the Institute for Social Research, University of Zambia, 1967.
———. *Politics, Law, and Ritual in Tribal Society.* Chicago: Aldine, 1965.
HOBHOUSE, LEONARD T. *Morals in Evolution: A Study in Com-*
parative Ethics (1906). 7th ed. With a new introduction by Morris Ginsburg. London: Chapman & Hall, 1951.
KOCH, KLAUS-FRIEDRICH. *War and Peace in Jalemo: The Management of Conflict in Highland New Guinea.* Cambridge, Mass.: Harvard University Press, 1974.
LLEWELLYN, KARL N., and HOEBEL, E. ADAMSON. *The Cheyenne Way: Conflict and Case Law in Primitive Jurisprudence.* Norman: University of Oklahoma Press, 1941.
MALINOWSKI, BRONISLAW. *Crime and Custom in Savage Society.* New York: Harcourt, Brace, 1926. Reprint. New York: Humanities Press, 1951.
NADER, LAURA. *Talea and Juquila: A Comparison of Zapotec Social Organization.* University of California Publication in American Archaeology and Ethnology, vol. 48, no. 3. Berkeley: University of California Press, 1964.
RADCLIFFE-BROWN, A. R. "Primitive Law." *Encyclopedia of the Social Sciences*, vol. 9. Edited by Edwin R. A. Seligman, Alvin Johnson, et al. New York: Macmillan, 1933, pp. 202–206.
SCHAPERA, ISAAC. "Some Anthropological Concepts of 'Crime.'" The Hobhouse Memorial Lecture. *British Journal of Sociology* 23 (1972): 381–394.
THODEN VAN VELZEN, H. U. E., and VAN WETERING, W. "Residence, Power Groups, and Intra-social Aggression: An Inquiry into the Conditions Leading to Peacefulness within Non-stratified Societies." *International Archives of Ethnography* 49 (1960): 169–200.
WHITING, BEATRICE B. "Sex Identity Conflict and Physical Violence: A Comparative Study." *American Anthropologist* 67, no. 6, part 2 (Special Publication: The Ethnography of Law. Edited by Laura Nader) (1965): 123–140.

4.
SOVIET UNION

Soviet criminal law is a mature, integrated, highly developed system, similar in many important respects to the systems of criminal law of most countries of Europe and of North and South America. Yet it also has many distinguishing characteristics. These are connected with the *political* role of Soviet criminal law in protecting the interests of the Communist one-party state and of the centralized planned economy; with the *philosophical* emphasis of Soviet criminal law on the nurturing of Soviet citizens in the moral values of socialist community life; and with the *historical* roots of Soviet criminal law in prerevolutionary Russian law, on the one hand, and in revolutionary and early postrevolutionary developments, on the other.

Criminal procedure

The preliminary investigation and the role of the procuracy. Soviet criminal procedure is similar to that of France, Germany, and many other countries in providing for a preliminary investigation of major crimes by an impartial official prior to indictment and trial. Called the *sledovatel'* ("investigator"), he is comparable to the French *juge d'instruction* and the German *Untersuchungsrichter*. Lesser crimes are subject to an inquiry by the police or by other agencies of inquiry. At the conclusion of the preliminary investigation, the accused is shown the entire record of the testimony to be used against him at trial.

A major difference, however, between the Soviet system of preliminary investigation and that of Western European countries is that the Soviet investigator is subordinate to the procuracy (*prokuratura*) rather than to the courts or the Ministry of Justice. This is true whether the investigation is conducted by the Ministry of Internal Affairs (which controls the regular police), by the Committee on State Security (which controls the security police), or by the procuracy itself. The Soviet procuracy is rooted historically in the prerevolutionary Russian procuracy, founded in the early eighteenth century by Peter the Great. It has the task of "general supervision" of legality, including the duty to "protest" to higher authorities concerning any illegal administrative act that is brought to its attention. It also conducts the prosecution of criminal cases. The procuracy's control over an impartial and extensive examination of the accused and of witnesses prior to the indictment has many important consequences. One is that the indictment, which contains a detailed record of the preliminary investigation, is apt to be accorded great respect by the trial court, whose functions include that of questioning the accused and the witnesses in order to corroborate or refute the evidence reported therein.

The prestige of the procuracy and its independence from other state agencies (although apparently not from the state security agency in many political cases) may also affect the accused in other, more favorable, ways. He may appeal to the procurator against illegal actions of the investigator. The procurator, through his power of general supervision, also has the duty to expose administrative illegalities that may be exonerating or mitigating factors in the prosecution of the accused. Moreover, higher agencies of the procuracy may and often do protest to higher courts convictions obtained by lower procurators.

The system of preliminary investigation may involve long periods of confinement of accused persons prior to indictment. Under the criminal procedure codes of the fifteen constituent republics of the USSR, a person who is arrested may be detained for twenty-four hours before being turned over to the procuracy.

He may be detained by the procuracy for another forty-eight hours—and in exceptional instances up to a total of ten days—before being formally charged. Thereafter he may either be detained or released under surveillance for a period of two months while the preliminary investigation takes place. However, this two-month period may be extended to three months by permission of a higher procurator, to three more months by permission of the procurator of the given republic, and to three additional months—making a total of nine months—by permission of the procurator general of the USSR. Detention is authorized not only when there is reason to believe that the accused will hide from the investigation or otherwise hinder it, but also when there is reason to believe that if released he will engage in criminal activity.

Partly in reaction against the massive abuses of legality that took place during the Stalin era, the Fundamental Principles of Criminal Procedure of the USSR and the Union Republics (enacted on December 25, 1958) and the criminal procedure codes subsequently adopted by the constituent republics emphasize the protection of the accused during the preliminary investigation as well as at the trial stage and thereafter. Special features of Soviet criminal procedure codes include the enumerating of certain "rights of the accused," which must be explained to him at the outset of the preliminary investigation, and the obtaining of his signature to a certification that such explanation has been given. These rights are "the right to know what he is accused of and to give explanations concerning the accusation presented to him, to present evidence, to submit petitions, to become acquainted with all the materials of the case upon completion of the preliminary investigation or inquiry, to have defense counsel [at a certain point in the preliminary proceedings], to participate in the [trial], to submit challenges, [and] to appeal from the actions and decisions of the person conducting the inquiry, the investigator, the procurator, and the court" (Fundamental Principles of Criminal Procedure, art. 21; Code of Criminal Procedure of the Russian Soviet Federated Socialist Republic [RSFSR] [Russian CCP], arts. 46, 149). Force may not be used to obtain testimony, and a person may not be convicted on the basis of his silence, or, indeed, of his uncorroborated confession. However, there is no "privilege against self-incrimination" in the Anglo-American sense, since adverse inferences may be drawn from a refusal to answer.

Prior to 1958, defense counsel were not permitted during the preliminary investigation, but only at trial. The 1958 Fundamental Principles of Criminal Procedure and the 1960 Russian CCP permit defense counsel to participate at the last stage of the preliminary investigation, after the investigator has presented the indictment to the accused. Defense counsel may then be called in for the first time, to study the indictment, talk with the accused, challenge the sufficiency of the indictment, challenge the investigator, petition that new witnesses be called, or take various other steps (Russian CCP, art. 51). Participation of defense counsel from the beginning of the preliminary investigation is obligatory in cases of minors, deaf, dumb, and blind persons, and other persons who by reason of psychological or physical defects cannot themselves exercise their right to defense.

Trial procedure. The trial commences with a reading of the summary of the detailed indictment, normally followed by interrogation of the accused by the court. The Soviet trial court consists of a professional judge, chosen for five years, and two lay judges, called people's assessors, chosen from the population to sit for two weeks a year for two and a half years. Decision is by majority vote. The court seeks to elicit from the accused, and thereafter from the various witnesses, confirmation or refutation of the evidence in the indictment. Interrogation by the court is normally followed by interrogation by the procurator and defense counsel. The accused and the victim (who may bring a civil action in the criminal proceeding) may also themselves, or through counsel, put questions to each other and to the witnesses. The proceedings are quite informal by American standards.

Participation of defense counsel is obligatory at trial—unless refused by the accused—in all cases in which a state prosecutor appears, and if such counsel is not engaged by the accused he must be appointed by the court (Russian CCP, art. 49). Defense counsel is required to present evidence tending to acquit the accused or to mitigate his responsibility. He is given "the right to copy necessary information [from the file of the case], to present evidence, to submit challenges, [and] to appeal from the actions and decisions . . . of the court" (art. 51).

Review of decisions. Either the accused or the procuracy may appeal an adverse decision to the next higher court, consisting of three professional judges, which reviews the facts as well as the law. If the accused appeals, the appellate court may not increase the punishment or apply the law for a graver crime. If, however, the procurator appeals, the judgment may be set aside and the case remanded on the ground of the mildness of the punishment or the applicability of the law for a graver crime.

The decision of the appellate court is, technically, final. However, it may be reviewed "by way of supervision" by higher courts, or upon protest of higher procurators or of the presidents or vice-presidents of higher courts. In fact, the supreme courts of the Soviet constituent republics and the Supreme Court of the USSR are continually reviewing, as a discretionary matter, "final decisions" of intermediate appellate courts at lower levels. At the hearings neither the accused nor his counsel may appear in person, although they may submit briefs.

The presumption of innocence. Whether there is a presumption of innocence in Soviet law depends on the definition of that phrase. There is certainly no presumption of guilt. It is expressly provided that the "obligation of proof" is not to be transferred to the accused, that the judgment of the court shall be based only on evidence considered in the trial, and that a conviction may not be based on assumptions but "shall be decreed only if the guilt of the accused is proved in the course of the trial" (Russian CCP, arts. 20, 301, 309). Soviet jurists uniformly state that doubts are to be resolved in favor of the accused, citing the Latin maxim *in dubio pro reo*. On the other hand, since the court interrogates the accused, and is itself under an "obligation" to expose the circumstances of the case, it is not meaningful to speak of the burden of proof in the Anglo-American sense of a risk of not going forward with evidence or a risk of failing to persuade the trier of fact.

The role of social organizations and of comrades' courts. A heavy emphasis is placed, both in legal theory and in legal practice, on the educational role (*vospitatel'naia rol'*; literally, "nurturing role") of law in Soviet society. The law, and especially criminal law, is considered to have the task of forming the character of people, inculcating values, and training people to think and act in desired ways. Thus, Article 3 of the 1958 Fundamental Principles of Court Organization of the USSR provides that "by all its activities the court shall educate citizens of the USSR in the spirit of devotion to the Motherland and the cause of communism, in the spirit of strict and undeviating execution of Soviet laws, care for socialist property, observance of labor discipline, an honorable attitude toward public and social duty, [and] respect for the rights, honor, and dignity of citizens [and] for the rules of socialist community life." The various republican codes of criminal procedure not only reiterate the duty of judges to conduct trials in such a way as to secure their educational influence, but also introduce new types of procedural devices to implement this duty.

Thus, in a criminal case the Soviet court is required

not only to determine the guilt or innocence of the accused and to pass sentence, but also, under Article 21 of the Russian CCP, to "expose the causes and conditions that have facilitated the commission of the crime and to take measures to eliminate them." Such causes and conditions are subject to proof (art. 68). Wide use must be made of the help of the public in bringing them to light (art. 128). The court is required to issue special rulings to directors of enterprises, heads of institutions or ministries, and other officials concerning improper situations that have been exposed during the trial (art. 321).

In addition, the educational role of the court is enhanced by the wide participation of so-called social organizations in judicial proceedings—the collective of colleagues in the factory or institution where the accused works or studies; the collective of his neighbors in the apartment house or district where he resides; units of volunteer auxiliary police called the People's Guard; the Young Communist League; Communist Party organizations; and other voluntary associations. A social organization may initiate a criminal case (art. 108), and its representatives may appear in court on one side or the other as "social accuser" or "social defender," with full rights of counsel (arts. 228, 236, 250, 251, 276, 288, 291, 293–298). The court may also release an accused person to the "suretyship" (poruka) of a social organization for supervision and reeducation (art. 9) or, after conviction, it may suspend the sentence and transfer the convicted person to such suretyship (art. 304). The trial may be held in the clubroom of a factory, apartment house, or other place where the accused works, lives, or studies. Wherever it is heard, the court may, "for the purpose of increasing the educational effect of a judgment . . . send a copy of [it] to the convicted person's place of work, study, or residence, upon its entry into legal effect" (art. 359).

In addition, minor offenses may be tried in comrades' courts, which are informal tribunals of neighbors or fellow workers of the accused that have power to issue warnings and reprimands and, in some cases, to impose small fines as well as civil damages.

Substantive criminal law

The General Part. The criminal code of each of the fifteen republics is divided, in the European style, into a General Part and a Special Part. The General Part is virtually identical with the Fundamental Principles of Criminal Legislation of the USSR and the Union Republics (enacted on December 25, 1958). In the 1960 Criminal Code of the Russian Soviet Fed-

erated Socialist Republic [RSFSR] [Russian CC], Article 1 states the "tasks" of the Code: "the protection of the Soviet social and state system, of socialist property, of the person and rights of citizens, and of the entire socialist legal order, from criminal infringements." Article 3 states the "basis of criminal responsibility": "Only a person guilty of committing a crime, that is, [one] who intentionally or negligently commits a socially dangerous act provided for by law, shall be subject to criminal responsibility and punishment. Criminal punishment shall be applied only by judgment of a court." Article 6 adopts the principles of nonretroactivity of laws establishing the punishability of an act or increasing a punishment. Articles 7 through 19, collectively entitled "Crime," define the concepts of crime, intent, negligence, responsibility of minors, nonimputability, self-defense, protection of social or personal interests, extreme necessity, preparation and attempt, voluntary refusal to bring a crime to completion, complicity, concealment, and failure to report a crime. The rules here follow the main lines of classical criminal law theory.

Articles 20 through 36 of the Russian CC deal with punishment. Article 20 states: "Punishment not only constitutes an atonement for a committed crime but also has the purpose of correcting and reeducating convicted persons in the spirit of an honorable attitude toward labor, of strict compliance with the laws, and of respect toward socialist communal life; it also has the purpose of preventing the commission of new crimes both by convicted persons and by others. Punishment does not have as a purpose the causing of physical suffering or the lowering of human dignity." Here the emphasis is on the distinction between what punishment *is*—namely, an atonement, a price to be paid, which inevitably involves suffering—and what it is *for*, namely, correction and deterrence. In the background of Article 20 is a rejection of an earlier Soviet theory which had altogether eliminated the word "punishment" from criminal legislation, substituting the phrase "measure of social defense of a judicial-correctional character."

Article 20 lists the kinds of punishment applicable to persons who commit crimes. The basic punishment is (1) deprivation of freedom, which under Article 24 may extend from three months to fifteen years. Deprivation of freedom is served in correctional labor colonies of various types or, less frequently, in prisons. Other punishments include: (2) exile to a certain locality; (3) banishment from a certain locality or localities; (4) "correctional tasks without deprivation of freedom," almost always meaning a deduction of 5 percent to 20 percent of monthly wages for a period of one month to one year; (5) deprivation of the right to hold specified offices or to engage in specified activity; (6) a fine; (7) dismissal from office; (8) imposition of the duty to make amends for harm caused; (9) social censure; (10) confiscation of property; and (11) deprivation of military or special rank and/or assignment of persons in regular military service to a disciplinary battalion. The death penalty is listed separately "as an exceptional measure of punishment, until its complete abolition" (art. 23). Nevertheless, the death penalty is applicable to a large number of crimes listed in the Special Part, discussed below.

Articles 37 to 57 are concerned with criteria for assignment of punishment and relief from punishment. Article 37 provides that in assigning punishment "the court, guided by socialist legal consciousness, shall take into consideration the character and degree of social danger of the committed crime, the personality of the guilty person, and the circumstances of the case that mitigate or aggravate responsibility." Article 38 lists nine circumstances that mitigate responsibility, adding that the court may also deem other circumstances as mitigating responsibility. Article 39 lists twelve circumstances that aggravate responsibility; this list is intended to be exhaustive. Other articles cover suspended sentences and probation, relief from criminal responsibility or from punishment if the act or the person has ceased to be socially dangerous, transfer of criminal cases for consideration by an informal tribunal of neighbors or fellow workers called a comrades' court, relief from criminal responsibility with release of the guilty person to the suretyship of a "social organization," parole, expunging of the record of conviction, and related matters.

Articles 58 to 63 deal with the commitment of accused persons who are mentally ill to psychiatric hospitals or to the care of relatives or guardians, the application of medical measures to accused persons who are alcoholics or drug addicts, and the application of compulsory measures of an educational character to accused persons who are minors.

Soviet legal theory stresses that an act, to be a crime, must be "socially dangerous." "Social danger" is called the "material" element, and prohibition by an enacted law the "formal" element, of the definition of crime. This distinction dates from the earliest period of Soviet legal development, and is considered an original and important contribution of socialist jurisprudence. Its significance, however, has altered substantially in the decades since Stalin's death in 1953. Under the Russian criminal codes of 1922 and 1926, the formal element was not a necessary element; that

is, if a particular type of socially dangerous act was not specifically proscribed in the Special Part of the Code, it could nevertheless be considered criminal and punished under a provision of the Special Part proscribing an analogous act. Thus, in the early 1920s economic misconduct was punished by the courts as a counterrevolutionary crime "by analogy." In the late 1930s and again in the late 1940s and 1950s the "doctrine of analogy," as it was called, came under sharp criticism and was finally abolished in 1958, leaving the element of social danger as a basis only for restricting punishability and not (as before) also for enlarging it. Acts that are not "socially dangerous" are not considered to be crimes, even if formally they fall within the statutory definition of crimes.

The concept of social danger is applied not only to the definition of crime but also to the determination of the relative gravity of particular crimes and to the assignment of punishment. In particular, the structure of the Special Part of the Code reflects a strong commitment to the proportioning of punishment to the social danger of the criminal act. Here too, however, there has been a reduction in the significance of the concept of social danger.

The Special Part. The Special Part of the criminal code of each of the fifteen Soviet constituent republics lists those acts that are punishable as crimes, and states the applicable punishment. There is uniformity among the codes with respect to those crimes that are covered by federal (USSR) law, namely, crimes against the state, military crimes, and certain individual crimes in other categories, for example, large-scale stealing of state or social property. With respect to nonfederal crimes, there are diversities among the republican codes. Nevertheless, the Russian CC may serve as a useful model for purposes of a general exposition.

As of 1980, the Special Part of the Russian CC contained 240 articles divided into twelve chapters. The first ten chapters are intended to be arranged in a descending scale of social danger: crimes against the state; crimes against socialist ownership; crimes against the life, health, freedom, and dignity of the person; crimes against political and labor rights of citizens; crimes against personal ownership; crimes against the socialist economy; crimes by officials; crimes against justice; crimes against the system of administration; and crimes against public security, public order, and public health.

Within each chapter the individual crimes are listed, so far as possible, in descending order of social danger. Thus, for example, the first chapter is divided into "especially dangerous crimes against the state" and "other crimes against the state." The first group begins with treason and espionage and goes on to terrorist acts, sabotage, wrecking, anti-Soviet agitation and propaganda, and propagandizing of war. Where a particular crime is placed in the Code—in what chapter and, within the chapter, in what position—is considered significant in terms of the stigma attached to it and, consequently, the punishment to be applied. It may also have other significance: for example, all especially dangerous crimes against the state must—theoretically—have a direct antistate intent, that is, they must be committed with a desire to undermine or weaken the state. (This requirement has often been violated in practice.) "Other" crimes against the state, however, may be committed through negligence. For example, negligent loss of documents containing state secrets is punishable by deprivation of freedom from one to three years, or, if it causes serious consequences, from three to eight years.

Sentencing. Soviet statistics concerning the incidence of crime, sentences, the number of persons in places of detention, and conditions in such places, are a state secret known only to a relatively few people, although occasionally certain partial statistics for particular cities or regions are published. Nevertheless, a considerable amount of information concerning such matters is available from former prisoners and former specialists in criminology who have emigrated from the Soviet Union. On the basis of such unofficial information, as well as of scattered published data, it is estimated that nearly half the persons convicted of crimes are sentenced to deprivation of freedom, and that the average term of such sentences is three years.

Under the Criminal Code parole is available, depending on the type of crime, after one-half, two-thirds, or three-fourths of the sentence is served. It is reliably reported that in one year in the early 1970s approximately 1.6 million persons were convicted, and that in another year during that period approximately 950,000 persons were sentenced to deprivation of freedom. On that basis, the population of the labor colonies and prisons would have been between 2 million and 3 million. On the other hand, a leading Soviet dissident, the physicist Andrei Sakharov, stated in 1975, on the basis of numerous reports from inmates and others, that the number of prisoners was about 1.5 million. Given a Soviet population of 253 million in 1975, Sakharov's estimate would yield a ratio of 593 prisoners per 100,000 people.

These figures compare with Western estimates of 7 to 20 million prisoners during the Stalin period, out of a total population of well under 200 million.

The contrast is made still sharper by the fact that the great majority of prisoners in the Stalin period were sentenced for so-called counterrevolutionary crimes, whereas the prisoners sentenced for political or ideological crimes at any one time in the post-Stalin period are numbered in the thousands (Sakharov's estimate in 1975 was between 2,000 and 10,000), and probably most of those were convicted for violating restrictions on religious activities.

Published Soviet sources state that the majority of convictions are for the crime of hooliganism, defined as "intentional actions violating public order in a coarse manner and expressing a clear disrespect toward society" (Russian CC, art. 206). The maximum punishment for simple hooliganism is deprivation of freedom for one year; however, malicious hooliganism is punishable by deprivation of freedom for one to five years, and either type of hooliganism committed with a weapon is punishable by a term of three to seven years.

As originally enacted in 1960, the Russian Republic's Criminal Code sought to make the severity of punishment for a given type of crime proportional to its social danger. Flexibility was maintained by giving the court discretion, within the minimum and maximum limits set by the Code, to vary the sentence according to the personality of the convicted person and in the light of mitigating or aggravating circumstances (Russian CC, art. 37). However, the concepts of what is more and what is less socially dangerous changed substantially as time went on. Less than two years after the Code went into effect it was amended to permit the death penalty for certain violations of currency regulations, for stealing state property or social property on an especially large scale, for the taking of a bribe by an official if committed under especially aggravating circumstances, and for "infringing" on (later defined by the USSR Supreme Court as taking or attempting to take) the life of a policeman or of a people's guard if committed under aggravating circumstances. Indeed, in the first decade after the 1960 Code took effect, some 60 of the 268 original articles were amended (some of them more than once), and over 25 new articles were added. Moreover, it has always been a necessary discrepancy within the original structure of the Code, based as it is on social danger, that a crime which in general is considered more serious (such as treason or armed robbery) may be committed under circumstances that render it less serious, and that a crime which in general is considered less serious (such as smuggling or theft) may be committed under circumstances that render it more serious.

Partly because of these considerations, Soviet law-makers in 1972 radically revised the original structure of the Criminal Code by introducing a new Article 7-1, entitled "The Concept of a Grave Crime." Its first paragraph states: "Intentional acts representing heightened social danger, listed in the second paragraph of the present Article, shall be deemed to be grave crimes." The second paragraph lists the kinds of crimes, with reference to the appropriate articles of the Code, that constitute grave crimes, namely, especially dangerous crimes against the state; banditry; acts disrupting work of correctional labor institutions; mass disorders; damaging of routes of communication and means of transport; making or passing counterfeit monies or securities; violation of rules for currency transactions or speculation in currency or securities under aggravating circumstances; stealing of state or social property in large amounts or in especially large amounts; overt stealing (*grabiozh*) under aggravating circumstances; assault with intent to rob; where committed under aggravating circumstances, intentional destruction or damaging of state or social property or personal property of citizens; intentional homicide; intentional infliction of grave bodily injury; and more than a dozen others.

The "heightened social danger" characterizing "grave crimes" under Article 7-1 seems also to be connected with the criminal act's degree of immorality. For example, although the interests of state ownership are given a position in the Code superior to that of the interests of personal ownership, overt stealing of personally owned property, committed by a group of persons in accordance with a preliminary plan, is regarded as a grave crime, whereas secret stealing, or theft (*krazha*), of state-owned property of the same value committed under the same circumstances is not regarded as a grave crime. The reason must be that *grabiozh* is considered "worse" than *krazha*, or that persons who commit *grabiozh* deserve more severe punishment than persons who commit *krazha*. Thus the concept of social danger has been expanded to include an important moral component. The convicted person is required to pay a price proportionate not to the harm he has done to certain social interests but to the immorality of his act.

The immediate practical significance of the creation of a new group of "grave crimes" is manifested in the simultaneous amendment of Article 24 of the Code to provide that punishment of persons sentenced to deprivation of freedom for grave crimes shall be served in corrective labor colonies that have a harsher regimen than those to which persons are sentenced for crimes that are not "grave."

Conditions of confinement

The substitution of "measures of social defense" for "punishment" in the earlier Soviet criminal legislation was associated with the establishment of so-called corrective labor colonies for persons who committed crimes ("socially dangerous acts"), in order to reeducate them through collective work. From the beginning of the Soviet regime, however, a sharp distinction was made between persons who committed political or ideological offenses, and other criminals. The former were to be placed in corrective labor "camps," which, unlike the "colonies," were subordinated to the state security agency. Eventually, under Stalin, corrective labor colonies were reserved chiefly for persons sentenced to deprivation of freedom for up to three years, and corrective labor camps were maintained by the state security agency for persons sentenced to deprivation of freedom for three years or more, regardless of the type of offense. In addition, Stalin restored the concept of punishment as infliction of suffering and as a price to be paid for violating the law. The conditions in the camps were extremely harsh for almost all types of prisoners, although those sentenced under the notorious Article 58 of the 1926 Criminal Code of the RSFSR, which dealt with counterrevolutionary crimes, were usually treated worse than others.

After Stalin's death there was a massive review of cases of persons previously sentenced to corrective labor camps, and some millions of such persons were rehabilitated, in many instances posthumously. At the same time the post-Stalin regime corrected many of the abuses of legality that had been systematically practiced in the camps during the Stalin era.

One of the most important reforms of the immediate post-Stalin era was the introduction of procuratorial control over violations of legality in corrective labor institutions. Under the 1955 Statute on Supervision by the Procuracy in the USSR, procurators were to visit the camps at any time in order to hear complaints of prisoners, with the power and duty to demand immediate rectification of illegal conditions. This provision was subsequently reaffirmed in the Fundamental Principles of Corrective Labor Legislation of the USSR and the Union Republics (enacted on July 11, 1969), which states that "the procurator shall be obliged to take timely measures to prevent and eliminate any violations of the law, from whomsoever these violations may emanate, and to bring the offenders to responsibility," and further, that "the administration of corrective labor institutions . . . shall be obliged to implement the orders and proposals of the procurator concerning the observance of the rules of serving punishment established by the corrective labor legislation of the USSR."

The 1970 Corrective Labor Code of the Russian Soviet Federated Socialist Republic, which incorporated the 1969 USSR legislation, established four different types ("regimens") of corrective labor colonies. (The word "camp" was eliminated from Soviet legislation after Stalin's death, although it has continued to be used in popular speech.) Colonies of general regimen (*obshchii rezhim*) are for first offenders sentenced for lesser crimes; colonies of stricter regimen (*usilennyi rezhim*) are for first offenders sentenced for grave crimes; colonies of severe regimen (*strogii rezhim*) are for recidivists and for persons convicted of especially dangerous crimes against the state; and colonies of special regimen (*osobyi rezhim*) are for recidivists convicted of dangerous crimes and for reprieved capital offenders. In 1977 a separate system of corrective labor colonies was established for persons who have committed crimes through negligence.

Female prisoners are placed in separate colonies of either general or severe regimen, and minors are placed in so-called educational labor colonies of either general or stricter regimen. Confinement in a prison (*tiur'ma*) is generally considered to be a more severe sanction than sentence to a labor colony and is usually reserved for certain persons who have committed especially dangerous crimes or for certain recidivists. Prisons are also divided into two types, "general" and "stricter."

The regimen in colonies and prisons is regulated by the all-union Fundamental Principles of Corrective Labor Legislation (1969) and by the various republican corrective labor codes. The latter contain provisions concerning certain aspects of working conditions, rewards and penalties, visits of relatives and lawyers, limits on correspondence and receipt of packages, and so on. Detailed implementation of these provisions, however, is left to the Rules of Internal Order of Corrective Labor Institutions, issued by the Ministry of Internal Affairs.

The harsh conditions of the Soviet corrective labor colonies are due chiefly to the hard physical labor that certain categories of prisoners are required to perform, inadequate food rations, and insufficient rest; and these aspects of the various penitentiary regimens are regulated not by legislation but by the Rules of Internal Order as interpreted by the administrative authorities. Moreover, even with regard to matters regulated by legislation, there is inevitably a great deal of administrative leeway. For example, the Russian Republic's Corrective Labor Code (art. 53) limits

solitary confinement of recalcitrant prisoners in a punishment-isolation cell (*izoliator*) to fifteen days. In actuality, the conditions of such confinement are left to administrative authorities to determine, and it is widely reported that prisoners are illegally kept in such "isolators" naked, cold, and without food. Similarly, the Code (art. 39) requires that prisoners be paid for work at the same rates as workers in the national economy generally; however, under the Rules of Internal Order substantial deductions are made for room, board, and clothing.

Nevertheless, despite the many great differences between law in books and law in action, it is significant that a very strong effort has been made to establish certain legal rights of prisoners and to maintain legal controls over abuses of such rights. The Corrective Labor Code (art. 23) requires that all prisoners be informed of the provisions of the Rules of Internal Order concerning conduct during work and rest, prohibited types of work, items prisoners may or may not have in their possession, checks on prisoners, receipt of visits and of packages and letters, and items of food and basic necessities that may be purchased. Article 36 provides: "Prisoners shall have the right to submit complaints, statements, and letters to state agencies, social organizations, and officials. [These] shall be transmitted in accordance with the Rules of Internal Order of Corrective Labor Institutions. . . ." The second paragraph of Article 36 contains the following interesting qualification: "Complaints, statements, and letters addressed to the procurator shall not be subject to examination and shall be transmitted within twenty-four hours."

HAROLD J. BERMAN

See also ADVERSARY SYSTEM; CRIMINAL LAW REFORM, *articles on* CONTINENTAL EUROPE *and* ENGLAND; CRIMINAL PROCEDURE: COMPARATIVE ASPECTS.

BIBLIOGRAPHY

BERMAN, HAROLD J. *Justice in the USSR: An Interpretation of Soviet Law.* Rev. ed., enlarged. Cambridge, Mass.: Harvard University Press, 1963.

———, ed. and trans. "Cases on Criminal Law and Procedure." *Soviet Statutes and Decisions* 1, no. 4 (1965): 1–154.

———, and SPINDLER, JAMES W., trans. *Soviet Criminal Law and Procedure: The RSFSR Codes.* 2d ed. Introduction and analysis by Harold J. Berman. Cambridge, Mass.: Harvard University Press, 1972.

BORODIN, STANISLAV V., and LEVITSKY, G. A. *Voprosy ugolovnogo prava i protsessa v praktike verkhovnykh sudov SSSR i RSFSR, 1938–1978.* Moscow: Iuridicheskaia Literatura, 1980.

A Chronicle of Human Rights in the USSR [Journal]. New York: Khronika Press, 1973—.

FELDBRUGGE, FERDINAND J. M., ed. *Encyclopedia of Soviet Law.* 2 vols. Dobbs Ferry, N.Y.: Oceana, 1973.

HAZARD, JOHN N.; BUTLER, WILLIAM E.; and MAGGS, PETER B. *The Soviet Legal System: Fundamental Principles and Historical Commentary.* 3d ed. Dobbs Ferry, N.Y.: Oceana, 1977.

JUVILER, PETER H. *Revolutionary Law and Order: Politics and Social Change in the USSR.* New York: Free Press, 1976.

KRIGER, G. A.; KURINOV, B. A.; and TKACHEVSKII, IU. M., eds. *Sovetskoe ugolovnoe pravo: obshchaia chast'.* Moscow: Izdatel'stvo Moskovskogo Universiteta, 1981.

——, eds. *Sovetskoe ugolovnoe pravo: osobennaia chast'.* Moscow: Izdatel'stvo Moskovskogo Universiteta, 1982.

KUDRIAVTSEV, P. I. *Voprosy ugolovnogo prava i protsessa v praktike prokurorskogo nadzora za sobliudeniem zakonnosti pri rassmotrenii sudami ugolovnykh del.* Moscow: Iuridicheskaia Literatura, 1976.

MAKEPEACE, R. W. *Marxist Ideology and Soviet Criminal Law.* Totowa, N.J.: Barnes & Noble, 1980.

PIONTKOVSKII, ANDREI A. et al., eds. *Kurs sovetskogo ugolovnogo prava: chast' obshchaia.* 6 vols. Moscow: Nauka, 1970—.

REKUNKOV, A. M., and ORLOV, A. K., eds. *Kommentarii k ugolovno-protsessual'nomu kodeksu RSFSR.* Moscow: Iuridicheskaia Literatura, 1981.

SEVERIN, IU. D., ed. *Kommentarii k ugolovnomu kodeksu RSFSR.* Moscow: Iuridicheskaia Literatura, 1980.

SIMONS, WILLIAM B., ed. *The Soviet Codes of Law: Status Jurisdiction, 1 August 1980.* Law in Eastern Europe, no. 23. Rockville, Md.: Sitjhoff & Noordhoff, 1980.

SOLOMON, PETER H. *Soviet Criminologists and Criminal Policy: Specialists in Policy Making.* New York: Columbia University Press, 1978.

SPIRIDONOV, BORIS MIKHAILOVICH. *Prokurorskii nadzor za sobliudeniem zakonnosti v ispravitel'no-trudovykh uchrezhdeniiakh.* Moscow: Izdatel'stvo Moskovskogo Universiteta, 1978.

STROGOVICH MIKHAIL S. *Kurs sovetskogo ugolovnogo protsessa.* 2 vols. Moscow: Nauka, 1968–1970.

COMPETENCY TO STAND TRIAL

Introduction

The notion that a mentally incompetent defendant may not be subjected to a criminal trial is deeply rooted in the common law. The common-law rule was expounded by Blackstone as follows: "If a man in his sound memory commits a capital offence, and before arraignment for it, he becomes mad, he ought not to be arraigned for it; because he is not able to plead to it with that advice and caution that he ought. And if, after he has pleaded, the prisoner becomes mad, he shall not be tried; for how can he make his defence?"(*24). This rule had a three-part rationale. First, it was an extension of the ban against trials in absentia. Second, the rule was deemed necessary to ensure against the conviction of innocent persons. Third, the trial of a mentally incompetent person was deemed to conflict with notions of common humanity.

In modern American law, the common-law rule has been elevated into a constitutional principle (*Drope v. Missouri*, 420 U.S. 162, 171–172 (1975)). The cornerstone of the Anglo-American criminal justice system is the entitlement of each litigant to an adequate hearing as embodied in the notion of due process. A necessary corollary of an adversary system that emphasizes the role of the individual litigant is the capacity of each party to participate meaningfully in the conduct of a trial. If the accused lacks the capacity to do so, his trial in such circumstances would deprive him of his entitlement to an adequate hearing.

The incompetency standard

Definition of the standard. The exact dimensions of the constitutional rule requiring competency on the part of a defendant in a criminal case are unclear. In *Dusky v. United States*, 362 U.S. 402 (1960), the standard applicable in all federal court proceedings was held to be whether the accused "has sufficient present ability to consult with his lawyer with a reasonable degree of rational understanding—and whether he has a rational as well as factual understanding of the proceedings against him." Although various state statutes contain standards at least textually at variance with the *Dusky* text, state courts generally adhere to the *Dusky* formulation. Moreover, it is likely that the Fourteenth Amendment due process clause obligates a competency test which incorporates at least the core elements of *Dusky*. The Supreme Court has quoted that standard in cases such as *Drope* (172), which involved a state proceeding, although the Court had occasion to rule only on the procedure followed by the state court.

The federal statute and numerous state laws require that the defendant be "insane or otherwise *mentally incompetent*" (18 U.S.C. § 4244 (1976); italics added). Notwithstanding such restrictive language, it is unlikely that a finding of incompetency could constitutionally be prohibited for incompetent persons suffering only from a physical disorder. Whenever the issue has arisen, courts have tended to ignore the statutory restriction and have focused instead on the degree of incapacitation (*People ex rel. Myers v. Briggs*, 46 Ill. 2d 281, 263 N.E.2d 109 (1970); *Jackson v. Indiana*, 406 U.S. 715, 735–736 (1972)).

Application of the standard. The element of the *Dusky* standard pertaining to the capacity of the defendant to consult with his attorney has been broadly construed to include the "ability to confer intelligently, to testify coherently and to follow the evidence presented." Thus, any substantial impairment that interferes with the defendant's ability either to communicate or to follow the proceedings with a "reasonable degree of rational understanding" will lead to a finding of incompetency (*Martin v. Estelle*, 546 F.2d 177, 180 (5th Cir. 1977), quoting Comment, p. 457).

It has been suggested that an ability to consult meaningfully with counsel necessitates a capacity "to remember the facts surrounding the occurrence of the alleged offense" (*United States v. Wilson*, 263 F. Supp. 528, 531 (D.D.C. 1966), *rev'd sub nom. Wilson v. United States*, 391 F.2d 460 (D.C. Cir. 1968)). This would mean that a defendant's inability to recall relevant events because of amnesia constitutes incompetency. For the most part, however, courts have rejected this argument (*United States v. Knohl*, 379 F.2d 427 (2d Cir. 1967); *United States v. Stevens*, 461 F.2d 317 (7th Cir. 1972); *Commonwealth v. Whitt*, 493 Pa. 571, 427 A.2d 623 (1981)). Some courts, however, have held that amnesia may be the basis for a finding of incompetency where the defendant's inability to recall events is deemed prejudicial to the construction of a defense. Among the factors to be considered in determining prejudice is whether the defendant is able, notwithstanding the amnesia, to reconstruct the "evidence relating to the crime and any reasonably possible alibi" (*Wilson v. United States*, 463–464; *United States v. Swanson*, 572 F.2d 523 (5th Cir. 1978)).

A similar lack of judicial consensus exists concerning competency achieved through the administration of maintenance doses of antipsychotic medication. Some state courts have held that a defendant receiving antipsychotic medication is per se incompetent (Winick, pp. 772–775), reasoning that the amelioration of symptoms produced by the medication may be prejudicial to a defendant who is relying on the insanity defense. This view also reflects the belief that chemically induced competency is artificial and insufficiently trustworthy. In most jurisdictions, however, the courts have approached the problem on a more pragmatic basis and have permitted the trial of the defendant receiving antipsychotic medication so long as he is otherwise competent.

Unless a defendant is able to comprehend the nature of the proceedings and the rules under which they are conducted, he may not be able to assess meaningfully whether or not to plead guilty or to "appreciate what information is relevant to the proof of his innocence" (*Martin*, 180). Consequently, *Dusky* established the additional requirement that the defendant have a rational, as well as a factual, understanding of the proceedings. This emphasis on rationality signals a requirement of comprehension going beyond surface knowledge (*People v. Swallow*, 60 Misc. 2d 171, 175, 301 N.Y.S.2d 798, 803 (1969)). But the rational understanding called for by *Dusky* means no more than some reasonable degree of comprehension; an understanding without any impairment is not required. Consequently, defendants who have some intellectual or emotional disturbance that prevents them from functioning at normal levels of effectiveness can still meet the standard. Even the presence of a psychosis does not compel a finding of incompetency (*Feguer v. United States*, 302 F.2d 214, 236 (8th Cir. 1962)).

The determination of competency: procedural aspects

Stage I: initiating the inquiry. The adjudication of incompetency entails a three-stage process. The first is essentially a pleading stage, involving a motion by either the defendant or prosecutor raising the issue. The issue may also be raised by the court; indeed, whenever "the evidence [presented] raises a 'bona fide' doubt as to the defendant's competence to stand trial, the trial court is under a constitutional obligation to raise the issue on its own motion and initiate a hearing" (*Pate v. Robinson*, 383 U.S. 375, 385 (1966)). Once the question has been raised, neither the defendant nor his attorney can waive the issue and demand that the case be brought to trial (384).

Due process requires that the defendant be competent throughout the trial (*Drope*, 172). As a consequence, an inquiry into competency may be initiated at any point in the proceeding and, in some jurisdictions, even after trial and sentencing. The issue may also be raised for the first time in a federal habeas corpus action months or even years after the trial (*Clark v. Beto*, 359 F.2d 554 (5th Cir. 1966); *United States v. Makris*, 535 F.2d 899, 904 (5th Cir. 1976)).

In most jurisdictions the initial motion raising the issue of competency automatically makes a psychiatric examination mandatory; elsewhere, the ordering of the examination is within the discretion of the judge. Only if there is sufficient evidence to raise a "bona fide doubt" as to the defendant's competency does the defendant have a constitutional right to a psychiatric examination. The testimony of one lay witness to the effect that the defendant had been acting in a "peculiar" manner has been held to meet the test of "substantial doubt" requiring a psychiatric referral (*Tyler v. Beto*, 391 F.2d 993, 997 (5th Cir. 1968)). The psychiatric examination usually is conducted by one or more experts who are appointed by the court and whose opinions are therefore regarded as impartial.

Stage II: preliminary determination of competency. The determination by the court as to whether there are sufficient grounds to hold a formal hearing constitutes a second stage in the process. As a practical matter, this determination is heavily influenced by the results of the psychiatric evaluation report. In the federal system, for example, if the psychiatric report indicates that the defendant may be incompetent, a hearing on the question is mandatory. Aside from any statutory requirement that may mandate a hearing, the Constitution itself requires a hearing whenever sufficient evidence pointing to incompetency has been presented to the court. Although the Supreme Court has declined to define the quantum of evidence that compels a hearing, it has held that a standard couched in terms of evidence raising a bona fide doubt satisfies constitutional requirements (*Drope*, 172–173). Lower court decisions, in turn, have held that a bona fide doubt exists where there is any substantial evidence of incompetency (*Chavez v. United States*, 656 F.2d 512, 517–518 (9th Cir. 1981)). In deciding whether there is substantial evidence, the trial court must accept as true all evidence suggesting incompetency; the issue of credibility is reached only if a competency hearing is held.

Stage III: the hearing. The determination of competency occurs at a hearing, separate from the trial, at which guilt is adjudicated. The principal witness will usually be the psychiatric expert who conducted the initial mental status examination. Both the defendant and prosecutor may introduce additional evidence, including the testimony of lay or expert witnesses.

The hearing is adversary in nature, and the defendant has the right to be represented by counsel and to cross-examine adverse witnesses. The defendant, however, does not have all the procedural rights that apply at a criminal trial, such as the constitutional right to have the issue decided by a jury. In most jurisdictions it is the trial judge who makes the determination. Moreover, the burden of proof is usually allocated to the defendant, and even when it rests with the prosecution (as it does in the federal system), it is the "preponderance of the evidence" standard, rather than the "beyond a reasonable doubt" standard, that governs (*Makris*, 906; *United States v. DiGilio*, 538 F.2d 972, 988 (3d Cir. 1976)). Finally, the privilege against self-incrimination applies in only limited

form at the competency hearing. For example, the privilege may not be invoked by the defendant to bar the testimony of the examining psychiatrist when the testimony is directed to the issue of competency (*Estelle v. Smith*, 451 U.S. 454 (1981)).

In determining whether the accused is competent, the trier of fact may take into account not only evidence introduced but also the defendant's appearance and demeanor during the proceedings (*United States ex rel. McGough v. Hewitt*, 528 F.2d 339, 344 (3d Cir. 1976)). Moreover, since the determination of competency involves the application of a legal standard, the trier of fact is not compelled to accept the medical expert's conclusions.

Effect of a finding of incompetency

The immediate effect of a finding of incompetency is that the defendant may not be tried and convicted until competency is restored. But such a finding does not preclude the adjudication of certain pretrial defenses, such as that the indictment is insufficient or that the statute of limitations has run its course. Neither does it bar the limited type of trial, authorized by some states, at which the defendant is provided with an opportunity to "establish his innocence without permitting his conviction" (*Jackson*, 741).

A finding of incompetency does not serve to dismiss the charge, and unless the charge is dismissed by the prosecutor, it remains pending. This, coupled with the fact that the statute of limitations is generally suspended during the period of incompetency, makes it possible to bring a defendant to trial whenever competency is restored, even if a substantial period of time has elapsed. To prevent this result, it has been suggested that the Sixth Amendment speedy trial guarantee should be applied to foreclose a trial where the delay has been substantial (*United States v. Geelan*, 520 F.2d 585 (9th Cir. 1975)). In general, however, the mere passage of time has not been held to bar the trial of a defendant upon his restoration to competency. Of course, where the incompetency is permanent, this means that the defendant can never be brought to trial.

Traditionally, the practice in most states was automatically to commit a defendant found incompetent to stand trial. Moreover, the commitment would be of indefinite duration; the defendant's release could only come about if he were restored to competency and brought to trial or if the charges were dismissed by the prosecutor. As a consequence, it was common for persons who had neither been convicted of a crime nor committed in accordance with the state's normal commitment procedures to be incarcerated for extended periods in institutions for the criminally insane. In 1972 the Supreme Court held that the period of automatic commitment cannot exceed a "reasonable period of time necessary to determine whether there is a substantial probability that he will attain that capacity in the foreseeable future." The Court imposed the additional condition that during this period of confinement the state must demonstrate "progress" in the attainment of competency. Thus, a defendant whose restoration to competency is not reasonably foreseeable must either be released or be subjected to "the customary civil commitment proceeding that would be required to commit indefinitely any other citizen" (*Jackson*, 738).

The "reasonable" period of commitment authorized by the Supreme Court has been variously construed. Some states restrict the period of automatic commitment to twelve months (Fla. R. Crim. P. 3.212(c) (1981 Supp.)). Others permit confinement for up to three years or a period not exceeding the maximum sentence for the offense charged, whichever is shorter (Cal. Penal Code § 1370(c)(1) (1981 Supp.)). The extent to which a state is free to enact commitment laws that differentiate in any way between incompetent defendants and others has not been authoritatively resolved, although the laws of a number of states make such a distinction.

RALPH REISNER

See also DIMINISHED CAPACITY; EXCUSE: INSANITY; MENTAL HEALTH EXPERT, ROLE OF THE; MENTALLY DISORDERED OFFENDERS.

BIBLIOGRAPHY

BLACKSTONE, WILLIAM. *Commentaries on the Laws of England* (1765–1769), vol. 4. Reprint. University of Chicago Press, 1979.
Comment. "Incompetency to Stand Trial." *Harvard Law Review* 81 (1967): 454–473.
PIZZI, WILLIAM T. "Competency to Stand Trial in Federal Court: Conceptual and Constitutional Problems." *University of Chicago Law Review* 45 (1977): 21–71.
WINICK, BRUCE J. "Psychotropic Medication and Competency to Stand Trial." *American Bar Foundation Research Journal* (1977): 769–816.

COMPLICITY

See ACCOMPLICES.

COMPULSION

See ACTUS REUS; EXCUSE: DURESS.

COMPUTER CRIME

Introduction

Computers have produced significant benefits to society. Industrialized countries rely on their continuous availability and integrity. Computers have introduced innovations into the business world, communications media, and scientific community. In addition, as computers have developed, new categories and methods of perpetrating crime have emerged that employ them. Computer crime was first observed in the United States, but it has spread to other countries as computer systems have been adopted throughout the world.

Computer programs and data files represent entirely new types of assets—assets that are subjected to theft, fraud, and unauthorized use. Data stored magnetically and electronically are compact, volatile, and only indirectly accessible, compared with the paper-based data in previous manual systems. This produces a different environment for the criminal and for investigators and prosecutors of crime.

A computer crime is defined as any illegal act requiring knowledge of computer technology for its perpetration, investigation, or prosecution (U.S. Dept. of Justice). It has two main categories. In the first, the computer is a tool of a crime, such as fraud, embezzlement, and theft of property, or is used to plan or manage a crime. In the second, the computer is the object of a crime, such as sabotage, theft or alteration of stored data, or theft of its services. In this category, data may represent money directly, as in electronic fund-transfer systems, or indirectly in the costs of replacing erased or altered data or the losses incurred if data are disclosed or used without authorization. Thus, underlying the definition of computer crime is the concept that data represent money. Although the computer may be used as a tool or as the object in these crimes, it is people, not computers, who commit these offenses. The computer cannot be manipulated without the instruction of a human being.

Computer crime and the new problems it creates have been subjects for research since the 1960s. The value of this research lies in describing abusive acts involving computers in qualitative, case-by-case terms and in learning from actual experience how to deal more effectively with the serious problems that such inquiry reveals. The focus of the research is on examining the changing nature of crime as computers are increasingly used and relied upon, not on collecting statistics. This research has revealed that definitive categories of computer crime must be established, security measures must be developed to prevent them, police investigators and prosecutors must be educated in means of detecting and investigating them, and penal codes must be updated to address computer crimes.

Categories of computer crime

The computer as a tool of crime. Large amounts of the assets of institutions and companies are recorded in computers as data that can be manipulated. For example, data on property can be erased or altered to indicate that the property has been destroyed or damaged or is obsolete, when in fact it has been stolen. In such crimes, the simplest, safest, and most common method is data diddling, which involves changing data before or during the input to computers. The changes can be made by anyone associated with, or having access to, the processes of creating, recording, transporting, encoding, examining, checking, converting, and transforming the data that ultimately enter a computer. Examples are forging or counterfeiting documents; exchanging valid computer tapes, cards, or disks with prepared replacements; and falsifying initial entries.

Embezzlement. The theft of property by someone who has access to it through some office or position of trust is embezzlement. Employees have discovered sophisticated methods of using the computer to steal money from their employers or customers. One of the methods is the *salami technique,* whereby small amounts of assets are stolen from a large number of sources, the principle being to take small slices without a noticeable reduction of the whole. For example, a bank's demand-deposit accounting system can be changed to reduce thousands of accounts randomly by a few cents through transferring the money to a favored account, from which the perpetrator makes withdrawals. The success of the theft is based on the idea that each account loses so little that the loss is seldom observed.

Fraud. The development of fictitious personal data, contracts, accounts, and companies is often more successfully accomplished in a computer system than in manually maintained records. Nonexistent individuals, companies, street numbers, and street names are easier to "hide" in a computer system because continuous evaluation by people is lacking after the data enter the computer, and because the controls in computer programs are often insufficient.

Employee-payment systems are particularly vulnerable to computer crime. Fictitious employees can be created, or the perpetrator can manipulate information on time cards or monthly and annual salaries for other employees. The individual employee will often not have the ability or desire to check the calculations in his payment. Welfare payments are another vulnerable area. Fictitious welfare claims have been presented in large numbers.

The computer as an object of crime.

Sabotage. Computers, computer facilities, data, and programs can be physically destroyed or damaged by arson, explosives, or other means. For example, people have thrown car keys and screwdrivers into computer equipment to destroy it. In France, Italy, and other countries, computers have become targets for terrorists, who burn and damage computer centers, including data and programs.

A sophisticated method of sabotage is the electronic destruction of data and programs. A *logic bomb* is a computer program that determines what conditions or states of the computer optimally facilitate perpetration of a malicious act. The logic bomb can be inserted in the computer system by the *Trojan horse method*—the covert placement of instructions in a program so that the computer will perform unauthorized functions as well as its intended functions. Programs are usually constructed sufficiently loosely that space can be found or created for inserting extra instructions.

An additional method takes advantage of *trapdoors.* In the development of large application and computer operating systems, programmers routinely insert debugging aids that provide breaks in the code for inserting additional codes and intermediate output capabilities. Although computer operating systems are designed to prevent access and insertion or modification of codes, a system programmer can insert a code that permits compromise of these safeguards during the debugging phases of program development and later when the system is being maintained and improved. Such trapdoors can purposely be left in to facilitate future access and modification, compromise of computer programs, or other unauthorized activities, such as the use of large amounts of computer time free of charge.

Theft.

1. Tangible Property. Computers, computer equipment, and other tangible property can be the object of theft. Magnetic tapes and disks can be tempting targets, especially if they contain data representing money, personal information, trade secrets, or other information that could be valuable to unauthorized people or companies.

2. Data. Of value to a computer crime perpetrator

are computer programs—the ordered sets of data that are coded instructions for processing other data, such as computer-accessible data on individuals, companies, trade secrets, and the like. In direct telephone communication systems with computers, perpetrators can obtain unauthorized access to the computer and send information to their own remote terminals. The transfer of magnetic recordings and electronic pulses make the property "taken" intangible.

One method of achieving such thefts is by *impersonation,* whereby the perpetrator illegally obtains and presents to the computer the user's positive identifications, passwords, magnetic-strip card, or metal key. In *electronic piggybacking methods,* a hidden computer terminal is connected to the same line as an authorized terminal through the telephone switching equipment. The hidden terminal is used when the authorized terminal is not in use. The computer cannot differentiate between or recognize the two terminals; it senses only one terminal and one user.

The potential for *wiretapping* increases as more computers are connected to communication facilities, and greater amounts of electronically stored assets are transmitted from computer to computer over communication circuits. So far, such cases have been rare because data usually can be obtained or modified more easily through the impersonation or electronic piggybacking methods.

3. Services. When people gain unauthorized access to a computer and use the services for their own purposes, the crime is also often described as theft of computer time. If the unauthorized use continues for an extended period, it can result in a considerable loss in terms of service value. Without permission from the employer, employees have established their own companies and have used the employer's computer for the new company. Sometimes the employer's existing data and programs have been used.

Security

The security of a computer system depends on that of the facility, on the protection afforded by the procedures used in operations and maintenance, on controls in the system, and on the trustworthiness of the people in key positions. The need for developing security measures to protect computers and their contents was only gradually recognized as computer use increased. This was easily accomplished for early computers, but problems arose when technical advances permitted the sharing of resources by more than one user at a time, continuous storing of data from job to job, and servicing of more than one user at a time.

In addition, computers are used for many more applications that offer the possibilities of gain through unauthorized or malicious acts and of serious losses through errors.

With the increasing sophistication of computer systems, security is continually upgraded. This requires controls over physical access, appropriate administrative procedures, and discipline in maintaining them. However, the security of older computer applications cannot be sufficiently upgraded, except in special cases and at high cost. Comprehensive technological and practical solutions to the security problem are only slowly being adopted in the design of new computer applications.

Protection of computers is afforded through such technical safeguards as electronic door locks, the control of terminal access by requiring passwords, the protection of data files by access controls and encryption, and the maintenance of the integrity of operating systems and application programs by program design and hardware functions. Analytical methods, such as risk analysis and safeguard selection, are useful in optimizing the allocation of limited funds for computer security. In addition, the introduction of the new occupations of electronic data processing (EDP) auditor and computer security specialist has helped to formalize the new discipline of computer security. Nevertheless, because security problems are caused by people, the security measures must be directed to controlling the people working in computer environments.

Computer crimes tend to be perpetrated by workers in computer-related occupations, for these people have the necessary skills, access, and knowledge to perform computer crimes. Perpetrators of sophisticated computer crime are generally young, energetic, highly motivated, and intelligent. One-third of those identified are managers. In some cases, their acts deviate only slightly from the accepted practices of their colleagues. The "Robin Hood" syndrome is common: they rationalize acts against organizations but believe that acts against individuals are immoral. The perpetrators apparently are challenged by the game of "beating the machine." In the absence of established ethical standards in new computer-related occupations, a personal philosophy conducive to unauthorized acts and to criminal acts can be created.

In the future, many security activities now performed by individuals will be automated. However, computers will still be vulnerable to a few systems-maintenance people who have sufficient skills, knowledge, resources, and access to commit a crime. This limited accessibility would nevertheless be a considerable improvement over the widely experienced situation in which large numbers of computer users have the capacity to subvert computers at both the system and application levels.

Detection and investigation

Detection of sophisticated computer crime is a serious problem. Most known cases are discovered by accident and are not caught by auditing. Often much time elapses between the commission of the act and its detection. Government, state, and local authorities, as well as officials in private industry, tend to be reluctant to report these cases because they fear adverse publicity.

Such problems are similar to those in white-collar crime but occur to a greater extent because the public still does not recognize computer crime as an ordinary offense involving money and records. In fact, the more sophisticated the computer crime, the more exciting the public finds it, and the victim is often blamed more than the perpetrator. Such attitudes can create serious effects on law enforcement, because early detection and reporting, and the victim's cooperation, are essential elements in the investigation.

To investigate sophisticated computer crime successfully, investigators and prosecutors must be specially trained. They must have technical skills so that they can control and direct the investigation of complex cases, using the services and assistance of computer experts. For less complex cases, investigators and prosecutors must have a basic understanding of how computers work and can be manipulated, and they must understand the technical terminology. The Federal Bureau of Investigation has given courses in computer crime investigation to more than a thousand of its agents, and state and local law enforcement officers have participated in similar courses, as have police in other countries.

In the investigation of computer crime, a team approach is recommended. Ideally, the team comprises an investigator, a prosecutor, a computer expert, and an EDP auditor. Investigations frequently require a search of a computer center or a remote computer terminal. The assistance of a data processing expert familiar with the particular computer center will be necessary to draft search warrants which include all pertinent systems and program components, so that the team can take possession of computer media, such as magnetic tapes and disks, to gain knowledge of their contents.

The investigation should be as far advanced as possible before an arrest is made. Search warrants and

affidavits should be completed, witnesses interrogated, and subpoenas prepared prior to arrest. The degree, type, and level of secrecy of the investigation must be decided, to avoid alerting the suspected perpetrator. This is important because within seconds the suspect can erase or damage such evidence as data and programs.

The investigator and the prosecutor can handle less complex cases routinely, especially those in which ordinary documents, checks, invoices, and the like suffice as evidence, even though these documents have been processed by computer.

Prosecution

New and proposed statutes. Forty statutes of the United States Code not written specifically for computers can be applied to such crimes. Beginning in 1977, repeated attempts have been made to expand federal statutes to cover more specifically the use for fraudulent or other illegal purposes of any computer owned or operated by the United States or certain financial institutions, or any that affects interstate commerce.

At the state level, as of August 1981 fifteen states had enacted computer crime legislation: Arizona, California, Colorado, Florida, Georgia, Illinois, Kentucky, Michigan, Montana, North Carolina, New Mexico, Rhode Island, Tennessee, Utah, and Virginia. Typical of state computer crime laws are the following paragraphs from Section 502 of the California Penal Code (1981 Supp.):

(b) Any person who intentionally accesses or causes to be accessed any computer system or computer network for the purpose of (1) devising or executing any scheme or artifice to defraud or extort or (2) obtaining money, property, or services with false or fraudulent intent, representations, or promises shall be guilty of a public offense.
(c) Any person who maliciously accesses, alters, deletes, damages, or destroys any computer system, computer network, computer program, or data shall be guilty of a public offense.
(d) Any person who violates the provisions of subdivision (a) or (b) is guilty of a felony and is punishable by a fine not exceeding five thousand dollars ($5,000), or by imprisonment in the state prison for 16 months, or two or three years, or by both such fine and imprisonment, or by a fine not exceeding two thousand five hundred dollars ($2,500), or by imprisonment in the county jail not exceeding one year, or by both such fine and imprisonment.
(e) This section shall not be construed to preclude the applicability of any other provision of the criminal law of this state which applies or may apply to any transaction.

Several other countries are aware of the legal problems in prosecuting computer crime, and some have made efforts to propose or enact specific statutes to fight such offenses—for example, West Germany, the United Kingdom, Sweden, and Norway. The international transborder flow of data through telephone systems, microwave facilities, satellites, and radio systems could create bilateral or multilateral problems if data were stolen through these channels. Since in any such case two or more countries would be involved, there is a need to harmonize the penal codes of the various nations through guidelines or recommendations to assure proper prosecution, which otherwise could be hampered by international jurisdictional problems.

Specific statutes covering computer crime produce a greater deterrent effect than existing criminal statutes, by creating a basis for ethical behavior within the computer society and by easing the evidentiary burdens in computer crime cases. With such specific statutes, prosecutors and courts need not stretch existing statutes to cover computer abuses.

Prosecution under existing statutes. Many computer crime cases can be successfully investigated and prosecuted under the existing theft and fraud statutes covering money and tangible property. The theft of data or computer services and the obliteration and alteration of data are, however, difficult to prosecute. The inadequacy of the existing statutes could result in no charges against the perpetrator or dismissal of some cases or counts in court. The mail fraud or wire fraud statutes have often been the only practical laws to use, even though the use of wire or mail may have been only incidental or peripheral to the case. For example, a computer programmer who had stolen a confidential program from his former employer's computer center was convicted of wire fraud because he had used a wire transmission across state lines in the scheme. The count involving interstate transportation of stolen property was dismissed in court on the theory that the electronic impulses transmitted by telephone lines across state lines did not satisfy the statute's requirement that stolen property be involved.

The principal defense strategy in a computer crime case is typically an attack on the admissibility of the computer materials involved and of computer-generated evidence. When the prosecutor attempts to introduce such evidence in court, the greatest care must be taken to prove its authenticity and relevance. The prosecutor must be prepared to present in court the "computer trail," which extends from the systems analyst who designed and specified the computer program that produced the evidence to the programmer,

the operator, the data entry personnel, and the job output clerk who was responsible for the manual handling of the output after the evidence was run in the computer. The prosecutor must also obtain the original material and not a copy, because of the difficulty in establishing the integrity of the copy. If the victim needs this material to continue conducting business, he can use copies of the material.

In both the investigation and prosecution, computer jargon (software, firmware, bits, bugs) should be avoided because the ambiguity of the terms tends to confuse the jury and the court.

Conclusion

The nature of crime is changing as computer technology alters the environments and methods of crime. There are no valid statistics on computer crime because no comprehensive mechanisms exist to collect the data. However, the size of losses in known cases is growing. Therefore, major efforts must be made to improve computer security, train auditors, and prepare the criminal justice community to deal with this crime phenomenon.

STEIN SCHJØLBERG
DONN B. PARKER

See also both articles under EMPLOYEE THEFT; SECURITY, INDUSTRIAL; THEFT; WHITE-COLLAR CRIME: HISTORY OF AN IDEA.

BIBLIOGRAPHY

BECKER, JAY. "Rifkin, A Documentary History." *Computer/Law Journal* 2, no. 3 (1980): 471–720.
COMER, MIKE J. *Corporate Fraud.* New York: McGraw-Hill, 1977.
GEIS, GILBERT, and STOTLAND, EZRA, eds. *White-collar Crime: Theory and Research.* Beverly Hills, Calif.: Sage, 1980.
JOHNSTON, NORMAN, and SAVITZ, LEONARD D. *American Legal Process and Corrections.* New York: Wiley, 1982.
Koba Associates. *Computer Crime: Expert Witness Manual.* Washington, D.C.: U.S. Department of Justice, Bureau of Justice Statistics, 1980.
KRAUSS, LEONARD I., and MACGAHAN, AILEEN. *Computer Fraud and Countermeasures.* Englewood Cliffs, N.J.: Prentice-Hall, 1979.
McKNIGHT, GERALD. *Computer Crime.* London: Joseph, 1973.
PARKER, DONN B. "Computer Abuse Research Update." *Computer/Law Journal* 2 (1980): 329–352.
———. *Computer Security Management.* Reston, Va.: Reston, 1981.
———. *Crime by Computer.* New York: Scribner, 1976.
———. *Ethical Conflicts in Computer Science and Technology.* Arlington, Va.: AFIPS Press, 1979.
SCHJØLBERG, STEIN. "Computer Crime in Norway." *A Decade*

of Computers and Law. Edited by Jon Bing and Knut S. Selmer. Oslo: Universitetsforlaget, 1980, pp. 440–459.

SEIDLER, LEE J.; ANDREWS, FREDERICK; and EPSTEIN, MARC J. *The Equity Funding Papers: The Anatomy of a Fraud.* Santa Barbara, Calif.: Wiley/Hamilton, 1977.

U.S. Department of Justice, Bureau of Justice Statistics. *Criminal Justice Resource Manual: Computer Crime.* Prepared by SRI International. Washington, D.C.: The Bureau, 1979.

WHITESIDE, THOMAS. *Computer Capers: Tales of Electronic Thievery, Embezzlement, and Fraud.* New York: Crowell, 1978.

CONDEMNATION

See CRIME: CONCEPT OF CRIME; GUILT; PUNISHMENT.

CONDITIONAL RELEASE

See PRETRIAL DIVERSION; *articles under* PROBATION AND PAROLE.

CONFESSIONS

The need for confessions

The need for confessions and the need to interrogate suspects in the absence of counsel and without advising them of their right to remain silent have often been asserted or assumed but also sharply disputed. In *Crooker v. California,* 357 U.S. 433 (1958), the defendant argued that every police denial of a suspect's request to contact counsel should be viewed as a constitutional violation of the right to counsel, rendering any resulting confession inadmissible. But a 5–4 majority of the Supreme Court dismissed this contention with the observation that it would have a "devastating effect on enforcement of criminal law, for it would effectively preclude police questioning—*fair as well as unfair*—until the accused was afforded opportunity to call his attorney" (*Crooker,* 441).

A few years later, in the course of a long plurality opinion designed to develop a "set of principles" for the "voluntariness" test, Justice Felix Frankfurter thought it self-evident that, despite modern advances in crime detection technology, police interrogation of those suspected of involvement in an offense is "often indispensable to crime detection" (*Culombe v. Connecticut,* 367 U.S. 568, 571 (1961)). It followed, he thought, that "whatever reasonable means are needed to make the questioning effective must also be conceded to the police." Thus, "often prolongation of the interrogation period will be essential";

"counsel for the suspect will generally prove a thorough obstruction to the investigation"; and even informing the suspect of his legal right to remain silent "will prove an obstruction" (*Culombe,* 579–580).

The deep division in the Supreme Court in the mid-1960s over the need to replace the traditional voluntariness test with new doctrines that imposed tighter restrictions on police interrogation may be explained to a considerable degree in terms of the Justices' differing views on the need for confessions. The majority in the famous case of *Escobedo v. Illinois,* 378 U.S. 478 (1964) observed that "history amply shows that confessions have often been extorted to save law enforcement officials the trouble and effort of obtaining valid and independent evidence" (490). The opinion strongly implied that a system which relies on "extrinsic evidence independently secured through skillful investigation" could, without seriously impairing police efficiency, replace a system "which comes to depend on the 'confession.'"

The four Justices who dissented in *Escobedo* also dissented two years later in the landmark *Miranda* opinion (*Miranda v. Arizona,* 384 U.S. 436 (1966)), and this time they made their disagreement even more emphatic. Justice Byron White, joined by Justices John Harlan and Potter Stewart, dissented, saying that the *Miranda* decision "will measurably weaken the ability of the criminal law to perform [its] tasks" and warning that in a significant number of cases "the Court's rule will return a killer, a rapist or other criminal to the streets [to] repeat his crime whenever it pleases him" (526, 541–542). Justice Thomas Clark's dissenting opinion expressed the fear that the Court's new "strict constitutional specific inserted at the nerve center of crime detection may well kill the patient" (500); and the dissenting opinion of Justice Harlan, joined by Justices Stewart and White, stated that the "social costs of crime are too great to call the new rules anything but a hazardous experimentation" (517).

The dire predictions of the *Miranda* dissenters find little support in any of the empirical studies evaluating the impact of that 1966 decision on the criminal justice system. For example, one study concluded that the need for confessions was important in only a small number of cases and that warning a suspect of his right to the assistance of counsel before answering any questions and of his right to remain silent was a factor in reducing the success of interrogation in only about 10 percent of the cases evaluated (Project).

Studies such as this, however, cannot be viewed as the last word on the need for confessions and the importance of police interrogation. For one thing, they suggest that suspects brought to the station house for questioning are in such a crisis-laden situation and are so often unable to grasp the full significance of what they are told that a system of police warnings is simply an inadequate means of fortifying a suspect's rights (Project, pp. 1572–1573, 1613). Moreover, the above study points out that despite the presence of student observers, suspects were given the full *Miranda* warnings less than one-fourth of the time and that when the police did give the warnings, they often did so in a tone and manner which gelded them of much of their meaning or incorporated some "hedging."

It may still be argued, therefore, that careful, unequivocal, and emphatic *Miranda* warnings or a more effective means of implementing a suspect's rights than police warnings (such as requiring the presence of an attorney before a suspect can waive his rights) would have had a devastating impact on law enforcement. This much, and perhaps only this much, can be safely said: Whatever the *actual* facts, "the *perceived* need [for confessions] surely has constituted the strongest force against attempts to abolish or restrict police interrogation" (Grano, 1979b, p. 896; italics added).

Historical background

The voluntariness test and its shortcomings. Until the 1940s, the rule that a confession was admissible if not "coerced" or "involuntary" was essentially an alternative statement of the rule that a confession was admissible if free of influences that made it untrustworthy or "probably untrue" (Berger, pp. 102–103). The "untrustworthiness" rationale—the view that the rules governing the admissibility of confessions were designed merely to protect the integrity of the fact-finding process—was adequate to explain the exclusion of the confession in the first Fourteenth Amendment due process confession case, *Brown v. Mississippi*, 297 U.S. 278 (1936), and in those cases that immediately followed, for they all involved threatened or actual police brutality or violence. But when cases involving the more subtle psychological pressures began to appear, it became more difficult to assume that the confessions excluded were unreliable as evidence of guilt.

The famous case of *Ashcraft v. Tennessee*, 322 U.S. 143 (1944) is instructive in this regard. A 6–3 majority reversed a murder conviction based on a confession obtained after thirty-six hours of almost continuous police interrogation. However, there was ample reason to think that Ashcraft had indeed been involved in the murder. The man he named as his wife's killer promptly admitted the killing and accused Ashcraft of hiring him to do the job. After the interrogation, when examined by his family physician, Ashcraft made an "entirely voluntary" statement explaining why he wanted to kill his wife. Thus, "it is fair to suggest that the result reached by the [*Ashcraft*] Court reflected less a concern with the reliability of the confession as evidence of guilt in the particular case than disapproval of police methods which a majority of the Court conceived as generally dangerous and subject to serious abuse" (Allen, 1959, p. 235).

In *Watts v. Indiana*, 338 U.S. 49 (1949) and two companion cases, the Court overturned three convictions resting on coerced confessions without disputing the accuracy of Justice Robert Jackson's observation (concurring in *Watts* and dissenting in the other two cases) that the confessions in each were "inherently believable" and "not shaken as to truth by anything that occurred at the trial." The Court responded by pointing out that "the Due Process Clause *bars police procedure* which violates the basic notions of our accusatorial mode of prosecuting crime and vitiates a conviction based on the fruits of such procedure" (italics added).

That the Court was applying two constitutional standards for the admissibility of confessions—a "police methods" test as well as a "trustworthiness" test—was made even clearer by subsequent cases. Thus, in *Spano v. New York*, 360 U.S. 315 (1959), the Court pointed out that the refusal to permit the use of involuntary confessions turned not only on their untrustworthiness but on "the deep-rooted feeling that the police must obey the law while enforcing the law" and on the premise that "life and liberty can be as much endangered from illegal methods used to convict those thought to be criminal as from the actual criminals themselves." The rejection of the untrustworthiness test as the exclusive rationale governing the admissibility of confessions was underscored in *Rogers v. Richmond*, 365 U.S. 534 (1961). The trial judge had found that the police pretense of bringing the defendant's wife in for questioning had no tendency to produce a false confession, and in his charge to the jury he had indicated that the admissibility of the confession should turn on its probable reliability. In reversing, the Court emphasized that the question whether the police tactics had produced an involuntary confession had to be answered "with complete disregard of whether or not [the defendant] in fact spoke the truth."

The voluntariness test left much to be desired. It soon became clear that the courts were not using such terms as *voluntariness* and *coercion* as tools of analysis but as "shorthands" or conclusions. When a court concluded that the police had resorted to intolerable or sufficiently offensive interrogation tactics (the conclusion often turned on the "totality of circumstances," for example, the particular suspect's age, background, or other characteristics), it characterized the resulting confession as "involuntary" and talked of "overbearing" or "breaking the will." When, on the other hand, a court concluded that the interrogation techniques were acceptable under the circumstances, it called the resulting confession "voluntary" and talked of "mental freedom" or "self-determination." Unfortunately, the courts shed insufficient light on the underlying analyses that led them to label a challenged confession "voluntary" or "involuntary" (Bator and Vorenberg, pp. 72–73; Kamisar, pp. 14, 25, 70–76).

Moreover, as the rationales for the Supreme Court's confession cases evolved, it became increasingly clear that terms such as *voluntariness, coercion,* and *breaking the will* were actually misleading. Such terms did not focus directly on either of the two critical concerns—the offensiveness of the interrogation methods and the tendency of these methods to produce a false confession (Kamisar, pp. 15–20; Paulsen, pp. 429–430; Schulhofer, pp. 867–878).

Another problem with the voluntariness standard was that because of its vagueness and the need to assess the "totality of circumstances" (including such factors as the age, intelligence, education, racial or ethnic background, and previous criminal experience of the suspect), it furnished very little guidance to police officers seeking to ascertain what interrogation tactics they could use or to trial judges seeking to ascertain what criteria they should apply in resolving confession claims (Berger, pp. 107–112; Schulhofer, pp. 869–870).

As police interrogators made greater use of psychological techniques over the years, the always difficult problems of proof facing the person so questioned became aggravated. Frequently, the defendant was inarticulate and his perceptions were not acute. The disputed events inevitably occurred in secret, with the suspect isolated and often frightened or confused. Moreover, the local courts almost always resolved the virtually inevitable "swearing contest" over what happened behind closed doors in favor of the police. Perhaps this was because any trial judge is so close to the scene that it is especially hard for him "to set apart the question of the guilt or innocence of a particular defendant and focus solely upon the procedural aspect of the case" (Schaefer, 1956, p. 7).

As Geoffrey Stone has observed, "Given the [Supreme] Court's inability to articulate a clear and predictable definition of *voluntariness,* the apparent persistence of state courts in utilizing the ambiguity of the concept to validate confessions of doubtful constitutionality, and the resultant burden on its own workload, it seemed inevitable that the [Supreme] Court would seek 'some automatic device by which the potential evils of incommunicado interrogation [could] be controlled' " (pp. 102–103). The Supreme Court's dissatisfaction with the elusive voluntariness test and its efforts to replace the test with a more concrete and workable standard were to culminate in the *Miranda* decision.

The right-to-counsel approach. The case of *Massiah v. United States,* 377 U.S. 201 (1964) arose as follows: After Massiah had been indicted for various federal narcotic violations, had retained a lawyer and pleaded not guilty, and had been released on bail, Massiah was invited by his codefendant, Colson, to discuss the pending case in Colson's car. Massiah assumed he was simply talking to a friend, his partner in crime, who had also been indicted, but unknown to him Colson had become a secret government agent. A radio transmitter had been installed under the front seat of Colson's car to enable a nearby agent equipped with a receiving device to overhear the Massiah-Colson conversation. As expected, Massiah made several damaging admissions.

Despite the fact that Massiah was neither in *custody* nor subjected to *police interrogation* as these terms are usually understood, a 6–3 majority of the Supreme Court held that his damaging admissions should have been excluded from evidence. The decisive feature of the case was that after he had been indicted—"and therefore at a time when he was clearly entitled to a lawyer's help"—government agents had "deliberately elicited" statements from him in the absence of counsel. *Massiah* stands for the proposition that once a person is formally charged or "judicial" or "adversary" criminal proceedings have otherwise been initiated against him, his right to the assistance of counsel has "begun" or "attached." Unless the defendant voluntarily and knowingly waives that right, the absence of counsel under such circumstances is alone sufficient to exclude any resulting incriminating statements.

Massiah was soon overshadowed by *Escobedo,* decided a short five weeks later in the same term. When Escobedo was taken into custody, the police told him that he had been named as the one who killed his brother-in-law. Escobedo repeatedly but unsuccessfully asked to speak to his lawyer. Instead, the police arranged a confrontation between him and his accuser, DiGerlando. In the course of denying that he had fired the fatal shots and claiming that DiGerlando had done so, Escobedo implicated himself in the murder.

Although Escobedo's interrogation had occurred before judicial or adversary proceedings had commenced against him, a 5–4 majority of the Court held that Escobedo's incriminating statements should have been excluded:

The interrogation here was conducted before petitioner was formally indicted. But in the context of this case, that fact should make no difference. When petitioner requested, and was denied, an opportunity to consult with his lawyer, the investigation had ceased to be a general investigation of 'an unsolved crime.' [Citation omitted] Petitioner had become the accused and the purpose of the investigation was to 'get him' to confess his guilt despite his constitutional right not to do so. At the time of his arrest, and throughout the course of the interrogation, the police told petitioner that they had convincing evidence that he had fired the fatal shots. . . . Petitioner, a layman, was undoubtedly unaware that . . . an admission of 'mere' complicity in the murder plot was legally as damaging as an admission of firing of the fatal shots. [Citation omitted] The 'guiding hand of counsel' was essential to advise [him] of his rights in this delicate situation. . . . It would exalt form over substance to make the right to counsel, under these circumstances, depend on whether at the time of the interrogation, the authorities had secured a formal indictment [485–486].

Until *Miranda* moved the decision off center stage two years later, the scope and meaning of *Escobedo* was a matter of strong and widespread disagreement. In large part this was the result of the accordionlike quality of the Court's opinion. Parts of the opinion suggest that a suspect's right to counsel comes into play whenever the investigation begins to focus on him, regardless of whether he is in custody or has asked for a lawyer. At some places the opinion launches so broad an attack on the use of confessions in general and so emphatically rejects the need for an "effective interrogation opportunity" that it threatens (or promises) to eliminate virtually all police interrogation. At other places, however, the opinion is quite confining, so much so that it arguably limits the case to its special facts (Escobedo had specifically and repeatedly requested, and had repeatedly been denied, an opportunity to seek advice from counsel; the police had failed to warn him of his right to remain silent; and he was in police custody).

The *Miranda* case

The Court in *Massiah* and *Escobedo* seemed to be moving in the direction of banning all incriminating statements obtained from a suspect, even "volunteered" statements, unless they were made knowingly and with the tactical assistance of counsel. Strongly protesting this development, the *Escobedo* dissenters maintained that it was "incongruous to assume that the Sixth Amendment right to counsel rather than the Fifth Amendment privilege against self-incrimination governed the admissibility of confessions" (497). The self-incrimination provision ("No person . . . shall be compelled in any criminal case to be a witness against himself"), they stressed, "addresses itself to the very issue of incriminating admissions and resolves it by proscribing only *compelled* statements" (497; italics added).

A remarkable feature of the American confessions law is that the self-incrimination provision was long deemed inapplicable to police interrogation. It was not until 1964 that the Supreme Court even held that Fourteenth Amendment due process "secures against *state* invasion the same privilege that the Fifth Amendment guarantees against *federal* infringement—the right of a person to remain silent unless he chooses to speak in the unfettered exercise of his own will, and to suffer no penalty [for] such silence" (*Malloy v. Hogan*, 378 U.S. 1, 8 (1964); italics added). But until *Miranda* the privilege against self-incrimination had not been deemed applicable in *federal* confession cases either—certainly not as it applied to judicial or other formal proceedings.

Why had the self-incrimination provision been excluded from the police station and other kinds of "custodial interrogation" until *Miranda*? The legal reasoning was that "compulsion" to testify against oneself meant *legal* compulsion. Thus, a legislative committee could not hold a witness in contempt for refusing to incriminate himself. Nor could a court hold a defendant in contempt for refusing to testify at his own trial. But a person subjected to police interrogation cannot *legally* be compelled to say anything, since he is threatened neither with perjury for testifying falsely nor with contempt for refusing to testify at all. Thus it could not be said, ran the pre-*Miranda* argument, that the interrogated suspect was being "compelled" to be a witness against himself within the meaning of the Fifth Amendment—even though he was likely to assume or be led by the police to believe that there were legal (or extralegal) sanctions for refusing to "cooperate" (Kamisar, pp. 45–46; Schaefer, 1967, pp. 16–18; Traynor, p. 674).

In *Miranda* a 5–4 majority, speaking through Chief Justice Earl Warren, concluded at long last that "all the principles embodied in the privilege [against self-incrimination] apply to informal compulsion exerted by law-enforcement officers during in-custody questioning" (461). Observed the Court:

An individual swept from familiar surroundings into police custody, surrounded by antagonistic forces, and subjected to the [tactics described in various police interrogation manuals, from which the Court quoted at length] cannot be otherwise than under compulsion to speak. As a practical matter, the compulsion to speak in the isolated setting of the police station may well be greater than in courts or other official investigations, where there are often impartial observers to guard against intimidation or trickery [461]. [The "interrogation environment"] carries its own badge of intimidation [and] is at odds with [the privilege against self-incrimination]. Unless adequate protective devices are employed to dispel the compulsion inherent in custodial surroundings, no statement obtained from the defendant can truly be the product of his free choice [457-458].

The "adequate protective" devices necessary to "neutralize" the "interrogation environment"—the coercive conditions surrounding or inherent in "custodial police interrogation"—are, of course, the now familiar "*Miranda* warnings:" Miranda's confession would have plainly been admissible a few years earlier, for he had confessed to a rape-kidnapping after only two hours of questioning. But what proved fatal for the government was that neither before nor during the questioning had the police advised him of his right to remain silent, his right to consult with an attorney (either retained or, if the defendant is indigent, as Miranda was, appointed) before answering questions, or his right to have an attorney present during the interrogation.

Although *Miranda* is grounded primarily on the privilege against self-incrimination, it also has a right-to-counsel component designed to protect and to reinforce the privilege. *After* he has been taken into custody "or otherwise deprived of his freedom of action in any significant way" and *prior* to any questioning, a suspect must be warned that he has a right to remain silent and to be advised that "anything said can and will be used against [him] in court" (469). But such a warning (and explanation) "cannot itself suffice" to "assure that the individual's right to choose between silence and speech remains unfettered throughout the interrogation process" (469). Thus, the suspect must also be told of his right to counsel, either retained or appointed. "The need for counsel to protect the Fifth Amendment privilege comprehends not merely a right to consult with counsel prior to any questioning, but also to have counsel present during any questioning if the defendant so desires" (470).

A suspect, of course, may waive his rights, provided he does so "voluntarily, knowingly and intelligently"

(444). But no valid waiver can be recognized "unless specifically made after the warnings [have] been given" (470). Moreover, the "mere fact that [a person] may have answered some questions or volunteered some statements on his own does not deprive him of the right to refrain from answering any further inquiries until he has consulted with an attorney and thereafter consents to be questioned" (445).

Miranda was the "high-water mark" of the Warren Court's "due process revolution" (Graham, 1970, p. 157). It plunged "the Warren Court into an ocean of abuse" and became "one of the leading issues of the 1968 presidential campaign" (Lieberman, p. 326). Nevertheless, the case may fairly be viewed as a compromise between the old voluntariness test (and the coercive interrogation tactics which that elusive test permitted in fact) and extreme proposals (based on an expansive reading of *Massiah* and *Escobedo*) that, as was feared (or hoped) on the eve of *Miranda*, would have "killed" confessions.

Miranda did not, and was not designed to, "kill" confessions. It allows the police to conduct "general on-the-scene questioning" or "other general questioning of citizens" (477-478) even though the citizen is neither informed nor aware of his rights. Moreover, according to *Miranda*, so long as the police do not question the suspect, they are free to hear and act upon volunteered statements even though the suspect has been brought to the police station or otherwise taken into custody. Custody does not in itself call for the *Miranda* warnings. It is only the *combination* of custody and interrogation that establishes the interrogation environment which is so at odds with the privilege against self-incrimination and which calls for *Miranda*'s protective devices (Kamisar, pp. 195-197).

On the eve of *Miranda*, fear was voiced that the Supreme Court might "project" counsel into the police station, and doubts were raised whether it would still be "possible to enforce criminal law" if that were to occur (Kamisar et al., p. 523; cf. pp. 498-514). But *Miranda* did not *fully* project counsel into the station house, for it did not require that a suspect actually consult with a lawyer in order for his waiver of constitutional rights to be valid.

Whether suspects are continuing to confess because they do not fully grasp the meaning of the *Miranda* warnings, because the promptings of conscience override the impact of the warnings, or because the police are hedging or undermining the warnings, it is plain that they are continuing to confess with great frequency (Stephens, pp. 165-200; Project; Medalie, Zeitz, and Alexander). It is difficult to believe that this would have been the case if *Miranda* had *fully* projected counsel into the interrogation room by requiring the advice of counsel or the presence of counsel before a suspect could effectively waive counsel and his right to remain silent.

Because *Miranda* was the centerpiece of the Warren Court's "revolution in American criminal procedure" and the prime target "of those who attributed the mounting wave of crime to the softness of judges" (Lieberman, p. 326), almost everyone expected the Burger Court to treat *Miranda* unkindly. And it did, for a decade. Thus, the new Court held that statements obtained by police who issued defective warnings or who refused to honor a suspect's assertion of his rights and continued to question him, although inadmissible in the presentation of the prosecution's own case, could be used to impeach the defendant's credibility if he took the stand (*Harris v. New York*, 401 U.S. 222 (1971); *Oregon v. Hass*, 420 U.S. 714 (1975); *Michigan v. Mosley*, 423 U.S. 96 (1975), in which a second interrogation session that occurred after a suspect initially refused to make a statement did not violate *Miranda* under the circumstances of the case; *Oregon v. Mathiason*, 429 U.S. 492 (1977), in which it was held that not all police questioning that takes place in a station house is necessarily "custodial interrogation").

However, in *Rhode Island v. Innis*, 446 U.S. 291 (1980), the Court gave *interrogation* within the meaning of *Miranda* a fairly generous interpretation, holding that the *Miranda* safeguards come into force "whenever a person in custody is subjected to either express questioning or its functional equivalent. That is to say, the term 'interrogation' refers not only to express questioning, but also to any words or actions on the part of the police (other than those normally attendant to arrest and custody) that the police should know are reasonably likely to elicit an incriminating response from the suspect" (300–301).

One may quarrel with the Court's *application* of its definition of *interrogation* to the *Innis* facts, as the three dissenters did. The majority held that Innis had not been interrogated when, after he had been arrested and put in a squad car, two police officers conversing with each other in the front of the car, but in Innis's presence, expressed concern that because the murder had occurred in the vicinity of a school for handicapped children, one of the children might find the missing shotgun and injure himself. At this point, Innis interrupted the officers and offered to lead them to where the shotgun was hidden. But *Innis* is a harder case than most because there was "a basis for concluding that the officer's remarks were made for some

purpose *other* than that of obtaining evidence from the suspect. An objective listener could plausibly conclude that the policemen's remarks in *Innis* were made solely to express their genuine concern about the danger posed by the hidden shotgun." The suspect might have viewed the purpose of the police conversation in the front of the car the same way, and if he did, "he would differentiate the speech or conduct from a 'direct question' because he would not see it as a demand for information" (White, 1980, pp. 1234–1235).

Considering the various alternatives, the *Innis* case's definition of *interrogation* seems more significant than the Court's questionable application of it in that case. The Court might have adopted a mechanical approach, as some lower courts had, and limited interrogation to those situations in which the police directly address a suspect. It might have limited interrogation to those instances in which the record establishes that the police intended to elicit an incriminating response, a rule that would have been very difficult to administer. But the Court did not adopt either of these approaches. Moreover, by explicitly including police tactics that do not involve verbal conduct, the Court appears to have repudiated the position taken by a number of lower courts that confronting a suspect with incriminating physical evidence or with an accomplice who has confessed and is seeking to put most of the blame on his cosuspect is not interrogation because it involves no verbal conduct on the part of the police (White, 1980, p. 1234).

Despite the fairly generous reading of *Miranda* in the *Innis* case, by holding the defendant's incriminating disclosures admissible the Court maintained its record of not excluding a single item of evidence solely on *Miranda* grounds since Warren Burger became Chief Justice in June of 1969. But that eleven-year record was broken the following year. Without a dissent, the Court excluded incriminating statements on the authority of *Miranda* in two 1981 cases decided the same day: *Edwards v. Arizona*, 451 U.S. 477 (1981) and *Estelle v. Smith*, 451 U.S. 454 (1981) (alternative holding).

In *Edwards*, the suspect asserted his right to counsel, but the police, without furnishing him a lawyer, returned the next day and reinterrogated him. The Court held that once a suspect requests a lawyer, he cannot be subjected to further interrogation until counsel has been made available to him "unless the [suspect] himself initiates further communication, exchanges or conversation with the police" (*Edwards*, 485). In *Smith*, the Court held that the death sentence imposed on the defendant was fatally tainted by the use, during the penalty phase of his trial, of a court-appointed psychiatrist's pretrial evaluation of the defendant's future dangerousness. The admission of the psychiatrist's testimony, ruled the Court, violated the defendant's privilege against self-incrimination, because he was not advised before the psychiatric examination that he had a right to remain silent and that any statement he made could be used against him at a capital sentencing proceeding.

The demise of *Escobedo* and the revivification of *Massiah*

Although the *Miranda* Court understandably tried to retain some continuity with the *Escobedo* opinion, it has become increasingly clear that *Miranda* actually marked a fresh start in describing the circumstances under which Fifth and Sixth Amendment protections come into play. *Escobedo* seemed to assign great significance to the *amount of evidence* available to the police at the time of questioning; the opinion therefore contains much talk about "prime suspects," "focal point," and the "accusatory stage." But *Miranda* attaches primary significance to *the conditions surrounding, or inherent in,* the interrogation setting; thus, the opinion includes much discussion of the "interrogation environment" and the "police-dominated" atmosphere. If an individual is subjected to custodial interrogation, *Miranda* applies whether or not the individual is a prime suspect or the focal point of the investigation. On the other hand, if a person is not subjected to custodial interrogation and the pressures generated thereby, despite the implications of *Escobedo* he is not entitled to be advised of his rights no matter how intensely the police have focused on him or to what extent they regard him as the prime suspect. In short, *Miranda* did not enlarge *Escobedo* as much as it displaced it (Kamisar, pp. 162–163).

The same cannot be said for *Massiah*. Although *Miranda* has dominated the confessions scene since the mid-1960s, *Massiah* has emerged as the other major Warren Court confessions doctrine. As clarified and strengthened by two Burger Court decisions, *Brewer v. Williams*, 430 U.S. 387 (1977) and *United States v. Henry*, 447 U.S. 264 (1980), *Massiah* holds that once adversary or judicial proceedings have commenced against an individual (by way of indictment, information, or "initial appearance" before a magistrate), government efforts to "deliberately elicit" incriminating statements from him, whether done openly by uniformed police officers (as in *Williams*) or surrepti-

tiously by "secret agents" (as in *Massiah* and *Henry*), violate the individual's right to counsel. The *Massiah* doctrine represents a "pure" or "straight" right-to-counsel approach. It comes into play regardless of whether a person is in custody or being subjected to interrogation in the *Miranda* sense. There need not be any "compelling influences," inherent, informal, or otherwise. In the *Massiah* case itself, of course, the defendant was free on bail and unaware that he was talking to a government agent. He thought he was merely chatting with a codefendant.

Massiah operates on the premise that "by its history, language, and function, the [Sixth Amendment] sought to draw a starting point after which counsel's assistance is generally required as an element of our adversary system" (Israel, p. 1368, n. 224). This starting point is reached when judicial or adversary criminal proceedings are initiated. At this point the criminal investigation has ended and the criminal prosecution, to which the pure right to counsel is applicable, has begun. The adverse positions of the government and the defendant have solidified. The parties, as the Court put it in the *Henry* case, are then "'arms length' adversaries" (273). At this point, it seems, the government has built its case. But if it has not, it may no longer elicit any information from the defendant himself. It may only proceed against him through his counsel.

The Burger Court decisions in *Williams* and *Henry* revitalized *Massiah;* one might even say they "disinterred" it (Grano, 1979a, p. 7). For until these decisions, there was good reason to think that *Massiah* had only been a stepping-stone to *Escobedo* and that it had been lost in the shuffle of fast-moving events that reshaped constitutional criminal procedure in the 1960s (Kamisar, pp. xvi, 160–164).

Actually, the *Henry* case not only reaffirmed the *Massiah* doctrine but expanded it, for it applied *Massiah* to a situation in which the Federal Bureau of Investigation had instructed its secret agent, ostensibly a fellow prisoner, not to question the defendant about the crime, and there was no showing that he had. But it sufficed that the FBI had "intentionally create[d] a situation likely to induce [the defendant] to make incriminating statements without the assistance of counsel" (*Henry*, 274). The government created such a situation, ruled the *Henry* Court, when an FBI agent instructed the undercover informant to be alert to any statements made by the defendant, who was housed in the same cellblock. "Even if the FBI agent's statement is accepted that he did not intend that [the defendant's] 'fellow inmate' would take affirmative steps to secure incriminating information, [he] must have known that such propinquity likely would lead to that result" (271).

Some final thoughts

Although few, if any, would have predicted it in the mid-1970s, in the second decade of the Burger Court, *Miranda* was not only very much alive but in some respects reinvigorated. Moreover, the *Massiah* doctrine had emerged as a much more potent force than it ever had been in the Warren Court era. Although at various times in the 1970s several members of the Burger Court seemed to be casting a longing eye at the old "voluntariness" test, the Court's action in *Edwards* and *Smith*, its generous reading of *Miranda* in the *Innis* case, and its even more generous reading of *Massiah* in the *Henry* case have, to borrow the language of one commentator, "reaffirmed its commitment to controlling police efforts to induce confessions by constitutional rules that look beyond the voluntariness test" (White, 1979b, p. 69).

Whatever chipping away or retreats from *Miranda* and *Massiah* are achieved by the Supreme Court, "one can be sure that the status quo ante will not be restored. By reason of what the Warren Court said and did, we now perceive as problems what too often were not seen as problems before. This is the dynamic of change, and that fact may well be more significant than many of the solutions proposed by the Warren Court" (Allen, 1975, p. 539).

YALE KAMISAR

See also COUNSEL: RIGHT TO COUNSEL; CRIMINAL PROCEDURE: CONSTITUTIONAL ASPECTS; EXCLUSIONARY RULES.

BIBLIOGRAPHY

ALLEN, FRANCIS A. "Due Process and State Criminal Procedures: Another Look." *Northwestern University Law Review* 48 (1953): 16–35.
———. "The Judicial Quest for Penal Justice: The Warren Court and the Criminal Cases." *University of Illinois Law Forum* (1975): 518–542.
———. "The Supreme Court, Federalism, and State Systems of Criminal Justice." *De Paul Law Review* 8 (1959): 213–255.
AMSTERDAM, ANTHONY G. "The Supreme Court and the Rights of Suspects in Criminal Cases." *New York University Law Review* 45 (1970): 785–815.
BATOR, PAUL, and VORENBERG, JAMES. "Arrest, Detention, Interrogation, and the Right to Counsel: Basic Problems and Possible Legislative Solutions." *Columbia Law Review* 66 (1966): 62–78.

BEISEL, ALBERT R. *Control over Illegal Enforcement of the Criminal Law: Role of the Supreme Court.* Boston University Press, 1955.
BERGER, MARK. *Taking the Fifth: The Supreme Court and the Privilege against Self-incrimination.* Lexington, Mass.: Heath, Lexington Books, 1980.
ENKER, ARNOLD N., and ELSEN, SHELDON H. "Counsel for the Suspect: *Massiah v. United States* and *Escobedo v. Illinois.*" *Minnesota Law Review* 49 (1964): 47–91.
GRAHAM, FRED P. *The Self-inflicted Wound.* New York: Macmillan, 1970.
GRAHAM, KENNETH W., JR. "What Is 'Custodial Interrogation'?: California's Anticipatory Application of *Miranda v. Arizona.*" *UCLA Law Review* 14 (1966): 59–134.
GRANO, JOSEPH D. "*Rhode Island v. Innis:* A Need to Reconsider the Constitutional Premises Underlying the Law of Confessions." *American Criminal Law Review* 17 (1979a): 1–51.
———. "Voluntariness, Free Will, and the Law of Confessions." *Virginia Law Review* 65 (1979b): 859–945.
HERMAN, LAWRENCE. "The Supreme Court and Restrictions on Police Interrogation." *Ohio State Law Journal* 25 (1964): 449–500.
INBAU, FRED E. "Police Interrogation: A Practical Necessity." *Journal of Criminal Law, Criminology, and Police Science* 52 (1961): 16–20.
———, and REID, JOHN E. *Criminal Interrogation and Confessions.* 2d ed. Baltimore: Williams & Wilkins, 1967.
ISRAEL, JEROLD H. "Criminal Procedure, the Burger Court, and the Legacy of the Warren Court." *Michigan Law Review* 75 (1977): 1319–1425.
KAMISAR, YALE. *Police Interrogation and Confessions: Essays in Law and Policy.* Ann Arbor: University of Michigan Press, 1980.
——— et al. "Has the Court Left the Attorney General Behind?: The Bazelon-Katzenbach Letters on Poverty, Equality, and the Administration of Criminal Justice." Symposium. *Kentucky Law Journal* 54 (1966): 464–524.
LEVY, LEONARD. *Against the Law: The Nixon Court and Criminal Justice.* New York: Harper & Row, 1974.
LIEBERMAN, JETHRO. *Milestones! Two Hundred Years of American Law: Milestones in Our Legal History.* St. Paul: West, 1976.
MEDALIE, RICHARD J.; ZEITZ, LEONARD; and ALEXANDER, PAUL A. "Custodial Interrogation in Our Nation's Capital: The Attempt to Implement *Miranda.*" *Michigan Law Review* 66 (1968): 1347–1442.
MELTZER, BERNARD D. "Involuntary Confessions: The Allocation of Responsibility between Judge and Jury. A Comment on *Stein v. People of the State of New York.*" *University of Chicago Law Review* 21 (1954): 317–354.
Note. "Developments in the Law: Confessions." *Harvard Law Review* 79 (1966): 935–1119.
PAULSEN, MONRAD G. "The Fourteenth Amendment and the Third Degree." *Stanford Law Review* 6 (1954): 411–437.
Project. "Interrogations in New Haven: The Impact of *Miranda.*" *Yale Law Journal* 76 (1967): 1519–1648.

SCHAEFER, WALTER V. "Federalism and State Criminal Procedure." *Harvard Law Review* 70 (1956): 1–26.

———. *The Suspect and Society: Criminal Procedure and Converging Constitutional Doctrines.* Evanston, Ill.: Northwestern University Press, 1967.

SCHULHOFER, STEPHEN. "Confessions and the Court." *Michigan Law Review* 79 (1981): 865–893.

STEPHENS, OTIS H. *The Supreme Court and Confessions of Guilt.* Knoxville: University of Tennessee Press, 1973.

STONE, GEOFFREY R. "The Miranda Doctrine in the Burger Court." *The 1977 Supreme Court Review.* Edited by Philip B. Kurland and Gerhard Casper. University of Chicago Press, 1978, pp. 99–169.

TRAYNOR, ROGER J. "The Devils of Due Process in Criminal Detection, Detention, and Trial." *University of Chicago Law Review* 33 (1966): 657–680.

WHITE, WELSH S. "Interrogation without Questions: *Rhode Island v. Innis* and *United States v. Henry.*" *Michigan Law Review* 78 (1980): 1209–1251.

———. "Police Trickery in Inducing Confessions." *University of Pennsylvania Law Review* 127 (1979 a): 581–629.

———. "*Rhode Island v. Innis:* The Significance of a Suspect's Assertion of His Right to Counsel." *American Criminal Law Review* 17 (1979 b): 53–70.

WIGMORE, JOHN HENRY. *A Treatise on the Anglo-American System of Evidence in Trials at Common Law,* vol. 3. 3d ed. Revised by James Chadbourne. Boston: Little, Brown, 1970.

CONFLICT THEORY

See CRIMINAL JUSTICE SYSTEM: SOCIAL DETERMINANTS; CRIMINOLOGY: MODERN CONTROVERSIES; DEVIANCE; POLITICAL PROCESS AND CRIME; VIOLENCE IN THE FAMILY: WIFE BEATING; YOUTH GANGS AND GROUPS.

CONFRONTATION AND CROSS-EXAMINATION

See CRIMINAL PROCEDURE: CONSTITUTIONAL ASPECTS; TRIAL, CRIMINAL.

CONSENT

See EUTHANASIA; RAPE: LEGAL ASPECTS; VICTIMLESS CRIME.

CONSPIRACY

Introduction

The crime of conspiracy is traditionally defined as an agreement between two or more persons, entered into for the purpose of committing an unlawful act.

At first carefully delimited in scope, conspiracy evolved through a long and tortuous history into a tool employed against dangerous group activity of any sort. The twentieth century in particular has witnessed an expansion of conspiracy law in the face of modern organized crime, complex business arrangements in restraint of trade, and subversive political activity. At the same time, indiscriminate conspiracy prosecutions have sparked great controversy, not only because the vagueness of the concept of agreement and the difficulty in proving it frequently result in convictions with only a tenuous basis for criminal liability, but also because conspiracy law involves a number of extensions of traditional criminal law doctrines. The principal extensions are the following:

1. Conspiracy criminalizes an agreement to commit a crime, even though an attempt conviction would not be permitted because of the highly preparatory nature of the act.

2. Although conspiracy is now generally limited in most jurisdictions to agreements to commit statutorily defined crimes, traditionally persons agreeing to commit tortious acts, or indeed any acts resulting in "prejudice to the general welfare," could be held liable for conspiracy.

3. All conspirators are liable for crimes committed in furtherance of the conspiracy by any member of the group, regardless of whether liability would be established by the law of complicity.

4. Contrary to the usual rule that an attempt to commit a crime merges with the completed offense, conspirators may be tried and punished for both the conspiracy and the completed crime.

5. Special procedural rules designed to facilitate conspiracy prosecutions can prejudice the rights of defendants. For example, all conspirators may be joined for trial, with resultant danger of confusion of issues and of guilt by association; and rules of evidence are loosened to alleviate the difficulties of proving the existence of a clandestine agreement.

In order better to understand and evaluate these doctrines, it is necessary to examine the elements of the crime of conspiracy. Like most crimes, conspiracy requires an act (actus reus) and an accompanying mental state (mens rea). The agreement constitutes the act, and the intention to achieve the unlawful objective of that agreement constitutes the required mental state.

The agreement

One of the fundamental purposes of the criminal law is to prevent conduct which is harmful to society.

Accordingly, the law punishes conduct that threatens to produce the harm, as well as conduct that has actually produced it. However, the law does not punish all persons shown to harbor a criminal intent. Everyone occasionally thinks of committing a crime, but few actually carry the thought into action. Therefore, the law proceeds only against persons who engage in acts that sufficiently demonstrate their firm intention to commit a crime.

The act of conspiracy.   The rationale of conspiracy is that the required objective manifestation of disposition to criminality is provided by the act of agreement. Agreement represents an advancement of the intentions that a person conceives in his mind. Intervention of the law at this point is said to be justified because the act of agreement indicates a firm intention to promote the crime, and because the agreement enhances the likelihood that unlawful action will ensue. The greater probability of action is believed to stem from the dynamics of group activity: the group exerts psychological pressure against withdrawal of its members, a single individual cannot deflect the will of the group as easily as he can change his own mind, and the group can bring greater resources to bear on its objective than could an individual acting alone. Conspiracy law, then, seeks to counter the special dangers incident to group activity by reaching back to incipient stages of criminal behavior.

Ironically, conspiracy was initially directed neither at preparatory activity nor at group crime in general. Rather, it was a narrowly circumscribed statutory remedy designed to combat abuses against the administration of justice. According to Edward Coke, it consisted of "a consultation and agreement between two or more to appeal or indict an innocent man falsely and maliciously of felony, whom accordingly they cause to be indicted and appealed; and afterward the party is lawfully acquitted" (p. 142). A writ of conspiracy would lie only for this particular offense, and only when the offense (including acquittal of the falsely indicted party) had actually taken place. However, in 1611 the Court of Star Chamber extended the law by upholding a conspiracy conviction even though the falsely accused party was not indicted (*Poulterers' Case*, 77 Eng. Rep. 813 (K.B. 1611) (Coke)). The court reasoned that the confederating together, and not the false indictment, was the gist of the offense. The ramifications of this decision were twofold. First, if it was not necessary that the intended injury occur, then conspiracy punished the attempted crime. Second, if the agreement and not the false indictment was the target of conspiracy law, then conspiracy was loosed from its mooring: subsequent decisions logically

could and in fact did hold that agreement to commit any unlawful act was criminal conspiracy.

There is a serious question as to whether the act of agreement is not too slender a reed to support such a vast extension of conspiracy law. First, agreement—a "conscious union of wills upon a common undertaking" (Developments in the Law, p. 926)—is an act primarily mental in nature. This is emphasized by the fact that parties to an agreement need not communicate directly; a tacit understanding may constitute an agreement. Conspiracy thus comes perilously close to criminalizing an evil state of mind without any accompanying act. Most jurisdictions have therefore bolstered the act element by requiring an overt act in pursuance of the conspiracy. The function of the overt act is "to manifest that the conspiracy is at work . . . and is neither a project still resting solely in the minds of the conspirators nor a fully completed operation no longer in existence" (*Yates v. United States*, 354 U.S. 298, 334 (1957)). However, this requirement rarely hinders a conspiracy prosecution because almost any act, however trivial, will suffice. For example, if two persons plan to rob a bank, the purchase of disguises would be a sufficient overt act. An act of this nature is highly equivocal; it would not support an attempt conviction because it is not a substantial act that sufficiently demonstrates the defendant's firm intention to rob the bank. There is reason, then, to support the position of a few states that set a stricter standard by requiring a substantial step in pursuance of the object of the conspiracy, and thereby render conspiracy more comparable to the law of attempt (Note, pp. 1153–1154).

Second, conspiracy is a clandestine activity. Persons generally do not form illegal covenants openly. In the interests of security, a person may carry out his part of a conspiracy without even being informed of the identity of his co-conspirators. Since an agreement of this kind can rarely be shown by direct proof, it must be inferred from circumstantial evidence of cooperation between the defendants. What people do is, of course, evidence of what lies in their minds. Since a person's acts might, by extension of this principle, create an inference concerning what he has agreed to do, it is fair to infer an agreement to join a conspiracy from the performance of acts that further its purpose. However, this evidentiary rule can obscure the basic principle that conspiracy is not established without proof of an agreement. Conspiracy is not merely a concurrence of wills, but a concurrence resulting from agreement. Even if a conspiracy between two parties is established, not every act of a third party that assists in accomplishment of the objective of the conspiracy is a sufficient basis to demonstrate his concurrence in that agreement.

For example, in *United States v. Alvarez*, 610 F.2d 1250 (5th Cir. 1980), the defendant was convicted of conspiracy to import marijuana into the United States. The evidence showed that other persons arranged with an undercover agent for a marijuana shipment to be made from Colombia to the United States. In the presence of the defendant, one of the others told the agent that the defendant would unload the shipment in the United States, and when the agent asked the defendant if that were so, he nodded his head affirmatively. The appellate court reversed the conspiracy conviction, stating that the evidence showing the defendant's intention to perform an act subsequent to importation (unloading the plane) supported an inference that he knew illegal activity was afoot, but was not sufficient to prove either that he knew of the agreement between the others or that he must have joined that illegal agreement. It is not enough that a defendant may have knowingly aided a criminal act or that he may have intended to do so in the future. To convict a person of conspiracy, the prosecution must show that he agreed with others that together they would accomplish the unlawful object of the conspiracy.

Unfortunately, many courts have not adhered this strictly to the requirement of an agreement. The decision of the United States Supreme Court in *Interstate Circuit Inc. v. United States*, 306 U.S. 208 (1939) is more representative of the courts' loose treatment of the requirement of an actual agreement. In this case, the manager of Interstate, a motion picture exhibitor that dominated the motion picture business in certain cities in Texas, sent a letter to eight motion picture distributors demanding certain concessions as conditions for continued exhibition of those distributors' films. He requested that, in selling their products to "subsequent run" theaters, the distributors impose the restrictions that the films never be exhibited below a certain admission price or in conjunction with another film as a double feature. Both of these restrictions constituted significant departures from prior practice.

The Court found that the distributors conspired with one another and with Interstate to impose the demanded restrictions in violation of the Sherman Antitrust Act. Agreement among the distributors was inferred from several strands of evidence. First, the letter named all eight distributors as addressees; hence each distributor was aware that the proposals were being considered by the others. Second, the distributors were in active competition; hence without

unanimous action with respect to the restrictions, each risked substantial loss of business, and, conversely, unanimity yielded a prospect of increased profits. Finally, the distributors did in fact act with substantial unanimity. However, since the actions of each distributor might just as easily have resulted from the exercise of self-interest in the absence of any illegal agreement, the Court had to take one step further. It declared, "We think that in the circumstances of this case such agreement for the imposition of the restrictions upon subsequent run exhibitors was not a prerequisite to an unlawful conspiracy. It was enough that, knowing that concerted action was contemplated and invited, the distributors gave their adherence to the scheme and participated in it" (*Interstate Circuit Inc.*, 226). Such a dilution of the requirement of agreement may be necessary in view of the special problems of enforcing the nation's antitrust policy. However, difficulties of proof lead courts to extend the principle to conspiracy prosecutions generally.

The scope of a conspiracy. Another large problem which arises in connection with the requirement of an agreement is that of determining the scope of a conspiracy—who are the parties and what are their objectives. The determination is critical, since it defines the potential liability of each defendant. Ascertaining the boundaries or scope of a conspiratorial relationship is crucial for resolving several major questions. Among these are (1) the propriety of joint prosecution; (2) the admissibility against a defendant of hearsay declarations of other conspirators; (3) the satisfaction of the overt-act requirement; (4) the liability of a defendant for substantive crimes committed by other conspirators pursuant to a conspiracy; and (5) the possibility of multiple convictions for conspiracy and substantive crimes.

The problems generated by the question of the scope of conspiracy are among the most troublesome in conspiracy law. They derive from the necessity of applying the theoretical idea of agreement to the reality of ongoing, fluctuating partnerships engaged in diverse criminal activity. Can a single agreement embrace persons unknown to one another in a sprawling, far-flung illegal operation? Can separate decisions made over a course of time to commit various crimes be said to stem from a single agreement? Generally, does the multiplicity of relationships making up a criminal organization constitute one large conspiracy or several smaller ones?

The law has developed several different models with which to approach the question of scope. One such model is that of a chain, where each party performs a role that aids succeeding parties in accomplishing the criminal objectives of the conspiracy. An illustration of such a single conspiracy, its parts bound together as links in a chain, is the process of distributing an illegal foreign drug. In one such case, smugglers, middlemen, and retailers were convicted of a single conspiracy to smuggle and distribute narcotics (*United States v. Bruno*, 105 F.2d 921 (2d Cir.), *rev'd on other grounds*, 308 U.S. 287 (1939)). On appeal, the defendants argued that there were separate conspiracies—one between the smugglers and the middlemen, and the other between the middlemen and the retailers. The court rejected this view and found a single overall conspiracy despite the absence of cooperation or communication between the smugglers and retailers, stating:

The smugglers knew that the middlemen must sell to retailers; and the retailers knew that the middlemen must buy of importers of one sort or another. Thus the conspirators at one end of the chain knew that the unlawful business would not, and could not, stop with their buyers; and those at the other end knew that it had not begun with their sellers. . . . The accused were embarked upon a venture, in all parts of which each was a participant, and an abettor in the sense that the success of the part with which he was immediately concerned, was dependent upon the success of the whole [922].

Another prototype, denominated the wheel conspiracy, exists where one central figure, the hub, conspires with several others, the spokes. The question is whether there is a rim to bind all the spokes together in a single conspiracy. A rim is found only when there is proof that the spokes were aware of one another's existence and that all promoted the furtherance of some single illegal objective. In the celebrated case of *Kotteakos v. United States*, 328 U.S. 750 (1946), one man, Brown, agreed with a number of different persons to obtain loans for each of them from the Federal Housing Authority through fraudulent means. Since each of these transactions was entirely distinct and independent of the others, there could not be a finding of a single conspiracy. Instead, there were a number of separate conspiracies consisting of Brown and each of his customers.

On the other hand, a single conspiracy may be found where each person's success depends on continued operation of the hub, which in turn depends on success of all the spokes. In this situation each spoke can be said to contribute to the separate objectives of all the other spokes. In the case of *Anderson v. Superior Court*, 78 Cal. App. 2d 22, 177 P.2d 315 (1947), a woman who referred pregnant women to a physician for abortions was indicted for a conspiracy to commit abortion with him and with other persons who referred pregnant women to him. She was also indicted for the illegal abortions committed upon the women she referred, as well as for the abortions committed upon women referred by the other persons who had made such referrals. The court held that the evidence permitted the inference of a conspiracy among all the referring persons and the physician, because the defendant knew that the others were referring business to him, and because his continued functioning and hence the woman's commission depended upon continuance of all these sources of referral. For these reasons it might be said that she contributed to each separate instance of abortion.

These models deal with situations in which various parties conspire to promote a single unlawful objective. The traditional concept of agreement can also accommodate the situation where a well-defined group conspires to commit multiple crimes; so long as all these crimes are the objects of "the same agreement or continuous conspiratorial relationship," a finding of one large conspiracy is appropriate (Model Penal Code, 1962, § 5.03(c)).

However, traditional conspiracy law is inadequate when applied to criminal organizations in which highly diverse objectives are pursued by apparently unrelated individuals. Hence, Congress enacted the Racketeer Influenced and Corrupt Organizations Act of 1970 [RICO] to cope with the growing problem of organized crime (18 U.S.C. §§ 1961–1968 (1976 & Supp. IV 1980)). This act facilitates conspiracy prosecutions by modifying the traditional idea of a conspiratorial objective. Instead of proving that each defendant conspired to commit a particular crime or crimes—a task that is exceedingly difficult in the context of a large, sprawling criminal organization—the prosecution need only show that each defendant conspired to promote the enterprise through his individual pattern of criminal activity. No matter how diverse the goals of a large criminal organization, there is but one objective: to promote the furtherance of the enterprise.

The problem with this tendency to view conspiracy as an ongoing criminal enterprise is that it beclouds the idea of an act of agreement. Many persons may thereby be snared in the coils of a single conspiracy whose nature and membership were unknown to them. The effect may be to convict people in circumstances where the traditional requirement of personal guilt is not present. The Model Penal Code has attempted to reformulate the definition of conspiracy to avoid this consequence. For each defendant, it would ask whether and with whom he agreed to commit which parts of the entire illegal scheme, thus reaffirming the centrality of the agreement in a conspiracy prosecution (Model Penal Code, 1960, commentary on § 5.03). A number of state criminal codes have now adopted this approach.

Mental state

The two elements of mental state required by conspiracy are the intent to agree and the intent to promote the unlawful objective of the conspiracy. The first of these elements is almost indistinguishable from the act of agreement. Agreement is in any case morally neutral; its moral character depends upon the nature of the objective of agreement. It is the intention to promote a *crime* that lends conspiracy its criminal cast.

Some crimes do not require an intention to cause the prohibited result. Manslaughter, for example, may be committed by a person who kills another by his act of driving carelessly. These crimes may not be the basis of a conspiracy, however, since two people could not be said to agree together to kill another carelessly. The nature of the requirement of agreement, therefore, limits the objectives of conspiracy to those crimes that are committed by intentional actions.

Problems arise, however, in determining the sense of intention that is required. Does it include acting with knowledge of the probable results of one's action, or is it confined to acting with a purpose to attain such results? The question has most frequently arisen in the case of suppliers who furnish goods to members of a conspiracy with knowledge of their intended illegal use. Examples include the supplying of yeast and sugar to a group known to be using them to engage in illegal production of whiskey (*United States v. Falcone*, 311 U.S. 205 (1940)), or the furnishing of medical drugs by a manufacturer that knows they will be used for nonmedical and illegal purposes (*Direct Sales Co. v. United States*, 319 U.S. 703 (1943)).

Some courts have found it enough to convict the supplier for an illegal conspiracy with the user when the supplier knew of the illegal use. The justification for this position is that the supplier has knowingly furthered a crime and has no interest in doing so that is worthy of protection (Model Penal Code, 1960, commentary on § 5.03). However, the majority view is to the contrary: the supplier must be shown to have had a purpose to further the illegal objectives of the user (Model Penal Code, 1962, § 5.03(1)). In the language of Judge Learned Hand, "he must in some sense promote their venture himself, make it his own, have a stake in its outcome" (*United States v. Falcone*, 109 F.2d 579, 581 (1949)). This might be demon-

strated by evidence of the sale of unusually large quantities of goods, particularly where such goods are legally restricted; by evidence of inflated charges or of the sale of goods with no legitimate use; or by evidence that sales to an illegal operation have become a dominant proportion of the seller's business.

The reasons for requiring a stake in the venture are twofold. First, the act of agreement necessarily imports a purpose; indifference to illegal use by another of what one supplies him for otherwise legitimate reasons does not constitute an agreement. Second, making the supplier liable in these situations whenever a jury decides that he knew of the illegal use imposes an undue burden on legitimate business since to avoid liability suppliers would be obliged to police the intended uses of their purchasers. By taking into account the social usefulness of the commercial activity and the magnitude of the seller's contribution to the crime, the majority rule strikes a balance between the needs of business enterprises to operate without oppressive restriction and of society to protect itself against crime.

The object of a conspiracy

Common-law conspiracy encompassed agreements to commit an unlawful act. The key word is *unlawful:* it refers not only to criminal, but also to tortious acts, or even to acts that, in the opinion of a court, result in "prejudice to the general welfare or oppression of an individual of sufficient gravity to be injurious to the public interest" (*Commonwealth v. Dyer*, 243 Mass. 472, 138 N.E. 296 (1922)). This rule owed its origin to seventeenth-century expansion of the scope of conspiracy, which was stimulated by impatience with the narrow technicalities of medieval law, coupled with a tendency to identify criminality with immorality. It was thought that courts had authority to correct

errors and misdemeanors extra-judicial, tending to the breach of peace, or oppression of the subjects, or to the raising of faction, controversy, debate, or to any manner of misgovernment; so that no wrong or injury, either public or private, can be done, but that it shall be here reformed or punished by due course of law [*Bagg's Case*, 77 Eng. Rep. 1271 (K.B. 1616) (Coke)].

The doctrine's most significant use in the United States occurred in the early nineteenth century, when many courts sustained criminal-conspiracy prosecutions against unions of workers seeking to organize in order to pressure employers to meet their employment demands by collectively withholding their labor (Wellington, pp. 7–46).

In affording discretion to judges to punish as a crime the group pursuit of any objectives they determined to be against morality and the public interest, the law of conspiracy contravened the classic principle of *nulla poena sine lege* (no punishment without law). It also went contrary to the principle forbidding ex post facto punishment (criminalizing conduct not previously declared to be criminal). Today, such discretionary criminal liability is vulnerable to constitutional attack as violative of due process of law (*Musser v. Utah*, 333 U.S. 95 (1948)). Although the common-law rule still prevails in some jurisdictions—notably in the federal provision directed against conspiracy to commit "any offense" against or to defraud the United States (18 U.S.C. § 371 (1976))—the modern approach limits the scope of conspiracy to statutorily defined criminal objectives, except where the legislature has identified and prohibited specific kinds of concerted activity.

Conspiracy and complicity

Conspiracy is not only a substantive crime. It also serves as a basis for holding one person liable for the crimes of others in cases where application of the usual doctrines of complicity would not render that person liable. Thus, one who enters into a conspiratorial relationship is liable for every reasonably foreseeable crime committed by every other member of the conspiracy in furtherance of its objectives, whether or not he knew of the crimes or aided in their commission. The rationale is that

criminal acts done in furtherance of a conspiracy may be sufficiently dependent upon the encouragement and support of the group as a whole to warrant treating each member as a causal agent to each act. Under this view, which of the conspirators committed the substantive offence would be less significant in determining the defendant's liability than the fact that the crime was performed as part of a larger division of labor to which the defendant had also contributed his efforts [Developments in the Law, p. 998].

This rationale, however, becomes attenuated in many situations in which the doctrine is applied. For example, in the leading case of *Pinkerton v. United States*, 328 U.S. 640 (1946), a defendant who had earlier conspired with his brother to operate an illegal still was held liable for his brother's later acts of operating the still, despite the fact that by the time those acts were committed, the defendant was in prison for another offense.

Although dilution of the strict concepts of causality

and intention may be required to cope with the dangers of organized crime, serious objections have been raised to this aspect of the law of conspiracy. Liability for substantive crimes is predicated on the loose evidentiary standards of conspiracy law; liability attaches for crimes not actually intended or even necessarily foreseen; and holding each member of a conspiracy liable for all crimes committed by the group without regard to the character of that person's role within the group yields overly broad liability without penal justification. This is particularly true in those jurisdictions that allow the finding of a single conspiracy, rather than several smaller ones, in cases of large, sprawling, and loosely confederated criminal enterprises. As a consequence, some states, following the lead of the Model Penal Code, have eliminated this feature of traditional conspiracy by declaring that one is liable for the criminal actions of another only if he is made liable by the doctrines of the law of complicity.

Procedural rules

Perhaps the most significant advantage of a prosecutor's decision to charge several defendants with conspiracy is that he may invoke special procedural rules which apply only to conspiracy cases. The major prosecutorial advantages of conspiracy are that it enables the prosecution to join all the conspirators for trial and to use out-of-court statements of each conspirator against all the others.

Joinder of conspirators for trial, coupled with relaxation of the rules of venue to allow the trial to take place wherever acts in pursuance of the conspiracy have occurred, is a measure designed to promote efficiency and convenience for courts, prosecutors, and witnesses. Where evidence pertaining to all defendants substantially overlaps, joinder avoids multiple trials involving the same issues and evidence. Even where the cases against various defendants are more distinct, the rule is helpful to the prosecution, since such constraining factors as prosecutorial resources and availability of witnesses often dictate a choice between joint trial and dismissal of charges against some of the conspirators.

In some situations, however, joinder may well yield not increased efficiency but rather a profusion of evidence, a multiplication of issues, and consequently much ambiguity and confusion. Moreover, joinder may substantially impair the rights of defendants. Where the jury is asked to hear a large amount of complex evidence, to remember which evidence applies to which defendant, and to make fine discriminations of individual guilt or innocence, there are several problems. First, there is serious danger of guilt by association. Second, conspirators may be hampered in their defense if optimal group strategy conflicts with the best course for an individual. Frequently, defendants attempt to cast the blame on someone else, and end up by convicting one another.

Loosened standards of admissibility of evidence prevail in a conspiracy trial. Contrary to the usual rule, in conspiracy prosecutions any declaration by one conspirator, made in furtherance of a conspiracy and during its pendency (hearsay), is admissible against each co-conspirator. For example, in a conspiracy prosecution of a sheriff and a magistrate for extorting money from a coal company, an executive of the company testified that the sheriff told him that the magistrate was his (the sheriff's) agent in the extortion scheme and would pick up the extortion payments (*United States v. Vinson*, 606 F.2d 149 (6th Cir. 1979)). This testimony would normally be inadmissible because it is hearsay as against the magistrate—that is, it is testimony by the declarant (the witness) of what someone else said (the sheriff), offered to prove the truth of the matter asserted by that other person (that the magistrate was his agent in the scheme). However, since there was enough evidence of a conspiracy, the hearsay testimony was admitted as further evidence of the conspiracy and of the magistrate's participation in it.

The conventional reason for the exclusion of hearsay evidence is that such evidence is thought to be untrustworthy. The witness may report it poorly, either from faulty memory or from motive to misstate, and more importantly, the jury has no means of evaluating the credibility of the declaration unless the original declarant is available for cross-examination. Despite the unreliability of hearsay evidence, it is admissible in conspiracy prosecutions. Explaining this rule, Judge Hand said, "Such declarations are admitted upon no doctrine of the law of evidence, but of the substantive law of crime. When men enter into an agreement for an unlawful end, they become ad hoc agents for one another, and have made 'a partnership in crime.' What one does pursuant to their common purpose, all do, and as declarations may be such acts, they are competent against all" (*Van Riper v. United States*, 13 F.2d 961, 967 (2d Cir. 1926)).

Thus conspirators are liable on an agency theory for statements of co-conspirators, just as they are for the overt acts and crimes committed by their confreres. Although this theory may explain why co-conspirators are liable for each other's declarations, it does not really dispel the concerns of the hearsay

rule regarding the trustworthiness of evidence. By requiring that the declarations be made within the scope of the agency relationship and with intent to advance the objectives of that relationship, the rule excludes declarations made before the agreement or after the termination of the conspiracy as peripheral and hence too unreliable. It thereby creates a nexus between the declarations and the criminal goals of the conspiracy, with whatever assurance of truth that might import.

However, the justification for circumventing the hearsay rule in conspiracy prosecutions is the practical need for such evidence—since conspiracy is a type of crime of which direct evidence is usually unavailable, the choice may be between admitting inferior evidence and admitting no evidence at all. Nevertheless, the practice of admitting this evidence conflicts with the policy of the hearsay rule.

The problems encountered in applying the exception to the hearsay rule for co-conspirators were aptly described by Justice Robert Jackson in his concurring opinion in *Krulewitch v. United States*, 336 U.S. 440, 453 (1949):

Strictly, the prosecution should first establish prima facie the conspiracy and identify the conspirators, after which evidence of acts and declarations of each in the course of its execution are admissible against all. But the order of proof of so sprawling a charge is difficult for a judge to control. As a practical matter, the accused often is confronted with a hodgepodge of acts and statements by others which he may never have authorized or intended or even known about, but which help to persuade the jury of existence of the conspiracy itself. In other words, a conspiracy often is proved by evidence that is admissible only upon assumption that conspiracy existed. The naive assumption that prejudicial effects can be overcome by instructions to the jury, . . . all practicing lawyers know to be unmitigated fiction.

Conclusion

Conspiracy, a crime special to common-law jurisdictions and largely unknown, except in modest forms, in continental European countries, is one of the most controversial of all substantive crimes. It affords great advantages to law enforcement, since it avoids multiple trials, permits prosecution of preparatory activity at an early stage, facilitates prosecution against organized criminality, and extends a number of evidentiary and procedural advantages to the prosecution. At the same time, it constitutes what Justice Jackson in *Krulewitch* termed an "elastic, sprawling and pervasive offense" (445) that departs from traditional requirements of liability: (1) the crime of conspiracy is vaguely defined and its contours are often unpredictable; (2) it permits conviction on acts largely mental in character; (3) its essential feature, an agreement, is often diluted to something approaching suspicion of agreement; and (4) it affords a highly tenuous basis for holding the defendant for substantive crimes committed by others. Moreover, the procedural advantages to the prosecution impose corresponding disadvantages on the defendant, disadvantages thought inappropriate and unfair when other crimes are charged.

The balance has been struck on the side of retaining the offense with modest revisions, despite long-standing criticism (Johnson). The crime of conspiracy will in all likelihood remain an integral part of the prosecutor's arsenal. Whether it will be kept within tolerable bounds depends on how sensitively and critically prosecutors employ it, courts administer and interpret it, and legislators act to preclude its excesses.

JAMES ALEXANDER BURKE
SANFORD H. KADISH

See also ACCOMPLICES; ATTEMPT; SOLICITATION.

BIBLIOGRAPHY

American Law Institute. *Model Penal Code: Proposed Official Draft*. Philadelphia: ALI, 1962.
———. *Model Penal Code: Tentative Draft No. 10*. Philadelphia: ALI, 1960.
COKE, EDWARD. *The Third Part of the Institutes of the Laws of England: Concerning High Treason, and Other Pleas of the Crown, and Criminal Causes* (1641). London: E. & R. Brooke, 1797.
Developments in the Law. "Criminal Conspiracy." *Harvard Law Review* 72 (1959): 920–1008.
FILVAROFF, DAVID B. "Conspiracy and the First Amendment." *University of Pennsylvania Law Review* 121 (1972): 189–253.
HARNO, ALBERT J. "Intent in Criminal Conspiracy." *University of Pennsylvania Law Review* 89 (1941): 624–647.
JOHNSON, PHILLIP E. "The Unnecessary Crime of Conspiracy." *California Law Review* 61 (1973): 1137–1188.
LEVIE, JOSEPH H. "Hearsay and Conspiracy: A Reexamination of the Co-conspirators' Exception to the Hearsay Rule." *Michigan Law Review* 52 (1954): 1159–1178.
MITFORD, JESSICA. *The Trial of Dr. Spock, the Rev. William Sloane Coffin, Jr., Michael Ferber, Mitchell Goodman, and Marcus Raskin*. New York: Knopf, 1969.
Note. "Conspiracy: Statutory Reform since the Model Penal Code." *Columbia Law Review* 75 (1975): 1122–1188.
SAYRE, FRANCIS. "Criminal Conspiracy." *Harvard Law Review* 35 (1922): 393–427.
TURNER, MARJORIE B. S. *The Early American Labor Conspiracy Cases—Their Place in Labor Law: A Reinterpretation.* San Diego, Calif.: San Diego State College Press, 1967.
U.S. National Commission on Reform of Federal Criminal Laws. *Final Report: A Proposed New Federal Criminal Code (Title 18, United States Code).* Washington, D.C.: The Commission, 1971.
———. *Working Papers,* vol. 1. Washington, D.C.: The Commission, 1970.
WELLINGTON, HARRY H. *Labor and the Legal Process.* New Haven: Yale University Press, 1968.
WRIGHT, ROBERT S. *The Law of Criminal Conspiracies and Agreements.* Philadelphia: Blackstone, 1887.

CONSTITUTION, CRIMINAL LAW AND THE

See CRIME: DEFINITION OF CRIME; CRIMINAL PROCEDURE: CONSTITUTIONAL ASPECTS.

CONSUMER FRAUD

Consumer fraud, which costs American consumers hundreds of millions of dollars annually, is a basic form of white-collar crime. The regulation of consumer fraud as a crime has been a relatively recent phenomenon, running counter to traditional caveat emptor ("let the buyer beware") philosophy and laissez-faire economic theory. Protection has been afforded to consumers primarily through federal and state legislation.

Historical development. Civil courts first recognized deceit in commercial transactions as a cause of action in the thirteenth century. A contractual relationship between the plaintiff and the defendant was initially required as a prerequisite to relief, but in 1789, *Pasley v. Freeman,* 100 Eng. Rep. 450 (1789) dispensed with this privity requirement. Although civil remedies were available to victims of fraudulent schemes, criminal sanctions generally were not.

Late-nineteenth-century writers such as James Bryce and Henry Demarest Lloyd documented and criticized the corruption endemic in the business world, and in 1939, Edwin Sutherland first used the term *white-collar crime* to describe such odious entrepreneurial behavior (Geis and Edelhertz, pp. 989, 994). With the strong development of consumerism during the 1960s and 1970s, courts and legislatures slowly began to recognize the propriety of using criminal sanctions to deter and punish conduct aimed at swindling consumers.

Cheats and frauds have not been indictable under

the common law except in limited circumstances, for example, in cases of obtaining property by false pretense as a form of theft. However, various statutes have been enacted that apply either to general kinds of fraud or to specific forms of deceit. Many of these statutes have merely provided civil remedies, but some have imposed criminal penalties for such conduct.

The most widely used enactment against consumer fraud has been the Mail Fraud Act of 1909, 18 U.S.C. § 1341 (1976), proscribing "any scheme or artifice to defraud" involving the use of the mails. The most common violation is the use of mail-order advertisements that falsely represent product quality, capability, or price. A few states have enacted laws that similarly proscribe fraudulent practices. For example, the Scheme to Defraud Statute (N.Y. Penal Law § 190.65 (1981)) imposes criminal sanctions upon any person who engages in conduct intended to defraud ten or more people by false or fraudulent misrepresentations or promises, when property is obtained from at least one victim. Other laws apply to specific types of fraud. The New York Odometer Tampering Law (N.Y. Gen. Bus. Law § 392-e (1981)), which is similar to the federal Odometer Rollback Act, 15 U.S.C. §§ 1984, 1990c (1976), prohibits odometer tampering. A District of Columbia law, the Fraudulent Advertising Law, D.C. Code §§ 22: 1411-13 (1973), has outlawed fraudulent advertising, as have the laws of several states. Other schemes have also been specifically proscribed, including securities, medical, and land-sales fraud.

Criminal consumer fraud is more difficult to establish than civil consumer fraud, which requires that grossly negligent, or in some cases negligent, misrepresentations have been made. Criminal sanctions, however, are usually imposed only where intentional misrepresentations have occurred, or where false representations have been made with a reckless disregard for their accuracy (*Sparrow v. United States,* 402 F.2d 826 (10th Cir. 1968)). Nonetheless, detrimental reliance on such misrepresentations by prospective customers and actual injury to customers need not be established in most criminal cases, as they must be in civil actions. As long as fraudulent misinformation has been conveyed with the intent to induce customer reliance and there is a reasonable likelihood that the desired effect might be achieved, criminal liability may usually be found (*United States v. Regent Office Supply Co.,* 421 F.2d 1174 (2d Cir. 1970)).

Facts and opinions. To be criminally cognizable, misrepresentations must generally relate to past or existing facts, not to future occurrences or to mere expressions of opinion. However, some courts have found unlawful misrepresentation of existing facts where, at the time people make their statements regarding future circumstances, they either know that they do not intend to act on their present promises, or simply do not believe the predictions they are making. Similarly, some courts have imposed criminal liability where parties falsely represent their true present opinions.

Acts and omissions. If an individual only partially discloses factual information in order to create a false impression concerning undisclosed facts, a fraudulent misrepresentation may be found. Although a party may be under no initial obligation to disclose the critical facts, once he decides to make a partial divulgence that is designed to deceive, an obligation to correct the resulting misimpression is generally imposed.

Mere silence does not constitute criminal fraud unless the silent party is under a legal duty to disclose the factual information being withheld. Statutes such as securities laws may require the disclosure of certain information prior to a sales transaction, in which case nondisclosure may be unlawful. Even in the absence of a statute, when one party knows that another party is laboring under a material misconception and the misunderstood fact is within the special knowledge of the first party, continued silence may be illegal if it is intended to deceive the other individual.

Dearth of prosecutions. Since consumer fraud generally does not involve the use or threat of violence and can theoretically be rectified through traditional civil remedies, criminal sanctions are not frequently sought. Where fraudulent practices are pervasive, state attorneys will often endeavor to alleviate the problem through civil injunctive actions or suits seeking restitution for the injured parties, rather than through resort to criminal prosecutions. There are several reasons for this. Because of the more stringent requirements of proof regarding intent and misrepresentation in criminal cases, prosecutors often find it difficult to prove their cases. Prosecutors also fear that successful criminal cases will diminish the victims' likelihood of obtaining restitution for their losses. The reluctance of judges to impose significant sentences upon the white-collar criminals who typically engage in consumer fraud also discourages the vigorous prosecution of such cases.

CHARLES B. CRAVER

See also CORPORATE CRIMINAL RESPONSIBILITY; MAIL: FEDERAL MAIL FRAUD ACT; *both articles under* STRICT LIABILITY; THEFT; VICARIOUS LIABILITY; WHITE-COLLAR CRIME: HISTORY OF AN IDEA.

BIBLIOGRAPHY

GEIS, GILBERT, and EDELHERTZ, HERBERT. "Criminal Law and Consumer Fraud: A Sociolegal View." *American Criminal Law Review* 11, no. 4 (1973): 989–1010.

GIVENS, RICHARD A. "Roadblocks to Remedy in Consumer Fraud Litigation." *Case Western Reserve Law Review* 24 (1972–1973): 144–161.

KIRSCHNER, NANCY M. "Criminal Consumer Fraud: Must the Goals of Deterrence and Compensation Be Mutually Exclusive?" *American Journal of Criminal Law* 7 (1979): 355–383.

OGREN, ROBERT W. "The Ineffectiveness of the Criminal Sanction in Fraud and Corruption Cases: Losing the Battle against White-collar Crime." *American Criminal Law Review* 11, no. 4 (1973): 959–988.

ROTHSCHILD, DONALD, and CARROLL, DAVID W. *Consumer Protection Reporting Service*, vol. 2. Rockville, Md.: CSG Press, 1979.

CONTRIBUTING TO THE DELINQUENCY OF MINORS

Statutes and judicial interpretations. Contributing to the delinquency of minors is a purely statutory offense, unknown to the common law, that exists in forty-two American states and the District of Columbia. The first such law was passed in Colorado in 1903 (Act of March 7, 1903, ch. 94, 1903 Colo. Sess. Laws 198), four years after the enactment of the nation's first juvenile court law (Act of April 21, 1899, 1899 Illinois Laws 131), and was part of the same broad child-protective movement. To achieve maximum protection, contributing-to-delinquency laws were designed to punish adults who not only directly caused a child's delinquency but also in any way exposed a child to conditions that might possibly have a baneful influence. Thus, the Colorado judge who was instrumental in securing passage of that state's juvenile court law wrote that if a child merely entered certain prohibited places, no matter how innocent his purpose, the person who had directed the child to go there, even to deliver a message or do an errand, contributed to the child's delinquency (Geis, p. 63).

Despite academic and judicial criticism, contributing laws not only remain on the books in most states but continue to be interpreted by courts to encompass an extremely wide range of adult conduct deemed harmful to children. Most jurisdictions classify contributing to the delinquency of a minor as a misde-

meanor punishable by fine or imprisonment of one year or less, although several consider it a felony, especially if aggravating circumstances are involved (Wis. Stat. Ann. § 947.15 (1958 & 1981–1982 Supp.)).

Statutes that prohibit contributing to the delinquency of a minor typically state that no person shall "aid, abet, induce, cause, encourage, or contribute to . . . the delinquency of a child . . . or act in a way tending to cause delinquency . . . in such child" (Ohio Rev. Code Ann. § 2151.41 (1976)). A variant punishes an adult who by any act "corrupts or tends to corrupt the morals" of a minor (Pa. Cons. Stat. Ann. tit. 18, § 6301 (1981–1982 Supp.)). At least four aspects of these statutes have caused problems of interpretation for the courts and have led to scholarly criticism: the kinds of adult conduct that may constitute contributing, the causal relationship between the adult's conduct and the child's delinquency, statutory definitions of delinquency, and the mental element, or mens rea, of the offense.

It is apparent from the Ohio statute cited above that although the offense of contributing to delinquency is defined in terms of a resulting harm (delinquency) and of a causal relationship between the adult's conduct and that harm, the statute does not specify or limit the kinds of adult conduct that may constitute the offense. Three cases illustrate the great range of conduct that has been condemned under contributing statutes. Before the United States Supreme Court ruled compulsory flag-salute legislation unconstitutional (*West Virginia State Board of Ed. v. Barnette*, 319 U.S. 624 (1943)), a father was convicted for directing his child, for religious reasons, to refuse to salute the American flag, since the refusal led to the child's expulsion from school (*State v. Davis*, 58 Ariz. 444, 120 P.2d 808 (1942)). An Ohio couple was convicted of conduct tending to cause delinquency when they took their eleven-year-old adopted daughter into West Virginia, allowing her to misrepresent her age and be married in an apparently legal ceremony—the "delinquency" being not the marriage but the probability that she would be truant from school (*State v. Gans*, 168 Ohio St. 174, 151 N.E.2d 709 (1958)). A hotel clerk was successfully prosecuted for allowing a minor to spend the night in the hotel with a sailor who was not her husband, even though the clerk had inquired and had been informed that the couple were married (*People v. Reznick*, 75 Cal. App. 2d 832, 171 P.2d 952 (1946)).

Despite this diversity of condemned conduct, most contributing cases have involved sexual contacts between adults and minors, of varying degrees of seriousness. Indeed, there is evidence that contributing to delinquency is often used by prosecutors as a plea bargaining device to obtain convictions on the lesser offense of contributing where prosecution for a more serious sexual offense would prove inexpedient (Geis, p. 68). Contributing prosecutions are also frequent in cases of providing liquor to minors or permitting minors to remain on premises where liquor is sold (*Loveland v. State,* 53 Ariz. 131, 86 P.2d 942 (1939)). It has been suggested that because states usually have criminal statutes punishing specific adult conduct deemed harmful to children, such as liquor or sex offense statutes, there is no need for the vague catchall offense of contributing to delinquency in order to protect children adequately, and that it would be fairer to defendants to proceed under the more clearly drawn criminal statutes (Model Penal Code, commentary on § 230.4).

A second unique aspect of contributing statutes is the imprecision of the causal relationship they require between the adult's conduct and the child's delinquency. The inexact language used in the statutes substantially attenuates the usual criminal law requirement that a defendant must have caused the proscribed harm before he may be convicted. The Ohio statute cited above, for example, does not require that an adult "cause" an act or condition of delinquency, but merely "contribute" to it. The statute thus leaves to the court's discretion just how much an adult must do to constitute "contribution" to delinquency. Further, courts interpreting contributing statutes have frequently held that in order to achieve their broad protective purposes it is not necessary for conviction that a child actually be adjudged delinquent or have committed delinquent acts; it is sufficient that, in the court's estimation, the adult's conduct merely *tends* to cause delinquency (*State v. Blount,* 60 N.J. 23, 286 A.2d 36 (1972)).

A very few jurisdictions, often following specific statutory wording, have held that to support a contributing conviction a child must be adjudged delinquent or at least have committed acts sufficient to establish delinquency. Thus, the Colorado Supreme Court has held that a defendant who took a fifteen-year-old-girl to Utah and married her could not be convicted of contributing, for two reasons: (1) the marriage, being valid in Utah, was recognized as valid by Colorado law, although it would have been void if it had been performed in Colorado; and (2) entering a marriage regardless of age was not a delinquent act within the statutory definition of delinquency (*Spencer v. People,* 133 Colo. 196, 292 P.2d 971 (1956)).

A third problem of contributing-to-delinquency laws is the amorphousness of the concept of delinquency itself. Although statutory definitions of delinquency invariably include violation of federal, state, or local laws that would be crimes for adults, they may also include such purely juvenile misbehavior as running away from home, being truant from school, habitually disobeying one's parents, endangering one's own or another's health or morals, or, most broadly, "by reason of being habitually wayward or habitually disobedient becom[ing] an incorrigible or uncontrollable child" (Miss. Code Ann. § 43-23-3(g) (1981)). Even if states limit the definition of delinquency to criminal law violation, they also frequently punish contributing to the "waywardness" or "unruliness" of children, concepts that include a broad range of noncriminal misbehavior. Given the all-encompassing nature of the concepts of delinquency and unruliness, virtually any conduct by an adult might be said to "contribute" or "tend to contribute" to the child's condition.

The fourth characteristic of contributing statutes that has spawned litigation is the imprecision of the mens rea of the crime. Contributing statutes often contain no mental element at all or else state generally that the act must be done "willfully," without making clear what that term means or to which elements of the offense it applies. In particular, courts have had to decide whether a defendant could be convicted of contributing if he or she did not know that the other person was a minor. In general, courts have held that ignorance of the minor's age is not a defense (*Anderson v. State,* 384 P.2d 669 (Alaska 1963)), although a few courts have intimated that knowledge of, or recklessness as to, age is necessary for conviction (*State v. Friedman,* 35 Ohio Op. 39, 74 N.E.2d 285 (1947)).

A related mens rea question is whether a defendant may be convicted of "willfully" contributing to delinquency if he or she is not present when, and indeed has no knowledge that, the act alleged to constitute contributing is taking place—what the law calls vicarious liability. This situation typically involves owners of establishments where minors purchase items, such as liquor or obscene literature, the sale of which is legally forbidden to them. Several cases have held that proprietors of such establishments may be convicted of contributing when their employees make illegal sales to minors or allow them to remain on forbidden premises, although the proprietor is not present at the time and may even have instructed the employee not to deal with minors (*State v. Sobelman,* 199 Minn. 232, 271 N.W. 484 (1937)). The United States Supreme Court has held, however, that the New Hampshire contributing statute, which prohibits "willfully" contributing to delinquency, requires that the owner of a store personally sell to a minor a button bearing an obscene printed slogan in order to be convicted under the statute (*Vachon v. New Hampshire*, 414 U.S. 478 (1974)).

The imprecision of contributing statutes has led scholars and a few courts to conclude that the laws, or sections of them, are constitutionally "void for vagueness." It is a basic principle of criminal law that a statute creating an offense must be sufficiently precise to inform those who seek to obey the law of the conduct that is prohibited; failure to do so violates the due process clause of the Fourteenth Amendment to the United States Constitution. Since the contributing statutes often condemn broadly any conduct contributing to delinquency, no matter how trivial, it may be impossible to know in advance what acts are prohibited. In effect, this results in a legislative delegation of discretion to the trial court or jury to define the offense (Comment, 1976, pp. 574–583; Model Penal Code, commentary on § 230.4; *Stone v. State*, 220 Ind. 165, 41 N.E.2d 609 (1942)). The Oregon Supreme Court, in holding that state's contributing law unconstitutional, has suggested that the statute's loose language offended due process because it enabled the prosecution "selectively to rid the community of individuals deemed subjectively less desirable than other offenders" (*State v. Hodges*, 254 Ore. 21, 28, 457 P.2d 491, 494 (1969)).

Most courts, however, have rejected arguments that contributing statutes are unconstitutionally vague (*State v. Cialkowski*, 193 Neb. 372, 227 N.W.2d 406 (1975)). Their arguments are twofold: (1) legislatures must use broad and general language because they cannot possibly enumerate all the ways in which adults might corrupt youths (*State v. McKinley*, 53 N.M. 106, 111, 202 P.2d 964, 967 (1949)); and (2) although a statute might admit borderline cases, the particular conduct in question is such that an ordinary person would know that the statute unquestionably applies (*Holton v. State*, 602 P.2d 1228, 1236 (Alaska 1979)).

Current developments. In response to the criticisms detailed above, the American Law Institute's Model Penal Code recommends that contributing-to-delinquency statutes be abandoned and that there be substituted an offense entitled "Endangering Welfare of Children" (§ 230.4), which reads: "A parent, guardian, or other person supervising the welfare of a child under 18 commits a misdemeanor if he knowingly endangers the child's welfare by violating a duty of care, protection or support." The proposed offense would still condemn a wide range of adult behavior,

but its scope would be narrowed by limiting the class of persons subject to the statute, by clearly specifying the mens rea required ("knowingly," which, the Model Penal Code commentary makes clear, would require knowledge of the child's age), and by specifying that a duty of care, protection, or support must exist in law. Although very few states have followed the Code's recommendation that contributing statutes be abolished, many states now have statutes that punish endangering the welfare of children. Some states define the crime as a violation of a duty of care that endangers the child (Haw. Rev. Stat. § 709-904 (1976)), and others condemn acts that may prove mentally, physically, or morally injurious to the child (Del. Code Ann. tit. 11, § 1102 (1979)). It is thus not uncommon for states to possess both a contributing-to-delinquency and an endangering-the-welfare-of-minors statute (Pa. Cons. Stat. Ann. tit. 18, § 4304 (1973); § 6301 (1981–1982 Supp.)).

Finally, states may also have a wide assortment of other statutes designed to protect children, including statutes prohibiting abandonment or neglect of a child, the selling of children, child abuse, and such specific acts as engaging in unlawful transactions with a child, allowing a child to observe sex acts, or permitting a minor to be in a house of prostitution, a gambling establishment, or a place where liquor is sold.

PETER D. GARLOCK

See also FAMILY RELATIONSHIPS AND CRIME; JUVENILE STATUS OFFENDERS; *both articles under* STRICT LIABILITY.

BIBLIOGRAPHY

American Law Institute. *Model Penal Code and Commentaries: Official Draft and Revised Comments.* Philadelphia: ALI, 1980.

Comment. "Contributing to Delinquency: An Exercise in Judicial Speculation." *Akron Law Review* 9 (1976): 566–583.

Comment. "Contributing to Delinquency Statutes: An Ounce of Prevention?" *Willamette Law Journal* 5 (1968): 104–120.

Comment. " 'Parental Responsibility' Ordinances: Is Criminalizing Parents when Children Commit Unlawful Acts a Solution to Juvenile Delinquency?" *Wayne Law Review* 19 (1973): 1551–1581.

GEIS, GILBERT. "Contributing to Delinquency." *St. Louis University Law Journal* 8 (1963): 59–81.

LOU, HERBERT H. *Juvenile Courts in the United States* (1927). Reprint. New York: Arno Press, 1972.

LUDWIG, FREDERICK. "Delinquent Parents and the Criminal Law." *Vanderbilt Law Review* 5 (1952): 719–745.

RUBIN, SOL. *Crime and Juvenile Delinquency.* 3d ed., rev. Dobbs Ferry, N.Y.: Oceana, 1970.

CONTROL THEORY

See CRIME CAUSATION: SOCIOLOGICAL THEORIES; EDUCATION AND CRIME; FAMILY RELATIONSHIPS AND CRIME.

CONVICTION

See DOUBLE JEOPARDY; GUILT.

CONVICTION: CIVIL DISABILITIES

Introduction

It is generally thought that when a person leaves prison, or is released from probation or parole, his punishment has ended. For many offenders, however, the most serious and long-lasting aspect of their punishment is only beginning, since every state, to a greater or lesser degree, prohibits the ex-felon from exercising some of the most basic rights of free citizens, ranging from the right to vote to the right to employment by the state. These barriers, called collateral consequences, are for many criminals—particularly for the 50 percent of convicted persons who are never imprisoned—anything but collateral; they are, in fact, the most persistent punishments that are inflicted for crime.

Historical background

The notion that those who have committed crimes forfeit their rights as citizens is not new. Both the Greeks and Romans imposed on a convicted person the punishment of "infamy," which forbade him to exercise the rights of a free citizen. Early English law followed the same principle. A person convicted of a felony was declared "attainted," losing all his civil rights and forfeiting his property; collectively, these sanctions were called "civil death." More dramatic was the notion of "corruption in the blood," which prohibited the felon's heirs from inheriting his estate. This doctrine was based on the fiction that the criminal's act evidenced his entire family's corruption.

The death penalty was abolished for many crimes in nineteenth-century England, and in America it was significantly limited from the earliest days after the Revolution. Thus, the heritage of the past might have been ignored. Indeed, the notion of attainder as such

was so repugnant that the United States Constitution specifically prohibited forfeiture and corruption of blood except in the case of a person convicted of treason. Nonetheless, the notion of civil death persisted, and many of the rights that would have died with the executed felon in medieval England continued to be denied to the felon who in nineteenth-century America was merely imprisoned and later released.

The vast majority of states have now rejected the idea of a blanket civil death as an adjunct of conviction for a crime; only thirteen continue to adhere to such a doctrine, and these generally apply it only to persons sentenced to life imprisonment. But every state, to some degree, still imposes civil disabilities on ex-offenders.

The bases for imposing civil disabilities

Considerable variation exists among the states (and sometimes even within a jurisdiction) as to what civil disabilities are and when they may be imposed. By far the most common basis for imposing civil disabilities is a conviction for a felony. Although the term *felony* is not always consistently defined, it typically means a crime for which a year or more of imprisonment may be imposed. Thus, the same civil disability may be visited both on a person convicted of first-degree murder and on one convicted of a relatively minor crime. But in some states only certain enumerated felonies may be the basis for imposition of general or specific civil disabilities. Conversely, in some states conviction of a "crime of moral turpitude" or of an "infamous crime," even if it is not a felony, suffices, thereby subjecting to civil disabilities a person convicted of a misdemeanor that is believed to reflect some weakness of morals or moral behavior. One court, for example, has ruled that the term *moral turpitude* includes any offense that is "contrary to justice, honesty, principle, and good morals" (*In re Hatch*, 10 Cal. 2d 147, 73 P.2d 885 (1937)). The ambiguity of this standard was revealed in a later decision by the same court, which held that failure to report for the Selective Service draft during World War II was not a crime of "moral turpitude" (*Otsuka v. Hite*, 64 Cal. 2d 596, 414 P.2d 412 (1966)).

Although conviction is usually a prerequisite for suffering the pains of civil disabilities, some states impose civil disabilities only if the convicted felon has been imprisoned. This exempts from the scope of civil disabilities the nearly 50 percent of all felons who are placed on probation. Some states, however, impose civil disabilities on those who are merely arrested for a certain crime or crimes.

Civil disabilities are usually imposed in a blanket fashion, without any connection between a specific disability and the crime that has been committed. Thus, a person convicted for a drug violation may find himself forbidden to vote or even to make contracts, even though his crime has no obvious bearing on his ability capably to engage in these activities. Although the issue is not clear, such provisions are probably constitutional (*Hawker v. New York*, 170 U.S. 189 (1898)). This is one reason why a number of organizations have suggested that if civil disabilities statutes are not totally repealed, they should be amended to require that the state or private employer be required to demonstrate that there is some "rational connection" between the crime and the specific disability imposed. For example, a person convicted of bribery might be disqualified from public employment or from serving on a jury, and an embezzler might be prohibited from working as a bank teller or in another capacity involving funds or records. But neither could be barred from exercising private rights, or suffer other disabilities unrelated to the crime for which he was convicted. These suggestions for reform, however, have met with little success in the legislatures.

Specific rights lost

Public rights. Apparently on the premise that violation of the criminal law indicates a general lack of respect for law and for the obligations of citizenship, most states, as well as the federal government, have barred former offenders from participating in a number of public activities normally open to citizens—some of which indeed are considered obligations of citizenship.

The right to citizenship. No right is more basic or all-encompassing than citizenship itself. In a number of decisions, the United States Supreme Court has either directly invalidated or cast substantial doubt upon attempts by Congress to revoke naturalized citizenship for such crimes as desertion in time of war or residing for three years in a foreign country of birth (*Trop v. Dulles*, 356 U.S. 86 (1958); *Schneider v. Rusk*, 377 U.S. 163 (1964)).

The right to vote. Next to citizenship itself, the right to vote is probably the single most important political right held by a citizen. Yet as of 1971 at least thirty-one states provided for disenfranchisement of those convicted of certain offenses. Many of these provisions are found in state constitutions rather than in statutes,

reflecting a deeply and widely held belief that the right to participate in democracy's most basic exercise is forfeited by criminal action. In 1974 the Supreme Court upheld such a provision in the California constitution, relying on a provision of the Fourteenth Amendment to the United States Constitution that was interpreted to allow such disenfranchisement (*Richardson v. Ramirez*, 418 U.S. 24 (1974)).

The right to hold public office. Most of the states have constitutional or statutory provisions disqualifying persons convicted of certain crimes from holding or retaining public office. These provisions generally apply to local as well as state public offices, and to appointive as well as elective positions. Court decisions have held, for example, that the term *public office* includes the positions of city manager, postmaster, school board member, county treasurer, and justice of the peace.

Congress has similarly enacted legislation providing that persons convicted of certain offenses cannot hold federal office (for example, 18 U.S.C. §§ 593, 1901, 2071). Yet nothing in the federal Constitution prohibits such persons from being elected to Congress itself or, for that matter, from being elected President.

Whether or not one agrees with the disqualification of former offenders from holding appointive office, barring them from elective public office seems particularly hard to defend. Theoretically, the electorate should be able to assess for itself both the severity of the offense and the offense's bearing on the candidate's ability to perform the job.

Judicial rights. Various provisions affect what might be called judicial rights. Some state laws provide that a person convicted of or imprisoned for certain offenses cannot litigate in the state's courts for the period of disability. In most instances these statutes allow the prisoner to bring his suit after the disability is lifted. However, this is far from a perfect remedy, since the passage of time may affect the memories or availability of witnesses, or result in other difficulties that the litigant would encounter on release. Moreover, it still leaves the offender, while encumbered with the disability, without the right to appear in court and to represent his own interests. Some state statutes make provision for the appointment of a substitute for the defendant or for counsel, but impediments to receiving the full protection of the courts and the legal system still remain substantial.

A second judicial right clouded by a criminal conviction is the right to testify in court. Most states do not automatically disqualify offenders from appearing as witnesses, unless the conviction was for perjury; these statutes are all that remains of the common-law doctrine that persons convicted of serious crimes were incompetent to testify. However, another substantial rule of evidence law significantly intrudes on the right to testify. In virtually every state, a previously convicted witness may be questioned about his past record. This rule has the valid purpose of informing the jury about facts that may be relevant to the witness's credibility. Such rules do, however, discourage witnesses—and particularly persons charged with new crimes—from testifying in court. Some states, as well as the federal courts, have restricted the use of such "impeachment" evidence to recent convictions, on the ground that older convictions are no longer significantly relevant.

A third judicial right sometimes rescinded is the right to perform fiduciary duties. A criminal conviction may prevent the offender from holding a court-appointed position of trust, from serving as the executor of a will or administrator of an estate, or from being a guardian of a person or estate. For example, a testamentary guardian named in a will by the parents of a minor or of an incompetent person must be approved by the court. A few jurisdictions disqualify any nominee who has been convicted of a felony or infamous crime.

By far the most symbolic disqualification from judicial rights is the barrier to serving on a jury. Although only a handful of states automatically prohibit such service, three-fourths of the states expressly exclude from jury service persons who have been convicted of certain crimes. Furthermore, where a state statute provides that a juror must have "good character," evidence of a conviction may be sufficient to result in disqualification. A requirement that a juror be a qualified elector will, of course, result in incapacity to be a juror in those states that disfranchise felons.

As with the issue of holding public office, the concern that motivates this disqualification is clear. Similarly, disclosure of the potential juror's criminal record should be sufficient to protect the interests of the parties.

Private rights.

Family and personal rights. Conviction of a crime may jeopardize the offender's relationship to his family in several ways. Incarceration, of course, severely hampers this relationship. But beyond this, in many states conviction alone, or conviction and imprisonment, may provide the impetus to legal dissolution of family ties. A convict subject to civil death may be forbidden to marry; many others, either while incarcerated or on conditional liberty, may find their right to marry subject to the scrutiny and approval of a probation or parole officer. More commonly, a conviction may be declared grounds for divorce; in fifteen states, a divorce will be automatically granted only if the convicted spouse is actually incarcerated. When civil death is incurred, conviction may be automatic grounds for divorce.

Conviction or imprisonment may result in the forfeiture of parental rights as well. Indirectly, imprisonment may serve as a basis for a finding of abandonment; in dependency and neglect proceedings in two states, a parent's criminality is an express ground for terminating parental rights. In virtually every state, a conviction is evidence of unfitness in a custody proceeding. Further, some states rule that a person's imprisonment renders unnecessary his consent to the adoption of his children by others, although most provide such a draconian penalty only in the event of lengthy incarceration.

At common law, the convicted felon generally possessed the right to inherit. The aversion of the colonists to bills of attainder generally ensured that this right would continue. But in the twentieth century many jurisdictions have legislated an exception, providing that a felonious slayer cannot inherit from his victim. This new doctrine has been universally upheld as constitutional.

A criminal conviction may also prevent the offender from participating in insurance, pension, and workmen's compensation programs. The federal government, for example, disqualifies Social Security recipients from annuity or retirement programs if they have been convicted of certain crimes. Similarly, eighteen states have enacted statutes that directly prohibit convicted criminals from benefiting from pension funds in some instances. Finally, a criminal conviction adversely affects the offender's right to receive workmen's compensation benefits; in most states, convicts are not entitled to such benefits for injuries sustained while they are incarcerated, even during the course of work at prison jobs.

Employment. Certainly the most pervasive disqualification is the exclusion, by statute or by administrative decision, of the convicted felon from specific types of employment. Because it significantly reduces the convicted offender's ability to reenter society as a working citizen, this exclusion is thought by many either to restrict offenders to menial jobs, or to impel them to return to crime.

Certain crimes, moreover, disqualify offenders from holding a job with the federal government. More importantly, government and private employers alike may generally refuse to hire any applicant who has been convicted, using the criminal conviction as the basis for such discretion. For example, the civil service provides that "criminal, infamous, dishonest, immoral or notoriously disgraceful" conduct may be grounds for refusal to hire an applicant.

State and municipal governments as well may bar convicted persons from official positions. Nearly half the states bar some convicted persons from certain official jobs, but the typical pattern is one of discretionary discrimination rather than statutory exclusion. At the other extreme lie municipalities and states that hire ex-offenders as police or, more typically, as correctional or parole officers. The latter help rehabilitate other ex-offenders and at the same time demonstrate to sentenced offenders that the state is concerned about their future employment.

Other provisions deal with the licensing of convicted persons for work at certain jobs. In the nineteenth and early twentieth centuries, only "professions" were licensed by the state, and the barring of convicted persons from such employment, although onerous, was not catastrophic. Today, however, literally thousands of jobs are open only to state-licensed persons. In one state, for example, brokers, dry cleaners, cosmetologists, embalmers, and trainers of guide dogs for the blind must be licensed. Another state licenses (among others) minnow dealers. In all, nearly six thousand occupations are licensed in one or more states; the convicted offender may find the presumption against him either difficult or impossible to overcome.

Access to licensed employment is usually determined by licensing boards, which are generally composed of persons engaged in the given occupation. Concerned with upholding the public image of their trade, many such board members tend to react adversely to any convicted applicant, even if the crime committed bears no relation to the trade in question. Furthermore, some of the most frequently licensed occupations are those taught in prison vocational rehabilitation programs. Thus, the released prisoner may find himself blocked from plying the very skills he was taught during incarceration, thereby frustrating both the prisoner and the correctional authorities.

Some courts have restricted the discretion of boards automatically to deny licenses on the basis of a criminal record, requiring that the board consider the circumstances of the criminal conviction and the extent of rehabilitation, the relation (if any) of the crime to the duties of the job, and the person's character at the time he applies. On the whole, however, courts have been extremely reluctant to interfere with the discretion of licensing boards, even when that discretion has thwarted rehabilitative goals both in and out of prison. In most states, therefore, ex-offenders remain barred from many licensed occupations.

Private employers, like their government counterparts, frequently simply refuse to hire ex-convicts. They usually fear that the ex-criminal will recidivate; neither clear indications that he has been rehabilitated nor the fact that the crime was unrelated to the job sought can erase that fear or the taint he allegedly retains. Although federal (and some state) statutes may prohibit discrimination in hiring on the basis of such factors as sex and race, a past criminal record is not among these factors.

Restoration of rights

Once a person has lost civil rights as a result of a conviction, he may never be able to regain them. Thus, disfranchisement in many states is lifelong; there is no mechanism for restoring the right to vote. A prospective employer, public or private, may use a decades-old conviction for a minor offense as grounds for denying employment to an applicant. The stigma of conviction lasts long after a sentence has been served, and it may constitute a permanent barrier to reintegration into the community. Some states limit the duration of at least some civil disabilities, usually providing for automatic restoration of certain rights at the end of imprisonment, probation, or parole. Many states take a middle ground, providing some discretionary mechanism, either judicial or administrative, for the restoration of at least some civil rights.

A substantial and growing number of states have enacted legislation providing for the "expungement" of a criminal conviction, under specific circumstances and for specific crimes. The statutes are usually vague about the scope of expungement and even less clear about its effect on those civil rights that would otherwise be lost or suspended. For example, it is uncertain whether a person whose conviction has been "expunged" may validly deny, on employment application forms or in other settings, that he has been convicted of a crime.

Similar difficulties arise with regard to specific rights that are generally lost upon conviction. In California, for example, the expungement statute provides that the defendant convicted of a misdemeanor "shall be released from all penalties and disabilities resulting from the offense or crime" (Cal. Penal Code § 1203.4a (1981 Supp.)). The California courts have interpreted this language in varying ways. Thus, expungement restores the voting franchise and releases the offender from the obligation to register with local police, but it does not restore either his right to possess a firearm or his right to regain professional licenses automatically. Nor does expungement prohibit the civil service from relying on evidence of a conviction in dismissing a public employee. Similar confusion has attended efforts to provide for the restoration of other civil rights that are lost as a result of conviction.

Analysis and future of civil disabilities

The imposition of collateral civil disabilities on those convicted of crime raises perplexing problems of both policy and law. The major problem encountered in analyzing civil disabilities is the existence of competing views concerning their purposes. If it is assumed that the primary purpose of the criminal justice system is to rehabilitate the offender, it follows that no civil disabilities should be imposed on him, at least after incarceration, since this will only jeopardize his reintegration into the community. Critics of civil disability laws and practices point out with particular anguish that it is often government itself, although allegedly seeking the rehabilitation of offenders, that refuses to hire ex-offenders, erects legal barriers to their reacceptance by the community, and allows private employers and others to indulge their fears about them. Such critics urge complete restoration of rights immediately upon release, as well as strict prohibition against any search for information about a person's past criminal record.

At the other extreme is the view that civil disabilities are merely additional components of the offender's sentence and punishment. However, imposing the same disabilities—in some cases lifetime ones—on all offenders regardless of the seriousness of their crimes seems to violate the cardinal principle of proportionality. It is, moreover, uncertain how much legal right licensing boards and other administrative agencies actually have in determining the length and impact of such punishments.

Resolving these differences would be formidable enough; the difficulty is compounded when one takes into account the additional view that nonoffenders have the right to inquire about an offender's past record in order to avoid becoming victims of his possible future crimes. Despite inconclusiveness in the data on recidivism, there is no doubt that some offenders do return to crime and that they are more prone to do so if the circumstances surrounding their first crime recur. Arguably, then, potential future victims should have the right to exclude the offender from situations in which they would be particularly vulnerable, or at least the right to know about the past conviction so that they can decide whether to take a risk such as that of employing him. Thus, even if only one out of every thousand former embezzlers might embezzle again, it seems at first blush questionable to prohibit a prospective employer from learning of an applicant's past background, including his past convictions, and from acting on that information. Prohibiting such an inquiry, however, could be supported on the grounds that (1) the fear of recidivism is greatly exaggerated and cannot outweigh, in utilitarian terms, the benefits that employment would bring to ex-offenders; and that (2) the offender has "paid the price" of his crime and should be allowed to reenter society without continuing impediments and burdens.

Balancing the rights of the ex-offender against the rights of others is no easy task. Where the conflict concerns such potential victims as the state, and the issue is the right to vote or to serve as a juror, perhaps the balance should be weighted differently than where the potential conflict is between the right of one individual—the ex-offender—and that of another individual—the potential employer as victim. This view, of course, runs counter to that of the "rehabilitationist" school, and it requires delicate judgments.

Numerous reforms have been suggested for dealing with these problems. The Model Penal Code (§ 306.6) provides for automatic restoration of all civil rights to any successful probationer or parolee, as well as to all persons who have completed their incarceration and have not committed a crime for two years; yet it does allow licensing boards to deny licenses when there is a prior criminal record. The National Advisory Commission on Criminal Justice Standards and Goals recommends automatic restoration of civil rights upon completion of sentence, and would require a licensing board to show a "direct relationship between the offense committed or the characteristics of the offenders and the license or privilege being sought" before denying a license. Similar standards adopted by the American Bar Association and the National Conference of Commissioners on Uniform State Laws extend the requirement to private employers as well. The National Council on Crime and Delinquency goes further, calling for automatic restoration of rights by a court on completion of parole, probation, or incarceration, and allowing licensing boards (and possibly private employers) to inquire only whether the applicant has ever been arrested for or convicted of a crime "which has not been annulled by a court."

Civil disability statutes are vague and uncertain of

application, and would seemingly provide fertile grounds for legal challenges in terms of both due process and equal protection. If change is to occur, however, it seems unlikely to come from the courts. A few sporadic judicial decisions have invalidated state actions, but the imposition of civil disabilities is within the province of the legislature, and except in extreme cases it does not violate the offender's constitutional rights.

In effecting change, the legislatures will have to confront the philosophic and policy dilemmas posed by civil disabilities laws, as well as the practices of private employers and others who seek information about a person's criminal background. The predicament of former offenders is unquestionably real, but public concern about their future behavior is equally real. This is the problem that will confront the legislatures in the future.

RICHARD G. SINGER

See also PRISONERS, LEGAL RIGHTS OF.

BIBLIOGRAPHY

American Bar Association. "Legal Status of Prisoner Standards." *Standards for Criminal Justice.* Washington, D.C.: ABA, 1981.

American Law Institute. *Model Penal Code: Proposed Official Draft.* Philadelphia: ALI, 1962.

DAMAŠKA, MIRJAN R. "Adverse Legal Consequences of Conviction and Their Removal: A Comparative Study." *Journal of Criminal Law, Criminology, and Police Science* 59 (1968): 347–360.

HUNT, JAMES W.; BOWERS, JAMES E.; and MILLER, NEAL. *Laws, Licenses, and the Offender's Right to Work: A Study of State Laws Restricting the Occupational Licensing of Former Offenders.* Washington, D.C.: National Clearinghouse on Offender Employment Restrictions for the ABA Commission on Correctional Facilities and Services and Criminal Law Section, 1974.

MILLER, HERBERT. *The Closed Door: The Effect of a Criminal Record on Employment with State and Local Public Agencies.* Prepared for the Manpower Administration, U.S. Department of Labor. Springfield, Va.: National Technical Information Service, 1972.

National Conference of Commissioners on Uniform State Laws. *Uniform Law Commissioners' Model Sentencing and Corrections Act.* Washington, D.C.: U.S. Department of Justice, Law Enforcement Assistance Administration, National Institute of Law Enforcement and Criminal Justice, 1979.

National Council on Crime and Delinquency. "Annulment of a Conviction of Crime: A Model Act." *Crime and Delinquency* 8 (1962): 97–102.

Note. "The Loss of Parental Rights as a Consequence of Conviction and Imprisonment: Unintended Punishment." *New England Journal on Prison Law* 6 (1979): 61–112.

RUBIN, SOL. *The Law of Criminal Correction.* 2d ed. St. Paul: West, 1973.

RUDENSTINE, DAVID. *The Rights of Ex-offenders.* New York: Avon Books, 1979.

Special Project. "The Collateral Consequences of a Criminal Conviction." *Vanderbilt Law Review* 23 (1970): 929–1241.

U.S. Department of Justice, Law Enforcement Assistance Administration, National Advisory Commission on Criminal Justice Standards and Goals. *Corrections.* Washington, D.C.: The Commission, 1973.

CORONER, ROLE OF THE

Introduction. Of all the offices in the Anglo-American legal system, that of the coroner—or medical examiner—probably has the greatest influence with respect to the investigation of death. An accused person may be exonerated by the cleverness of his defense lawyer or the mistakes of police investigators or prosecutors. However, without the coroner's approval the cause of a death may never be investigated, and a homicide may therefore be deemed a case of natural, accidental, or suicidal death. By the nature of his office, a coroner can prevent investigations from taking place or initiate one against the wishes of attending physicians, hospital staffs, and relatives. Often he can insist on a complete autopsy, convene a coroner's inquest, initiate grand jury proceedings, and cause arrest warrants and subpoenas to be issued. In many states he is the only official empowered to arrest the high sheriff of the county.

The coroner also seeks information to protect the community against diseases, identifies remains, notifies survivors, and helps settle estates and insurance claims. He assists in the completion of official records and aids other law enforcement officers in their investigations of deaths.

History. The office of coroner was established in England in 1194. It was a fiscal rather than a medical office, its purpose being to raise funds to ransom King Richard I from captivity. A coroner was appointed for each shire, or county, and was required to impound the goods of felons and to fine communities in which the bodies of slain Normans were discovered. If he decided that a death had resulted from murder, negligence, or accident, the instrument by which the death had occurred (and sometimes the property on which it had occurred) was forfeited to the Crown. In 1487 the coroner was given authority to deduct the fees for inquests from the proceeds of the sale of a condemned felon's property. During succeeding centuries the quality of the office's incumbents tended to deteriorate (Mant, 1973). Only in 1926 was the Coroner's (Amendment) Act enacted in Great Britain, abolishing property ownership as the sole qualification for the office of coroner and instead requiring that only a physician or attorney of five years' standing be appointed (16 & 17 Geo. 5, c. 59 (repealed in part)).

Until the late nineteenth century in America, the office of coroner was either appointive or elective, and it required no particular training or competence. Autopsies, if legally justified and approved, were performed by local general practitioners and even veterinarians—and, in many states, they still are.

The first significant change in the United States took place in Massachusetts in 1877, when the county coroner was replaced by a physician called the county medical examiner. The jurisdiction of the office was confined to cases of death through "violence," and in such cases only the district attorney was authorized to order an autopsy. In 1915, New York City established the first modern medicolegal investigatory system empowered to perform autopsies on its own authority. The first statewide medical examiner system was established in Maryland in 1939. But as late as 1946 the only requirements for holding the office in another state (North Carolina) were belief in God and a certification of never having participated in or arranged a duel.

Powers and duties of the medical examiner. For many years after World War II, autopsies were virtually routine procedures in hospitals. In 1950, half of all patients dying in hospitals were autopsied. By 1978, however, fewer than 20 percent were autopsied. In the 1980s many states required that the next of kin grant permission for an autopsy in the event of a hospital death. The high cost of autopsies—varying from $750 to $2,500—and religious prohibitions against the desecration of the body have helped reduce the number of postmortem examinations. But although hospital autopsies may not seem to be within the purview of the coroner, many states give him authority to order such an examination if the deceased appears to be the victim of some criminal act, an omission, or even certain diseases ("Dying Autopsy").

Reflecting recommendations of the National Association of Medical Examiners, a California statute gives coroners particularly broad power (Cal. Gov.

Code §§ 27460–27471, 27490, 27491 (1968 & 1982 Supp.)). California coroners must inquire into all violent, sudden, unusual, or unattended deaths. These include all deaths in which the deceased had not been attended by a physician within the preceding ten days, suicides, self-induced or criminal abortions, and deaths resulting from hanging, wounds, poisonings, accidents, fires, exposure, starvation, alcoholism, drug addiction, or aspiration (inhaling of noxious substances). The coroners are also obliged to investigate deaths occurring in connection with rape, assault, or "crimes against nature" while the deceased was in prison or under sentence, as well as deaths that may be linked to public-health hazards and occupational diseases. Finally, a catchall section requires coroners to investigate all known or suspected deaths resulting from the criminal acts of another.

The statutes of forty-nine states mandate a postmortem examination in deaths involving criminal violence, but only thirty-eight make this a requirement in the event of suicide. Thirty-four states mention accidents as one of the types of death requiring an autopsy; twenty-five states insist on autopsies for persons dying in a public institution or hospital, but only five do so for persons dying in police custody. Autopsies are necessary in twenty-four states in the event of sudden death for no visible cause, often including unattended deaths, so that medical examiners must often perform numerous autopsies in cases of natural death.

Sixteen states require autopsies for deaths resulting from possible public-health hazards, and ten states, for deaths from occupational causes. In seven states it is mandatory that an autopsy be performed when the body is to be cremated; since cremation precludes a subsequent autopsy, this requirement is an important factor in preventing the surreptitious disposal of homicide victims. Several states have catchall provisions requiring autopsies in all suspicious, unusual, or unattended deaths; in five states these include unattended stillbirths.

Status of the medical examiner. There is no nationwide standard of qualifications for holding the coroner's office, and in the early 1980s many states' qualifications were still uncertain. Only thirteen states had a statewide medical examiner's office for which a medical degree was required. In ten states, medical examiners with a medical degree were provided for only in large urban areas. In the twenty-seven remaining states, the county-based system remained in effect, with standards set on the county level; only thirteen of these states required a medical degree, and only seven provided for appointment rather than election. As a result, more than one-third of the United States population resided in places where the county coroner was not required to be a qualified medical examiner. Haphazard methods of selection mean that the ineptitude of some coroners poses real obstacles to the proper investigation of serious crimes; in certain states, killers may have little difficulty hiding their deeds.

By far the weakest of the systems by which deaths are investigated in the United States is that of elected county coroners. Frequently such an official is also the county sheriff, district attorney, or local mortician. Usually the laws defining his duties are vague. In most states he is empowered to hire others to perform autopsies, although limited funds or penury frequently prevent him from doing so.

The system of medical examiners' offices prevailing in several states and in some heavily populated counties is clearly superior to the traditional system of county coroners, although it is not ideal. Depending on the size of the community, medical examiners' staffs comprise one or two pathologists, a chemist, a forensic toxicologist, and various laboratory technicians and investigators. The office is usually directed by a career medical examiner trained in scene investigation as well as forensic autopsy procedures.

The most desirable system, that of a statewide medical examiner's office, unfortunately is found in only thirteen states. Under this system, each county has a medical examiner, assisted by forensic pathologists and toxicologists who can travel throughout the state. Community hospitals, general practitioners, and other pathologists also perform autopsies. A few states with a medical examiner statute still have very little system uniformity, quality control, or central guidance, all of which can only be developed over time.

In most states where a statute empowers the coroner to conduct an investigation, it is usually provided that the body not be disturbed or moved from its position without permission of the coroner or his deputy. This has caused many problems for investigating officers, for it often takes an hour or more for a coroner or his deputy to arrive at the scene. Frequently a memorandum of understanding or a working agreement allows law enforcement officers to resolve this matter with the local coroner. In almost all states, coroners have been given the power to have a body exhumed if subsequent evidence shows that an autopsy should have been performed.

Under common law a coroner's verdict was equivalent to the findings of a grand jury and was sufficient for prosecution for murder and manslaughter. This power has been modified by statute in most states. The coroner is not allowed to conduct an inquest arbitrarily and capriciously in the majority of the states. An autopsy is an integral part of the coroner's inquest, and it may be conducted without the consent of the deceased's family where the statutes so provide. An inquest can and perhaps should be public, but professional ethics stipulate that inquests not be arranged for teaching or training purposes or used to embarrass the deceased's kin. In 1982 a well-known coroner who was a medical examiner and forensic pathologist was replaced because he had been too talkative about the injuries and deaths of celebrities he had examined.

The office of the coroner is still a powerful one—and an essential one for the criminal justice system. It would not be stretching the point to argue that continual upgrading of the coroner or medical examiner system is necessary for achieving a civilized, safety-conscious society.

RUSSELL VORPAGEL

See also CRIMINALISTICS; HOMICIDE: LEGAL ASPECTS.

BIBLIOGRAPHY

CHILDS, RICHARD S. "Best States for a Murder: A Report of Progress." Mimeographed. New York: National Municipal League, 1970.
"Dying Autopsy." *Time Magazine,* 18 September 1978, pp. 90–91.
MANT, A. KEITH. "Official Medico-Legal Investigation under the Coroner's System in London, England." *Medico-Legal Bulletin* 223 (1971): 1–8.
———. "A Survey of Forensic Pathology in England since 1945." *Journal of Forensic Science and Society* 13 (1973): 17–24.
National Association of Medical Examiners. *Standards for Inspection and Accreditation of a Modern Medicolegal Investigative System.* St. Louis: The Association, 1974.
PRESSWALLA, F. B. "Historical Evolution of Medico-Legal Investigative Systems." *Medico-Legal Bulletin* 25 (1976): 1–8.
———. "The Philosophy of Classification of Deaths." *Medico-Legal Bulletin* 26 (1977): 1–5.
SPITZ, WERNER U., and FISHER, RUSSELL S., eds. *Medicolegal Investigation of Death: Guidelines for the Application of Pathology to Crime Investigation.* 2d ed. Springfield, Ill: Thomas, 1980.
STUART, FRANK P. "Progress in Legal Definition of Brain Death and Consent to Remove Cadaver Organs." *Surgery* 81 (1977): 68–73.
U.S. Department of Health, Education, and Welfare, Public Health Service, Bureau of Community Health Services. *Death Investigation: An Analysis of Laws and Policies of the United States, Each State and Jurisdiction (as of January 31, 1977).* Rockville, Md.: The Bureau, 1978.

CORPORAL PUNISHMENT

Corporal punishment is the infliction of physical pain as a penalty for an infraction. Past forms of corporal punishment included branding, blinding, mutilation, amputation, and the use of the pillory and the stocks. It was also an element in such violent modes of execution as drowning, stoning, burning, hanging, and drawing and quartering (in which offenders were partly strangled and, while still alive, disemboweled and dismembered). In most parts of Europe and in the United States such savage penalties were replaced by imprisonment during the late eighteenth and early nineteenth centuries, although capital punishment itself remained. Physical chastisement became less frequent until, in the twentieth century, corporal punishment was either eliminated as a legal penalty or restricted to beating with a birch rod, cane, whip, or other scourge. In ordinary usage the term now refers to such penal flagellation.

Prevalence. Although corporal punishment has been widely banned, the extent to which it continues to be used is difficult to determine. Countries that strictly observe Islamic law inflict both amputation and whipping as penalties. In South Africa, males under twenty-one years of age may be whipped for any offense in lieu of other punishment, and adult males between the ages of twenty-one and thirty may be whipped either in addition to or instead of other punishment for many offenses, including robbery, rape, aggravated or indecent assault, burglary, and auto theft.

In the 1970s an annual average of 335 adults were sentenced to "corporal punishment only." Whipping was used more extensively to chastise juveniles, but official statistics have not been kept. In Singapore and Malaysia, caning may be added to other punishments for drug trafficking and for rape and certain other violent crimes.

In Great Britain the Cadogan Committee, appointed in 1937 to review the application of corporal punishment, reported that this penalty had been abolished for criminal offenses by adults in every "civilized country" in the world except those whose criminal code was influenced by English criminal law—that is, in some of the British dominions and American states, where it could still be legally imposed for offenses by juveniles and for violations of prison discipline (Cadogan Committee, pp. 59–60, 143–144). The committee's recommendation that corporal punishment be abandoned as a judicial penalty in England was adopted in the Criminal Justice Act, 1948, 11 & 12 Geo. 6, c. 58 (Great Britain), which abolished the pen-

alty for all offenses except serious violations of prison discipline; in 1967 it was also eliminated for these. The Advisory Council on the Treatment of Offenders (ACTO) reported in 1961 that corporal punishment had not been reintroduced in any country which had abolished it and that in those few countries which continued to prescribe such penalties various limitations had been introduced, so that infliction had become uncommon (ACTO, pp. 12–13). The last two American states to use corporal punishment as a judicial penalty were Maryland, where it was seldom inflicted before being abolished in 1952, and Delaware, where the last flogging took place in 1952 although formal abolition did not occur until 1972. Corporal punishment remains available, however, as a penalty for serious breaches of prison discipline in a number of states.

A retributive penalty. Corporal punishment satisfies demands for reprisal and is seen as a fitting penalty for certain kinds of offenses. Both sentiments are resurgent among the public in countries in which such punishment has been abolished. Apparent or real increases in crime, particularly violent offenses, spark public demands for the restoration of corporal punishment. A 1960 poll in England revealed that 74 percent of the population thought it an appropriate penalty for some crimes. The idea that corporal punishment is peculiarly fitting for certain offenses—for example, those involving personal violence—is ultimately a moral or political judgment that reflects the retributive theory of punishment. Various modern expressions of human rights policy, however, condemn corporal punishment. Article Three of the European Convention on Human Rights declares that "no one shall be subjected to torture or to inhuman or degrading treatment or punishment" (Council of Europe, p. 25), and in 1978 the European Court of Human Rights found corporal punishment to be "degrading" under the terms of this article (*Tyrer v. United Kingdom*, 2 Eur. Human Rights R. 1, 58 I.L.R. 339 (Eur. Ct. Human Rights 1978)). Moreover, the United Nations' "Standard Minimum Rules for the Treatment of Prisoners" specifically states that "corporal punishment . . . shall be completely prohibited as punishment for disciplinary offenses" (United Nations Secretariat, Rule 31, p. 69).

Effectiveness. Advocates of corporal punishment argue that it is more likely than any alternative to prevent offenders from committing further criminal acts, and that it is also an exceptionally strong deterrent to potential offenders. These claims have been subjected to some empirical investigation, especially by the Cadogan Committee, whose research was continued in 1960 by the Home Office Research Unit for ACTO.

Individual deterrence. Part of the research carried out by the Cadogan Committee and ACTO covered 3,023 cases of robbery with violence (virtually the only offense for which corporal punishment was imposed) between 1921 and 1947. Offenders were divided into two groups: those previously convicted of serious crimes and those not previously convicted. In both categories, offenders who were not flogged showed slightly better subsequent records. Those who were flogged seemed slightly more likely to be convicted again of robbery with violence, although the numbers were small and the differences not statistically significant (Cadogan Committee, pp. 131–140; ACTO, pp. 53–57). These findings suggested that flogging was not especially effective as an individual deterrent, but they were not conclusive: the groups of those flogged and not flogged were not properly matched, nor were the sentences randomly assigned, for some judges habitually made more use of the penalty than others.

General deterrence. The Cadogan Committee devoted special attention to five cases of corporal punishment used as an exemplary sentence in response to major outbreaks of crimes for which, according to public opinion, the penalty was particularly suitable. The committee found that in some cases the facts plainly contradicted such beliefs and that reductions in crime could just as plausibly be attributed to causes other than the penalties imposed on offenders. It also noted that the incidence of robbery with violence in England and Wales had declined steadily in the years before World War I notwithstanding infrequent and decreasing use of corporal punishment, whereas in the postwar years it had tended to increase despite a much greater and increasing resort to floggings. It was also shown that between 1890 and 1934 the incidence of robbery in England and Wales (where corporal punishment might have served as a deterrent) declined more slowly than in Scotland, where corporal punishment was not inflicted for those offenses (Cadogan Committee, pp. 83–87, 89–90).

ACTO also compared the incidence of robbery with violence in England and Wales before and after corporal punishment was abolished as a judicial penalty in 1948. The number of robberies reported to the police increased steadily during and after World War II, although corporal punishment was employed more frequently than before the war. After 1948, however, there was a marked downward trend, and until 1957 instances of robbery remained well below the 1948 level. The causes of this reduction were unknown, but ACTO inferred that corporal punishment had not

been a strong deterrent immediately before its abolition and noted that abolition was not followed by an increase in the offenses for which it had previously been imposed (Advisory Council on the Treatment of Offenders, p. 15). In short, no evidence proved that corporal punishment provided more deterrence than imprisonment, to which it commonly served as an alternative penalty before abolition. Canadian and New Zealand studies confirmed these findings (Canada, Parliament, pp. 39–59; New Zealand Department of Justice, pp. 216–234).

Conclusion. Repudiation of the infliction of pain as a penal method and the substitution of corrective incarceration for physical punishment have been conspicuous features of penal history since the late eighteenth century. Corporal punishment has come to be seen as incompatible with "modern" penal methods and as likely to militate against the success of reformative or rehabilitative treatment. The decline of corporal punishment was once hailed as a sign of the progress of humanitarianism, enlightenment, and civilization. In the latter part of the twentieth century, however, such optimism has been questioned by certain writers, notably Michel Foucault, who have argued that the rehabilitation theory and the creation of "noncorporal" penal systems generally meant only the insidious expansion and refinement of penal repression. However, neither Foucault nor other critics of the rehabilitative ideal have expressed approval of earlier penal practices or recommended that corporal punishment be revived as a penal method.

GORDON HAWKINS

See also CAPITAL PUNISHMENT; COMPARATIVE CRIMINAL LAW AND ENFORCEMENT: ISLAM; CRUEL AND UNUSUAL PUNISHMENT; PUNISHMENT; TORTURE.

BIBLIOGRAPHY

Advisory Council on the Treatment of Offenders. *Report: Corporal Punishment.* Cmnd. 1213. London: Her Majesty's Stationery Office, 1961.

Cadogan Committee. *Report of the Departmental Committee on Corporal Punishment.* Cmnd. 5684. London: Her Majesty's Stationery Office, 1938. Reprint, 1963.

CALDWELL, ROBERT G. "The Deterrent Influence of Corporal Punishment on Prisoners Who Have Been Whipped." *American Sociological Review* 9 (1944): 171–177.

Canada, Parliament. *Reports of the Joint Committee of the Senate and House of Commons on Capital Punishment, Corporal Punishment, Lotteries.* Ottawa: Queen's Printer and Controller of Stationery, 1956.

Council of Europe. *The European Convention on Human Rights.* Strasbourg, France: Directorate of Information, 1968.

FOUCAULT, MICHEL. *Discipline and Punish: The Birth of the Prison.* New York: Pantheon, 1977.

New Zealand Department of Justice. *Crime in New Zealand.* Wellington, New Zealand: Government Printer, 1968.

SCOTT, GEORGE RYLEY. *The History of Corporal Punishment: A Survey of Flagellation in Its Historical, Anthropological, and Sociological Aspects.* Reprint. London: T. Werner Laurie, 1942.

United Nations Secretariat. "Standard Minimum Rules for the Treatment of Prisoners." *First United Nations Congress on the Prevention of Crime and the Treatment of Offenders, Geneva, 22 August–3 September 1955.* New York: United Nations, Department of Economic and Social Affairs, 1956, pp. 67–73.

CORPORATE CRIMINAL RESPONSIBILITY

Introduction

In the majority of American jurisdictions the corporation is criminally responsible for illegal acts of its agents that are (1) committed within the scope of their employment and (2) intended to benefit the corporation ("Developments in the Law," pp. 1246–1250). This simple black-letter rule represents, however, an uneasy marriage of civil and criminal concepts of responsibility that has long proved troubling to legal scholars (Comment, 1975; Miller; U.S. National Commission on Reform of Federal Criminal Law). Indeed, although the use of criminal sanction against the corporate entity is now relatively common in American courts, the concept of corporate criminal responsibility is accepted to a far more modest extent in Great Britain, and not at all in civil law jurisdictions (Leigh; Mueller).

The debate over corporate criminal liability has had two distinct levels, conceptual and pragmatic. On the first level, the American common-law rule of corporate liability for an agent's crimes has been criticized both on the ground that it entails an acceptance of vicarious responsibility (that is, the acts of the agent are imputed to a corporate principal—here, the employer) and because it arguably downgrades the significance of intent and blameworthiness in the criminal law. On the pragmatic level, much skepticism has been expressed about the efficacy of corporate criminal responsibility: Is the corporation an apt or appropriate target for criminal sanctions? Would civil remedies be more effective? Does corporate liability tend to deflect attention from the responsibility of the individual actors? Indeed, can the corporation be deterred at all, if the financial penalties imposed on it can be passed on to others as a business cost?

Development of corporate criminal liability

The case law. The early English common law denied that a corporation could commit a crime (*Anonymous Case* (No. 935), 88 Eng. Rep. 1518 (K.B. 1701)). Four distinct barriers inhibited judicial recognition of corporate criminal liability. First, until the maturation of the doctrine of *respondeat superior* (the principle that an individual was civilly liable for the acts of his agents) as a concept of tort law in the nineteenth century, a conceptual basis was lacking for the imputation of acts committed by an individual to the corporation (Leigh, pp. 4–5). Second, where specific intent was an element of the crime, it struck early jurists as an obvious contradiction to speak of the corporation as having the requisite mens rea—in effect, to look for a guilty mind in the case of the corporation seemed a search for the ghost in the machine. Third, the doctrine of *ultra vires* posed a further conceptual impediment since until well into the nineteenth century this doctrine limited the corporation's powers to either those expressly authorized by its charter or those necessarily implied by such express powers. Thus, because the charter would formally empower the corporation only to commit lawful acts, the corporation logically lacked any power to commit a crime. Fourth, a corporate prosecution could not be squared with the rigid procedural requirements of the time, which required, for example, that the defendant be personally brought before the court for an arraignment; again, since the corporation was not an individual, it could only appear through its agents or attorneys—a concept that was entirely foreign to the English law, which disfavored criminal prosecution in absentia.

These obstacles, however, did not totally preclude corporate criminal liability. As industrialization began to spread across England in the mid-nineteenth century, the English courts were confronted with violations of law committed by railroads, and they responded by holding that the corporate entity could be prosecuted for a criminal omission (*Regina v. Birmingham & Gloucester Railway*, 114 Eng. Rep. 492 (Q.B. 1842)). Initially, the rationale was narrow: the case of omissions was different, it was held, because no individual agent of the corporation was responsible for the corporation's omission. That is, because only the corporation was under a duty to perform the specific act in question, no individual had violated the law; hence there was no imputation of guilt from agent to principal, and the supposed evil of vicarious responsibility was thus avoided.

Nonetheless, as the tort doctrine of *respondeat superior* became established, this initial category of corporate crimes was soon expanded to include, first, nuisance offenses and, by the end of the nineteenth century, public welfare and similar regulatory offenses generally. In these cases, because specific intent was not an element of the offenses, the problem of defining the corporate mens rea was evaded, and the liability could be rationalized as essentially civil in character. For the most part, American courts followed in the path of their English brethren, and by the end of the nineteenth century it was generally established that the corporation could at least be convicted of those crimes that did not require proof of specific intent as an element of the offense.

With the advent of the twentieth century, however, the paths of American and English courts parted dramatically. American courts responded to the political climate of the Progressive era, both by expanding corporate liability to include mens rea offenses and by making irrelevant the level of the agent within the corporate hierarchy. In contrast, English courts articulated a much narrower "alter ego," or "organ," theory of corporate criminal liability in the case of mens rea offenses, under which only the acts of the most senior corporate officers—who constituted the corporation's "brain"—could, for criminal law purposes, be imputed to the corporate entity.

The landmark American case was the Supreme Court's decision in *New York Central & Hudson River R.R. v. United States*, 212 U.S. 481 (1909), which upheld the constitutionality of the prohibition on the granting of rebates by common carriers in interstate commerce set forth in the Elkins Act of 1903, 49 U.S.C. §§ 41–43 (1976 & Supp. III 1979) (mostly repealed). In the Elkins Act, Congress had specifically provided that acts and omissions of an officer functioning within the scope of his employment were to be deemed those of the corporation employing him. Thus, the Court was faced with a clear legislative intent to impose vicarious liability for a crime that required specific intent. At the same time, the political context of the decision was undoubtedly also clear to the Court: railroad rebates had been a central tactic used by the industrial trusts to acquire monopoly power, and their elimination had been a rallying cry for Progressive era reformers, whose efforts had culminated in the Elkins Act.

Against this historical backdrop, the Court not only accepted the possibility of corporate criminal liability but proclaimed the need for it in emphatic terms. The "public history of the times" showed, the Court wrote, that if only individuals were subject to the criminal law, "many offenses might go unpunished." Seeing "no good reason why corporations may not be held responsible," the Court used the tort law doctrine of *respondeat superior* to justify such a result (*New York Central*, 494–495). This step had significant doctrinal consequences because, by offering this analogy to tort law, the Court opened the door to corporate criminal liability in cases where the legislature had not explicitly intended to impose it.

Although *New York Central* could in principle have been confined to instances where the legislature had found corporate responsibility essential to its regulatory scheme, the tone of the decision invited a more expansive reading. Lower courts were not long in accepting this invitation. Statutes that forbade "any person" to commit an act were soon read to include any corporation, and distinctions were quickly dismissed between "regulatory" crimes, such as the paying of a rebate, and traditional *mala in se* offenses. Indeed, within a decade of the *New York Central* decision, Judge Learned Hand held that a corporation could be convicted of violating the Espionage Act of 1917, ch. 30, title I, § 3, 40 Stat. 217—ironically, an offense similar to the crime of treason, which William Blackstone (*476) had said a corporation could not commit (*United States v. Nearing*, 252 F. 223 (S.D.N.Y. 1918)). In so finding, Judge Hand wrote that no distinction should be drawn between the civil and criminal liability of the corporation, each being "merely an imputation to the corporation of the mental condition of its agents" (231).

In marked contrast, English courts during this same period shrank from any acceptance of vicarious criminal liability and instead developed a theory that held the corporation liable only for the acts of its "alter ego," but not for those of its agents generally (Leigh, pp. 91–108). Under this formulation, the corporation's liability was (at least in theory) not vicarious, because the criminal act or intent was not imputed from agent to principal, but rather the corporate entity was in effect defined for criminal law purposes to mean the limited class of its senior officers and directors. This distinction was rationalized through an anthropomorphic analogy: the lower-level agents were seen as merely the corporation's hands, whereas the senior officials were viewed as its "mind," or "will," and hence were the corporation itself. As a result, under the British rule only the acts of senior officials within the corporate hierarchy would be imputed to the corporation when mens rea offenses were involved. Even in the case of statutes that contain a strict liability standard, contemporary English law has permitted the corporation to show as a defense that the act of the agent was against the corporation's policy and hence unauthorized. Conversely, under the prevailing American rule, the corporation can be held criminally liable for the acts of even its lowest subordinates (cf. *Tesco Supermarkets, Ltd. v. Nattrass,* [1972] A.C. 153 and *United States v. George F. Fish, Inc.,* 154 F.2d 798 (2d Cir. 1946)).

Statutory developments. Although the British "alter ego" theory of liability has never been accepted by the federal courts, its influence appears discernible in the American Law Institute's Model Penal Code, which has been substantially adopted by a number of states. The Model Penal Code takes an essentially tripartite approach with respect to corporate criminal liability. First, for those crimes of intent where no "legislative purpose to impose liability on corporations plainly appears" (that is, common-law crimes such as fraud and manslaughter), the Code essentially adopts the British "alter ego" theory by providing that a corporation may be held liable for the criminal acts of an agent only if the offense was performed, authorized, or recklessly tolerated by the board of directors or a high managerial agent (§ 2.07(1)(c)). The critical term *high managerial agent* is broadly defined, however, to mean an officer or other agent "having duties of such responsibility that his conduct may fairly be assumed to represent the policy of the corporation" (§ 2.07(4)(c)). In a comment, the Code indicates that corporate liability would not therefore result from the unauthorized conduct "of a foreman in a large plant or of an insignificant branch manager" (1955, commentary on § 2.07).

In contrast, for crimes of intent where a legislative intent to penalize the corporation is plain, such as price-fixing and securities violations, the 1962 Code expressly accepts the principle of *respondeat superior* and makes the corporation liable for crimes committed by agents acting within the scope of their employment and with an intent to benefit the corporation (§ 2.07(1)(a)). However, in contrast to the federal rule, the Code permits an affirmative defense: the corporation can still avoid liability by proving that a high managerial agent with supervisory responsibility over the subject matter of the offense acted with "due diligence" to prevent it (§ 2.07(5)).

Still a third basic form of criminal liability is recognized by the Model Penal Code if the crime is one of strict liability, that is, if it lacks any requisite element of intent. In such cases, the Code assumes that the legislature intended to hold the corporation liable on a theory of *respondeat superior* "unless the contrary plainly appears" (§ 2.07(2)). Here, the defense of due diligence would not be available.

More a liberalized version of the British "alter ego" theory than a statutory expression of the federal rule, the Model Penal Code assumes that the basic purpose of corporate criminal liability is to encourage managerial diligence in supervising corporate obedience to law, rather than to punish or deter corporate violations generally. This premise in turn rests on the belief that the criminal law has no other realistic aim in punishing the corporation and should not impose losses on innocent stockholders for acts that their managerial agents sought reasonably to prevent. Accordingly, by creating an incentive to encourage managerial supervision through its provision of an affirmative defense of "due diligence," the Code seeks to accomplish what it believes can be achieved—increased supervision and oversight within the entity—without imposing the potentially high cost of general deterrence on shareholders.

In overview, British and American federal courts have responded in predictably divergent fashion to the conceptual problems posed by corporate criminal responsibility. More legal realists than formalists, American courts have for the most part rationalized a relaxation of the usual substantive limits on criminal liability, because to do otherwise seemed to threaten important regulatory policies and also to invite a sharp conflict with the legislature. More legal formalists than realists, and never prodded by their legislature, English courts instead constructed an elaborate, if sometimes crudely anthropomorphic, rationale by which to distinguish primary from vicarious corporate liability.

Current state of the American law: some complexities in *respondeat superior*

The rule of *respondeat superior* should not be confused with strict liability. The corporation is not liable simply because an agent commits the actus reus of an offense. Rather, three elements must be proved: that an agent (1) has committed a crime (2) while acting within the scope of his authority and (3) with an intent to benefit the corporation. Close questions can arise in each of these areas.

The first of these requirements would seem to imply that the corporation could not be convicted if the agent committing the actus reus lacked the requisite intent. However, federal case law has relaxed this intent requirement in several respects. First, intent may be imputed to the corporation from a person distinct from the one who commits the actus reus, such as a supervisory official who realized the significance of the act. Nor has it been necessary for the prosecutor to identify the actual agent who committed the crime if the prosecutor can show that some person within the corporation must have so acted. Even more significantly, inconsistent verdicts are tolerated under which the corporation is convicted but all conceivable individual agents are acquitted. Finally, some decisions have accepted a theory of "collective knowledge," under which no single individual had the requisite knowledge to satisfy the intent requirement, but various individuals within the organization possessed all the elements of such knowledge collectively (*United States v. T.I.M.E.-D.C., Inc.,* 381 F. Supp. 730 (W.D. Va. 1974)).

Normally, an agent's scope of authority is limited by express instructions from his principal. Yet in the context of corporate criminal prosecutions, the requirement that the agent act within the scope of his authority has also been eroded. Virtually any act engaged in by an employee in a job-related activity will satisfy this requirement ("Developments in the Law," pp. 1249–1250). Obviously, such a result has a strong policy justification, for if express restrictions could negate corporate liability, the board of directors could immunize the corporation simply by adopting formal policies to the effect that employees not fix prices, make materially misleading statements, pollute the air or water, or tolerate unsafe products. In general, good-faith efforts by the corporation to prevent the crime will not constitute a defense in the federal courts. In contrast, English decisions have found discretionary acts by lower-echelon officials to have been beyond the scope of their delegated power, even in the case of strict liability offenses. In *Tesco Supermarkets, Ltd.,* for example, a corporation was not held liable for the ministerial acts of a store manager not authorized by the corporation, even in the case of a strict liability regulatory statute.

Similarly, an intent to benefit the corporation remains a precondition of liability, but the federal courts have downgraded it from an essential element of the crime to merely an evidentiary consideration. No actual benefit need be received by the corporation so long as an intent to benefit it can be reasonably inferred by the fact finder. However, where an employee acts adversely to the corporation's interests but within the scope of his authority, it remains a valid defense for the corporation to assert that its agent was on a frolic and detour. Thus, in *Standard Oil Co. of Texas v. United States,* 307 F.2d 120 (5th Cir. 1962), evidence that employees of one corporation were acting to ben-

efit a rival corporation (which had bribed them) when they violated a regulatory statute was sufficient to exonerate the employer corporation. Even in such cases, however, liability to the employer corporation might result if it was found to have ratified or tolerated the act.

The majority of state courts now subscribe to the federal rules set forth above. Exceptions, of course, exist in those jurisdictions that have enacted the Model Penal Code and in a small number of cases that have accepted corporate good faith and due diligence as a defense. Pending legislation to recodify the Federal Criminal Code also adopts the federal rule intact and would in substance codify it for the first time.

Other special problems with the theory of corporate liability arise where the analogy breaks down between the fictional person of the corporation and real individuals. For example, can a dissolved corporation be prosecuted? Despite the view that the defendant is civilly dead, the answer appears to be in the affirmative (as in *Melrose Distillers, Inc. v. United States,* 359 U.S. 271 (1959)). Similarly, can the corporation be convicted of conspiring with its subsidiaries or with its employees? Here, legal realism appears to be triumphing, and the case law (at least in the antitrust context) has begun to reject the idea of such "bathtub conspiracies," recognizing that the corporation must necessarily act through its agents (as in *Sunkist Growers, Inc. v. Winckler & Smith Citrus Products Co.,* 370 U.S. 19 (1962)). A consensus appears to have developed that any other rule would give undue significance to such fortuitous factors as whether corporate subunits were denominated as subsidiaries or only as unincorporated divisions. However, this same realism has also prevented parent corporations from insulating themselves against criminal liability through the use of subsidiaries. In such instances, the corporate subsidiary can itself be viewed as an agent and its action imputed to the parent corporation, if the subsidiary appears to have been acting to benefit the parent and has little independent reality apart from the parent corporation.

A policy appraisal: is corporate criminal liability useful?

"Corporations don't commit crimes; people do." This theme (borrowed, of course, from the opponents of gun control) has been implicit in a substantial body of legal commentary that has criticized the idea of corporate criminal liability. The criticism has had two quite different focal points: (1) the asserted injustice of vicarious criminal liability; and (2) the alleged inefficiency of corporate liability. The following critiques have been repeatedly made. First, with respect to the rationale underlying corporate liability, it has been claimed that:

1. Vicarious liability is appropriate only as a principle of tort law since its justification lies in its allocation of the loss to the party more able to bear it (or at least more deserving of the burden), but it is unrelated to the purposes of retribution, deterrence, prevention, and rehabilitation that underlie the criminal law (Leigh, p. 15).
2. Vicarious liability is unjust because its burden falls on the innocent rather than the guilty—that is, the penalty is borne by stockholders and others having an interest in the corporation, rather than by the guilty individual (U.S. National Commission, p. 163; Comment, 1975, p. 920).
3. Vicarious liability results in a disparity between businesses conducted in the corporate form and those run as a proprietorship, since the individual proprietor will not be criminally liable for the independent acts of his employees (Leigh, p. 118).
4. Vicarious liability for the corporation may in the future open the door to expanded vicarious criminal liability for individuals as well.

Second, a number of arguments have been advanced to claim that corporate punishment is inefficient or even counterproductive:

1. Corporations are largely undeterrable; fines are ineffective, and only the imprisonment of guilty individuals achieves real deterrence (U.S. National Commission, p. 163; Leigh, pp. 154–155).
2. Prosecution of the corporation may lead courts, juries, and prosecutors to acquit or dismiss charges against individual defendants, and thus corporate liability serves as a shield behind which the truly guilty can hide ("Developments in the Law," pp. 1248–1249).
3. Civil remedies are more flexible and potentially as severe, and they also avoid the constitutional restrictions associated with a criminal prosecution ("Developments in the Law," pp. 1369–1375).
4. No additional deterrence is achieved under the federal rule, since the Model Penal Code's affirmative defense will also give the corporation an incentive to monitor and police its employees (Miller, pp. 66–68).

Although none of these arguments is frivolous, each on closer examination seems seriously overbroad or

at least unconfirmed by the relatively slim empirical evidence available. Each will be assessed below, as will the equally debatable arguments for corporate liability.

The debate over rationale. Should vicarious liability be limited to the context of tort law as a device for equitable allocation of losses? This argument has a surface plausibility to the extent that tort and criminal law are thought to have substantially different concerns: the former with compensation, the latter with deterrence. Still, vicarious liability may be more closely related to the goal of deterrence than its critics concede. Economists have asserted that the most efficient way to deter organizational crime is to focus on the organization, not the individual (Elzinga and Breit, pp. 132–138). Although others have objected to aspects in this analysis (Coffee, 1980), it does seem likely that the organization has a greater capacity than do public authorities to monitor and police its own internal processes. Thus, if it could be deterred, it would in turn more effectively supervise its agents. Indeed, the corporation could undertake preventive measures in advance of any crime's commission, whereas the state is essentially forced to restrain its own hand until afterward because its right to act (at least insofar as the criminal law is concerned) is initiated only by the commission of the crime.

Conversely, in the absence of corporate penalties, the corporation may, consciously or otherwise, encourage noncompliance by its agents and even pressure for it (Coffee, 1981, pp. 413–415). Thus, a twofold answer seems possible to those who object to corporate vicarious criminal liability for criminal acts of an agent: (1) such vicarious liability may well be closely related to the criminal law's chief aim of prevention, both by deterring individual offenders and by encouraging the corporation to install incapacitative monitoring controls; and (2) victim compensation might also be a legitimate goal of the criminal law, both through sentences such as restitution (which the corporation almost uniquely is able to afford) and through the potential collateral estoppel impact of a criminal conviction on civil litigation brought by the victims of the crime.

Still, the argument that the penalty falls on the innocent remains troubling. The traditional answer to this criticism of corporate liability has been that a penalty imposed on the corporation simply eliminates unjust enrichment: since the stockholders indirectly benefited from the crime, they should indirectly bear the penalty (Edgerton, p. 837). This defense of corporate liability seems oversimple, however, because frequently the penalty will greatly exceed the gain (if any) from the crime. Indeed, many economists believe that adequate deterrence can only result if the expected penalty exceeds the expected gain by a margin sufficient to adjust for limited risk of apprehension and conviction. For example, if the expected gain were $1 million and the risk of apprehension were as low as 10 percent, only a penalty of $10 million would in theory remove the incentive to commit the crime.

This observation heightens the dilemma stemming from the fact that innocent parties suffer when the corporation is punished. But ultimately, the claim that corporate criminal liability is unjust because of the injury caused by the overspill of corporate penalties onto nonculpable shareholders proves too much. First, society does not face this issue exclusively in the context of the criminal law. If avoidance of punitive burdens on shareholders is taken as a first principle, it should also require the elimination of punitive damages in tort cases, treble-damage awards in civil antitrust cases, civil penalties, and possibly the very concept of *respondeat superior* as well. Equally important, the loss imposed on shareholders is generally mitigated through "cost spreading." That is, if a penalty of $10 million were imposed on a company having 100,000 shareholders holding its securities on a pro rata basis, the penalty per shareholder would be only $100 apiece—a loss that is considerably less significant than if the corporation had only a few shareholders. In reality, shareholders protect themselves from such risks through diversification of their investment portfolios, so that their exposure to such penalties is minimal. In short, the problem is not that the impact of a corporate penalty is unjustly severe, but rather that it is so negligible (on a per shareholder basis) that it gives shareholders little incentive to seek to hold management accountable.

The argument that corporate vicarious liability creates an unfair disparity between proprietorships and corporations also seems less than compelling. To be sure, the individual proprietor is not normally criminally liable on a vicarious basis for the criminal acts of his agents, but he is subject to incarcerative penalties if the prosecutor can convince a jury that he conspired with such agents. This risk is real, even if he is innocent, since conspiracy may be proved on circumstantial evidence. One suspects that if a disparity exists here, it favors the corporate shareholder, who seldom will be exposed to a threat of incarceration.

Finally, there remains the "open floodgates" argument: will vicarious liability for the corporation lead to similar liability for individuals? This ominous possibility might well have chilled commentators in 1909, immediately after the *New York Central* case, but in

the years since that decision, no rush by the legislature to adopt statutes imputing criminal liability from one individual to another has been evident.

In any event, one answer to the "open floodgates" argument may be to redefine corporate criminal responsibility so that it is not truly a species of vicarious criminal liability. At bottom, vicarious liability rests on the imputation of evil intent from one juristic person to another. But such an imputation is not necessary to justify the application of a sanction. Alternatively, one can focus on the negligence or recklessness of the entity in suffering or permitting the act of its agent, and thereby omit the conceptually troublesome fiction of transferring the agent's intent to the entity.

Although this theory—which for the sake of convenience might be called a suretyship rationale—has received little attention from courts, it has been advanced by commentators. One writer has made the interesting suggestion that the corporation should be viewed not as a legal personality but as a "committable common fund" whose "members incur [a] diminished or derivative liability that penalizes them only through their common fund" (Stoljar, p. 172). Conceptually, such a rationale avoids personifying the corporation, instead focusing on the granting of the corporate franchise by the state and construing it as having been conditioned upon an obligation to act as surety for defined criminal acts of its agents.

Under this implied-consent theory, the suretyship is a voluntarily accepted responsibility, to which the stockholder consents in return for the grant of the charter. In contrast, the English law's emphasis on culpability involving an "alter ego" of the corporation sees the corporation not as simply an insurer but as itself morally blameworthy. In essence, then, the English law on corporate responsibility is closely tied to a retributive rationale for punishment. Yet only a few commentators (for example, Fisse, "Reconstructing Corporate Criminal Law") see the corporation as a suitable vehicle for retributively motivated punishment, and there is some risk that in imposing retributive punishment on the corporation the law will appear to many to have been blinded by its own fiction. If so, the special moral and educative force that the criminal law possesses may be compromised.

A surety rationale is also potentially broader than the concept of vicarious liability. Under such a theory, the entity could be held liable for suffering an act by another, even though the individual actor would not necessarily be criminally liable. Thus, if the corporation's agent acts without the requisite level of intent—recklessly but not willfully, for example—the corporation cannot today be held liable under a vicarious theory of liability since under such a theory the corporation simply stands in the shoes of its agent, who is not here guilty. Yet it is far from self-evident that the legislature should be denied the power in all cases to so hold the corporation criminally liable; for example, the legislature might wish to hold the corporation more strictly accountable than its agent for tolerating a life-threatening safety hazard to exist, or for suffering an inadequately trained employee to operate a nuclear power plant. These cases can be reached today by making the offense one of strict liability and by enforcing the statute, as a practical matter, only against the corporate principal and not the agent. But a suretyship rationale permits a more formalized distinction between the liability of the individual and that of the entity by creating different standards of culpability for the individual and the entity, thus enabling the legislature to enact substantial deterrent penalties for the entity without permitting incarceration of individuals for behavior that was only negligent.

Similarly, the reach of a vicarious theory of liability may fall short of the surety theory in those cases where the actual actor cannot be identified or where the actor pursues his own ends rather than those of the corporation. For example, sexual harassment of female employees by their male superiors could be criminalized, but corporate liability would not normally follow under current law since the agent did not act to benefit the entity. Of course, it is possible to legislate the crime of suffering an act by another, either negligently or as a matter of strict liability, but initially it seems anomalous to create a lower threshold of criminal liability for the party who suffers the act by its agent than for the agent who actually commits it. Yet under a surety rationale it is at least comprehensible that society might, in some limited class of cases, wish to impose a higher standard of intent for the accused individual actor than for the entity employing him, in part because the entity is only being held liable as a guarantor but not "punished" in any retributive sense. This argument raises in turn a more basic question: to the extent that a suretyship rationale is legislatively adopted, should its use be confined to civil rather than criminal sanctions?

As a legal theory, a surety rationale would expand to its logical limits the idea, already inherent in the current federal law of vicarious corporate liability, that a person can be blameworthy for suffering an act by his agent. In practice, such a rationale would modify American law by eliminating the need for the act to be in the interests of the corporation or within the agent's real or apparent authority, and it would permit

different levels of intent to govern the liability of the agent and the entity. Yet, although such an expansion of criminal liability is probably constitutional (since strict liability statutes have been upheld), it would leave little remaining distinction between civil and criminal concepts of legal responsibility. From either a civil libertarian perspective or from one that seeks to conserve and protect the special educative force of the criminal law as a legal sanction, it can be questioned whether the gains in deterrence generated by such an expansion justify the potential costs that are risked through overuse of society's most powerful (and theatrical) sanction. The corporation is an anomaly in the criminal process, and the requirement that the agent act to benefit the corporation may well help to rationalize that anomaly and help society conceive of the corporation as a "true" offender.

The utility of corporate punishment. Some critics of corporate liability have doubted whether the corporation itself can be deterred. Such an evaluation seems premature, however, given another conclusion which virtually every commentator on the subject has reached: that corporations tend to receive very small fines in relation to their size, their earnings, or even their expected gain from the criminal transaction (Comment, 1975, pp. 921–922; Note, 1961, pp. 285–287). Thus, it is logically difficult to assert simultaneously that corporations are not punished and that they are not deterrable.

But here a problem noted earlier resurfaces: corporate punishment tends to fall on the innocent—not only on stockholders but also on employees (who may be laid off), creditors, the surrounding community, and, of course, the consumer, who may in effect indemnify the corporation if the fine can be passed on as a cost of doing business. Thus, an apparent paradox is reached: the economist's model asserts that only the imposition of severe fines in an amount well in excess of the expected gain will generate adequate deterrence, since it is necessary to compensate for a risk-of-apprehension factor that invariably falls well below 100 percent. But if corporate penalties are escalated in this fashion, the remedy may be worse than the disease, because layoffs, plant closings, and the threatened insolvency of major corporate institutions may be a more adverse result than the financial loss suffered by consumers or the government as a result of price-fixing or tax fraud (Coffee, 1981, pp. 415–422).

This problem suggests the desirability of corporate penalties that minimize "overspill." A number of proposals have been made in this regard: for example, the use of an equity fine levied in common stock would avert corporate insolvency and eliminate injury to nonstockholders, while also threatening a change of corporate control in order to activate management (Coffee, 1981, pp. 427–439). Similarly, a sentence of corporate probation has been recommended as a vehicle for public intervention in the internal decision-making of delinquent corporations (Note, 1979). Others have recommended increased use of a publicity sanction and a sentence to render community service (Fisse, 1971, 1981). These proposals suggest that the issue of corporate liability can and should be divorced from that of the optimal form of corporate punishment.

An argument frequently made against corporate liability is that it may interfere with the assignment of individual liability. Here, anecdotal evidence does suggest that juries have sometimes compromised, acquitting all individual defendants while convicting the corporation (Comment, 1975, p. 923). The pervasiveness of this pattern cannot be estimated. Still, public-opinion surveys suggest that many white-collar crimes are no longer viewed as mere "regulatory" or technical violations but are ranked relatively high on a scale of seriousness, and consequently this pattern of jury reluctance to convict individual defendants for white-collar crimes may be a declining phenomenon. In any event, the prosecution always has the option of not prosecuting the corporation—or, at least, of not doing so in the same proceeding.

Conversely, corporate liability may make it easier to convict the individual defendants. In any multidefendant prosecution, the interests of the defendants are at least potentially adverse, since each can generally gain concessions by implicating another. The corporation is no exception to this rule and is in a position to provide evidence against individual defendants or to discipline them, in return for leniency for itself. Drafts of the pending federal criminal code have appropriately recognized this by instructing the sentencing court, when levying a fine against the corporation, to consider the degree to which the corporation has undertaken internal disciplinary measures (S. 1722: A bill to codify, revise, and reform title 18 of the United States Code, and for other purposes, § 2202(a)(4), 96th Cong., 1st sess. (1979)). In short, such an invitation to mitigate the fine if the corporation will dismiss or discipline responsible officials makes it desirable from a law enforcement perspective to prosecute the corporation along with the individual defendants.

Still another perspective on the potential utility of corporate criminal liability begins from the much-repeated observation that it is frequently difficult to identify the "true" culprit within a firm. Although the point is undoubtedly correct, its truth may lie less in the ability of the "true" culprit to hide his identity than in the absence of any such "true" offender in a broad range of cases. From a social-science perspective, it is virtually a truism that knowledge may exist collectively within an organization, even though it is not localized within any one individual. This theory proceeds from a view of the corporation as a bureaucratic institution, and from this organizational perspective it is frequently argued that information flows poorly and in a selectively biased fashion within the corporate hierarchy. Lower echelons do not wish to communicate adverse information to those above, and those above filter out information that does not confirm their prior expectations. In addition, upper echelons within the corporation tend increasingly to speak a very different language than those at operating levels—one focused on financial results and unfamiliar with a production or operational vocabulary (Coffee, 1977). Thus it is likely that information will exist at one level of an organization that would alter decisions at another, but no mechanism will necessarily force the transmission of this information to where it is needed. Some federal decisions appear to have responded already to such considerations by recognizing a "collective knowledge" doctrine, under which the corporation may be held liable even though no single individual had the requisite information (T.I.M.E.-D.C., Inc.).

These problems indicate one inadequacy of an exclusive focus on the individual decision-maker: recurrently, it is unlikely that any single individual within the corporate hierarchy will have the requisite intent, and yet the firm as an entity may have knowledge of an unsafe design, a carcinogenic risk, or a dangerous side effect that its products can cause. In this light, the argument for corporate liability rests not only on the evidentiary problems of identifying the "true" culprit but on the organizational reality that there may be no actual individual culprit at all, because of the diffusion of responsibility within the corporate hierarchy. Moreover, an insistence on finding a responsible individual decision-maker might produce a scapegoat system of criminal justice, in which lower-echelon operating officials would probably bear the primary responsibility and risk of exposure.

The foregoing arguments focus on the problem of cognitive failures within the corporation's internal information processing as a justification for corporate liability. An alternative justification proceeds from the motivational failures that also accompany the corporate form. Almost inevitably, there is an incongruence between the interests of the manager and those of the firm as an entity: criminal behavior may be attractive to the pressured or ambitious manager, even if it is not to the corporation. Compounding this problem is the tendency for conflicting signals to issue from the senior levels of the corporate hierarchy to the middle echelons, which tend to be the locus of criminal behavior. Such signals may formally require obedience to law, but they also demand and reward short-term profit maximization. The implicit signal may thus be read by middle-level managers as meaning only "don't get caught." Of course, individual criminal liability may partially countervail this pressure on the middle manager. But even if the severity of the criminal sanction vastly exceeds that of the counterthreats the corporation can make, such as dismissal, demotion, or foregone promotion, the absolute severity of the sanction must be discounted by its probability of imposition (Coffee, 1981). This means that the discounted threat of apprehension and conviction by the state for a criminal offense may be less than that of the strong likelihood of internal discipline or dismissal by the corporation for failure to maximize profits. Thus, the manager faces both public and private sanction, and the latter, although lesser in gravity, tend to be higher in probability, making the outcome uncertain and possibly dependent on the level of risk-aversion of the individual manager.

The alternative of civil remedies. Corporate sanctions may be necessary, but it is far from clear that such sanctions must be criminal in nature. Civil penalties are now utilized by many, if not most, administrative agencies. Moreover, a system of civil penalties offers some obvious advantages to the prosecutor. First, the corporation could not claim the protection of constitutional rights, such as the "reasonable doubt" standard or double jeopardy, that are applicable only to criminal proceedings. Second, the possibility of judicial or jury nullification is reduced because of the lesser stigma. Third, courts of equity traditionally have been more able than criminal courts to fashion flexible and novel forms of relief. Thus, from the standpoint of specific deterrence and incapacitation, some have concluded that civil penalties offer significant advantages over criminal law enforcement in the case of the corporation ("Developments in the Law," pp. 1365–1374).

In this light, what arguments remain for the use of the criminal law as a preferred legislative strategy? Little agreement exists here, but the following arguments deserve consideration. First, the criminal law has long been thought uniquely capable of performing an educative role in defining and reinforcing the boundaries of acceptable conduct. The civil law's quieter, less theatrical character limits its ability to perform this socializing function. Closely allied to this point is the criminal law's ability to stigmatize and employ publicity as a sanction. The highly publicized prosecution of the Ford Motor Company in 1979 for the allegedly unsafe design of the Pinto illustrates this capacity of the criminal process. Second, the criminal law characteristically moves at a faster pace than the civil law. Thus, to the extent that restitution is an authorized sentence, the criminal law can serve as the engine by which to obtain victim compensation more quickly. In addition, because the double jeopardy clause does not preclude a successive civil prosecution after an acquittal in a criminal trial, the prosecutor can in effect obtain a second chance by proceeding first criminally and then civilly.

Third, courts of equity have traditionally been barred from imposing penalties, and although this does not amount to a constitutional barrier, there may linger a reluctance on the part of courts when operating in a civil mode to pursue deterrent objectives. The basic format of the civil enforcement proceeding also has yet to be resolved, and the fairness and reliability of administratively determined civil penalties is a matter of serious dispute.

Finally, joint prosecutions of the corporation and its agents require a criminal forum if the threat of incarceration is to be used to deter individuals. From a law enforcement perspective, such joint trials are desirable both because they are less costly than separate prosecutions and because they permit one prosecutor to pursue the case in an integrated fashion; a separate prosecution, particularly if pursued in a different forum, might require a different prosecutor.

At most, these arguments suggest that corporate prosecutions for truly significant violations might best remain in a criminal courtroom, but they do not deny that corporate prosecutions for many regulatory and strict liability offenses, which today fit awkwardly at best within the criminal process, could be safely transferred to the civil process.

Affirmative defenses. As noted earlier, the Model Penal Code permits the corporation to prove as an affirmative defense that it exercised adequate diligence to supervise its employees (§ 2.07(5)). The underlying premise here, which is shared by British law, is that the function of corporate criminal liability is more to deter criminality by executives and encourage supervision of subordinates than to punish the corporation generally for all misdeeds caused by its agents ("Developments in the Law," p. 1252). Yet it is questionable whether recognition of such a defense advances or frustrates its announced purposes. Without such a defense, the corporation would still have an incentive to monitor and police its employees since, as a practical matter, it will probably be held strictly liable for any offense committed by employees in the course of their work. But by recognizing the defense, one raises the possibility of feigned compliance and thus encourages cosmetic attempts at monitoring. Worse yet, there is the danger that honest efforts at monitoring and compliance will be mistaken by middle-level management as only a cynical attempt to prepare a due-diligence defense in advance.

On a more theoretical level, once such a defense is recognized, the corporation might invest less funds in monitoring and detecting illegal and potentially illegal behavior since, once the minimal standard of diligence is met, the corporation becomes legally immune and has no remaining incentive to prevent criminal acts by its agents, even though further investment might prevent such crime. In theory, the ideal position for the corporation would be to invest just enough to establish the defense but not to prevent those crimes profitable to the corporation. Yet without the defense, the rational corporation would invest in crime prevention by any means (including research or experimentation with new techniques) up to the level at which such expenditures equaled the expected penalty—that is, the likely fine discounted by the likelihood of apprehension and conviction. In short, the absence of the defense creates an incentive to seek new methods of prevention not yet established or required by a due-diligence standard. Ironically, the more diligence is made a defense, the less it is encouraged.

Still, a total refusal to recognize any role for corporate due diligence may seem unjust. Thus, a role might be created for such a defense that would be less likely to result in reduced deterrence. This would be done by reducing the role of due-diligence efforts from an affirmative defense to a sentencing consideration (S. 1722, § 2202(a)(4) so provided in its attempt to recodify the Federal Criminal Code). The legislature could provide that the court shall consider at sentencing any corporate efforts directed at internal reform or at the discipline of employees. In particular, such a step would give the corporation an incentive to seek out guilty individuals in order to reduce its own penalty, whereas otherwise there might exist a desire to avoid such an inquiry for fear of detecting still-undiscovered violations. The threat of individual liability would thus be increased since corporate employees would come to expect that their employer would turn them in if it faced conviction itself.

Making due diligence a sentencing consideration rather than an affirmative defense has other desirable consequences as well. First, it ensures that violation by an agent will result in a corporate conviction, thereby authorizing the court to order restitution to victims and to consider interventionist strategies that might be implemented through a sentence of corporate probation. Second, the conviction would have a res judicata effect on civil litigation brought by injured victims of the crime; such civil liability in turn increases the corporate incentive to monitor. Finally, the court would gain a wider angle of vision in determining the adequacy of corporate monitoring efforts since it could consider developments subsequent to the offense that would be legally irrelevant at trial.

Summary

As noted at the outset, the problem of corporate criminal responsibility has a conceptual and a pragmatic dimension. On the conceptual level, the majority American rule of *respondeat superior* has troubled those who understandably fear vicarious liability and a reduction in the role of intent in the criminal law, but it has evoked little concern on the part of the public. On a theoretical level, a different rationale—the surety rationale—might respond to these concerns by adopting a less fictional justification for punishing the corporation, but such a rationale (focused as it is on suffering an act rather than on vicariously being the actor) fits awkwardly at best with the public's conception of criminal responsibility.

On a pragmatic level, the lack of empirical scholarship about corporate behavior clouds all efforts to understand the impact of corporate criminal liability, but much of the criticism of the contemporary federal rule seems overstated. To immunize the corporation from criminal liability and to focus only on the individual actor could significantly reduce the deterrent threat underlying the criminal law insofar as (1) the corporation can implicitly threaten its agents with private sanctions (such as dismissal) that have a higher likelihood of being imposed than the state's penalties; (2) no single individual may have acted with sufficient specific intent to justify conviction; and (3) such a step invites the corporation to relax its efforts at monitoring its agents. In addition, corporate liability can potentially serve other purposes, such as victim compensation, and it offers a vehicle for interventionist strategies directed at the corporation that are not realizable through prosecutions of individuals.

Although a focus on the firm, as opposed to the individual actor alone, thus seems prudent, the case for corporate criminal liability is problematic and, as civil enforcement procedures are formalized and enhanced, it may diminish significantly. Ultimately, it must rest either (1) on practical considerations which suggest that the prosecutor obtains tactical advantages or can succeed in imposing greater penalties in a criminal context; or (2) on the greater visibility of the criminal process and the consequent utility of the criminal trial as a means of communicating an essentially moral and educative lesson about the boundaries of acceptable conduct. Neither foundation is today secure, but, correspondingly, adequate alternatives are unproved and largely unauthorized.

JOHN C. COFFEE, JR.

See also articles under ECONOMIC CRIME; *both articles under* STRICT LIABILITY; VICARIOUS LIABILITY; WHITE-COLLAR CRIME: HISTORY OF AN IDEA.

BIBLIOGRAPHY

American Law Institute. *Model Penal Code: Proposed Official Draft.* Philadelphia: ALI, 1962.

———. *Model Penal Code: Tentative Draft No. 4.* Philadelphia: ALI, 1955.

BALL, HARRY V., and FRIEDMAN, LAWRENCE M. "The Use of Criminal Sanctions in the Enforcement of Economic Legislation: A Sociological View." *Stanford Law Review* 17 (1965): 197–218.

BLACKSTONE, WILLIAM. *Commentaries on the Laws of England* (1765–1769), vol. 1. Reprint. University of Chicago Press, 1979.

CLINARD, MARSHALL B., and YEAGER, PETER C. *Corporate Crime.* With the collaboration of Ruth Blackburn Clinard. New York: Free Press, 1980.

COFFEE, JOHN C., JR. "Beyond the Shut-eyed Sentry: Toward a Theoretical View of Corporate Misconduct and an Effective Legal Response." *Virginia Law Review* 63 (1977): 1099–1278.

———. "Corporate Crime and Punishment: A Non-Chicago View of the Economics of Criminal Sanctions." *American Criminal Law Review* 17 (1980): 419–476.

———. "No Soul to Damn; No Body to Kick: An Unscandalized Inquiry into the Problem of Corporate Punishment." *Michigan Law Review* 79 (1981): 386–459.

Comment. "Corporate Criminal Liability." *Northwestern University Law Review* 68 (1973): 870–892.

Comment. "Is Corporate Criminal Liability Really Necessary?" *Southwestern Law Journal* 29 (1975): 908–927.

"Developments in the Law—Corporate Crime: Regulating Corporate Behavior through Criminal Sanctions." *Harvard Law Review* 72 (1979): 1229–1375.

EDELHERTZ, HERBERT. *The Nature, Impact, and Prosecution of White-collar Crime.* Washington, D.C.: U.S. Department of Justice, Law Enforcement Assistance Administration,

National Institute of Law Enforcement and Criminal Justice, 1970.

EDGERTON, H. W. "Corporate Criminal Responsibility." *Yale Law Journal* 36 (1927): 827–844.

ELKINS, JAMES R. "Corporations and the Criminal Law: An Uneasy Alliance." *Kentucky Law Journal* 65 (1976): 73–129.

ELZINGA, KENNETH G., and BREIT, WILLIAM. *The Antitrust Penalties: A Study in Law and Economics.* New Haven: Yale University Press, 1976.

FISSE, BRENT. "Community Service as a Sanction against Corporations." *Wisconsin Law Review* 81(1981): 970–1017.

———. "Reconstructing Corporate Criminal Law: Deterrence, Retribution, Fault and Sanctions," forthcoming.

———. "Responsibility, Prevention, and Corporate Crime." *New Zealand Universities Law Review* 5 (1973): 250–279.

———. "The Social Policy of Corporate Criminal Responsibility." *Adelaide Law Review* 6 (1978): 361–412.

———. "The Use of Publicity as a Criminal Sanction against Business Corporations." *Melbourne University Law Review* 8 (1971): 107–150.

FRIEDMAN, HOWARD M. "Some Reflections on the Corporation as a Criminal Defendant." *Notre Dame Lawyer* 55 (1979): 173–202.

GEIS, GILBERT. "Criminal Penalties for Corporate Criminals." *Criminal Law Bulletin* 8 (1972): 377–381.

———, and STOTLAND, EZRA. *White-collar Crime: Theory and Research.* Beverly Hills, Calif.: Sage, 1980.

KADISH, SANFORD H. "Some Observations on the Use of Criminal Sanctions in Enforcing Economic Regulations." *University of Chicago Law Review* 30 (1963): 423–441.

LEIGH, L. H. *The Criminal Liability of Corporations in English Law.* London School of Economics and Political Science, 1969.

MILLER, SAMUEL R. "Corporate Criminal Liability: A Principle Extended to Its Limits." *Federal Bar Journal* 38 (1979): 49–68.

MUELLER, GERHARD O. W. "Mens Rea and the Corporation: A Study of the Model Penal Code Position on Corporate Liability." *University of Pittsburgh Law Review* 19 (1957): 21–46.

NAFTALIS, GARY P., ed. *White-collar Crimes.* Philadelphia: American Law Institute, American Bar Association Committee on Continuing Professional Education, 1980.

Note. "Corporate Criminal Liability for Acts in Violation of Company Policy." *Georgetown Law Journal* 50 (1962): 547–565.

Note. "Decision-making Models and the Control of Corporate Crime." *Yale Law Journal* 85 (1976): 1091–1129.

Note. "Increasing Community Control over Corporate Crime: A Problem in the Law of Sanctions." *Yale Law Journal* 71 (1961): 280–306.

Note. "Structural Crime and Institutional Rehabilitation: A New Approach to Corporate Sentencing." *Yale Law Journal* 89 (1979): 353–375.

ORLAND, LEONARD. "Reflections on Corporate Crime: Law in Search of Theory and Scholarship." *American Criminal Law Review* 17 (1980): 501–520.

STOLJAR, SAMUEL J. *Groups and Entities: An Inquiry into Corporate Theory.* Canberra: Australian National University Press, 1973.

STONE, CHRISTOPHER D. "The Place of Enterprise Liability in the Control of Corporate Conduct." *Yale Law Journal* 90 (1980): 1–77.

———. *Where the Law Ends: The Social Control of Corporate Behavior.* New York: Harper & Row, 1975.

U.S. National Commission on Reform of Federal Criminal Law. "Staff Memoranda on the Responsibility for Crimes Involving Corporations and Other Entities." *Working Papers* 1 (1970): 163–215.

CORPUS DELICTI

Corpus delicti literally means the body or substance of the crime. In law the term refers to proof establishing that a crime has occurred, that is, proof establishing each of the necessary elements of the offense in question.

Although misunderstanding about corpus delicti has been common among lawyers and laymen alike, it can be seen that the term does not refer to a dead body. There is a corpus delicti of robbery, arson, perjury, tax evasion, and, indeed, of every criminal offense. Moreover, even in a homicide case, a "dead body" is neither necessary nor sufficient to establish the corpus delicti. Testimony that a ship's passenger deliberately pushed the deceased overboard on the high seas can establish the corpus delicti of murder even if the body is never recovered. Conversely, the body of a child killed in a fire would *not* establish the corpus delicti of murder in the absence of proof that the fire was caused by some criminal act (Perkins).

When a failure to prove some fact essential to the charge (such as a failure to prove intercourse in a rape case) implies that the offense was not committed by anyone, the courts sometimes say that reversal of the conviction is required by the absence of a corpus delicti (*Azbill v. State,* 84 Nev. 345, 440 P.2d 1014 (1968)). It would be equally accurate, and perhaps less mysterious, to say simply that the reversal results from the prosecutor's failure to prove an essential element of the case.

The principal significance of the corpus delicti is its effect on the admissibility of evidence. It is generally held that certain relatively suspect kinds of evidence (confessions, for example) are not admissible unless there is some independent evidence of a corpus delicti. Once the prosecution has introduced such evidence, it can then use the confession either to strengthen its evidence that a crime was committed or to prove that the defendant was the person responsible.

Many murder convictions have been obtained even though the body of the alleged victim was never found. In at least three early cases, dating from the seventeenth century and before, the "deceased" turned up alive and well shortly after the defendant had been executed (Perkins). Such miscarriages of justice contributed to the development of the rule requiring independent corroboration of any confession and, of course, to insistence on proof beyond a reasonable doubt. In the modern era, numerous murder convictions continue to be found by juries and upheld by the courts even in the absence of a dead body. In nearly all of these cases the defendant confessed, and the proof of corpus delicti, together with the defendant's direct admissions, afforded strong evidence of guilt. A recent example is *People v. Manson,* 71 Cal. App. 3d 1, 139 Cal. Rptr. 275 (1977), involving one of the murders committed by the notorious Charles Manson "family."

More troublesome, and much less common, are murder prosecutions in which there is no dead body, no confession, and no eyewitness to the alleged crime. In these cases the proof of guilt is necessarily "circumstantial"—that is, based entirely on inferences drawn from such suspicious facts as the sudden disappearance of the alleged victim. Although the potential for a miscarriage of justice in such a case is evident, the legal system must have some means for dealing with the offender who is able to obliterate all trace of the victim (Morris). In at least four modern cases the circumstantial evidence of guilt was held sufficiently strong to warrant conviction of murder, even though neither a dead body, a confession, nor an eyewitness was available (*People v. Albert Scott,* 274 Cal. App. 2d 905, 79 Cal. Rptr. 587 (1969); *People v. Leonard Scott,* 176 Cal. App. 2d 458, 1 Cal. Rptr. 600 (1959); *Regina v. Onufrejczyk,* [1955] 1 Q.B. 388 (C.C.A.); *Rex v. Horry,* [1952] N.Z.L.R. 111 (C.A.)).

STEPHEN J. SCHULHOFER

See also CONFESSIONS; DISCOVERY.

BIBLIOGRAPHY

MORRIS, NORVAL. "Corpus Delicti and Circumstantial Evidence." *Law Quarterly Review* 68 (1952): 391–396.

PERKINS, ROLLIN M. "The Corpus Delicti of Murder." *Virginia Law Review* 48 (1962): 173–195.

CORRECTIONAL REFORM ASSOCIATIONS

"Americans of all ages, all conditions, and all dispositions constantly form associations," wrote Alexis de Tocqueville in his *Democracy in America,* first published in 1839. For the cause of prison reform, which is as old as the prison itself, Americans have indeed formed associations. The first eighteenth-century prison-aid association—the Philadelphia Society—has been succeeded by many modern counterparts.

The reform spirit in American penology derived from the Enlightenment thought of the Old World and the republican fervor of the New. Cruel punishments seemed a monarchical holdover from British rule, and, some thought, the ideals of the new nation might actually overcome the natural depravity of man. The historian David Rothman notes that "the rhetoric of the Revolution had prepared Americans to fulfill a grand mission, and now they would demonstrate . . . how to uplift the criminal class" (p. 60). Thus, statutes were amended, usually with the support of benevolent societies, substituting prison sentences for the penalties of death or other physical abuse.

Perhaps because Americans hoped that the penitentiary would remedy all of society's evils, many able and successful people supported or joined the reform associations during the eighteenth and nineteenth centuries. Benjamin Franklin participated in meetings that resulted in the founding of the Philadelphia Society in 1787. Prominent Quakers led the movement against capital and corporal punishment. Such reformers as Dorothea Dix, the well-known crusader for humane treatment of the mentally ill, engaged in fierce disputes over the congregate (New York) and separate (Pennsylvania) systems of penitentiary organization.

Americans' faith in the possibility of improving human behavior through institutional reform, at its height during the Jacksonian Era (approximately 1820–1850), dimmed thereafter, when the role of prison reform associations changed to some extent. Although the aim of reforming prisoners was not forgotten, it took second place to reform in such issues of prison policy as the convict lease system, under which prisoners were leased to private persons to work for a minimal fee, paid to the state rather than to the worker. In the early twentieth century, some of the reform associations also assumed responsibility for services to prisoners. For example, the Pennsylvania Prison Society (successor to the Philadelphia Society) sought to prepare prisoners for release, and the Prison Association of New York supervised prisoners on parole.

Modern American correctional reform associations bear little resemblance to their predecessors. Whereas the nineteenth-century prison societies focused on making penal institutions effective and humane, contemporary organizations are often skeptical that traditional penal goals can be realized, and therefore do not necessarily focus on improving institutional life. The National Prison Project of the American Civil Liberties Union has used litigation in its fight for improved prison conditions and prisoners' rights, and the Pennsylvania Prison Society seeks the same end through advocacy and public education. Offender Aid and Restoration and the Fortune Society, however, concentrate their efforts on services to those leaving prison; the American Friends Service Committee and the National Council on Crime and Delinquency advocate alternatives to incarceration for many offenders. In the 1970s some reform groups, notably the Prison Research Education Action Project, for the first time actually advocated the abolition of prisons. Other organizations work on a single issue—for example, the National Moratorium on Prison Construction and the National Coalition Against the Death Penalty—or provide a single specialized service, such as assistance to inmates' families.

The diversity of activities of today's correctional reform groups reflects, in part, the diversity of sources of pressure on corrections. The Attica rebellion of September 1971 brought American prisons under a scrutiny more intense than any they had known since the mid-nineteenth century. For the first time the courts have entered the field, finding entire state correctional systems unconstitutional and prescribing standards with which they must comply. Presidential commissions have looked closely at the correctional system and found it seriously deficient. In 1973 the report of the National Advisory Commission on Criminal Justice Standards and Goals, entitled *Corrections,* declared that American prisons are places of "crippling idleness, anonymous brutality, and destructive impact" (p. 1). Legislatures have contributed to the prisons' problems by enacting "get-tough" policies in the form of longer and mandatory sentences. By the 1980s, prison reformers and prison administrators alike were openly voicing doubts that incarceration could ever accomplish what society expected it to do, namely, to "correct" the offenders in its charge and to send an effective message to potential criminals that crime does not pay.

If the American prison has not been able to control

crime or reduce recidivism, how does this failure reflect upon the effectiveness of prison reform movements? The correctional reform associations were undoubtedly effective in instituting what were considered reforms during the first fifty years of the republic; the Quakers and others active in benevolent societies forced legislative changes restricting the range of capital offenses. In the mid-nineteenth century, the associations could take at least partial credit for abolishing imprisonment for debt, and later they had some influence on the demise of the convict lease system. In subsequent years the correctional reform groups' principal achievement has probably been their exposure of the oppressive nature of imprisonment to a public otherwise protected from that knowledge. Noting the importance of prison riots as pressure for reform, Jessica Mitford has written in *Kind and Usual Punishment* that "protest behind the walls, when heeded and acted on by outside agitators, has historically been the only significant factor in calling public attention to the prisoner's plight and in wresting from the prison authorities any sort of amelioration of conditions" (p. 231).

This is hardly a triumphant legacy. After two centuries of prison reform, prison sentences in the United States are lengthening, conditions remain deplorable, and the public seems willing to incur the tremendous social and economic costs of confining at least those who commit major crimes. As *Struggle for Justice,* an influential report to the American Friends Service Committee, concluded in 1971, "The quest for justice will necessarily be frustrated so long as we fail to recognize that criminal justice is dependent upon and largely derives from social justice" (Bacon, p. 13).

DIANA R. GORDON

See also CAPITAL PUNISHMENT; CORPORAL PUNISHMENT; CORRECTIONAL TREATMENT; CRUEL AND UNUSUAL PUNISHMENT; JAILS; *articles under* PRISONS; REHABILITATION.

BIBLIOGRAPHY

BACON, G. RICHARD et al. *Struggle for Justice: A Report on Crime and Punishment in America.* Prepared for the American Friends Service Committee. New York: Hill & Wang, 1971.

ERIKSSON, TORSTEN. *The Reformers: An Historical Survey of Pioneer Experiments in the Treatment of Criminals.* New York: Elsevier, 1976.

MAESTRO, MARCELLO T. *Cesare Beccaria and the Origins of Penal Reform.* Philadelphia: Temple University Press, 1973.

MITFORD, JESSICA. *Kind and Usual Punishment: The Prison Business.* New York: Knopf, 1973.

ROTHMAN, DAVID J. *The Discovery of the Asylum: Social Order and Disorder in the New Republic.* Boston: Little, Brown, 1971.

SILBERMAN, CHARLES E. *Criminal Violence, Criminal Justice.* New York: Random House, 1978.

TOCQUEVILLE, ALEXIS DE. *Democracy in America* (1835), vol. 2. Translated by Henry Reeve, as revised by Francis Bowen and further corrected and edited by Phillips Bradley. New York: Random House, Vintage Books, 1954.

U.S. Department of Justice, Law Enforcement Assistance Administration, National Advisory Commission on Criminal Justice Standards and Goals. *Corrections.* Washington, D.C.: The Commission, 1973.

CORRECTIONAL TREATMENT

Correctional treatment embraces all those procedures and services intended to induce the convicted offender to lead a law-abiding life after his release from control and to assist him in doing so. For many offenders, the deterrent effects of incarceration and surveillance by a probation or parole officer undoubtedly contribute substantially to the achievement of this objective. This article, however, will focus on correctional programs provided to offenders with the aim of enhancing their ability to survive in the community. Such an expectation rests on the assumption that substantial changes will be needed in the attitudes, psychological condition, and educational status of the individual. This assumption has been accepted penological doctrine for two centuries, during which many programs have been attempted, usually with high hopes at the outset but seldom with commensurate results.

Four general conditions help explain the disappointing results of correctional treatment initiatives. First, there is the intractable difficulty of managing beneficial services within a coercive setting, in which the requirements of custodial control and those of treatment services frequently conflict. Second, and probably more important, is the inadequate application of good ideas by personnel who are too often insufficient in numbers and training, working without appropriate equipment and facilities, and accountable to a management that places a low value on their services. Third, the person who is to be assisted has been seriously damaged by the stigma attached to the convicted criminal and by his loss of confidence in the possibility of living as a law-abiding citizen on any terms. Fourth, nearly all offenders are handicapped by limited education and by frequent failures at conventional living.

These obstacles to the effectiveness of correctional treatment in conditions of captivity have yet to be overcome for either adult or juvenile offenders. They must be kept in mind in any review of the potentialities of correctional treatment in custody. The greater success attained with offenders placed on probation, as measured by their lower rate of recidivism, may be partly attributed to treatment services that have been provided, but it is also true that probationers are generally less serious offenders than prisoners and that their lives have been less disrupted.

Although there are wide differences in the ability of institutions and agencies to surmount these obstacles, failure has been neither inevitable nor universal. In the history of treatment as an element of the penal process, many improvements in the care of convicted offenders have been made, in spite of the unsatisfactory results of particular programs. Finally, although disappointments have generally outnumbered successes, there have been enough verifiable successes to justify persistence with correctional treatment.

Conceptual development

Early history. Even in the time of Plato (c. 428–c. 348 B.C.), the divergent purposes of the punishment of offenders were subjects of debate. In the *Protagoras* and later in the *Gorgias,* Plato asserted that punishment should aim to prevent crime rather than to exact vengeance. Reasoning that a crime cannot be undone, he held that the offender's punishment should be corrective. In his last work, the *Laws,* Plato prescribed punishments of great severity, but he also urged that the elders of the city, its most respected leaders, counsel prisoners in the interest of reforming them. Plato never abandoned his belief that punishment should be for the benefit of the city; he believed that the reform of citizens who had committed crimes must be to the general advantage.

Despite Plato's recognition of the reformative purposes of punishment, there is no evidence that his guidance in this matter was followed by courts and prisons, either in Athens or elsewhere. It was not until the eighteenth century, the age of the Enlightenment, that influential writers considered the preventive purposes of penal sanctions and won acceptance for their views.

The idea of prevention as the purpose of the criminal law became ascendant with Cesare Beccaria (1738–1794), whose *On Crimes and Punishments* was published in 1764. Beccaria was closely followed by Jeremy Bentham (1748–1832), the founder of the utilitarian school of ethics, who devoted a long and industrious career to the reform of the English common law. One of his projects was the creation of a new kind of prison, the Panopticon, in which prisoners would work at constructive labor, be educated in schools, and have other opportunities for improvement. The Panopticon was never built to Bentham's design, but the idea of reform through treatment became a dominant concern in the prison reform movement that began in the early nineteenth century.

The Pennsylvania system. In the United States, concern about crime prevention through reform of the criminal followed a parallel track. The Society of Friends was the founding nucleus of the Commonwealth of Pennsylvania. Severe and protracted persecution in England and in several of the American colonies had awakened in the Friends a practical concern about the purposes of punishment and its administration. It was clear to them that prisons should provide services which aimed to restore the offender to the community as a productive citizen. To this end, the famous Walnut Street Jail, in actuality the first penitentiary, was built in 1776. There, as well as at the Eastern State Penitentiary, opened in 1829, the Pennsylvania system of correction was developed with such thoroughness and fidelity to principle that its example was followed throughout Europe. The Pennsylvania system was the first application of a treatment concept in practice. The concept may seem primitive and naive to contemporary eyes, but the very formulation of a reformative concept was a novelty without much precedent at the time.

The Eastern State Penintentiary was designed to put into practice the theory of correctional treatment expounded by the Philadelphia Society for Alleviating the Miseries of Public Prisons, founded in 1787. This theory held that crime was caused by the influence of a vicious environment: young and impressionable persons were led astray by confirmed criminals and by such other misfits as drunkards, prostitutes, and vagrants. It followed that once the offender was committed to the penitentiary, where criminals were concentrated, he should be kept apart from them. The prisoner would then be aided by his keepers to show penitence, in the most literal sense of the word—hence the name of the institution. It was clear that he should work hard, as befitted the ethos of post-Revolutionary America; moreover, to prevent association with confirmed criminals, the work had to be performed in solitary confinement. Care was taken to keep prisoners separate, even to the extent of providing separate exercise yards outside each cell. Even at Sunday worship services, prisoners were prevented from seeing one another. In European adaptations of the Pennsylvania system, chapels were built in which the hooded prisoners could only see the preacher and watch the service.

Although contacts with fellow prisoners and with members of the community from which they came were to be firmly prevented, prisoners subject to the Pennsylvania system were given religious instruction by ministers and lay visitors. Friendly visits by members of the Pennsylvania Prison Society (as the Philadelphia Society was renamed) were encouraged. The founders and early administrators of the system were certain that offenders could be reformed and that theirs was the way to accomplish that end. The opponents of the system who chose the Auburn silent system, discussed below, were equally sure that years of solitary confinement could only damage, if not destroy, the mental and physical faculties of the prisoner. Attempts to carry out the Pennsylvania system ceased long before the rise of the twentieth-century vogue for evaluating results: the enormous expense of maintaining the system, the formidable difficulties of administering it, and the skill with which convicts evaded its rigors gradually brought it to an end. Its physical facilities remained intact, and were difficult to adapt to other kinds of treatment.

The Pennsylvania system has often been derided, and even more often denounced. Nevertheless, the original concept focused on the offender as an individual who had to be treated purposefully. Corporal punishment was forbidden, and aside from their enforced solitude, the prisoners were apparently well treated. The privacy of their life could well have reduced the sense of shame felt by convicts living in congregate prisons. Although the Pennsylvania prisoner may have left prison debilitated by years of rigorous restriction, he had not been subjected to the degradation of the lockstep, the whip, and the other features that proved necessary to the Auburn silent system, the rival penal regime of the nineteenth century.

The Auburn silent system. In the competition of ideas, the Auburn silent system emerged victorious over its Pennsylvania rival, but the contest was won on economic rather than conceptual grounds. Nevertheless, the victory had a lasting influence on the development of correctional treatment. Although they were primitive even for their own time, the assumptions on which the Auburn system rested have had a pervasive effect on corrections in the United States and have been the primary force in shaping the conceptual development of American penology. Until af-

ter the Civil War no one questioned their validity, despite many protests against the harshness of their application. The Auburn system's principles lingered long after the repudiation of their practice. They shaped the nature of American correctional treatment, influencing the architectural design of prisons and the organization of custodial operations, and contributed to the uniquely immense size of the American megaprison.

Unlike the Pennsylvania system, the Auburn silent system is not associated with the names of any early nineteenth-century intellectual or religious leaders. Early in its development it came under the domination of Elam Lynds (1784–1855), a veteran of the War of 1812 and a firm believer in rigorous discipline as the most appropriate method for the reform of criminals. The Auburn system was housed in a prison that Lynds did not design, but everything else about the system bore his indelible imprint. Among Lynds's assumptions about criminals were the views that they were inferior to the general run of humanity and that hard labor was necessary to their reform. When Gustave de Beaumont and Alexis de Tocqueville interviewed him during their survey of American prisons, Lynds frankly said that the first step in the reform of criminals was to break their spirit. He used the whip to reduce prisoners to the proper level of submissiveness and required them to move in lockstep from their cellblocks to the mess hall and the workplace. Any attempt by a prisoner to communicate with another was severely punished. Long hours of unpaid work were required, and Lynds boasted that the prisons he administered not only paid for themselves but made a profit for the state.

Emulation of Lynds's methods and results would be impossible in twentieth-century America, but his view of the nature of criminal man continues to be influential. For generations the belief persisted that criminals were mentally defective, and many still regard them as inferior owing to emotional or mental abnormality. Rather than attempt to treat them as individuals—an aim that clinicians and scholars alike have urged—prisoners are handled in the mass, sometimes by the hundreds, and correctional treatment is still administered under conditions of humiliating degradation.

Because the Auburn system was efficient in controlling large numbers of convicts, it was possible to build immense prisons. Great economies of scale have been claimed by their managers, but effective programs of correctional treatment are extremely difficult to administer under the conditions that necessarily prevail in such facilities. The legacy of the Auburn silent system is evident not only in the many surviving prisons that were designed in accordance with its principles, but also in its sedulous application to prison design decades after the abandonment of the system itself.

The reformatory movement. The ascendancy of brutality and the mass management of convicts throughout the nineteenth century did not go unopposed. Reformers exposed these conditions and brought before the courts various perpetrators of exceptional abuses of prisoners, including the redoubtable Warden Lynds—who was exonerated, as were most of his contemporaries. The reform movement eventually conceded that strong measures were needed to maintain control of convicts. Protests continued, but the progress of prison reform in the United States languished for want of alternatives to excessively harsh regimes.

After the Civil War, perspectives changed. Travelers returning from Europe reported innovations in the management of prisons that challenged reformers to propose adaptations suited to the American scene. The first result was the Elmira Reformatory, which became an archetype for American prisons.

Maconochie and the Norfolk experiment. The idea of training prisoners for freedom had been implicit in the thought of Beccaria and Bentham. It remained for an imaginative Scottish naval captain, Alexander Maconochie (1787–1860), to put their ideas into practice, although it is doubtful that he had read their works before he applied their ideas. Assigned to the office of the governor of New South Wales in 1840, he was given charge of the convict prison at Norfolk Island, an isolated spot in the Pacific Ocean more than 900 miles from Sydney.

At that time, Norfolk was reserved for convicts who had committed crimes after being transported to Australia. As recidivists, they were considered to deserve the utmost in severe punishment, and Maconochie's predecessors saw to it that they received it. On arriving at Norfolk, Maconochie immediately stopped the barbarous practices being inflicted on the convicts. He instituted a "mark" system that provided incentives for good conduct and application to work. By accumulating a sufficient number of marks a convict could gain amenities and eventually a "ticket of leave" that entitled him to live on the island as he pleased, within the limits of good conduct. The system seems to have been remarkably effective in preparing convicts for a return to free society, but it aroused the hostility of the colonial establishment. It was thought that any leniency practiced on Norfolk Island would compromise the presumed deterrent effect of commitment to that notoriously rigorous penal outpost. Penal

officials in New South Wales did not take kindly to Maconochie's liberal principles of prison governance, regardless of their success, and he was dismissed in 1844. He returned to England, convinced of the value of what he had done, and spent the remainder of his life writing and lecturing on prison management.

Crofton and the Irish mark system. One of Maconochie's disciples was Walter Crofton (1815–1897), who became the director of the Irish prison administration in 1854. In that capacity he was responsible for the development of the "Irish mark system," which became the model for the Elmira Reformatory and for the reformatory movement that swept through the United States in the latter part of the nineteenth century and the early twentieth century.

The Irish mark system was inspired by Maconochie's ill-fated Norfolk Island experiment. Crofton was a skillful administrator and an effective exponent of his ideas to superior officials and to the general public. In charge of Irish prisons for twelve years, he had the time and freedom to develop a system that eventually attracted worldwide interest. It was based on a recognition of society's right to punish, but Crofton insisted that prisoners must be trained for their return to society. The "marks" on which Maconochie had set store were given as incentives for satisfactory work and school performance. A certain number of marks would qualify the prisoner for transfer from the rigors of maximum security to an "intermediate" prison near one of several major cities of Ireland, where employment in agriculture or industry could be arranged. The eligible prisoner was awarded a ticket of leave and was transferred to the supervision of the police, who would ensure that his conduct justified his freedom. This last feature of the Irish system constituted the first aftercare program in penal history. Police supervision was criticized as harsh and stigmatizing, but it remained an integral element of the system.

The Elmira Reformatory. Crofton's ideas attracted prison reformers from many countries, including Gaylord Hubbell, warden of Sing Sing Prison in New York, who studied the Irish system in 1863. Reporting to the New York Prison Association on his observations, he aroused the enthusiastic interest of its members, who then formed a nucleus of reformers with a plan of action. A prison under construction at Elmira was designated a "reformatory," and a detailed plan of administration was drawn up for the new system of penal treatment. Admission was limited to first-offender felons between the ages of sixteen and thirty. The Irish system was followed methodically, with marks given for satisfactory behavior and industry, three graded levels of accommodation and privilege, and a period of aftercare supervision. To this imported structure of programs was added the original idea of the indeterminate sentence, which, wrote Frederick Wines, a sympathetic contemporary, "gave to the whole a wonderful vitality."

At Elmira, the superintendent decided on the prisoner's readiness for release. The accounts of Frederick Wines and of Zebulon Brockway (1827–1920), the first superintendent of the new reformatory, show that experience and intuition were generally relied on in making these decisions; the prisoner's fitness for release could not be judged solely by the marks he had accumulated. The institutional system of rewards and punishments served as incentives for the offender to cooperate in his own reform. The system could not predict the conditions that would confront the released offender in the community, but the reformatory did not intend to release anyone who had not responded appropriately to its program.

The Elmira regime was meant to be an active one. Vocational training, an educational program, hours of military drill, athletics and gymnastics, and moral and religious instruction filled the days of the prisoners. There was no industrial program in the original Elmira model; Brockway had to yield to the public sentiment that honest workmen should not be deprived of their livelihood in order that prisoners might be employed at useful labor. In spite of this concession—which penal administrators were to make many times during the next century—the Elmira regime was rigorous and exacting. One critic commented that its object seemed to be "to tire the man out with a strict daily routine to the point that he longs to go to bed early." Although principles were lofty, practice often fell far short. The mark system was allowed to decay, to the point that the compliant prisoners were assigned to the first graded level and the unruly to the third, with hardly any in the second. Corporal punishment was administered (with a paddle), but only by Brockway himself. Idealism was gradually eroded by realities, a process that has always confronted those who administer correctional facilities. Brockway retired from his reformatory disillusioned and disappointed.

Nevertheless, Brockway's influence was enormous. He had served as superintendent of Elmira from its opening in 1876 until his retirement in 1900. Earlier, in 1870, he had joined with Enoch Cobb Wines (1806–1879) in organizing the first meeting of the National Prison Association, later called the American Correctional Association. On this climactic occasion authorities from Europe, including the famous Walter Crof-

ton, addressed delegates from most of the states on the new, more hopeful concepts of penology. Wines and Brockway described in great detail the plan for the Elmira Reformatory, receiving an enthusiastic endorsement. The assembled wardens and reformers joined in adopting a Declaration of Principles: thirty-seven precepts that stressed the responsibility of prison administrators to undertake the reform of prisoners. Of these principles, it has often been said that they are as appropriate for the guidance of penology a century after their adoption as they were when written, but as difficult to apply. In spite of the disparity between principles and practice, the declaration of 1870 marked the beginning of a preoccupation with the standards of correctional treatment that has persisted throughout the subsequent history of American penology.

The first meetings of the National Prison Association spurred the dissemination of the reformatory idea throughout the United States. Before the end of the century twelve states had built facilities on the Elmira model, and by 1933 there were eleven more. Like the Irish prisons, where the mark system was developed, Elmira became a magnet for reformers from all over the world. One visit which was especially significant for the future of correctional treatment was that of Evelyn Ruggles-Brise (1857–1935), who arrived in 1897, two years after his appointment as chairman of the British Prison Commission. Ruggles-Brise was determined to change the character of the harsh and repressive British prisons. Deeply impressed with the Elmira system, he returned to England and began preparations for a reformatory system for young offenders that was to become famous as the Borstal system.

The Borstal system. Borstal is a small town in Kent where a prison was converted into a reformatory under plans originally drawn up by Ruggles-Brise and later elaborated under the charismatic leadership of Alexander Paterson (1884–1947), for many years a member of the Prison Commission. Admission to the Borstal training was limited to youths between the ages of sixteen and twenty-one. The Borstal system rapidly grew to a circuit of more than twenty small facilities to which boys (called "lads" in the Borstal terminology) were sent from a reception center in London. Diagnostic procedures were developed to facilitate decisions as to the specific Borstal destination, since some Borstals were designated for boys of limited intelligence, some specialized in vocational training, and some offered remedial education. One celebrated Borstal was a camp on the North Sea where boys who were expected to be unskilled laborers worked at a land reclamation project jointly with the Borstal staff. Another Borstal was reserved for youths who had failed in aftercare. In contrast to the Elmira-style reformatories in the United States, whose populations sometimes exceeded 1,500, all the Borstals were small, seldom housing more than 200 "lads."

Throughout his long career, Paterson was convinced that it was "men and not buildings that will change the ways of misguided lads. The foundations of the Borstal system are first the recruitment of the right men" (quoted in Fox, p. 356). Many of the men Paterson recruited for Borstal service eventually transferred to prisons, where they fostered programs more constructive than the demeaning make-work that had characterized British prisons in the years before Ruggles-Brise. The treatment programs administered in the Borstals varied widely, and the overall success of the system in its "golden age" was unquestionably attributable to a staff that created environments favorable to correctional treatment.

The Borstal system was adapted in the Scandinavian countries and in the Netherlands. Its influence is also to be seen in many of the youth training schools established in the United States after World War II, especially those that were organized into state systems under the model Youth Corrections Act formulated by the American Law Institute and published in the early 1940s.

In England there has been a gradual decline in the perceived effectiveness of Borstal training since the early 1960s. Many causes for the decline have been suggested. The Criminal Justice Act, 1961, 9 &10 Eliz. 2, c. 39 (Great Britain) required that all youths between the ages of sixteen and twenty-one who are to serve terms of more than six months but less than three years be committed to Borstals regardless of their suitability for training, a requirement that made it impossible to reject boys for whom the system had no appropriate program. Perhaps because of the statutory changes of 1961, Borstals are now distinguishable from one another more by the length of the terms to be served in them than by what the boys do while serving their terms. It has also been suggested that the profound changes taking place in the English class structure may account for the apparent erosion of the system's effectiveness. Working-class youths, especially those of the racial minorities, are no longer as amenable to the guidance of upper-middle-class Borstal governors and housemasters as they were in the age of Paterson.

In England, other approaches to the treatment of the youthful offender have supplemented the Borstal system. Youthful offenders with more than three years to serve are sent to the Young Prisoners' Centers, where specialized programs of work and training are administered separately from those for adult prisoners in the same facility. Youths whose crimes do not warrant a Borstal assignment are committed to the Detention Centers, where strenuous work and athletics are emphasized. In the Attendance Centers, youths spend Saturday afternoons working under the direction of police officers.

The Borstal system is no longer a model emulated throughout the world. It survives as a structure for the incarcerative punishment of moderately serious young offenders. Like the reformatory everywhere else, it has yet to find a plan for treatment that is suited to delinquent youth in an age when social values and economic opportunities have changed dramatically.

Probation and parole. Probation had its origin in ordinary philanthropy, innocent of any pretensions to conceptual depth or juridical principle. The familiar story of John Augustus (1784–1859), a shoemaker in Lexington, Massachusetts, serves to illustrate the strengths and weaknesses of probation as a vehicle for correctional treatment. Augustus became interested in court procedure in his community and was impressed with the destructive futility of incarceration for drunkards, prostitutes, and petty offenders. Gradually he developed a system whereby he would bail out an offender after conviction and undertake to supervise his conduct in the community. Augustus's highly personal approach included aid to the offender's family, arrangements to find him employment, and friendly counseling over a reasonable period of time. At an agreed point, Augustus would report the offender's progress to the court, and sentence on the original offense would be pronounced. Usually it was a fine of one cent, and the offender would be sent home.

Augustus began his work in 1827. By 1858, a year before his death, he had bailed out nearly two thousand offenders, with what lasting success we cannot know. It was not until 1878 that the first public probation agencies were authorized by statute in Massachusetts, and only in 1899 did the practice of probation gather real momentum with the inception of the juvenile court movement, for which a probation service was an obvious necessity. Since that time the assistance that John Augustus gave out of his pocket as a volunteer has been rendered almost exclusively by official agencies in most communities.

The strength of the probation idea lies in the economy afforded by maintaining offenders in the community instead of sending them to prison or jail, and in the humane assistance provided by the probation officer. If the supply of talented and resourceful volunteers were sufficient, it would be hard to justify the creation of official agencies. Unfortunately, the supply is neither sufficient nor reliable. Accordingly, the state has set up probation agencies, manned by civil servants, to carry out community correctional treatment. To the tasks of treatment and assistance to offenders, responsibilities have been added for presentence investigations, surveillance of the probationer, and reports to the court on probation violations. The problems involved in carrying out all these functions properly can be dealt with only by probation officers with exceptional personal qualities.

An identical conflict confronts the parole officer, who works under different auspices in most jurisdictions. The history of parole began with the ticket of leave granted to transported prisoners in Australia in Maconochie's time, a procedure adopted by Crofton as part of the Irish mark system. The released offender was kept under surveillance and was to be returned to custody if he violated the terms of his ticket of leave. The Elmira and Borstal systems elevated the surveillance principle into a requirement that the released prisoner be assisted as well as watched. Ever since, correctional theorists have attempted to reconcile surveillance with treatment by asserting that surveillance confronts the offender with reality by making him face the consequences of his actions, whether good or bad. In proposing this principle, the theoreticians of probation and parole do not instruct the practitioner as to how a relationship of trust between the agent and the offender may be created.

Although the differences between probation and parole are important in legal and social contexts, the treatment problems are identical. Most offenders find themselves in difficult social and economic straits. They need work, as well as help in finding it. For such assistance most are willing enough to turn to the probation or parole agency, which generally provides these services.

As the social-work profession took shape in the 1920s, a movement began that sought to adapt casework principles to the correctional setting. The monitor of probation compliance and the friendly benefactor were to be replaced by the impersonal professionalism of the counselor-therapist. None of these patterns has prevailed. The probation officer and the parole officer have found themselves in the uneasy position of balancing all three roles. Their predicament has been complicated by inadequate training, indiscriminate recruiting policies, and case

loads that are usually far too heavy to allow efficient fulfillment of any of these functions.

The development of juvenile correctional treatment. Long before the establishment of the first juvenile court in Illinois in 1899, many states had built reform schools for juvenile delinquents that sometimes housed children as young as seven or eight years of age. These schools had the indisputable merit of keeping children out of prisons and jails, but their positive achievements were usually minimal. Most superintendents had great difficulty keeping their charges occupied; hence the easily rationalized allocation of many hours each day to military drill on the pretext that this discipline was invaluable for developing the self-control that delinquent boys needed to keep out of trouble when they were returned to the community. Before the creation of the juvenile court apparatus, no other official response to the delinquency of a minor was available. A number of states had no juvenile institutions at all, relying on prisons for older children and admonitions for younger ones.

The juvenile court was intended to change the entire philosophy of criminal justice as applied to children. Instead of requiring minors charged with crimes to be subjected to common-law procedures in a criminal court, the juvenile court was expected to act in the best interests of the child, under the chancery principle of *parens patriae*. The child's interests might still require residential treatment in a public institution, but it was expected that less drastic intervention would be more effective for most children in trouble. The early years of the juvenile court in Chicago, where the juvenile justice movement had its origins, coincided with the early years of professional social work. It was natural that the probation officers would be men and women who had been exposed to the concepts of social diagnosis and social casework. Treatment was to be based on the identification of each child's social and psychological needs. Not long after the creation of the Cook County juvenile court, the associated Institute for Juvenile Research, established in Chicago, began conducting diagnostic procedures on an interdisciplinary basis.

The principle that a delinquent child needs remedial services rather than punishment was often distorted in practice but never abandoned. Much was made of the function of the juvenile detention facility for the juvenile in trouble, pending development of a plan for his rehabilitation. The resemblance of many juvenile detention facilities (especially those in metropolitan centers) to the jails from which children had been removed was glossed over. What was considered important was that within the detention centers the child's life history was compiled and diagnostic procedures were worked out.

As case studies became more comprehensive and diagnosis more precise, treatment procedures could not match them in fitting remedies to the conditions to be corrected. Education, vocational training, counseling, and group therapy constituted the gamut of juvenile correctional treatment. Each of these approaches could be beneficial in the hands of gifted and sensitive professionals, but such persons are scarce in juvenile corrections, where working conditions are usually unpleasant and failure of the best efforts is all too probable. In a searching study of life in such an institution, Howard Polsky discovered that the brutally exploitative life in the "cottages" where boys resided had little relation to the carefully tuned therapy offered by counselors and psychologists in the central treatment clinics. This finding was emphatically confirmed by the observations of Clemens Bartollas, Stuart Miller, and Simon Dinitz, who described the endemic violence of a small, treatment-oriented institution for serious juvenile offenders in which the treatment had become virtually irrelevant to the residents' present and future ways of life.

From the time of the Supreme Court's decision in *In re Gault,* 387 U.S. 1 (1967), juvenile justice has been preoccupied with the constitutional and moral issues presented by the special structure of the juvenile court. Acknowledging these perplexities, critics believe that the most serious problem in juvenile justice reform is the disposition of young offenders. In view of the unreliability of the treatment programs in use, it has been said that the best course of action is to do nothing at all. Inactivity may be the best policy for many children, but for the occasional violent children who must be subjected to residential control, effective treatment has yet to be designed. Neither community treatment on probation nor special care during incarceration has yielded enough consistent success to justify optimistic expectations.

Summary. There have been many false starts since attempts at correctional treatment began in the late eighteenth century. Although official commitment to treatment concepts has been firm, actual practice has been found wanting. Correctional clinicians are often capable of applying a high polish to offender social histories and to the interpretation of projective psychological tests, but treatment has been limited mainly to education and psychological intervention. It has frequently been asserted that the uneven performance of correctional treatment is primarily attributable to a lack of adequate funds, personnel, and other resources. Although resources have indeed been mea-

ger, it is also true that reliable programs for treatment of offenders have not emerged from the subtle diagnostic procedures that have been in use.

Faced with ineffectual programs and chronically inadequate support, the practice of correctional treatment is heavily influenced by the nature of the offender's experience while he is under control. This ranges from the intimidation of harsh incarcerative control to the relatively benign climate of individualized assistance. The evidence suggests that neither approach is reliably successful, and the failures are sometimes so dramatic as to shake public confidence in the entire criminal justice system.

The practice of correctional treatment

The legacy of Zebulon Brockway and the Elmira Reformatory was a system of correctional diagnosis and treatment that became the standard for American corrections. A sequence of diagnosis, classification, treatment, and assessment of progress was eventually to lead the offender to such improvement in attitudes and behavior that a paroling authority could release him to the community under supervision. After a suitable period of favorable adjustment, supervision could be terminated.

The same progressive system was suited to the administration of probation. A presentence investigation would advise the court regarding the offender's eligibility for a community treatment program. With the court's approval, a plan for the probationer's reinstatement in the community would be made. The probation officer would act as a counselor and monitor, and would report to the court on the success or failure of the plan.

The indeterminate sentence. The concept of the indeterminate sentence was considered essential to correctional treatment. Release of the offender from control depended not so much on the gravity of the crime as on his individual need for treatment. The indeterminate sentence was originally intended for the young first-term convict assigned to reformatories, but its principle soon spread to all correctional programs. The logic was obvious: a person convicted of a felony would not have committed his crime if he were not affected by some deficiency of character or education that had to be corrected. If released without remedial treatment, he could be expected to repeat his offense. It followed that release under the indeterminate sentence laws could not be allowed when a change for the better had not taken place. From the first, it was agreed that there also had to be an improvement in the social conditions of the home or neighborhood to which the prisoner would return.

The logic was plausible enough, but the realities of crime and the surrounding social conditions were such that results seldom matched expectations. The treatment administered as a precondition to release was seen as treatment under duress: resisted by some, manipulated by others, and benefiting principally those who needed it least. In most correctional facilities, programs were insufficient to meet the needs identified by diagnosis and were usually administered by personnel with minimal qualifications.

Treatment in American correctional institutions must be understood in the context of the indeterminate sentence. By the coercive effect of relating release to the offender's progress toward rehabilitation, the indeterminate sentence effectively deprived him of any volition in an effort toward self-improvement. In addition, the indeterminate sentence furnished the keepers with their most powerful instrument for the control of the kept. Compliance with prison discipline was always a primary determinant of the duration of a prisoner's confinement.

In European countries, most of which did not adopt the indeterminate sentence, other patterns have prevailed. The procedures of diagnosis and classification are faithfully carried out, but as a rule only work and compliance with regulations are mandatory; efforts at self-improvement are optional with the prisoner himself. Except for prisoners suffering from serious mental disturbances, few attempts at psychological intervention are made.

Although there is a consensus on the futility of coerced treatment, the years in which it was attempted saw the introduction of a wide variety of programs intended to assist or reform prisoners. Some experimental research has been attempted in an effort to evaluate them. Most of these studies have yielded inconclusive (or, occasionally, negative) findings. Policies resulting from these conclusions have yet to be formulated; in the meantime, correctional treatment survives in many forms.

Religious instruction. The professional service that first found its way into the prison was the chaplaincy. Priests and ministers saw their responsibility to preach, to counsel, and to teach the elements of religion to the men and women who inhabited the prisons and jails. They were still more concerned with ministering to the spiritual needs of children in correctional institutions. Even the stern Auburn silent system conformed to the accepted requirement that criminals in prison must be provided with religious services. In the Pennsylvania system, worship services were the only occasions when prisoners could be allowed to assemble, even though they were not permitted to communicate with one another. Ministers and elders of the Society of Friends were also expected to visit prisoners in their cells for counseling and instruction.

The response of the prisoners to these efforts is unknown, but the employment of chaplains, usually at state expense, has always been standard in American and British prisons. Attendance at services has long been optional, and it is generally low, owing to the clergy's inadequate preparation for their duties in prison, the inappropriateness of the services that are offered to prison populations, the absence of a curriculum for religious education, and the prisoners' lack of religious background. The overidentification of some chaplains with the interests of the prison administration has alienated many prisoners.

The success of the Black Muslim movement in gaining converts among prisoners suggests that when clergymen from the community are allowed to proselyte and to conduct services in which prisoners can play true congregational roles, religious participation increases. Unfortunately, clergy from most denominations are not prepared for this kind of pastoral care.

Academic education. It has always been recognized that most offenders come to prison with substantial educational deficiencies. The average educational level of prisoners reflects the condition of the school systems of the states in which they live. In no state does the average school achievement score of arriving prisoners exceed the ninth-grade level, and in some states the average score will approximate the fifth or sixth grade. Many convicts are either functionally or totally illiterate.

Little is known of the effect of prison education on the reduction of recidivism. In a study of 1,051 prisoners released from federal prisons in 1956, Daniel Glaser found that those prisoners who had not attended prison school committed fewer crimes after release than those who had. Glaser tentatively concluded that for most prisoners, the prevailing prison education program was associated with higher-than-average post-release failures. This study has never been replicated, in spite of Glaser's view that its conclusions should be regarded with caution.

A study conducted by John Conrad in 1981 found wide differences in the quality and value of correctional education. Some states, most notably Minnesota and Texas, have been remarkably innovative in their use of computer-assisted instruction and other advanced technology. The experience of these correctional systems is seen as a significant contribution to the development of adult education in prisons.

The lack of authoritative evaluation of academic education is a serious handicap to its further development. Because programmed activity is essential to the orderly and humane administration of the contemporary prison, it is vital that educational programs be offered as effectively and attractively as possible, but in an era of lost confidence in correctional rehabilitation, some administrators tend to assume that funds allocated to education will be wasted. Nevertheless, through intuition and reliance on experience and the available research, they continue to provide extensive educational programs in order to keep prisoners constructively busy. The urgent need to maximize return on this investment in education can only be met by more vigorous study of its results.

Vocational training. As with academic education, little has been done to evaluate vocational training. The logic supporting it is as persuasive as that which is advanced for academic education. Almost all prisoners are educable and trainable, but very few have any regular experience of work or any demonstrable skill at a trade. Clearly, investment should be made in practical instruction aimed at enabling prisoners to obtain steady, remunerative employment after their release. This proposition was embodied in the Declaration of Principles formulated at the first meeting of the National Prison Association in 1870. The consensus as to its validity has been nearly unanimous among penologists ever since.

Realization of the principle has fallen sadly short of expectations. Some excellent training programs have achieved remarkable results, but they are isolated examples. For the most part, vocational training is conducted with inadequate or obsolete equipment, and instructors are poorly prepared. Too often the training is intended to meet institutional maintenance needs rather than the formal requirements of an apprenticeship.

A more formidable problem is the great expense of equipment necessary for many training programs that can prepare prisoners for entry into a skilled trade. Even when this investment can be made, it is often found that many unions are reluctant to accept released prisoners as members. The most difficult problem of all is the insufficient time for training that a prison term allows. The average term of two or three years does not permit the completion of apprenticeship requirements for most trades, even when the prisoner has had an adequate level of preparatory education. Waiting lists for entry into training programs, assignment of unpaid inmate trainees to industrial programs that offer wages, and the inertia inherent in prison life often keep offenders from participating in training until it is too late to learn enough to make participation worthwhile.

Some impressive reports suggest that when liaison with an outside industry is established and when competent instruction in modern prison shops is offered, remarkable successes are achieved in placing prisoners in good jobs, with very low recidivism reported. However, successes are usually achieved with those individuals whose post-release success would be probable in any event. In sum, whether for adult or juvenile offenders, vocational training must be regarded as a costly program of most benefit to individuals with good educational preparation whose intelligence and motivation are consistent with a law-abiding life.

Industrial employment. A persistent theme in the history of the modern prison has been the requirement that the convicted criminal serve a period of "hard labor," a term that has never been adequately defined. Nineteenth-century English prisons kept convicts busy at sewing mailbags or cleaning hemp by hand. Sometimes completely unproductive tasks were set: prisoners were required to turn a resistant crank or to walk for hours on a treadmill. In nineteenth-century America, on the other hand, there was a chronic labor shortage, and hard but productive work could usually be found for convicts. Where farming was the usual employment, convicts were kept at work from sunrise to sunset. Road gangs worked in the same way, as did prisoners in factories and prison mines.

Public sentiment put an end to the crank and the treadmill in England. Contemporary English prisoners are generally employed, although not at recognizable levels of industrial efficiency. In the United States, hard labor has been replaced by overmanned dawdling and outright idleness. The cause is not hard to find. Neither employers nor organized labor welcomes the intrusion of the unpaid prison laborer in the free and competitive market. Both federal and state legislation have generally limited the sale of goods produced by prison labor, however paid, to a portion of the state-use market, or, in the case of the federal prisons, to the larger federal government market.

Even within these limits, much more could be done in most states. Initial outlays of capital are necessary for any industry, and for most, these outlays must be large. Few legislatures have been willing to make sufficient funds available for efficient production. A more enlightened policy has been adopted by the United States Congress, which has allocated funds to support relatively advanced industries producing goods for various federal operations, including those of the Department of Defense. For many years the Federal Prison Industries has been able to report a modest profit. Although federal government needs are large enough to permit it to purchase from state prison industries as well, little has been done to open this market to any correctional agencies except the United States Bureau of Prisons.

Many European prisons, on the other hand, produce not only for the state market but for the free market as well. In some systems, notably in Scandinavia, wages comparable to those in the free market are paid to prisoners. This trend is less general in the United States, but some progress has been made toward raising American prison wages to an acceptable level.

Since the mid-1970s a few state departments of corrections have sought to emulate private-sector standards in prison industry operations. Under the Free Venture Program initiated by the Law Enforcement Assistance Administration in 1976, state prison industries, which previously had existed as alternatives to complete idleness, were encouraged to become economically self-sufficient by adopting industrial standards of productivity, management, and marketing. In 1979 Congress passed the Justice System Improvement Act of 1979, Pub. L. No. 96-157, 93 Stat. 1167 (codified in scattered sections of 5, 18, 41, 42 U.S.C.), which authorized pilot projects that would contract with the private sector to produce goods for interstate commerce. Through such efforts, industries in some prisons have become productive operations providing benefits to the public, the prison, and the prisoner-employee.

These programs are vulnerable to the same economic vicissitudes confronting the private sector, and they must also face the criticism that in times of high unemployment, prisoners should be less eligible for wage-earning jobs than citizens who are out of work. Further, it has yet to be shown that all work in any prison system can be put on a Free Venture basis. Some critics argue that Free Venture and similar programs create an elite of favored prisoners who enjoy the privilege of well-paid employment that is denied to those who lack the education or skills required in Free Venture shops. These justified criticisms throw into bold relief the agonizing dilemma of penal policy. The destructive effects of chronic idleness are not mitigated by assigning prisoners to make-work jobs or by arranging for several men to labor all day at tasks that a single one could finish in an hour. But any plan for full employment for convicts in a society in which full employment for all citizens is seldom achieved is an anomaly that the state cannot easily justify. The few cautious experiments, such as the Free Venture Program, are welcome steps toward an end to the intolerable idleness that has prevailed in American prisons, but it remains to be seen whether this growth can be appreciable. Until useful labor with effective pay incentives for diligence and care can be provided for inmates, order and safety in American prisons will be precarious, and the deterioration of prisoners during their confinement must be expected.

Social and psychological intervention. The interest of volunteers in assisting offenders has persisted throughout the history of American prisons and has been responsible for many important reforms. No estimate has ever been made of the success of such friendly contact, but its value is indicated by the numbers of prisoners who accept these relationships wherever they are encouraged by prison management. This level of intervention, based on simple friendship, was the only kind of social assistance available to prisoners until the rapid growth of modern psychiatry in the twentieth century.

Modern psychiatric concepts aroused expectations that criminals, generally regarded as psychopaths, might be "cured" by psychiatric intervention. The concept of psychopathy, as developed over a century of clinical work, is still "slippery." The attributes of psychopaths, such as lack of conscience, inability to form personal attachments, and indifference to the feelings of others, are viewed by psychiatrists as major obstacles to treatment. Indeed, many clinicians regard psychopathy as an essentially untreatable condition because of the subject's inability to form lasting relationships. Nevertheless, some clinicians have persisted in attempts to create methods of therapy that would reach the attitudes and behavior of the *sociopath*, as psychopaths are now generally designated. Such names as William Healy, August Aichhorn, Franz Alexander, Fritz Redl, and Karl Menninger have been associated, beginning in the 1920s, with the development of psychological approaches to the treatment of offenders. Although they and many others have added greatly to the understanding of offenders and the drives that propel them into delinquency, no generally established regimen of treatment has resulted.

Treatment approaches have been divided between individual and group therapy; the range of professional sophistication in each has varied widely. Individual treatment of offenders has generally consisted of practical counseling conducted by persons with meager professional preparation, although there have also been some adaptations of classical psychoanalysis. The economics of professional psychiatric care have limited its availability to offenders. Counseling is generally restricted to adaptations of social casework, usually addressed to personal emergencies or plans for the future.

Group treatment has been much more popular, especially in incarcerative settings. As with individual counseling, the quality varies from professionally led psychotherapeutic treatment groups to group counseling conducted by personnel with minimal training. Many of the methods applied have been highly idiosyncratic, based on such vogues as those of "guided group interaction," "therapeutic communities," and "reality therapy," as well as some treatment activities developed by persons with few, if any, professional credentials.

Anecdotal evidence of the benefits of these kinds of intervention is abundant, but statistical evaluation has been inconclusive. This state of affairs is likely to continue. There has never been successful proof of the value of psychotherapy in general practice, except the case studies of clinicians. It is probable that this kind of treatment is not susceptible to statistical evaluation.

Summary. The presence of clinical personnel within the correctional apparatus has undoubtedly conferred secondary benefits outweighing their success in achieving behavior changes in offenders. The professionalization of corrections and an insistence on minimum standards of care and on the individual treatment of offenders have coincided with the introduction of clinicians in correctional facilities. When the offender is seen as a person to be treated clinically, he ceases to be merely an object for control. If clinical approaches and a sense of fairness are to prevail in the criminal justice system, the system must accommodate itself to the needs of the persons under control rather than to economies of scale and the convenience of management. To the extent that the correctional experience can be attuned to the needs of individuals rather than to those of the system, the destructive impact of incarceration and intrusive social control will be mitigated.

JOHN PHILLIPS CONRAD

See also CORRECTIONAL REFORM ASSOCIATIONS; CRIMINAL JUSTICE SYSTEM: OVERVIEW; INCAPACITATION; JAILS; PREDICTION OF CRIME AND RECIDIVISM; *articles under* PRISONS; *articles under* PROBATION AND PAROLE; REHABILITATION.

BIBLIOGRAPHY

American Institute of Criminal Justice. *Guide to Effective Prison Industries.* 7 vols. Philadelphia: The Institute, 1979.

BARNES, HARRY ELMER, and TEETERS, NEGLEY K. *New Horizons in Criminology.* 3d ed. Englewood Cliffs, N.J.: Prentice-Hall, 1959. Still by far the most comprehensive textbook of criminology, this volume traces in detail the history and development of the principles and practice of correctional treatment.

BARRY, JOHN VINCENT. *Alexander Maconochie of Norfolk Island: A Study of a Pioneer in Penal Reform.* Foreword by Sheldon Glueck. New York: Oxford University Press, 1958.

BARTOLLAS, CLEMENS; MILLER, STUART J.; and DINITZ, SIMON. *Juvenile Victimization: The Institutional Paradox.* Beverly Hills, Calif.: Sage, 1976. An unsparing account of the contrast between the principles of correctional treatment and their application in a youth correctional institution in Ohio.

BECCARIA, CESARE. *On Crimes and Punishments* (1764). Translated with an introduction by Henry Paolucci. Indianapolis: Bobbs-Merrill, 1963. Along with the work of Jeremy Bentham, this essay must be counted as the beginning of modern penology, and the basis for the adoption of the prison as the alternative to torture and the death penalty.

BROCKWAY, ZEBULON R. *Fifty Years of Prison Service: An Autobiography* (1912). Montclair, N.J.: Patterson Smith, 1969. Most of this volume is an apologia for the Elmira Reformatory, written by the architect of its original program and its first superintendent.

CONRAD, JOHN P. *Adult Offender Education Programs.* Washington, D.C.: National Institute of Justice, 1981.

DUNLOP, ANNE B., and MCCABE, SARAH. *Young Men in Detention Centers.* New York: Humanities Press, 1965.

ERIKSSON, TORSTEN. *The Reformers: An Historical Survey of Pioneer Experiments in the Treatment of Criminals.* Translated by Catherine Djurklou. New York: Elsevier, 1976.

FOX, LIONEL W. *The English Prison and Borstal Systems: An Account of the Prison and Borstal Systems in England and Wales after the Criminal Justice Act, 1948, with a Historical Introduction and an Examination of the Principles of Imprisonment as a Legal Punishment.* London: Routledge, 1952.

GLASER, DANIEL. *The Effectiveness of a Prison and Parole System.* Indianapolis: Bobbs-Merrill, 1964.

HOOD, ROGER. *Borstal Re-assessed.* London: Heinemann, 1965.

HUSSEY, FREDERICK A., and DUFFEE, DAVID E. *Probation, Parole, and Community Field Services: Policy, Structure, and Process.* New York: Harper & Row, 1980.

JACOBS, JAMES B. *Stateville: The Penitentiary in Mass Society.* University of Chicago Press, 1977.

KASSEBAUM, GENE G.; WARD, DAVID A.; and WILNER, DANIEL L. *Prison Treatment and Parole Survival: An Empirical Assessment.* New York: Wiley, 1971. A carefully designed evaluation of the California group-counseling program which found that its impact on prisoners did not have any statistically discernible effects.

LEMERT, EDWIN M., and DILL, FORREST. *Offenders in the Community: The Probation Subsidy in California.* Lexington, Mass.: Heath, Lexington Books, 1978.

LEWIS, WALTER DAVID. *From Newgate to Dannemora: The Rise of the Penitentiary in New York, 1796–1848.* Ithaca, N.Y.: Cornell University Press, 1965. A full and detailed account of the development and eventual eclipse of the Auburn silent system.

LIPTON, DOUGLAS; MARTINSON, ROBERT; and WILKS, JUDITH. *The Effectiveness of Correctional Treatment: A Survey of Treatment Evaluation Studies.* New York: Praeger, 1975. A review of all treatment evaluations conducted prior to 1967. It concludes that few programs were effective, and has been influential in discrediting rehabilitation programs and concepts.

MACK, MARY PETER, ed. *A Bentham Reader.* New York: Pegasus, 1969.

McCLINTOCK, FREDERICK H.; WALKER, MONICA A.; and SAVILL, N. C. *Attendance Centres: An Enquiry by the Cambridge Institute of Criminology on the Use of Section 19 of the Criminal Justice Act, 1948.* New York: St. Martin's, 1961.

PALMER, TED. *Correctional Intervention and Research: Current Issues and Future Prospects.* Lexington, Mass.: Heath, Lexington Books, 1978. A response to Lipton, Martinson, and Wilks, contending that the findings reported do not accurately represent the effectiveness of correctional treatment.

PLATO. *Collected Dialogues.* Edited by Edith Hamilton and Huntington Cairns. New York: Pantheon Books, 1961. In the *Protagoras* and the *Gorgias*, Plato established his view that punishment should be administered to correct the offender, rather than for "blind vengeance." In the *Laws* he prescribed a severe regime intended to change the behavior of offenders by counseling and intimidation.

POLSKY, HOWARD W. *Cottage Six: The Social System of Delinquent Boys in Residential Treatment.* New York: Russell Sage, 1962. Valuable for a discussion of the disparity between program intentions and realities.

STUDT, ELLIOT; MESSINGER, SHELDON L.; and WILSON, THOMAS P. *C-Unit: The Search for Community in Prison.* New York: Russell Sage, 1968. An account of a project designed to create a therapeutic community setting in a youth-training facility. Especially valuable for its insights into the obstacles to effective treatment.

WINES, ENOCH C., ed. *Transactions of the First National Congress on Penitentiary and Reformatory Discipline, Cincinnati, Ohio, October 12–18, 1870.* Reprint. Washington, D.C.: American Correctional Association, 1970. Of considerable historical interest, containing addresses by Brockway, Crofton, and other penal authorities. Includes the original version of the Declaration of Principles.

CORRECTIONS

See CAREERS IN CRIMINAL JUSTICE: CORRECTIONS; CORRECTIONAL REFORM ASSOCIATIONS; CORRECTIONAL TREATMENT.

CORRUPTION

See BRIBERY; FEDERAL CRIMINAL LAW ENFORCEMENT; ORGANIZED CRIME: OVERVIEW; POLICE: MISCONDUCT.

COSTS OF CRIME

See CRIME STATISTICS: COSTS OF CRIME.

COUNSEL

The RIGHT TO COUNSEL *article explores the dimensions of the constitutional right to counsel in criminal cases provided in the Sixth Amendment to the United States Constitution. The article on* ROLE OF COUNSEL *discusses the various functions which the defense attorney, whether retained or appointed, should perform in the criminal process.*

1. RIGHT TO COUNSEL   Arval A. Morris
2. ROLE OF COUNSEL   Peter W. Tague

1.
RIGHT TO COUNSEL

American criminal procedure is founded upon the adversary system of justice. To function properly, the adversary system must be balanced, for the essence of the system is challenge—an incessant searching and a rigorous questioning of each governmental accusation, assertion, or decision at every stage of the criminal law process. Consequently, a vigorous defense role played by the accused during a criminal trial is as important to the proper functioning and well-being of the adversary system as are the roles played by an active prosecutor and an astute, impartial judge. Since all prosecutors are professional criminal law lawyers but defendants are not, the adversary system is seriously out of balance initially. A necessary remedy that partially redresses the balance is the right of the accused to the effective assistance of counsel. This right is "the most pervasive" of all rights a defendant has because "it affects his ability to assert any other rights he may have" (Schaefer, p. 8).

The Sixth Amendment to the Constitution of the United States provides that "in all criminal prosecutions, the accused shall enjoy the right . . . to have the Assistance of Counsel for his defence." Despite this clear, mandatory, and unequivocal language, only accused persons charged with death-penalty crimes in federal courts have been guaranteed this right throughout American history, and then only because of a federal statute passed before the Sixth Amendment became part of the Constitution (Judiciary Act of 1789, ch. 20, 1 Stat. 73).

The historical right to assistance of counsel of all defendants in state cases has depended on a defendant's capacity to pay for his own attorney and on state law. This situation existed because the Sixth Amendment initially was applied only to protect the right to privately hired counsel and then only to criminal trials prosecuted in federal courts. Today, however, the right to the assistance of privately retained counsel is "unqualified," so that any denial of a defendant's right to the assistance of his privately retained lawyer on any issue in any criminal prosecution, state or federal, is a per se violation of "fundamental fairness" and a denial of due process of law (*Chandler v. Fretag,* 348 U.S. 3 (1954); *Reynolds v. Cochran,* 365 U.S. 525 (1961); *Ferguson v. Georgia,* 365 U.S. 570 (1961)).

Appointed counsel for trial

Nature of the charge. In the 1930s, the Supreme Court began to enlarge the class of persons guaranteed the assistance of a lawyer, paid by the state if necessary. In 1932, after first analyzing the need to balance the adversary system, the Court declared that the right to counsel was so fundamental to our adversary system that the due process clause of the Fourteenth Amendment required states to provide the effective assistance of counsel during the trial of all defendants charged with state death-penalty crimes (*Powell v. Alabama,* 287 U.S. 45 (1932)). Six years later, in *Johnson v. Zerbst,* 304 U.S. 458 (1938), the Court ruled that federal courts must appoint lawyers for all indigent defendants during the trial of every federal felony case, stating that "the Sixth Amendment . . . embodies a realistic recognition of the obvious truth that the average defendant does not have the professional legal skill to protect himself when brought before a tribunal with power to take his life or liberty, wherein the prosecution is represented by experienced and learned counsel" (462–463).

Four years later, in 1942, the Supreme Court refused to extend the Sixth Amendment's guaranteed right to counsel to all state felony trials. Oddly, the Court did not focus on the requirement of balance in the adversary system in state criminal trials but instead addressed itself to various classes of cases, ruling that a lawyer was not required in every state felony trial. In addition to death-penalty cases, the Court held, a lawyer must be provided by the state only in those complex state criminal cases having "special circumstances" where a lack of counsel would produce a trial devoid of "fundamental fairness." The Court ruled that an "asserted denial [of fundamental fairness] is to be tested by an appraisal of the totality of facts in a given case" to see if they "constitute a denial of fundamental fairness, shocking to the universal sense of justice" (*Betts v. Brady,* 316 U.S. 455 (1942)). This approach was unsound for several reasons. For example, a trial judge could not know until after the completion of the trial whether the "totality of facts" was such that appointment of counsel at the beginning of the trial was warranted! The Supreme Court overruled *Betts* in *Gideon v. Wainwright,* 372 U.S. 335 (1963), holding the Sixth Amendment's right to the effective assistance of counsel to be so "fundamental and essential to a fair trial" that in all felony cases it must be "made obligatory upon the States by [the due process clause of] the Fourteenth Amendment."

Left open was the question of the rule that governed the availability of counsel for indigent accuseds during trial of misdemeanors. In addition to the right to the assistance of counsel, the Sixth Amendment provides that an accused shall have the right to a jury trial "in all criminal prosecutions." However, this provision has always been interpreted to mean that juries are not required in trying "petty offenses" (*Duncan v. Louisiana,* 391 U.S. 145 (1968)). An offense is not "petty" if it carries a possible penalty of more than six months' imprisonment (*Baldwin v. New York,* 399 U.S. 66 (1970)) or if its character carries a particular "moral quality" in relation to the common-law crimes (*District of Columbia v. Clawans,* 300 U.S. 617 (1937)). The Supreme Court rejected "the premise that since prosecutions for crimes punishable by imprisonment for less than six months may be tried without a jury, they may also be tried without a lawyer." The Court did not delineate the constitutional scope of an indigent's right to counsel in petty offense cases, but merely concluded that "no imprisonment [for a misdemeanor or other petty offense] may be imposed, even though local law permits it, unless the accused is represented by counsel" (*Argersinger v. Hamlin,* 407 U.S. 25 (1972)).

Seven years after *Argersinger,* in *Scott v. Illinois,* 440 U.S. 367 (1979), the Supreme Court ended most speculation about the right of an indigent accused to appointed counsel in petty offense cases when, by a 5–4 vote, it ruled "that the central premise of *Argersinger*—that actual imprisonment is a penalty different in kind from fines or the mere threat of imprisonment—is eminently sound and warrants adoption of actual imprisonment as the line defining the constitutional right to appointment of counsel" for indigent defendants. The Court did not analyze the adversary system to determine its balance requirements under the due process clause in a petty offense context. It provided no theoretical underpinning. Instead, it simply accepted as a constitutional principle the distinction revealed by the facts in *Argersinger*. Justice Lewis Powell, concurring, provided the fifth vote in *Scott* solely in order to "provide clear guidance to the hundreds of courts across the country that confront this problem daily." Justices William Brennan, Thurgood Marshall, and John Paul Stevens dissented, focusing on the adversary system. They noted that "the services of a professional prosecutor were considered essential" by the state in all misdemeanor prosecutions and that "nonindigent defendants charged with this offense would be well advised to hire the 'best lawyers they can get.'" The Justices concluded that "Scott's right to the assistance of appointed counsel is thus plainly mandated by the logic of the court's prior cases, including *Argersinger* itself." *Scott* is not soundly grounded in principle or reason and may not endure.

Indigency. Although the Supreme Court has used language describing defendants as "indigent" or lacking sufficient "funds to hire a lawyer," it has never defined an indigency standard, leaving the problem of definition to lower courts and to other branches of government. In close cases, trial judges tend to appoint counsel rather than risk a possible reversal on appeal because of a later finding that the accused was "indigent." Lower appellate courts have ruled that separate financial resources of relatives or spouses cannot be considered when determining whether an accused is indigent (*People v. Gustavson*, 13 Ill. App. 2d 887, 269 N.E.2d 517 (1971)), that an accused cannot be forced to choose between liberty and a lawyer and thus is indigent if he lacks sufficient funds both to hire a lawyer and to post a bail bond (*People v. Eggers*, 27 Ill. 2d 85, 188 N.E.2d 30 (1963)), and that when determining indigency, authorities are limited to considering an accused's current financial condition, not his future earning capabilities (*March v. Municipal Court*, 7 Cal. 3d 422, 498 P.2d 437 (1972)). On the other hand, the Supreme Court has upheld the right of the government to recoup its costs of providing a defense lawyer for an indigent if he later becomes financially able to make reimbursement. A recoupment statute cannot make arbitrary discriminations among convicted indigent defendants, for exam

ple, by applying to those who are imprisoned but not to those placed on probation or parole (*Rinaldi v. Yeager*, 384 U.S. 305 (1966)). But if such a statute applies evenly to all indigents who have been convicted, irrespective of whether they are imprisoned or placed on parole or probation, it is constitutional (*Fuller v. Oregon*, 417 U.S. 40 (1974)).

Prejudice presumed. A state's failure to provide the effective assistance of counsel to an indigent accused during all aspects of the actual trial requires, according to *Gideon* and *Scott*, automatic reversal of any subsequent conviction; actual prejudice to the accused is constitutionally presumed. Moreover, such a failure makes the conviction void, so that at a later trial on a different charge it may not be used by the prosecution to impeach the defendant's testimony (*Loper v. Beto*, 405 U.S. 473 (1972)) or to increase the sentence under a recidivist statute (*Baldasar v. Illinois*, 446 U.S. 222 (1980)).

Counsel at other times

Pretrial stages. The Sixth Amendment's right to the assistance of counsel, that is, the "pure" right, is limited to adversary "criminal prosecutions," a limitation that has been interpreted somewhat narrowly by the Supreme Court. Although much of importance to a criminal prosecution can occur in the police station or before the grand jury, the Sixth Amendment's right to counsel "attaches only at or after the time that adversary judicial proceedings have been initiated . . . whether by way of formal charge, preliminary hearing, indictment, information, or arraignment" (*Kirby v. Illinois*, 406 U.S. 682, 688–689 (1972)). The "initiation of judicial criminal proceedings," the Supreme Court stated in *Kirby*, "is the starting point of our whole system of adversary criminal justice" because "it is only then that the Government has committed itself to prosecute, and only then that the adverse positions of Government and defendant have solidified" (689). It is at this time that "a defendant finds himself faced with the prosecutional forces of organized society" and "immersed in the intricacies of substantive and procedural criminal law."

At the very beginning of American criminal law processes, certain important preliminary stages occur that technically are not part of the Sixth Amendment's formal "criminal prosecution" and that therefore are not governed by the amendment. Chief among these is police custody, interrogation, and investigation. In *Miranda v. Arizona*, 384 U.S. 436 (1966), the Supreme Court ruled that the right to counsel was required in order to safeguard the Fifth Amendment's privilege against self-incrimination and that the detained individual "must be clearly informed that he has the right to consult with a lawyer and to have the lawyer with him during interrogation" whenever police take a person into custody. Both custody and interrogation are required before *Miranda* applies. An arrested person who is not interrogated and is without counsel can be required to permit a physician to take a blood sample for purposes of alcohol analysis because this situation presents "no issue of counsel's ability to assist petitioner in respect of any rights he did possess" (*Schmerber v. California,* 384 U.S. 757 (1966)).

Grand jury proceedings are another early stage in criminal law processes. The government *may* permit witnesses—that is, potential defendants—before a grand jury to interrupt their testimony in order to confer in another room with a privately retained lawyer. But counsel can be excluded from the grand jury room itself, and no lawyer need be provided to confer with indigent witnesses. Under "settled principles the [grand jury] witness may not insist upon the presence of his attorney in the grand jury room." "That," declared four Justices in *United States v. Mandujano,* 425 U.S. 564 (1976), reaching a conclusion not arrived at by others, "was plainly a correct recital of the law" because "no criminal proceedings had been instituted" and "the Sixth Amendment right to counsel had not come into play" (cf. *In re Groban,* 352 U.S. 330 (1957)).

Although the Court in *Kirby* stated that adversary "judicial criminal proceedings" can be initiated "by way of formal charge, preliminary hearing, indictment, information, or arraignment," there remains some uncertainty about exactly what constitutes the initiation of adversary judicial proceedings. Clearly, the Sixth Amendment's guaranteed right to counsel in a "criminal prosecution" is not applicable simply because a person has become "the prime suspect" or "focal point" of a police investigation, or even immediately after an arrest without a warrant on probable cause. Equally clearly, after the filing of a formal charge (an indictment or information) in criminal court against an accused, adversary judicial criminal proceedings have been instituted. Thereafter, a state cannot require an indigent accused either to submit to police interrogation (*Brewer v. Williams,* 430 U.S. 387 (1977); *Massiah v. United States,* 377 U.S. 201 (1964)) or to a pretrial psychiatric or other interview (*Estelle v. Smith,* 451 U.S. 454 (1981)) if either is a "critical stage" in the process, without first affording him the assistance of counsel.

Not all pretrial judicial hearings constitute the initiation of adversary "judicial criminal proceedings" im-

plicating an indigent's right to counsel. A preliminary hearing to determine whether the evidence presented by the prosecutor justifies going to trial or presenting the case to a grand jury can involve fine resolutions of conflicting evidence and credibility determinations about witnesses' testimony. The presence of defense counsel is essential "to protect the indigent accused against an erroneous or improper prosecution" or to learn enough to prepare a defense for the trial. Defense counsel can cross-examine witnesses presented by the prosecutor and may "expose fatal weaknesses in the State's case," "preserve testimony favorable to the accused of a witness who does not appear at the trial," or "discover the case the State has against his client and make possible the preparation of a proper defense to meet that case at trial" (*Coleman v. Alabama,* 399 U.S. 1 (1970)). On the other hand, if a preliminary hearing is held immediately after an arrest without a warrant solely to determine "whether there is probable cause for detaining the arrested person pending further proceedings," it requires neither an adversary hearing nor counsel because the basic decision is similar to the one made when determining whether to issue an arrest warrant (*Gerstein v. Pugh,* 420 U.S. 103 (1975)).

The Supreme Court has not ruled directly on the question of whether a judicially issued arrest warrant institutes adversary judicial criminal proceedings. But it has ruled that adversary judicial criminal proceedings had begun where a judicial "warrant had been issued for [the defendant's] arrest, he had been arraigned on that warrant before a judge . . . and had been committed by the court to confinement in jail" pending further proceedings (*Brewer,* 399). Lower courts disagree as to whether an arrest warrant issued by a judicial officer in an ex parte hearing on information and oath, but without subsequent arraignment and jailing, constitutes the beginning of adversary "judicial criminal proceedings" (*United States v. Duvall,* 537 F.2d 15 (2d Cir. 1976); cf. *Commonwealth v. Richman,* 458 Pa. 167, 320 A.2d 351 (1974)).

The arraignment occurs in court after a formal criminal charge has been filed. The charge is read to the accused, who is obliged to enter a plea of guilty, not guilty, or nolo contendere. Arraignment is a "critical stage"; it takes place after adversary judicial criminal proceedings have been instituted, and an indigent accused is entitled to appointed counsel. But failure to appoint counsel does not automatically constitute reversible error if the defendant pleads not guilty or if he pleads guilty and that plea can later be withdrawn without being used against him at trial. However, if an uncounseled accused's plea at arraignment operates to bar any defenses (such as insanity) or objections (for example, to the legal sufficiency of the charge) at trial, then failure to appoint counsel at arraignment requires automatic reversal of any conviction that might occur later. The reason, the Court stated, is that the degree of prejudice "can never be known" because only counsel present at the time of pleading "could have enabled the accused to know [all of the ramifications of] all the defenses available to him and to plead intelligently" (*Hamilton v. Alabama*, 368 U.S. 52, 55 (1961)). In this situation, actual prejudice to the accused is constitutionally presumed. By contrast, actual prejudice to the accused owing to a lack of counsel at other "critical stages" where rights are not automatically lost must be shown before a reversal of a subsequent conviction will occur (*Coleman*).

Some rather important stages of the criminal law process have been characterized as not being "critical stages," although they fall within the Sixth Amendment's "criminal prosecution" phase. Postcharge police lineups are "critical stages" requiring the assistance of counsel (*United States v. Wade*, 388 U.S. 218 (1967)). Excluded from consideration as a "critical stage," however, is the use of such scientific procedures as taking handwritten or spoken exemplars; fingerprinting; taking blood or hair samples or items of clothing; photographing, weighing, or measuring the accused; or requiring him to stand, assume a stance, or walk. The Court has reasoned that "knowledge of the techniques of science and technology is sufficiently available, and the variables in the techniques few enough, that the accused has the opportunity for a meaningful confrontation of the Government's case at trial through the ordinary processes of cross-examination . . . and the presentation of the evidence of his own experts" (227–228; cf. *Gilbert v. California*, 388 U.S. 263 (1967)).

Post-trial stages. The Sixth Amendment's right to the assistance of counsel extends beyond the conclusion of the trial. In *Mempa v. Rhay*, 389 U.S. 128 (1967), the Supreme Court held that sentencing after trial and conviction is a "critical stage" of the criminal prosecution, requiring appointed counsel. A parole or probation revocation, by comparison, is not based on the original criminal charge made at trial and, strictly speaking, is not part of the "criminal prosecution" controlled by the Sixth Amendment. But the Fourteenth Amendment's due process clause applies to such hearings, and it requires appointment of counsel in cases where the probation or parole violation is disputed or it is claimed that "there are substantial reasons which justified or mitigated the violation and

make revocation inappropriate and . . . the reasons are complex or otherwise difficult to develop or present" (*Gagnon v. Scarpelli*, 411 U.S. 778, 790 (1973)).

Neither the federal government nor the states are required by the Constitution to provide any system of criminal appeals (*McKane v. Durston*, 153 U.S. 684 (1894)). If the government does provide a system of appellate courts and grants a first appeal as a matter of right, then the Fourteenth Amendment's "equal protection" clause requires the government to afford counsel to an indigent defendant on the first appeal as of right (*Douglas v. California*, 372 U.S. 353 (1963)). Appointed counsel may request to withdraw from "wholly frivolous" appeals, but that request must be accompanied by a thorough brief on the merits discussing all items in the trial record "that might arguably support the appeal," and only after finding none of the items to be legally "arguable" may an appellate court dismiss an indigent's appeal (*Anders v. California*, 386 U.S. 738 (1967)).

On the other hand, the Supreme Court has ruled that the due process and equal protection clauses do not "require appointment of counsel for indigent state defendants . . . for [direct] discretionary state appeals and for applications for review in this Court" (*Ross v. Moffitt*, 417 U.S. 600 (1974)). The Court reasoned that a lawyer was not necessary in direct discretionary appeals at a higher appellate level, after the first direct appeal as of right, because in such a situation a "defendant needs an attorney on appeal not as a shield to protect him against being 'haled into court' by the State and stripped of his presumption of innocence, but rather as a sword to upset the prior determination of guilt" (610–611).

The Supreme Court has yet to rule squarely on whether appointed counsel must be afforded an indigent who seeks to challenge his conviction through such collateral proceedings as habeas corpus, as distinguished from direct appeals. But the Court's reasoning in cases such as *Ross* is grounded in the general view that government need not provide counsel for collateral attacks on convictions—at least not for the preparation and filing of the documents initiating collateral proceedings. In practice, indigent prisoners themselves generally prepare the documents initiating collateral attack proceedings, and most courts do not provide counsel for that purpose. They generally do, however, appoint counsel for the hearing whenever a prisoner's petition for collateral proceedings raises complex issues that "by their nature and character, indicate the necessity for professional legal assistance" (*Honore v. Board of Prison Terms and Paroles*, 77 Wash. 2d 660, 466 P.2d 485 (1970)).

"Effective assistance"

The tests. An accused's right to counsel, the Supreme Court declared in 1932, means more than merely having an attorney physically present at trial. It is the right to receive "effective aid in the preparation and trial of the case" (*Powell*). Thus, the failure of either appointed or privately retained counsel to provide adequate legal services to his client, for whatever reason, is a denial of the accused's constitutional right to "effective" counsel, and requires a reversal of a subsequent conviction. "Since the State's conduct of a criminal trial implicates the State in the defendant's conviction," the Supreme Court ruled, "we see no basis for drawing a distinction between [privately] retained and [state] appointed counsel . . ." (*Cuyler v. Sullivan*, 446 U.S. 335, 344–345 (1980)).

The law is in flux on precisely what constitutes the "effective" assistance of counsel. The Supreme Court has yet to set forth a definitive standard, and lower courts have adopted differing ones. Prior to the 1970s the most common standard was the "mockery of justice" standard, under which counsel's assistance was "ineffective" only when it was so inadequate that it reduced the trial "to a farce" or rendered it a "mockery of justice." Since that time, most courts have abandoned this formulation in favor of more stringent requirements, stipulating, for example, that "counsel must exercise [the] customary skill and knowledge which normally prevails at the time and place" (*Moore v. United States*, 432 F.2d 730 (3d Cir. 1970)), that counsel must render the "reasonably competent assistance of an attorney acting as his diligent conscientious advocate" (*United States v. Decoster*, 487 F.2d 1197 (D.C. Cir. 1973)), or that counsel's representation must be "within the range of competence demanded of attorneys in criminal cases" (*Marzullo v. Maryland*, 561 F.2d 540 (4th Cir. 1977)). All of these new standards beg the questions of what traditional level of practice is to be regarded as "customary," "diligent," or "reasonable." Thus, little has been definitively resolved by the new, higher standards.

Conflict of interest. However, one area is clear. If a convicted defendant can show that his lawyer "actively represented conflicting interests" at trial, he is automatically entitled to a reversal without having to show that his lawyer's performance was "ineffective" and to his substantial prejudice (*Cuyler*). A defendant's right to the undivided loyalty of his lawyer is "too fundamental and absolute to allow courts to indulge in nice calculations as to the amount of prejudice resulting from its denial" (*Glasser v. United States*, 315 U.S. 60 (1942)).

Conflicting interests most frequently arise when a lawyer represents multiple defendants. During plea bargaining, for example, if the prosecutor offers one, but not all, of a lawyer's multiple clients a "deal," the defense lawyer is placed in a most difficult position. If he advises one client to accept the deal, he may later be confronted at the trial with that ex-client as a prosecution witness against his remaining clients. Problems of multiple representation at trial also can be severe, for example, when a defendant's testimony would be beneficial to him but damaging to a codefendant. A lawyer representing multiple defendants may resolve such difficulties by pursuing only those trial strategies that benefit all defendants, which means that the conflict may never appear on the court's record and may be lost from sight forever. For this reason, there is much to be said for the proposition that, in the absence of special circumstances, counsel should never be permitted to represent multiple defendants. Nevertheless, the Supreme Court has ruled that such representation "is not *per se* violative of constitutional guarantees of effective assistance of counsel" (*Holloway v. Arkansas*, 435 U.S. 475 (1978)). *Holloway* also holds that if counsel calls the judge's attention before or during trial to the probable risk of a conflict of interests because of counsel's representation of multiple defendants, "special circumstances" exist, and the judge then must either "appoint separate counsel or . . . take adequate steps to ascertain whether the risk was too remote to warrant separate counsel." Failure of the judge to do either deprives multiple defendants "of the guarantee of the assistance of counsel" (484).

The burden is on counsel. They have an ethical obligation to avoid conflicting representations and to advise the court promptly when a conflict of interest arises during the course of a trial. Nothing "in our precedents," declared the Supreme Court, requires "courts themselves to initiate inquiries." In the absence of "special circumstances" showing that the "trial court knows or reasonably should know" that a possible conflict of interests exists, "trial courts may assume either that multiple representation entails no conflict or that the lawyer and his clients knowingly accept such risk of conflict as may exist" (*Cuyler*). If a trial court determines that an actual conflict of interests exists, it can disqualify reluctant defense counsel from continued multiple representation even though a defendant objects and executes an informed waiver because, presumably, the constitutional right is to "effective" counsel and the power to waive that right does not create an inferior constitutional right to "ineffective" counsel (*United States v. Dolan*, 570 F.2d 1177 (3d Cir. 1978)).

In a case in which there are no "special circumstances" obligating a trial court to inquire about conflict of interest in a multiple representation case, a convicted multiple defendant seeking to reverse his conviction has the burden of showing that such a conflict actually existed. A violation of the Sixth Amendment right to the effective assistance of counsel is not established simply by showing that a potential or possible conflict of interests existed, because a "possible conflict inheres in almost every instance of multiple representation" (*Cuyler*).

Legal restrictions on counsel. A clear-cut categorical approach has emerged in a second area, that is, whenever the "effective" assistance of counsel is denied by the operation of the law. For example, if a statute permits a witness to make an unsworn statement but prohibits that statement from being elicited by counsel on direct examination, the law denies the "effective" assistance of counsel (*Ferguson*). Similarly, a denial of the "effectiveness" of counsel occurs if a law prevents defense counsel from deciding when to put the defendant on the witness stand (*Brooks v. Tennessee*, 406 U.S. 605 (1972)), if a law denies defense counsel a closing summation in a nonjury trial (*Herring v. New York*, 422 U.S. 853 (1975)), or if a trial court's order prohibits a defendant from consulting with his lawyer during an overnight recess between direct and cross-examination (*Geders v. United States*, 425 U.S. 80 (1976)).

Preparation, tactics, omissions. For the aid of counsel to be "effective," a lawyer obviously must first have adequate time to prepare an accused's case. But the Supreme Court has refused to adopt a categorical "per se rule requiring reversal of every conviction following tardy appointment of counsel" (*Chambers v. Maroney*, 399 U.S. 42 (1970)). In such circumstances a defendant must establish "a serious incompetency that falls measurably below the performance ordinarily expected of fallible lawyers" and must prove that "counsel's inadequacy affected the outcome of the trial." Thereafter "the burden passes to the government, and the conviction cannot stand unless the government demonstrates that it is not tainted by the deficiency, and that in fact no prejudice resulted" (*United States v. Decoster (Decoster III)*, 624 F.2d 196, 208 (D.C. Cir. 1979)). A categorical rule for indigent defendants would better comport with the fact that the state controls the time when appointed counsel are made available.

A variable, judgmental, and noncategorical rule requiring actual prejudice to the accused is applied to the remaining large number of ineffectiveness-of-counsel cases in which claims are based on such common complaints as the inexperience of counsel, the failure to conduct a full and complete investigation, or, probably the most common complaint, trial errors—the failure to cross-examine a witness vigorously or to use certain alternative procedures at trial. Appellate courts are disinclined to second-guess defense counsel in trial situations, especially because decisions by counsel that seem like errors may in retrospect have been legitimate trial strategy. Consequently, unless counsel's statements or actions clearly show that his trial performance was outside "the range of competence demanded of attorneys in criminal cases," courts tend to hold that "mistakes" in legal "judgment" or mistaken "trial strategy" or legal advice, as well as counsel's failure to advance a particular defense, are not errors of constitutional dimension unless they are totally without foundation (*Frand v. United States*, 301 F.2d 102 (10th Cir. 1962)).

Waiver: self-representation

An accused can waive his right to the effective assistance of counsel if that waiver is not only "voluntary but constitutes a knowing and intelligent relinquishment or abandonment of a known right or privilege, a matter which depends in each case 'upon the particular facts and circumstances surrounding that case, including the background, experience and conduct of the accused'" (*Edwards v. Arizona*, 451 U.S. 477 (1981)). Courts "indulge every reasonable presumption against waiver of fundamental rights" and "do not presume acquiescence in the loss of fundamental rights" (*Johnson*). "Presuming waiver from a silent record is impermissible," and the "record must show that an accused was offered counsel but intelligently and understandably rejected the offer" (*Carnley v. Cochran*, 369 U.S. 506, 516 (1962)).

If an accused waives his right to counsel, he "has a constitutional right to proceed *without* counsel when he voluntarily and intelligently elects to do so." The "right to self-representation—to make one's defense personally—is . . . necessarily implied by the structure of the [Sixth] Amendment," and "to force a lawyer on a defendant can only lead him to believe that the law contrives against him" (*Faretta v. California*, 422 U.S. 806, 819, 834 (1975)). This implied Sixth Amendment right to defend oneself is given directly to the accused, and it does not permit him to choose another nonlawyer to present his defense (*United States v. Whitesel*, 543 F.2d 1176 (6th Cir. 1976)). Once a trial has started, courts are most reluctant to permit an accused to discharge his counsel and proceed *pro se.*

Because *Faretta* holds that the implied right to self-representation is "independently found in the structure and history of the constitutional text," it may be that an accused cannot be forced to choose between his right to represent himself and his additional right to the effective assistance of counsel. If this is so, an accused could have the active assistance of counsel and also actively participate. In any event, even if the accused rejects an offer of appointed counsel and elects to proceed *pro se,* the trial court wisely will appoint standby counsel in all except the simplest cases, because an uncounseled defendant may quickly recognize the value of having a lawyer.

Systems of representing indigents

Three basic methods are used to provide the assistance of counsel to indigent defendants: (1) the public defender method; (2) the assigned counsel method; and (3) the mixed method, which combines aspects of the first two.

Public defender method. There is a growing trend toward the use of public defenders. Under the "pure" public defender method a professional office is established which, like that of the public prosecutor, has the advantages of efficiency and expertise resulting from specialization. The work load is large and concentrated, justifying the employment of investigators and other useful paraprofessionals. Moreover, like prosecutors who are paid from public funds but unlike private attorneys who must dispose of a case and earn a fee as quickly as possible, public defenders can put more time into a difficult and complex case. Because of the nature of their office, they come to know police practices well and may be better able to identify deficiencies that may help their indigent clients. Public defenders enter a case earlier than assigned counsel, and usually they are in the courtroom when the indigent defendant makes his first appearance. Consequently, they can be of early assistance in many matters, including the setting of bail. On the other hand, most offices of public defenders have inadequate budgets and are understaffed, so that, some observers contend, they are under pressure to concentrate on their stronger cases while encouraging guilty pleas in their weaker ones. Many indigent defenders believe that public defenders are bureaucrats rather than "real" lawyers; one study showed that little time was spent with clients and that "nearly half (49 percent) of the public defender clients thought their attorney was 'on the side of the state' " (Casper, p. iv). This perception may change if states appropriate adequate funds for public defenders or provide that "where there are no countervailing considerations of comparable weight, it is an abuse of sound judicial discretion to deny the defendant's request to appoint the counsel of his preference" (*Harris v. Superior Court,* 19 Cal. 3d 786, 567 P.2d 750 (1977)).

Assigned counsel method. Under the "pure" assigned counsel method, a private practicing lawyer is assigned by a court, usually the magistrate, to represent an indigent defendant. Although the state pays the attorney, the amount usually is substantially less than private practitioners generally earn. Moreover, some judges appoint less capable lawyers who are friends or political allies of the judge or who are young and inexperienced. To avoid this problem, some jurisdictions assign counsel to indigent defendants by rotation, using a list of all the criminal law practitioners in the community. The rotation scheme ensures experienced criminal law attorneys for indigents, but it places a heavy burden on the criminal law bar and diminishes the incentive of those lawyers by paying them a substantially lower fee than they would otherwise receive in private practice.

Mixed method. The mixed method is the most common form. Under it, an assigned counsel system is supplemented by a public defender office, which is usually a private, nonprofit organization. The organization is paid a fixed fee by the state each time it receives an appointment. If the jurisdiction also uses the rotation system to assign private criminal law practitioners to indigents, the mixed method can alleviate some of the burden that otherwise is put on them under the "pure" assigned counsel method.

ARVAL A. MORRIS

See also COUNSEL: ROLE OF COUNSEL; CRIMINAL PROCEDURE: CONSTITUTIONAL ASPECTS.

BIBLIOGRAPHY

American Bar Association. *Standards for Criminal Justice,* vols. 1 and 4. 2d ed. Prepared with the assistance of the American Bar Foundation. Boston: Little, Brown, 1980.
BAZELON, DAVID L. "The Defective Assistance of Counsel." *University of Cincinnati Law Review* 42 (1973): 1–46.
———. "The Realities of *Gideon* and *Argersinger.*" *Georgetown Law Journal* 64 (1976): 811–838.
BEANEY, WILLIAM M. *The Right to Counsel in American Courts.* Ann Arbor: University of Michigan Press, 1955.
BRENNAN, WILLIAM J., JR. "The Criminal Prosecution: Sporting Event or Quest for Truth?" *Washington University Law Quarterly* (1963): 279–295.
CASPER, JONATHAN D. *American Criminal Justice: The Defendant's Perspective.* Englewood Cliffs, N.J.: Prentice-Hall, 1972.

FINER, JOEL JAY. "Ineffective Assistance of Counsel." *Cornell Law Review* 58 (1973): 1077–1120.

GOLDSTEIN, ABRAHAM S. "The State and the Accused: Balance of Advantage in Criminal Procedure." *Yale Law Journal* 69 (1960): 1149–1199.

KADISH, SANFORD H. "Methodology and Criteria in Due Process Adjudication: A Survey and Criticism." *Yale Law Journal* 66 (1957): 319–363.

KAMISAR, YALE; LAFAVE, WAYNE R.; and ISRAEL, JEROLD H. *Modern Criminal Procedure: Cases, Comments, and Questions.* 5th ed. St. Paul: West, 1980.

KERPER, HAZEL B., and ISRAEL, JEROLD H. *Introduction to the Criminal Justice System.* 2d ed. St. Paul: West, 1979.

MEADOR, DANIEL J. *Prelude to Gideon: Notes on Appellate Advocacy, Habeas Corpus, and Constitutional Litigation.* Charlottesville, Va.: Michie, 1967.

National Legal Aid and Defender Association. *Guidelines for Legal Defense Systems in the United States: Final Report.* Washington, D.C.: The Association, 1976.

PACKER, HERBERT L. *The Limits of the Criminal Sanction.* Stanford, Calif.: Stanford University Press, 1968.

SCHAEFER, WALTER V. "Federalism and State Criminal Procedure." *Harvard Law Review* 70 (1956): 1–26.

SKOLNICK, JEROME. *Justice without Trial: Law Enforcement in Democratic Society.* 2d ed. New York: Wiley, 1975.

TAGUE, PETER W. "An Indigent's Right to the Attorney of His Choice." *Stanford Law Review* 27 (1974): 73–99.

———. "Multiple Representation and Conflicts of Interests in Criminal Cases." *Georgetown Law Journal* 67 (1979): 1075–1130.

U.S. Attorney General's Committee on Poverty and the Administration of Federal Criminal Justice. *Poverty and the Administration of Federal Criminal Justice.* Washington, D.C.: The Committee, 1964.

2.
ROLE OF COUNSEL

Introduction

The societal and legal perception of the criminal defense attorney's role is one of sharp contrasts. Admired by the public as the epitome of the trial lawyer and hailed by the courts as the champion of his client, the criminal defense attorney stands between his client and the government's attempt to convict him. Regardless of his client's conduct, counsel acts as a guard, ensuring that the government has not violated the defendant's intricate web of constitutional and statutory rights and that the criminal justice system will not punish the defendant unless the government has proved him guilty or he has elected to plead guilty. Counsel's help is considered so indispensable that almost every defendant, regardless of wealth, educa-

tion, or experience, is constitutionally entitled to retain an attorney or to demand that the court appoint one at state expense.

There are, however, conflicting views of the criminal defense attorney's work. The public, fearing that counsel succeeds in protecting too many guilty defendants, may extend its moral condemnation of the defendant's conduct to defense counsel. Courts criticize defense attorneys on the different ground that too frequently they fail to provide the effective representation the criminal justice system and the adversary process demand.

Underlying these contrasting views of defense counsel's work is uncertainty over the appropriate answer to a host of nettlesome questions that confront the defense attorney. May counsel represent a guilty defendant? If so, what sort of defense should counsel mount? How does counsel provide constitutionally effective representation? If counsel disagrees with his client over some matter, should counsel override or accede to his client's demand? Must counsel disclose to the prosecutor evidence that incriminates his client? What must counsel do when his client intends to commit perjury? Questions such as these lie at the core of defense counsel's work; they pose problems for counsel quite apart from whether he is technically able to examine a witness or to persuade the jury in final argument. Before examining several of these questions, it is useful to sketch the topography of defense counsel's work.

The criminal defense attorney's role

The defense attorney rarely provides preventive counseling by advising the client concerning his intended future conduct. Instead, he usually begins his representation after the government has begun to investigate his client's conduct, or, even more typically, after the government has charged his client with a crime. Counsel immediately enters a formal adversarial relationship with the government.

Within this adversarial context, counsel's role is to help his client avoid sanction or receive the most limited sanction. Counsel explains to his client the elements of the crime, the evidence the government must adduce, and the range of sanctions the court may impose. If the defendant is in jail, counsel seeks his release on bail or personal recognizance. He investigates whether his client is guilty by searching for information from leads provided by the client and by discovering information through formal or informal means from the government. He asserts his client's constitutional and statutory rights so as to prevent the government from using improperly obtained evidence against the defendant or otherwise to impede the prosecution. He bargains with the prosecutor to obtain a favorable plea offer, and in some jurisdictions he discusses the plea bargain with the judge to influence the latter's choice of sanction to impose. He advises his client whether to accept the plea offer or to run the risk of being convicted of additional crimes or of being sanctioned more severely if the defendant is convicted at trial. If his client elects to go to trial, counsel challenges the persuasiveness of the government's evidence and, with the defendant's help, decides whether to present defense evidence.

This outline of counsel's work, however, does not reveal the orientation of many defense attorneys. They are usually uninterested in the guilt of the defendant; in fact, many assume that the client is guilty, an assumption that enables them to limit their role solely to one of challenging the government's evidence rather than undertaking proof of the defendant's innocence. Many never ask the defendant whether he is guilty; those attorneys who do frequently continue to question a defendant who initially admits incriminating information until he says something that makes his guilt more problematic. Many defense attorneys are not troubled if a jury acquits a client who they know (or at least strongly suspect) is guilty.

This orientation is a product of the fact that defense counsel's role is derivative, defined by the principles of the adversary system and by the constitutional and statutory rights of persons charged with a crime. The American criminal justice system simultaneously imposes the burden of proof solely on the government and restricts the ways in which the government may gather and use evidence to satisfy its proof burden. This reflects not only the value which we place upon individual autonomy, but also the fact that the government's resources in investigating criminal conduct are far greater than those of the defendant. Imprisonment of the defendant is a significant sanction, and there is a reluctance to allow such punishment to be too readily inflicted. This bias in favor of the defendant is attributable not only to a distrust of government power and uncertainty over the societal purpose in imposing such a sanction, but also to the concern for accurate guilt determinations by juries in criminal cases. All these considerations are together viewed as providing a justification for defense counsel to seek the most favorable result for his client.

Defense counsel's efforts to impede the government's attempt to prove the defendant guilty are also justified by other values. For example, by moving to suppress evidence that the government seeks to use—the heroin the police seize when, without judicial authorization, they break into the defendant's apartment; the confession the police wrench from a fearful, overwhelmed defendant; or the identification they obtain by biasing the eyewitness's choice—counsel protects the specific defendant from an intrusion made in violation of the Constitution. Moreover, counsel's attempts on behalf of his client to exclude evidence are one way of achieving the long-run utilitarian result of protecting each person's constitutional rights. Society's acceptance of these justifications is severely tested when counsel's successful suppression of evidence has the short-run result of freeing an apparently guilty defendant. But objection to counsel's actions in impeding the government in this way is more properly redirected to the content of the individual rights that counsel seeks to protect.

Barriers to effective representation

Despite the theoretical slant of the defense attorney toward his client, he may not always act as loyally or work as effectively as expected. Defendants frequently complain that the attorney was aligned more with the prosecution than with them, citing as evidence the attorney's pressure on them to plead guilty. Courts worry that defense attorneys do not always prepare themselves to make informed decisions. Defense attorneys candidly admit that they do not aggressively represent certain clients.

The structure of the criminal justice process contributes to counsel's failure to satisfy his obligation. Loyalty is often a function of friendship or of continuous personal interchange. But a defense attorney usually represents a criminal defendant only once, and then only for a short time. Most defendants, especially the indigent, are of a different social class than the defense attorney, who frequently feels closer communion with the prosecutor and the judge.

Defense attorneys also feel that they must maintain friendly relations with the prosecutor because of the difficulty of obtaining information about the client's conduct and the government's evidence. Many defendants do not provide counsel with the information he needs because they forget, they do not recognize the significance of certain information, or they distrust counsel. A client who is unable to retain an attorney may believe that he has no control over the court-appointed attorney. Fearing that such an attorney's allegiance runs to the judge who authorizes his compensation, the client may refuse to disclose information. Many attorneys find that, despite their assurance to the client that the attorney-client privilege bars them from disclosing almost anything the client says, they cannot learn what the client wants or what he knows. The discovery rules in criminal litigation are usually quite restrictive, and do not provide counsel with an alternative way of obtaining information from the government. If the prosecutor is obliged to disclose, his disclosure obligation commonly arises only immediately before or during the trial itself, and thus at a time when defense counsel has scant opportunity to capitalize on what he learns. To obtain information informally from the prosecutor, defense counsel sometimes feels that he must modify the aggressiveness of his representation. If he acts too aggressively, the prosecutor may sanction him by refusing to disclose information.

The economics of criminal defense work also tends to separate counsel from his client. Criminal defense work is usually not very remunerative. Few defendants are able to pay a high fee; many refuse to pay the contracted price. Defense attorneys are driven to obtain the fee in advance and to conduct a volume practice, representing as many clients as they can and concluding each case as quickly as possible in order to maximize the return. The busier an attorney is, the less time he can spend in preparing himself to help each client. The quickest way to end a case is to convince the client to plead guilty. From defense counsel's point of view, a trial is economically inefficient.

Different economic considerations may affect an attorney appointed to represent an indigent defendant. A court-appointed attorney depends upon the judge to select him from among his colleagues and to establish the total compensation he will receive for his services. Such an attorney may structure his representation to avoid offending the judge for fear of jeopardizing both his compensation in the particular case and his appointment in future cases. An attorney who thinks that the judge believes his client is guilty may not ask for money to investigate, may not raise objections that lengthen the proceeding or that threaten the prosecution's case, and may pressure his client to plead guilty.

Finally, courts have failed to define how counsel provides the effective representation to which the defendant is constitutionally entitled. Understandably, courts have refused to define effective representation in terms of the outcome. Most defendants are convicted of some crime; if they were not, one would have reason to question whether the government was properly deciding which defendants to prosecute. As a result, courts have begun to define "effective representation" in terms both of counsel's efforts to prepare himself to make informed decisions and of the reasonableness of his decisions.

But such a standard is not self-explanatory. For example, must counsel try to interview every government witness? Must he search for an alibi witness whom his client cannot identify? Must he seek legal relief that he is convinced the judge will refuse? Courts have not explained when counsel may forego some act whose marginal utility, in counsel's judgment, is outweighed by the unlikelihood of success, by its additional cost, or by counsel's responsibility to other clients.

Neither have courts found a way to monitor counsel's work. Courts understandably hesitate to ask counsel to explain what he has done before his client pleads guilty or the jury returns with a verdict. Apart from the economics of such an inquiry, many defendants would protest that counsel might reveal confidential, privileged matters which could unfairly bias the judge or arm the prosecutor with information that he could use against the defendant. Appellate courts find it difficult to decide after the defendant's jury conviction or guilty plea whether counsel provided effective representation. Compounding the problem of determining what counsel did or did not do is the question of the remedy. Unless appellate courts use a preventive rule and reverse the defendant's conviction whenever counsel has acted ineffectively, regardless of the impact of counsel's failure they must devise a different way to prod defense counsel to provide effective representation. They have not yet succeeded in that search.

Two ethical questions for the defense attorney

Lawyers continue to debate a variety of questions that go to the core of the criminal defense attorney's orientation and justification for his work. Two representative questions concern the division of decision-making responsibility between attorney and defendant, and the attorney's disclosure obligation when he learns that his client intends to commit perjury or when his client gives him incriminating physical evidence.

The allocation of decision-making responsibility. Some criminal defense attorneys demand complete power to decide every tactical and legal question other than the defendant's decision whether to plead guilty. To protect that power, they neither inform the defendant of the substantive and tactical decisions the defense must make nor try to convince the defendant of the correctness of counsel's choice. These attorneys argue that the justifications supporting the constitutional right to counsel of every indigent defendant who faces a jail sanction—the attorney's dispassion and his greater experience and education—also support recognition of this power.

The counterposition stresses the defendant's right to autonomy. The defendant, not his attorney, risks being sanctioned if he is convicted. If we believe the convicted defendant's rehabilitation is affected by his feeling that he was treated fairly by the criminal justice system, do we not want to give him the power to override counsel? Defense counsel's paternalistic demand to decide also appears inconsistent with the defendant's constitutional right to represent himself. If we permit the defendant to reject counsel's assistance even while we fear that the choice of self-representation is folly, should we not also authorize the defendant to structure the work of an attorney whose assistance the defendant wants? At the least, should not the defendant make the major decisions: whether to plead guilty, to waive a jury trial, to call a particular witness, to testify himself, to move to suppress certain evidence, and so forth? Moreover, when counsel has time to let the defendant decide an issue, arguably he should do so because counsel's unilateral decision to forego some procedural protection usually prevents the defendant from raising that issue for the first time on appeal after he is convicted.

Most defense attorneys believe that the defendant should decide and that they should prepare him to make an informed decision. Most also believe that they can convince the defendant to accept the course of conduct they prefer. Occasionally, however, an attorney confronts the dilemma of whether to override a client whose choice appears suicidal. For example, in *Taylor v. State*, 291 Ala. 756, 287 So. 2d 901 (1973), the defendant, charged with murder, denied having killed the victim and claimed to have an alibi that counsel could not corroborate. Considerable evidence indicated that the defendant had killed the victim during a fight. Defense counsel wanted to argue self-defense based on the description of the fight provided by several witnesses. The defendant rejected that defense; he insisted that he had been elsewhere and demanded that counsel let him testify that he had not killed the victim. Counsel did not believe the defendant's explanation and feared that the defendant would perjure himself in denying the act. Moreover, counsel thought the self-defense theory might convince the jury to acquit.

Counsel sought help from the trial judge, who told him to follow the defendant's demand. Immediately after his conviction, however, the defendant appealed, objecting that counsel should have overridden his

choice of the alibi defense. The intermediate state court of appeals agreed and reversed the conviction. The state supreme court disagreed, holding that the defendant could select his defense, and reinstated his conviction. This judicial disagreement over the allocation of decision-making responsibility carries over into every major decision the defense must make. Although the eventual result in *Taylor* suggests that counsel should accede if he is unable to convince his client to choose counsel's preferred course of conduct, that result will not convince every defense attorney, and it will not free counsel from the burden of justifying his assent on postconviction challenge by a disappointed defendant.

Perjury and incriminating physical evidence. If we can accept counsel's attempts to expose the weaknesses in the government's evidence, can we permit counsel to assist his client in committing perjury or to withhold from the fact finder physical evidence that establishes his client's guilt? In all three instances the fact finder may err; but in the latter two, counsel knows that a jury acquittal of the defendant is factually erroneous. Our failure to define counsel's obligation in either instance illustrates tensions inherent in the adversary system. Counsel's ethical obligation not to mislead the fact finder drives us to require counsel to disclose in each instance; the defendant's constitutional right to loyal and effective representation and the protection the client enjoys under the attorney-client privilege suggest that we should not require counsel to disclose (and perhaps that we should forbid counsel from disclosing).

Commentators and courts suggest three solutions when counsel learns that his client will commit or is committing perjury and when he is unable to withdraw or to convince the client not to so testify. The first solution is for counsel to notify the court; the polar opposite is for counsel to permit the client to testify and argue his testimony in jury summation as if he had spoken the truth. The intermediate solution is for counsel to permit the defendant to testify without disclosing his perjury, but for counsel neither to assist the defendant as he testifies nor to argue the truth of his testimony in jury summation.

Each alternative has its supporters. To require counsel to disclose is consistent with counsel's obligation to further the truth-determination process; but several courts have nonetheless held that counsel should not disclose if he thereby converts himself into a witness against his client and if his disclosure would overly influence the fact finder. To require counsel not to disclose is consistent with his obligation to provide loyal representation. Advocates of this second solution argue that by not disclosing, counsel enables the client to act in the same way as would the attorney if he were the defendant. The intermediate solution threatens to penalize the defendant indirectly if the judge and the jury recognize that counsel's conduct implies that he knows his client is committing perjury. But advocates of the intermediate solution argue that it does not clash with the defendant's right to effective representation as much as does the first position, and that it does not require counsel to assist in the perjury as much as does the second position. Supporters of disclosure criticize this intermediate solution as morally indefensible; supporters of nondisclosure criticize the intermediate solution as inconsistent with counsel's obligation of loyal representation.

In the absence of a clear directive, attorneys frequently sidestep the problem by questioning the defendant until he retracts his stated intention to commit perjury and instead claims that his "perjured" testimony is in fact "truthful" testimony. The attorney thereby "solves" his ethical problem by arguing that he does not "know" whether his client will perjure himself and that, in the absence of such knowledge, he must treat his client like any other witness.

Counsel's obligation to comply with a government subpoena to produce a murder weapon received from his client is somewhat clearer. Counsel's obligation turns on the hypothetical obligation his client would have had if instead he had been served with the subpoena duces tecum to deliver the weapon to the government. If the defendant could not have successfully asserted his Fifth Amendment protection against self-incrimination had he received the subpoena, he has no constitutional basis to oppose his attorney's compliance.

Counsel's obligation, however, is much less clear when the government has not subpoenaed the item from him. Courts have occasionally held that counsel must voluntarily produce the item because his refusal to do so would overly impede the government's efforts to prosecute the defendant. However, this rationale, which served as a way to circumvent those courts' understanding of the defendant's Fifth Amendment privilege, is no longer as persuasive as it was before the United States Supreme Court reinterpreted the Fifth Amendment to hold that the government could subpoena items from the defendant and his attorney (*Fisher v. United States*, 425 U.S. 391 (1976)). Moreover, we may not want to require counsel to disclose voluntarily if by doing so we discourage attorneys from taking possession of a murder weapon to prevent the defendant from destroying it. By taking possession of the weapon but not disclosing it, counsel at least

enables the government to seek a subpoena for it.

Pragmatic considerations, however, pressure the attorney to disclose voluntarily. Attorneys worry that they risk being charged with the crimes of obstruction of justice or of illegal possession of contraband (for example, if the item is heroin). As a result, judicial treatment of counsel's disclosure obligation has usually involved the defendant's challenge to counsel's voluntary disclosure; in this setting, courts have held that counsel may disclose, a holding that unfortunately does not resolve the question of whether counsel must disclose. Because counsel must withdraw from representing his client if he elects to disclose voluntarily, many attorneys also try to sidestep this problem by refusing to accept the murder weapon or the heroin from the client. Such a decision, however, may lead to the societally undesirable result of encouraging the defendant to destroy the evidence, even if counsel urges him not to do so to avoid committing the separate crime of destroying evidence. On balance, courts probably should not require counsel to disclose voluntarily.

PETER W. TAGUE

See also ARRAIGNMENT; CAREERS IN CRIMINAL JUSTICE: LAW; CONFESSIONS; COUNSEL: RIGHT TO COUNSEL; CRIMINAL JUSTICE SYSTEM: OVERVIEW; GRAND JURY; *both articles under* GUILTY PLEA; PRELIMINARY HEARING; SENTENCING: PROCEDURAL PROTECTION; TRIAL, CRIMINAL.

BIBLIOGRAPHY

BAZELON, DAVID L. "The Defective Assistance of Counsel." *Cincinnati Law Review* 42 (1973): 1–46.

BLUMBERG, ABRAHAM S. *Criminal Justice.* 2d ed. New York: New Viewpoints, 1979.

CASPER, JONATHAN D. *American Criminal Justice: The Defendant's Perspective.* Englewood Cliffs, N.J.: Prentice-Hall, 1972.

CURTIS, CHARLES P. "The Ethics of Advocacy." *Stanford Law Review* 4 (1951): 3–23.

FRANK, JEROME. *Courts on Trial: Myth and Reality in American Justice.* Princeton, N.J.: Princeton University Press, 1949.

FRANKEL, MARVIN E. "The Search for Truth: An Umpireal View." *University of Pennsylvania Law Review* 123 (1975): 1031–1059.

FREEDMAN, MONROE H. *Lawyers' Ethics in an Adversary System.* Indianapolis: Bobbs-Merrill, 1975.

MITCHELL, JOHN B. "The Ethics of the Criminal Defense Attorney: New Answers to Old Questions." *Stanford Law Review* 32 (1980): 293–337.

PACKER, HERBERT L. *The Limits of the Criminal Sanction.* Stanford, Calif.: Stanford University Press, 1968.

PATTERSON, L. RAY, and CHEATHAM, ELLIOTT E. *The Profession of Law.* Mineola, N.Y.: Foundation Press, 1971.

PYE, A. KENNETH. "The Role of Counsel in the Suppression of Truth." *Duke Law Journal* (1978): 921–959.

ROSENTHAL, DOUGLAS E. *Lawyer and Client: Who's in Charge?* New York: Russell Sage Foundation, 1974.

SEVILLA, CHARLES M. "Between Scylla and Charybdis: The Ethical Perils of the Criminal Defense Lawyer." *National Journal of Criminal Defense* 2 (1976): 237–285.

WASSERSTROM, RICHARD. "Lawyers as Professionals: Some Moral Issues." *Human Rights* 5 (1975): 1–24.

WICE, PAUL B. *Criminal Lawyers: An Endangered Species.* Beverly Hills, Calif.: Sage, 1978.

COUNTERFEITING

It is critical for a government to ensure the integrity of its obligations, securities, and currency, and it is also necessary that citizens have confidence in the currency, securities, and obligations of their government. Therefore, the United States Congress, in the Comprehensive Act of June 30, 1864, defined the various crimes against currency and prescribed a uniform set of punishments for those crimes. Prior to this legislation, Congress, when creating a new form of debt, typically had provided a sanction against its forgery. However, this method created much confusion stemming from the fact that these various penal sections were not grouped together even though they were interrelated. The Comprehensive Act of June 30, 1864, which was reenacted in 1873, combined the crimes of counterfeiting and forgery into a single area of federal statutory law (18 U.S.C. §§ 471–509 (1976)).

The present federal law defines counterfeiting as occurring when "the fraudulent obligation bears such a likeness or resemblance to any of the genuine obligations or securities issued under the authority of the United States as is calculated to deceive an honest, sensible and unsuspecting person of ordinary observation and care dealing with a person supposed to be upright and honest" (*United States v. Lustig*, 159 F.2d 798, 802 (3d Cir. 1947), *rev'd on other grounds*, 338 U.S. 74 (1949)).

Related to the offense of counterfeiting, and included within the same chapter of the United States Code, is the crime of forgery. This offense involves the false making or alteration of any writing, with the intent to defraud. The term *forgery* is generally limited to writing, whereas *counterfeiting* refers principally to the unauthorized duplication of money, stamps, or official documents.

Under Title 18 of the United States Code, sections 471 and 509, it is a crime to counterfeit, forge, or alter United States obligations and securities; coins and minor coins; foreign bank notes; foreign obligations and securities; foreign coins; federal credit agency bonds, obligations, and instruments; certificates of discharge from United States military and naval service; contractors' bonds, bids, and related public records; letters patent granted by the President of the United States; military and naval passes and permits; money orders and postal notes; naturalization and citizenship papers; paper bearing the watermark of any stamped envelope or postal card; papers relating to customs matters; passports; United States postage stamps; foreign postage stamps; postmarking stamps; any United States government or agency seal; a ship's papers; transportation requests of the government; visas, permits, and other entry documents; and the seal of any United States court, department, or agency.

In order to counterfeit something, the original object that is to be copied must be valid on its face: a void instrument cannot be counterfeited (*Moss v. Arnold*, 63 Okla. Crim. 343, 75 P.2d 491 (1938); *People v. Kramer*, 352 Ill. 304, 185 N.E. 590 (1933)). Counterfeit objects must sufficiently resemble the genuine objects so that a person of ordinary caution would be deceived. Similarity becomes a question for the trier of fact.

Jurisdiction and elements. Both the state and the federal courts have the right to hear counterfeiting cases, because both have distinct interests to protect. The federal government must protect the currency's purity, whereas the states are obligated to protect their citizens against fraud (*State v. Scarano*, 149 Conn. 34, 175 A.2d 360 (1961)). One does not have to cross a state line in order to invoke federal jurisdiction: federal and state jurisdiction in these offenses are concurrent within a state's geographic boundaries.

The elements of this crime may vary slightly from state to state; however, under the federal statute, the key element is intent. This need not be directed at the government: the mere intent to defraud anyone is sufficient. When one unknowingly possesses a counterfeit note or coin, it is a defense that the money was received innocently in the course of trade (*Paz v. United States*, 387 F.2d 428 (5th Cir. 1967); *United States v. Sheiner*, 410 F.2d 337 (2d Cir. 1969)). Therefore, in order for the prosecution to convict someone of counterfeiting under the federal code, it must show that the defendant knew the bills were counterfeit and had the intent to use them in order to defraud another (*United States v. Lorenzo*, 570 F.2d 294 (9th Cir. 1978)). Although there are many avenues for the government to present evidence so as to prove intent, the case of *United States v. Haggins*, 545 F.2d 1009

(5th Cir. 1977) provides a clear example of how that can be done. To infer the requisite intent, the prosecution in *Haggins* presented evidence that showed (1) a rapid series of passing bills; (2) passing these bills at several establishments; (3) the repeated use of large bills rather than of the change received from the previous transactions; and (4) an attempt to destroy the remaining notes when capture was imminent.

In addition to possessing, passing, and making counterfeit things, it is contrary to federal law to possess the paraphernalia used in counterfeiting, such as the distinctive paper, dies, devices, plates, or other items used for counterfeiting. These prescriptions apply regardless of whether the item to be counterfeited is a United States or a foreign obligation.

Several ancillary offenses are included within the counterfeiting and forgery sections of the United States Code. These involve not the making of a counterfeit obligation but what is done with it after it has been produced. When one, with the requisite intent to defraud, passes, utters, or sells currency or attempts to do so, that person acts in violation of the law. In this context, *to pass* is defined as the delivery of a counterfeit substance in payment or exchange for something else. To complete the act, there must be acceptance by another party. *To utter* is to declare that the instrument is good or to offer to pass it as good (*United States v. Wolfe*, 307 F.2d 798 (7th Cir. 1962)).

Finally, possession of counterfeit objects, with the appropriate intent to defraud, is a crime. The prosecution, with regard to this offense, need not show an intent to pass, but only an intent to defraud (*Barbee v. United States*, 392 F.2d 532 (5th Cir. 1968)). Either actual or constructive possession satisfies the requirements of this statute (*United States v. Pitts*, 508 F.2d 1237 (8th Cir. 1974)). If one is in possession of more than one forged bank note, he cannot be prosecuted separately for each note since possession is a single offense (*State v. Benham*, 7 Conn. 414 (1829)). However, as ruled in *McConlogue v. Aderhold*, 56 F.2d 152 (5th Cir. 1932) and *Ross v. Hudspeth*, 108 F.2d 628 (10th Cir. 1939), forgery and uttering constitute separate offenses for each instance, as do uttering and possession.

ROBERT L. BOGOMOLNY

See also FEDERAL CRIMINAL JURISDICTION; FEDERAL CRIMINAL LAW ENFORCEMENT; FORGERY.

BIBLIOGRAPHY

CHADMAN, CHARLES E., ed. *A Treatise on Criminal Law and Criminal Procedure, Including Criminal Evidence and Criminal Pleading; Also a Treatise on the Law of Evidence and Leading Cases* (1906). Reprinted with a new preface by John J. Sullivan. New York: AMS Press, 1976.

Federal Reserve Bank of Atlanta. *Counterfeit?* Federal Reserve Bank of Atlanta, 1968.

———. *Fundamental Facts about U.S. Money.* Federal Reserve Bank of Atlanta, 1982.

Federal Reserve Bank of Boston. *Dollar Points.* Federal Reserve Bank of Boston, 1975.

Law Commission. *Criminal Law: Report on Forgery and Counterfeit Currency.* London: Her Majesty's Stationery Office, 1973.

SCOTT, KENNETH. *Counterfeiting in Colonial America.* New York: Oxford University Press, 1957.

WHARTON, FRANCIS. *Wharton's Criminal Law,* vol. 4. 14th ed. Edited by Charles E. Torcia. Rochester, N.Y.: Lawyers Co-operative, 1978.

COURT-MARTIAL

See articles under MILITARY JUSTICE.

COURTS

See APPEAL; COURTS, ORGANIZATION OF; *both articles under* CRIMINAL COURTS; *articles under* JUVENILE JUSTICE.

COURTS, ORGANIZATION OF

Structure of the courts. There are fifty-one separate judicial systems in the United States, the federal system and one for each state. Generally, state courts are concerned with litigation involving state law, whereas federal courts apply federal law. With respect to criminal law, this means that prosecutions for crimes created by Congress are brought in federal courts, and prosecutions for crimes enacted by state legislatures are brought in state courts. Federal law provides for the transfer of a state prosecution to a federal court in limited circumstances, as where a federal officer has been charged with a state crime in connection with his federal duties.

Each judicial system has both trial and appellate courts. The trial court hears the evidence in a case, determines the applicable law, and then applies the law to the facts or else directs the jury to do so. By contrast, the appellate court reviews the trial court's actions to ensure that it did not err; it does not hold an evidentiary hearing, but instead reviews the case by examining a transcript of what occurred in the trial court. Appellate courts ordinarily can hear all types of cases, although in some states there are separate appellate courts for civil and criminal appeals.

Some trial courts are specialized in that they handle only cases involving certain types of legal questions; for example, a probate court would deal only with wills and estates. Most trial courts are not so limited, and criminal cases have traditionally been assigned to these trial courts of general jurisdiction. Virtually all judicial systems are structured so that civil and criminal cases of a minor nature are assigned to one group of courts and more serious cases to another. The trial courts limited to minor cases are commonly described as magistrate courts. In some jurisdictions magistrates may try all misdemeanors, whereas in others they may only try lesser misdemeanors.

The federal system. The federal system does not have a separate magistrate court, but one or more United States magistrates are employed by each of the general trial courts, the United States district courts. The magistrates, who must be lawyers, are selected by the district court judges. Full-time magistrates serve for eight years, and part-time magistrates have a four-year term. Federal magistrates are empowered to try all misdemeanor cases, but any misdemeanor defendant may elect to be tried in the district court instead. Magistrates also perform various other functions in both misdemeanor and felony cases, such as issuing search warrants and arrest warrants and presiding at the first court appearance of an arrested person. Magistrates also hold preliminary hearings in felony cases.

The general trial court of the federal system is the district court. There are ninety-four judicial districts, and each state contains at least one. Each district is described by reference to the state or geographic segment thereof in which it is located, for example, the United States District Court for the Northern District of Illinois. The district court has jurisdiction over all civil suits brought under federal statutes and all prosecutions brought under federal criminal law. But this federal court also has an impact upon state criminal prosecutions because a state prisoner, tried and convicted under state law in state court, may obtain relief in the federal district court if he shows that his conviction was obtained in violation of his federal constitutional rights. This relief is obtained by the state prisoner petitioning the federal court for a writ of habeas corpus.

The intermediate appellate court of the federal judicial system is the United States Court of Appeals. The court is divided into twelve circuits; one has jurisdiction solely over federal cases arising in the District of Columbia, and each of the others covers a geographic area of several states. All cases decided by the district court are appealable as a matter of right

to the Court of Appeals for the circuit within which the district court is located. Appeals are ordinarily heard by a panel of three randomly selected judges of the circuit. On occasion, however, an appeal will be heard *en banc*, that is, before all the judges of the appellate court in that circuit. If two different panels in that circuit have reached inconsistent results on the same legal issue, *en banc* review is particularly likely.

The United States Supreme Court is the appellate court of last resort in the federal system. That Court, composed of nine Justices, hears every case *en banc*. The Supreme Court can review any case decided by any of the circuits of the Court of Appeals, but appeal to the Supreme Court is not a matter of right. A litigant who has lost in the Court of Appeals must petition for review, and only a small percentage of the petitions are accepted by the Supreme Court.

The state systems. The courts of first instance in the administration of state criminal justice ordinarily are the courts of limited jurisdiction. These courts are usually referred to as magistrate courts, although in some jurisdictions they have such other titles as justice of the peace courts, municipal courts, district courts, police courts, and recorder's courts. These courts have jurisdiction over lesser criminal offenses. In some states, this trial jurisdiction extends to all misdemeanors (usually defined as all offenses punishable by a jail term not exceeding one year). Elsewhere the trial jurisdiction is more limited, for example, applying only to misdemeanors punishable by no more than six months' imprisonment or those punishable by no more than ninety days in jail. Magistrate courts also have limited jurisdiction extending to preliminary proceedings concerning offenses that are beyond their trial jurisdiction. The preliminary matters customarily handled by a state magistrate include the issuance of search and arrest warrants, the first appearance of the arrested person before a court, the setting of bail, the appointment of counsel for indigent defendants, and the determination at a preliminary hearing of whether there is probable cause for the case to proceed to trial.

There is considerable variation from state to state in the staffing and structure of magistrate courts. Some states have divided the state into districts each of which has the same type of magistrate court, whereas others have districts coinciding with such political subdivisions as a city or township. In the latter circumstance, there are likely to be many different types of magistrate courts, each with different attributes, in the same state. About half of the states have at least one kind of magistrate court that is "not of record," which originally meant the lack of capacity to provide a complete transcript of the trial. Because of that lack (and, in more recent times, because of a belief that in any event the defendant should have an opportunity for a more thorough and formal trial), a defendant convicted in such a court is likely to be afforded a right to trial de novo (that is, an entirely new trial) in a higher court. In most states, at least some magistrates serve part-time and need not be lawyers; such circumstances are more likely to be found in rural areas.

The general trial courts in state judicial systems are known by various names, such as superior court, circuit court, district court, and court of common pleas. Typically, the state is divided into a number of judicial districts, and at least one general trial court judge will sit in each district. The most common pattern is for there to be one district in every county of the state. The trial jurisdiction of these general trial courts usually begins where the trial jurisdiction of the magistrate court ends. These courts also hear appeals from minor cases tried in the magistrate court. Except where there is a right to trial de novo, this review involves examination of the record in magistrate court for possible error.

Nearly half of the states have intermediate appellate courts, commonly referred to as courts of appeals. Most of these states have a single court of intermediate appeals that hears appeals from all trial courts in the state, but some divide this court into divisions, each of which serves a district made up of several counties. These courts usually sit in panels of three. In a state which has an intermediate appellate court, a defendant convicted in the general trial court will have a right of appeal to that court.

The highest appellate court in the state is usually called the supreme court, and it consists of five, seven, or nine justices. With rare exceptions, these justices sit *en banc* rather than dividing into panels. If the state lacks an intermediate appellate court, the state supreme court is the first available appellate level for a defendant convicted in the general trial court, and thus he usually has an automatic right of appellate review in that court. But if the state has an intermediate appellate court, then the state supreme court usually has discretion to grant only those petitions for review that it believes merit additional judicial consideration. However, even in a state with a two-tiered appellate system, there is likely to be review as a matter of right in the highest court for certain cases, such as those in which the sentence is capital punishment.

The state supreme court is the court of last resort in state cases as to matters of state law. But where the matter involves an issue of federal law, further review can be sought from the United States Supreme Court. The Supreme Court's appellate jurisdiction in this respect is largely discretionary, and the Court refuses to accept jurisdiction in most cases coming from state courts. However, many of the most famous decisions of the Supreme Court have involved the federal constitutional claims of defendants who were convicted in a state court and had their objections rejected by the state appellate courts.

WAYNE R. LaFAVE

See also both articles under CRIMINAL COURTS; CRIMINAL JUSTICE SYSTEM: OVERVIEW.

BIBLIOGRAPHY

KERPER, HAZEL B., and ISRAEL, JEROLD H. *Introduction to the Criminal Justice System.* 2d ed. St. Paul: West, 1979.

RYAN, JOHN P.; ASHMAN, ALLAN; SALES, BRUCE; and SHANE-DuBow, SANDRA. *American Trial Judges: Their Work Styles and Performance.* New York: Free Press, 1980.

SILBERMAN, LINDA J., with the assistance of PRESCOTT, ELIZABETH, and CLARK, MATTHEW. *Non-attorney Justice in the United States: An Empirical Study.* New York: Institute of Judicial Administration, 1979.

U.S. Bureau of the Census. *National Survey of Court Organization.* Washington, D.C.: U.S. Department of Justice, Law Enforcement Assistance Administration, National Criminal Justice Information and Statistics Service, 1973.

CRIME

CONCEPT OF CRIME *discusses various approaches to identifying the essential elements of the concept of a criminal action and considers the different consequences of characterizing conduct as criminal or as a civil wrong.* DEFINITION OF CRIME *explores the analytic elements that enter into the prohibition of conduct, the agencies responsible for defining crime, and the requirements of specificity, clarity, and prospectivity that definitions of crime must meet.*

1. CONCEPT OF CRIME   Graham Hughes
2. DEFINITION OF CRIME   Edward L. Kimball

1.
CONCEPT OF CRIME

The natural concept

Two concepts of crime overlap, and it is important to elucidate the relations between them. First, there is an idea of crime that might be called *natural* and that is intuitively understood by most people. It embodies a sense of an act that is deeply wrong, that evokes strong communal disapproval, and that is thought to deserve, indeed to call for, a punitive sanction. The nature of what is perceived as wrong in this way may vary to some extent with time and culture. Thus, blasphemy or deviant sexual behavior may be considered grave wrongs in some places and at some times.

This restricted understanding of a crime as a grave wrong calling for a deeply censorious response is present in popular speech. The adjective *criminal* is often used in conversation to refer to conduct thought to be very reprehensible, even though it may not be obviously illegal. On the other hand, most people do not regard overtime parking as a crime even though the legal procedures followed for parking violations may have features in common with those found in the prosecution of acts that are popularly accounted crimes.

Besides this natural concept of crime there is a second, broader one that derives from the enactments of a particular legal system. This idea of crime is connected with a particular set of procedures and with special officials, special courts, and perhaps special rules of evidence and special avenues of appeal. This body of law is usually called criminal, or penal, law (from the Latin *poena*, "punishment"), and it always has as a possible outcome the imposition on the defendant of some disadvantage—such as imprisonment, a fine, or probation—for engaging in prohibited conduct. In the United States the classification of a proceeding as "criminal" takes on a heightened significance since the Constitution of the United States, and the constitutions of individual states, require that special rights and protections be accorded a defendant in a criminal prosecution.

The Sixth Amendment to the United States Constitution guarantees trial by an impartial jury in a criminal prosecution and assures the accused of the right to counsel and the right to confront the witnesses against him. Because of such provisions, the question of whether a proceeding is to be classified as criminal takes on legal and constitutional importance and may have to be decided by the courts. Even in a society without such written constitutional guarantees for criminal defendants, the question of whether proceedings are criminal may be a substantial one that must be adjudicated. In Great Britain, for example, special rules of evidence and burdens of proof apply in a criminal case, and a special appellate process is prescribed.

For these reasons, lawyers and courts need a concept of crime for internal, legal purposes. One commentator, Glanville Williams, has suggested that this concept must be a purely procedural one that cannot be illuminated by any discussion of the elements that constitute the natural concept of crime (pp. 107–130). Williams argues that neither popular nor criminological concepts of crime are helpful to the lawyer since they are clearly repudiated by legal doctrine. Petty offenses are in many respects handled under the special legal rules for criminal cases even though most people do not think of them as crimes, and criminologists would generally consider them outside the ambit of their discipline. The courts have frequently declared that conduct must be recognized as a crime if it has been procedurally stamped in a certain way by the legislature even though no keen sense of moral wrong is associated with the conduct in popular judgment.

Crimes and civil wrongs. A further objection often made to attempts to describe crimes in terms of the inherent wrongness of the prohibited conduct is that such efforts fail to distinguish between crimes and civil wrongs since the same act may amount to both. A murderer may be sued for damages by his victim's family in a civil action separate from the criminal prosecution. It has been argued that there is nothing in the nature of the act done that helps differentiate between the criminal prosecution and the private suit. In some cases even the outcome of the two processes will be identical—an order to pay money, although in one case the payment will be to the state in the form of a fine, and in the other to the victim in the form of damages.

One answer to this objection is that the wrong and the financial penalty have a different character in the criminal case and the civil case. In the criminal case the wrong is perceived as violating a collective interest that must be vindicated through a public process, and the sanction imposed is seen as an expression of reprobation rather than as a way of affording compensation to an individual. Critics have retorted that the use of such adjectives as *public* or *reprobative* merely restates in an uninformative fashion the assertion that a process is criminal or that an act is a crime without contributing to the elucidation of a distinction. But this criticism, which, if valid, would destroy the importance of the natural concept of crime, is misguided.

The defect in the objection is that it fails to acknowledge the differentiating power of the way in which acts and processes are perceived in society. Sociologists have sometimes referred to accusation and conviction as a social degradation ceremony, an observation that throws light on the contrast between a criminal prosecution and a suit for damages. It is the public understanding of a process and its outcome as punitive, evidenced by the language of blame and condemnation, that distinguishes a criminal proceeding from a civil one, in which liability is often divorced from any notion of bad intent or even culpable negligence. If the act is a morally bad one and may lead to both civil and criminal proceedings, the two procedures are still regarded as separate precisely because of the different perceptions of their nature and aims. This public understanding is more important, even to courts, than are the details of the procedural differences in any particular jurisdiction. Indeed, in continental Europe the two processes are often largely fused, and the victim participates in the criminal prosecution as the "civil party," asking for damages which may be awarded in the same judgment that fixes the criminal penalty. It is not the procedural differences in the modes of trial and judgment that distinguish a crime from a civil wrong; rather, it is the natural perception of the differences between a criminal process and a means for fixing compensation that has led to the growth of different legal procedures.

Regulatory offenses. A more serious objection to the utility of the natural concept of crime might seem to reside in the scope of modern criminal law, which includes a mass of regulatory provisions not popularly associated with any idea of moral wrong. A distinction between natural wrongs and wrongs created by special duties applicable to regulated groups has long been recognized in the language of the law. There is an ancient contrast between *mala in se* (acts wrong in themselves) and *mala prohibita* (acts wrong because they are prohibited), and this remains helpful in understanding the nature of modern criminal law. Murder, assault, and theft are natural wrongs, but a real estate developer's failure to file on time all the forms required by a federal agency is an offense intelligible only in the context of the whole setting of regulated building procedures. Although the need for such regulation may be understood and it may be agreed that a fine or loss of permit can sometimes be the most effective method of enforcement, society may feel neither the reaction of deep condemnation nor any stirring of the demand for punishment that is excited by the commission of natural wrongs.

Part of the explanation for these differing responses may be that in the case of natural wrongs each individual act is perceived as a complete and serious wrong in itself. The death of the murderer's victim and the trepidation and injury caused by theft are either irreparable or imperil cherished personal interests. But with regulatory offenses the injury is often only to be found in some concept of the disorder or damage that would be caused by a general lack of observance or by some extreme case of exploitation by an individual. One person's overparking at a meter causes no shock, although a total absence of parking regulations might lead to chaotic and intolerable conditions. One negligent failure to file an accurate report with a government agency might be shrugged off as morally undisturbing, but a general absence of any reporting system would lead to fraud and corruption. Thus, the social harms whose avoidance is sought through regulation may often be as serious as those that are inflicted by some traditional crimes. The difference is that the harm done by the individual who infringes a regulation is often in itself minuscule or nonexistent.

The procedural concept

If some critics reject the concept of wrongdoing as the key to an understanding of the concept of crime, what can they put in its place? Williams has suggested that society must be content with an elucidation of the exact legal usage and that a crime must be defined by reference to the legal consequences of the act: "A crime then becomes an act that is capable of being followed by criminal proceedings, having one of the types of outcome (punishment etc.) known to follow these proceedings" (p. 123).

This substitution of "criminal proceedings" as the concept in need of elucidation points in a helpful direction. It calls for close attention to a special segment of a legal system distinguished by a special vocabulary and institutions. Thus, in criminal proceedings statutes speak of "conviction" and "sentence," special offices such as that of the prosecutor are mentioned, and special procedures such as indictment by a grand jury may be required. In any modern legal system these procedural marks are so distinct that only rarely can there be any doubt as to whether a legal matter is criminal. But to conclude from this that the identification of conduct as criminal ends with the citation of the title of the code in which it is to be found, and that a natural concept of crime is superfluous, would be to ignore the marginal cases, analysis of which illuminates the central understanding of the concept.

Difficulties begin to appear when a provision found in a particular section of the code, or the procedures that are actually followed in carrying out a transaction, are not accepted as determining the question. A party may argue that a proceeding ought to be treated as criminal even though the usual setting and vocabulary of the criminal process have been carefully eschewed by the legislature or executive. The argument here will be that certain measures have an inherently penal character and that it is therefore unfair to permit them to be carried out under procedures that are different from those required in criminal cases. This position requires recognition of the importance of an underlying, natural concept of crime.

Conversely, it may be argued that once conduct is legislatively classified in a way that invokes consequences of a kind generally associated with the criminal procedures of a particular jurisdiction, it will be unfair not to accord the defendant all the principles of excuse and defense generally associated with criminal cases. This position is another assertion of the underlying axiom that the imposition of punishment must be attended with certain safeguards demanded by principles of fairness. These difficulties will be better understood after considering some examples.

Marginal cases

American courts have had to decide at times whether the constitutional guarantees reserved for criminal cases ought to be applied to legal proceedings that possess only some, if any, of the usual procedural characteristics of criminal matters. Proceedings against a juvenile for delinquency are one example. Since the late nineteenth century the reform movement in criminal justice wisely preached the necessity of protecting juveniles from the corrupting clutches of adult offenders in adult penal institutions. The very idea that a juvenile could be a criminal in the same sense as an adult was challenged.

As a result, proceedings against juveniles came to be governed by special statutes and procedures with a vocabulary quite unlike that of the criminal law. Special courts were set up, convictions became "findings," sentences were transformed into "dispositions," and prisons and correctional facilities were given such euphemisms as "training schools." For all this, juveniles were often judged to have committed acts that would be serious crimes if committed by adults, and the consequences for the juvenile might involve several years' confinement in an institution. Yet most of the constitutional guarantees accorded to criminal defendants, such as the rights to counsel, confrontation, and jury trial, were not provided in the very informal atmosphere of the juvenile court.

Delicate questions of principle and policy are involved in this conflict between the old reform ideal of juvenile proceedings as a nonadversary inquiry into a young person's "condition" that should be cured by therapeutic treatment and, on the other hand, the reality of confinement as a consequence of a finding of acts that are generally condemned as serious crimes. The Supreme Court delivered a crucial judgment on this question in *In re Gault*, 387 U.S. 1 (1967). In that case the Court held that since delinquency proceedings had sufficiently severe consequences for the juvenile, due process therefore demanded that at least some of the constitutional guarantees associated with criminal proceedings must be accorded the young person. These included adequate notice of charges, the right to counsel, the protection of the privilege against self-incrimination, and the rights of confrontation and cross-examination.

But the language in *Gault* and in later cases shows that the Court did not intend simply to classify juvenile proceedings as criminal. For example, in *McKeiver v. Pennsylvania*, 403 U.S. 528 (1971) the Court held that jury trial was not constitutionally required in a juvenile case. The natural concept of crime does not insist that every element of conventional criminal procedure is indispensable, but it does demand the procedural guarantees required by basic fairness. In this way, *Gault* and *McKeiver* create a curious legal hybrid of proceedings that are not to be called criminal and yet partake so substantially of the nature of accusation and punishment that large segments of the Constitution's requirements for criminal prosecutions are made applicable.

Such decisions demonstrate irrefutably that the courts make use of a concept of crime that transcends procedural settings and legislative placement and vocabulary. The basis of *Gault* is the social reality of delinquency proceedings and their consequences, which cannot be erased by benevolent intentions and studious language. That reality may entail the imposition of a highly disadvantageous consequence (confinement) of a kind familiar as a response to serious wrongdoing and as a result of a finding of conduct that is generally accounted criminal in an adult.

In its explanations of modern juvenile proceedings, the legislature has given earnest assurances that juveniles are not regarded as wrongdoers and that confining them is not intended as punishment. Although the legislative intent is not to be ignored, the courts have rightly said that a justified popular perception of the resemblances between juvenile detention and the imprisonment of an adult criminal must in some contexts count for more than the legislature's profession of ideals. In this way these cases testify to the enduring importance of a publicly held concept of accusation and punitive disposition that identifies a criminal matter, whose reality may be visible underneath the forms in which a legislature may clothe a particular proceeding.

Punishment as a test. The importance of possible confinement as contributing to the criminal nature of delinquency proceedings was stressed in *Gault*. But it is not the threat of confinement alone that always makes a proceeding a criminal one, nor is a proceeding necessarily only civil when confinement is not a possible outcome. The essential feature of the concept of crime is the use of a sanction that is traditionally *punitive* and not merely compensatory. This means that it must be imposed for reasons that have to do with a judgment that the defendant's behavior was wrong in a way deserving of public rebuke and sanction, going beyond a mere judgment of the justice of making reparation to a victim. In *Middendorf v. Henry*, 425 U.S. 25 (1976), the Supreme Court held that summary court-martial procedures in the military forces were not criminal cases that required counsel under the Sixth Amendment. Even though the proceedings could result in brief detention, the Court reasoned that the military code performed regulatory functions for reasons that were often peculiar to the concept of military discipline. Therefore, the code should not be understood as establishing a set of wrongs felt to be worthy of punishment in the sense in which that idea is comprehended in the community at large. Similarly, confinement of a person who is seriously emotionally ill and dangerous is not thought of as punishment.

People suffer unpleasant consequences every day because someone with power or authority over them believes they have fallen short of a certain standard, but not all such incidents can be thought of as criminal proceedings. Losing a job because of a judgment of one's incompetence formed by a superior is unpleasant, but one will not be regarded as a criminal because of it. But if an employer dismisses an employee after accusing him of theft, what is involved is the imposition of a serious harm as a response to what is charged as a serious wrong. Why should this not be viewed as a criminal proceeding, and why should the employer not be compelled to give the employee a hearing with all the attributes of a criminal trial? One answer is that society's notion of a criminal proceeding or prosecution is that of a process instituted by the state. In the example given, a private employer would indeed be accusing the employee of committing a crime, but the process of dismissal could not be thought of as a criminal prosecution since there would be no official accusation by the state.

If the state is the employer, a dismissal will still not ordinarily have connotations of punishment for crime, since loss of employment is not normally considered a specially inflicted deprivation such as a fine or imprisonment imposed by a court. Nor is the loss of employment in itself equivalent to the publication of a judgment of wrongdoing that is always apparent in a conviction by a court, even when there is no fine or imprisonment. But exceptional cases may arise.

In *United States v. Lovett*, 328 U.S. 303 (1946), a statute provided that no salaries should be paid to certain named government employees. This followed a congressional debate in which those employees had been described as affiliated with communist-front organizations. The employees sued for their salaries. When the case reached the Supreme Court, the Court interpreted the statute as permanently proscribing the employees from government service. This, joined with the reasons publicly stated in the congressional debate, constituted more than the loss of a job, and could only be understood as punishing the employees for their political beliefs. Such retroactive statutory imposition of punishment was held to be unconstitutional. The *Lovett* decision again denotes a natural concept of crime in terms of the combination of an opprobrious accusation with the possibility of a punitive sanction.

It is difficult to distinguish *Lovett* from the later case of *Flemming v. Nestor*, 363 U.S. 603 (1960). Here, the appellant was an alien who, after forty years' residence in the United States, had been deported for having been a member of the Communist party some decades earlier. Under a section of the Social Security Act his old-age benefits were terminated because of his deportation. In a 5–4 decision, the Supreme Court held that this termination was constitutional because it did not amount to a punishment that would necessitate the guarantees of the criminal process. The majority read the statute not as aiming at individuals in retribution for their past conduct, but rather as setting rational standards for the disbursement of Social Security funds, thus distinguishing it from the decision in *Lovett*.

The decision is regrettable. Action was taken against Nestor for exactly the same reason as against Lovett. In both cases the consequence imposed would not always be punitive, but it clearly was when coupled with the reason for imposition in the particular case. To impose a deprivation or ban because of a stated reason that amounts to a public accusation of what is considered to be a seriously wrongful act converts the consequence into punishment, and *Nestor* should have been decided in the same way as *Lovett*.

These cases are of help in elucidating the concept of punishment. It is not possible to explain the concept solely in terms of a special kind of deprivation; rather, it can only be understood in the light of special reasons for imposing a deprivation. Whether a deprivation is a punishment depends upon the way in which the reason for its imposition is understood by society at a particular time, and upon how close that understanding comes to the central perception that constitutes the core of the concept of crime. This perception involves the identification of a serious accusation, proof of which elicits a demand for a censorious and retributive response.

Impact of the Constitution

In a jurisdiction that lacks the American system of constitutional guarantees for criminal proceedings, the reasons for classifying a procedure as criminal or not may be less dramatic. In England the leading case in this area is *Amand v. Home Secretary,* [1943] A.C. 147. The appellant was a Netherlands citizen who had been arrested in England as a deserter from the Netherlands army. A statute established procedures under which such persons might be handed over by the magistrates to the Netherlands military authorities. After such an order had been made against him, the appellant had unsuccessfully applied for a writ of habeas corpus. The Court of Appeals denied the appeal from the refusal of the writ on the ground that this was a criminal case over which the Court of Appeals had no appellate jurisdiction. A further appeal to the House of Lords was rejected on the same ground.

The House of Lords admitted that the distinction between a habeas corpus in a civil matter as compared with one in a criminal case was not easy to draw. The test of whether a case was criminal, they held, was that the proceedings might put the applicant in jeopardy of being punished by a court having jurisdiction over him. In *Amand* the process before the magistrates entailed the possible surrender of the defendant to a military court before which he might be charged and punished. It was therefore a criminal case.

Although the House of Lords in such a marginal case used the same yardstick as would the United States Supreme Court (an analysis of whether punishment was a possible outcome), a British court cannot defend the natural concept of crime as resolutely as an American court may and must do with its constitutional mandates. If Parliament provides that juvenile delinquents need not be afforded counsel at public expense, or that a deported alien should be denied social security payments, that is likely to be the end of the matter. In the United States it is only the beginning of the inquiry.

The natural concept of crime often serves in Great Britain only to criticize the actions of the legislature in a political or social forum. In the United States the natural concept is fully converted into a legal one through the alchemy of the Constitution. This does not diminish the importance of sensitivity to the elements of the natural concept in a country such as Great Britain, but it illustrates the tighter fusion of moral and legal ideas in a constitutional system of fundamental rights.

Strict liability

In modern times the widespread use of the criminal law to enforce business and social regulations whose violation is not generally perceived as moral wrongdoing has tended to separate the natural and procedural concepts of crime. Such offenses are usually not found in the penal code but may be collected in statutes that deal with the commercial or other activity in question. If the infractions are of a very minor nature they are more usually referred to as offenses or violations rather than crimes, and carry only a fine as a possible penalty. Indeed, some penal codes define a crime as a felony or misdemeanor, and describe petty violations as "noncriminal offenses" or by some similar phrase. But at the same time, in other respects these offenses do resemble the classical core of the criminal law. Sometimes they are not trivial but may be misdemeanors. They may result in the taking away of the defendant's money or property by the state; they may sometimes have grave consequences in the loss of licenses or permits; they may have a bad effect on commercial reputation; and they may retain much of the criminal vocabulary of prosecution, sentence, and conviction.

An important process of interaction takes place here. It was the rough congruence between the natural concept of crime and the content of the classical criminal law that invested the legal system's criminal process with many of its connotations of obloquy and degradation. As the expanded criminal law system threw its procedural cloak over many acts that were not crimes in the natural sense, it nevertheless inevitably subjected those who were prosecuted for these offenses to some shadow of the disrepute that falls on those convicted of serious crimes. Whether this development can be defended is a much-debated question.

In the first place one may ask whether the criminal process is always the best method of enforcing regulatory structures. Certainly a financial exaction often seems the most suitable sanction, but, as has often been pointed out, the fine imposed in cases of regulatory offenses sometimes seems more of a penalty than a punishment. It is a levy exacted for not doing business or conducting a licensed activity according to standards that are deemed desirable. Often the defendant will have acted only negligently and not with any bad intent, so that a punitive response (as opposed to a penalty) may seem exaggerated. Where this is so it would be better strictly to separate such proceedings both in vocabulary and procedure from the general body of the criminal law.

But if the regulatory offense is pursued according to conventional criminal process, especially in the case of a misdemeanor, the accompanying connotations demand that the usual principles of fairness inherent in a just criminal procedure be applied. The idea of punishment is the obverse of blame or culpability. Negligent conduct may sometimes deserve punishment; however, behavior that is neither intentional nor negligent but that is the result of unavoidable accident or the uncontrollable acts of another should never be punished. Yet in many regulatory offenses the courts have imposed "strict liability," holding that the defendant may not escape conviction even by showing that he was not in any way negligent.

Some kind of strict accountability may be a helpful means of enforcing a regulatory system, but it has no place in a penal system. The remedy is either to purge the regulatory enforcement of any serious ties with criminal prosecution, or else to abandon strict liability. Here again it is the natural concept of crime that furnishes an invaluable moral standard for evaluating and criticizing the state of the law.

Early and prelegal societies

The analysis of primitive societies provided by anthropologists casts no serious doubts on the validity of a natural concept of crime, although it does show that the nature referred to is the social nature of mankind and that over long periods of time important shifts may occur in social attitudes and the quality of judgments. For example, all societies have shared the concept of a wrong that, for one reason or another, is serious enough to be a source of communal concern, but the gravity of the wrong has not always been judged by the bad intent of the culprit. Acciden-

tal violation of taboo, as by quite innocently stumbling upon a sacred and exclusive ceremony, might be a reason for sanctions against the offender. The rank or social status of the victim might be taken to be an important aggravating or mitigating circumstance, as has also been the case with the killing of members of minority groups by members of the dominant group in some modern societies.

Although the intentional or deliberate nature of the act was often seen in earlier societies to be one aggravating circumstance, it certainly did not dominate the inquiry as it would in moral judgments today. But the distinction does sometimes appear in a very modern form, as when an accidental killing might necessitate a purification ceremony but not any sanctions against the innocent actor. This is a recognition of the inappropriateness of punishment and a simultaneous perception of a need for correction of the situation through a ritualistic restoration of the balance of natural and supernatural forces.

The notion of what kinds of harm are properly the concern of the society as a whole may also shift dramatically with the passage of time. In some early societies offenses such as theft or even killing were seen as less important than violations of divinely ordained observances or ceremonies of a propitiatory or placatory nature. This was a reasonable position since such violations were considered as endangering the whole community, whereas theft and killing were not so clearly seen in that light but were taken to be more the concern of the individual victim and his immediate family. Thus, publicly initiated consequences in the way of condemnation and sanctions against the person of the offender might be reserved for the former set of acts, but actions such as theft might be left either to self-help or at least to privately initiated dispute settlement. But if the details of the distinction between crimes and civil wrongs have not been exactly the same in all societies at all times, the total absence of any version of that distinction seems unknown.

A concept of crime may be said to exist whenever certain acts are regarded as deeply wrong and elicit a censorious response, even if it is unstructured. Criminal law emerges when the censorious response leads to a process, whether initiated publicly or by a private citizen, culminating in a publicly imposed sanction that is perceived as something other than an award of compensation to a victim. In many societies, including the sophisticated legal world of ancient Rome, criminal punishment was slow to emerge for many natural wrongs; the law of theft in particular was long left largely to compensatory remedies. By contrast, Anglo-Saxon law early developed a powerful sector devoted to the infliction of punishment by royal officers. It should be noted that it is not the initiation of the process by a public officer that is so vital. Until very recent times most prosecutions in England were theoretically instituted by private complaints. What sets criminal law apart is the public understanding of the process as aiming at the protection of a public interest by the imposition of a punitive sanction.

Conclusion

To say, as Glanville Williams did, that a crime is any conduct followed by certain procedures and consequences turns out in the end to say both too little and too much. It says too little because it does not accord enough significance to the natural elements in the concept of crime. It says too much because it implies a virtually unlimited legislative power to create crimes without regard to any restraining principles.

There is of course one sense in which this is true. A capricious dictatorship might put persons to death as a "punishment" for uncontrollably sneezing, and such a process could be dressed up in statutes that mimicked the language of traditional criminal procedure. But the attempt would be self-defeating, for to invoke the notion of punishment is to summon up (like it or not) its essential counterpart—the foundation of guilt or blame. When someone tries to pass off inflicting an injury on another as punishment without being able to point to guilt or blame, it is obvious that what is happening is unjustified force hypocritically seeking to legitimize itself. Even in a system lacking express constitutional guarantees, judges could find a principle for refusing to enforce such edicts, namely, that the concept of guilt or culpability is legally necessary to the concepts of crime and punishment. This would simply be to read or interpret a statute in the light of general principles of fairness, a duty that judges should always acknowledge. The requirement of fairness is entailed in the natural concept of crime.

GRAHAM HUGHES

See also CRIME: DEFINITION OF CRIME; GUILT; MENS REA; PUNISHMENT.

BIBLIOGRAPHY

ALLEN, CARLETON K. "The Nature of a Crime." *Journal of Comparative Legislation and International Law*, 3d series, 13 (1931): 1–25.
AUSTIN, JOHN. *Lectures on Jurispurdence; or, The Philosophy of Positive Law* (1861), vol. 1. 5th ed. Revised and edited by Robert Campbell. London: John Murray, 1911.
BLACK, DONALD, and MILESKI, MAUREEN, eds. *The Social Organization of Law.* New York: Seminar Press, 1973.
COHEN, MORRIS R. "Moral Aspects of the Criminal Law." *Yale Law Journal* 49 (1940): 987–1026.
CRESSEY, DONALD R., and WARD, DAVID A. *Delinquency, Crime, and Social Process.* New York: Harper & Row, 1969.
FEINBERG, JOEL. "The Expressive Function of Punishment." *Doing and Deserving: Essays in the Theory of Responsibility.* By Joel Feinberg. Princeton, N.J.: Princeton University Press, 1970, pp. 95–117.
FITZGERALD, PATRICK J. *Criminal Law and Punishment.* Oxford: Clarendon Press, 1962.
GLASER, DANIEL. *Social Deviance.* Chicago: Markham, 1971.
GLUCKMAN, MAX. *The Ideas in Barotse Jurisprudence.* New Haven: Yale University Press, 1965.
HUGHES, GRAHAM. "The Concept of Crime: An American View." *Criminal Law Review* (1959): 239–249, 331–339.
KADISH, SANFORD H. "Some Observations on the Use of Criminal Sanctions in Enforcing Economic Regulations." *University of Chicago Law Review* 30 (1963): 423–449.
MAINE, HENRY. *Ancient Law: Its Connection with the Early History of Society and Its Relation to Modern Ideas* (1861). Introduction by C. K. Allen. World's Classics, vol. 362. London: Oxford University Press, 1931.
PERSHITS, A. I. "The Primitive Norm and Its Evolution." *Current Anthropology* 18 (1977): 409–417.
RICHARDS, DAVID A. J. *The Moral Criticism of Law.* Encino, Calif.: Dickenson, 1977.
WILLIAMS, GLANVILLE. "The Definition of Crime." *Current Legal Problems* 8 (1955): 107–130.

2.
DEFINITION OF CRIME

Crime is a set of circumstances for which the law permits imposition of a criminal penalty. Thus, crime is not a natural phenomenon but a legal one: whatever the lawmaker defines as crime is crime. In the United States, the Constitution and considerations of practicality impose limitations on the lawmaker's choices, but the concept of "crime" does not.

Crime is not intrinsic; that is, one cannot identify characteristics other than the lawmaker's fiat from which it is possible to distinguish criminal from noncriminal circumstances. Acts hurting others in very direct ways—murder, rape, theft, battery, and arson—are almost universally criminal, but even these are socially determined and may change from time to time and place to place. The list of universal crimes is short indeed.

By its nature, treason cannot be noncriminal: no

society can tolerate it. Similarly, killing and robbing at random will be criminal if there is any developed criminal law. The last qualification must be added because in some societies, such as England before the Norman Conquest of 1066, there is almost nothing we would recognize as criminal law, but only a scheme of victim compensation.

Few kinds of conduct have not been permitted at one time and place and forbidden at another. At the extremes, capital offenses in one culture may not even be criminal in another. A father's deliberate killing of his child, which would be a capital offense in the United States, was permissible in ancient Greece. Blasphemy and filial disobedience, which were capital offenses in the law of Moses, are not even criminal in the United States today. We include incest and exclude witchcraft from our canon of crimes, whereas other cultures have reversed those value judgments. Even within a culture, change occurs. Gambling, abortion, drug use, and consensual extramarital sexual acts have shifted back and forth between criminal and noncriminal in American legal history.

Elements of crime

The circumstances that constitute crime will ordinarily, but not always, involve (1) an actor (2) with a guilty mind (mens rea) (3) who causes (4) harm (5) in a particular way or setting, and (6) a lawmaker who has decreed that these circumstances expose the actor to imposition of fine, imprisonment, or death as a penalty. For example, (1) a person who (2) intentionally (3) causes (4) damage (5) to the property of another to the extent of less than $250 is guilty of criminal mischief and (6) subjects himself upon conviction to imprisonment for ninety days (Utah Code Ann. § 76-6-106 (1978)).

Conduct. The most common element of crime is action. Shooting, kidnapping, raping, shoplifting, burning—these are the sorts of conduct one first thinks of as crimes. Whenever action is involved, it must be "voluntary." That leaves some difficult borderline situations, such as movement that is habitual, nearly reflexive, under hypnosis, or in a semiconscious state.

In addition to actions, there are crimes of words (such as extortion, libel, or threat), of omission (nonsupport or failure to report an abortion, to register for the draft, or to file income-tax reports), of possession (possession of drugs, burglary tools, or concealed weapons), or of status (being an addict or a common drunk or vagrant).

Punishing omissions poses no theoretical problems,

provided the law imposes an obligation to act. The offender must, however, have the capacity to act, so that his omission can be said to flow from his will. Possession is not strictly either act or omission, yet it is punishable so long as there was awareness that the thing possessed was within the offender's control. However, there are problems in punishing status. The United States Supreme Court has ruled, for example, that one cannot be punished merely for being a narcotic addict (*Robinson v. California*, 370 U.S. 660 (1962); cf. *Powell v. Texas*, 392 U.S. 514 (1968), in which an alcoholic was intoxicated in public) or a vagrant (*Papachristou v. City of Jacksonville*, 405 U.S. 156 (1972)).

Mental element. Most crime involves conscious disregard for the legal rights of others, as when a person intentionally wrongs another or recklessly does so, that is, acts with an awareness that his conduct is likely to have such effect. But this is not true of all crimes. Crime may also involve negligence, which is a blameworthy failure to consider the rights of others, or it may involve no mental state at all and incur punishment despite ignorance of any wrongdoing. In addition, a single crime may involve several mental elements, one for each factual element, and the mental elements may vary, with any combination of intention, recklessness, negligence, and strict liability being found in one crime.

The mental element in crime is variously described. The commentaries to the proposed Federal Criminal Code point out that some eighty words or phrases describing required mental states have been used in federal statutes. The Model Penal Code and the federal code would reduce those to a very few—purpose, knowledge, recklessness, negligence, and strict liability.

Strict liability. Strict liability exists when no fault need be shown, not even negligence. It is not presumed, but rather is recognized only when it seems to be required by the language or clear purpose of the statute. However, the Supreme Court has in several cases upheld the constitutionality of imposing criminal penalties on persons not shown to have acted with "guilty mind" (*United States v. Balint*, 258 U.S. 250 (1922); *United States v. Dotterweich*, 320 U.S. 277 (1943)).

A problem with strict liability is its dilution of the moral aspect of criminal law. It permits some "innocent" persons to be caught up in the criminal law net. Such use of criminal law for "social engineering" purposes, where there is no community indignation to support it, deprives the criminal law of some moral quality and substitutes expediency. It encourages people to feel that their only concern need be with getting caught.

Strict liability tends to be used where proof of mental state is difficult or costly and where penalties are small. Other legal systems have managed to deal with those problems by using a negligence standard or by shifting the burden of proof to the defendant to show that he was nonculpable. Negligence has only infrequently been used by American legislatures, and where the statute is silent about mental state the courts have assumed that the offense is either one of strict liability or requires the government to prove at least recklessness. So far as the burden of proof is concerned, the Supreme Court has held that the state cannot shift the burden of establishing every element of a crime beyond a reasonable doubt (*Mullaney v. Wilbur*, 421 U.S. 684 (1975)), although the state may constitutionally require the accused to bear the burden of proof on affirmative defenses, such as extreme emotional disturbances (*Patterson v. New York*, 432 U.S. 197 (1977)).

Consequences. Often the crime is basically in the harm done, not in the means by which it is accomplished. Causing death with the requisite mental state is the crime of murder, however it is caused. Destroying the eye is mayhem, irrespective of the method used. Torturing an animal is the crime of cruelty, whatever the means.

Sometimes the harm done is included in the definition as a clearly separate element, such as the physical harm of "serious bodily injury" or the psychic harm of "fear of imminent serious bodily injury." Other crimes are aimed at tendency to do harm, whether or not the harm occurs, such as providing a prisoner with anything that might facilitate escape (whether or not there is an escape), impersonating an officer (whether or not anyone is fooled), giving out false information tending to expose another to ridicule (whether or not ridicule follows), or conspiracy to rob (even if the plan is abandoned).

The harm may be done to intangible community interests, as in bribing a public official or committing consensual incest or sodomy. But there must be some threat or harm to a legitimate social interest, or the law will be struck down as arbitrary. There is long-standing debate regarding whether it is enough that the actor directly harm only himself, as in failing to wear a motorcycle helmet. Some urge that the law cannot be used to protect individuals against their own bad judgment, but others point out the indirect costs to the community if people who injure themselves become a public charge (*State v. Lee*, 465 P.2d 573 (Haw. 1970)).

Causation. There must be a causal connection between the conduct and the harm which is close enough that the law will recognize it as sufficient, or "proximate." The requirement in the criminal field is closely analogous to the same concept in personal-injury litigation.

Circumstances. The circumstances often determine the existence of crime or its gravity. Bribery requires involvement of a public servant; bigamy is marrying when one is already married; burglary is "aggravated burglary" if the burglar is armed; and unlawful sexual intercourse is committed if the female is under sixteen and is not the offender's wife.

Penalty. Although fine, imprisonment, or death are the usual penalties for crime in the United States, there are others, such as probation and disqualification for public office (Utah Code Ann. § 76-3-201 (1978 & 1981 Supp.)). Still other penalties have been imposed in the past, such as whipping (held constitutional in Delaware in *State v. Cannon*, 190 A.2d 514 (Del. 1963)), mutilation, the pillory, forfeiture of estate, and exile. The United States Constitution prohibits some punishments as "cruel and unusual."

The death penalty is rarely imposed, even for the most grievous crimes. Imprisonment is the chief penalty used today for crime, but imprisonment, in the sense of involuntary incarceration, is also used for a number of noncriminal purposes—commitment of the juvenile delinquent, the mentally ill, the tubercular, the drug-addicted, the contumacious, the intoxicated, and the alien awaiting deportation. Slavery and imprisonment for debt are not so very far in our past. Conscription for military service also involves governmentally imposed loss of freedom.

Finding the definition of crimes

Statutes. The criminal law defines crime, and a large part of that law is to be found in the statute books. Whatever the legislature has designated as crime will be crime unless the statute is unconstitutional and therefore invalid. Typically, the statute books will contain a criminal code or penal code that states general principles of interpretation and application and that specifies the elements of a long list of major and minor crimes. Although the felonies tend to be concentrated in the criminal code, most of the other criminal provisions are found elsewhere. For example, in Wisconsin Statutes (1953) only 34 percent of all the criminal provisions were in the criminal code. Scattered outside the criminal code are the hundreds of criminal provisions in the motor vehicle code, food and drug laws, licensing requirements, tax laws, and so on. Most offenses committed in the community are violations of these noncode criminal provisions.

Constitution. Although a state's constitution is likely to be much more concerned with criminal procedure, it will deal somewhat with substantive criminal law. The Utah Constitution, for example, defines the crimes of treason (art. I, § 19) and blacklisting (art. XII, § 19) and prevents the legislature from legalizing gambling (art. VI, § 28) or polygamous marriage (art. III). Concepts of cruel and unusual punishment, equal protection, and due process of law also impose more general limitations upon what the legislature can make criminal. By and large the constitution operates negatively, controlling the legislature rather than positively making something a crime.

Court decisions. The decisions of the state's courts constitute important acts of further definition of statutory crimes, whether in interpreting the language of the statutes or in applying a general form of words to varying combinations of facts. If the court decisions are unreported, they have only local impact; if they are reported—whether trial or appellate court decisions—they become accessible to lawyers, who cite them as authority to other judges.

In addition to interpreting and applying statutes, the courts may occasionally find the definition of crimes in the customary, or "common," law. In the Middle Ages, English judges conceived of the common law as existing outside human judgment; they undertook to discover the common law by consulting tradition and by applying principles of reason and policy that seemed self-evident to them. The list of felonies under English common law was short: homicide, mayhem, arson, rape, robbery, burglary, prison breach, and rescue of a felon. Statutes greatly enlarged the number of felonies. Common-law misdemeanors constituted a much longer list. As new situations arose, they might be found to fit under an existing criminal definition, or the judge might discover a new category of crime. In the United States most legislatures have decreed that there shall be no crimes which are not defined by statute. In those jurisdictions the common-law understanding of crime continues to be relevant, but only to interpreting the statutory language, because the statutes are the exclusive source of definition. Even without legislative abolition, the common law has rarely been the source of new crimes in the twentieth century. One of the few instances is the decision, in *Commonwealth v. Mochan,* 177 Pa. Super. 454, 110 A.2d 788 (1955), that the maker of obscene telephone calls had committed a misdemeanor. (This decision may be compared with that of the House of Lords in *Knuller Publishing, Ltd.*

v. Director of Public Prosecutions, [1972] 3 W.L.R. 143 (H.L.(E)), which discussed whether it is a common-law crime to agree to publish advertisements for homosexual contacts that are not themselves illegal.) Modern courts would tend to think of newly recognized common-law crimes as judge-made law that violated the spirit of the maxim *nullum crimen sine lege,* that persons should not be punished for conduct they could not know was criminal.

Administrative application. Administrative agencies have an important role in defining crimes. Sometimes the legislature explicitly delegates power to them by making it a crime to violate administrative regulations on a particular subject. If the regulation is within that delegation and the delegation was itself proper, then the agency has lawfully specified some of the elements of the crime. In effect, the administrative regulation is incorporated in the statute by reference.

Law enforcement agencies define crime in a less openly acknowledged way. The enforcement agency by its policy or practice, or any individual enforcement agent by his own action in ignoring conduct or in treating conduct as criminal, gives practical meaning to the formally defined law. For example, the statute may purport to make all gambling a crime, but if the police department instructs its officers to ignore private or petty or noncommercial games of chance, in one sense such gambling is not a crime despite the language of the statute. If an officer made an arrest in spite of instructions to the contrary, the court would reject a defendant's direct claim that his gambling was not a crime, but it might consider that the defendant was entitled to a defense of estoppel or mistake of law if he relied on the instructions (*Cox v. Louisiana,* 379 U.S. 559 (1965) (overturning the conviction of demonstrators parading "near" a courthouse when they were told by the police officials that their parading 100 feet away was permissible); cf. *Hopkins v. State,* 193 Md. 489, 69 A.2d 456 (1949)). If the officer acted in violation of department policy, the prosecutor and the court and jury, all of whom have power to release the defendant, might well dismiss or acquit him if they believed he was unjustifiably singled out for punishment for violation of a generally unenforced law.

The agency or agent can only narrow the criminal law, not expand it. That is to say, the police should never arrest anyone for conduct outside the statute. If that occurs, every other actor in the system who deals with the case has definite responsibility to free the accused: the prosecutor should refuse to file charges, the court should dismiss the charges, the jury should acquit, or the appellate court should vacate the conviction.

Even if in theory the enforcement agency were to act only ministerially, without acknowledged power to define crime, from a citizen's viewpoint the policies, judgments, and actions of the police or other enforcers are critical. In a colloquial sense, that conduct which does not run a genuine risk of conviction and punishment can be said to be not criminal. Some statutes have been so long unenforced that they are widely violated without concern. In the civil law there is a concept of desuetude—that is, a law long unenforced becomes unenforceable—but this concept has been rejected in the common-law system. Theoretically, then, a statute is enforceable no matter how obsolete (*District of Columbia v. John R. Thompson Co.,* 346 U.S. 100 (1953)).

Modern code definitions

Categories of offenses. Modern codes tend to have three categories of violations: (1) felonies, which typically authorize imprisonment for more than one year; (2) misdemeanors, with imprisonment up to one year; and (3) infractions, offenses, or violations (the terminology varies). Infractions may or may not be characterized as criminal.

There are other categories as well. Treason is sometimes listed as more than a felony, and there may be a high misdemeanor or an indictable misdemeanor category. Both felonies and misdemeanors are commonly divided into several grades. A category of "petty offense" or "summary offense" designates crimes for which the full panoply of procedural protections, such as jury trial, is not available.

Limitations on legislative power to define crime

Although the legislature is the source of nearly all new criminal definitions, its power is not unlimited. Statutes are subject to judicial interpretation and judicial evaluation of constitutionality.

Canons of interpretation. Ambiguity exists in most statutes, whether from the limitations inherent in communicating by symbols, from unforeseen fact situations, from error in formulating the provisions, or even from deliberate generality to give the enforcement agency ample room for exercising discretion in enforcement. The task of the court is to interpret the statute as it thinks the legislature intended, or as it thinks the legislature would have intended if it had considered the issue. The court relies on a number of established principles of interpretation. One is that the court does not look for ambiguity but takes words in their ordinary meaning rather than speculating about fanciful alternatives. Another is that the statute should be construed to meet the problem which gave rise to it and to accord with common sense; sometimes there are mechanical errors in the statute which the court can correct in this way. Where there is substantial doubt, it is resolved in favor of the accused; some states have expressly abandoned this rule of strict construction by statute, but the courts tend to apply it nonetheless. Differences in wording are presumed to import different meanings. Words—especially catchall expressions—are interpreted from their context, and notably by the illustrations used; the listing of some items (such as available defenses) implicitly excludes other items not listed. Where there is a conflict, the more specific provision or the one later enacted governs.

Constitutional limitations. Some limitations upon legislative crime-making derive from the Constitution. Statutes may be unconstitutional because they are excessively broad, narrow, late, vague, harsh, or obscure.

Outside legislative competence. Some enactments are simply too broad and outside the legislative power. For example, Congress cannot legislate in areas outside those enumerated in the Constitution. Some federal "peg" therefore must exist on which to hang these matters. For example, the federal crime is not stealing cars, but transporting them across state lines; not sale of marijuana, but failure to pay the federal tax on sale; and not killing a black, but depriving him of his civil right to life. Even state legislatures, which have plenary power, cannot legislate arbitrarily. For example, a New York statute made it a crime knowingly to sell any magazine from which the cover had been removed. The statute was designed to protect wholesalers who had given credit to retailers upon return of the cover of unsalable magazines. But in *People v. Bunis,* 9 N.Y.2d 21, 172 N.E.2d 273, 274 (1961), the court held the statute unconstitutional because "it is unreasonable and beyond the legitimate exercise of the police power for the Legislature to interdict all sales, permissible and illicit alike, in order to prevent those which are illicit."

Some rights of citizens cannot be interfered with. For example, rights of "privacy" or "personal autonomy" have caused invalidation of statutes relating to such things as abortion, use of marijuana, wearing motorcycle helmets, contraception, many consensual sexual activities between adults, and possession of pornography. The constitutional basis often is "due process of law" or an implied constitutional "right of privacy." Other constitutional rights—freedom of speech, freedom of religion, freedom of movement, the right to bear arms, and the right of assembly—can also be invoked to invalidate statutes that interfere unduly with those rights.

Bills of attainder and equal protection. A statute may be too narrow. If it is aimed at a particular person it will be a constitutionally proscribed bill of attainder; if it creates unfair categories it will be held to deny equal protection of the laws to those groups specified in the law.

Ex post facto laws. A statute may be too late in the sense that it is intended to be applied to conduct which occurred before the statute's enactment. Such a statute would be unconstitutional as ex post facto or retroactive in effect.

Fair notice. A statute must be knowable. It once was possible for a citizen's act to occur between the enactment of a new law and knowledge of the enactment coming to his community. In an era of instant communication it is theoretically possible for a citizen to know immediately when a law becomes effective. But it is still possible for a statute to be so obscure that the citizen cannot fairly be charged with notice of its provisions. In *Lambert v. California*, 355 U.S. 225 (1957), the Supreme Court held that Lambert could not be convicted for violation of a Los Angeles law requiring a person convicted of a felony to register with the police within five days of coming into the city, unless it could be shown that she probably had knowledge of the law. The Supreme Court distinguished situations where the activity itself (such as engaging in business) might have suggested to Lambert that she inquire about regulations governing her activity.

Proportionality. A reasonable relationship between the crime and the penalty is required. In *Coker v. Georgia*, 433 U.S. 584 (1977), the Supreme Court held that the death penalty could not be imposed for a rape which did not involve bodily harm. The conduct is criminal, but the death penalty is too severe. Imprisonment for possession of a small amount of marijuana has similarly been held beyond legislative power in some jurisdictions. This means that the statute is unconstitutional insofar as it allows imposition of an excessive penalty.

Voluntariness. No one can be punished for doing things beyond his control. One cannot be punished solely for being an addict (*Robinson*). In *Powell*, the Supreme Court explored the question of whether an alcoholic could be punished for being drunk in public, but it found that the particular alcoholic defendant was not wholly lacking in self-control.

Vagueness. The limitation most frequently relied on is that a statute may not be too vague. Perfect clarity is too much to expect, but the citizen who wishes that his conduct conform to the law must have a reasonable understanding from reading the statute or the cases interpreting it of what he may or may not do.

Where the statute deals with some aspect of conduct that is specially protected by the Constitution, such as free speech or the right of privacy, the statute must be clearer than when it deals with conduct that could be wholly forbidden. For example, a statute forbidding the sale of religious literature in the pedestrian areas at a state fair must be clearer than a statute forbidding the sale of used furniture at a state fair.

The void-for-vagueness doctrine exists under the general concept of due process of law. Fair notice is required. For example, the Supreme Court has held language unduly vague that forbade "membership in a gang," selling books with stories of bloodshed "so massed as to incite to crime," and "raising prices above what the market value would be under conditions of fair competition."

Legislative process and enforcement mechanisms. Some limitations do not flow from external constraints but from the nature of the legislative process. Legislators must respond to the views of their constituents or suffer politically.

Statutes are enacted and many more are left unrepealed because the legislator does not want to appear to condone the proscribed conduct, even though his personal view may be that the criminal law should not be used in the situation. Such laws are intended to be little enforced or not enforced at all, and no monies are likely to be appropriated for enforcement.

Similarly, the legislature's effort to make conduct criminal must still run the hurdle of the willingness of prosecutor, court, and jury to enforce the law. Jurors have the practical power of nullification. Their decision to acquit a person, however clear his guilt, is final because the accused is protected against retrial by the constitutional guarantee against double jeopardy. Jurors interpret the law and apply their own sense of fairness and economy to the task. Jurors may acquit because they think the individual defendant does not deserve punishment or because they think the law is unwise; they may feel that some departures from social norms are better left to religion and education and social pressures, without wheeling out the cannon of the criminal law.

EDWARD L. KIMBALL

See also ACTUS REUS; CRIME: CONCEPT OF CRIME; MENS REA.

BIBLIOGRAPHY

American Law Institute. *Model Penal Code: Tentative Draft No. 4.* Philadelphia: ALI, 1955.

BENTHAM, JEREMY. *An Introduction to the Principles of Morals and Legislation* (1789). Oxford: Clarendon Press, 1907.

BLACKSTONE, WILLIAM. *Commentaries on the Laws of England* (1765–1769). 4 vols. Reprint. University of Chicago Press, 1979.

FLETCHER, GEORGE P. *Rethinking Criminal Law.* Boston: Little, Brown, 1978.

HALL, JEROME. *General Principles of Criminal Law.* 2d ed. Indianapolis: Bobbs-Merrill, 1960.

LaFAVE, WAYNE R., and SCOTT, AUSTIN W., JR. *Handbook on Criminal Law.* St. Paul: West, 1972.

MILSOM, STROUD F. C. *Historical Foundations of the Common Law.* London: Butterworths, 1969.

PACKER, HERBERT L. *The Limits of the Criminal Sanction.* Stanford, Calif.: Stanford University Press, 1968.

PERKINS, ROLLIN M. *Criminal Law.* 2d ed. Mineola, N.Y.: Foundation Press, 1969.

WILLIAMS, GLANVILLE. *Criminal Law: The General Part.* 2d ed. London: Stevens, 1961.

CRIME CAUSATION

1.

THE FIELD

Causal explanation is one of those primarily verbal activities by which humans represent the world to themselves. Because thought is dependent upon language, people make sense of their experiences by using words to designate and interrelate persons, places, and things. Causation is one such type of interrelationship.

As the eighteenth-century philosopher David Hume pointed out in his classic *Treatise of Human Nature,* the priority and the closeness of what is called the cause to what is called its effect can usually be observed, but a necessary connection between them can only be inferred. Theories of causation express these inferences; the theories not only identify alleged causes, but also concentrate on describing the nature and necessity of connections between causes and their effects.

Concepts, modern philosophers assert, are verbal tools for coping with the world and for solving problems. In deliberating about difficulties, description is logically the first step and explanation the next; only after these steps is it rational to propose solutions. Of course, in practice these three steps are often intermingled. Types of causal theories may differ either because they address different problems, focus on different aspects of one problem, adopt alternative perspectives on the same problem, or use different terminology for similar ideas. A tremendous variety of causal theories have been formulated to explain crime and to justify policies for dealing with it.

New causal theories usually are created by what Donald Schon calls "displacement of concepts." This displacement is the use of causal terms as metaphors that transfers them from the types of problems that they seem to fit satisfactorily to new types of problems where at first they fit more crudely and where they usually acquire new connotations. This process is perhaps most frequent with words from direct mechanical causation, such as *push, make, control,* or *release;* these are mingled as metaphors with terms for more subjective mental processes—such as *choose, plan, justify, influence,* or *motivate*—to explain human conduct (Lakoff and Johnson).

Each of these causal concepts and many more have been used to explain crimes. All such terms convey distinctive images of the criminal act, embellished by the other words accompanying them in the sentences that comprise theories of crime causation. Thus, some biological theories describe criminals as pushed by instinctual or hormone-generated drives, or as handicapped by deficient capacity to learn noncriminal conduct or self-control. Economic theories, on the other hand, convey an image of the criminal as rational calculator, and this is the image usually implied by the law in holding persons responsible for their illegal acts. Indeed, in the ethical and legal judgment of criminals there is often a shift from the determinist language of causal theories to a freewill frame of reference, which implies that each person is the sole cause of his own acts. Yet when imposing sentences there is frequently a return from freewill to determinist causal theories in deciding what experiences will reduce the probability of the offenders' committing further crimes (Glaser, 1956, 1976).

In contrast to the images conveyed by biological and economic theories of crime causation, political theories recognize that any behavior is officially criminal only because that is how government agents define and react to it. Such theories evoke a view of the offender as purely a pawn of the state. Psychological theories are extremely diverse, but most emphasize the individual's early learning experience as producing a personality that is conducive to crime. Sociological theories also vary, but all conceive of crime as the result of relationships among people, rather than of purely personal actions, even in those offenses that the culprit commits alone. There are also integrative theories that purport to unify several of the types of theories discussed here (Glaser, 1980).

The choice of a causal theory determines what is looked at and what is overlooked in explaining particular crimes. The theory selected may also guide what is done about the offenses. A biologist usually looks at the crime problem in a much different way than an economist, and the theories of each imply different solutions to the crime problem. Indeed, many distinct and contrasting theories may be valid, but apply to different aspects of offenses and have different uses. For example, one theory may mainly suggest programs to reduce the probability of people ever becoming criminal; another, to make it less likely that prisoners will repeat their crimes; and still another, to argue for redefining an offense so that it is no longer illegal. Moreover, in each of these types of practical actions several varieties of theories may be useful.

Thus, the various types of theories that survive tests by scientific research are more likely to complement than to contradict each other. Just as the operation of an automobile's engine may be validly explained in a mechanic's broad terms, a chemist's analysis, and a physicist's mathematical formulas, different aspects of a crime problem are illuminated by different kinds of theories. However, one theory may be most useful for a particular category of crime or criminal, whereas other theories contribute more to our understanding of another category.

The foregoing comments imply that it is futile to argue about the superiority of one or another of the five types of theories to be discussed below. Biological, economic, political, psychological, and sociological theories each have advantages for particular problems and purposes. Perhaps the best preparation for effectively using any type of theory is awareness of the potential uses of all the others and of their interrelationships.

DANIEL GLASER

See also CRIMINOLOGY.

BIBLIOGRAPHY

GLASER, DANIEL. "The Compatability of Free Will and Determinism in Criminology: Comments on an Alleged Problem." *Journal of Criminal Law and Criminology* 67 (1976): 486–490.

———. "Criminality Theories and Behavioral Images." *American Journal of Sociology* 61 (1956): 433–444.

———. "The Interplay of Theory, Issues, Policy, and Data." *Handbook of Criminal Justice Evaluation.* Edited by Malcolm W. Klein and Katherine S. Teilmann. Beverly Hills, Calif.: Sage, 1980, pp. 123–142.

HUME, DAVID. *A Treatise of Human Nature* (1739). 2d ed. Edited with an analytical index by L. A. Selby-Bigge. With text revisions and variant readings by P. H. Nidditch. New York: Oxford University Press, 1978.

LAKOFF, GEORGE, and JOHNSON, MARK. *Metaphors We Live By.* University of Chicago Press, 1980.

SCHON, DONALD A. *Displacement of Concepts.* London: Tavistock Publications, 1963.

2.
BIOLOGICAL THEORIES

Historical theories

Two theories on the connection between biological factors and crime are primarily of historical interest. These theories focused almost exclusively on the relationship between gross, observable physical characteristics and criminality; neither explicitly acknowledged the importance of social factors in the etiology of criminality.

Atavisms. In 1876, Cesare Lombroso proposed a biological theory of criminality, hypothesizing that atavistic physical features characterized criminals. According to Lombroso, the physical characteristics of criminals resembled those of apes: both had protruding jaws, receding foreheads and chins, and asymmetrical facial features. However, subsequent empirical research invalidated Lombroso's hypothesis. The atavistic features he described as unique to criminals were also frequently characteristic of noncriminals.

Somatotypes. William Sheldon postulated in 1949 that specific temperamental traits uniquely characterized persons with different body builds, or somatotypes. According to Sheldon, three basic somatotypes are identifiable in the human population. Endomorphs are plump, round individuals with warm and affable personalities. Ectomorphs are tall and thin persons with reflective, sensitive personalities. The muscular, athletic mesomorph is socially assertive and vigorous. Some research findings suggest that delinquents tend to be mesomorphs, but the relationship is weak. In general, empirical research has revealed little evidence for the unique temperamental traits that Sheldon ascribed to the three somatotypes. Although studying somatotypes in relation to criminality may be an interesting adjunct to other studies, it is unlikely that this theory will significantly influence future research on biological factors in criminality.

Genetic factors

Studies of families, twins, and adoptees indicate the influence of genetic factors in antisocial behavior, and the findings suggest that biological predispositions may partially explain crime.

Family studies. It has long been observed that antisocial parents raise a high proportion of children who become antisocial. In classic studies such as that by Sheldon Glueck and Eleanor Glueck, the father's criminal behavior has been identified as one of the best predictors of crimes committed by the son. In terms of genetics, however, researchers can conclude very little from family data because it is difficult to disentangle hereditary and environmental influences; the biological parents are also the rearing agents.

Twin studies. Identical, or monozygotic (MZ), twins have the same genetic makeup; fraternal, or dizygotic (DZ), twins share only 50 percent of their genes. Comparisons of criminality in MZs and same-sex DZs provide one method for estimating the relative influences of genetic and environmental factors in criminality. If MZ twins show a greater concordance of criminal behavior than DZ twins, the hypothesis of a genetic influence would be bolstered.

At least eight studies of criminality in twins were conducted between 1929 and 1962. In these studies, drawing upon data from Germany, the Netherlands, Great Britain, Finland, Japan, and the United States, the proportions of MZ and DZ twin-pair members who received criminal convictions were compared. The results indicated that between 60 percent and 70 percent of the MZ twins were concordant for criminality, whereas only 15 percent to 20 percent of the DZ twins were concordant. These results supported the genetic hypothesis. Many of these studies, however, suffered sampling biases that inflated the probabilities of detecting criminality among MZ twins. Thus, such studies overestimated the influence of genetics in the etiology of crime.

The largest twin study was not limited by sampling biases. Karl Christiansen studied criminality among all 3,586 twins born in a certain region of Denmark between 1881 and 1910. The results were consistent with the genetic hypothesis. If one male MZ twin was convicted for criminal behavior, the probability that the other would also be convicted was 35 percent; for male DZ twins the corresponding figure was only 12 percent. This *population* study permits a more realistic assessment of the strength of the genetic effect in criminality, and the results show the genetic effect to be weaker than was reported in the older studies. Results similar to Christiansen's were obtained in a Norwegian study by Odd Dalgaard and Einar Kringlen. These investigators suggested that because identical twins look more alike than fraternal twins, identical twins receive more similar treatment by others in their rearing environment. Thus, higher criminal concordance rates for MZ twins could be ascribed to environmental influences, not just to genetic effects. Since twins are usually raised together, it is impossible to infer a strictly genetic basis for any behavior, owing to similarities in the environments they experience.

Adoption studies. Because of the limitations of the twin method in decisively separating genetic and environmental effects, researchers have turned to the study of adoptees. Adoption studies allow a more powerful separation of environmental and genetic factors. If adoptees who were separated from their biological parents at birth exhibit criminal behaviors that are more similar to those of their biological, rather than their adoptive, parents, then a hereditary influence can be inferred. This is especially true since the typical adoptee has almost never seen his biological parents, does not know who they are, and may not even realize that he has been adopted.

Findings from two American adoption studies support the hypothesis that heredity influences crime. Raymond Crowe found an elevated rate of criminality in eighteen Iowa adoptees with criminal biological mothers. Remi Cadoret studied the antisocial behaviors of 246 Iowans adopted at birth, and found significant relations to their biological parents' antisocial behaviors. In a study of Swedish adoptees, Michael Bohman originally reported no significant relationship between adoptees and their biological parents' criminal status. Additional analyses completed by Bohman have, however, yielded evidence of a genetic relationship: there was a significant relationship between the adoptees and their biological parents' severity of criminality.

Three adoption studies have been completed in Denmark. American and Danish researchers at the

Psykologisk Institut in Copenhagen gathered information on all nonfamilial adoptions in Denmark that took place between 1924 and 1947. Information on a total of 14,427 adoptees and their biological and adoptive parents was obtained. Fini Schulsinger studied 5,483 of these adoptees. He identified 57 psychopaths by the consistency of their inadequately motivated impulse-ridden acts, which persisted beyond adolescence; but he excluded neurotics and psychotics. He also studied 57 matched nonpsychopath individuals as controls, and found that the biological relatives of psychopathic adoptees had the highest rates of psychopathy. In the 1970s, Barry Hutchings and Sarnoff Mednick studied the arrest records of 1,145 male adoptees born in Copenhagen between 1924 and 1941. Of these, 185 adoptees had been convicted of a violation of the Danish Penal Code. Forty-nine percent of the biological fathers of the criminal adoptees were also criminal, compared to only 28 percent criminality among biological fathers of matched noncriminal adoptees (Mednick and Volavka).

Mednick, William Gabrielli, and Barry Hutchings subsequently completed the largest-scale adoption study of criminality ever made. It included information on *all* 14,427 adoptions in Denmark between 1924 and 1947. With court convictions serving as an index of criminal involvement, criminality among the 14,427 adoptees was studied in relation to their biological and adoptive parents' criminal status.

It was possible to study the criminality rates of subgroups of male adoptees who had criminal and noncriminal biological and adoptive parents. For the adoptee subgroup in which the biological and adoptive parents were not criminal, only 13.5 percent of the sons were criminal. If the adoptive parents exhibited criminality and the biological parents did not, the adoptees' criminality rate rose to 14.7 percent. If at least one biological parent was criminal but the adoptive parents were not, the criminality rate among sons was 20 percent. If the biological and adoptive parents were both criminal, the rate of criminality in the sons reached 24.5 percent, the highest rate observed. Although crime rates among females were lower, similar results emerged when these analyses were repeated for adoptee daughters. These findings favor the hypothesis of genetic influence in the etiology of crime.

The chronic offender. In the Danish adoption study conducted by Mednick, Gabrielli, and Hutchings, chronic offenders were defined as those with more than two court convictions. Danish male adoptees defined as chronic offenders according to this criterion constituted only a small proportion of the adoptees studied: 4.09 percent. But these chronic offenders were responsible for a great deal of crime: their criminal behavior accounted for 69.4 percent of the court convictions received by all Danish male adoptees studied.

Genetic factors may be especially important in explaining the behavior of the chronic offender. A total of thirty-seven chronic offenders—comprising only 1 percent of adoptees studied—had biological parents who received more than two court convictions. The criminal behavior of these thirty-seven adoptees was responsible for 30 percent of the court convictions received by all adoptees.

These findings, derived from a variety of nations and research designs, offer rather strong evidence for the existence of a genetic component in the etiology of antisocial behavior.

Studies of sex chromosome abnormalities. Ascription of crime to the XYY chromosome may have been one of the most publicized events in twentieth-century criminology. Men usually have forty-six chromosomes; two are sex chromosomes, one X and one Y, and the notation for this configuration is XY. Men who have two Y chromosomes (XYY) are extremely rare.

Surveys undertaken in the 1960s suggested that XYY men are disproportionately represented in maximum-security hospitals, but other studies contradicted these findings. It was soon realized that the inconsistencies resulted from small, arbitrarily selected sample sizes. In order to overcome the sample bias introduced by limiting such studies to observations on men already incarcerated, it was necessary to study XYY subjects in the general population.

Precisely such a study was undertaken at the Psykologisk Institut in Copenhagen (Witkin et al.). Investigators identified a cohort consisting of all 31,436 men born in the municipality of Copenhagen between 1944 and 1947. After extensive search, 12 XYY men were found in a subgroup of the 4,139 tallest members of the cohort. (XYY men have above-average height.) The XYYs and controls were checked in the official Danish criminal records. There was no recorded evidence of violent behavior among the XYY men. These men, however, manifested significantly more criminal behavior than did XY men of their age, height, intelligence, and social class. Because this study selected all of the XYYs from among a total birth cohort of Danish men, the results are reliable despite the small number of XYYs, and the findings can be generalized to the population represented by the cohort.

Summary of genetic research. The evidence reviewed supports the hypothesis that genetic factors play an etiological role in antisocial behavior. If one accepts this hypothesis, then a necessary implication is that *biological* factors play an etiological role in criminal behavior, or at least in some forms of criminal behavior. Both the autonomic and the central nervous systems are influenced by genetic factors. It is conceivable that part of the genetically transmitted predisposition to criminal behavior is biologically mediated by the nervous system. Genetic findings in criminal behavior may be significant chiefly in that they point to the importance of studying biological factors in the causation of crime.

Accordingly, the focus of this discussion shifts to consideration of the role of biological factors in crime, including aspects of central and autonomic nervous system functioning, and biochemical states. However, it should be emphasized that the relevance of biological factors to crime does not necessarily imply genetic determination, since many nervous system functions are susceptible to significant alteration by the environment. In addition to the study of genetic influences, the interpretation of human biological research requires careful consideration of the health and other conditions of the organism and of environmental events.

Central nervous system studies

The central nervous system (CNS) encompasses all nervous systems enclosed within the bony portions of the skull and spine. The CNS is mainly involved in the processing of complex sensory information and the control of voluntary muscle movements. The two most widely used techniques for the assessment of CNS functioning have been the electroencephalogram and neuropsychological testing. Both have produced considerable amounts of information and a number of theories concerning the brain functioning of criminals.

Electroencephalographic research. Electrochemical processes in the brain produce minute electric voltage oscillations that can be detected through the human scalp. These fluctuations form the basis of electroencephalographic (EEG) recording. The rhythmic oscillations are described by their rates (usually expressed in cycles per second) and amplitudes.

Research has established that incarcerated individuals tend to have higher proportions of abnormal EEGs than do individuals in the general population: approximately 50 percent, as opposed to 10 percent (Mednick et al., 1982). The EEG abnormalities exhibited by the majority of prisoners are not diagnostically indicative of any one particular brain syndrome. The most frequent type of abnormality characteristic of criminals is an excess of slow-wave EEG activity. It has long been known that as normal persons mature from infancy to adulthood, EEG-wave rates increase. Criminals exhibit slower EEG frequencies than would be expected on the basis of their chronological age. Therefore the hypothesis has been advanced that criminals suffer from a maturational lag in cerebral development (Forssman and Frey) that retards their socialization learning.

The cortical-immaturity hypothesis has been an important stimulus to research. Some have questioned whether the excessive amount of slow EEG activity is the cause or the consequence of criminals' activities. Criminals may sustain brain damage during the course of their illicit activities, which could cause EEG slowing; alternatively, it is possible that criminals exhibited slower EEGs *before* they committed offenses. Evidence for the latter hypothesis would suggest that certain brain states are important etiological factors in criminal behavior.

Two independent prospective research studies suggest that children who *later* become criminal have excessive slow-wave EEG activity. In one study, EEG records were obtained for a group of persons twelve years of age. Eight years later their delinquency and criminality were ascertained from official records. The children who later evidenced antisocial behavior exhibited slower EEG activity than did the control group (Mednick et al., 1981). Similar findings were obtained in a prospective EEG study of criminality in a large Swedish population (Petersen et al.).

Another hypothesis regarding the slow EEG characteristics of antisocial individuals is that such persons are underaroused (Hare). As an individual proceeds from a state of heightened alertness to one of relaxation and sleep, the EEG slows. (The hypoarousal hypothesis is treated more fully below, in the discussion of the autonomic nervous system.)

Epilepsy. Temporal-lobe epilepsy (also termed psychomotor seizure) has been extensively investigated in relation to crime, especially violent crime. The earliest link between temporal-lobe epilepsy and violence resulted from an individual case study: an Englishman who had committed an unmotivated murder manifested epileptic-like paroxysms in his EEG. Much evidence has subsequently been collected in hopes of clarifying the connection between epilepsy and violence.

One set of studies explored the prevalence of temporal-lobe epilepsy among violent individuals, whereas a second series of studies examined the prevalence of violent behavior among groups of temporal-lobe epileptics. Evidence regarding the relationship between nonviolent crime and epilepsy has also accumulated. The evidence is quite contradictory, and has been interpreted both for and against the association of epilepsy and crime: no definite conclusions are yet possible (Mednick et al., 1982). In any case, the number of epileptics is small, and it is unlikely that they account for a significant proportion of the total criminal behavior in the population.

Neuropsychological examination. In addition to the EEG, a variety of other medical and psychological procedures can be used to assess brain functioning. Most of these are used to test for brain damage. Medical examinations include X rays, CAT scans (computerized axial tomography), and spinal taps (which examine spinal fluid for signs of infection or internal bleeding). Neuropsychological procedures can be used to probe for behavioral indications of localized brain damage, provided the subject cooperates. Results of neuropsychological tests administered to criminals suggest that violent, impulsive individuals suffer from damage to specific brain areas.

Lorne Yeudall used neuropsychological examinations to study prisoners, primarily violent offenders. His work suggests that prisoners suffer from damage to anterior brain regions. The specific brain areas Yeudall identified were the frontal and temporal lobes. Research posits that the psychological processes mediated by the frontal lobes are the ability to plan, to foresee the consequences of actions, and to inhibit impulses. The temporal lobes are linked to emotional functioning. Yeudall's findings in this area must be considered tentative, but they have been independently confirmed by some other investigators.

Pierre Flor-Henry has proposed a comprehensive theory of brain laterality and psychopathology. Two predictions derived from this theory are relevant to criminality, but they depend on the sex of the offender and the type of offense committed. According to the theory, male criminals guilty of serious crimes exhibit greater impairment of the dominant cerebral hemisphere (for approximately 97 percent of the population, dominant refers to the left cerebral hemisphere). Female criminals should be more likely to exhibit diffuse or nondominant hemisphere dysfunction (nondominant usually refers to the right cerebral hemisphere). Empirical evidence supports the prediction that males incarcerated for violence, sexual offenses, and persistent criminality frequently exhibit dominant-hemisphere dysfunction. Results of studies on female criminals also tend to support Flor-Henry's theory, although there is less research evidence.

Daisy Schalling suggested that antisocial males are less analytic and foresightful, and tend to be emotional and impulsive. Such observations are consistent with Flor-Henry's work, and belie possible dominant-hemisphere dysfunction. Schalling's hypothesis was evaluated by examining laterality preferences (handedness and footedness) among delinquents. The laterality hypothesis predicts a lesser degree of right-hand and right-foot preference in delinquents. The empirical evidence supports Schalling's position (Gabrielli and Mednick).

The origin of the hypothesized brain dysfunction in the antisocial individual is seldom explicitly stated. Two types of environmental events that damage the CNS have special import for the study of criminal behavior. First, prisoners report a very high incidence of earlier head injury, accompanied by loss of consciousness. Both the EEG and neuropsychological studies indicate that abnormalities in brain functioning among prisoners are localized to anterior brain regions, especially the frontal and temporal lobes (Mednick et al., 1982). Of all brain areas, the frontal and temporal lobes are the most vulnerable to damage when closed cerebral injury occurs.

Second, brain damage can occur during pregnancy or delivery. In an unpublished study conducted by Mednick and Terrie Moffitt in Denmark, delinquents convicted of more than one *violent* offense were characterized by significantly worse neurological status than other delinquents immediately after birth and at one year of age. Recidivist violent offenders showed the most severe neurological problems at one year of age.

Two major findings emerge from CNS research on criminality. The EEG work, based on prospective studies of normal populations as well as research on prisoners, demonstrated a slowing of brain waves in antisocial individuals. This has been interpreted as indicating cortical immaturity or low arousal, either of which leads to deficits in socialization learning. Meanwhile, neuropsychological research reveals that criminals, especially impulsive and violent ones, may suffer from brain damage in the frontal and temporal regions, and that such damage might be lateralized to the right or left cerebral hemisphere. This brain damage may result from perinatal problems or closed cerebral injury.

Neuroendocrinology and neurochemistry

Brain development and functioning are heavily dependent on complex biochemical reactions involving critical chemical substances. These reactions and substances may be influential in the etiology of antisocial behavior.

Testosterone. Since criminality is an activity dominated by young males, it had been posited that high levels of the male sex hormone, testosterone, induce "super-maleness" and increase the likelihood of criminal behavior. An opposing view holds that sex-role learning accounts for reduced criminality in women.

The importance of gender differences in ascribing aggressive criminal behavior to learned sex roles has been challenged. Developmental studies indicate that children's imitation of the behavior of like-sexed adults does not begin before the age of six. In a review of thirty-two studies on children under six years of age, no instances of girls manifesting greater aggression than boys were reported (Maccoby and Jacklin). Statistically, boys are significantly more aggressive in 75 percent of the studies. Males are more active in general, but this factor does not account for the gender difference in aggression. The evidence from cross-cultural studies (including study of the free-ranging chimpanzee) all points in the same direction. Nor is it likely that sex differences can be explained by differential punishment or reinforcement rates for aggressive behaviors of boys and girls; no early differences were observed. These data strongly suggest that greater male aggressiveness is present in children before social learning occurs. One possible causal explanation is that higher levels of the male sex hormone testosterone increase aggression.

There are two ways in which testosterone may influence behavior. During adolescence and young adulthood, males have high levels of this hormone. These high levels may have immediate effects on behavior. Moreover, testosterone levels in the fetus affect brain development. Female monkeys that are experimentally exposed to high levels of testosterone during prenatal development exhibit more aggressive behavior and masculine sexual behaviors when they reach adulthood (Ehrhardt and Meyer-Bahlburg). Perhaps excessively high circulating testosterone in the fetus shapes brain development in directions that predispose the individual to violent behavior.

Empirical research on testosterone and crime has proceeded along two tracks. One method has related testosterone levels to psychological measures of aggression. The psychological measures usually consist of asking the subjects how they would behave in hypothetical situations. This research has been completed with normal males and with prisoners. In both cases the results have been equivocal, with positive and negative findings alike reported. The second method relates testosterone levels to the severity of actual criminal or aggressive behavior; with this method, significant associations emerge. Prisoners with histories of violent crimes have higher levels of testosterone than do prisoners without such histories (Rubin, Reinisch, and Haskett). In longitudinal studies, Dan Olweus and his colleagues found that testosterone levels correlate positively with physical and verbal aggressiveness in sixteen-year-old males. An important study that has yet to be conducted would examine the role of fetal testosterone on later criminal and aggressive behavior.

Neurotransmitters. Most of the research on brain chemicals that might be relevant to criminality has been undertaken through studies of aggression among animals (Rubin). Thus far, the results of animal studies suggest that at least three neurotransmitters—dopamine, serotonin, and norepinephrine—help regulate expression of aggressive behavior. Territorial and intermale aggression may be precipitated by increased norepinephrine and dopamine levels, but these chemicals simultaneously inhibit predatory aggression. Serotonin seems to inhibit all aggression.

There has been little research on the role of these brain chemicals as mediators of aggression in humans, but the findings that have emerged thus far support those derived from animal studies. Among eight recidivists, there was an association between violence rankings and ratios of norepinephrine to epinephrine; the correlation appears to be the result of higher norepinephrine levels among violent recidivists (Brown, Ballanger et al.). Similarly, in a study of twenty-six adult men, those who had higher norepinephrine levels tended to have more of a lifetime history of aggressive behavior. In the same study, a negative correlation of serotonin with a lifetime history of aggressive behavior was found, indicating that higher levels of serotonin characterize less aggressive men (Brown, Goodwin et al.).

Autonomic nervous system studies

Psychophysiologists have developed precise techniques for the systematic study of emotions and emotional learning. Descriptions of psychopaths and recidivist criminals have emphasized such characteristics as lack of affect, inability to feel guilt or to love, callousness, and deficiencies in emotionally mediated learning (failure to learn from punishment or to anticipate negative consequences, as well as failure to become socialized). It was inevitable that the psychophysiologist would be tempted to determine whether this clinically described diminished emotionality was expressed in lower levels of objectively measured *physiological* indexes of emotional expression.

Some psychophysiologists are especially interested in studying peripheral signs of autonomic nervous system (ANS) activity. Among other functions, the ANS mediates the physiological activity that is associated with emotion. Examples of peripheral manifestations of ANS activity include changes in heart rate, blood pressure, respiration, muscle tension, pupil size, and electric activity of the skin.

The measurement of electric properties of the skin (called GSR, for galvanic skin resistance, or skin conductance) is the most commonly used peripheral indicator of ANS activity, both in general psychophysiology and in criminology. The skin conductance response, as it is usually measured, generally depends on the sweat gland activity of the palms. Individuals who are often emotionally aroused tend to have clammy, wet handshakes because their emotional responsiveness is reflected in the overactive glands of their palms. Very calm, unemotional individuals typically have dry skin and very low skin conductance.

If a weak current generated by a battery is leaked through an individual's fingers, one can monitor the electrical resistance (or, inversely, the conductance) of the skin to the passage of this current. Stimulating the individual to become emotionally aroused (for example, by firing a gun behind his back) causes his ANS to activate the sweat glands of his palms. The skin will be soaked with perspiration, which will increase its conductance; if this conductance is monitored on a polygraph, deviations will be observed proportional on the recording to the extent of ANS arousal experienced by the subject.

Skin conductance studies. Investigation of the skin conductance of delinquents, criminals, prisoners, and psychopaths have produced remarkably consistent results. Antisocial individuals reliably display diminished responsiveness, slow latency of response, and slow recovery of skin conductance (Mednick and Volavka). Psychophysiological research has made it clear that these results reflect underlying ANS activity.

Failure to learn from punishment. The clinical characteristic of the psychopath that is perhaps most critical to understanding the origins of his condition is his reputed inability to learn from punishment. This failing certainly bears upon his recidivism. Even more importantly, it suggests a mechanism that would make the young psychopath-to-be relatively unresponsive to one of society's important moral training forces: namely, family and peer punishment for acts that transgress moral and legal norms.

A theory has been proposed that attempts to ex-

plain some individuals' inability to learn from punishment (Mednick and Volavka). The theory explains the development and learning of morality and law-abiding behavior by postulating an interaction of specific social factors with specific ANS characteristics.

The important injunctions of moral behavior that are critical for everyday activities are essentially negative and inhibitory. They begin, "Thou shalt *not*. . . ." How are these inhibitions taught to children? Mednick and Jan Volavka postulate that the avoidance of transgression (that is, the practice of law-abiding behavior) demanded by the moral commandments is learned through the punishment of antisocial responses. Such punishment is administered by society, family, and peers, as well as by the child's own capacity to *learn to inhibit* antisocial responses. For example, when child A steals from child B, A is often punished by a peer or a parent. Eventually, after enough punishment, the mere thought of stealing should produce a bit of anticipatory fear in A. If the fear response is strong enough, the reaching fingers will drop and the stealing response will be successfully inhibited.

This theory suggests that what happens in this child after he has successfully inhibited such an antisocial response is critical for his learning of civilized behavior. Let us consider the situation in more detail. First, child A contemplates stealing. Second, because of previous punishment or the threat of punishment, he suffers fear. Third, because of fear, he inhibits the stealing impulse. Fourth, *because he no longer entertains the stealing impulse, the fear will begin to be reduced and to dissipate.*

Fear reduction is the most powerful naturally occurring reinforcement that psychologists have discovered. The reduction of fear that immediately follows the inhibition of the stealing impulse can act as a reinforcement for this *inhibition,* and it will result in learning the inhibition against stealing. The powerful reinforcement associated with the reduction of fear increases the probability that inhibition of the stealing impulse will recur. After many such experiences, the normal child will learn to inhibit his stealing impulses. Each time such an impulse arises and is inhibited, the inhibition will be strengthened by reinforcement, since the fear elicited by the impulse will be reduced following successful inhibition.

In order to learn social norms effectively, a child thus needs (1) a censuring agent (typically family or peers); (2) an adequate fear response; (3) the ability to learn the fear response in anticipation of an antisocial act; and (4) rapid dissipation of fear to provide a natural reinforcement for the inhibitory response.

As already mentioned, the antisocial individual exhibits an abnormally diminished ANS response to frightening or neutral stimuli (point 2 above), and he is relatively unable emotionally to anticipate negative events (point 3). But what of the antisocial individual's ability to experience normally rapid dissipation of fear response and to be reinforced for inhibiting the antisocial response?

The speed, size, and quality of reinforcement determine its effectiveness. An effective reinforcement is one that is delivered immediately after the relevant response. The swifter the reduction of fear, the swifter the delivery of the reinforcement. The fear response is, to a large extent, controlled by the ANS. ANS activity can be studied by the use of peripheral indicators, such as skin conductance.

A child whose ANS characteristically recovers very quickly from fear will receive a swift and strong reinforcement for inhibiting the stealing response, and he will learn inhibition quickly. If his ANS recovers very slowly, he will learn to inhibit stealing slowly, if at all. Mednick and Volavka's theory predicts that if critical variables such as family training, social status, criminal associations, poverty level, and similar factors are held constant, many of those who commit antisocial acts will be characterized by slow ANS recovery. The slower the recovery, the less the learned inhibition, and the more serious and repetitive the antisocial behavior is likely to be.

A number of tests, conducted in many laboratories and in nations with different definitions of antisocial behavior, definitively conclude that transgressors evince slower ANS recovery than less antisocial individuals. In three prospective longitudinal investigations (Mednick et al., 1982), slow ANS recovery predicted later antisocial behavior. This biosocial theory has been useful in generating research, and it has also proved surprisingly robust in empirical tests.

Implications

The findings of genetic, central and autonomic nervous system, and hormonal studies suggest that biological factors are useful in helping to understand the origins of antisocial behavior. These biological variables must be seen as supplementing research on the social and familial antecedents of crime. Perhaps more importantly, researchers must account for interactions of biological and social criminogenic factors. Study of these biosocial interactions seems likely to yield information needed for the creation of new treatment and prevention strategies.

Consideration of both biological and social factors and their interaction holds promise for the develop-

ment of methods in the early detection of serious criminal offenders. Since a small group of recidivists is responsible for the majority of crimes (including the more serious, violent crimes), even moderately successful primary intervention with this group would yield dramatic reductions in the levels of crime in society.

VICKI POLLOCK
SARNOFF A. MEDNICK
WILLIAM F. GABRIELLI, JR.

See also DIMINISHED CAPACITY; INTELLIGENCE AND CRIME; MENTALLY DISORDERED OFFENDERS; PSYCHOPATHY; VIOLENCE.

BIBLIOGRAPHY

BOHMAN, MICHAEL. "Some Genetic Aspects of Alcoholism and Criminality: A Population of Adoptees." *Archives of General Psychiatry* 35 (1978): 269–276.

BROWN, GERALD L.; BALLANGER, JAMES C.; MINICHIELLO, MARCIA D.; and GOODWIN, FREDRICK K. "Human Aggression and Its Relationship to Cerebrospinal Fluid 5-Hydroxyindoleacetic Acid, 3-Methoxy-4-Hydroxyphenyllglycol, and Homovanillic Acid." *Psychopharmacology of Aggression.* Edited by Merton Sandler. New York: Raven Press, 1979, pp. 131–148.

BROWN, GERALD L.; GOODWIN, FREDRICK K.; BALLANGER, JAMES C.; GOYER, P. F.; and MAJOR, LESLIE F. "Aggression in Human Correlates with Cerebrospinal Fluid Amine Metabolites." *Psychiatric Research* 1 (1979): 131–139.

CADORET, REMI J. "Psychopathology in Adopted-away Offspring of Biologic Parents with Antisocial Behavior." *Archives of General Psychiatry* 35 (1978): 176–184.

CHRISTIANSEN, KARL O. "A Preliminary Study of Criminality among Twins." *Biosocial Bases of Criminal Behavior.* Edited by Sarnoff A. Mednick and Karl O. Christiansen. Foreword by Marvin E. Wolfgang. New York: Gardner Press, 1977, pp. 89–108.

CROWE, RAYMOND R. "An Adoptive Study of Psychopathy: Preliminary Results from Arrest Records and Psychiatric Hospital Records." *Genetic Research in Psychiatry: Proceedings of the Sixty-third Annual Meeting of the American Psychopathological Association.* Baltimore: Johns Hopkins University Press, 1975, pp. 95–103.

DALGAARD, ODD S., and KRINGLEN, EINAR A. "A Norwegian Twin Study of Criminality." *British Journal of Criminology* 16 (1976): 213–232.

EHRHARDT, ANKE A., and MEYER-BAHLBURG, HEINO F. L. "Effects of Prenatal Sex-hormones on Gender-related Behavior." *Science* 211 (1981): 1312–1318.

FLOR-HENRY, PIERRE. "Laterality, Shifts of Cerebral Dominance, Sinistrality, and Psychosis." *Hemisphere Asymmetries of Function in Psychopathology.* Edited by John Gruzelier and Pierre Flor-Henry. Amsterdam and New York: Elsevier/North-Holland Biomedical Press, 1979, pp. 3–19.

FORSSMAN, H., and FREY, T. S. "Electroencephalograms of Boys with Behavior Disorders." *Acta Psychiatrica et Neurologica Scandinavica* 28 (1953): 61–73.

GABRIELLI, WILLIAM F., JR., and MEDNICK, SARNOFF A. "Sinistrality and Delinquency." *Journal of Abnormal Psychology* 89 (1980): 654–661.

GLUECK, SHELDON, and GLUECK, ELEANOR. *Unraveling Juvenile Delinquency.* New York: Commonwealth Fund, 1950.

GOLDSTEIN, MURRAY. "Brain Research and Violent Behavior: A Summary and Evaluation of Biomedical Research on Brain and Aggressive Violent Behavior." *Archives of Neurology* 30 (1974): 1–35.

HARE, ROBERT D. "Electrodermal and Cardiovascular Correlates of Psychopathy." *Psychopathic Behavior: Approaches to Research.* Edited by Robert D. Hare and Daisy Schalling. New York: Wiley, 1978, pp. 107–144.

HUTCHINGS, BARRY, and MEDNICK, SARNOFF A. "Criminality in Adoptees and Their Adoptive and Biological Parents: A Pilot Study." *Biosocial Bases of Criminal Behavior.* Edited by Sarnoff A. Mednick and Karl O. Christiansen. New York: Gardner Press, 1977, pp. 127–141.

LOMBROSO, CESARE. *L'uomo delinquente in rapporto all'antropologia, alla giurisprudenza ed alle discipline carcerarie* (1876). 5th ed. 3 vols. Turin: Fratelli Bocca, 1896–1897.

MACCOBY, ELEANOR E., and JACKLIN, CAROL NAGY. "Sex Differences in Aggression: A Rejoinder and Reprise." *Child Development* 51 (1980): 964–980.

MEDNICK, SARNOFF A. *Learning.* 2d ed. With the collaboration of Howard R. Pollio. Englewood Cliffs, N.J.: Prentice-Hall, 1973.

————; GABRIELLI, WILLIAM F., JR.; and HUTCHINGS, BARRY. "Genetic Influences in Criminal Behavior." Unpublished manuscript. Los Angeles: University of Southern California, 1982.

MEDNICK, SARNOFF A.; POLLOCK, VICKI E.; VOLAVKA, JAN; and GABRIELLI, WILLIAM F., JR. "Biology and Violence." *Criminal Violence.* Edited by Marvin E. Wolfgang and Neil A. Weiner. Beverly Hills, Calif.: Sage, 1982, pp. 21–81.

MEDNICK, SARNOFF A., and VOLAVKA, JAN. "Biology and Crime." *Crime and Justice: An Annual Review of Research,* vol. 2. Edited by Norval Morris and Michael Tonry. University of Chicago Press, 1980, pp. 85–158.

————; GABRIELLI, WILLIAM F., JR.; and ITIL, TURAN M. "EEG as a Predictor of Antisocial Behavior." *Criminology* 19 (1981): 219–229.

OLWEUS, DAN; MATTSON, AKE; SCHALLING, DAISY; and LOW, HANS. "Testosterone, Aggression, Physical, and Personality Dimensions in Normal Adolescent Males." *Psychosomatic Medicine* 42 (1980): 253–269.

PETERSEN, INGEMAR; MATOUSEK, MILOS; MEDNICK, SARNOFF A.; VOLAVKA, JAN; and POLLOCK, VICKI. "EEG Antecedents of Thievery." *Acta Psychiatrica Scandinavica* 65 (1982): 331–338.

RUBIN, ROBERT T. "The Neuroendocrinology and Neurochemistry of Antisocial Behavior." *Biology and Antisocial Behavior.* Edited by Sarnoff A. Mednick and Terrie E. Moffitt. The Hague: Kluwer-Nijhoff, 1984.

————; REINISCH, JUNE M.; and HASKETT, ROGER F. "Postnatal Gonadal Steroid Effects on Human Behavior." *Science* 211 (1981): 1318–1324.

SCHALLING, DAISY. "Psychopathy-related Personality Variables and the Psychophysiology of Socialization." *Psychopathic Behavior: Approaches to Research.* Edited by Robert D. Hare and Daisy Schalling. New York: Wiley, 1978, pp. 85–106.

SCHULSINGER, FINI. "Psychopathy: Heredity and Environment." *Biosocial Bases of Criminal Behavior.* Edited by Sarnoff A. Mednick and Karl O. Christiansen. New York: Gardner Press, 1977, pp. 109–125.

SHELDON, WILLIAM H. *Varieties of Delinquent Youth: An Introduction to Constitutional Psychiatry.* With the collaboration of Emil H. Hartl and Eugene McDermott. New York: Harper & Row, 1949.

TRASLER, GORDON. "Relations between Psychopathy and Persistent Criminality: Methodological and Theoretical Issues." *Psychopathic Behavior: Approaches to Research.* Edited by Robert D. Hare and Daisy Schalling. New York: Wiley, 1978, pp. 273–298.

WITKIN, HERMAN A. et al. "Criminality, Aggression, and Intelligence among XYY and XXY Men." *Biosocial Bases of Criminal Behavior.* Edited by Sarnoff A. Mednick and Karl O. Christiansen. New York: Gardner Press, 1977, pp. 165–187.

YEUDALL, LORNE T. "Neuropsychological Assessment of Forensic Disorders." *Canadian Journal of Mental Health* 25 (1977): 7–15.

3.
ECONOMIC THEORIES

Beginning in the 1960s, economists have developed a number of theoretical conceptions, which they call models, to explain criminal behavior. These models, which are expressed as mathematical equations, have the basic premise that those who commit criminal acts respond to incentives just as the rest of us do. Economists believe that most people commit crimes because they expect to be better off doing so than using their time and other resources in alternative activities. Given this assumption that criminals are rational, economists can apply to crime the mathematical tools they have developed to study other individual decisions.

Economists do not deny that there are differences in individual attitudes toward the law or even that there might be inherently criminal persons, but they believe that such attitudes do not change very rapidly. If attitudes change slowly, then short-run changes in criminal activity must be explained mainly by differences in opportunities. In their theoretical work, economists generally focus their models on incentives rather than on attitudes. They have attempted to separate out statistically a large number of factors believed to be associated with differences in attitudes (such as race, age, addiction, and education) so that they can accurately measure the distinct effect of certain incentives on the level of criminal activity.

The economists' approach

Economists see individuals as spending time and other resources to commit crimes if such a resource allocation will make their level of well-being higher than any alternative allocation. For example, consider the individual deciding how much time to give to illegal activities and to legitimate work. Economists see this individual behaving as if he compares the level of well-being achieved by all alternative allocations of time and chooses that which maximizes his overall level of well-being. To compare the level of well-being associated with different time allocations, the individual must mentally evaluate all cost and benefit factors affecting well-being in a single unit of measurement, such as money. One obviously cannot observe this mental process, but economists represent it in their mathematical equations as though it actually occurred. The mathematical equation that represents this hypothesized mental process is called a *utility function*. According to the economic model, individuals behave as if they can determine the level of well-being of every possible time allocation and choose that which produces the highest level.

There are a number of interesting aspects of this representation of individual decision-making. First, economists generally see relatively few factors as affecting the individual's level of well-being. This is not done out of naiveté concerning human nature, but rather to represent the essence of the particular decision by as simple a model as possible. In their modeling efforts, economists do not seek to mirror reality but to develop equations that both represent the central aspects of, and accurately predict the results of, the process being studied. Second, individual differences in tastes are not explicitly represented in the utility function, but rather are implicit in the mathematical form. Because economic models are concerned primarily with incentives, they represent tastes in this very general and abstract way. Obviously, it would be useful to combine sociological and psychological representations of individual tastes and taste formation with economic models, which have a richer representation of the effect of incentives.

Next, consider the way in which the level of income or wealth is determined. For individuals who allocate some time to illegal activities, the level of income or wealth from a particular time allocation is uncertain, since such persons might be subject to actions of the criminal justice system that will affect their levels of wealth. If one assumes, as is commonly the case in economic models, that the individual either succeeds or fails completely in criminal activity, he is faced with two possible levels of wealth. If successful, this level equals the sum of the individual's prior wealth, labor income, and any income derived from illegal activities. Economic models generally assume that labor income is certain, but some models introduce an unemployment rate and allow labor income to be uncertain.

Economic models represent the gains from illegal activities and the cost of criminal justice sanctions either as monetary or as if they could be monetized. This monetizing is central to economic models but has been the subject of much debate and speculation. Both the gains from illegal activity and the cost of the criminal justice sanction are believed to increase with the time spent in illegal activity. Individual levels of wealth are assumed to be reduced by the monetary value of any criminal justice sanctions. When any factor affecting the individual's level of well-being is uncertain, as it is in economic models of criminal behavior, the individual is seen as acting to maximize expected well-being or utility.

Economists determine the time allocation that will maximize expected utility. Having determined the individual's optimal use of time, they explore the way in which such time allocations change when there is a change in factors that are beyond individual control. In the above model, these factors include the individual's wage rate, the level of gains available in illegal activity, the individual's level of beginning wealth, the probability of criminal justice action, and the "cost" of criminal justice sanctions. Results obtained in this analysis are referred to as *comparative static results* because they represent and compare different stable equilibrium positions rather than the process of change from one position to another. These comparisons permit one to determine the nature of individual adjustments to changed incentives but do not permit one to infer anything about the process of adjustment or allow one equilibrium solution to affect another, as dynamic models might. Such models obtain results by comparing different static states.

Economic models of criminal behavior

The above description provides the tools needed to compare and assess modern economic models of criminal behavior. There was relatively substantial interest in criminal activity among economists during the nineteenth century (Ehrlich, 1979), but twentieth-century economists largely ignored criminal behavior until the 1960s, preferring to refine and formalize their models of business and consumer decisions.

Becker's model. In 1968, Gary Becker produced a pioneering work that has formed a basis for most subsequent economic models. He resurrected the eighteenth- and nineteenth-century insights on deterrence of Cesare Beccaria (1738–1794) and Jeremy Bentham (1748–1832), expressing them in the mathematical form developed in modern consumer demand theory. As part of a larger model designed to explore optimal criminal justice policy, he developed the "supply of offense" function, which indicates the factors affecting the number of crimes an individual commits. Becker formally analyzed the effect of the probability of conviction and the level of criminal justice sanctions, finding that an increase in either reduces the supply of offenses. Further, he noted that whether increases in the probability of convictions or in sanction levels are relatively more effective in deterring offenses depends critically on the individual's attitude toward risk. He claimed that for those who like risky endeavors (the gamblers among us), increases in the probability of conviction will be relatively more effective, while for those who dislike risk (most individuals), increases in sanction levels will be relatively more effective.

Becker's results were extremely important, for they provided a theoretical basis for the widely discussed "deterrence hypothesis"—that criminal justice sanctions reduce crime—and stimulated much additional research. Becker saw the level of well-being of individuals as depending only on their levels of income or wealth and as not affected directly by their allocations of time. His model assumes simply that individuals allocate their resources so as to maximize wealth, which incorporates all psychic costs and benefits emanating from both work and criminal activity. In this model, it makes no difference whether wealth is obtained legally or illegally; the model represents the potential criminal as a true economic person whose feelings about lawbreaking may be simply monetized, with a level of well-being that should be exactly the same with earnings of $20,000 (assuming these earnings incorporate all psychic costs and benefits) as an extortionist or as a lawyer. This strikes one as being at odds with the behavior of many, if not most, persons. However, as noted above, economists do not seek to mirror reality in their models but rather to capture its essence. The question becomes: Does this model accurately predict individual behavior? Do people basically behave as economic persons?

Becker's reduction of all factors directly affecting individual well-being to a single item—wealth—has a number of modeling advantages. First, it allows a simple and straightforward analysis of the way in which individual attitudes toward risk affect the extent of illegal behavior. For example, it implicitly suggests that the gamblers among us will participate more extensively in illegal acts, other things being equal, since this is a risky venture. Second, the reduction allows one, with very few and common assumptions, to predict explicitly the way in which the actions of the criminal justice system will affect the extent of illegal behavior.

Further developments of Becker's model. Becker did not fully develop his insights concerning the supply-of-offense function, since this was only one portion of his larger model of optimal sanction of, and protection against, crime. Isaac Ehrlich (1974) and, apparently independently, David Sjoquist elaborated and extended Becker's insights while maintaining his basic assumption that it is only the level of wealth that directly affects the individual's level of well-being. Their essential contribution was to analyze explicitly the effect of the level of illegal gains and legal opportunities on the individual's level of criminal activity. Both Ehrlich and Sjoquist assume that returns from legal and illegal activities depend only on the time spent on them, although factors beyond the control of the individual may change the level of rewards in either activity. They both also generally assume that legal returns are certain—that is, that there is no unemployment. Ehrlich (1974) does, however, explore the effect of unemployment in his more extended works. Both Ehrlich and Sjoquist find that the time allocated to illegal activity will increase with an increase in wealth (the rich participate more than the poor) or in illegal gains and will decrease with an increase in the probability of apprehension, the size of the penalty if apprehended, or the legal wage rate.

To obtain these comparative static results, Ehrlich and Sjoquist make a number of rather common assumptions concerning the nature of individual preferences, specifically, that utility, illegal gain, legal gain, and penalty functions have appropriate mathematical forms; that people dislike risk; and that they dislike it most when they are poorer. The last assumption is probably most open to question but is required in order to determine unambiguously that illegal activity increases with wealth and with illegal gains and decreases with an increase in the legal wage rate. If people's dislike of risk changes in a more complex way with income, then these comparative static results are not forthcoming. For example, if it is at middle income levels that risk is most distasteful, one might expect to see principally the poor and the rich participating in illegal activities. The type of offense in which these two classes participate may, of course, be quite different, with the rich participating in organizational offenses (for example, price-fixing) and white-collar offenses (for example, tax evasion), and the poor participating in more traditional offenses, such as larceny, burglary, and robbery.

Ehrlich's and Sjoquist's work also indicates, like Becker's, that increases in sanctions are relatively more effective than increases in the probability of their imposition if people dislike risk. J. M. Heineke (1978a) has shown that this result requires that the penalty function have a particular mathematical form.

In his extended work, Ehrlich (1974) is unable to determine unambiguously the effect of increased unemployment on the level of illegal activity. However, he is able to show that increased unemployment increases the incentive to participate in illegal activity.

Ehrlich's and Sjoquist's work is important because it not only reinforces Becker's results concerning deterrence but also suggests that improved legal opportunities or decreased levels of illegal gain may reduce crime.

Criticism of models based on Becker; alternative approaches. Theoretical economists became intrigued by the emerging literature on criminal behavior because it yielded so many unambiguous predictions; most economic models do not do so. In the beginning, economists assumed that all costs associated with working, committing illegal acts, and criminal justice sanctions could be monetized. Later work indicated that this may not be possible if individual feelings or tastes concerning work, crime, or sanctions are sufficiently strong or if income is sufficiently low. Thus, an extremely law-abiding citizen may find illegal activity so distasteful that no amount of money is adequate compensation for a substantial time allocation to crime. If all penalties and feelings about work and crime cannot be monetized, economic modeling becomes more complex.

Michael Block and Heineke see the amount of time the individual allocates to work and crime as directly affecting well-being. They find that this alteration of the basic economic model destroys the ability to obtain comparative static results with generally accepted assumptions, because changes in time allocation will now be affected by individual tastes as well as by rewards and by attitudes toward risk. One must make assumptions on how the individual valuation of an extra hour in any activity varies with wealth (including how valuation of an extra hour in illegal activity changes when one is wealthier) and how it varies with a change in the level of participation in another activity (for example, how valuation of an extra hour in illegal activity changes when one increases working time). Economic theory provides no guidance on the direction of these effects; hence, one is forced either to make arbitrary assumptions or to turn to empirical models for guidance. However, even here, the modeling effort indicates what factors are important to measure and how to specify models of crime commission.

Later, Heineke (1978a) found that increases in legal returns caused decreases in illegal activities in Ehrlich's and Sjoquist's models because in these models the time allocated to leisure activities was assumed to be fixed. When one allows the time in leisure activity to vary, one finds that increases in returns to legal activity actually cause increases in illegal activities. Legal and illegal activities become gross complements rather than substitutes. One might expect such a situation for some types of offenses (such as employee theft or the use of an expanded legitimate business by a "fence" as a front), but it seems a somewhat peculiar result for most situations.

Extension of the basic models. There are three basic ways in which the models discussed above have been extended. First, the rather simple assumption that there is a single criminal justice outcome—failure—has been relaxed. Second, researchers developed models concerned primarily with violent offenses, whereas prior models primarily explained offenses against property. Finally, economists have relaxed the implicit assumption that time-allocation decisions are relatively simple (for example, that time may be allocated to only two uses) and are made independently of other individual decisions on consumption and investment.

More complex criminal justice outcomes. Both Ehrlich (1975) and Ann Witte, instead of assuming a single criminal justice outcome, allowed for three different probabilities of outcomes: arrest, conviction, and severe penalty (execution for Ehrlich, restriction on freedom for Witte). For his model, Ehrlich is able to show that increases in all three probabilities will deter. Further, a given increase in the probability of arrest will be a more effective deterrent than the same increase in the probability of conviction, which will be a more effective deterrent than a similar increase in the probability of severe sanctions. Witte obtains no comparative static results for her original model, which includes time allocations in the utility function; she obtains results similar to, but not as strong as, Ehrlich's for a simpler model that contains only wealth in the utility function.

Models of violent behavior. Ehrlich (1975); Lachman; and Karr, Long, and Witte have developed models for certain types of violent crimes. Ehrlich developed a model for murder in which the murderer's level of well-being is highest when the victim's level of consumption is reduced to zero—that is, when the victim is dead. Lachman's model of interpersonal disputes makes use of response functions similar to those used to represent the behavior of firms with few competitors. Lachman sees the level of harm inflicted by two combatants as interdependent. Low levels of harm inflicted by one party will tend to make the other party become more aggressive and inflict more harm. After a point, additional harm causes the victim to display fear rather than aggression. The precise outcome depends on the nature of the response function for the two combatants.

Karr, Long, and Witte seek to model family violence by combining insights from the literature on the economics of crime and the "economics of marriage." They see the family as run by a dictator who inflicts harm on other family members because he benefits from doing so. The amount of harm that the dictator can inflict is constrained by the fact that the victim may choose to leave the family (for example, through separation or divorce if the victim is the spouse) and by the fear of criminal justice sanctions. Given these constraints, the dictator chooses an "optimal" amount of harm to inflict.

Largely because of the interpersonal interaction, these models yield fewer comparative static results than do more traditional economic models of crime. For example, Karr, Long, and Witte can say that criminal justice sanction will deter only if the individual's valuation of harm increases with income.

Interactions of crime and other decisions. Most economic models of crime see the individual deciding how to allocate time to two uses (legal and illegal activities), without regard to other decisions. Heineke (1978b) developed a model that allows the individual to decide how to allocate time between work and three income-producing offenses (burglary, larceny, and robbery). He sees this time-allocation decision as determined simultaneously with total consumption expenditures. As is usually the case with such general economic models, he was not able to obtain comparative static results. However, he found empirically that the time an individual would allocate to the activities considered depended primarily on two factors: the gain from the particular activity being considered (such as the loot from robbery) and the individual's level of wealth. He also found that the time devoted to all illegal activities considered decreased rather markedly as wealth increased, that property crime is only a poor substitute for work, and that substitution even among property crimes is rather limited.

Evaluation. What one can conclude from economic models developed to date depends on what one is willing to assume. If one is willing to assume that people obtain utility directly only from income or wealth (they are economic persons), that the psychic costs of time allocations and criminal justice penalties may be monetized, and that people dislike risk and dislike it most when they are poorer, then the economic model provides a priori support for the deterrence hypothesis and for the level of returns to an activity affecting the time allocated to it. If one is not willing to make these assumptions, economic models tell us little about how criminal justice system operations or legal and illegal opportunities affect crime.

One should not conclude from this that the development of general economic models of criminal behavior is all for naught. Even when these models produce no comparative static results, they provide rather strong and valuable guidance to empirical work. For example, the general model developed by Block and Heineke suggests that the time allocated to illegal and legal activities is determined interdependently and, thus, that empirical work will need to develop equations for both legal and illegal activities and use estimation techniques which allow these equations to interact. Further, their model suggests that the time allocated to illegal activities will be affected by the following factors: time allocated to legal activity, how the criminal justice system functions, the level of penalties, the gains from illegal activities, the individual's wage rate, the individual's attitude toward risk, the individual's level of wealth, the individual's "law-abidingness," the individual's attitudes toward work, and other factors affecting individual tastes.

Results of empirical tests of economic models

Obtaining insights about individual behavior from aggregate data on cities, states, or countries requires very strong assumptions, such as that all individuals are identical. Individual data have their own limitations (such as limited generalizability), but they are far more appropriate for testing economic models.

The results of empirical studies using aggregate data are at least consistent with the prediction of the simpler economic models concerning deterrence. Philip Cook (p. 173) summarizes: "There is strong evidence . . . that an increase in the threat of punishment can reduce the amount of some crimes in some circumstances, but very little evidence about the long-term effects, the typical magnitudes involved, the relevance of process, the responsiveness of juveniles to threats, or the extent to which some important crime categories (such as murder) are responsive to changes in the threat level." Further, the strength and consistency of the evidence supporting the deterrent effect of high probabilities of apprehension and punishment is much greater than that supporting the deterrent effect of longer prison sentences. However, this type of empirical work is so flawed that one must doubt (along with Nagin and with Brier and Fienberg) that it warrants definitive conclusions or that much will result from further attempts to model the effect of punishment on crime with the type of aggregate data used thus far.

As far as we are aware, there has been, to date, only one attempt to test the deterrence hypothesis using individual data (Witte). Although this work can only be considered a beginning, it provides some interesting results. The work finds that the deterrent effect of criminal justice sanctions varies markedly across types of crime, although sanctions do seem to reduce some types of offenses in the particular circumstance studied. However, estimates of the strength of the deterrent effect are very sensitive to the specific measures one assumes are appropriate for some of the variables in the model. Changes in the probabilities of conviction and imprisonment have a greater effect on crime rates than do changes in expected sentence length, but in contrast to the aggregate studies, effects from expected sentence length are slightly more significant than from the probability of sanctions.

Work with aggregate data shows a clear-cut relationship between the statistical indexes for legitimate income and crime rates only when both a measure of very low income or poverty (such as the percentage of families with income below $3,000) and median or average income are included in the equations. This work finds both greater poverty and higher average income to be significantly related to higher crime rates. Effects are generally more significant for offenses against property than for those against persons.

Studies of natural variations in noncriminal economic opportunities provide consistent but weak support for the hypothesis that higher wages deter crime, and weak, if any, support for unemployment being associated with higher levels of illegal activity. These studies suggest that it is job satisfaction, measured by such factors as work stability, that is most consistently and strongly associated with lower levels of criminal activity. The highly diverse results from the relevant literature suggest that to reduce crime, it may be necessary to provide both monetary and psychological support to individuals making the transition from lawbreaking to stable, legitimate work.

Taken as a whole, existing empirical studies support the simpler economic models of crime but not all of the comparative static predictions of these models. The empirical literature suggests that human behavior is much more complex, adaptive, and dependent on previous circumstances than is reflected thus far in the economists' models. For example, the literature suggests that job satisfaction, which is not fully reflected in wage rates, may lead to lower levels of criminal activity. It also suggests that the effectiveness of criminal sanctions depends critically on the individual's ability to consider possible outcomes rationally when committing an offense but that certain types of violent offenders, and offenders addicted to drugs, may not always be able to do this.

Summary and conclusions

Economists studying criminal behavior have done two basic things. First, they have developed simple but rigorous deductive models that are consistent with both the deterrence hypothesis and with the assumption that individual actions are affected by the relative gains available in legal and illegal activities. Second, economists have provided more sophisticated and systematic statistical tests of these hypotheses than were to be had prior to their reentry into the study of criminal behavior.

Economists have alerted others studying criminal behavior to the fact that incentives are important and that one should at least consider the possibility that many offenders behave quite rationally. Much research effort during the 1960s had concentrated rather myopically on the effect of mental states and of social institutions and groups on criminal behavior. This work had often led to a conclusion that either the individual or society was diseased and that the cure for crime lay in treating the individual offender or changing the way society operated. Economists suggested a different approach. Change the incentives facing the offender. Make crime less profitable either by changing the way in which the criminal justice system operates or the way in which potential victims behave. Make legitimate endeavors more lucrative and satisfying.

These suggestions, which come both from economists' simple deductive models and from their empirical work, are valuable. Economists' models provide hypotheses to be tested empirically, guidance for empirical work, and insights that can be incorporated into eclectic models of criminal behavior. To obtain unambiguous results, economists are forced to make their deductive models too simple to form a basis for policy prescription, but they provide useful insights that could, in combination with insights from other disciplines, form a basis for understanding the complex phenomena of criminal behavior.

Perhaps the greatest flaw in economists' empirical study of crime has been the use of low-quality data for legal jurisdictions such as cities and states. Researchers in other disciplines tend to be much more alert to the need, in the study of criminal behavior, for carefully collected data on individuals. However, economists have considered the type of statistical techniques needed to analyze their data much more attentively than have most other researchers. For example, when they estimate the effect of criminal justice sanctions, they generally try to control for many more additional factors affecting crime rates than have researchers in other disciplines. It appears that economists provide a useful challenge but that the understanding of criminal behavior can now best be advanced by research which considers and incorporates the insights of several disciplines.

Given the simplicity of their deductions and the often unavoidable flaws in their empirical tests, the work of economists should be viewed as giving policy insights rather than guidance. Their research suggests that the perceptions of potential criminals are extremely important and that if offenders can be convinced that they are rather certain to be appreciably punished, they will be less likely to commit offenses. Further, it suggests that increasing the perceived probability of more general events, such as arrest, is likely to be more effective than increasing the perceived probability of less general events, such as imprisonment. The research also suggests that society should try to increase the relative advantages of legal alternatives to illegal behavior. This may consist either of decreasing expected gains from illegal behavior (for example, improving vehicle ignition locking systems or training potential victims in self-defense) or of improving prospects for legal satisfaction (for example, decriminalizing certain types of behavior such as gambling or using certain drugs, or improving the availability and quality of jobs). The best policy, of course, would be one that combined a number of these factors.

ANN DRYDEN WITTE

See also CLASS AND CRIME; RACE AND CRIME; UNEMPLOYMENT AND CRIME.

BIBLIOGRAPHY

BECKER, G. S. "Crime and Punishment: An Economic Approach." *Journal of Political Economy* 76 (1968): 169–217.

BLOCK, M. K., and HEINEKE, J. M. "A Labor Theoretic Analysis of the Criminal Choice." *American Economic Review* 65, no. 3 (1975): 314–325.

BRIER, S. S., and FIENBERG, S. E. "Recent Econometric Modeling of Crime and Punishment: Support for the Deterrence Hypothesis?" *Evaluation Review* 4 (1980): 147–191.

COOK, PHILIP J. "Punishment and Crime: A Critique of Current Findings concerning the Preventive Effects of Punishment." *Law and Contemporary Problems* 41 (1977): 164–204.

EHRLICH, I. "The Deterrent Effect of Capital Punishment: A Question of Life and Death." *American Economic Review* 65, no. 3 (1975): 397–417.

———. "The Economic Approach to Criminal Behavior: A Preliminary Assessment." *Criminology Review Yearbook*, vol. 1. Edited by Sheldon L. Messinger and Egon Bittner. Beverly Hills, Calif. and London: Sage, 1979, pp. 25–60.

———. "Participation in Illegitimate Activities: An Economic Analysis." *Essays in the Economics of Crime and Punishment.* Edited by Gary Stanley Becker and William M. Landes. New York: Columbia University Press for the National Bureau of Economic Research, 1974, pp. 68–134.

HEINEKE, J. M. "Economic Models of Criminal Behavior: An Overview." *Economic Models of Criminal Behavior.* Edited by J. M. Heineke. Amsterdam: North-Holland, 1978a, pp. 1–33.

———. "Substitution among Crimes and the Question of Deterrence: An Indirect Utility Function Approach to the Supply of Legal and Illegal Activity." *Economic Models of Criminal Behavior.* Edited by J. M. Heineke. Amsterdam: North-Holland, 1978b, pp. 153–209.

KARR, PATRICE; LONG, SHARON K.; and WITTE, ANN D. "Family Violence: A Microeconomic Approach." Paper presented at National Conference for Family Violence Researchers, July 1981, at University of New Hampshire.

LACHMAN, JUDITH. "A Theory of Interpersonal Conflict with Applications to Industrial Disputes." Working paper, Yale University, School of Law, 1978.

LONG, SHARON K., and WITTE, ANN D. "Current Economic Trends: Implications for Crime and Criminal Justice." *Crime and Criminal Justice in a Declining Economy.* Edited by Kevin N. Wright. Cambridge, Mass.: Oelgeschlager, Gunn & Hain, 1981, pp. 69–143.

NAGIN, DANIEL. "General Deterrence: A Review of the Empirical Evidence." *Deterrence and Incapacitation: Estimating the Effects of Criminal Sanctions on Crime Rates.* Edited by Alfred Blumstein, Jacqueline Cohen, and Daniel Nagin. Washington, D.C.: National Academy of Sciences, 1978, pp. 95–139.

SJOQUIST, DAVID L. "Property Crime and Economic Behavior: Some Empirical Results." *American Economic Review* 63, no. 3 (1973): 439–446.

WITTE, ANN D. "Estimating the Economic Model of Crime with Individual Data." *Quarterly Journal of Economics* 94 (1980): 57–84.

4.
POLITICAL THEORIES

Introduction

Political theories of crime causation rest on certain assumptions about how the exercise of a state's power relates to the occurrence of crime. Together with other theories of crime causation, they attribute crime to the nature of the human organism or to the social, cultural, or economic character of human relations. Inasmuch as the power of the state does not operate in a vacuum, a purely political theory of crime causation does not exist. This article describes not a unique body of theory, but rather the political nature of different notions of crime causation.

The political nature of crime

In its ordinary usage, *crime* means a violation of law punishable by officials of the state. Strictly speaking, without a state whose officials make and apply penal law there can be no crime (Kennedy). Since the question of whether crime exists is a matter of the exercise of power by officials of the state, it is an inherently *political* matter.

Unfortunately, even among criminologists, the political nature of crime has often been obscured by equating crime with inherently wrongful behavior, or, as Leslie Wilkins has expressed it, by confusing crime with "sin." In the case of homicide, for example, the Bible commands simply that "thou shalt not kill," but nowhere is all killing considered criminal. In fact, it can be a crime not to kill, as in wartime. German soldiers who refused to kill Jews and other civilians during World War II were liable to punishment by officials of the Nazi regime, and later, at the Nuremberg trials, they were held liable to punishment for having carried out Nazi orders. A person who fails to take reasonable action to save another from drowning is liable to criminal prosecution in France, but not in England or the United States. Similarly ambiguous is the issue that has arisen in the United States of whether a husband is legally entitled to sexual relations with his wife or is guilty of rape for forcing her to engage in such relations against her will.

The political ambiguity is a matter not simply of legislation but also of how the law is applied. For example, it is unheard of to prosecute doctors for homicide in the death of patients as a consequence of unnecessary surgery, or employers for the death of workers in unsafe working conditions. Jeffrey Reiman has argued, however, that such persons can and should be prosecuted as murderers. The homicide rates and trends that Americans normally accept as authoritative consist of what law enforcement agencies decide to report, based on their interpretation of Federal Bureau of Investigation guidelines. These guidelines nominally call for the reporting of all intentional killing except by law enforcement officers—even killing in self-defense—as "murder or non-negligent manslaughter."

The political nature of crime extends to property offenses. The Bible also commands people not to steal, but once it is acknowledged that one cannot steal something unless it is considered another's property, the dependence of the theft on state definition becomes obvious. The bank employee who is today called an embezzler may become the hero of tomorrow's revolution for having taken what was only his due from a criminally oppressive employer. This could occur even without changing criminal theft statutes, if officials changed their definition of ownership (Pepinsky, 1976, pp. 25–43).

A political typology of theories of crime causation

Relation of people to the state. There is good reason for every theory of crime causation to rest on assumptions about the relation of people to a state. For some, crime implies a dearth or failure of state control, as by not punishing offenders severely enough. For others, crime implies poorly functioning state control, as in failure to enforce the laws equitably. For yet others, too much state activity breeds crime, however disciplined the government's criminal procedure. These three categories will be referred to, respectively, as state vacuum, state dysfunction, and state excess.

Theorists of crime causation in all categories assume both that the behavior of officials can be changed at will, and that crime rates can be made to rise or fall accordingly. State vacuum theorists assume that crime occurs because officials do too little. State dysfunction theorists assume that the occurrence of crime depends not on the amount but rather on the kind of official activity. Theorists of state excess assume that crime occurs because officials do too much.

Within each of these three categories there exists considerable variation that resists neat classification. Most of the theorists popularly perceived as conservative fall within the state vacuum group; the state dysfunction rubric encompasses most self-styled liberals; and most of what is called *radical criminology* has a state excess perspective on crime in capitalist countries. However, it is best to minimize use of such right-to-left labels and simply to describe the variations within these three broad categories.

Radical criminology. To many criminologists, political theory has come to be equated with "radical" or "critical" criminology. The term *radical* is used to refer to criminologists who trace their perspective to the nineteenth-century work of Karl Marx and who ascribe crime and crime control to the structure and dynamics of what they generally call *late monopoly capitalism*. In this view, the drive toward maximizing profit by creating large, criminal multinational corporations leaves human waste (street criminals) in its wake and spawns an increasingly repressive criminal justice apparatus. It remains for ordinary working people to unite to overthrow capitalism in favor of *socialism*, a rather loose term for a political system that distributes resources according to need rather than according to private ownership of the means of producing goods and services.

Critical is a term originally applied to members of the Frankfurt School of social thought, which arose in the 1930s and included such scholars as Theodor Adorno, Jürgen Habermas, and Max Horkheimer. They in turn trace their work to the eighteenth-century philosophy of Immanuel Kant, who argued that we can know the world only as human minds construct it, not as the world really exists. Critical criminologists seek to expose and explain popular and legal myths about crime and crime control. Much of their work suggests that crime and punishment are born of self-serving myths perpetuated by officials, the wealthy, and the powerful—myths born of economic and political selfishness.

In the 1970s, within the Association for Humanist Sociology, some criminologists began to call themselves *humanist* criminologists. By humanist, they meant the kind of spiritual imperative proclaimed by Karl Marx and in the *Humanist Manifestos I and II* (American Humanist Association), which called for maximizing the pooled creative potential equally inherent in all healthy human beings. In 1980, with the publication of *The Struggle to Be Human* by Larry Tifft and Dennis Sullivan, the first text of its kind, *anarchist* criminology also became established in the field. The anarchists assume that governments and law cause more problems than they solve.

These groups' critical analyses of the crime problem are in many if not most respects similar. They all criticize the conventional assumption by criminologists that the essence of the crime problem lies in the convicted offender; instead, they all assume that offenders are victims of larger economic and political forces represented by repressive government apparatus. It is, however, doubtful that most adherents of this viewpoint can decide with certainty whether to characterize themselves as Marxist, radical, critical, humanist, or anarchist, since criminologists seldom bother to attribute their analyses exclusively to particular origins. Although such labels as *radical* are applied to increasingly prominent and important studies of crime causation, they can be misleading.

State vacuum theories

The late eighteenth century was an era of political optimism in the Western world. The French and American revolutions claimed to have made government rational at last. Utilitarian theorists of the time, such as Jeremy Bentham, forecast that rational government would make crime virtually disappear as a social problem. The Bolsheviks were similarly optimistic after 1917.

Crime, however, remained chronic. The poor filled modern penal institutions in the early nineteenth century in Western Europe, as did socially dislocated "parasites" in the Soviet Union a century later. Once released, many young offenders are arrested again on new charges. Rather than criticizing their governments, biologically and psychologically oriented criminologists ascribe offenses to defects in the personal or family upbringing of offenders that impede their responding to the laws as "rational" citizens should. The crime problem to them is simply that some mentally defective persons are unresponsive to the reasonable exercise of state power.

A middle ground exists between questioning the legitimacy of state crime control and attributing crime to the personal defects of identified offenders: it can be argued that industrialization or modernization creates strain in individuals as well as social disorganization. Debate continues as to whether the chief cause of strain or disorganization is the growth of cities, the movement of people, clashes among diverse groups, the frustration that results from not being able to attain a better life, or the contamination that is caused by association with bad people or bad conditions. Whatever the cause or causes, crime is viewed as an unavoidable price of social progress (Shelley).

Although the "strain" or "social disorganization" theorists lay the blame for crime on the social order rather than on identified offenders, they provide little basis for a critique of industrializing societies. It is inevitable that some crime will take place in the best-functioning modern states, both because much crime is similarly defined and caused in all modern states, and because there is no possibility of modern states regressing to primitive ways. Both those who believe crime is caused by personal defects and those who ascribe it to social disorganization assume that crime occurs in a *vacuum* created by the organization of the modern state and society.

The most conservative of those who build their theories on the assumption that the state is simply not powerful enough to prevent crime believe that state officials identify criminals without class, ethnic, or other bias. Hence, they assume that most criminals really are poor or dispossessed. Since they presume that officials accurately reflect universal values about wrongdoers, such state vacuum theorists are said to be value-neutral (Pepinsky, 1980, pp. 67–80).

Just as theorists of state vacuum are prone to ambivalence over whether offenders are blameworthy, so in making pragmatic suggestions they have not been able to decide whether officials can best prevent crime by helping, hurting, or incapacitating offenders. This ambivalence is dramatically reflected in the role that American Quakers (the Society of Friends) have played since the early nineteenth century in the evolution of the modern science of treating and punishing offenders, originally termed penology and now known as corrections.

The Quakers are committed to pacifism and forgiveness. In order to shift the emphasis of crime control from exacting society's revenge to facilitating the redemption of offenders, Quakers developed in Philadelphia one of the first modern prisons. Their benevolence, however, took the form of isolating offenders so that they could reflect quietly on their sins—a treatment that proved so devastating to inmates that it has since been abandoned in the United States except as a disciplinary measure.

A century and a half later, the American Friends Service Committee sponsored a study concluding that coerced help was a contradiction in terms and hence that, regardless of official intentions, prisons serve only to punish. Such attacks on rehabilitation efforts in prison led in the 1980s to a punitive trend toward record-high incarceration rates. Similar increases in the total number of persons restrained by the state characteristically follow movements to divert offenders away from prison and jail and into other rehabilitative programs (Pepinsky, 1980, pp. 78–83).

Many state vacuum theorists favoring retribution, such as the psychoanalyst Ernest Van den Haag, advocate punishing offenders more severely, for example, by imposing longer prison terms or the death penalty. Others, notably the political scientist James Wilson,

emphasize the deterrent effect of increased certainty and celerity of punishment. They contend on pragmatic grounds that the awareness of prospective punishment would keep citizens law-abiding out of fear and out of respect for the state. The abstract philosophical argument that a state's officials should not tolerate failure of virtue can be traced to Thomas Aquinas. The proponents of deterrence by certainty and swiftness of punishment, who assert that citizens will remain law-abiding if they know that crime does not pay, employ an argument advanced by such eighteenth-century utilitarians as Jeremy Bentham. Those who call for the incapacitation of offenders typically become prominent in periods when punitive policies replace the rehabilitative ideal. They call for longer periods of incarceration for repeat offenders (Kramer), reasoning that a small group of hard-core offenders are responsible for most serious crime.

Harold Pepinsky (1980) has pointed out that the vacuum perspective has dominated Western criminal justice policy and practice since the eighteenth century. Its attraction is that it limits the problem of crime to dealing with offenders. Thus, apart from paying the salaries and expenses of criminal justice officials, citizens can detach themselves from responsibility for crime or its prevention. Such a perspective is particularly compatible with the value that Americans place on individualism, since it detaches each citizen's social fate from that of others, including the alleged offenders. Those who run afoul of the law can simply be left to face the degradation they have achieved for themselves.

The attractive simplicity of state vacuum theories is also their limitation; they offer a very narrow range of options for trying to control crime. Practical applications of the theory were by and large exhausted by the late nineteenth century. Since then, as the crime problem has grown worse, anticrime efforts by proponents of the state vacuum view have returned to the old punitive and rehabilitative approaches to criminals, in alternating waves of enthusiasm and disenchantment.

In the United States, where attempts to fill the state vacuum have been particularly vigorous, the criminal justice system has grown apace. The American incarceration rate is one of the world's highest, and so is the American crime rate. Crime control practices, from which the lives of supposedly law-abiding citizens have been insulated, have had consequences analogous to those of the law of entropy in physics: the more energy that is introduced into a closed system, the more disordered the system becomes. It appears that the more energetically officials try to help, hurt, or confine offenders, the more crime the officials create and the less they prevent. As will be seen, state excess theories may indicate a solution to the problem.

State dysfunction theories

It is possible to assume that people create crime by the way they enforce the law. When questionable law enforcement behavior is assumed to have no relation to the kind of political system in which law enforcement occurs, the resultant theories of crime causation may be said to be theories of state dysfunction.

Most state dysfunction theorists straddle the boundary between supposed value-neutrality and manifest political criticism. At one extreme, the French sociologist Emile Durkheim declared in the late nineteenth century that crime was a normal feature of a social system. He supposed that members of any society would select a quota of wrongdoers to punish, for the sake of affirming their commitment to behaving properly and to holding the society together. In an almost paradoxical way, law-abiding members of society needed to find and punish law violators in order to affirm the collective identity of the law-abiding community. The existence of crime, therefore, was not a reflection of state powerlessness but rather was requisite to state officials' maintenance of social stability. At the same time, Durkheim assumed that crimes were harmful, and in this sense, that state officials and the members of society who supported them in fact helped maintain socially dysfunctional behavior.

Durkheim was aware that he was dealing with an issue of profound moral and political significance. Still, when discussing it in *The Rules of Sociological Method*, he seemed to adopt the detached viewpoint of the politically disinterested scientist, that is, he remained value-neutral about crime causation. •

Another kind of explanatory theory of state dysfunction became prominent late in the Depression Era in the United States. In this era, when "social security" had become a right, a number of criminologists concluded that it was politically unfair to associate crime and its causes with poverty (Pepinsky, 1980, pp. 198–201).

Sophia Robison wrote in 1936 that poor youths committed offenses not because of inherent criminal tendencies but because they came from "the wrong side of the tracks." Two years later, in *Culture Conflict and Crime*, Thorsten Sellin asserted that what was criminal behavior to the law enforcer might well be "normative," or socially acceptable, to the offender. Such "criminals," then, simply had the misfortune of belonging to a less powerful subculture than that represented by state officials.

In 1940, Edwin Sutherland, who coined the term *white-collar crime*, presented more forcefully the implication of discriminatory law enforcement for theories of crime causation. If, as it appeared, the rich were as dishonest as the poor but were politically more insulated from being identified as criminals, then all theories of crime causation resting on an association between poverty and criminality were invalid.

Frank Tannenbaum took this argument a step further, arguing that discriminatory law enforcement created a self-fulfilling prophecy. By being labeled as deviants, the generally law-abiding, casual offenders who happened to be caught would find their life chances and their self-concept so restricted that they would turn into confirmed delinquents or criminals. If so, then not merely society's picture of crime, but crime itself, is caused by unwarranted political discrimination.

Implicit in the criticism leveled by these dysfunction theorists was the assumption that it was not the existence of the state itself but the unfair ways in which officials made and enforced law that created crime as it was popularly known. Such an assumption conformed to an older tradition of liberal theorizing that was more purely pragmatic in its concerns, and that inquired into how crime should be attacked through achieving greater efficiency and fairness within existing state resources.

The classic Western work in this tradition is *On Crimes and Punishments*, published in 1764 by the Italian nobleman Cesare Beccaria. Criticizing the harsh punishments of the time, Beccaria argued that the certainty of prospective punishment would suffice to deter rational people from committing offenses. State penalties that were more severe than the minimum necessary to deter, Beccaria contended, promoted disrespect for law and caused crime.

If the Beccarian theory held true and his system were perfected, state officials would practically never be called upon to act, and prisons and jails would be nearly empty. A trend in this direction would be the measure of progress toward Beccarian crime control. Beccaria's emphasis on deterrence, and his argument that too much official action against crime is dysfunctional, contrast with the views of such contemporary deterrence pragmatists as James Wilson. Writing about a society—the United States—whose relatively high severity of punishment coincides with relatively high crime rates, Wilson argues that crime is caused by failure to punish enough (Pepinsky, 1980, pp. 129–131).

By the 1980s, theorists' only substantial bow in the Beccarian direction was an advocacy of selectivity about the kinds of offenses that should receive punishment. Norval Morris and Gordon Hawkins, for example, argued that respect for law and order, as well as crime control efficiency, would be increased if such victimless offenses as drug use, gambling, and prostitution were no longer treated as crimes, or "decriminalized." Officials could then concentrate on enforcing the law against offenders who manifestly injured other persons.

There are two major difficulties with state dysfunction theory. First, criminal justice officials, historically, have responded to attempts at decriminalization and diversion by increasing their activity in new directions. The net result has been that arrests, convictions, and confinement have increased. Second, if officials were to initiate change by enforcing the law more selectively, they would give the appearance of being less responsive to crime, thereby suggesting that people could commit more crime without being caught.

These problems can only be solved if members of private communities somehow control crime on their own initiative and find less occasion to call on officials to respond to crime. Private initiative is on the agenda of state excess theorists.

State excess theories

If it is possible to criticize officials for causing crime by perverting their mandate, it is also possible to go a step further. Crime can be seen as caused simply by the creation of the state or of law. Implicit in such a position is the assumption that people can maintain satisfactory social relations without state control.

This assumption has underlain the cross-cultural studies of a number of anthropologists. They have found that making an act punishable by the state, which Mark Kennedy called "incrimination," is only one among a number of alternative ways of handling disputes. Many of the alternatives, such as mediation, are achieved informally. This cross-cultural research has been surveyed by Donald Black, an American sociologist who treats "law" as something societies can have in varying quantities according to the extent to which they use state control. Such a perspective suggests that members of any society can arrange to have more or less law and more or less crime, as they please. But the state excess theorists who conduct historical research within single societies seem to find that the growth of state and law is inevitable, if regrettable.

The most prominent state excess theorists have developed the political and economic analyses propounded in the mid-nineteenth century by Karl Marx and Friedrich Engels. In the Marxist view, the modern Western state exists to serve the interests of those controlling the means of production, that is, the ruling class or the bourgeoisie. The law functions largely to keep workers on the job in order to make profits for the ruling class. In the "advanced" or "late" stage of capitalism in which Western societies exist, laws of confinement, and law enforcement, increasingly serve also to keep unneeded or "surplus" workers from making trouble while they are out of work. Members of the working class who violate capitalist law are seen as driven to crime, either as a means of coping with or as a way of rebelling against their exploitation by the ruling class.

When, as is historically inevitable, according to Marxism, the workers become sufficiently united and aware of their plight, they will overthrow the bourgeoisie. Then, under a dictatorship of the proletariat, they will eliminate dependence on private ownership for production and consumption. This in turn will eliminate both the causes of working-class crime and the possibility of ruling-class crime and corruption. Ultimately, in a socialist or communist society, crime will practically disappear.

Other explanatory theorists of state excess, commonly known as conflict criminologists, take a more limited view of historical development. They ascribe either particular legislation or law enforcement patterns to the ability of the more powerful persons or groups to make their own interests prevail over those of weaker persons or groups. Thus, a study by William Chambliss traces the law of vagrancy and the punishment of vagrants to the rise of capitalism in England, when feudal landowners began to lose control of the national economy. Similarly, the origins of crime legislation in the United States since about 1880 have been explained as a response to the interests of powerful groups (Galliher and Pepinsky).

Some theorists of state excess point to the many ways in which people in various societies can control and handle disputes other than by treating disputes as crimes. These theorists, unlike others in the state excess group, assume that neither historical forces nor a ruling class preclude a citizenry from working out private substitutes for resort to state power.

When crime is defined as acts punishable by the state, the level of crime reflects the extent to which disputes are handled publicly rather than privately. Or, as the anthropologist Philip Parnell has asserted, the crime rate is a matter of competition between state adjudicators and private mediators of disputes.

Rather than being harmful or sinful behavior, "crime" becomes just one among a number of possible definitions of a dispute. This raises the obvious question of the connection between levels of violence and predation on the one hand, and levels of crime on the other.

Some state excess theorists foresee that elimination of the state, and hence of crime, may mean an end to violence and predation. This group includes anarchist criminologists as well as some atypical Marxist criminologists who believe that the requisite political revolution is within the control of the popular will. An interesting twist has been given to the Marxist theory by Richard Quinney (1980), who argues that those carrying out the revolution must be imbued with Paul Tillich's conception of the Christian spirit. Quinney's view, as well as Marx's early idea of human emancipation, is virtually identical to that of such anarchist criminologists as Tifft and Sullivan. This common vision is one of a world in which people understand that personal fulfillment comes of giving freely of one's talents and abilities to others, with everyone assuming that as a consequence of such universal sharing the greatest quantity of resources will be available to all, to be taken by all persons in proportion to their needs. The pool of resources and capacity for cooperation increase as the scale and planning of production arrangements diminishes, promoting flexibility and accommodation to diverse and changing human needs and circumstances. Because it is assumed that future human contingencies are unpredictable, our standardized organization of production (based on private ownership), laws and regulations, and state maintenance of order are viewed as counterproductive.

Marxists and such anarchists as Tifft and Sullivan disagree about the strategy for achieving the ideal society that they portray. The Marxists maintain that a disciplined cadre will have to lead a violent overthrow of the ruling class and its servant, the state, setting up a socialist state in its place in order to eradicate all remnants of bourgeois thought and action and to enforce a transition to stateless communism. The anarchists offer the objection that the Marxist revolution would only substitute one state and set of rulers for another. Instead, in Tifft and Sullivan's version of anarchism, those who understand the virtues of a stateless society must first establish and then live and work in autonomous communities, attracting defectors from state society by their example.

Other theorists, notably Parnell, are less sanguine about the possibility of achieving a communist or anarchist millennium. Informal control systems can eas-

ily promote violence and predation among groups, and oppression within them. One promising direction, examples of which are found both in isolated, small, and technologically underdeveloped societies and in urban areas in industrialized societies, is to promote the development of what anthropologists call cross-cutting ties. When, for example, a shop customer who lives outside a neighborhood has a dispute with a resident, the shop owner, whose ties cut across residence and commerce, may be able to negotiate a peaceful resolution of their conflict.

In this kind of community, with informal controls more active than those of the state, several effects relevant to violence, predation, and crime can be expected (Pepinsky, 1980, pp. 107–110):

1. People will exercise more restraint about hurting those on whose future cooperation they are likely to depend.
2. The odds of intervention in attempts at violence and predation will increase.
3. People will be deterred from engaging in such antisocial conduct by perceiving these high odds of intervention.
4. People in trouble will be more likely to refer their problems to those with whom they live and work rather than to strangers, including the police and other officials.
5. Those matters still referred to officials will be more serious problems, in which community cooperation will facilitate successful prosecution and the imposition of sanctions.

Pragmatic state excess theory offers no panaceas for human conflict, and it is the least developed of the various political theories of crime causation. Whether application of the theory could lead to substantial reductions in crime in societies with high crime levels remains to be seen.

Conclusion

The spectrum of theories ranging from those of state vacuum to those of state excess can be said to move from right to left. There is also a tendency for the more abstract of these theorists, as well as for those closest to the state vacuum perspective, to label adherents of rival theories as unscientific and overly "political." Those focusing on applications of theory and those closest to state excess perspectives often label their counterparts as politically naive and, more harshly, as morally bankrupt lackeys of the state and of the ruling class.

It is difficult for debate among theorists belonging

to various categories to rise above polemics. Superficially, the assumptions underlying each category of theory appear arbitrary and mutually exclusive. Theorists of state vacuum presume that crime and social harm increase as the state fails to exert enough force to make citizens obey orders; those of state dysfunction presume that crime and social harm reflect a lack of self-discipline among state officials, and focus on enforcement priorities. State excess theorists presume that crime and social harm are promoted by government action, whether disciplined or not, and focus on political repression and ways by which citizens might avoid it.

There may be a way to transcend the rhetoric that divides these groups of crime causation theorists. No group of theorists loses by acknowledging its investment in the perspectives it advocates, or the impact of this investment on its inquiry. To all groups, crime signifies some kind of failure in the relationship of citizens to states. All groups seek a more solid understanding of that failure and recognize that the strength of their understanding is measured by how well their theories survive the test of human experience. Together, these shared beliefs imply that the value of each group's ideas depends on whether, in practice, shifts in the relationship of citizens to states cause the rates of crime or criminality to rise, to fall, or to remain untouched.

The fruitfulness of social theory—its contribution to knowledge—rests on its success in predicting what people will do or what consequences may arise from such behavior. If, for example, state vacuum theorists commit fewer errors than other theorists in predicting who will become a criminal despite official efforts, or if they accurately predict that crime will decrease as a result of greater state aggressiveness, then the partial validity of their theory should be acknowledged by the other theorists. Theorists of crime causation have a vital interest in the results of every political experiment with crime control. Insofar as such experiments fail, the force of reason should impel some theorists advocating the failed effort to give way to others. It is only by acknowledging a stake in the success or failure of political efforts at crime control that theorists of crime causation can transcend the parochialism that results from strict adherence to any of the various political categories of crime causation theory.

HAROLD E. PEPINSKY

See also ASSASSINATION; CLASS AND CRIME; CRIMINAL JUSTICE SYSTEM: SOCIAL DETERMINANTS; POLITICAL PROCESS AND CRIME; TERRORISM; WAR AND VIOLENT CRIME.

BIBLIOGRAPHY

American Humanist Association. *Humanist Manifestos I and II.* Buffalo, N.Y.: Prometheus Books, 1973.

BACON, G. RICHARD et al. *Struggle for Justice: A Report on Crime and Justice in America.* Prepared for the American Friends Service Committee. New York: Hill & Wang, 1971.

BENTHAM, JEREMY. *Of Laws in General* (1839). Atlantic Highlands, N.J.: Humanities Press, 1970.

BECCARIA, CESARE. *On Crimes and Punishments* (1764). Reprint. Translated with an introduction by Henry Paolucci. Indianapolis: Bobbs-Merrill, 1963.

BLACK, DONALD J. *The Behavior of Law.* New York: Academic Press, 1976.

CHAMBLISS, WILLIAM J. "A Sociological Analysis of the Law of Vagrancy." *Social Problems* 12 (1964): 67–77.

DURKHEIM, EMILE. *The Rules of Sociological Method* (1895). 8th ed. Translated by Sarah A. Solovay and John H. Mueller. Edited by George E. G. Catlin. New York: Free Press, 1964.

GALLIHER, JOHN F., and PEPINSKY, HAROLD E. "A Meta-study of Social Origins of Substantive Criminal Law." *Crime, Law, and Sanctions: Theoretical Perspectives.* Edited by Marvin D. Krohn and Ronald L. Akers. Beverly Hills, Calif.: Sage, 1978, pp. 27–38.

KENNEDY, MARK C. "Beyond Incrimination: Some Neglected Facets of the Theory of Punishment." *Catalyst,* no. 5 (1970): 1–37.

KRAMER, RONALD C. "From 'Habitual Offenders' to 'Career Criminals': The Historical Construction and Development of Criminal Categories." *Law and Human Behavior: Special Issue on Contemporary Lessons from Historical Research* 5 (1982): 273–294.

MARX, KARL, and ENGELS, FRIEDRICH. *Marx and Engels: Basic Writings on Politics and Philosophy.* Edited by Lewis S. Feuer. Garden City, N.Y.: Doubleday, Anchor Books, 1959.

MORRIS, NORVAL, and HAWKINS, GORDON J. *The Honest Politician's Guide to Crime Control.* University of Chicago Press, 1970.

PARNELL, PHILIP C. "Village or State?: Competitive Legal Systems in a Mexican Judicial District." *The Disputing Process: Law in Ten Societies.* Edited by Laura Nader and Harry F. Todd, Jr. New York: Columbia University Press, 1978, pp. 315–350.

PEPINSKY, HAROLD E. *Crime and Conflict: A Study of Law and Society.* New York: Academic Press, 1976.

———. *Crime Control Strategies: An Introduction to the Study of Crime.* New York: Oxford University Press, 1980.

QUINNEY, RICHARD. *Criminology: Analysis and Critique of Crime in America.* 2d ed. Boston: Little, Brown, 1979.

———. *Providence: The Reconstruction of Social and Moral Order.* New York: Longmans, 1980.

REIMAN, JEFFREY H. *The Rich Get Richer and the Poor Get Prison: Ideology, Class, and Criminal Justice.* New York: Wiley, 1979.

ROBISON, SOPHIA M. *Can Delinquency Be Measured?* (1936). Reprint. Montclair, N.J.: Patterson Smith, 1972.

SELLIN, THORSTEN. *Culture Conflict and Crime.* New York: Russell Sage, 1938.

SHELLEY, LOUISE I. *Crime and Modernization: The Impact of Industrialization and Urbanization on Crime.* Carbondale: Southern Illinois University Press, 1981.

SUTHERLAND, EDWIN H. "White-collar Criminality." *American Sociological Review* 5 (1940): 1–12.

TANNENBAUM, FRANK. *Crime and the Community.* Boston: Ginn, 1938.

TIFFT, LARRY, and SULLIVAN, DENNIS. *The Struggle to Be Human: Crime, Criminology, and Anarchism.* Sanday, Orkney, Scotland: Cienfuegos, 1980.

VAN DEN HAAG, ERNEST. *Punishing Criminals: Concerning a Very Old and Painful Question.* New York: Basic Books, 1975.

WILKINS, LESLIE T. "Putting 'Treatment' on Trial: Efficiency, Equity, and the Clinical Approach to Offenders." *Hastings Center Report* 5, no. 1 (1975): 35–36, 39–48.

WILSON, JAMES Q. *Thinking about Crime.* New York: Basic Books, 1975.

5.
PSYCHOLOGICAL THEORIES

Psychology and the concept of crime

This article reviews psychoanalytic theory, frustration-aggression theory, behavior theory, and social-learning theory in terms of their relevance to the genesis of aggressive, criminal, and delinquent behavior. These four approaches either have been historically influential or are based on the firmest evidence and represent the best that psychology has to offer at this time.

Although they may be relatively simple concepts to define in the legal sense, crime and delinquency are very complex in terms of the actual behavior they subsume. Bootleggers, burglars, and bank robbers little resemble one another in what they actually *do.* Criminals constitute a class of individuals only insofar as they all break the law; they are far from being a class in the psychological sense of being homogeneous in their behavior or motivations for crime. However, much early empirical work by psychologists treated criminals as though they were homogeneous by undertaking largely fruitless attempts to show that "criminals" were different from "normals" in various psychological characteristics.

Psychological subgroups of offenders

Some psychological researchers have taken as their starting point the fact that even those engaging in the *same* criminal act are not necessarily alike in regard to their psychological or behavioral characteristics.

For example, theft of an automobile may be for the purpose of joyriding and subsequently junking the car, for selling the car to a buyer who is part of a network, or for using the car to "escape" to California. In each case the instigation for the same crime is clearly different, and the personal characteristics and psychological state of the offender are also likely to be different.

Empirical research attempting to develop behavioral classification systems for offenders, despite differences in approach and in labels, has yielded categories having many common features (Quay, 1979; Megargee and Bohn). Almost without exception a pattern of hostile, overtly aggressive, predatory, uncaring, and thrill-seeking behavior has been found. This pattern has been given such labels as "unsocialized aggressive," "conduct disordered," or "psychopathic." Offenders who are at the extreme in this pattern have been the subject of considerable theory and research (Hare and Schalling).

Particularly among juveniles, a pattern labeled "socialized delinquent," "socialized aggressive," or "subcultural" has also frequently been identified. The most common characteristics are gang membership, group deviant activities, and the endorsement of values and standards of behavior that are seen as deviant by the larger community but not by the delinquents themselves.

Despite the rather common misconception that all offenders are aggressive, a constellation of characteristics that include social withdrawal, anxiety, and guilt has also been found. Labels for this pattern have included "neurotic" and "anxious." A fourth pattern subsumes such characteristics as social ineptness, passivity, indecisiveness, lack of perseverance, and incompetence. The labels applied here have been "immature," "inadequate," and "dependent."

Finally, there is a group of offenders with a very limited, if any, history of criminal behavior, who are married and support a wife and often a family, and who claim that their (often) single offense was a result of family problems or financial reverses. These individuals lack the "deviant" behavioral characteristics of the first four patterns. The labels most often applied here are "situational" or "normal" offender.

These subgroups of offenders, encompassing as they do such disparate patterns of behavior, should engender some skepticism with regard to the likelihood of finding a single causative factor for crime. However, demonstration of the existence of these subgroups has had little influence on the development of theories of crime causation, from either a psychological or sociological viewpoint. One obvious reason is that the rise of many theories of aggression and crime antedates the development of the typologies. Second, modern psychological theories emphasize that all behavior is learned by the same principles. For behavior theory and social-learning theory, *what* behavior patterns are learned is not as important as *how* they are learned. These patterns of offender behavior have more obvious relevance to what has been learned than to how learning has taken place. However, research on these differing subgroups has been at least suggestive of differences in psychophysiological, motivational-incentive, and learning mechanisms among the subgroups (Quay, 1979, 1982). So far, the ways in which processes important to these theories *may* differ among the subtypes has yet to be directly addressed.

Requisites for a psychological theory of crime causation

Psychological theories that deal with crime causation may be characterized as either broad or narrow. The broad theories represent attempts to explain all, or almost all, of human behavior; psychoanalytic theory, behavior theory, and social-learning theory are of this type. The narrower theories attempt to explain some more limited aspects of behavior, such as aggression or hostility; an example is frustration-aggression theory. The more circumscribed patterns of behavior with which a narrower theory deals may have obvious relevance to crime, but there is clearly less than perfect correspondence; thus, all aggressive people are not criminal and all criminals are not aggressive.

Psychological theories also vary in their formal properties as theories. Perhaps most important is the extent to which a theory relies on internal, unobservable, hypothetical entities as explanatory constructs, as does psychoanalytic theory, or eschews unobservables altogether, as does strict behaviorism. A corollary to this is the extent to which the theory is open to disconfirmation by observations of the phenomena to which it refers or by the falsity of predictions made from it. Theories also vary in the specificity of the psychological characteristics and mechanisms that they adduce and in their concern with physiological variables.

The "ideal" theory of crime causation and control should describe (1) the processes by which criminal behavior is acquired; (2) the social contexts in which this learning is most likely to take place; (3) the motivations of criminal behavior; (4) the means by which patterns of criminal behavior may be changed; and

(5) the ways in which the development of criminal behavior can be prevented.

Psychoanalytic theory

Basic concepts. The term *psychoanalysis* is used to refer both to Sigmund Freud's theory of personality development and to his method of treatment. However, neither Freud nor his immediate circle had criminal behavior in mind when psychoanalytic theory was being formulated. Freud's efforts were directed toward understanding neuroses and developing ways to rid patients of their neuroses through uncovering the unconscious bases of their symptoms. The theory ultimately became one of total human personality development.

The basic concepts of psychoanalytic theory are familiar to many people. The theory asserts that much of man's behavior is motivated unconsciously and that early experiences can have lasting effects, even in the absence of one's ability to recall these experiences. Also basic are the psychosexual stages of development—oral, anal, and genital—through which one must pass in order to avoid fixations at earlier stages, as well as the "layers" of personality expressed in terms of id, ego, and superego. The struggle between the primitive urges of the id and the "morality" of the superego has particular relevance for crime causation. Pertinent too are the various mechanisms of ego defense such as repression, projection, and rationalization, which protect the individual from unacceptable impulses and the anxieties arising out of them, albeit by symbolic and often distorted behavior.

With respect to aggression, Freud's final (1933) position was that aggression is an inborn drive originating in the death instinct, and that it is fruitless to attempt to *eliminate* aggression, although its intensity and its form can be modified. Although there has been a general reluctance among psychoanalysts to accept the death instinct, aggression is still treated as an instinctual drive that originates internally, as do hunger, thirst, and sex.

Crime causation. The psychoanalytic view of delinquency first put forth by August Aichhorn (p. 4) is that every child is at first asocial, demanding "direct primitive instinctual satisfaction without regard for the world around him." The normal course of child rearing leads to an adulthood in which such conduct is unacceptable. However, this training cannot be successful unless "the libidinal development of the child pursues a normal course." If there are disturbances in the libido organization, the child "remains asocial or else behaves as if he had become social without having made an actual adjustment to the demands of society." This means that the "instinctual wishes" have not been repudiated, but are suppressed so that "they lurk in the background awaiting an opportunity to break through to satisfaction." This state Aichhorn calls "latent delinquency," which can become "manifest" on provocation.

Although utilizing the methods of psychoanalytic psychotherapy, Aichhorn described its application to the delinquent child as remedial education: "It becomes possible for the remedial educator to discover the motivation of delinquency and then to obtain a point of attack for treatment . . . [the educator's] task is to bring into consciousness those unconscious processes which determine the undesirable behavior" (p. 9).

Since the time Aichhorn published his work there have been extensive writings presenting the psychoanalytic view of delinquency and crime. The various theorists do not always agree with one another—or, sometimes, with their own earlier writings. There are, however, some basic formulations that are generally regarded as relevant to the genesis of antisocial behavior.

Since it is the task of the superego to control impulse gratification, too weak a superego, or none at all, clearly sets the stage for crime. Individuals with such impairments are likely to belong to the unsocialized or psychopathic subgroup discussed above. However, particularly in adolescence, the superego may also be weak only in certain areas, especially if the resulting behavior is overtly or tacitly approved by the parents (Johnson). Furthermore, under dammed-up pressure from instinctual drives even a normally well-functioning superego can be overwhelmed.

Ego defects that impair contact with, and realistic interpretation of, the environment can also lead to crime. Individuals with weak egos and those seeking punishment because of unconscious guilt feelings are likely to fall into the anxious or immature group. The influences of the environment are generally viewed as precipitating factors in already heavily predisposed individuals. Crime-causing conflicts, as well as ego and superego defects, are generally ascribed to disturbed parent-child relations, usually resulting from psychological problems of the mother.

In many ways these explanations are appealing, if only for their simplicity. Weak superegos can often be "found" in criminals, particularly if criminal behavior is accepted as evidence for the weakness. Also, many criminals seem to show unconscious desires for punishment by leaving fingerprints or other incriminating evidence at the scene of the crime; but this may also be explained by the empirical finding that a high level of anxiety impedes deliberate thinking. Psychoanalytic theory, in addition to the unobservable nature of its basic explanatory constructs and its reliance on instinctual drives, including aggression, does not provide adequate room for the empirically well-demonstrated role of environmental factors and the processes of learning. Therefore, those aspects of psychoanalytic theory that have been utilized as explanatory in criminal behavior are now accepted as viable only by the minority of psychologists still close to Freud in their thinking. Yet the impact of many psychoanalytic concepts and ideas is lasting. The drive notion of aggression was incorporated into the frustration-aggression theory, although the assumption that it is an innate drive is dropped in modern learning theories. The basic idea that humans must become socialized by environmental influences was clearly carried over into modern learning (as well as sociological) theories. It is little debated that long-forgotten early events can have lasting influence. However, these events are now seen as having produced behavior that can be unlearned at any time with the proper application of the principles of learning.

Crime control. Little, if any, attention has been given to crime control in the psychoanalytic literature beyond assertions that many criminals can be remolded into law-abiding citizens by psychoanalytic treatment. Even so, those with very weak superegos—that is, with character disorders—are seen as not motivated for psychoanalysis and as resistant to treatment. Furthermore, the efficacy of psychoanalysis, as well as other forms of psychotherapy, in treating even less difficult problems remains to be convincingly demonstrated.

Frustration-aggression theory

The basic assertion of frustration-aggression theory is that aggression is *always* the consequence of frustration and that frustration always leads to some form of aggression. Frustration is defined as interference with response to a goal and is ascribed to three factors: (1) the strength of the motive or goal whose satisfaction is being interfered with; (2) the degree of the interference; and (3) the number of frustrated responses. This third factor suggests that the effects of frustration both persist and are cumulative. Thus, a high degree of frustration would occur where there is strong motivation toward a goal, where interference completely blocks the person from attaining that goal, and where there has been continual frustration (Dollard et al.).

Environmental conditions of economic disadvantage and discrimination would be expected to engender a high level of frustration and violence, thus explaining the link between economic conditions and violence. Research suggests that the arbitrariness of the frustration (as in racial discrimination) increases aggression.

Frustration-aggression theory has been criticized on a number of points: (1) frustration does not always lead to aggression; (2) there are other demonstrable antecedents to aggression; and (3) the definition of frustration has become so broadened in attempts to account for experimental findings that it now lacks specific meaning (Bandura, 1973, pp. 31–39). Edwin Megargee (p. 11) points out that social programs which attempt to reduce aggression by "buying off" potentially violent people fail to take into account the complexity of aggressive and criminal behavior and the varying ways in which it may be instigated and carried out.

Catharsis, a concept derived from psychoanalytic theory but prominent in theorizing about aggression, refers to the reduction of accumulated aggressive drive by its expression in aggressive behavior. Yet an ingenious series of experiments casts doubt on the catharsis notion by showing that the physiological arousal accompanying aggression-inducing events can be reduced not only by aggressive behavior but also by nonaggressive and even self-punishing behavior (Hokanson). Thus, there is little need to believe that opportunities must be provided to behave aggressively in order to "drain off" aggressive drive, or that aggression must be channeled into socially less disapproved forms of behavior in order to diminish the likelihood of more damaging forms of aggression.

Behavior theory

Modern behavior theory had its roots in the early behaviorism of John Watson during the 1920s and 1930s, but its leading modern figure is the psychologist B. F. Skinner. It emphasizes observable events and makes no use of the hypothetical constructs so prominent in psychoanalytic theory. The basic assumption is that almost all human behavior is learned, and the theory is directed toward explaining *how* it is learned and performed. Its primary principle is that behavior is controlled by its consequences. This contingent relationship between behavior and ensuing events is the heart of both behavior theory and behavior modification, which is the theory's application to behavior change.

Reinforcement. An event that serves to increase the frequency of a behavior that it follows is a *positive reinforcer*, more commonly called a reward. However, a reward is *not* a positive reinforcer unless it actually increases the likelihood of the occurrence of the behavior it follows. *Primary reinforcers* do not depend upon previous training for their reinforcement value; to a thirsty person, water is a primary reinforcer. *Secondary reinforcers*, which control most of human behavior, have acquired their value by association with other reinforcers. Parental attention becomes reinforcing to a child because it has been paired with the delivery of a primary (food) reinforcer. *Generalized reinforcers* have acquired their value by being paired with many other reinforcers; the best example is money, but social approval and affection are also in this category. These generalized reinforcers control a great deal of adult human behavior, and to function effectively in a complex society an individual must be responsive to generalized reinforcers. In *shaping*, complex new behavior is learned by reinforcing separately each small step toward learning it, which is how animals are taught to perform such unnatural acts as jumping through fire. In *chaining*, only the last step in a sequence is reinforced, for example, in payoffs only for completed tasks.

The concept of *negative reinforcement* refers to an increase in the frequency of a behavior as a function of the *removal* of an event when the behavior occurs. Although some events may be seen as unpleasant and undesirable, they meet the criteria for a negative reinforcer only if their removal after a response makes that response more likely. Negative reinforcement requires an ongoing *aversive* event that can be removed or terminated when some specific response is made.

Persons can develop persistence in any behavior that has been successful in reducing aversive experiences. Indulgence in alcohol or drugs is a form of behavior that may be made more frequent because its consequence is the reduction of worry and anxiety. Avoidance of aversive events may be negatively reinforcing, as is escape from them. Most persons do not commit crimes, even those that would readily be rewarding, because they learn crime-avoidance behaviors from experience with aversive events, or punishments.

Schedules of reinforcement. Since in the natural setting reinforcers rarely follow the response to be changed, the effects of various *schedules* of reinforcement have been the focus of much research. There are four basic schedules of reinforcement, but that which is especially relevant to crime is called a *variable ratio*. The operation of a slot machine is an excellent example: sometimes one or two pulls yield a payoff, but sometimes many more are required. Variable-ratio schedules generally result in high rates of responding, for the faster the responses the more quickly reinforcement comes. Most activities that are a "gamble" are on some sort of variable-ratio reinforcement schedule. Many forms of crime, including street robberies or burglaries, may be reinforced on such a schedule.

An additional factor in the delivery of reinforcement is the time that elapses between the response and the reinforcer. The early stages of learning are impeded by too great a time lapse. Delay is of great practical importance when there is a "choice" between an immediate or delayed reinforcer (a dollar now versus ten dollars at the end of the week) and when there are both positive and aversive consequences accruing to the same behavior (freedom from worry tonight but a hangover tomorrow). Criminal activity very often seems to produce an immediate positive consequence as opposed to work or study, whose effects are temporally more distant. Furthermore, the potential aversive consequences of crime, also on a variable-ratio schedule, can be long in coming.

Punishment. A concept in behavior theory which is particularly relevant to the control of crime is that of punishment. Its definition in behavior theory does *not* carry with it the notions of revenge, retribution, and just deserts that are linked with this concept in criminal justice. Punishment is defined as either the presentation of an aversive event or the removal of a positive event following a behavior which decreases that behavior's frequency. In behavior theory, an event is punishment *only* if the conduct it follows is made less likely: it is defined solely by its effect on behavior.

There are two different forms of punishment. In the first, an aversive event follows a response; reprimands and painful physical consequences are common examples. The second type of punishment involves contingent removal of a positive reinforcer after a response. Fines represent removal of a positive reinforcer, whereas imprisonment entails removal of freedom as well as the opportunity to obtain positive consequences.

Since it is often desirable to reduce rather than increase the frequency of certain behavior, there has been much research on how to make punishment work most efficiently. This has yielded a set of "rules" for the effective use of punishment (Azrin and Holz). One rule for maximizing the effect of penalties is that the intensity of the initial and subsequent punishments should be as great as possible. The second principle

has to do with certainty: the punishment should be delivered for every occurrence of the undesired behavior. Third, the temporal delay should be minimized. In fact, the best time to punish may be at the very onset of the prohibited behavior. A fourth principle is that there should be no unauthorized means of escape from the punishment: any "way out" will lessen the effect. Moreover, whatever behavior succeeds in avoiding the punishment will be negatively reinforced and thus increased in frequency. Certainty and swiftness of penalties are frequently cited objectives of the criminal justice system. However, initially high levels of sanctions are generally not employed on humanitarian grounds.

These first four principles are more or less common knowledge. The subsequent rules are more subtle. Although no unauthorized escape from penalties should be allowed, conditions should be arranged so that an alternative, nonpunished response can be positively reinforced by the same event that has previously reinforced the punished response. A permissible alternative response to obtain the same goal makes the punished response less necessary. Concomitantly, the level of motivation to make the punished response should be decreased. (It may be noted in passing that offender rehabilitation as a technique of crime control has the aim both of providing alternative means to obtain positive consequences and of reducing the motivation for criminal behavior.) Finally, if mild intensities of punishment are used, long periods of punishment should *not* be used. Adaptation to mild intensities can occur over time, diminishing their effect.

Another important aspect of punishment is that previously neutral stimuli which are paired with punishment themselves acquire punishing characteristics: they become secondary or acquired punishers. Those persons in the environment associated with punishment are tarred with the same brush, and, as with primary punishers, avoiding them is reinforcing. Thus, the chronic offender seeks to avoid any aspect of the criminal justice system—even those parts designed to "help" him.

Extinction. *Extinction* is a method of decreasing the frequency of behavior without punishment. It means the cessation of reinforcement, and it results in the reduction and eventual elimination of the behavior. In everyday life, extinction often takes the form of ignoring and not responding to the conduct of others. In order to extinguish unwanted behavior it is, of course, necessary to know what *is* reinforcing the behavior, so that these events can be prevented from occurring. The speed with which extinction occurs is, in part, dependent upon the prior schedule of reinforcement. Variable-ratio schedules lead to greater resistance to extinction since the individual becomes accustomed to making large numbers of nonreinforced responses, and the onset of extinction may not represent, at least for a while, a perceptible change in circumstances.

Discrimination and stimulus control. In some situations (more precisely, in the presence of a certain stimulus) behavior may be reinforced, whereas in other situations (presence of other stimuli) it is not. When such instances recur, the situation comes to signal the consequences to follow. The result is that the behavior is likely to occur only in those situations that signal reinforcement. When the person behaves differently in the presence of different stimuli, a *discrimination* has been made. When responses are differentially controlled by different situations, behavior is said to be under *stimulus control*. Most behavior is under some form of stimulus control: we eat yellow grapefruit but not green ones, and open doors when the bell rings. Crime-preventive measures are often those that try to signal a low probability of reinforcement, such as barred windows and doors on a residence, and collected bus fares kept in an unbreakable box. Criminal behavior is not always under good stimulus control; the activities of the socialized-aggressive delinquents mentioned earlier may be reinforced on the inner-city street corner but not in the schoolroom; hence, failure to discriminate between the two settings may lead to behavior labeled "delinquent" in school. Seemingly "stupid" crimes such as robbing a store with a patrol car outside may also be failures of discrimination.

Generalization. *Stimulus generalization* refers to the extension of behavior to situations other than those in which it has been trained: it is the opposite of discrimination. The extent to which the behavior will generalize to a new setting is a function of the similarity of the new setting(s) to those in which reinforcement has occurred. Clearly, generalization has both positive and negative consequences. One's behavioral effectiveness would be limited if one could not generalize one's actions to new but similar settings.

Response generalization refers to the reinforcement of one response increasing the likelihood that similar responses will also occur more frequently. Thus, successful assaults may increase the likelihood of an individual committing robberies as well, since the behaviors involved are similar. One factor that may operate here is that people possess patterns of related behavior. What happens to one particular behavior may affect the frequency of others in its pattern. An impor-

tant practical aspect of response generalization is that each behavior in the pattern need not itself be the focus of behavior change efforts in a one-after-the-other order for all to change, a process that would obviously be very time-consuming and inefficient.

Behavior theory and crime causation. For behavior theory, crime is learned and performed according to the same principles as any other behavior. Criminality does not result from unconscious forces, hypothetical antecedent events, or the aggressive nature of humans, but from an individual's past reinforcements for crime and for alternatives to crime. Thus, *any* environmental circumstances that reinforce acquisition and performance of behavior defined as criminal are the "causes" of crime. It is obvious that very often crime does pay, often on a variable-ratio schedule that makes it resistant to extinction. It is also clear that the positive consequences of crime occur much sooner after the criminal act than do the negative consequences—if the latter occur at all.

The behavioral approach to understanding crime has obvious appeal and in many respects coincides with common sense. However, the all-too-frequent desire of both criminal justice professionals and the man on the street to deal with crime only in terms of imposing negative consequences is too limited an application of behavior theory, one that has not succeeded and is unlikely to do so. Behavior theory holds that rearranging the contingencies of the environment to teach and maintain noncriminal behavior is the only approach likely to be truly effective over the long term in crime prevention.

Behavior theory and crime control. Behaviorists have generally directed their attention to *changing* the behavior of offenders, especially juveniles. One reason for this emphasis is that, for behavior theory, cause and remediation are not interdependent; there is really no cause to be removed before cure can be effected. The task is to extinguish criminal behavior by nonreward, by the positive reinforcement of new behavior, and, in some instances, by the application of aversive consequences for crime coupled with positive reinforcement for new behavior.

The fact that behavior theory has relatively few concepts, all of which are operational and easily communicable, has facilitated its application. Moreover, insistence on continuous monitoring of the behavior that is being changed makes evaluation of the effectiveness of change efforts continuous, easy, and an integral part of the treatment.

There have been, however, some problems with the application of behavioral principles in changing criminal behavior. To control response-reinforcement contingencies, the person who is modifying behavior must have considerable control over the situation in which the treatment is to take place. This is not always easy, even in closed institutions whose avowed purpose is correcting criminal behavior, for the staff may not have the desirable degree of control. As has been demonstrated, a great deal of reinforcement is available in correctional institutions for undesired, rather than desired, behavior.

Another difficulty has been that complex chains of criminal behavior, such as finding a likely target, putting it under observation, circumventing alarms, and entering and removing property, are difficult to extinguish because they do not occur in the treatment setting. The behaviorist must almost always try to attain his goals by reinforcing acceptable forms of behavior that will, it is hoped, achieve the same goals as criminal conduct. In many instances the behavior that is desirable in the setting in which it is trained either is too "simple" to be functional, such as keeping one's room clean, or is actually nonfunctional in the offender's real-life circumstances.

There is also the problem that newly learned behavior is subject to extinction if it is not reinforced in the natural environment. Nor is the individual insulated against relearning criminal behavior in its old form, or in new forms, if these behaviors are those that are reinforced in the real-life setting. An environment that does not reward, or actually punishes, "reformed" behavior can and does counteract the behaviorist's rehabilitation efforts. Although these problems limit the theory they in no way invalidate it. Such outcomes are exactly what the theory predicts, since they are forms of behavior controlled by their consequences.

Social-learning theory

Like psychoanalytic and behavior theory, social-learning theory represents an attempt to understand the acquisition and performance of all complex forms of human behavior. Social-learning theory has, however, been somewhat more specifically concerned with aggression; many empirical studies have been directed toward understanding how aggression is instigated, learned, and performed.

Acquisition of aggressive and criminal behavior. As a theory in the behavioral tradition, social-learning theory assumes that man is not born with a repertoire of aggressive behavior but that all aggressive responses are learned. It is, however, explicitly recognized that biological factors set limits on the types of responses that can be developed, influence the rate

at which learning can proceed, and make organisms more likely to perceive and learn certain critical features of their environment. Specific neurophysiological systems that probably mediate aggressive behavior are also recognized. However, as Albert Bandura, the leading theorist in the field, has stated, "In the social learning view, people are endowed with neurophysiological mechanisms that enable them to behave aggressively, but the activation of these mechanisms depends on appropriate stimulation and is subject to cognitive control. Therefore, the specific forms that the aggressive behavior takes, the frequency with which it is expressed, the situation in which it is displayed, and the specific targets selected for attack are largely determined by social learning factors" (1979, p. 201).

Although behavior theory emphasizes performance and reinforcement, social-learning theory emphasizes the vast extent to which learning takes place vicariously. Observing the behavior of others and its consequences for them permits people to acquire patterns of complex behavior by using other persons as models without the need to shape and chain elements of their own conduct through trial and error. Learning by observation involves attention to the model, memory of the model's behavior, and the motor reproduction of the observed behavior (Bandura, 1973). In this process, behavior can be learned but not necessarily practiced. Individuals learn to respond in an aggressive or criminal fashion and retain the capacity to do so, but they may not put these behavior patterns into action unless there are incentives and motivations to do so. Lack of incentive or the presence of negative sanctions may result in such behavior being dormant in the repertoire until incentive conditions change. This may explain why a long-docile individual can suddenly commit a highly aggressive act.

Social-learning theory also recognizes that from observing others, people can abstract general strategies and tactics of conduct and then apply them to new forms of behavior. Those extrapolations and recombinations of what has been observed are generally labeled "creative" and can include both legal and illegal activities; the same principles are involved in both cases.

Although modern social-learning theory has emphasized learning by observation, there is also a place for learning by direct experience, through trial and error. Complex patterns of behavior can be shaped and chained out of more rudimentary responses. Although recognizing the importance of consequences in shaping and making responses more probable, Bandura (1979) has reinterpreted the role of reinforcement to make it less a mechanistic than a cognitive process. Consequences allow one to observe the effects of one's actions and those of others in bringing about beneficial outcomes and avoiding punishing ones. Learning of aggressive and criminal behavior also results from practice and reinforcement; one can directly teach aggressive behavior to passive children (Patterson, Littman, and Bricker).

Motivation for aggression. Social-learning theory distinguishes between two broad classes of motivators of behavior (Bandura, 1979). Biologically based motivators include aversive stimulation from both body conditions and external sources, either of which can motivate efforts to reduce these unpleasant experiences when one reacts to physical irritations. The second source of instigation to aggression is a mental one, consisting in a person's capacity to imagine *future* material, sensory, or social consequences of behavior. Goal setting and self-evaluations operate here as acquired reinforcers to create self-inducements to act and persist until one's own standards are met.

Frustrating events can all be seen as aversive. In social-learning theory, aversive events are deemed to produce a general state of physical arousal that can elicit different forms of behavior, which *may* include aggression. Responses actually used to deal with such arousal depend on past learning and on their reinforcement by a subsequent reduction in the arousal.

An additional factor of some importance is the interpretation placed by the individual on his physiological state of arousal. An aversive event can be "reconciled" by giving it a particular interpretation that does not call for an aggressive response: an insult can be turned away by "considering the source." It would appear that past learning determines what cognitive interpretation will be given to the aversive event and the arousal it produces. As Bandura has pointed out, "Frustration tends to provoke aggression mainly in people who have learned to respond to aversive experiences with aggressive attitudes and conduct" (1979, p. 210). When aggression is practiced in new circumstances and is rewarded by the termination of the aversive event and the subsequent reduction of arousal, the aggressive response is further strengthened.

When anger becomes the most frequent cognitive interpretation of the arousal, and aggression the most likely response, the individual will be perceived as chronically hostile. He will, in turn, be a source of aversive stimulation to others, leading them either to counteraggress or to avoid. Both consequences would serve to remove the overly aggressive person from many sources of positive social reinforcement.

In turn, this lack of positive reinforcement (sometimes called frustrative nonreward) is itself aversive, provides arousal, and facilitates more aggression. Gerald Patterson has provided data on the development of such vicious circles within the family setting that may lead to child abuse, and he has discussed the reciprocal nature of parent-child behavior in initiating and maintaining deviance.

Adverse changes in the conditions of one's life can be aversive and provoke aggression. Socioeconomic disadvantage is frequently cited as a major cause of crime. However, since most impoverished people do not aggress or become criminals, this instigative factor requires more detailed analysis. As Bandura (1979) has noted, a sizable majority of the impoverished are apathetic and have lost the belief that there is anything they can do about their situation; their experience has been that the environment is either punishing or nonresponsive. Why some aggress when the majority do not is a complex question that, as one might expect, involves prior learning. Those whose assertive efforts have periodically been rewarded (variable-ratio schedule) are more apt to aggress; those who have almost never been reinforced for aggression will not. Thus, since most people who are and who feel deprived are not criminal, the aversive nature of economic disadvantage itself is not a sufficient cause of crime.

Aversive events are not the only instigators of aggression. Social-learning theory recognizes the capacity of humans to "see" into the future and to represent future events symbolically in the present. According to Bandura, "A great deal of human aggression, in fact, is prompted by anticipated positive consequences" (1979, p. 214). These expected consequences are generally derived from prevailing conditions of reinforcement. However, expectation and the actual consequences do not always coincide; it has been suggested, for example, that habitual offenders tend to overestimate their chances of success. The opportunity to observe others acting aggressively can serve as an instigator as well. Research has suggested that the activation potential of modeling is enhanced if the observer is angered, if the modeled aggression is socially justified or is shown to be successful in securing rewards, and if the victim invites attack through being associated with prior aggression (Bandura, 1979).

Aggression can also be instigated by instruction. In their upbringing most people are trained to obey orders. Once this form of behavior has been established, what Bandura calls "obedient aggression" can be secured (1979, p. 216). Pressures from both peers and legitimate authorities can instigate aggression.

Finally, aggressive behavior can be prompted by erroneous or frankly delusional beliefs. Although very few criminal individuals are mentally ill to this extent, in some instances—usually dramatic ones, such as the murder of public figures—there is clearly delusional instigation.

Maintenance of behavior. Social-learning theory, like behavior theory, is cognizant of the extent to which behavior is maintained by its consequences. Three types of consequences are considered that not only operate independently but interact to enhance or weaken their effects.

External reinforcement, or positive incentives, may take a variety of forms. Tangible rewards, such as goods and money, are reinforcers clearly available for much criminal behavior. Social-status rewards come in the form of approbation and approval: parents of aggressive children frequently condone, approve, and reinforce aggressive behavior outside the home. Much socialized-aggressive behavior is maintained, at least in part, by peer approval for fighting and for such delinquent behavior as truancy and stealing.

As noted earlier, the reduction of aversive consequences coming from others may reinforce counteraggression. Social-learning theory emphasizes that this defensive aggression is reinforced more by anticipated consequences than by immediate effects: people will suffer pain from the reprisals of others in the expectation that their own aggression will eventually remove noxious conditions imposed by others. The anticipated cost of timidity may also sustain aggression even in the face of immediate aversive consequences.

Punishment also plays a role in social-learning theory by restraining behavior. Social restraints derive from threats of external punishment, but personal restraints "operate through anticipatory self-condemning reactions toward one's own conduct" (Bandura, 1979, p. 222). The need to have learned nonpunished alternative behavior that evokes positive reinforcement is particularly important in making punishments effective. Law-abiding behavior is maintained more by having socially approved options than by the threat of legal sanctions.

The second general type of consequence is that of vicarious reinforcement. Its function in maintenance is the same as in acquisition: by observation it provides information about the likely consequences of one's own behavior. There are a number of factors that have been experimentally shown to make both vicarious reinforcement and vicarious punishment effective (Bandura, 1973). These include the status of the person observed, whether this person's behavior is rewarded or punished, the nature of the behavior observed, the perceived comparability of the person observed to the observer, and the nature of the behavior already in the observer's repertoire. The factors that influence the effectiveness of modeling and vicarious consequences are obviously relevant to crime control by publicizing desirable conduct and by general deterrence.

Self-regulatory mechanisms are an important facet of social learning. According to Bandura, "People are not simply reactors to external influences. Through self-generated inducements and self-produced consequences, they can exercise some influence over their own behavior. In this self-regulating process, people adopt through tuition and modeling certain standards of behavior and respond to their own actions in self-rewarding or self-punishing ways. An act therefore includes among its determinants self-produced influences" (1979, p. 224). The processes whereby one observes one's own performance according to such criteria as quality and ethics, makes judgments about that performance, and then self-reinforces are complex. They are not, however, controlling psychic "agents" but rather are cognitions learned through experience.

Thus, one's self-generated consequences can either reinforce or punish aggressive and criminal behavior, depending upon the nature of one's thinking. It is likely that the same set of contexts that provide for the acquisition of criminal behavior also lead to the acquisition of thought patterns that provide for self-reward, or at least for the absence of self-punishment and antisocial behavior.

Even in individuals who have self-regulatory processes that inhibit criminal behavior, there are lapses in the control mechanism; these mechanisms are not invariant and may be disengaged. One mechanism of disengagement is cognitive restructuring, for example, "the end justifies the means" or "compared to what the politicians steal, what I take is nothing." Another method involves obscuring or distorting the relationship between actions and the effects they cause, thus displacing responsibility for, or minimizing, the effects of one's actions. Moreover, aggression toward persons who are devalued or dehumanized is less apt to arouse self-condemnation than is aggression toward those perceived more sympathetically. Conditions of life that lead both to impersonal and anonymous relations among people and to estrangement foster the development of these devaluative mechanisms. Although not specifically a part of social-learning theory, disengagement can also result from physiological changes brought about by the use of alcohol and drugs.

The contexts of acquisition. According to social-learning theory, the origins of aggressive and illegal behavior lie in the family, in the subculture in which people reside, and in the symbolic modeling provided by the media. Investigators have empirically demonstrated that children become aggressive when aggression is modeled by family members, when aggression in children is reinforced—wittingly or unwittingly—by family members, and when aggression is instigated by frustration and by aversive stimuli (Hetherington and Martin).

The subculture, which has been the focus of so much theory and research for the sociological point of view, provides a larger context in which the family is embedded. Although the cohesion and reality of subcultures is debated among sociologists, there is agreement that a disproportionate number of delinquents and criminals come from social circumstances in which models of aggression and criminality are in high profile. In these environments there are both tangible and intangible rewards for crimes, such as peer approval (Conger), limited opportunities to learn alternative forms of behavior, and impediments to developing self-regulation.

Research has demonstrated that television—clearly the most influential of the media with regard to children and adolescents—has four different effects on social behavior. According to Bandura (1979), these are (1) the teaching of aggressive styles of conduct; (2) the lessening of restraints on aggression; (3) desensitization and habituation to violence; and (4) the shaping of images of reality upon which people base their actions. All of these effects are likely to occur when aggression and violence are constantly modeled by television characters, when aggression is portrayed as an acceptable and successful—if not actually preferred—solution to life's problems, when violent and aggressive acts parade almost unendingly across the screen, and when many people are portrayed as unscrupulous, hedonistic, untroubled by material needs, and unburdened by responsibilities to family, workplace, or society at large.

It is of interest that the pattern of delinquent and criminal behavior which has been labeled "unsocialized aggressive," "conduct disordered," or "psychopathic" seems to have its origins most clearly in the family context and in the interaction (at least in the most extreme cases) of this context with physiological factors. The development of the anxious and immature patterns would also seem clearly to take place in the family. On the other hand, the socialized-ag-

gressive pattern seems to have its origins in the deviant subculture. It may be that the media function equally well as a context for learning aggression among everyone, but one could speculate that their reality-shaping function has more effect on the economically disadvantaged.

The social contexts that appear to be criminogenic have been extensively studied from other points of view and by disciplines other than psychology. What social-learning theory offers is an understanding of the mechanisms by which these contexts exert, or fail to exert, their predicted influences.

Issues in the psychological analysis of crime causation

Two other issues relevant to the role of psychological theories in the explanation of crime have often been raised by those whose perspective is not psychological. These issues are the relation of crime to mental illness and to the "medical model." The extent to which theory and data from psychology are relevant to these concerns is not always clearly understood.

Crime and mental illness. Debates about whether or not offenders are "mentally ill" or have "psychiatric disorders" are frequent. In fact, about 7 percent of *incarcerated* offenders who are mentally ill suffer from a major psychotic disorder. Furthermore, the rates for offenders are no higher than for their counterparts in society (Monahan, pp. 78–79). A larger proportion of offenders have been diagnosed as suffering from less serious disorders, especially personality disorders that do not legally affect competency. There are those who maintain that *all* offenders are psychiatrically disordered in some way, but this assertion reveals more about the looseness of the concept of psychiatric disorder than about the personality of offenders.

Research into possible causal relationships between mental illness and crime is plagued by imprecision in defining and diagnosing mental illness and in determining what crimes persons have committed. Patients suffering from a major mental disorder may be arrested *because* of their bizarre behavior although no crime has been committed, yet other persons known to be mental patients may *not* be arrested even though they have committed a crime. Criminal behavior may also contribute to the patient's being defined as mentally ill in the first place.

One research strategy has been to follow discharged mental patients to determine how their subsequent arrests compare with non–mentally ill samples. Judith Rabkin's detailed review of such studies has ascertained: (1) since 1959, mental patients discharged from public facilities have total arrest records for all crimes that equal or exceed public rates with which they have been compared; (2) a small subset of patients who have prior criminal records accounts for a large majority of post-discharge arrests; (3) the predictors of post-discharge arrests include being male, young, and unmarried, factors that tend to be associated with arrest rates in the general population; and (4) mental patients are more likely to be arrested for assaultive and sometimes lethal behavior than are other people. With respect to mental illness causing crime, Rabkin concluded, "At the present time there is no evidence that their [discharged patients'] mental status as such raises their arrest risk; rather, antisocial behavior and mentally ill behavior apparently coexist, particularly among young, unmarried, unskilled, poor males, especially those belonging to ethnic minorities" (p. 25).

Crime and the medical model. Motivated by the questionable results attained in many attempts to rehabilitate offenders by psychologically oriented methods, some writers have rejected both the medical model of treatment and other attempts to change offenders. Indeed, they seem to suggest that changing the behavior of offenders requires acceptance of the medical model, which assumes that there is a cause for criminality *within the individual* and that the removal of the cause is necessary for a "cure."

As has been pointed out, behavior and social-learning theory reject this notion with respect to *all* behavior considered deviant, and behavior *modification* deals directly with behavior rather than with "underlying" disease factors that "cause" symptoms. Behavior theory and social-learning theory are both concerned with how behavior is determined through the interaction of a biological organism with an environment. Understanding these determinants can guide environmental interventions to extinguish criminal behavior or to prevent its occurrence in the first place. Attempts to change offenders by using the principles of behavior theory and social-learning theory in no way imply the acceptance of any underlying disease process, even though the behavior change effort may well be based on a "diagnosis" of what must be changed.

Learning theory and individual biological differences

Biological factors influence the learning *process.* Thus, poor conditionability in extraverts (Eysenck), a combination of hyporesponsiveness and slow recovery of the autonomic nervous system (Mednick), a

failure to learn to respond to signals of impending punishment (Trasler), and a deficiency in the behavioral inhibition system (Fowles) all relate to learning, particularly to learning *not* to engage in prohibited behavior. Although these approaches emphasize a failure to learn to inhibit criminal behavior, they do not deal with the other side of the coin: how such behavior is energized, acquired in particular forms, performed, and maintained. Furthermore, they tend to be directed toward exploring the behavior of unsocialized or psychopathic criminals, who probably constitute less than 25 percent of all offenders.

Psychological theory and crime control

Both behavior theory and social-learning theory imply that crime will occur as long as there are (1) unmet needs available to instigate criminal behavior; (2) opportunities to learn such behavior by instruction or observation; (3) environmental and intraindividual circumstances that facilitate crime; and (4) positive reinforcements for criminal behavior. Therefore, crime control involves (1) reducing unmet needs; (2) providing fewer examples of successful criminal behavior; (3) decreasing the number of contexts in which criminal behavior can be learned; (4) lessening the opportunities for criminal behavior and the availability of the instruments of crime; and (5) reducing the likelihood that criminal behavior will be positively reinforced. Concomitantly, there must be opportunities to learn alternative behavior, which is then consistently reinforced by success in meeting both primary and social needs.

Although many have repeatedly recognized the necessity of all these goals, social-learning theory provides a tested explanation *why* these things need to be done and why failure to accomplish them makes it unlikely that crime will be reduced. Behavior theory and social-learning theory also warn that any form of intervention that, however unwittingly, actually reinforces criminal behavior is likely to have an effect opposite to its avowed purpose. For example, providing delinquent gangs with adult attention and tangible rewards more often when they are delinquent than when they are not gives unwitting reinforcement to their misconduct and may explain the failure of many delinquency prevention efforts.

Behavior theory and social-learning theory also aid in analyzing approaches to crime control from other points of view. What is sometimes referred to as specific deterrence does not, in psychological terms, differ from punishment. However, the criminal justice system is too constrained by constitutional safeguards and by the practical problems of detection, apprehension, and adjudication of offenders to follow the psychological "rules" for the best use of punishment. The lack of certainty and swiftness in the application of sanctions is only too evident. Current practice also escalates the magnitude of the aversive consequence (sanctions) over time rather than the reverse. Escape from aversive consequences by some manipulation of the system is rampant. Thus, given a democratic society and a criminal justice system of limited efficiency and capacity, behavior theory indicates that specific deterrence is not a promising means of crime control. A no less important point is that although under ideal conditions punishment may suppress or possibly extinguish criminal behavior, punishment does not *teach* anything except ways to avoid it. No one can learn to read or write, to acquire a vocation, or to develop effective social behavior *solely* by being punished for criminal behavior.

One may also view general deterrence in the light of behavior theory and social-learning theory. To be effective, deterrence requires that the potential offender (1) attend to deterrence "messages," taking note of sanctions being imposed on others; (2) comprehend these observations as relevant to himself; (3) recall this information at the appropriate time; and (4) use it to guide his own behavior. Such deterrence clearly relies on observational learning and vicarious reinforcement for the subsequent nonperformance of the prohibited behavior. What researchers in social-learning theory have discovered about conditions that enhance modeling effects is clearly relevant to general deterrence.

The prediction of individual criminality

Despite the obvious relevance of social-learning theory to both causation and control, it cannot be overemphasized that the actual performance of aggressive or other criminal acts by a particular person at a given time can be strongly influenced by factors both in the immediate environment and within the individual. The former relate to the concepts of stimulus control in behavior theory and of disinhibition and disengagement in social-learning theory. Inherent intraindividual influences include general intelligence as well as the ingestion of alcohol and drugs. The influence of these immediate factors operating on persons who apparently have both the motivation and response capabilities for aggression makes individual violent behavior very difficult to predict with

an acceptable degree of accuracy (Monahan). Even repeat criminality of any type among incarcerated offenders is difficult to predict, especially in the face of generally favorable outcomes for the group of which the individual is a member.

Conclusions

Social-learning theory provides the most complete and accurate explanation available as to how *all* social behavior is acquired and performed. It has incorporated and expanded upon the most viable concepts of psychoanalytic theory and earlier forms of learning theory. Its propositions are open to test, and its empirical foundations are firm.

Aggressive and criminal behavior are clearly special cases of general social behavior, and it can be argued that sociological theories of crime causation are related to particular propositions of social-learning theory, especially those having to do with modeling, reinforcement, and disinhibition. The biological theories all relate to problems in the *processes* of learning, and any that turn out to be correct will only require that social-learning theory pay particular attention to these process problems and how they may be circumvented or overcome.

The particulars of social-learning theory will be further honed, and the experimental study of its propositions will probably continue to provide support for it. In the largely political arena of criminal justice, greater attention will have to be paid to what social-learning theory has to say about causation, deterrence, and the unlearning of criminal behavior in offenders if there is to be real progress in crime control. In fact, the major "problem" with the theory is that criminal justice policymakers have failed to understand both the theory and its implementations.

HERBERT C. QUAY

See also DIMINISHED CAPACITY; EXCUSE: INSANITY; INTELLIGENCE AND CRIME; MENTALLY DISORDERED OFFENDERS; PREDICTION OF CRIME AND RECIDIVISM; PSYCHOPATHY; REHABILITATION.

BIBLIOGRAPHY

AICHHORN, AUGUST. *Wayward Youth.* New York: Viking Press, 1935.
AZRIN, NATHAN H., and HOLZ, WILLIAM C. "Punishment." *Operant Behavior: Areas of Research and Application.* Edited by W. K. Honig. New York: Appleton-Century-Crofts, 1966, pp. 380–447.

BANDURA, ALBERT. *Aggression: A Social Learning Analysis.* Englewood Cliffs, N.J.: Prentice-Hall, 1973.

———. "The Social Learning Perspective: Mechanisms of Aggression." *Psychology of Crime and Criminal Justice.* Edited by Hans Toch. New York: Holt, Rinehart & Winston, 1979, pp. 198–236.

CONGER, RAND. "Juvenile Delinquency: Behavior Restraint or Behavior Facilitation." *Understanding Crime: Current Research and Theory.* Edited by Travis Hirschi and Michael Gottfredson. Beverly Hills, Calif.: Sage, 1980, pp. 131–142.

DOLLARD, JOHN; MILLER, NEAL E.; DOOB, LEONARD W.; MOWRER, O. HOBART; and SEARS, ROBERT R. *Frustration and Aggression.* New Haven: Yale University Press, 1961.

EYSENCK, HANS J. *Crime and Personality.* Boston: Houghton Mifflin, 1964.

FOWLES, DON C. "The Three Arousal Model: Implications of Gray's Two-factor Learning Theory for Heart Rate, Electrodermal Activity, and Psychopathy." *Psychophysiology* 17 (1980): 87–194.

FREUD, SIGMUND. *New Introductory Lectures on Psycho-analysis.* Edited and translated by James Strachey. New York: Norton, 1933.

HARE, ROBERT D., and SCHALLING, DAISY, eds. *Psychopathic Behaviour: Approaches to Research.* New York: Wiley, 1978.

HETHERINGTON, E. MAVIS, and MARTIN, BARCLAY. "Family Interaction." *Psychopathological Disorders of Childhood.* 2d ed. Edited by Herbert C. Quay and John S. Werry. New York: Wiley, 1979, pp. 247–302.

HOKANSON, JACK E. "An Escape-Avoidance View of Catharsis." *Criminal Justice and Behavior* 1 (1974); 195–223.

JOHNSON, ADELAIDE M. "Sanctions for Superego Lacunae of Adolescents." *Searchlights on Delinquency: New Psychoanalytic Studies Dedicated to Prof. August Aichhorn on the Occasion of His Seventieth Birthday, July 27, 1948.* Edited by Kurt R. Eissler. New York: International Universities Press, 1949, pp. 225–245.

MEDNICK, SARNOFF A. "A Biosocial Theory of the Learning of Law-abiding Behavior." *Biosocial Bases of Criminal Behavior.* Edited by Sarnoff A. Mednick and Karl O. Christiansen. Foreword by Marvin E. Wolfgang. New York: Gardner Press, 1977, pp. 1–8.

MEGARGEE, EDWIN I. *The Psychology of Violence and Aggression.* Morristown, N.J.: General Learning Press, 1973.

———, and BOHN, MARTIN J., JR. *Classifying Criminal Offenders: A New System Based on the MMPI.* Beverly Hills, Calif.: Sage, 1979.

MONAHAN, JOHN. *The Clinical Prediction of Violent Behavior.* Rockville, Md.: U.S. Department of Health and Human Services, Public Health Service, Alcohol, Drug Abuse, and Mental Health Administration, National Institute of Mental Health, 1981.

PATTERSON, GERALD R. "Children Who Steal." *Understanding Crime: Current Research and Theory.* Edited by Travis Hirschi and Michael Gottfredson. Beverly Hills, Calif.: Sage, 1980, pp. 73–90.

———; LITTMAN, ROBERT A.; and BRICKER, WILLIAM. "Assertive Behavior in Children: A Step toward a Theory of Aggression." *Monographs of the Society for Research in Child Development* 32, no. 5, serial no. 113, 1967.

QUAY, HERBERT C. "Adolescent Aggression." *Review of Human Development.* Edited by Tiffany M. Field, Aletha Huston, Herbert C. Quay, Lillian Troll, and Gordon E. Finley. New York: Wiley, 1982, pp. 381–394.

———. "Classification." *Psychopathological Disorders of Childhood.* 2d ed. Edited by Herbert C. Quay and John S. Werry. New York: Wiley, 1979, pp. 1–42.

RABKIN, JUDITH G. "Criminal Behavior of Discharged Mental Patients: A Critical Appraisal of the Research." *Psychological Bulletin* 86 (1979): 1–27.

REDL, FRITZ, and TOCH, HANS. "The Psychoanalytic Perspective." *Psychology of Crime and Criminal Justice.* Edited by Hans Toch. New York: Holt, Rinehart & Winston, 1979, pp. 183–197.

TRASLER, GORDON. "Relations between Psychopathy and Persistent Criminality: Methodological and Theoretical Issues." *Psychopathic Behaviour: Approaches to Research.* Edited by Robert D. Hare and Daisy Schalling. New York: Wiley, 1978, pp. 273–298.

6.
SOCIOLOGICAL THEORIES

Types of theories

Societies and groups of lesser scale—referred to collectively as social systems—have different rates of crime; their crimes are variously distributed among their regions, age groups, genders, social classes, and other social positions and sectors; and their kinds, quantities, and distributions of crime vary over time.

Some sociological theories of crime causation ask: What is it about social systems that explains these variations in crime? Other theories are directed to another set of questions: What is the connection between crimes and the personalities of those who commit them? How do people acquire the personalities that are prone to commit crimes, or crimes of some particular sort? How do people acquire the habits, skills, and values that facilitate and support criminal behavior? What motivates criminal behavior? That is, what states of mind and what external stimuli—opportunities, provocations, threats—lead people to commit crimes? Although psychologists have also addressed these questions, sociologists have typically placed more emphasis on the ways in which personality, learning, and motivation are affected by the actor's participation in, and dependence upon, larger systems of social relationships and the surrounding culture.

These two sets of theories are independent in the

sense that they are answers to different questions, but they are also interrelated in important ways. Theories about personality, learning, and motivation have implications for theory on the social-system level. For example, if theories claim that crimes are the result of certain kinds of personalities, learning experiences, or motivating circumstances, it would then follow that the distribution of crime in the society or group would correspond to a like distribution of those personality types, learning experiences, or motivating circumstances. The task of a system-level theory would then be to identify the properties *of the system*—those aspects of its structure and functioning—that generate these distributions of personality, learning, or motivation among the various sectors of the system.

In short, theories about personality, learning, and motivation suggest strategies for the construction of theories on the social-system level. Approaching the matter from the other direction, theories about the social-system level make assumptions about personality, learning, or motivation—that is, about what is sometimes called "models of man" or "human nature."

Modern beginnings: Shaw and McKay

The work of Clifford Shaw and Henry McKay provides an appropriate introduction to modern sociological thinking about crime. These researchers coordinated in a clear and cogent way many of the most important sociological ideas about crime that had emerged from the nineteenth and early twentieth centuries. Looking ahead, they presented sharp and often original statements of theoretical positions that are very much part of the contemporary criminological scene.

Like others of the Chicago school of American sociology, Shaw and McKay approached their subject from the point of view of the ecology—the distribution in space—of juvenile delinquency, mainly in Chicago but also in several other American cities. They observed that delinquency rates were highest in the zone surrounding the central business district and declined systematically as one moved outward to the suburbs, as did poverty, deteriorated housing, illness, and economic dependence. These ecological phenomena, they concluded, were natural products of urban growth. As cities grow, the commercial and industrial center expands and invades the surrounding residential areas. These areas become less desirable as places to live, and those who can afford to leave move out, but usually not very far; their arrival prompts others in the areas where they resettle to move still farther

out, and so on. There is a continuous spatial redistribution of population. The mix of persons in the area surrounding the center—the "zone in transition"—creates a milieu conducive to high rates of delinquency and crime. High mobility, social and cultural diversity, limited resources, and the struggle to make a living hamper people's efforts to achieve a sense of community, to maintain strong organizations and institutions, to work together for the common good, and to insist on better government services. Even the bonds between parents and children, who may be separated to some degree by language and culture, tend to break down. A condition of social disorganization prevails.

A specific manifestation of social disorganization is a breakdown in social control. First, a divided neighborhood cannot provide its children with clear and consistent rules or guides for conduct; second, the reduced capacity for concerted action means that supervision and sanctioning are less effective. In short, social conditions promote delinquency by failing to inhibit it. This is a major and recurrent theme in criminological theory.

Another major theme is that these communities provide positive incentives toward delinquency. In high-delinquency areas, "various forms of lawlessness have become more or less traditional aspects of social life and are handed down year after year through the medium of social contacts" (Shaw and McKay, p. 126). Delinquency is infraction, but it is also conformity to the codes and ideals of the delinquent and criminal groups. The persistence of these traditions helps to explain the continuous high rates of delinquency and crime in certain areas while their ethnic composition undergoes complete transformation. Patterns of criminal behavior, wrote Shaw and McKay, "are acquired through group contacts just as any cultural form is disseminated and transmitted through social groups" (p. 390). These patterns are what a later generation of criminologists was to call delinquent and criminal subcultures.

Underlying Shaw and McKay's sociology are some explicit assumptions about personality, motivation, and learning. Contrary to the then-prevailing view, especially in psychology and psychiatry, they did not consider delinquents abnormal or pathological. The delinquent has the same "desires for recognition, approbation and esteem of his fellows, for stimulation, thrill and excitement, for intimate companionship, and for security and protection" as the nondelinquent (p. 250). The difference is that the delinquent finds satisfaction of these desires in groups with delinquent patterns and traditions, and his dependence on those groups provides the incentive to learn and conform to their codes. This too has proved to be a strong theme of sociological criminology.

The work of Sutherland

Differential association. No sociologist has left a stronger impression on American criminology than Edwin H. Sutherland, whose most important works were published in the 1930s and 1940s. Although these works touched on a great variety of criminological subjects, his greatest impact was through his theory of differential association. Part of the appeal of this theory derived from its claim to constitute, in a few parsimonious propositions, a general and comprehensive explanation of crime, as contrasted to multiple-factor theories, which have many explanations for crimes but no general rule applicable to all crimes.

Differential association theory—the notion that crime is culturally patterned behavior and that it is learned in the same way as any other element of culture—represented an extreme development of one theme in Shaw and McKay's work. In the course of interaction with others, primarily within intimate personal groups, individuals are presented with definitions of legal codes as rules to be observed and with other definitions favorable to violations of the legal codes. "A person becomes delinquent because of an excess of definitions favorable to violations of law over definitions unfavorable to violations of law" (Cohen, Lindesmith, and Schuessler, p. 9). This is the principle of differential association. The amount of association with criminal and anticriminal definitions, and therefore the excess of the one over the other, depends on the frequency, duration, priority, and intensity of the respective associations.

The theory asserts that criminal behavior is learned by all of the mechanisms involved in any other learning. It also claims that "though criminal behavior is an expression of general needs and values, it is not explained by those general needs and values since non-criminal behavior is an expression of the same needs and values" (Cohen, Lindesmith, and Schuessler, p. 10). Thus, people might commit offenses because of frustration or a desire for happiness, status, or money, but a theory of crime must explain why they express these moods and desires in criminal rather than lawful ways.

Sutherland acknowledged that other factors, not included in the theory of differential association, affected crime, but he did not see this as a problem. The effect of such factors on crime was indirect, by

fostering criminal and anticriminal associations. Associations explain crime, declared the theory; it was not the job of the theory to explain associations.

The theme originated by Shaw and McKay and amplified by Sutherland might be called the "cultural transmission" theory or approach to criminal behavior. Sutherland's theory represents the most radical statement of the cultural transmission approach because it sets forth what it claims are the necessary and sufficient conditions for the explanation of all crime, at least on the level of the individual.

On the social-system level, the theory implies that the distribution of crime must correspond to the distribution of the patterns of differential association through which crime is learned. The features of the system that explain the distribution of crime, then, are those that explain differences in access to criminal and noncriminal patterns at different locations in the system. Thus, for example, because of the sexual division of labor and the greater restriction of females' freedom of movement, which might vary by social class or ethnic group, females are less exposed than men to procriminal associations and therefore are less likely to become criminal. Sutherland himself did not elaborate the system-level implications of differential association theory in a clear and consistent way. Donald Cressey has developed this line of explanation more systematically and has used it to explain many facts about the distribution of crime.

Sutherland explained crime in terms of certain characteristics of the learning process. He did not explain it in terms of personality characteristics, poverty, stress, or biological or psychological abnormality. In this way his theory was an attack on most of the popular criminological theories of his time. The attack was reinforced when he turned his attention away from those offenders with whom criminology had been almost exclusively concerned, those of predominantly lower-class background who populate the prisons, and focused on crimes committed by persons of high economic status in the course of their occupations.

White-collar crime. Sutherland's *White Collar Crime* called attention in a forceful way to the huge scale and high cost of such lawbreaking, especially the crimes of large business corporations, although these most respectable of all criminal offenders were rarely punished by the criminal courts. Sutherland pointed out that since these offenses did not figure in the criminal statistics and in the data of criminology, the theories of criminology did not take them into account. If they had, it would have been obvious that most criminological theories, based on information about lower-class offenders, break down because they do not fit the facts of white-collar crime. Although Sutherland's work on white-collar crime has attracted much attention, actual research and theory on the subject were modest until the mid-1970s. Since then, they have gathered considerable momentum, probably reflecting an increasing awareness and appreciation of the growth of gigantic corporations and their enormous power in modern society.

Differential association and learning theory. There have been efforts, notably by Robert Burgess and Ronald Akers, to reformulate the theory of differential association in terms of modern learning theory. This so-called Skinnerian theory ascribes a person's development of new types of behavior, called "operants," to the immediacy, intensity, and recurrence schedule of rewards and punishments—called positive and negative "reinforcements"—that the behavior evokes. This process is called "operant conditioning," and Burgess and Akers claimed that it provides the mechanism that accounts for the effects of associations. However, the attempt to translate Sutherland into this learning theory has had no great impact in criminology. Yet Skinnerian learning theory itself, having achieved great success in the field of psychology, appears with increasing frequency in sociological criminology.

Merton and anomie theory

In sharp contrast to Sutherland's theory of differential association was Robert Merton's approach to deviance and crime as formulated in his famous essay "Social Structure and Anomie." Differential association theory was concerned with the way in which individual actors adopted behavior patterns from models in their intimate environments. It did not leave much room for originality—the development of new forms of criminal conduct as a means of solving a problem.

Merton's theory dealt with the way in which a society's characteristics determine the distribution of behavior within that society. Behavior itself was conceived of as problem-solving. Crime must, therefore, be distributed as it is because the problems to which it is a solution are distributed that way. The characteristics of the system that explain the distribution of those problems will explain the corresponding distribution of crime within the system.

A society's culture instills in its members goals that may be the same for all members or may be different for persons in different positions. Society also equips its members with regulative norms, that is, with rules

that specify the means that may legitimately be used in the pursuit of these goals. These are the institutionalized means, and they too are distributed diversely. At some social positions, the means will be fully adequate to achieve the goals; at others, there will be a gap or disjunction of some magnitude. Where the institutionalized means are adequate, there will be no incentive to employ forbidden means. Where there is a disjunction, there will be strain, which, if serious or sustained, may erode attachment to the regulative norms and produce a condition of "deregulation" that the French sociologist Emile Durkheim (1858–1917) called anomie.

In this condition of anomie, people may either accept or reject culture goals and institutionalized means and may replace rejected goals or means with culturally disapproved goals or means. The result is a set of logically possible alternative adaptations to strain; one is conformity, and the others are modes of deviance. (Theories like Merton's are often called strain theories.) Merton had little to say about the determinants of choice among the disapproved adaptations, and in this respect his scheme falls short of being a rounded theory. Although it is presented as a theory of deviance, it is clear that deviance is meant to include criminality.

In the terms of this theory it is possible to describe and compare different societies, different sectors of the same society, and a given society at different times. Primarily, however, the theory has been applied to American society. Here Merton emphasized a relative agreement throughout the system on a cultural goal of material success, but a very unequal distribution of means for achieving it, so that strain was chronically present in the lower classes. This purported to explain the higher crime rates in those classes.

Merton's criminals and deviants are, then, people seeking relief from strain resulting from socially structured problems of adjustment. Sutherland's criminals are not distinguished by the nature or intensity of their problems. They are simply people who have learned that criminal behavior is appropriate to certain situations, and they behave accordingly.

Subcultural theory

Delinquent subcultures: Cohen. Albert Cohen was a student of Merton and later of Sutherland. His *Delinquent Boys* reflects these contrasting traditions. He was persuaded by Sutherland that people become criminals, for the most part, by being exposed to and taking over the criminal subcultures in their environments. However, he asked a characteristically Mertonian structuralist question: Why are such subcultures there to be taken over? What is it about the society that accounts for the existence and distribution of its subcultures?

Cohen first sketched out his plan for a general theory of subcultures. Human behavior involves a constant process of problem-solving. To most of the problems of everyday life there are culturally patterned, socially approved, and reasonably satisfactory solutions. But problems arise for which there are no culturally patterned solutions, or for which there are no means at hand for making effective use of culturally approved solutions. One is then in the market, so to speak, for an alternative solution. Up to this point, Cohen walks in the footsteps of Merton, but now he raises a question that reflects the concerns of the Chicago school of American sociology, of which Sutherland was a representative: Since human beings are so dependent upon others for help, approval, acceptance, and standards of morality and truth, how is it possible for people to depart from the culturally established ways and to make use of solutions for which there is no precedent and support in the world around them? It is possible, said Cohen, when people with problems to which there are no culturally approved solutions do not stand alone, that is, when a number of actors in close communication with one another share the same problems. If they collectively and simultaneously adopt a novel solution, then no individual actor need stand alone. Each continues to enjoy the support of a group of people, although this group may be limited to those who share the problem. A deviant, perhaps a criminal, subculture has emerged.

Cohen explains the delinquent subculture as a special application of this general theory of subcultures. He assumes that the delinquent gang is primarily a male, lower-class phenomenon. The democratic ethos of American society, he says, holds that lower-class boys are entitled to, and indeed ought to aspire to, the same goals as middle-class boys. They are encouraged to achieve, and the rewards are supposed to be assigned on the basis of performance without regard to family background or other ascribed statuses. In fact, however, although the culture prescribes similar goals, the society does not provide everyone with the same means for achieving them. In short, lower-class boys are judged by the same standards as middle-class boys, but are denied the material and cultural resources necessary to compete effectively with them. When lower-class boys turn out to be failures in the society of young people, especially in the school, they draw together and elaborate alternative life-styles,

codes, and criteria for judging themselves and others—in short, a subculture—in which they can do well. They create a game, so to speak, in which they can be winners, and this game is the delinquent subculture.

Illegitimate opportunity: Cloward and Ohlin. The fusion of two traditions in Cohen's work was developed further by Richard Cloward and Lloyd Ohlin in *Delinquency and Opportunity*. Cloward was a student of Merton; Ohlin, a student of Sutherland. The book sought to explain why, as the authors claimed, there were three different delinquent subcultures, not just one. The importance of their work lies in the introduction of the notion of illegitimate opportunities. Cloward and Ohlin pointed out that just as institutionalized means, which may be read as legitimate opportunities, were not equally available throughout the system, neither were the means for pursuing goals illegitimately. The occurrence of deviant behavior and the form that it would take depend on the *illegitimate* opportunity structure: the opportunity to learn, to practice, and to perform deviant and criminal codes. The opportunity to learn comes from one's association with others who display and approve the illegitimate behavior. Thus, the relevant opportunity structure includes the way in which the organization of social life determines the distribution of differential association.

Cloward and Ohlin described three different delinquent subcultures that they called the criminal, the violent, and the retreatist subcultures. Each is the result of community characteristics that determine the illegitimate opportunity structure and, therefore, the form that delinquency will take. For example, in some neighborhoods there are many successful criminals who interact and communicate freely with young people. These criminal adults also have ties to local people and institutions and a stake in the tranquillity of their neighborhoods. Therefore they provide youth with opportunities to learn criminal attitudes and skills but block their opportunities to engage in violent gang activity. Under these conditions, said Cloward and Ohlin, one finds the delinquent subculture of the criminal type. It is contrasted with the conflict type, exemplified by fighting gangs, of youths with little access to professional criminals. It contrasts also with the retreatist type, exemplified by drug addict groups, who are thwarted in both criminal and conflict, as well as conventional, adaptations.

Although Cloward and Ohlin's object was to explain delinquent subcultures, the principal effect of their work was to establish the concept of the illegitimate opportunity structure as part of the basic vocabulary of criminology, with no necessary reference to its role in the theory of subcultures.

Lower-class culture: Miller. Walter Miller, an anthropologist, denied that delinquency was the product of a subculture created by some lower-class male youths as a way of coping with a special set of problems. In fact, there was no delinquent subculture. Delinquency was a product of lower-class culture, not of the subculture of a subpopulation within the lower class. Lower-class culture can, however, be described in terms of a distinctive set of "focal concerns," or preoccupations, such as "trouble," "smartness," "fate," "toughness," "excitement," and "autonomy." These focal concerns are not per se delinquent, but preoccupation with them may, under some circumstances, require or encourage delinquent conduct. For example, if his masculinity is derided, a lower-class boy may have to defend his claim to toughness by aggressive behavior that is illegal. This is a rather different view of the relationship between culture and delinquency from the views discussed thus far.

Subterranean values: Sykes and Matza. A still different view was presented by Gresham Sykes and David Matza. They too denied the existence of a delinquent subculture. Delinquency is made possible by certain features of the culture common to most Americans that Sykes and Matza called "subterranean values" because they are not acknowledged and do not enjoy much respectability or official status. They include the high valuation of such elements of a leisure-class life-style as extravagant spending and the pursuit of excitement. When lower-class youth pursue these values in the same spirit as upper-class adults do, the result is often delinquency. Because delinquent children are not indifferent to legality and morality, before they can perform delinquent acts they must find a way of neutralizing the prohibitions of the dominant culture. Here the dominant culture itself plays a role, for the justifications or techniques of neutralization that these children invoke, which make it possible for them to violate the law with a clear conscience, are similar to those that operate in courts of law and elsewhere in adult society to defend infractions of rules. In short, the subterranean values and the techniques of neutralizing the dominant culture play a part in Sykes and Matza's work very similar to that of the lower-class culture in Miller's work.

Subculture of violence: Wolfgang and Ferracuti. Marvin Wolfgang and Franco Ferracuti have advanced the hypothesis of the "subculture of violence," an idea more compatible with Sutherland's theory. The subculture of violence is a set of norms that condone or require recourse to violence when one's courage, manhood, or honor are challenged by insults, threats, or display of weapons. This subculture is found in many countries but is more heavily concentrated in certain parts of the population. In the United States, for example, it is most common in the South, among blacks, and among lower-class males. This is a kind of "pure" cultural transmission theory, for the origins of the subculture are left unexplained, structural pressures are ignored, and the culture's persistence from one generation to another is explained only by association and exposure of the culture bearers.

Labeling theory

Labeling and the definition of crime. All the theories considered thus far have two elements in common. First, they all define deviance as infraction—that is, the violation of rules. In the case of crime, it is the violation of the criminal law. Second, they tend, by and large, to treat as completely separate matters the causes of crime and the societal reaction to crime, that is, social control. The most conspicuous exception to this practice is the common notion that prisons, one of the instruments of social control, are schools for crime.

There is a set of views, lumped together under the heading "labeling theory" or, more modestly, the "labeling perspective," that breaks with one or both of these assumptions. The definitions of crime as infraction and of the criminal as lawbreaker are rejected in favor of the definition of the criminal as one who bears the label of "criminal" and is publicly identified as a criminal. It is then possible for persons who have violated no law to be criminals and for persons who have violated the law not to be criminals. The most influential statement of this view was made by Howard Becker in *Outsiders*. Becker's reasoning is that human action is determined not by the intrinsic properties of things but rather by the ways in which they are socially defined: what they are called and the connotations that their names evoke.

If, as labeling theory asserts, being labeled a criminal in a particular society makes one a criminal there, then explaining criminality is a matter of explaining how people acquire the label. By arresting, convicting, and incarcerating people, the criminal justice system certifies to their criminality and thereby literally produces criminals. Explaining criminality is, therefore, principally a matter of elucidating the ways in which the criminal justice system selectively ensnares people and, at each stage of processing, selectively lets some of them go and moves others along for further processing and labeling. Important variables affecting such production of criminals include the staffing (police, prosecutors, and judges) available to do the work necessary to transform citizens into criminals, the capacity of prisons and jails to house certified criminals, the popular demand for more-vigorous law enforcement and punishment, and the vulnerability—the weakness or strength—of the citizen versus the authority and power of the police and the courts. This approach has generated extensive research into determinants of the movement of the population into, through, and out of the criminal justice system.

Labeling as the cause of crime. The thesis of most labeling theorists is that the societal reaction to crime, of which labeling is the chief but not the only part, engenders processes that produce crime. The pioneer of labeling theory in this sense was Frank Tannenbaum, who in 1938 stated the position very forcefully in *Crime and the Community*. The societal reaction may produce crime in several ways. By assigning criminal identities to people and by treating them as such, it may eventually induce them to define themselves as criminal, to accept the identity and role of the criminal, and to behave in ways that are expressive of that role (Lemert). It may reduce their access to legitimate opportunity and encourage them to turn to illegitimate opportunities to achieve their goals. In addition, it may reduce their attractiveness to conventional persons as friends and associates; rejected by such persons, they may turn to delinquents or criminals for recognition and response, and through association with the latter may progress in a criminal direction. As this occurs, they become even further estranged from conventional persons; the cycle repeats itself, and with each repetition there is a corresponding "amplification of deviance" (Wilkins). The activities of society that are intended to *reduce* crime and delinquency have, ironically, the opposite effect. Even if the evidence does not support the conclusion that this is the typical outcome of official intervention, labeling theory has usefully sensitized criminology to the unintended effects of the criminal justice system upon criminal careers.

Labeling theory lends itself to certain ideological uses, since it strongly suggests that the criminal as a person is not very different from noncriminals before his encounters with the law. It evokes sympathy for the lawbreaker as an underdog and a victim—perhaps an object of oppression by the state through the massive, powerful, unfeeling apparatus of the criminal justice bureaucracy. Of course, these ideological implications should not affect one's judgment of the theory's validity, but they may explain why labeling theory surged into prominence during the 1960s,

when it appealed to the countercultural themes that government and indeed all forms of authority were instruments of oppression and enemies of freedom.

Labeling theory has also had a strong impact on criminal justice policy. It implies that to reduce crime the most useful policy for the criminal justice system is to do as little as possible. Especially for juveniles, ways of responding to lawbreaking other than through official intervention should be found. This might be achieved by closing down institutions and by diverting offenders away from the criminal justice system and into nongovernmental, noncoercive treatment contexts, usually within the community. There has been much movement in these directions, and labeling theory has contributed to it.

Control theory

Bonds to society: Hirschi. The theories surveyed above assume that there is no natural inclination to crime or delinquency: people are by nature more or less benign or, at least, neutral—clean slates on which culture and experience can write almost any script. Conformity does not have to be explained; it is crime that is puzzling. According to control theory, by contrast, people do not have to be schooled by their cultures or subcultures or otherwise induced to commit crimes. Crimes are often the quickest, the cheapest, and the easiest way to satisfaction—sometimes the only way. From this perspective, the task of crime causation theory is to explain why people do *not* commit crimes.

The most influential statement of control theory is found in Travis Hirschi's *Causes of Delinquency*. Hirschi follows in the footsteps of Durkheim, who argued in *Suicide* that control and discipline of one's desires and the subordination of inclinations to the expectations of others derive above all from integration into the group—that is, from the strength of one's bonds to the group and the intensity of one's involvement in its life. For Hirschi, "control theories assume that delinquent acts result when an individual's bond to society is weak or broken" (p. 16). The bonds are of four kinds: (1) *attachment* to others, such as parents, peers, or the school; (2) *commitment* to conventional lines of action, for example, the pursuit of and desire to achieve conventional goals, so that one has a stake in adhering to lines of action leading to those goals; (3) *involvement* in conventional activity, such as work, sports, recreation, hobbies, and school-related activities; and (4) *belief* in norms that forbid delinquent and criminal conduct. These bonds inhibit deviance because they represent things of value that might be lost or jeopardized by deviance, they reduce time and other resources that might be available for deviance, or they make people feel guilty when they misbehave.

Hirschi's focus is on the actor's motivation to conformity. A system-level theory in the spirit of Hirschi's work would deal with the ways in which the social organization produces the attachments, commitments, involvements, and beliefs of Hirschi's theory and their distribution within the system. Although the individual ideas that go to make up Hirschi's theory are not new, his statement is the most successful effort to bring together in a single compact and coherent system the many strands of one kind of control theory.

Disciplining others: Wilson. There is another kind of control theory whose primary focus is not, as in Hirschi's work, on the discipline the actor imposes on himself in order not to jeopardize the things he values, but on the incentive and capacity of people to exercise control over others. The political scientist James Wilson argues that neighborhoods with high crime rates are neighborhoods in which social control has broken down because those who live there lack either the incentive or the capacity to employ sanctions against other members of the community who depart from the community's standards of acceptable conduct. Population composition and other characteristics of the community and of the larger society affect this incentive and capacity and therefore the crime rate. The residents themselves vary in their vulnerability to other people's sanctions. Wilson would have provided a theory of the ecology of crime from another kind of control perspective if he had described, in a systematic way, how the structure of society determines the spatial distribution of (1) the incentive and capacity to exercise control over one's neighbors, and (2) vulnerability to other people's discipline.

Deterrence theory and economic theory. Two developments in criminology are closely related to control theory. Deterrence theory is a body of research and speculation on the deterrent effect of punishment on crime. It seeks knowledge about the effects on different types of crime of varying the kind, severity, celerity, and other characteristics of punishment, and also seeks to determine to what extent people refrain from crime because they fear punishment.

The economic theory of crime applies the concepts and theory of contemporary economics to the analysis of crime and punishment. It is concerned with choosing among lines of conduct, insofar as choosing consists of the rational allocation of scarce means to alternative ends. This implies weighing criminal options and then deciding among them on the basis of the costs and benefits to be expected from criminal, as opposed to noncriminal, lines of conduct. Both the deterrence and the economic theories of crime assume that for most people criminal conduct is often attractive and that people refrain mainly because of the possible costs. In this respect the theories are quite compatible with control theory of the Hirschi variety. A major difference, however, is that Hirschi is more sensitive to certain costs that are not easily quantifiable, that is, those that consist of damage to social relationships, jeopardy to conventional commitments, and the psychic costs of violating one's own moral beliefs. In Hirschi's scheme, the contributions to control of the penalties imposed by the criminal justice system—those emphasized by deterrence theory and economic theory—are of secondary importance.

Radical criminology: Marxism. Radical criminology views the state and law as instruments used by the wealthy and powerful to dominate and exploit the weak, and it views traditional criminological theory as an ally of the wealthy and powerful because it concentrates on the offenders and assumes that they, rather than the "system," are the problem (Taylor, Walton, and Young). There are many varieties of radical criminology; among them, the Marxist theories (Greenberg) are the most radical in the sense that they see crime as the inevitable product of a system which functions for the benefit of one class. Marxist criminology has experienced a great growth in both Europe and the United States since the late 1960s. Marxist theories see crime and law as expressions or effects of the economic mode of production and the conflict between social classes, with each class defined by its relationship to ownership and control of the means of production and distribution.

Marxist theories are preeminently social-system theories. Otherwise, however, they vary considerably. Some are essentially versions of labeling theory: the state and the criminal justice systems are simply instruments employed by the capitalist class to promote its own interests and to keep the working class under control by the threat of criminal labels. This kind of "instrumental" Marxism is not much interested in the causes of crime, since it views the criminal as the hapless victim of an oppressive system; by this theory the system, not the criminal, needs to be explained and transformed. Other Marxist theories are more complex and recognize the need to explain crime itself. Some of the themes to be found in the Marxist literature are the following.

First, capitalism produces crime because it fosters in people, especially in businessmen, a spirit of competitiveness, acquisitiveness, and egotism. The same preoccupation with taking care of oneself and indifference to others that make for business success in a capitalist world also make for criminality. Second, capitalism seeks to create and maintain a surplus army of labor—a reserve pool of unemployed or underemployed labor whose presence "in the wings" makes it possible to keep wages down and profits high. Third, the victims of capitalism turn to crime for a number of reasons, variously emphasized by different Marxist authors.

1. The poor, since they have no property, do not respect property as do the bourgeoisie. Lacking both economic and political power and enjoying none of the fruits of the system, they feel little compunction about violating its laws.
2. Degraded, thwarted, and humiliated by the system, the poor sometimes express their alienation and rage by attacking their oppressors. Such crimes may be thought of as political acts.
3. Treated like brutes and preoccupied with the struggle for existence, the poor become coarse, brutish, and violent and turn upon one another, so that they become their own chief victims.
4. Capitalism ensures that many hard-working parents will fail to realize their aspirations for themselves and their children, will become permanently or intermittently dependent, and will lose hope, pride, cohesion, and harmony. Such parents produce delinquent children.
5. Men need steady work to validate their manhood. Capitalism ensures that many of them will work only intermittently and at despised jobs. They will feel that they are failures as men and will seek other pursuits that are illegal or conduce to illegality but that carry the social meaning of masculinity, such as deeds of violence, daring, and defiance.
6. Some crime is simply an effort to meet one's basic needs or protect one's livelihood where legitimate means fail. The poor may steal because they refuse to starve. They may commit acts of violence against workers who accept employment during a strike because their own jobs, incomes, and unions are at stake. They may destroy labor-saving machinery in order to protect their jobs. These crimes are all part of the class struggle.

The Marxist theories incorporate many ideas about the proximate causes of crime from non-Marxist theories, for example, masculine protest, the importance of the family, and crime as the only available way to satisfy elementary needs. However, the Marxist theories see these motivations and other circumstances conducive to crime as the inevitable products of capitalism; they accuse non-Marxist theory of complicity with the status quo through avoiding inquiry into the role of capitalism and thereby protecting capitalism from criticism and change.

Role-self theory. What is variously called self theory, identity theory, and role-self theory interprets behavior as an effort to construct, test, validate, and express one's self (Wells). The self is the person as one would describe oneself to oneself—that is, what one believes oneself to be, or the self-image. Related to people's self-images are the aspirations and expectations they have of themselves (self-demands) and how they feel about themselves (self-judgment)—results of the congruence between the self-demands and the self-image. How people present themselves and how they appear to others are not identical with how they appear to themselves, but it is difficult to maintain a concept of the self that is at variance with how one is defined by others.

The self is largely constructed from role categories present in the cultural setting, such as (1) those identified with age, sex, occupational, and kinship designations; or (2) social types—persons who are labeled by a distinctive attribute, such as tough, honest, fearless, loyal, hip, cool, or generous. Together with these roles go culturally standardized meanings, that is, images and expectations. As individuals come to identify with these roles, they take over the cultural standards for judging adequacy in the roles and therefore the adequacy of their selves. Behavioral choices are always determined to an important degree by the anticipated consequences for the self. In fact, according to the symbolic interactionist tradition in sociology, one's humanity consists largely in one's ability to become an object to oneself, to respond to that object, and to find one's greatest satisfactions and disappointments in the qualities and performances of that object: the self one credits oneself with having.

Behavior is determined by the self principally in two ways. It may express some aspect of the self, in the sense that it directly embodies the images and expectations that go with the roles of which the self is constructed. The small boy with an image of himself as a tough cowboy does not cry. Behavior may also support the self, in the sense that it is instrumental to, or facilitates, conduct that is role-expressive. The small boy saves his money to buy a catcher's mitt. Walking around with the catcher's mitt is role-expressive; saving money to make this possible is role-supportive.

The choice of criminal or noncriminal behavior, like any other behavioral choice, depends on its consequences for the self. The self may include roles that are intrinsically deviant or criminal—that is, that require deviant or criminal behavior to validate and express them. Membership in a pickpocket mob or in an illegal political movement is an example. There are roles that may be alternatively expressed through criminal or noncriminal conduct, depending on circumstances. For example, to be tough or to be a "real man" will not necessarily call for illegal violence, but there may be situations in which one's claims can be expressed in no other way.

It is not only to others but to themselves as well that people make and defend claims about their selves. Sometimes people's criminal projects can go forward only after they have worked out some formula that seems to reconcile their criminal conduct—shoplifting, tax evasion, or embezzlement from employers—with their conventional role claims. Sykes and Matza's "techniques of neutralization" and what others have called rationalizations may be seen as ways of accomplishing this. They are rhetorical devices for altering the role-expressive meanings of illegal conduct.

Applications of role-self theory run through the sociological literature on crime. Some of them bear on the linkages between the constituents of the self and behavior, and some with the determinants of the choice of self. Containment theory, developed by Walter Reckless and others, emphasizes the part played by the self in insulating the actor from deviance and crime. One's identity may include a component: "I am the kind of person who does *not* do that sort of thing." The implications of role-self theory have not been elaborated on the larger-system, or macrosociological, level. One can easily imagine, however, a scheme, similar to Merton's anomie scheme, that calls for a mapping of the social distribution of aspirations for, and demands upon, the self; a corresponding mapping of the availability of legitimate and illegitimate opportunities for expressing and supporting the self; and propositions about the ways in which behavior depends on the relationship between the two mappings.

The integration of theories

Differential anticipation: Glaser. There is no sociological theory of crime that draws upon only one of the above themes. For example, the ideas of opportunity, the expression and validation of the self, and socially structured strain occur in many different theoretical systems. Several efforts at integration of a number of strands deserve particular attention. One is Daniel Glaser's theory of differential anticipation, developed in an attempt to account for success and failure upon release from prison. The theory states that, when choosing between criminal and noncriminal courses of action, people are constrained by the legitimate and nonlegitimate opportunities available to

them. From the available alternatives, they choose that from which they anticipate the most favorable concepts of themselves.

Whether people anticipate that they will feel better or worse about themselves in consequence of a given course of action will depend on the nature of their selves—the sort of persons they think they are and are trying to become—and on the perspectives from which they judge the adequacy of those selves. These in turn depend very much on people's histories of what appears to be differential association with criminal and noncriminal persons. The anticipated consequences depend also, however, on how rewarding or disappointing for the self these courses of action have turned out to be in comparable situations in the past—in other words, on people's reinforcement histories. Here there is an interweaving of opportunity structure, role-self, differential association, and social-learning theories. Glaser draws the inference for policy: "The correctional treatments of maximum reformative effect are those that enhance a prisoner's opportunities in legitimate economic pursuits and those that improve his conception of himself when he identifies with anti-criminal persons" (p. 29).

Routine activities: Cohen and Felson. The distinctive feature of the routine-activities approach is the idea that almost any of the routine activities of daily life, indeed any feature of the social system, however innocent its purpose or how remote it might seem from the world of crime, may be an embodiment or indicator of the variables that determine crime. For example, it is possible to approach any event or condition with the question, How does this enlarge or reduce illegitimate opportunities?

This perspective on opportunity and, indeed, on any other constituents of a theory of crime has been most systematically developed by Lawrence Cohen and Marcus Felson. Most criminal acts require the coming together in space and time of likely offenders (individuals who are motivated to commit crimes), suitable targets (things that are valuable, visible, accessible, and easily transported), and an absence of capable guardians. Much has been written on each of these under the headings of motivation, opportunity, and social control. The most original aspect of Cohen and Felson's work is not their recognition of the need for all three and for their convergence at the same time and place, but rather their demonstration that this convergence is produced by the patterning of routine activities and that crime rates change with shifts in routine activity patterns.

According to Cohen and Felson, "we would expect routine activities performed within or near the home and among family or other primary groups to entail lower risk of criminal victimization because they en- hance guardianship capabilities" (p. 594). Since World War II, however, the United States has experienced a major shift of routine activities away from the home and into jobs and other activities away from home. Between 1960 and 1970 there was a striking decline in the physical weight of such highly valued consumer goods as television sets and record players, resulting in an increase of suitable targets. Cohen and Felson find significant and sometimes impressive correlations between crime rates and a number of such indicators of routine features of everyday life. They suggest that the great increase in crime rates since World War II is not a result of a corresponding increase in human wickedness but of demographic and other changes reflected in changes in routine activities. They suggest also that in the future the routine-activities approach might be applied to the analysis of offenders and their inclinations as well.

The present state of theory

One could form the impression that the sociology of crime is an arena of numerous contending and mutually exclusive theories; that these theories come and go like fads and fashions; and that since truth is unitary and the theories are legion, they cannot all be right and most of them must be wrong. This, however, would not be a correct assessment.

Most of the theories discussed represent an attempt to enhance the explanatory value of a single idea. They often claim to be general, comprehensive, and sufficient theories, not even distinguishing between the different kinds of questions to which theory may be addressed. No theory, under fire, has been able successfully to defend such claims. Sutherland's theory addresses itself to the kinds of people who commit crimes; it does not deal with the properties of situations that engender crimes, and it has been attacked on the ground of being untestable because of the vagueness of its critical terms. Merton has been criticized by Cohen for neglecting the role of interaction in choosing an adaptation to socially structured strain. Cohen's theory of the delinquent subculture has been criticized on the ground that it too is untestable because opposite research outcomes can be interpreted as evidence for the theory. James Short and Fred Strodtbeck evaluated the theories of Cohen, Cloward and Ohlin, and Miller in the light of a massive research project on juvenile gangs in Chicago and found all of them wanting.

The evidence for a subculture of violence has alternatively been interpreted as evidence for the crimino- genic effects of poverty and its correlates, without benefit of subculture. Research on whether labeling and stigma produce crime seems to conclude, "Sometimes, maybe." Marxist theory, which has so many explanations of why capitalism produces crime, has few explanations of why socialist countries also produce crime. Yet the charge is seldom leveled against any one of these theories that there is nothing of value in it. Most of the criticism is to the effect that the theories try to explain too much and that the set of contained ideas is too weak to carry the burden of all the explaining.

Even the theories that stand up best do not seem to explain much of the variation in crime and delinquency. It is virtually certain that every theoretical idea discussed above has something to do with crime and should somehow be taken into account in a satisfactory theory—but a list of things that have something to do with crime is not a theory. A theory directs one to obtain certain information about a situation, a person, or a social system and provides one with a set of rules for putting this information together and coming up with a statement: "In the light of this information, this is what should be expected in the way of crime." There are no demonstrably powerful theories in this sense. Novel ideas of real importance will surely continue to crop up, but it may be that the chief task of theory now, and perhaps the one that requires the most powerful imagination, is to integrate several strands into a coherent, parsimonious, and testable system of theoretical propositions.

Theory and social control

A theory of crime causation implies that crime may be controlled by manipulating the conditions that, according to the theory, produce crime. Thus, cultural transmission theories suggest that we try to direct people's associations away from procriminal and toward anticriminal cultures, and to transform deviant into conforming cultures. Control theory suggests that we try to counterbalance the appeal of crime by strengthening attachments, commitments, and other bonds to conventional institutions. Economic theories suggest that we attempt to increase the costs of deviance and the rewards of conformity. Theories that emphasize opportunity suggest that we try to increase access to legitimate, and to reduce access to illegitimate, opportunity structures. Other theories suggest still other strategies of crime control. In every case, however, the question arises of whether society has the knowledge, the resources, and the authority to implement these strategies, and also the question of whether it is prepared to pay the costs that these strategies would entail. What we propose to do about crime will, therefore, depend on our theories about the causes of crime, but never on our theories alone.

ALBERT K. COHEN

See also CLASS AND CRIME; DELINQUENT AND CRIMINAL SUB-CULTURES; DEVELOPING COUNTRIES, CRIME IN; DEVIANCE; FAMILY RELATIONSHIPS AND CRIME; MASS MEDIA AND CRIME; RACE AND CRIME; RIOTS: BEHAVIORAL ASPECTS; UNEMPLOY-MENT AND CRIME; WHITE-COLLAR CRIME: HISTORY OF AN IDEA; YOUTH GANGS AND GROUPS.

BIBLIOGRAPHY

BECKER, HOWARD S. Outsiders: Studies in the Sociology of Deviance. Reprint. New York: Free Press, 1973.

BURGESS, ROBERT L., and AKERS, RONALD L. "A Differential Association-Reinforcement Theory of Criminal Behavior." Social Problems 14 (1966): 128–147.

CLOWARD, RICHARD A., and OHLIN, LLOYD E. Delinquency and Opportunity: A Theory of Delinquent Gangs. New York: Free Press, 1960.

COHEN, ALBERT K. Delinquent Boys: The Culture of the Gang. New York: Free Press, 1955.

———; LINDESMITH, ALFRED R.; and SCHUESSLER, KARL, eds. The Sutherland Papers. Bloomington: Indiana University Press, 1956.

COHEN, LAWRENCE E., and FELSON, MARCUS. "Social Change and Crime Rate Trends: A Routine Activity Approach." American Sociological Review 44 (1979): 588–608.

CRESSEY, DONALD R. "Crime." Contemporary Social Problems. 2d ed. Edited by Robert K. Merton and Robert Nisbet. New York: Harcourt, Brace & World, 1961, pp. 21–76.

DURKHEIM, EMILE. Suicide: A Study in Sociology (1899). Translated by John A. Spaulding and George Simpson. Edited with an introduction by George Simpson. New York: Free Press, 1951.

GLASER, DANIEL. The Effectiveness of a Prison and Parole System. Indianapolis: Bobbs-Merrill, 1964.

GREENBERG, DAVID F., ed. Crime and Capitalism: Readings in Marxist Criminology. Palo Alto, Calif.: Mayfield, 1981.

HIRSCHI, TRAVIS. Causes of Delinquency. Berkeley: University of California Press, 1969.

LEMERT, EDWIN. Social Pathology: A Systematic Approach to the Theory of Sociopathic Behavior. New York: McGraw-Hill, 1951.

MERTON, ROBERT K. "Social Structure and Anomie." American Sociological Review 3 (1938): 672–682.

MILLER, WALTER G. "Lower-class Culture as a Generating Milieu of Gang Delinquency." Journal of Social Issues 14, no. 3 (1958): 5–19.

RECKLESS, WALTER C.; DINITZ, SIMON; and MURRAY, ELLEN. "Self-concept as an Insulator against Delinquency." American Sociological Review 21 (1956): 744–746.

SHAW, CLIFFORD R., and MCKAY, HENRY D. Social Factors in Juvenile Delinquency: A Study of the Community, the Family, and the Gang in Relation to Delinquent Behavior. Report on the Causes of Crime, vol. 2. U.S. National Commission on Law Observance and Enforcement [Wickersham Commission]. Washington, D.C.: The Commission, 1931.

SHORT, JAMES F., and STRODTBECK, FRED L. Group Process and Gang Delinquency. University of Chicago Press, 1965.

SUTHERLAND, EDWIN H. White Collar Crime. New York: Dryden Press, 1949.

SYKES, GRESHAM M., and MATZA, DAVID. "Techniques of Neutralization: A Theory of Delinquency." American Sociological Review 22 (1957): 664–670.

TANNENBAUM, FRANK. Crime and the Community. Boston: Ginn, 1938.

TAYLOR, IAN; WALTON, PAUL; and YOUNG, JOCK. The New Criminology: For a Social Theory of Deviance. London: Routledge & Kegan Paul, 1973.

WELLS, L. EDWARD. "Theories of Deviance and the Self-concept." Social Psychology 41 (1978): 189–204.

WILKINS, LESLIE. Social Deviance: Social Policy, Action, and Research. Englewood Cliffs, N.J.: Prentice-Hall, 1965.

WILSON, JAMES Q. Thinking about Crime. New York: Basic Books, 1975.

WOLFGANG, MARVIN E., and FERRACUTI, FRANCO. The Subculture of Violence: Towards an Integrated Theory in Criminology. Translated from the Italian. London: Tavistock, 1967.

CRIME COMMISSIONS

The emergence of crime as a national issue in America dates back to the early 1920s. The Volstead Act, providing for federal enforcement of the Eighteenth Amendment (which prohibited the manufacture, sale, or transportation of intoxicating liquors), went into effect in January 1920. This was followed by the rapid growth of organized crime in the form of large-scale smuggling, manufacture, and sale of alcoholic beverages. The open and well-publicized violence and lawlessness involved inspired a widely held belief that the nation was undergoing a crime wave.

This led President Calvin Coolidge in November 1925 to appoint the first national crime commission to investigate what steps could be taken to reduce crime. Members of the executive committee of the commission included Franklin D. Roosevelt (former assistant secretary of the Navy), Charles Evans Hughes (former United States Supreme Court Justice and later the Court's Chief Justice), Richard Washburn Child (former ambassador to Italy), Hubert Hedley (chancellor of Washington University), and Hugh Frayne (representing the American Federation of Labor).

The establishment of the commission was criticized

on the grounds that its members lacked "expert knowledge" or "special experience" of the crime problem; that it had "no power"; and that consequently there was "little hope of any practical results from such a commission" (Wigmore, pp. 313–314). That prediction appears to have been fulfilled. The commission "met with little success and much opposition and jealousy from state counterparts" (Cronin, Cronin, and Milakovich, p. 28).

The commission did, however, make one significant discovery. As Roosevelt put it in 1929: "On the word of the National Crime Commission which has been studying the matter for three years . . . no one can today state with any authoritative statistics to back him, whether there is or is not a crime wave in the United States . . . as to whether or not there is a total increase in the number of crimes committed we have no knowledge whatever." No one could tell "even in the most inaccurate way" how many murders took place per year (p. 369).

The second national crime commission was also the product of presidential concern that a crime wave had swept the country. President Herbert Hoover, who had campaigned in part on a law-and-order platform, declared in his inaugural address on March 4, 1929, that "the most malign of all these dangers today is disregard and disobedience of law. Crime is increasing. Confidence in rigid and speedy justice is decreasing."

Hoover added that he would "appoint a national commission for a searching investigation of the whole structure of our Federal system of jurisprudence, to include the method of enforcement of the 18th amendment and the causes of abuse under it" (1974, pp. 2, 4). Accordingly, in May 1929 he established the United States National Commission on Law Observance and Enforcement, with former attorney general George W. Wickersham as chairman, and requested it to "investigate and recommend action upon the whole crime and prohibition question" (1951–1952, p. 277).

Within the next two years the commission, which included among its members Roscoe Pound of the Harvard University Law School and Ada Comstock, president of Radcliffe College, issued fourteen separate reports totaling almost three and a half million words. The reports were the product of an exhaustive investigation of all aspects of national law enforcement, and they made numerous recommendations for reform.

Unfortunately, what attracted most attention were the commission's contradictory and inconclusive findings in its *Report on the Enforcement of the Prohibition Laws of the United States.* By a large majority, the commission opposed the repeal of the Eighteenth Amendment, but at the same time it presented substantial evidence that effective enforcement was unattainable (U.S. National Commission on Law Observance and Enforcement, vol. 2).

As a result, the commission was attacked by both supporters and opponents of Prohibition. It was ridiculed by the press and even criticized by Hoover himself. In the national debate on Prohibition that culminated in the 1932 election, the commission's other recommendations were forgotten. Nevertheless, it is generally credited with exerting substantial influence in bringing Prohibition to an end.

Otherwise, the Wickersham Commission's reports and recommendations had little impact on the administration of criminal justice. But it was a first-rate effort that, for the first time in American history, attempted to present to a national audience a body of research into the problems of crime and its control. The reports have proved to be of enduring value to the community of criminal justice and criminological scholars.

Since 1920 there have been eight major national crime commissions under presidential authority or that of the attorney general. But the Wickersham Commission was the last national crime commission appointed until the mid-1960s. After a lapse of more than three decades, the next four commissions were created, between 1965 and 1971. These were the President's Commission on Law Enforcement and Administration of Justice (1965); the United States National Advisory Commission on Civil Disorders (the Kerner Commission) (1967); the United States National Commission on the Causes and Prevention of Violence (1969); and the Justice Department's National Advisory Commission on Criminal Justice Standards and Goals (1971). The most recent entries into this forest of blue-ribbon advice have been the Justice Department's National Advisory Committee for Juvenile Justice and Delinquency Prevention (1980) and the Attorney General's Task Force on Violent Crime (1981), arising out of a promise made during Ronald Reagan's presidential campaign.

The four national efforts that were reported between the mid-1960s and the early 1970s deserve briefer individual attention, at least in this context, because they overlap substantially in time and topic coverage. The first and most serious was a product of the 1964 presidential election, when Senator Barry Goldwater and the Republicans campaigned on a "law and order" "crime in the streets" platform. After his election victory, President Lyndon Johnson responded in 1965 to citizen concern about crime by creating the President's Commission on Law Enforcement and Administration of Justice, calling upon it to "give us the blueprints that we need . . . to banish crime" (Johnson, p. 983).

Although it cannot be said to have fulfilled that demand, the President's Commission, with Attorney General Nicholas Katzenbach as chairman and James Vorenberg of the Harvard University Law School as executive director, produced a report, *The Challenge of Crime in a Free Society*, which is perhaps the best official expression of modern America's crime dilemmas ever produced. That report, together with the nine task force volumes which supplement it, has been described as constituting "the most comprehensive description and analysis of the crime problem ever undertaken" (Caplan, pp. 596–597).

The next two "crime commissions" were responses to emergencies. The Kerner Commission reacted to the race riots of the mid-1960s with a highly ideological document that probably reflected the correct ultimate conclusion: the United States was unsuited for apartheid. Living as two societies (one black, one white) would be totally destructive of the American national mission. The National Commission on the Causes and Prevention of Violence appeared in June 1969, in the aftermath of the assassination of Robert Kennedy. This commission delegated to a body of scholars, task forces, and assistants the independent responsibility of producing volumes on the causes and prevention of violence in American life. The commission's report itself was not a tower of strength. The substantial body of scholarly knowledge in the task force reports was a tribute, as was the Wickersham Commission's report, to serious work and good intentions. The emphasis on task force efforts represented a deliberate departure from the procedure of the President's Commission on Law Enforcement and Administration of Justice, where the main report was the focus of the commission's senior staff effort.

The National Advisory Commission on Criminal Justice Standards and Goals issued its major report, *A National Strategy to Reduce Crime*, in 1973. It was a Nixon commission and a Nixon document. The commission's standards for immediate reform were too high. For example, most forms of predatory crime were to be cut in half by 1983 (p. 7). "Standards" and "goals" abounded in the report, the former including many platitudes and the latter awash in numerical fantasies.

By contrast, the last two federal commissions to report on crime have been low-budget affairs. The National Advisory Committee for Juvenile Justice and Delinquency Prevention reported in 1980. Its major contribution was a set of standards for the administration of juvenile justice. No scholarly tomes were at the foundation of this volume, and no great ambitions informed it. It was an intense and sincere effort, but as Oscar Wilde remarked about sincerity, a little of it "is a dangerous thing and a great deal of it is absolutely fatal."

Compared to the other commissions, Attorney General William French Smith's 1981 Task Force on Violent Crime was a more modest, "no-nonsense" undertaking. Its report stood in sharp contrast to the basic strategy of crime commissions since their inception: seek expert advice and report on basic knowledge. Wickersham and the 1960s national crime commissions had taken years and produced large volumes; Attorney General Smith's task force was given 120 days, and during this period the task force members interrupted their deliberations to travel to seven cities for public hearings. Nevertheless, the task force produced a volume of ninety-six pages, documenting sixty-four individual recommendations. Many of the sixty-four were off-the-shelf conservative bromides; others were hastily conceived in an atmosphere of high enthusiasm and substantial misinformation.

The political context of the crime commissions. Nationally chartered blue-ribbon commissions on the causes and prevention of crime have generated enough reports since 1925, and particularly since the mid-1960s, to empty major Canadian forests. The question is, Why? The answers are manifold.

The federal government is only a 10 percent partner with the states in direct crime control. When direct intervention is unavailable as a federal option, the appeal to national expertise and the capacity to recommend are immensely attractive. As a general matter, when the government does not know what to do, the tendency to turn to blue-ribbon commissions is irresistible.

Crime commissions and their causes cannot be understood without substantial awareness of the politics of crime control at the national level in the United States. In national politics, violent crime is a candidate's dream but an incumbent's nightmare. Running for office, the candidate confronts a national consensus against crime in the streets. Once he is President, the issue before him is no longer whether the American public would rather not be mugged, but what the federal government can do about street crime. The answer that has emerged over sixty years—encompassing both free-spending and frugal administrations—is that the federal government cannot do much.

Why is American national government a Prometheus Bound when it comes to the control of street crime? The central problems are two. The first, while important, is elementary. At any level of government there are limits to the capacity of Western democracies to control crime without sacrificing the freedom of the general citizenry. Combining urban interdependence with Western liberty is a risky task in Europe as well as in the United States.

The American federal government operates under a second handicap unknown to other nations. The division of power between different levels of government in the United States stacks the deck against direct federal initiatives to counter street crime. The limited criminal justice role of the American national government has few parallels in the developed world. Aside from drug trafficking and bank robbery, street crime in the United States is the province of local police, county courts, and state prison systems.

A few comparative statistics make the point. The United States has more than half a million accused or convicted criminals behind bars—but fewer than one in fifteen are in the federal system. Several states have larger prison systems than the federal government. Prisons, moreover, are only the beginning. Decisions to arrest, prosecute, and send to prison are even more decentralized than decisions about prison administration. Here, cities and counties make the decisions, while state governments pay the prison bills. In criminal law enforcement there is nothing new about what has been called the "New Federalism," but much that frustrates the electorate.

The essential frustration is that street crime is a national problem without a federal solution. Jammed between these elevator doors, the remarkable fact about national crime commissions is not that there have been so many but so few. These documents, relying on recommendation where no power exists, range from deplorable to extraordinarily good. Almost invariably, a national crime commission is a response to a specific problem, a high crime period, a change in presidential leadership, or all three. The timing of these documents, their contents, and their legacies vary widely. But serious study of the relationship between the federal government and crime cannot ignore the blue-ribbon commission as a device for coping with the national dimensions of what the public perceives as the crime problem.

Whatever fault may be found with the national crime commissions, they have not been niggardly in making recommendations. Most prodigal was the National Advisory Commission on Criminal Justice Standards and Goals, which contributed 494 recommendations to a grand total of more than 1,200 for all the commissions. The National Advisory Commission's summary report referred to "the sweeping range of its proposals." Yet many of those proposals (such as those to "establish mandatory retirement for all judges at age 65" or to "open church facilities for community programs") seem unlikely to contribute greatly to crime reduction (pp. 153–158, 164).

So great a profusion of proposals has a tendency to be counterproductive, weakening the impact that four or five targeted priorities might have. At the same time, proclaiming such unrealistic objectives as the reduction of robbery by "at least 50 percent" within ten years (U.S. Department of Justice, National Advisory Commission, p. 7) tends to undermine whatever credibility these documents might otherwise possess.

It is not at all clear to whom all the admonitions and injunctions in the various commission reports were addressed. Who, for example, was supposed to respond to the 1967 President's Commission's exhortations to "expand efforts to improve housing and recreation" or to "create new job opportunities" (pp. 293–294)? Sometimes unspecified "civic and business groups and all kinds of governmental agencies" are apostrophized (p. xi). Or, even less specifically, "all Americans" or "the citizens of this country" are called on to "work to bring about the necessary changes" (U.S. Department of Justice, National Advisory Commission, p. 4). Most often the recommendations seem, like Longfellow's arrow, to be shot into the air to fall to earth "I know not where."

How is it that intelligent and responsible people produce these grandiose manifestos? The trouble is that national commissions are invariably problem-specific. Yet the intractability of the American crime problem lies in its intimate connection with a multitude of other problems, such as race, poverty, unemployment, and drug abuse. It requires a leap of faith to believe that the criminal justice system can somehow surgically remove all the criminogenic elements from this complex of interrelated problems.

There is another aspect to the matter. Crime commissions are assigned to study a single problem in a world where problems are multiple. In the course of their studies they learn how serious *their* problem is, but they acquire little knowledge of the other ills that beset society. Thus the competition for scarce resources between national afflictions is almost invariably overlooked. This creates a disjunction between the blue-ribbon commission and the national political process, a process that must consider the multiplicity of problems in a multiproblem United States.

To summarize: some crime commissions take years to complete their work, others take months. Some issue huge numbers of volumes, and others produce slim reports. Their common problem is that the federal government can only serve as a limited partner in the administration of criminal justice. No matter how urgent a national issue mugging becomes, the federal response must be limited: when this is the case, it is time to call for the experts and hope they will help. Sometimes they have done so and sometimes they have not. It would be an occasion for amazement rather than surprise if the United States has seen its last national commission on crime and justice.

FRANKLIN E. ZIMRING
GORDON HAWKINS

See also CRIMINAL JUSTICE SYSTEM, *articles on* MEASUREMENT OF PERFORMANCE *and* PLANNING; CRIMINAL LAW REFORM, *articles on* CURRENT ISSUES IN THE UNITED STATES *and* HISTORICAL DEVELOPMENT IN THE UNITED STATES; POLITICAL PROCESS AND CRIME; PUBLIC OPINION AND CRIME.

BIBLIOGRAPHY

CAPLAN, GERALD. "Reflections on the Nationalization of Crime, 1964–1968." *Law and the Social Order* 3 (1973): 583–635.

CRONIN, THOMAS E.; CRONIN, TANIA; and MILAKOVICH, MICHAEL E. *U.S. v. Crime in the Streets.* Bloomington: Indiana University Press, 1981.

HOOVER, HERBERT C. *Memoirs.* 3 vols. New York: Macmillan, 1951–1952.

———. *Public Papers of the Presidents of the United States: Herbert Hoover, 1929.* Washington, D.C.: Office of the Federal Register, National Archives and Records Service, General Services Administration, 1974.

JOHNSON, LYNDON B. *Public Papers of the Presidents of the United States: Lyndon B. Johnson, 1965,* vol. 2. Washington, D.C.: Office of the Federal Register, National Archives and Records Service, General Services Administration, 1966.

MOWRY, GEORGE E. "Wickersham, George Woodward." *Dictionary of American Biography,* vol. 11, supp. 2. Edited by Robert Livingston Schuyler and Edward T. James. New York: Scribner, 1958, pp. 713–715.

President's Commission on Law Enforcement and Administration of Justice. *The Challenge of Crime in a Free Society.* Washington, D.C.: The Commission, 1967.

ROOSEVELT, FRANKLIN D. *The Public Papers and Addresses of Franklin D. Roosevelt* (1938), vol. 1. Special introduction and explanatory notes by President Roosevelt. Compiled by Samuel I. Rosenman. Reprint. New York: Russell & Russell, 1969.

U.S. Department of Justice, Attorney General's Task Force on Violent Crime. *Final Report.* Washington, D.C.: The Department, 1981.

U.S. Department of Justice, Law Enforcement Assistance Administration, National Advisory Commission on Criminal Justice Standards and Goals. *A National Strategy to Reduce Crime.* Washington, D.C.: The Commission, 1973.

U.S. Department of Justice, Office of Juvenile Justice and Delinquency Prevention, National Advisory Committee for Juvenile Justice and Delinquency Prevention. *Standards for the Administration of Juvenile Justice: Report.* Washington, D.C.: The Committee, 1980.

U.S. National Advisory Commission on Civil Disorders [Kerner Commission]. *Report.* Washington, D.C.: The Commission, 1968.

U.S. National Commission on Law Observance and Enforcement [Wickersham Commission]. *Reports* (1930–1931). 15 vols. Reprint. Montclair, N.J.: Patterson Smith, 1968.

U.S. National Commission on the Causes and Prevention of Violence. *To Establish Justice, To Insure Domestic Tranquility.* Washington, D.C.: The Commission, 1969.

WICKERSHAM, GEORGE W. "The Work of the National Crime Commission." *Report of the Forty-ninth Annual Meeting of the American Bar Association Held at Denver, Colorado, July 14–16, 1926.* Reports of the American Bar Association, vol. 51. Baltimore: Lord Baltimore Press, 1926, pp. 233–237.

WIGMORE, JOHN H. "The National Crime Commission: What Will It Achieve?" *Journal of the American Institute of Criminal Law and Criminology* 16 (1925): 312–315.

CRIME PREVENTION

The first article, COMMUNITY PROGRAMS, *describes efforts to apply knowledge from sociological study of the subcultural and social-group aspects of crime causation.* ENVIRONMENTAL AND TECHNOLOGICAL STRATEGIES *focuses on the distribution of lawbreaking in relation to its physical environment. Such strategies include planning the routes and schedules of offenders and law-abiding persons in order to keep them apart, and designing buildings and landscapes for defense against crime.* JUVENILES AS POTENTIAL OFFENDERS *analyzes recent and prospective efforts to prevent crime by early detection of delinquents, neighborhood programs for juveniles, deinstitutionalization of juvenile status offenders, diversion from police or courts, and juvenile gang interventions. The concluding article,* POLICE ROLE, *investigates collaboration with citizens' groups and private security systems, as well as the use of computers and other technology, for surveillance of citizens. The reader is warned, however, that such efforts at crime suppression may frequently oppress the general public, in addition to alleged offenders.*

1. COMMUNITY PROGRAMS   Anthony Sorrentino
2. ENVIRONMENTAL AND TECHNOLOGICAL STRATEGIES   C. R. Jeffery
3. JUVENILES AS POTENTIAL OFFENDERS   Malcolm W. Klein
4. POLICE ROLE   Thomas C. Gray

1.

COMMUNITY PROGRAMS

Despite the wide variety of methods that have been employed to prevent delinquency and crime, law-violating behavior has continued undiminished for many decades. Rates of arrests, court appearances, and commitments to correctional institutions continue to soar, not only in depressed inner-city areas but in suburban communities as well. Moreover, violent crime is more rampant than ever.

No one seems to offer adequate measures to ameliorate or eliminate these problems. Nor will they be eliminated by magic, simplistic solutions, or harsh punishment. Instead, new approaches and methods must be tried and tested empirically.

Correctional institutions have not been notably successful in rehabilitating offenders. Follow-up studies based on official records show that 60 percent to 80 percent of delinquents dealt with by institutions have continued in delinquency despite a wide variety of treatment methods. At the same time, the costs to the taxpayer have been astronomical. The annual per capita cost of treatment in a juvenile institution is estimated to range between $15,000 and $20,000, much more than the annual cost of education in the best private schools and universities.

An alternative to reliance on correctional institutions is experimentation with neighborhood programs of prevention and rehabilitation. Such community-based programs attract support today as never before.

Nature of the problem. In 1926, Clifford Shaw, Henry McKay, and their associates at the Institute for Juvenile Research in Chicago began studying both the ecological aspects of delinquency and the sociopsychological dynamics of individual and gang delinquents. Their studies of communities in Chicago and other cities revealed that for many decades certain areas had produced a disproportionate volume of delinquency. These "delinquency areas" were located around the central business district and adjacent to industrial areas.

During the early twentieth century these areas were occupied successively by various European immigrant groups who at the time were lowest in status—economically, socially, and politically. Neighborhood institutions, so important in the development of community morals and controls, were associated mainly with religious and mutual-aid groups and were only moderately successful in attracting the younger generation.

These areas were later occupied by new migrant groups, many of them from depressed areas of the United States and its territories. However, the original patterns of delinquency have remained basically the same, passed on from youth to youth and from gang to gang. The delinquent world provides sanctions, awards, and approvals for the delinquent, just as conventional society provides them for the nondelinquent.

Problems such as juvenile delinquency, street crime, and narcotic addiction have extended to many more urban neighborhoods than formerly. As waves of new migrants arrive, additional neighborhoods succumb. Many absentee property owners, seeing opportunities for increased profits, divide large apartments into smaller units and reduce maintenance. As a result the physical condition of rental properties deteriorates, causing further decay of the communities and general demoralization of the newcomers. Furthermore, many established institutions that formerly lent stability to these communities, such as churches and clubs, have become weak and inadequate in meeting the needs of the residents. Others have closed their doors and left. As a result, juveniles have no local haven or hangout where they can spend their spare time and energies pursuing legitimate activities with law-abiding adults. In turn, truancy and delinquency increase.

The youth in trouble is not necessarily antisocial, destructive, and cruel by nature, but he is a growing youngster with the same needs and aspirations that other youngsters have. Moreover, delinquent and criminal groups usually do not regard themselves as "problems" and hence do not seek treatment. Because the neighborhood—its residents and their expressed attitudes, behavior patterns, and cultural norms—molds the life of those who grow up there, the solution to juvenile delinquency and youth crime lies with the community's residents and institutions.

Community-based programs. Two diametrically opposed trends appear to prevail in the criminal justice field. The first is a continuation of the age-old "get tough with the criminals" approach. Recommendations are being made to give lawbreakers longer sentences and to transfer certain types of juvenile offenders from the jurisdiction of juvenile courts to that of criminal courts.

The second trend, more humane and optimistic, is represented by the proliferation of community-based programs for treating both juvenile and adult offenders. Since such measures have as their goal the reduction of recidivism, they can also be considered as secondary prevention. Many of these programs, launched in the early 1970s, ushered in what Harold

Finestone has called "the era of community corrections."

Community-based programs for prevention or correction are not panaceas, but they unquestionably do make intelligent use of available resources and are usually based on sound principles. They utilize small group homes and work-release programs, in addition to intervention strategies that provide special counseling, alternative schools, volunteers in juvenile courts, police diversion to social-service agencies, and other special services aimed especially at juveniles. Status offender programs handle juveniles charged with such offenses as truancy, running away, and minor acts of delinquency.

These new measures undertaken by juvenile courts and departments of corrections appear to be reducing commitments to juvenile correctional institutions. In Illinois, for example, the state training school for girls has been closed, and delinquent girls are now placed in private group homes or foster homes. The small number of serious offenders are placed in a state-operated facility. Similarly, Massachusetts in the early 1970s closed down its juvenile correctional institutions; offenders are now treated through a variety of group homes and community-based services. Vermont has followed the Massachusetts pattern completely, and other states have done so to a lesser extent.

The Chicago Area Project model. Since 1934 the Chicago Area Project has assisted local residents in initiating and developing their own community welfare enterprises, especially but not exclusively those concerned with preventing crime. This method is based on the belief that the most effective institutional form for dealing with many human problems is one that originates with neighborhood residents, derives its vitality from the intelligent use of their talents and leadership, and seeks to ensure the physical, social, and moral well-being of their own and their neighbors' children. The Area Project has sought especially to change the community situations that mold the values of children. It is the longest-running community-based program in the United States.

Many years' experience in many localities has demonstrated the validity and feasibility of carrying on welfare programs in local communities on this model. Where this program has long been in operation, experience has shown that responsible citizens' groups become vital instruments in meeting the needs of children, especially youths in difficulty. This method of cooperative self-help has mobilized the neighborhood for concerted and collective attacks on human problems. Citizens and local leaders know their community

intimately, have personal contacts and relationships with the social environment of the offenders, and can therefore make distinctive contributions toward the solution of local delinquency and crime problems.

The principles and the strategy of the area projects, established in 1934 by Clifford Shaw, may be summarized as follows: (1) the neighborhood is the unit of operation; (2) planning and management are in the hands of local residents; (3) local workers are on the staff; (4) community resources are more fully utilized and coordinated; and (5) credit is given to local residents. Clearly, these principles sharply contradict the current practices of most philanthropic and social work in this country, which is oriented toward perpetuating professional organizations and their leadership positions outside the neighborhoods they serve.

Forty separate community committees have developed in Chicago, and one hundred similar programs operate in downstate Illinois. They are independent, self-governing citizens' groups, functioning under their own local names and charters. The areas that they represent vary in size from approximately one-half a square mile to two-and-a-half square miles, with populations ranging from ten to twenty thousand. These citizens' committees, as well as the board of directors of the specific area project and the governmental agencies that furnish personnel, represent the enterprise generally referred to in northeastern Illinois as the Chicago Area Project. In downstate Illinois the Quincy Area Project also operates on this basis. Many municipalities, townships, and counties in other parts of the United States have organized similar youth and community programs that embody some of the features of the Chicago Area Project.

The resources usually needed to establish self-directed organizations of residents in specific urban neighborhoods are as follows: (1) trained personnel made available by a municipal, state, or other group-work or community development agency; (2) initial financial assistance by an outside government or foundation source, such as the Chicago Area Project, often offered on condition that matching amounts be raised by local community committees; and (3) assistance to local committees in their search for other sources of funds.

State personnel in Illinois, functioning as consultants and community workers, help the independent citizens' groups attain their objectives. As the committees approach the point of self-sufficiency, they are encouraged to dispense with the services of the state-employed personnel in favor of their own paid staff. When this is achieved, the state personnel are available only as consultants.

Each of the local community organizations identified with the Chicago Area Project is an autonomous unit chartered as a nonprofit corporation. Each has a headquarters and office, and some committees have developed subcenters or branches. Although programs and, to some degree, the organizational structure of specific groups may vary, each community committee conducts a wide range of programs. The committees have promoted recreation and sports programs involving thousands of children and young people and, in two instances, have purchased or built their own summer camps. They have secured space for their activities from churches and other local institutions and groups that is usually not available for neighborhood welfare programs. They have improved relationships between the schools and communities by helping to organize parent-teacher associations and adult education classes. They have also given leadership to campaigns for community improvement and, in several instances, have initiated the formation of housing boards.

Especially encouraging has been the treatment of delinquents and older offenders. In an effort to help as many delinquents as possible, the citizens' groups have established regular working arrangements with youth officers of local police departments, with probation officers of the juvenile and adult courts, and with parole systems. When preventive neighborhood measures have failed, local residents seek to maintain contact with the offender in court, in the institution if he is committed, and again in the community when he is released on parole. Work with young parolees has been one of the most promising aspects of this program. In four or five neighborhoods where intensive work has been carried on, local residents have had unusual success in procuring jobs and school entry for released offenders and in persuading them to join neighborhood groups. Thus, in many instances the parolees become members of the local community committees, eventually serve on the board of directors, and sometimes are elected as officers of the committee.

Work with individual delinquents has been supplemented by efforts to deal with gangs as a whole through the intermediary of local leaders. In fact, before a neighborhood program is launched, the local worker has often approached the area's gangs and street-corner groups. This has enabled the workers and the citizens' committees to obtain information necessary for the planning and development of the program. Young adult workers who symbolize values meaningful to the youngsters are in a strategic position to guide them into constructive activities.

Each year the local committees have raised money for neighborhood enterprises and spent these funds carefully and wisely with minimum overhead. The local residents and private groups involved in the program have almost matched the state's financial contribution. More important, perhaps, are the voluntary services of hundreds of persons, contributions in kind, and free access to facilities in churches, schools, and police stations.

Other models. Many programs have been influenced by the Chicago Area Project. Its philosophy of self-help and its utilization of local leadership and indigenous institutions are employed by many agencies, notably the community organization projects sponsored by the Industrial Areas Foundation under the leadership of Saul Alinsky.

Another type of program, which developed in New York and other cities after World War II, identified corner groups and gangs and worked with them outside the traditional institutional framework. Adopting the slogan "reaching the unreached," "detached workers" who represented conventional values interacted with the corner groups and tried to redirect them to legitimate activities.

Community councils have been organized in many cities since the early 1930s. Composed largely of social workers and other professionals, such organizations attempt to coordinate their efforts in order to avoid duplicating services. They aim at improving existing programs and at developing new resources to aid youth in trouble and bring about community improvement.

Local residents in many communities began banding together in the 1970s, organizing block clubs and citizens' patrols to help in guarding against crime and reporting offenses to the police. In suburban communities, where delinquency and crime have increased, new private agencies and local governmental units have organized a variety of programs to cope with these problems. These have included youth service bureaus and municipal or township commissions on youth. The agencies accept referrals from the police and plan and conduct a variety of programs to prevent crimes.

Problems in evaluation. The effectiveness of programs such as those developed by the Chicago Area Project should, of course, be appraised. However, relatively reliable data are difficult to secure, and it is virtually impossible to ascertain the relationship between crime rate trends and specific prevention programs.

Students of community organization raise searching questions about the Shaw-McKay, or Area Project, model of crime prevention. They have pointed out, for example, that the target of such a neighborhood organization—a high-crime, impoverished urban area—is often powerless to deal with the root causes of its crime and delinquency, for it cannot exert any significant impact on underlying social, economic, and political conditions, which usually transcend the neighborhood itself. It has been proposed instead that large-scale community organizations encompassing a more extensive geographic area are needed to deal with the larger factors that create crime-prone neighborhoods. In some cases, community organizers have forged coalitions of special-interest groups on a citywide basis to cope collectively with problems, such as youth unemployment, that foster delinquency and youth crime in all neighborhoods.

Perhaps the best example of such a citywide model of community organization is Saul Alinsky's Industrial Areas Foundation. Alinsky utilized some of Shaw's basic ideas, especially the concept of the "indigenous worker"—a resident of the area who may not be professionally trained but who has rapport with the people there. However, Shaw believed essentially in working "within the system," although he urged that community committees confront the power structure of the city when necessary. On the other hand, Alinsky organized people so that they might influence governmental and other institutions within and outside the community. Both agreed that residents of delinquency areas needed to win power, but their strategies were quite different. To Shaw, power was to be used to remedy community problems by attracting resources or concessions from influential persons or agencies outside the high-crime area. Alinsky, militant and radical in his approach, used the power of people who represented churches, labor unions, and other community institutions to fight basic injustices by attacking the dominant politicians and economic interests.

A recent Chicago Area Project self-study, conducted with the aid of outside consultants, concluded that the two theories of community organizing should no longer be regarded as conflicting. Rather, they are complementary, and the key to understanding them lies in recognizing the appropriate sphere for each. In Chicago, for example, both types of community organization coexist, with interesting variations in program content. The Alinsky model tends to focus on the social, economic, and political problems of community areas with populations of more than 100,000, which it represents in dealing with metropolitan, state, and federal agencies. The Area Project model utilizes the neighborhood, usually covering an urban area comprised of approximately 10,000 to 20,000 residents within a large city, as the unit of operation. A strategy of conflict characterizes the Alinsky approach, whereas the Shaw-McKay methods respect area residents' capacity for compromise and growth, and seek cooperation with outside sources of aid. In a rapidly changing society, with its multitude of social ills, both approaches have a useful place.

In several communities where area projects have been in operation for a number of years, the incidence of crime and delinquency has decreased. The difficulty is in deciding whether the program causes this trend, since data fluctuate widely in small areas and since the decrease may be explained by other influences in the community or by changes in administrative procedure.

There are other ways, however, of appraising local neighborhood programs. When the people of a neighborhood band together and work collectively in a community welfare program, new and basic resources are brought to bear on local problems. As residents work on behalf of their children and community, positive attitudes are reinforced. The children begin to live in a better milieu and respond to constructive social influences. It seems reasonable to assume that these influences, as well as the improvements in general living conditions that the residents are able to effect, advance both the prevention of delinquency and the treatment of delinquents. Of course, all prevention programs should be more rigorously reexamined and critically evaluated. Without continuing experimentation and testing, new methods of community prevention are not likely to be developed.

ANTHONY SORRENTINO

See also CRIME CAUSATION: SOCIOLOGICAL THEORIES; DISPUTE RESOLUTION PROGRAMS; ECOLOGY OF CRIME; FEAR OF CRIME.

BIBLIOGRAPHY

ALINSKY, SAUL. *Reveille for Radicals.* New York: Random House, Vintage Books, 1969.
CARNEY, FRANK J.; MATTICK, HANS W.; and CALLAWAY, JOHN D. *Action on the Streets: A Handbook for Inner City Youth Work.* New York: Association Press, 1969.
FINESTONE, HAROLD. *Victims of Change: Juvenile Delinquents in American Society.* Westport, Conn.: Greenwood Press, 1976.
FISH, JOHN HALL. *Black Power/White Control.* Princeton, N.J.: Princeton University Press, 1973.
KNAPP, DANIEL, and POLK, KENNETH. *Scouting the War on Poverty.* Lexington, Mass.: Heath, Lexington Books, 1975.
KOBRIN, SOLOMON. "The Chicago Area Project: A Twenty-five-year Assessment." *Annals of the American Academy of Political and Social Science* 322 (1959): 19–29.
MCKAY, HENRY D. "Report on the Criminal Careers of Male

Delinquents in Chicago." *Task Force Report: Juvenile Delinquency and Youth Crime.* President's Commission on Law Enforcement and Administration of Justice, Task Force on Juvenile Delinquency and Youth Crime. Washington, D.C.: The Commission, 1967, pp. 107–114.

——. *Subsequent Arrests, Convictions, and Commitments among Former Juvenile Delinquents.* Washington, D.C.: President's Commission on Law Enforcement and Administration of Justice, 1967.

President's Commission on Law Enforcement and Administration of Justice. *The Challenge of Crime in a Free Society.* Washington, D.C.: The Commission, 1967.

SHAW, CLIFFORD R., and McKAY, HENRY D. *Juvenile Delinquency and Urban Areas.* Rev. ed. University of Chicago Press, 1969.

SHORT, JAMES F., ed. *Delinquency, Crime, and Society.* University of Chicago Press, 1976.

SORRENTINO, ANTHONY. *How to Organize the Neighborhood for Delinquency Prevention.* New York: Human Sciences Press, 1979.

——. *Organizing against Crime: Redeveloping the Neighborhood.* New York: Human Sciences Press, 1977.

SPERGEL, IRVING A., ed. *Community Organization: Studies in Constraint.* Beverly Hills, Calif.: Sage, 1972.

WITMER, HELEN L., and TUFTS, EDITH. *The Effectiveness of Delinquency Prevention Programs.* Children's Bureau Publication No. 350. Washington, D.C.: U.S. Department of Health, Education, and Welfare, 1956.

2.
ENVIRONMENTAL AND TECHNOLOGICAL STRATEGIES

Criminology and crime prevention. Although two of the pioneers of criminology, Cesare Beccaria (1738–1794) and Enrico Ferri (1856–1929), made prevention a key concept in crime control, the hitherto dominant classical and positivist schools of criminology have tended to stress punishment and the study of the individual offender as a psychological or sociological type. Since the 1970s a new approach has arisen that advocates crime prevention through environmental design (Jeffery, 1977). Its proponents have linked prevention to the physical environment, maintaining that the crime patterns encountered in the United States could be explained in terms of such ecological issues as population growth, industrialization, and technological change. They have asserted that crime prevention differs from either punishing or treating the offender in that it takes place before the crime, involves direct control over criminal behavior, and demands consideration of the physical environments within which crime occurs.

Ecological criminology. The prevention of crime through analysis and control of the physical environment is an extension of ecology, which examines the relationship of man to his environment, making use of concepts of population, organization, physical environment, and technology (Duncan and Schnore). Ecological criminology is the theoretical base for crime prevention through environmental design.

The basic proposition of ecology holds that different physical environments support different species possessing different adaptive techniques, including different behavioral systems. To survive, the organism must adapt to its environment. Crime is a behavioral response to a given environmental situation, and the key concept in ecological criminology is that crime is spatially distributed, that is, crime is more prevalent in some environments than in others. In fact, some areas are almost crime-free, whereas others are highly crime-prone. Seventy-five percent of certain crimes take place in 25 percent or less of the environments (Jeffery, 1977). This observation forces the behavioral scientist to ask why some environments are relatively crime-free and others are not. Knowing that yellow fever occurs near the swamps that are breeding grounds for mosquitoes and hence sources of disease, we can drain the swamps and stop swatting flies. Similarly, knowing that crimes are prevalent in certain environments, we can ask how such environments may be redesigned so as to prevent crime.

Criminology was originally an ecological science, as exemplified in the work of Adolphe Quételet (1796–1874) and André Guerry (1802–1866). This ecological approach was revived during the 1920s by sociologists at the University of Chicago, headed by Robert Park and including Ernest Burgess, Clifford Shaw, and Henry McKay (Voss and Peterson). However, whereas Park used biological concepts to analyze social systems, his students and most other American sociologists generally followed the lead of Emile Durkheim (1858–1917) in rejecting biology and psychology in the analysis of human ecology (Baldwin and Bottoms). In criminology, the shift from bioecology to social ecology occurred with the publication of work by Shaw and McKay that analyzed delinquency rates in terms of social variables rather than of the physical environment. Shaw and McKay interpreted delinquency as a product of cultural conflict, norms, and values, and the cultural transmission of social values (Baldwin and Bottoms; Morris). Their findings were incorporated into criminological thought by Edwin Sutherland's theory of differential association, which held that criminal behavior was a product of the differential learning of criminal—as opposed to noncriminal—attitudes and values. The resulting eco-logical approach, known as social-area analysis, focused on the social character of the offender rather than on the physical environment in which crime is committed.

Since the mid-1950s, however, social-area analysis has been challenged by a group of British ecologists, notably Terence Morris, John Baldwin, and A. E. Bottoms. Morris concluded from Shaw's data that crimes are committed where the opportunity is most favorable, not because of the attitudes of others in the community. The new emphasis on environment shifts the focus of research to the place where crimes occur and away from the place where offenders reside, and it reexamines the problem of analyzing individual events in terms of group, or statistical, data. The location or setting that is important to the occurrence or nonoccurrence of a crime is missing when one looks at data on a national, regional, state, or city level. Such data provide little information as to why specific crimes occur where they do. What is needed is an analysis of crime at the block or building level. It has been shown that an analysis of burglary or murder at the block level is quite different from an analysis of the same crimes at a state or regional level (Brantingham, Dyerson, and Brantingham).

The reemergence of the physical environment. From about 1930 to 1970, the theories of traditional criminology seemed to imply that nonphysical individuals were operating in nonphysical environments. The effect of the physical environment—streets, parks, buildings, terminals, and highways—on crime rates was ignored. However, in the 1970s a concern for the physical environment reappeared in behavioral science literature.

In psychology a new field called ecological, or environmental, psychology emerged (Stokols) to study the effect on behavior of the physical environment or of such specific locales as airports, prisons, and universities. At the same time, environmental sociology was developing, stressing both the physical and the social environment. As early as 1959, Otis Duncan and Leo Schnore (p. 134) had written that "one searches the literature in vain for more than superficial reference to the brute fact that men live in a physical environment and that they employ a material technology in adapting to it." Environmental sociology, under the leadership of William Catton and Riley Dunlap, has challenged the Durkheimians and the symbolic interactionists, who reject both the physical organism and the physical environment. "Within mainstream sociology the environment is used to refer to social and cultural influences on the entity being examined

. . . . Environment seldom denotes the physical properties of the settings in which individuals participate, or the characteristics of the biophysical region" (p. 22).

The physical environment affects human behavior, and hence criminal behavior, at several different levels. In genetics, the genotype interacts with the physical environment to produce the phenotype, or organism. The ability of the individual organism to function depends on this interaction of genetics and environment because the size and complexity of the brain depend upon it. A "starved brain," one deprived of nutrients, proteins, and sensory stimulation, will be smaller and less complex than the brain of an individual reared in an enriched environment. Historically, crime and poverty have been linked in criminology; it is possible that one of the linking variables is the lack of protein in the diets of those reared in poverty. Hypoglycemia, brain and hormonal defects, and learning disabilities are also related to environmental as well as genetic conditions. Consequently, basic crime prevention should include ensuring a proper diet for children, providing proper neurological examinations, limiting the intake of refined sugar, and environmentally controlling genetic defects. It may be that population growth, food supply, and other basic ecological relationships are the most critical aspects of crime rates and thus of future crime control.

Moreover, the physical environment is closely linked to human behavior, including criminal behavior, as a setting within which behavior takes place. Behavior is a response to an internal or external environmental setting, which in modern psychology is often referred to as the stimulus aspect of behavior.

The physical environment and crime. The study of environmental criminology has been an interdisciplinary effort uniting criminologists (Jeffery), architects (Newman), geographers (Georges-Abeyie and Harries), and urban planners and lawyers (Brantingham and Brantingham). From this interdisciplinary research, which is still in its childhood, we can conclude that crime patterns are aspects of evolving ecological conditions, which in turn reflect changing population distributions, rural-urban developments, industrialization, and technological advances.

The work of the architect Oscar Newman set the tone for much crime prevention thought during the 1970s. From a study of public housing in New York City and elsewhere, Newman concluded that crime rates vary according to territoriality, surveillance, image, and environment. *Territoriality* is the sense of possessiveness for land and the tendency to defend one's territory against invaders, a behavioral trait found by ethologists among many birds, fishes, and mammals. *Surveillance* means the ease with which human activities can be observed around the buildings or streets where crimes are likely to occur. *Image* refers to the stigma or reputation of a housing project or building, since crimes are more likely to occur in projects with an unfavorable image. *Environment* constitutes the environs—the streets, parks, and adjacent buildings—that make a zone safe or unsafe. By the term *defensible space*, Newman meant an area where the residents exhibited a high feeling of territoriality, where surveillance and image were good, and where the surrounding environment was safe and protective of the residents.

According to the defensible-space theory, crime could be reduced by enhancing territoriality and improving surveillance, image, and environment. This would involve creating clear demarcations of public and private space through the use of shrubbery, sidewalks, signs, lawns, and the like, increasing surveillance opportunities through lighting and the removal of hidden pathways, and improving the image and environment within which public-housing projects are located.

Evaluations of defensible-space concepts have for the most part concluded that they are not successful in deterring crime (Mayhew). The criticisms of Newman's work include British findings that surveillance and the size of buildings are not as pertinent to crime rates as defensible-space theory assumes. Social and ownership variables (for example, private versus public housing) are more relevant than territoriality and surveillance. Newman's later work on crime prevention has shifted from physical design to the social character of the housing project, centering on such factors as the size of the family and the number of families on welfare. This raises the question of whether Newman is an architectural or a social-environment determinist. Pat Mayhew has concluded that social and physical variables interact in the development of a crime prevention model. The defensible-space theory ignores the behavioral aspects of environmental design—that is, those aspects of genetics, brain functioning, and learning theory which are basic to what in environmental psychology are called the cognitive processes that individuals use to adapt to physical environments. In the architectural view of behavior, the organism is somehow lost or left out.

Patricia Brantingham and Paul Brantingham have analyzed crime rates in terms of the occupational and economic specialization of urban areas (Georges-Abeyie and Harries). Most crimes against the person, such as murders and assaults, are committed under conditions of poverty and urban slum life. Burglary

and larceny tend to take place in cities specializing in finance, insurance, real estate, and government, where the targets are concentrated and the opportunities for such crimes exist. There is a different crime pattern in such insurance and financial centers as Hartford or Jacksonville than in a government center such as Washington, D.C. or the manufacturing cities of Gary and Detroit. Entertainment centers, such as Miami and Las Vegas, have high rates for the crimes of murder, assault, rape, robbery, and burglary, because they attract high numbers of potential victims. Robbery and auto theft are relative to the density of target distribution, and such university cities as Tallahassee, Boulder, and Gainesville have a high incidence of rape resulting from the concentration of females in the area. Convenience stores, liquor stores, gas stations, and student housing are high-crime areas as well (Jeffery).

Crime rates have also been analyzed in terms of the interaction of criminals with the work, residential, and entertainment areas of a city. Human activity pathways from residence to work, entertainment, and shopping areas are the corridors along which criminal activity takes place (Brantingham and Brantingham).

The pathways ("trips") that criminals follow from their residences to crime sites have been studied extensively in several cities (Jeffery, 1977; Georges-Abeyie and Harries). Personal crimes, such as rape and murder, are perpetrated near the residence of the criminal, whereas property offenses involve longer trips of one or two miles. One can anticipate that as urban sprawl continues and as freeways link more distant parts of a city, as in Los Angeles, criminal trips will increase in length.

Environmental analysis has been particularly fruitful in studying the high crime rates characteristic of Sunbelt cities. Such rapidly growing cities as Atlanta, Jacksonville, Miami, Tampa, Houston, Dallas, Tucson, Phoenix, Los Angeles, and San Diego display the ecological patterns of urbanization, migration, and population density. The mobility made possible by the automobile and the airplane, and the crime targets created by these new technologies, share a major responsibility for the crime pattern prevailing in the Sunbelt.

Environmental and technological strategies for crime prevention. From the above discussion it may be concluded that crime prevention has been ignored in favor of criminal justice and crime control; the few preventive efforts have been sporadic, untested, and largely unproductive. In an attempt to remove the environmental opportunities for crimes, however, architectural principles for crime prevention have been applied to the design of buildings, streets, parks, terminals, subways, and malls. Lighting has been used to increase surveillance. Shrubbery, trees, and fences have been placed so as to minimize hazards, to maximize the sense of territoriality, and to smooth the transition from public to private space. Lobbies, elevators, and stairwells have been relocated or guarded with alarm systems, television cameras, and police patrols.

Other preventive measures have entailed redesigning the structure of parking meters or coin boxes in telephone booths or on buses and taxis. Vandalism of streetlights or school buildings has been reduced by using construction materials that are difficult to break or deface. Many bus drivers now do not give change, and the customer must deposit the exact amount of the fare.

The police are the most active criminal justice agency engaged in crime prevention. Law enforcement efforts have focused on crime prevention lectures to high school students and community action groups, the distribution of crime prevention pamphlets, crime surveys, property identification, and the creation of citizen groups for block patrols and other crime prevention efforts. Yet, most police officers still regard their real work as responding with "guns, red lights, and patrol cars" to a crime that has already taken place.

Much of the crime prevention effort has been at the level of "target hardening"—providing alarms, streetlights, watchdogs, more-secure doors and windows, and the like. This effort is to be commended and encouraged, since many crimes are committed in places where even minimal security precautions have not been taken, but it is not the most important part of crime prevention. Advocates of environmental approaches to crime control maintain that a more imaginative and research-oriented effort is needed if prevention is to alleviate the crime problem. They argue that crime prevention must be interdisciplinary and behavioralist in orientation, emphasizing research *before* application, and enlisting behavioral genetics, the neural sciences, psychobiology, biological psychiatry, criminology, sociology, systems analysis, urban planning, and bioecology. They deplore the political sentiment in favor of more police, prisons, and executions that emerged in the United States in the early 1980s. They are convinced that prisons are not the solution to the problem—that, indeed, they *are* the problem, creating dangerous criminals and later releasing them into society. Instead of merely replacing locks on windows and doors, advocates of environmental control call for preventing crime through the redesign of cities, highways, recreational facilities, and industrial systems.

C. R. JEFFERY

See also CRIME CAUSATION: SOCIOLOGICAL THEORIES; ECOLOGY OF CRIME; GUNS, REGULATION OF; SECURITY, INDUSTRIAL.

BIBLIOGRAPHY

BALDWIN, JOHN, and BOTTOMS, ANTHONY E., in collaboration with WALKER, MONICA A. *The Urban Criminal.* London: Tavistock, 1976.

BRANTINGHAM, PATRICIA L., and BRANTINGHAM, PAUL J. "Notes on the Geometry of Crime." *Environmental Criminology.* Edited by Paul J. Brantingham and Patricia L. Brantingham. Beverly Hills, Calif.: Sage, 1981, pp. 27–54.

BRANTINGHAM, PAUL J.; DYERSON, DELMAR A.; and BRANTINGHAM, PATRICIA L. "Crime Seen through a Cone of Resolution." *American Behavioral Scientist* 20 (1976): 261–273.

CATTON, WILLIAM R., JR., and DUNLAP, RILEY E. "A New Ecological Paradigm for Post-exuberant Sociology." *American Behavioral Scientist* 24 (1980): 15–47.

DUNCAN, OTIS DUDLEY, and SCHNORE, LEO F. "Cultural, Behavioral, and Ecological Perspectives in the Study of Social Organization." *American Journal of Sociology* 65 (1959): 132–153.

GEORGES-ABEYIE, DANIEL E., and HARRIES, KEITH D. *Crime: A Spatial Perspective.* New York: Columbia University Press, 1980.

HARRIES, KEITH D. *Crime and the Environment.* Springfield, Ill.: Thomas, 1980.

HIRSCHI, TRAVIS, and GOTTFREDSON, MICHAEL, eds. *Understanding Crime: Current Theory and Research.* Beverly Hills, Calif.: Sage, 1980.

JEFFERY, C. R. *Crime Prevention through Environmental Design.* Rev. ed. Beverly Hills, Calif.: Sage, 1977.

————. "Criminal Behavior and the Physical Environment: A Perspective." *American Behavioral Scientist* 20, no. 2 (1976): 149–174.

MANNHEIM, HERMAN, ed. *Pioneers in Criminology.* Montclair, N.J.: Patterson Smith, 1972.

MAYHEW, PAT. "Defensible Space: The Current Status of a Crime Prevention Theory." *Howard Journal of Penology and Crime Prevention* 18 (1979): 150–159.

MICHELSON, WILLIAM M. *Man and His Urban Environment: A Sociological Approach.* Reading, Mass.: Addison-Wesley, 1976.

MORRIS, TERENCE. *The Criminal Area: A Study in Social Ecology.* London: Routledge & Kegan Paul; New York: Humanities Press, 1958.

NEWMAN, OSCAR. *Defensible Space: Crime Prevention through Urban Design.* New York: Macmillan, 1972.

STOKOLS, DAVID. "Environmental Psychology." *Annual Review of Psychology.* Edited by Mark R. Rosenzweig and Lyman W. Porter. Palo Alto, Calif.: Annual Reviews, 1978, pp. 253–295.

Voss, Harwin L., and Peterson, David M. *Ecology, Crime, and Delinquency.* New York: Appleton-Century-Crofts, 1971.

3.
JUVENILES AS POTENTIAL OFFENDERS

Most people during their juvenile years break laws for which they could be arrested—for example, by shoplifting or by habitual truancy from school. Therefore, the issue of the potential offender is one of predicting which juveniles will become serious, chronic, or adult lawbreakers. The critical questions become these: (1) How accurately can such predictions be made? (2) Can this identification of potential offenders be translated into prevention activities? (3) Can such prevention activities succeed?

The early-identification paradox

Most of the attempts to identify future delinquents have failed. This is because a predictive accuracy of over 90 percent is required to predict the 10 percent who will be the most serious offenders and yet correctly separate future delinquents from nondelinquents with fewer errors than would result from predicting nondelinquency for all cases. The most serious or chronic 10 percent are in the minority as well as hard to identify beforehand. Thus, much intervention effort will perforce be expended on incorrectly labeled cases (commonly called "false positives").

But the difficulties of early identification and prediction, accompanied by the logical consequence of inefficient or ineffective interventions, do not constitute the whole problem, for they involve only the false positives. Equally problematic is the effect of early identification on those who might be accurately identified as potential offenders.

Paradoxically, the process of early identification and subsequent treatment may be perceived by the juvenile as a negative process: it may create a public stigma as well as a concept of oneself as "sick" or "bad." Thus, balanced against the presumed advantages of early identification—the opportunities to treat and deter—are the risks of "fixing" a juvenile in a deviancy; predictions of delinquency may thus be self-fulfilling prophecies.

Standard prevention

Despite the difficulties of accurate prediction and its possibly negative consequences, treating potential offenders individually is the standard method of trying to prevent delinquency. However, every major review of such programs has found them designed with limited conceptual clarity and ineffective in reducing offenses (Wright and Dixon; Walker, Cardarelli, and Billingsley).

Additional problems of standard prevention programs have included the following:

1. Inconsistent diagnosis and treatment
2. Failure to base intervention strategies and outcome expectations on theories of delinquency causation or control appropriate to the clients selected
3. Reliance principally on counseling therapies and recreational activities, despite evidence that there are many causes of delinquency quite independent of individual or interpersonal pathology
4. Absence of a policy guided explicitly by data on program effectiveness
5. "Skimming" or "creaming"—that is, selecting as program clients those youngsters least likely to become chronic or serious offenders

Alternative approaches

Although these and other impediments have hampered standard prevention approaches, federal aid has fostered alternative strategies, some of which merit coverage here.

School programs. The widely demonstrated correlation between school failure and delinquency, and the availability of almost all youths as a "captive audience" of students, justify preventive work in the schools. Furthermore, about one-third of teenage robbery and assault victimization, as well as much other delinquency, occurs within the schools. This was revealed by a study that advocates, for delinquency prevention, the improvement of school discipline, coordination, personal student-staff relationships, and relevance of courses to student interests (National Institute of Education). Another major study called also for combining work with study for high-risk youths, education on juvenile laws, and cooperative liaisons with youth-service agencies (Brodsky and Knudten).

Highly contrasting levels of school involvement with potential offenders have proved rather ineffective. A project using teachers only to refer disruptive children to therapy programs had no effect on recidivism (Rodman and Grams). Neither could the effect of maximum involvement on recidivism be shown. This was exemplified by attempts at major restructuring of inner-city schools in New York City, Atlanta, and Indianapolis with private and federal financial support as well as the personal backing of President

Jimmy Carter's family (Murray, Bourque, and Mileff). These schools typically resisted social and educational innovation, family service, and delinquency prevention. Thus, the case for delinquency prevention in the schools has not yet been demonstrated.

Deinstitutionalization of status offenders. Status offenders—those whose offenses, such as running away from home, could not lead to arrest if committed by an adult—are thought to be particularly prone to committing more serious offenses in the future. To many, status offenders epitomize "potential offenders," and most states have developed procedures to remove them from pre- and post-adjudication incarceration. When eight special projects of diverse size and location were funded as models of deinstitutionalization, independent evaluation (Kobrin and Klein) concluded:

1. All projects provided alternative treatment and increased deinstitutionalization.
2. Rather uniformly, they "widened the net" of the juvenile justice system by providing services to youths with low potential as future offenders (false positives).
3. The services provided tended to be very narrow—primarily counseling—and minimal in amount.
4. Recidivism among the youths in the eight projects showed a slight but statistically significant increase, rather than the anticipated decrease, when compared to similar, but institutionalized, youths.

Thus, the effectiveness of status offender programs remains undemonstrated.

Diversion. The most characteristic approach to potential offenders from the late 1960s through the early 1980s was to divert them from the juvenile justice system into alternative community treatment services. A major review of this movement (Klein, 1979) concluded:

1. Although diversion is supposedly for offenders who would otherwise be processed further into the justice system, most diversion programs have been applied disproportionately to minor offenders who would otherwise merely be warned and released.

2. Diversion programs defined and justified their concerns ambiguously, offered a very limited range of services, were resisted by practitioners in the justice system, and "widened the nets" of agencies outside the juvenile justice system. Thus, they relabeled minor offenders, using other categories of deviance, and provided mental health services that diverted juveniles from one stigmatizing system into another.

3. Evaluators have been unable to document significant positive changes of any sort in the clients of most diversion programs. Some programs have produced harmful effects, including higher official recidivism rates. As with other alternative approaches to the potential offender, the case for diversion has yet to be demonstrated.

Gang intervention. Juvenile street gangs comprise the highest-risk pool of potential offenders. Most gang members eventually accumulate police records, and many also reach the courts and correctional programs. Therefore, intervention with them seems to minimize criminalization through early identification.

From the mid-1950s to about 1970, many major cities had programs that assigned to the gangs what were called detached workers. The workers sought to transform gang values and organization through individual counseling, manipulation of interactions within the gang, and the development of alternative activities for the gang members. Evidence from several cities suggested, however, that detached-worker programs had inadvertently solidified the gangs. No firm evidence demonstrated positive results from this transformation approach (Klein, 1971).

In the 1970s and early 1980s, emphasis shifted from transformation to control. Workers became less oriented toward dealing with specific gangs and more toward controlling particular extremely violent areas. They showed less concern for delinquency prevention and more for intervention whenever violent incidents occurred or seemed imminent. Programs stressed surveillance and mediation of intergang conflicts, along with community control almost to the point of vigilantism. Thus, the potential offender was replaced as a target by the potential violent episode, and prevention as a goal was replaced by violence reduction. There was no longer much concern for the consequences of labeling youths as potential offenders, for the early-identification paradox, or for false positives.

Future trends

Until successful intervention methods can be clearly demonstrated, there must be considerable doubt about how well the causes of delinquency are understood. Even so, programs aimed at potential offenders will continue, as will research that may illuminate both sources and impediments of success. As support for nonintervention wanes, there may be more punishment of first-time offenders, reflecting a movement toward deterring specific individuals rather than general deterrence of all persons (Klein, 1981).

Now that many of the impediments to program implementation are well documented, more attention may be focused on overcoming them. Consequently, more emphasis may be placed on understanding whether intervention is feasible and on knowing the likelihood of such unintended consequences as extending control over larger numbers of youths (net-widening), as well as the results of the early-identification paradox.

Finally, greater attention may be paid to the available and substantiated knowledge about patterns of delinquent behavior. For example:

1. Since most juvenile offenders engage in diverse rather than specialized types of offenses, to treat them as types—for example, as auto thieves or assaulters—is fallacious.
2. Because juvenile offenders do not progress markedly from minor to serious crimes, early intervention will not prevent later violence by reducing escalation from nonviolent offenses.
3. Almost all juveniles have committed acts for which an arrest could be made; therefore, the exercise of police or judicial intervention must be highly selective.
4. Since a relatively small number of delinquents commit a disproportionately large number of repeated offenses, for the sake of efficiency attention should be shifted from the potential offender to the developing chronic offender.

These findings, together with what has been learned about program impediments and failures, give reason to believe that the future holds promise. Thoughtful planning, continual evaluation, and resolute implementation can reasonably be expected to yield results more fruitful than those of the past.

MALCOLM W. KLEIN

See also CHILDREN, CRIMINAL ACTIVITIES OF; EDUCATION AND CRIME; FAMILY RELATIONSHIPS AND CRIME; articles under JUVENILE JUSTICE; JUVENILE STATUS OFFENDERS; POLICE: HANDLING OF JUVENILES; PREDICTION OF CRIME AND RECIDIVISM; PRISONS: CORRECTIONAL INSTITUTIONS FOR DELINQUENT YOUTHS; SCHOOLS, CRIME IN THE; YOUTH GANGS AND GROUPS.

BIBLIOGRAPHY

BRODSKY, STANLEY L., and KNUDTEN, RICHARD D. Strategies for Delinquency Prevention in the Schools and Other Recommendations for Phase III in Criminal Justice Programs and Planning. University: University of Alabama, Department of Psychology, 1973.
KLEIN, MALCOLM W. "Deinstitutionalization and Diversion of Juvenile Offenders: A Litany of Impediments." Crime and Justice: An Annual Review of Research, vol. 1. Edited by Norval Morris and Michael Tonry. University of Chicago Press, 1979, pp. 145–201.
———. "A Judicious Slap on the Wrist: Thoughts on Early Sanctions for Juvenile Offenders." New Directions in the Rehabilitation of Criminal Offenders. Edited by Susan E. Martin, Lee B. Sechrest, and Robin Redner. Washington, D.C.: National Academy Press, 1981, pp. 376–393.
———. Street Gangs and Street Workers. Englewood Cliffs, N.J.: Prentice-Hall, 1971.
KOBRIN, SOLOMON, and KLEIN, MALCOLM W. National Evaluation of the Deinstitutionalization of Status Offender Programs. Washington, D.C.: U.S. Department of Justice, Law Enforcement Assistance Administration, National Institute for Juvenile Justice and Delinquency Prevention, 1981.
MURRAY, CHARLES A.; BOURQUE, BLAIR B.; and MILEFF, SUSAN J. The National Evaluation of the Cities in Schools Program. Prepared for the National Institute of Education, U.S. Department of Education. Washington, D.C.: American Institutes for Research, 1981.
National Institute of Education. Violent Schools–Safe Schools: The Safe School Study Report to the Congress. Washington, D.C.: U.S. Department of Health, Education, and Welfare, NIE, 1978.
RODMAN, HYMAN, and GRAMS, PAUL. "Juvenile Delinquency and the Family: A Review and Discussion." Task Force Report: Juvenile Delinquency and Youth Crime. President's Commission on Law Enforcement and Administration of Justice, Task Force on Juvenile Delinquency and Youth Crime. Washington, D.C.: The Commission, 1967, pp. 188–221.
WALKER, JERRY P.; CARDARELLI, ALBERT P.; and BILLINGSLEY, DENNIS L. The Theory and Practice of Delinquency Prevention in the United States: Review, Synthesis, and Assessment. Columbus: Ohio State University, Center for Vocational Education, 1976.
WRIGHT, WILLIAM E., and DIXON, MICHAEL C. "Community Prevention and Treatment of Juvenile Delinquency: A Review of Evaluation Studies." Journal of Research in Crime and Delinquency 14 (1977): 35–67.

4.
POLICE ROLE

Police efforts to control crime suggest three broad categories: prevention, suppression, and oppression. Prevention is marked by the direct participation of citizens and police in a cooperative effort to protect the community and individuals from criminals. Suppression is primarily the legitimate use of police power and authority in reaction to crime, and is marked by the investigation and apprehension of criminals. Oppression is the illegitimate use of power and authority to control noncriminal conduct and is marked by a disregard of individual rights. Each of these categories of prevention is examined here in terms of the inherent conflict between democratic ideals and the need for social control.

Prevention. Police-sponsored crime prevention programs deal with the involvement of citizens in protecting themselves from crime. They tend to center on such politically sensitive offenses as burglary, crimes against children, and crimes against the elderly. Besides thematic and content similarities, most crime prevention programs were once funded by the federal government and thus have had some degree of centralized political control. Together, these commonalities of theme, content, and funding suggest the importance of crime prevention to the public, the police, and politicians.

Effective crime prevention by citizens generally requires a relatively stable and culturally homogeneous population, in which neighbors know and trust each other. Moreover, the members of stable, homogeneous populations frequently share common ideas about what constitutes suspicious activities, and neighbors know one another well enough to ascertain if something is suspicious and should be reported to the police. Such notions of a homogeneous and stable society may apply in small towns and villages, but their relevance is doubtful in major metropolitan areas, where population shifts and differing values are the norm.

Urban areas have populations made up of people of diverse cultural and ethnic backgrounds and do not have the degree of social cohesiveness found in small towns and villages. This often gives rise to special-interest groups that have close ties with the media, politicians, and public administrators. The closer these ties, the greater the special-interest group's influence in formulating public policy. A low degree of community cohesiveness adds to the strength of special-interest groups and makes police administrators sensitive to their needs. Frequently, such groups have an interest in preventing certain kinds of crimes. For example, homeowners' associations may be interested in preventing burglary, business associations may seek to prevent vandalism, and women's groups may support rape prevention. These interests are expressed to city managers, city councils, or the press, who in turn suggest in memos or editorials that the police do something about "the problem." Police administrators frequently respond by seeking a crime prevention grant to address the problem and simultaneously to hold down the cost of policing.

Illustrative of this kind of crime prevention effort is Operation Identification. A number of these programs exist across the United States on the premise that marked property is less likely to be stolen and, if stolen, easier to recover. In most cities, however, this merely means that people can borrow an electric engraver from the police department, mark their property with it, and place a decal in their window announcing their membership in Operation Identification. Participation in the program is predictably minimal. Yet if asked, police administrators and politicians will point to Operation Identification as something tangible being done by the police to prevent burglaries.

Crime prevention, seen in this context, is a public-relations tool. Objectively, such programs are not cost-effective, but for some citizens, they serve the important psychological function of providing a sense of confidence in the police. Other citizens, however, gain the impression that the police are understaffed and underequipped. The police, when trying to involve citizens in crime prevention programs, foster this belief by referring to increased crime rates, low police-citizen ratios, and inadequate equipment. There is some justification for police to point to these problems, because too often the existing conditions motivate some citizens to become involved in police-sponsored crime prevention. This kind of appeal also serves the police by fostering a climate in which increases in police budgets and additional police personnel are supported by the community.

The perception of inadequacy generated by the police in trying to motivate people to help protect themselves, however, has several unanticipated consequences. Believing that the police are understaffed and underequipped, some citizens have formed self-help groups to prevent crime in their neighborhoods. These groups range in character from anonymous informant systems to quasi-military groups that focus on community street crimes, such as muggings and purse-snatchings. As disparate as these groups are, they share at least five points in common: (1) they fear crime; (2) they are essentially an urban phenomenon; (3) they cooperate with, but are not controlled by, the police; (4) they are highly organized; and (5) the leadership tends to be socially and politically conservative.

The degree of direct involvement in the prevention of crime determines the degree to which each of the five points applies. In addition, the amount of direct involvement in crime prevention determines the character of the organization. The more direct the involvement, the more the group resembles the police both in appearance and in attitude. Those groups that organize to prevent crimes such as muggings and purse-snatchings often adopt uniforms and have radio communications, a high degree of organization, and discipline. This kind of structure reflects a need of those directly involved in preventing crime to impose order on an apparently disorderly world. It also serves to set these groups apart from other people on the street and make them instantly recognizable to one another and to potential criminals. The more like the police these groups become, the more they perceive certain other persons as potential threats to themselves. The thinking of such groups, then, implies the notion of symbolic assailants, because those to whom the groups react with apprehension dress and walk differently and have facial expressions different from those of ordinary persons in the neighborhood.

Public perceptions of police inadequacy have also helped swell the ranks of private security firms and turned them into a multibillion-dollar industry. The sales argument of these firms is a subtle variation of the police effort to involve citizens in crime prevention. Private security firms point to the lack of police personnel and equipment. They claim that they can fill in where the police cannot, because the firm can give specialized attention to a specific business or individual. Frequently, however, private security firms and the police duplicate each other's efforts. Moreover, the cooperation between the two is occasionally strained because of a confusion of roles and because of the lower hiring, training, and retention standards of most private security firms.

Suppression. Undermining police-sponsored crime prevention programs and their public-relations effect are police officers' and police administrators' perceptions that "real police work" is investigating crimes and arresting criminals. Given this perception, crime prevention programs become lodged in specialized units of the police department. Frequently, these are the same units responsible for such things as community relations, school programs, public information, and police cadet programs. By placing crime prevention in this organizational context, the police administrator is tacitly admitting that crime prevention per se is a secondary factor in the day-to-day management and deployment of police resources.

Further handicapping crime prevention efforts is a lack of personal contact between citizens and the police. This lack of contact often means that the police do not know who is committing crimes, simply because they do not know the people they are policing. A further problem is the mobility of criminals, who may live in one police jurisdiction and commit crimes

in another. Consequently, in highly mobile urban areas, determining who is committing crimes and where and how they are being committed increasingly requires the use of computers to apply a probabilistic model of prediction. This model is based on volumes of computerized historical data about criminal individuals and groups and their methods of committing crimes. Because of the mobility of criminals, this information necessarily cuts across jurisdictional boundaries. In part, it compensates for the lack of a stable resident population traditionally relied on for information in the investigation and apprehension of criminals.

Without computers, the investigation of crimes and the arrest of criminals depend primarily on the deployment of police in areas with the highest incidence of reported crime and calls for services. This practice tends to reduce crime in specific geographic areas while displacing the incidence of crime to other areas. The most common result of this pattern is a disproportionate allocation of police resources to poor and minority sections of a city, because these areas often have a high crime rate and the largest number of calls for service. The cycle seems to stop when police budgets can no longer accommodate this pattern or when specific crimes are targeted for reduction by the police.

The widespread emergence of crime-specific programs designed to reduce such crimes as robberies, burglaries, rapes, and auto thefts coincides with an increase in the use of computers by police departments, and tends to reduce dependence on the cyclical allocation of police personnel. This cycle is broken by computer use because specific crimes, and not just the number of reports from a given area, are examined more closely to see how the police can increase the effective investigation, identification, and arrest of criminals. This kind of analysis requires large volumes of information that could be correlated and ordered in some rational sequence. A natural extension of these requirements is the use of computers for analysis as well as information storage and retrieval.

The application of computer technology to the analysis of crime, however, requires the use of information that can be fed directly into a computer. This necessitates a change in police reports from an essentially narrative style detailing what, where, when, how, and who, to coded reports detailing additional specific information. Thus, information on the date, time, place, and type of crime, as well as specific information about the suspect, is coded for input into a computer. This kind of analysis gives police more useful and detailed information. Consequently, it has become common to see computer-generated information used by neighborhood watches, truancy-reduction programs, crime-specific projects, and specialized crime task forces working on a common problem.

From these crime-specific efforts a computer technology has emerged that allows police to correlate an unknown criminal's method of operation with information about individual criminals and crimes. These developments have also made it possible to identify and locate criminals and vehicles by using only their physical descriptions and methods of operation.

The computer developments have led to programs designed to coordinate police activities and apprehend serious criminal offenders. The basic model for these programs relies on the correlation of all information available to the police about specific crimes and individuals. The programs assume that the more information available, the better, because the amount and quality of information leads to superior tactical and managerial decisions. Computers also provide needed information for estimating when, where, how, and what crimes are likely to occur. Such knowledge assists in the allocation of police resources and in administrative control of these resources. The application of computers—unlike programs dependent on civilian participation, such as the neighborhood watch—affirms the police notion of police work.

The state of California in the late 1970s developed a computer-based program that emphasizes the apprehension of career criminals. In focus and intent, it concentrates efforts on serious and habitual offenders, and has made the computer-aided identification and apprehension of serious and habitual offenders equal in importance to the computerized deployment of police resources. The emphasis of the California program on the criminal, however, requires a more specific use of information and a different order of intelligence information than that needed for the purely managerial and deployment functions of a police agency. Suggestive of its potential intelligence function is the attempt to reduce parolees' physical descriptions to discrete numerical descriptors for inclusion in a computer data bank. In addition, parolee vehicles, vehicles to which they have access, and known associates of parolees are reduced to numerical concrete descriptors.

The federally funded programs and the California program are at the cutting edge of crime suppression development, and current use is restricted to experimental sites. Like any new development in policing, these programs have both advocates and critics within the police ranks. The advocates are generally found in the upper administration of police agencies. The programs are supported because they provide a data base for the rational deployment of resources, as well as data justifying additional personnel and larger operating budgets. The programs also increase the accountability of the rank-and-file police officer, providing police administrators with a rationalized basis for transfers and promotion.

Critics of the programs are found primarily among the rank and file of the police agency. The programs compel police officers to learn new reporting procedures and new ways of processing reports. However, the results of these changes are not visible to the officer in the field for six months to a year. Additionally, other changes not supported by the rank and file may accompany the use of computers. These changes may include abandoning the use of tape recorders or narrative reports in favor of hand-printed reports with multiple fields and categories arranged in a check-off format. From the detective's point of view, the new reports may be more difficult to read (especially descriptions of suspects and vehicles) and may not contain all the information they think essential in developing leads in a case. In any event, it is argued that computers do not necessarily lead directly to arrests, nor do they cause a reduction of work.

Oppression. In developing computer-based crime suppression programs, the police tread a fine line between suppression and oppression. Suppression of crime is the reasonable use of power or authority to control criminal behavior; oppression is the abusive use of power or authority to control noncriminal conduct. Historically, the police (with the indifference or support of the public) have from time to time oppressed various groups that were not in political favor. Examples include the use of police to enforce Jim Crow laws, break union strikes, or spy on private citizens who protest specific political policies. Although these practices seem remote from the day-to-day work of modern police departments, scandals recurrently are in the news, indicating that the problem is persistent; frequently exposed are abuse of minority prisoners and other "undesirables" such as illegal aliens in police custody, and the use by department intelligence units of electronic surveillance and infiltrating agents to gather information on deviant but legal political groups.

At the heart of such historical and current excesses is a fundamental conflict between the need for social control and the need for individual freedom in a democratic society. The police exist for the purpose of social control. Democratic ideals exist to maximize individual freedom. The police in a democratic society are consequently caught between incompatible philosophies. Like any organization caught in a double bind, one course of action will become dominant. For the police, social control is the rationale of their existence and, consequently, the course of action they most frequently take.

Given the historical and philosophical outlook of the police, some critical questions arise concerning modern developments in crime prevention. Clearly, the mass of information available to the police and the application of computers to correlate and analyze this information raise questions about how, and by whom, this information will be used. These questions become particularly relevant when one realizes that the majority of people contacted by the police are innocent of any crime but become part of official police documents because they are victims or witnesses, or simply because they report crimes.

Fear of crime and the mystique of police as experts in crime have, however, created a milieu more supportive of social control than of democratic principles. Indicative of the public support for social control is the behavior of some neighborhood watches and self-help groups that frequently see strangers as suspicious persons. The greater the difference between the strangers' appearance and what is most customary in the neighborhood, the greater the suspicion. Thus, the presence of teenage blacks in a white middle-class neighborhood is seen as more suspicious than that of teenage whites in the same neighborhood. This kind of perception by citizens makes it easier for the police to stop and question persons whom they consider suspicious, or to tell strangers to "move along." Such actions also give the police "cause" to write on a field interview card the suspect's name, physical description, address, vehicle description, and license plate number. Like other reports, every such card becomes a part of the police record system. This information is computerized and used to compare descriptions of unidentified criminals with the names and descriptions of persons on the field interview cards. The danger of this practice lies in simply calling to the attention of the police an innocent person as a potential criminal. In and of themselves, these measures are not oppressive; however, when taken together, their effect is to reduce freedom of movement, the right to protest, and even the right to express dissenting opinions.

Police efforts to prevent and suppress crime have led to elaborate information systems that are open to potential abuse. The rationale for these systems is an increasing crime rate and the mobility of persons committing crimes. These concerns are real and need to be addressed. Yet this rationale means that the social control activities of the police are seldom made public, and suppression and oppression are generally compartmentalized rather than seen in the larger context of social control. This kind of compartmentalization may benefit the police but not necessarily the public, for it obscures the potentially oppressive nature of the police. Unable to prevent crime without public support but fearful of direct citizen involvement, police frequently use crime prevention programs to gain increased budgets that may be used for excessive control over the daily lives of the citizenry.

Consequently, in maintaining a balance between social control and democratic ideals, technology and police methods for addressing crime prevention both need to be measured against the potential loss of individual freedoms and of citizen involvement in the political process. The danger is that freedom will be traded for security.

THOMAS C. GRAY

See also CRIMINAL JUSTICE SYSTEM: SOCIAL DETERMINANTS; ECOLOGY OF CRIME; articles under POLICE.

BIBLIOGRAPHY

PACKER, HERBERT L. *The Limits of the Criminal Sanction.* Stanford, Calif.: Stanford University Press, 1968.
SKOLNICK, JEROME H. *Justice without Trial: Law Enforcement in Democratic Society.* 2d ed. New York: Wiley, 1975.

CRIME RATES AND PATTERNS

See AGE AND CRIME; CLASS AND CRIME; *articles under* CRIME STATISTICS; ECOLOGY OF CRIME; EDUCATION AND CRIME; INTELLIGENCE AND CRIME; RACE AND CRIME; RURAL CRIME; URBAN CRIME; WOMEN AND CRIME.

CRIME REPORTING

See *articles under* CRIME STATISTICS.

CRIMES AGAINST HUMANITY

See INTERNATIONAL CRIMES AGAINST THE PEACE; INTERNATIONAL CRIMINAL LAW; WAR CRIMES.

CRIMES AGAINST NATURE

See HOMOSEXUALITY AND CRIME; *both articles under* SEX OFFENSES.

CRIMES AGAINST THE PEACE

See INTERNATIONAL CRIMES AGAINST THE PEACE; INTERNATIONAL CRIMINAL LAW; WAR CRIMES.

CRIME STATISTICS

To understand the nature and dimensions of the crime problem and to devise effective policies for crime control and prevention, we need to know many facts about crime. Most of the questions for which we seek answers require analysis of aggregated data on specific criminal events, offenders, and victims, or actions taken by the criminal justice system. Our understanding and effective response to crime depend heavily, therefore, on the adequacy of the basic statistical data on which such judgments are grounded. We need valid and reliable data to know how much crime of different types there is, the characteristics of offenders, victims, and crime-generating situations, the costs and benefits of alternative policies, and the way all of these are changing in response to major historical events or more basic long-term trends in society. This section on crime statistics focuses on three major questions. What have been the major trends in the volume and distribution of crimes against persons or property? What are the relative strengths and weaknesses of various methods for assembling crime data? How can we develop a more effective cost-accounting system to guide the allocation of scarce crime-control resources?

Our ability to chart the effect of specific historical events on crime, such as wars or economic depressions, or the impact of long-term trends such as industrialization and urbanization, depends on the availability of comparable crime data over many years. As one might expect, such data are very limited and highly variable in quality. Yet, as the article on HISTORICAL TRENDS IN WESTERN SOCIETY indicates, many useful insights can be gained. These help place the events and trends of recent years in better perspective and suggest significant differences that require more concentrated attention.

However, to avoid the misinterpretation or misuse of crime statistics it is essential to understand the limitations, as well as the relative advantages, of different methods for compiling crime data. The article on REPORTING SYSTEMS AND METHODS provides such a guide. It identifies the primary sources of data on crime, ranging from officially collected statistics to surveys of victims and confidential self-reports of crime from general or special population samples. Each of these sources provides a unique contribution to our total understanding of the crime problem. The self-report and victim surveys launched in recent years have greatly assisted in illuminating the "dark figure," or hidden volume, of crime that escapes official notice

or clearance. As the article notes, however, analysis of these new sources of information about crime has shown a convergence with official data for frequent and serious crimes and offenders. This has strengthened confidence in the use of official data for studying the correlates of those crime patterns which are of most concern to the public.

Efforts to assess the total cost of crime and public and private control measures have been unsuccessful and of little practical value. What is needed instead is a system of cost accounting that takes advantage of cost-benefit forms of analysis developed in application to other social problems by economists. The article on COSTS OF CRIME explores the possible application of these methods to guide analysis of alternative crime-control policies and allocations of resources.

1. COSTS OF CRIME   Philip J. Cook
2. REPORTING SYSTEMS AND METHODS   Joseph G. Weis
3. HISTORICAL TRENDS IN
   WESTERN SOCIETY   Theodore N. Ferdinand

1.
COSTS OF CRIME

Introduction

Crime reduces our standard of living. The prices of consumer goods are inflated by shoplifting, employee theft, embezzlement, antitrust violations, and extortion of legitimate businesses by organized crime. The fear of household burglary and street crime motivates us to make large expenditures on self-protection and insurance. Our tax bills reflect the pervasive crimes of income-tax evasion and government program fraud, as well as the necessity of supporting public law enforcement efforts. Perhaps even more important than such financial losses associated with criminal activity is the loss of peace of mind that is a consequence of contending with inebriated drivers on the highways, muggers and rapists in the city parks and alleys, and heavily armed neighbors.

For some purposes, it is useful to quantify the effect of crime on our standard of living. The best-known comprehensive effort to quantify the "costs of crime" was reported by the President's Commission on Law Enforcement and Administration of Justice. The commission estimated that in 1965 the total costs of crime and the criminal justice system (CJS) equaled about 3 percent of the gross national product. Unfortunately, the commission's accounting procedures were not guided by a clear conceptual framework, and they were at odds with the principles of cost-benefit analysis in several important respects.

This article sketches an economic accounting framework for evaluating the costs of crime. It does not attempt to calculate revised estimates of the "total costs of crime," a task that may be impossible and is in any event artificial in the absence of any known technique for accomplishing the elimination of crime. Public policies often do have some marginal impact on the costs of crime, however, and evaluating these policies requires a systematic method for quantifying such effects.

The social-cost accounting framework

Most of the resources employed in preventing crime, avoiding crime, and committing crime have alternative uses in society. The value of these alternative uses is by definition their "opportunity cost." The social cost of crime should therefore be measured in terms of the loss to society of resources that are destroyed or diverted as a result of criminal activity, and that otherwise would be used in legitimate, productive activity.

The total social cost of crime includes the *direct* cost to victims (net of benefits to criminals) and the indirect costs associated with public- and private-sector responses to crime. Both types of cost are expressed in a quantifiable unit of measure, for example, the dollar. A valid accounting framework for calculating both types of costs is provided by cost-benefit analysis, a technique for evaluating public-sector choices that was developed by economists and that has been applied in a wide variety of contexts since the 1930s. The practical application of this technique in the crime area is difficult in several respects, not the least of which is finding a method for valuing the disparate crime-related harms in a common unit of account, such as dollars. But even when the statistical application of this approach poses practical difficulties, the theoretical framework is useful in clarifying the basic issues in criminal justice policy evaluation.

Direct social costs of crime. The most common class of serious crimes involves the illegal taking of money or goods from an unwilling victim, as in embezzlement, larceny, and fraud. Viewed dispassionately, in this type of crime the victim's monetary loss is equal to the criminal's monetary gain; on balance, then, there is no direct social cost to the *transfer itself.* (If merchandise rather than cash is stolen, however, there may be some social cost from the transfer if the criminal places a lower value on the merchandise than does the victim.) From the larger perspective of society, the direct social cost of such crimes is equal to the loss of the criminal's time (as well as the other resources he devoted to perpetrating the crime), which would otherwise have been used in legitimate activity. This of course presumes that the criminal is properly viewed as a member of society. The theft of $100 in cash from an unattended purse has essentially no direct social cost, since the victim's loss is equal to the thief's gain.

Other crimes against property, including vandalism and arson, destroy productive resources, and in this respect they are fundamentally different from thefts. Although there may be some psychic gain to the perpetrators of such crimes, it is reasonable to assume that this psychic gain is usually much smaller than the productive loss to the victims. The destruction of $100 worth of property by vandals has a direct social cost of approximately $100 and may be a more serious crime than the theft of $100 in cash, which has a direct social cost near zero.

It is certainly possible for the benefit of a criminal act to exceed its direct cost. Plausible examples include some instances of double parking, substance abuse, antitrust violations, and crimes of conscience or protest against injustice.

Such accounting of the direct costs of crime is useful in evaluating the relative seriousness of different types of offenses. This, in turn, allows for the enlightened setting of priorities within the CJS and for the establishment of a rational sentencing structure for various offenses.

Indirect social costs of crime. The threat of crime diverts resources into public and private activities that are designed to reduce or protect against this threat. The bulk of public-sector expenditures to combat crime goes to support the police, courts, and other agencies of the CJS. Budgeted CJS expenditures at all levels for this purpose account for about 1.1 percent of the gross national product. A complete accounting of such CJS costs should include some items that do not appear in any budget—among them the uncompensated (or only partially compensated) value of services provided by civilian witnesses and jurors and the costs imposed by the system on suspects, defendants, and convicts. For example, the cost of imprisoning a man for one year includes, in part, the cost to the taxpayers of maintaining him, as well as the value the prisoner places on his freedom.

The private-sector response to the threat of crime is much more costly than that of the CJS and is much more difficult to measure. Obvious crime-related expenses in business include private guards, inventory control systems, and alarm systems. More subtle expenses are also incurred. Retailers employ extra clerks because self-service displays are vulnerable to shop-lifters; firms design accounting systems to protect against embezzlement by employees; and insurance companies employ claims investigators to discourage and detect fraudulent claims.

Costs to households include the purchase of such defensive hardware as locks, handguns, and alarm systems. In addition, people living in high-crime areas may, to reduce their exposure to criminal victimization, give up such valued activities as going out at night or walking in public places, with a resulting degradation in the social life of the community. Those who can afford it may move to safer but more expensive neighborhoods or may decide to incur the costs of sending their children to private schools.

The threat of theft weakens effective claims to the use and enjoyment of private property and may thereby reduce the incentive to engage in productive activities or to make major purchases. For example, a teenager's incentive to work toward the purchase of an auto will be undermined by a high auto-theft and vandalism rate. Generally speaking, the threat of theft is similar in effect to a tax on consumer durables; such a "tax" will cause consumers to reduce their purchases of theft-vulnerable items in favor of commodities less easily stolen.

All these examples illustrate a basic point: the threat of crime engenders a variety of costly adaptations on the part of potential victims. Resources are diverted into self-protective activities; production and consumption decisions are distorted to reduce potential loss in the event of criminal victimization. These adaptations are clearly very costly in the aggregate, but so varied and intertwined with other resource allocation decisions as to defy ready measurement.

Since self-protective efforts are never completely effective, households and businesses continuously confront the risk of criminal victimization. Potential loss can be reduced by the purchase of insurance, which also serves the valuable function of reducing anxiety. But insurance coverage is costly, and it is also usually less than complete, especially with respect to violent crime. Medical expenses and even future earnings can be insured, but pain and psychological trauma cannot. Thus anxiety, uncertainty, and the expense of insurance are all indirect consequences, and therefore costs, of the threat of crime.

Policy evaluation

An accurate assessment of the social costs of crime (both direct and indirect) should underlie crime-related policy decisions. If the maximization of total wealth (broadly construed) is a proper objective for social policy, then criminal justice policy should be guided by the criterion of minimizing the social cost of crime. Some commentators object to the use of this single criterion on the ground that it ignores the distribution of these costs among different groups: cost-benefit analysis is concerned with the size of the economic pie, rather than how it is divided among members of society.

Minimizing the social cost of crime is, of course, not the same as minimizing the "amount" of crime. For example, increased crime prevention efforts may cost more than they are perceived to be worth. Airport security measures to deter hijacking have been criticized—despite their notable effectiveness during the 1970s—on the ground that many passengers would rather accept a higher risk of being hijacked than be subjected to the inconvenience and higher ticket prices resulting from these security measures. The proper objective is to minimize the *sum* of the direct and indirect costs of crime.

Accounting and measurement problems for specific crimes

An enormous variety of offenses are covered by the criminal law. The special problems associated with determining the social costs of three major categories of crime are discussed below.

Predatory crime. Rates of "predatory crime," including burglary, robbery, rape, vandalism, assault, and personal larceny, differ widely among geographic areas. Some neighborhoods within a large city are much safer than others. Differences in the risk of victimization from this type of crime are reflected in property values. Other things being equal, home buyers or renters are willing to pay more for a residence in a relatively safe neighborhood than for one located in a neighborhood with a higher crime rate. Crime-related differences in property values thus indicate the value placed by the public on a marginal reduction in crime, which in turn is closely related to the social cost of crime. Richard Thaler, among others, has attempted to extract estimates of this sort from data on property values, crime rates, and neighborhood-specific amenities. The practical difficulties with this statistical procedure are enormous, however.

A more direct method of estimating the social cost of predatory crime is through sample surveys that elicit judgments from respondents concerning how much they would be willing to pay for specified reductions in victimization risks. Responses from a carefully constructed questionnaire should give an indication of the cost the public attaches to some of the more subtle crime-related harms, such as anxiety and restrictions on life-style, in addition to the more tangible costs of self-protection. For example, suppose that the average household indicated in such a survey that it would be willing to pay $20 to reduce the risk of being robbed by half for a year. In such a case, the economic benefit of a program that cut the noncommercial robbery rate in half would be properly estimated at about $1.6 billion, given about 80 million households in the United States.

Consensual crimes. For some types of offenses, including the sale and purchase of a wide range of vice-related goods and services, all parties directly involved are voluntary participants in the illegal activity. Since their participation in such activities is voluntary, the perpetrators evidently believe that the benefits derived from such activities outweigh the cost. Presumably, legislators outlaw these consensual activities because their constituents view them as immoral and destructive; that is, people who are not directly affected by the consumption of these commodities object to them on moral and paternalistic grounds. The net social costs of such activities are therefore related to the strength of these "third party" feelings.

It should be noted that the measure of the direct social costs of illegal gambling used by the President's Commission on Law Enforcement and Administration of Justice—revenues net of payoffs—is not appropriate as a measure of social cost, although it does give an indication of this industry's contribution to the gross national product. Nor is it appropriate to include the costs of violence, political corruption, and so on that often are associated with providing illegal goods and services if the objective is to calculate the direct social costs of the consumption of these commodities (although these ancillary crimes are part of the indirect costs of bringing vice within the purview of the criminal law). In any event, a dominant coalition of political actors perceives that the benefits of suppressing a variety of consensual activities through use of the criminal sanction warrant the indirect social costs of adopting this approach. Conducting a cost-benefit analysis that would help confirm or refute this judgment would require clear definition of the *nature* of the social benefits to be derived from legal suppression.

Income-tax evasion. Government tax revenues are reduced by billions of dollars each year as a result of criminal evasion. The result of reduced tax collection is either a reduction in government expenditures, an increase in tax rates, or an increase in government borrowing. Higher tax rates and increased borrowing alike tend to discourage economic activity in the private sector, resulting in a reduction in the national income. The direct social cost of tax evasion is closely related to this reduction in national income. Income-tax evasion also has a redistributional effect, of course, with evaders gaining at the expense of honest taxpayers. This redistributional effect is not reflected in the social-cost accounting framework, which, as discussed above, is concerned with the *average* standard of living rather than its distribution.

Distribution of crime costs

The cost-benefit framework developed above takes no account of the distribution of the costs of criminal activity. Distributional concerns should and do influence criminal justice policy. It is not always obvious who ultimately "pays" the costs of crime, however.

How, for example, are the costs of shoplifting distributed? Retailers will locate in a high-crime neighborhood only if they expect to earn as high a rate of return on an investment there as they could in other locations. As a result, prices are often higher and retail outlets scarcer in high-crime areas. Predictable shoplifting costs are thus borne by residents of the neighborhood, rather than the retailers. But if the shoplifting rate increases unexpectedly, the owners of retail outlets will suffer a corresponding loss in wealth. A similar analysis applies to owners of real estate in high-crime neighborhoods. Housing and land prices reflect expected rates of predatory crime. Much of the benefit of an unexpected reduction in the rates of predatory crime in a neighborhood will come in the form of a windfall gain in property values. Renters will not benefit so much since rents will tend to increase, reflecting the reduced risk of victimization.

Inefficiency in law enforcement

Criminal justice system policies and resource allocation decisions influence the amount of crime (direct cost), as well as determining the level of public and private expenditures on crime (indirect cost). The CJS is inefficient to the extent that a modification in its policies could reduce crime without increasing crime prevention costs, or that crime prevention costs could be reduced without a resulting increase in crime. Efficiency questions arise at three levels in CJS policy: (1) the choice of techniques employed within the CJS to pursue crime control objectives; (2) the allocation of resources among different organizations within the CJS and also among competing priorities (different types of crimes); and (3) the division of crime control activity between public agencies and the private sector. Each of these questions is discussed briefly below.

Choice of technique. A police chief allocates his financial resources among a variety of crime control methods, including preventive patrol units, specialized patrol and investigation units, public relations and education efforts, data processing, and training. These allocation decisions are influenced above all by the objective of crime prevention. Unfortunately, little is known about the relationship between policing techniques and crime prevention. The first careful evaluations of police crime control efforts, conducted by The Rand Corporation, the Kansas City Police Department, and other organizations, have yielded some intriguing findings. Two traditionally important uses of police resources—preventive patrol and detective units—appear to be ineffective in controlling crime, whereas increased use of hidden cameras in commercial places, and increased aggressiveness in crime detection and investigation by police, appear to be highly productive.

Other CJS organizations must also make choices about which techniques are best suited to achieving their objectives. Failure to seek out and employ the most productive techniques results in the waste of economic resources. One representative example helps illustrate the wide range of issues here. Punishment in the form of a fine or other pecuniary assessment is less costly socially than incarceration; a fine is simply a transfer payment, with no direct social cost (except the cost of collection), whereas incarceration imposes costs on both taxpayers and the convict that are of no direct benefit to others. If a fine can be imposed in place of a jail term without loss of deterrent effect, then the fine is a relatively efficient mode of punishment.

Resource allocation among CJS organizations and types of crime. Even if each CJS organization chooses efficient techniques for combating each class of crime, another source of economic waste may still exist: the inefficient allocation of resources among different organizations or among different types of crime.

One general rule for the efficient allocation of resources among different activities is that the last dollar's worth of resources allocated to each activity be equally productive. If resources are not allocated in this way, then a transfer of resources from one activity to another would increase total "output." For example, if an additional assistant prosecutor can be hired for the *same cost* as an additional patrolman, and at the same time be more productive, then the system

as a whole can be made more productive by transferring resources from policing to prosecution. Of course, the decentralized nature of the CJS does not provide any simple procedure for achieving such a reallocation.

A similar issue arises with respect to dividing CJS resources among the control of different types of crime. Prosecutors, for example, must decide how much priority to give violent crimes as opposed to nonviolent crimes, such as burglary, larceny, substance abuse, and white-collar crime. Emphasizing one of these crime categories inevitably comes at the cost of reduced emphasis for other categories. An efficient allocation of resources across crime types is also governed by the "last dollar" rule. In this case, the rule requires that allocation be guided by the relative social cost of each type of crime, as well as by the degree to which the rate of each type of crime is responsive to prosecutorial activities.

Allocation of crime control resources between the public and private sectors. The third level at which the efficiency question arises is with respect to the overall size of the CJS. Resources employed by the system are not available for other socially valued uses, such as education, public transportation, and private consumption. If additional resources would have greater value in combating crime than in other uses, then the system is too small.

One consequence of providing inadequate resources to CJS activities may be an inefficiently large private expenditure on self-protection against crime. For example, suppose a high commercial robbery rate induces half of the retailers in a city to hire private guards. These private expenditures will probably displace robberies to other commercial targets without significantly reducing the overall rate of robbery. If, however, the same resources were instead devoted to an antirobbery unit in the city police force, then it is plausible to expect the overall commercial robbery rate to fall.

Conclusion

The main accomplishment of research on the social costs of crime has been the creation of a conceptual framework for analyzing public decisions relating to the law and law enforcement. First, this framework suggests a precisely defined objective for criminal justice policy: minimize the sum of the direct and indirect social costs of crime. Second, the framework gives some guidance for evaluating the relative seriousness of different types of crime and for evaluating the consequences of decriminalizing certain activities.

Third, the framework provides a method for evaluating changes in CJS enforcement policies and budgets. This social-cost accounting framework is derived from the principles of cost-benefit analysis, a technique that has proved useful in a wide variety of applications. Its major shortcoming is that it ignores the *distributional* consequences of policy innovations.

PHILIP J. COOK

See also CRIME STATISTICS: REPORTING SYSTEMS AND METHODS; CRIMINAL JUSTICE SYSTEM: MEASUREMENT OF PERFORMANCE; RESEARCH IN CRIMINAL JUSTICE.

BIBLIOGRAPHY

BECKER, GARY S. "Crime and Punishment: An Economic Approach." *Journal of Political Economy* 76 (1968): 169–217.

CLOTFELTER, CHARLES T. "Public Services, Private Substitutes, and the Demand for Protection against Crime." *American Economic Review* 67 (1977): 867–877.

DEMMERT, HENRY G. "Crime and Crime Control: What Are the Social Costs?" Technical Report CERDCR-3-79. Stanford, Calif.: Stanford University, Hoover Institution, Center for Econometric Studies of the Justice System, 1979.

DENISON, EDWARD F. "Effects of Selected Changes in the Institutional and Human Environment upon Output per Unit of Input." *Survey of Current Business* 58, no. 1 (1978): 21–44.

FRIEDMAN, LEE S. "An Interim Evaluation of the Supported Work Experiment." *Policy Analysis* 3 (1977): 147–170.

GILLESPIE, ROBERT W. "Heroin Addiction, Crime, and Economic Cost: A Critical Analysis." *Journal of Criminal Justice* 6 (1978): 305–313.

GRAMLICH, EDWARD M. *Benefit-Cost Analysis of Government Programs.* Englewood Cliffs, N.J.: Prentice-Hall, 1981.

GRAY, CHARLES M., ed. *The Costs of Crime.* Beverly Hills, Calif.: Sage, 1979.

LANDES, WILLIAM M. "An Economic Study of U.S. Aircraft Hijacking, 1961–1976." *Journal of Law and Economics* 21 (1978): 1–32.

President's Commission on Law Enforcement and Administration of Justice. *The Challenge of Crime in a Free Society.* Washington, D.C.: The Commission, 1967.

ROTTENBERG, SIMON. "The Social Cost of Crime and Crime Prevention." *Crime in Urban Society.* Edited by Barbara N. McLennan. Foreword by Ramsey Clark. New York: Dunellen, 1970, pp. 43–58.

THALER, RICHARD. "A Note on the Value of Crime Control: Evidence from the Property Market." *Journal of Urban Economics* 5, no. 1 (1978): 137–145.

THUROW, LESTER C. "Equity vs. Efficiency in Law Enforcement." *Public Policy* 18 (1970): 451–459.

U.S. National Commission on Law Observance and Enforcement. *Report on the Cost of Crime.* Washington, D.C.: The Commission, 1931.

2.

REPORTING SYSTEMS AND METHODS

Introduction

In order to better understand, explain, and control crime, one needs accurate counts of its occurrence. *Crime statistics* represent the counts of criminal behavior and criminals. They are typically uniform data on offenses and offenders and are derived from records of official criminal justice agencies, from other agencies of control, and from unofficial sources such as surveys of victimization or criminal involvement. Particularly in the case of official crime statistics, they may be published annually or periodically in a relatively standard format of data presentation and analysis.

Official crime statistics are generated at different levels of government (municipal, state, and federal) by a variety of criminal justice agencies (police, court, and corrections) and at different stages in the criminal justice process (arrest, prosecution, conviction, imprisonment, and parole). Official statistics are also produced on the violation of laws, codes, and standards of a variety of administrative and regulatory agencies of control, primarily at the federal level. Official crime statistics are based on the records of those agencies that are the official registrars of criminal behavior and criminals.

Unofficial crime statistics are produced independently of the records of official agencies of crime control. The sources of these statistics are the records of private security and investigative agencies and the data collected by social scientists through experiments and observations, as well as through surveys of victimization and of self-reported criminal involvement.

Crime statistics emerged in the early nineteenth century as an adjunct to the administration of justice, the primary purpose being the measurement of the *amount* of crime, particularly "to know if crime had increased or decreased" in order to inform crime control policy and practice (Sellin and Wolfgang, p. 9). Early researchers pointed out the ultimately more important purpose of measuring the *distribution* of crime by a variety of social, demographic, and geographic characteristics. Both official and unofficial crime statistics have distinctive problems and sources of error, but a major one they share is the underestimation of the actual amount of crime. However, it is probable that the various measures generate similar distributions of crime, meaning that there is convergence rather than discrepancy in their depictions of the characteristics and correlates of crime. It is also likely that multiple indicators of crime best inform research, theory, policy, and practice.

The major types of official and unofficial crime statistics are discussed here in terms of their history and contemporary sources; their role as measures of crime; methodological and utilization issues and problems; and the general issue of discrepancy or convergence among crime statistics regarding the distribution and correlates of crime.

History of crime statistics. Simultaneously with the emergence of the discipline of statistics in the seventeenth century, the fledgling discipline's luminaries began to call for crime statistics in order to "know the measure of vice and sin in the nation" (Sellin and Wolfgang, p. 7). It was not until the nineteenth century that the measurement of a nation's moral health by means of statistics led to the development of the branch of statistics called "moral statistics." France began systematically collecting national judicial statistics on prosecutions and convictions in 1825. For the first time, comprehensive data on crime were available to the overseers of moral health, as well as to researchers. The French data became the source of the first significant statistical studies of crime, by the Belgian Adolphe Quételet and the Frenchman André Michel Guerry, who have been called the founders of the scientific sociological study of crime. Soon afterward, similar analytical and ecological studies of crime were carried out by other Europeans who were influenced directly by, and made frequent references to, the work of Quételet and Guerry.

In the United States, the earliest crime statistics were state judicial statistics on prosecutions and convictions in court and on prisoners in state institutions. New York began collecting judicial statistics in 1829, and by the turn of the twentieth century twenty-four other states had instituted systems of court data collection. Prison statistics were first gathered in 1834 in Massachusetts, and twenty-three other states had begun the systematic collection of prison data by 1900 (Robinson). The early state data on imprisonment were augmented by the first national enumeration of persons institutionalized in prisons and jails as part of the 1850 census and by subsequent decennial (taken every ten years) population counts thereafter. These early United States Bureau of the Census statistics are relatively complete and informative, including for each prisoner the year and offense of commitment, sex, birthplace, age, race, occupation, and literacy status.

By the end of the nineteenth century, most European countries and a number of states in the United States were systematically collecting judicial and prison statistics, and concomitantly most of the problems relating to these statistics and the measurement of crime in general had been identified. Numerous critics pointed to the fact that judicial and prison statistics were "incomplete" measures of the actual amount and distribution of crime in the community, primarily because of the "dark figure" of undetected, unreported, unacted upon, or unrecorded crime. It has always been clear that not all crimes committed in the community come to the attention of the police, that only a portion of crimes known to the police eventuate in arrest, that not all offenders who have been arrested are prosecuted or convicted, and that only a small fraction of the cases where there is a conviction lead to imprisonment. This underestimation of the volume of crime is not necessarily problematic if, as Quételet suggested, we "assume that there is a nearly invariable relationship between offenses known and adjudicated and the total unknown sum of offenses committed" (p. 18). In other words, if there is a constant ratio between the actual amount of crime (including the dark figure of unknown offenses) and officially recorded crime, whether recorded by arrest, prosecution, conviction, or imprisonment, then the latter is "representative" of the former and acceptable as a measure of crime. Later research showed this to be a fallacious assumption, but during the nineteenth century and through the first quarter of the twentieth century, scholars and practitioners alike generally operated under this assumption in using and defending judicial statistics as the true measure of crime in a society. Critics pointed to the fact that judicial statistics were not representative of the actual number of crimes or criminals in their proposals that police statistics, particularly of "offenses known to the police," be used in the measurement of crime.

Beginning in 1857, Great Britain was the first nation to systematically collect police data, including offenses known to the police. The significance of this type of data was appreciated by only a few nineteenth-century scholars, among them Georg Mayr, the leading criminal statistician of the time. In 1867, he published the first statistical study using "crimes known to the police" as the primary data source, proposing that crimes known to the police should be the foundation of moral statistical data on crime (Sellin and Wolfgang, p. 14). A few researchers called for utilization of police statistics, but judicial statistics on prosecution and conviction remained the crime statistic of choice in studies of the amount and distribution of crime.

Although the origin, utilization, and defense of judicial statistics were a European enterprise, the emergence of police statistics as a legitimate and eventually favored index of crime can be characterized as an American endeavor. As a result of a growing dissatisfaction with judicial statistics and of the fact—axiomatic in criminology—that "the value of a crime rate for index purposes decreases as the distance from the crime itself in terms of procedure increases" (Sellin, p. 346), the American criminologist August Vollmer in 1920 proposed a national bureau of criminal records that, among other tasks, would compile data on crimes known to the police. In 1927 the International Association of Chiefs of Police made this suggestion an actuality by developing a plan for a national system of police statistics, including offenses known and arrests, collected from local police departments in each state. The Federal Bureau of Investigation became the clearinghouse for these statistics and published in 1931 the first of its now-annual Uniform Crime Reports (UCR). That same year, "offenses known to the police" was accorded even more legitimacy as a valid crime statistic by the Wickersham Commission, which stated that the "best index of the number and nature of offenses committed is police statistics showing offenses known to the police" (U.S. National Commission on Law Observance and Enforcement, p. 25). Ever since that time, "offenses known to the police" has generally been considered the best source of *official* crime data. However, most of the European countries which had developed national reporting systems of judicial statistics did not include police statistics, particularly crimes known, until the 1950s, and ironically, Great Britain did not acknowledge that crimes known to the police was a valid measure of crime until the mid-1930s, although these data had been collected since the mid-nineteenth century (Sellin and Wolfgang, pp. 18–21).

According to Thorsten Sellin's axiom, "crimes known to the police" has the most value of all official measures of crime because it is closest procedurally to the actual crime committed, probably as close as an official crime statistic will ever be. Even so, as with each and every measure and crime statistic, there are problems regarding even this best of official crime statistics.

Official crime statistics

Contemporary official crime statistics, proliferating with the growth of crime-control bureaucracies and their need to keep records, are more comprehensive and varied than nineteenth-century judicial statistics and early twentieth-century police statistics. The purposes and functions of crime statistics have also changed. Whereas the early judicial statistics were utilized to measure a nation's moral health or the social and spatial distribution of crime, many of the more contemporary official statistics are the by-products of criminal justice "administrative bookkeeping and accounting." For example, data are collected on such matters as agency manpower, resources, expenditures, and physical facilities, as well as on warrants filed and death-row populations. Consequently, in the United States there are hundreds of national—and thousands of state and local—sources of official statistics, most of which are best characterized as data on the characteristics and procedures of the administration of criminal justice and crime control.

Unfortunately, even with this wealth of information available to them, the editors of the annual *Sourcebook of Criminal Justice Statistics*—the most comprehensive and useful reference work on consolidated nationwide crime data—concluded that there are fundamental data gaps in a number of important areas, that coverage is not systematic, uniform, or comparable, and that many of the data are uneven in quality (Flanagan, van Alstyne, and Gottfredson, p. x). Given the different histories of judicial and police statistics in Europe and the United States, it is not surprising that in the latter there are relatively good police data compiled on a nationwide annual basis and relatively poor judicial data. In fact, the United States is one of only a few developed countries that publishes no national court statistics. Reflecting the unique history of corrections in the United States, where the state prison and local jail are differentiated by jurisdiction, incapacitative functions, type of inmate, and record-keeping practices, there are relatively comprehensive annual national data on the number and characteristics of adults under correctional supervision in state and federal prisons, but no national statistics on jail populations are published. A review of sources of criminal justice statistics concluded that "the absence of regular annual data on jail inmates is, along with the absence of court statistics, the most glaring gap in American criminal justice statistics" (Doleschal, p. 123).

Official crime statistics measure crime and crime control. Clearly, the historically preferred source of official statistics on the extent and nature of crime is police data, particularly crimes known to the police. Other official data gathered at points in the criminal justice system that are procedurally more distant from the crime committed are less valid and less useful measures of crime. However, these data can serve as measures of the number and social characteristics of those who are arrested, prosecuted, convicted, or imprisoned; of the characteristics, administration, and procedures of criminal justice within and between component agencies; and of the socially produced and recognized amount and distribution of crime. Official statistics, except for data on crimes known to the police, are more correctly regarded as measures of crime control because they record a social-control *reaction* of the criminal justice system to a known offense or an offender. For example, a crime known to the police is typically reported to the police by a complainant, and the record of it is evidence of the *detection* of a crime. If the police clear the offense through arrest, the arrest record is evidence of the *sanction* of a criminal, a measure of crime control (Black). In other words, a crime known to the police registers acknowledgment of an offense; an arrest, of an offender. Arrest, prosecution, conviction, and disposition statistics, as well as administrative bookkeeping and accounting data, are best thought of as information on the characteristics, procedures, and processes of crime control. The focus in this article will be the official statistics of crime, specifically police statistics on offenses known.

A measure of crime: offenses known to the police. From the beginning, the primary objective of the Uniform Crime Reports was made clear in 1929 by the Committee on Uniform Crime Records of the International Association of Chiefs of Police—to show the number and nature of criminal offenses committed. At the time it was argued that among the variety of official data, not only were "offenses known" closest to the crime itself, but a more constant relationship existed between offenses committed and offenses known to the police than between offenses committed and other official data—assumptions shown to be erroneous by victimization surveys some fifty years later. Nevertheless, the UCR have always been the most widely consulted source of statistics on crime in the United States.

The UCR are published annually by the FBI, and they provide statistics on the amount and distribution of crimes known to the police and arrests, with other, less complete data on clearances by arrest, average value stolen in a variety of property offenses, dispositions of offenders charged, number of law enforcement personnel, and officers assaulted or killed. The statistics are based on data submitted monthly by some fifteen thousand municipal, county, and state law enforcement agencies, which have jurisdiction over approximately 98 percent of the United States population.

For crimes known and arrests, data are collected on twenty-nine categories of offenses, using standard-ized classifications of offenses and reporting procedures. Crimes known and arrests are presented for the eight "index crimes"—murder, rape, robbery, aggravated assault, burglary, larceny, motor-vehicle theft, and arson—and arrests only, for the remaining (nonindex) crimes. (Arson was designated as an index crime in 1978, with the first data on arson collected by the UCR program in 1979. However, the most recent available statistics for 1981 are still based on incomplete reporting data for arson. The arrest data on arson are complete beginning in 1979, and are included in arrest statistics for arson and the Total Crime Index and property index.) For each index crime, crimes known to the police are presented by number of crimes reported, rate per hundred thousand population, clearances, nature of offense, geographical distribution (by state, region, size, and degree of urbanization), and number of offenders arrested. Arrests are presented by total estimate for each index and nonindex crime, rate per hundred thousand population, age, sex, race, and decade trend.

The index crimes are intended to represent serious and high-volume offenses. The Total Crime Index is the sum of index crimes, and subtotals are provided on violent (the first four) and property (the last four) index crimes. The Total Crime Index, and to a lesser extent the violent- and property-crime indexes, are often used to report national trends in the extent and nature of crime.

The statistics presented in the UCR of crimes known to the police are records of "reported" crime, and since reporting and recording procedures and practices are major sources of methodological and utilization problems, they deserve further attention. Crimes known to the police are typically offenses reported to the police by a victim or other person and are recorded as such unless they are "unfounded," or false. For property crimes, one incident is counted as one crime, whereas for violent crimes one victim is counted as one crime. Except for arson, the most serious of more than one index crime committed during an incident is counted; arson is recorded even when other index crimes are committed during the same incident. For example, stealing three items from a store counts as one larceny, but beating up three people during an altercation counts as three assaults.

Larceny and motor-vehicle theft account for the largest proportion of index crimes, for reasons pointed to by critics. Both are the least serious of the index crimes, with larceny of any amount now eligible to be counted and motor-vehicle theft having one of the highest rates of victim reports to the police because theft must be established to file for insurance claims. On the other hand, many crimes that could be considered more serious because they involve physical injury and bodily harm to a victim are not index crimes. Moreover, completed and attempted crimes are counted equally for more than half of the index crimes. Robbery is counted as a violent crime and accounts for almost one-half of all reported violent index crimes. Most other countries classify robbery as a major larceny, as did the United States before the inception of the UCR. Of course, this difference in classification explains in part the relatively higher rate of violence in the United States. A number of other serious offenses are not counted at all in the reporting program, including a variety of victimless, white-collar, and organizational crimes, as well as political corruption, violations of economic regulations, and the whole array of federal crimes. One might characterize the Total Crime Index as a measure of the extent, nature, and trends of relatively ordinary street crime in the United States.

There are also some problems in the presentation of these data. The Total Crime Index, as a simple sum of index offenses, cannot be sensitive to the differential seriousness of its constituent offense categories and to the relative contributions made by frequency and seriousness of offenses to any index of a community's crime problem (Sellin and Wolfgang). Rudimentary summations of data also mask potentially important variations among offenses and other factors. Comparisons of data from year to year, and even from table to table for the same year, may be hampered in some cases because data may be analyzed in various ways (for example, by aggregating data in different ways for different tables). Comparisons are also made difficult by the use of inappropriate bases (or denominators) in the computation of the *rates* that are presented both for crimes known to the police and for arrests.

The crime rates given in the UCR, as well as in most criminal justice statistical series, are computed as the number of crimes per year per hundred thousand population. This type of "crude" rate can lead to inappropriate inferences from the data. The use of crude rates can conceal variation in subgroups of the population, so it is desirable to standardize rates for subgroups whose experience is known to be different, for example, by sex, race, and age. These subgroup-specific rates also facilitate comparisons between groups—male-female rates, white-black rates, and juvenile-adult rates.

At times, inappropriate population bases are used in calculating rates. A crime rate represents the ratio of the number of crimes committed to the number of persons available and able to commit those crimes; this ratio is then standardized by one hundred thousand of whoever is included in the base. For some offenses, the total population is an inappropriate base. For example, a forcible-rape crime rate based on the total population is less appropriate than a rate based on the number of males available and able to commit rape. Similarly, the juvenile crime rate should reflect the number of crimes committed by the population of juveniles.

Crime rates can be interpreted as victimization rates, depending on who (or what) is included in the base. If the total population base can be considered potential criminals, they can also be considered potential victims. For crimes where the victim is a person, the calculation of surrogate victimization rates using crime data is relatively straightforward—the number of available victims becomes the base. Again, in the case of forcible rape, the total population and the male population would be inappropriate bases—here the population of available victims is essentially female. Therefore, the surrogate victimization rate would be calculated as the number of forcible rapes known to the police per hundred thousand female population.

For property crimes it is more difficult, but not impossible, to calculate surrogate victimization rates. Here the denominator may have to be reconceptualized not as a population base but as a property base. For example, Sarah Boggs, and later Lawrence Cohen and Marcus Felson, included "opportunities" for property theft in the bases of their analyses, including, for example, the number of cars available to steal. They reported that the subsequent opportunity-standardized rates were very different from the traditional population-standardized crime (or victimization) rates. Opportunity-standardized rates may sometimes differ even in direction. For example, rather than showing the rate of motor-vehicle-related theft increasing, a corrected rate showed it to be decreasing (Wilkins; Sparks). Ultimately, of course, much more precise victimization rates are available from victimization survey data.

Finally, the total population base may be used incorrectly if the decennial Bureau of the Census counts of the population are not adjusted for projected population estimates on a yearly basis. For example, if the 1970 census data are used in the base to calculate 1979 crime rates, the rates will be artificially inflated simply as a consequence of using too small a population base. Obviously, 1979 population estimates are more appropriate in the calculation of 1979 crime rates.

Overall, the data presented in the UCR are "representative." However, the greatest threat to the validity of these statistics is differential reporting—to the FBI by local police, within participating departments, and to local authorities by citizen victims or other complainants. There is underreporting both *by* and *to* the police.

The reports of participating law enforcement agencies to the FBI can be affected in a variety of ways, leading to variations in the uniformity, accuracy, and completeness of reporting. In spite of efforts to standardize definitions of eligible offenses, police in different states with different statutory and operational definitions of offense categories may classify crimes differently. There may be internal and external pressures on police agencies to demonstrate reductions in community crime or specific targeted offenses, and these pressures may induce police to alter classification, recording, and reporting procedures. Such changes can have a dramatic impact on the amount and rate of crime. A classic example was the reorganization of the Chicago police department. As part of the reorganization, more efficient reporting and recording procedures were introduced, and reported crime increased dramatically from 57,000 offenses in 1959 to 130,000 in 1960 (Rae).

To make the problems with the UCR even more complicated, the reported statistics can vary across time and place as policies change, police technology becomes more sophisticated, laws and statutes are modified, commitment to the program waivers, demands for information change, available resources fluctuate, and so on (Hindelang). Unfortunately, even if all the difficulties of validity, reliability, and comparability were eliminated and the statistics became completely and uniformly accurate, there would remain the more serious problem of differential reporting *to* the police by victims and other citizens. There is evidence of substantial underreporting and nonreporting to the police by victims of crime; in fact, the majority of crimes committed are *not* reported to the police.

The assumption of the originators of the UCR that there is a constant ratio between crimes known to the police and crimes committed has been shown to be fallacious by studies using unofficial crime statistics. One may never know the *actual* volume of crimes committed, and therefore the true base remains indeterminate. But more importantly, underreporting or nonreporting to the police varies by offense type, victim and offender characteristics, perceptions of police

efficiency, and the like. In short, the dark figure of undetected and unreported crime limits the adequacy of even the historically preferred crimes-known-to-the-police index of the amount and distribution of crime.

Unofficial crime statistics

Even though most of the fundamental problems with official crime statistics had been identified before the end of the nineteenth century, including the major problem of the dark figure of unknown crime, it was not until the mid-twentieth century that systematic attempts to unravel some of the mysteries of official statistics were initiated. Turning to data sources outside of the official agencies of criminal justice, unofficial crime statistics were generated in order to explore the dark figure of crime that did not become known to the police, to create measures of crime that were independent of the official registrars of crime and crime control, and to address more general validity and reliability issues in the measurement of crime.

There are two categories of unofficial data sources: social-science and private-agency records. The first of these is much more important and useful. Among the social-science sources, there are two major, significant measures, both utilizing survey methods. The first is *self-reports* of criminal involvement, which were initially used in the 1940s to "expose" the amount of hidden crime. The second is surveys of *victimization,* the most recent and probably the most important and influential of the unofficial crime statistics. Victimization surveys were initiated in the mid-1960s to "illuminate"—that is, to specify rather than simply to expose—the dark figure and to depict crime from the victim's perspective. There are also two minor, much less significant sources of social-science data: observation studies of crime or criminal justice, and experiments on deviant behavior. Among the sources of private-agency records are those compiled by firms or industries to monitor property losses, injuries, or claims; by private security organizations; and by national trade associations. The focus here will be on the social-science sources of unofficial crime statistics, particularly victimization and self-report surveys.

Victimization surveys. Recognizing the inadequacies of official measures of crime, particularly the apparently substantial volume of crime and victimization that remains unknown to, and therefore unacted upon by, criminal justice authorities, the President's Commission on Law Enforcement and Administration of Justice initiated relatively small-scale pilot victimization surveys in 1966. One was conducted in Washington, D.C. A sample of police precincts with medium and high crime rates was selected, within which interviews were conducted with residents. Respondents were asked whether in the past year they had been a victim of any of the index crimes and of assorted nonindex crimes. Another surveyed business establishments in the same precincts in Washington, D.C., as well as businesses and residents in a sample of high-crime-rate precincts in Boston and Chicago. The instruments and procedures used in the first pilot survey were modified and used to interview residents in the second study. Owners and managers of businesses were asked whether their organization had been victimized by burglary, robbery, or shoplifting during the past year. The third pilot survey was a national poll of a representative sample of 10,000 households. Again, respondents were interviewed and asked whether they or anyone living with them had been a victim of index and nonindex crimes during the past year. They were also asked their opinions regarding the police and the perceived personal risk of being victimized.

These pilot studies verified empirically what criminologists had known intuitively since the early nineteenth century—that official crime statistics, even of crimes known to the police, underestimate the actual amount of crime. However, these victimization studies showed that the dark figure of hidden crime was substantially larger than expected. In the Washington, D.C., study, the ratio of reported total victim incidents to crimes known to the police in respondents' precincts was more than twenty to one (Biderman). This dramatic ratio of hidden victimizations to reported crimes was replicated among the individual victims in the Boston and Chicago study (Reiss) and in the national pilot survey, which showed that about half of the victimizations were not reported to the police (Ennis). The survey of business establishments discovered the inadequacy of business records as measures of crime, showed higher rates of victimization than police records indicated, and verified the valid reporting of business victimization by respondents (Reiss). These studies also demonstrated that the discrepancy between the number of victimizations and of crimes reported to the police varies importantly by the type of offense and by the victim's belief that reporting a crime will have consequences. In general, the more serious the crime, the more likely a victim is to report it to the police; minor property crimes are reported least frequently. As a result of the startling findings of these pilot victimization surveys and of the subsequent recommendations of the President's Commission, an annual national victimization survey

was initiated in the National Crime Survey (NCS).

In 1972 the United States became one of the few countries to carry out annual national victimization surveys. The NCS is sponsored by the Bureau of Justice Statistics (within the United States Department of Justice) and is conducted by the Bureau of the Census. Its primary purpose is to "measure the annual change in crime incidents for a limited set of major crimes and to characterize some of the socioeconomic aspects of both the reported events and their victims" (Penick and Owens, p. 220). In short, the survey is designed to measure the amount, distribution, and trends of victimization and, therefore, of crime.

The survey covers a representative national sample of approximately sixty thousand households, and through 1976 it included a probability sample of some fifteen thousand business establishments. Within each household, all occupants fourteen years of age or older are interviewed, and information on twelve- and thirteen-year-old occupants is gathered from an older occupant. Interviews are conducted every six months for three years, after which a different household is interviewed, in a constant process of sample entry and replacement.

The crimes measured in the NCS are personal crimes (rape, robbery, assault, and theft), household crimes (burglary, larceny, and motor-vehicle theft), and business crimes (burglary and robbery). These crimes were selected intentionally for their similarity to the index crimes of the UCR in order to permit important comparisons between the two data sets. The only two index crimes missing are murder, for which no victim can report victimization, and arson, the ostensible victim of which is often the perpetrator.

The questionnaire used in the interviews consists of two parts, screening questions and crime incident reports. The screening questions ascertain basic household information and the sociodemographic characteristics of the occupants. They also make inquiries about crime that are designed to determine whether a respondent has been a victim of one of the survey crimes during the preceding six months. For each crime incident discovered during the screening, a crime incident report is administered. The report contains almost one hundred questions on the number of victimizations, time and place of occurrence, relationship between the victim and perpetrator, extent of physical injury or monetary loss, perception of the offender's sociodemographic characteristics, and whether and why the crime was or was not reported to the police.

The statistics on victimization generated by the NCS

provide an extremely important additional perspective on crime in the United States. Ever since they were first published, the survey's reports have forced a revision in thinking about crime. For example, a report on victimization in eight American cities, using data from 1972 and 1975, provided striking confirmation of the magnitude of the underreporting and nonreporting problem identified in the pilot projects. Comparing the rates of victimization and crimes known to the police, the victimization data showed fifteen times as much assault, nine times more robbery, seven times the amount of rape, and, surprisingly, five times more motor-vehicle theft than reported in the UCR for the same period (U.S. Department of Justice).

Some of the discrepancy in the two rates can be accounted for by the practices of the police—not viewing a reported offense as a crime, failing to react, and not counting and recording it. But since the time of the pilot research it has been clear that the major reason for the discrepancy is the reporting practices of victims: the pilot national survey reported that approximately 50 percent of victimizations are not reported to the police (Ennis). An analysis of preliminary data from the first NCS in 1973 concluded that nonreporting by victims accounted for much more of the difference between victimization and official crime rates than did nonrecording by the police. Almost three-fourths (72 percent) of the crime incidents were not reported to the police, ranging from a nonreporting rate of 32 percent for motor-vehicle theft to a rate of 82 percent for larceny (Skogan).

The primary reasons for citizen hesitancy to report a crime to the police are relatively clear—the victim does not believe that reporting will make any difference (35 percent) or that the crime is serious enough to bring to the attention of authorities (31 percent) (U.S. Bureau of the Census). The less serious crimes, particularly minor property crimes, are less often reported to the police, and the more serious ones are reported more often. Paradoxically, some of the more serious personal crimes, including aggravated assault and rape, are not reported because a personal relationship between victim and perpetrator is being protected or is the source of potential retribution and further harm (Hindelang, Gottfredson, and Garofalo). Another crime, arson, presents the problems of potential overreporting and of distinguishing between victim and perpetrator, since collecting insurance money is often the motive in burning one's own property.

The NCS does not merely provide another national index of crime, a view of crime from the perspective of the victim, and illumination of the dark figure of hidden crime. It has also contributed to a better understanding of crime in the United States, forcing scholars and criminal justice professionals alike to question many basic assumptions about crime. Perhaps most perplexing are the implications of the victimization trend data. Since 1973, the overall victimization rate has remained relatively stable from year to year, whereas the UCR show a more inconsistent and upward trend. There are a number of possible interpretations for this difference, centering around the relative strengths and weaknesses of official records of crimes known to the police, as compared to unofficial victim reports.

In general, victimization surveys have the same problems and threats to validity and reliability as any other social-science survey, as well as some that are specific to the NCS. Ironically, there is a "double dark figure" of hidden crime—crime that is not reported to interviewers in victimization surveys designed to uncover crimes not reported to the police! Such incomplete reporting of victimization means that victimization surveys, like official data sources, also underestimate the true amount of crime. Of course, this suggests that the discrepancy between the crime rate estimates of the NCS and of the UCR is even larger than reports indicate.

A number of factors contribute to this doubly dark figure of unreported victimization. One of the most difficult problems in victimization surveys is to anchor the reported crime within the six-month response frame. A respondent not only has to remember the crime incident, but must also specify when it took place during the past six months. Memory may be faulty: the longer the period of time between crime and interview, the more likely is memory to fail a respondent, who either forgets an incident completely or does not remember some important details about his victimization. The less serious and more common offenses are less worth remembering because of their more trivial nature and ephemeral consequences. The concern and tolerance levels of victims may also affect their recollection of crime incidents. Moreover, telescoping may take place: the victimization may be moved forward or backward in time, from one period to another. A victim knows that a crime took place but cannot recall precisely when.

Another source of inaccurate and inconsistent responses is deceit. Some respondents may simply lie, or at least shade their answers. There are many reasons for deceit, including embarrassment, social desirability (wish to make a socially desirable response), interviewer-respondent mistrust, personal aggrandizement, attempts to protect the perpetrator, disinterest, and lack of motivation. Memory decay and telescoping are neither intentional nor manipulative, and are therefore more random in their effects on responses. They are likely to contribute to the underestimation of victimization. However, deceit is intentional and manipulative, and it is more likely to characterize the responses of those who have a reason to hide or reveal something. The effects on victimization estimates are more unpredictable because deceit may lead to underreporting among some respondents but to overreporting among others. One can assess the extent of underreporting through devices such as a "reverse record check," by means of which respondents who *have* reported crimes to the police are included in the survey sample (Turner; Hindelang, Hirschi, and Weis, 1981). Comparing a respondent's crime incidents reported in the victimization interview with those reported to the police provides a measure of underreporting. A problem, though, is that underreporting can be validated more easily than overreporting. One "underreports" crimes that actually took place. For every official crime known to the police of a particular offense category, one can be relatively certain of underreporting if no victimization is reported for that offense category. If more victimizations are reported for an offense category than are known to the police, one cannot know whether the respondent is overreporting. A person may "overreport" crimes that never took place—they cannot be known, verified, or validated.

One of the strengths of the NCS, namely, that the crimes included in the questionnaire are FBI index crimes, is also a problem. In addition to the fact that two of the index crimes (murder and arson) are not included, many other important crimes are not measured in the victimization surveys. Obviously, the whole array of crimes *without* victims are excluded, as well as the nonindex crimes and crimes not included in the UCR program. The result is that the victimization statistics are somewhat limited in their representativeness and generalizability.

An important limitation of the design of the NCS is a strength of the UCR—its almost complete coverage (98 percent) of the total United States population and the resultant ability to examine the geographic and ecological distribution of crime from the national level to the levels of regions, states, counties, Standard Metropolitan Statistical Areas, cities, and local communities. Data on victimization are collected from a sample of approximately 132,000 respondents, distributed geographically throughout the United States. There are simply not enough data to generate meaningful and useful statistics for each of the geographic and ecological units represented in the UCR. This would require a comprehensive census of households, the cost of which would be prohibitive.

Another design problem is referred to as bounding, or the time frame used as the reference period in interviews, which is established at the first interview on a six-month cycle for "household location." This is done to fix the empirically determined optimum recall period of six months and to avoid double reporting of the same crime incident by respondents. The bounding of household locations rather than of the occupants of the household has also been a problem. If the occupants move, the new occupants are not bounded, and it has been estimated that about 13 percent of the sample in 1974–1975 consisted of unbounded households. This factor, coupled with the mobility of the sample, creates a related problem: complete data records covering the three-year span of each panel are available for perhaps only 20 percent of the respondents. This restricts general data analysis possibilities, particularly the feasibility and utility of these data for longitudinal analyses of victimization experiences (Fienberg).

Finally, there are the inevitable counting problems. When there is more than one perpetrator involved in a crime, it is particularly difficult for respondents to report the number of victimizers with accuracy. The typical impersonality of a household burglary makes it impossible for a victim to know the number or characteristics of the burglars. Even as personal a crime as aggravated assault often presents the victim with problems in accurately recalling his perceptions when more than one person attempted or did physical injury to his body. The respondent's reports, then, may be less accurate when the perpetrator could not be seen or when there was more than one observable perpetrator. If a respondent reports multiple victimizers in a crime incident, whether a property crime or violent crime, it counts as one victimization event—the general counting rule is "one victim, one crime." By itself this is not necessarily problematic, but if one compares victimization rates and official crime rates for property offenses (for which the UCR counting rule is "one incident, one crime"), there may be sufficient noncomparability of units to jeopardize the validity of the comparison. For example, a three-victim larceny would yield three reports of victimization but only one crime known to the police. A three-victim assault would yield three of each and present fewer problems of comparability. The perspectives of the victim and the police are different, as are those of the NCS and the UCR in counting and recording crime incidents with different statistical outcomes and interpretations.

A more serious counting problem involves series victimizations or rapid, repeated similar victimization of an individual. For a victim, it can be very difficult to separate one crime from another if they are very similar and happen within a compressed time period. The consequence is that validity suffers and there is a tendency to "blur" the incidents and to further underestimate the number of victimizations. The questionnaire separates single and series incidents, which are defined as three or more similar crimes that the respondent cannot differentiate in time or place of occurrence. Early publications of the NCS excluded these series victimizations from the published victimization rates, raising the possibility that the rates are underestimations. For the first (1973) survey, 5 percent of the reported victimizations for crimes against the person were series victimizations, with the respondents suffering an average of five victimizations per series. Thus, the extent of underestimation may be as high as 20 percent for crimes against the person and perhaps 33 percent for violent crimes (Fienberg). Even more of the dark figure of hidden crime might be illuminated. If this and other problems with victimization surveys are resolved, the discrepancy between the amount of crime committed and the amount eventually reported to the police may become more substantial. There is little evidence that victims (except those of forcible rape) are changing their patterns of reporting crimes to the police, but there is mounting and more rigorous evidence that our ability to measure the amount and distribution of the dark figure of unreported crime is improving.

Self-report surveys. Surveys of self-reported criminal involvement are an important part of the improved capacity to illuminate the dark figure, in this case from the perspective of the criminal (or victimizer). The origin of self-report surveys predated victimization surveys by more than twenty years. Preliminary, groundbreaking research on self-reported hidden crime was conducted in the 1940s, but the method of simply asking someone about the nature and extent of his own criminal involvement did not become a recognized standard procedure until the late 1950s, with the work of James Short and Ivan Nye.

This variation of the survey research method of "self-disclosure" by a respondent was first used by Austin Porterfield in 1946, to compare the self-reports of college students regarding their delinquent activities while they were in high school with self-reports of delinquents processed through the juvenile court. Not only were more offenses admitted than detected,

but more significantly, it appeared that the college students had been involved in delinquency during their adolescence in ways similar to those of the officially defined delinquents. These findings suggested that the distinction between delinquent and nondelinquent was not dichotomous, but rather more continuous, and that crime was perhaps distributed more evenly in the American social structure than official statistics would suggest. Fred Murphy, Mary Shirley, and Helen Witmer reported in 1946 that the admissions of delinquent activities by boys who participated in a delinquency prevention experiment significantly surpassed the number of offenses that came to the attention of juvenile authorities. A study that remains unique in self-report research because it surveyed a sample of adults was conducted by James Wallerstein and Clement Wyle in 1947. They discovered that more than 90 percent of their sample of about fifteen hundred upper-income "law-abiding" adults admitted having committed at least one of forty-nine crimes included in the questionnaire.

These early self-report survey findings confirmed empirically what criminal statisticians, law enforcement authorities, and even the public had known since the time of Quételet—that a substantial volume of crime never comes to the attention of the criminal justice system. The hint that some of this invisible crime is committed by persons who are not usually considered candidates for official recognition as criminals was even more revelatory and intriguing, but it remained dormant for a decade.

Heeding suggestions that criminology needed a "Kinsey Report" on juvenile delinquency, Short and Nye in 1957 developed an anonymous, self-administered questionnaire that contained a checklist of delinquent acts, which was administered to populations of students and incarcerated delinquents. Their research had a more profound and longer-lasting impact because it was tied to theory-testing and construction (Nye) and, more importantly, because it provocatively verified the hint only alluded to in the earlier self-report studies—that crime is not disproportionately a phenomenon of the poor, as suggested by official crime statistics. The self-report data were apparently discrepant with the official data because they showed that self-reported delinquency was more evenly distributed across the socioeconomic status scale than official delinquency. This one provocative finding called into question the correlates and theories of juvenile delinquency and crime because most were based on official crime statistics and their depiction of crime and delinquency as a phenomenon of the poor. The controversy set off by the work of Short and Nye still continues (Hindelang, Hirschi, and Weis, 1981).

Literally hundreds of similar studies have been carried out since Short and Nye's pioneering work, most with similar results: there is an enormous amount of self-reported crime that never comes to the attention of the police; a minority of offenders commits a majority of the offenses, including the more serious crimes; the more frequently one commits crimes, the more likely is the commission of serious crimes; and those most frequently and seriously involved in crime are most likely to have official records. Self-report researchers have tended to assume that self-reports are valid and reliable—certainly more so than official measures. Ever since the mid-1960s, work critical of criminal justice agencies and of official crime statistics generated further support for these assumptions. A few theorists, such as Travis Hirschi, even constructed and tested delinquency theories based on self-report measures and their results.

It has been suggested that "confessional data are at least as weak as the official statistics they were supposed to improve upon" (Nettler, p. 107). This criticism is damning to the extent that the statistics produced by the self-report method and official statistics are valid and reliable measures of crime: if one rejects official statistics, then one should also question the adequacy of self-report statistics. Furthermore, as with official records and victimization surveys, there are a number of problems with the self-report method. Some of these are problems shared by victimization surveys and self-report surveys, and others are unique to the latter. The shared problems are the basic threats to the validity and reliability of responses to survey questions, including memory decay, telescoping, deceit, social-desirability response effects, and imprecise bounding of reference periods. The unique problems fall into four categories: inadequate or unrepresentative samples, unrepresentative domains of behavior measured, validity and reliability of the method, and methods effects.

Whereas the national victimization surveys cannot provide refined geographical and ecological data because of the dispersion of the probability samples across the United States, self-report surveys have other problems of representativeness and generalizability because they do *not* typically use national samples. Practically all self-report research is conducted with small samples of juveniles attending public schools in a community that, characteristically, is relatively small, often suburban or rural, and modally middle-class and white. This, of course, restricts the ability to generalize beyond these kinds of sample characteristics to adults, juveniles who are not in school, those

who refuse to participate, urban inner-city juveniles, and poor and nonwhite youngsters. Such "convenience" samples also create analytic problems because data on those variables that are correlated with delinquency are simply unavailable or underrepresented in the sample. In short, most self-report research has somewhat limited generalizability because of typical sample characteristics. On the other hand, unlike the NCS or UCR, self-report surveys were not intended originally to produce national or even generalizable estimates of the amount of juvenile delinquency (or crime) in the United States.

They were intended, however, to produce data on a variety of delinquent behaviors. Compared to the restricted range of index crimes included in the NCS, the domain of behavior measured in self-report surveys is expansive, with as many as fifty illegal acts in a questionnaire not being uncommon. Such expansiveness, however, creates other problems. Historically, the juvenile court has had jurisdiction over both crimes and offenses that are illegal only for juveniles, usually referred to as status offenses and including truancy, incorrigibility, curfew violation, smoking, and drinking. Self-report surveys have correctly covered crimes and status offenses alike in studying juvenile delinquency, but in some cases there has been an overemphasis on the less serious offenses. To the extent that there is an overrepresentation of less serious and perhaps trivial offenses, self-report measures are inadequate measures of the kind of serious juvenile crime that is likely to come to the attention of authorities. This is important in describing accurately the characteristics of juvenile offenders and their behavior, as well as in comparing self-report and official data. Such comparison is crucial to validation research, where one needs to compare the same categories of behavior, including both content and seriousness, in order to assess the reciprocal validity of self-report and official measures. In criminology as elsewhere, one should not compare apples with oranges!

Unfortunately, there has been a dearth of this kind of careful validation research, as well as of systematic research on reliability. The accuracy and consistency of self-report surveys have been assumed to be quite acceptable, or, if questions have been posed, they have typically come from validity and reliability research on general social-science survey methods. For example, it has been assumed that anonymous surveys are more valid than signed surveys and that interviews are preferred over self-administered questionnaires. Yet no study had directly compared the validity, and only one had compared the reliability, of two or more self-report methods within the same study (Kulik, Stein, and Sarbin) until the work of Michael Hindelang, Travis Hirschi, and Joseph Weis in 1981. In those isolated studies where validity and reliability were addressed, external validation criteria such as official record data have been used too infrequently.

Of course, critics have remained skeptical about the accuracy of responses from liars, cheaters, and thieves, as well as from straight and honorable persons. The latter are not motivated by deception or guile, but they may respond incorrectly because a questionnaire item has poor face validity, meaning that it does not make sufficiently clear what is being asked and that the respondent is consequently more free to interpret, construe, and attribute whatever is within his experience and imagination. For example, a common self-report item, "Have you ever taken anything from anyone under threat of force?" is intended to tap instances of robbery. However, respondents might answer affirmatively if they had ever appropriated a candy bar from their kid sister. This problem of item meaning and interpretation is chronic in survey research, but it only remains problematic if no validation research is undertaken to establish face validity. Unfortunately, this has been the case in the development of self-report instruments.

There has been a basic inattention to the psychometric properties of self-report surveys and attendant methods effects on measurement. From the psychometric research that went into the development of the NCS, it is more clear that the bounding practices in self-report research have been inadequate: the reference periods are typically too long and variable from study to study. Most self-report surveys ask whether a respondent has "ever" committed a crime, a few use the past "three years," some use the past "year," but very few use the past "six months" (or less), which was established as the optimum recall period for the national victimization surveys. This poses threats to the accuracy of responses since it is established that the longer the reference period, the more problems with memory decay, telescoping, and misinterpretation of events.

A related problem arises when the self-report researcher wants to find out how often within a specified period a respondent has committed a crime. A favored means of measuring the frequency of involvement has been the "normative" response category. A respondent is asked, "How often in the past year have you hit a teacher?" and is given a set of response categories that includes "Very often," "Often," "Sometimes," "Rarely," and "Never." One respondent can check "Rarely" and mean five times, whereas another

can check the same response and mean one time. They each respond according to personal norms, which are tied to their own behavior, as well as to that of their peers. This creates analytic problems because one cannot norm (that is, accurately compare) the answers of each respondent, obviating meaningful comparisons. A great deal of information is thus lost. These problems can be solved simply by asking each respondent to record the actual frequency of commission for each offense.

Finally, unlike the NCS and the UCR, there is very little about self-report surveys, whether their samples, instruments, or procedures, that is "standardized." This restricts the kinds of comparisons across self-report studies that could lead to more improvements in the method and provide a more solid empirical foundation for theory construction and testing, as well as the possibility of nationwide self-report statistics comparable to those of the NCS and the UCR.

This lack of standardization, inadequacies of samples, and the question of the differential validity and reliability of self-report and official measures of crime have led to two important developments in the research on crime statistics. The first is the initiation of surveys of national representative samples of juveniles for the purpose of estimating the extent and nature of delinquency and of substance abuse in the United States. The second is the conducting of more rigorous and comprehensive research on the differential validity and reliability of official, as compared to self-report, measures of crime and delinquency. In 1967, the National Institute of Mental Health initiated the first of an interrupted but relatively regular series of National Youth Surveys of a representative sample of teenage youths, who were interviewed about a variety of attitudes and behaviors, including delinquent behavior. This survey was repeated in 1972, and in 1976 the National Institute for Juvenile Justice and Delinquency Prevention became a co-sponsor of what has become an annual self-report survey of the delinquent behavior of a national probability panel of youths aged from eleven to seventeen years in 1976. The two major goals are to measure the amount and distribution of self-reported delinquent behavior and official delinquency and to account for any observed changes in juvenile delinquency.

In 1975, the National Institute on Drug Abuse began an annual self-report survey of drug use among high-school seniors, Student Drug Use in America. Again using a national representative sample of youths, the survey attempts to estimate the yearly prevalence of drug use and trends, as well as to provide data on a variety of attitudes, values, and experiences related to drug use. The National Institute on Drug Abuse also conducts what is perhaps the only relatively regular national survey of illegal behavior among adults in the United States, the National Survey on Drug Abuse. Beginning in 1971 and continuing on an almost biennial basis, a national sample of persons twelve years of age and older has completed questionnaires on drug abuse. The survey focuses on the extent and correlates of drug use among adults, young adults, and juveniles, as well as on trends from survey to survey.

These periodic national self-report surveys allow more rigorous estimation of the nature and extent of delinquent behavior. It is ironic, however, that the validity, reliability, and viability of the self-report method as an alternative *or* adjunct to official measures was not assessed rigorously until Hindelang, Hirschi, and Weis began a study of measurement issues in delinquency research, focusing on the comparative utility of self-report and official data (1979, 1981). This two-phase study, begun in 1976, included comprehensive literature reviews and secondary data analyses, as well as primary data collection.

Within an experimental design, a comprehensive self-report instrument was administered to a random sample of 1,600 youths from fourteen to eighteen years of age, stratified by sex, race (white or black), socioeconomic status (high or low), and delinquency status (nondelinquent, police contact, or court record). Officially defined delinquents, boys, blacks, and lower-socioeconomic-status subjects were oversampled in order to facilitate data analysis within those groups that are often underrepresented in self-report studies. Subjects were randomly assigned to one of four test conditions that corresponded to four self-report methods of administration: anonymous questionnaire, signed questionnaire, face-to-face interview, and blind interview. A number of validation criteria were utilized, including the official records of those subjects identified in a reverse record check, a subset of questions administered by the randomized response method, a deep-probe interview for face-validity testing a subset of delinquency items, and a follow-up interview with a psychological-stress evaluator to determine the veracity of responses. The subjects were brought to a field office, where they answered the questions within the method condition to which they were randomly assigned (Hindelang, Hirschi, and Weis, 1981). This experimental design, coupled with a variety of external validation criteria and reliability checks, ensures that the findings and conclusions can be drawn with some confidence—undoubtedly with more confidence than in any prior

research on validity and reliability in the measurement of delinquency.

Hindelang, Hirschi, and Weis's study produced a variety of findings on the whole range of previously identified methodological problems and issues. Official crime statistics, it concluded, generate valid indications of the sociodemographic distribution of delinquency. Self-reports, indeed, measure a domain of delinquent behavior that does not overlap significantly with the domain covered by official data, particularly for the more serious crimes. However, self-reports can measure the same type and seriousness of delinquent behaviors as are represented in official records. Within the domain of delinquent behavior that they do measure, self-reports are very reliable, and basically valid. Self-report samples have been inadequate in that they do not include enough officially defined delinquents, nonwhites, and lower-class youths to enable confident conclusions to be drawn regarding the correlates of the more serious delinquent acts for which a juvenile is more likely to acquire an official record. Delinquency, whether measured by official or self-report data, is not equally distributed among all segments of society—there are real differences between those youngsters who engage in crime and those who do not. Methods of administration have no significant effects on the prevalence, incidence, validity, or reliability of self-reports. There is apparently less validity in the self-reports of those respondents with the highest rates of delinquency—male, black, officially defined delinquents. Perhaps the most significant finding of the research is related to this finding of differential validity for a small subpopulation of respondents. As originally proposed by Hindelang, Hirschi, and Weis in 1979, the empirical evidence shows that there is *no discrepancy* in the major correlates of self-reported *or* official delinquency, except for race, which may be attributable to the less valid reponses of black subjects, particularly males with official records of delinquency.

The finding that self-reports and official measures do not produce discrepant results regarding the distribution and correlates of delinquency, but rather show convergence, is a critical piece of evidence in the controversy that has existed among criminal statisticians since the dark figure was identified at the beginning of the nineteenth century. Does the distribution of crime look the same when those crimes *not* known to the police are included in the overall distribution *and* compared with the distribution of crimes known to the police? Are the different sources of crime statistics producing *discrepant* or *convergent* perspectives of crime?

Conclusion: discrepancy or convergence?

Returning to the two primary purposes of crime statistics, to measure the "amount" and "distribution" of crime, it is clear that there has been, and will probably continue to be, discrepancy among the estimates of the amount of crime that are generated by the variety of crime statistics. The dark figure of crime may never be completely illuminated, the reporting practices of victims will probably remain erratic, and the recording of crimes by authorities will continue to be less than uniform.

However, the ultimately more important purpose of crime statistics is the measurement of the distribution of crime by a variety of social, demographic, and geographic characteristics. Fortunately, the major sources of crime data—crimes known to the police, victimization surveys, and self-report surveys—generate similar distributions and correlates of crime, pointing to convergence rather than discrepancy among the measures of the basic characteristics of crime and criminals. The problems associated with each of the data sources remain, but they diminish in significance because these imperfect measures produce similar perspectives of crime. As Gwynn Nettler concluded, "Fortunately, despite the repeatedly discovered fact that more crime is committed than is recorded, when crimes are ranked by the frequency of their occurrence, the ordering is very much the same no matter which measure is used" (p. 97).

Comparisons of data from the UCR and the NCS program show that they produce similar patterns of crime (Hindelang; Maltz). There is substantial agreement between the two measures in the ordering of the relative frequencies of each of the index crimes. Comparisons of self-reports of delinquency with crimes known to the police show that each provides a complementary rather than a contradictory perspective on juvenile crime (Hindelang, Hirschi, and Weis, 1981; Belson). Self-reports do not generate results on the distribution and correlates of delinquency that are contrary to those generated by police statistics—or, for that matter, by victimization surveys. The youngsters who are more likely to appear in official police and court record data—boys, nonwhites, low achievers, youths with friends in trouble, urban residents, and youths with family problems—are also more likely to self-report higher rates of involvement in crime.

This message should be of some comfort to a variety of people interested in crime and delinquency, from researchers and theorists to policymakers, planners, program implementers, and evaluators. The basic facts of crime are more consistent than many scholars and authorities in the past would lead one to believe. In fact, the major sources of official and unofficial crime statistics are not typically inconsistent in their representations of the general features of crime, but rather provide a convergent perspective on crime. The characteristics, distribution, and correlates of crime—and, therefore, the implications for theory, policy, and programs—are not discrepant by crime measure, but convergent. The data generated by a variety of measures are compatible and confirming sources of information on crime. The study and control of crime can best be informed by these complementary sources of crime statistics.

JOSEPH G. WEIS

See also CRIMINOLOGY: RESEARCH METHODS; RESEARCH IN CRIMINAL JUSTICE.

BIBLIOGRAPHY

BELSON, WILLIAM A. *Juvenile Theft: The Causal Factors—A Report of an Investigation of the Tenability of Various Causal Hypotheses about the Development of Stealing by London Boys.* New York: Harper & Row, 1975.

BIDERMAN, ALBERT D. "Surveys of Population Samples for Estimating Crime Incidence." *Annals of the American Academy of Political and Social Science* 374 (1967): 16–33.

BLACK, DONALD J. "Production of Crime Rates." *American Sociological Review* 35 (1970): 733–748.

BOGGS, SARAH L. "Urban Crime Patterns." *American Sociological Review* 30 (1965): 899–908.

COHEN, LAWRENCE E., and FELSON, MARCUS. "Social Change and Crime Rate Trends: A Routine Activity Approach." *American Sociological Review* 44 (1979): 588–608.

DOLESCHAL, EUGENE. "Sources of Basic Criminal Justice Statistics: A Brief Annotated Guide with Commentaries." *Criminal Justice Abstracts* 11 (1979): 122–147.

ENNIS, PHILIP H. *Criminal Victimization in the United States: A Report of a National Survey.* University of Chicago, National Opinion Research Center, 1967.

Federal Bureau of Investigation. *Crime in the United States.* Uniform Crime Reports for the United States. Washington, D.C.: U.S. Department of Justice, FBI, annually.

FIENBERG, STEPHEN E. "Victimization and the National Crime Survey: Problems of Design and Analysis." *Indicators of Crime and Criminal Justice: Quantitative Studies.* Edited by Stephen E. Fienberg and Albert J. Reiss, Jr. Washington, D.C.: U.S. Department of Justice, Bureau of Justice Statistics, 1980, pp. 33–40.

FLANAGAN, TIMOTHY J.; VAN ALSTYNE, DAVID J.; and GOTTFREDSON, MICHAEL R., eds. *Sourcebook of Criminal Justice Statistics, 1981.* Washington, D.C.: U.S. Department of Justice, Bureau of Justice Statistics, 1982.

GUERRY, ANDRÉ MICHEL. *Essai sur la statistique morale de la France, précédé d'un Rapport à l'Académie des Sciences, par MM. Lacroix, Silvestre, et Girard.* Paris: Crochard, 1833.

HINDELANG, MICHAEL J. "The Uniform Crime Reports Revisited." *Journal of Criminal Justice* 2 (1974): 1–17.

————; GOTTFREDSON, MICHAEL R.; and GAROFALO, JAMES. *Victims of Personal Crime: An Empirical Foundation for a Theory of Personal Victimization*. Cambridge, Mass.: Ballinger, 1978.

HINDELANG, MICHAEL J.; HIRSCHI, TRAVIS; and WEIS, JOSEPH G. "Correlates of Delinquency: The Illusion of Discrepancy between Self-report and Official Measures." *American Sociological Review* 44 (1979): 995–1014.

————. *Measuring Delinquency*. Beverly Hills, Calif.: Sage, 1981.

HIRSCHI, TRAVIS. *Causes of Delinquency*. Berkeley: University of California Press, 1969.

KULIK, JAMES A.; STEIN, KENNETH B.; and SARBIN, THEODORE R. "Disclosure of Delinquent Behavior under Conditions of Anonymity and Nonanonymity." *Journal of Consulting and Clinical Psychology* 32 (1968): 506–509.

MALTZ, MICHAEL D. "Crime Statistics: A Mathematical Perspective." *Journal of Criminal Justice* 3 (1975): 177–193.

MURPHY, FRED J.; SHIRLEY, MARY M.; and WITMER, HELEN L. "The Incidence of Hidden Delinquency." *American Journal of Orthopsychiatry* 16 (1946): 686–696.

NETTLER, GWYNN. *Explaining Crime*. 2d ed. New York: McGraw-Hill, 1978.

NYE, F. IVAN. *Family Relationships and Delinquent Behavior*. New York: Wiley, 1958.

PENICK, BETTYE K. EIDSON, and OWENS, MAURICE E. B., III, eds. *Surveying Crime*. Washington, D.C.: National Academy of Sciences, National Research Council, Panel for the Evaluation of Crime Surveys, 1976.

PORTERFIELD, AUSTIN L. *Youth in Trouble: Studies in Delinquency and Despair, with Plans for Prevention*. Fort Worth, Tex.: Leo Potishman Foundation, 1946.

President's Commission on Law Enforcement and Administration of Justice. *The Challenge of Crime in a Free Society*. Washington, D.C.: The Commission, 1967.

QUÉTELET, ADOLPHE. *Recherches sur le penchant au crime aux différens âges*. 2d ed. Brussels: Hayez, 1833.

RAE, RICHARD F. "Crime Statistics, Science or Mythology." *Police Chief* 42 (1975): 72–73.

REISS, ALBERT J., JR. *Studies in Crime and Law Enforcement in Major Metropolitan Areas*. Field Surveys III, vol. 1. President's Commission on Law Enforcement and Administration of Justice. Washington, D.C.: The Commission, 1967.

ROBINSON, LOUIS N. *History and Organization of Criminal Statistics in the United States* (1911). Reprint. Montclair, N.J.: Patterson Smith, 1969.

SELLIN, THORSTEN. "The Basis of a Crime Index." *Journal of the American Institute of Criminal Law and Criminology* 22 (1931): 335–356.

————, and WOLFGANG, MARVIN E. *The Measurement of Delinquency*. New York: Wiley, 1964.

SHORT, JAMES F., JR., and NYE, F. IVAN. "Reported Behavior as a Criterion of Deviant Behavior." *Social Problems* 5 (1957–1958): 207–213.

SKOGAN, WESLEY G. "Dimensions of the Dark Figure of Unreported Crime." *Crime and Delinquency* 23 (1977): 41–50.

SPARKS, RICHARD F. "Criminal Opportunities and Crime Rates." *Indicators of Crime and Criminal Justice: Quantitative Studies*. Edited by Stephen E. Fienberg and Albert J. Reiss, Jr. Washington, D.C.: U.S. Department of Justice, Bureau of Justice Statistics, 1980, pp. 18–32.

TURNER, ANTHONY. *San Jose Methods Test of Known Crime Victims*. Washington, D.C.: U.S. Department of Justice, Law Enforcement Assistance Administration, National Institute of Law Enforcement and Criminal Justice, 1972.

U.S. Bureau of the Census. *Criminal Victimization Surveys in the Nation's Five Largest Cities: National Crime Panel Surveys of Chicago, Detroit, Los Angeles, New York, and Philadelphia*. Washington, D.C.: U.S. Department of Justice, Law Enforcement Assistance Administration, National Criminal Justice Information and Statistics Service, 1975.

U.S. Department of Justice, Law Enforcement Assistance Administration, National Criminal Justice Information and Statistics Service. *Criminal Victimization Surveys in Eight American Cities: A Comparison of 1971/1972 and 1974/1975 Findings*. Washington, D.C.: NCJISS, 1976.

U.S. National Commission on Law Observance and Enforcement [Wickersham Commission]. *Report on Criminal Statistics*. Washington, D.C.: The Commission, 1931.

VOLLMER, AUGUST. "The Bureau of Criminal Records." *Journal of the American Institute of Criminal Law and Criminology* 11 (1920): 171–180.

WALLERSTEIN, JAMES S., and WYLE, CLEMENT J. "Our Law-abiding Law-breakers." *Probation* 25 (1947): 107–112.

WILKINS, LESLIE T. *Social Deviance: Social Policy, Action, and Research*. Englewood Cliffs, N.J.: Prentice-Hall, 1965.

3.

HISTORICAL TRENDS IN WESTERN SOCIETY

The extent of crime in Western societies is an issue of grave concern to public officials and criminologists alike. Those who are projecting police budgets and building prisons need to know about the levels and kinds of crime that are likely to affect society in future years, just as those who think more broadly about the causes of crime need to know how it has bored through society in years past. Many publics seek information about the trends of criminality, and many groups develop such information. The problems inherent in determining the distribution of crime in society, as well as its historical trends, are substantial, and before a reasonable estimate of its extent in Western society can be provided, the difficulties in gathering such information must be considered.

Some problems of measurement

Since the incidence of crime is an unpredictable phenomenon, akin to a volcano, it can be measured in its natural habitat only after it has taken place. All measurement of crime is to some extent remote from its incidence, and subject to all the errors that indirect measurement entails. All attempts to measure crime, therefore, omit some cases, record some that are not criminal, and incorrectly classify others. Accordingly, all attempts to measure crime reflect not simply the underlying incidence of criminal behavior, but also biases inherent in the measurement process itself.

Three common sources of information about crime include data gathered and compiled by official crime control organizations (the police, the courts, and correctional agencies), data collected by individual researchers in contact with offenders (self-report studies), and victimization data collected by such survey organizations as the United States Census Bureau. Most of what is known about crime is derived from one or more of these three sources. Each assesses a distinct facet of crime and experiences distinctive problems. Crime data issued by the courts and police, however, have been the source of much information regarding criminality, especially before the modern era, and one must be aware of the biases that creep into such data.

Police departments in particular are subject to a variety of pressures beyond their control that distorts the picture of crime they present. Many police departments enjoy a reputation of excellent service in their communities and have the full confidence of their citizens. But some departments are seen by their communities as unresponsive or ineffective, and some citizens are less willing to report crime, particularly minor crime, to the police. This reluctance is especially sharp in minority, working-class, and lower-class neighborhoods, where a long history of poor police relations has left a legacy of little confidence in the police. Insofar as this reluctance to report minor crime is a factor, it results in a decrease in the criminal complaints brought to the police and increases the amount of unreported crime in the community.

Another difficulty that plagues those who would use police data about crime is the fact that certain departments are more effective in solving criminal cases than are others. Some of this difference reflects such qualities as leadership, morale, recruitment, or training, which are controllable by the departments, but some of it is inherent in the communities they serve.

Smaller cities, that is, those with a population of less than forty thousand, often display a degree of neighborliness and community identity that larger cities rarely exhibit. This sense of community, however, has a special significance for crime data reported by police agencies. When crimes are committed in small towns, the suspect is often known, and evidence and other information are made readily available to the police. In larger cities, the citizens are less involved with one another, are less likely to have knowledge of crimes, and, even if willing, are less able to offer evidence and information to the police.

This difference between small towns and larger cities probably accounts for the fact that police in small departments clear a higher percentage of certain minor crimes than do the police in major cities. In towns in the United States with populations of less than ten thousand, 29 percent of motor-vehicle thefts and 16.5 percent of burglaries were cleared in 1979. In that same year, in cities with a population of more than one million, only 8.2 percent of motor-vehicle thefts and 11.1 percent of burglaries were cleared (Federal Bureau of Investigation, 1980, pp. 179–180).

This differential effectiveness has important implications for the crime data these departments report. Crimes cleared by arrest serve as the basis for detailed descriptions of offenders, which in turn provide data for reports on such problems as juvenile delinquency. If auto thefts are not cleared by arrests, the police have no basis for knowing what portion was committed by juveniles. In 1979, 12.9 percent of motor-vehicle thefts and 14.5 percent of burglaries cleared in cities of one million population or more were committed by juveniles. In towns of ten thousand population or less, on the other hand, 29.4 percent of motor-vehicle thefts and 38.5 percent of burglaries were committed by juveniles (FBI, 1980, p. 184). Motor-vehicle thefts and burglaries were solved in small towns at rates more than twice those found in larger metropolitan centers, and accordingly, information on auto thieves and burglars derived from police arrest data in small towns is more precise than that in larger cities. The scope of delinquency in larger cities, therefore, is probably underestimated, and to compare the delinquency problem in larger cities and small towns without keeping this fact in mind is a serious mistake.

A similar problem plagues comparisons of criminality during different epochs in the history of a city. It is commonly acknowledged that there are several different styles of policing and that these distinctive styles often exhibit different levels of effectiveness. James Wilson has identified three common patterns among modern police departments: the watchman, the legalistic, and the service types. This typology, although criticized, has been widely used in police research.

The watchman department is one weak in leadership, lax in discipline, low in morale, and ineffective in both recruitment and training. It often has a poor reputation in the community and therefore receives relatively little help from citizens. It typically exhibits a poor clearance rate, particularly in property crimes.

The legalistic department, on the other hand, has aggressive leadership, tight discipline, good morale, careful recruit screening, and intensive training. The legalistic department usually enjoys a better reputation in the community, but its bureaucratic isolation inhibits close citizen cooperation. Other factors being equal, it is usually more effective than the watchman department in solving crimes. The service department, however, is close to its community, and even though it cannot compare with the legalistic department in most measures of professionalism, it regularly receives substantial citizen cooperation in cases involving both major and minor crimes, and it achieves the highest clearance rate of all—particularly for minor property crimes.

But as a community and its police department develop, their relationship changes, and the style of policing alters accordingly. Often the department becomes more formal and distant, that is, it evolves from a service to a legalistic or watchman pattern, and in so doing its overall effectiveness and its clearance rate may decline. It has already been seen that such changes can have a sharp effect on complaints known to the police and on estimates of delinquency.

To some extent, secular changes in the crime rates of a city over several decades reflect organizational changes of this sort. The long-term fluctuations in violent crime in Boston and Salem, cited below, probably reflect in part such changes, that is, shifts in the relationship between the police department and the community. Thus, the frequency of complaints brought to the police, as well as citizen cooperation and ultimately the clearance rate, vary over time. In using police data to estimate long-term criminal patterns, it is essential that long-term changes in police organization be considered.

Court data must also be used with an eye to the peculiarities of a changing court system. Different criminal courts, of course, have jurisdiction over different segments of the criminal spectrum. City courts cover minor crimes and violations of city ordinances; state courts handle crimes covered by the common law, and federal courts dispose of a heterogeneous

collection of serious crime and administrative crime. No single court can provide a comprehensive estimate of the crime in a community, because each has only limited jurisdiction. Two courts at different levels in the same system, however, may follow different policies in prosecuting crime, and their jurisdictions may not overlap exactly. The city courts may cover only the immediate urban area; the state court may cover the county; and the federal court may cover a specific district. It is not always feasible, therefore, to assemble an estimate of crime in the community from the activities of two or more related courts at different levels in the same system.

Pitfalls also await those who would compare the activities of a single court over time. For example, the same court may change its jurisdiction, with the result that the comparison may inappropriately relate a lower court with a higher court. The Boston Municipal Court was established in 1800, but in 1859 it became the Superior Court of Suffolk County. The Boston Police Court was founded in 1822, and in 1859 it became the Municipal Court of Boston! A comparison of the Municipal Court in 1850 with the Municipal Court in 1870 would be inappropriate, because it would compare a higher court with a lower one.

Despite these problems, the courts and the police are very useful sources of information regarding the incidence of and distribution of crime, and in historical periods they offer virtually the only systematic data available. It is well to become aware of their weaknesses.

Criminality in the premodern era

Since criminal justice agencies did not issue regular reports of their activity before the modern era, knowledge of premodern criminality is limited. It is based for the most part on studies of early court records, and requires careful efforts to collect and interpret useful data from handwritten documents.

Studies of medieval European towns generally report very high levels of violent personal crime but lower levels of property crime. A study of thirteenth-century England found homicide rates varying between 64 per 100,000 in Warwick and 4 per 100,000 in Bristol (Given, p. 36). Another study, of coroner's rolls in fourteenth-century London, revealed an annual homicide rate of about 44 per 100,000, or 100 times the modern rate of 0.4 per 100,000 (Hanawalt, p. 98). Few infanticide cases were reported in the latter study, and only about 2 percent involved intrafamily violence, which suggests that this estimate is actually conservative. Similarly, appraisals of violence in medieval England (Bellamy) and in Venice (Rug-giero), based on contemporary documents, report a heightened concern, even alarm, among citizens regarding the level of violence. There is near-unanimity among scholars that medieval communities from the Baltic to the Mediterranean were dangerous places. James Given, for example, estimates that "every person in England in the thirteenth century, if he did not personally witness a murder, knew, or knew of someone who had been killed" (p. 40).

By the end of the sixteenth century, crime was still a matter of concern in England: judges and others regularly lamented the rising tide of lawlessness, although one wonders what inspired their concern since neither authoritative crime statistics nor long-term studies of crime trends were available. Indeed, the best evidence indicates that violent crime had not increased significantly in England since the fourteenth century. In rural areas, crime was more typical of yeomen, that is, prosperous farmers, than of peasants, although the gentry regularly defied the courts and were rarely punished.

Justice was usually swift in Tudor England, but it was by no means sure (Baker). Those convicted of capital crimes and sentenced to die were, in the absence of a reprieve, marched out of the courtroom and promptly hanged. But there were many legal detours on the way to the gallows. Pardons, both special and general, were one way of cheating the hangman; insanity, pregnancy, and childhood were others. The most common loophole was benefit of clergy, which by the sixteenth century had been extended to all who could read, but this was limited to cases of minor theft.

With the growth of commercial civilization in seventeenth-century England, violent crime seems to have receded. A study of seventeenth-century Surrey and Sussex counties indicates that the annual homicide rate between 1663 and 1694 was about 5.7 per 100,000, but that by the years between 1722 and 1724 it had dropped to 2.3 per 100,000. Property crime, however, increased slightly, from 53 per 100,000 in the 1690s to 65 per 100,000 by the 1760s. As might be expected, property crimes were more common in urban areas during this period (Beattie).

Colonial New England experienced an even higher level of recorded criminality. The rate of violent crime in Boston in the early decades of the eighteenth century was about equal to that found for Surrey and Sussex, that is, 37 per 100,000 between 1703 and 1732; but property crime in Boston was roughly twice as common, the rate being 123 per 100,000 (Ferdinand, 1980a). This contrast is particularly striking in that puritan New England had a reputation among the American colonies for sober conventionality and little crime.

Overall, one can probably place some confidence in these early studies of criminality, particularly those of homicide, for it is likely that violent death was treated seriously and formally by the legal institutions. But medieval definitions of homicide embraced a broader range of violent deaths than is the case today. They included, for example, many forms of accidental death that would not have found their way into a modern criminal court, and it may be that the very high rates of homicide reported for the medieval period reflect this difference of definition.

The figures for lesser crime, however, are difficult to evaluate since legal institutions generally played a limited role in the adjudication of minor offenses in deference to the Church and to other mechanisms for controlling minor deviance. An unknown but still considerable number of property crimes were also settled informally by the victim and offender that today would appear in the lower criminal court. Any estimate of premodern property crime, therefore, probably seriously underestimates its actual incidence. Many victims were reluctant to take their complaints to the courts, which did not have a reputation for sure-handed justice. Many offenders went free through misfeasance or malfeasance, and many victims preferred to settle matters themselves. Unless there was a powerful reason, such as revenge, to report a criminal offense to the court, many victims simply suffered in silence or settled matters in their own way.

A question might be raised about the criminal nature of unreported violations. If the victims were not sufficiently annoyed to make a formal complaint to the criminal court, some might argue that unreported violations do not warrant being classified as crimes. But if the basic reason was simply that private action was more effective, it would seem that these violations were indeed recognized as criminal by the parties. They went unreported because of the poor reputation of the courts, not because they were regarded as inconsequential.

Estimates of crime in the modern era

Studies of property crime during the late eighteenth and early nineteenth centuries present a similar problem. The picture these studies offer is inevitably colored to some degree by the place of legal institutions in the community. Where the courts were merely formal instruments for carrying out the informal will of the community, or where, in addition to the courts, the Church and other nonlegal institutions played a major part in sanctioning wrongdoers, as in colonial New England, the picture of crime provided by studies of court records probably seriously underestimates the actual level of minor deviance. Where the courts had already achieved a high degree of independence and authority in a largely secular society, as in eighteenth-century England, estimates of criminality based upon court records are probably more accurate.

As the estimates of crime for modern societies are examined, the pattern becomes more interesting. Much more is known about the sociopolitical and legal forces that produced the reported crime patterns. The strains that modernization created in these societies are well understood: artisans and craftsmen generally found their economic skills becoming obsolete, whereas laborers and businessmen encountered a more favorable climate. Immigrants to urban centers from less developed regions often confronted an alien social experience and a criminal justice system committed to curbing their more exotic forms of behavior, and from time to time businessmen invented new ways of illegally pursuing profits.

In the midst of these changes, the legal institutions themselves were often straining to develop the structures, methods, and procedures of a modern court system. The training of lawyers and judges was improved, criminal procedures were sharpened and rationalized, and new policies and methods for coping with a mounting volume of minor crime were invented, so that as the character of criminality changed in response to modernization, the legal institutions for coping with it were simultaneously rationalized and bureaucratized. Since both processes were occurring simultaneously, it is sometimes difficult to know which picture the crime studies represent: crime as a changing social reality, or crime as a reflection of evolving criminal courts. In most cases, the picture is a double exposure portraying both aspects of the crime scene.

Nineteenth-century criminality

There have been a number of studies of crime in nineteenth-century cities and nations. Researchers have been forced to rely largely on court reports, but police data became available by the middle of the nineteenth century, and several investigators have utilized this important source.

Virtually every study reports a steady decline in serious crime throughout the nineteenth century. In France, for example, serious crime fell by nearly 90 percent between 1826 and 1954 (Lodhi and Tilly). In England and Wales, indictable offenses declined by 79 percent between 1842 and 1891, and in London they declined by 63 percent between the 1820s and 1870s (Gatrell and Hadden). Much of the decline in London derived from a sharp drop in violent crime—about 68 percent between the 1830s and the 1860s. Larceny indictments also decreased in London, from about 220 per 100,000 in the 1830s and 1840s to about 70 per 100,000 in the 1850s, again by 68 percent. This decline, however, stems at least partially from a revision of the criminal code in 1855, which removed most larcenies from the indictable category and permitted courts to deal with them summarily. Although this revision treated simple assaults similarly, nearly all the decline in assaults had occurred by 1855. Other property crimes, particularly robbery, burglary, fraud, and embezzlement, increased during this period or remained relatively steady. In Stockholm, the trend was much the same (Gurr, Grabosky, and Hula, pp. 256–257). The number of persons accused of theft fell from about 75 per 100,000 in the 1840s to about 22 in 1900, a 71 percent decline; and the number of persons sentenced for assault or breach of the peace dropped from about 400 per 100,000 in the 1840s to about 60 in the 1920s, an 85 percent decrease.

One of the few studies to reveal a different criminal pattern focused on the Black Country in England, that is, the region around Birmingham, which became a major steel-producing region in the late eighteenth and early nineteenth centuries. As the Black Country industrialized, it experienced steady increases in criminality. Larceny committals to trial rose from 91 per 100,000 in 1835 to about 262 in 1860, an increase of 188 percent, and committals to trial for offenses against the person increased from about 6 per 100,000 to about 14, a 133 percent increase (Philips, p. 143). This study suggests that rural areas and small towns exhibited sharply higher levels of criminality as they industrialized, whereas it is clear from other studies that more heavily urbanized areas such as London and Stockholm experienced declines in serious criminality as they and their surrounding communities developed.

Studies of criminality in nineteenth-century American cities tend to bear out this thesis. In Boston, the peak of recorded serious crime during the nineteenth century occurred in 1824 and was not exceeded until the turbulent decade of the 1970s. In 1824 there were 1,430.5 prosecutions per 100,000 for crimes against the person in the Boston Police Court, a figure nearly four times the comparable 387.8 per 100,000 arrest figure for 1967. There were fluctuations, of course, corresponding to the wars and economic cycles that beset Boston over the years, but the low mark in serious violent crime in modern Boston was recorded in the period from 1928 to 1930, when the rate was only 28 percent of the 1824 peak. Property crime during the nineteenth century rose only slightly, from 859.4 per 100,000 in 1824 to 878.2 in 1884 and 1885 (Ferdinand, 1980a).

Similar long-term declines in violent crime have been found during the nineteenth century in Buffalo, New York (Powell), and Salem, Massachusetts (Ferdinand, 1972). On the other hand, a study of crime in Rockford, Illinois, which was founded in the 1840s, revealed that violent crime rose sharply from 1882–1884 to 1905–1907 (Ferdinand, 1976). After declining slightly in the first half of the twentieth century, it rose sharply again during the 1950s and 1960s. Thus, established cities like Boston and Salem, and to some extent Buffalo, exhibited declining serious crime rates as they modernized, whereas relatively new communities and rural areas showed increasing serious crime rates as they industrialized and became more urbanized.

The distinctive crime pattern of old cities undergoing industrialization has been explored in a series of historical studies of European and American communities (Zehr; Boutelet; Gégot; Ferdinand, 1978). Old established communities in France and Germany, for example, experienced a rapidly increasing level of violent personal crime relative to their property-crime level as they developed an industrial base. Old cities that did not industrialize maintained a low level of violent personal crime, and new cities and rural areas exhibited rising levels of property crime as they industrialized. These same studies have shown, however, that as an older city became industrialized, its violent crime rate receded, and property crime became the dominant form of criminality. Thus, as older cities began to industrialize, the ratio of violent personal to property crimes increased rapidly, often to the point where violent crimes clearly outnumbered property crimes. But when these cities completed the process of industrialization, the ratio of violent personal to property crimes receded once again to a point where property crimes outnumbered violent crimes by three or four to one. Older cities exhibited a transitional increase in their ratio of violent to property crimes, which newer communities, as they industrialized, did not regularly display. In the United States, this transitional pattern has been discovered in Boston, Salem, and New Haven, all old cities, but not in the new city of Rockford, Illinois (Ferdinand, 1978).

Although this transitional pattern is surprisingly general, a definitive explanation has not yet been proposed. It seems that the dislocations erupting in a newly developing industrial economy are more wrenching to an older, established urban center than to a newer community that is still evolving. At the same time, a growing body of evidence indicates that legal institutions begin to assume a much broader role in controlling minor crimes when communities modernize. As the criminal courts displace other institutions, most notably the Church, in monitoring and sanctioning minor crime, they attempt to maintain much the same standard of public behavior that the other institutions had established in an earlier era. Thus, recorded crime exhibits a rapid increase, although why the rise is concentrated particularly in violent crime against the person remains to be explained.

It may be that after some years of attempting to maintain a high standard of public behavior, the courts begin to lose interest in minor criminal offenses, and particularly in minor violent offenses, with the result that recorded violence declines. Property crime, however, does not seem to exhibit the same sharp fluctuation as a community industrializes. Thus, the swings in violent crime levels found in the older cities of both Europe and America on the threshold of industrialization probably reflect both basic changes in their social structure and economy and adjustments in the criminal courts as they attempt to meet the demands of a changing society.

Criminality in the modern era

During the late nineteenth and early twentieth centuries, criminality in Western societies, particularly property crime, fluctuated primarily in response to economic conditions. Although wars had a significant impact on crime rates, reducing them during hostilities and elevating them afterward, their effect was not long-lasting. But periods of economic distress usually result in higher levels of property crime, especially burglaries, whereas periods of prosperity typically produce lower levels. Oddly enough, juvenile delinquency rates seem to follow a very different path: they rise during prosperity and fall during depressions (Glaser and Rice). Throughout this period, the late nineteenth century and the first half of the twentieth century, delinquents constituted a small but growing part of the crime problem. Overall, the trends in property crime were downward, at least through World War II.

The well-documented decline in criminality during

the late nineteenth and early twentieth centuries has sparked a controversy among historians and criminologists, some of whom believe that the decline represents a gradual adaptation of nineteenth-century immigrants to urban living (Lane, 1968). Others argue that the decline reflects basically the improved effectiveness of urban police departments (Gatrell). These are not necessarily competing explanations, since both could be correct.

Nevertheless, there are basic difficulties with the thesis that declining urban crime rates between 1830 and 1950 resulted from growing police efficiency. The earliest police departments—that is, centralized police organizations without an overt political mission—were organized during the early decades of the nineteenth century. The first to be established was the London Metropolitan Police, in 1829, followed in the United States by police departments in Philadelphia (1833), Boston (1838), New York (1844), and Baltimore (1857). Their primary responsibility was to contain the civil disturbances that swept English and American cities during the early decades of the nineteenth century. During this period the middle classes were accumulating property rapidly, and they feared the destructiveness of urban mobs that gathered periodically in the summer months. Constables had held crime in check in American cities during the early nineteenth century, but they were too few in number, and were not organized to cope effectively with the riots that broke out with increasing frequency. Political support for a mobile, centralized police force grew in these cities on the eve of the American Civil War.

If the decline in criminality after 1830 is to be attributed to the police and their growing effectiveness, it must be explained why the sharpest drop was in violent personal crime and not in property crime. Property crimes are more difficult to police because good witnesses are rarer, but it would seem that the emerging bourgeois civilization of the late nineteenth century would have demanded of its police greater attention to property crime than it was receiving. Moreover, it is difficult to understand why violent crime should continue to drop long after establishment of a centralized police force in the city. After an initial period of trial and error, one might expect that the crime rate would have stabilized as the police and the underworld in its many forms found a level of accommodation that neither could effectively change. But in Boston, as has been seen, violent crime declined from 1824 (before a modern police force was established) to a level from 1928 to 1930 which was only 28 percent of that prevailing a century earlier. Those who see the police as primarily responsible

for this decline must explain why the impact of a modern police force should extend for so long after its introduction during the early decades of the nineteenth century. There is some evidence that conviction rates improved during the nineteenth century in London, which could indicate a greater effectiveness on the part of the police (Gatrell), but this may only reflect a tendency on the part of the police to neglect the weaker cases.

The thesis that declining urban crime rates reflect a growing police effectiveness suffers by virtue of the close relationship between declining crime rates and the progressive bureaucratization and isolation of the police in the twentieth century. A sharp decline in arrests followed closely on the heels of a shift from foot patrols to motorized patrols in Salem, Massachusetts, and in Rockford, Illinois. As patrol became mainly a motorized function in these and other cities, arrests per officer dropped to very low levels. For example, in Boston several officers made more than 1,000 arrests in 1850, and in Salem the mean number of arrests per officer per year rarely fell below 30 during the latter half of the nineteenth century. In 1907 it reached 48.2 arrests per officer in Salem.

When the Salem police force began to patrol in cars, however, annual arrests per officer dropped sharply, and throughout the 1920s and 1930s the rate never rose above twenty-one. By the 1950s and early 1960s the rate had slipped below ten arrests per officer per year. Some of the decline in criminality noted in the first half of the twentieth century probably stems from secular shifts in deployment policies in urban police departments, rather than from any improvement in their ability to suppress crime.

Secular shifts in urban police organization may also help to explain the decline in crime rates between 1830 and 1950. The early police departments in American cities were often headed by men of considerable reputation and integrity. Benjamin Pollard, appointed Boston's first city marshal in 1823, was a Harvard graduate, a lawyer, and a man of distinction. His immediate successors, who ultimately served as the first police chiefs when the department was formed in 1838, were also Harvard graduates or lawyers, and the early Boston department was an effective instrument of city policy. After the Civil War, the Boston department declined under the combined impact of fierce ethnic rivalry, intense political struggles, and the corrupting influence of organized vice. Other urban departments, most notably New York's, suffered under the same burdens, and in general the quality of urban police departments, particularly in the old cities of the Northeast, seriously eroded in the post–

Civil War period. To some extent, the decline in crime rates in late-nineteenth-century American cities can probably be attributed to a widespread demoralization and loss of effectiveness as the patronage system and corruption infected major urban police departments. There are several good reasons, therefore, to question the conclusion that the increasing efficiency of American police departments caused crime rates to fall in the nineteenth century and the first half of the twentieth century.

A better explanation may well be that urban immigrants, who had recently arrived from rural societies, were becoming better adapted to their communities as they gained experience of urban life. Settling into urban occupations and learning the techniques of city life and established urban neighborhoods, they were drawn toward a more stable, relatively crime-free life by the institutions of urban society—churches, ethnic clubs, labor unions, political groups, informal social groups, family, and relatives. For the most part it was the rootless poor who fell into crime, and as the decades passed, the tramps, hoboes, and wanderers of the nineteenth century began slowly to disappear. During the 1930s a mobile army of rootless men reappeared, but all through the late nineteenth and early twentieth centuries their ranks had been shrinking in favor of a stable working class that increasingly established itself in distinctive neighborhoods throughout the major cities of America. It is probably no coincidence that such offenses as drunkenness and prostitution have also declined steadily in America since the 1920s. As the working classes have assumed a settled, stable pattern of life, criminality in America, particularly criminality bespeaking a disorganized lifestyle, has declined.

The post–World War II crime wave

With the end of World War II and the economic recovery in Europe in the 1950s, crime rates and particularly rates of violent crime began to climb once again throughout the Western world. In England and Wales, murder and assault cases increased from 13 per 100,000 in 1950 to 144.3 per 100,000 in 1975, an elevenfold increase (Gurr, p. 363). During the same period, the rate of thefts rose from 847 per 100,000 to 3,659 per 100,000, a more than fourfold increase. Throughout Scandanavia much the same pattern unfolded, with Finland experiencing the worst explosion. Between 1960 and 1974–1975, assaults and murders in Finland more than doubled, from 127.9 to 282.0 per 100,000, and thefts more than tripled, from 886 to 2,850 per 100,000 (Gurr, p. 364). These increases in Europe were concentrated in the cities; between 1950 and 1971, the rate of thefts, assaults, and murders in Stockholm more than quadrupled.

A similar pattern prevailed in the United States. Between 1960 and 1980, violent crime arrests shot up from 97.4 to 241.4 per 100,000, and property crime arrests rose comparably, from 403.3 per 100,000 to 841.4 per 100,000 (FBI). The sources of this crime wave in the 1960s and 1970s are clear: an ethic of personal emancipation became established in several hitherto closely controlled groups—young people, females, and blacks—as well as in hitherto peripheral rural areas. The pattern is by no means general, but it is sufficiently widespread to be suggestive. Between 1960 and 1976, for example, arrests of youths under eighteen years of age for violent crimes increased by 331 percent; in rural areas, arrests for violent crimes increased by 150 percent over the same period; and for blacks the comparable figure was 115 percent. By contrast, arrests for violent crimes in cities above 250,000 population increased by 121 percent during the same period (FBI, 1961–1977).

Property crime in the United States showed similar increases in the 1960s and 1970s. From 1960 to 1976, the number of females arrested for property crimes rose by 259 percent; arrests of youths under eighteen increased by 204 percent; and arrests of blacks for property crimes climbed by 176 percent. Rural areas made little contribution to the overall increase in property crime, since arrests there rose least of any demographic category, a relatively low 65 percent (FBI, 1961–1977).

The ethic of emancipation seems also to have affected the young people of Europe. After World War II, several delinquent and near-delinquent groups became prominent features of European urban life: the Teddy Boys and Rockers in London, the Provos in Amsterdam, and the Raggare in Stockholm. It is interesting in this regard that, in contrast to the pattern in the United States, the increase in crime found so prominently among the young people in Europe seems to have been concentrated among young adults from eighteen to twenty-five years of age instead of youths under eighteen.

There are several additional reasons for this sharp increase in youth crime. The mere fact of their disproportionate increase in the populations of Western nations as the birthrate rose dramatically after World War II has resulted in strong upward pressures on youth crime and delinquency. By the 1960s, the babies born after the war were becoming teenagers and young adults, and as their numbers grew, so did their criminality. A study of the impact of the dispropor- tionate growth of the adolescent population in post- war America revealed that 11.6 percent of the rise in serious crime between 1950 and 1965 was due sim- ply to changes in the age structure of the population. Auto theft and forcible rape were affected most dra- matically, up 13.8 percent and 47.1 percent, respec- tively; homicide and aggravated assault rose much less sharply—5.5 percent and 9.2 percent, respectively (Ferdinand, 1970).

But the young people of the 1960s made an impact on Western society not simply by virtue of their grow- ing numbers. They were becoming increasingly con- scious of their social and political influence, and the dissenting voices of young people in Berkeley, Paris, and elsewhere demanded changes in the policies of their leaders (Keniston). This aggregation of young people into groups—political, social, and even delin- quent—is a relatively modern development and is un- doubtedly a major factor in the elevated crime rates of young people at all levels in society.

Young people are learning the attitudes and tech- niques of delinquency and crime from one another through their youth culture, and as their social net- works expand, delinquency and youth crime become a serious national problem. Thus, the rapid rise in youth crime in the postwar period is to a large extent a consequence of a growing youth culture whose dom- inant themes are the virtues of personal emancipation and the rejection of traditional bourgeois values (Fer- dinand, 1980b).

The theme of emancipation was probably inspired by the civil rights struggles of American blacks in the 1950s and 1960s, but the ideals of emancipation were embraced by other groups as well, notably by young people and, somewhat later, by feminists. The emanci- pation of these three groups in American life was ac- companied by considerable political turmoil, by an expansion of their sense of moral propriety, and, ulti- mately, by an upsurge in their criminality. The youth of Europe seized on this theme as well, and by the late 1960s it had become an important aspect of West- ern culture.

Conclusion

The above discussion has identified several patterns in the history of criminal behavior. First, evolving le- gal institutions in Western society have contributed importantly to a secular decline in violent offenses. The long secular decline in homicide from fourteenth- century London to the seventeenth-century counties of Surrey and Sussex, near London; the decline in

violent offenses from nineteenth-century Boston to Boston in the 1920s; and similar declines in nine- teenth-century London and Stockholm undoubtedly owe much to the long evolution of rational legal insti- tutions in the West.

Before the ninth century, in much of Europe per- sonal losses suffered at the hands of another were considered private matters to be settled by the parties, and one rash act often led to a series of escalating violent reactions. No one knows for certain why the ruling classes decided to step into this situation and administer justice in the community, but during King Alfred's reign in ninth-century England the Crown assumed some responsibility for domestic tranquillity, and the King's peace became the cornerstone of En- glish criminal justice.

It is easy to see how private justice could breed violence, and how the King's peace would discourage it, but it was not possible to institute the King's peace everywhere at once. Rather, a civilizing of the people was required—a maturation of public culture to an extent that individuals were willing to submit their personal quarrels to the King and his officers. In short, the legitimacy of the instruments of public justice had to be sufficiently strong and widespread to guarantee that those who accepted their authority were not sys- tematically plundered by those who did not. Accep- tance of the King's peace was a gradual process de- pending as much upon a growing awareness of the efficacy of public justice as upon the pains attending its violation.

No controlled experiment can establish that emerg- ing legal institutions played a part in civilizing the peoples of the West, but it seems likely that the long- term decline of violence in medieval England owes much to the widening jurisdiction of the King's courts and to the long-term rationalization of the instru- ments of public justice. As the fairness with which justice was administered improved, the legitimacy of the King's courts in the eyes of the people was strengthened. Nevertheless, as trial courts replaced trials by ordeal and as royal officers assumed responsi- bility for serious crime in the twelfth and thirteenth centuries, they encountered a people accustomed to more violent methods of settling their differences, and the courts recorded a very high level of violent crime. As victims turned increasingly to the King's courts, however, the overall level of violence fell. Under the impact of evolving legal institutions, a civic temper was cultivated among the English people, and as this civic temper gained a wider sway, serious crime, and particularly violent crime, slowly receded.

At the same time, opposing forces were also at work

counteracting the civilizing effects of royal justice and its institutions. As English society evolved from a folk-communal society based on handicrafts to an urban commercial society and later to an urban industrial one, the legal institutions of the West began to displace other important institutions, such as the Church, in sanctioning deviance (Ferdinand, 1978). The expanding jurisdiction of the criminal courts at first drove crime rates higher. These highs were probably recorded as each major innovation in the criminal justice system made its appearance, for example, when the police courts assumed full responsibility for minor crime, or when a centralized police force replaced a scattered constabulary. Important developments in the organization of criminal justice or in its relationship to such private institutions as the Church were often accompanied by sharp but transitory increases in measured criminality.

A second conclusion focuses on the social bases of criminality. During much of the nineteenth century and the first part of the twentieth century, crime trends, particularly for property crimes, were closely attuned to economic conditions. Moreover, criminality as recorded by the courts and the police was largely a working-class or lower-class phenomenon; relatively few middle-class individuals were implicated in common-law violations.

During the 1960s, however, this close association between poverty and crime weakened. Prosperity was widespread in America, and living standards improved generally; but criminality rose even more rapidly, especially among the economically favored classes. It is now apparent that the values of broad segments of the people shifted during the 1960s and that new styles of behavior arose, some of which violated the criminal law. But the crime pattern of the 1960s challenged economically based explanations of crime that had dominated the thinking of policymakers and criminologists for decades. Culturally based crime had become a major factor in the crime picture of Western nations.

Ironically, during the 1960s the United States initiated a major campaign to eliminate poverty and to prevent crime and delinquency; but despite a massive nationwide effort, few (if any) projects demonstrated that relieving poverty reduced crime. Theories that worked well in explaining crime during the nineteenth century could not explain it in the 1960s.

A historical survey of crime patterns provides an excellent basis for projecting future trends, particularly if it is theoretically informed. There is reason for optimism. The levels of crime in the West should decline over the intermediate term, that is, during the 1980s, compared to that of the 1960s. The most prominent forms of crime in the coming years will probably be those spawned by modern youth's ethic of emancipation. The forms of youth crime—property crime, minor violent crimes, sex crimes, and crimes of political protest—will continue to follow the model of the 1960s and 1970s. Nothing can reverse the momentum of youth culture, and the implications of this for criminality are inescapable. A sizable segment of youth will continue to engage in criminal behavior. Declining birthrates in the West, however, will ultimately help to shrink the numbers of young people, and the level of youth crime in Western societies should fall somewhat in the 1980s and 1990s.

The emancipation of blacks in the United States has also reached a plateau, so that black crime as well should moderate in the coming years. The migration of blacks from the rural South (an area of low crime rates) to the urban North and West (areas of high crime rates) has slowed, and a black middle class with significant economic and political influence has begun to emerge. Some of the pressures behind the surge in black crime in the 1960s have begun to moderate, and in response the rise in black crime has begun to slacken. In 1976, 47.5 percent of the violent crimes and 30.9 percent of the property crimes were committed by blacks, but in 1980 the corresponding figures were 44.1 percent and 29.9 percent (FBI, 1977, 1981). Since 1976, the increase in black crime has not kept pace with that of the society as a whole. The heaviest contributors to the crime upsurge of the 1960s and 1970s—young people and blacks—will in all probability be less significant contributors to criminality in the United States in the coming decades. Serious crime rates should fall from 10 percent to 15 percent between 1980 and 1990.

The emancipation of women still has some way to go, however. The ethic of emancipation is only now beginning to reach young women, and the full implications of this trend have yet to be seen in crime rates. Nevertheless, female crime is only a small part of the overall picture, and increases here, although large in percentage terms, will not alter significantly the prediction of a 15 percent reduction in serious crime.

Young women, like blacks, are intensely involved in the youth culture, and the emancipation of women must be distinguished from that of youth in general. The emancipation of young women assumes a form distinct from that exhibited by adult women. The former focuses more heavily on a liberation of sexual mores and male-female relationships (Carns); the latter is less concerned with gender relationships and more with social and economic equality. The young female is more deeply involved in a male-dominated youth culture; the adult female is more independent and less imitative of the values of male society. Thus, young women will exhibit sizable percentage increases in criminality in the intermediate future, but their contribution should be minor in seriousness as well as in numbers.

All the other components contributing to criminality in American cities—for example, organized crime, professional crime, and Hispanic immigration—should continue with only minor deviation from levels displayed in the 1960s. Thus, declines projected for blacks and youths should reduce the overall level of criminal activity in the United States by about 15 percent. Cities with heavy Hispanic immigrations, such as Miami, Chicago, and Los Angeles, will not show declines as great as those in cities like Minneapolis or San Jose, which have little such immigration. Added to these adjustments is the continued long-term integration of the economic underclass into the urban social fabric, which should contribute to a slow decline in lower-class crime.

Social dislocations such as severe depressions or political divisions can seriously aggravate the crime problem, but the crime pattern of the nineteenth century, in which economic conditions in the lower classes broadly affected the level of crime in society, is being replaced by a pattern more closely affected by the values and morale of distinctive social and political groups. Some of these groups—women, blacks, and youths—are influenced more by their social prospects than by their immediate economic condition. Accordingly, the economic explanation of crime advanced by theorists in the 1930s and 1940s (Kornhauser) will be of less value in the 1980s than theories focusing more on the existential and *social* conditions of groups central to the crime problem.

THEODORE N. FERDINAND

See also CRIME STATISTICS: REPORTING SYSTEMS AND METHODS; DEVELOPING COUNTRIES, CRIME IN; ECOLOGY OF CRIME; RURAL CRIME; URBAN CRIME; WOMEN AND CRIME.

BIBLIOGRAPHY

BAKER, J. H. "Criminal Courts and Procedure at Common Law, 1550–1800." *Crime in England, 1550–1800.* Edited by J. S. Cockburn. Princeton, N.J.: Princeton University Press, 1977, pp. 15–48.
BEATTIE, J. M. "The Pattern of Crime in England, 1660–1880." *Past and Present* 62 (1974): 47–95.
BELLAMY, JOHN G. *Crime and Public Order in England in the Later Middle Ages.* London: Routledge & Kegan Paul, 1973.
BOUTELET, B. "Etude par sondage de la criminalité du bailliage de Pont-de-l'Arche (XVIIe–XVIIIe siècles); de la violence au vol: en marche vers l'escroquerie." *Annales de Normandie* 4 (1962): 236–262.
CARNS, DONALD E. "Identity, Deviance, and Change in Conventional Settings: The Case of 'Sexual Revolution.'" *Our American Sisters: Women in American Life and Thought.* 2d ed. Edited by Jean E. Friedman and William G. Shade. Boston: Allyn & Bacon, 1976, pp. 401–416.
Federal Bureau of Investigation. *Crime in the United States.* Uniform Crime Reports for the United States. Washington, D.C.: U.S. Department of Justice, FBI, 1961–1981.
FERDINAND, THEODORE N. "Criminal Justice: From Colonial Intimacy to Bureaucratic Formality." *Handbook of Contemporary Urban Life.* Edited by David Street. San Francisco: Jossey-Bass, 1978, pp. 261–287.
———. "Criminality, the Courts, and the Constabulary in Boston: 1702–1967." *Journal of Research in Crime and Delinquency* 17 (1980a): 190–208.
———. "Delinquency in Developing and Developed Societies." *Critical Issues in Juvenile Delinquency.* Edited by David Shichor and Delos H. Kelly. Lexington, Mass.: Heath, Lexington Books, 1980b.
———. "From a Service to a Legalistic Style Police Department: A Case Study." *Journal of Police Science and Administration* 4 (1976): 302–319.
———. "Politics, the Police, and Arresting Policies in Salem, Massachusetts since the Civil War." *Social Problems* 19 (1972): 572–588.
———. "Research and Methodology: Demographic Shifts and Criminality: An Inquiry." *British Journal of Criminology* 10 (1970): 169–175.
GATRELL, V. A. C. "The Decline of Theft and Violence in Victorian and Edwardian England." *Crime and the Law: The Social History of Crime in Western Europe since 1500.* Edited by V. A. C. Gatrell, Bruce Lenman, and Geoffrey Parker. London: Europa, 1980, pp. 238–370.
———, and HADDEN, T. "Criminal Statistics and Their Interpretation." *Nineteenth Century Society: Essays in the Use of Quantitative Methods for the Study of Social Data.* Edited by Edward A. Wrigley. Cambridge, England: Cambridge University Press, 1972, pp. 336–396.
GÉGOT, J. C. "Etude par sondage de la criminalité dans le bailliage de Falaise (XVIIe–XVIIIe siècles): Criminalité diffuse ou société criminelle?" *Annales de Normandie* 16 (1955): 103–164.
GIVEN, JAMES B. *Society and Homicide in Thirteenth Century England.* Stanford, Calif.: Stanford University Press, 1977.
GLASER, DANIEL, and RICE, KENT. "Crime, Age, and Employment." *American Sociological Review* 24 (1959): 679–686.
GURR, TED ROBERT. "On the History of Violent Crime in Europe and America." *Violence in America: Historical and Comparative Perspectives.* Rev. ed. Edited by Hugh Davis Graham and Ted Robert Gurr. Beverly Hills, Calif.: Sage, 1979, pp. 353–374.
———; GRABOSKY, PETER N.; and HULA, RICHARD C. *The Politics of Crime and Conflict: A Comparative History of Four Cities.* Beverly Hills, Calif.: Sage, 1977.

HANAWALT, BARBARA A. *Crime and Conflict in English Communities, 1300–1348.* Cambridge, Mass.: Harvard University Press, 1979.

JOHNSON, DAVID R. *Policing the Urban Underworld: The Impact of Crime on the Development of the American Police.* Philadelphia: Temple University Press, 1979.

KENISTON, KENNETH. *Young Radicals: Notes on Committed Youth.* New York: Harcourt Brace, 1968.

KORNHAUSER, RUTH ROSNER. *Social Sources of Delinquency: An Appraisal of Analytic Models.* University of Chicago Press, 1978.

LANE, ROGER. "Crime and Criminal Statistics in Nineteenth-century Massachusetts." *Journal of Social History* 2 (1968): 156–163.

———. *Policing the City: Boston 1822–1885.* Cambridge, Mass.: Harvard University Press, 1967.

LODHI, ABDUL QAIYUM, and TILLY, CHARLES. "Urbanization, Crime, and Collective Violence in Nineteenth-century France." *American Journal of Sociology* 79 (1973): 296–318.

PHILIPS, DAVID. *Crime and Authority in Victorian England: The Black Country, 1835–1860.* London: Croom Helm, 1977.

POWELL, ELWIN H. "Crime as a Function of Anomie." *Journal of Criminal Law, Criminology, and Police Science* 57 (1966): 161–171.

RUGGIERO, GUIDO. *Violence in Early Renaissance Venice.* New Brunswick, N.J.: Rutgers University Press, 1980.

WILSON, JAMES Q. *Varieties of Police Behavior: The Management of Law and Order in Eight Communities.* Cambridge, Mass.: Harvard University Press, 1968.

ZEHR, HOWARD. *Crime and the Development of Modern Society: Patterns of Criminality in Nineteenth-century Germany and France.* Totowa, N.J.: Rowman & Littlefield, 1976.

CRIMINAL CAREERS

1. ORDINARY OFFENDERS   Peter W. Greenwood
2. SPECIALIZED OFFENDERS   James A. Inciardi

1.
ORDINARY OFFENDERS

Interest in criminal careers. Self-reporting studies have shown that most people break the law at least once in their life (Gold and Reimer). However, only about one-third of the population ever commit the more serious crimes of homicide, assault, rape, robbery, or burglary, and less than 10 percent continue to commit these crimes over an extended period of time (Wolfgang, Figlio, and Sellin). It is the latter group that is the focus of criminal-career research. What is the life-style of these offenders? At what age

do they begin their crimes? What kinds of crime do they commit as juveniles, and how does their pattern of criminal behavior change as they grow older? How many crimes do they commit in a year? What is their employment pattern? What is their involvement in drugs? What distinguishes those with long careers from those whose careers are brief? What distinguishes high-rate offenders from those who commit crimes infrequently?

These are not just idle questions of academic concern. They have a direct relevance to how convicted offenders should be sentenced. Answers to these questions can serve as a guide in determining which offenders are more suitable for probation and which should be incarcerated, as well as which should receive short sentences and which should be incarcerated for longer periods of time.

In most criminal cases, the relative severity of the sentence is justified at least partly by its preventive effects on future crime. To the extent that sentencing practices are justified by their possible influence on the amount of future crime, they invoke theories of either deterrence, rehabilitation, or incapacitation. A harsh sentence for a particularly notorious crime may be justified on the ground that it will deter others. A particular form of custody and treatment may be recommended for a particular offender on the ground that it is required for his rehabilitation. Another offender may be sentenced to a long term in prison (incapacitation) in the belief that he would represent an undue risk to society if he were released.

Although there are many well-developed theories about how deterrence, rehabilitation, and incapacitation should work, empirical evidence as to their actual effects is quite limited. Reviews of the research on rehabilitation (Sechrest, White, and Brown) and deterrence (Blumstein, Cohen, and Nagin) have concluded that the case for neither of these effects has been proved. A variety of experimental studies involving various forms of treatment have failed to find any consistent rehabilitation effects. Deterrence studies, on the other hand, generally find an inverse correlation between crime and sanctions that is consistent with deterrence theory, but they are unable to rule out other competing hypotheses that would also explain the observed relationships. The only crime-reduction effect of sentencing for which there is reliable information is incapacitation (Blumstein, Cohen, and Nagin).

The primary assumption of most incapacitation theories is that the criminal career is unaffected by sentencing practices (Shinnar and Shinnar). This assumption is supported by the fact that the rehabilitation literature shows no positive or negative effects of imprisonment on subsequent recidivism (Sechrest, White, and Brown). If the "no treatment effect" assumption holds, then prison terms merely subtract time from the overall length of the career. If an offender is incarcerated for 30 percent of his career, the number of crimes he commits will be 30 percent less than he would have committed if he were never incarcerated. The number of crimes prevented by locking up any given offender is proportional to the rate at which he commits crime when he is free. In order to maximize the incapacitation effect (crime-reduction effect) achieved for any given population size, it is necessary to maximize the average offense rate of the offenders who are incarcerated, not by changing anyone's rate but by attempting to select those offenders with higher rates for longer terms.

Criminal-career research. Information about the characteristics of criminal careers comes from a variety of sources. Between 1930 and 1950, when criminal justice research centered mainly on prevention and rehabilitation, a number of studies collected extensive information on the family background and social environment of delinquent youths but did not focus explicitly on their criminal activities (Shaw and McKay; Glueck and Glueck). Other studies described the activities of particular adult offenders, based on extensive interviews, without attempting to draw a representative picture of adult criminality.

Later research on criminal careers, which has been more responsive to sentencing issues, has followed three different approaches. The first is the birth-cohort study pioneered by Marvin Wolfgang, Robert Figlio, and Thorsten Sellin in 1972 at the University of Pennsylvania and replicated by Lyle Shannon in 1978. The Philadelphia cohort consisted of all males born in the city in 1945 who lived there between the ages of ten and eighteen, and the study assembled and analyzed data on all police contacts experienced by the cohort, in addition to social and economic variables. The cohort study is the most accurate means of determining the prevalence and distribution of criminal activity across the general population, as reflected in official records. It is also a good means for examining such issues as the age of onset of criminality and the age of desistance as a function of social and economic factors.

The second method of studying criminal careers involves collecting self-reported information from a sample of known offenders, usually while they are incarcerated. This method of research was pioneered at the Rand Corporation by Joan Petersilia, Peter Greenwood, and Marvin Lavin in 1977, in a study

of 49 incarcerated robbers, and by Mark Peterson and Harriet Braiker in 1980, in a study of 625 California prison inmates. These self-report studies have the advantage of providing a more complete picture of an offender's criminal activities than solely those known to the police.

Studies conducted in the early 1980s (Hindelang, Hirschi, and Weis; Marquis) have shown that although there is considerable variation between self-reports and official records (that is, police contacts or convictions), there is no systematic bias toward either over- or underreporting across different types of offenders, categorized by age, race, or conviction offense. The primary problem with self-reported studies is the sample bias, inevitably introduced by criminal justice processing decisions, when the sample is drawn from an incarcerated population.

The third approach to criminal-career studies involves the analysis of longitudinal criminal-history data (arrests, indictments, convictions) for a sample of known offenders in a given geographic area. This form of research has been pursued by Alfred Blumstein and Jacqueline Cohen at Carnegie-Mellon University. The use of arrest histories has the advantage of avoiding the expensive data collection required for self-report studies (all of the studies to date have used computerized contact files) and avoids the problems of respondent veracity, although criminal justice records have their own reliability problems. Their disadvantage is that they provide information on only a fraction of each individual's crimes and nothing about his social background. Both self-report and official-record studies are superior to cohort studies in focusing on the most serious types of offenders, who are rarely encountered in cohort studies.

Prevalence of criminal activity. One of the critical questions underlying crime-control policies is the distribution of criminal activity among the general population. If participation in crime is widespread, with arrestees representing only a small fraction of those actually engaged in crime, then any attempts to control crime by rehabilitating or incapacitating convicted offenders cannot be effective, since only a small portion of the active offenders will be reached. If, on the other hand, most crimes are the product of a relatively small number of chronic or habitual offenders who are repeatedly arrested, then either rehabilitation or incapacitation strategies could have some effect, since the target population is small and potentially identifiable.

A number of criminologists have argued that the first situation prevails—that the incidence of criminality is widespread. The evidence usually cited to support this position is twofold. First, only a small fraction of offenses are ever cleared by arrest; therefore, many offenders are never detected. The characteristics of the arrestee population are influenced heavily by police enforcement practices rather than by actual offending patterns (Petersilia).

Second, self-reporting studies of general-population samples indicate that the number of people who commit crimes is quite high and much more evenly distributed across racial and economic classes than arrest figures would support. The discrepancies between arrest figures and self-report data are attributed to biases in the criminal justice system. It has been argued that the overrepresentation of blacks among arrestees and prison inmates is caused by biases in the system, by harassment, or by greater police presence in the black community, rather than by actual differences in criminality (Gold and Reimer).

Later studies, including the Philadelphia cohort study, have refuted this line of reasoning and brought the findings from self-report studies into much closer alignment with those derived from official records (Hindelang, Hirschi, and Weis). The key to resolving this discrepancy was to focus more closely on crime seriousness. If every possible infraction is counted (truancy, defying parents, petty theft), everyone is a criminal. But that begs the question. The general public is not concerned with every possible law violation. Its concern is primarily with those acts affecting public safety—homicide, rape, assault, robbery, burglary, and theft. If one asks what percentage of the general population has engaged in these crimes, as opposed to any other type of violation, the answer is very different. Assuming that all offenders have roughly similar chances of being arrested for any particular type of crime, arrest statistics can provide a reasonably accurate picture of the active offender population.

In the Philadelphia cohort study, 47 percent of the males born in 1945 had at least one police contact for a nontraffic criminal offense before the age of thirty; 22 percent had a contact for a felony (Wolfgang, Figlio, and Sellin). About one-third of those with one contact had no further contact by age thirty. For those with multiple contacts, the probability of further contacts increased with the number already recorded. The older an offender at the time of first contact, the lower the probability of subsequent contacts.

The most interesting group in the Philadelphia cohort study was the 6 percent labeled as chronic offenders, each of whom had five or more contacts before his eighteenth birthday. These offenders accounted for 51 percent of all juvenile police contacts by the

entire cohort. Expanding the definition to include all those with five or more contacts prior to age thirty (15 percent of the cohort), Wolfgang, Figlio, and Sellin found that chronic offenders accounted for 74 percent of all crimes charged to the cohort members, 84 percent of the personal-injury offenses, and 82 percent of the serious property offenses. From these figures, it is clear that frequent offending also means, on the average, more-serious offending.

Other factors found to be associated with frequent police contacts were race (nonwhites offended more frequently), low socioeconomic status, frequent residential or school moves, low school grades, and low intelligence quotient.

The Philadelphia cohort study highlighted the important relationship between juvenile criminality and adult criminal careers. About 43 percent of those boys with juvenile arrests were subsequently arrested between the ages of eighteen and twenty-six, but only 12 percent of those without. The peak age for first arrest is seventeen. The earlier the first arrest, the greater the likelihood of subsequent arrests and the more serious these subsequent offenses are likely to be.

Another finding of the Philadelphia cohort study was the general lack of specialization among repeat offenders. The pattern of subsequent police contacts demonstrated no correlation with respect to the number or nature of prior contacts. The criminal activities of most offenders appeared to be a random mixture of various types.

Intensity of criminal activity. The length of the career and its intensity are two different issues. A given offender may lead a basically legitimate lifestyle, only occasionally engaging in unplanned acts of theft or violence, possibly induced by depression or anxiety over some external event. This behavior pattern could last for ten to twenty years and result in occasional periods in jail or even in prison. Nevertheless, while free, this type of offender would commit only one or two crimes per year.

Another offender might have a much shorter career, perhaps only five to seven years, but would pursue it far more intensely. He might commit robberies or burglaries several times a week, regularly sell and use drugs, and be armed and prepared to use violence. Such an offender could commit hundreds of crimes a year. His career would be marked by frequent periods of incarceration, interspersed with periods of intense criminal activity.

Studies involving self-reports of incarcerated offenders (Petersilia, Greenwood, and Lavin; Peterson and Braiker) or arrest histories (Blumstein and Cohen) have shown that the distribution of individual offense rates is heavily skewed to the low end. Most offenders, even those in prison, commit crimes at fairly low rates—only one or two per year. Only a small percentage commit as many as twenty serious crimes per year. In the Rand inmate survey (Peterson and Braiker), among those California prison inmates who committed armed robberies (34 percent of the sample), half committed fewer than 1.5 armed robberies per year; about 8 percent reported committing more than 30 per year. The average number of armed robberies committed by active robbers was about 5 per year. This same general pattern held for every type of offense studied.

As in the Philadelphia cohort study, the Rand survey found no strong patterns of specialization. Most inmates reported engaging in a number of different types of crime during any particular time in their lives. There was no strong correlation among offense rates for different types of crime. An offender who committed robberies frequently, as well as burglaries, was not more likely to commit burglaries frequently than one who committed robberies infrequently or not at all. Obviously, the most serious types of offenders were those few who engaged in many types of crime—including robbery, burglary, theft, assault, and drug sales—many of them at high rates.

Although the high-rate offenders could not be easily distinguished, there were some characteristics that tended to identify them. High-rate offenders were more likely than others to have committed serious crimes at a very early age—thirteen or fourteen. Their juvenile crimes were both more frequent and more serious than those of other offenders. They were more likely to be using hard drugs at an early age and to continue using and selling them throughout their careers.

High-rate offenders were also more likely to see themselves as criminals and to have adopted a set of values and an outlook consistent with their criminal life-style. Although recognizing that any offender faced some risks of being caught, they believed that they could successfully avoid this outcome. They rejected what they saw as the boredom and frustration of a "straight" existence, opting instead for the excitement available through drugs and crime. They believed that they were more likely to achieve the status and material goods they desired through crime rather than through legitimate employment.

These offenders did not have experiences consistent with their expectations. Although they may have gained some excitement from their criminal escapades, they earned very little money. Most street crimes are not very rewarding—providing less than $100 per offense—and the risks are high. Many of the offenders spent a substantial portion of their lives behind bars. Few achieved stable living arrangements with family or friends.

One of the expected attributes of extended participation in crime that did not turn out to be significant was criminal sophistication or skill. Many people believe that continued involvement in crime, or exposure to other criminals in prison, will make an offender more sophisticated in the execution of crimes or skillful in avoiding arrest.

Such is not the case: there is no evidence that offenders become more skillful as they grow older (Petersilia, Greenwood, and Lavin). Most offenses are unplanned and opportunistic. Those offenders who show some degree of sophistication in their criminal pursuits, by selecting targets more carefully or planning their escapes, do so at an early age. Those who typically do not learn well in school also apparently do not learn much in prison. For most offenders, the likelihood of arrest for any one crime does not decline with age. The literature on prison behavior suggests that the principal concern of most prisoners is not planning for the future but simply surviving the prison experience or improving their status within the prison culture. In fact, lack of any planning or interest in the future is one of the most salient characteristics of the criminal mentality.

Implications for crime-control policy. In 1967 the President's Commission on Law Enforcement and Administration of Justice concluded that the way to reduce crime was to improve the ability of the criminal justice system to treat convicted offenders. Community corrections and individualized treatment were the wave of the future. Improved treatment programs and more-skilled treatment personnel would lead to lower recidivism rates.

This viewpoint has not been sustained by experience. Rehabilitative treatment is still seen as an important objective of the criminal justice system, but only for those offenders who choose to accept it. There is no longer a consensus that forced treatment can significantly change recidivism rates.

The primary objectives of sentencing are shifting from rehabilitation to punishment and public protection. In state after state, sentencing laws and procedures are being revised or modified to reduce the discretion of courts and parole boards and thereby the resulting sentence disparities that discretion produces among similar offenders. The principal factors determining the severity of punishment are the seriousness of the conviction offense and the prior record of the offender, both of which are thought to reflect the culpability of the offender and his potential threat to society. How can knowledge about criminal-career patterns assist in this line of policy development?

Although criminal-career research offers little guidance in determining the relative degree of punishment deserved by different offenses, it is much more helpful in determining how sentences should be adjusted to maximize the degree of community protection afforded by a given incarceration capacity. It can provide a rational basis for a policy of selective incapacitation.

Selective incapacitation need not be based on any predictions about a particular offender's future behavior. Rather, it can be based upon actuarial evidence concerning the relative degree of risk posed by different categories of offenders, where the categories are defined by such characteristics as current offense, prior adult record, juvenile record, and history of drug abuse. Every state's sentencing laws make some explicit provision for adjusting sentences based on all or some of these characteristics. Yet in most cases, no attempt is made to articulate whether the time added to a convicted defendant's sentence for prior convictions is justified on the basis of additional punishment or public protection. In most instances, differences in length of term are determined by political consensus rather than by empirical evidence as to which offenders actually pose the greatest risk. In California, for example, a prior prison term can be used to add one or three years to a defendant's base sentence, depending on whether it was for a nonviolent or violent offense. The extreme variability in individual offense rates and their strong association with prior behavioral characteristics suggest that selective incapacitation provides a means of holding down the mounting demand for increased prison capacity while still providing some protection to the public.

Research issues. Criminal-career research has focused primarily on estimating the prevalence of criminal activity among the general population, charting the age of onset or desistance of criminal activity, and determining patterns of individual crime rates and their association with various predictor variables. Now that the basic outlines of criminal-career patterns have been established, there is a need to explore many other related issues in more specific detail, especially if incapacitation is to become an explicit consideration in shaping future sentencing policy.

More knowledge is required about how various interventions may affect criminal-career patterns. Are there particular age groups or categories of offenders for whom incarceration may extend the criminal career, simply postponing future criminal activity, rather than preventing it, as current incapacitation theory now assumes? How do juvenile career patterns compare with those of adults? In particular, more research needs to be conducted on major juvenile offenders, since studies focusing on serious offenders have dealt exclusively with adults.

Can anything be predicted about an offender's potential future criminal behavior from a study of whether his prior offenses were committed alone or in groups? Juveniles are much more prone to group activity than adults (Greenwood, Petersilia, and Zimring). Is there a shift from group crime to individual crime with age, or are juveniles who commit crimes alone more likely to continue into adult criminal careers? What happens when part of an operational criminal group is incarcerated? Does the remainder of the group, as Albert Reiss suggests, recruit new members to replace those who are lost?

If there is a marginal increase in deterrent effects caused by harsher penalties, how is it distributed? That is, do fewer people engage in crime, or is there a reduction in the rate of activity among those who are active? To what degree do increased penalties for one crime displace the activity of offenders to other crimes? Does knowledge of criminal-career patterns provide a more effective means of devising or testing intervention strategies designed to curtail criminal activity?

During the 1970s, criminal-career research has provided a new perspective from which to view various criminal justice problems. There is now some empirical foundation for differentiating among offenders on the basis of their offense patterns and rates. Further research on criminal careers will require more detailed and accurate information on various cohorts of offenders who have contact with the criminal justice system.

PETER W. GREENWOOD

See also DELINQUENT AND CRIMINAL SUBCULTURES; PREDICTION OF CRIME AND RECIDIVISM; TYPOLOGIES OF CRIMINAL BEHAVIOR.

BIBLIOGRAPHY

BLUMSTEIN, ALFRED, and COHEN, JACQUELINE. "Estimation of Individual Crime Rates from Arrest Records." *Journal of Criminal Law and Criminology* 70 (1979): 561–585.
———, and NAGIN, DANIEL, eds. *Deterrence and Incapacitation: Estimating the Effects of Criminal Sanctions on Crime Rates.* Washington, D.C.: National Research Council–National Academy of Sciences, 1978.
GLUECK, SHELDON, and GLUECK, ELEANOR. *Unraveling Juve-*

nile Delinquency. New York: Commonwealth Fund, 1950.

GOLD, MARTIN, and REIMER, DAVID J. "Changing Patterns of Delinquent Behavior among Americans Thirteen through Sixteen Years Old: 1967–72." *Crime and Delinquency Literature* 7 (1975): 483–517.

GREENWOOD, PETER W.; PETERSILIA, JOAN; and ZIMRING, FRANKLIN E. *Age, Crime, and Sanctions: The Transition from Juvenile to Adult Court.* R-2642-NIJ. Prepared under a grant from the National Institute of Justice, U.S. Department of Justice. Santa Monica, Calif.: Rand Corporation, 1980.

HINDELANG, MICHAEL J.; HIRSCHI, TRAVIS; and WEIS, JOSEPH G. *Measuring Delinquency.* Sage Library of Social Research, vol. 123. Beverly Hills, Calif.: Sage, 1981.

MARQUIS, KENT H., with the assistance of EBENER, PATRICIA. *Quality of Prisoner Self-reports: Arrests and Conviction Response Errors.* R-2637-DOJ. Prepared for the National Institute of Justice. Santa Monica, Calif.: Rand Corporation, 1981.

PETERSILIA, JOAN. "Criminal Career Research: A Review of Recent Evidence." *Crime and Justice: An Annual Review of Research,* vol. 2. Edited by Norval Morris and Michael Tonry. University of Chicago Press, 1980, pp. 321–379.

———; GREENWOOD, PETER W.; and LAVIN, MARVIN. *Criminal Careers of Habitual Felons.* Reprint. Washington, D.C.: U.S. Department of Justice, National Institute of Law Enforcement and Criminal Justice, Law Enforcement Assistance Administration, 1978.

PETERSON, MARK A., and BRAIKER, HARRIET B., with POLICH, SUZANNE M. *Doing Crime: A Survey of California Prison Inmates.* R-2200-DOJ. Santa Monica, Calif.: Rand Corporation, 1980.

President's Commission on Law Enforcement and Administration of Justice. *The Challenge of Crime in a Free Society.* Washington, D.C.: The Commission, 1967.

REISS, ALBERT J., JR. "Understanding Changes in Crime Rates." *Indicators of Crime and Criminal Justice: Quantitative Studies.* Edited by Stephen E. Fienberg and Albert J. Reiss, Jr. Washington, D.C.: U.S. Department of Justice, Bureau of Justice Statistics, 1980.

SECHREST, LEE B.; WHITE, SUSAN O.; and BROWN, ELIZABETH D., eds. *The Rehabilitation of Criminal Offenders: Problems and Prospects.* Washington, D.C.: National Academy of Sciences, 1979.

SHANNON, LYLE W. "A Longitudinal Study of Delinquency and Crime." *Quantitative Studies in Criminology.* Edited by Charles Wellford. Sage Research Progress Series in Criminology, vol. 8. Beverly Hills, Calif.: Sage, 1978, pp. 121–146.

SHAW, CLIFFORD R., and McKAY, HENRY D. *Juvenile Delinquency and Urban Areas: A Study of Rates of Delinquents in Relation to Differential Characteristics of Local Communities in American Cities* (1942). With a new introduction by James F. Short, Jr. and new chapters updating delinquency data for Chicago and suburbs by Henry D. McKay. Rev. ed. University of Chicago Press, 1969.

SHINNAR, SHLOMO, and SHINNAR, REVEL. "The Effects of the Criminal Justice System on the Control of Crime: A Quantitative Approach." *Law and Society Review* 9 (1975): 581–611.

WOLFGANG, MARVIN E.; FIGLIO, ROBERT M.; and SELLIN, THORSTEN. *Delinquency in a Birth Cohort.* University of Chicago Press, 1972.

2.
SPECIALIZED OFFENDERS

Crime is among the most ancient of human phenomena, and its manifestation as a career with focused levels of specialization has been known for many millennia. In the Old Testament, Abimelech, King of Shechem around 1108 B.C., contracted professional killers to dispose of his seventy legitimate brothers. Hophni and Phineas, referred to in the Scriptures as the "sons of Belial" because of their brutal rapacity, may have been the originators of extortion; and observations of banditry and prostitution as specialized careers were noted in the recollections of Moses. Theft and prostitution were depicted in the *Lives* of Plutarch and the *Annals* of Tacitus, the craft of the pickpocket was portrayed in the *Satyricon* of Petronius, and after the first millennium A.D. both history and literature vividly described crime as a structured and focused career enterprise.

The systematic analysis of criminal behavior that accompanied the growth of the science of criminology soon noted the levels of specialization and career transformation that were characteristic of offender populations. To the late nineteenth-century criminologist Cesare Lombroso, career offenders were "criminaloids," and his distinguished pupil Enrico Ferri devoted close study to the nature of the career criminal. Even before these pioneering contributions to the scientific study of crime, numerous descriptions of the underworld of Paris during the 1840s explored the attitudes, habits, and ways of life of what were referred to as the "dangerous and criminal classes."

Subsequent analyses of criminal life-styles and careers have gone well beyond the early descriptions and classifications. Contemporary criminology has focused on offenders' occupational career patterns, placing special emphasis on initiation and maturation in crime and on the social organization and survival of specific criminal behavior patterns. These studies have demonstrated that although most varieties of offenders evince elements of a career orientation, the manifestation of crime as a career is apparent within only limited segments of lawbreaking. Furthermore, the term *career crime* (often called professional crime) typically relates only to those offenders who have developed a high degree of specialization. As such, it refers to offense behavior that is pursued as an occupation for the purpose of obtaining a steady flow of income. The development of the specialized criminal career begins with an initiation and socialization into the world of crime, followed by a maturation process involving the acquisition of needed skills, knowledge, and associations. The most highly developed criminal careers are those of professional theft, professional "heavy" crime, and illegal enterprise.

Professional theft. The concept of professional theft was introduced to the social-science literature in 1937 with the publication of Edwin Sutherland's *The Professional Thief, by a Professional Thief*. Sutherland's use of the term referred to nonviolent forms of criminal activity pursued with a high degree of skill in order to maximize financial gain and minimize the possibility of arrest. The professional thief made a regular business of stealing and was the graduate of a developmental process that included the acquisition of specialized attitudes, knowledge, skills, and experience. Furthermore, in organizing his life around the pursuit of theft he identified himself with an exclusive criminal fraternity that extended friendship, understanding, security, and respect. Finally, the professional thief was able to steal for long periods of time without extended terms of incarceration. He committed crimes in a manner that reduced the risks of apprehension, and was able to deal effectively with police and the courts. Professional thieves typically have engaged in pickpocketing, shoplifting, burglary, sneak theft, forgery, and confidence swindling.

The term *professional thief* was not Sutherland's own creation; it had been in use for centuries. To Edward Crapsey, a New York journalist who had extensive contacts with the underworld during the 1860s and 1870s, professional thieves were the pickpockets, shoplifters, sneak thieves, and forgers who depended exclusively on the fruits of theft for a livelihood and represented a class that was immune from punishment. In 1800 the British magistrate Patrick Colquhoun noted that "professed thieves" were members of a fraternity who could buy their freedom by bribing witnesses. William Harrison's *Description of England* (1577) noted the unity of specialized thieves as members of a "profession." In the writings of the Elizabethan rogues and vagabonds of the fifteenth and sixteenth centuries, the term *professional theft* was invariably used to describe persistent stealing pursued with a high level of skill. Thus, the term *professional thief* seemingly had in-group origins: it was and continues to be applied *by* professional thieves *to* other professional thieves.

Studies by Sutherland in the 1930s, David Maurer in the 1940s and 1950s, Bruce Jackson in the 1960s, and James Inciardi in the 1970s have demonstrated that although the number of professional thieves in the United States has drastically declined since the early twentieth century, their criminal career patterns have remained largely unchanged.

Professional theft manifests many characteristics of legitimate occupations: recruitment and training, maxims and rules, a code of ethics, and an organization, however informal. Crucial to the initiation and development of a career of theft is the interactional setting in which the amateur becomes a professional.

The habitat of the professional thief falls within the traditional locales of urban vice and crime: amusement centers, red-light districts, and rooming-house and skid-row areas. Of central importance are the hangouts, or meeting places where thieves of all types congregate for leisure or to make business arrangements. Hangouts may be taverns, poolrooms, cafeterias, cabarets, the lobbies of cheap hotels, or other places where an informal atmosphere allows thieves to interact. Amusement centers and skid rows also provide the short-term housing that facilitates inconspicuous living and that is appropriate to the life-style of professional predators, who are primarily rootless transients. This milieu, furthermore, is isolated both socially and psychologically, and communication often occurs by means of a specialized argot that binds the thieves together in a fraternity.

Recruitment and training typically take place within this interactional setting. It is here that amateur thieves, as well as prostitutes, waiters, cab drivers, and hotel clerks, come in contact with professional thieves. Prisons as well can be active centers for recruitment and training. The induction process begins when the professional recognizes the necessary "larceny sense" that a potential recruit may have, and training involves the development of new skills, acquaintance with new rackets, and exposure to new associates in the world of crime.

The neophyte becomes a professional by mastering techniques and becoming aware of the need for caution and precaution. He learns the specialized argot, establishes connections for the safe disposal of stolen goods, and is put in contact with those who can "fix" criminal cases, that is, make payoffs to police and court officials in order to prevent arrest or prosecution. He may also begin to specialize in one specific area of theft. Fledgling pickpockets, for example, may graduate from being "handbag openers" to "pants-pocket workers"; small-time street hustlers may become astute confidence swindlers; and snatch-and-grab thieves may develop into precision burglars, shoplifters, and safe-openers.

Julian Roebuck's study of criminals in the District of Columbia Reformatory demonstrated that many professional thieves had associated with specific criminal types at a youthful age. He found, for example, that confidence men typically came from urban slum areas where criminal tutelage started early in life. They had delinquent companions before the age of ten and criminal companions before the age of eighteen, yet these peer groups characteristically avoided violence. Their childhood experiences taught them that deceit was rewarded and, on the other hand, that violence did *not* pay.

The careers of professional thieves tend to be longer than those of most other offenders, and their careers end in varied ways. Many become too old to steal successfully and thus retire to skid rows; others are expelled from the profession for some serious violation of the underworld code. Exit from the profession can result from a loss of protection, not only for a breach of the code but also for poor relations with case fixers. Extremely long prison sentences, in turn, may shock a thief into reform or inactivate him until old age. On the other hand, thieves may become fixers, move into illegal enterprise, or transfer their profits into a legitimate business. Finally, physical disability and drug addiction have forced many from their careers as professional thieves.

Professional "heavy" crime. The category of career crime often includes professional "heavy" crime, which involves skilled offense behavior for monetary gain yet employs the use or threat of force, violence, and property damage.

Central to a conceptualization of professional "heavy" crime is the historical notion of banditry. In its purest form, as the sociologist James Inciardi has noted, banditry involves marauding by organized or semiorganized groups of outcast or oppressed persons emerging from the fringes of organized society. Banditry endures until its arena is encroached upon by civilization, and it is suppressed or dispersed when advancing society can no longer tolerate it.

Banditry as professional "heavy" crime was manifest in the piracy of Blackbeard, Henry Morgan, and Captain Kidd. After the Spanish discovery of America in 1492, the West Indies became a frontier of Europe and remained so for some three hundred years. Trade, with cargoes often in excess of $100 million per ship, found a natural right-of-way through the Caribbean, made highly navigable by Gulf Stream currents, the prevailing winds, and the sheltering islands of the West Indies, whose topography was well suited for piracy. The islands provided landside strongholds, and the endless number of coves offered natural opportunities for ambush followed by swift and secure retreat.

During the seventeenth and eighteenth centuries the West Indies became a dumping ground for transported convicts and social, political, economic, and religious outcasts from Great Britain, France, and Spain, as well as a sanctuary for the runaway indentured servant and the unemployed "free willer" who had sold himself under an indenture agreement.

The grand era of piracy began in 1714, when Captain Henry Jennings and three hundred seamen descended upon the salvage crew of a grounded Spanish galleon, looting the vessel of some three hundred thousand gold coins. News of the event galvanized the social pariahs and displaced mariners on the Caribbean waterfronts, and ships were seized and manned, becoming pirate vessels.

The decline of piracy began with the march of civilization into the maritime frontier of the West Indies. During the latter part of the eighteenth century, Great Britain strengthened its navy, conquered the West Indies, and began systematic colonization. Pirate vessels flying the Jolly Roger were no match for the Royal Navy's warships, and maritime plunder was quickly put to rest.

The buccaneers and pirates of the Caribbean were comparable to the desperadoes of the American West. Professional outlaws emerged during the decade after the Civil War. Many were Union and Confederate veterans who wandered the country as penniless vagabonds searching for excitement. They drifted to the Southwest when Congress opened millions of acres there for settlement and development. Herds of cattle had been left untended and free to roam in these lands during the war years. Much of this stock was also unbranded, proof of ownership was practically impossible, and "possession was nine points of the law." Surpassing the efforts of the cattle thieves and adding to professional organized banditry were the robbers of stagecoaches, trains and banks—all of whose crimes were made profitable by the gold dust and solid currency that were accumulating in the developing West. Western banditry began to decline as the nineteenth century drew to a close. The growing population demanded security, and law enforcement quickly responded.

The modern bandits of the Depression era were the latter-day counterparts of the earlier outlaw breed. Their frontier was more social than natural—public apathy and rapid social change. The crash of 1929 had slashed the national income; hundreds of banks had collapsed, and thirteen million Americans were left jobless. Urban centers had grown so large that local law enforcement had become unwieldy and inefficient, and areas of vice and corruption were unbounded. The changes in law, science, and community organization, although they had led to the demise of the rustler and the robber of stagecoaches, banks and trains a few decades previously, failed to adjust to the new criminality. Armed with machine guns, the new professional "heavies" re-created the frontier pattern of rapid assault, followed by immediate and elusive retreat. Fast cars and intricate highways replaced the desert and canyon escape routes. Like commuters, the outlaws now shuttled between distant cities or to adjoining states for sanctuary. Local police were helpless: they had few modern weapons; their patrol vehicles were old and often disabled; and they were understaffed and poorly paid, often having to provide their own guns and transportation. New political administrations frequently changed police chiefs at the cost of morale and efficiency. County officials were equally ineffective, state police were little more than paper organizations, and federal authority was subject to local political pressure and states' rights.

Such was the setting for the crime wave of the 1930s, whose leading figures included John Dillinger, George "Machine Gun" Kelly, and Charles "Pretty Boy" Floyd. But their frontier also was quickly curtailed, primarily by the growth of a new national law enforcement agency, the Federal Bureau of Investigation.

Contemporary professional "heavy" criminals include the organized armed robbers and million-dollar cargo hijackers of urban post-industrial America. Their careers usually begin in a juvenile gang where techniques and rationalizations for criminal behavior are gradually learned. Individuals begin with vandalism, gang fighting, and petty theft, move on to street muggings and purse-snatching, and ultimately progress to burglary, auto theft, armed robbery, and hijacking. As young adults, their experiences with police, courts, and reformatories add to their sophistication in criminality. Living on the fringes of society, members of the "heavy" rackets view robbery, burglary, and auto theft not as careers but as ways to "get rich quick" and to become socially mobile. Yet they do not operate within a social and interactional setting similar to that of professional thieves, where knowledge is shared and case fixers are available. Thus, "heavy" criminals develop an ethos of "easy come, easy go": they are arrested and convicted frequently, and they often fail to advance economically. Consequently, they lock themselves into the "heavy" criminal career.

Illegal enterprise. Business undertakings directed toward illicit economic gain are referred to as illegal enterprise. They provide unlawful goods and services through such activities as arson, gambling, loansharking, commercialized vice, bootlegging, trafficking in narcotics, and disposing of stolen merchandise. Illegal enterprise also infiltrates legitimate business.

The term *illegal enterprise* is used here rather than the more traditional *organized crime* since the latter has become hopelessly compromised by its use as a synonym for all the criminal activities engaged in by Sicilians and other Italians. At the heart of what is meant by organized crime, however, are the types of enterprises noted above that provide illegal goods and services to customers. Such activities are not always highly organized, and consequently they may result in disparate criminal career patterns. Those perpetrating these activities range from free-lance neighborhood numbers men to members of regionally organized gambling or drug syndicates.

Criminal careers involving illegal enterprise tend to be numerous and diverse, primarily owing to the many levels of organization and types of racketeers. Donald Cressey has pointed out that in the more traditional organized-crime "families" there are many positions. These include bosses, underbosses, corrupters, enforcers, executioners, and soldiers, each with a specific role in the syndicate hierarchy. "Soldiers," for example, run small illegal enterprises on a sharecropping basis. Enforcers and executioners are syndicate "toughs" who maintain discipline and mete out punishments. All three types generally begin their criminal careers as delinquents in urban slums. They see racketeering as a means of upward mobility, but until they become members of a syndicate their criminal careers are essentially similar to those of professional "heavy" offenders. Potential racketeers are actively sought out and trained, and once they become trusted members of the mob their criminal careers diverge. Some become full-time workers and are salaried by the syndicate. Others work on specific illicit operations on a percentage basis. The remainder are only part-timers and work at legitimate jobs obtained for them by the upper-status members of the mob. In some organized-crime families, however, these part-time workers commit armed holdups as a source of income during times of financial pressure.

Other syndicate operatives include accountants, lawyers, and mature college graduates who are recruited to manage the large-scale business operations of the syndicate. Generally these managers have only minor, if any, prior criminal contacts, and are known to the syndicate through friendship or kinship.

Formal recruitment and entry into a "family" takes place for both "workers" and "managers" when a syndicate "opens its books." New members are then brought in and serve in a probationary role, ultimately moving up the hierarchy on the basis of friendship, kinship, and performance.

"Corrupters" (typically attorneys who fix cases and pay bribes to government officials), underbosses, and others in high-ranking positions generally have kinship ties to the "boss" of the family. Other individuals within the underworld of illegal enterprise may have only the weakest of ties, or perhaps none, to the local syndicate or family. Their criminal lives develop in varying ways. Numbers men and bookmakers establish their careers through associations with the world of gambling. Brothel owners may have entered commercialized vice through successful apprenticeships as prostitutes or pimps. Traffickers in narcotics may have begun as local drug merchants. In short, the paths of entry to illegal enterprise are as numerous and divergent as the criminal types that exist within its ranks.

Conclusion. Career crime begins with initiation and socialization into the world of crime, attended by a maturation process involving the acquisition of skills, knowledge, and associations appropriate for maintaining the desired occupational market value. Career crime is also vocational in nature, since the participants view their offense behavior as their "calling." It is this commitment that distinguishes the career offender from the non-career-oriented criminal. Beyond these broad conceptual similarities, the different types of career criminals—the professional thief, the professional "heavy," and the racketeer—have little in common.

A most important distinction among the three is that the length of careers tends to vary. Professional theft, for example, is often of a low-risk nature. Victims and offenders may act in collusion with one another, as in confidence games; the expertise with which the crimes are committed often leaves few clues for investigators; and the nonviolent nature of the thefts evokes only minimal societal reaction. In addition, professional thieves often develop ties that enable them to fix cases. These immunities perpetuate contacts among members of the profession, strengthening the unique subcultural organization that has been structured to ensure its further preservation. Codes of ethics; argot; self-segregation into vice areas; isolation; and association combine to further the protective structure and to lengthen the careers of professional thieves.

Professional "heavy" criminals, such as armed robbers, operate without this informal structure. Furthermore, their crimes are violent and have high visibility, thus diminishing the possibilities for case fixing. Their careers are short-lived, and many of them are designated as habitual offenders and receive long prison sentences.

Illegal enterprise, like professional theft, is organized in a self-perpetuating manner. Immune from sanction and providing goods and services that meet the demands of legitimate society, illegal enterprise tends to have a somewhat limited ecology of risk, resulting in relatively long careers for its members. However, this can vary, depending upon a racketeer's kinship ties and role. "Workers" do not always receive the same levels of protection as do those in the upper echelon of a syndicate; the careers of executioners and enforcers may be short-lived owing to the more violent nature of their work; and independent operators may fail to develop the political ties and financial base needed to secure immunity from sanction.

JAMES A. INCIARDI

See also DELINQUENT AND CRIMINAL SUBCULTURES; ORGANIZED CRIME: OVERVIEW; PREDICTION OF CRIME AND RECIDIVISM; *both articles under* PROFESSIONAL CRIMINAL; WHITE-COLLAR CRIME: HISTORY OF AN IDEA.

BIBLIOGRAPHY

COLQUHOUN, PATRICK. *A Treatise on the Police of the Metropolis, Containing a Detail of the Various Crimes and Misdemeanors by Which Public and Private Property and Security Are, at Present, Injured and Endangered; and Suggesting Remedies for Their Prevention.* 6th ed., corrected and enlarged. London: Mawman, 1800.

CRAPSEY, EDWARD. *The Nether Side of New York; or, The Vice, Crime, and Poverty of the Great Metropolis.* New York: Sheldon, 1872.

CRESSEY, DONALD R. *Theft of the Nation: The Structure and Operations of Organized Crime in America.* New York: Harper & Row, 1969.

EINSTADTER, WERNER J. "The Social Organization of Armed Robbery." *Social Problems* 17 (1969): 64–83.

HARRISON, WILLIAM. *Harrison's Description of England in Shakespeare's Youth: Being the Second and Third Books of His Description of Britaine and England* (1577, 1587). Edited by Frederick J. Furnivall. London: N. Trübner for the New Shakespeare Society, 1877–1881.

INCIARDI, JAMES A. *Careers in Crime.* Chicago: Rand McNally, 1975.

JACKSON, BRUCE. *A Thief's Primer.* New York: Macmillan, 1969. Reprinted as *Outside the Law: A Thief's Primer.* New Brunswick, N.J.: Transaction Books, 1972.

MAURER, DAVID W. *The Big Con: The Story of the Confidence Man and the Confidence Game.* Indianapolis: Bobbs-Merrill, 1940.

———. *Whiz Mob: A Correlation of the Technical Argot of Pickpockets with Their Behavior Pattern.* Gainesville, Fla.: American Dialect Society, 1955.

ROEBUCK, JULIAN B. *Criminal Typology: The Legalistic, Physical-Constitutional-Hereditary, Psychological-Psychiatric, and Sociological Approaches.* Springfield, Ill.: Thomas, 1967.

SUTHERLAND, EDWIN H., ed. and annotator. *The Professional Thief, by a Professional Thief.* University of Chicago Press, 1937.

CRIMINAL COURTS

1. LOWER CRIMINAL COURTS   Malcolm M. Feeley
2. FELONY DISPOSITIONS   Peter W. Greenwood

1.

LOWER CRIMINAL COURTS

In the United States, trial courts are usually divided into two types: courts of first appearance, or lower courts with limited jurisdiction, and superior courts, or courts of general jurisdiction. Although the precise criminal jurisdiction of lower courts varies significantly from state to state, their powers are usually restricted to cases involving local ordinances, violations, traffic offenses, misdemeanors, and lesser felonies in which a sentence cannot exceed one year. A similar bifurcation is found in most other countries, although the division of authority varies widely. In many areas in the United States, there are even further subdivisions among lower courts, for example, justice of the peace courts, police courts, traffic courts, or special violations courts with still more limited authority. Often these lowest-level courts do not allow jury trials and do not maintain records of their proceedings, and "appeals" from them are in the form of a trial de novo—a new trial in a higher-level court of record. Even those jurisdictions with a "unified" (that is, one-level) trial court system are likely to be separated into formally recognized divisions, some of which are assigned duties traditionally handled by lower courts in bifurcated systems. Prosecutors' offices are usually organized along parallel lines.

In the United States, these various courts of first appearance dispose of well over 90 percent of all criminal cases, excluding traffic and local violations (Alfini; Vera Institute of Justice), and the proportion is even higher in England and Wales, Scotland, and most countries on the Continent (McBarnet; Felstiner). Only a minute fraction of cases handled in these courts are transferred to superior courts or are appealed, so for most criminal defendants, victims, and witnesses, they are the courts of first and last resort.

Traditional functions of lower courts

Although the duties of lower courts vary widely, typically they include (1) serving as the arraignment court for all criminal cases; (2) setting conditions for pretrial release for all criminal defendants arraigned before them; (3) reviewing evidence prior to binding over or transferring more serious cases to superior courts; and (4) serving as the trial court for charges of misdemeanors and lesser felonies where sentences will not exceed one year or so. Thus not only are they the final trial court for the vast majority of all criminal cases, but they also serve important gatekeeping functions for upper-level courts.

Arraignment. The overwhelming majority of arrests are made by police officers in the field without a warrant. Most other arrests are obtained upon issuance of a sworn complaint or warrant. In either situation, new arrestees are usually taken to these courts within a day or so for arraignment. (Increasingly in minor criminal cases, arresting officers are following practices long used in traffic cases—issuing citations in the field, and giving a date for appearance in court.) At first appearance, arrestees are formally charged with a criminal offense by the prosecutor, apprised of their rights by the judge, and asked how they plead. A great many cases are terminated at this stage, either because the prosecutor or judge decides to drop the charges outright or because the defendant pleads guilty. In the United States and Great Britain, roughly one- to two-thirds of all criminal cases are terminated at this first appearance (Alfini; McBarnet).

Pretrial release. If the accused has not been released by the police prior to arraignment or if the case is not terminated at this time, the judge will set conditions for pretrial release. Conditions can range from release on recognizance (ROR) to bail of thousands of dollars, although in a few instances bail can be denied altogether. If bail is set, the defendant can be released if he posts the specified amount with the court. In recent years in the United States, the vast majority of the criminally accused are released on their own recognizance, and many others secure their release on bail (Thomas). Still, a significant minority of arrestees remain in jail, unable to post bond, until their cases are disposed of. The British practice is to release on recognizance or, if the accused is judged a bad risk or dangerous, to detain without bail. Continental countries rely heavily on noncustodial arrests (citations), but have authority to detain without bail.

Preliminary hearings. Defendants generally have a right to an early hearing to review evidence against them, and even those charged with serious offenses well beyond the arraignment court's jurisdiction have this right before their case is transferred to the higher-level court or sent to a grand jury. Although in practice there are very few probable-cause or preliminary hearings that formally review evidence, the *possibility* of this review is enough in many cases to cause prosecutors to reduce charges or drop them altogether. For this reason, lower courts often dispose of many cases where originally there were serious charges beyond their trial and sentencing jurisdictions. Those cases in which the charges remain ones of serious felony are sent to the superior courts.

Adjudication. In many courts of most limited jurisdictions, jury trials are not permitted, and a defendant must petition to have his case removed to a court with more authority if he wishes a jury trial. But even where they are permitted, trials—court or jury—are rare. By far the most common modes of disposition in lower courts are dismissals of all charges or pleas of guilty.

History

Origins. Trial courts throughout the world have long been bifurcated into lower and upper courts. Exodus (18:13–26) records that Moses assigned assistants to handle lesser cases and reserved larger issues and appeals for himself. Imperial administrations—before and since the Roman Empire—have permitted indigenous courts to deal with many petty criminal matters according to indigenous law, but have attempted to assume authority over more serious, and often politically sensitive, issues (Burman and Harrell-Bond; Shapiro). This same division of labor is found within sovereign countries as well. As the modern nation-state emerged in the West, central political authority usually permitted indigenous law governing minor criminal offenses to continue, and recognized the authority of local courts to handle these issues (Stephen; Maine). Even when a uniform national law was imposed, locally selected officials often continued to preside over local courts. This deference to local autonomy no doubt served an important symbolic function, giving appearances of local control at a time when there was likely to be local resistance to remote authority.

The magistrates' courts in England and Wales and in Scotland have their roots in the local feudal and justice of the peace courts of the fourteenth century (Stephen). Although financed by national funds, they remain locally controlled and often continue to be staffed by laymen. However, the magistrates do not provide investigative functions for higher-level courts in serious criminal cases, as they once did. This function was assumed by the police and prosecutors as their role expanded in the nineteenth century. The structure of contemporary American state courts has its origin in the early colonial courts, which in turn were imported from Great Britain in the seventeenth and eighteenth centuries (Goebel and Naughton; Pound). Although likely to be centrally staffed and administered, the lower courts in the various European countries can also be traced to early local courts.

Well into the twentieth century, there was also an important practical reason for this dual court system. Of the vast numbers of minor criminal cases that reach the authorities, only a few involve serious or politically sensitive charges that may bring severe consequences. Most are charges of drunkenness, disorderliness, petty theft, minor assaults without permanent injuries, and the like. Because of the infrequency of serious cases, legally trained professional judges handling them were usually assigned to large areas, rotating their courts from place to place and only occasionally appearing in a given locale. Lower courts with part-time magistrates who were often unpaid and untrained were expected to fill in during the interim, conducting investigations, handling preliminary matters in serious cases, and quickly disposing of the large numbers of lesser cases by themselves. Even with the growth of large metropolitan areas, which has necessitated the creation of full-time lower and higher courts alike, this traditional division has been maintained.

Evolution of the lower courts in the United States. Throughout the nineteenth century and well into the twentieth century, most states made provision for locally elected justices of the peace, mayors, or police officials to have summary jurisdiction over a variety of petty criminal offenses. In the urban centers, justices of the peace were often supplemented by police courts or magistrates' courts with similar jurisdiction. Those who presided over these courts usually had no formal legal training, were often uncompensated or paid a percentage of the fines they imposed, and frequently held part-time positions. These lower courts were not required to make a record of their proceedings, did not permit jury trials, and were constrained by few formal procedures. Rarely were defendants represented by counsel. At times the accused were let off after a warning by a justice who knew them personally; at other times, they would meet with swift and arbitrarily imposed punishments. More typically, however, sentences were small fines or brief stays in jail. Those contesting the judge's determination of guilt or wishing to be tried by a jury had to appeal for a trial de novo in a higher court of record, a process that, according to many, led to waste and delay since it meant in effect that cases would have to be tried twice. However, few defendants took advantage of this option because they were likely to incur harsher punishments if convicted in the upper courts.

During the early twentieth century, one of the major goals of court reformers was the abolition of inferior courts of no record, such as justice of the peace courts, police courts, and other similar courts, and by the mid-twentieth century such courts were in sharp decline. In the United States, justice of the peace courts possessing substantial criminal jurisdiction still exist only in some sparsely populated regions of a few (mostly western) states, although elsewhere in the United States they continue to exist in large numbers, handling minor traffic cases and the like. For the most part, lower criminal courts in the United States are now courts of record, and criminal defendants have the right to trial by jury in them, although some states prohibit a trial by jury for some very minor offenses. Lower-level courts in Great Britain possess similar jurisdiction.

Decision-making in lower courts

Decision-making in lower courts bears scant resemblance either to the popular image of trial courts portrayed in the media or to the practices of higher trial courts, which handle far fewer cases. As the general arraignment court for all criminal offenses, they are usually busy every morning (especially Mondays), processing the batch of suspects who have been arrested the day (or weekend) before. These proceedings are usually fast-paced and highly routinized. Defendants are often herded before the bench in a group and informed of their rights en masse. Arraignments take place at a rapid pace. Unless they have been released prior to this first appearance or have retained a private attorney, it is unlikely that defendants will have consulted with a defense attorney prior to this appearance, and it is at this stage that defendants may make application for publicly appointed defense counsel.

First appearance. In some communities, prosecutors have briefly reviewed the arrest report and charges prior to the accused's first appearance, and at arraignment they often announce that they are going to drop the charges altogether because of lack of evidence, the reluctance of the complainant to press the case, or "in the interests of justice"—a catchall phrase signifying that they believe the case is too insignificant to bother with. In the United States, roughly one-third of all cases are disposed of through the prosecutor's decision to drop the charges, and most of these decisions in minor cases are made on the spur of the moment, at or just prior to arraignment. In the remaining cases, the prosecutor might press the accused to plead guilty, asking, "Do you want to get this matter over with today or do you want to plead not guilty?" Such a question is usually accompanied by hints that the sentence will be lenient—a suspended sentence, a small fine, or at most a few days in jail.

Court officials vary in their propensities to encourage defendants to plead guilty at first appearance. Some actively encourage it in almost all minor cases, whereas others are reluctant to do so if the accused is charged with an offense likely to lead to a jail sentence, has a history of prior arrests, or appears disoriented or confused. In these situations, prosecutors and judges may encourage the accused to plead not guilty and to confer with an attorney. Still, most court officials are anxious to get rid of petty cases (often involving domestic disputes) without delay, and many defendants also have a strong incentive to extricate themselves as quickly as possible. Whatever the merits of the state's case, many defendants plead guilty to avoid the necessity of having to post bond, obtain an attorney, and return to court. Nationwide, roughly 50 percent or more of all criminal cases are formally disposed of at first appearance (Alfini). In Great Britain, duty solicitors are available for quick consultation prior to arraignment, but they are generally more difficult to obtain for representation in court. The lower number of dismissals of charges and the higher rate of guilty pleas at first appearance are no doubt related to this more restrictive policy on publicly provided defense services, although of course numerous other factors account for differences in practice in the United States and Great Britain (McBarnet). In West Germany and other northern European countries, where most minor offenses are handled by a noncustodial citation, the comparable figures for pleas of guilty through the mail are still high (Felstiner).

Pretrial release. In some jurisdictions, arrestees can be released on their own recognizance or on bail by the police, or by special release agencies immediately after arrest and before their first appearance in court. In others, however, arrestees are detained until arraignment, usually the following day, at which time conditions of release are set by the court. Wherever made, these decisions are usually quickly and routinely determined according to some standardized consideration of the nature of the offense, the accused's prior record, and his ties to the community.

In the United States, 90 percent or more of arrestees whose cases continue beyond this first appearance secure their release, either on their own recognizance or by posting bond (Thomas). Of those who do not, many are held without bond or on very high bond because of outstanding warrants in other jurisdictions, parole violations, or prior bail-jumping. Those who post bond often rely upon bail bondsmen, who charge a fee of about 10 percent of the value of the bond. (A fee for posting a $5,000 bond is likely to be $500.) Often the bondsman's fee is higher than the fine a convicted defendant will have to pay, and it is to avoid this fee that some arrestees plead guilty at arraignment (Feeley).

Numerous studies have documented that those defendants who are unable to post bond are more likely to be convicted than those who are released, and, if convicted, are more likely to receive longer sentences (Rankin; Flemming). Some explain this pattern by the fact that a detainee probably does not have the same ability as a released defendant to aid in developing his defense or to meet with attorneys. Others point to the subtle prejudicial effects created by a defendant entering the courtroom from the "holding cell" and appearing before the bench in handcuffs and jail garb.

Traditionally, the purpose of bail has been to ensure appearance in court, yet research reveals that bail is often used for punitive purposes, to impose immediate sanctions on the accused, or to detain arrestees thought to be dangerous. By setting bail beyond the means of the accused, judges can easily accomplish these goals without having to acknowledge them. Indeed, in many minor cases, defendants unable to afford bond plead guilty in order to obtain their release and a suspended sentence.

Courts also have a problem with defendants who fail to appear in court. Although few arrestees willfully flee the jurisdiction, a great many neglect to arrive for scheduled court appearances. This problem is greatest among those charged with misdemeanors, where the failure to appear (FTA) rate may be as high as 10 percent to 20 percent in some big cities. Since most of these cases involve petty nonviolent charges, neither the court nor the police generally search vigorously for nonappearants, preferring instead to wait and see if they will reappear on their own or be rearrested. Even here, however, prosecutors do not actively seek conviction on the additional charge of failure to appear, and the courts are relatively tolerant of it. In money bond cases, presumably

the bail bondsmen are liable if their clients fail to appear, but most states provide various ways for bondsmen to avoid this liability, and in nonpublicized low-bond cases, they often have little incentive to actively shepherd their clients to court.

Defense services. For the most part, criminal defendants are poor and unable to afford counsel. However, with the expansion of publicly financed defense services and the United States Supreme Court's landmark decision in *Argersinger v. Hamlin*, 407 U.S. 25 (1972), right to counsel even in minor criminal cases is constitutionally guaranteed, and is routinely offered to those who qualify for it. Some communities make this service readily available to criminal defendants in minor cases by employing a staff of full-time public defenders who have offices in or near the courthouse, whereas others rely upon specially appointed private attorneys, who are not so readily available for consultation at arraignment. There is considerable debate about which of these two types of publicly provided counsel is best. However, there is general agreement that this expansion of right to counsel for the accused in minor criminal offenses has improved the quality of justice dispensed in the lower courts.

Although publicly appointed counsel have long been criticized for providing second-rate service, numerous studies comparing public and private defense attorneys do not reveal any clear-cut differences in effectiveness (Hermann, Single, and Boston). Overall, publicly paid counsel appear to perform as well—or as poorly—as privately retained counsel. Indeed, for some offenses there is evidence to suggest that the presence or absence of an attorney makes no significant difference. However, it would be a mistake to conclude that defense attorneys are irrelevant in the lower courts, since as a group their presence helps shape the standard operating procedures for these courts. For example, many more cases are dropped by the prosecutor or dismissed in lower courts in the United States than in England and West Germany, and this may result, in part, from the larger role and more frequent appearance of defense attorneys in the lower courts in the United States than in England and West Germany.

Adversary processes in lower courts. It is often said that the adversary process has all but collapsed under the weight of heavy case loads in the lower courts. The low rate of trials is usually offered as evidence here. Yet it would be a mistake to attribute the lack of trials or of adversariness to increased arrest rates and case loads. Historical studies of lower courts reveal that trials have been rare in American lower courts since the late nineteenth century (Heumann;

Moley), and comparative studies of various types of jurisdictions reveal few trials even in communities where the case load is relatively light. Further, accounts of trials in lower courts where they were held, or continue to be held with some frequency, reveal these proceedings to be brief rituals not unlike the fast-paced and routine dismissal and guilty-plea proceedings in today's lower courts (Friedman; Mather). In the nineteenth century, it was common for several trials to take place in one day; rarely did the accused mount a careful defense. Although trials are rarely part of contemporary proceedings, one key difference is that the accused is more likely to be represented by counsel who is familiar with his case and who can represent the accused's interests in negotiations with the prosecutor.

Indeed, the demise of the trial in criminal cases may have been facilitated by the expansion of defense counsel and professionalization of the lower courts. The rise of full-time prosecutors and judges during the twentieth century has given officials the resources to review cases prior to court proceedings, and it may be this expansion of services and resources—rather than the rise in case loads or any other factor—that has contributed most to the decline of the trial.

It is also commonly said that plea bargaining has become the standard form for disposing of criminal cases in the lower courts. Strictly speaking, this is not correct. As noted above, a great many cases in lower criminal courts are dropped outright, either through a nolle prosequi decision by the prosecutor or through the dismissal of *all* charges by a judge. Although occasionally conditions are placed upon these decisions by the prosecutor (for example, "Stay out of trouble," or "Join Alcoholics Anonymous"), there is usually no waiver of right to trial or agreement to plea, a practice that is usually implicit in the meaning of the term *plea bargaining.*

Plea bargaining is conventionally understood as an arrangement whereby the accused waives his right to trial and pleads guilty in exchange for a guarantee of reduced sanctions. This process does not accurately describe the reality of decision-making in many lower courts. These courts are more akin to supermarkets, in which prices for various items are clearly known. Typically in the lower courts, cases are assessed by the courtroom work group (the judge, prosecutor, defense attorney, and so forth, who work with one another on a regular basis), who establish the "worth" or "going rate" for each type of offense. This is not plea bargaining in the conventional sense, in that decisions about dropping charges, judgments about the nature of the charges, and sentence need not be conditioned upon explicit agreements to plead guilty. What prosecutors and defense attorneys often refer to as plea bargaining is often actually a normative endeavor—a joint assessment of the seriousness of the incident, the facts, the actions, and the character of the largely dependent accused (Ericson and Baranek; Feeley; McBarnet).

Still, such decisions may take on the *appearance* of vigorous plea bargaining. This is a symbolic device, often engineered by defense attorneys to give clients the impression that they are obtaining favorable treatment. Observers of attorney-client discussions report that defense attorneys often present prosecutors' recommendations about sentences in ways that magnify or exaggerate their own achievements (Skolnick; Feeley). Although lower courts rarely impose anything approaching the maximum sentence, defense attorneys are able to give the impression of securing great bargains for their clients by contrasting statutory maximum terms with what the prosecutor is in fact willing to settle for if the defendant pleads guilty.

There is, however, one important group of lower-court cases in which the standard plea bargaining process often operates. In that large group of moderately serious felony cases in which the accused, if convicted, stands some chance of receiving a sentence longer than one year, there is a strong incentive for him to plead guilty in lower court in order to avoid the possibility of a longer sentence in the higher court. Lower-court prosecutors, as well as officials in the superior courts, have a strong incentive to see these cases disposed of in the lower courts. This expedites case processing, avoids grand jury indictments, reduces the number of preliminary hearings, and reserves the superior courts for "truly serious" cases. Such a process encourages many felony defendants to plead guilty to avoid the possibility of harsher punishment in a higher court, but at the same time it encourages police and prosecutors to overcharge in order to create this inducement.

Data on the pattern of dispositions support this conclusion. One important study of *felony* arrests in New York City (where sentences *could* exceed one year) revealed that less than 30 percent of the convictions were on felony charges and only one-third of these felony convictions led to felony-length (more than one year) sentences. In sum, the study found that only 5 percent of the felony arrests (and 10 percent of all convictions in felony arrests) led to felony convictions *and* felony time. The overwhelming bulk of all these serious cases were disposed of by the lower-level courts (Vera Institute). Figures for other communities are similar (Eisenstein and Jacob).

Alternative procedures of adjudication. In several northern European countries, most minor criminal cases are handled routinely without even a single court appearance by the accused (Felstiner). There, police officers issue suspects a written citation in lieu of a custodial arrest, and later the court mails to the accused a summary of charges and a statement of a proposed fine. This notification also informs the accused that he has the choice of pleading guilty and remitting the specified amount of the fine by mail, or appearing in court for trial at a specified time and place. The vast majority of all defendants in these minor cases choose to plead guilty and pay their fines by mail. In such situations, the court bears a close resemblance to an administrative agency routinely processing noncontested orders.

A similar practice has emerged informally in some American lower courts. Increasingly defendants in minor cases are ordered to post bond shortly after arrest and then encouraged *not* to show up at their appointed court date. In these cases their bonds are forfeited and their cases closed. For years this has been the routine way most motorists pay their traffic "fines." Although quite convenient for the court and for some accused, such practices also structure the process so as to strongly discourage formal hearings and active defenses.

Perennial problems of lower courts

Lower courts have long been a source of popular dissatisfaction (Pound). Specific complaints vary in time and place, but the underlying concerns are ubiquitous. They include complaints that lower courts lack standards and professionalism, are unduly influenced by particularism and political considerations, and are charged with handling intractable social problems better diverted from the criminal courts.

Lack of standards and professionalism. The lower courts have long been criticized for their perfunctory and humiliating treatment of the criminally accused. Accounts of the operations of magistrates' courts in medieval England describe the circuslike atmosphere of the proceedings and the insults and ridicule heaped upon the accused (Stephen). Indeed, there are reports that courts were convened out of doors in the town square to accommodate the boisterous crowds who viewed the judges' humiliation of defendants with amusement. Similar practices have been recorded in the United States (Robertson). Ever since the late nineteenth century, hundreds of local, state, and national reform-inspired commissions have issued reports critical of the lower courts, pleading

for more decorum, more and better-trained personnel, and more evenhanded treatment of witnesses and defendants. Specific proposals have called for full-time, adequately compensated personnel, merit selection, state rather than locally administered courts, expanded due process guarantees for criminal defendants, and more deliberateness in handling cases. Many of these reforms have been accomplished in form, if not in practice. Even in England, which retains a substantial lay magistracy, these officials are supplemented by legally trained clerks who are active advisers; in busy jurisdictions, they are supplemented by full-time, legally trained magistrates who are available to assume responsibility of the more difficult cases. In the United States, almost all judicial and prosecutorial positions are now filled by full-time lawyers. By the late twentieth century, most of the rights available to the accused in serious felony cases have been extended to those accused of lesser offenses as well.

Still, critics of the lower courts have not been satisfied. One reason is that these improvements have brought about heightened standards and increased expectations. There continues to be a glaring and persistent gap in resources and decorum between lower- and upper-level trial courts. The low visibility and pettiness of the charges, as well as the powerlessness of most of the accused, leads officials to adopt perfunctory and routinized proceedings even when the courts are well staffed and financed.

Political influences. Another source of concern to reformers has been the close connection between politics and the administration of justice in lower courts. Throughout history, courts have been criticized for being tools of the dominant political authorities. In the seventeenth century, English magistrates were castigated as instruments of the aristocracy and landed gentry in their harsh enforcement of laws prohibiting wood gathering, trespassing, and poaching. But in other times and places, local magistrates and juries have been celebrated for disregarding unpopular laws (such as Prohibition) imposed by remote authority. The active exercise of discretion by prosecutors and judges has long been used to achieve rough justice in order to temper the rigors of the formal law, although notions of what constitutes appropriate rough justice vary considerably with time, place, and political influence.

In the United States, the lower courts have been criticized for their association with local political organizations. Urban political machines throughout the late nineteenth and early twentieth centuries used appointments to positions in these courts for the purposes of patronage. This practice had spillover effects;

well-connected attorneys, defendants, or victims could often expect preferential treatment as a result of favoritism or bribes. Although now muted, this political connection survives, and these courts continue to serve as important sources of patronage.

Intractable problems. Cases involving public drunkenness and domestic disputes have always constituted a large proportion of lower-court case loads, and observers have long lamented the frequency with which defendants in such cases reappear in courts (Robertson). Various proposals have been advanced to curb what has come to be known as turnstile justice. Decriminalization has reduced the number of people charged with public drunkenness, although many are now arrested on other charges. Increasingly, courts are referring people with chronic alcohol problems to detoxification and substance-abuse programs, rather than processing them as *criminal* cases. Frequently, lower courts divert cases involving nonsupport and other types of domestic disputes to an auxiliary staff that administers specialized treatment and counseling programs. These pretrial diversion programs are justified on the ground that although the behavior precipitating the arrest might technically involve criminal violations, dealing with the underlying causes and cures for this behavior is beyond the capacity of the courts and the criminal sanction. But as attractive as the *idea* for such diversion programs is, there is substantial evidence to suggest that they are no more effective than the courts, and that they are even more obtrusive in imposing sanctions and more careless about due process considerations than are the courts.

Another recent and popular lower-court-related reform has been the development of mediation and neighborhood justice centers as alternatives to criminal prosecution in the courts. Justifications for these centers abound, but they often rest upon the complaint that courts are too rigid and too formal to deal effectively with problems which, although technically arising out of allegations of criminal conduct, also involve parties who have long histories of prior personal relationships or whose behavior stems from various personal problems. Proponents of these reforms argue that informal, community-based mediation is more effective in resolving certain types of disputes than are the courts. Ironically, many (although by no means all) of the features of these new informal alternatives bear a striking resemblance to the very institutions that reformers of the lower courts in the early twentieth century so vigorously sought to eliminate. Thus, for example, just as the American Bar Association could claim victory in its battle to eliminate non-

lawyer justice of the peace courts, it embraced the idea of informal, nonlawyer-administered neighborhood justice centers.

Conclusion

Many of the complaints against, and remedies for improvements in, the lower courts are similar to popular adages, which, although they contain much truth, also contradict one another (compare "Haste makes waste" and "A stitch in time saves nine"). It is for this reason that many of the problems of the lower courts in the West are perennial and perhaps insoluble, at least within the existing social structure. These courts are asked to pursue contradictory goals. On one hand, society demands careful and deliberate adjudication, but on the other, it wants swift and speedy justice. It wants justice to be administered in a dispassionate, evenhanded manner, but it also wants compassion, as well as representation for the interests of the local community. It is no wonder, then, that lower courts have been a perennial source of problems throughout much of recorded history.

MALCOLM M. FEELEY

See also ARRAIGNMENT; *both articles under* BAIL; COURTS, ORGANIZATION OF; CRIMINAL COURTS: FELONY DISPOSITIONS; *both articles under* GUILTY PLEA; INFORMAL DISPOSITION; PRELIMINARY HEARING; PRETRIAL DIVERSION; *articles under* SENTENCING; SPEEDY TRIAL; TRIAL, CRIMINAL.

BIBLIOGRAPHY

ALFINI, JAMES J., ed. "Symposium on Misdemeanor Courts." *Justice System Journal* 6 (1981): 5–148.

BURMAN, SANDRA B., and HARRELL-BOND, BARBARA E., eds. *The Imposition of Law.* New York: Academic Press, 1979.

EISENSTEIN, JAMES, and JACOB, HERBERT. *Felony Justice: An Organizational Analysis of Criminal Courts.* Boston: Little, Brown, 1977.

ERICSON, RICHARD V., and BARANEK, PATRICIA M. *The Ordering of Justice: A Study of Accused Persons as Defendants in the Criminal Process.* University of Toronto Press, 1982.

FEELEY, MALCOLM M. *The Process Is the Punishment: Handling Cases in a Lower Criminal Court.* New York: Russell Sage Foundation, 1979.

FELSTINER, WILLIAM L. F. "Plea Contracts in West Germany." *Law and Society Review* 13 (1979): 309–325.

FLEMMING, ROY B. *Allocating Freedom and Punishment.* New York: Longman, 1982.

FRIEDMAN, LAWRENCE M. "Plea Bargaining in Historical Perspective." *Law and Society Review* 13 (1979): 247–259.

GOEBEL, JULIUS, JR., and NAUGHTON, T. RAYMOND. *Law Enforcement in Colonial New York: A Study in Criminal Procedure (1664–1776).* New York: Commonwealth Fund, 1944.

HERMANN, ROBERT; SINGLE, ERIC; and BOSTON, JOHN. *Counsel for the Poor: Criminal Defense in Urban America.* Lexington, Mass.: Heath, Lexington Books, 1977.

HEUMANN, MILTON. *Plea Bargaining: The Experiences of Prosecutors, Judges, and Defense Attorneys.* University of Chicago Press, 1977.

MAINE, HENRY SUMNER. *Ancient Law: Its Connection with the Early History of Society and Its Relation to Modern Ideas* (1861). Introduction by C. K. Allen. London: Oxford University Press, 1950.

MATHER, LYNN M. *Plea Bargaining on Trial: The Process of Criminal-case Disposition.* Lexington, Mass.: Heath, Lexington Books, 1979.

MCBARNET, DOREEN J. *Conviction: Law, the State, and the Construction of Justice.* London: Macmillan, 1981.

MOLEY, RAYMOND. *Politics and Criminal Prosecution.* New York: Minton Balch, 1929.

POUND, ROSCOE. *Criminal Justice in America* (1930). Reprint. New York: Da Capo Press, 1975.

RANKIN, ANNE. "The Effect of Pretrial Detention." *New York University Law Review* 39 (1964): 641–655.

ROBERTSON, JOHN A., ed. *Rough Justice: Perspectives on Lower Criminal Courts.* Boston: Little, Brown, 1974.

SHAPIRO, MARTIN M. *Courts: A Comparative and Political Analysis.* University of Chicago Press, 1981.

SILBERMAN, LINDA J., with PRESCOTT, ELIZABETH, and CLARK, MATTHEW. *Non-attorney Justice in the United States: An Empirical Study.* New York: Institute of Judicial Administration, 1979.

SKOLNICK, JEROME H. *Justice without Trial: Law Enforcement in Democratic Society.* New York: Wiley, 1966.

STEPHEN, JAMES FITZJAMES. *A History of the Criminal Law of England,* vol. 2. London: Macmillan, 1883.

THOMAS, WAYNE H. *Bail Reform in America.* Berkeley: University of California Press, 1976.

Vera Institute of Justice. *Felony Arrests: Their Prosecution and Disposition in New York City's Courts.* Rev. ed. New York: Longman, 1981.

2.
FELONY DISPOSITIONS

Each year more than 1.5 million adults are arrested on felony charges and enter the funnel (or sieve, depending on one's viewpoint) that is called the felony disposition process. Fewer than 10 percent go to trial, and only about half of those arrested are convicted. Fewer than 10 percent of those convicted serve time in prison.

These figures are subject to several different interpretations. Conservative critics of the process can charge that the statistics indicate either ineffectiveness on the part of the individual agencies involved in the process, or a pattern of undue leniency. They would like to see conviction and incarceration rates raised. Liberal critics of the system can charge that the figures indicate both the futility of attempting to control crime through the criminal justice system, because it is so ineffective, and the arbitrariness of the process, which singles out only a small percentage of the cases to receive the most severe type of sanction.

Each of the agencies that plays a role in the process can use these figures to defend its own performance. When charged with failure to control crime, the police can blame the courts for letting too many defendants off. When their case settlement policies are attacked for being too lenient, prosecutors can charge the police with using poor judgment in making arrests, or failing to collect sufficient evidence to win a conviction.

There are several factors that make it difficult to evaluate this process, the first problem being one of definitional ambiguity. The most frequent forms of criminal behavior fall within broad statutory categories that encompass wide variations in actual seriousness. Robbery can involve many things, for example, a dispute with an acquaintance over gambling debts, riding in a car with someone who commits a robbery, or an armed assault on a pedestrian or retail establishment. Burglary can involve anything from poking through a neighbor's garage to the surreptitious entering of an occupied dwelling. Few people believe that all of the behaviors encompassed under such broad statutory categories deserve either the same attention or punishment. Therefore, some of the confusion encountered in interpreting case disposition data, which rely on these categories, is caused by the ambiguity of the legal labels involved.

Another factor contributing to the difficulty of interpreting or changing case disposition patterns is the complex adversarial nature of the process. It is not just a matter of the prosecution versus the defense. The prosecutor cannot afford to initiate proceedings in every case in which the police have made an arrest, and the court cannot allow every case filed to go to trial. Each of these agencies uses its own set of standards and procedures to evaluate the merit of cases and establish priorities. One prosecutor may concentrate on screening out difficult cases, whereas another focuses on identifying defendants with serious records for special attention. A prosecutor who receives a large percentage of cases that have involved fairly thorough investigative work by the police will be in a stronger plea bargaining position than one who receives many cases that are weak on evidentiary grounds.

Finally, the ambiguity of the process serves all of

the routine participants, but not necessarily the general public, by shrouding both the nature of their activities and the quality of their performance from outside review. In fact, the quality with which specific functions are performed is seldom subject to objective measurement, although they are frequently a topic for political debate.

The felony disposition process is the heart of the criminal justice system. First, the pattern of felony dispositions represents the central and most visible outcome of the entire criminal justice system. It is the primary reason for the system's existence. To the extent that the system has any effect on crime through deterrence, rehabilitation, or incapacitation, these effects are determined by the pattern of case dispositions. Second, the quality of justice in any particular site depends largely on how well individual actors in the felony disposition process perform their roles. Finally, although the legislature may in theory determine the minimum or maximum sentence for any particular crime, the felony disposition process determines in fact what sentences will apply. Even where sentences are narrowly prescribed for specific acts, the felony disposition process can circumvent the expressed intent of the legislature by what charges it chooses to find the defendant guilty of. Any policy intervention designed to alter sentencing patterns must deal with this informal process.

Felony disposition procedures

Arrest. Most felony cases begin with the arrest of a suspect. The arrest need only be based on probable cause—that is, reasonable cause to believe that the person to be arrested has committed a felony, whether or not a felony has actually been committed. Conviction requires proof beyond a reasonable doubt. For example, a police patrol unit responding to a call that a robbery is in progress may apprehend two suspects as they are leaving the scene of the robbery. The subsequent investigation may reveal that only one of the suspects entered the store and robbed the proprietor. The other suspect may claim that he did not know about the robbery and was only waiting for his friend. By interviewing both suspects, and any witnesses to the crime, the police will attempt to establish whether the second suspect was really not involved or was acting as a lookout for his partner. When the police have completed their investigation, usually within forty-eight hours, they must either release the suspect or present the case to the prosecutor for filing.

Charging. Formal legal proceedings against a suspected offender are initiated when the prosecutor files a complaint charging the suspect with specific criminal acts. Not all felony arrests result in the filing of a complaint. In at least 10 percent of the cases, the police will decide on the basis of their investigation that they have insufficient proof and release the suspect. The prosecutor may decide that there is insufficient evidence, or that the alleged crime was too trivial, to file charges. In the example of the two robbers caught in the act, the police would probably bring both cases to the prosecutor for his review.

Prosecutors in most large jurisdictions maintain a special unit or specific deputies who specialize in the filing of cases. They review all of the facts in each case brought to them by the police, to determine what specific crimes, if any, a potential defendant will be charged with.

In the early 1970s the filing of complaints was not looked upon as an important prosecutorial function. In some cities the police could file complaints directly; in others, the deputy prosecutors who were assigned to this function were the ones deemed least suitable for appearance in court. Thereafter, the picture changed considerably. Now, most prosecutors are aware that filing decisions have an important impact on the performance of their office. Cases involving crimes of a trivial nature or cases in which the evidence is weak are screened out early. If further investigation by the police is required, the case will usually not be filed until the investigation is complete. Since most prosecutors do not have any investigators of their own, one way they can provide an incentive to keep the police working on a case is to refuse to file it until the work is complete.

Careful case screening serves other functions as well. By weeding out the weak cases early in the process, the prosecutor avoids wasting scarce court resources on cases that have a low probability of conviction. In difficult cases, careful screening can alert the prosecutor to potential problems, such as a difficult witness, that can be overcome with special effort.

In offices that screen cases carefully, the charging process is more than a mere formality. It puts the defendant on notice as to what charges the prosecutor realistically thinks he can prove. A defendant may be charged with five robberies by the police, but the prosecutor will only file the strongest two. A defendant may be arrested for the possession of a small amount of drugs, a crime that is technically a felony. The prosecutor may file it as a misdemeanor, placing the defendant in jeopardy of a substantially less severe penalty than if the case were handled as a felony.

In screening cases, as in later steps in the process, the prosecutor attempts to anticipate how the court will react. If the court routinely dismisses cases involving the possession of small amounts of drugs, the prosecutor will not file them. If in cases of defendants with no prior record the court routinely reduces simple burglary from a felony to a misdemeanor, the prosecutor will file them as misdemeanors (Greenwood, Wildhorn et al.).

Pretrial detention. If a complaint is to be filed, the next step is to determine under what conditions the defendant will be released pending his trial. The two options are money bail or release on his own recognizance (ROR). The choice is made by a magistrate. At issue are two matters: whether a defendant will appear for trial if he is not held in custody, and what danger the community risks if he is released. The stronger the defendant's ties to the community—through residence, family, and job—the greater his chance of being granted ROR or having bail set at a low figure that he can meet.

The use of ROR was introduced in the 1970s to improve the chances of poorer defendants being released pending their trial. It is not available in all jurisdictions, and requires some agency to investigate the defendant's background to determine the likelihood that he will appear at trial.

Preliminary hearing. All jurisdictions have at least two levels of court: a lower, or municipal, court for misdemeanors and civil cases involving small amounts of money, and an upper, or superior, court for felonies and larger civil cases. The Constitution requires that in order for a felony case to be initiated in the superior court, there must be some type of hearing to evaluate the state's case. This is the function of the preliminary or grand jury hearing.

The preliminary hearing takes place in the lower court. The prosecutor is required to present sufficient evidence to establish a prima facie case—that is, sufficient evidence to convict the defendant if it is unchallenged by the defense. In the course of the preliminary hearing, the lower court judge may eliminate or modify any of the charges. If the case is dismissed on a defense motion, without prejudice, the prosecutor can file it again. If the dismissal is with prejudice, the case is closed. In practice, dismissed cases are seldom refiled unless the prosecutor obtains substantial new evidence.

The alternative to the preliminary hearing as a means of reviewing the people's case is the grand jury, a panel of lay persons who perform basically the same function as a judge in the preliminary hearings. The special feature of grand jury proceedings is that they are secret. Even witnesses are sworn to secrecy, and defense counsel is not present. In all

but a few jurisdictions, grand jury proceedings are only used in those cases that involve complicated conspiracies or charges against political figures. The end result of either a preliminary hearing or a grand jury hearing is that the defendant is bound over to the superior court or the felony charges are dropped.

Negotiated pleas. After a defendant has been bound over, he is formally arraigned in the superior court and required to enter a plea. Defense counsel is appointed if the defendant is indigent. Even though the defendant may have been represented by a public defender at his bail hearing or preliminary hearing, he is not usually assigned a permanent counsel of record (one who will handle the case through final disposition) until the superior court arraignment. This is the first time that defense counsel seriously reviews the case and contemplates a defense. At some point between the arraignment and start of a trial, most defendants decide to plead guilty. Most do not plead guilty to all of the allegations in the complaint. Defendants who plead guilty receive, on the average, less severe sentences than defendants who go to trial.

Plea negotiations can take a variety of forms, depending on the jurisdiction (Eisenstein and Jacob). In some, there is an almost explicit discount for every offense. Unarmed robbers can plead to assault. Burglars can plead to possession of stolen property. In New York City, very few burglary arrests result in burglary convictions; they are invariably bargained down to lesser charges (Vera Institute). In other jurisdictions, plea bargaining is on a case-by-case basis. The prosecutor may only give up those charges that will be difficult to prove. In jurisdictions in which a mandatory prison sentence is required for certain offenses, such as robbery with a firearm, the prosecutor may be willing to give up those elements of the offense that invoke the mandatory sentence. In other jurisdictions, the prosecutor may be willing to stipulate "no felony time" for a first offender. In still others, the court may merely indicate what the sentence will be if the defendant pleads guilty.

In plea negotiations, the defense counsel tries to limit the severity of the sentence his client will receive. The weaker the evidence or the more congested the court, the better his bargaining position. If the case against his client is strong, all that may be necessary to induce a plea is to have the court indicate the maximum sentence it will impose.

Trials. If a satisfactory plea bargain cannot be reached, the case proceeds to trial. If the defense moves to have certain items of evidence excluded from the trial on the ground that they were illegally obtained, its motions are heard in a separate hearing before the trial begins. With the exception of murder cases, most felony trials require only a few days to complete. As in earlier phases of the felony process, the trial can result in conviction or acquittal on each of the charges for which the defendant has been held to answer.

Sentencing. In most jurisdictions a presentence investigation report is prepared by the probation department and submitted to the court prior to sentencing. Of course, if all parties have agreed to a sentence as part of a plea bargain, the presentence report may be waived. Alternatively, the court may agree to a plea bargain that is contingent on no aggravating factors (such as a prior prison term) appearing in the presentence report. The presentence report typically describes the defendant's background, education, work experience, family life, and prior criminal record. It may also contain statements from either the victim or the defendant about the current offense that clarify the defendant's role or motives.

The severity of the sentence that can be imposed is limited by the seriousness of the charges to which the defendant pleaded or of which he was found guilty. With the exception of a very few capital offenses, the most severe sentence that can be imposed for a felony conviction is a term in state prison, the maximum term being specified for each offense category. If the court decides to place a defendant on probation rather than in prison, it can require, as a condition of probation, that the defendant pay a fine, make restitution to the victim, engage in some community service project, or serve some specified term in the county jail.

Unless the conviction offense is one for which a prison commitment is mandatory, the court has complete discretion in deciding whether to impose a prison term or a term of probation. Prison terms may be legislatively mandated for specific acts, such as the use of a firearm, or for defendants with serious prior records.

Case attrition

One way of describing the felony disposition process in a particular jurisdiction is to recount which variation of the procedures discussed above is normally followed. That is how two prosecutors from different sites would have compared their offices in the early 1970s. An alternative way of describing the process is to indicate the outcomes statistically: What fraction of felony arrests are filed? What fraction of defendants plead guilty to the most serious charge? What fraction of cases go to trial? What fraction of defendants convicted of robbery are sentenced to prison?

A term sometimes used to describe felony disposition data is the *case attrition pyramid.* The name comes from the shape of the graph that plots the fraction of cases surviving each step in the process. The case attrition pyramid for felony arrests in California is shown in Figure 1. Out of 150,004 felony arrests in 1978, 82 percent were referred to the prosecutor for filing and 68 percent were actually filed, 34 percent as felonies. Fifty-seven percent of the arrests resulted in conviction on some charge, and 39 percent resulted in some form of incarceration. Six percent of the arrests resulted in confinement in some state institution—the California Youth Authority, a narcotic rehabilitation facility, a mental health facility, or a prison. Of the 102,281 cases filed, 84 percent resulted in a

FIGURE 1. *Case attrition pyramid for California adult felony arrests (1978)*

Number		Percentage of arrests
9,188	Prison	6
58,000	Incarcerated	39
84,918	Convicted	57
102,281	Complaint filed	68
127,270	Complaint requested	82
150,004	Adult felony arrests in California (1978)	100

SOURCE: Deukmejian.

TABLE 1. *Arrest dispositions for robbery, burglary, and drug offenses in California (1978)*

		Robbery	Burglary	Drugs
Arrests		10,832	27,745	31,754
Complaints filed	Total	69	82	76
(as a percent-	Felony	58	47	37
age of arrests)	Misdemeanor	11	35	39
Convictions				
Percent of arrests		54	69	52
Percent of cases filed		93	84	68
Incarcerated				
Percent of arrests		50	55	31
Percent of convictions		93	80	60
Prison commitment				
Percent of arrests		20	7	2
Percent of convictions		37	10	4

SOURCE: Deukmejian.

conviction on some charge, and 7 percent resulted in a prison sentence. Fewer than 2 percent of these arrests resulted in a jury trial in the superior court.

It should be readily apparent that no one statistic, such as conviction rate, provides an adequate measure of a prosecutor's performance. If the conviction rate is based on all arrests, it will be greatly affected by police arrest practices (Feeney, Dill, and Weir). If it is based on cases filed, it reflects both the amount of case screening and the quality of case preparation.

It is generally assumed that a prosecutor can increase the fraction of cases in which defendants plead guilty by accepting pleas to lesser charges. Therefore, in comparing offices, one also needs to know the fraction of cases that result in conviction for the most serious charge contained in the complaint. In order to monitor trends over time, to compare one site against another, or to evaluate the impact of some specific policy changes, one needs to know the complete felony disposition pattern, with all its subsidiary branches from arrest to sentencing. Anything less is likely to lead to erroneous conclusions.

Table 1 shows how the pattern of case dispositions varies across three types of crime in California—robbery, burglary, and drug offenses. The disposition patterns reflect differences in both public and official perceptions of the seriousness of these three offense types. Robbery has the lowest filing rate—69 percent—probably because police investigations subsequent to arrest are more likely to find that the witnesses cannot positively identify the suspect. Conviction for burglary or drug charges can be based on the defendant's possession of stolen property or

drugs, but conviction for robbery normally requires a victim or witness identification.

Table 1 also shows that robbery arrests are more likely to result in the filing of a felony complaint, and that once filed, robbery arrests are more likely to result in conviction, incarceration, and imprisonment: 93 percent of the arrested robbers who are convicted on any charge are incarcerated in jail or prison. Of those defendants convicted of robbery (28 percent of robbery arrests), 69 percent are committed to state institutions. Although robbery, burglary, and possession or sale of narcotics are all legally defined as felonies punishable by imprisonment, Table 1 shows how the system reacts to different degrees of crime seriousness. Since convictions for burglary or drug offenses are much less likely to result in imprisonment than robbery convictions, they are more likely to be filed as misdemeanors by the prosecutor.

Knowing how one jurisdiction disposes of its felony cases gives little information about what to expect in another. Table 2 shows considerable cross-site variation in the frequency with which incarceration is im-

TABLE 2. *Variation in incarceration rate across cities (percent of convicted defendants incarcerated)*

Convicted offense	Detroit	New Orleans	Los Angeles	Indianapolis
Rape	52	—	75	82
Robbery	73	91	66	91
Assault	26	—	50	62

SOURCE: Brosi, appendixes.

posed. There is no theory based on organizational or procedural differences to explain why defendants in Indianapolis are consistently sentenced more-harshly than those in Los Angeles or Detroit. Nor is there a clear explanation of why robbery defendants in Detroit are sentenced more harshly than robbery defendants in Los Angeles, whereas assaulters and rapists are not.

The judges in one jurisdiction may view a particular type of offense as less serious than judges elsewhere. The average offense within any particular crime category, such as robbery, may in fact be less serious in the degree of force involved or the degree of injury to victims. The prosecutor in one jurisdiction may be more willing to grant sentencing concessions in return for a guilty plea by the defendant. In a study of the Los Angeles District Attorney's Office, it was found that the percentage of convicted defendants who were sentenced to state prison varied by more than a factor of two across branch offices of the court (Greenwood, Wildhorn et al.).

Explaining the disposition of felony cases

It was pointed out above that there are substantial variations in the disposition patterns for different types of offenses. Since 1970 a number of statistical studies have attempted to identify other case characteristics that might explain differences in the probability of conviction or imprisonment among defendants charged with the same offense. A group of researchers from the Vera Institute of Justice examined a 1971 sample of adult felony arrests from New York City, and another group, from the Institute for Law and Social Research (Williams; Williams and Lucianovic; Forst, Lucianovic, and Cox), studied a sample of cases prosecuted in the District of Columbia between 1971 and 1975. Philip Cook and Daniel Nagin also analyzed a sample of robbery cases from Washington, D.C., to determine the effect of weapon use on case outcomes. Peter Greenwood, Joan Petersilia, and Franklin Zimring have examined the impacts of age on disposition patterns in several cities. Floyd Feeney, Forrest Dill, and Adrianne Weir conducted a study of case attrition in arrests made by the San Diego, California, and Jacksonville, Florida, police departments. From these studies, several consistent findings have emerged.

The most important factor associated with the probability of conviction is the strength of the evidence (Williams; Williams and Lucianovic; Vera Institute; Forst, Lucianovic, and Cox; Feeney, Dill, and Weir). Cases based on physical evidence or testimony of sev-eral witnesses are much more likely to result in conviction. Cases in which there was a previous relationship between the defendant and victim are less likely to result in conviction, apparently because there is a strong probability that the victim will become uncooperative with prosecutors, either because of a reconciliation with the defendant or fear of retribution (Vera Institute). The exclusion of evidence by the court because of illegal police methods accounts for only a small number of dismissals or acquittals (Feeney, Dill, and Weir). It appears that in some jurisdictions dismissals are used as an informal method of diversion for less serious cases against young first-time offenders (Greenwood, Petersilia, and Zimring).

Among those defendants who are convicted, the probability of imprisonment is consistently affected by the seriousness of their prior records (Vera Institute; Cook and Nagin) and the presence of certain aggravating features in the current offense. Both the Vera Institute and Cook studies found that robberies in which there was a prior relationship between victim and offender were less likely to result in incarceration than robberies involving strangers. In the only study that looked at the issue of arming directly, Cook and Nagin found that robbers who used firearms were more likely to be incarcerated than those who did not. The presence of other weapons had no consistent effect. Greenwood, Petersilia, and Zimring found that in some sites the youngest adult defendants were less likely to be incarcerated than older offenders who had committed similar crimes.

For many years it has been the conventional wisdom that pretrial detention increased the likelihood of conviction. It was hypothesized that defendants who were held in custody would be less able to prepare their defense and more ready to plea bargain. Furthermore, since cases involving defendants in custody normally take priority over other cases in court scheduling, it was believed that increased delays experienced by defendants not in custody would improve their chances of acquittal. In reviewing the evidence on this issue, the Feeney, Dill, and Weir study concluded that previous studies neither deny nor confirm this hypothesis. Although detained defendants are more likely to be convicted, it is not possible to tell whether their higher conviction rate is caused by their detention or simply a result of the fact that courts are less likely to detain those for whom the probability of conviction is low.

Some reforms in processing procedures

In 1920, Roscoe Pound and Felix Frankfurter were invited by the city fathers of Cleveland to undertake a comprehensive study of that city's criminal justice sytem. The heart of Pound and Frankfurter's report was a series of tables showing a pattern of case dispositions not unlike that described above. The Cleveland study was interpreted as showing a complete breakdown in the system, and sweeping reforms were called for.

In 1967, the President's Commission on Law Enforcement and Administration of Justice, in its review of the criminal courts, also found much to be unhappy with: overworked and in many cases undertrained personnel; congested calendars; assembly-line processing; undisciplined discretion; lack of many rudimentary management techniques; and high case attrition rates. Many of the commission's recommendations were aimed at general improvements in the entire court process: unification of felony and misdemeanor courts; increased manpower and modernization of facilities; increased training; and the development of case processing standards.

Since then, the direction of reforms in felony case processing has shifted away from wholesale attempts at improving the entire process to more focused attempts at solving particular problems. Probably the most significant innovation has been the growth in research and administrative statistics concerning the felony disposition process. A number of studies have documented patterns of filing, case settlement, and sentencing. Others have investigated factors leading to case attrition or affecting sentence severity. Many prosecutors and courts have adopted computerized case tracking systems, which can provide administrators with information on the status of any particular case, or summary statistics on overall work load or disposition patterns. These research efforts, unlike more general indictments of the entire process offered by earlier studies, have helped to identify some tractable problems.

Another major reform movement under way is the shift toward more structured sentencing procedures. For many years the sentencing of felony defendants was governed by indeterminate-sentencing procedures. The court sentenced a defendant to prison for an indeterminate term, such as from five years to life for robbery. The actual term served was then determined by a parole board, based in part on the conviction offense but also on the defendant's perceived potential for rehabilitation or danger to the community.

Indeterminate sentencing has, however, been challenged by several lines of research that have attacked its underlying principles. Research on prison rehabilitation programs has refuted claims that they are of any success in changing criminal behavior, and examination of clinical prediction accuracy has shown that judgments about future dangerousness are highly inaccurate. Finally, studies of the sentencing patterns that result from indeterminate sentencing have revealed wide disparities between similar types of offenders. In other words, the discretion granted decision-makers under the indeterminate-sentencing schemes was not being guided by any rational principles. These accumulated research findings have in turn generated a search for new principles on which to base sentencing decisions.

One such development is a procedure known as sentencing guidelines, which provide judges with a matrix of presumptive sentences for different combinations of offenses and defendant characteristics (primarily the prior record). These guidelines can be normative, by being based on an analysis of past sentencing decisions, or prescriptive, by being based on an analysis of sentencing goals and projections of future crime rates and prison capacity. Most guideline systems have been adopted by the judiciary as a voluntary means of reducing sentencing disparity. A 1982 evaluation of the effects of guidelines in several sites did not find that they had yet had a significant impact on sentencing patterns (Rich et al.).

Determinate sentencing represents another approach to reducing sentence disparity. Under determinate sentencing, the legislature establishes a narrow range of sentences for each offense type; the sentencing judge then selects the appropriate term for a particular offender, within a fairly narrow range of discretion based on the seriousness of the case and the defendant's background. Most states provide grounds for increasing the base term by specific increments upon the pleading and proof of specific facts, such as that the defendant has served a prior prison term. As of 1982, about six states had adopted some form of determinate sentencing. In those that have not, many parole boards have established parole guidelines intended to achieve similar results.

A procedure that has been developed by many prosecutors to overcome the problems of growing case loads and court congestion is known as career-criminal prosecution. In most large court systems, individual prosecutors specialize at any given time in one particular phase of the process—complaints, arraignments, preliminary hearings, or trials. No one individual is responsible for any particular case. This method of organization invariably leads to some cases falling between the cracks. They end up by being dismissed or plea bargained away because a witness is not prepared or because the deputy handling the negotiations is not aware of the severity of the defendant's prior record.

Career-criminal prosecution was developed and funded by the Justice Department's Law Enforcement Assistance Administration as a method of giving more attention to cases against serious defendants. As adopted in most sites, it usually involves a special unit that handles career-criminal cases. Incoming cases are screened at intake to determine whether they meet the career-criminal criteria, usually some combination of serious current offenses and prior record. If the case is accepted by the career-criminal unit, a single deputy is assigned to handle the case through every step of the process. The case loads of deputies in the special unity are substantially lower than in other parts of the office, in order to give the deputies adequate time to prepare the cases. Since each case is prepared for trial, plea bargaining is minimal and strictly controlled. In some units special police liaison officers are assigned to expedite the handling of evidence. Career-criminal cases are frequently given priority on the trial calendar.

A different legislative approach to controlling the scheduling of felony cases is embodied in various "speedy trial" acts passed by the Congress and many state legislatures. These acts typically require that a defendant be brought to trial within a specified time period after arrest or indictment.

Most speedy-trial acts are designed to protect the interests of both the public and the defendant in a speedy trial, interests that are not symmetrical. The public's interest is to ensure that criminal defendants are punished promptly and not allowed to go free on bail for long periods of time while awaiting trial. If a defendant foresees a high probability of conviction and he is free on bail, it is usually in his interest to postpone trial as long as possible. The strength of a case invariably weakens over time, and even if the defendant is found guilty, his punishment is delayed.

Although the prosecutor is theoretically interested in a speedy trial, in practice, delays help him balance his case load. The speedy-trial requirement is also an imposition on the court, which must postpone its civil calendar in order to give criminal cases priority. Since none of the parties to a criminal case normally have a vested interest in a speedy trial, and since most, if not all, speedy-trial acts provide for exceptions "in the interests of justice," these acts consequently have very little if any effect. In uncongested courts they are not needed, and in congested courts they are nullified by the practice of granting exceptional continuances (Misner, p. 234).

Another area in which some reform has occurred is in the handling of victims and witnesses. Historically, victims and witnesses have been the most neglected participants in the trial process. They were frequently called to appear when their presence was not required—for instance, when both parties knew the case would be continued. They were frequently condemned to wait long hours in noisy hallways and frequently were unprepared by the police or prosecutor for their appearance. If a witness failed to appear, it was usually assumed that he was uncooperative, and the case was dropped (Cannavale and Falcon).

Prosecutors have gradually come to understand that victims and witnesses are important allies. Some have "on call" procedures whereby a witness is allowed to stay at home or work until the exact time of his appearance is known. Many have established special units to guarantee that victims and witnesses are only called when their presence is required. Some of these units also keep track of witnesses to ensure that their failure to appear is not caused by the simple fact that their court papers were sent to the wrong address. These may seem like fairly mundane matters, but in a busy courthouse handling a large number of defendants and witnesses from poor inner-city neighborhoods, they can constitute quite a challenge.

In summary, since the early 1970s the courts have either adopted or been saddled with a number of procedural and administrative reforms intended to improve their efficiency or increase the quality of justice that they provide. Since criminal proceedings invariably involve several parties with divergent interests, it is not surprising that many of the reforms have been modest in scope and of limited success.

PETER W. GREENWOOD

See also ARRAIGNMENT; *both articles under* BAIL; CRIMINAL JUSTICE SYSTEM, *articles on* MEASUREMENT OF PERFORMANCE, OVERVIEW, *and* SOCIAL DETERMINANTS; *both articles under* GUILTY PLEA; JURY: JURY TRIAL; *articles under* SENTENCING; SPEEDY TRIAL; TRIAL, CRIMINAL.

BIBLIOGRAPHY

BROSI, KATHLEEN B. *A Cross-city Comparison of Felony Case Processing.* Washington, D.C.: Institute for Law and Social Research, 1979.
CANNAVALE, FRANK J., JR., and FALCON, WILLIAM D. *Witness Cooperation: With a Handbook of Witness Management.* Lexington, Mass.: Heath, Lexington Books, 1976.
COOK, PHILIP, and NAGIN, DANIEL. *Does the Weapon Matter?: An Evaluation of a Weapons Emphasis Policy in the Prosecution of Violent Offenders.* PROMIS Research Project, Publication No. 8. Washington, D.C.: Institute for Law and Social Research, 1978.

DEUKMEJIAN, GEORGE. *Adult Felony Arrest Dispositions in California.* Sacramento: California Department of Justice, Division of Law Enforcement, Criminal Identification and Information Branch, Bureau of Criminal Statistics and Special Services, 1979.

EISENSTEIN, JAMES, and JACOB, HERBERT. *Felony Justice: An Organizational Analysis of Criminal Courts.* Boston: Little, Brown, 1977.

FEENEY, FLOYD; DILL, FORREST; and WEIR, ADRIANNE. *Analysis of the Rate and Reasons for Dismissals of Criminal Cases.* Davis: University of California, Center on Administration of Justice, 1981.

FORST, BRIAN; LUCIANOVIC, JUDITH; and COX, SARAH J. *What Happens after Arrest?: A Court Perspective of Police Operations in the District of Columbia.* Washington, D.C.: U.S. Department of Justice, Law Enforcement Assistance Administration, National Institute of Law Enforcement and Criminal Justice, 1978.

GREENWOOD, PETER W. "The Violent Offender in the Criminal Justice System." *Criminal Violence.* Edited by Marvin E. Wolfgang and Neil Alan Weiner. Beverly Hills, Calif.: Sage, 1982, pp. 320–346.

————; PETERSILIA, JOAN; and ZIMRING, FRANKLIN E. *Age, Crime, and Sanctions: The Transition from Juvenile to Adult Court.* R-2642-NIJ. Prepared under a grant from the National Institute of Justice, U.S. Department of Justice. Santa Monica, Calif.: Rand Corporation, 1980.

GREENWOOD, PETER W.; WILDHORN, SORREL; POGGIO, EUGENE C.; STRUMWASSER, MICHAEL J.; and DeLEON, PETER. *Prosecution of Adult Felony Defendants: A Policy Perspective.* Lexington, Mass.: Heath, Lexington Books, 1976.

MISNER, ROBERT L. "Delay, Documentation, and the Speedy Trial Act." *Journal of Criminal Law and Criminology* 70, no. 2 (1979): 214–234.

POUND, ROSCOE, and FRANKFURTER, FELIX, eds. *Criminal Justice in Cleveland: Reports of the Cleveland Foundation Survey of the Administration of Criminal Justice in Cleveland, Ohio.* Cleveland Foundation, 1922.

President's Commission on Law Enforcement and Administration of Justice, Task Force on the Administration of Justice. *Task Force Report: The Courts.* Washington, D.C.: The Commission, 1967.

RICH, WILLIAM D.; SUTTON, L. PAUL; CLEAR, TODD R.; SAKS, MICHAEL J. *Sentencing by Mathematics: An Evaluation of the Early Attempts to Develop and Implement Sentencing Guidelines.* Williamsburg, Va.: National Center for State Courts, 1982.

Vera Institute of Justice. *Felony Arrests: Their Prosecution and Disposition in New York City's Courts.* New York: The Institute, 1977.

WILLIAMS, KRISTEN M. *The Prosecution of Sexual Assaults.* PROMIS Research Project, Publication No. 7. Washington, D.C.: Institute for Law and Social Research, 1978.

————, and LUCIANOVIC, JUDITH. *Robbery and Burglary: A Study of the Characteristics of the Persons Arrested and the Handling of Their Cases in Court.* PROMIS Research Project, Publication No. 6. Washington, D.C.: Institute for Law and Social Research, 1979.